THE CAMBRIDGE HISTORY OF EGYPT

VOLUME 1

Islamic Egypt, 640–1517

Volume 1 of THE CAMBRIDGE HISTORY OF EGYPT addresses the period from the Arab invasion in 640 to the Ottoman conquest of 1517. The volume opens with a discussion of the preceding centuries to illustrate the legacy of ancient Egypt, and then progresses chronologically according to the major dynastic episodes. While the focus of the volume is not restricted to politics, questions of political process and changes in regime are interpreted by the relevant experts in the light of recent research. Authors have been encouraged to conceptualize their topics around a variety of rubrics including communal interaction, financial development, diplomatic relations, and religious trends.

CARL F. PETRY is Professor of History at Northwestern University, Evanston, Illinois. His research has focused on pre-modern Egypt, and his publications include *Protectors or Praetorians? The Last Mamluk Sultans and Egypt's Waning as a Great Power* (1994), *Twilight of Majesty: The Reigns of al-Ashraf Qaytbay and Qansuh al-Ghawri in Egypt* (1993), and *The Civilian Elite of Cairo in the Later Middle Ages* (1981).

THE CAMBRIDGE HISTORY OF EGYPT

General editor

M. W. DALY

Kettering University, Michigan

THE CAMBRIDGE HISTORY OF EGYPT offers the first comprehensive English-language treatment of Egyptian history through thirteen centuries, from the Arab conquest to the end of the twentieth century. The two-volume survey, written by international experts, considers the political, socio-economic and cultural history of the world's oldest state, summarizing the debates and providing insight into current controversies. Implicit in the project is the need to treat Egypt's history as a continuum and at the heart of any regional comparisons. As Egypt reclaims a leading role in the Islamic, Arab and Afro-Asian worlds, the project stands as testimony to its complex and vibrant past. Its balanced and integrated coverage will make an ideal reference tool for students, scholars and general readers.

VOLUME 1

Islamic Egypt, 640–1517

Edited by

CARL F. PETRY

VOLUME 2

Modern Egypt, from 1517 to the end of the twentieth century

Edited by

M. W. DALY

THE CAMBRIDGE HISTORY OF EGYPT

VOLUME 1

Islamic Egypt, 640–1517

EDITED BY

CARL F. PETRY

CAMBRIDGE
UNIVERSITY PRESS

PUBLISHED BY THE PRESS SYNDICATE OF THE UNIVERSITY OF CAMBRIDGE
The Pitt Building, Trumpington Street, Cambridge CB2 1RP, United Kingdom

CAMBRIDGE UNIVERSITY PRESS
The Edinburgh Building, Cambridge, CB2 2RU, United Kingdom
http://www.cup.cam.ac.uk
40 West 20th Street, New York, NY 10011–4211, USA http://www.cup.org
10 Stamford Road, Oakleigh, Melbourne 3166, Australia

First published 1998

Printed in the United Kingdom at the University Press, Cambridge

Typeset in Sabon 9.5/12 pt [CE]

A catalogue record for this book is available from the British Library

ISBN 0 521 47137 0 hardback

CONTENTS

List of illustrations to chapter 13 *ix*
List of contributors *x*
Preface *xiii*
Note on transliteration *xv*
Maps *xvi*

1 Egypt under Roman rule: the legacy of Ancient Egypt *1*
ROBERT K. RITNER

2 Egypt on the eve of the Muslim conquest *34*
WALTER E. KAEGI

3 Egypt as a province in the Islamic caliphate, 641–868 *62*
HUGH KENNEDY

4 Autonomous Egypt from Ibn Ṭūlūn to Kāfūr, 868–969 *86*
THIERRY BIANQUIS

5 The Ismāʿīlī Daʿwa and the Fāṭimid caliphate *120*
PAUL E. WALKER

6 The Fāṭimid state, 969–1171 *151*
PAULA A. SANDERS

7 The non-Muslim communities: Christian communities *175*
TERRY G. WILFONG

8 The non-Muslim communities: the Jewish community *198*
NORMAN A. STILLMAN

9 The crusader era and the Ayyūbid dynasty *211*
MICHAEL CHAMBERLAIN

10 The Baḥrī Mamlūk sultanate, 1250–1390 242
LINDA S. NORTHRUP

11 The regime of the Circassian Mamlūks *290*
JEAN-CLAUDE GARCIN

12 The monetary history of Egypt, 642–1517 *318*
WARREN C. SCHULTZ

13 Art and architecture in the medieval period *339*
IRENE A. BIERMAN

14 Culture and society during the late Middle Ages *375*
JONATHAN P. BERKEY

15 Historiography of the Ayyūbid and Mamlūk epochs *412*
DONALD P. LITTLE

16 Egypt in the world system of the later Middle Ages *445*
R. STEPHEN HUMPHREYS

17 The military institution and innovation in the late Mamlūk period *462*
CARL F. PETRY

18 The Ottoman occupation *490*
MICHAEL WINTER

The rulers of Egypt, 254–922/868–1517 *517*
Glossary *521*
Bibliography *540*
Index *619*

ILLUSTRATIONS TO CHAPTER 13

1 The mosque of al-Ḥākim. From *Description de l'Egypte* (1820) *342*

2 The mosque of Aḥmad ibn Ṭūlūn. From Robert Hillenbrand, *Islamic Architecture* (Columbia University Press, 1994), p. 75 *351*

3 The *miḥrāb* area in the mausoleum of Sultan al-Ṣāliḥ Najm al-Dīn Ayyūb. With the permission of the German Archaeological Institute, Cairo *355*

4 A minbar donated to the Friday mosque in Qūṣ by the Fāṭimid wazīr al-Ṣāliḥ Ṭalāʾiʿ *356*

5 The Luʾluʾa mosque, Qarāfa *359*

6 A Coptic screen (detail) *362*

7 A metalwork door revetment from the mosque-*madrasa* of Sultan Ḥasan *364*

8 A page of the Qurʾān, from the reign of Sultan Shaʿbān *366*

9 The facade of the mosque of al-Aqmar *371*

10 The lion emblem of Sultan al-Ẓāhir Baybars, Citadel, Cairo. Photo: Nairy Hampikian *373*

CONTRIBUTORS

JONATHAN P. BERKEY, Associate Professor of History, Davidson College, North Carolina, is the author of: "Women and Education in the Mamlūk Period" (1991), *The Transmission of Knowledge in Medieval Cairo: A Social History of Islamic Education* (1992), and "Tradition, Innovation and the Social Construction of Knowledge in the Medieval Islamic Near East" (1995).

THIERRY BIANQUIS is Professeur d'histoire et civilisation islamiques, Université Lumière-Lyon II. Among his publications are "Les derniers gouverneurs ikhschīdides à Damas" (1970), "L'Acte de succession de Kāfūr d'après Maqrīzī" (1974), *Damas et la Syrie sous la domination fatimide (359–468/969–1076)*, 2 vols. (1986, 1989), and "L'espace ismailien et le régime du vizirat militaire en Égypte, le Yémen ṣulayḥide et l'Ifrīqiya zīride" (1995).

IRENE A. BIERMAN is Associate Professor of Art History and Director of the Middle East Center, University of California Los Angeles. Among her publications are "Urban Memory and the Preservation of Monuments" (1995), "Inscribing the City: Fāṭimid Cairo" (1997), and *Writing Signs: The Fatimid Public Text* (1998).

MICHAEL CHAMBERLAIN is Associate Professor of History, University of Wisconsin. He has written *Knowledge and Social Practice in Medieval Damascus, 1190–1350* (1994).

JEAN-CLAUDE GARCIN is Professeur in the Centre des Lettres et Sciences Humaines, Université de Provence, Aix-Marseille I. His writings include "Histoire, opposition politique et piétisme traditionaliste dans le Ḥusn al-Muḥāḍarat de Suyūṭī" (1967), *Un centre musulman de la Haute-Égypte médiévale: Qūṣ* (1976), *Espaces, pouvoirs et idéologies de l'Égypte médié-*

vale (1987), and "The Mamluk Military System and the Blocking of Medieval Muslim Society" (1988).

R. STEPHEN HUMPHREYS is ʿAbd al-ʿAzīz al-Saʿūd Professor, Department of History, University of California Santa Barbara. His writings include *From Saladin to the Mongols: The Ayyubids of Damascus, 1193–1260* (1977), *Islamic History: A Framework for Inquiry* (1991), and *Between Memory and Desire: The Middle East in Recent Times* (in press).

WALTER E. KAEGI, Professor of Byzantine History at the University of Chicago, is the author of *Byzantine Military Unrest, 471–843: An Interpretation* (1981), "Byzantine Logistics: Problems and Perspectives" (1993), and *Byzantium and the Early Islamic Conquests* (1995).

HUGH KENNEDY is Professor of Middle Eastern History, University of St Andrews. His publications include *The Prophet and the Age of the Caliphates: the Islamic Near East from the Sixth to the Eleventh Century* (1986), and *Muslim Spain and Portugal: A Political History of al-Andalus* (1996).

DONALD P. LITTLE is Professor of Arabic Language and Islamic History, Institute of Islamic Studies, McGill University, Montreal. He is the author of *An Introduction to Mamlūk Historiography: An Analysis of Arabic Annalistic and Biographical Sources for the Reign of al-Malik al-Nāṣir Muḥammad ibn Qalā'ūn* (1970), *A Catalogue of the Islamic Documents from al-Ḥaram aš-Šarīf in Jerusalem* (1984), "Notes on the Early *naẓar al-khāṣṣ*" (1998), and "Documents Related to the Estates of a Merchant and his Wife in Late Fourteenth Century Jerusalem" (1998).

LINDA S. NORTHRUP, Associate Professor in the Department of Near and Middle Eastern Civilizations, University of Toronto, is the author of "Muslim–Christian Relations during the Reign of the Mamluk Sultan al-Mansur Qalawun, AD 1278–1290" (1990), "Life in Jerusalem during the Mamluk Period as Portrayed in the Documents of al-Ḥaram al-Sharīf" (in Arabic) (1994), and *From Slave to Sultan: The Career of al-Manṣūr Qalāwūn and the Consolidation of Mamlūk Rule in Egypt and Syria (678–689/1279–1290)* (1998).

ROBERT K. RITNER is Associate Professor of Egyptology at the Oriental Institute, University of Chicago. His publications include *The Mechanics of Ancient Egyptian Medical Practice* (1993) and "Egyptian Magical Practice under the Roman Empire: the Demotic Spells and their Religious Context" (1995).

PAULA A. SANDERS, Associate Professor of History, Rice University, Houston, is the author of *A Mediterranean Society*, VI (Cumulative Indices), with S. D. Goitein (1993), *Ritual, politics and the city in Fatimid Cairo* (1994), and "Writing Identity in Medieval Cairo" (1995).

WARREN C. SCHULTZ, Assistant Professor of History, DePaul University, Chicago, is the author of: "Maḥmūd ibn ʿAlī and the New *Fulūs*: Late Fourteenth-Century Mamlūk Egyptian Copper Coinage Reconsidered" (1998) and "Mamlūk Monetary History: The State of the Field" (in press).

NORMAN A. STILLMAN is Schusterman/Josey Professor of Judaic Studies, University of Oklahoma. Among his books are *The Jews of Arab Lands: A History and Sourcebook* (1979) and *The Jews of Arab Lands in Modern Times* (1991).

PAUL E. WALKER is a research affiliate of the Middle East Center, University of Chicago. Among his publications are *Early Philosophical Shiism: The Ismaili Neoplatonism of Abū Yaʿqūb al-Sijistānī* (1993), "The Ismaili Daʿwa in the Reign of the Fatimid Caliph al-Ḥākim" (1993), and *The Wellsprings of Wisdom* (1994).

TERRY G. WILFONG is Assistant Professor of Egyptology in the Department of Near Eastern Studies and Assistant Curator for Graeco-Roman Egypt, Kelsey Museum of Archaeology, University of Michigan, Ann Arbor. His publications include *Women and Gender in Ancient Egypt: From Prehistory to Late Antiquity* (1997), "Agriculture among the Christian Population in Early Islamic Egypt: Theory and Practice" (1998), "Constantine in Coptic: Coptic Constructions of Constantine the Great and his Family" (1998), and "Reading the Disjointed Body in Coptic: From physical modification to textual fragmentation" (1998).

MICHAEL WINTER, Professor in the Department of Middle Eastern and African History, Tel Aviv University, has written *Society and Religion in Early Ottoman Egypt: Studies in the Writings of ʿAbd al-Wahhāb al-Shaʿrānī* (1982) and *Egyptian Society under Ottoman Rule, 1517–1798* (1992).

PREFACE

The *Cambridge History of Egypt* attempts to fill a gap in English-language treatment of Egyptian history since the Arab conquest. Given the long and continuing outside interest in Egypt, that such a treatment is overdue seems surprising; the very length of Egyptian history has inevitably led to its compartmentalization and to the increasing specialization of scholars interested in it. Essential, underlying continuities have sometimes therefore been obscured, while superficial points of demarcation have sometimes been exaggerated.

Advances in research in the last half-century amply justified the editors in undertaking this task. An explosion of interest in Egypt, the development of new disciplines and methods of academic research and the increasing availability of Egyptian archival sources have led not only to important progress in the understanding of Egypt's past, but also to ever-increasing specialization in outlook, method, and, therefore, in the audiences to which historical writing has been addressed.

The *Cambridge History* is therefore an attempt to present a comprehensive survey for a general audience, to make use of recent advances in historical knowledge, and to synthesize from discrete sources – increasingly from fields beyond the traditional bounds of history – Egypt's political and cultural history since the coming of Islam.

Volume 1 of the *History* addresses the period from the Arab invasion in 640 to the Ottoman conquest of 1517. The volume proceeds according to the major chronological and dynastic episodes demarcating this lengthy era. The focus of individual chapters is not restricted to politics but questions of political process and reasons for changes of regime remain significant subjects of scholarly interest and debate, and continue to warrant explanation in the light of recent research. Chapter authors have been encouraged to conceptualize their topics under broad rubrics such as cultural pluralism, communal interaction, financial developments, military organization, diplomatic relations, intellectual controversy, popular culture and religious currents. Contributors were invited to incorporate recent scholarship on these issues rather than to summarize previous syntheses.

No such survey has been attempted, or at any rate published, in a European language since Gaston Wiet's *L'Égypte arabe*, part 4 of Gabriel Hanotaux's *Histoire de la nation égyptienne* (Paris, 1937). This new assessment balances solid political history and contemporary theory so that the interests of both the informed general reader and the specialist are considered. The volume begins with discussions of conditions in Egypt during the centuries preceding the Arab invasion, on the assumption that the rapid consolidation of Arab power in the Nile valley cannot be understood without a summary of the late roman and Byzantine legacies.

An enterprise of this nature draws upon the experience and assistance of colleagues and collaborators too numerous to acknowledge individually. But the advice of Fred Donner and Bruce Craig at the University of Chicago, Jere Bacharach at the University of Washington, and Ulrich Haarmann at the University of Kiel was too significant to pass over without comment. None of these colleagues was in a position to contribute a chapter for this project, but the editor found their opinions valuable at both its conceptual and procedural stages nonetheless. It has been a pleasure to work with Martin Daly and Marigold Acland in the transformation of an appealing idea into a finished product which, it is hoped, will serve to encourage those interested in the history of Islamic Egypt to explore this rich and complex era in greater depth.

CARL PETRY

NOTE ON TRANSLITERATION

The system of Arabic transliteration employed is that of the *International Journal of Middle East Studies*. Terms in other languages and styles of elision have been rendered according to the usages of individual chapter contributors.

The glossary in volume 1 and the maps throughout have been prepared by the volume editors in consultation with chapter contributors. The dynastic tables in volume 1 rely on C. E. Bosworth's *The New Islamic Dynasties. A Chronological and Genealogical Manual* (New York, 1996).

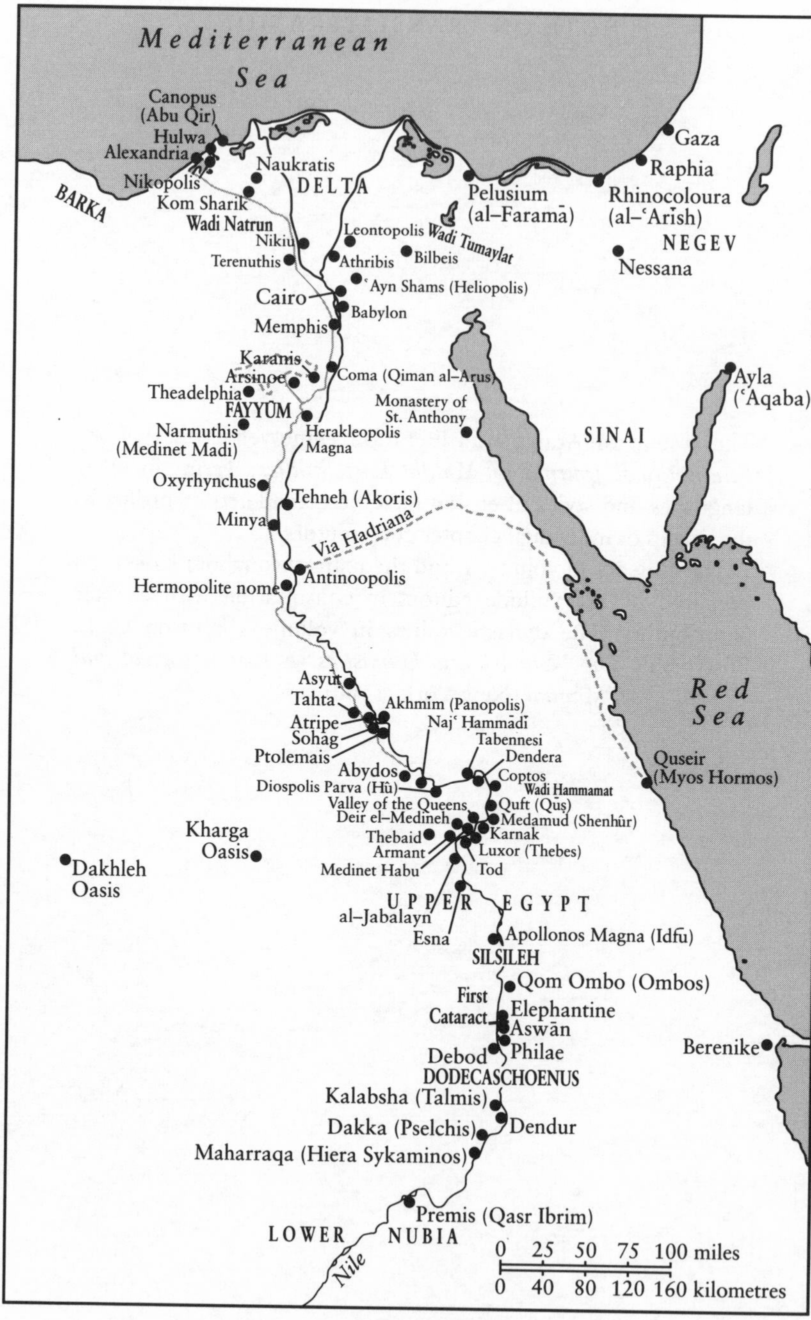

Map 1 *Ptolemaic and Byzantine Egypt*

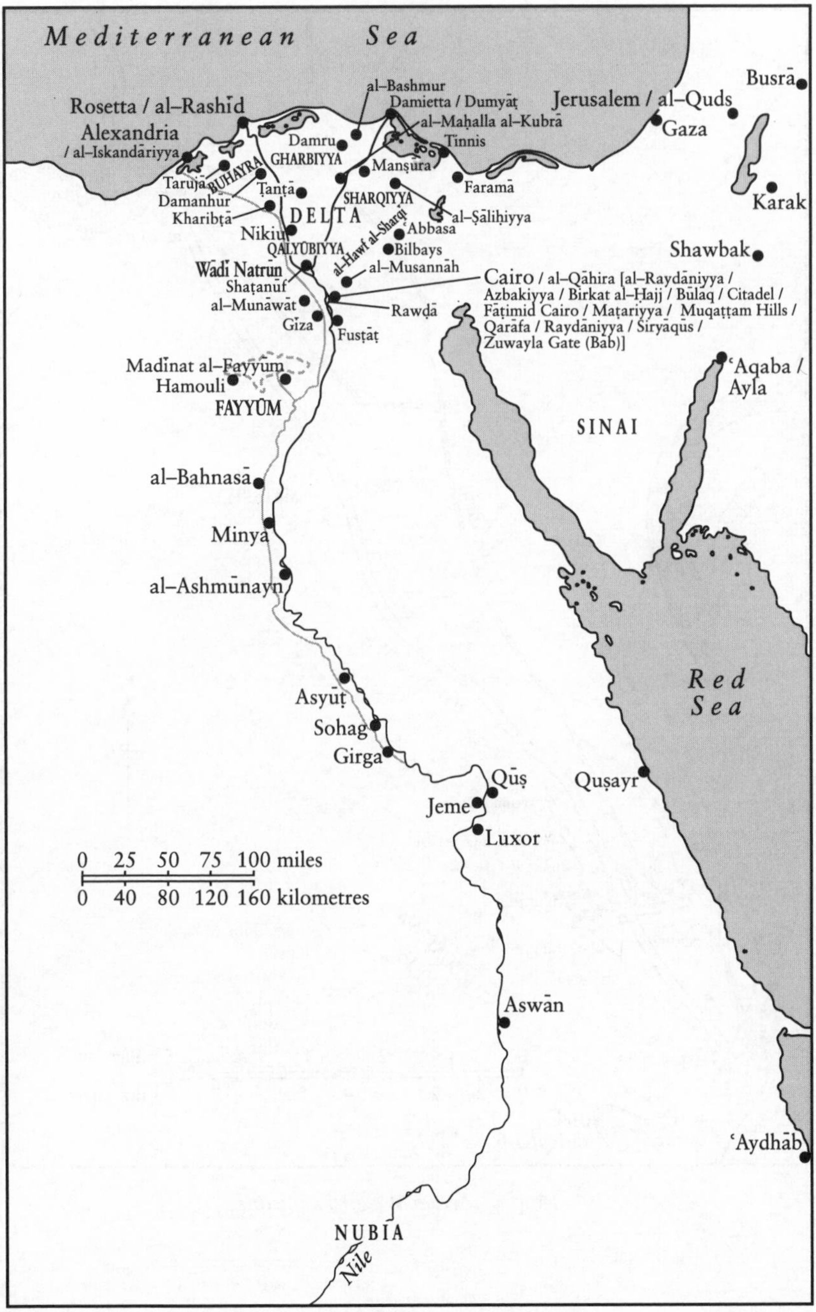

Map 2 *Islamic (post-conquest) Egypt*

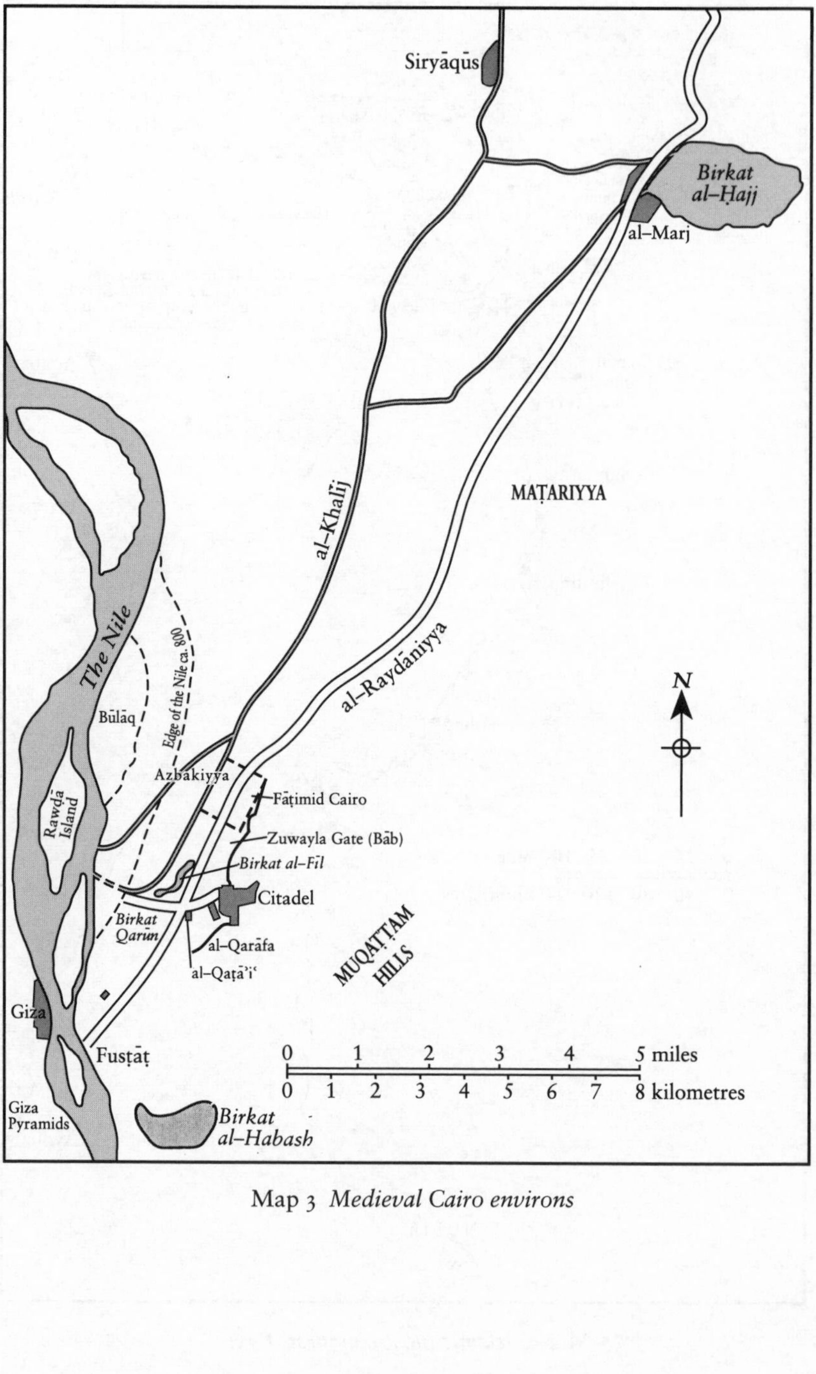

Map 3 *Medieval Cairo environs*

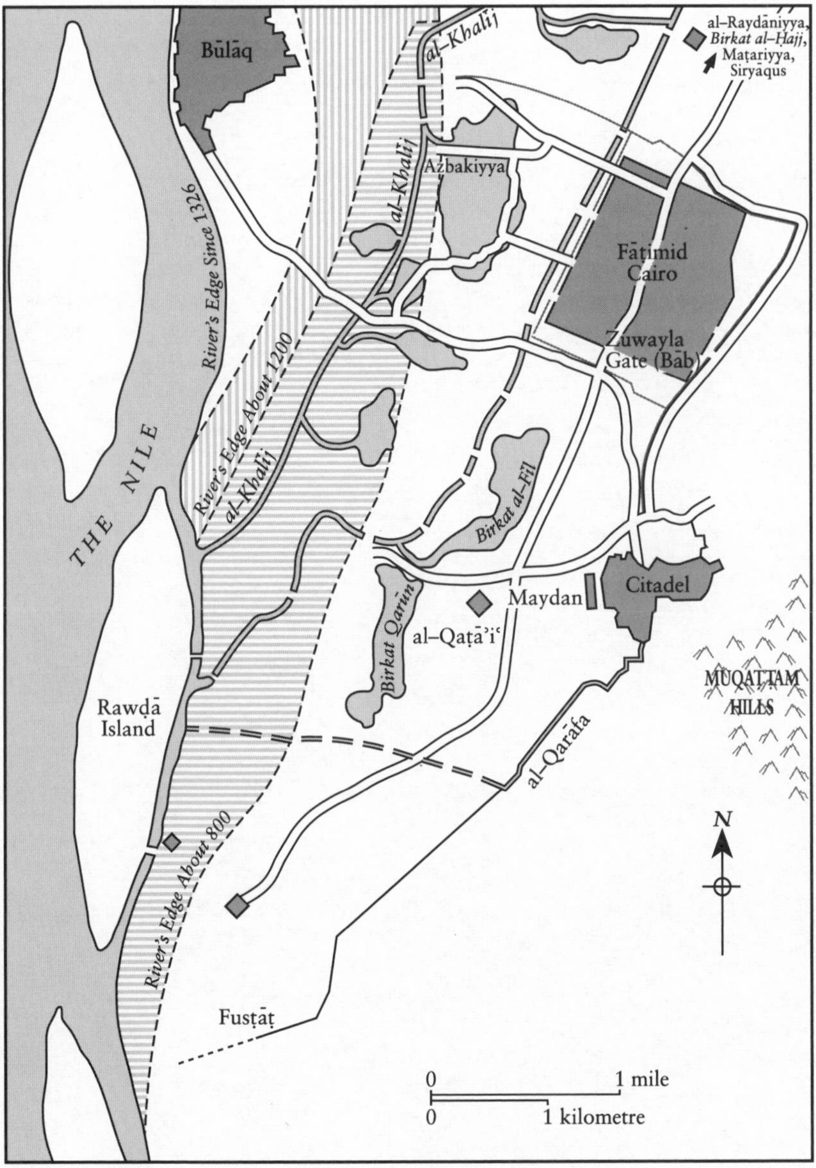

Map 4 *Medieval Cairo*

1

Egypt under Roman rule: the legacy of ancient Egypt

ROBERT K. RITNER

The death of Cleopatra the Great (VII) in 30 BC marked a pivotal moment in Egyptian history and indigenous culture. Long accustomed to foreign political domination after a succession of Libyan, Nubian, Assyrian, Persian and Macedonian rulers, Egyptian society had nonetheless proved remarkably resilient, assimilating its resident conquerors to varying degrees, while patiently enduring the brief ascendancy of those who ruled from a distance. When, however, the conquering Octavian "added Egypt to the empire of the Roman people,"[1] Egypt was forever relegated to the periphery of political power, and pharaonic society could no longer command extraordinary accommodation from alien rulers. If the Ptolemies were compelled to mollify Egyptian sensibilities for fundamental reasons of national stability, the Romans might do so for mere political expediency.

Although there is now some dispute regarding the degree to which Egypt differed from other Roman provinces,[2] certain unique features have long been noted. Octavian specifically excluded Egypt from customary senatorial control. Rather, he placed the province under the direct "dominion [*kratēsis*] of Caesar," a phrase traditionally interpreted to indicate Egypt's status as a "personal estate" of the emperor.[3] Unlike other provinces, Egypt was administered by a prefect (Latin *praefectus*; Greek *eparchos*) of equestrian rank, accountable exclusively to the emperor, rather than by a proconsul of senatorial rank, with potentially divided loyalties.[4] Indeed, senators or even prominent equestrians were formally prohibited from entering Egypt

1 *Res Gestae Divi Augusti*, 27. For a translation of this passage of the "Acts of Augustus," see A. H. M. Jones, *A History of Rome through the Fifth Century* (London, 1970), 21.

2 N. Lewis, "The Romanity of Roman Egypt: A Growing Consensus," in *On Government and Law in Roman Egypt, Collected Papers of Naphtali Lewis*, American Studies in Papyrology 33 (1984; reprint, Atlanta, 1995), 298–305.

3 See also A. Bowman, *Egypt After the Pharaohs* (Berkeley, 1986), 37 (with caveats); N. Lewis, *Life in Egypt under Roman Rule* (Oxford, 1983), 15.

4 For the adminstration, see Tacitus, *Annals*, XII.60, and Strabo, XVII.1.12.797, in Jones, *History of Rome*, 135, 179.

without the explicit approval of the emperor. As in the Ptolemaic regime, Egyptian currency remained a closed system, isolated within the empire. Until the reforms of Diocletian (AD 296), the export of Alexandrian coinage was prohibited, and the exchange of all foreign currency obligatory.[5]

The administrative isolation of the province is most likely to be explained by Egypt's designated role as the imperial granary, responsible for providing approximately one-third of the annual grain supply for the city of Rome.[6] The need to ensure the consistent production and delivery of the harvest determined virtually all aspects of Roman policy in Egypt. If restrictions on suspect visitors safeguarded Egypt's great wealth from potential imperial challengers, so the establishment of a particularly large, permanent garrison at Nikopolis near Alexandria was necessitated less by the threat of foreign invasion than by the fear of a Roman insurgent.[7] By the death of Augustus in AD 14, Egypt housed two of the three African legions. Moreover, a variety of social restrictions on local inhabitants enforced a governmental policy of keeping the natives "down on the farm" without the possibility of disruptive social advancement.

Long-standing assumptions regarding the unique status of Egypt have been based upon a perceived uninterrupted continuity of agricultural life for the great mass of the Egyptian peasantry:

> The passing of Ptolemaic rule was probably unmourned, perhaps even largely unnoticed, by the majority of the inhabitants of the Nile valley for whom the replacement of a Macedonian monarch by a Roman emperor heralded no obvious or dramatic change.[8]

Always primarily an agricultural society, Egypt was uniquely dependent for its survival upon the Nile flood waters, harnessed by an extensive network of local irrigation canals. Across the millennia of Egyptian history, even the most disruptive changes in regime and religion brought only minimal impact upon the daily work of the peasant farmers, or fallahin. Some innovations do appear late in pharaonic history, and these persist throughout Roman and medieval times and still survive in contemporary rural Egypt. Thus the saqīa, an ox-driven water wheel of likely Persian origin (ca. 525–404 BC),[9]

5 See Bowman, *Egypt After the Pharaohs*, 92–93.

6 So explicitly Tacitus, *Annals II*, LIX. See Geoffrey Rickman, *The Corn Supply of Ancient Rome* (Oxford, 1980), 61, 67–71; Lewis, *Life in Egypt*, 165; cf. Bowman, *Egypt After the Pharaohs*, 38–40.

7 R. C. C. Law, "Egypt and Cyrenaica under Roman Rule," in J. D. Page (ed.), *The Cambridge History of Africa*, vol. II (Cambridge, 1978), 192, 194; cf. Bowman, *Egypt After the Pharaohs*, 40. See further Michael P. Speidel, "Augustus' Deployment of the Legions in Egypt," *Chronique d'Égypte*, 57, no. 113 (1987), 120–24. Pertinent documents on army life appear in Jones, *History of Rome*, 148, 151–53, 179. Nikopolis was located about four miles east of Alexandria.

8 Bowman, *Egypt After the Pharaohs*, 37.

9 See the sources gathered in Karl W. Butzer, *Early Hydraulic Civilization in Egypt*

and the Archimedes screw introduced in the Ptolemaic era (ca. 287–212 BC)[10] continue to assist Egyptian farmers in company with the ancient shadūf, a simple water-hoist attested from New Kingdom times (ca. 1346–1334 BC).[11] In the fields of modern Najʿ Ḥammādī (Nag Hammadi), each of these devices has been repeatedly captured by tourist photographs, as have the wooden ox-drawn plows seemingly identical to those depicted in ancient tomb representations. The static necessities of existence in the Nile valley overwhelm each of its conquerors, as even later Arab settlers would discover.[12]

There can be little doubt that the essential features of this agrarian lifestyle exerted great influence upon the resident Greco-Roman population in Egypt, as is made evident by the predominant calendrical system, one of the few instances where an Egyptian institution effectively displaced its Greek counterpart. Closely associated with the rural life of the countryside, the ancient calendar comprised three seasons, corresponding to the recurring agricultural cycle: "Inundation" (ꜣḫ.t), "Seed-time" (pr.t), and "Harvest" (šmw). Each season contained four thirty-day months, making a total of twelve months with five intercalary days. So pervasive was the influence of this calendar that it survived repeated attempts at modification by foreign conquerors, easily replacing the Macedonian calendar for both Greeks and Egyptians in Ptolemaic Egypt,[13] and serving as the basis for the Roman (Julian) calendar introduced by Julius Caesar on the advice of the Alexandrian scientist Sosigenes.[14] Despite preserving the names and festivals of ancient deities, the month names survived the transition to Coptic Christianity as well.[15] Regardless of language, ethnicity or religion, scribes of Ptolemaic, Roman and Byzantine Egypt utilized almost exclusively the indigenous system. Although the Muslim lunar months were introduced

(Chicago, 1976), 46. Fitted with a series of stationary pots (qadus) on a rotating wheel, the saqīa can lift a continuous supply of water over 3.5 m in elevation.

10 Diodorus V.37.3; see P. M. Fraser, *Ptolemaic Alexandria* (Oxford, 1972), vol. I, 399, vol. II, 577–78, n. 174.

11 Earliest attestations in the Theban tomb of Neferhotep from the Amarna period; see Butzer, *Early Hydraulic Civilization*, 44, 46. By use of a weighted counter-pole, the shadūf can lift individual buckets of water over 1 m in elevation. For the saqīa and shadūf in nineteenth-century Egypt, see Edward W. Lane, *An Account of the Manners and Customs of the Modern Egyptians* (London, 1860; reprinted, New York, 1973), 327–28.

12 Succinctly stated, "the Arab settlers were absorbed into the age-old pattern and way of life of the Nile valley"; Bernard Lewis, "The Contribution to Islam," in J. R. Harris (ed.), *The Legacy of Egypt*, 2nd edn. (Oxford, 1971), 458–59.

13 See M. David and B. A. van Groningen, *Papyrological Primer*, 4th edn. (Leiden, 1965), 34*–36*.

14 Richard A. Parker, "The Calendars and Chronology," in Harris, *The Legacy of Egypt*, 13.

15 Walter C. Till, *Koptische Grammatik* (Leipzig, 1955), 87–88.

during the Islamic conquest and are cited in early rural documents,[16] the same pattern still prevails in the colloquial Arabic of modern Egypt.[17] A table of the Egyptian months follows:

Arabic	Coptic	Greek	Egyptian
tūt	ⲐⲞⲞⲨⲦ	Θωυθ	Ḏḥwty
bāba	ⲠⲀⲞⲠⲈ	Φαωφι	Pn-ỉp.t
hatūr	ϨⲀⲐⲰⲢ	Αθυρ	Ḥw.t-ḥr
kiyahk	ⲔⲞⲒⲀϨⲔ	Χοιακ	Kȝ-ḥr-kȝ
ṭūba	ⲦⲰⲂⲈ	Τυβι	Tȝ-ʿb.t
amshīr	ⲘϢⲒⲢ	Μεχειρ	Mḫr
baramhāt	ⲠⲀⲢⲘϨⲞⲦⲠ	Φαμενωθ	Pn-ʾImn-ḥtp
barmūda	ⲠⲀⲢⲘⲞⲨⲦⲈ	Φαρμουθι	Pn-Rnnwt.t
bashens	ⲠⲀϢⲰⲚⲤ	Παχων	Pn-Ḫnsw
baūna	ⲠⲀⲰⲚⲈ	Παυνι	Pn-ʾın.t
abīb	ⲈⲠⲎⲠ	Επιφι	ʾIpʾıp
misra	ⲘⲈⲤⲞⲢⲎ	Μεσορη	Msw.t-Rʿ

The five intercalary days are simply described as "added" to the year:
aiyām en-nasi <ⲈⲠⲀⲄⲞⲘⲈⲚⲎ< αι επαγωμεναι < 5 ḥry.w rnp.t

As the basic patterns of humble village life seemed unaffected by the change from Ptolemaic to Roman rule, so Rome's social impact was deemed minimal. Recent studies, however, have recognized that Ptolemaic society comprised far more than rural peasants, and have emphasized the distinct impact of Roman authority upon the urban Greek population and its institutions.[18] However, the corresponding impact upon the elite Egyptian class has not been investigated thoroughly. For these individuals, the formal custodians of native Egyptian culture, the change from Ptolemaic to Roman authority was surely notable, dramatic and a cause for mourning.

Deprived of most civil and military offices during the long centuries of foreign domination, prominent Egyptian families had turned instead to the temples as their source of income and prestige. In marked contrast to earlier practice, priestly elites of the "Late Period" accumulated a multiplicity of real or nominal temple offices, with corresponding financial benefices. By

16 E.g., within tenth-century private contracts from the Faiyum; see Nabia Abbott, *The Monasteries of the Fayyum*, Studies in Ancient Oriental Civilizations (SAOC) 16 (Chicago, 1937), 15, 21 (Jumādā; 946–947 AD).

17 For the Arabic forms, see Till, *Koptische Grammatik*, 87–88. The anglicized transcriptions that follow are derived from Karl Baedeker, *Baedeker's Egypt 1929*, (1929; reprint, London, 1974), xl.

18 N. Lewis, "Romanity of Roman Egypt", 300–01. Contrast the received opinion stated by Law, "Egypt and Cyrenaica", 194: "Roman rule did not involve any considerable degree of 'Romanization' for Egypt."

this stratagem such priests retained both wealth and authority in the face of foreign control and the intrusion of an alien, supposedly dominant, class.

Far from being cloistered, otherworldly mystics divorced from their surrounding communities, Egyptian sacerdotal elites actively participated in the economic and political life of the kingdom. It is these individuals who comprise the bulk of the parties engaged in the often brisk land and property speculation recorded in the numerous Demotic contracts.[19] Generally ignored in older studies of Ptolemaic society compiled by classicists, the Egyptian elite was sharply distinct from the rural fallahin, and hardly a second-class citizenry cowed by the perception of a Greek "master race." Taking these privileged Egyptians into consideration, the very notion of official ethnic discrimination becomes quite dubious for the Ptolemaic period.[20] Upper-class Egyptians often were fluent in the administrative language of Greek, an expediency that should not be mislabeled "assimilationist," as the same individuals did not need to forsake either an Egyptian identity or a fluency with native Demotic, also accorded official recognition as an administrative language.[21]

Mixed marriages between Egyptians and Greeks were increasingly common, particularly in the countryside, and the resulting families maintained conscious connections to both ethnicities, often expressed in the form of double names (one Greek, one Egyptian) accorded their children. By late Ptolemaic times, a number of such Hellenized Egyptians – or Egyptianized Hellenes[22] – had risen to prominence in civil and military positions, and the accelerating process would surely have continued but for the ha[illegible]crees of social separation imposed by Octavian himself.

As recorded in a surviving second-century copy of the regulations of the *idios logos*, or imperial "private account"[23] established by the deified

[19] Janet H. Johnson, "The Role of the Egyptian Priesthood in Ptolemaic Egypt," in L. H. Lesko (ed.), *Egyptological Studies in Honor of Richard A. Parker* (Hanover, NH, 1986), 70–84.

[20] See Robert K. Ritner, "Implicit Modes of Cross-Cultural Interaction: A Question of Noses, Soap, and Prejudice," in J. H. Johnson (ed.), *Life in a Multi-Cultural Society*, SAOC 51 (Chicago, 1992), 283–90, esp. 289–90.

[21] Contra N. Lewis, *Greeks in Ptolemaic Egypt* (Oxford, 1986), 154, there is no reason why exalted Egyptians should need or desire Greek status. For middle-class Egyptian indifference to Greek status, see J. H. Johnson, "Ptolemaic Bureaucracy from an Egyptian Point of View," in M. Gibson and R. D. Biggs (eds.), *The Organization of Power. Aspects of Bureaucracy in the Ancient Near East*, SAOC 46, 2nd edn. (Chicago, 1991), 123–31.

[22] Unconsciously following the racial distinctions imposed by Octavian, classical historians invariably designate the descendants of mixed Greco-Egyptian parentage as Hellenized *Egyptians*, rather than Egyptianized *Greeks*. A corrective is found in Bowman, *Egypt After the Pharaohs*, 124.

[23] BGU 1210; see A. S. Hunt and C. C. Edgar, *Select Papyri II* (Cambridge, MA, 1934), 42–53; Jones, *History of Rome*, 262–66; N. Lewis, *Life in Egypt*, 32–34; Bowman, *Egypt After the Pharaohs*, 127–28.

Augustus, the government now enforced a strict hierarchy of ethnic classes, divided into privileged Roman citizens, favored urban Greeks, and disenfranchised Egyptians. Only those able to demonstrate citizenship in the exclusive "Greek cities" (*poleis*) of Alexandria, Naukratis, Ptolemais, and, after AD 130, Antinoopolis, were eligible for the status of Greek. Greco-Egyptian families were all stigmatized as Egyptian, a class burdened by extraordinary restrictions and fines:

§43. If Egyptians after a father's death record their father as a Roman, a fourth (of the estate) is confiscated.

§44. If an Egyptian registers a son as an ephebe [of a polis], a sixth is confiscated.

§45. If an urban Greek marries an Egyptian woman and dies childless, the fisc appropriates his possessions; if he has children, it confiscates two-thirds. But if he has begotten children of an urban Greek woman and has three or more children, his possessions go to them . . .

§49. Freedmen of Alexandrians may not marry Egyptian women.

§53. Egyptians who, when married to discharged soldiers, style themselves Romans are subject to the provision on violation of status.[24]

No Egyptian could attain Roman citizenship without first acquiring elusive Alexandrian citizenship,[25] and the normal route to Roman citizenship, service in the legions, was effectively barred to all Egyptians. Any Egyptian who might enter the legion by ruse was denied this standard retirement benefit upon discovery.

§55. If an Egyptian serves in a legion without being detected, he returns after his discharge to the Egyptian status.[26]

As Roman or Greek citizenship conferred exemption from certain taxes, obligations and punishments, some restrictions on social advancement could be justified on a purely practical basis. However, the unparalleled severity of this "veritable ancient apartheid" has suggested to many a more sinister terpretation, deriving from Octavian's personal animosity to Cleopatra an ll things Egyptian.[27] More charitably, the system could be viewed as a dispa ionate guarantee of generations of serf labor for the critical grain supp . As once noted by Milne, "Egypt supplied corn, not men, to

24 N ewis, *Life in Egypt*, 33; Jones, *History of Rome*, 265.

25 Se e letter of Pliny the Younger imploring Trajan on behalf of his Egyptian chi ctor, cited in N. Lewis, *Life in Egypt*, 18; and Bowman, *Egypt After the Pha* 127.

26 Hunt lgar, *Select Papyri II*, 50–51; Jones, *History of Rome*, 265.

27 N. Lew n *Egypt*, 33–34.

Rome."[28] In any case, there can be little dispute that the Augustan social regulations effectively served as "an instrument of fiscal oppression."[29]

For the native sacerdotal elite, fiscal and social restrictions came quickly. Under the Ptolemies, the wealthy Memphite family of high priests had dominated ecclesiastical bureaucracy and economy and maintained intimate relations with the royal house. Like medieval popes, these Egyptian "pontiffs" crowned the succeeding rulers and controlled extensive territories attached to religious institutions. At the moment of Octavian's invasion, the Memphite priesthood was held by Petubast IV, whose sudden death in 30 BC at the age of sixteen is quite suspicious, particularly since his official interment was delayed by some six years. His successor, Psenamoun II, disappears after this ceremony in 23 BC, and the line comes to an abrupt end.[30] Thereafter, temple matters were subject to the secular authority of the imperial "private account." By the reign of Hadrian, religious authority was centralized under an appointed civil bureaucrat of equestrian rank, "the High Priest of Alexandria and all Egypt."[31]

The regulations of the *idios logos* provide a clear picture of the new arrangement. Priesthoods are reduced in number, temple holdings are decreased, and the civil bureaucracy now monitors the order and tenure of the hierarchy, their duties, dress and personal finances. Higher clergy were forbidden to engage in any financial activities outside their designated religious duties. All priests were required to wear linen (but never wool) and to be circumcised, unblemished and, subject to a 1,000-drachma fine, shaven bald.[32] As early as 4 BC, the prefect Gaius Turranius had demanded a registry of temple functionaries, their duties and their children, with the expressed intent of removing all individuals "not of priestly origin."[33] A further registry of the property of individual priests was introduced in the reign of Nero, becoming an annual report on temple and priestly finances (*graphai hieron*).[34] Admission to the priestly caste now required official

28 J. G. Milne, *A History of Egypt under Roman Rule* (London, 1898), v.

29 T. Rice Holmes, as cited in Lewis, *Life in Egypt*, 33.

30 E. A. E. Reymond, *From the Records of a Priestly Family from Memphis* (Wiesbaden, 1981), 220–21, 231; with corrections in Jan Quaegebeur, "The Genealogy of the Memphite High Priest Family in the Hellenistic Period," in Dorothy J. Crawford, Jan Quaegebeur and Willy Clarysse (eds.), *Studies on Ptolemaic Memphis*, Studia Hellenistica 24 (Leuven, 1980), 43–81.

31 M. Stead, "The high priest of Alexandria and all Egypt," in R. S. Bagnall et al. (eds.), *Proceedings of the XVIth International Congress of Papyrology 1980* (Ann Arbor, MI, 1981), 411–18; vs. Milne, *A History of Egypt under Roman Rule* (2nd revised edn., London, 1924), 11, 181, who attributes this title to the reign of Augusus.

32 N. Lewis, *Life in Egypt*, 92–93; Bowman, *Egypt After the Pharaohs*, 179–81.

33 BGU 1199; N. Lewis, *Life in Egypt*, 180.

34 J. E. G. Whitehorne, "P. Lond. II, 359 and Tuscus' list of temple perquisites," *Chronique d'Égypte*, 53 (1978), 321–28; O. Montevecchi, "*Graphai hieron*," *Aegyptus*, 12 (1932), 317–28.

certification before the provincial administrator (*strategos* of the nome) that the candidate was of priestly descent and unblemished, and thus entitled to the restricted rite of circumcision.[35] In return for such social isolation, the temple hierarchy was provided with a government subvention (*syntaxis*), and the upper echelons were exempt from taxation and compulsory public service.[36] From these Roman restrictions derives the later stereotyped image of cloistered, ascetic Egyptian priests, devoted to purity and contemplation and "enduring hunger and thirst and paucity of food during their whole life."[37]

The restricted acceptance accorded the native clergy parallels that granted to Demotic, the indigenous language and script. Unlike the Ptolemies, the Roman emperors never authorized trilingual decrees, which would have certified the official legitimacy of the Egyptian language. While no formal policy against Demotic is known, the use of Demotic contracts declines precipitously after AD 50, with only isolated examples continuing into the reign of Marcus Aurelius. Roman administration, conducted in Latin and Greek, probably discouraged the recognition of documents in a third language incomprehensible to imperial officials. To be valid in cases of lawsuit, contracts had to be registered with the official archives, and such registries operated exclusively in Greek. Native courts were also discontinued, so that legal proceedings and relevant instruments were necessarily in Greek, or in Greek translation. For purely practical reasons, Egyptians increasingly switched from Demotic to Greek scribes. "Demotic documentation was a victim, or casualty, of the Roman annexation of Egypt."[38]

Despite bureaucratic restrictions, written Demotic flourished, and in some genres actually expanded, until the Christianization of the province in the late fourth century. Religious texts, formerly confined to hieroglyphs or hieratic, first appear in the "secular" Demotic script in the final years BC.[39] The second century in particular witnessed a resurgence of Demotic writings in religious, literary, and scientific fields associated with temple scriptoria.[40]

[35] David and van Groningen, *Papyrological Primer*, 127–28.

[36] Richard Gordon, "Religion in the Roman Empire: the civic compromise and its limits," in Mary Beard and John North (eds.), *Pagan Priests* (Ithaca, 1990), 241–42.

[37] Chaeremon, frags. 10–11, in P. W. van der Horst, *Chaeremon*, Etudes préliminaires aux religions orientales dans l'Empire romain 101 (Leiden, 1984), 16–23.

[38] See N. Lewis, "The demise of the Demotic document: when and why," *Journal of Egyptian Archaeology*, 79 (1993), 276–81 (quote on p. 277), and the present author's comments therein. Further late Demotic documents in K.-Th. Zauzich, "Spätdemotische Papyrusurkunden III," *Enchoria*, 4 (1974), 71–82; and idem, "Spätdemotische Papyrusurkunden IV," *Enchoria*, 7 (1977), 151–80.

[39] For one of the first examples, see Mark Smith, *The Mortuary Texts of Papyrus BM 10507*, Catalogue of Demotic Papyri in the British Museum III (London, 1987), 19.

[40] W. J. Tait, "Demotic Literature and Egyptian Society," in Janet H. Johnson (ed.), *Life in a Multi-Cultural Society. Egypt from Cambyses to Constantine and Beyond*, SAOC 51 (Chicago, 1992), 303–10.

Proficiency in Demotic and the older scripts was expected of priestly candidates, and the ancient hieroglyphic system was maintained beyond the prohibition of Pagan cults. During the reign of Trajan, in 107, the prominent town of Oxyrhynchus employed five hieroglyphic carvers for its temples to native deities.[41] By the second century, priests of the Fayyum metropolis of Narmuthis (Medinet Madi), who provided services to smaller regional shrines, conducted internal business in mixed Demotic and Greek.[42] Experimentation with the Greek and Egyptian scripts continued in priestly circles. Devised to record vowels in Pagan incantations, the resulting "Coptic" script was ultimately adopted by Christian writers to facilitate the spread of biblical literacy among the indigenous population.[43]

The vitality of Egyptian religious culture in the face of official hostility or lack of interest is manifest in its contemporary penchant for adaptability. For the Latin state, the official cult of the Roman emperor was readily absorbed within pharaonic ruler worship.[44] For the Hellenistic population, Egyptian themes predominated in funerary contexts such as the Alexandrian catacombs of Kūm al-Shiqāf (Qom es-Shugafa),[45] while Greek residents in the Fayyūm and Oxyrhynchus revered as city patrons the crocodile Sobek (Souchos) and the hippopotamus Taweret (Thoeris).[46] For the native elite, Greek portraiture replaced traditional burial masks to produce the celebrated "Fayyūm portraits" of the first to fourth centuries.[47] Syncretistic terra-cotta figurines of deities occupied the household shrines of both sections of the population.

Not all religious reaction was so harmonious. Priestly rancor at Roman misrule appears both in isolated revolts (as in AD 71–175) and in apocalyptic literature like "The Potter's Prophesy," decreeing the downfall of Roman

41 P. Oxy. 1029; see Bowman, *Egypt After the Pharaohs*, 179.

42 Paolo Gallo, "The Wandering Personnel of the Temple of Narmuthis in the Faiyum and Some Toponyms of the Meris of Polemon," in Johnson, *Life in a Multi-Cultural Society*, 119–31.

43 R. K. Ritner, "Coptic," in Peter T. Daniels and William Bright (eds.), *The World's Writing Systems* (Oxford, 1996), 287–90.

44 Elanor Huzar, "Emperor Worship in Julio-Claudian Egypt," *Aufstieg und Niedergang der römischen Welt*, II, §18.5 (Berlin, 1995), 3092–143; Heinz Heinen, "Vorstufen und Anfänge des Herrscherkultes im römischen Ägypen," *Aufstieg und Niedergang der römischen Welt*, II, §18.5, 3144–80; and Jean-Claude Grenier, "L'Empereur et le Pharaon," *Aufstieg und Niedergang der römischen Welt*, II, §18.5, 3181–94.

45 Françoise Dunand, "Pratiques et croyances funéraires en Égypte romaine," *Aufstieg und Niedergang der römischen Welt*, II, §18.5, 3216–32.

46 Cf. John Whitehorne, "The Pagan Cults of Roman Oxyrhynchus," *Aufstieg und Niedergang der römischen Welt*, II, §18.5, 3050–91.

47 Lorelei H. Corcoran, *Portrait Mummies from Roman Egypt (I–IV Centuries AD)*, SAOC 56 (Chicago, 1995); idem, "Evidence for the Survival of Pharaonic Religion in Roman Egypt: The Portrait Mummy," *Aufstieg und Niedergang der römischen Welt*, II, §18.5, 3316–32.

authority and the reinstitatement of pharaonic rule.[48] Though of certain Egyptian origin, the prophesy circulated in Greek copies until the end of the third century.

All Egyptians had cause to resent the oppressive Roman system of taxation. At the instigation of Augustus, a new capitation tax was levied upon male Egyptians between the ages of fourteen and sixty. The full rate of this poll tax, or *laographia*, varied greatly between districts, from 12 drachmas in the Hermopolite nome to 40 drachmas in the prosperous Fayyūm. Only natives paid the full amount. Romans, citizens of Greek cities and certain priests were exempt, and nome metropolites paid a reduced rate. Egyptians alone contributed an additional dike tax of $6\frac{2}{3}$ drachmas and a "pig tax" of about 2 drachmas. Such taxes were paid to the state, upon which most regional services were financially dependent. For purposes of collection, a formal "house by house" census was instituted at fourteen-year intervals, corresponding to the age of male majority. All individuals registered in their home districts, indicating heads of households, inhabitants and distinguishing marks.[49] Births and deaths required individual registration.[50]

Corresponding cadastral surveys listed agricultural properties and owners, with tax and irrigation categories. Paid in kind, the land tax provided the primary source of revenue for the province and was often ruthlessly collected by zealous tax farmers, who profited personally from any surplus. To these basic taxes were added well over 100 further charges and surcharges upon individual goods and services, sales and transport. Further impositions came in the form of "liturgies," compulsory acts of public service entailing either physical labor ("corporeal") or payment ("patrimonial"). Roman use of liturgies in Egypt was unparalleled in the empire, affecting all residents except the privileged classes and fathers of five or more children. Elite priests, veterans, women, the aged and infirm were freed from corporeal liturgies. The liturgic system was expanded throughout the Roman era, replacing even tax-farming by AD 117.

In aggregate, the taxes were exceptionally burdensome upon the native cultivators, and in time affected even the prosperous elite. A distinctive response among the Egyptian population was the unusual custom of

48 P. Oxy. 2332; in E. Lobel and C. H. Roberts, *The Oxyrhynchus Papyri, Part XXII*, Graeco-Roman Memoirs 31 (London, 1954), 89–99; Ludwig Koenen, "Die Prophezeiungen des 'Töpfers'," *Zeitschrift für Papyrologie und Epigraphik*, 2 (1968), 178–209; idem, "The Prophecies of a Potter: A Prophecy of World Renewal Becomes an Apocalypse," in Deborah H. Samuel (ed.), *Proceedings of the Twelfth International Congress of Papyrology*, American Studies in Papyrology 7 (Toronto, 1970), 249–54; idem, "A Supplementary Note on the Date of the Oracle of the Potter," *Zeitschrift für Papyrologie und Epigraphik*, 54 (1984), 9–13; and Robert K. Ritner, *The Mechanics of Ancient Egyptian Magical Practice*, SAOC 54 (Chicago, 1993), 152.

49 Examples in Jones, *History of Rome*, 256–57, 259–60.

50 Robert K. Ritner, "Poll Tax on the Dead," *Enchoria*, 15 (1988), 205–07.

brother–sister marriage, specifically forbidden to resident Romans by regulation 23 of the "private account." Sibling marriage preserved inherited properties from fragmentation, ensuring some degree of family prosperity. While religious and other influences have been invoked to explain the custom,[51] a neglected ancient Egyptian text makes the financial motive explicit. The "Chester Beatty Dream Book" explains that "if a man see himself in a dream copulating with his sister: Good. It means the transferal to him of property."[52] Consanguineous marriage was ultimately prohibited throughout the empire by a decree of Diocletian in AD 295, as part of a general reorganization of an empire on the verge of political collapse.

On the political level, Roman efforts to enforce security in Egypt were largely successful until the third century, and an overview of the official history of the province is fairly straightforward. After the conquest of Egypt by Octavian in 30 BC, the first prefect, C. Cornellius Gallus (30–29 BC), faced the only significant external threat to Roman authority in Egypt for three centuries. Inspired and abetted by the Meroitic kingdom to the south, a revolt in the Upper Egyptian Thebaid was rapidly suppressed. The prefect's subsequent arrogation of imperial prerogatives – including the erection of a trilingual victory decree at Philae following Ptolemaic royal precedent – resulted in his summary dismissal, disgrace and suicide.[53]

Deriving from pretensions to the Egyptian crown extending back to the Nubian Twenty-Fifth Dynasty (ca. 751–656 BC), the Meroitic threat continued under Gallus's successor Petronius, when in 25 BC a force of 30,000 Meroitic troops captured the border settlements of Aswan, Elephantine and Philae.[54] The counterinvasion by Petronius, with 10,000 infantry and 800 cavalry, extended as far south as the old Nubian capital of Napata above the Fourth Cataract and induced the enemy queen (Meroitic "kandake") to sue for peace. Petronius withdrew, stationing 400 men at the fortress of Premis (Qasr Ibrim). A new Meroitic assault on Premis brought Petronius south again in 23 BC, and his successful defense of that fort led to a formal treaty at Samos two years later. Rome maintained the "Dodecaschoenus" extending

[51] See J. Černý, "Consanguineous Marriages in Pharaonic Egypt," *Journal of Egyptian Archaeology*, 40 (1954), 23–29; Schafik Allam, "Geschwisterehe," in W. Helck and E. Otto (eds.), *Lexikon der Ägyptologie*, vol. II (Wiesbaden, 1977), cols. 568–69; K. Hopkins, *Comparative Studies in Society and History*, 22 (1980), 303–54; N. Lewis, *Life in Egypt*, 43–44, 216.

[52] P. BM 10683, col. 3/8, in A. Gardiner, *Chester Beatty Gift*. 2 vols. (HPBM 3) (London, 1935), 12, plate 5.

[53] H. G. Lyons and L. Borchardt, "Eine trilingue Inschrift von Philae," *Sitz. Berl. Akad.* (1896), 469–82; H. Schäfer, "Zur Inschrift des C. Cornelius Gallus," *Zeitschrift für Ägyptische Sprache und Altertumskunde*, 34 (1896), 91.

[54] For Meroitic–Roman relations, see Derek A. Welsby, *The Kingdom of Kush* (London, 1996), 67–70; William Y. Adams, *Nubia: Corridor to Africa* (London, 1977), 338–44; and P. L. Shinnie, *Meroe: A Civilization of the Sudan* (London, 1967), 43–52.

to Maharraqa (Hiera Sykaminos), 80 km south of the First Cataract, while Meroe controlled the greater portion of Nubia. With the conclusion of these hostilities, the southern border area of Egypt remained calm until the scattered raids of the nomadic Blemmyes, beginning under Decius (AD 249–51). Meroe itself became an active trading partner of Rome, maintaining a pharaonically inspired kingdom well after Egypt itself was largely Christianized.[55]

The disputed Nubian territory preserves most of the official construction projects credited to Augustus. At Kalabsha (Talmis), a small Ptolemaic shrine was completed in the name of the new conqueror, designated simply as "The Roman." The larger adjacent temple, erected by the late Ptolemies, was first decorated under the emperor. With the developed titulary of "Autocrator Caesar, living forever, beloved of Ptah and Isis," the cartouche of Augustus was added to sites at Philae and Debod, with variant forms at Dakka and Elephantine. A more elaborate undertaking was the newly erected Dendur temple, dedicated to two divinized "heroes" who had drowned in the Nile. In Egypt itself, Augustus appears at Armant, Dendera, Deir el-Medineh and Shenhūr.

Little need be said of the succeeding reigns of Tiberius (AD 14–37), Caligula (AD 37–41) or Claudius (AD 41–54), which are characterized by a relative tranquility marred only by simmering unrest between Greek and Jewish factions in Alexandria. An unauthorized visit to Egypt by the eastern governor Germanicus provoked censure from Tiberius.[56] Caligula flirted with Egyptian religious cults in Rome, formally restoring the worship of Egyptian deities banished from the capital since the days of Augustus.[57] Claudius tactfully rebuffed Alexandrian requests for a self-governing senate, while cautioning Greeks to tolerate Jewish customs and Jews to cease agitation for privileged status.[58] The Greco-Egyptian reaction is preserved in the "Acts of the Pagan Martyrs," emphatically anti-Roman tracts popular in both Alexandria and the countryside, which prefigure literary martyrdoms

[55] For the limits of Hellenization in Meroe, see S. Burstein, "The Hellenistic Fringe: The Case of Meroë," in P. Green (ed.), *Hellenistic History and Culture* (Berkeley, 1993), 38–66. For Meroitic religion, see Inge Hofmann, "Die meroitische Religion. Staatskult und Volksfrömmigkeit," *Aufstieg und Niedergang der römischen Welt*, II, §18.5, 2801–68; and Janice Yellin, "Meroitic Funerary Religion," *Aufstieg und Niedergang der römischen Welt*, II, §18.5, 2869–92.

[56] Tacitus, *Annals*, II.LX–LXI. Cf. Hunt and Edgar, *Select Papyri II*, 76–79; Jones, *History of Rome*, 197–98, §86; and L. Kákosy, "Probleme der Religion im römerzeitlichen Ägypten," *Aufstieg und Niedergang der römischen Welt*, II, §18.5, 2908.

[57] E. Köberlein, *Caligula und die ägyptischen Kulte* (Meisenham am Glan, 1962); M. Malaise, *Les conditions de pénétration et de diffusion des cultes égyptiens en Italie*, Études préliminaires aux religions orientales dans l'Empire romain 22 (Leiden, 1972), 397; Kákosy, "Probleme der Religion," 2910.

[58] See Hunt and Edgar, *Select Papyri II*, 78–89; Jones, *History of Rome*, 223–26.

of the Christian persecutions.[59] As patron of Egyptian monuments, Tiberius is well represented at Armant, Aswan, Athribis, Coptos, Debod, Dendera, Diospolis Parva (Hū), Edfu, Karnak, Kom Ombo (Ombos), Luxor, Philae and Shenhūr. Caligula appears at Coptos and Dendera, as does Claudius, who is further attested at Aswan, Athribis, Esna, Kom Ombo and Philae.

The reign of Nero (AD 54–68) witnessed a "scientific" expedition to Meroe, perhaps intended as a scouting mission for an aborted military invasion.[60] If so, any plans for conquest were halted by the Judean revolt of AD 66. Nero's interest in the south may have been sparked by his tutor Chaeremon, an Egyptian priest, Stoic philosopher and extraordinary example of social advancement accorded to a member of the native Egyptian elite.[61] Nero's official sponsorship of the Egyptian elite is recorded at Aswan, Coptos, Dendera, Karanis, Kom Ombo, Tehneh (Akoris) and in the Dakhleh Oasis.

With the death of Nero and the end of the Julio-Claudian dynasty in AD 68, local authority resided in the hands of the first Alexandrian-born prefect, Tiberius Julius Alexander, descended from a Hellenized Jewish family related to the theologian Philo. Securely in office during the brief reigns of Galba (68–69), Otho (69) and Vitellius (69), it was this prefect who formally proclaimed Vespasian emperor in Alexandria on July 1, 69. If somewhat diminished, the Egyptian harvest was still viewed as "key to the grain supply" (*claustra annonae*) of Rome, and Vespasian's acquisition of this resource contributed to his victory and the establishment of the Flavian dynasty.[62] In Egypt, the transitory Galba and Otho both appear in reliefs at the small Eighteenth Dynasty temple of Medinet Habu. Of Vitellius there is no trace.

During his momentous visit to Alexandria, the first by an emperor since Augustus, Vespasian (AD 69–79) was welcomed into the hippodrome as a proper Egyptian Pharaoh, being proclaimed the son of the creator Amon and Serapis incarnate. The designation "son of Amon" evokes not only phar-

59 H. A. Musurillo, *The Acts of the Pagan Martyrs. Acta Alexandrinorum* (Oxford, 1954); N. Lewis, *Life in Egypt*, 199–201.

60 Accounts are found in Seneca (VI.8.3) and Pliny (*Natural History* VI. XXXV, 181–87). F. Hintze, "Meroitic Chronology: Problems and Prospects," *Meroitica*, 1 (1973), 131, posits two expeditions, one in AD 62, another in 66 or 67. For interpretations, see Welsby, *Kingdom of Kush*, 70; Adams, *Nubia*, 341–42; and Karl-Heinz Priese, "Zur Ortsliste der römischen Meroe-Expedition unter Nero," *Meroitica*, 1 (1973), 123–26. Pliny's statement that Nero's expedition was preparatory to "an attack on Ethiopia" (*Natural History VI*, XXXV, 181) has generally been interpreted as hostile to Meroe, but Milne, *History of Egypt*, 22–23, suggests that the expedition was intended to support Meroe against the rising power of Auxum.

61 van der Horst, *Chaeremon*.

62 Rickman, *Corn Supply of Ancient Rome*, 67.

aonic precedent, but the famous greeting accorded Alexander the Great at the Siwa Oasis. The identification with the Greco-Egyptian deity Serapis, chief patron of Alexandria and the former Ptolemaic kingdom, catered to more local and contemporary taste. Vespasian demonstrated the validity of these claims by healing a blind and a crippled man by means of magical spitting and trampling, both traditional native ritual techniques.[63] The family's interest in Egyptian religion was demonstrated again by Vespasian's son Titus in AD 70, when he formally attended the consecration of a new Apis bull at Memphis following his suppression of the Judean revolt and the destruction of the Jerusalem temple. Reprisal for the Jewish rebellion affected Egypt directly in AD 73, with the sacking of the Leontopolite temple, founded by the fugitive High Priest Onias in the reign of Ptolemy VI (180–145 BC). In contrast, Vespasian favored native temple construction at Esna, Kom Ombo, Medinet Habu, Silsileh and in the Dakhleh Oasis.

The succeeding reigns of Titus (79–81), Domitian (81–96) and Nerva (96–98) left a lesser imprint upon the country, though official Alexandrian coinage now recognized Egyptian deities of the provincial nomes, evidence of a pro-Egyptian policy attested in Italy as well. Domitian founded temples to Isis and Serapis in Benvenuto and Rome itself, utilizing pharaonic trappings to add further legitimacy to imperial pretensions. In Rome, Domitian's emphasis on absolute authority, with scorn for the senate, led to his assassination and the end of the Flavian dynasty. The throne passed to the former consul and likely conspirator Nerva, who abandoned the principle of imperial heredity in favor of the adoption of qualified heirs. In Egypt, ongoing temple projects recorded the sponsorship of Titus at Dakhleh and Esna, Domitian at Akhmim, Armant, Dendera, Esna, Kom Ombo, Philae, and Silsileh, with Nerva attested uniquely at Esna.

With the accession of Trajan (98–117), native cults received continued support at Dendera, Esna, al-Jabalayn (Gebelein), Kalabsha, Kom Ombo, Medinet Habu and Philae. A temple at Dendera to Nea Aphrodite, identifying the empress Plotina with Hathor, represents the first direct association of the imperial family (beyond the person of the emperor) with native deities. More in evidence, however, was religious disharmony in the form of new Jewish revolts sparked by the appearance of a supposed "messiah" in Cyrene. An initial outbreak in Alexandria in 114 was quickly suppressed, but the transferal of troops in the following year for a Parthian campaign ignited three years of vicious guerrilla warfare throughout the countryside (115–17). Massacres of Greeks by roving Jewish terrorists led to the arming of the Egyptian peasantry, an act of desperation echoing Ptolemaic policy prior to the battle of Raphia in 217 BC. The revolt was crushed, and the

63 The practice parallels both ancient Egyptian healing techniques and that used by Jesus; see Ritner, *Mechanics of Magical Practice*, 90, nn. 429–30.

Jewish community in Egypt was effectively extinguished until the third century. So great was the social impact of the hostilities that the city of Oxyrhynchus still celebrated its deliverance from Jewish brigands more than eighty years later. The end of Trajan's reign marks as well the full development of the liturgy system, with its extension to tax collection and the elimination of tax-farming.

To Hadrian (117–138) fell the task of restoring stability to the country, and in 118 he decreed a reduction in land taxes in reaction to poor agricultural production during the insurrection (resulting both from destruction and conscription). A brief native revolt during the consecration of an Apis bull in 122, a far less successful counterpart to the native revolts against the Ptolemies after Raphia, may also be attributable to the arming of the peasantry. In his fourteenth and fifteenth years (130–31), Hadrian and his court paid a state visit to Egypt lasting some eight to ten months. Touristic aspects of the trip included a lion hunt in the Libyan desert, a Nile cruise, and a morning visit to the colossi of Memnon in western Thebes, where Balbilla, attendant of Empress Sabina, carved commemorative graffiti on the left leg of the "singing" colossus.

The most significant testament to the journey was the founding of the Greek city of Antinoopolis, memorializing the drowning of Hadrian's youthful lover, Antinous. According to Egyptian theology, such a death entailed a special identification with the drowned Osiris, god of the underworld. Under Augustus, "deification by drowning" had provided the rationale for the native hero cults at the remote temple of Dendur, but Hadrian's Egyptianizing cult of Antinous was extended throughout the empire. The receipt by Antinous of traditional rituals ("opening the mouth") was duly recorded in hieroglyphs on the last commissioned obelisk, thereafter erected in Rome.[64] Hadrian's religious advisor was perhaps the Egyptian poet and priest Pancrates, later associated with the emperor in magical writings.[65] Antinoopolis became the fourth Greek *polis* with citizenship rights in Egypt, and its debt to indigenous religion seems acknowledged in a special privilege accorded its citizens, who were free to intermarry with Egyptians.

To ensure the financial success of his foundation, Hadrian in 137 ordered the construction of a road linking the new city with the Red Sea port of Berenike, in competition with the older trade route to the Nile at Coptos.[66]

64 The Barberini Obelisk, see M. Smith, *Mortuary Texts*, 25–26.

65 See Antonio Garzya, "Pancrates," in *Atti del XVII Congresso Internazionale di Papyrologia*, vol. II (Naples, 1984), 319–25; H. D. Betz (ed.), *The Greek Magical Papyri* (Chicago, 1986), 83 (PGM IV, 2446–55), and R. Ritner, "Egyptian Magical Practice under the Roman Empire," in *Aufstieg und Niedergang der römischen Welt*, II, §18.5, 3358. For the theme of the Egyptian magician, see Fulvio De Salvia, "La figura del mago egizio nella tradizione letteraria greco-romana," in A. Roccati and A. Siliotti (eds.), *La Magia in Egitto* (Milan, 1987), 343–65.

66 OGIS 701; in Jones, *History of Rome*, 198–99, §88.

The "Via Hadriana" may well have diverted the valuable Indian spice trade from the Wadi Hammamat, as the associated Red Sea port at Quseir (probably to be identified with Myos Hormos) declined following the reign of Hadrian.[67] Aside from Antinoopolis, Hadrian's patronage is recorded at Armant, Dendera, Esna and Philae. Hadrian's reign produced a contemporary vogue for "Egyptomania," epitomized by the "Canopus" section of the emperor's villa on the Tiber.

The reign of Antoninus Pius (138–161), first of the Antonines, began auspiciously with the "millennialist" celebration in 139 of a completed Sothic Cycle, signaling the return to accuracy of the wandering civil calendar.[68] The substantial reign witnessed the last significant temple construction in Egypt, with additions at Armant, Dendera, Coptos, Esna, Medamud, Medinet Habu and Tod. Local peace was broken only by an Alexandrian riot in 153 that resulted in the unprecedented slaying of the prefect. Nevertheless, the emperor reportedly visited the city subsequently and sponsored the construction of a new hippodrome and city gates.

Alexandrian prosperity was enhanced by its control of the Indian mercantile trade, passing through the Red Sea and the Nile valley. In contrast, the countryside now entered upon a period of prolonged economic decline, owing to years of social disruption, over-taxation and desultory maintenance of critical irrigation systems. Liturgical service, theoretically a voluntary honor, was made compulsory for lack of willing volunteers. Impoverished nominees sought to evade the system's financial burden by simply abandoning their agricultural property and fleeing (*anachorēsis*).[69] In 154, the prefect's New Year's edict denounced as outlaws those "who fled from certain liturgies because of the poverty all about them," offering an amnesty to these delinquents "still living away from home in fear."[70] As the government failed to lower the grain assessments against such shrinking villages, remaining families were increasingly unable to meet the state's obligations and fled themselves, producing a downward spiral of declining production and population.[71] Whole villages became abandoned, and the

[67] Sources and discussion in Donald Whitcomb, "Quseir al-Qadim and the Location of Myos Hormos," *Topoi*, 6 (1996), 747–72.

[68] Lacking a "leap day", the native calendar strayed over time, so that its New Year's day no longer coincided with the theoretical new year, marked by the heliacal rising of the star Sirius. The official and theoretical cycles intersected every 1,460 years. Alexandria commemorated the Antonine celebration by issuing special coins displaying the phoenix.

[69] For the phenomenon, see N. Lewis, "Μερισμὸς ἀνακεχωρηκότων: an aspect of the Roman oppression in Egypt," *Journal of Egyptian Archaeology* 23 (1937), 63–75; and idem, "A reversal of a tax policy in Roman Egypt," *Greek, Roman, and Byzantine Studies*, 34 (1993), 101–18.

[70] N. Lewis, *Life in Egypt*, 183. For an example of avoidance of nomination from AD 192, see Jones, *History of Rome*, 230–31.

[71] N. Lewis, *Life in Egypt*, 181– 84, 203–04.

desert reclaimed once productive sites throughout the Faiyum. Conditions were set for a popular rebellion.

Social tensions erupted during the tenure of Marcus Aurelius (161–80) with a fierce revolt (171–75) waged by native "herdsmen" (*boukolai*) led by the priest Isidorus. Having routed the resident Roman forces, the Egyptians were subdued only after the arrival of fresh detachments under Avidius Cassius, governor of Syria and son of a former Egyptian prefect. Once successful, however, Cassius caused his troops to proclaim him emperor after a false report of the death of Aurelius. Recognized in Egypt and much of the east for three months in 175, Cassius was murdered by a centurion. Aurelius toured the repentant provinces and Alexandria in 176, granting pardon to the city and the family of Cassius. Revolutionary devastation was augmented by an outbreak of plague in Egypt, as in much of the empire, from 165 to 180. Physical evidence of the pestilence has now come to light in the Theban Valley of the Queens, where a mass grave (Tomb 53) contained some 276 bodies covered in quicklime.[72] The dramatic fate of these individuals is in marked contrast to that of most Roman-era high-status native burials in the area, which give evidence of a sedentary population with little trauma and a prolonged survival of the elderly and infirm.

Despite the revolt of Isidorus, Egyptian religion had come to the aid of Aurelius during the Danube campaign of 172 in the person of Harnuphis, a priestly magician who reportedly brought rain to rescue the Roman troops.[73] As Pharaoh, Aurelius is noted at Dendera, Esna, Kom Ombo and Philae. Perhaps in response to the native revolt, however, the reign of Aurelius marks the last use of Demotic ostraca to record official tax receipts; all subsequent receipts are in Greek.[74] The latest Demotic papyrus contract is attested in the same reign (175/76).[75]

Commodus (180–192), less gracious than his predecessor, promptly ordered the murder of the pardoned family of Cassius. The incident may be reflected in the last of the "Acts of the Pagan Martyrs," in which the unpopular emperor is rebuked as "tyrannical, boorish and uncultured."[76]

[72] André Macke and Christiane Macke-Ribet, "Paléopathologie osseuse de la population égyptienne d'époque romaine provenant de la Vallée des Reines," in S. Curto et al. (eds.), *Sesto Congresso Internazionale di Egittologia: Atti*, vol. II (Turin, 1993), 299–306.

[73] J. Guey, "Encore la 'pluie miraculeuse', mage et dieu," *Revue de philologie, de littérature et d'histoire anciennes*, 3me sér., vol. XXII, (Paris, 1948), 16–62. A belated attempt to "Christianize" the miracle was made by Eusebius, *The History of the Church*, v. 5.

[74] For private transactions, isolated examples of Demotic ostraca continue into the reign of Septimius Severus; see P. W. Pestman, *Chronologie égyptienne d'après les textes démotiques (322 av. J.-C.–453 ap. J.-C.)*, Papyrologica Lugduno-Batava, 15 (Leiden, 1967), 109–11.

[75] P. Tebtunis Botti 3; see N. Lewis, "Demise of the Demotic Document," 276.

[76] See Bowman, *Egypt After the Pharaohs*, 43; Milne, *History of Egypt*, 55.

The economic decline of the country, already noted under Antoninus, had become sufficiently critical that the annual grain supply to Rome required supplementation by a north African grain fleet. A lowered silver standard with a corresponding discontinuation of bronze coinage are yet further indications of financial ills. Commodus is the last emperor widely attested as pharaonic patron, appearing at Armant, Esna, Kom Ombo and Philae. The subsequent decrease in pharaonic representations does not signal an official change in attitude toward native culture, but rather a general lack of resources available for clergy and temple construction, at first exacerbated by the murder of Commodus and uncertain succession.

In 193, as in 69 a year of four emperors, claim to the throne was made by Pertinax, Didius Julianus, Pescennius Niger and Septimius Severus. Though proclaimed emperor in Rome on January 1, Pertinax was recognized in Egypt only twenty-two days before his assassination on March 28, and news of his death did not reach the countryside until after mid-May. His Roman successor, Didius Julianus, was never acknowledged. By June, dating protocol and an issue of Alexandrian coinage show that local allegiance had been given instead to Piscennius Niger, general of Syria and former popular commander at the Egyptian border fortress of Aswan.

The successful contender to replace the Antonine dynasty was Septimius Severus (193–211), who occupied Rome, north Africa and Egypt before defeating Niger at the battle of Cyzicus on the Propontis. Egyptian adherence to the Severan cause was secured by February 13, as proved by a papyrus from Arsinoe in the Fayyūm. Severus and his family toured the province in his eighth year (199–200), following the itinerary of Hadrian. The visit of Severus is recorded by a prominent relief at Esna, where the emperor is shown accompanied by his wife Julia and his sons Caracalla and Geta.[77] The tour included the obligatory visit to the colossus of Memnon, which the emperor repaired so that it never sang again. More significant, if equally flawed, were the proposed administrative and legal reforms. Alexandria and the nome capitals were granted long-desired senates, villagers were exempted from compulsory service in the Greek cities, and nominees to liturgies might avoid service without imprisonment or loss of status by ceding all real property to the state.[78] The new senates had little independent authority, however, and the reforms seem rather an attempt to improve tax collection.

At the outset of the imperial visit (199), the prefect Q. Aemilius Saturninus issued a decree against processional oracles, banning a central feature

[77] S. Sauneron, "Les querelles impériales vues à travers les scènes du temple d'Ésné," *Bulletin de l'Institut Français d'Archéologie Orientale*, 51 (1952), 111–21.

[78] See Bowman, *Egypt After the Pharaohs*, 44, n. 41, 66; N. Lewis, *Life in Egypt*, 183. For typical acts of city councils, see Jones, *History of Rome*, 232–35.

of native temple cult.[79] The ban was largely unsuccessful, though official condemnation ultimately did drive the procedure underground; later Demotic oracles are all private procedures disguised by cipher. The Greek tale of Thessalos recounts the events of such an oracle conducted secretly by a priest in Thebes. Immediately following the visit (201), a more portentous religious controversy erupted in Egypt, with the first of many anti-Christian persecutions. As chronicled by Eusebius, the martyred included not only Alexandrians, but converts "from the whole of Egypt and the Thebaid," suggesting an initial spread of Christianity among the native population.[80] The theologian Origen, orphaned during this Severan purge, is the first author to distinguish "Egyptian" and "Greek" Christians, and biblical papyri begin to appear upcountry about the same time.[81]

If the reign of Severus was characterized by increased social division within the Roman state, that of his son Caracalla (211–17) began with an unprecedented extension of Roman citizenship to all inhabitants of the empire (212). Adopted by Caracalla as a sign of descent from Marcus Aurelius, the family name Aurelius (feminine Aurelia) was assigned as a hereditary forename to all new "Romans" and thus became particularly common among Egyptians. Aside from this formal dignity, citizenship now carried few prerogatives and some tax liabilities (such as the inheritance tax). Like his father's extension of city councils, Caracalla's grant seems more a matter of symbolism than substance.

The accession of Caracalla ignited a rivalry with his brother and joint emperor Geta, whose murder in 212 was followed by a general *damnatio memoriae* and the erasure of his image at Esna. References to Geta could prove a liability, as demonstrated during Caracalla's Egyptian visit in 215. Alexandrians had mocked the emperor's pretensions of heroism and publicly scoffed at his claim of self-defense in Geta's murder. In retaliation, Caracalla ordered the death of the prominent delegation that had come out to welcome him and allowed several days of indiscriminate plunder and murder by his troops throughout the city. Thereafter, public gatherings were suspended, the police presence was increased, and native Egyptians were expelled from the city except on matters of business and religion. Earlier attempts to excuse Caracalla's savagery for reasons of "public security" seem rather dubious,[82] but the expulsion of natives was motivated less by

79 P. Yale inv. 299; see Ritner, *Mechanics of Magical Practice*, 217–20.

80 Eusebius, *The History of the Church*, vi.1; see Colin H. Roberts, *Manuscript, Society and Belief in Early Christian Egypt* (London, 1979), 5, 65. See further E. A. E. Reymond and J. W. B. Barns, *Four Martyrdoms from the Pierpont Morgan Coptic Codices* (London, 1973), 16.

81 See Roberts, *Manuscript, Society and Belief*, 64–73.

82 Milne, *History of Egypt*, 64.

simple racism than by the traditional desire to maintain rural productivity through serf labor:

> The ones to be prevented are those who flee the countryside where they belong in order to avoid farmwork, not those who converge upon Alexandria out of a desire to view the glorious city or come here in pursuit of a more cultural existence or on occasional business.[83]

True rustics, Caracalla noted, could be detected by their rude speech, dress and manners. Caracalla's naïve assessment notwithstanding, fugitive laborers had fled not from farmwork, but from ruinous taxation and prolonged governmental mismanagement.

Following the murder of Caracalla, the imperial throne was contested by his assassin Macrinus (217–18) and by Elagabalus (218–22), putative son of Caracalla and priest of the Syrian solar deity El-Gabaal at Emesa. More significantly, Elagabalus was the protégé of the influential Julia Maesa, his natural grandmother and Caracalla's maternal aunt. Breaking the Augustan prohibition on senatorial interference in Egypt, Macrinus sent a prefect and senator to administer the ruined province, which was no longer relevant to Roman survival.[84] News of the defeat and subsequent death of Macrinus at Antioch precipitated fierce rioting in Alexandria, in which the senator was killed and the prefect expelled. Macrinus is noted once at Kom Ombo;[85] Elagabalus is unattested in native sources. Scandalizing Roman convention regarding religion, sexuality and dress, Elagabalus was murdered by the praetorian guard on the orders of his grandmother, and his cousin Severus Alexander (222–35) became emperor.

Aside from protocols in Greek papyri, the new ruler is unnoted in Egypt, although he might have visited Alexandria. Clearly signaling Egypt's political insignificance, he appointed a mutineer from the Praetorian Guard as prefect (Epagathus, ca. 228). In the Persian war of 232, mutinous Egyptian contingents proved equally unreliable, reflecting the deteriorating state of the resident legions. Following a defeat by the Alamanni on the Rhine, Alexander was slain by his own troops, ending the Severan dynasty and

[83] N. Lewis, *Life in Egypt*, 202; see Hunt and Edgar, *Select Papyri II*, no. 215, 90–93. This critical passage is eliminated from the excerpted translation in Bowman, *Egypt After the Pharaohs*, 126, producing a somewhat distorted impression.

[84] One cannot accept Rickman's rejection of economic recession (*Corn Supply of Ancient Rome*, 233), loosely following Sherman L. Wallace, *Taxation in Egypt from Augustus to Diocletian* (New York, 1938), 350–52. Wallace does not deny the country's ruin, but reattributes the cause to corrupt officials rather than to inherent defects in the taxation system itself. See still J. Milne, "The Ruin of Egypt by Roman Mismanagement," *Journal of Roman Studies*, 17 (1927), 1–13.

[85] With his son Diadumenianus; see H. Gauthier, *Le Livre des Rois d'Égypte*, vol. V, "Les Empereurs Romains," MIFAO 21 (Cairo, 1917), 212.

beginning a succession of rival emperors of as little consequence to Egypt as was the province to them.

Elected by the army in Germany, Maximinus (235–238) was opposed for seventy-two days in 238 by the senatorial candidates Gordian I and his son Gordian II, and then by their successors, the co-emperors Balbinus and Pupienus (238). These last outlived the military assassination of Maximinus only to fall victim to Praetorian Guards after a ninety-nine-day reign. The throne then passed to the youth Gordian III (238–44), whose victorious campaign against Shapur I of Iran was cut short by his sudden death, probably at the instigation of his deputy Philip the Arab (244–49). As noted by Milne:

> The only way in which Egypt exercised any influence on the course of imperial policy about this time was through its poverty; the inability of the central government to collect the revenues in the Eastern provinces compelled Philip to make peace with the Goths on the Danube.[86]

The cartouche of Philip appears unobtrusively on the inner rear wall of Esna temple, where it has been supplanted by the name of the next military usurper, Trajanus Decius (249–51).[87] The last attestation of an emperor at Esna, this erasure constitutes as well the final instance of "surcharged cartouches," a traditional feature of dynastic quarrels throughout pharaonic history.

In contrast to the waning instances of imperial temple sponsorship was the pervasive growth of rural Christianity, first evident under Severus. The Alexandrian Patriarch Dionysus (247–64) became notable for actively recruiting converts from the indigenous, or "Coptic," inhabitants. Traditional cults were elaborate, expensive and increasingly arcane. Roman interference had crippled temple funding and marginalized the social role of the native priesthood and the written Demotic language. Projecting an enhanced status quo into the afterlife, Egyptian religion was inherently life-affirming, centered upon a royal intermediary equally human and divine. As life in Roman Egypt became increasingly onerous and the emperors remote and irrelevant, traditional theology proved less attractive. It is significant that the ancient pharaonic paradise became the Coptic Christian Hell (Amente). As temples were abandoned for economic or social reasons, Christianity filled the void with a comparable intermediary, a simplified theology[88] and a rejection of earthly bonds. No practice underlines the

[86] Milne, *History of Egypt*, 69.

[87] Sauneron, "Les querelles impériales," 118–21; R. Lepsius, "Der letzte Kaiser in den hieroglyphischen Inschriften," *Zeitschrift für Ägyptische Sprache und Altertumskunde*, 8 (1870), 25–30.

[88] Robert K. Ritner, "Horus on the Crocodiles: A Juncture of Religion and Magic in Late Dynastic Egypt," in W. K. Simpson (ed.), *Religion and Philosophy in Ancient Egypt* (New Haven, 1989), 114.

distinction so sharply as the martyrdoms actively sought by fervent Christian converts. The profession of Christianity became a form of social protest, with pagans castigated as alien "Hellenes."

Under Decius (250), an attempt was made to curtail the growing Christian disaffection by requiring proof of sacrifice before communal deities, stipulating that each citizen "made sacrifice and libation and tasted the victim's flesh." Numerous certificates of sacrifice (*libelli*) survive from Egypt, and while some Christians complied, many others were executed.[89] External as well as internal disturbances threatened. For the first time since the reign of Augustus, the southern border of Egypt came under attack, with raids by the nomadic Blemmyes along the Dodecaschoenus of Lower Nubia.[90] At Kalabsha, Roman occupation is last attested by an inscription dated to Philip.[91] In 251, Decius was slain by the Goths and the anti-Christian persecution lapsed. St. Antony (ca. 251–356), the father of monasticism, was born about the same time in the Egyptian village of Coma (Qiman al-Arus), some 75 km south of modern Cairo. Despite the general impression of economic hardship, certain regions did prosper in the middle of the third century. The vast Heroninos archive (ca. 247–70) from Theadelphia in the Fayyūm documents the flourishing properties of Appianus, "the best attested large private estate from the Roman empire."[92]

The turbulent reigns of Trebonianus Gallus (251–53) and Aemilian (253) are attested almost exclusively by Alexandrian coinage and Greek documentary protocols. In the final year of Gallus, an envoy of Meroe to Rome recorded his mission at Philae in the longest known graffito in Demotic.[93] Beset by constant Germanic invasions in the West and by renewed assaults of the Persian Shapur I in the East, Valerian (253–60) effectively partitioned the empire with his son Gallienus (253–68), anticipating the formal division under Diocletian. To divert attention from external disasters, Valerian reinstituted the Christian persecutions, requiring sacrifice and authorizing the seizure of clerical property.[94] If demonized by the Christian clergy, Valerian appears as a proper Pharaoh at Armant, acting as patron of the burial of Buchis, the resident sacred bull of the Thebaid. Valerian's capture by Shapur in 260 marks the nadir of Roman imperial history, thereafter styled the "Year of the Thirty Emperors," an estimate only somewhat exaggerated. In Syria, the legions proclaimed Macrianus and Quietus

89 Jones, *History of Rome*, 327.

90 See Karim Sadr, *The Development of Nomadism in Ancient Northeast Africa* (Philadelphia, 1991), 121–25.

91 I. G. R. 1356.

92 Dominic Rathbone, *Economic Rationalism and Rural Society in Third-Century* AD *Egypt* (Cambridge, 1991), quote on p. 3.

93 Philae no. 416, in F. Ll. Griffith, *Catalogue of the Demotic Graffiti of the Dodecaschoenus* (Oxford, 1937), 114–19 (AD 253).

94 See Jones, *History of Rome*, 327–30.

(260–61), who were recognized in Egypt as far south as Coptos. With their defeat, the Alexandrian mob compelled the prefect Aemilianus to accept imperial honors. Aemilianus successfully repelled Blemmye raids, which now extended beyond Lower Nubia into the Thebaid. By August 262, he had been defeated by the forces of Gallienus in pitched street battles across Alexandria that devastated the city and reduced its population by approximately two-thirds.[95]

Following the murder of Gallienus, the reigns of Claudius Gothicus (268–70), Quintillus (270) and Aurelian (270–75) found Egypt a source of contention between Rome and Zenobia, Queen of the rebellious state of Palmyra. Zenobia's son Vaballathus was proclaimed joint ruler in the East by Aurelian, but Palmyra declared independence in 271 and held Egypt for much of that year before it was recaptured by the Roman general, and future emperor, Probus. Palmyra and Alexandria revolted again in 272, now at the instigation of Firmus, a wealthy Alexandrian merchant with reputed economic ties to the Blemmyes.[96] After reducing Palmyra, Aurelian besieged Alexandria and forced the suicide of Firmus. In gratitude, Oxyrhynchus presented a golden statue of victory to the emperor.[97]

The reign of Tacitus (275–76) is unnoted in Egypt, and the elevation of his brother Florian (276) was successfully contested by Probus (276–82), backed by the Egyptian legions. Blemmye raiders continued to threaten Upper Egypt, penetrating as far north as Coptos and Ptolemais before they were defeated by Probus. The victorious Roman legions were then assigned to ignominious dike repair, reflecting the deterioration of the local infrastructure which continued unabated in the reigns of Carus (282–83), Carinus (283–85) and Numerian (283–84).

The first systematic reorganization was undertaken by Diocletian (284–305), who in 293 converted the empire into a "Tetrarchy" under two Augusti (Diocletian in the East, Maximian in the West) assisted by two Caesars (Galerius and Constantius Chlorus, respectively). Provinces throughout the empire were subdivided so that they doubled in number. These smaller units were grouped into thirteen dioceses under vicars (*vicarii*), with primary control granted to four praetorian prefects, each subject to a tetrarch. In Egypt, the Thebaid was made a distinct province. This fractioning of administrative units continued throughout the fourth and fifth centuries, while Egypt was reunited as a diocese of six provinces by about 371.[98] With smaller provinces, traditional nomes lost their administrative significance, and by 308 these were supplanted by subunits labeled *pagii*.

[95] See J. Grafton Tait, "Aemilianus the 'Tyrant'," *Journal of Egyptian Archaeology*, 10 (1924), 80–82.
[96] So Milne, *History of Egypt*, 76.
[97] Bowman, *Egypt After the Pharaohs*, 39–40 and 44.
[98] Bowman, *Egypt After the Pharaohs*, 78–81.

Financial reform was also attempted on a wide scale. In an effort to combat inflation, Diocletian decreed maximum limits upon prices and salaries throughout the empire, and the system of taxation was revised to give consideration to differences in soil and harvest. Adopted in Egypt in 297, the new taxation system had a variable rate determined annually, "the first budget in the history of finance."[99] After the reforms of Diocletian, Egypt lost much of the idiosyncratic character that it had retained since Augustus. For the first time in Roman Egypt, authority was divided between a civil administrator (*praeses*) and a military governor (*dux*), and Egyptian coinage was now integrated within the broader imperial system. Nevertheless, Egypt proved restive, and in 293, while Diocletian proposed his reforms, Coptos revolted and was destroyed by Galerius, the new Caesar of the East.

An Alexandrian revolt followed (297–98), instigated by one Lucius Domitius Domitianus and his deputy Achilleus. Diocletian personally supervised the eight month siege of the ravaged city. The conclusion of the revolt was commemorated by the erection of the column erroneously known today as "Pompey's Pillar," which once bore an equestrian statue of the emperor.[100] Diocletian's visit continued with an inspection of the southern frontier post at Philae, where a defensive gateway was constructed in his name. Acknowledging Rome's inability to eradicate Blemmye razzias in Lower Nubia, Diocletian formally withdrew from the Dodecaschoenus, fixing the new border at Aswan. The lost territory, accompanied by annual subsidies, was ceded to the Noba tribe as a buffer against further Blemmye encroachment. A record of the emperor's visit, and the inadequacy of the local administration's preparations for it, survives in a papyrus from Panopolis dating to 298.[101]

In 302, Diocletian returned to Egypt. In the last visit by a reigning emperor, he distributed free bread to the population of Alexandria and inveighed against the alien religion of Manichaeism. The following year, the emperor's fear of seditious cults prompted the bloodiest assault against Christianity, after a hiatus of some forty years. Known as the "Great Persecution" to Christian authors, the purge was particularly virulent in Egypt under prefects Sossianus Hierocles (310), noted by Eusebius, and Satrius Arrianus (304–07), the caricatured villain of numerous Coptic maryrdoms.[102] Later Coptic church estimates of 144,000 to 800,000 martyrs may well be inflated but clearly reveal the intensity of the persecu-

[99] Jones, *History of Rome*, 267–68.

[100] Cf. the explanations in Milne, *History of Egypt*, 82, and Bowman , *Egypt After the Pharaohs*, 45.

[101] P. Beatty Panop. 1.167–79; see Bowman, *Egypt After the Pharaohs*, 77–78. For the suggestion that this territory was ceded to Meroe, rather than to the Noba, see Welsby, *Kingdom of Kush*, 71.

[102] Reymond and Barns, *Four Martyrdoms*, 7, 145.

tion. From the sixth century to the present,[103] the Coptic calendar has dated not from the birth of Christ, but from the "Era of the Martyrs," calculated retrospectively from Diocletian's accession in 284. In stark contrast, Diocletian received full pharaonic honors at Armant on the Buchis stela of 295, and in later years an artificial "Era of Diocletian" would be used reverentially to avoid mention of Christian emperors.[104] Following the abdication of Diocletian and Maximian in 305, the persecutions continued unrelentingly until a deathbed decree of religious toleration by Galerius (305–11).[105]

After a generation, the fragile Tetrarchy rapidly succumbed to personal rivalries in both West and East. In Italy, Maxentius had ousted Severus II as Augustus in 307, before his own defeat by "Caesar" Constantine at the celebrated battle of Milvian Bridge in 312. Maximin Daia (310–313), who had been Eastern Caesar from 305 to 310, contested the office of Augustus with Licinius (308–24), a military associate of the deceased Galerius. Ruling from Egypt to Asia Minor, Maximin strongly encouraged traditional cults throughout the East, creating a new hierarchy of the Pagan clergy under provincial high priests. Although this clerical reform is often assumed to have been modeled upon Christian practice, strong Egyptian influence has been noted in the role of priestesses and the stipulation that clerical vestments be of white linen.[106] Such Egyptian influence in the broader Pagan defense is to be expected, as the native clergy increasingly dominated Alexandrian "Greek" philosophical schools, producing the hybrid "Hermetic" Corpus of theoretical speculation and the "Magical" collections of practical theurgy.[107]

As the last aggressively Pagan emperor in the East, Maximin Daia is correspondingly the final emperor to be officially acknowledged in hieroglyphic texts. At the site of Tahta in Middle Egypt, blocks from a ruined temple preserve his cartouches beside a fragmentary offering scene.[108] With

103 The earliest known use of the Era of the Martyrs dates to 522/23; see Jean-Claude Grenier, "La stèle funéraire du dernier taureau Bouchis (Caire JE 31901 = Stèle *Bucheum* 20)," *Bulletin de l'Institut Français d'Archéologie Orientale*, 83 (1983), 205, n. 2.

104 Grenier, "La stèle funéraire," 204–5; Bagnall and Worp, *The Chronological Systems of Byzantine Egypt* (Zutphen, 1978), 43–49.

105 Eusebius, *History of the Church*, VIII.17; see Jones, *History of Rome*, 335–36.

106 Henri Grégoire, "L'Énigma de Tahta," *Chronique d'Égypte*, 15, no. 29 (1940), 122, 123, n. 2.

107 Garth Fowden, *The Egyptian Hermes* (Cambridge, 1986), 167–68, 182–86; Brian P. Copenhaver, *Hermetica* (Cambridge, 1992), li–lix; Jean-Pierre Mahé, *Hermès en haute-Égypte*, 2 vols. (Quebec, 1978–82); Ritner, "Egyptian Magical Practice," 3358–71; Jean Maspero, "Horapollon et la fin du paganisme égyptien," *Bulletin de l'Institut Français d'Archéologie Orientale*, 11 (1914), 163–95.

108 Jean Capart, "L'Énigma de Tahta," *Chronique d'Égypte*, 15, no. 29 (1940), 45–50; and Henri Grégoire, "L'Énigma de Tahta," 119–23.

the full titulary Valerius Maxi(mi)nus *Caesar*, it is suggested that these blocks date from 305 to 310, before his proclamation as Augustus,[109] but hieroglyphic texts are not scrupulous regarding titular distinctions of the Tetrarchy.[110] A stela at Aberdeen (no. 1619) recording the burial of a mother of Buchis at Armant is dated to year eight of Caesar Maxi(mi)nus, his penultimate year as Augustus (311/12).[111]

In 313, Maximin crossed with his army into Thrace, but was defeated by Licinius at Tzirallum beside the Erghen river. Retreating to Tarsus, Maximin became ill and died, yielding authority to the first pro-Christian emperor in the East. The same year, Constantine issued the Edict of Milan in the West, granting religious toleration for Christians and Pagans, and Licinius adopted the new policy that summer.[112] For Egyptian Christianity, 313 marks the baptism of Pachomius (ca. 292–346), the former soldier who would devise the first coenobitic monastic regulations at the abandoned village of Tabennesi, a former cult site of the goddess Isis.

The reign of Licinius in Egypt (313–324), while relatively long, is little documented. It is during his rule that the Pagan "Era of Diocletian" is first noted in dates of the Buchis bull born in 316/317 ("year 33 of Diocletian") and enthroned in 322/323 ("year 39 of Diocletian").[113] Diocletian's Nubian strategy proved unsuccessful, and Blemmye plundering resumed, so that the new monastery of Tabennesi was harassed between 323 and 346.[114] Licinius is said to have turned against the Christian clergy with restrictive measures in 320 and 321,[115] and worsening relations with Constantine provoked open hostilities from 316. Defeated by Constantine in 324, Licinius was captured and executed.

During the reign of Constantine as sole emperor (324–337), the transformation of the "Roman" into the "Byzantine" empire was all but complete. The radical reforms of the army, finance and administration begun by Diocletian were pursued and extended, and the divide between East and West intensified. A new taxation system was introduced in 313, with fifteen-year tax-cycles termed "indictions" calculated retrospectively from 312. In 331, the emperor formally transferred the imperial capital from Rome to Constantinople, the former Byzantium, on the Bosphorus, and the Latin principate conceived by Augustus evolved into an empire increasingly Greek.

[109] Grégoire, "L'Énigma de Tahta," 119.

[110] For Augustus Diocletian as Caesar, see Grenier, "La stèle funéraire," 203, n. 3.

[111] Capart, "L'Énigma de Tahta," 47–50.

[112] Eusebius, *History of the Church*, X.5; see Jones, *History of Rome*, 336–39.

[113] Grenier, "La stèle funéraire," 197–208.

[114] Jehan Desanges, "Les raids des Blemmyes sous le règne de Valens, en 373–374," *Meroitic News Letter*, 10 (1972), 34.

[115] Ibid., 206, n. 3.

Most importantly, Constantine's empire increasingly favored Christianity, though the emperor himself was baptized only a week before his death.

In 325, shortly after his accession as sole emperor, Constantine acted as arbiter during the Council of Nicaea, convened to determine the divinity of Christ. The need for the council might have halted an intended visit by the emperor to Egypt, as suggested by texts from Oxyrhynchus detailing preparations for an imperial reception. Attended by 220 bishops, the council issued the Nicene Creed, thereby vindicating Athanasius of Alexandria against the "heretic" Arian, who had denied that Christ was "of one substance with the Father." The subsequent refusal by Athanasius to reinstate the humbled Arian led to a feud with Constantine, exacerbated by reports that Athanasius had presumed to levy taxes for his church. The banishment of the Alexandrian bishop in 335, associated with a revolt led by one Philumenos, established a pattern of hostility that would characterize church–state relations in Egypt for the remainder of the Byzantine occupation. Athanasius would be expelled from his see five times before his death in 373. His zeal for orthodoxy further aggravated the local Meletian schism, concerning the rehabilitation of Christians who had recanted during the former persecutions.[116]

Notwithstanding the new doctrinal conflicts, Egyptian monasticism expanded with official patronage, and in 330 Macarius ("the Great") founded the complex of monasteries still thriving in the Wadi Natrun. On the basis of onomastics, 330 has been considered a watershed year in Egypt, with Christianity claiming 50 percent of the population, increasing to 80 or 90 percent by the end of the century. This estimate seems excessive; other tabulations suggest less than 25 percent conversion by 350, with 50 percent by 388.[117]

Despite the rapid growth of Christianity under Constantine, centers of Paganism persisted in Alexandria and the Egyptian countryside. Thebes lost in stature to Panopolis, home of the philosopher Zosimos (*floruit* ca. 300) and several distinguished sacerdotal families.[118] The religious complexity of the period is epitomized by the fortunes of the Panopolite family of Aurelius Petearbeschinis, whose eldest son, Aurelius Horion, was high priest of the ithyphallic local deity Min, while his brother Harpocration was official panegyrist at the imperial court in Constantinople.[119]

116 Bowman, *Egypt After the Pharaohs*, 49.

117 R. Bagnall, "Religious conversion and onomastic change in early Byzantine Egypt," *The Bulletin of the American Society of Papyrologists*, 19 (1982), 105–23; but cf. Ramsay MacMullen, *Christianizing the Roman Empire (AD 100–400)* (New Haven, 1984), 156–57, n. 41; and Bowman, *Egypt After the Pharaohs*, 47.

118 For the decline of Thebes, see John Tait, "Theban Magic," in S. P. Vleeming (ed.), *Hundred-Gated Thebes* (Leiden, 1995, 169–82. For Zosimos, see Howard M. Jackson, *Zosimos of Panopolis on the Letter Omega* (Missoula, MT, 1978), 3–5.

119 Sources in Fowden, *The Egyptian Hermes*, 174.

Constantius (337–61), the son and successor of Constantine in the East, was a committed follower of Arianism, and his repeated quarrels with Athanasius dominated imperial policy toward Egypt. The emperor's non-conciliatory religious views did, however, affect the legacy of pre-Christian Egypt. At Armant, the Buchis bull who had been born in the unrecognized reign of Licinius was buried in 340, in "year 57 of Diocletian." This is the last preserved royal cartouche and certainly the last interred Buchis as well. The catacombs were subsequently ransacked and this stela "exorcised" by the painted addition of three red crosses and the repeated name of Jesus Christ.[120] While such outrages probably date from the proscription of Pagan cults under Theodosius I, it is under Constantius in 341 that official toleration for Christianity devolves into formal persecution of traditional religions: "Let superstition come to an end, and the insanity of sacrifices be abolished."[121] From 353, a series of imperial edicts resulted in prohibitions on cultic ceremonies and enforced temple closings. In 359, an oracle of the god Bes at Abydos foretold the end of his reign, and Constantius decreed an (unsuccessful) abolition of oracles throughout the empire. He died two years later, marching against his rebellious cousin Julian.[122]

At the accession of Julian (361–63), Paganism regained the official patronage of the imperial court. In Egypt, the Alexandrian mob used the occasion to murder the Arian bishop George, who had been imposed upon the city by Constantius in 357. Throughout the empire, Julian attempted to defend and rehabilitate deteriorating temples. The military commander Artemius, accused of plundering the Alexandrian Serapeum, was recalled to court and executed. Athanasius was now banished not merely from Alexandria, but from the whole of Egypt. He withdrew instead into the Thebaid until the death of Julian while on campaign against the Persians.

The short reign of Jovian (363–64) allowed the return of Athanasius, who thereafter maintained his see despite the elevation of the Arian emperor Valens (364–78), co-founder of the Valentinian dynasty. Less daunting than his predecessor, the next bishop, Peter, was imprisoned and replaced by an Arian. The ensuing schism was further compounded by an attempted military draft of monks. Among the new monks in 370/71 was Shenute of Atripe (ca. 348–466), a future abbot of the White Monastery at Sohag and preeminent Coptic stylist and zealot.[123] In 373, a Demotic inscription at the temple of Philae ("year 90 of Diocletian") recorded an incursion of the

[120] Grenier, "La stèle funéraire," 207–08.

[121] Jones, *History of Rome*, 344; Pierre Chuvin, *A Chronicle of the Last Pagans* (Cambridge, MA, 1990), 36–38.

[122] Ammianus Marcellinus, XIX.12. 3–16; see Alexandre Piankoff, "The Osireion of Seti I at Abydos during the Greco-Roman Period and the Christian Occupation," *Bulletin de la Société d'Archéologie Copte*, 15 (1958–60), 125–49.

[123] David N. Bell, *The Life of Shenute by Besa* (Kalamazoo, MI, 1983), 7–8.

Blemmyes into the Kharga Oasis.[124] Perhaps encouraged by the Persian Shapur II, both Blemmyes and Saracens raided monasteries in the Sinai during the same year. Valens disappeared during a rout of the Roman army by invading Visigoths in Thrace.

Theodosius I (379–395) announced in 380 that the Nicene faith propounded by Alexandria and Rome was the only true religion, thus ending imperial support for Arianism, which now spread among the Germanic tribes in the West. The emperor's subsequent campaign against various "heresies" was championed in Alexandria by the Patriarch Theophilus (385–412). On February 24, 391, by an edict addressed to Rome from Milan, Theodosius abruptly banned all expressions of Paganism throughout the empire.[125] A second edict of June 16 was addressed specifically to Alexandria and Egypt.

In an act of provocation, Theophilus attempted to convert a local temple into a church. Sacred relics were discovered and paraded in the streets, instigating riots between Christians and Pagans. Theophilus now sacked the prestigious Alexandrian Serapeum, into which the Pagans, led by the philosopher Olympius, had fled.[126] The suburban Serapeum at Canopus (Abu Qir) was also pillaged, and monks settled amid its ruins. Later Coptic legends romanticized the bishop's ability to reap gold from ruined temples.[127] In time, the Serapeum was converted into a church of Saint John the Baptist, while the Canopus temple became the church of Saints Cyril and John. Throughout Egypt, the same fate was visited upon the ancient temples, and the remains of intrusive churches are clearly evident at Dendera, Esna, Luxor, Medinet Habu and elsewhere. The policy was officially sanctioned by Shenute and examples were extolled in Coptic legend:

Thus then at the site of a shrine to an unclean spirit, it will henceforth be a shrine to the Holy Spirit. And if previously it is prescriptions for murdering man's soul that are therein . . . the dogs and cats, the crocodiles and frogs, the foxes, the other reptiles, the beasts and birds, the cattle, etc. . . . it is the soul-saving scriptures of life that will henceforth come to be therein.[128]

124 Philae, no. 371; in Jehan Desanges, "Les raids des Blemmyes," 32–34. The graffito is one of four dated to 373 after a gap of a century; see Griffith, *Catalogue of Demotic Graffiti*, 10, 103–5 (nos. 369–372).

125 Jones, *History of Rome*, 345.

126 For the five versions of the story, see John Holland Smith, *The Death of Classical Paganism* (New York, 1976), 168–73. See also the papyrus illustration in R. E. Witt, *Isis in the Graeco-Roman World* (Ithaca, NY, 1971), 230, fig. 68.

127 László Kákosy, "A Christian Interpretation of the Sun-disk," in M. Heerma Van Voss, et al. (eds.), *Studies in Egyptian Religion Dedicated to Professor Jan Zandee* (Leiden, 1982), 70–75; Georgio Zoega, *Catalogus Codicum Copticorum Manuscriptorum*, 2nd edn. (Leipzig, 1903), 50–51.

128 Dwight W. Young, "A Monastic Invective Against Egyptian Hieroglyphs," in Dwight W. Young (ed.), *Studies Presented to Hans Jakob Polotsky* (East Gloucester, MA, 1981), 348–60; quote on pp. 353–54. For legends of temple destructions, see François

The summer after the dismantling of the Serapeum there was an exceptionally high Nile and, in consequence of this perceived blessing, a large number of conversions.

Many of Alexandria's Pagan intellectuals thereafter fled the city, including Ammonius, "priest of the ape (Thoth)" and the poet Claudian, whose work bears the stamp of native theology.[129] Though proscribed, Paganism was not yet dead. On August 24, 394, the last dated hieroglyphic inscription was carved at the frontier temple of Philae, recording the birth festival of Osiris in year 110 (of Diocletian).[130]

Arcadius (395–408), the eldest son of Theodosius, further formalized the distinctions between the Eastern and Western empires and is often credited with being the first true Byzantine emperor. Traditional worship at Philae continued unabated, as evidenced by a Demotic graffito of year 124 of Diocletian (407/08) memorializing the worship of a "Chief of Secrets of Isis."[131] The reign of Theodosius II (408–50) was dominated by a new doctrinal struggle between Cyril "the Great" of Alexandria and the court prelate Nestorius, who denied to Mary the title of "Theotokos," or "Mother of God." As a result of the rhetorical skills of Cyril and the physical backing of Shenute and his monks, Nestorius was condemned at the Council of Ephesus in 431 and banished to the Kharga Oasis in 435. He died in Egypt after 451, having survived captivity during Blemmye raids that had sent 20,000 refugees to Shenute's White Monastery. More significant for Coptic history was the "Monophysite" controversy at the Second Council of Ephesus in 449. Officially appointed to resolve a dispute regarding the humanity of Christ, the council was rather the setting for a political contest between Alexandria, Rome and Constantinople, whose Patriarch Flavian had initiated charges against a local archimandrite, Eutychus. Backed by the Alexandrian Patriarch Dioscorus I (444–454/58), Eutychus was vindicated over objections outlined in a tardily sent "Tome" of Pope Leo. Marking the pinnacle of Alexandria's theological influence, the council would be repudiated by Rome and Constantinople in the following reign.

The intemperate fury directed against perceived heretics fell upon prominent Pagans as well. In 415, the philosopher Hypatia was dragged naked through the streets of Alexandria before she was murdered by a mob of

Lexa, *La Magie dans l'Égypte Antique*, vol. II (Paris, 1925), 217–22; Zoega, *Catalogus Codicum*, 533–34, 100–102; and Piankoff, "The Osireion of Seti I," 125–49.

129 Philippe Derchain, "A propos de *Claudien* Eloge de Stilichon, II, 424–436," *Zeitschrift für Ägyptische Sprache und Altertumskunde*, 81 (1956), 4–6; Fowden, *The Egyptian Hermes*, 183.

130 Philae, no. 436; Griffith, *Catalogue of Demotic Graffiti*, 126–27, and pl. 69.

131 Philae, no. 364; Griffith, *Catalogue of Demotic Graffiti*, 102.

monks in the church of Saint Michael, the official seat of the Patriarch. Pagan philosophy survived under the direction of the native Panopolite scholar Horapollo the elder (ca. 408–50) and his descendants Asklepiades, Heraiskos (both ca. 425–90) and Horapollo the younger (ca. 450–500).[132] In a Philae Demotic graffito of 435 (year 152 of Diocletian), one of the last known Egyptian priests, Esmet the elder, first prophet of Isis, documented his role as "scribe of the divine books."[133] Among the clients of the ancient cults were the Blemmyes and the Noba, whose renewed military actions were recorded in barbaric Greek. At the temple of Kalabsha, Silko, king of the Noba, left a victory scene and text, while a letter from Qasr Ibrim preserves the boasts of the Blemmye king Phonen to Abourni, king of the Noba.[134] Though a scourge to Christians, the Blemmyes were romanticized heroes to traditionalists. Olympiodorus of Thebes visited them and wrote of his pleasant experiences (ca. 425), and the nomads are the subject of a fragmentary epic of the late fifth century.[135]

Emperor Marcian (450–57) made two decisions pivotal for Egyptian history in 451. A peace treaty was concluded with the Blemmyes, allowing them yearly access to the temple of Philae and the right to borrow the cult statue for processional oracles. Thus Philae was spared the ravages of conversion for almost a century. The Council of Chalcedon was convened in retaliation for the Second Council of Ephesus. Dioscorus was now condemned and exiled, ensuring the permanent schism with the Coptic Church that persists to this day. Disharmony among the victors of the conference led to the further break between Rome and Constantinople only thirty-three years later. In 452, the last dated Demotic inscriptions were carved at Philae. On December 2, in "year 169 of Diocletian," Esmet the elder and his like-named junior partner recorded their continued service in the temple, probably at the time of the Blemmye visitation.[136] On December 11, the final Demotic inscription was carved, labeling "the feet of Petinakht junior," who attended the festivities.[137] Knowledge of Demotic may have lasted much later, as suggested by hagiographies of the seventh-century bishop Pisentius of Quft, whose "thirty-second wonder" entailed the reading of an ancient funerary scroll, prior to his conversation with a resurrected

132 Fowden, *The Egyptian Hermes*, 184–86; Roger Rémondon, "L'Égypte et la suprême résistance au Christianisme (Ve–VIIe siècles)," *Bulletin de l'Institut Français d'Archéologie Orientale*, 51 (1952), 63–78; Maspero, "Horapollon," 163–95.

133 Philae, no. 366; Griffith, *Catalogue of Demotic Graffiti*, 103.

134 T. C. Skeat, "A Lettter from the King of the Blemmyes to the King of the Noubades," *Journal of Egyptian Archaeology*, 63 (1977), 159–70.

135 Rémondon, "L'Égypte et la suprême résistance,", 76–77; Ludwig Stern, "Fragmente eines griechisch-ägyptischen Epos," *Zeitschrift für Ägyptische Sprache und Altertumskunde*, 19 (1881), 70–75.

136 Philae, no. 365; Griffith, *Catalogue of Demotic Graffiti*, 102–03.

137 Philae, no. 377; Griffith, *Catalogue of Demotic Graffiti*, 106.

mummy.[138] The Demotic tale of Seta I was reportedly discovered in the grave of a Coptic Christian.[139]

At the accession of Leo I (457–74), the Alexandrian mob tore to pieces the court-imposed bishop, Proterius, despised successor to Dioscorus. In conformity with the pattern now customary in the Coptic Church, a new Patriarch was selected from among the monks. Timothy ("the Cat") was rejected by Leo and Zeno (474–91), continuing the imperial rift with Alexandria healed briefly during the interregnum of the monophysite Basiliscus (475–76). Zeno returned to power in 476, as the Western empire fell to the German Odoacer. In 482, Zeno made an attempt at reconciliation by promulgating the "Henoticon," which rejected both Chalcedon and the teachings of Eutychus. The edict was considered a rebuke to papal authority, and in 484 the pope excommunicated the Byzantine emperor. In the same year, a new revolt against Zeno by the general Illus implicated the nationalistic Egyptian intellectuals of Alexandria, leading to the interrogation of Heraiskos and Horapollo the younger, the probable author of the *Hieroglyphica*, a treatise on the symbolic value of hieroglyphs.[140]

In the reign of Anastasius (491–518), the Persians invaded the Delta but failed to occupy Alexandria and withdrew. Pagan authority over the Alexandrian university ended in 517, when John Philoponus assumed its leadership.[141] Blemmye raids resumed against Upper Egypt, continuing under Justin I (518–27). In 540, during the reign of Justinian (527–65), the Noba were converted to Christianity in a contest between the missionaries of the emperor and those of his monophysite wife, Theodora. Won to the Coptic cause, the Noba joined the Byzantine army in crushing the power of the Blemmyes. In 543, Justinian dispatched Narses the Persarmenian to close the temple of Philae, imprison its priests, and carry off the divine statues to Constantinople. The final stronghold of Egyptian religion was rededicated as a church, by a ruse according to Coptic legend.[142] As late as 552, a citizen of Ombos (Kom Ombo) was discovered repairing sanctuaries for the Blemmyes.[143]

From the perspective of traditional Egypt, little need be said of the

138 Gawdat Gabra Abdel Sayed, *Untersuchungen zu den Texten über Pesyntheus Bischof von Koptos (569–632)* (Bonn, 1984), 309–10; E. A. Wallis Budge, *Coptic Apocrypha in the Dialect of Upper Egypt* (London, 1913), 326–30.

139 F. Ll. Griffith, *Stories of the High Priests of Memphis* (Oxford, 1900), 67.

140 Jürgen Osing, "Horapollo," in W. Helck and E. Otto (eds.), *Lexikon der Ägyptologie*, vol. II (Wiesbaden, 1977), col. 1275; George Boas, *The Hieroglyphics of Horapollo* (New York, 1950).

141 Henry Chadwick, *The Early Church* (London, 1967), 172.

142 E. A. Wallis Budge, *Miscellaneous Coptic Texts in the Dialect of Upper Egypt* (London, 1915), Part I, 445–47; Part II, 961–63.

143 P. Maspero 67004; see Ulrich Wilcken, "Papyrus-Urkunden," *Archiv für Papyrusforschung*, 5 (1913), 443–44.

anarchic reigns of Justin II (565–78), Tiberius II (578–82), Maurice (582–602), Phocas (602–10) or Heraclius (610–41). Philae was refortified against the Blemmyes in 577, internal brigandage severed the grain supply to Alexandria under Maurice, and war returned to Egypt in 609, with the revolt of Heraclius against Phocas. In the seventh year of Heraclius (616), the Persians successfully invaded Egypt and held it for about ten years. The return of Heraclius in 627 ignited older doctrinal differences, which may have encouraged Coptic acquiescence or compliance during the Arab conquest directed by ʿAmr ibn al-ʿĀs from 640 to 642. To the latter should be attributed the final destruction of the remnants of the Alexandrian library.

Following the conquest, the ancient Egyptian legacy survived through the intermediaries of Coptic art, eschatology, folklore, and particularly the Coptic language, which dominated most local environments even after 705 when the Umayyad viceroy ʿAbd-Allāh ibn ʿAbd al-Malik required the use of Arabic in all state affairs.[144] As a vehicle for literary and documentary texts, Coptic remained in use until the fourteenth century. In the symbolism of the modern Coptic Church, Egyptian features still live.

144 See Budge, *Coptic Apocrypha*, lxi–lxxii; Marvin Meyer and Richard Smith (eds.), *Ancient Christian Magic: Coptic Texts of Ritual Power* (New York, 1994); and R. K. Ritner, "Egyptians in Ireland: A Question of Coptic Peregrinations," *Rice University Studies*, 62 (1976), 65–87.

2

Egypt on the eve of the Muslim conquest

WALTER E. KAEGI

Egypt's population in the early seventh century AD cannot be determined with any certainty, but it probably numbered less than the five million persons frequently attributed to the province at the height of the Roman Empire in the Early Principate. By the year 600, the population may have declined to three million; mortality resulting from plagues erupting during Justinian's reign in the sixth century cannot be accurately estimated.[1] Many Egyptians were designated "Chalcedonians" or "Monophysites," but this distinction did not represent a genuine cleavage of ethnic identity in Egyptian society.[2] An assumption that "Chalcedonian" referred exclusively to Greeks rather than to native Egyptians is erroneous. Greek remained an important spoken and written language in Egypt, although by the early seventh century Coptic was used increasingly in written records. Subliterary texts in Coptic dated back to the early third century.[3]

Many other aspects of Egypt's economy, social structure and spiritual outlook during Late Antiquity persisted into the early seventh century. But the privatization of public functions by owners of great estates intensified from the fourth century, a process that significantly altered institutional

1 I wish to acknowledge the indispensable aid of a fellowship of the American Research Center in Egypt in 1979 and from valuable critical comments of Todd M. Hickey, and the help of Professor John F. Oates and the Papyrology Room, Perkins Library, Duke University. Fundamental is R. S. Bagnall, *Egypt in Late Antiquity* (Princeton, 1993). On population: Hans-Albert Rupprecht, *Kleine Einführung in die Papyruskunde* (Darmstadt, 1994), 158.

2 Ewa Wipszycka argues against any nationalist thesis, in "Le nationalisme a-t-il existé dans l'Égypte byzantine?" *The Journal of Juristic Papyrology*, 22 (1992), 83–128, reprinted in Wipszycka, *Études sur le christianisme dans l'Égypte de l'antiquité tardive*, Studia Ephemeridis Augustinianum, 52 (Rome, 1990), 9–61.

3 L. S. MacCoull, *Coptic Perspectives on Late Antiquity* (Aldershot, 1993); E. M. Isḥaq, "Coptic Language, Spoken," in A. S. Atiya (ed.), *Coptic Encyclopedia*, II, (New York, 1991), 604–7; T. G. Wilfong, "Coptic," in E. M. Meyers (ed.), *Oxford Encyclopedia of Archaeology of the Near East*, II (Oxford, New York, 1997), 65–7.

structures during the remaining periods of Byzantine administration.[4] Members of the social elite could still acquire some familiarity with the repertory of Greek authors of antiquity, as testified by the writings of the poet Dioskoros of Aphrodito in the sixth century or the historian Theophylact Simocatta in the early seventh.[5] Theatrical performances in Alexandria during the early seventh century continued to entertain audiences that included high officials.[6]

The general population was probably quite young, its numbers restricted by plague epidemics and widespread infant mortality. Agriculture continued as the foundation of the economy.

The Patriarch of Alexandria, Egypt's largest city,[7] controlled extensive properties and functioned as a prominent communal leader as well as head of the Church. The ecclesiastic institution itself changed over the period from the fourth to the seventh centuries. The Patriarchate, monasteries and religious foundations continued to mature, developing their institutional sophistication and acquiring more landed wealth through bequests and gifts. By the year 600, the ecclesiastic establishment was more elaborate than it had been in the fourth century. Forbidden to alienate its properties, the Church rarely lost its landed holdings. Many papyrological, hagiographic or historical narrative sources refer to the accumulation of vast wealth by ecclesiastical institutions in Egypt. The Patriarchate of Alexandria was the prime beneficiary, but several monasteries amassed large estates as well.[8] Many civilian and military officials envied this growth in ecclesiastic wealth, and disputed its propriety.[9]

Among religious minorities, the Jewish community was prominent. However, Jews do not appear to have figured significantly in either the Persian or Islamic conquests. If they had, Byzantine apologists would probably have attempted to attribute the loss of Egypt to them. In contrast

4 J. Gascou, "Les grands domaines, la cité et l'état en Égypte byzantine," *Travaux et Mémoires*, 9 (1985), 1–90; J. G. Keenan, "Papyrology and Byzantine Historiography," *Bulletin of the American Society of Papyrologists*, 30 (1993), 137–44; cf. I. F. Fikhman, "De nouveau sur la colonat du Bas-Empire," *Miscellanea papyrologica in occasione del bicentenario dell'edizione della Charta Borgiana, Papyrologica Florentina*, 19 (Florence, 1990), 159–179.

5 L. MacCoull, *Dioscorus of Aphrodito: His Work and His World* (Berkeley, 1988); Julian Krüger, *Oxyrhynchos in der Kaiserzeit: Studien zur Topographie und Literaturrezeption* (Frankfurt, Bern, New York, 1990), 144–52.

6 *Miracles of St. Artemios*, ed. trans. V. S. Crisafulli and John Nesbitt (Leiden, 1997), 108–115.

7 C. Haas, *Alexandria in Late Antiquity. Topography and Social Conflict* (Baltimore, 1997), 46–7.

8 Jean Gascou and Leslie MacCoull, "Le cadastre d'Aphroditô," *Travaux et Mémoires*, 10 (1987), 102–58; Gascou, *Un codex fiscal Hermopolite (P. Sorb. II 69)*, American Studies in Papyrology, 32 (Atlanta, 1994), 57; Wipszycka, *Études sur le christianisme.*

9 See the bibliographic additions of P. M. Fraser to A. J. Butler, *Arab Conquest of Egypt* (Oxford, 1978), xlvi–xlviii.

with assignations of blame in Palestine-Syria, there were no allegations of Jewish complicity or incidents of anti-Jewish hostility mentioned as causes for the failure of Byzantine forces to bar the Muslims from Egypt.

Although the intellectual horizons of its rural population may have been narrow, Egypt had maintained extensive ties with the external world long before the seventh century.[10] Egypt possessed renowned pilgrimage sites. Its Mediterranean ports of Alexandria and Pelusium were flourishing. Inhabitants of its coastal towns and river ports had access to news from around the empire, if on a delayed basis because of slow communications. Egypt possessed significant transportation hubs, even though the majority of its inhabitants were rustics who lived by agriculture and, to a lesser extent, pastoralism.[11] The remaining pagan elements on its periphery had probably been converted to Christianity by the late sixth century, and its cities no longer harbored pagans who were willing to declare their allegiances openly. Egypt's coasts and river shores provided opportunities for contact with travelers and merchants from other shores of the Mediterranean. Egyptians were still making pilgrimages in the early seventh century to venerate relics and religious sites in Palestine. Their visits contributed a measure of cosmopolitanism to the province. Those regions were still part of a larger late antique cultural world. Some rough and non-Christianized tribes still occasionally raided and terrorized communities such as Scete on the western edge of the desert as late as the 630s.[12]

While Egypt was not the catalyst for the seminal political and military events of the early seventh century,[13] it did assume an important role in the broader Byzantine imperial economy in terms of agriculture, commerce and artisanal production. Egypt may have contributed as much as 30 percent of total imperial tax revenues from the Prefecture of the East.[14] Egypt was an integral part of the broader Byzantine and Mediterranean economy, and its financial contributions were essential to Byzantine fiscal integrity at the start of the seventh century; its grain contributions were crucial to feeding Constantinople until about 617. During that year Emperor Heraclius

[10] *P. Oxy.* LVI 3872 is an unusual documentary example of travel between Alexandria, Babylon (Old Cairo) and Constantinople; see J. G. Keenan, "A Constantinople Loan, AD 541," *Bulletin of the American Society of Papyrologists* 29 (1992), 175–82.

[11] J. G. Keenan, "Pastoralism in Roman Egypt," *Bulletin of the American Society of Papyrologists* 26 (1989), 175–98.

[12] Ugo Zanetti, "La vie de Saint Jean Higoumène de Scété au VIIe siècle," *Analecta Bollandiana* 114 (1996), ch. 20, pp. 338–41, 382–3; Anthony Alcock (ed., trans.), *The Life of Samuel of Kalamun by Isaac the Presbyter*, c. 17–18 (Warminster, 1983), 90–2. Pilgrimages: Papyrus 55, *Greek Papyri of the Byzantine Period*, ed. G. Fantoni [Griechische Texte, X, CPRF, XIV], 107–9.

[13] For overviews, see A. Stratos, *Vyzantion ston z' aiona*, 6 vols. (Athens, 1965–1978); J. Haldon, *Byzantium in the Seventh Century*, 2nd edn. (Cambridge, 1997).

[14] M. Hendy, *Studies in the Byzantine Monetary Economy* (Cambridge, 1985), 171–2, 613–18.

(610–41), reacting to the Persian conquest of Egypt, suppressed this ancient entitlement. The cancellation of the grain dole, following the loss of Egypt, inflicted hardships on Constantinople's inhabitants. There is no scholarly consensus as to whether Egyptian contributions of grain to Constantinople were temporarily restored after the Byzantine recovery of Egypt in 629 from the Persians.

The Byzantines did care about the fate of Egypt. If one looks at later seventh-century scapegoating, Egypt and its loss loomed large in their eyes. Whether everyone else of importance in the late 630s and 640s concurred is open to question. But a variety of sources attest to the significance of Egypt from Constantinople's point of view, and to acrimonious disputes about why and how it fell to the Muslims. There was, however, another perspective.[15] The Byzantine Empire had already begun to learn what it was like to do without Egypt during the era of the Persian occupation. The empire had managed to survive, but at a great cost in terms of lost prestige, foodstuffs, population, intellectual life, commerce and craft wealth.

Egypt experienced widespread disruption in the final decades of Byzantine administration. The province had become aware of consequences of events outside its borders. First came news of the violent overthrow of Emperor Maurice in 602 by the usurper Phokas. According to the *Life of the Patriarch John the Almsgiver* by Leontios of Neapolis (Cyprus), the report allegedly took only nine days to reach Alexandria from Constantinople, its rapidity an indicator of its urgency. Egypt experienced more fighting and consequent loss of life and property by civilians as well as the military, in conflicts between the armies and partisans of the usurper Phokas and the rebel Heraclius, Exarch of Africa, and his son Heraclius, whose rebellion against Phokas commenced in 608, than did any other Byzantine province in the years 608–610.[16] Only half a dozen years later the Persian invasion interrupted the restoration of stability in Egypt. Egypt returned to Byzantine authority in late 629 but in another five years the Muslim menace became apparent and cast its shadow over Egypt well before Muslim armies actually invaded the province.

A detailed review of the Muslim conquest of Egypt between late 639 and 645 is inappropriate here. The analysis of A. J. Butler is still valuable, but has been superseded with respect to Byzantine sources by new papyrological discoveries, and by a new understanding of the larger Byzantine context and of late Roman history overall. In the case of Arabic sources, many texts have been edited – such as the critical work of Ibn ʿAbd al-Ḥakam: *History of the*

15 W. E. Kaegi, *Byzantium and the Early Islamic Conquests* (revised paperback, Cambridge, 1995), 205, 217. See also D. M. Olster, *Roman Defeat, Christian Response, and the Literary Construction of the Jew* (Philadelphia, 1994).

16 D. M. Olster, *The Politics of Usurpation in the Seventh Century* (Amsterdam, Las Palmas, 1993).

Conquest of Egypt, about which Butler and Leone Caetani had only imperfect knowledge – and newer critical methodologies in approaching the texts and their tradents have been developed.[17]

Egypt's Byzantine defense forces in the early seventh century, including irregulars, may have numbered 25–30,000 – roughly the same size as earlier Roman contingents stationed there. These were not elite troops; most were probably of Egyptian origin. Maritime communications were the principal means by which Egypt and Constantinople remained in contact. Byzantium controlled the Mediterranean and had the capacity to shift elite troops by sea to Egypt from districts surrounding Constantinople. Other strong forces might be sent from Numidia overland or from Syria-Palestine, either by land (the Via Maris) or by sea, in ships that skirted the Mediterranean coast.[18] One may wonder how easily troops from the Balkans or Thrace could have adjusted to unfamiliar military service conditions in Egypt (climate, health, terrain, diet, availability and quality of water). Byzantine military forces garrisoned in Egypt had never been the empire's best troops, who were not recruited from or stationed there. Egypt was not a major center of Byzantine military unrest, which mostly occurred on its eastern frontier with Persia or in the Balkans.[19]

Echoes of spirituality in Egypt on the eve of the conquest appear in some writings of the hagiographer John Moschus, and in the biographies of Patriarch John the Almsgiver (610–19) and the Coptic Patriarch of Alexandria, Benjamin (626–55). Scattered remarks by them indicate the founding of new churches and dedications in Egypt, and the appeal of Christian saints, festivals and bishops. At the end of Byzantine rule, Christian values still caused a banker to drop his career for an ecclesiastic calling.[20]

The Heraclian dynasty (610–11), or some of its members, hoped for assistance from north Africa, just as Heraclians had previously resisted the usurper Emperor Phokas (602–10) and had stood firm against the Persians who had overrun Egypt (617–29). In Egypt it is possible that some might

[17] Ibn ʿAbd al-Ḥakam, *Futūḥ Miṣr*, ed. Charles C. Torrey (New Haven, 1922). The absence until 1922 of this critical edition is significant. See esp. vol. 4 of L. Caetani, *Annali dell'Islam*, 10 vols. (Milan, U. Hoepli, 1905–26; reprint, Hildesheim, 1972).

[18] Kaegi, *Byzantium and the Early Islamic Conquests*, 40; J. Maspero, *Organisation militaire de l'Égypte byzantine* (Paris, 1912), 117–18; Kaegi, "Byzantine Logistics: Problems and Perspectives," in J. Lynn (ed.), *Feeding Mars* (Boulder, 1993), 39–55; Jean Gascou, "L'Institution des bucellaires," *Bulletin de l'Institut français d'Archéologie Orientale au Caire*, 76 (1976), 143–56; O. Schmitt, "Die *Bucellarii*. Eine Studie zum militärischen Gefolgschaftswesen in der Spätantike," *Tyche*, 9 (1994), 147–74.

[19] W. E. Kaegi, *Byzantine Military Unrest, 471–843: An Interpretation* (Amsterdam, Las Palmas, 1981).

[20] Stephanos Efthymiadis, "Living in a City and Living in a Scetis: The Dream of Eustathios the Banker," *Byzantinische Forschungen*, 21 (1995), 11–29.

have regarded north Africa as a possible bulwark against invasion, because the Persians had not overrun that region. The Heraclian dynasty had, after all, emerged from north Africa to seize imperial power, and this last fact might have encouraged some observers to look west, however unrealistically, for military rescue.

With due regard for lacunae in the primary sources on the Islamic conquest, many scholars would argue that they are superior to those for the conquest of Syria or Mesopotamia. In some respects historians of the Arab conquest of Egypt are better informed because of more diverse primary sources than for Syria and Palestine; some papyri have survived, as have contemporary Christian sources such as John of Nikiu.[21] On the other hand, the Muslim Iraqi tradents did not pay as much attention to Egypt as to Iraq.

[21] Jean Gascou, "De Byzance à l'Islam," *Journal of the Economic and Social History of the Orient*, 26 (1983), 97–109. It is inappropriate here to survey papyri in detail, but among the important ones of relevance, there are esp. *P. Oxy.* LVIII3959, in J. R. Rea (ed.), *The Oxyrhynchus Papyri*, Egypt Exploration Society, Graeco-Roman Memoirs, 78 (London, 1991), 58: 116–18, dated to 620 CE; but see also others in series 3940–62, esp. 74–129; also papyrus 4132 in T. Gagos et al. (eds.), *Oxyrhynchus Papyri*, vol. 61, Graeco-Roman Memoirs, 81 (1995), 137–38; *P. Sorb.* II 69 in Jean Gascou, *Un codex fiscal Hermopolite (P. Sorb. II 69)*, American Studies in Papyrology, 32 (Atlanta, 1994); *P. Hamb.* 56 (on which see Roger Rémondon, "P. Hamb. 56 et P. Lond. 1419 (notes sur les finances d'Aphrodito du VIe siècle au VIIIe siècle)," *Chronique d'Égypte* 40 (1965), 401–30; early seventh-century archive of Makarios, Arsinoite nome, on which see Georgina Fantoni (ed.), vol. 10, *Greek Papyri of the Byzantine Period, Corpus Papyrorum Raineri* (*CPRF*) XIV, 62–75 and papyrus 55, 107–8 (Vienna 1989); archive of Philemon and Thekla (622–47 CE), on which see A. A. Schiller, "The Budge Coptic Papyrus of Columbia University and Related Greek Papyri of the British Museum," *Actes du Xe Congrès International des Papyrologues* (Warsaw, 1964), 193–200; early seventh-century archive of John the *apaitêtês*, Arsinoite nome, on which see Monika Hasitzka, Michael Müller, B. Palme et al., *Corpus Papyrorum Raineri* vol. 10, *Griechische Texte* 7 (1986), 21–56; early seventh-century archive of Aurelius Pachymios, Panopolis [Akhmīm, in upper Egypt, north of Luxor], in Friedrich Preisigke et al. *Sammelbuch griechischer Urkunden aus Ägypten* (*SB*) 1: 4503–5, 374–376 (Strasbourg, 1915); and papyri from the Monastery of Epiphanius published by W. E. Crum, H. E. Winlock, *The Monastery of Epiphanius* (New York, 1926), I–II; *BGU* 314 [Herakleopolis]; 370 [Arsinoe] = *Ägyptische Urkunden aus den Königlichen Museen zu Berlin, Griechische Urkunden* (Berlin, 1895–98), I, II; *P. Ross.* iii, 51; *SB* 4662, 9461; *P. Lond.* i, 113, 6 (b), F. G. Kenyon (ed.), *Greek Papyri in the British Museum* (London, 1893), 1: 214–15; *P. Flor.* 306 in Girolamo Vitelli (ed.), *Papiri Greci Egizii*, 3: *Papiri Fiorentini* (Milan, 1915), No. 306, p. 40 [Oct/Nov 635] *SB* 4488; *P. Lond.* 1012, in Kenyon, *Greek Papyri in the British Museum*, 3, 265–267; *P. Lond.* 113, 10, in Kenyon, *Greek Papyri in the British Museum*, 1: 222–224; *SB* 6271 (Berlin, 1926): 44–45, which is dated 640/641, from Apollonos Magna [Idfu, in the Thebaid]; esp. *P. Lond.* 113, 10; *CPRF* 556; *SB* 9748=*CPRF* 552; *SB* 9749=*CPRF* 553; *SB* 9755=*CPRF* 554; *SB* 9751=*CPRF* 559; *SB* 9752=*CPRF* 560; *SB* 9753=*CPRF* 561, from Friedrich Preisigke, F. Bilabel, contd. by Emil Kiessling, *Sammelbuch griechischer Urkunden aus Ägypten* (Wiesbaden, 1965), 8: 86–9, 89–90; all of these last are from Herakleopolis Magna, or modern Ihnāsīyat al-madīna, in the Fayyūm area.

Similar problems emerge in evaluating Muslim traditions concerning Egypt as in other early Islamic traditions. Ibn ʿAbd al-Ḥakam (d. 871) is a relatively early compiler, and his account depends on an Egyptian school of traditionists. As we learn from Ibn ʿAbd al-Ḥakam's *History*, Ibn Lahīʿa (715–790) preserved early traditions of this school for the final moments of Byzantine Egypt.[22]

Christian historians in Egypt were writing long after these events. John of Nikiu, a contemporary, was an exception, but his text has survived in a faulty Ethiopic transmission.[23] Byzantine chroniclers such as Nikephoros and Theophanes[24] do not draw directly on Egyptian sources, but instead use materials such as the work of Theophilus of Edessa that were probably compiled in northern Syria or Constantinople. These sources transmit traditions that tend to represent events in terms of personalities. Latin sources are of little assistance. However important they are for other aspects of seventh-century history, Armenian sources, such as Sebeos, barely mention Egypt. Greek hagiography provides broader information, but does not clarify aspects of the context of the Islamic conquests. Archaeology and its ancillary disciplines – epigraphy, sigillography, and numismatics – illuminate some of this context but do not clarify complex questions of chronology or historical interpretation. The result is an impressionistic picture. Ibn ʿAbd al-Ḥakam provides traditions that correlate with those of Theophanes (so-called Theophanes, or George the Syncellus).

Ibn ʿAbd al-Ḥakam claims that Heraclius stiffened Byzantine resistance in Egypt, while Theophanes reports that Heraclius had replaced civilian leaders such as John Kateas in Osrhoene with Ptolemais and Patriarch Kyros with Manuel. Ibn ʿAbd al-Ḥakam provides names of traditionists who preserved that memory. His tradents from the Egyptian school provide a powerful group tradition, although the numbers of its practitioners do not necessarily insure its accuracy. These include Yaḥyā ibn Ayyūb, who died in 784, and Khālid ibn Ḥumayd, who died in 785/6. These last two are early and well regarded. The tradition that Heraclius sought to forbid civilian authorities from making separate peace terms with the Muslims without previous explicit approval from him is plausible. Such traditions, of course, also helped to preserve the prestige of the Heraclian dynasty, foisting blame on

22 R. G. Khoury, *ʿAbd Allāh Ibn Lahīʿa (97–174/715–790). Juge et grand maître de l'École égyptienne* (Wiesbaden, 1986).

23 John, Bishop of Nikiu, *Chronicle*, trans. R. M. Charles (Oxford, 1916). On Oriental Christian sources see Micheline Albert, R. Beylot, et al., *Christianismes orientaux. Introduction à l'étude des langues et des littératures* (Paris, 1993).

24 Nikephoros, *Short History*, ed. and trans. C. Mango (Washington, 1990); Theophanes, *Chronographia*, ed. C. de Boor, 2 vols. (Leipzig, 1883); *Chronicle of Theophanes the Confessor*, trans. C. Mango and R. Scott (Oxford, 1997). L. I. Conrad, "Theophanes and the Arabic Historical Transmission: Some Indications of Intercultural Transmission," *Byzantinische Forschungen*, 15 (1990), 1–45.

others for the military reverses and disasters – and the loss of territory, and human or financial resources, but Ibn ʿAbd al-Ḥakam was no tool of a Heraclian propaganda machine. Nevertheless, there may be some relevance of this tradition to later juridical claims that the Muslims acquired Egypt by conquest, making those territories subject to higher taxes.

The sources warrant caution. They do not give reliable statistics and are frequently vague. No direct archival material survives in Egypt, Constantinople or Cyprus that treats the critical communications between the Byzantine imperial government and its leaders in Egypt on the eve of the conquests. Nor are there archival materials that indicate policy decisions of ʿAmr ibn al-ʿĀṣ, commander of the Muslim victors. Instead we have later compilations of traditions which often reflect the tradents' other agenda or their sources. These traditions are often overly simplistic and tend to attribute too much responsibility to personalities. There is also a tendency for Muslim sources to report, at a later date, events in a scheme of classification that makes sense only in terms of later juridical interpretations or disputes that were historically inappropriate for Egypt in the 630s and 640s. Noth plausibly believes that ʿAmr invaded Egypt on his own initiative, not on the authorization of Caliph ʿUmar.[25]

Surviving Byzantine sources at Constantinople probably owe some of their information to Arab Christian traditions and transmission. They are so fragmentary in their coverage that it would be impossible to understand the Muslim conquests of Egypt by relying exclusively on them.[26] Nor do collections of Greek epistolography, sermons, speeches, or other literature fill in the gap. Muslim sources, for their part, do not rely on credible Christian or Byzantine sources. Coptic Christian sources reveal their own biases. John of Nikiu provides the most reliable account, which may be supplemented with the histories of Ibn ʿAbd al-Ḥakam and al-Ṭabarī, saints' lives or papyri. The Christian Arab historian Eutychius (Saʿīd ibn Baṭrīq) provides a late and confused version of the conquest. Although some hagiographic traditions exist, they do not celebrate any Christian martyrs who fought to the death defending Egypt against the Muslims. The only such traditions are from Gaza and they provide no new insights. In contrast to the Martyrs of Gaza, there is no record of Christian martyrs of the initial Muslim invasion of Egypt.[27]

[25] A. Noth, with L. I. Conrad, trans. M. Bonner, *The Early Arabic Historical Tradition: A Source-Critical Study* (Princeton, Darwin, 1994), 183–4. Important also is Av. Cameron and L. I. Conrad (eds.), *Problems in the Literary Source Material*, The Byzantine and Early Islamic Near East, 1 (Princeton, 1992), for many relevant papers.

[26] F. M. Donner, *The Early Islamic Conquests* (Princeton, 1981).

[27] H. Delehaye, "Passio sanctorum sexaginta martyrum," *Analecta Bollandiana*, 3 (1904), 289–307; J. Pargoire, "Les LX soldats martyrs de Gaza," *Échos d'Orient*, 8 (1905), 40–3.

The Emperor Heraclius did not visit Egypt, nor had any of his recent predecessors. How did that fact affect Egypt's fate? Heraclius's family was of Armenian extraction, with some familiarity with conditions of service in northern Syria, Mesopotamia, the upper Euphrates and Africa Proconsularis, but not Egypt. Presumably, Heraclius's impression of Egypt would have relied in part on information from his cousin Niketas, who had reconquered it in 608–10, taking it from partisans of the usurper Phokas. Niketas presumably also reported to Heraclius his observations about the positive and negative features of Egypt with respect to war against an opponent from the east who occupied Syria-Palestine. Niketas's opinions derived from his recent experiences in winning a civil war against Bonosus, Phokas's general, and his own abandonment of Egypt to the Persian invaders.[28] Whether the historian Theophylact Simocatta, who hailed from Egypt and wrote at the court, spoke with Heraclius and his entourage about Egypt cannot be ascertained. But there were probably other Egyptians in Heraclius's entourage. Heraclius probably acquired better information from Niketas about Egypt than had his predecessors, who did not benefit from a trusted cousin's recent service there. Toward the end of his life, Heraclius was probably exercising his authority as emperor only intermittently: a worsening medical condition impeded his efforts to make rational decisions.

Egypt remained a vital source of revenues to Constantinople, despite the loss of grain for the city, but one ponders the accuracy of information to the government in Constantinople about Egypt's situation, political, military or ecclesiastical. How much the Byzantine leadership knew about the Muslim invaders and their leadership in Medina is speculative, and the predominant perceptions of the Byzantine leaders probably derived from rumors, fear and confused reports from refugees. The Senate emerged as an important institution at Constantinople during this era, but the nature of its members' knowledge about Egypt is a mystery.

The consequences of the Persian occupation are complex.[29] The initial invasion inflicted little physical damage. The Persians' evacuation of Egypt was peaceful, following the July 629 agreement at Arabissos (southeast Anatolia) between Heraclius and Shahrbarāz, the Persian general who had conquered Egypt but who then nurtured other ambitions in Persia. The Persians seem to have departed swiftly, perhaps within two months of the

[28] On Niketas 7, sv. Nicetas, see F. R. Martindale, *Prosopography of the Later Roman Empire III* (Cambridge, 1992), 940–943; C. Mango, "A Byzantine Hagiographer at Work: Leontios of Neapolis," *Sitzungsberichte, Österreichische Akad. d. Wiss., philosoph.-hist. Kl.*, 434 (1984), 25–41.

[29] I owe much to the 1992 University of Chicago seminar paper of T. M. Hickey, "Observations on the Sasanian Invasion and Occupation of Egypt," now being revised for publication.

629 agreement.[30] The dearth of primary sources prohibits a more precise date, and the size of the Persian military occupation force also defies estimation. The best Persian troops had probably left Egypt by July 629 to accompany Shahrbarāz to the Cilician Gates and the vicinity of Alexandretta. No more than a skeletal occupation force of Persians remained in Egypt, even at the time of Shahrbarāz's meeting with Heraclius at distant Arabissos in that month. Impending friction between Shahrbarāz and the Sasanian monarch Khusraw II probably imperiled shipment of supplies to the Persian forces in Egypt, who feared reprisals or being cut off there, when their situation would have become untenable. Egyptians did not participate in any known effort to cast off Persian rule, and no fear of them caused Shahrbarāz to evacuate Egypt. His decision was part of his larger plan to seize control of Persia for himself and his partisans.

The Persian occupation was disruptive politically, interrupting the continuity of Roman–Byzantine rule, and causing some deterioration of the infrastructure. We have few details on the precise organization of the Byzantine army in Egypt after the Byzantines reoccupied the province. If the situation in Egypt parallels that in Palestine, there may have been an effort to restore the situation to what it was immediately before the Persian invasion, but not to reimpose any radical reorganization or reform. Unlike their presence in Syria or upper Mesopotamia, there are no reports of Persian troops remaining in Egypt, even as renegades. Egypt was physically more remote from Persia, and Persian soldiers would have been more vulnerable there if they had wished to remain.

No question persists over Shahrbarāz's conquest of Egypt, although many specifics are unclear. The chronology of his dispute with Khusraw II is poorly understood: in all likelihood tensions grew unbearable for Shahrbarāz after the end of the 626 siege of Constantinople by Avars and the Persians. It is also uncertain how Shahrbarāz's overtures to Heraclius and alienation from Khusraw II affected Egypt and its population, but they probably resulted in a reduction of violence on the part of Persian troops. This cannot be documented, however. While Shahrbarāz's actions probably aroused both Melkite and Coptic hopes, his eyes were on Heraclius and a return on his part to triumph in Persia rather than on local improvements in relations with Egyptians. No one claims that Egyptian geopolitical issues motivated Shahrbarāz's dispute with Khusraw II or his decision to cooperate with Heraclius. Heraclius could not easily ignore Shahrbarāz's overtures, although it is plausible that he remained skeptical of Shahrbarāz's sincerity or future decisions. Shahrbarāz shifted his tactics in the Byzantine–Persian

30 W. E. Kaegi and P. M. Cobb, "Heraclius, al-Ṭabarī and Shahrbarāz," to appear in the proceedings of the 1995 University of St. Andrews conference on al-Ṭabarī, ed. H. Kennedy.

conflict when he departed Egypt and drew near to the war's centers. Egypt remained important, but its strategic significance did not equal that of northern Syria or upper Mesopotamia for expeditionary armies of the two protagonists. The news of Shahrbarāz's assassination in Persia (633) probably evoked no reaction in Egypt, where he no longer wielded any power.

Egypt remained relatively prosperous after the Persian departure. The resumption of coastal trading and the end of the Persian occupation helped to revive the economy of Alexandria and other coastal towns, and trade also facilitated the spread of news both true and false. Egyptians had not considered the Persians to be welcome masters. One can speculate that various Arabs, some of whom may have served as couriers and interpreters, had learned much about the Persian occupation and evacuation of Egypt. The Persian troops under Shahrbarāz who had formerly served in Egypt but subsequently moved to northern Syria and Mesopotamia, had probably disseminated information, exposing vulnerabilities and opportunities. Arab communities which lay astride the lines of Persian communications between Egypt and Mesopotamia probably learned about conditions in Egypt and passed on some of that information.[31] It is uncertain whether tentative Byzantine efforts to open gold mines in the Eastern Desert (most notably, Biʾr Umm Fawākhīr) in Justinian's reign had continued into Heraclius's. But the abortive efforts of the sixth century may have left some expectation of great mineral wealth in Egypt even after the mining ceased. Rumors about it could have added to the material temptations for a Muslim invasion.[32]

The leading church officials in Egypt were Cyrus/Kyros, the Monothelete Patriarch of Alexandria, who arrived from Phasis in 630/31 – the Muqawqis of Arabic traditions – and Benjamin, the Coptic Patriarch of Alexandria after 626. The two intensely disliked each other. Because he is remembered as an oppressor, it is difficult to assess Kyros accurately. There is no way to evaluate the veracity of later reports that the Prophet had summoned Kyros, among other political leaders, to Islam. However, it is plausible that Kyros, as Byzantine governor and patriarch, paid tribute to the Muslims to forestall invasion. It is also plausible that ʿAmr ibn al-ʿĀṣ, who led the Muslim conquest, accepted such funds. Kyros's efforts to make peace with ʿAmr necessitated commercial taxes. The fact that Kyros could contemplate raising so much money through these taxes is an indication of the vitality and volume of commerce in the 630s. Furthermore, the dozen or so years of Sasanian occupation had not irrevocably damaged such trade. Stories that ʿAmr first saw Egypt while on a trading visit underscore the commercial

[31] Fundamental on the Arabs on the eve of the Muslim conquests, including their roles as intermediaries: I. Shahid, *Byzantium and the Arabs in the Sixth Century*, 2 vols. (Washington, 1995).

[32] Carol Meyer, "A Byzantine Gold-Mining Town in the Eastern Desert of Egypt: Bir Umm Fawakhir, 1992–1993," *Journal of Roman Archaeology*, 8 (1995), 192–224.

importance of Egypt and the familiarity of some Arabs with it. Trade had revived sufficiently by the end of the 630s that Kyros believed he could garner substantial funds from it. In his own mind, raising taxes would not do undue damage to life, stability or values in Egypt. The later Christian Arab historians Agapius and Severus also claim that Kyros secured a truce for three years in return for tribute payments. Their source presumably derived from the work of Theophanes/George Syncellus. An early tradent, Ḥārith ibn Yazīd al-Ḥaḍramī (d. ca. 700), reports via Ibn Lahīʿa, according to Ibn ʿAbd al-Ḥakam, that Abū Bakr made a peace arrangement with Kyros for Egypt immediately before the conquests of Syria.[33] This would not be inconsistent with other reports in the histories of Nikephoros, Theophanes, Michael the Syrian, and Agapius, who draw on Theophilus of Edessa.[34]

It is significant that the Persian evacuation of Egypt did not result from any Byzantine campaign from north Africa or from any Byzantine naval actions against its coasts, let alone any naval landings. Instead it resulted from actions at the center of gravity – in upper Mesopotamia and northern Syria and the Caucasus – and a political revolution that brought the Emperor Heraclius and the Persian general Shahrbarāz together. So other than offering troops, supplies, and other resources from the defense of Palestine and Syria against the Persians, earlier historical precedents did not offer any clear indication as to how Egypt might defeat the new Muslim conquerors of Syria. There was no easy formula to grasp.

The role of religious strife in Byzantine Egypt deserves attention, especially given Kyros's prominence in it. Coptic memory of the end of Byzantine rule is filled with recollections of persecution during Benjamin's long patriarchate. Coptic literature contains hostile references to Arabs, before and after the conquest, indicating that not every Copt welcomed Arabs as deliverers. And some who originally did soon changed their opinions. It is risky to assume that later Coptic attitudes were also those of the time of the original conquest. Ibn ʿAbd al-Ḥakam includes a tradition in his history that the dissident Patriarch, Benjamin, made separate arrangements with ʿAmr ibn al-ʿĀṣ. We know from him and from the Byzantine historians Theophanes and Nikephoros that Heraclius rejected the terms Kyros had made and deposed him, probably early in 640.[35] The inclusion of this tradition in Ibn ʿAbd al-Ḥakam's history does not guarantee its truth, but merely that it was deemed worthy of reporting in light of the late ninth-century situation. Some Copts of this later period may have interpreted events in the same

33 Ibn ʿAbd al-Ḥakam, *Futūḥ Miṣr*, 53.

34 Nikephoros, *Short History* 23, 70–73, 189 (Mango); Theophanes, A.M. 6126 (De Boor I, 338); 469–71 (Mango); Michael the Syrian, *Chronique*, ed. trans. J.-B. Chabot, 4 vols. (Paris, 1899–1910), II, 425; Agapius of Membij, *Patrologia Orientalis* 8: 471–74.

35 Nikephoros, *Short History*, 189.

way, as the contemporary testimony by John of Nikiu suggests. Respective transmissions of traditions may have distorted what really happened.

As the Muslim conquest of Palestine progressed between 634 and 637, separation of Egypt by land from the core of Byzantine territory in western Asia only made it more difficult to devise a solid land defense. Such a tactic had not worked when the Persians overran Palestine and Syria in the early 600s, and while the Byzantines did not learn from this experience, the Muslims had. ʿAmr had conquered Gaza in 637, if we believe the account of the Sixty Martyrs of Gaza. While in southern Palestine ʿAmr had time to learn about Egypt and was strategically placed to take advantage of Persian vulnerabilities there. He could also prevent any other Muslim commander from exploiting the situation. It is conceivable that ʿAmr had made a provisional arrangement with Kyros of Alexandria, and that in return for monetary payments he held off from invading or raiding Egypt. The logistical problems of maintaining communications and supplies for troops operating in Egypt were not insuperable when the Muslims controlled Gaza and its environs. Outposts such as Nessana on the edge of the Negev may no longer have been manned. Some of their occupants were of partial Arab background, if one can trust their known names. Possession of Palestine gave the potential initiative and a range of options to the Muslims.

Some Byzantine troops from Palestine fled into Egypt after the Byzantine defeat there at the hands of the Muslims between 634 and 637, but we neither know their precise numbers nor can identify their units. Given their defeat by the Muslims, those Byzantine troops and their leaders were too demoralized to repel the Muslims from Egypt, nor had they learned from their debacles in Syria and Palestine to make any significant contribution to their forces defending the province. Their behavior when they retreated into Egypt is unclear. The Muslim invasion itself followed the Byzantine loss of most of Palestine and Syria;[36] only a few coastal points were still holding out against the Muslims on the Syro-Palestinian coast at its inception. The invasion of Egypt made their retention even more perilous and ultimately irrelevant, and a dynamic of Muslim military success was already evident.

The Byzantine government faced another challenge. There was no great general whom it could trust to devise a successful defense. No officer emerged from the disarray of Byzantine forces to win renown or to show leadership potential. Admittedly, conditions in Egypt contrasted with those in Syria, nor were the soldiery similar. Armenians had served prominently in Syria and Mesopotamia, and friendly Arab tribesmen constituted a large portion of the Byzantine forces there. In Egypt, the ethnic mix seems to have differed. Many local levies were of dubious quality. Some troops from

[36] For a summary of events see P. M. Fraser, "Arab Conquest of Egypt," in A. S. Atiya (ed.), *Coptic Encyclopedia*, 8 vols., I (New York, 1991), 183–89.

adjacent parts of north Africa served in Egypt, although not as many as the government had wished. Some forces were transported by sea from Thrace, but their adjustment to local conditions may have been difficult.

The overall effect of the Muslim successes in Palestine and Syria, especially the fall of Jerusalem and other holy places, cannot have been positive, especially after Heraclius had restored the presumed fragments of the Cross to their rightful places. Problems of morale were probably created within Egypt for both the army and civilians.[37]

Byzantine military commanders were at odds personally, and disagreed over whether to make terms with the Muslims or to persist in violent resistance. Domentianus, brother-in-law to Kyros, concurred with him about the advisability of trying to reach an accommodation with the Muslims, but these commanders were occasionally inconsistent, or at least opportunistic. Domentianus was later inclined to honor General Valentinus and the advisors surrounding the eleven-year-old Emperor Constans II at Constantinople, who took a hard line. John of Barka, Marianos and others also favored resistance, as did Manuel when he was dispatched to Egypt.[38] The rationale within the military for Egypt's defense is not well understood. The existence of cleavage is clearly important because it drained support and strength for a coherent resistance, and also convinced Muslims that theirs was the winning side.

Disputes among civilian, ecclesiastical and military leaders did not account for all internal Byzantine divisions. Serious problems had emerged at the imperial capital, Constantinople. The death of Heraclius at the beginning of 641 paralyzed Byzantine resistance.[39] Even the Muslim tradents Yaḥyā ibn Ayyūb (d. 784) and Khālid ibn Ḥumayd reported such a tradition. The regency of Heraclius's widow, Martina, preferred a more moderate stance toward the Muslims than did some other factions at the court. No confidential memoranda or archival materials survive from Constantinople or Egypt concerning this important policy issue. The position taken by Martina's faction can be explained by a fear that her regency was vulnerable to deposition at the hands of a soldier-emperor if fighting intensified or if the government suffered further defeats on the battlefield. Martina, her sons and partisans could ill afford another Yarmūk, yet there was a real danger of another occurring. The regency, in that dangerous period when there were minor children of a controversial union, needed an interval in which stability could be gained and consolidated. In addition the government did not want to be in the position of having to assume responsibility for the further loss of important territory. The personal

37 See B. Flusin, *Saint Anastase le Perse et l'histoire de la Palestine au début du VII siècle* (Paris, 1992), II, 151–72.

38 On these generals, see Martindale, *Prosopography*, 408–9, 704, 829, 811.

39 D. Misiu, *He diatheke tou Herakleiou* (Thessaloniki, 1985).

opinions about Egypt on the part of the Constantinopolitan Patriarch Pyrrhos, Empress Martina or her sons are unknown.[40] Martina's attitudes were probably formed in the circles of Heraclius's family. She had personal knowledge of Syria, but not of Egypt.

Philagrios, the powerful Koubikoularios (imperial palace chamberlain) and Sakellarios (treasurer), urged support for Heraclius's son, Heraclius Constantine III, and grandson, Constans II (descending from his first marriage to the late Fabia/Eudocia).[41] He used his financial influence to win support of critical military elements with the help of his aide, the ambitious Armenian officer Valentinos. This individual was based at Constantinople in the service of Heraclius Constantine and Constans.[42] The treasury of the *sacellum* was in the ascendant in the seventh century, following the disintegration of the old praetorian prefecture and its financial structure. The struggle for succession was acrimonious, and distracted the imperial government from any coherent effort to save Egypt.

It is unclear whether Philagrios ever managed to enforce a new census for the entire empire ordered by Heraclius just before his death, or whether he even implemented it in Egypt.[43] Its likely date, 640, happens to coincide approximately with the recall of Kyros and his ensuing exile. The issue at hand was not simply the loss of revenues to the Muslims, but also a powerful internal bureaucratic quarrel about the effort to initiate a new census. Kyros claimed that he would impose a new commercial tax to compensate for the loss of revenues to the Muslims. However, any expedient would have weakened the bureaucratic controls of Philagrios in Constantinople, and so met resistance. There thus was a complex set of fiscal factors involved.

Heraclius's wrath against Kyros may have been intensified by Philagrios pressing him, for his own reasons, to reject any initiatives devised by Kyros, since they would enable local officials in Egypt to gain more autonomy. If true, this perspective was myopic. But Kyros and other local officials might well have resented Philagrios's efforts to extend such an unfamiliar measure as a census to Egypt. The creation of a new census would have offered many opportunities for the central bureaucracy in Constantinople to consolidate its control over Egypt, and would have threatened many constituencies that extended beyond Kyros's circle. No Egyptian source mentions this measure. Philagrios and Kyros were opponents for reasons probably connected to

[40] On Martina see Martindale, *Prosopography*, 837–38; on Pyrrhos see J. L. Van Dieten, *Geschichte der Patriarchen von Sergios I bis Johannes VI* (Amsterdam, 1972), 57–105.

[41] F. R. Martindale, s.v. Philagrius, *Prosopography*, 1018.

[42] Nikephoros, *Short History* 29, 78–81, 188–89.

[43] See *Synopsis Chronike*, ed. C. Sathas, in his *Mesaionike Bibliotheke* 7, VII (Paris, 1894) 110 (reprint Athens, 1972, VII, 1–556); Kaegi, *Byzantium and the Early Islamic Conquests*, 257–258, 287. On Philagrios' support for Constans II see Nikephoros, *Short History*, 189.

rivalries over control of revenues and spheres of influence. There is no reason to doubt John of Nikiu's information about this antagonism. Philagrios supported members of the Heraclian family whose support depended on military leaders who found it in their interest to advocate strong military resistance to the Muslims, especially in Asia Minor. These disputes in Constantinople distracted the government, and contributed to the failure of a sound defense strategy for Egypt.

Egypt's size and remoteness from Constantinople also complicated its defense. One may reasonably ask whether any strategy would have succeeded once the loss of Palestine, Syria and Mesopotamia blocked contact by land between Egypt and Anatolia and Constantinople. That loss also deprived Byzantium of contact with friendly Arab Christian tribes who in the past had served as a shield against hostile Arabs. If Egypt was to be protected from Muslim Arab invaders, it would be necessary to find the right troops and to devise effective strategies. Judging from the Mauricius *Strategikon* of ca. 600, the extant military manuals provided no easy formulae.

The Blue and Green circus factions of Constantinople also existed in late Byzantine Egypt, as literary texts and inscriptions attest. Some scholars have emphasized religious sectarianism and the role of these factions, identifying the Greens with resistance to Islam and the Blues with readiness to avoid a military confrontation. These interpretations are simplistic and unpersuasive. An argument that those previous partisans of the Circus Factions explain the fall of Egypt is unconvincing.[44] It is incorrect to attribute to the factions any significant role; they may not have made any positive contribution to Egypt's defense, but they were not the cause of its failure.

It is incorrect to assume that all Monophysite Egyptians supported the Muslims against the Byzantines.[45] The situation was more complex. Some Egyptians did collaborate and rapidly converted to Islam, but Muslim victories cannot be simply ascribed to help from Egyptian collaborators. The Muslims possessed excellent military commanders and a coherent purpose, while everyone agrees that the Byzantine political, ecclesiastical and military authorities in Egypt and Constantinople were mired in bitter rivalries that proved ruinous to their chances. Previous massacres of Christians by the Persians, and the rapid surrender of many Palestinian towns to Muslims in

[44] J. Jarry, "L'Égypte et l'invasion musulmane," *Annales Islamologiques*, 6 (1966), 1–29; Z. Borkowski, *Alexandrie II: Inscriptions des factions* (Warsaw, 1981); A. Cameron, *Circus Factions* (Oxford, 1977); but cf. Jean Gascou, "Les institutions de l'hippodrome en Égypte byzantine," *Bulletin de l'Institut français d'archéologie orientale au Caire*, 76 (1976), 185–212.

[45] Correct is F. Winkelmann, "Ägypten und Byzanz vor der arabischen Eroberung," *Byzantinoslavica*, 40 (1979), 161–82, reprinted in his *Studien zu Konstantin den Grossen und zur byzantinischen Kirchengeschichte*, ed. W. Brandes and J. Haldon (Birmingham, UK, 1993).

the 630s probably induced the Byzantines to reach a peaceful settlement with the Muslims in Egypt. Rumors about possible atrocities may have intensified this propensity.

There was no coherent plan to arm the Egyptian population, or for rapid training in the use of arms so that the populace could resist. Acquiring sufficient wood for fashioning weapons itself posed problems. Civilians were most likely to participate in local defense by helping to repair canals or man walls against invaders. There were precedents in Palestine, Syria and Upper Mesopotamia of local authorities making separate peace during the Persian invasions of the sixth and early seventh centuries, as well as during the Muslim invasions of the 630s. It is not surprising that Egyptians behaved similarly. There was no desire among the local population for fighting to the death to save their town or district from occupation. One cannot trust later traditions about terms of surrender, which may involve post-hoc juristic reasoning rather than historical realities.

Their long-held conviction that the Arabs were unable to besiege walled towns may have blinded the Byzantines to their own vulnerabilities during the Muslim invasion. In Egypt, as in Syria, some walled towns held out longer against the invaders than did regions. The early fall of the fortress of Babylon (Old Cairo) to the Muslims placed them in a strong strategic position; they were able to cut off Upper Egypt from the Delta. Again by a process of "blinding," they made it virtually impossible for any defense of Upper Egypt to be conducted coherently, since those who might resist in the south could learn only with difficulty about the central government's efforts in Constantinople. Egypt had to attempt its defense in the absence of good communications with other Byzantine forces, except by land and sea with Numidia or other parts of north Africa.

Egypt had provided financial support for military operations in Syria and many earlier campaigns. The imposition of a heavy tribute on the province temporarily forestalled a Muslim invasion. But the payment of such a huge tribute deprived Byzantine Syria of the means previously available to aid its defense. In this way, the fortunes of Egypt and Syria were intertwined during the early Islamic conquests. Whether this was a conscious plan on the Muslims' part or not, its consequences were serious.

In May 655, the Monotheletic government of Emperor Constans II (641–68) accused the zealous Chalcedonian monk Maximus the Confessor, exiled in Africa since 633, of discouraging a Byzantine commander, Peter, from moving Numidian troops to rescue Egypt. He was held responsible for the loss of that great province to the Muslims.[46] Such scapegoating is a reminder of how important was Egypt's loss. It is plausible that the

[46] *Relatio motionis factae inter domnum abbatem Maximum et socium ejus atque principes in secretario*, ed. J. P. Migne, Patrologia Graeca 90, 112–113.

government of Heraclius had attempted to move troops from Numidia against the Muslim invaders of Egypt in response to the first reports of restiveness among Arabs in nearby regions of the Arabian peninsula, on the eve of the more powerful Muslim penetrations into Palestine and Syria. This indicates that there was some perceived Arab threat to Egypt as early as 633, even though there was no substantial invasion until 639. This threat further reinforces the veracity of reports that Patriarch Kyros purchased some temporary relief from Muslim invasions.

The defeat and death of General John Barkaines (Barka was one Byzantine term for al-Marj, in Cyrenaica) early in the Muslim invasion may provide another indication that some troops from areas west of Egypt participated in its defense at the end of Heraclius's reign. John Barkaines died at the battle of ʿAyn Shams (Heliopolis), near modern Cairo, probably in July 640. The reported size of both Muslim and Byzantine armies are suspect. Some scholars doubt that John Barkaines came from Barka or that his presence indicated any participation of troops from Byzantine-controlled regions west of Egypt. But given the earlier Heraclian conquest of Egypt from coastal areas in Libya and Carthage, and given accusations that efforts to send relief forces from the west (with which Maximus the Confessor allegedly interfered) were sabotaged, that skepticism seems excessive.

Niketas had already quarreled with John the Almsgiver, Patriarch of Alexandria, about taking control of church funds to help the beleaguered empire and its government.[47] The quarrels between Kyros and Heraclius, or Kyros and Philagrios, seem to have been similar. Tensions were inherent between a wealthy church and a military with an unquenchable thirst for funds. Thus the tensions of 641 paralleled those during the Persian invasion. Niketas had directed the earlier defense of Egypt against the Persians. That had involved a battle at Caesarea, resulting in a truce (613). He had also fought the Persians in northern Syria, near Antioch. Such clashes were part of Syria's defense, but also outer skirmishes to protect Egypt. It was presumably after the failure of those actions that Niketas withdrew into Egypt and then fled by ship from Alexandria in the face of the Persian invasion. It is unclear what military lessons he learned from his experience.

The loss of Egypt to the Constantinopolitan government had twice negatively affected Syria's defense earlier in the seventh century, by diverting the attention of its protectors and by removing Egypt's financial resources from its support in 610 during Heraclius's revolt against Phokas. The occupation by Shahrbarāz and the Arab conquest soon followed. However, in neither case did the loss of Egypt permanently impair the defense of

[47] Leontios of Neapolis, *Vie de Syméon le Fou et Vie de Jean de Chypre*, ed. trans. A. J. Festugière (Paris, 1974), 356; V. Déroche, *Études sur Léontios de Néapolis*, Studia Byzantina Upsaliensia, 3 (Uppsala, 1995), 33–36.

Anatolia. The Arab menace with respect to Egypt was always seen as a problem emanating from the Sinai Peninsula, and in addition there was the threat of nomadic incursions from Nubians in the south. Those had imperiled travel, overland commerce and agriculture in certain important regions, but they did not endanger the control of Egypt by the central government, except in the direst moments of the third-century crisis of the Roman Empire when the aggression of Palmyra was at its zenith. Egypt had long maintained contact with Arabs, including those from Sinai. Literary references to Arabs in religious texts do not reveal any new trend culminating in the late sixth or early seventh centuries.[48] Such references are often stereotypic and should be regarded with caution.

Control of the sea and of Egypt's waterways was always essential to the administration of Byzantine Egypt. The sea was the medium for dominating the church in Egypt, for recalling and communicating with patriarchs, for sending troops and supplies, and for extracting funds from Egypt to Constantinople. Egypt was navigationally linked to Cyprus, which remained in Byzantine hands even after Syria fell. That link progressed from Egypt through Cyprus to Rhodes, and from Rhodes to Constantinople. Control of the littoral and such ports as Alexandria/Alexandretta in Syria or western Asia were also of importance, permitting the Byzantines to strike at coastal areas in Egypt occupied by hostile forces. This control did not, however, secure the Egyptian interior very well, especially if a district were distant from Egypt's waterways, since the Byzantines do not appear to have developed techniques of large-scale warfare away from them.

Jean Maspero once observed that the Byzantines lacked unity of command in trying to devise a defense of Egypt.[49] Modern scholars' doubts about Maspero's thesis are unwarranted. There were poor coordination of relief forces, disagreements between their leaders and local defense levies. Maspero noted that the Byzantine forces in Egypt were sufficient for their normal military duties, but that they were inadequate for the task of securing it against the Muslims in the early seventh century. The fortresses and fortifications in themselves were satisfactory.

Modern historians have praised Heraclius for not risking the loss of his remaining armies by trying to retain Egypt. The emperor thus implicitly conceded that the loss of Palestine and Syria doomed the province. The perspective of those who give such praise is, of course, that of Constantinople – not that of Alexandria or Cairo. The Byzantine Empire's strategic needs caused it to concentrate its better troops in northern Syria and upper

[48] Michael Lapidge, *Biblical Commentaries from the Canterbury School of Theodore and Hadrian* (Cambridge, 1994), 324–325. Hadrian may have been born in Cyrenaica in the late 630s.

[49] J. Maspero, *Organisation militaire*, 119–23.

Mesopotamia rather than in Egypt.[50] Ordinarily, few elite expeditionary troops of maneuver were stationed there. We know little about events along the Egyptian Red Sea coast in this period, and their significance for broader developments. It is unlikely, for example, that the early negotiation of terms with the Muslims at the northern Red Sea port of Ayla (ʿAqaba) by its bishop would have escaped notice by some Egyptians, but there is no recorded evidence of this.[51] Nor is there evidence about the movement of Byzantine troops or vessels along the Red Sea coast in response to the movement of Muslims in the northern Ḥījāz. Likewise, although the Red Sea could have been a conduit for valuable information about events in Arabia to reach Byzantine officials in Egypt, no record has survived that they received such reports and revised their policies accordingly.

Most material in Byzantine military manuals concerning maneuvers and battle formations was inappropriate for conditions in Egypt, especially the Delta.[52] But it was equally so for other parts of the province, in particular the harsh, dry regions away from the Nile. We have no manuals on the use of canals, waterways, marshes or arid districts to deter invaders. On the other hand, the Muslims benefited from knowing more about the Byzantines than their opponents knew about them. Given their control of Palestine, the Muslims were able to keep the Byzantines guessing about their intentions, and whether they planned to strike against Egypt or against Byzantine outposts on the edge of northern Syria, or the route to Anatolia. Byzantium thus faced a strategic dilemma: where does one concentrate the limited supply of remaining troops that requires time and expense to deploy? In Syria-Palestine there is marginal evidence, some epigraphic or parenthetical anecdotes in literary sources, that local elites repaired walls or patrolled districts, activities continuing from the sixth century, but there is no similar evidence for Egypt. Egypt lacked raw materials, especially iron and wood, for manufacturing weapons and military machinery. Supplies of wood probably came from forested areas of the empire, such as southwest Anatolia, the Adriatic coasts, or the Black Sea littoral and its interior.

Urban unrest certainly contributed to the fall of Egypt to the Muslims. Yet what could such unrest have accomplished against them? There were Muslim traditions that the population of Alexandria had twice risen against

[50] Kaegi, *Byzantium and the Early Islamic Conquests*, 26–87; see also the volume of papers from the 1992 conference on *States, Resources and Armies*, ed. A. Cameron (The Byzantine and Early Islamic Near East, vol. 3) (Princeton, 1996), esp. J.-M. Carrié, "L'État à la recherche de nouveaux modes de financement des armées (Rome et Byzance, IVe-VIIe siècles)," 27–60.

[51] P. M. Cobb and D. Whitcomb in their respective publications, including Whitcomb's excavations, are elucidating much about this important port.

[52] See G. T. Dennis's editions of *Three Byzantine Military Treatises* (Washington, 1985), and the Maurikios *Strategikon*, trans. G. T. Dennis (Philadelphia, 1984), and his edition of the Greek original, published by the Austrian Academy, Vienna 1981.

the Arabs after the signing of peace terms. Some have imputed the settlement with the Muslims to fatigue on the part of Egypt's leadership stemming from the volatility of local public opinion and exasperation over shifting imperial policies. These views may be credible.

One may guess that, as in Syria, few in Egypt at the beginning believed that the Muslim conquest was irrevocable. But unlike in Syria, the possibility of flight by civilians was not easy. The swift Muslim conquest of the Pentapolis by 643 effectively eliminated the opportunity for overland flight west to Byzantine Africa. It was possible by sea but there was a limit to the number of those ready to take the risk. The earliest attitudes towards Arab Muslims took shape at all levels of Byzantine society in Palestine-Syria, not in Egypt, in the light of the initial contacts between Christians and Muslims. Whatever their accuracy, these attitudes would circulate rapidly in Egypt as well.

The Muslims' invasion of Egypt came at a propitious time for them, when the imperial government found itself rent by internal strife over the succession. Although unintended, the timing was perfect for the Muslims to apply maximum pressure with minimal troops. The conflict between the Treasurer Philagrios and Patriarch Kyros also worked to their advantage. While not causing the political crisis, they profited from it. The imperial postal system was still partially operative in Anatolia early in the seventh century, but whether it still linked Egypt with Constantinople is unclear.[53] There is no evidence for the creation of a new Byzantine "theme" system in Egypt during Heraclius's reign, even though the appointment of Manuel to replace Kyros signified a stronger Byzantine commitment to a military response during the crisis.[54]

The sequence of events throughout the Muslim conquest poses some problems but is less ambiguous than that of the conquest of Syria. ʿAmr led his troops past Pelusium (al-Faramā), which he took after a siege of one month, and then through Wādī Tūmīlāt to the eastern side of the Delta. He sought to capture the strategically vital fortress of Babylon so that he could isolate the Delta. Copts reportedly aided him in his capture of Pelusium. After taking Bilbeis and Tendunias, he requested reinforcements from Caliph ʿUmar, who sent him another 4,000 troops. (One should suspect reports of round numbers such as 4,000 in Arab historical traditions.) When they arrived, his forces totaled perhaps 15,000. ʿAmr triumphed at the battle of ʿAyn Shams north of Tendunias and then besieged Babylon from August/

[53] Jean Gascou, "Les grands domaines," 53–59; Andrea Jördens, *P. Heidelberg* V, in *Vertragliche Regelungen von Arbeiten im späten griechsprachigen Ägypten* (Heidelberg, 1990), 43–48.

[54] W. Kaegi, *Byzantium and the Early Islamic Conquests*, 279–85. On the themes, see J. Haldon, "Military Service, Military Lands and the Status of Soldiers," *Dumbarton Oaks Papers*, 45 (1993), 1–67.

September 640 until its surrender in April 641. The Patriarch Kyros made a provisional treaty with the Muslims that Heraclius rejected. ʿAmr's initial raids into the Delta encountered problems, so he returned to the siege of Babylon. He then proceeded north along the western edge of the Delta, capturing Terenuthis, Nikiu, Kom Sharīk and Sultays before reaching the suburbs of Alexandria at Ḥulwa. The city was placed under siege.

Meanwhile, Kyros returned from temporary exile to Babylon, via Rhodes. Kyros negotiated a general peace in return for payment of tribute and two dīnārs per unconverted male. He was granted an armistice period of eleven months to evacuate all Byzantine troops. ʿAmr then extended his control over upper Egypt as far as the Thebaid. Kyros died in March 642. Four years later, Manuel returned with troops to restore Byzantine authority in Alexandria, but he was slain. After their defeat, his troops were again evacuated, leaving the Muslims in permanent control.

It is impossible to estimate accurately the civilian or military casualties on either side during the operations resulting from the conquest. Massacres of civilians on a large scale are unlikely, but smaller ones surely spread terror. There were scattered reports of individuals accepting Islam.

It would be equally futile to attempt an estimate of financial and economic consequences. Intercity trade was surely affected negatively, as was the movement of agricultural products from region to region. No immediate health disaster ensued from refugees crowding into a few densely packed towns.

The Byzantines probably retained their best military units at Constantinople to protect the capital and confront the threat of civil war posed by the ambitious General Valentinos.[55] Other troops would have been concentrated in Anatolia, to stave off a Muslim invasion through the Taurus Mountains. Anatolia was more important to the Byzantine government than Egypt, and the retention of Anatolic and Armenian forces was essential for its defense, so that there could be no option of sending them to Egypt's rescue. Thus the Muslim push on to the Anatolian plateau in 644 may have deterred any serious effort to recover Egypt.

Internal strife in Egypt on the eve of the conquest cannot be ascribed to a single factor. Several sources testify to disagreements between the Melkite Patriarchate and military officials such as Niketas or General Isaakios, on the eve of the Persian invasion several decades previously. These conditions had worsened by the 630s and early 640s. Patriarch John the Almsgiver sought to negotiate a peace between the Persians and the imperial government, but encountered popular and military opposition. Leontios of Neapolis's *Life of John* was composed on Cyprus in 641/2 under Archbishop Arkadios, an ally of the embattled Patriarch Kyros.

[55] Martindale, *Prosopography*, 1354–55.

The *Vita* and its epitomes' information regarding events in 619 may contain not accurate reports but distortions that reflect the perspectives of Kyros and Arkadios in the early 640s. Then, as in 619 and the 650s, controversy flared over responsibility for the loss of Egypt. In both instances, the Patriarch of Alexandria was the object of hostility to at least one important military commander. John fled Egypt for Cyprus. He may have been accompanied by Niketas or Isaakios, who allegedly betrayed Alexandria to the Persians.[56] Kyros's abortive attempt to negotiate peace with the Arabs paralleled John's earlier approach to the Persians. One other epitome of the *Life of John* reports that Saracens (Arabs) fled to Alexandria when the Persians invaded.[57] One wonders whether they were Sinai Arabs or arrivals from Palestine. John also ransomed some families from Madianites who appear to have been Arabs from Trans-Jordan or somewhere east of the Dead Sea. Use of a Septuagint term like Madianites implies that they were Bedouin from the Dead Sea region. They were probably pursuing opportunities for enrichment in the aftermath of the chaos following the Persian defeat of the Byzantines.[58]

Those negotiating the return of captives from the Bedouin raids in 619 were the Bishop of Rhinocolura (al-ʿArīsh), the Archbishop of Constantia in Cyprus and the Abbot of St. Anthony's Monastery. Involvement of the Cypriot Archbishop on behalf of Patriarch John may indicate a coastal location for a meeting and return of ransomed captives. All of these texts depict friction between the Patriarch of Alexandria and its military leadership over money or willingness to negotiate peace. John is represented as accompanied by Niketas, Heraclius's cousin. In both cases, it seems that some inhabitants of Alexandria opposed their Patriarch's settlement with the respective invader.

The "Saracens" who had fled to Alexandria before the Persian advance were a source of information about the city to the Muslim Arabs two decades later. The inclusion of a reference to them may indicate that in the past their presence in Alexandria was unusual and thus worthy of mention in the *Vita* epitome composed by Sophronios. The presence of Saracens in Alexandria created a pool of personnel of whom some spoke Arabic and could serve as translators familiar with Arab negotiating techniques.

[56] H. Delehaye, "Une vie inédite de Saint Jean l'Aumônier," *Analecta Bollandiana*, 45 (1927), 5–74, esp. 25.

[57] E. Lappa-Zizicas, "Un épitomé inédit de la vie de S. Jean l'Aumônier," *Analecta Bollandiana*, 88 (1970), 272.

[58] Delehaye, "Une vie inédite de Saint Jean l'Aumônier," 23–24; Lappa-Zizicas, "Un épitomé inédit de la Vie de S. Jean l'Aumônier," 276. Dawes and Baynes's commentary on the translation (in their *Three Byzantine Saints*) referred to Midian, but not to Arabs, hence the reason why many scholars have probably overlooked this passage: E. H. Dawes, N. H. Baynes, commentary on *Vita* of John in *Three Byzantine Saints* (Oxford, 1948), 265.

Finger-pointing over responsibility for the loss of Alexandria thus occurred at least twice in the seventh century. The accusations against Maximus the Confessor were another aspect of that controversy and its recriminations. A. J. Butler wrote his *Arab Conquest of Egypt* prior to the publication of either epitome of John's Life. He therefore could not assess its information in his otherwise competent history.

It is essential to consider the role of controversies about Kyros and Arkadios, Philagrios and Martina, and the imperial succession crisis in the composition of Leontios's *Vita* in its present form. These controversies also reinforce the need to contemplate events in Cyprus and their relationship to Alexandria and Constantinople. The earlier controversies about Patriarch John and the surrender of Alexandria belonged to recent memory. This memory probably inclined Patriarch Kyros to caution in his negotiations with ʿAmr ibn al-ʿĀṣ. The need to shield himself from allegations of treachery and betrayal may have complicated Kyros's role even further at the end of the 630s and early 640s.

An atmosphere of mistrust arose from more than differences about Christology. An earlier Patriarch was believed to have been the object of conspiracy and even murder by the military commander Isaakios. These controversies hampered decision-making. They also contributed to the breakdown of confidentiality. Heraclius's reaction to Kyros's unauthorized treaty with the Muslims was consistent with his deposition of John Kateas, curator of Osrhoene, for negotiating a similar truce with the Muslims after the battle of Yarmūk. There is a logic in Heraclius's policies of restraint over administrators attempting to make separate terms, whether in northern Syria, upper Mesopotamia or Egypt.[59]

Patriarch John the Almsgiver played an uncertain role in negotiating an obscure peace settlement between the naval commander Aspagurios and the Cypriot port of Constantia in 619. It is possible that dissident and disgruntled Byzantine military forces on Cyprus had considered the rejection of imperial authority in the wake of Persian victories and Byzantine defeats. That strife in 619 had further complicated Byzantine efforts to defend Egypt from the Persians.[60]

The controversial stance of Archbishop Arkadios of Constantia towards the imperial succession crisis at the death of Heraclius could have made Egypt's lines of communication at the difficult moment of 641/2 even more tenuous. It probably discouraged the leadership in Egypt from taking further risks. It jeopardized communications and logistics at the worst possible moment for Egypt's security. Those who sailed between Constantinople and

[59] Kaegi, *Byzantium and the Early Islamic Conquests*, 160–9, 202, 253.

[60] On ties with Cyprus see M. Rodziewicz, *Alexandrie* I: *La céramique romaine tardive d'Alexandrie* (Warsaw, 1976), 55.

Egypt via Cyprus could not have been ignorant of these frictions. They adversely affected the Byzantine army's morale. The murky case of Aspagurios thus underscores strife in Cyprus in the second decade of the seventh century, a prelude to difficulties stemming from Heraclius's death and the resultant succession crisis in the early 640s that compromised Egypt's security.

Three ecclesiatical leaders – Patriarchs John and Kyros of Alexandria, and Archbishop Arkadios of Constantia – died in the midst of the events of 619 and 641 respectively. General Isaakios, involved like John in the earlier controversy, also died in Cyprus during the course of events. Their deaths exacerbated the rapid turnover of imperial leadership at Constantinople and prohibited a continuity of leadership.

The precedent of negotiations with Arabs about captives does not in itself confirm the veracity of other reports about negotiations to forestall the Muslim invasion. But there is testimony that Patriarch John had planned to turn away the Persians by negotiation, and that General Isaakios, after betraying Alexandria to them, sought to murder John when he was fleeing to Cyprus. These events foreshadowed Kyros's actions. Butler doubted whether the Muslims would have accepted money in return for some temporary respite of three years. Yet the payment of a substantial sum to them would have denied it to the Byzantines for their defense of Syria and Anatolia. Thus a decision by the Muslims to accept it would be perceptive. It would reinforce their position while denying vital resources to their opponents at a critical moment. The strategic situations on these different fronts were interrelated.

The interest of Niketas, according to the *Vita* of John the Almsgiver, in associating John with Heraclius is noteworthy, if the account is accurate. By inference, Patriarch John may have sought to avoid implying his approval of Heraclius in those desperate moments of the emperor's reign that were clouded by questions over his imperial legitimacy and doubts over divine protection for the empire. Echoes of civil–ecclesiastical strife are discernible even in the story of Niketas and John. This story had odd resonances at the end of Heraclius's reign. The *Vita*'s author emphasizes the close relationship between Niketas and John, and subsequently between him and the dynasty. The author may have worried about new efforts by the government to seize still more ecclesiastical wealth. He accordingly invoked the prestigious names of both John and Niketas to discourage more expropriations or forced loans in the early 640s, even if they were to finance the restoration of Byzantine control over Egypt. Hagiographic memory reflected genuine ecclesiastical fears of further confiscations after 641.

As Nikephoros mentions in his *Short History*, the relationship between Niketas and his daughter, Gregoria, is significant. She married the Emperor Heraclius Constantine (III). Niketas was celebrated for victories over

Persians in Constantinopolitan statuary and one inscription, but there is no evidence that he defeated the Persians in Egypt. Presumably, he was long deceased. Whatever the genetic consequences of these ties, the nature of illnesses suffered by Fabia/Eudocia and Heraclius are unclear. The role of Empress Gregoria, who had strong ties with the neighboring Cyrenaican Pentapolis, is uncertain. She may have exerted influence at the imperial court in support of hardline policies that would protect Africa by seeking to prevent the Muslim conquest of Egypt (such as moving more troops to Egypt from other parts of Africa) or she may have reluctantly accepted the terms negotiated by Kyros in the hopes that peace in Egypt would protect Africa. Heraclius's north African heritage may have reinforced the already strong connection of Constans II to the remaining members of the Heraclian dynasty. The connection may also have reinforced his commitment to retain north Africa. Despite his limited resources, this relationship could have influenced Constans to travel west to Italy and Sicily. He murdered his brother some time after the loss of Egypt, but this act reflected the larger context of internal strife that had plagued the imperial house since Heraclius's later years.

Severus's late account of the patriarchs of Alexandria contains material on the seventh century that is compatible with Theophanes' and Nikephoros' versions. It also accords with the Christian Arab *History* of Agapius of Membij, despite religious differences. Severus also repeats the story that Egypt paid three years' tribute to stave off the Muslim invasion, an assertion made by Nikephoros and Theophanes. So even a Coptic tradition, or one passed down by a Monophysite tradent, accepts the tradition of an arrangement to buy off the Muslims from their invasion. It may have derived from what Theophilus of Edessa passed on to Nikephoros and Theophanes. These accounts were consistent with the activities of Patriarchs like John the Almsgiver, who also sought to make arrangements in lieu of warfare and the consequent loss of life and property.

It is difficult to escape the conclusion that the Byzantines could have fashioned a better defense of Egypt than they did. The fall of Egypt was not inevitable, although at some point reversal of the process became difficult. Internal Byzantine strife was worse during the empire's attempts to defend Egypt than during its unsuccessful efforts to hold Syria. The initial capture of Alexandria in 641 marked a threshold, if that had not already been crossed when Babylon surrendered to the Muslims. The caliber of the generals sent to direct the resistance was low. The accession in late 641 of a leadership in Constantinople that favored resistance to the end did not substantially alter Egypt's position. That new leadership needed to consolidate its grip on power, and while seeking to deflect criticism, it could not afford to take big risks. It did send Manuel the Augustulis with a large force in a last attempt to retrieve the deteriorating situation. But that expedition ended in ignominious failure, although there was no naval disaster comparable to that of 468 when the Byzantine fleet failed to recover Africa from the Vandals. The Byzantines suffered no serious losses from their Egyptian operations. Recriminations about the defeat reverberated for decades in many literary genres, but these charges did not illuminate the complex context of decisions and actions. There does not appear to have been any great longing for a return to Byzantine rule among Egyptians, and unlike in northern Syria, that was not an option since Byzantine power rapidly receded westward across north Africa.

From the perspective of the Byzantine regime, it was a success simply to have extricated its elite forces by sea after the likelihood of Muslim victory was obvious. Accordingly. there was little hope for a reversal of conditions that would allow a Byzantine recovery. In the early 640s, the government could afford the loss of no more elite troops to the Muslims. How much equipment they did abandon in the evacuation is unknown. Byzantine forces in Egypt suffered no battle of annihilation, nor were they trapped under siege and destroyed. Thus in conclusion, the Byzantines won no victory, but avoided a disaster that would have weakened their defenses in Anatolia and the Balkans. On balance, the Byzantines lamented the Muslim conquest as "the Egyptian destruction."[61] For Ibn ʿAbd al-Ḥakam and his sources, it was the Emperor Heraclius who was the backbone of Byzantine resistance and with him perished Byzantine power in Egypt.[62]

A tentative chronology of important events during the Muslim conquest

633 Maximus the Confessor discourages the dispatch of troops from Numidia to Egypt to reinforce Byzantine defenses against real or perceived threats of Arab military action.

637 Patriarch Kyros agrees to pay 200,000 dīnārs or their equivalent in Byzantine gold solidi annually to the Muslims to deter them from invading Egypt.

[61] Anastasius the Sinaite, *Sermo adversus Monothelatas* 3.1, 86–92, in: *Anastasii Sinaitae Opera. Sermones duo in constitutionem hominis secundum imaginem Dei necnon Opuscula adversus Monothelatas*, ed. Karl-Heinz Uthemann, Corpus Christianorum, Series Graeca, 12 (Brepols-Turnhout, 1985), 60.

[62] See Ibn ʿAbd al-Ḥakam, *Futūḥ Miṣr*, 76, relying as always on Yaḥyā ibn Ayyūb, who died in 784, and Khālid ibn Ḥumayd, for traditions about Heraclius stimulating resistance to the Muslims. These traditions are valuable, because only the Egyptian school has left identification of tradents of traditions about Heraclius's refusal to accept locally inspired peace treaties. Such treaties occurred in northern Syria, and were rejected by him, but Theophanes or his oriental source does not identify the Syrian source for such traditions in the north. In any case they were not unique to the last days of Byzantine Egypt.

December 639	ʿAmr ibn al-ʿĀṣ commences his invasion, from southern Palestine.
End of January 640	Pelusium falls to the Muslims after a one-month siege.
July 640	The Muslims win an important victory at Heliopolis or ʿAyn Shams.
640	The Emperor Heraclius summons Patriarch Kyros to Constantinople and criticizes his negotiations with the Muslims.
Late 640 or early 641	Miṣr or the town of Babylon (Old Cairo) falls to the Muslims. The Muslims begin to invade the upper delta of the Nile.
February 11, 641	The death of the Emperor Heraclius.
April 9, 641	The citadel of Babylon or Old Cairo falls to the Muslims.
May 13, 641	Nikiu falls to the Muslims.
May 24, 641	The death of Emperor Heraclius Constantine III, when power temporarily devolves to the regency of Empress Martina and Patriarch Pyrrhos of Constantinople; Philagrios is exiled to north Africa.
September 641	The coronation of Constans II after the deposition of Martina and her sons; Philagrios is recalled from exile.
September 14, 641	Kyros returns to Alexandria.
September 29, 641	Muslim troops enter Alexandria.
November 28, 641	The Byzantine treaty, signed at Babylon, surrenders Egypt.
December 10, 641	The first payment of tribute from Egypt to the Muslims after this treaty.
March 21, 642	The death of Patriarch Kyros.
September 17, 642	Byzantine troops under the command of Theodoros evacuate Alexandria, but leave a prefect, John, to coordinate the transition to Muslim rule.
644/45	There is an abortive effort by the eunuch Manuel to recover Egypt with the assistance of a Byzantine fleet. Manuel is slain.

3

Egypt as a province in the Islamic caliphate, 641–868

HUGH KENNEDY

The Muslim conquest of Egypt followed naturally from that of Syria.[1] The sources for the early Muslim conquests are extremely problematical, and it would be wrong to be too categorical about specific details.[2] The Arabic sources are generally agreed that the first attack was launched from southern Palestine at the end of 18/639 or the beginning of 19/640. The leader and inspiration for this expedition was ʿAmr ibn al-ʿĀṣ as a member of the powerful Umayyad clan. The force he led was very small, perhaps 3,500–4,000 troops, but as the conquest progressed they were joined by further reinforcements, notably 12,000 led by Zubayr ibn al-ʿAwwām, a senior companion of the Prophet ʿAmr, however, remained in command.

The invasion force headed southwest along the eastern fringes of the desert to the Byzantine stronghold of Babylon (Old Cairo). Here they besieged the garrison of the fortress, which surrendered after some seven months in Rabīʿ II, 20/Easter 641. Alexandria, not Babylon, was the Byzantine capital and, after securing his position ʿAmr marched through the Delta to attack the city. Divisions among Byzantines and the loss of so much territory seem to have led to a spirit of defeatism among the defenders. At the end of the year 30 (November 641) a treaty was made in which the Byzantines agreed to give up the city by Shawwāl 21/September 642. This meant the end of serious resistance: it was now up to the small army of

[1] The best discussion of the conquest in general remains A. J. Butler, *The Arab Conquest of Egypt*, which should be consulted in the second edition, P. M. Fraser (ed.), (Oxford, 1978); see also D. R. Hill, *The Termination of Hostilities in the Early Arab Conquests* (London, 1971) and V. Christides, "The Conquest of Egypt," "*Misr*," *EI2*.

[2] In addition, to the general sources discussed below, two works deal with specifically with the conquests, the Coptic *Chronicle* of John of Nikiou, which survives only in an Ethiopic translation, and the anonymous *Futūḥ Bahnasā*, which contains information on the conquest of the Fayyūm and Upper Egypt, largely neglected by other sources. For these problems in general see A. North in L. I. Conrad (ed.), *The Early Arabic Historical Tradition* (Princeton, 1994).

conquerors to establish a working government over the rich lands they had so swiftly acquired.

Our understanding of the history of Egypt in the two centuries which followed the conquest is restricted by the nature of the sources at our disposal. The affairs of Egypt do figure in the general chronicles of the Muslim world, the most important of which is the *Taʾrīkh al-rusul waʾl-mulūk* of al-Ṭabarī (d. 310/923), but the references are usually short and sporadic and, while they sometimes contribute details not found elsewhere, they would not allow us to reconstruct the general history with any conviction.

Fortunately for the historian, whether medieval or modern, a local historical tradition developed early in Muslim Egypt. The first major figures seem to have been Ibn Lahīʿa (d. 790) and al-Layth ibn Saʿd (d. 791).[3] Their works have now been lost but, along with other early authorities, they form the basis of the first surviving book, the *Futūḥ Miṣr* of Ibn ʿAbd al-Ḥakam (d. 871).[4] This is a collection of traditions about the conquest and early settlement of Egypt with additional material on north Africa and Spain. The material was collected for legal rather than historical reasons, but it nonetheless provides a wealth of information about the conquest and settlement.

The most important source for the period, however, are the two works of Muḥammad ibn Yūsuf al-Kindī, the *Kitāb al-Wulāt* or *Book of Governors* and the *Kitāb al-Quḍāt* or *Book of Judges*.[5] As their titles imply, both these works deal with the history of rulers rather than being a more wide-ranging account of the whole country, but al-Kindī was a meticulous chronicler and his work, though sometimes dry, provides the basis for the reconstruction of the Muslim political system of the period. Subsequent historians of Egypt were largely dependent on Ibn ʿAbd al-Ḥakam and al-Kindī for their accounts of this early period and offer little which is new.

While they are in many ways excellent, these Arabic accounts have a very limited focus, and their interests are almost entirely confined to the activities of the ruling group in the capital, Fusṭāṭ, with occasional references to Alexandria. To understand anything of life outside this charmed circle, we have to look at Christian sources.

Of the Christian sources, the most useful for this period is the *History of the Patriarchs of the Egyptian Church*, usually ascribed to Sawīrus ibn al-Muqaffaʿ, Bishop of Ashmūnayn. In fact this is a composite work, and

3 On whom see R. G. Khoury, "Al-Layth ibn Saʿd (94/713–175/791), grand maître et mécène de l'Egypte," *JNES*, 40 (1981), 189–202.

4 On this see the English introduction to his edition of the Arabic text by C. C. Torrey (New Haven, 1922).

5 On this see the English introduction to his edition of the Arabic text by R. Guest (London, 1912).

Sawīrus probably translated earlier biographies from Coptic to Arabic and edited them. The biographies of the patriarchs are vigorously partisan, hostile alike to the Muslims and to Christians of other sects. Their chronology and detail are often confused, but they do give us a wholly different perspective, including the opinions of taxpayers, and there is more material from Alexandria, where the patriarchs usually resided.

In the aftermath of the final Byzantine surrender of Alexandria in 22/642, the most important decision facing ʿAmr was the settlement of the victorious troops. There is an old tradition that ʿAmr himself wished to establish Alexandria as the capital but the Caliph ʿUmar intervened to forbid this. He argued that the Arabs should not establish a city on any site which was separated from Medina by water and, of course, the Nile ran to the east of Alexandria.[6] Like many anecdotes about the second caliph, this must be treated with some caution, yet we can be certain that in Egypt, as in Iraq and initially in Syria, the Muslims did not settle in the existing administrative centres but in new towns on the edge of the desert. The Muslims may also have been concerned to avoid the Mediterranean coast, where there was always a danger of Byzantine raids.

The site eventually chosen was just north of the Roman fortress of Babylon, at a site which came to be known as Fusṭāṭ possibly in memory of the fact that ʿAmr's tent had been pitched on the site during the Arab siege.[7] The settlement of the site began with the foundation of the mosque which, though much altered, is still known as Mosque of ʿAmr. Around this were settled the *Ahl al-Rāya* or People of the Standard, men from Quraysh and the *anṣār, or other Companions of the Prophet, who formed the elite of the army. Khiṭṭa*s (parcels of land) were then allotted to or acquired by tribal groups. The vast majority of these early settlers came from the south Arabian or Yemeni tribes; of these Azd, Ḥimyar, including Maʿāfir, Kinda, including Tujīb, and Lakhm seem to have been the most important. Members of these South Arabian tribes formed the *jund* of Egypt. They were to dominate the political and intellectual life of Muslim Egypt for the next two centuries, and it was from their ranks with the *wujūh* (notables) were drawn. By contrast, the north Arabian (Qays) Bedouin, so powerful in Syria, were hardly represented at all.

Muslim settlement seems to have been confined to Fusṭāṭ, though troops were sent out for periods of duty in Alexandria and probably other areas as well. Fusṭāṭ was their *miṣr* and it was here that the *dīwān* which recorded their names was housed. In the years following the conquest there was continuing immigration of Arabs who came to join friends and relatives. The

[6] W. Kubiak discusses the tradition in *Al-Fustat: its Foundation and Early Urban Development* (Cairo, 1987), 58, n.4.

[7] For the early history of Fusṭāṭ see A. R. Guest, "The Foundation of Fustat and the Khittahs of that Town," *JRAS* (1907), 49–83, and Kubiak, *Al-Fustat*.

army of the conquest is said to have numbered 15,500.[8] By the Caliphate of Muʿāwiya (41–60/661–80) the number of names on the *dīwān* had allegedly reached 40,000,[9] but thereafter the register was effectively closed and only with difficulty could further names be added to it. As in other provinces of the early Islamic state, the members of the *jund* whose names appeared in the *dīwān* and who received the ʿaṭāʾ or monthly pay were fiercely jealous of their privileged position. They were determined to protect their status from encroachments either by caliphs who wished to acquire a larger share of the revenue for themselves, or from fellow Muslims trying to acquire a position on the *dīwān*. Much of the political agitation and violence in the first two centuries of Muslim Egypt was concerned in one way or another with these issues.

The most important figure in the political life of the province was the governor or *wālī*. He was in charge of leading the prayers in the mosque on Fridays – at which the *khuṭba* was pronounced and the name of the caliph proclaimed – and of making sure that the *kharāj* (tax) was collected. Sometimes these two functions were divided and separate officials placed in charge of taxation. In theory the powers of the governor were absolute; in practice they were more limited and differed from one individual to another. Some, like Maslama ibn Mukhallad al-Anṣārī (47–62/667–82) or the Umayyad ʿAbd al-ʿAzīz ibn Marwān (65–86/685–715) enjoyed long terms of office and were effectively viceroys. Others held the position for much shorter periods, a tendency which became more pronounced in the early ʿAbbāsid period (132–193/750–809), when governors were changed much more frequently. In these circumstances, a governor on a short-term appointment who was an outsider to the province had very little opportunity to establish his position.

The governor did not have an easy task. On one hand he had to keep the confidence of the caliph by keeping the province peaceful and forwarding as large a proportion of the revenue as was practical to Damascus or Baghdād. On the other hand, he also had to satisfy the demands of the *jund* of Fusṭāṭ who constituted the only military force at his disposal, and who reacted violently if their pay was not provided. From 107/725–26 on there were also repeated rebellions of the Copts, protesting at over-taxation. Caught as they were between the various conflicting pressures, it is hardly surprising that some governors lost their jobs fairly quickly.

After the governor, the most important figure in the political administration was the *ṣāḥib al-shurṭa*. This official was in charge of maintaining law and order and of leading the *jund*: it is also probable that he was responsible

[8] Muḥammad ibn Yūsuf al-Kindī, *The Governors and Judges of Egypt*, ed. R. Guest (London, 1912), 8–9.

[9] *Futūḥ Miṣr*, ed. C. C. Torrey (New Haven, 1922), 102. Kubiak, *Al-Fustat*, 79.

for paying the *ʿaṭāʾ* to those whose names were on the *dīwān*, which provided opportunities for patronage and building up a following. The *ṣāḥib al-shurṭa* in Egypt was almost always a local man, chosen by the governor from the *wujūh* of Fusṭāṭ and the office often ran in families. The most conspicuous of these local dynasties was the family of Muʿāwiya ibn Ḥudayj al-Tujībī. Muʿāwiya himself seems to have been in the original army of conquest, and some held that he was a companion of the Prophet. In the civil wars which followed the murder of ʿUthmān, he played an important part in securing Egypt for the Umayyads. His son ʿAbd al-Raḥmān and grandsons ʿAbd al-Wāḥid and ʿAbd Allāh served as *ṣāḥib al-shurṭa* and as *qāḍī*. Their influence seems to have been unaffected by the ʿAbbāsid Revolution. ʿAbd Allāh became *ṣāḥib al-shurṭa* in 143/760 and held office for nine years until 152/769, when he was appointed governor (a rare example of a local man holding this office). On his death three years later his status was inherited by his son Hāshim and then by his grandson Hubayra, both of whom served as *ṣāḥib al-shurṭa*. The family remained one of the most important in the province until most of them were massacred in the civil wars of the year 200/815.

The family of Muʿāwiya ibn Ḥudayj held office through five generations and were leading figures among the *wujūh* of Fusṭāṭ for a century and a half, but they were not exceptional. The families ʿAmr ibn Qaḥzam al-Khawlānī, ʿAssāma ibn ʿAmr al-Maʿāfirī and ʿUlayy ibn Ribāḥ al-Lakhmī are other examples of the tightly knit oligarchy which dominated Egypt in this period. Their power was based on their property, the support they could command from the *jund* and their knowledge of the country and its administration, which was indispensable to an incoming governor.

The third major figure in the life of the community was the *qāḍī* or judge. In the Umayyad period these were usually chosen by the governor from the leading families of Fusṭāṭ, and it was not unknown for the same man to serve as both *qāḍī* and *ṣāḥib al-shurṭa*. In the early ʿAbbāsid period this slowly began to change: *qāḍīs* were chosen from the *fuqahā* and were increasingly specialists. The caliphs began to take a more active interest in their appointment, and in 164/780 al-Mahdī appointed Ismāʿīl ibn al-Yasaʿ al-Kindī, who was not only an outsider from Kūfa in Iraq but also followed the law school of Abū Ḥanīfa which was then completely unknown in Egypt; this was a clear attempt to assert central authority.[10] Despite this, however, most *qāḍīs* were respected local men, at least until the reassertion of caliphal control by ʿAbd Allāh ibn Ṭāhir in 211/826.

In the years which followed the conquest the Muslim community in Egypt was involved in two major developments, expanding Muslim rule in north Africa and responding to the major political upheavals in the rest of the

[10] Al-Kindī, *Governors and Judges*, 371.

Muslim world. There was also a problem they did not have to face: rebellions among the local population. The reasons for this absence of local resistance are something of a puzzle. It seems clear that the local Monophysite Copts, whether or not they had actually aided the Muslim invasion, saw Muslim rule as no worse or more oppressive than the rule of the Chalcedonian Byzantines. More important, perhaps, was the fact that Muslim rule intruded little into the everyday lives of most native Egyptians. The Muslims lived apart from them, they did not take possession of houses or fields. Of course, they did collect taxes, but so had their predecessors, and the tax collectors with whom most people came in contact were the same sort of local officials who had collected taxes for the previous administration. Very few Copts seem to have converted to Islam at this early stage. It was only when tax collection became harder and conversion increased in the later Umayyad period, that Coptic revolts broke out for the first time.

After the conquest ʿAmr was accepted as governor by the Caliph ʿUmar. After ʿUmar's death, however, the new Caliph ʿUthmān dismissed him in 25/645 and replaced him by ʿAbd Allāh ibn Saʿd ibn Abī Sarḥ, who had previously been sub-governor of the Ṣaʿīd (Upper Egypt). ʿUthman was determined to centralise the administration of the caliphate, and a semi-independent ruler like ʿAmr would want to keep all the resources of the province for himself and his followers. ʿAbd Allāh was to be his agent in this and he set about reforming and tightening up the financial administrative system the Muslims had inherited from the Byzantines.[11] As a result of this he was unpopular among many in the province. He successfully drove off a Byzantine counter-attack on Alexandria in 25/646, and he began the development of a Muslim navy which defeated the Byzantines at the Battle of the Masts off the coast of Lycia in 34/654.[12] ʿAmr had led the first Muslim expedition to Tripolitania, and Ibn Abī Sarḥ followed this up with a major expedition which resulted in the defeat of the Byzantines near Subaytila in 27/647. The Muslims withdrew after the Byzantines had paid very substantial sums in tribute. In 31/651–52. Ibn Abī Sarḥ led an expedition south to

11 The literature on the fiscal administration of early Islamic Egypt is extensive: for introductory discussions see H. I. Bell, "Organisation of Egypt under the Ummayad Khalifs," *Byzantinische Zeitschrift*, 28 (1929), 278–86; A. Grohmann, *From The World of Arabic Papyri* (Cairo, 1952); K. Morimoto, *The Fiscal Administration of Egypt in the Early Islamic Period* (Tokyo, 1981); G. Frantz-Murphy, "Land tenure and social transformation in early Islamic Egypt," in T. Khalidi (ed.), *Land Tenure and Social Transformation in the Middle East* (Beirut, 1984), 131–39; J. B. Simonsen, *Studies in the Genesis and Early Development of the Caliphal Taxation System* (Copenhagen, 1988). For a recent bibliography of the papyrological literature, see Butler, *Arab Conquest*, xlv–liv, lxxvi–lxxxiii, and the succinct overview in Christides, "Islamic Egypt".

12 For the development of Muslim naval power, largely based on Egyptian evidence, see A. M. Fahmy, *Muslim Sea Power in the Eastern Mediterranean from the 7th to the 10th Cent.* (London, 1950).

Nubia. The Muslims were unable to conquer the country and a treaty was made between them and the Nubians, known as the *baqṭ* (from the Latin *pactum*). According to this, there was to be peace between the two peoples, and the Nubians were to send gifts of slaves while the Arabs responded with gifts of food. The treaty effectively established the southern frontier of Muslim Egypt at Aswān. With only occasional interruptions, relations remained peaceful throughout the early Islamic period.[13]

Ibn Abī Sarḥ's determination to forward revenue from Egypt to the caliph in Medina provoked opposition among the Muslims, who felt that it was theirs by right of conquest.[14] Matters were made worse by the arrival of more Arab settlers which put further pressures on local resources. This resentment finally exploded in Rajab 35/January 656 when the governor was out of the country on a visit to Medina. It was led by one Muḥammad ibn Abī Ḥudhayfa who openly rejected the governor's authority. He was supported by a party drawn mostly from those groups which had participated in the first conquest but now found that their monopoly of wealth and power had been undermined. Like Ibn Abī Ḥudhayfa himself, these were not important tribal leaders. According to the well-known story, some 400 of these protestors set out to demand redress from ʿUthmān. They accepted his assurances but on their journey back they intercepted a messenger who was carrying the caliph's orders to Ibn Abī Sarḥ, then at Ayla (modern ʿAqaba), to deal with them. Furious at this apparent deceit, they returned to Medina and played a leading role in the siege and murder of ʿUthmān in 35/656.

Meanwhile in Egypt Muḥammad ibn Abī Ḥudhayfa was opposed by a group of pro-ʿUthmān notables led by Muʿāwiya ibn Ḥudayj al-Tujībī and including Maslama ibn Mukhallad al-Anṣārī, soon to be governor, and ʿAmr ibn Qaḥzam al-Khawlānī. When news of the caliph's murder reached Fusṭāṭ, the ʿUthmānī party took the oath of allegiance to Muʿāwiya ibn Ḥudayj and came out in open opposition. In Ramaḍān 36/February 657 the two sides fought at Kharibtā, between Fusṭāṭ and Alexandria. The ʿUthmānī party was victorious but was unable to take Fusṭāṭ. The next month, Muʿāwiya ibn Abī Sufyān came from Syria and captured some of the leading insurgents, including Ibn Abī Ḥudhayfa, by a ruse and transported them to Syria where they were soon killed.

At this stage ʿAlī ibn Abī Ṭālib was still generally accepted as caliph, but his attempts to establish his power in Egypt were dogged by difficulties. His first governor, Qays ibn Saʿd al-Anṣārī, was dismissed in 37/late 657 because he was suspected of preparing to defect to Muʿāwiya. The next governor was one of ʿAli's most devoted supporters, Mālik al-Ashtar, but he died at

13 See P. Forand, "Early Muslim Relations with Nubia," in *Der Islam*, 48 (1972), 111–21, updated with full bibliography by V. Christides "Nuba," *EI2*.

14 For the revolt in Egypt see M. Hinds, "The Murder of the Caliph ʿUthman," *IJMES*, 3 (1972), 450–69.

Suez before he was able to enter the province. ʿAlī then appointed Muḥammad ibn Abī Bakr, son of the first caliph, who took office in 37/early 658. He attempted to take strong measures against the pro-ʿUthmānī party at Kharibtā, burning their houses in Fusṭāṭ and imprisoning their families, but this inevitably drove them to seek the support of Muʿāwiya ibn Abī Sufyān in Syria. In response Muʿāwiya despatched ʿAmr ibn al-ʿĀṣ, who had long sought to regain his old position in the province he had conquered, with a Syrian army. In Ṣafar 38/July–August 658 a bloody battle was fought at al-Mussannāh, between Fusṭāṭ and ʿAin Shams. ʿAmr's forces were victorious and soon after they took Fusṭāṭ: Muʿāwiya ibn Ḥudayj personally ordered the execution of Abū Bakr's son.

Egypt was now firmly attached to the Umayyad cause. Until his death at the ʿĪd al-Fiṭr 43/January 664, ʿAmr was undisputed ruler of the province. It is said that he was allowed to keep all the surplus revenue, after the payment of the *ʿaṭāʾ* of the *jund* and other expenses, for himself.[15] His ascendance was also a triumph from the *wujūh* of Fusṭāṭ, confirming them in their position. The affair shows how the Sufyānid regime attracted and relied on the support of local Muslim notables in the provinces and was prepared to confirm their privileged status in return for political support.

ʿAmr did not, however, establish a hereditary governorate. On his death the caliph appointed his own brother, ʿUtba ibn Abī Sufyān. During his short governorate, he seems to have tried to increase the Muslim presence in Alexandria: 12,000 *jund* were sent there and a Dār al-Imāra was constructed. However, the commander complained that they were too few and that he felt threatened, presumably by the the local Christian population.[16] He in turn was succeeded for a short while by one ʿUtba ibn ʿĀmir, who had been the Prophet's muleteer. In 49/669 he in turn was replaced by a local notable, Maslama ibn Mukhallad al-Anṣārī, who had petitioned Muʿāwiya for the job.

Maslama was to remain governor for the rest of Muʿāwiya's caliphate. Unusually for a member of the *anṣār* (people of Medina), he had long been a leader of the Umayyad party. We have little information on his long governorate apart from the names of his *aṣḥāb al-shurṭa*; his extension of the mosque of ʿAmr, and the absence of incident in the Arabic chronicles or of vigorous complaint in the Christian sources probably point to a period of peace and calm. On the main political issue of the day, Maslama remained firmly loyal to the Umayyad cause: when Muʿāwiya died in the spring of 680, he had no hesitation in having the oath of allegiance taken to his son Yazīd, threatening the only objector, ʿAbd Allāh ibn ʿAmr ibn al-ʿĀṣ, with death by fire.

[15] Al-Kindī, *Governors and Judges*, 31.
[16] Ibid., 36.

Maslama's own death in 62/682 was followed by renewed signs of conflict and discontent in the province. The main issue was one which was to recur throughout the early Islamic period. The *wujūh* and *jund* of Egypt wanted a governor chosen from their own ranks who would make the safeguarding of their interests his priority. The new Caliph Yazīd appointed Saʿīd ibn Yazīd al-Fihrī from Palestine. Despite the fact that he continued his predecessor's *ṣāḥib al-shurṭa*, ʿĀbis ibn Saʿīd al-Murādī, in office, he was met with vigorous opposition from ʿAmr ibn Qaḥzam al-Khawlānī, a leading member of the *wujūh*, who remonstrated with him that there were a hundred young men as good as he in Egypt. As a result the new governor was generally unpopular.

In 64/683 Yazīd ibn Muʿāwiya died, and the caliphate was immediately claimed by Ibn al-Zubayr in Makka. He attracted the support of the Kharijites in Egypt (who appear for the first time at this stage) and they pledged their allegiance to him. In return he dispatched a new governor, ʿAbd al-Raḥmān ibn ʿUtba al-Fihrī, supported by many of the Kharijites who were with him in Makka. The governor, Saʿīd ibn Yazīd, simply retired, but the *ashrāf* of Egypt would not accept this Khariji-dominated regime, and when the Umayyad Marwān ibn al-Ḥakam was proclaimed caliph in Syria at the end of 64/summer 684, they secretly began to make approaches to him.

Marwān and his supporters, among them his son ʿAbd al-ʿAzīz, immediately set out for Egypt. The governor imagined that the Egyptians were behind him and ordered the fortification of Fusṭāṭ and a trench was dug whose traces could still be seen in al-Kindī's time, three centuries later. He also sent a fleet and armies to oppose ʿAbd al-ʿAzīz at Ayla, but the army retreated and the fleet was dispersed by a storm.

When Marwān arrived at Fusṭāṭ there were one or two days of fierce fighting and then a group of the leading figures in the city arranged a capitulation. Ibn Zubayr's governor was to be allowed to leave with his possessions. In Jumādā I 65/December 684 Marwān entered the Egyptian capital and settled there, building a palace for himself. A few leading members of the *jund*, including al-Akdar ibn Ḥamām, the *sayyid* of Lakhm, refused to abandon their oath of allegiance to Ibn Zubayr, and around eighty of them were executed. This in turn provoked widespread discontent and some 30,000 of the *jund* gathered outside Marwān's residence to protest, but they were soon dispersed.

Before he returned to Syria, Marwān made arrangements for the government of Egypt. He appointed his son ʿAbd al-ʿAzīz as governor, and according to the accounts in al-Kindī, gave him careful instructions to rule in cooperation with the leaders of the *jund*. Marwān's takeover of Egypt marked a major victory in the struggle between the Umayyads and Ibn Zubayr, but it was also a victory for the *jund* of Fusṭāṭ and its leaders: it was not a Syrian takeover and no significant numbers of Syrian soldiers came to settle. The local elite retained its privileged position and, as a sign of this continuity, ʿAbd al-ʿAzīz appointed as his first *ṣāḥib al-shurṭa* ʿĀbis ibn Saʿīd al-Murādī, who had also served all of the three previous governors in that capacity. When ʿAbd al-ʿAzīz left the province to visit his brother, ʿĀbis unilaterally decided to increase the *ʿaṭāʾ* of the *jund* and when the governor returned he had no choice but to acquiesce in the decision.

ʿAbd al-ʿAzīz ibn Marwān was to remain governor for twenty years until his death in 86/705, a period which coincided almost exactly with the caliphate of his brother, ʿAbd al-Malik. He was the most important figure in the history of Umayyad Egypt and ruled as a virtual viceroy. Relations with his brother were unusually cordial but the caliph does not seem to have interfered in the internal affairs of the province at all, while ʿAbd al-ʿAzīz sent 3,000 Egyptian soldiers to help in the final siege of Ibn al-Zubayr in Makka. The only source of tension seems to have occurred over the succession, when ʿAbd al-Malik wanted his brother to take the oath of allegiance to his son al-Walīd but ʿAbd al-ʿAzīz refused, hoping apparently to leave open the possibility that his own son al-Aṣbagh would succeed.

ʿAbd al-ʿAzīz's reign was a period of almost uninterrupted peace. The governor spent most of his time in Fusṭāṭ visiting his brother in Syria on two occasions and making four trips to Alexandria. He extended the mosque in Fusṭāṭ and built a large palace. When the plague struck in 70/689–90 he left the capital and established a new government center at Ḥulwān.[17] This was also a period of Muslim expansion in the Maghrib, and ʿAbd al-ʿAzīz was determined that this enterprise should be controlled from Fusṭāṭ and that the booty taken should be brought there rather than to Damascus. In around 74/694 ʿAbd al-Malik had sent a large Syrian army under Ḥassān ibn Nuʿmān al-Ghassānī to the Maghrib but, after winning a number of victories, he was dismissed by ʿAbd al-ʿAzīz and replaced by the governor's nominee, Mūsā ibn Nuṣayr, who was to complete the conquest of north Africa and command the Muslim invasion of Spain.

ʿAbd al-ʿAzīz's long governorate came to an end in the spring of 86/705. It seems that he had been grooming his son al-Aṣbagh for the succession.[18] He hoped no doubt to make Egypt into a hereditary appanage for his branch of the Umayyad family, but the son predeceased his father by a few months. Though this plan failed, ʿAbd al-ʿAzīz's descendants seem to have continued to live in the province and to have made an attempt to seize control in early ʿAbbāsid times.

The caliph was determined to assert his right to select a governor and he

17 For his role as a builder see al-Muqaffaʿ, *History of the Patriarchs of the Coptic Church of Alexandria*, ed with English trans. B. Evetts, Patarologia Orientalis, 296–7.

18 Noted in Sawīrus, *History of the Patriarchs*, 304–5 where al-Aṣbagh is said to have been very grasping towards the Copts.

appointed his own son, ʿAbd Allāh, with instructions to remove all traces of ʿAbd al-ʿAzīz's administration. He dismissed all the officials, including the *ṣāḥib al-shurṭa*, ʿAbd al-Raḥmān ibn Muʿāwiya ibn Ḥudayj, who was placed in charge of the garrison (*murābiṭa*) in Alexandria, a position of honor but well away from the capital. He also made another important change: in 87/706 he ordered that the *dīwāns* be compiled in Arabic rather than in Coptic, while the Copt in charge was dismissed and replaced by a Syrian from Ḥimṣ. In this way the Egyptian administration was brought into line with a practice which had been introduced by ʿAbd al-Malik in Syria, and it is clear that Arabic was increasingly widely used. It also meant that Copts who wanted a post in the administration now had to learn Arabic and this in turn may have encouraged conversion to Islam. Christians however, continued to be influential; in the governorate of Qurra ibn Sharīk, for example, one Theodore seems to have been in charge of the administration of Alexandria, though not, of course, of leading the Muslims in prayer,[19] and as late as the reign of al-Maʾmūn a Copt, Isḥāq ibn Andūna al-Sayyid, was *sāḥib dīwān al-sulṭān*.[20]

ʿAbd Allāh's short governorate was marred by a severe famine, the first recorded under Muslim rule. Many people blamed the food shortage on the governor, accusing him of corruption. The Copts saw him as grasping and oppressive, increasing the taxes and decreeing that the dead could not be buried before their taxes were paid.[21] Whether it was because of complaints about his conduct or simply because the new Caliph al-Walīd (86–96/705–15) wanted to appoint his own man, ʿAbd Allāh was dismissed in 90/709 and replaced by Qurra ibn Sharīk al-ʿAbsī.

In some ways Qurra is the best-known of all the Umayyad governors of Egypt. In a sense this is by chance, since it is from his period of office that the richest collection of administrative papyri survive,[22] but both Christian and Muslim chronicle sources also suggest that the administration was becoming increasingly efficient at collecting taxes and dues. Qurra is also said to have reorganised the *dīwān* (*dawwana al-dīwan*)[23] which may mean that he added new names to it. For al-Kindī, however, his main achievements were the rebuilding of the mosque in Fusṭāṭ on the caliph's orders and irrigating an area of desert near the city at Isṭabl.[24]

[19] Sawīrus, *History of the Patriarchs*, 311–12, 326. There is no mention of this in the Arabic sources.

[20] Sawīrus, *History of the Patriarchs*, 591.

[21] Sawīrus, *History of the Patriarchs*, 307–10.

[22] In addition to the general works listed in n. 7 above, see N. Abbott, *The Kurrah Papyri from Aphrodito in the Oriental Institute*, Studies in Ancient Oriental Civilisation 15 (Chicago, 1938), and Y. Ragib, "Lettres nouvelles de Qurra ibn Sarik," *JNES*, 49 (1981), 173–88.

[23] Al-Kindī, *Governors and Judges*, 65.

[24] Al-Kindī, *Governors and Judges*, 63–6.

Qurra died in office in 96/715. Perhaps because of a concern for experience and administrative efficiency, the new governor was not an Umayyad grandee but a local man. ʿAbd al-Malik ibn Rifāʿa al-Fahmī had succeeded his uncle as *ṣāḥib al-shurṭa* in 91/710. He was now appointed governor in his own right, the first, but by no means the last, occasion on which such a promotion was made.[25] Sawīrus[26] paints a picture of increasing fiscal oppression at this time, the most marked feature of which was a regulation that all travellers had to carry an official passport (*sijil*) presumably to prevent them from escaping taxation and forced labor. The author claims that this policy had a very damaging effect on the economic life of the country and virtually brought trade to a standstill. The papyri from Qurra's rule also show the authorities making strenuous efforts to control the free movement of people, with drastic penalties for local officials who did not arrest and return fugitives.

In 99/717 the Caliph Sulaymān was succeeded by his cousin ʿUmar, son of that ʿAbd al-ʿAzīz ibn Marwān who had been governor of Egypt. The Egyptian sources support the picture given elsewhere of ʿUmar as the originator of major reforms. Al-Kindī notes that he took advice about the appointments of a governor and enquired who in Egypt was the most suitable man. Two names were mentioned, those of Muʿāwiya ibn ʿAbd al-Raḥmān ibn Muʿāwiya ibn Ḥudayj and Ayyūb ibn Shurāḥbīl, whom the caliph chose. For the Muslims in the *dīwān* ʿUmar's accession meant an increase in salaries on the caliph's orders, and the numbers in the *dīwān* were also to be increased by 5,000. Various pious measures of Islamization were also decreed: wine shops were to be closed and the stocks destroyed. Money was set aside to pay the debts of Muslims who had fallen on hard times and Christian village headmen (*mawāzīt*) were to be replaced by Muslims. From the Christian point of view too there were benefits, and churches and monasteries had their fiscal privileges confirmed. But Christians also found themselves under pressure to convert and the poll tax was made a universal obligation.[27]

As elsewhere, ʿUmar's death meant a reversal of most of these policies. The new caliph, Yazīd II, appointed a new governor, Bishr ibn Ṣafwān al-Kalbī, an Umayyad supporter from Syria, who appointed his own brother Ḥanẓala as *ṣāḥib al-shurṭa*; the salary increases for Muslims and the fiscal immunities of churches were both cancelled. When Bishr was sent to Ifrīqiya as governor in 721, Ḥanẓala was appointed to succeed him.

As usual, the accession of a new caliph meant a new governor and when Hishām in turn succeeded in 105/724 he began by appointing his brother

25 Sawīrus, *History of the Patriarchs*, 321, has Qurra succeeded by one Usāma.
26 Sawīrus, *History of the Patriarchs*, 322–5.
27 Sawīrus, *History of the Patriarchs*, 235–6. The classic discussion of Umar's fiscal policy is H. A. R. Gibb, "The Fiscal Receipt of Omar II," *Arabica*, 2 (1955),1–16.

Muḥammad. The new governor arrived in Egypt to find the plague raging, took one look and resigned his office, retiring to his estate in al-Urdunn. After this failed attempt at family government, Hishām decided on a major change in the administration of the province. He appointed ʿUbayd Allāh ibn al-Ḥabḥāb, not as governor but as *ṣāḥib al-kharāj* or head of taxation.[28] Until his transfer to north Africa in 117/734 ʿUbayd Allāh was the real ruler of Egypt: when the governor al-Ḥurr ibn Yūsuf quarrelled with him in 108/727, ʿUbayd Allāh simply wrote to the caliph, who dismissed the governor; his successor soon suffered the same fate.

The Christian sources used by Sawīrus saw Hishām as a just, if strict, ruler. He is described as "God fearing after the manner of the Muslims." He was especially praised for allowing the restoration of the Jacobite Patriarchate of Antioch and for ordering that receipts should be given for the payment of taxes so that none might be unfairly treated.[29] Ibn al-Ḥabḥāb is given a less good press. He conducted a major cadastral survey of the country, measuring lands, counting beasts and obliging all men to wear numbered badges. His cruelty to the aged Patriarch Alexander is recorded with all the pathos of a martyr's agony.

ʿUbayd Allāh was appointed to increase the tax revenues of the province. This he did by increasing the *kharāj* by a *qirāṭ* (or an eighth of a *dīnār*) per *dīnār* collected.[30] This move provoked a violent reaction in 107/725–6. For more than eighty years since the conquest the Coptic population, certainly still the overwhelming majority in Egypt, had peaceably borne the burden of taxation. Now, because of this most recent increase and the fact that tax-gathering was increasingly in the hands of the Muslims, not their own people, revolts began. These seem to have been leaderless and without any developed political programme. They never came near to overthrowing Muslim rule, but they tested the military ability of the *jund* and could destroy a governor who had lost the confidence of the local militia. This first revolt was centered in the Eastern Hawf and was put down with great loss of life.

The governor, meanwhile, remained responsible for conducting the prayers and leading the *jund*; some of these were local notables, including ʿAbd al-Malik ibn Rifāʿa (108/726), who had been a previous governor, and his brother al-Walīd (108–17/726–35). Politically the most important event was the transfer of a number of Qaysī Arabs to the Saʿīd, beginning in 109/727–28. As already mentioned, most of the Arabs in the *jund* came from south Arabian tribes. Under Umayyad rule, and particularly since the battle

[28] On ʿUbayd Allāh see N. Abbott, "A new papyrus and a review of the administration of ʿUbaid Allah ibn al-Ḥabḥāb," in G. Makdisi (ed.), *Arabic and Islamic Studies in honor of Hamilton A. R. Gibb* (Leiden, 1965), 21–35.

[29] Sawīrus, *History of the Patriarchs*, 327–28.

[30] Sawīrus, *History of the Patriarchs*, 340.

of Marj Rāhiṭ (65/684) when the Umayyads, supported by the Yemenis, had defeated their Qaysī Syrian rivals, a major rivalty had developed between Qays and the Yemen which threatened to tear the Umayyad state apart.

During the reign of Hishām there was a large scale migration of Qaysīs into north Africa and, later, Spain. The transfer of Qaysīs to Egypt is said to have been suggested by ʿUbayd Allāh ibn al-Ḥabḥāb. The caliph agreed to it on the condition that they were not permitted to settle in Fusṭāṭ, presumably because he realised that their presence would provoke a confrontation with the locals, and that their *dīwān* should be transferred to Egypt. Ibn al-Ḥabḥāb arranged that some 3,000 of them be recruited in the Syrian desert and they were settled in the Eastern Ḥawf: money from the tithes was given to them to buy horses and camels and they made a living by carrying food to Suez, presumably to go by sea from there to the Ḥijāz. Other Qaysī bedouin followed from Syria until there were some 5,000 at the end of Hishām's reign.

The purpose of this move is obscure, but Ibn al-Ḥabḥāb probably wanted to relieve pressure on the resources of Syria and to provide a counter-balance to the monopoly of power held by the *jund*. It marks an important stage in the Arabization of the province because, for the first time, Arabs settled in considerable numbers outside Fusṭāṭ and Alexandria.

This period of comparative stability was brought to an end with the death of the Caliph Hishām in 125/743, and there followed almost a decade when the growing weakness of the Umayyad caliphate led to intense rivalries and open hostility in Egypt. The governor at the time was Ḥafṣ ibn al-Walīd al-Ḥaḍramī, a member of a well-established local family who had previously served as *ṣāḥib al-shurṭa* and briefly as governor. He seems to have been determined to reestablish the position of the *jund* of Fusṭāṭ. His first action was to expel all the Syrians who had drifted into Fusṭāṭ, which he only accomplished by the use of force. Next he raised a new military force in Egypt of 30,000 men recruited from the *maqāmiṣa* and the *mawālī*: exactly who these were is not clear, but it is likely that they were recruited among the non-Arab Muslims of the country, perhaps as a counter to the Qaysīs. This new force was known as the Ḥafṣīya, after the governor who had raised it.

When the pro-Qaysī Caliph Marwān ibn Muḥammad established his power in 127/744 there was an immediate reaction: Ḥafṣ resigned and the caliph ordered that the Ḥafṣīya be disbanded. He appointed a new governor, Ḥassān ibn ʿAṭāhiya. These measures provoked a violent response, the Ḥafṣīya refused to disband and the *jund* of Fusṭāṭ besieged the new governor's house. In the end Ḥassān and the *ṣāḥib al-kharāj* were obliged to leave the country and the unwillingly Ḥafṣ was restored.

Marwān could not afford to let Egypt slip from his grasp. In 128/745 he dispatched a large force of Syrian troops and a new governor, Ḥawthara ibn

Suhayl al-Bāhilī, described as a Bedouin Arab well known for his eloquence.[31] Some of the Egyptian *jund* and the Ḥafṣīya wanted to resist him but Ḥafṣ was unwilling to lead them and after some negotiation, Ḥawthara entered Fusṭāṭ. He immediately began a purge of the opposition leaders, including the commander of the Ḥafṣīya and Ḥafṣ himself. He also set about recruiting 2,300 more troops from the Umayyad *mawālī* and Qays to bolster his position. There was a marked contrast between this brutal takeover and the much lighter hand shown by Marwān ibn al-Ḥakam when he took over the province in 65/684.

Meanwhile, the Umayyad caliphate was collapsing rapidly under the onslaught of ʿAbbāsid armies from the east. In Jumādā I 131/January 749 Ḥawthara was ordered to go the Wāsiṭ to help Ibn Hubayra resist the invaders. His successors in Egypt were unable to prevent many Egyptians from declaring their support for the ʿAbbāsids in Alexandria, the Ḥawf and Aswān. As far as we can tell, these ʿAbbāsid supporters were all Egyptian Arabs, not Khurāsānīs or other ʿAbbāsid supporters from the east. In Shawwāl 132/May–June 750 the Caliph Marwān himself arrived, hotly pursued by ʿAbbāsid forces led by Ṣāliḥ ibn ʿAlī and Abū ʿAwn. He and his supporters attempted to establish control over the province but time was not on their side, and in Dhū'l-Ḥijja 132/August 750 he and many of his followers were killed at Būṣīr.

Egypt under the early ʿAbbāsids, 132–193/1750–809[32]

At the beginning of 133/Summer 750, Ṣāliḥ ibn ʿAlī and the ʿAbbāsid troops entered Fusṭāṭ and a new era had begun. The most striking characteristic of early ʿAbbāsid administration in Egypt is its continuity with the Umayyad period. As before, the governors were mostly outsiders, chosen from among the leaders of the Khurāsānī military or minor members of the ʿAbbāsid family on short-term postings, while the *aṣḥāb al-shurṭa* continued to be chosen from the leading families, the *wujūh*, of Fusṭāṭ, families such as the descendants of Muʿāwiya ibn Ḥudayj al-Tujībī, ʿAmr ibn Qaḥzam al-Khawlānī and ʿAssama ibn ʿAmr al-Maʿāfirī remained as important as they had in Umayyad times. There was no attempt to settle large numbers of Khurāsānī troops in the province and the ʿAbbāsids ruled in cooperation with the local elite.

The first governor of this province was Ṣāliḥ ibn ʿAlī ʿAbbāsī, an uncle of the first two ʿAbbāsid caliphs. He may have hoped to establish a position in Egypt as ʿAbd al-ʿAzīz ibn Marwān had done: he was certainly ruthless in

31 Al-Kindī, *Governors and Judges*, 89.

32 For Egypt under the early Abbāsids see H. Kennedy, "Central government and provincial elites in the early ʿAbbasid caliphate," *BSOAS*, 44 (1981), 26–38.

hunting down ʿAbd al-ʿAzīz's descendants in the province. However, after the defeat of his brother ʿAbd Allāh's rebellion in 137/754, he turned his attention to Syria, which became the base for his branch of the dynasty.

He was succeeded by four leading members of the Khurāsānī military in turn, Abū ʿAwn (137–141/755–758), Mūsā ibn Kaʿb (141/758–9), Muḥammad ibn al-Ashʿath (141–2/759–60) and Ḥumayd ibn Qaḥṭaba (143–4/760–762). They all used local men as *ṣāḥib al-shurṭa* to maintain contact with the local *jund*. Ḥumayd is said to have brought some 20,000 soldiers with him, but it seems that these were in transit to Ifrīqiya where Muḥammad ibn al-Ashʿath was now in bitter conflict with the Ibāḍī Kharijites. Among them was al-Aghlab ibn Sālim, whose descendants were to be independent rulers of Ifrīqīya through the third/tenth century until the Fāṭimid conquest of 296/909.

The next governor, Yazīd ibn Ḥātim, held the post for eight years, longer than anyone else in the early ʿAbbāsid period. He was a member of the famous Muhallabī family of Baṣra and he and his brother Rawḥ were also to play an important role in the government of Ifrīqiya. He was one of the Caliph al-Manṣūr's inner circle, and may have been appointed to secure Egypt in the event of an attempted takeover by the ʿAlids. Al-Manṣūr was always aware of the history of the Umayyad Caliphate, and he would have remembered how crucial the control of Egypt had been to both Muʿāwiya and ʿAbd al-Malik when they were establishing themselves as caliphs.

The main ʿAlid rebellions were led by Muḥammad the Pure Soul in Medina and his brother Ibrāhīm in Baṣra in 145/763. It seems that a member of the ʿAlid family had arrived in Fusṭāṭ when Ḥumayd ibn Qaḥṭaba was governor and he had failed to take any action against him. Al-Manṣūr became aware of this and dismissed Ḥumayd. There was no established pro-ʿAlid party in Egypt and the ʿAlid leader, ʿAlī ibn Muḥammad ibn ʿAbd Allāh, attracted little support in the province, apart from that of some descendants of ʿAbd al-ʿAzīz ibn Marwān, the Umayyad governor, who saw it as an opportunity to re-establish their position, and a handful of discontented members of the *jund*. The rebels planned to take over the mosque in Fusṭāṭ and summon the people to their cause, but the plot was soon betrayed to Yazīd, who sent his *ṣāḥib al-shurṭa*, ʿAbd Allāh ibn ʿAbd al-Raḥmān ibn Muʿāwiya ibn Ḥudayj, to deal with it. There was a short struggle and the conspirators fled, trying to seek refuge in the city. In the end, there were only thirteen deaths, a marked contrast with the battles and bloodshed in Baṣra and Medina at the same time; the alliance of the governor and the local *jund* kept the province secure. This incident shows how the local elite was now bound to the new ruling dynasty. As for ʿAlī ibn Muḥammad, he escaped and his fate was uncertain, but according to one source he was concealed by a leading member of the *wujūh*, ʿAssāma ibn ʿAmr, and died in hiding. ʿAssāma himself was taken to Baghdād and imprisoned but was released on the accession of the Caliph al-Mahdī and returned to Egypt. His exploits do not seem to have affected the status of his family in the province.

Yazīd ibn Ḥātim was removed from office in 152/769 and the Caliph al-Manṣūr seems to have decided on a new policy for the government of the province. With the appointment of ʿUbayd Allāh ibn al-Ḥabḥāb as financial controler in Umayyad times, the caliphs had been trying to increase the revenue yield of the province. In 141/758 the governor Muḥammad ibn al-Ashʿath had been asked to sign a *ḍamān*, a guarantee that he would be responsible for any shortfall in the reveue from the province. When he refused to do so, the financial administration was entrusted to one Nawfal ibn al-Furāt, who removed the *dīwān*s from the governor's palace. From the appointment of ʿAbd Allāh ibn ʿAbd al-Raḥmān ibn Muʿāwiya ibn Ḥudayj al-Tujībī in 152/769 until the arrival of ʿĪsā ibn Luqmān in 161/778, the governors were chosen from among the members of the local *wujūh* families, but they were not given charge of the financial administration, which was entrusted to officials sent out from Baghdād; clearly the Caliph intended to break the stranglehold that people of the *dīwān* had on the revenues while continuing to rely on the *jund* for security purposes.

By and large, al-Manṣūr's measures seem to have secured the peaceful government of the province. Under his son, al-Mahdī (158–69/775–85), there were renewed attempts to increase the revenues but his financial demands, coupled with the appointment of unsuitable outsiders as governors, resulted in a major rebedllion against the government. The trouble began when one Diḥyā ibn Muṣʿab, a descendant of the famous Umayyad governor ʿAbd al-ʿAzīz ibn Marwān launched a rebellion in the Ṣaʿīd. He is said to have claimed the caliphate for himself, but this was essentially an anti-tax movement. The governor, a minor member of the ʿAbbāsid family called Ibrāhīm ibn Ṣāliḥ, failed to respond effectively and was unceremoniously sacked in 167/784. In his place the caliph sent Mūsā ibn Muṣʿab al-Khathʿamī. He had already served as governor of al-Jazīra, where his ruthless taxation policies had led to widespread unrest. He attempted to implement a similar agenda in Egypt, raising taxes on the land and imposing taxes on the *sūqs* and riding animals. He soon alienated all sections of Egyptian society. In the Ḥawf, Qaysī and Yemeni Arabs put aside their ancient feuds and combined against him. They made contact with the *jund* of Fusṭāṭ, who were infuriated by the new taxes on their urban properties and who promised not to fight for the governor. In Shawwāl 168/April 784 Mūsā led the *jund* out to meet the Ḥawfī rebels. As agreed, the *jund* and its leaders abandoned him to his fate, he was killed and the *jund* returned to Fusṭāṭ without striking a blow. There was no clearer indication of the limits of the caliphal government, which simply could not function without the cooperation of the local elite.

The caliph responded by sending a new governor, al-Faḍl ibn Ṣāliḥ al-ʿAbbāsī, with a large army of Syrian soldiers. In a fierce battle at Buwīṭ, Diḥyā and his supporters were defeated. Diḥya himself fled to the western oases where he took refuge with the Kharijite Berbers, but they accused him of favoring the Arabs over them and abandoned his cause, leaving him to be killed by the governor's troops. By the time al-Faḍl ibn Ṣāliḥ left the province the next year, order had been restored.

The accession of Hārūn al-Rashīd in 170/786 inaugurated a period of rapid turnover of governors, few lasting more than a year. In the twenty-three years of his reign, there were twenty-two changes (in contrast to only eight in the twenty-two years of al-Manṣūr's reign). Since almost all the governors were outsiders – members of the ʿAbbāsid family or court functionaries who brought few troops with them – they were heavily dependent on the *ṣāḥib al-shurṭa* and the local *wujūh* to enforce their authority. The government in Baghdād, dominated until 187/803 by the Barmakids, was largely concerned with revenues and seems to have been constantly frustrated by the poor yields from Egypt. Various stratagems were tried: in 176/792 a special investigator, ʿUmar ibn Mihrān, was sent in disguise to investigate corruption, and his report survives in the accounts of Iraq-based sources such as those of al-Ṭabarī and al-Jahshiyārī,[33] but not the Egyptian al-Kindī. In 183/799 and 185/801, the governor, al-Layth ibn al-Faḍl, was ordered to bring the revenue to Baghdād in person.

Apart from the lack of will in Fusṭāṭ, the main obstacle to increasing revenue was the persistent refusal of the Arab settlers in the Ḥawf to pay anything and the reluctance of the *jund* in Fusṭāṭ to force them to do so. In 186/802 for example, the Ḥawfīs rebelled in protest at what they claimed were corrupt surveyors who had shortened the measuring rods, and threatened to march on Fusṭāṭ. A force of 5,000 *jund* was sent against them but, faced with the enemy, all except 200 deserted without striking a blow. Despite being heavily outnumbered, the governor drove the rebels back; the capital was saved but the Ḥawfīs still refused to pay. In the administrative chaos after the fall of the Barmakids in 183/803, Hārūn seems to have been prepared to allow large-scale tax-farming, one Maḥfūẓ ibn Sulaymān giving a *ḍamān* that he would collect taxes from the Ḥawfīs without using any troops. History does not tell us if he was successful.

The final years of Hārūn's reign saw increased tensions in the province. This was partly a reflection of the widespread insecurity of the period. The Ḥawfī Arabs continued to defy the governor. On occasion Egypt was effectively cut off from Baghdād by unrest in Syria. In 190/806 there was a

[33] Al-Ṭabarī, Muḥammad ibn Jarīr, *Taʾrīkh al-rusul waʾl-mulūk*, ed. M. J. de Goeje et al. (Leiden, 1879–1901), iii, 626–28; al-Jahshiyārī, *Wuzarā* (ed. El-Sakka), 217–20; see also Grohmann, *Arabic Papyri*, 116, for documentary confirmation.

rebellion in the Aqaba area, and in 193/809 money being sent to Baghdād was intercepted by the people of Ramla in Palestine who took it as their *ʿaṭāʾ* which had not been paid. When the governor al-Ḥasan ibn al-Takhtākh left office in 194/810 he had to go through the Ḥijāz because of the disturbed state of Syria.

The death of Hārūn al-Rashīd in 193/809 made matters much worse. He was succeeded by his son al-Amīn, who was almost immediately challenged by his own brother, al-Maʾmūn, governor of Khurāsān. This dispute meant that there was an alternative focus for loyalty to which dissidents could turn. The succession war fought out in Iran and Iraq provided the occasion for the outbreak of a prolonged struggle for power in Egypt.

The political situation in the province had been changing in the last decade of Hārūn's reign. The monopoly of military power enjoyed by the *jund* of Fusṭāṭ was being challenged by newcomers. The failure of the *jund* to suppress the Ḥawfī rebels led the caliph to send troops from the *abnāʾ* (troops of Khurāsānī origin resident in Baghdad, who formed the backbone of the early ʿAbbāsid armies), and when al-Layth ibn al-Faḍl was appointed governor in 183/799 he brought with him a force which included al-Sarī ibn al-Ḥakam. Al-Sarī is said by al-Kindī[34] to have been a man of no importance when he arrived in the province, but he soon established himself as one of the leaders of the *abnāʾ*.

The other groups of Arabs in Egypt also sought to challenge the power of the traditional *wujūh*. The most successful of these was ʿAbd al-ʿAzīz ibn al-Wazīr al-Jarawī. He seems to have had his power base among the Yemeni tribes of Lakhm and Judhām in the northern part of the country, and in 190/806 he had been one of the commanders sent against the rebels in Aqaba.

Between the death of Hārūn in 193/809 and the reestablishment of the authority of the Caliph al-Maʾmūn by ʿAbd Allāh ibn Ṭāhir in 211/826, Egypt was the scene of a prolonged power struggle between these groups. The events are complicated by a number of factors: the attempts of outsiders, like the ʿAbbāsid al-Faḍl ibn Mūsā ibn ʿĪsā and his family in 198–99/814–15 to establish themselves in the province, the takeover of Alexandria by a group of Andalusī exiles[35] in 199/815, and the constantly shifting political groupings as individual leaders sought to build up their power base.

Several clear trends do, however, emerge from this confusion. Governors continued to be nominated, first by al-Amīn and then, after his death in 198/813, by his brother al-Maʾmūn, but their authority was minimal and they were no more than one player in the complex power politics of the country. By 197/813 Egypt had effectively been divided between ʿAbd al-ʿAzīz al-

[34] Al-Kindī, *Governors and Judges*, 148.

[35] These Andalusīs seem to have left Spain because of discontent with the authoritarian rule of the Umayyad Amīr al-Ḥakam ibn Hishām (180–206/796–822).

Jarawī who had taken control of the north, from Shaṭanūf 30 km north of Fusṭāṭ to Faramā, with intermittent control of Alexandria, while al-Sarī ruled the south, from Fusṭāṭ to Aswān.[36] Both collected the *kharāj* for themselves and acknowledged Caliphs and pretenders to the throne as they wished. A *ṭirāz* of 197/812–13 survives with an inscription saying that it was made by al-Sarī and al-Jarawī on the orders of al-Faḍl ibn Sahl, al-Ma'mūn's wazīr.

The losers in this complex struggle were the old-established *wujūh* and *jund* of Fusṭāṭ. For reasons which are not clear, they seem to have been unable to sustain their power or produce leaders who could challenge al-Sarī and al-Jarawī. In 200/816 most of the leading members of the Banū Ḥudayj, the most distinguished of the old *wujūh* families, perished when their palace in Alexandria was attacked by a mob of Andalusīs and Lakhmī tribesmen, an event which seems to have meant an effective end to their power. In 204/819 al-Sarī had a number of the senior leaders of the *jund* drowned in the Nile "because he was afraid of them."[37] The failure of the old *jund* to establish themselves in power, or even to retain their existing status, marks a major break in the history of early Islamic Egypt. The tightly knit group of *wujūh* who had dominated it since their ancestors had come in the armies of the first conquest was now broken, and it was left to others to struggle over the spoils.

Both ʿAbd al-ʿAzīz al-Jarawī and al-Sarī died in 205/820, but their conflicts were inherited by their sons, ʿAlī ibn ʿAbd al-ʿAzīz and ʿUbayd Allāh ibn al-Sarī. Neither was able to achieve any permanent advantage over the other. It was this divided and war-ravaged country which ʿAbd Allāh ibn Ṭahir entered in Rabīʿ I, 211/June–July 826 as governor of the ʿAbbāsid Caliph al-Ma'mūn. It was not the first time al-Ma'mūn had attempted to restore the province to ʿAbbāsid control: in 206/822 he had sent Khālid ibn Yazīd ibn Mazyad. However, despite the support of ʿAlī ibn Jarawī, he had been completely outmaneuvered by ʿUbayd Allāh ibn al-Sarī and was forced to leave the province in humiliation. Ibn Ṭāhir was in a much stronger position, having just restored Syria and Palestine to ʿAbbāsid rule. He came with a large military force and brought ships from Syria to help in the amphibious warfare in the Delta.

Ibn al-Jarawī immediately approached him with gifts, and ʿAbd Allāh appointed him in command of the ships. Ibn al-Sarī decided to resist but at the same time sent a messenger to the caliph to request an *amān*. The surrender document was negotiated by al-Sarī's secretary Muḥammad ibn Asbāṭ, and witnessed by the most prominent *fuqahā* of the province. He was

[36] Sawīrus, *History of the Patriarchs*, 428. Al-Jarawī's takeover of the Delta area is described in al-Kindī, 151; for the final establishment of al-Sarī's control of Fusṭāṭ, ibid., 161–62.

[37] Al-Kindī, *Governors and Judges*, 171.

then given 10,000 *dīnārs* and sent to the caliph in Baghdād. He never returned to Egypt but lived peacefully in Sāmarrā until his death in 251/865. It remained only to subdue Alexandria where the Andalusīs were still holding out. ʿAbd Allāh sent a large force against them and accepted their surrender on condition that they abandon the city and take no-one or nothing with them. Most of them sailed to Crete, which they conquered and used as a base for raids on the Byzantine Empire.

The conquest of Egypt by ʿAbd Allāh ibn Ṭāhir marked the beginning of a new phase in the history of the province. It was still ruled by governors but, after 213/829, these ceased to be appointed directly by the caliph. The western provinces were entrusted to "super-governors," members of the ruling family or leading figures in the Turkish military establishment. These seldom visited the province but remained in the capital. From there they sent governors to conduct the administration and send the revenues directly to them. From 213/819 until his accession as caliph in 218/833 the super-governor was al-Ma'mūn's brother Abū Isḥāq (the future Caliph al-Muʿtaṣim). When he became caliph he appointed one of his trusted Turkish soldiers Ashinās, who held office until his death in 229/843, when he was succeeded by another Turk, Ītākh. In 235/849, as one of a series of moves to reduce the influence of leading Turks, al-Mutawwakil removed Ītākh, whom he had arrested, and replaced him with his own son, al-Muntaṣir, who remained as "super-governor" until he in turn became caliph in 247/861. There is no evidence that Ashinās, Ītākh or al-Muntaṣir ever visited Egypt during his term of office.

Instead, they appointed governors from the ruling class of the Sāmarrā caliphate. They were Arabs, Turks or Armenians by descent, but all of them were outsiders. Terms of office were longer than under Hārūn and three or four years were not uncommon. They continued to appoint *aṣḥāb al-shurṭa*, but these were no longer members of the local elite but soldiers of Turkish or eastern Iranian origin and, like their masters, incomers to the province.

The army ʿAbd Allāh had used to subjugate Egypt was composed of two elements, members of the *abna'* of Baghdād, many of whom took service with the Ṭahirids at the end of the civil war in Iraq, and Iranians or Turks from further east. Alexandria, for example, was governed by Ilyās ibn Asad ibn Sāmān Khūdā from Samarqand, after its conquest. Few of these troops were Arab in origin and none of them were Egyptians. From now onwards Egypt was to be ruled not by a native Muslim elite but by outsiders from far to the east.

ʿAbd Allāh ibn Ṭāhir governed Egypt for seventeen months. In this period he restored peace and found the resources for a major enlargement of the mosque in Fusṭāṭ. In 212/827 he left for Iraq, leaving his second-in-command, ʿĪsā ibn Yazīd al-Julūdī to govern the province. In 213/829 there was a reorganisation of the high command of the caliphate: ʿAbd Allāh ibn

Ṭāhir went east to succeed his brother as governor of Khurāsān and at the same time the western provinces were entrusted to the overall supervision of the caliph's brother, Abū Isḥāq.

The new regime seems to have been very oppressive in its early stages. The effective exclusion of local people from power, combined with heavy tax demands, assured widespread rebellions in the Ḥawf and Delta regions. As often before, the problems began with the refusal of the Ḥawfīs to pay the *kharāj*. Abū Isḥāq's new governor, ʿUmayr ibn al-Walīd, was entrusted with the task of forcing them to do so. In 214/830 he led an army against them. At first things went well and the Ḥawfīs , the Yemenis led by ʿAbd al-Salām ibn Abī'l-Māḍī and the Qaysīs led by ʿAbd Allāh ibn Ḥulays al-Hilālī, were forced to retreat; they laid an ambush, and the governor and many of his men were killed. His successor, ʿĪsā al-Julūdī, was obliged to fortify his dwelling in Fusṭāṭ.

At this stage Abū Ishāq himself decided to take matters in hand, and arrived in Egypt with 4,000 of the much feared Turkish troops he was using to establish his power. This time the Ḥawfīs were soundly defeated and their leaders captured and executed. Nonetheless, as soon as he left, trouble began again. By 216/831 there was a general rebellion of Arabs and Copts combined against the government, an unprecedented alliance of local interests. They chose as their leader one Ibn ʿUbaydūs, a descendant of ʿUqba ibn Nāfiʿ, one of the original Muslim settlers in Egypt and conqueror of much of north Africa. They were opposed by al-Afshīn, one of al-Muʿtaṣim's most senior commanders who had come to Egypt to try to recover the treasure allegedly hidden by Ibn al-Jarawī. Afshīn now set out through the Delta and won a series of victories over the opposition there. Everywhere his progress was followed by execution. In Alexandria, which seems to have been the last stronghold of the old elite, the *ru'asā* (chiefs), led by a descendant of Muʿāwiya ibn Ḥudayj, were driven out and their influence destroyed. The military power of the new regime was irresistible, and the Egyptians were forced to accept this alien domination.

In Muḥarram 217/February 832 the Caliph al-Ma'mūn visited the province in person. Apart from Marwān ibn al-Ḥakam when he was consolidating his power, al-Ma'mūn was the only reigning caliph to do so during the two and a half centuries in which Egypt was part of the caliphate. He only stayed for forty-nine days but his visit seems to have marked something of a turning-point. He accused the governor of concealing the true state of affairs from him and of allowing his tax collectors to oppress the people. For Sawīrus, al-Ma'mūn was a just ruler who respected the Christians and put an end to many abuses, but he was sometimes overruled by the evil genius of his brother al-Muʿtaṣim. At the same time Afshīn extinguished the last of the revolts: among the Copts, the men were killed and the women and children sold into slavery, while Ibn ʿUbaydūs al-Fihrī was taken and executed. After this, open resistance effectively ceased and no further rebellions are reported in the next quarter of a century.

When al-Muʿtaṣim became caliph in 218/833, he completed the destruction of the early Islamic order. He ordered that all the Arabs be dropped from the *dīwān* and that their *ʿaṭā*ʾ be stopped.[38] The influence of the *jund* of Egypt had long been in decline, but this move finally destroyed its economic foundation and marked the end of the system that had been in operation since the time of the conquest. There were protests and small-scale disturbances among the Lakhm and Judhām, led by Yaḥyā ibn al-Jarawī. They claimed that the payments were "our right and our *fay*ʾ (i.e. the booty acquired at the time of the conquest)," but they were speaking the language of a vanished age and their protest cut no ice with the ʿAbbāsid government of the third/ninth century.

The governors themselves do not emerge as distinctive personalities, though al-Kindī notes, perhaps with sadness, that ʿAnbasa ibn Isḥāq al-Ḍabbī (238–42/852–56), besides being respected for his justice and the tight rein he kept on his tax officials, was the last Arab governor of Egypt and the last to lead the people in prayer in the mosque in Fusṭāṭ.[39] It was also during his period of office that the Byzantines began to raid the Egyptian coast again. They took Damietta and captured many Muslims and non-Muslims in 239/853. After the raid was over, the Caliph al-Mutawwakil ordered that the city be fortified.

This assertion of political control from Sāmarrā was matched by the ideological control represented by the *miḥna*, or inquisition, which aimed to force all officials and *fuqahā* to acknowledge the createdness of the Qurʾān. This inquisition was not vigorously enforced under al-Muʿtaṣim but with the accession of al-Wāthiq in 227/842, the *qāḍī*, Muḥammad ibn Abīʾl-Layth al-Khwārazmī, was ordered to take stern measures against anyone who refused to accept the doctrine of the created Qurʾān. This led to resistance by several leading religious figures supported by popular sentiment which can, perhaps, be seen as an expression of local opposition to ʿAbbāsid autocracy. When al-Mutawwakil reversed this policy in 235/850, the unfortunate *qāḍī* was imprisoned and publicly cursed.[40]

This period of comparative peace was brought to an end by a rebellion in 248/862. The rebellion seems to have begun as a protest by the ʿAlids against the punitive measures taken against them by the Caliph al-Muntaṣir. On previous occasions the ʿAlids had attracted little support in the province, but it seems on this occasion as if their grievances touched a chord in other sections of the population. The chaos in Sāmarrā, where one caliph followed

38 Al-Kindī, *Governors and Judges*, 193–94.
39 Al-Kindī, *Governors and Judges*, 200–2.
40 For the *miḥna* in Egypt and the popular reaction see al-Kindī, 449–67.

another in rapid succession after the assasination of al-Mutawwakil in 247/861, meant that government control weakened rapidly throughout the caliphate at this time.

The rebellion began among the Banū Mudlij, led by Jābir ibn al-Walīd, in Alexandria, but they were soon joined by the surviving remnants of the old *wujūh* and many others, both Christian and Muslim. Soon most of the Delta was in the hands of the rebels, tax collectors were driven out and the leadership was assumed by an ʿAlid pretender, Ibn al-Arqaṭ. The governor, Yazīd ibn ʿAbd Allāh al-Turkī (242–253/856–867) struggled to contain the rebellion, but it was difficult, even after substantial reinforcements of Turkish soldiers under Muzāḥim ibn Khāqān arrived from Iraq. It was not until Muzāḥim himself took over as governor that Jābir ibn al-Walīd was finally induced to surrender. Shortly after Muzaḥim's death at the beginning of 254/868 news arrived of the appointment of Aḥmad ibn Ṭūlūn as the new governor. Probably no one at the time realized it, but a new era in the history of Islamic Egypt had begun.

The years since the arrival of ʿAbd Allāh ibn Ṭāhir (211/826) had seen the total domination of the political and military life of the province by Turkish soldiers. Not only were the governor and his army Turkish, it was even the Turkish *ṣāḥib al-shurṭa*, Azjūr who ordered the Imām and congregation of the great Mosque in Fusṭāṭ to abandon their ancient practices and adopt new ways introduced from the east. A Persian, armed with a whip, stood by to make sure they did as they were told.[41]

The event is symbolic of the way in which the Muslim population of Egypt had become a subject group which had lost control of its own destiny. The reasons why Egypt did not develop a native political elite at this time, as for example happened in much of Syria, the Jazīra, Yemen or the Maghrib, are not clear. The slow pace of conversion and the determination of the *wujūh* and *jund* of Fusṭāṭ to maintain their exclusive position must have played a part: the Muslim elite could maintain itself against the Copts, but not against the powerful and effective Turkish military organization of the third/ninth century, determined to capture the resources of the country for their alien masters. The collapse of the early Islamic system left a power vacuum. In the rest of the Islamic world, ambitious warlords were rejecting the authority of the strife-torn Sāmarrā government. It was only a matter of time before some ambitious Turkish soldier decided to exploit the resources of Egypt to establish his own autonomous rule.

[41] Al-Kindī, *Governors and Judges*, 210.

4
Autonomous Egypt from Ibn Ṭūlūn to Kāfūr, 868–969

THIERRY BIANQUIS

The emergence of an autonomous Egypt

From 850, the attention of Arab chroniclers ceased to focus on the eastern provinces of the Dār al-Islām, the ʿAbbāsids' primary concern for a century. Southern Iraq, potentially so rich because of its high-yielding agriculture, its vast port of Baṣra, its convergence of caravans and riverine navigation (the main route directing the Iranians toward Mecca and the commodities of the Indian Ocean toward the Byzantine markets), was nonetheless shaken by unrest. From 820 to 834 the disturbances engendered by the undisciplined Zuṭṭ, buffalo breeders who had arrived from India during the Sassanid period, compelled the ʿAbbāsid caliphs in 222/837 to relocate them in northern Syria, confronting the Byzantines. Subsequently, the general uprising of the Zanj erupted, a rebellion of black slaves imported from Zanzibar to cultivate the southern Iraqi plantations of sugar cane and rice under unbearable climatic conditions. Inspired by an ʿAlid pretender, they were initially victorious. The Zanj temporarily occupied Baṣra and, after 255/869, menaced all the fertile agrarian lands of southern Mesopotamia. Although they were vanquished in 270/883, the region's agriculture did not recover from the devastation that was inflicted on it. A group of Ismāʿīlī agitators, the Carmatians, had inaugurated their programs of indoctrination in the region of Kūfa around 264/877. After founding a state at Baḥrayn on the southern shore of the Persian Gulf in 286/899, they instigated revolts among the poor peasants of southern Iraq and the Arab tribes of the Syro-Iraqi steppe at the beginning of the fourth/tenth century. Central and southern Iraq were simultaneously threatened from 865 to 900 by the Ṣaffārid revolt, an insurrectionary movement which first appeared in western Iran, and whose leaders were prepared to march against Baghdād itself. The disorders in lower Iraq compromised the primacy of the maritime commercial route toward India, Ceylon and southeast Asia via the Gulf, consequently enhancing the appeal of the land route across Iran, Jazīra and Anatolia known as the "Silk Road."

In Iraq, the demographic explosion of the cities was more a burden than a dynamic growth factor for the economy. The caliphs had already created Sāmarrā, recognizing that the failure of coexistence between a large Turkish army and an urban civil population that was constantly expanding posed insurmountable problems of supply and security. To maintain tranquility, responsible officials of the state had to assure the regular provision of grain, olive oil, sugar, meat and fuel to the bakeries and the public baths for the enormous city of Baghdād. The implications of this formidable demand for media of transport, storage facilities, initial processing of goods and management of their distribution across myriad local markets were intimidating. The activities of merchants would clearly not suffice to meet this demand, and it was therefore necessary for state officials to pressure the governors of Mawṣil and other regional centers in Jazīra and eastern Syria to despatch vast quantities of grain to the capital.

Syria and Egypt witnessed a number of brief military revolts or tribal rebellions during the second half of the ninth century. But the security of property and persons was nonetheless maintained with more assurance than in Iraq. In 827 Crete had been occupied by the Cordobans of Alexandria. In 830 Sicily also came under Muslim domination. From 870 to 960, the Arab navy based in Crete joined with fleets sailing out of Syria to disrupt shipping in the Aegean and Adriatic seas. Arab navigation was reestablished between Syria and Egypt, and between Egypt and the Maghrib and al-Andalus. At the same time, the caravan trade between Aghlabid Ifrīqiya, a region experiencing widespread prosperity, and Egypt expanded significantly. The importance of economic ties between north Africa and the Andalus on one hand, and Egypt, the Arabian Peninsula and Syria on the other, is attested in the fourth/tenth century by the Jewish archives of the Geniza. Such ties indeed predated the Geniza information by a century according to a text of Ibn Khurradādhbih (d. 272/885 or 300/912) that mentions Jewish traveling merchants. The maritime itinerary via the Gulf route, progressively less protected, was therefore abandoned in favor of direct navigation between the Yemen and India. Aden and the Red Sea once again experienced frequent shipping after a depressed period during the Umayyad epoch. On the western coast of the Red Sea, the port of ʿAydhāb, fifteen days' journey from Aswān and thirteen from Qūṣ, is mentioned by al-Yaʿqūbī in the ninth century. Later, ʿAydhāb was supplanted by the port of Quṣayr, further north and only three days away from Qūṣ. Via the upper Nile valley and the Oases, Egypt remained in contact with eastern, tropical and equatorial Africa. Imports of black slaves were directed through Qūṣ, where influential merchants were based. Some slaves were destined for civilian domestic service, the *ḥarīm* or work in the vast agricultural projects, while others were reserved for military training, primarily as infantrymen. Gold dust, imported through the same route, bolstered the capacity of the province to strike coins. The pharaonic tombs were also methodically plundered to garner this precious metal.

The wealth of agriculture in the Nile valley and the Delta, and its high level of productivity assured by Byzantine fiscal institutions whose function had been reorganized in certain details but preserved in its basic forms, served to provide this province with vast and varied resources. Yet the province's daily requirements were not as great as those of Iraq. With the exception of Fusṭāṭ, an important urban center during this period but not of the same size or stature as Baṣra, there were no large cities. Alexandria, Tinnis and Damietta remained only modest port towns by the mid-third/ninth century. Their significant development would occur at the end of the fourth/tenth century; this situation left Egypt with a substantial agrarian surplus that enabled the holy cities in Arabia to be fed. In this way, Egypt influenced public opinion within the Islamic world during the annual pilgrimage. An artisan class skilled in textile manufacture, distributed throughout numerous sites, produced a variety of woven cloths of which the most costly were exported. Through its traveling merchants, Egypt was well informed about the economic and political life of Iraq and the Andalus.

The ʿAbbāsid caliphate in Iraq was hardly more than a symbol. Struggles between its factions steadily intensified. Initiated by the ʿAbbāsids after 750, the process of disbanding the Arab tribal army and professionalizing the military institution – now reserved primarily for peripheral ethnic groups – was vigorously advanced in the decade between 830 and 840. Throughout the second quarter of the third/ninth century, the caliphate in Baghdād (later in Sāmarrā) and its state apparatus were dominated by Iranian or Arab civilians and supported by Turkish military slaves. This palatine elite, part Shīʿite, part Ḥanafite and Muʿtazilite, promoted a policy of expedience that was posited on a rationalist approach to royal rights in the unifying spirit of the Qurʾān. By contrast, the majority of the Arabic-speaking Sunnī *ʿulamāʾ*, Mālikīs and Shāfiʿīs, rigorously defended their influence over society. This influence was based on memorization of minute juridical norms derived from traditions of the Prophet (*Ḥadīth*), myriad and thus beyond regulation. They increased their opposition after the death of the Caliph al-Maʾmūn in 833. The protest of Ibn Ḥanbal against the imposition, in the name of state-sponsored reason, of the doctrine of the created Qurʾān, resonated favorably among the men of the Sunnī mosques, even if they did not accept every extreme literalist opinion held by those who bore the designation *Ahl al-Ḥadīth*.

Abu'l-Faḍl Jaʿfar ibn Muḥammad al-Mutawakkil, caliph after 847, was the first to cede support of the state to Ḥanafism; he sided with Ibn Ḥanbal. His assassination in 247/861 inaugurated a period of weakness on the part of the caliphate and a struggle for power between Arab or Persian viziers and Turkish amīrs. As with the Praetorian Guard at Rome during the declining Empire, the Turks of the palatine guard installed and deposed the caliphs at their pleasure, taking care to collect at each new oath of obedience (*bayʿa*) a higher bonus. It is not possible to analyze Egypt from 868 to 969 without considering politics in Sāmarrā or Baghdād, since the increasing debility of ʿAbbāsid central authority provoked the eruption of several provincial revolts. These led to a new style of managing Muslim territories.

The governor of Egypt collected substantial taxes in grain or gold, while his expenses remained modest. He could hasten or delay, direct to whom he wished, or even cancel, the transfer to Iraq of the tribute awaited by the caliph's brother al-Muwaffaq for financing the supression of rebellions. During an epoch that witnessed the professionalizing of warfare and the rising costs of purchasing and supplying military slaves, their horses and arms, this fiscal advantage allowed first Ibn Ṭūlūn and subsequently Muḥammad ibn Ṭughj to occupy the whole of Syria up to the region of Aleppo and the frontier sites, and to impose their conditions on the ʿAbbāsids. They were obliged, however, to husband their treasury and to continue to support their army. For after tensions subsided in the east, the ʿAbbāsid authority, still militarily effective, attempted to reassert its control over the rich provinces of Syria and Egypt.

The hundred years between 264/868 and 358/969 thus marked a turning-point in the history of Arabic Egypt. Until that time, it was essentially passive, except during the period of ʿUthmān and ʿAlī, dominated and colonized by the Arabs – as it had been previously under the Achaemenid Persians, Ptolemies, Romans and Byzantines. During this century, Egypt gradually become a center of power radiating outside its territory, and commanding a position of central authority on his own, the amīr of Egypt finally found himself threatened as well. The numerous members of his family or the governors of his provinces might set off rebellions at any moment. The phenomena that had proved ubiquitous for other power centers: the burden of expenses and the immobility of the central army garrisoned in the capital, made their appearance in Egypt also.

The chronicles that focus on the Arab east from 860 to 970 present a series of violent campaigns led by non-Arab Muslims. These episodes are difficult to follow because of the large number of protagonists involved. Sketchily presented to the reader, most of these men were brutally eliminated, to be replaced by others emerging from the same background of warriors. The conflicts described by the chronicles occurred at every level. At the ʿAbbāsid court in Sāmarrā or Baghdād, they either brought together or placed in confrontation the caliph, members of his family, viziers, senior Turkish officers who frequented the palace, or even secretaries of the central administration. In the provincial capitals, the authority of the military governors was contested by the tax farmers or the senior officers appointed to control towns or districts, as well as by the chieftains of tribes whose territories intruded into their provinces.

ʿAbbāsid authority was called into question everywhere, and as soon as a local power initially delegated by the caliph became entrenched it took on a separate personality. The image of the *wālī*, the governor who could be readily nominated and subsequently revoked, gave way to that of the amīr, who regarded himself as a legitimate prince and strove to designate his own son as his heir. The amīr refused to acknowledge the central government's authority to dismiss him or to name his successor. From the caliph's entourage to that of the lowest soldier of fortune, loyalty was demanded from subordinates but denied to superiors. Familial competition, either for position or for succession, instigated dangerous conflicts as well. Thus may be explained the minimal duration of certain offices, such as the prefecture of police (*ṣāḥib al-shurṭa*) or even the *qāḍīs* of Egypt, who often held their posts for a few months only. The chroniclers soberly noted these disorders – without revealing the social psychology of the period, or the emotions of these men, their expressions of loyalty, their brotherhood in arms or even the simple camaraderie which could unite them.

One acquires or loses personal political power solely by force. As a temporary and fragile possession, one must take profit from it rapidly to enrich oneself and one's family by exploiting taxation of real estate, confiscating via the *kharāj* the major portion of income from agrarian land. A substantial portion of such gains must, in any case, be expended on the pay of those soldiers who protect this power and who all too often threaten it. The long-term political goal in the Islamic lands became indistinct during this period: power seemed only to function for itself, to appropriate to itself all sources of profit and thus to assure its own perpetuation with no higher purpose.

Egypt, however, proved to be the exception. Ibn Ṭūlūn and his son, Khumārawayh, then al-Ikhshīd and his successor, Kāfūr, openly favored this province and attempted to develop its economic potential – notably its agrarian productivity – by restoring its system of irrigation. They simultaneously sought to enhance the quality of daily life by reforming taxation policies and the operation of institutions in ways favorable to the indigenous inhabitants. A special kind of rapport between the local government of Egypt and its subjects was thereby established. From the end of the pharaonic period, this province had been dominated from a distant capital such as Rome, Constantinople or Ctesiphon, or one nearby but culturally quite distinct, such as the Alexandria of the Ptolemies. From the time of the Arab conquest, Egypt had played a passive role, but between 868 and 969, Ibn Ṭūlūn and his successors radically transformed this state of affairs, and thereby created a powerful autonomous regime. The Fāṭimids would subsequently benefit from their foundation.

The Ṭūlūnids

Ṭūlūn, Aḥmad's father, had belonged to a tribute corps of Turkish slaves sent by the governor of Bukhārā to the Caliph al-Maʾmūn. He became captain of the caliph's elite guard. Born in Ramaḍān 220/September 835 in Muslim territory, Aḥmad had never been a slave. He received his military training at Sāmarrā, his religious instruction at Ṭarṣūs in Cilicia where the role of the *ribāṭ* was accentuated by the duty of holy war (jihād) against the Byzantines. The *muḥaddithūn* and men of piety congregated there, attracted by the sums expended by al-Muʿtazz and his mother that guaranteed the subsistence of the *murābiṭūn* in the town.

Exhibiting the physical and moral qualities that had enabled his ethnic group to monopolize senior ranks in the army, Ibn Ṭūlūn distinguished himself above all for his sense of duty by organizing the defense of a caravan that was attacked by Bedouins near Edessa, while his fellow officers in the escort stood by. This episode won Ibn Ṭūlūn the affection of the Caliph al-Mustaʿīn, who made a gift to him of a female slave who would be Khumārawayh's mother. Ibn Ṭūlūn accompanied the Caliph al-Mustaʿīn to exile in 251/865, but he was unable, or possibly did not seek, to avert his execution in 252/866.

Having acquired the religious and literary culture worthy of an Arab civil administrator, Ibn Ṭūlūn bestowed the names of Arab tribes on several of his sons. He enjoyed the company of the *ʿulamāʾ*, poets, architects and physicians. He maintained a certain distance with regard to his comrades in arms and was never regarded as a military ruffian. He exhibited a keen political acumen. Exceedingly self-confident, he began to design long-term projects. Capable of concealing his emotions until the moment when he could give them free rein without damaging consequences, he rarely submitted to fits of temper. He withheld his reaction to any aggression directed against him, in order to control the situation and thus to force his rival to fall into the trap he had prepared for him. Then his revenge was swift and terrible. According to the sources, Ibn Ṭūlūn was responsible for the deaths of more than 18,000 persons executed by his order or expiring in his jails.

In 254/868 the Caliph al-Muʿtazz bestowed Egypt as an appanage on Bākbāk, the second spouse of Aḥmad ibn Ṭūlūn's mother. Having been delegated authority over the country by his step-father, Ibn Ṭūlūn entered Fusṭāṭ on 23 Ramaḍān 254/15 September 868, accompanied by Aḥmad ibn Muḥammad al-Wāsiṭī. The arrival of Ibn Ṭūlūn in Egypt was described in the Arabic sources as a propitious event, with reference to the astronomic circumstances of his ceremonial day of entry into Fusṭāṭ and predictions pronounced by a youthful blind seer. This was not the simple installation of a new governor but the first official act of a quasi-sovereign dynasty. Ibn

Ṭūlūn was credited with laying the foundations of a new Egypt, not merely a dependent province of a distant ʿAbbāsid capital but the seat of a new center of political and economic power. All the omens were favorable, as they were a century later when the *qāʾid* Jawhar laid out Cairo for the Fāṭimid Imām.

The governors appointed over Fusṭāṭ bore the title *wālī al-jaysh waʾl-ṣalāt*, overseer of the army and the Friday prayer (*al-jumʿa*). At the same time, they might or might not receive supervision of the *kharāj* – the collection of the country's agrarian property taxes. In general, they immediately appointed a prefect of police (*wālī al-shurṭa*) and a deputy governor of Alexandria. Initially charged with authority only over Fusṭāṭ, *al-qaṣaba* or capital of the province excluding Alexandria, Aḥmad found as incumbent supervisor of the *kharāj* an eminent fiscal secretary. This was Ibn al-Mudabbir Aḥmad ibn Muḥammad al-Rastisānī, who had already completed a lengthy career. Director in Sāmarrā of the *dīwān al-jaysh* under al-Wāthiq, and then administrator of seven dīwāns under al-Mutwakkil, but cast into prison in 240/854, he was subsequently named director of finances in the two Syrian *junds* (provinces) of Damascus (central and southern Syria) and Tiberiad/Urdunn (northern Palestine). Preceding the arrival of Ibn Ṭūlūn, most likely in 247/861, he had assumed the same duties in Egypt. Finding the fiscal yield of the province far too small, he doubled the *kharāj* and the *jizya*, deprived the Christian clergy and monks of their traditional exemptions, and created new taxes – to be collected according to the lunar year (*hilālī*). He also imposed non-Qurʾanic tariffs (*maks/mukūs*) on pasturelands, fisheries and beds of caustic soda. He thus was considered the most hated man in Egypt, which explains the escort of 100 young guardsmen who accompanied him on all occasions. Because Ibn Ṭūlūn was henceforth responsible for maintaining order but had refused any cash donation, he demanded that Ibn al-Mudabbir turn his guards over to him. Despite Ibn al-Mudabbir's unpopularity, Ibn Ṭūlūn had to spend four years directing intrigues on the part of his agents in Sāmarrā in order to arrange the transfer of the fiscal intendant to Syria in Ramaḍān 258/July 871. He took the opportunity to rid himself of Shukayr, postmaster of Egypt (responsible for the mail [*barīd*] and information services), and personally assumed collection of the *kharāj* in 259/872.

In 256/869–70 Bākbāk was put to death, and during the summer of 257/871 the appanage of Egypt devolved upon Yārjūkh (alt. Yārūj), whose daughter Ibn Ṭūlūn had married. From this time on, administration over the whole of Egypt, including Alexandria and Barka, was conferred upon the governor of Fusṭāṭ. Ibn Ṭūlūn proceeded solemnly to assume power in Alexandria, the government of which he turned over to his son al-ʿAbbās two years later.

Ibn Ṭūlūn was occupied with suppression of a series of disorders, for which mission he had been appointed. Because of its rapid Islamization and

Arabization, Upper Egypt was marginally controlled by the governor of Aswān. It was also menaced by the Nubians, who had stubbornly remained Christian, by the Budja[1] and by the turmoil surrounding the exploitation of the local gold mines directed by the Banū Rabīʿa. After 255/868 the Budja, having converted to Islam, were able to help the Egyptians resist the Nubians. Berber tribes rampaged in the oases that formed the termini for the trade routes to northern and Saharan Africa. The Delta was unsettled by the semi-sedentarized Arab tribes who were grappling with raids by the nomadic Berbers from Libya. An ʿAlid, Bughā al-Aṣghar Aḥmad ibn Muḥammad Ibn al-Ṭabāṭabā, revolted during Jumādā I 255/spring 859 in the territory between Alexandria and Barka, proclaiming himself caliph. He was captured and executed in Upper Egypt during the summer of 255/869. Subsequently, another ʿAlid, Ibn al-Ṣūfī, Ibrāhīm ibn Muḥammad, a descendant of ʿUmar ibn ʿAlī ibn Abī Ṭālib fomented rebellions over two years and massacred the inhabitants of Esna at the end of 255/869. Having defeated a Ṭūlūnid general in Rabīʿ I 256/winter 870, he was forced to seek refuge in the Oases during the spring. In Muḥarram 259/autumn 872 he emerged from his retreat to attack another self-proclaimed chieftain in Nubia, al-ʿUmarī.[2] Suffering defeat, Ibn al-Ṣūfī ravaged the district of Aswān where he cut down tens of thousands of palm trees. He then sought refuge in Mecca where he was captured and turned over to Ibn Ṭūlūn, who imprisoned him in Fusṭāṭ before allowing his return to Medina. Abū ʿAbd Allāh ibn ʿAbd al-Ḥamīd al-ʿUmarī, a descendant of the second caliph and the individual who had confronted Ibn al-Ṣūfī, carved out a principality in the vicinity of the Nubian gold mines. Following an encounter that resulted in the rout of the Ṭūlūnid army, al-ʿUmarī was tolerated in Nubia. He proceeded to sell his gold and slaves in the market of Aswān until his own officers assassinated him. In 260/873–874, Abū Rūḥ Sukun, a former partisan of Ibn al-Ṣūfī, revolted in the oases and made life hard for Ibn Ṭūlūn's cavalrymen. The latter was compelled to offer him a truce (*amān*).

In 261/874–875 the governor of Barka, Muḥammad ibn al-Farāj al-Farghānī, declared his rebellion. The army despatched by Ibn Ṭūlūn achieved no success by soft tactics, and was forced to use siege engines to storm the city. The suppression was moderate, however: Ibn Ṭūlūn displayed great restraint in his dealings with the western limits of his territory. Relations between Egypt and north Africa were enhanced. According to the exaggerated account of Ibn al-Athīr, once lighthouses were built along the coast a message sent from the minaret of the Sabta Mosque on the coast of Ifrīqiya in the evening could reach Alexandria the same night. However, when the Aghlabid

[1] Hamitic-speaking populations partially Christianized and living in the Nubian Nile valley. See *EI2*, "Bedja," I, 1157b, and "al-Ṣaʿīd," VIII, 893.

[2] Cf. *EI2*, "al-Ṣaʾīd," VIII, 893.

Ibrāhīm ibn Aḥmad sought to protect a route between Ifrīqiya and the Ḥijāz for commerce and the pilgrimage, he feared that Ibn Ṭūlūn would not permit a sustained continental link across Egypt. He therefore fortified the port of Sousse and arranged a maritime passage via Sicily.

ʿIsā ibn al-Shaykh al-Shaybānī, known as Ibn al-Shaykh, governor of Ramla (southern Palestine) and Tiberiad/Urdunn (northern Palestine), was arrested by his own commander in Damascus for having pilfered from the tribute of 750,000 dīnārs, some three tons of fine gold that Ibn al-Mudabbir during his tenure as fiscal collector in Egypt had sent to Iraq. Ibn Ṭūlūn, while maintaining relations with Ibn al-Shaykh, immediately set about recruiting Greek and black soldiers. He equipped an army in Ṣafar 256/winter 869–870. But since the caliphal establishment announced its displeasure, Ibn Ṭūlūn cut short his march on Syria and returned to Fusṭāṭ in Shaʿbān 256/summer 870. That year, the Caliph al-Muʿtamid appointed an officer, Amājūr, as governor of Damascus. This individual took possession of the city despite an abortive resistance by Ibn al-Shaykh who submitted to accepting a command post in Armenia.

At this time the situation in Iraq was tense. Al-Wāthiq's son, al-Muhtadī, had acceded to the caliphate upon the demise of al-Muʿtazz in July of 869. Pious and energetic, he sought to restore the caliph's authority in the face of Turkish opposition. Relying on the civil administration's backing, he succeeded in removing several Turkish military commanders – in particular the powerful Muḥammad ibn Bughā. The latter's brother, Mūsā ibn Bughā, returned to Sāmarrā with a formidable army, however. After inflicting a defeat upon al-Muhtadī, Mūsā put him to an atrocious death in 256/June 870. Abu'l-ʿAbbās Aḥmad ibn al-Mutawakkil, al-Muʿtamid ʿalā Allāh, succeeded him as caliph. Compelled to reside in Sāmarrā, he never exercised any genuine authority since real power remained in the hands of his brother, Abū Aḥmad al-Muwaffaq, who was serving as viceroy of the eastern caliphate and had been designated his successor. Al-Muʿtamid's son, Jaʿfar, had theoretically received sovereign primacy in the ʿAbbāsid west, notably Syria, but had never in fact managed to command obedience in that province. Based in Baghdād, al-Muwaffaq had to rely on his Turkish generals, and consequently required ready access to all the fiscal revenues of the empire to deal with rebellions: Saffārids in Fars Province (southwest Iran), Zanj in Lower Iraq, Khārijites in Jazīra and Mawṣil, Ḥasanids in the Ḥijāz, Zaydites in Ṭabaristān. He also had to deal with conspiracies plotted against him closer to home, in Baghdād or Sāmarrā. This situation thus facilitated Ibn Ṭūlūn's takeover of Egypt. Indeed, while Syria could be counted on as a refuge into which the caliph might retreat to await a rearrangement of alliances in the aftermath of his defeats following the struggles for power in Iraq, Egypt, because of its distance, enjoyed a greater measure of autonomy with respect to palace intrigues in Baghdād.

During his first eight years in power in Egypt, Ibn Ṭūlūn took advantage of the financial and military dilemmas confronting al-Muwaffaq to extend his sphere of influence and to nurture his autonomy. He ultimately intended to transfer the center of power from the ʿAbbāsid zone to Egypt. Of the 4.3 million dīnārs in fiscal rents collected within Egypt in 263/876, Ibn Ṭūlūn sent 1.2 million to al-Muwaffaq to support his war effort and 2.2 million to al-Muʿtamid. Counting on the Caliph al-Muʿtamid's friendship in return for the tribute he sent him directly and discretely but which he denied al-Muwaffaq, Ibn Ṭūlūn assumed the title of Mawlā Amīr al-Muʾminīn after 265/878.

In 258 or 259/872 or 873, following Yārjūkh's death, the Egyptian appanage devolved upon al-Muʿtamid's son Jaʿfar, the designated future Caliph al-Mufawwaḍ. Beholding al-Muwaffaq occupied with repression of the Zanj revolt, Ibn Ṭūlūn kept Egypt aloof and withheld his allegiance from his new suzerain, who had refused to reconfirm him in his office. In 262/875–876, al-Muwaffaq sought to recruit a volunteer to assume the governorship of Egypt. All the senior officers serving in Baghdād had been secretly bought off by Ibn Ṭūlūn, however, and thus declined his offer. Al-Muwaffaq then wrote a threatening missive to Ibn Ṭūlūn demanding his resignation, which provoked a brusque refusal. Ibn Ṭūlūn proceeded to fortify his frontier towns and coastal ports. Al-Muwaffaq named Mūsā ibn Bughā governor of Egypt and despatched him with a contingent to Syria. Ibn Bughā tarried some ten months at Raqqa, however, and possessing insufficient money to pay his soldiers, he was forced to return to Iraq.

Having performed his initial military service at Tarsus by participating in the jihād, Ibn Ṭūlūn wished to establish himself in this city with authority over Cilicia as a whole, in order to direct its defense against the Byzantines. He requested al-Muwaffaq to confer its command upon him, but the regent predictably refused. However, a series of events had seriously eroded the capacity of the Muslims to hold off the Byzantines, and in 263/876–77 the Caliph al-Muʿtamid therefore pressed al-Muwaffaq to confer upon Ibn Ṭūlūn responsibility for Syria and Cilicia, the frontier districts (*al-thughūr*). He was charged with protection of the Anatolian frontier. Henceforth, Ibn Ṭūlūn regarded Amājūr, ʿAbbāsid governor of Damascus, as his subordinate. When this individual died in 264/877–78, Ibn Ṭūlūn summoned his son and compelled him to acknowledge Ṭūlūnid authority, to which the latter submitted. Ibn Ṭūlūn marched upon Syria himself, appointed Ibn Amājūr commander in Ramla, and then took possession of Damascus, Homs, Hama and Aleppo.

Ibn al-Mudabbir had been the fiscal bursar (*ʿāmil*) of Damascus, Tiberiad/Urdunn and Palestine-Ramla since 258/871–872. In 264/877, after occupying Damascus, Ibn Ṭūlūn fined him 600,000 dīnārs and cast him into prison, where he remained until his death in 270/883–84. At the same time,

Ibn al-Mudabbir's brother, involved with the Zanj rebellions from 255 to 270/868 to 883, was arrested in Baṣra, but was able to escape from his jail cell.

Ibn Ṭūlūn retained Amājūr's officers in their posts. He was then forced to subdue the opposition of Sīmā al-Ṭawīl, governor of Aleppo, who had sought refuge in Antioch. Ibn Ṭūlūn mounted an assault on that city, during which the governor was killed, possibly by a woman's hand. Ibn Ṭūlūn then marched on Tarsus, and upon entering the town began preparing for a jihād. The presence of his army in such high numbers caused prices to rise, and the inhabitants of Tarsus proceeded to his camp to demand either his departure or a reduction of his contingent to a few soldiers. Heated words were exchanged. As the incident threatened to escalate, Ibn Ṭūlūn feigned a retreat before the hostility of Tarsus's populace, ostensibly wishing to impress upon the Byzantines the capacity of Tarsus to resist a siege. In fact, he was anxious to return to Egypt where his own son al-ʿAbbās was preparing to revolt. However, reassured by subsequent messages attesting to the solidity of the caretaker regime he had left behind in Fusṭāṭ, he decided not to depart the region before clearly demarcating his territory. After restoring the assets that Sīmā had unjustly seized from the notables of Aleppo and reconfirming the *qāḍī* in his office, he installed his *ghulām* Lu'lu' there in command of an army. He was supported in this venture by Ibn al-ʿAbbās, chief of the Banū Kilāb. He also based another contingent at Ḥarrān. In order to capture the audacious Mūsā ibn Atāmish, who had challenged his progression through the district, Ibn Ṭūlūn was obliged to recruit the service of a Bedouin. This individual devised a stratagem that Ibn al-Athīr, intrigued by its shrewdness, described at length. In 269/ 883, Ibn Ṭūlūn placed Lu'lu', who was already serving as governor of Diyār Muḍar, in charge of Ḥoms, Aleppo and Qinnasrīn. Of the towns occupied by Ibn Ṭūlūn, only al-Qarqīsiyā was retaken by al-Muwaffaq in 268/881. Ibn Ṭūlūn thus had established a principality whose frontiers broadly defined the territory which Ṣalāḥ al-Dīn and the Mamlūks would later dominate.

Exploiting the absence of his father, whom he had replaced as the titular head of Egypt, al-ʿAbbās declared open rebellion. Pliable of mind, he was easily manipulated by his military comrades. The steadfastly loyal vizier, al-Wāsiṭī, prior to being bound and carried off as a parcel, had managed to alert Ibn Ṭūlūn who returned in Ramaḍān 265/April 879. Al-ʿAbbās left Fusṭāṭ leading a contingent of 800 mounted warriors and 10,000 infantrymen and absconding with the state treasury. He reached Alexandria and then Barka, where he demanded that the Aghlabid Ibrāhīm III step down in his favor. He claimed to possess a certificate of nomination to the leadership of Ifrīqiya emanating from al-Muʿtamid. Al-ʿAbbās put the town of Labda to sack after routing the army of the Aghlabid governor Muḥammad ibn Qurhub. He besieged Tripoli, but the Ibadite Ilyās ibn Manṣūr al-Nafūsī, governor of Jabal Nafūsa and Tripoli on behalf of the Rustamid of Tahert, led a force of 12,000 men and defeated him in 266/879–880 or 267/winter 880–81. Having lost all his resources, al-ʿAbbās retreated toward Egypt. He was captured near Alexandria and conducted on a mule back to Fusṭāṭ, where his father ordered him to gouge out the eyes and cut off the hands of his fellow conspirators. This he did, much to Ibn Ṭūlūn's consternation, since he had secretly expected his son's refusal. Weeping profusely, he ordered his son to be lashed and then cast into prison. From this date of 268/881–82, al-ʿAbbās's brother, Khumārawayh, became Ibn Ṭūlūn's successor-designate.

Prior to Ibn Ṭūlūn, only al-Sarī ibn al-Ḥakam ibn Yūsuf al-Balkhī had attempted to establish an autonomous dynasty in Egypt. He had been named governor in Ramaḍān 200/April 816, but was deposed in Rabīʿ I 201/September 816. Reappointed in Shaʿbān 201/March 817, al-Sarī remained in office until his death in Jumādā II 205/November 820. His sons temporarily occupied the position of governor until 211/September 826.

The existence of numerous public ministries (dīwāns) is documented in Egypt prior to Ibn Ṭūlūn's arrival. The texts indicate an administration to deal with the *kharāj* or real estate tax, the *barīd* or postal and information service, a *dīwān al-ahrāʾ* which managed the public granaries, a *dīwān asfal al-arḍ* that controlled the Delta in 143/761. A *dīwān al-khāṣṣ* (privy fund) may have existed to rearrange the financial services responsible for administering the governor's assets. With regard to the *dīwān al-inshāʾ*, it possibly preceded Ibn Ṭūlūn although it may have been created by his director of administration, Abū Jaʿfar Muḥammad ibn ʿAbd al-Kān (d. 278/891). Ibn Ṭūlūn set up a chancellory in Fusṭāṭ, essentially on the model of Sāmarrā, by exploiting the talents of Ibn ʿAbd al-Kān, four brothers of the Banū al-Muhājir and Ibn al-Dāya. In 266/879, Abū Bakr al-Atrash (the Deaf) Aḥmad ibn Ibrāhīm al-Mādharāʾī (*nisba* relating to a village in the vicinity of Wāsiṭ) was proclaimed governor of finances in Egypt and Syria. He died in 270/884. His descendants continued to hold the high financial offices in Egypt under Ibn Ṭūlūn's successors and to amass one of the largest personal fortunes of the medieval Arab east. Most of the personnel appointed to these dīwāns had been trained in Sāmarrā. Several heads of financial dīwāns would attain positions of the highest responsibility, but subsequently suffer imprisonment or the obligation of paying steep fines. Some of these amounted to several million dīnārs,[3] levied either under Ibn Ṭūlūn or his successors.

As in Baghdād, members of the great families of viziers and public administrators, most of whom had originated in Iraq, could handle the *qalam* quite well. Later, when Muḥammad ibn Ṭughj wrote to the Emperor

[3] A million gold dīnārs corresponds to approximately 4.25 tonnes of fine gold.

Romanus I, he had several secretaries draw up drafts of letters. He chose the example of al-Najīramī. Throughout the century which is our concern, marriages between families of Turkish or Farghānian militarists and Arab or Iranian viziers frequently occurred. Thus as an example, Abu'l-Fatḥ al-Faḍl Ibn Ḥinzāba, son of Abu'l-Khaṭṭāb Jaʿfar ibn al-Furāt, supervisor of property taxes in the east, and under al-Rāḍī, fiscal inspector of Egypt and Syria, married the daughter of Muḥammad ibn Tughj and gave to his own son as a second wife the daughter of the *amīr al-umarā'*, Ibn Rā'iq.

Like their predecessors in Iraq, some of these officials were men of letters who wrote poems or histories, but because of their more provincial status, they counted no philosophers among themselves, unlike in Baghdād. They recorded facts, practical affairs and conventional knowledge, but made no inquiries into the ethics of domestic life or of political practice or theory. From Ibn Ṭūlūn's epoch until the end of the Mamlūk period, Fusṭāṭ, and subsequently Cairo, was an, if not the most, important center of Muslim and Arab culture, especially with regard to historical writing. Yet no individual of high stature in rational or speculative thought, philosophy or logic, was mentioned as an Egyptian or as a long-term sojourner in Egypt. Such persons frequently emerged in Baghdād, Syria, Mā Warā al-Nahr (Transoxiana), al-Andalus or other remote Muslim provinces. To be sure, some Jewish thinkers who were born in Egypt – such as Saʿadyā al-Fayyūmī in the ninth–tenth centuries, or al-Muʿizz ibn Maymūn (Maimonides) in the twelfth–thirteenth centuries who spent part of his life in Cairo – attained wide renown in the realm of intellectual endeavor.

Accordingly, the secretary Aḥmad Ibn al-Dāya (b. 245 or 250/859 or 864, d. 330–340/941–951), wrote a history of Ibn Ṭūlūn, subsequently abridged by Ibn Saʿīd, and a history of physicians. Abū Muḥammad al-Farghānī ʿAbd Allāh ibn Aḥmad ibn Jaʿfar (283–362/895–973) settled in Egypt where he served as a soldier and wrote an appendix, *al-Ṣila*, to the History of al-Ṭabarī. His son, Abū Manṣūr Aḥmad ibn ʿAbd Allāh (327–398/939–1007), was born in Egypt and similarly became a senior officer and probably a historian.

Due to the restored security, sound administration and projects undertaken to enhance the irrigation system, the annual tax yield from agrarian land had reached 4,000,000 dīnārs by Ibn Ṭūlūn's demise. A reserve of 10,000,000 dīnārs had been accumulated.

Ibn Ṭūlūn's army allegedly numbered some 24,000 Turkish *ghulāms*, in addition to 42,000 black slaves and free men. In 263/876–877, when he noted that the ʿAbbāsid menace was becoming more pronounced, Ibn Ṭūlūn built a war fleet. He began to construct a fortified redoubt on Rawḍa Island between the two bridges to protect his treasury and his wives, although these projects were rapidly engulfed by Nile floods. He had restored the walls of the military port in the city of Alexandria, which was maintained from an independent budget. He docked his fleet in the Palestinian port of ʿAkka which he also fortified, this last project employing a high level of technical competence and amphibious masonry. It was carried out by the grandfather of the geographer al-Muqaddasī who describes in detail the construction of its docking facilities. By contrast, Qaysariyya, despite its Palestinian location, was left abandoned and covered with sand.

Fusṭāṭ was already an extensive city when Ibn Ṭūlūn established himself there, and it was divided into *khiṭṭa*s, each with its own mosque. The descendants of the Syrian Christians and Jews who had accompanied the numerous Yemenis during the conquest, now largely Islamized, dwelled in the three *ḥamra* that constituted the town's central quarter. It was bounded on the west by the Nile, which was gradually shifting westward. This quarter surrounded the great mosque which had been founded immediately after the conquest, the *Jāmīʿ ʿAmr* or *Jāmiʿ al-ʿAtīq*. To the south were located the heights of *al-Rasad*, to the north the heights of *Yashkur*. To the east, between Fusṭāṭ and the Muqaṭṭam, was the Qarāfa cemetery. The city was divided into two cantons: *ʿamal fawq*, the upper district, consisting of the heights to the south and east, and *ʿamal asfal*, the lower district, embracing the rest. Until the Fāṭimid era, each canton possessed its own administration and police. The ʿAbbāsid governors no longer resided in al-Ḥamrā' al-Quṣwā. They had founded, atop a hill to the northeast, *al-ʿAskar*, a military town with a *jāmiʿ al-ʿaskar* or the *jāmiʿ sāḥil al-ghalla* ("the mosque at the quay (on the *khalīj*) for agrarian produce") and a commercial quarter.

The inhabitants of Fusṭāṭ complained to Ibn Ṭūlūn of being disturbed at Friday prayer (*jumʿa*) by the excessive number of soldiers, in particular those who were black. The mosque, packed and cramped within a densely built up area, could not be enlarged or opened to fresh air. Ibn Ṭūlūn therefore ordered the construction in 264/878 of his own great mosque. Work was begun the following year and completed in 266/880. In consequence of the mosque project, the new town of al-Qaṭā'iʿ was created at the northeastern extremity of the Jabal Yashkur, on the site of abandoned Christian and Jewish cemeteries. The excessive number of soldiers in Baghdād had induced the ʿAbbāsid Caliphs to build Sāmarrā, and Ibn Ṭūlūn followed their precedent. Construction of the mosque allegedly cost 120,000 dīnārs, a sum implausibly small given its scale. Several houses had been placed in trust (*waqf*) to finance the mosque's operations. Ibn Ṭūlūn, and subsequently his son Khumārawayh, installed twelve muezzins, in three groups of four, in a room near the minaret. Both day and night they continuously recited the Qur'ān and sang praises to the Prophet, the *qaṣā'id*.

The mosque's plan and structure were Egyptian and its bell-shaped capitals were inspired by the ʿAmr Mosque, but Iraqi influence was shown in its use of fired bricks, its decoration with molded or carved stucco and its utilization of three *ziyāda* (external courtyards), all as in Sāmarrā. The original minaret must have been modeled on Sāmarrā examples, as is the present structure. An attractive dome, no longer extant, supported by two superimposed colonnades, sheltered a font in the center of the courtyard for the performance of minor ablutions. The lavatories and facilities for major ablutions, along with a pharmacy, had been built outside the mosque enclosure wall for reasons of sanitation. The architect was most probably a Mesopotamian Christian, Ibn Kātib al-Farghānī. In order to avoid the common practice of transferring columns from Christian churches, he had false columns carved into the brick pillars. A *dār al-imāra*, or palace of government adjoined the mosque on its eastern side. It was connected by a small door through the *qibla* wall, as was the practice at Baṣra or Damascus.

Ibn Ṭūlūn also founded the *mashhad* of Sayyida Nafīsa and the aqueduct. He built a mosque up on the Muqaṭṭam Heights at Tannūr Firʿawn.

According to al-Maqrīzī, Ibn Ṭūlūn laid out al-Qaṭāʾiʿ on a surface grid of 1,000 plots within an area of one square mile. Each unit of his polyglot army – regular troops, Bedouin allies, Byzantine mercenaries, Nubian infantry, black slaves, Turkish ghulāms and other soldiers of varied origins – was assigned as its residence a *qaṭāʾiʿ* or concession which bore its name. The whole, distributed around the amīr's palace and the great mosque, constituted the *Qaṭāʾiʿ*. A veritable amīral city thus surrounded the religious, political and military complex. The market of money-weighers (*sūq al-ʿayyārīn*) brought together drugs sellers and grain dealers, the peas market (*fāmiyyīn*) gathered butchers, vegetable sellers, roasters and spice purveyors, the cooks' market (*ṭabbākhīn*) assembled moneychangers, bakers and confectioners. All these markets were selling commodities of better quality than had the old markets of Fusṭāṭ.

Ibn Ṭūlūn also built a hippodrome and a hospital, *al-bīmāristān*, between 259 and 261/872 and 874. One facility was reserved for men, the other for women; neither slaves nor soldiers were granted access. As for Ibn Ṭūlūn himself, he preferred to reside in the Christian monastery of Quṣayr just north of Fusṭāṭ.[4] Indeed, even though he had at one time imprisoned the Patriarch Shanūda I who reigned between 859 and 880, and Khāʾil III, Patriarch from 880 to 890, following Coptic intrigues, Ibn Ṭūlūn and his successors, including the Ikhshīdids, elected to maintain positive relations with the Christians of Egypt. They had suppressed the excessive poll taxes that Ibn al-Mudabbir had imposed on this community.

In the autumn of 269/882, following the repression of al-ʿAbbās's rebellion, Ibn Ṭūlūn learned that his *ghulām* Luʾluʾ, whom he had appointed commander of an important military contingent in northern Syria, had been

[4] On this monastery see al-Shabushtī, *Kitāb al-Diyārāt*, ed. Kurkis ʿAwwād (Beirut, 1986), 284.

recalled by al-Muwaffaq. He departed immediately for Syria with al-ʿAbbās in tow and bound in chains, leaving Egypt under the regency of Khumārawayh. The situation at Tarsus also threatened to slip from Ibn Ṭūlūn's control, since in the aftermath of its governor's demise, his replacement, the eunuch Yazmān, was very popular with the inhabitants but refused to acknowledge his suzerain's authority. Passing through Damascus en route to the frontier districts, he received a message from the Caliph al-Muʿtamid, informing him that on the pretext of departing on a hunting expedition, he had surreptitiously departed from Sāmarrā for Syrian territory. Ibn Ṭūlūn decided to await the caliph at Damascus and to conduct him triumphantly back to al-Qaṭāʾiʿ. There he would find a palace and a great mosque whose stature and luxury would rival those of the vast official buildings in Sāmarrā. But al-Muwaffaq, discovering his brother's scheme, despatched a contingent led by Isḥaq ibn Kundāj, the governor of Mawṣil, who was able to defeat the officers escorting al-Muʿtamid at al-Ḥadītha on the Euphrates and to force the caliph's return to Sāmarrā in Shaʿbān 269/February 883. Al-Muwaffaq named Ibn Kundāj governor of Syria and Egypt, a post he would never take up.

By achieving sole mastery over Egypt and extending his power in Syria up to the Byzantine frontier, Ibn Ṭūlūn had fulfilled his first two objectives. He endured the failure to achieve his third and most ambitious goal: to install on the shores of the Nile the ʿAbbāsid dynasty, which in a prosperous and peaceful setting would regain its original glory. But he tenaciously refused to abandon his hopes. Ibn Ṭūlūn had the governor of Damascus convene the *qāḍīs*, *faqīhs* and *sharīfs* of all Ṭūlūnid territories and assemble them in a congress most probably held in the glorious Umayyad Mosque. The Egyptian delegation, comprising nine individuals of premier rank and an entourage of less distinguished persons, was headed by Bakkār ibn Quṭayba. This man was an Iraqi Ḥanafī with an austere demeanor of high reputation who had served as *qāḍī* of Egypt since 248/862–863. *Khuṭbas* were pronounced from all the minbars of the principality, luridly depicting the disarray and disgrace of the Caliph al-Muʿtamid who languished, confined as a prisoner, and the treason of Abū Aḥmad al-Muwaffaq who had defied the conditions of his *bayʿa* or oath of loyalty that he had sworn to his brother. Before these senior authorities on Islam assembled in Damascus during the spring of 269/883, Ibn Ṭūlūn demanded that they proclaim the jihād against al-Muwaffaq and thereby obliged the ʿummaʾ to deny its pledge of his enthronement. He managed to obtain a general agreement among the participants, but the *qāḍī* Bakkār, with the support of two Egyptians, refused to pronounce it formally since he claimed to be insufficiently informed. In fact, even despite the texts' silence on this issue, the obligation of jihād could not be invoked in a conflict among Sunnīs, since the dispute did not weaken the capacity of the *Dār al-Islām* to confront non-Muslims or heretics. Thus it was al-Muwaffaq rather than al-Muʿtamid who defended, arms in hand, public order in Iraq. Ibn Ṭūlūn, so close to his goal, had failed once again.

However, the convention of so large a body of senior mosque functionaries and legal practitioners to attempt to reach a consensus on policy was an innovation, an act unique since the ʿAbbāsid Revolution. It is no coincidence that it was assembled at Damascus, for here under al-Muʿāwiya a tradition had been inaugurated of an exchange of opinions about the distribution of Muslim authority between the caliph and his advisors at the *jumʿa*, which included women, that occurred every Friday at the conclusion of prayer. The public call for the views of civilians with regard to political matters rarely occurred in the eastern Arab world after 750. There were exceptions, at the beginning of the fifth/eleventh century on the occasion of the Caliph al-Qādir's denunciations of the Fāṭimids, and at the end of the sixth/twelfth century on the occasion of Caliph al-Nāṣir's desperate attempt to salvage the unity of Islam from the threat of its appropriation by non-Arab militarists.

Al-Muwaffaq, informed of the Damascus congress, ordered the proclamation from all ʿAbbāsid minbars of the following statement: "Almighty God, Confounder of a malediction that will promote the erosion of his power and denigrate his renown, make of him [Ibn Ṭūlūn] an example for those who will come after, for You will not permit the Scheme of Corrupters to succeed!"

Despite his previous triumphs, Ibn Ṭūlūn suffered an extremely onerous final year. He had appointed ʿAbd Allāh ibn al-Fatḥ with authority over Aleppo in place of Lu'lu', who, on the side of al-Muwaffaq, fought brilliantly against the Zanj. Ibn Ṭūlūn wished to drive Yazmān from Tarsus, and placed the city under siege in the autumn of 270/883. Yazmān diverted part of the Baradān River, inundating the Egyptian camp. Ibn Ṭūlūn retreated to Adana and then Massissa. There he became ill and was taken back to Egypt in a wheeled vehicle (*ʿajala*), a remarkable medium of transport for the period, arriving at Fusṭāṭ in a serious condition at the end of the year 883. He gave orders for the imprisonment of Bakkār and the verification of the *qāḍī*'s accounts. This individual was responsible for managing the assets of widows and orphans and controlling the charitable trusts (*awqāf*) as well as the striking of coinage. Ibn Ṭūlūn named a new judge, Muḥammad ibn Shādhān al-Jawharī, and conferred supervision over the *awqāf* or *ḥubus* upon the prefect of police, Saray ibn Sahl. Finding Bakkār culpable of no embezzlement since he had scrupulously accounted for all the sums that Ibn Ṭūlūn had remitted to him over fifteen years, Ibn Ṭūlūn ordered his release. But the aging *qāḍī*, now gravely ill himself, had no desire to leave his prison cell. Ibn Ṭūlūn's condition worsened. Muslims, Christians and Jews, including women and children, converged separately upon the flank of the Muqaṭṭam to implore God to save him. He died in Fusṭāṭ on the tenth of Dhu'l-Qaʿda 270/10 May 884, eleven-and-a-half months after the congress of Damascus, and less than sixteen solar years after his solemn entry into the city.

The government of Egypt by Aḥmad ibn Ṭūlūn was a pivotal act that affected the history of Egypt for centuries to come. For the first time in the Islamic world a Turkish general created an autonomous dynasty that was solidly anchored in a province. He appropriated the limited authority delegated to him by the caliph as an appanage holder in order to realize its full potential. He did so less for military purposes than for an intelligent manipulation of politics in the Arab east. He remained loyal, and Ṭūlūnid coins that were struck at Fusṭāṭ, Ramla, Aleppo, Antioch and probably Damascus, bore the caliph's name. He administered a province which, despite the period's indistinct grasp of the Orient's ancient past, exhibited many pharaonic manifestations attesting to the extreme antiquity of its civilization, comparable with that of Mesopotamia. His amirate's most notable characteristic was the quality of relations it maintained with Christians and Jews, and the position held by Jerusalem. Under the Ṭūlūnids, Syro-Egyptian territory was deeply imbued with the concept of an extraordinary role devolving upon Jerusalem in Islam as al-Quds, Bayt al-Maqdis or Bayt al-Muqaddas, "the House of Holiness," the seat of the Last Judgment, the Gate to Paradise for Muslims, as well as for Jews and Christians. In the popular conscience, this concept established a bond between the three monotheistic religions. If Aḥmad ibn Ṭūlūn was interred on the slope of the Muqaṭṭam, ʿĪsā ibn Mūsā al-Nāshārī and Takīn were laid to rest in Jerusalem in 910 and 933, as were their Ikhshīdid successors and Kāfūr. To honor the great general and governor of Syria, Anūshtakīn al-Dizbirī, who died in 433/1042, the Fāṭimid Dynasty had his remains solemnly conveyed from Aleppo to Jerusalem in 448/1056–57.

During the reign of Ibn Ṭūlūn, Theodore, Patriarch of Jerusalem, praised him for his benevolent exercise of power. According to Moshe Gil, it is possible that a Christian had been appointed governor of Ramla.[5] The situation began to change in the fourth/tenth century, after the fall of the Ṭūlūnids. Conflicts between Muslims and Christians in Jerusalem multiplied, with Jews occasionally taking the Muslims' side. Especially after 960, when the Byzantines were defeating Muslims in Cilicia and northern Syria and had regained Cyprus and Crete, Muslim antipathy toward Christians erupted in Antioch and Fusṭāṭ. In 355/966, the Patriarch of Jerusalem was executed by the Kāfūrid governor. Conditions became graver still at the outset of the fifth/eleventh century, when the Fāṭimid Caliph al-Ḥākim, alert to the rancor of Sunnīs in Fusṭāṭ and seeking to force his vision of religious unity

[5] Moshe Gil, *A History of Palestine, 634–1099* (Cambridge, 1992), 348.

on his subjects whether they wished it or not, severely persecuted Christians and Jews. He changed his attitude prior to his death, and permitted the return of Muslim converts to their former religion, restoring a portion of their confiscated possessions. The Dhimmīs' condition revived so rapidly that their restored status provoked a reaction among the ʿAbbāsid Sunnīs in Baghdād, less tolerant than their counterparts in Fusṭāṭ. Indeed, a substantial portion of the wealth generated in Egypt and Syria could have been produced only because of the harmonious division of economic activities among the diverse communities.

Between Iraq, progressively more oriented toward Iran, and al-Andalus, confronted by militant Christian chivalry, Ibn Ṭūlūn had created a new zone of power facing Constantinople in the eastern Mediterranean. The abortive attempt by his son al-ʿAbbās, despite its failure, substantiated the inclusion of Libya and Ifrīqiya within the southern region of the central Mediterranean. In the future, either Egypt would penetrate north Africa or, conversely, there would be an invasion of Egypt from the west. Ibn Ṭūlūn contributed to a process that, over the course of several centuries, separated the former Byzantine lands once again. Egypt, Syria, western Jazīra, and Cilicia were divided from the former Sassanid territories of Iraq and Iran – all of which Islam had sought definitively to unite during the first/seventh century.

For this grandson of a nomad from the steppes of central Asia, founding a new capital between the pyramids and the Muqaṭṭam that could rival Baghdād accomplished a grandiose ambition. From his perspective, Ibn Ṭūlūn had fulfilled the essential objective of the Arab conquest: he had reunited immense regions, diverse ethnic groups, venerable religions, and complementary economies to form a new urban-based civilization that was viable without being standardized, and was ready to accommodate the harmonious integration of its identities and differences.

Following the death of Ibn Ṭūlūn in 270/884, his son Khumārawayh, who was born in Sāmarrā in 250/864, succeeded him without requesting the caliph's endorsement. His brother al-ʿAbbās was executed, quite probably by his order, immediately before his assumption of power. This was the first time in ʿAbbāsid history with regard to the government of so large and rich a territory that a *wālī*, whose legitimacy derived from the caliph who had designated him, was succeeded openly by an amīr who claimed his legitimacy by inheritance. Khumārawayh's designation by his father as his successor had rendered any caliphal confirmation irrelevant in his eyes. Moreover, Ibn Ṭūlūn had left 10,000,000 dīnārs in the public treasury, a sum that facilitated the peaceful accession of his son.

But the regent al-Muwaffaq elected to take advantage of the transition to restore Egypt and Syria within the ʿAbbāsid orbit, and in particular to recoup unpaid tribute. He had been encouraged to pursue this goal by Aḥmad ibn Muḥammad al-Wāsiṭī, the loyal Ṭūlūnid general who nonetheless betrayed the dynasty. Several contingents commanded by Isḥāq ibn Kundāj and Muḥammad ibn Abi'l-Sāj entered Syria where they were joined by the army of Aḥmad ibn al-Muwaffaq, the future al-Muʿtaḍid. At the Battle of the Mills in Palestine during 271/winter 885, Ibn al-Muwaffaq and Khumārawayh took flight in opposite directions. But Saʿd ibn Aysar, the Ṭūlūnid commander, held his composure and won the battle. In consequence of his ignominious performance, Khumārawayh was thereafter continually obliged to prove his personal bravery to an ever-greater extent. He created a multi-ethnic army in which alongside the Turks served blacks, Iranians, Greeks and an elite bodyguard, *al-mukhtaṣṣ*. This last unit was recruited from the most obstreperous Bedouin of the Delta and was augmented by black slaves. Its loyalty to the amīr was unquestioned.

Khumārawayh conferred the custodianship of finances on the family of al-Mādharā'ī, who would perform the same function under the Ikhshīdids. He regained the support of Ibn Kundāj and Ibn Abi'l-Sāj, took control over most of the Jazīra and compelled Yazmān, master of Tarsus, to acknowledge him as suzerain. His domain thus exceeded his father's. In 273/886, a peace treaty was concluded between Khumārawayh and al-Muwaffaq, who agreed to recognize the Ṭūlūnids' right to govern Syria and Egypt for thirty years. To improve relations between Egypt and Syria, Khumārawayh improved the roadway through the pass (*ʿaqaba*) that permitted entry to the Jordanian plateau from Ayla.

Upon al-Muwaffaq's demise in 278/spring 892, al-Muʿtamid proceeded to Baghdād to exercise his caliphal authority. But al-Muwaffaq's son, Aḥmad al-Muʿtaḍid, continued to hold power. Al-Muʿtamid died in 279/autumn 892. Al-Mufawwaḍ, his son and heir-designate, who had served as governor of the west, was readily eliminated by al-Muʿtaḍid billāh. The new caliph recognized the Ṣaffārids in Khurāsān as sovereign in Fars and later Rayy, and subsequently the Ṣāmānids in Transoxiana after 900. With no hope of vanquishing Khumārawayh militarily, al-Muʿtaḍid was obliged to tolerate Ṭūlūnid autonomy in Egypt, Syria and along the Anatolian frontier. Concentrating his efforts henceforth on Iraq and its periphery, he reoccupied Isfahān in western Iran, and drove Ibn al-Shaykh from Mawṣil. A large portion of the eastern Jazīra was regained from Khumārawayh.

A new accord was reached with the caliph in Rabīʿ I 280/spring 893. Khumārawayh and his descendants received for three decades the right to direct Friday prayer (*al-ṣalāt*), to levy the land tax (*al-kharāj*), and to appoint judges and civil/fiscal administrators (*al-quḍā' wa jāmiʿ al-aʿmāl*) for their amirate, which now extended from Hīt on the Euphrates to Barka in Libya. The accord decreed as compensation to the ʿAbbāsid caliph an annual tribute of 200,000 dīnārs cumulatively calculated for those previous years in which none had been turned over, and 300,000 dīnārs per annum for future years. Khumārawayh surrendered the Diyār Rabīʿa and the Diyār

Muḍar surrounding Rāfiqa. The caliphal workshops for fine textiles (*ṭirāz*) in Fusṭāṭ and Alexandria were to continue production for the ʿAbbāsid caliph.

In 272/892, the Caliph al-Muʿtaḍid married Qaṭr al-Nadā, "Dew Drop," Khumārawayh's daughter. He provided her with a dower of 1,000,000 dīnārs, a wedding gift that was considered the most sumptuous in medieval Arab history. Abū ʿAbd Allāh al-Jawharī Ibn al-Jaṣṣāṣ, broker in jewelry to Khumārawayh's *ḥarīm*, negotiated Qaṭr al-Nadā's marriage to the caliph. Having held her gems on deposit, he enriched himself upon the princess's death, which occurred shortly afterwards, and was forced to pay a fine of several million dīnārs. He died much later in 315/927.

Khumārawayh now imagined himself almost as the caliph's equal. Moreover, one of the greatest and quintessentially Arab poets of the age, Abū ʿUbāda al-Buḥturī, who had been an intimate of every caliph from al-Mutawakkil to al-Muʿtaḍid, entered into a close relationship with him in 279/892. In contrast with the demeanor of numerous *ghulāms* and mamlūks later on, the inclination of Ibn Ṭūlūn and his son toward Arab civilization and literature was immediate and profound.

Nonetheless, the luxury and dissipation indulged in by Khumārawayh ultimately overwhelmed him, and he was assassinated in Damascus in Dhu'l-Qaʿda 282/January–February 896 by his court eunuchs, who had taken advantage of his absence to satisfy the insatiable sexual appetites of his harem women. He left an empty treasury, the dīnār having lost a third of its value as a result of his excessive prodigality. He had lived in luxury, and was rumored never to have mounted the same horse twice.

The decline of the dynasty accelerated under the rule of his two sons, Jaysh and Hārūn. Abu'l-ʿAsākir Jaysh ibn Khumārawayh was only fourteen when he acceded in 282/early 896, but he was already a drunkard. He put to death his uncle, Muḍar ibn Aḥmad ibn Ṭūlūn, under the lash. Several months later, in 283/July 896, the *faqīhs* and the *qāḍīs* of the realm declared his deposition and he died in prison.

Confronting the decadent Ṭūlūnid amirate, the ʿAbbāsid regime regained a measure of its former authority. Al-Muʿtaḍid, caliph after 279/spring 892, sealed the definitive return of the caliphate to Baghdād. He was served as vizier by ʿUbayd Allāh ibn Sulaymān ibn Wahb, and after his death in 288/901 by his son al-Qāsim. The faithful Badr al-Muʿtaḍidī was in command of the army. The Shīʿī family of the Banu'l-Furāt, followed by the Sunnī house of the Banu'l-Jarrāḥ, administered the taxes of Iraq. Al-Muʿtaḍid, named caliph from 278/June 892, died in 289/902; his reign was relatively brief but effective. The caliphate nonetheless was forced to deal with a new threat more terrible than it had faced from the Zanj: the Carmatian revolt.

Around 261/874 a group of Ismāʿīlīs in the *sawad* of Kūfa gathered behind a missionary, Ḥamdān Qarmaṭ, who preached the resumption of a radical assault on the urban civilization of the ʿAbbāsids. The Pilgrimage was denounced as a resurgence of Meccan idolatry focused on the Black Stone of the Kaʿba, an idolatry that Muḥammad himself had formerly attacked. The enrichment of urban elites and the impoverishment of peasants and Bedouin were imputed to a deviation from Islamic doctrine that was linked to the abandonment of the legitimate political primacy of the descendants of ʿAlī and Fāṭima. After 284/897 the Carmatian revolt directly threatened ʿAbbāsid power in lower Iraq, the *sawad* of Kūfa, and subsequently in Baḥrayn. The rebels inflicted a serious defeat on the ʿAbbāsids in 287/900. The movement endorsed the Fāṭimid family of ʿUbayd Allāh, which depicted itself as issuing from the Ḥusaynid ʿAlid Sharīfs who derived from the seventh Imām Ismāʿīl, son of Jaʿfar al-Ṣādiq. The Fāṭimids settled first in Syria, at Salamiyya at the edge of the steppe traversed by the tribes that had converted to Carmatianism. In 286/899, they broke away from the power center established by the Carmatians at al-Aḥsāʾ in Baḥrayn on the southeastern Gulf.[6] Because their existence was threatened in Salamiyya, they later passed by stealth through Egypt to settle anonymously in southern Ifrīqiya, modern Tunisia, where they set up a counter-caliphate in opposition to the Aghlabids in 297/909–10.

Throughout the final years of the third/ninth century the Carmatians harassed the towns, zones of sedentary agriculture and the caravan traffic in the Gulf, lower Iraq and Syria. Every governor of a Muslim province had to guarantee its security. The Carmatians, who quite probably prayed for a time toward Jerusalem, now launched an expedition into Syria. In 289/902, having defeated near Raqqa Ṭūlūnid troops under the command of Ṭughj ibn Juff, governor of Damascus, the Carmatians besieged the Syrian capital and refused to desist until they were paid tribute. After their leader, Ṣāḥib al-Nāqa, was killed, a new chief, al-Ḥusayn Ṣāḥib al-Shāma, induced them to ravage Ḥomṣ, Ḥamā, Baʿlabakk, Maʿarrat al-Nuʿmān, and Salamiyya, where they massacred ʿUbayd Allāh's family. Only at Aleppo were they finally brought to bay. The impotence of the Ṭūlūnid Dynasty prevented the imposition of any measure to preserve order. From the ʿAbbāsid perspective, Syria's defense depended on the replacement of the Ṭūlūnids. A dynamic response was imperative.

Following the Carmatians' ravages in Syria, the Caliph al-Muktafī dispatched Muḥammad ibn Sulaymān al-Kātib to Ḥomṣ. The ʿAbbāsid navy won out over the Ṭūlūnid fleet stationed at Dumyāṭ and Tinnīs. Subsequently, an ʿAbbāsid squadron over which al-Muktafī had placed the same

[6] See Farhad Daftary, "A Major Schism in the early Ismāʿīlī Movement," *SI*, 77 (1993), 123–39, which presents the current state of the question, and bibliography. For an alternate point of view see Thierry Bianquis, "L'Espace ismaïlien et le régime du vizirat militaire en Égypte, le Yémen sulayhide et l'Ifriqiya ziride," in J.-C. Garcin (ed.), *Clio, États, sociétés et cultures du monde musulman médiéval* (Paris, 1995), 81–117.

Muḥammad ibn Sulaymān, crushed the Carmatian force at Raqqa in Muḥarram 291/on November 29, 903. The senior Carmatian leaders were executed in Baghdād two months later. After the fall of the Ṭūlūnids in 293/906, the Kalb tribe, under the Carmatian Abū Ghānim Naṣr, attacked Damascus after pillaging Bosra, Derʿa, and Tiberiad. Naṣr was ultimately killed and Carmatian operations in later years continued at the expense of the Euphrates valley.

Abū Mūsā Hārūn ibn Khumārawayh had succeeded his brother Jaysh while still under the age of fourteen. His uncle, Rabīʿa ibn Aḥmad ibn Ṭūlūn, and his soldiers had rebelled in Alexandria with Berber support. Defeated and captured, Rabīʿa was executed by lashing in Fusṭāṭ in Shaʿbān 284/autumn 897. Since Ṭūlūnid debility was obvious, the ʿAbbāsid caliphate intervened in Cilicia to resurrect its administration over the Thughūr and the Jazīra. Henceforth, it exacted an annual tribute of 450,000 dīnārs.

Two other sons of Aḥmad ibn Ṭūlūn, ʿAlī and Shaybān, united against their nephew Hārūn and killed him while he was drunk in Ṣafar 292/December 904. He was only twenty-two, but had reigned for almost nine years. Shaybān assumed power and returned to Fusṭāṭ. Ṭughj ibn Juff, in consort with other officers, revolted in the aftermath of Hārūn's murder, and appealed to Muḥammad Sulaymān, a former secretary (*kātib*) of Luʾluʾ, Ibn Ṭūlūn's *ghulām*. They escorted Muḥammad to Fusṭāṭ. In Ṣafar 292/January 905, Shaybān abandoned his soldiers by night. Fusṭāṭ had to be surrendered to the victorious ʿAbbāsid troops who razed al-Qaṭāʾiʿ to the ground, with the exception of Ibn Ṭūlūn's great mosque. The destructive rage of the ʿAbbāsid soldiers is doubtlessly explained by the affluence of the nouveaux riches who had erected the recent districts of Fusṭāṭ while Baghdād had already begun its decline. ʿIsa ibn Muḥammad al-Nūsharī was appointed governor of Egypt.

At the conclusion of his discussion of the Ṭūlūnids, Maqrīzī inserts a nostalgic text evoking their splendid military processions and the luxury that Fusṭāṭ had enjoyed under their patronage.[7] The district of al-Qaṭāʾiʿ, before its second destruction under al-Mustanṣir, would contain tens of thousands of houses, gardens and orchards.

[7] See G. Wiet, *L'Égypte arabe*, vol. 4 of Gabriel Hanotaux (ed.), *Histoire de la nation égyptienne* (Paris, 1937) 80–179, and Maqrīzī, *Khiṭaṭ* (Cairo, 1270 AH), 1, 612: "During the night of the Fiṭr in the year 292/July 905, its events recalled how this evening was celebrated under the Ṭūlūnids: parades, handsome uniforms, magnificent arms, multicolored banners, flags streaming, numerous cavalry, the sound of trumpets, rolling of drums. The secretary Muḥammad ibn Abī Yaʿqūb fell asleep convinced that the realm, the reign and the elegance had disappeared [from Egypt] along with the House of Ṭūlūn. After the total destruction of the district of al-Qaṭāʾiʿ under al-Mustanṣir, Abu'l-Khaṭṭāb ibn Daḥiyya wrote that the number of dwellings that had vanished then counted more than 100,000 structures, each surrounded by gardens and orchards."

The Ikhshīd-Kāfūrid regime

From 292/905 to 323/935, after the collapse of the Ṭūlūnids and before the entrenchment of al-Ikhshīd at Fusṭāṭ, Egypt was officially under the direct control of the ʿAbbāsids in Baghdād. The country suffered a continuous series of disorders. Insecurity was so rampant that in 300/912, ʿIsā ibn Muḥammad al-Nūsharī had to lock the Mosque of ʿAmr except for prayer hours because the *bayt al-māl*, or public treasury, had been deposited there. Indeed, the mosque was the site for reconstituting the *dīwān al-māl* under the direction of the fiscal supervisor, Abū Bakr Muḥammad ibn ʿAlī al-Mādharāʾī. This public building was also the locale for auctioning the tax-farms and thus housed considerable sums. Probably for the same reason of insecurity, the Festival Prayer, which heretofore had been celebrated in the Muṣallā outside the town, was for the first time, at the outset of the fourth Hijra century, recited at the Mosque of ʿAmr.

The cause of such widespread unease was the perennial difficulty of paying the soldiers, since the tribute now left the country for Iraq. Moreover, the troops pillaged the property of civilians, who requested that their barracks be transferred to Giza on the western shore of the Nile, ostensibly to confront the principal danger, that of an attack by the Berber nomads or the Fāṭimid armies. Some Berbers had been incorporated into the ʿAbbāsid army stationed in Egypt. Disputes sporadically erupted between different military corps, strife that presaged the fundamental hostility between "easterners" and "westerners" that would so compromise the effectiveness of the Fāṭimid army. Incapable of guaranteeing the soldiers' regular stipends, the regime resolved upon apportioning *iqṭāʿāt* from Egypt's agrarian land. These were fiscal districts from which the *kharāj* was allotted to a particular officer who then paid and equipped his soldiers with the revenues. Certain secretaries and viziers were also granted *iqṭāʿāt* to guarantee the sums they forwarded to the state dīwāns. They also managed to amass fortunes exceeding several hundred thousand dīnārs, if not millions. The regime routinely tapped these fortunes through fines and confiscations to restore monies to the public treasury that should never have been removed from it. To escape such reprisals, the financiers resorted to placing their estates in pious trusts (*awqāf*), protecting them in the name of divine charity against the bureaucrats' malevolence. These two institutions – the *iqṭāʿāt* and the *awqāf* – augmented the revenues withdrawn from the countryside on behalf of the urban populace, leaving no medium available for the development of agrarian capitalism. They prevented the free movement of the economy and paralyzed the state's capacity to act.

It is pointless to list in detail events whose sequence is difficult to reconstruct. Sources such as al-Kindī and Ibn al-Athīr differ on the number of names and the dates of governors after 905.[8] Muḥammad ibn Sulaymān stepped down on behalf of a governor appointed from Baghdād. ʿIsā ibn Mūsā (or ibn Muḥammad) al-Nūsharī, compelled to seek refuge in Alexandria, abandoned Fusṭāṭ to a rebel named Ibrāhīm al-Khalanjī. Aḥmad Kayghalagh or Kayghulugh, a brilliant officer sent from Baghdād against this individual, was defeated and departed to combat the Byzantines successfully on the Cilician frontier. Al-Khalanjī recruited new soldiers from the jails of Fusṭāṭ.

In 293/905–06, the Caliph al-Muktafī decided to take the field himself against Egypt but, upon his arrival at Takrīt he learned that al-Khalanjī was being sent to him as a prisoner and he returned to his palace. ʿIsā al-Nūsharī subsequently had to deal with a pro-Ṭūlūnid rebellion instigated by Muḥammad ibn ʿAlī al-Khalij. This insurrection brought on pillaging and destruction in Fusṭāṭ and its environs, aggravated by a serious food shortage. The Aghlabid Ziyādat Allāh then arrived at Fusṭāṭ in 297/May 909, having been forced from his amirate by the Fāṭimids. He found a sparse reception and departed for Baghdād, but died in Palestine in 912 before he could prepare for an attempt at reconquering his principality.

Al-Nūsharī died in 297/May 910 and was interred in Jerusalem. He was replaced by Takīn, a Turkish freedman. In 301/913–14, the policy of bestowing appanages was temporarily resumed in Baghdād. Al-Muqtadir's son, Abu'l-ʿAbbās, the future al-Rāḍī billāh, at the age of four received north Africa, which in reality was occupied by the Fāṭimids, and Egypt over which he delegated his authority to Takīn. This individual had to deal with the first Fāṭimid attack in 914. A new prefect, Dhakā al-Aʿwar, the One-Eyed, succeeded Takīn at the beginning of 915. The general Mu'nis, having arrived from Iraq, was victorious against the Fāṭimid armies, for which he merited the *laqab* of al-Muẓaffar. Dhakā and his son, each named al-Muẓaffar as well, proceeded to restore Alexandria in 916. Dhakā died of an illness during the second Fāṭimid invasion in September 919. The Fāṭimids' presence induced Takīn to return in January 920. Mu'nis came back himself in May of 920 with 3,000 men and proved victorious once again in June 921. He dismissed Takīn and named Hilāl, who was supplanted by Aḥmad ibn Kayghulugh in July 923. This Aḥmad was also a brilliant officer but he was compelled to confront a revolt by his soldiers, who had not been paid.

Takīn was appointed governor for a third time in April 924. Insecurity was now so widespread that he performed his prayers in the governor's palace, since the mosques of ʿAmr and al-ʿAskar were too dangerous. Takīn died in March 933 and was buried in Jerusalem. His son Muḥammad was driven out by the troops. A former protégé of Takīn, Muḥammad ibn Ṭughj,

[8] See the attempt to construct a coherent summary by Wiet, *L'Égypte arabe*, 111–36, and the contrasting listings of these individuals in the *Encyclopaedia of Islam*.

was appointed his successor but could not assume his office since it had been preempted by Aḥmad ibn Kayghulugh. The army split into factions, one supporting Ibn Kayghulugh, the other endorsing Muḥammad ibn Ṭughj. Ibn Kayghulugh ultimately stepped down, to be replaced by Ibn Ṭughj who had been appointed a second time; by conducting an amphibious operation he had succeeded in forcing his rival's submission. This period was extremely unsettled because of external events, most notably the Carmatian robbery of the Kaʿba Black Stone of Mecca in January 930 and the struggle in Baghdād between Mu'nis and the Caliphs. Al-Qāhir had Mu'nis put to death in April 934.

Alongside the military governors, the civilian tax administrators played an important role. Abū ʿAlī al-Ḥusayn al-Mādharā'ī, known as Abū Zunbūr, served as director of finances in Egypt and later in Syria, following the reconquest. Dismissed and recalled to Baghdād in 304/916, he became the new financial director in Egypt in 306/919. Dismissed once again in 310/922, he had to pay an enormous fine of 5,000,000 dirhams. In 313/926, he appeared in Fusṭāṭ holding the same fiscal office for Egypt and Syria. He died in 917/929. Abū Bakr Muḥammad ibn ʿAlī al-Mādharā'ī, who lived from 258/871 to 345/957, was serving as vizier to Hārūn ibn Khumārawayh in 283/890. After the dynasty's fall, he was exiled to Baghdād from 293 to 301/905 to 913. In 304/916 he returned to Egypt as director of finances. He placed the Birkat al-Ḥabash and Suyūṭ in *waqf* to support the great mosque, the first documented example of agrarian land listed in such a charitable trust. Subsequently, he returned to private life and accumulated wealth. Highly pious, he went on the Pilgrimage every year from 301/914 to 322/934. In 318/930, he again took over the office of financial director in Egypt and held it until Takīn's death in 321/933. The Mādharā'īs would prevail in confrontation with Muḥammad ibn Takīn in 322/934.

The power vacuum of this period invited hostile activities. The Fāṭimid Imāms had established themselves in Ifrīqiya and sought to occupy affluent Egypt in order to set up a power base there more proximate to their ʿAbbāsid enemies. As previously noted, they had attempted to conquer the country three times. In 301/914–15, an initial expedition led by the son of Imām al-Mahdī,[9] Abu'l-Qāsim, the future Caliph al-Qā'im bi-Amr Allāh, succeeded in occupying Alexandria but failed to take Fusṭāṭ. Unable to confront Mu'nis, the Fāṭimids retreated to Ifrīqiya. In 919–21/307–09, a second expedition was organized under the same commander. Alexandria and the Fayyūm were occupied but the Fāṭimid fleet met disaster at Rosetta

[9] For an account of al-Mahdī's trip to Africa via Fusṭāṭ in 903–4, see A. Fu'ad Sayyid, "Nuṣūṣ ḍa'īʿa min Akhbār Miṣr li'l-Musabbiḥī," *AI* 27 (1981), 7–8, Arabic section. He was accompanied by his son, al-Qā'im, and was disguised as a merchant. He had considered proceeding directly to Yemen but, fearing exposure, he traveled west and crossed the Nile at the Miṣr bridge.

and Mu'nis proved victorious at Fusṭāṭ. The Fāṭimids called in vain upon the eastern Shiʿis to rebel on behalf of the dynasty that descended from ʿAlī and Fāṭima. The third campaign, organized by al-Mahdī, but launched after his death in 323/935 by al-Qā'im, utilized troops based in Ifrīqiya and Barqa. A Berber contingent took over Rawḍa Island and burned its arsenal. Al-Ikhshīd, who had just arrived in Egypt, was thus immediately compelled to confront the Fāṭimid invasion. ʿAlī ibn Badr and Bajkam, admirals of the Ikhshīdid fleet, and al-Ḥabashī, commandant of the Alexandria garrison, turned traitors together and placed themselves under al-Qā'im's orders. He sent Zaydān and ʿAmīr al-Majnūn to join them. In Jumādā I 324/April 936, the Kutāma tribe occupied Alexandria for the third time in fewer than twenty years. However, Ibn Ṭughj regained the city and the Fāṭimid army withdrew to Barka. There would be no more significant Fāṭimid forays against Egypt before the end of Ikhshīdid authority, following Kāfūr's death.

Muḥammad ibn Ṭughj Abū Bakr al-Ikhshīd was born in Baghdād in 268/882 and died in 334/946 at sixty-four years of age. Son of a Ṭūlūnid officer who originated from Farghāna, Muḥammad grew up in Ṭūlūnid territory. Following the dynasty's fall, he and his father were imprisoned in Baghdād in 292/905, but were released a year later. He was appointed governor of Palestine/Ramla in 316/928 and subsequently of Damascus in 319/931. Abu'l-Fatḥ al-Faḍl ibn Ḥinzāba, the son of Abu'l-Khaṭṭāb Jaʿfar ibn al-Furāt, the supervisor of property taxes in the east and, under al-Rāḍī, fiscal inspector of Egypt and Syria, had given his daughter in marriage to the son of Ibn Rā'iq. He was favorably disposed toward Muḥammad ibn Ṭughj, who was designated as governor of Egypt in 321/933 but was not installed until 323/summer 935. In 327/939, Muḥammad ibn Ṭughj obtained from the Caliph al-Rāḍī confirmation of his appointment as military and fiscal governor, receiving the *laqab* of *al-Ikhshīd* or "servant," a princely title from Farghāna.

After three decades of costly disorders in an Egypt administered by appointed governors, the caliphate had reached the conclusion that only an autonomous prince who, along with his descendants, assumed personal responsibility for this province, would be capable of defending it effectively against the Fāṭimids. And in fact, no significant incursion would occur over the thirty-two years intervening between the Fāṭimid defeat of 324/936 and Kāfūr's death in 357/968.

Al-Mādharā'ī, the director of finances in Egypt, regarded himself as all-powerful and sought to prevent al-Ikhshīd from assuming his post, but his troops abandoned him and rallied to the new governor. Al-Mādharā'ī had to refund his fortune to the Treasury. Confined in prison until 327/939, he was released to become regent for Ūnūjūr, al-Ikhshīd's son. Imprisoned once again in 335/946, he was set free by Kāfūr and allowed to resume his private life until his death in 345/957.

According to Ibn Saʿīd, Ibn Ṭughj was clearly less cultivated than Ibn Ṭūlūn, whom he nonetheless strove to imitate. He was a choleric and gluttonous man, yet shrewd and inclined toward avarice. Having newly arrived at riches, he had experienced prison life and poverty. He had a special passion for perfumes; in Damascus, his house wafted its fragrance throughout the center of the town. He appreciated beautiful objects. The sources indicate moreover that in this period consumer fashions in Fusṭāṭ among the upper classes were marked by a taste for luxury that inclined them to prefer imported commodities at high prices over local products that were too readily available. This proclivity induced Egyptian artisans to refine the style of their commodities and to draw their inspiration from foreign craft techniques and aesthetic forms.

Al-Ikhshīd, as previously noted, had immediately to confront a Fāṭimid invasion. His victory bolstered his authority over Egypt. Following 325/936–37, al-Ikhshīd occupied Syria as far as Aleppo. Like Ibn Ṭūlūn he relied on the Banū Kilāb and selected one of them as amīr of Northern Syria. His authority was disputed by Baghdād, which supported Muḥammad ibn Rāʾiq in Syria and Palestine against him. However, a son of this individual, Muzāḥim ibn Muḥammad, had married one of al-Ikhshīd's daughters. In 327/938, al-Ikhshīd threatened to bestow another of his daughters in marriage on the Fāṭimid Imām al-Qāʾim and to have the *khuṭba* preached in his name. Ibn Rāʾiq, who had failed in his attempt to assume power in Baghdād, set himself up in Damascus and entered into conflict with al-Ikhshīd. He subsequently sought al-Ikhshīd's confirmation of his authority over Syria and Ramla, but the peace initiative of 328/940 came to nothing. Ibn Rāʾiq was killed in 330/942 at Mawṣil, and Abū ʿAbd Allāh al-Ḥusayn ibn Saʿīd al-Ḥamdānī occupied Aleppo in 332/944 on behalf of the Amir of Mawṣil, Nāṣir al-Dawla.

In 332/944, the Caliph al-Muttaqī, the protégé of Nāṣir al-Dawla, proceeded to Raqqa. Al-Ikhshīd had reoccupied Damascus and driven al-Ḥusayn ibn Saʿīd from Aleppo, and agreed to meet him there. The Caliph refused to take up residence at Fusṭāṭ, but confirmed al-Ikhshīd's authority over Egypt, the Ḥijāz and Syria and returned to Baghdād. Sayf al-Dawla, al-Nāṣir's brother, then made his entry into Aleppo in 333/October 944 at the side of Abu'l-Fatḥ ʿUthmān ibn Saʿīd al-Kilābī. This leader of the Banū Kilāb had a brother, Abu'l-ʿAbbās Aḥmad, who was then serving as governor of Aleppo, a post he had previously occupied himself on behalf of al-Ikhshīd. In 333–334/spring–autumn 945, al-Ikhshīd took the field against Sayf al-Dawla. Winning a victory at Qinnasrīn, he eventually signed a treaty with him.

A mutually recognized frontier would henceforth separate a Ḥamdānid sphere of influence in northern Syria, comprising the *Jund* (military and fiscal province) of Qinnasrīn-Aleppo and the *Jund* of Ḥomṣ including ʿArqa and Jūsiyya, from an Ikhshīdid sphere of influence in the south, comprising the *Jund* of Damascus including Tripoli and Baʿlabakk, the *Jund* of Tiberiad/Urdunn and the *Jund* of Ramla/Palestine. In addition, the amīr of Egypt pledged himself to pay an annual tribute in compensation for Ḥamdānid abandonment of designs on Damascus. Sayf al-Dawla was to marry the daughter of ʿUbayd Allāh ibn Ṭughj, al-Ikhshīd's brother. The signed accord of 335/946 permitted the Caliph al-Muṭīʿ to confirm the commander of Aleppo as amīr of northern Syria and his use of Sayf al-Dawla's *laqab*. Not having the same personal tie to the *ribāṭ* of Tarsus as had Ibn Ṭūlūn, al-Ikhshīd wisely renounced his claim to suzerainty over this region on behalf of the Ḥamdānids. They would then assume the honor of confronting the Byzantines in Cilicia and would bear the expenses entailed by this war.[10]

Al-Ikhshīd was dismayed after his visit to the Caliph al-Muttaqī at Raqqa in Muḥarram 333/September 944, to whom he had offered his services in vain. He realized that he would have to abandon forever his plan to install the ʿAbbāsid Caliphate at Fusṭāṭ and his ambition for power over northern Syria and the frontier. These regions, tied to the Jazīra and Iraq, were thus threatened with disturbances as soon as Baghdād reasserted its claims of authority. They could not be controlled from Fusṭāṭ. Because of their proximity to the Byzantines, they were defended by well-equipped garrisons and thus posed the risk of offering a victorious officer the opportunity to mount an armed challenge against the central authority. Years later, Ibn Killis would counsel the Fāṭimid Imām al-ʿAzīz in like fashion.

In Dhu'l-Ḥijja 335/July 946, al-Ikhshīd died in Damascus. The regional context was shifting. The Carmatian leader Abū Ṭāhir had died in 332/944; his nephew al-Ḥasan ibn al-Aʿṣam succeeded him and restored the Black Stone to Mecca in 339/950. The Būyids, Imāmī Daylamite officers of Iranian culture who arrived from the mountains of the southern Caspian, had set up a group of allied familial principalities in Iran. They occupied Baghdād in 334/945 and subsequently took charge of the caliph's "protection," despite his stubborn commitment to Sunnism. Soon thereafter the Carmatians abandoned their traditional opposition to the ʿAbbāsids and agreed to hire their superb army out to the Caliph's new masters.

Ūnūjār succeeded his father and retained the black eunuch Abu'l-Misk Kāfūr as commander of his armies. Upon learning of al-Ikhshīd's death, Sayf al-Dawla immediately marched upon Damascus and then ventured into Palestine where Kāfūr defeated him. Sayf al-Dawla withdrew to Ḥomṣ and in the spring of 947 regrouped his troops with the ʿUqayl, Numayr, Kalb and Kilāb tribes. He made a foray down to Damascus and again suffered

[10] On the confrontation between al-Ikhshīd and Sayf al-Dawla, there is a detailed summary in the article "Sayf al-Dawla," *EI2*, IX,: 102a–110a.

defeat. Profiting from the absence of the Ikhshīdid army in Syria, Ghabūn, governor of Ashmūnayn and Middle Egypt, revolted, and menaced Fusṭāṭ. He actually invaded the capital before he met his death in July of 947. In the autumn of 336/947, Sayf al-Dawla permanently occupied Aleppo. Kāfūr pursued the Ikhshīdid policy of appeasement and negotiated terms with Sayf al-Dawla. The preceding treaty was reconfirmed but the Egyptians retained Damascus and no longer paid any tribute to the Ḥamdānids. This frontier between northern Syria, inclined toward Iraq, the Jāzīra and Anatolia, and southern Syria, with ties to Egypt and Arabia, would remain intact almost continuously until the Mamlūk seizure of the province in 658/1260.

Throughout the remainder of his life, Sayf al-Dawla would no longer confront the Ikhshīdids. The Egyptian state, now challenged on its western front by the Fāṭimids, resigned itself to the loss of northern Syria. It adhered to the sound principle of abandoning a peripheral province as less costly than maintaining an army on permanent war footing and less dangerous to the amīr's authority. The state would remain master over a vast territory, the traditional bulwark of Egypt comprising the Mediterranean coast from western Tripoli to Syrian Tripoli and the Red Sea all the way to Yemen. Al-Ikhshīd's son thus preserved the essential foundations of his father's power and wealth, leaving to the Ḥamdānid amīr the expensive defense of the frontier against a rearmed Byzantium.

Following al-Ikhshīd's death in 946, the black eunuch Kāfūr wielded real authority, even though he received the title of *Ustādh* only in 966 after the demise of ʿAlī ibn al-Ikhshīd. The historians have painted a highly contrasting portrait of him. They concur on his physical repulsiveness, the contradiction between his perfumed white camphor (*Kāfūr*) and his perfumed black musk (thus his kunya *Abuʾl-Misk*) which evoked his name, and the dark hue of his skin and the stench he emitted according to his enemies. His gross figure, deformed and clumsy, effectively disguised his military ability, intelligence and political acumen. The Ikhshīd had noticed when, as a little African boy in his service whose comrades had rushed to behold the arrival of exotic animals from Nubia in Fusṭāṭ, Kāfūr was unaffected, having eyes only for his master and ready to jump to any order he might give.

The texts also uniformly insist on Kāfūr's piety. He was more comfortable with the *ʿulamāʾ* than with poets, as indicated by his sorry experience with al-Mutanabbī. This individual, the most eminent poet of the fourth/tenth century, had come to him when fortune turned against his glorious and rich protector, Sayf al-Dawla. There was more money to be had in Fusṭāṭ than in Aleppo. Yet the poet could not forgive the *Ustādh* for compelling him to render homage to a black eunuch, a former slave of pitiful countenance, while he had sung the praise of the most eminent Arab warriors.

Surrounded by religious men whom he showered with gifts, Kāfūr made much of his constructing, in addition to a palace, a mosque in Giza and another on the Muqaṭṭam. However, this did not mean that he had relinquished his superstitions: he considered that a *jinn* or demon had once chased him from a house he had built at the Birkat Qārūn.

This was a difficult period. Kāfūr was suspicious of Ūnūjūr, who had once stood up to him. He recruited black soldiers, *al-kāfūriyya*, who engaged in street brawls with soldiers from the east, *al-Ikhshīdiyya*, who had been recruited previously. Egypt was struck by famines in 338/949 and 341/952, there was a devastating fire in Fusṭāṭ in 344/955, and yet another food shortfall and an earthquake in 343/955. These disasters were followed, after Ūnūjūr's death, by the extended and debilitating famine of 352–357/963–968. The grain shortages affected Fusṭāṭ ever more frequently and severely, providing an indication of overpopulation in a city still complacent from its copious supply under Ibn Ṭūlūn. Moreover, the dignity and honesty that characterized actions by the Qāḍī Bakkār in the third/ninth century were no longer apparent in the fourth/tenth. Accusations of embezzlement lodged against the *qāḍīs* and their legal witnesses, predictable in an environment of easy money, multiplied in Fusṭāṭ. By contrast, they remained exceptional in a modest city like Damascus, more provincial in character and subject to closer moral scrutiny. Richly detailed texts that deal with the *qāḍīs* have been preserved which allow a clearer understanding of the changes affecting a society undergoing rapid urbanization and enrichment. A separate and more specifically focused chapter would be necessary to treat the judiciary and religious establishment in Egypt and Syria during this century. Upon the demise of his brother Ūnūjūr in 349/961, ʿAlī ibn al-Ikhshīd officially succeeded him. But Kāfūr retained his grip on real power.

From 338/950, a Nubian incursion reached the oases, and in 343/March 956 a more serious invasion of Aswān and its environs subjected the region to massacres, pillage and capture of prisoners. This invasion was probably supported covertly by the Fāṭimids. In reprisal, Kāfūr despatched an expedition of extermination into Nubia 200 km south of Aswān. Nonetheless, a second Nubian invasion of Egypt occurred in 351–352/963. To the west and north, infiltrations of Berber nomads were reported in the Delta and the Oases. To the northeast, the Bedouin Arabs of the Sulaym, ʿUqayl, Ṭayy, and Kalb tribes were becoming ever more aggressive in southern and central Syria. The Carmatians also reappeared in the region, henceforth collecting an annual tribute and reinforcing their power around Damascus and throughout Palestine. In the overpopulated cities, tensions between religious communities led to grave incidents. Between 348/960 and 351/963, the Ikhshīdid navy was destroyed by the Byzantine fleet. This catastrophe provoked support for a jihād in Egypt, accompanied by spontaneous assaults on Christians by Muslims. The Melkite Christians, aroused by the Byzantine resumption of the offensive in Cilicia, Cyprus and Crete, took an opposing stand to the Jacobite Coptic Christians who were always hostile toward Constantinople.

A second danger, embedded within the ruling system, threatened Kāfūrid power. Professional soldiers, either slave or freeborn, increasingly interfered with the administrative process. The increase in expropriations from the tax yield and the collaboration between military holders of *iqṭā*ʿ and civilian financiers assigned tax collection – both combined to weaken the state. In the absence of a clear legitimizing principle – designation or recognition by the ʿAbbāsid caliph, or birthright – the incessant struggles for political power by senior officers presaged Mamlūk Egypt. Since the strong man, Kāfūr, was a black eunuch without issue, his demise could only set off a major crisis. By contrast, the familial and dynastic rationale for succession among the Daylamite Būyids in Iraq and Iran, or among the Ḥamdānids who were Arabs but strongly influenced by the Kurds of Jazīra and Northern Syria, foreshadowed the Ayyūbid period. In neither case was Arab Sunnī opinion consulted to establish a common rule for political behavior. The attempt by Aḥmad ibn Ṭūlūn at Damascus in 269/883 to appeal via notables to civil public opinion would have no sequel.

Upon the death of ʿAlī ibn al-Ikhshīd in 355/January 966, Abu'l-Misk Kāfūr succeeded him without making the pretense of protecting a prince of the family. Since Aḥmad ibn ʿAlī was too young, at the age of ten, to rule, Kāfūr received an official diploma from the caliph in Baghdād and assumed the title of *ʿUstādh* or "Master," due to his eunuch status. During this period of grave financial crisis, Kāfūr noted the qualities of Ibn Killis. He was a Jewish merchant born in Baghdād in 318/930 and who was subsequently a money dealer in Syria. Having survived a fraudulent bankruptcy, he became the administrator of agrarian lands in Egypt and then entered Kāfūr's private service. He rapidly memorized the yields of principal agricultural districts in the Nile valley as well as all the information regarding their irrigation and tax policies. To ensure his designation as vizier, Ibn Killis converted to Sunnī Islam with great fanfare. But Kāfūr died shortly thereafter, and the wazīr Abu'l-Faḍl Jaʿfar ibn al-Furāt, moved quickly to arrest a potential competitor. Upon his release, Ibn Killis traveled to Fāṭimid Ifrīqiya in September 968, where he espoused Ismāʿīlism with equal enthusiasm and provided vital assistance to technical preparations for the conquest of Egypt. Kāfūr died in 357/April 968 and was buried in Jerusalem. His death was rumored several times, so that various dates given for it have been retained.

The situation in Fusṭāṭ was desperate. From 963 to 969, a series of low Nile floods brought on a famine that Egypt had not experienced within living memory. The vizier Jaʿfar Ibn al-Furāt and the Ikhshīdid-Kāfūrid officers pulled in different directions. The senior commanders of the army reunited to prepare the succession and drafted a manifesto.[11] The governor of Palestine, al-Ḥasan ibn ʿUbayd Allāh ibn Ṭughj, uncle of the little Ikhshīdid prince, arrived in Fusṭāṭ in 357/autumn 968. He seemed ready to install himself as regent, and ordered the construction of a palace-garden on Rawḍa Island. But he abruptly departed for Palestine in 358/969, releasing Ibn al-Furāt whom he had had imprisoned. The Ikhshīdid possessions in Syria were now vulnerable, since the Ḥamdānid state had been unsettled from 349/960. After Sayf al-Dawla's death nothing any longer seemed to block the Byzantines who were ravaging northern Syria and were not concealing their ambitions towards Tripoli, Damascus and Jerusalem. Central Syria and Palestine were simultaneously coveted by the Carmatians, who exacted tribute payments to leave Damascus. A power vacuum prevailed in Egypt. Alerted to this situation, the Fāṭimid Caliph al-Muʿizz gave Jawhar, his white slave and the general-in-chief of his forces, the order to depart for Egypt at the head of an army in 358/February 969. In June, Jawhar stood before Fusṭāṭ. The senior Ikhshīdid and Kāfūrid officers hesitated over accepting his offer of peaceful submission and eventually decided to fight. Suffering heavy casualties after a fierce resistance, the surviving officers of the former regime escaped to Syria at the beginning of July 969.

Aware of the caliphate's inability to implement effective political policies in the Islamic world, al-Ikhshīd at the end of his life, and Kāfūr subsequently, would abandon Ibn Ṭūlūn's plan to transfer the capital of ʿAbbāsid power to Egypt. They rather attempted to build around Fusṭāṭ and the Nile valley a sound principality that, if it could not take over the whole of the Levant, Arabia, the Yemen, Nubia, and the Libyan zone, could effectively control central and southern Syria, the pilgrimage route, commercial traffic between the Nile valley and the Indian Ocean via the Red Sea, the outlets of trails leading into eastern equatorial Africa, and the coast west of the Delta to dominate the major routes across the central Sahara and north Africa.

They could rely on the support of Fusṭāṭ's population for their objective, and quite likely those of towns in the Delta, Qūṣ and Upper Egypt. The Syrians remained indifferent, but showed no open hostility. From the year 308/920, Egypt's rulers realized that the true danger to them was posed by the eastern ambitions of the Fāṭimid Imāms in Ifrīqiya. Their victory over the ʿAbbāsid caliphate depended on the prerequisite seizure of Egypt. Armed with the fanaticism of their Berber partisans and the highly prosperous economy in north Africa, they would concentrate their propaganda operations on Egypt. Due to the confluence of commercial networks among

[11] On this highly complex period, see the three articles by Thierry Bianquis: "Les derniers gouverneurs ikhchīdides à Damas," *BEO*, 23 (1970), 167–196; "La prise du pouvoir en Egypte par les Fatimides," *AI*, 11 (1972), 50–108; "L'Acte de succession de Kafur d'après Maqrizi," *AI*, 12 (1974), 263–269, and the works of Yaacov Lev.

merchants and financiers, Sunnīs, Imāmīs, Ismāʿīlīs, Jews and Christians, they were able to infiltrate the ranks of cultural notables, fiscal officials and movers of the economy in Fusṭāṭ. To win over the Sunnī masses whom they could not hope to convert to Shiʿism but who they knew were disaffected with the ʿAbbāsids, they played upon the general feeling at this time of fervor toward the People of the Prophet's Family.[12] An intensive period of psychological and political preparation, abetted by the malaise of the Ikhshīdid regime after Kāfūr's death, is more responsible for the Fāṭimids' successful settlement in Egypt than the modest military capacity of the army commanded by Jawhar. Their political agenda in the East was made easier by their predecessors' actions as Egypt's rulers, and by the growing consciousness of the Egyptians throughout the hundred years between 254/868 and 358/969 of the opulent future that was offered their country.

[12] Jere L. Bacharach in, "The Career of Muḥammad ibn Ṭughdj al-Ikhshīd," *Speculum*, 50 (1975), 594, reports a pro-Shiʿite revolt in Egypt during 330/942. See in this article, pp. 604 et seq., his remarks on Ikhshīdid monetary issues.

5

The Ismāʿīlī Daʿwa and the Fāṭimid caliphate

PAUL E. WALKER

With the proclamation of his caliphate in January 910, al-Mahdī, the first of the Fāṭimid rulers, celebrated the culmination of a clandestine struggle that had deep roots and varying fortunes in many Islamic territories far from the north African scene of his ultimate triumph. His rise to power occurred not in the eastern areas of Iran and Iraq, where his immediate ancestors were born, or at his recent headquarters at the town of Salamiya in north central Syria, or in the Yemen or any of the other regions where his followers had been active. Al-Mahdī was already recognized as the supreme religious leader, the imam, of the Ismāʿīlī Shiʿites by his loyal adherents, but he had not, until then, governed a politically defined realm; nor had there been in Islam as a whole another Shiʿite caliph except for ʿAlī ibn Abī Ṭālib two and a half centuries earlier. Al-Mahdī's ascension was, in his own view and that of his followers, a restoration, a revolution in which the wrongs of 250 years were redressed by the combining at last of the divinely sanctioned imamate and the caliphate in one office. He would henceforth guide the Islamic community as God had always intended, and as his ancestors the Prophet Muḥammad and Muḥammad's sole legitimate heir ʿAlī had done. His immediate goal was to return Islam to its true and proper form by bringing those who most loved the family of the prophet back into positions of authority. He would, moreover, fight against the enemies of Islam both abroad and at home; the ʿAbbāsid usurpers were thus served notice that their own claim to rule would no longer be without a rival. The Fāṭimids, although then in control of only parts of what constitute modern Tunisia, Algeria, Libya and Sicily, aimed at an empire as large as Islam itself.

In 969 the dream expressed in their earliest proclamations was to be sustained by a second culmination. In that year the fourth of the Fāṭimid caliphs, al-Muʿizz, saw his commander-in-chief, Jawhar, conquer Egypt and found there a new capital, al-Qāhira, the modern Cairo. Although it was not necessarily the primary purpose of its foundation, Cairo became thereafter the center of the Fāṭimid empire; and Egypt became an independent state for the first time since the coming of Islam. The new city Cairo was also to become the headquarters of an even greater religious network. As imāms, the Fāṭimids were the infallible arbiters of Islam and, for their followers everywhere, they were the single focus and the absolute core of religious devotion. The true meaning of Islam, which resided in the person of the imam-caliph, would henceforth also radiate from Cairo and remain there as long as the Fāṭimids were to rule from Egypt.

Naturally, these developments meant, and in a sense continue to mean, a variety of things according to the religious inclinations of those who observed them. The Fāṭimid caliphate began, as its name indicates, as a restoration of the rights of ʿAlī's family as descended from ʿAlī's sons by the prophet's daughter Fāṭima (and not by the offspring of his son Muḥammad whose mother was a Ḥanafite woman). In asserting this claim, al-Mahdī and his descendants indicated the sacred lineage that tied them directly back to the prophet and to ʿAlī and Fāṭima. The term "Ismāʿīlī" was not used by the Fāṭimids except informally, although it has become, in more recent periods, a proper name for modern adherents of these same imams – especially now for the followers of the Agā Khāns, who are themselves said to be direct lineal descendants of the first eight Fāṭimid caliphs. Nevertheless, even in the medieval Islamic literature about Shiʿite sectarian divisions, the term *Ismāʿīlī* or *Ismāʿīliyya*, was commonly employed as a name for those Shīʿa who upheld the imamate of Ismāʿīl the son of the imam Jaʿfar al-Ṣādiq, who was himself the great-grandson of ʿAlī's son al-Ḥusayn. The actual conditions of the succession to Jaʿfar, however, about which not much is known in any case, are not easily described by a single term, and the origin of the Fāṭimids, which was never clear and which became a subject of intense polemical debate, requires more detail than is afforded by the singular designation "Ismāʿīlī."[1]

The origin of the Ismāʿīlī Daʿwa

Our oldest and presumably most reliable authorities agree that Jaʿfar designated his second son Ismāʿīl to succeed him as imam.[2] Ismāʿīl, however, died before his father and yet he was not replaced, at least not

[1] On the name *Ismāʿīlī*, see F. Daftary, *The Ismāʿīlīs: Their history and doctrines* (Cambridge, 1990), 93–97; H. Halm, *Das Reich des Mahdi: Der Aufstieg der Fāṭimiden (875–973)* (Munich, 1991), 25, trans. M. Bonner as *The Empire of the Mahdi: The Rise of the Fāṭimids*, (Leiden, 1996), 17. For a general overview of the origin and development of the Ismāʿīlīs as a sect, see Wilferd Madelung's article "Ismāʿīliyya," in *EI2* as well as the work of Daftary just cited. Madelung's pioneering study of the Ismāʿīlī doctrine of the imāmate in its various phases ("Das Imamat in der Frühen ismailitischen Lehre"), *Der Islam*, 37 (1961), 43–135) remains basic although carefully summarized and revisited by Daftary and Halm.

[2] al-Ḥasan ibn Mūsā al-Nawbakhtī, *Firaq al-Shīʿa*, ed. H. Ritter, (Istanbul, 1931), 55;

explicitly. Upon the death of Jaʿfar, the Shiʿite community fell into confusion concerning the person of the imām, although in theory an imām must exist at all times. The possibilities proposed at the time varied considerably but among them two are of particular importance in regard to the Fāṭimids. Many followers of Jaʿfar quickly accepted his oldest son ʿAbdallāh as the imam. However, he, according to these same reports, died shortly thereafter without male issue and thus his imamate was denied since he had obviously failed to pass it on as required by theory. Most of his Shīʿa (his "followers") reverted to another son of Jaʿfar, Mūsā. Nonetheless, what makes ʿAbdallāh's initial succession of special interest is the claim by al-Mahdī, long afterward, in a letter to his followers in the Yemen, that he was actually a direct descendant of this same son of Jaʿfar.[3] A second group argued, in contrast to the others, that the imamate, once given to Ismāʿīl by explicit designation, could not move laterally to another of Jaʿfar's sons. Rather, for them, it continued from Ismāʿīl to Ismāʿīl's own son Muḥammad. In their view, Muḥammad ibn Ismāʿīl had assumed the imamate either at his father's death or at that of his grandfather Jaʿfar. There were also several variations of such a succession, each with adherents, and the names of some leaders for these factions are known, notably al-Mubārak ibn ʿAlī al-ʿAbdī and the group called after him al-Mubārakiyya.[4]

Jaʿfar al-Ṣādiq died in 765 and the conditions just outlined apply to the period immediately thereafter. Nothing appears in our sources about any of this, however, until well over a century later. When finally the claims concerning Muḥammad ibn Ismāʿīl and these alternate avenues of succession to Jaʿfar first resurface, they are associated with the term *Qarmaṭī*, the earliest instance of which occurs in the title of an Imāmī Shiʿite refutation of Qarmatian doctrines written prior to 873–4. Despite this evidence, in Islamic historical writings, the word *Qarmaṭī* begins as an adjective from the name Qarmaṭ as applied to a mysterious propagator of Ismāʿīlī religious teachings called in these sources simply Ḥamdān Qarmaṭ. He was active in

Saʿad ibn al-Qummī, *al-Maqālāt wa'l-firaq*, ed. M. J. Mashkūr (Tehran, 1963), 78; Daftary, *Ismāʿīlīs*, 93–94.

3 For the text of the letter and an analysis of it, see first Husayn F. Hamdani, *On the Genealogy of the Fāṭimid Caliphs* (Cairo, 1958), and second Abbas Hamdani and F. de Blois, "A Re-examination of Al-Mahdī's Letter to the Yemenites on the Genealogy of the Fāṭimid Caliphs," *JRAS* (1983), 2, 173–207, as well as Daftary, *Ismāʿīlīs*, 108, 128.

4 The Mubārakiyya and their leader were recognized by, among other early sources, al-Nawbakhtī (*Firaq*, 58) but later Fāṭimid claims insisted that Mubārak was a pseudonym for Muḥammad ibn Ismāʿīl himself. See the discussion by Daftary, *Ismāʿīlīs*, 96–97, 102–3, 112. However, a newly discovered source from an early period, written by Ibn al-Aswad, a north African Shīʿī who later supported the Fāṭimids, not only mentions this group but gives the full name of the *mawla* of Ismāʿīl ibn Jaʿfar who instigated it, strongly suggesting thereby that al-Nawbakhtī's information is correct. See Paul E. Walker, "The Resolution of the Shīʿah," in L. Clarke, (ed.) *The Party of Ali*, (forthcoming).

the rural Sawād around the Iraqi city of Kūfa from 877 onward.[5] The *Qarāmiṭa* (plural of *Qarmaṭī*) – presumably his followers – believed, according to the accounts taken from captives and renegade informants at a slightly later period, that the current imām was the same Muḥammad ibn Ismāʿīl who had succeeded Jaʿfar. According to them, he was at that time in occultation but about to return and lay claim to supreme lordship over the Islamic realm. When he does, acting as the messiah, he will, they also believed, end the imposition of religious law and usher in the form of paradise that once existed for Adam.[6]

The connection between the "Ismāʿīlī" groups of the eighth century, from which the name derives, and these later manifestations is, however, quite uncertain. It is known, nevertheless, that Ḥamdān Qarmaṭ and his brother-in-law ʿAbdān, the first recorded advocates for the cause of Muḥammad ibn Ismāʿīl in this later form, were acting on instructions from a single central leadership. From among those recruited in Iraq and those who joined the movement elsewhere, more agents were dispatched by this same leadership to yet other territories in subsequent years. Ibn Ḥawshab, later called Manṣūr al-Yaman ("Conqueror of the Yemen"), and his associate ʿAlī ibn al-Faḍl were sent to open an Ismāʿīlī mission in the Yemen in 880. From there yet another "missionary" went on to India in 883. More such agents began to penetrate northern Iran and then, later, Khurasan.

The general term for these missionaries is *dāʿī*, which means one who appeals for adherence and loyalty to a specific cause. The general concept is subsumed in the word *daʿwa*, which here preserves its Qur'ānic sense of "summons" as in Muḥammad's summoning his followers to Islam (Muḥammad was God's *dāʿī*), as well as the appeal for devotion to a particular leader as imam. Even more, for the Ismāʿīlīs, it denotes a tightly controlled organization that served to propagate a religious message and spread the movement. All members entered the *daʿwa* by swearing an oath of allegiance and accepting a covenant of obedience to its leader. By the time of its rapid proliferation in the final decades of the third/ninth century, the Ismāʿīlī mission recognized a resident of Salamiya in Syria as supreme head;

5 The most important modern study of the Qarmatians is Wilferd Madelung's "Fāṭimiden und Bahrainqarmaten," in *Der Islam*, 34 (1959), 34–88, trans. (slightly revised) as "The Fāṭimids and the Qarmaṭīs of Baḥrayn," in F. Daftary (ed.), *Mediaeval Ismaʿili History & Thought* (Cambridge, 1996), 21–73. Much of this material was summarized by Madelung in the articles in "Ḥamdān Ḳarmaṭ" and "Ḳarmaṭī" *EI2*. There are also good general accounts by Daftary, *Ismāʿīlīs*, ch. 3: "Early Ismāʿīlism," and, the most up to date, by Halm, *Reich des Mahdi*, "Der geheime Orden,"15–60, "The Secret Order," 5–57.

6 This information about Qarmatian doctrines has been collected and summarized most recently by Daftary, *Ismāʿīlīs*, 104–5; Daftary, "Carmatians," *EIR*; Halm, *Reich des Mahdi*, 24–9, 33–38, 225–26, trans. 16–22, 26–31, 250–52.

he was, in the terminology of that period, the *ḥujja*, which apparently did not mean imām but rather his highest visible representative.[7]

Along with the other missions of the period, including the important effort of the Qarmaṭian Abū Saʿīd al-Jannābī in Baḥrayn, yet another, begun even prior to 893, was eventually to become crucial in the foundation of the Fāṭimid empire. Abū ʿAbdallāh al-Shīʿī and his older brother Abu'l-ʿAbbās were recruited in their home town of Kūfa by an agent named Abū ʿAlī and sent to Egypt in about 891. Abu'l-ʿAbbās entered service in the *daʿwa* as a courier between Egypt and Salamiya, while Abū ʿAbdallāh set off for Mecca and then Yemen where he was to be trained by Ibn Ḥawshab. In the year 893, he and another *dāʿī* went north from the Yemen on the pilgrimage and, while in Mecca, befriended a group of Berber Muslims from the tribe of Kutāma. The two Ismāʿīlī agents then accompanied the returning Berbers, first to Egypt and then, at the urging of the Kutāma pilgrims themselves, onward across north Africa toward their home region in the Lesser Kabylia mountains of eastern Algeria. It is hard to say now whether Abū ʿAbdallāh had planned his venture in accord with fairly explicit instructions from his supervisors or whether, as our only source seems to insist, he simply followed the course of expediency in response to opportunities that presented themselves. In any case he had reached and established an independent base in the middle of Kutāma territory at a place called Īkjān by the end of 893.[8]

The spread of the Ismāʿīlī *daʿwa* by this time was impressively wide, reaching and included significant cells in Iraq, Iran, Syria, Baḥrayn, the Yemen, and the Maghreb; the number of Ismāʿīlīs in all these places was growing rapidly, particularly in rural Iraq, the Yemen and north Africa, but also with large pockets in many cities and other regions. Despite these undeniable successes, in 286/899, which is probably the death date of the leader in Salamiya, a new figure assumed charge of the *daʿwa* and announced to the many varied Ismāʿīlī communities that, henceforth, rather than use the title *ḥujja*, which had indicated the chief agent of the absent Muḥammad ibn Ismāʿīl, he intended now openly to claim the imamate for himself as the true lineal descendent of the only valid line of imams. He announced that the imamate, instead of depending on the reemergence of the long absent Muḥammad ibn Ismāʿīl, had, in reality, actively continued in his family all along. The newly revealed imam was by name, at least

[7] On the use of this term in this context, see Daftary, *Ismāʿīlīs*, 127–8; Halm, *Reich des Mahdi*, 29–30, 61–64, trans. 22, 62–64.

[8] Qāḍī al-Nuʿmān, *Iftitāḥ al-daʿwa wa ibtidāʾ al-dawla*, ed. Wadad Kadi (Beirut, 1970), and by Farhat Dachraoui (Tunis, 1975). The exact location of Īkjān is now known only approximately, in part because no direct physical evidence of it outlasted its use in this one relatively brief period. However, it was east of, and perhaps fairly near, Setif and certainly west-northwest of Constantine in what is modern Algeria.

according to some sources, Saʿīd ibn al-Ḥusayn, and he was the nephew of the previous leader. But he was also the grandson of Aḥmad and his father ʿAbdallāh, who were the leaders prior to his uncle. Moreover, his uncle had properly designated him as the new leader and therefore his right to lead was not in question. His claim to the imamate, however, was met with immediate skepticism and rejection by some Ismāʿīlīs while at the same time receiving support and acceptance by others. Many of the eastern groups broke away thereafter, preferring to maintain the imamate of Muḥammad ibn Ismāʿīl in occultation, who they believed, moreover, was then about to return as the messiah. ʿAbbāsid authorities, who had begun to be alarmed by the increasing strength of the Ismāʿīlīs, now found ways to ascribe reprehensible antinomian excesses to groups they continued to call the Qarmatians, a term that stuck and was later used to cover all of the non-Fāṭimid Ismāʿīlīs. Originally, these were, in the main, the Ismāʿīlīs who rejected Saʿīd ibn al-Ḥusayn's imamate in 899, as well as his subsequent assumption of the caliphate in 910 as al-Mahdī, the first of the Fāṭimids.[9]

An ambiguity among members of the *daʿwa* in respect to these troubling circumstances is also attested by our sources. On behalf of the *daʿwa* in Iraq, ʿAbdān, for example, declined to give support for the change, but others remained loyal to Salamiya, including among them his brother-in-law Ḥamdān Qarmaṭ, who now disappears from Qarmatian sources, having left Iraq and changed his name.[10] As yet another sign of the conflict, a loyal Iraqi *dāʿī* Zikrawayh arranged ʿAbdān's murder to silence him. Farther east the *daʿwa* likewise wavered, and it is not clear which of the *dāʿī*s, if any at all, were partial to the new Ismāʿīlī doctrine as opposed to the older Qarmatian teaching. Most significantly, the recently formed Qarmatian community of Baḥrayn ceased to accept the leadership of Salamiya altogether, and repercussions of this separation remained serious for the Fāṭimids up to and including the conquest of Egypt and the founding of Cairo.[11]

Therefore, although faced with an internal revolt, Saʿīd could nevertheless depend on crucial support in certain quarters. Ibn Ḥawshab and much of the Yemen held firm, as did Abū ʿAbdallāh in the Maghrib. The *dāʿī* Zikrawayh, however, although not necessarily completely hostile, began on his own an adventure that was certainly not condoned by Salamiya. Three of his sons went into the Syrian desert and converted substantial numbers of tribesmen either in the name of the new imām or of that of one of themselves as if,

[9] Daftary, *Ismāʿīlīs*, 125–30; Halm, *Reich des Mahdi*, 61–7, trans. 58–66.

[10] Apparently Ḥamdān Qarmaṭ at first sided with his brother-in-law in rejecting the new initiative but, not long after this revolt began, changed his position and resumed his former loyalty to the central leadership.

[11] Halm, *Reich des Mahdi*, 225–36, 334–35, 337–41, trans. 250–63, 377–78, 380–85, and Daftary, *Ismāʿīlīs*, 126.

according to one version, one of the brothers was actually Muḥammad ibn Ismāʿīl himself reappeared at last. The goal of this revolt was Salamiya, and ʿAbbāsid intelligence sources quickly made a connection between it and the person they were intended to see as merely a rich and noble merchant who happened to live in that city. Saʿīd's position was compromised and the previously clandestine Ismāʿīlī movement was about to be fully exposed. Possibly, the ʿAbbāsids already knew about Salamiya; in any case they could now no longer afford to delay action. While the Syrian Qarmatian followers of the sons of Zikrawayh marched to Ismāʿīlī headquarters in Salamiya in an effort to coopt the leadership, an ʿAbbāsid army moved from Iraq against them.[12]

Unable to trust the Qarmatians, Saʿīd decided to flee Salamiya and did so in haste, leaving behind family and much of the accumulated wealth and possessions that had been acquired in secret over the years as the contributions of the Ismāʿīlīs were passed up through the *daʿwa* to the supreme leadership. His home in Salamiya had become the material as well as the intellectual center of Ismāʿīlism. Now, with a few servants and with his young son and eventual successor, he traveled south to Ramla where he awaited the outcome of the Syrian revolt. Even then he obviously hoped to recover his hold over most of his former following.[13]

The prematurely violent confrontation by the sons of Zikrawayh with ʿAbbāsid authorities, however, not only ended badly for them but soon forced Saʿīd to continue his flight into Egypt. The ʿAbbāsids were determined to capture him. In Egypt, he eluded them and was carefully shielded by his local *daʿwa*, then directed by a man named in most sources simply as Abū ʿAlī but who was clearly a major figure. In fact, although one Fāṭimid source, the personal memoirs of Saʿīd's manservant, Jaʿfar, places the main *dāʿī* from Salamiya, someone named simply Fīrūz, in the position of chief of the *daʿwa* (the *bāb al-abwāb*), other sources having greater credence state that the head of the *daʿwa* was then, in fact, this same Abū ʿAlī. The geographer Ibn Ḥawqal, moreover, who was himself a Fāṭimid supporter, later knew Abū ʿAlī's son personally. He reports that Abū ʿAlī was none other than Ḥamdān Qarmaṭ, a piece of information that is hard to reject

[12] On this revolt and the imam's departure from Salamiya, see Halm, *Reich des Mahdi*, 67–89, trans. 66–91, and Daftary, *Ismāʿīlīs*, 132–35.

[13] From this point in the story of the imam's travels, the main source is the *Sīrat Jaʿfar al-Ḥājib*, a memoir dictated long afterwards by the manservant who accompanied him from Salamiya to Sijilmasa and finally to Raqqada. The Arabic text was published by W. Ivanow in the *Bulletin of the Faculty of Arts*, University of Egypt (Cairo, 1936), 107–33; Eng. trans. by Ivanow in *Ismaili Tradition Concerning the Rise of the Fāṭimids*, (London/Calcutta/Bombay, 1942), 184–223; French trans. by M. Canard, "L'autobiographie d'un chambellan du Mahdî 'Obeidallâh le Fâṭimide," *Hespéris*, 39 (1952), 279–330 (reprinted in *Miscellanea Orientalia*, London, 1973). See also Halm, *Reich des Mahdi*.

given both the crucial role of Abū ʿAlī and his prominence.[14] He is said, moreover, to have converted the brothers Abū ʿAbdallāh and Abu'l-ʿAbbās in Kūfa, and Abu'l-ʿAbbās obviously worked for him in Egypt later. That the head of the *daʿwa* – the famous Ḥamdān Qarmaṭ – was stationed in Egypt by this time may well be significant. Does it indicate that a plan to take Egypt was already under contemplation even as far back as this? More likely, because the *daʿwa* had not achieved in Egypt numbers comparable to those in the Yemen and north Africa, Abū ʿAlī's role was that of head gatekeeper, controlling messages and instructions coming and going from Salamiya to the Yemen and north Africa.

According to the testimony of the manservant Jaʿfar, the party traveling with the imām thought they would all proceed from Egypt to the Yemen, where Ibn Ḥawshab and ʿAlī ibn al-Faḍl had earlier subjugated most of the country. For reasons that are not clear, however, when the threat of ʿAbbasid capture loomed again, the imām announced instead that they would set off for the Maghreb. Fīrūz, reports Jaʿfar, refused and, despite his position, abandoned the imām and went instead to the Yemen on his own. In contrast, Abū ʿAlī asked to accompany the imām but was told to remain at his post in Egypt until the situation in the west was resolved satisfactorily. Egypt obviously was a key element in the imām's plan. Perhaps, significantly, although he was now regarded as a rebel, Fīrūz, who was said to have converted Ibn Ḥawshab originally, went to him in the Yemen and reported that the Yemeni *daʿwa* should be ready to march against Egypt when the imam returned there with the troops he was about to raise in north Africa.[15]

The imām went first to Alexandria where, disguised as a wealthy merchant, he joined a caravan headed west early in the summer of 905. Among those who accompanied him was Abu'l-ʿAbbās, the brother of Abū ʿAbdallāh. The baggage belonging to the party was obviously considerable and Saʿīd's ability to avoid detection was unlikely in the long run. From Tripoli, as he approached the territory of the Aghlabid rulers of Qayrawan and central north Africa, he requested that Abu'l-ʿAbbās go on alone in order to determine whether the rest of the party could safely expect to pass through and ultimately reach the Kutāma region where a thriving Ismāʿīlī

[14] Ibn Ḥawqal, *Ṣūrat al-arḍ*, ed. J. H. Kramers (Leiden, 1938), 96; French trans. by G. Wiet, *Configuration de la terre* (Beirut/Paris, 1964), 94. The son of Abū ʿAlī (Ḥamdān Qarmaṭ), who was also the grandson of the same Fīrūz, later himself became the chief *dāʿī* under al-Qā'im, al-Manṣūr, and al-Muʿizz. See the *Sīrat Jaʿfar*, 114. The authenticity of Ibn Ḥawqal's information about Ḥamdān Qarmaṭ, though often rejected, has been recently accepted by Wilferd Madelung in an extremely interesting paper, "Ḥamdān Qarmaṭ and the Dā'ī Abū ʿAlī," *Proceedings of the Seventeenth Congress of the UEAI (Union Européenne des Arabisants et Islamisants)*, (St Petersburg, 1997), 115–24.

[15] These details are reported in the *Sīrat Jaʿfar*, 113–15, Eng. trans. 291–94, French trans. 194–97. Cf. Halm, *Reich des Mahdi*, 88–89, trans. 90–91.

community awaited them. By then, however, the activities of Abū ʿAbdallāh were of considerable concern to the Aghlabids. He had forged out of the contentious Berber clans and tribes a solid army; his constant preaching of the Ismāʿīlī cause over more than a decade had steadily multiplied his following, which now constituted a formidable menace to the rulers in Qayrawān. Abu'l-ʿAbbās was immediately arrested on suspicion of complicity with Abū ʿAbdallāh. Aghlabid authorities may also have had good reason to suspect that the two were related.

The imām's purpose was served, however, in that he was warned away. Nevertheless, with messages from the ʿAbbāsids ordering his capture coming from the direction of Egypt, the imām had no choice but to continue westward. The only logical route, however, lay south of where he had hoped to go and the farther end of that path was some two months' travel away in the distant Maghribi town of Sijilmāsa.[16] Once there, moreover, he was not necessarily safe. Still, for the time being, he was compelled to remain in Sijilmāsa and hope for the best. He could easily keep pretending to be nothing more than a merchant, and his access to funds allowed him to buy the tolerance of the local ruler. In addition, he was never out of touch with his *daʿwa*, including now, most importantly, Abū ʿAbdallāh and the Kutāma.[17]

Aghlabid ability to govern depended ultimately on secure control over the towns of their region.[18] For them Qayrawān was a natural base since it was dominated by Arabs. The hinterland, however, fell progressively farther away from their immediate sway as the proportion of Arabs declined. Abū ʿAbdallāh had established his refuge, his *dār al-hijra*, in an area where there were no cities and where an Aghlabid army could not easily reach him and his Ismāʿīlī flock. The Aghlabids were also slow to react. Not until 902 did they move against the Ismāʿīlīs, and their first attempts failed. Patiently, Abū ʿAbdallāh built his small but growing kingdom of Ismāʿīlīs and waited before attacking major towns until he knew his Berber forces were likely to find success. It was not until 904 that he began to capture cities and, even then, he was hesitant to exploit his successes. By 908, the last government of Aghlabids, many members of which were then incompetent and morally bankrupt, had begun to destroy themselves. They had lost even the support of the Arabs who were increasingly impressed by Abū ʿAbdallāh's movement and his personal dedication, abstinence, self-control and obvious piety. Finally, in March 909, the Aghlabid ruler packed up and absconded toward Egypt. Kutāma troops arrived at the government enclave of Raqqāda just

16 An important town of pre-modern Islamic Morocco some 190 m/300 km south of Fez, now in ruins.

17 Halm, *Reich des Mahdi*, 89–92, trans. 91–95.

18 In addition to the other sources cited, see the study by F. Dachraoui, *Le Califat fatimide au Maghreb, 296–362/909–973: histoire, politique et institutions* (Tunis, 1981).

south of Qayrawān two days later and found that the local population had already had time to plunder what the Aghlabids had left behind.[19]

Abū ʿAbdallāh immediately assumed control; he was well received by those he had just defeated, many of whom hoped for an end to the injustice of the last Aghlabid, but some also were themselves already Shiʿite and they anticipated profound changes from a fellow Shiʿite. His most pressing problem, however, was to create a government which he could not easily do with only his Berber colleagues of the previous seventeen years. They, for their part, however, expected the fruits of victory in the form of plundered riches and prestigious appointments.

Another urgent task was the rescue of the imām from Sijilmāsa. After settling affairs in Qayrawān and Raqqāda, he wrote to his brother who was by then in Tripoli after having escaped Aghlabid detention. Abu'l-ʿAbbās came at once and together with the Berber leader Abū Zākī, who had been associated with the cause since the beginning, he was appointed co-regent for the interim while Abū ʿAbdallāh and his army marched west to retrieve the imam. Six months later the imām, now in full command, arrived in Raqqāda and assumed the caliphate under the name ʿUbayallāh, al-Mahdī bi-Allāh on January 6, 910.[20]

The elevation of al-Mahdī brought to power an Ismāʿīlī imām who had little reason to expect widespread acceptance from his non-Shiʿite subjects. A significant portion of the Berbers were already Kharijite – implacable enemies of the Shiʿites – and the majority of town dwelling Arabs belonged to the Maliki legal *madhhab* which was equally hostile. Still, initially, the new regime found support not only from the converted Kutāmas but from others, especially from the non-Maliki Arabs, some of whom were Shiʿite and some who were Sunnīs but were Hanafi in their *madhhab*. Eventually, however, religious difference rose to the surface and created enormous difficulties. The citizens of the new state had no choice but loyalty, reluctant or otherwise, or exile. Only a minority ever became Ismāʿīlī or were known as Ismāʿīlīs as the Kutāma were from the beginning. Rule by the Fāṭimids thus had two aspects: religious and political. One was the domain of the *daʿwa* acting on behalf of the imam; the other was more secular and involved a kind of recognition and obedience which never went deeper than the allegiance Muslims elsewhere pledged to the ʿAbbāsid caliphs. It is quite likely that from the first the overwhelming majority of those who lived

[19] Halm, *Reich des Mahdi*, 104–15, trans. 107–21, and M. Talbi, *L'Émirat Aghlabide (184–296/800–909)* (Paris, 1966).

[20] All non-Ismāʿīlī sources give al-Mahdī's name as ʿUbaydallāh whereas most Ismāʿīlī works prefer ʿAbdallāh, as if the diminutive ʿUbayd might be pejorative and demeaning. But the diminutive/endearing form "Ḥusayn" hardly implies less status for Ḥusayn ibn ʿAlī than for his brother Ḥasan.

under Fāṭimid government accepted their rulers with a similar if not the same sentiment as they had accorded previous political governors.

Within the total citizenry, however, the Ismāʿīlīs held a special position. For them, unlike the rest, the caliph was the single infallible representative on earth of God Himself. What the caliph decreed, therefore, was divine law, pure and simple; his understanding of all matters whether religious or otherwise was definitively true and valid without question or argument. Thus, while the establishment of the state brought about the rule of the righteous party in the political sense, continuing access to the imām as the divine guide in religious affairs gave the Fāṭimid state an additional dimension for its Ismāʿīlī inhabitants. The *daʿwa* for them remained a constant requirement; and the *dāʿīs* went on teaching Ismāʿīlīs within the state just as they also tried to expand the number of adherents by propagating their cause both at home and abroad.

In setting the course of his empire, al-Mahdī soon encountered a serious setback. Less than two years after achieving the finally victory over the Aghlabids and barely more than a year after his enthronement, Abū ʿAbdallāh, his brother Abu'l-ʿAbbās, and a number of the earliest Kutāma converts, turned against him. The cause of their dissatisfaction is not clear, but al-Mahdī apparently could not act otherwise than order their execution. As in many situations that were to occur later, the Kutāma proved as difficult to keep in check when they chose to go their own way as they were valuable when loyal. Many of them apparently regarded Abū ʿAbdallāh and his victory as theirs; they were disappointed with al-Mahdī and a style of rule largely foreign to their traditions and expectations.[21]

The first attempts to conquer Egypt.[22]

The empire, however, was not to be limited within the narrow territory won by Abū ʿAbdallāh and his Berbers, either politically or religiously. There is no doubt that al-Mahdī hoped soon to return eastward and to complete his empire by toppling the ʿAbbāsids. Berber forces were sent in that direction almost immediately. By 913 the Fāṭimids had already fought and defeated rebels in Tripoli. Early in 914, they began a campaign to add the region of Barka and not long afterward troops moved from there into Egypt.[23] By late summer of the same year, an advance force of Berbers had taken Alexandria, and the main army under the personal command of Abu'l-Qāsim, the heir to

[21] Idrīs ʿImād al-Dīn, *ʿUyūn al-akhbār*, ed. al-Yaʿlāwī as *Tārīkh al-khulafāʾ al-faṭtimiyyīn bi'l-maghrib: al-qism al-khāṣṣ min kitāb ʿuyūn al-akhbār* (Beirut, 1985), 180–88.

[22] See especially Halm, *Reich des Mahdi*, 180–94, trans. 196–213.

[23] Tripoli is a major city in western Libya; Barka is some 708 m/1141 km by road east of it in the Cyrenaica region, also in Libya.

the imamate, reached the city in early November. Alexandria was immediately put under Shiʿite rule.[24]

These victories so close to home awakened the ʿAbbāsids to the threat posed by the Fāṭimids who were not, it was now obvious, merely renegade dissidents in the far away province of Ifriqiyya, but were rebels with a grand agenda that aimed at the overthrow of the Sunnī caliphate. With Abu'l-Qāsim and his army stationed first in Giza opposite Fusṭāṭ and later in the Fayyum, the ʿAbbāsid ruler began sending reinforcements to Egypt. Ultimately, the Fāṭimids ran out of provisions before they could force a crossing to the east bank of the Nile. They did not fare well in pitched battles either. Finally, Abu'l-Qāsim retreated to Alexandria. There he maintained resolutely his intent to take the fight to the ʿAbbāsids. His attitude is clearly expressed both in a poem he sent back to his father and in the sermons he delivered in the mosque of Alexandria, the text of one of which survives.[25] As the ʿAbbāsids poured funds and personnel into Egypt, however, he could not hold out; by May of 915 he had returned to Raqqāda.[26]

The dream of eastern conquest was not over, however. Almost at once preparations were resumed, although it was not until a few years later that Abu'l-Qāsim and his army again reached Alexandria, where he spent most of 919 as reinforcements followed him into Egypt, an important contingent of which was the Fāṭimid fleet of some eighty ships. The ʿAbbāsids were already on the alert, having observed these developments carefully. They countered with a fleet of their own sent from Cilicia far to the north. In March 920 the two squadrons fought a sea battle near Abukir which ended in a disaster for the Fāṭimids. That summer Abu'l-Qāsim marched, as he had before, past Giza into upper Egypt where he assumed the posture of ruler, collecting taxes and controlling commerce. For a while a stalemate ensued; neither side possessed sufficient resources to dislodge the other. Instead they engaged in an exchange of rhetorical propaganda.[27] On being offered ʿAbbāsid recognition of Fāṭimid hegemony over the former Aghlabid domains, Abu'l-Qāsim replied with a denunciation of ʿAbbāsid legitimacy. He made his objective quite clear: the replacement of the ʿAbbāsids themselves. Neither north Africa nor Egypt would satisfy him if he were

[24] Idrīs, *ʿUyūn*, 194–5.

[25] Halm, *Reich des Mahdi*, 185–87, trans. 203–05, and Idrīs, *ʿUyūn*, 197–98 (poem) and 198–202 (sermon). This material from the *ʿUyūn al-akhbār* was published previously by S. M. Stern in his "Al-Mahdī's Reign According to the *ʿUyūn al-Akhbār*," *Studies in Early Ismāʿīlism* (Jerusalem, 1983, 96–145), 115–21.

[26] Idrīs, *ʿUyūn*, 196–209.

[27] On the details of this incident as well as the whole character of Fāṭimid propaganda against their various opponents including the ʿAbbasids, see the article by M. Canard, "L'impérialisme des Fāṭimides et leur propagande," *Annales de l'Institut d'Etudes Orientales de la Faculté des Lettres d'Alger*, 6 (1942–47), 156–93 (reprinted in *Miscellanea Orientalia*, no. II).

deprived of the ultimate goal of destroying the godless usurpers in Baghdad.[28]

The Fāṭimid position in Egypt was precarious, however. In the spring of 921, the ʿAbbāsid fleet recaptured Alexandria and their troops managed to blockade the Fayyūm, in effect trapping Abu'l-Qāsim. By traveling north through the desert route along the Wādī Naṭrūn, he escaped, but with huge losses. Once back at the court of his father, the damage done to Fāṭimid morale and its grand purpose was concealed by friendly propaganda. The jihād – the sacred struggle – and the *daʿwa* must be pursued regardless of the impossibility of immediate success; a just cause was a duty imposed by God and victory would come when and if He should will it.[29]

The two expeditions by the heir apparent against Egypt were not the only attempts of this kind by the Fāṭimids. On several other occasions, even during the reign of al-Mahdī, their troops entered Egyptian territory although with few or no consequences. Early in the reign of al-Mahdī's son Abu'l-Qāsim, who had adopted the throne name al-Qā'im bi-Amr Allāh in continuation of the messianic theme of the initial Fāṭimid rise to power, a large army again marched to Alexandria. This time al-Qā'im was trying to gain from internal Egyptian confusion and infighting. A group of Maghribi soldiers there had seized Alexandria and invited him to send troops. Although the Fāṭimids managed to capture Alexandria yet again, they could not hold it. Their army was soon defeated by Ikhshidid forces.[30]

Despite this evidence of Fāṭimid preoccupation with Egypt, it would be wrong to ignore their persistent attempts to expand westward into the farthest Maghrib or northward from Sicily, which they had inherited from the Aghlabids and which served as a base of jihād against Christian Italy and Byzantium. Nor did they neglect to extend their *daʿwa* in the same directions. Missionaries were sent, for example, to Spain to spread Shiʿism there; the former *dāʿī* of Egypt, Abū ʿAlī (Ḥamdān Qarmaṭ), who had been allowed to come to north Africa after the victory, was later dispatched to Constantinople. Spreading Ismāʿīlism among the citizenry of the Byzantine capital was, admittedly, an unlikely adventure, and he subsequently spent five years in detention there prior to freedom and a return to Qayrawān.[31] *Dāʿīs* loyal to the Fāṭimids were also active throughout all of the eastern Islamic territories. Fāṭimid interest in Egypt must be regarded therefore as

[28] Idrīs, *ʿUyūn*, 206–7; Canard, "L'impérialisme," 172–73.

[29] Idrīs, *ʿUyūn*, 208; Halm, *Reich des Mahdi*, 193, trans. 212–13.

[30] Ibn al-Athīr, ʿAlī ibn Muḥammad, *al-Kāmil fi'l-ta'rīkh*, ed. C. J. Tornberg (Beirut, 1965–67), viii, 285; Halm, *Reich des Mahdi*, 194, trans. 213.

[31] Idrīs, *ʿUyūn*, 237–38. This information appears with his obituary notice; he died in 321/933. He had been in Constantinople when the crisis with Abū ʿAbdallāh al-Shīʿī and his brother occurred. It is material that was not included for some reason in the earlier editions of Idrīs's text.

but one stage in their planned domination of Islam; for them control of the Nile was crucial but only as a preparation for this larger goal.

As it turned out, in the short term that all-consuming goal was soon put aside in response to a mortal threat from a new revolt among the Berbers. In a way not unlike Abū ʿAbdallāh on behalf the Ismāʿīlī Shiʿites against the Aghlabids, a Kharijite rebel named Abū Yazīd Makhlad ibn Kaydād inspired the Zanāta Berbers and fashioned out of them a formidable army which, beginning in 943, he used all but to destroy the Fāṭimid state. Known as the Man on the Donkey (*Ṣāḥib al-Ḥimār*) in standard sources, or simply as al-Dajjāl in Fāṭimid writings, Abū Yazīd rampaged through most of central Tunisia, took Qayrawān and Raqqāda, and ultimately reached the walls of al-Mahdiyya the coastal capital city of the Fāṭimids at the time.[32] Although first al-Qā'im and then his son and successor al-Manṣūr after him were safely ensconced within al-Mahdiyya, their North African state crumbled before the onslaught of Abū Yazīd. From 944 to 947, the Fāṭimids were completely preoccupied with reversing the damage and eradicating the Dajjāl and his influence. Only upon his final victory, in fact, did the new imām announce his own succession to the imamate, even though his father had died months before; appropriately, in honor of the occasion, he adopted the throne name al-Manṣūr, the Victor. The short reign of al-Manṣūr, however, though victorious, did not allow time for further expansion of the empire. That fell to his son, al-Muʿizz li-Dīn Allāh, who succeeded in March of 953.

Al-Muʿizz's plan for Egypt

The experience of the first three Fāṭimids constituted an inheritance well understood by al-Muʿizz who had personally witnessed most of it. Their aspirations were his own but he had the benefit of their mistakes and failures. His own approach was careful and cautious; his preparations were protracted and meticulously planned. Basically, his policy consisted of three distinct initiatives. One involved a new interpretation of Ismāʿīlī doctrine especially as it pertained to the application of law. A second was the creation of a professional core of administrators who would not bring with them the conflicts often carried over from previous tribal loyalties. This was particularly important for the army. Finally, he made an attempt to win back many of the eastern Ismāʿīlīs who had been Qarmatian and who had refused earlier to recognize Fāṭimid suzerainty.

Shiʿite law was already practiced in Fāṭimid domains prior to the

[32] Al-Mahdiyya, the capital city of the Fāṭimids from its founding until the building of al-Manṣūriyya, still exists on the coast. It lies approximately 120 m/200 km southeast of Tūnis and 60m/100k east of Qayrawān.

accession of al-Muʿizz, but it had never been systematically formulated by the Ismāʿīlīs.[33] In Ismāʿīlī theory the imām is the sole authority for all law and for all religious understanding, and each newly succeeding imam automatically replaces the former. Only by acknowledging and following the word of the living imām can an Ismāʿīlī be assured of salvation. Written documents by their very nature record the past and not the living present; to remain current, they require constant oral re-interpretation. ʿAbbāsid propaganda against the Ismāʿīlīs claimed, in fact, that they (here read, perhaps, Qarmaṭians) believed that for every literal wording of the law, for example, there is an esoteric interpretation that is its true meaning and that once a believer knows the secret inner reality behind the surface of the scripture or the law, the exterior no longer applies. Accordingly, the Ismāʿīlīs are free of legal obligations since they need follow only the hidden message of the scripture or the law. In part this assessment is accurate. Sunnī authorities, however, exaggerated its implications; almost no Ismāʿīlī author ever advocated abandoning the law but instead resolutely insisted that both the letter and the meaning of the law must be followed strictly. Islamic law must be observed in every detail; this form of the teaching was repeated by all Ismāʿīlī authorities for whom there now exists direct and unbiased evidence.

However, anti-Ismāʿīlī propaganda had hurt the Fāṭimid cause and al-Muʿizz realized that an Ismāʿīlī state would require a written and publicly accessible constitution, if only to put to rest fears of an impending irreligious lawlessness connected to a Fāṭimid assumption of power. To that end he commissioned the chief legal expert among the Ismāʿīlīs in North Africa, the famous Qāḍī al-Nuʿmān, to assemble and rationalize a complete corpus of Ismāʿīlī religious law. The Ismāʿīlī community in particular, and by direct implication the Fāṭimid state in general, would thereafter have a recognized written body of legal material and thus a constitution; and they would become a *madhhab* like the Malikis and Hanafis among the Sunnīs or the Twelvers among the non-Ismāʿīlī Shīʿīs.[34]

A secondary feature of this same initative had Qāḍi al-Nuʿmān and other writers begin to record the history of the Fāṭimid imams as if that history were exemplary and was itself a basis for what to expect from Ismāʿīlī imams in the future. All this was done as a matter of public policy ostensibly for an Ismaʿīlī audience but with a view toward those citizens of the Islamic

[33] On the background, see Madelung's study "The Sources of Ismaʿili Law," in *JNES*, 35 (1976), 29–40.

[34] Qadi al-Nuʿmān's legal compilations began with a massive collection of material called *Kitāb al-īḍāḥ*, which is almost entirely lost now, but he also produced several summaries and handbooks as well, most notably the *Daʿāʾim al-islām* (ed. by A. A. A. Fyzee, 2 vols., Cairo, 1963 and 1960) which subsequently became the standard text in Fāṭimid law. On his role in the entourage of al-Muʿizz, see Halm, *Reich des Mahdi*, 302–04 , trans. 340–42.

community who were not. While most of the literature produced by the *daʿwa* was guarded in secrecy, the works of Qāḍi al-Nuʿmān, except for a rare few, could and would be read by non-Ismāʿīlīs as al-Muʿizz had intended. Those who did found statements that were to reassure them that a Fāṭimid government was as solidly Islamic and orthodox as any other, certainly more so than that of the rival ʿAbbāsids.

Al-Muʿizz also recognized that the strength of the Fāṭimid appeal had been seriously weakened by the long standing defection of eastern Qarmatian Ismāʿīlīs. Had the Fāṭimid state been able to count on the support of Iraqi and Baḥraynī Ismāʿīlīs, the two together, acting in concert, might well have destroyed the ʿAbbāsids long before. Even had the first Fāṭimid invasion of Egypt been supported by a sizable force from the Yemen, as al-Mahdī evidently hope it would, the outcome would have been different. By the time of al-Muʿizz, however, the Yemeni *daʿwa* was no longer as vigorous as it had once been and some other portions of the *daʿwa* abroad had been weakened considerably. Nevertheless, the Qarmatians of the east, in contrast, remained formidable.

This old division in the Ismāʿīlī legacy was not easily mended despite the willingness of al-Muʿizz to compromise. Still, by judicious adjustments in the public teaching offered by his *daʿwa*, he succeeded in part. The messiahship of Muḥammad ibn Ismāʿīl was again admitted, for example, and the heady intellectual speculations of thinkers like the Neoplatonist *dāʿī* Abū Yaʿqūb al-Sijistānī and his predecessors, were now recognized as valid. Gradually, the dissidents rallied to his side, most notably al-Sijistānī himself.[35]

The more obdurate of the Qarmatians, however, refused to accommodate al-Muʿizz. They were unrepentant. Moreover, their successful predatory raids against ʿAbbāsid Iraq and the Ḥijāz gave them virtual hegemony over a large part of Arabia, with complete control of the eastern pilgrimage route. Many cities and governing entities paid them tribute even as they also despised them. When Abū Ṭāhir al-Jannābī seized Mecca in January of 930 and removed the Black Stone from the Kaʿba, this massive sacrilege – though hardly that in the eyes of the Qarmatians – constituted a disaster for the Ismāʿīlīs at large. The term *Qarmaṭī* was by then commonly pejorative; it now became doubly so. Even after the incident in which a false messiah fooled Qarmatian leadership and made a mockery of their doctrine, they could still threaten their enemies and force them to pay tribute. And the

35 Daftary, *Ismāʿīlīs*, 176–80, and Halm, *Reich des Mahdi*, 257–65, 335–37, trans. 288–97, 378–80. On the thought of al-Sijistānī, see Paul E. Walker, *Early Philosophical Shiʿism: the Ismāʿīlī Neoplatonism of Abū Yaʿqūb al-Sijistānī* (Cambridge, 1993); Walker, *The Wellsprings of Wisdom* (Salt Lake City, 1994); and Walker, *Abū Yaʿqūb al-Sijistānī: Intellectual Missionary* (London, 1996).

Fāṭimids, although sharing a common Ismāʿīlī heritage, were no exception; the Qarmatians were their enemies as well.

In the administration of the state, the Fāṭimids learned quickly that, although the Kutāma had put them in power and were the bedrock of their military, the Berbers – either as individuals or as a group – seldom succeeded in breaking away completely from their tribal past. There were frequent examples of friction between Berber commanders or governors and the non-Berber populations of occupied towns and cities. Some of the Kutāma, moreover, proved far too independent and uncontrollable. Early on the caliphs began to rely instead, not only on the experienced administrators of the regime they had supplanted, but on a growing cadre of purchased slaves, some of whom they subsequently freed and thereafter employed as they would other mercenaries and salaried retainers. Even though freed, the status of a former slave preserved a close sense of dependence and loyalty that freeborn Arab blood or Berber ancestry seemed often to prevent. The most famous of these slaves was Jawhar, who was originally of slavic extraction. After several masters, Jawhar finally was given to the Caliph al-Manṣūr who set him free and for whom he worked thereafter as a secretary (a *kātib*). Under al-Muʿizz, Jawhar acquired even greater responsibility as the commander of military expeditions, first to the farthest Maghreb which he subdued for the Fāṭimids all the way to the Atlantic ocean.[36] Al-Muʿizz's purpose was best served by such able planners who were sensible and methodical rather than impetuous and unpredictable.

There can be no doubt, given the history of previous Fāṭimid interest, that al-Muʿizz intended the conquest of Egypt from early in his reign, his expansion to the west and his complicated dealings with the Byzantines notwithstanding. In fact a Byzantine ambassador who had come to Tunisia and who witnessed there a show of Fāṭimid military might was told that he would next see al-Muʿizz in Egypt. (And when he actually arrived later in Egypt, al-Muʿizz predicted that their next meeting would be in Baghdād.)[37]

With a caution that was not characteristic of his immediate predecessors, al-Muʿizz organized his approaching conquest of Egypt as if it were not only sure to succeed but would ultimately result in a reconfiguration of the empire itself. His propaganda apparatus leaned heavily on the need to bring strong leadership to the jihād against the Byzantines in northern Syria. This was a theme designed to appeal in the east and was something the ʿAbbāsids, by implication, were not doing. Agents of the *daʿwa* were numerous in Fusṭāṭ, including among them the director of the local *daʿwa*, a wealthy

36 There is a biography of Jawhar in al-Maqrīzī's massive *al-Muqaffā al-kabīr*, ed. M. al-Yaʿlāwī, 8 vols. (Beirut, 1991), iii, #1102,83–111). See also H. Monés, "Djawhar al-Ṣiḳillī," in the *Encyclopaedia of Islam*, and Halm, *Reich des Mahdi*, 302, trans. 339–40, and 352–54, trans. 396–401 for Jawhar's campaign in the farthest Maghreb.

37 Ibn al-Athīr, *al-Kāmil*, viii, 663.

merchant named Abū Jaʿfar Aḥmad ibn Naṣr, who had befriended and perhaps also bribed many Egyptian officials, among them the wazīr, the chief judge and the heads of the local ʿAlid families.[38] As economic conditions along the Nile deteriorated because of unusually low water for several years in succession in the 960s, many Egyptians wondered if the Fāṭimids would not be preferable to the distant and increasingly impotent ʿAbbāsids who were represented in Egypt by surrogate military commanders. Moreover, the Qarmatians now began to dominate Syria, making Baghdad even less important.

By 966, Jawhar had been ordered to commence recruiting an army. Throughout 968, al-Muʿizz collected special taxes and amassed matériel of all kinds. His accumulation of monies alone was enormous and stunning: one report says he brought together 24,000,000 *dinars* for the purpose. The road to Egypt was also prepared meticulously, with new wells dug at regular intervals along the route. In early February 969, Jawhar and his army left Raqqāda. Al-Muʿizz had made sure that everyone knew the importance of this venture and equally the rank of its chief commander. The governors of towns en route were to dismount for the freedman Jawhar and kiss his hand.

Upon his arrival in Egypt, there was little or no sign of resistance. Jawhar quickly assumed control over the west bank of the Nile all the way into the Fayyum and waited for a reaction from the Egyptians. The wazīr, the heads of both Ḥasanid and Ḥusaynid *ashrāf*, the chief *Qāḍi*, and other notables soon came to see him in company with the local director of the Ismāʿīlī *daʿwa*. Surrender and occupation seemed a foregone matter. Jawhar grandly issued a proclamation of safe conduct (*amāna*) and arranged a treaty of capitulation in which he spoke of the need to recommence the jihād, secure the pilgrimage routes, end illegal taxes, restore mosques, and return to the true *sunna* of the prophet. Some unanticipated resistance by Ikhshīdid military units interrupted the expected bloodless transition, but this minor disturbance proved shortlived. By July, Jawhar's forces were peacefully crossing the pontoon bridge from Giza into Fusṭāṭ and setting up camp to the north of the mosque of Ibn Ṭūlūn on the site of what was later to become the city of Cairo. On July 9, Jawhar himself led prayers in the Old Mosque of ʿAmr in Fusṭāṭ and the preacher, dressed now in Fāṭimid white in place of ʿAbbāsid black, recited the *khuṭba* for the first time in Egypt in the name of al-Muʿizz li-Dīn Allāh.[39]

Although Jawhar's conquest had been largely peaceful, the task of

[38] Bianquis, "La Prise du pouvoir par les fatimides en Egypte (357–363/968–974)," *Annales Islamologiques*, 11 (1972), 48–108; 62–63 provides the details and sources for the activities of this agent. See also Halm, *Reich des Mahdi*, 362–64, trans. 409–10 and Daftary, *Ismāʿīlīs*, 171–72.

[39] On the Fāṭimid takeover of Egypt, in general, see Halm, *Reich des Mahdi*, 361–72, trans. 408–20, and Bianquis, "La Prise du pouvoir," 48–108.

governing Egypt in the name of his Shiʿite master was not quite as simple. There is almost no doubt that the Fāṭimids had planned in advance for the general initiatives undertaken by Jawhar, such as the building of a separate capital as a residential enclave for the troops and much of the government. Also, as they had done sixty years earlier in north Africa, they re-employed the administration of the previous regime in the bureaucracy and in the judiciary. Ibn al-Furāt, the former wazīr, was confirmed in place as were the chief *qāḍī* and the *khaṭīb* of the Old Mosque in Fusṭāṭ. Jawhar also tried whenever possible to reenlist the officers of the Ikhshīdid and Kāfūrid armies. Still, the acquisition of Egypt was, for the Fāṭimids, only a step – albeit a major step – towards Baghdād; their goal remained universal in respect to the Islamic world and Egypt was thus, for them, one more province of a wider empire. Equally, they hoped to convert to Shiʿism as much of the population as possible, since only in that way could they gain the true loyalty of their new subjects and engage them in the larger common cause, but, as in north Africa, this task would be difficult if not impossible.

Jawhar's efforts to stabilize the Egyptian economy, then in a shambles, and to restore prosperity were immeasurably aided by preserving administrative continuity with the older regime along with an aggressive military campaign against both rebels and brigands who had previously added to the suffering and general chaos. Once he had assured himself of his position, however, the sizable Fāṭimid army of imported Berber troops and commanders were quickly apt to become a burden both in terms of provisioning and unruly interaction with the local populations. In line with the original aim of further expansion, they were dispatched fairly soon in the direction of Syria.

Under the command of a Berber chieftain, Jaʿfar ibn Falāḥ, they marched swiftly and successfully through Palestine to Damascus, which they seized for the Fāṭimids prior to raiding northward. Whether the Fāṭimids were ultimately headed toward Baghdād or merely conducting the promised jihād against the Byzantine Christians, or both, northern Syria had to be taken first. By 971 Ibn Falāḥ had come within range of the great city of Antioch. A Fāṭimid army that far north constituted a major penetration into the Byzantine sphere of influence but this initial raid collapsed almost at once.[40] Fāṭimid attempts to conqueror and control Syria failed then as they would countless times again.[41]

Ibn Falāḥ not only suffered a defeat by the Byzantines in northern Syria but had to face an enraged Qarmatian foe shortly thereafter in front of Damascus, where he was killed and his army soundly beaten. The Qarmatians, having no allegiance to their fellow Ismāʿīlīs, had gathered a broad

[40] Walker, "A Byzantine Victory Over the Fāṭimids at Alexandreta (971)," *Byzantion*, 42 (1972), 431–40.

[41] Bianquis, *Damas et la Syrie sous la domination fatimide (359–468/969–1076)*, 2 vols., (Damascus, 1986, 1989).

coalition of tribal forces out of the east and added to them renegade former soldiers from Ikhshīdid territories. This coalition now invaded Egypt, rampaging throughout the eastern Delta, and finally confronted Jawhar at his new encampment near what is now the site of the modern city of Heliopolis. The luck of the Fāṭimid commander held, however, and in late December 971, he ultimately forced the Qarmatians and their allies back and out of Egypt.

Already of great benefit to Jawhar was the increasingly fortified enclave he was building along the Nile north of the mosque of Ibn Ṭūlūn. It was, in fact, rapidly becoming a city and was then called al-Manṣūriyya in direct imitation of the city in Tunisia where the imām resided, named for its builder the Caliph al-Manṣūr, father of al-Muʿizz. The plan for the new capital was brought with Jawhar, and like its namesake it was given a northern gate called al-Futūḥ, a southern gate called al-Zawīla, and a central congregational mosque named al-Azhar.[42]

Separation of the Shiʿite army of occupation from the crowded Sunnī city of Fusṭāṭ also proved useful. Jawhar, like most of the Fāṭimids, was fully conscious of differences between the two religious parties. Egypt was then strongly Sunnī despite an observable respect for the members of the *Ahl al-Bayt* and their corporations of *ashrāf*-nobility. The heads of both Ḥasanid and Ḥusaynid families readily acquiesced in the rule of Fāṭimid imams whom they apparently accepted as blood relatives and family, but they showed little or no sign of adopting Ismāʿīlī Shiʿism. Minimal steps were made by Jawhar to introduce Shiʿite ritual and those with care and suitable caution. The Shiʿite formula in the call to prayer was used first in the mosque of Ibn Ṭūlūn (March 970) and only later in the Old Mosque of ʿAmr in Fusṭāṭ.[43] The Ismāʿīlī method of determining the end of Ramaḍān caused difficulties in the earliest instance because the Shiʿites at al-Manṣūriyya broke the fast one day ahead of the Sunnīs in Fusṭāṭ. Later, however, more Shiʿite practices entered Egypt, such as celebration of the event of Ghadīr Khumm and the elaborate emotional mourning of ʿĀshūrāʾ. If and when the Sunnīs were separated physically from the Shiʿites, the friction was relatively small; if the regime tried to force the issue publicly, troubles and violence always ensued.

In Egypt many loyal subjects of the Fāṭimids accepted them as valid caliphs with full and legitimate rights to lead the Muslim community, but not in the absolute sense demanded in the Shiʿite theory of the imamate. Rather, the Fāṭimids were rulers like the ʿAbbāsids and, in this view, the claims of each were more or less comparable. True Ismāʿīlīs, called the

[42] On al-Manṣūriyya as the capital of the north African Fāṭimids, see Halm, *Reich des Mahdi*, 305–07, trans. 342–46. On its connection to the plan for Cairo, see 307 and 368, trans. 346 and 415–16.

[43] Ibn al-Athīr, *al-Kāmil*, VIII, 590.

"saints" (*awliyā'*), belonged to a more narrow spectrum of the population. They were, in their own view, the "believers" (*mu'minūn*) as opposed to the uninitiated masses who were simply "muslims" (*muslimūn*). Membership in this Ismā'īlī inner circle implied total devotion to the imam and to his orders and directives. Most Ismā'īlīs also attended regular sessions of prayer and instruction which gradually assumed greater importance, eventually becoming in Egypt the *majlis al-ḥikma* or *majlis al-da'wa*. Those who attended paid a fee called the *najwā* ("fee for a confidential discourse") or the *fiṭra* (contributions paid on the feast days), depending on the occasion.

Still, it is impossible to determine accurately what percentage of the population was actually Ismā'īlī, although, in Egypt as a whole, the numbers tended to remain small. There may have been an exception to this observation in the earliest phase of Fāṭimid rule. The chroniclers report waves of enthusiasm for the Ismā'īlī religious appeal during al-'Azīz's and the first portion of al-Ḥākim's reigns. On several occasions, attendance at the *da'wa*'s *majlis* session produced such large crowds that, twice in this early period, men died in the crush. From about the middle of al-Ḥākim's period, however, the numbers apparently began to decline markedly.[44] Thus Shi'ism remained the faith of a minority although the *da'wa* and its program of appeals and conversion continued its activity to the end of the Fāṭimid period. The most important institution of Ismā'īlī education, the *majlis al-ḥikma*, still under the supervision of the chief *dā'ī* of the empire, ceased in Egypt only when finally abolished by Ṣalāḥ al-Dīn in 1171, 200 years later.

Jawhar's ability to defeat the Qarmatians and generally to regulate the affairs of Egypt, coupled with the construction of a palace in the new capital city, convinced the Caliph al-Mu'izz that the moment had come finally to transfer the court. Like the conquest itself, this move was meticulously prepared. Revolts by the Zanāta Berbers in the central Maghrib caused serious difficulties at first and the Ḥamdūnids of Masīla,[45] once quite loyal to the Fāṭimids, went over to the Umayyads. Zīrī ibn Manād and other commanders sent after the rebels failed; Zīrī himself was killed by them. Only when Buluggīn[46] the son of Zīrī had won full revenge did quiet return to the western territories. It was Buluggīn, moreover, to whom the responsibility for the western domains of the Fāṭimid fell when al-Mu'izz departed.[47] Sicily was to remain under its long-time amīr from the family of al-Ḥasan

44 Walker, "The Ismā'īlī Da'wa in the Reign of the Fāṭimid Caliph al-Ḥākim," *JARCE* 30 (1993), 160–82.

45 M'sila (in currrent orthography) is located some 75m/125km southwest of Setif in Algeria. On its connection with the Fāṭimids, see F. Dachraoui, "Masīla," *EI2*.

46 There is a short notice on Buluggīn (in Arabic Buluqqīn or sometimes Bulukkīn) by H. R. Idris, *EI2*.

47 Daftary, *Ismā'īlīs*, 170–71; Halm, *Reich des Mahdi*, 368–69, 370, trans. 416–17, 418.

al-Kalbī.[48] As with the previous departure of Jawhar, large sums were collected and made ready for transport, along with great quantities of valuables and, most symbolic of the finality of this move, the coffins of the deceased Fāṭimid imāms. In November 972, the party set out, some by sea but most by land. They proceeded slowly and along the way several important figures died, including Ustādh Jawdhar, whose memoirs, the *Sīrat Ustādh Jawdhar*, are a vital source of information, and the famous Andulusian poet Ibn Hāniʾ.[49] In late May, al-Muʿizz reached Alexandria where he was met by a party of distinguished notables. Traversing the Delta en route to the capital, he was greeted by additional groups who came to him from the Egyptian capital, all of whom extended him the highest honors and recognition. Finally, in June 973, the imām entered the new al-Manṣūriyya which now became the City of al-Muʿizz's Victory, al-Qāhira al-Muʿizziyya, or more simply, Cairo.[50]

Cairo as the center of the Daʿwa

In one sense the arrival of the imam, which transformed the new city of Cairo into the seat of an empire, was itself an event that signalled the ultimate achievement of the Fāṭimids, especially of al-Muʿizz but also of his immediate predecessors, all of whom envisioned just this goal. However, in another sense, although for al-Muʿizz, who died only two and a half years later, it was the culmination of a long period of personal commitment, for the Ismāʿīlīs and the Shiʿites, Cairo was still not Baghdad and the hated ʿAbbāsid usurpers yet held power there. As they embellished their new headquarters, the Ismāʿīlīs were reaffirming its central importance as the residence of the living imam both politically and religiously. But the *daʿwa* would not cease, neither within the empire nor outside; if anything the triumph in Egypt encouraged expectations of total victory and spurred on the *dāʿīs* in distant lands to add their own individual contributions to the common vision of a total Shiʿite victory.

Away from the safety of direct Fāṭimid protection, the *daʿwa* continued to operate in secret as it had previously. The Egyptian Fāṭimid state grew as a

48 Daftary, *Ismāʿīlīs*, 156–7.

49 Halm, *Reich des Mahdi*, 370–71, trans. 419. Ibn Hāniʾ was murdered under mysterious circumstance en route. On him see Muḥammad al-Yaʿlāwī, *Ibn Hāniʾ al-Maghribī al-Andalusī* (Beirut, 1985) and the articles by F. Dachraoui, "Ibn Hāniʾ al-Andalusī," *EI2* and by Yalaoui (al-Yaʿlāwī), "Ibn Hâniʾ, poète Shîʾite et chantre des Fâtimides au Maghreb," *Les Africains*, VI (Paris, 1977) 99–125. Jawdhar died of old age. His *Sīra* is a rich source of documents and other information about the North African period, particularly for the reign of al-Muʿizz. The Arabic text was published by M. K. Husayn and M. ʿAbd al-Hādī Shaʿīra (Cairo, 1954); French trans. by M. Canard, *Vie de l'ustadh Jaudhar* (Algiers, 1958). See also Canard, "Djawdhar," *EI2*.

50 Halm, *Reich des Mahdi*, 371–72, trans. 419–20, and Daftary, *Ismāʿīlīs*, 175–76.

menace in the eyes of the ʿAbbāsids, and the danger to Ismāʿīlī agents and partisans in areas under Sunnī control increased accordingly. Still, we know that the agents of Fāṭimid Ismāʿīlism existed nearly everywhere, many now in close and direct contact with Cairo.

The non-Fāṭimid Qarmatian dissidents remained uncooperative, however, and threatened Egypt yet again. Their attack on Egypt during 974 was serious enough. With allies among the Syrian Bedouin tribes and with disaffected members of the Egyptian *ashrāf* under the leadership of Akhū Muḥsin, brother of the loyal Husaynid *sharīf*, they advanced against the Fāṭimids both in the Delta and near Akhmīm in Upper Egypt. With difficulty al-Muʿizz eventually defeated both contingents.[51] Only then did the Qarmatians all but disappear. Their decline occurred fairly rapidly and by the end of the tenth century they existed as no more than a small localized power. For a while they were even said to have recognized the Fāṭimids, although with little change in their doctrine, and they never accepted the Fāṭimid version of the imāmate.[52]

Many eastern Ismāʿīlīs did, however, and those who acceded to the Fāṭimid imamate now regarded Cairo as a destination of pilgrimage and as the center of Ismāʿīlī doctrine and teaching. *Dāʿīs* traveled to Egypt from distant regions, often carrying with them the fiscal contributions of far-off Ismāʿīlī communities, and they returned homeward with instructions and other orders from headquarters. Sizable groups of loyal supporters continued to exist in the Yemen, India and in parts of Arabia, as well as in areas of Iraq, Syria, and Iran.

Occasionally, the *dāʿīs* who visited Cairo were already or were later to become especially noteworthy in their own right. As an example the great philosophically minded theologian, Ḥamīd al-Dīn al-Kirmānī, who normally taught in Baghdād and Baṣra, was brought to Cairo late in the reign of al-Ḥākim. The chief of the *daʿwa*, Khatkīn al-Ḍayf, had requested his help and al-Kirmānī obliged, bringing to Egypt and to the *daʿwa* in Cairo much needed intellectual sophistication and rigor.[53] Al-Ḥākim's imamate had produced an unwanted and uncontrollable enthusiasm among a number of the *dāʿīs*, especially some from the east who arrived in Cairo with strange ideas about the divine nature of the imām. Al-Ḥākim himself had adopted an inexplicable style and an ascetic behavior quite at odds with that of either himself in his earlier years or that of any of his predecessors. As these

[51] Bianquis, "Prise du pouvoir," 98–102.

[52] On the end of the Qarmatians, see Madelung, "Ḳarmaṭī," *EI2*; and Daftary, *Ismāʿīlīs*, 220–22, 183–84, and 175–76.

[53] On al-Kirmānī's role in Cairo, see J. van Ess, "Biobibliographische Notizen zur islamischen Theologie," *WO*, 9 (1977/78), 255–61, and *Chiliastische Erwartungen und die Versuchung der Göttlichkeit. Der Khalif al-Ḥākim (386–411)* (Heidelberg, 1977). 2 Abhandlung; and Walker, "The Ismāʿīlī Daʿwa," 160–82.

enthusiasts began to ascribe to him ever more elaborate powers, including eventually outright divinity, al-Ḥākim either refused to take notice of them or possibly deliberately and knowingly tolerated their exaggerations. The *daʿwa* was, however, horrified; these preachers had after all once been *dāʿīs* themselves but had now gone seriously astray. Their arguments about the divinity of the imām were, moreover, quite familiar among the Shīʿa who had seen doctrines like this advocated by extremists (*ghulāt*) on many earlier occasions. Al-Kirmānī, on behalf of the central *daʿwa*, wrote several tracts against them refuting vigorously their absurd claims and they were soon forced underground, partly through his efforts and partly as a result of mob action and military force. In its general outlines but with later doctrinal modifications and additions, the original movement of those who tried to recognize the divinity of al-Ḥākim survived as the Druze. They failed or were suppressed in Egypt quickly but not long afterward found a home among some rural communities of the Lebanese mountains.[54]

Al-Kirmānī had returned to his home base in Iraq even before the Druze affair ended and was already there, in fact, prior to the disappearance of al-Ḥākim in 1021. Characteristically, we know almost nothing else about his life and career except for this one visit to Cairo. Were it not for a surviving body of writings that are, however, impressive for their contribution both to philosophy and to theology, his role in defending the imamate of al-Ḥākim might be the only evidence of his career in the *daʿwa*.[55]

The two main instigators of the trouble that had spawned the Druze, Hamza ibn ʿAlī and Muḥammad ibn Ismāʿīl al-Darazī, were, like al-Kirmānī, *dāʿīs* from the east, the one Persian, the other Turkish. Many others like them traveled to Cairo over the course of the dynasty, attracted there both by Ismāʿīlī devotions and by its Shiʿism. Thirty years after al-Kirmānī's visit, two of the most famous, Nāṣir-i Khusraw and Mu'ayyad fi'l-Dīn al-Shīrāzī, arrived in Cairo almost at the same moment, although both had come separately from different areas of Iran. Both men subsequently wrote personal accounts of their travels and adventures, both became poets, and both authored major books of Ismāʿīlī doctrine. Their respective careers in the Ismāʿīlī *daʿwa*, which resembled each other sharply in many respects, were, however, quite distinct in the long run. Yet both were distinguished representatives of the *daʿwa* and they well illustrate how it performed its larger mission in the middle of the eleventh century when they were most active.

[54] On the Druze origins in Fāṭimid Cairo, see D. Bryer, "The Origins of the Druze Religion," *Der Islam*, 52 (1975), 47–83, 239–62, and 53 (1976), 5–27; Daftary, *Ismāʿīlīs*, 195–200.

[55] On the philosophical contribution of al-Kirmānī, see now D. De Smet, *La Quiétude de l'Intellect: Néoplatonisme et gnose ismaélienne dans l'oeuvre de Ḥamīd ad-Dīn al-Kirmānī (Xe/XIe s.)* (Leuven, 1995).

Al-Shīrāzī came from an Ismāʿīlī family and his father was previously a *dāʿī*. Nāṣir's entry into the *daʿwa* is a matter of speculation and it is not certain exactly when he became Ismāʿīlī. Both men had grown dissatisfied or disaffected with conditions where they then lived – al-Shīrāzī had fallen into disfavor because of his activities and influence on behalf of the *daʿwa* with the Buyid Amir – and they set off for Cairo at about the same time, arriving there in 1046 and 1047 respectively. Each of them was then in his forties. At the time the head of the *daʿwa* in Cairo was the great-grandson of Qāḍi al-Nuʿmān, a man of minimal distinction and hardly the intellectual match of either of these two younger Persian immigrants. Al-Shīrāzī already prided himself on his command of Arabic style which he employed with skill both to promote himself and to embarrass his detractors. Nāṣir had made his journey, so he says in his own account, purely as a pilgrimage to Mecca. Significantly, that pilgrimage took him also to Cairo for an extended stay in between visits to the holy cities.[56]

From this point the careers of al-Shīrāzī and Nāṣir diverge. Nāṣir-i Khusraw returned to Khurāsān, where his activities on behalf of the Ismāʿīlī *daʿwa* brought him endless trials and tribulations and eventually forced his exile to the remote back-country of Yumgān. Still, he wrote a full dīwān of Persian poetry, which though often containing allusions to his Ismāʿīlī leanings, earned him a deserved literary reputation in itself. In addition he managed to write a number of important works on Ismāʿīlī doctrine which are themselves noteworthy, in part because Nāṣir composed them in Persian rather than Arabic. In contrast, al-Shīrāzī was sent as a special agent to Syria and Iraq where he was to support a major uprising against the ʿAbbāsids. He then returned to Cairo and held various posts in the *daʿwa* until ultimately becoming the *dāʿī al-duʿāt* or chief *dāʿī* of the empire, a position he retained for twenty years with a few minor interruptions. His writings included, besides an autobiography and a dīwān of Arabic poetry, a massive collection of some 800 lectures that he, as head of the *daʿwa*, had given in the weekly sessions of the *majlis al-ḥikma* in Cairo.[57]

Except for their literary attainments, the career pattern of these two *dāʿī*s was repeated by many others. Two more like them are particularly impor-

[56] Daftary, *Ismāʿīlīs*, 213–18.

[57] On the writings of both men, particularly their Ismāʿīlī works, see Ismail Poonawala, *Biobibliography of Ismāʿīlī Literature* (Malibu, 1977). The major titles by Nāṣir are his *Diwan*, of which there are numerous editions and English translations of some individual poems, the *Safar-nāma*, ed. with French translation, Charles Schefer, as *Sefer nameh: relation du voyage de Nassiri Khosrau* (Paris, 1881), with several later editions; English translation, W. M. Thackston Jr., *Nāṣer-e Khosraw's Book of Travels* (Albany, NY, 1986), the *Zād al-musāfirīn, Wajh al-dīn, Shish Faṣl, Khwān al-ikhwān, and Jāmiʿal-hikmatayn.* Mu'ayyad's *Dīwān* and *Sīra* were edited and published by M. Kāmil Ḥusayn in Cairo, 1949. Portions of his *al-Majālis al-Mu'ayyadiyya* were published by M. Ghalīib in Beirut, vols. I and III, 1974–84.

tant: Ḥasan ibn al-Ṣabbāḥ from Iran and Lamak ibn Malik al-Ḥammādī from the Yemen. Lamak was the chief Ismāʿīlī *Qāḍi* of the Yemen and a *dāʿī* when he was sent to Cairo by the Ismāʿīlī ruler and himself chief *dāʿī*, ʿAlī ibn Muḥammad al-Ṣulayḥī. He arrived in Egypt in 454/1062 and remained there five years.[58] Ḥasan ibn al-Ṣabbāḥ had been active in the Iranian *daʿwa* under ʿAbd al-Malik ibn ʿAṭṭāsh, who likewise dispatched his subordinate to Egypt where he was to spend three years (1078–1081). Both these cases are especially relevant because the future direction of the international *daʿwa* eventually depended on these same agents at a major juncture in the history of Ismāʿīlīsm. In the aftermath of the Nizārī-Mustaʿlī schism, it was Ḥasan who engineered the secession of the eastern, especially Iranian, *daʿwa*, and it was Lamak, by contrast, who played a key role in preserving Yemeni loyalty to Cairo and to the imamate of al-Mustaʿlī.[59]

Eastern successes

The purpose of these *dāʿīs* and the *daʿwa* for which they worked was not primarily to promote Ismāʿīlī loyalty in Egypt, of course, but rather to spread it abroad. Although *dāʿīs* continued to preach and convert Muslims to Ismāʿīlīsm inside Fāṭimid territory, the *daʿwa* scored its major successes elsewhere. The old goal of supplanting the ʿAbbāsid caliphate never disappeared but, as the possibility of sending an army from Cairo to Baghdad faded, the *daʿwa* had to fulfill a similar task. Syria receded more and more from the grasp of Cairo. As it did, the *daʿwa* became the only hope. Agents expended great effort and funds to convert and enlist allies near the ʿAbbāsid capital. On one occasion in 401/1010–11, for example, the ʿUqaylid Amir Qārwash ibn al-Muqallad, who controlled the Iraqi cities of Mawṣil and Kūfa, among others, proclaimed his allegiance to the Fāṭimids. This particular success of the *daʿwa*, although spectacular and certainly a glaring affront to the ʿAbbasids, was quite temporary. The ʿAbbāsids, moreover, retaliated not only by convincing Qārwash to renounce his Fāṭimid allegiance in short order, but in the following year, by assembling in Baghdād a distinguished group of Twelver Shiʿite authorities and members of the Ahl al-Bayt who, under government prodding, promptly issued a stinging denunciation of Fāṭimid genealogy which, according to this manifesto, was entirely bogus: the Fāṭimids were not descendants of ʿAlī and Fāṭima at all. This was a theme the ʿAbbāsids returned to frequently; another similar proclamation was issued from Baghdād in 444/1052.

[58] Daftary, "Hasan-i Ṣabbāḥ and the Origins of the Nizārī Ismaʿili Movement," in Daftary *Mediaeval Ismaʿili History*, 181–204; Daftary, *Ismāʿilis*, 209–10; Abbas Hamdani, "The Dāʿī Ḥātim Ibn Ibrāhīm al-Ḥāmidī (d. 596 H./1199 AD) and his Book *Tuḥfat al-Qulūb*," *Oriens*, 23–24 (1970–71), 258–300.

[59] Daftary, *Ismāʿilis*, 284–5.

It should be noted that the Fāṭimids in a similar way had often circulated derogatory rejections of ʿAbbasid "genealogy," in which they did not, of course, deny descent from the prophet's uncle ʿAbbās but pointed out, instead, that such lineage was practically worthless in term of religious merit and legitimacy. ʿAbbās had simply been of little or no consequence, certainly none that counted.

Fāṭimid influence outside their political domain, however, depended on the success of the *daʿwa* against the counter-propaganda of their various enemies of which the Baghdād Manifesto of 402/1011–12 was but one example. It also fell victim to the vagaries of local conflicts, some religious and others political, military or economic. In 440/1048, for example, the Zīrīd Amir of north Africa, al-Muʿizz ibn Bādīs, succumbed to various pressures exerted internally by the Maliki *fuqahāʾ* of his realm, and he renounced the Fāṭimids by declaring for the ʿAbbāsids. Although the actions in that year did not result in an irreversible break, they signalled a shift in sentiment and symbolically indicated the end of Fāṭimid influence in north Africa.[60] In the Yemen, the *daʿwa* fared better. After Ibn Ḥawshab, the original mission languished for a long time but revived dramatically in the middle of the eleventh century under the Ṣulayḥids who came to dominate Yemen as a whole and who remained a major force there until 532/1138.[61]

Still, given that the old dream of the Fāṭimids was to take Baghdād, the most impressive success of its *daʿwa* must surely be the victory of the Amīr al-Basāsīrī, who captured the ʿAbbāsid capital in 450/1058. Al-Basāsīrī and those who joined his cause were, moreover, the beneficiaries of direct Fāṭimid support and encouragement. Mu'ayyad fi'l-Dīn al-Shīrāzī was, in fact, the agent plenipotentiary responsible for orchestrating an elaborate scheme to thwart a Seljuk takeover in Iraq and Syria, as well as to ensure Shiʿite dominance in Baghdad. The ardently Sunnī Seljuk Sultan Ṭughril, for his part, had fully intended to eradicate Shiʿite influence and march all the way to Egypt to bring Fāṭimid rule to an end. Although al-Basāsīrī was himself Turkish in origin, he evidently had Shīʿī leanings, as did a number of the Arab tribal leaders in Iraq who aided him. Al-Mu'ayyad carried large sums of money and great numbers of weapons from Cairo and donated them to the effort. In this case the *daʿwa* was backed heavily and directly by the government in Egypt, at least in the initial phase of this undertaking.[62]

At a critical moment, the Seljuks were weakened temporarily by internal quarrels. Although Ṭughril had already seized Baghdād, he found it necessary to leave in order to put down a rebellion by his own brother who, like

[60] Daftary, *Ismāʿīlīs*, 211–12.

[61] Daftary, *Ismāʿīlīs*, 208–11.

[62] al-Maqrīzī, *Ittiʿāẓ al-hunafāʾ bi-akhbār al-aʾimma al-fātimiyyīn al-khulafāʾ*, I, ed. J. al-Shayyāl (Cairo, 1967); II–III, ed. M. Hilmī M. Aḥmad (Cairo, 1971, 1973), II, 232–237, 251–258; M. Canard, "al-Basāsīrī," *EI2*.

other amīrs in this complex conflict between Seljuks and Fāṭimids, toyed with the emissaries of Cairo to gain whatever advantage and support they might offer him. Several times various cities of Iraq and Syria announced allegiance to Cairo, only to fall away almost immediately. The crowning moment, however, came when al-Basāsīrī entered Baghdād in late December 1058. Shortly thereafter, in January 1059, he attacked and ransacked the palace of the ʿAbbāsid caliph. Subsequent to al-Basāsīrī's takeover, the *khuṭba* was offered in the name of al-Mustanṣir the Fāṭimid imam for almost a year. Baghdād belonged to the Fāṭimids, at least nominally, and the pleasure of the imām al-Mustanṣir at this victory was dampened only by al-Basāsīrī's failure to seize and then transport the ʿAbbāsid Caliph al-Qā'im to Cairo.

By then all parties must have begun to re-assess the situation. The Fāṭimids had expended vast resources to back a doubtful venture for which they soon found reason to express regret; al-Basāsīrī's main interests were local and, when Ṭughril was free again to concentrate his might against him, the amīr fled Baghdād and was killed shortly afterward. The Seljuks and the Sunnīs came out of the affair stronger than before and the Shīʿīs, in general, lost ground to them everywhere except in Egypt. Two of the most formidable enemies of the Ismāʿīlīs, the wazīr Niẓām al-Mulk and the theologian al-Ghazzālī, rose to prominence in the wake of this Seljuk restoration of Sunnī power.[63]

The rise of the Seljuks did not, however, diminish the resistance of the eastern Ismāʿīlīs, whose *daʿwa* began to take the lead in opposition to the widely perceived oppression of the Sunnī Turks against the indigenous Persians. The same Ḥasan ibn al-Ṣabbāḥ who had visited Cairo in the late 1070s now assumed a major role by going over to open revolt against the Seljuks. In September 1090, he seized the fortress of Alamūt in northern Iran and began to piece together an Ismāʿīlī state out of disparate and often isolated communities and mountain castles. His was a political territory largely without either a center or a land connection between its parts. At the time of his revolt, Ḥasan, as he had been since his conversion to the Ismāʿīlī faith, was loyal to the imām in Cairo, al-Mustanṣir. He never wavered in that allegiance and, for a period, the Fāṭimids through him controlled, in theory, a string of fortresses and other Ismāʿīlī holdings throughout Iran. They would likewise bear some remote credit for Ḥasan's successful assassination of the fervently anti-Ismāʿīlī wazīr Niẓām al-Mulk in October of 1092.[64]

[63] Later medieval Egyptian historians observed about this temporary triumph of al-Basāsīrī that "This incident was the last success of the Fāṭimid dynasty." Ibn Muyassar, *Akhbār miṣr*, ed. A. F. Sayyid (Cairo, 1981) 21; al-Maqrīzī, *Ittiʿāẓ*, II, 257.

[64] M. G. S. Hodgson, *The Order of Assassins* (The Hague, 1955); B. Lewis, *The Assassins: A Radical Sect in Islam* (New York, 1968); Daftary, *Ismāʿīlīs*, 335–71.

Schisms and survival

The revival of a strong *daʿwa* in the east, however, did not bear the fruit it promised when it began. At the death of al-Mustanṣir after a reign of over sixty years, several of his sons claimed the imāmate, and the Ismāʿīlīs both in Egypt and abroad now suffered a severe succession crisis. In Cairo the local strong man al-Afḍal, son and heir of Badr al-Jamālī, supported the youngest of al-Mustanṣir's many sons who assumed the imamate with the name al-Mustaʿlī. Of the other sons who felt they possessed a claim, Nizār, the oldest, immediately countered by declaring his own imāmate and going into open revolt against the Cairene establishment which was, however, firmly in the hands of al-Afḍal.

This dispute, the first real succession crisis in the Fāṭimid dynasty, resulted in a dramatic breakup of the *daʿwa* outside Egypt. Internally, al-Afḍal put down the supporters of Nizār, had Nizār himself killed, and forced the Nizāriyya, as the partisans of his imamate came to be called, including Nizār's descendants, to flee the country. In Iran, Iraq and parts of Syria where Ḥasan ibn al-Ṣabbāḥ directed the *daʿwa*, the outcome was quite different. Ḥasan had quickly declared for Nizār and once on that course refused to change. He would not accept a *daʿwa* on behalf of al-Mustaʿlī, whom he regarded thereafter as a usurper. He and his immediate successors continued to act in the name of Nizār or of Nizār's descendants. There were, in fact, a number of Nizār's sons as well as brothers who escaped Egypt and some of them rose in rebellion in later years.[65]

Ḥasan's rejection of al-Mustaʿlī and his line was not merely a sign of eastern independence. The Nizārīs retained an interest in Egypt and pursued there a campaign for revenge at least until the death of Ḥasan himself in 1124. Nevertheless, the eastern Nizārī Ismāʿīlī state, which now became entirely separated from the Cairo caliphate, was itself coterminous with the Seljuk empire. To emphasize the newness of their role, Ḥasan described the doctrines he advocated as the New *Daʿwa* (*al-daʿwa al-jadīda*) and, with the exceptions of the Ismāʿīlīs who followed him in Syria, most if not all began to use Persian rather than Arabic and they progressively lost contact with much of the older Ismāʿīlī literary heritage.

The imāmate in Cairo, which lost a sizable portion of its world-wide following because of the Nizārī–Mustaʿlī schism, held on to the important Ismāʿīlī communities of the Yemen and India which accepted the succession that had been decreed by the authorities in Egypt. In contrast to the distant provinces of Iran and Iraq, the Yemen had been carefully cultivated by Cairo in the latter period of al-Mustanṣir, after Badr al-Jamālī assumed control over the *daʿwa*. In the aftermath of al-Basāsīrī and the rise of the Seljuks, the

[65] Walker, "Succession to Rule in the Shiʿite Caliphate," *JARCE*, 32 (1995), 239–64, 254–6.

Fāṭimids, or at least those who ran their affairs in Egypt, focused their attention on the Yemen and India while allowing the Iranian *daʿwa* to function more and more on its own. That is evident from a number of governmental decrees, now preserved in the collection called *al-Sijillāt al-Mustanṣiriyya*,[66] dispatched to the Yemen after Badr al-Jamālī had taken power. It is also plainly borne out by the loyalty of the Yemeni *daʿwa* to al-Mustaʿlī and his son al-Āmir rather than to Nizār or his descendants.

When al-Āmir was murdered, however, this connection between Cairo and the Yemen was finally broken. What lay behind this latter rupture may not be more than the accident of not having a visible and properly designated claimant to the imamate. Al-Āmir had announced the succession of his only male child, who happened to be born only months prior to his own untimely death. The infant, called al-Ṭayyib, was immediately recognized in the Yemen and accepted as the new imam. The death of al-Āmir confirmed this fact; there could be no other result. In Cairo matters proceeded differently; al-Ṭayyib was ignored or forgotten. Eventually, a cousin of al-Āmir was proclaimed imam with the name al-Ḥāfiẓ and his partisans became thereafter the Ḥāfiẓiyya.[67] They comprised the main support of the last Fāṭimids. Ḥāfiẓī Ismāʿīlīs, based primarily in Egypt and parts of Syria with some pockets in the Yemen, were thus pitted now against Ṭayyibī Ismāʿīlīs who were mainly Yemeni with a secondary population in India.

Although Ḥāfiẓī Ismāʿīlism continued actively in Egypt until the end of the Fāṭimid dynasty and slightly beyond, it eventually died out, leaving almost no record of its doctrinal position except in regard to the arguments for its version of the imamate. Nizārī Ismāʿīlism, in contrast, flourished from its inception under Ḥasan ibn al-Ṣabbāḥ until it was virtually eradicated by the Mongols in 1256. It was never totally wiped out, however, and thus survived, its later adherents becoming the modern Ismāʿīlīs of Iran, India, and Syria who recognize the Aga Khans as their imams. Ṭayyibī Ismāʿīlīs are represented now by groups in the Yemen and in India where they are called Bohras. Unlike the Nizārī branch which broke with its Arabic past, the Ṭayyibīs, moreover, preserved an Arabic literary tradition that runs continuously from modern times back to the earliest years of the Fāṭimids. In the post-Fāṭimid period, Ṭayyibī scholars in the Yemen were especially active collectors and preservers of older Ismāʿīlī works of all kinds. Nearly

[66] Edited by ʿAbd al-Munʿim Mājid (Cairo, 1954).

[67] The best and most complete account of Ḥāfiẓī Ismāʿīlism is Daftary, *Ismāʿīlīs*, 264–69, 273–84, but see also Samuel M. Stern, "The Succession to the Fāṭimid Imam al-Amir, the Claims of the later Fāṭimids to the Imamate, and the Rise of Tayyibi Ismāʿīlism," *Oriens*, 4 (1951), 193–255; and Paula Sanders, "Claiming the Past: Ghadīr Khumm and the Rise of Ḥāifiẓī Historiography in Late Fāṭimid Egypt," *SI*, fasc. 75 (1992), 81–104.

all of the Ismāʿīlī sources for Fāṭimid history or doctrines that now exist are due to this effort; almost without exception they owe their preservation to the concern of Yemeni Ṭayyibīs for their own Fāṭimid past. Particularly for the Ṭayyibīs, who prefer the designation *Fāṭimī* (i.e. Fāṭimid) for themselves rather than *Ismāʿīlī* but also for the Nizārīs, Fāṭimid Egypt remains the land where the imāms they recognize lived and died and it continues therefore to constitute sacred territory until today.

6

The Fāṭimid state, 969–1171

PAULA A. SANDERS

Fāṭimid political history

At the heart of the Fāṭimid state lay the imamate, which challenged both the political hegemony and the religious authority of the Sunnī ʿAbbasid caliphate. The Fāṭimids were a sect of Shīʿīs, that is, one of several groups who argued that ʿAlī ibn Abī Ṭālib should have succeeded the Prophet Muhammad as head of the Islamic community of believers. These partisans of ʿAlī (*shīʿa*, hence the term *Shīʿī*) also eventually claimed that the headship of the Islamic community should rest with the descendants of ʿAlī and his wife Fāṭima, the daughter of the Prophet. They also believed that the descendants of ʿAlī and Fāṭima had inherited special authority to interpret the Qurʾan and religious law and belief. Disputes among different groups of Shīʿīs often centered, therefore, around genealogy. The Fāṭimids traced their own descent through Ismāʿīl, one of the early Shīʿī imams, and thus we call them Ismāʿīlī.

When the Fāṭimids came to Egypt, they had already worked out their genealogical claims in detail, moved from being a secret missionary group to an openly declared caliphate, and founded a state in Ifriqiyya (modern-day Tunisia).[1] The turning-point for the dynasty came with the accession of the fourth Fāṭimid imām-caliph, al-Muʿizz li-dīn Allāh in 342/953. In 358/969, he succeeded in conquering Egypt after three unsuccessful attempts by his predecessors. The relatively bloodless campaign was led by his general Jawhar, who founded a new capital city, Cairo, just two miles north of the original Arab capital Fusṭāṭ. Several years later, al-Muʿizz moved his court from north Africa to Cairo, and Egypt remained the center of the Fāṭimid empire until the end of the dynasty in 1171. Al-Muʿizz also carried out a successful program of propaganda in the holy cities of Mecca and Medina, where local rulers recognized Fāṭimid rule until the eleventh century.

[1] For these developments, see chapter 5 above.

The reign of al-Muʿizz's successor al-ʿAzīz (ruled 365–86/975–96) was dominated by his ambition to control southern and central Syria, and in this period the Fāṭimid empire reached its greatest extent. Egypt flourished under al-ʿAzīz, who introduced a series of military reforms. He fixed the rates of pay for his army and court personnel, and he brought Turkish slave troops into the army. These Turkish troops rose to prominence at the expense of the Berbers who had brought the Fāṭimids to power. They were often at odds with both the Berbers and new regiments of black slave troops, beginning a history of factional strife that would continue to plague the Fāṭimid army.

Al-ʿAzīz was succeeded by al-Ḥākim (ruled 386–411/996–1020), perhaps the best-known Fāṭimid caliph. His reign has been the object of much study, and modern scholars have puzzled over his often erratic behavior. In a state that had been marked by its tolerance of Jews, Christians, and Sunnīs, al-Ḥākim introduced numerous repressive measures against those groups. However, he often repealed those measures as suddenly as he announced them. His eccentricities were a source of encouragement to a small group who believed him to be an incarnation of divinity. This group, the Druze, believed that when he disappeared in 411/1020, he had gone into concealment and would return at a later time. It appears, however, that al-Ḥākim was murdered by his own sister, Sitt al-Mulk, not only because of the threats his unpredictable behavior posed to the dynasty, but also because of his plan to make a cousin his successor, a move that would have violated the fundamental Ismāʿīlī principle of father-to-son succession. Sitt al-Mulk also did away with the troublesome cousin and ensured the accession of al-Ẓāhir (ruled 411–27/1020–35) to the throne, averting what could have become an early schism, and acted as regent. Al-Ẓāhir's undistinguished reign was marred by famine and internal unrest as well as by a series of foreign relations failures, most notably with the Byzantines. Nonetheless, in the early years of the long reign of al-Mustanṣir (ruled 427–87/1035–94), the Fāṭimid state was prosperous and its rulers had access to considerable financial resources.

The Persian traveler Nasir-i Khusrau reported, in the aftermath of a visit to Egypt in 1047–48, that the caliphs owned all the shops in Cairo – numbering 20,000 (an inflated figure, to be sure), and collected rent of between 2 and 10 *dinars* each month from each one – the caravanserais and bath-houses in Cairo, and an additional 8,000 revenue-producing buildings in Cairo and Fusṭāṭ. However, starting in the 1060s, a series of low Niles resulted in intermittent famine for nearly twenty years and compelled the caliph to appeal to the Byzantine emperor for grain. In addition, the factional fighting of rival Turkish and black slave soldiers escalated into open warfare, inaugurating a period called by medieval chroniclers *al-shidda* (the calamity). The Caliph al-Mustanṣir was forced to sell the dynasty's immense treasuries of costumes, jewelry, and ceremonial arms in order to placate the army. But the situation continued to deteriorate, and in 465/1073, al-Mustanṣir asked the governor of Acre, Badr al-Jamālī, for help.

Badr, a freed slave of Armenian origin, arrived in Egypt in the winter of 1073 and restored order in a matter of months. With a private army composed largely of Armenian soldiers, he crushed the Turkish troops in the capital. Drought and factional fighting in the provinces had prevented the cultivation of agricultural land for several years; there was famine; parts of Cairo had been decimated by looting; poverty was widespread, affecting even the Fāṭimid family. Badr crushed the fighting factions in the provinces, cultivated the support of the merchant class in pursuing a policy of law and order, and suspended taxes for three years in order to allow the peasants time to begin cultivating their land again. His policies succeeded in restoring order and creating the conditions which, once the drought was over, allowed the economic recovery of the country.

Badr's power, unlike that of previous wazīrs, did not depend upon the direct patronage of the caliph; he had an independent base of power, his army, and his title *amīr al-juyūsh* (commander of the armies) was no mere honorific. Badr's arrival inaugurated a century of rule by military wazīrs with their own armies that persisted until the end of the Fāṭimid state. He assumed leadership of the civil bureaucracy, the military, and the propaganda mission. After Badr, Fāṭimid wazīrs were almost exclusively military officers, and they were the real rulers of the state.

Badr died in 487/1094, only a few months before the Caliph al-Mustanṣir, and was succeeded in the wazīrate by his son al-Afḍal. Al-Afḍal installed the younger son of al-Mustanṣir as the Caliph al-Mustaʿlī (ruled 487–95/1094–1101). The first five Egyptian Fāṭimids (al-Muʿizz, al-ʿAzīz, al-Ḥākim, al-Ẓāhir, al-Mustanṣir) were eldest sons, and the Fāṭimid family itself appeared to have adhered to the succession of the eldest son. The Nizārīs, or supporters of the dispossessed elder son Nizār, never accepted the legitimacy of al-Mustaʿlī and his line, and they worked actively, but unsuccessfully, to overthrow the Fāṭimid government. The short reign of al-Mustaʿlī was dominated by the Nizārī threat and by al-Afḍal's relatively successful attempts to recapture lost territories. In 495/1101, al-Afḍal raised a five-year-old son of al-Mustaʿlī to the throne. This caliph, al-Āmir (r. 495–524/1101–30), remained under the thumb of al-Afḍal until the latter's death in 515/1121.

After al-Afḍal's death, al-Āmir was able to reassert some of the power of the caliph, and he ruled directly after imprisoning his wazīr al-Ma'mūn al-Baṭā'iḥī in 519/1125. But al-Āmir's rule was challenged constantly by the Nizārīs, as well as by marauding Berber tribes. In 516/1125 he issued a proclamation that asserted the legitimacy of al-Mustaʿlī's line, but in 524/1130 he was assassinated by the Nizārīs. At his death, al-Āmir is said to have left an infant son, al-Ṭayyib. A cousin of the late caliph, ʿAbd al-Majīd, was named as regent by factions of the army. However, the son of al-Afḍal, Abū ʿAlī Kutayfāt, overthrew the government, confiscated the palace treasuries, and imprisoned ʿAbd al-Majīd. He also deposed the Fāṭimid line in favor of the expected imam of the Twelver Shīʿīs. Abū ʿAlī Kutayfāt remained in power for a little over a year and was murdered in 526/1131. At that time, ʿAbd al-Majīd was restored as regent; but the infant al-Ṭayyib had disappeared, and there was no apparent heir. ʿAbd al-Majīd thus proclaimed himself the imam with the title al-Ḥāfiẓ (ruled 524–44/1130–49). His authority was contested both by the Nizārīs, who opposed the Mustaʿlian line altogether, and by the Ṭayyibīs, who maintained that al-Ṭayyib was in concealment in the Yemen.

The last three Fāṭimid caliphs, al-Ẓāfir (ruled 544–49/1149–54), al-Fā'iz (ruled 549–55/1154–60) and al-ʿĀḍid (ruled 555–66/1160–71) came from the Ḥāfiẓī line. All were children, and the last few years of Fāṭimid rule were essentially a contest for power between generals and wazīrs. The last wazīr of the Fāṭimid caliphs was Ṣalāḥ al-Dīn, best known to modern readers as the heroic figure who successfuly recaptured Jerusalem from the crusaders. But he also dealt the final blow to the Fāṭimid caliphate. In 566/1171, Ṣalāḥ al-Dīn had the name of the ʿAbbāsid caliph read in the mosques of Cairo for the first time in over 200 years. A few days later, the last Fāṭimid caliph died.

The military and its role in the Fāṭimid state

Over the course of some 200 years of rule, the Fāṭimid military underwent dramatic changes in its structure and composition, and these changes were accompanied by equally important changes in the army's role in Fāṭimid society. The central position of the military was not restricted to its role in expanding the realm or defending its territories. By the late Fāṭimid period, the state itself had become militarized so that the army was involved in almost every aspect of Fāṭimid government and administration. Thus, understanding the military and its role is fundamental to understanding the character of the Fāṭimid state.

The Fāṭimids had come to power in north Africa and conquered Egypt largely on the strength and loyalty of a Berber tribal army. One Berber tribe, the Kutāma, were so central to the army that their affairs were administered by a special Office of the Kutāma, and they received many privileges, including exemption from taxation. Their loyalty was an enormous boon to the Fāṭimids, but they exhibited one distinct shortcoming: they were not skilled in archery. Therefore, when the Berber Fāṭimid army began to expand into Syria and encountered Turkish troops who were skilled archers, they suffered defeat. The need for archers was clear, particularly since Turks dominated the armies of the ʿAbbāsid caliphs, whose lands the Fāṭimids coveted. So the second Fāṭimid caliph, al-ʿAzīz billāh (ruled 365–86/

975–96), introduced Turkish troops into his army. At the same time, the *ḥujra* (barracks) system for training slave soldiers, first introduced by the ʿAbbāsids in the late ninth century, was incorporated into the Fāṭimid military structure. In the barracks, the new Turkish military slaves learned archery. Following a pattern that was already familiar in the Islamic world, these Turkish troops soon rose to prominence, playing a central role in defining the character of the Fāṭimid state.[2]

The diversification of the army continued under Caliph al-Ḥākim, who increased the numbers of black slaves in his army (*ʿabīd al-shirā'*). By the middle of the eleventh century, the Fāṭimid army included several different ethnic groups with martial specialties: the Berbers were cavalry fighting with lances, the blacks were heavy infantry, the Daylams (a group originating in the area southwest of the Caspian Sea) were light infantry using bows and javelins, and the Turks were mounted archers.[3]

These changes in the composition of the army were accompanied by shifting alliances. The Kutāma Berbers, the original mainstay of the army, felt sufficiently threatened by the growing power of the Turks to insist that one of their own, Ibn ʿAmmār, become the chief of the *dīwāns* upon the death of al-ʿAzīz. The blatant favoritism that Ibn ʿAmmār showed to the Kutāma provoked the Turks to depose him and install their own candidate in office. A few years later, in 1020, the Turks and the Kutāma formed a coalition against the black troops, who rioted to protest against the favors granted to the other groups. The black troops pillaged and burned Fusṭāṭ, where both Kutāma and Turkish soldiers had put down roots, even marrying into the local population. In this period, the Fāṭimid army was a multi-ethnic force, plagued by competition and factionalism that was kept in check by maintaining a delicate balance among its different elements, and between the army as a whole and the dynasty.

By the 1060s, however, this balance had begun to fail, and factional fighting culminated in a civil war between the black and Turkish troops. Desperate and unable to restore order, the Caliph al-Mustanṣir summoned the governor of Acre, Badr al-Jamālī, who arrived in Egypt with his own army in 1073. Badr's army was composed of several different ethnic groups, including Armenians. In his restructuring of the Fāṭimid army, Armenian Christians, serving in both infantry and cavalry units, came to predominate. These Armenian soldiers had no local ties and, therefore, their loyalty could be assured by their dependence upon Badr's patronage.[4] Badr also brought in large numbers of military slaves, whose loyalty could also be assured

[2] For these developments, see Yaacov Lev, *State and Society in Fatimid Egypt* (Leiden, 1991), 81–92; William Hamblin, "The Fāṭimid Army during the Early Crusades" (Ph.D. dissertation, University of Michigan, 1984), 32–36.

[3] Lev, *State and Society*, 89; Hamblin, "The Fatimid Army," 147–54.

[4] Hamblin, "The Fatimid Army," 19–27.

owing to their dependence upon him. These troops formed several regiments, the most important of which, the Juyūshiyya (so called after Badr's title *amīr al-juyūsh*), continued to play a significant role in the Fāṭimid army until they were suppressed by Ṣalāḥ al-Dīn in 1171.

From the time of Badr until the end of the dynasty, the Fāṭimid army remained a multi-ethnic force organized into a number of large regiments, each with its own quarter in Cairo, and held together by a complex system of patronage. Badr's son and successor, al-Afḍal ibn Amīr al-Juyūsh, maintained and elaborated the system his father established. But he faced an even more serious challenge than his father, namely the Crusaders. After suffering a crushing defeat in Palestine in 1099 and a series of minor humiliations, al-Afḍal established the Ḥujariyya, a regiment comprised of the freeborn sons of Fāṭimid soldiers who were trained in the barracks (*ḥujra*, pl. *ḥujar*) as mounted archers. In spite of the resources devoted to these troops, al-Afḍal's military reforms had little effect on the success of the Fāṭimid army, and the lost Syrian territories were not recovered from the Franks definitively until the 1160s.

Throughout the twelfth century the army provided a power base for a series of military wazīrs who were the effective rulers of the state. Only one Fāṭimid caliph, al-Āmir, was able to reassert any measure of political and military authority, and then only briefly. The last thirty years of Fāṭimid rule were marked by nearly continuous factional fighting among the regiments, by competition between caliphs and wazīrs for the loyalty of powerful regiments whose support was fundamental to the exercise of power, and by the manipulation of military factional politics through both patronage and purging.

The commanders themselves appear to have become increasingly independent, particularly in the provinces, owing in large part to the growth of the *iqṭāʿ* system, which can generally be described as allocating the revenues from designated lands to military personnel. While *iqṭāʿ* grants had certainly been used to supplement salaries for the army throughout the previous century, they began in the twelfth century to replace cash payments from the central government. The financial strain of this unwieldy army on a weakened economy and the priority given to the interests of the army by the succession of military wazīrs resulted in the significant loss of control by the central government over *iqṭāʿ*s, and by the late Fāṭimid period, many soldiers exercised direct control over their *iqṭāʿ*s. This situation had important implications for Fāṭimid governance, for the reliance on *iqṭāʿ*, which increasingly replaced cash payment from the central government, also undermined the elaborate system of patronage that was fundamental to maintaining order.[5]

[5] Lev, *State and Society*, 124–30.

The military came to play a significant role also in the broader administration of the state. From the time of Badr al-Jamālī, the Fāṭimid wazīrs were men who had risen to power through the military. The late Fāṭimid administrative hierarchy placed the wazīr at the head of both the civilian and the military bureaucracies. The wazīr, who was a "man of the sword," wielded much broader powers and prerogatives within even the civilian administration than earlier wazīrs, who had been men "of the pen." He crossed the boundaries between civil, religious, and military authority. The wazīr in the late Fāṭimid period, for example, was addressed by the title "judge of judges" (*qāḍī al-quḍāt*), although he exercised no judicial functions. He occupied a crucial position as the person responsible for executing the caliph's commands, and he often spoke for the caliph. Theoretically, his authority derived from the caliph, but his ability to act in the political arena was not a function of his investiture by the caliph; rather, it was constituted in large part by the loyalty he commanded from his own troops and from the various factions of the army that supported him. This, of course, often placed the wazīr at odds with the caliph. But the interests of the caliph and the wazīr did not conflict entirely. Both shared an interest in preventing a breakdown of order among the factionalized army, and both knew that the loyalties of the troops fluctuated according to their perception of their self-interest. The twelfth-century Fāṭimid army was diverse in its loyalties as well as in its ethnic and racial composition. It contained the remnants of personal troops of various commanders, wazīrs, and caliphs (or their descendants). These groups were powerful constituents and rivals, and much of the work of the late Fāṭimid administrative structure was devoted to providing resources to keep them in check.

Fāṭimid administration and administrative culture

Like other contemporary Islamic dynasties, the Fāṭimids created a sizable bureaucracy to organize and carry out the administration of their empire. The Fāṭimid state apparatus was divided into a number of departments called *dīwāns*. These *dīwāns* handled the fiscal, military, diplomatic and administrative affairs of the Fāṭimid state. The sources for their history, however, are highly disjointed, making it difficult to trace their development systematically. One of the obstacles to analyzing these *dīwāns* is that the names of the departments changed over time, and we cannot be certain to what extent the nominal changes reflected functional changes as well. Nonetheless, it is possible to characterize the history of Fāṭimid administration as one of progressive centralization and consolidation.

The earliest feature of Fāṭimid administration in Egypt was its continuity with the skeletal and highly decentralized Ikhshīdid administration. Like many other conquerors, Jawhar maintained local administrative practices and personnel, employing many Sunnī Muslims and Copts. The former Ikhshīdid wazīr, Ibn al-Furāt, kept his post, as did the tax collectors. The presence of a new dynastic authority was visible mainly in the attachment of north African inspectors and supervisors to the tax collectors and the bureaus managing the estates of the defeated Ikhshīdid regiments.

Upon his arrival in Egypt in 363/973, Caliph al-Muʿizz initiated a massive reorganization of Egyptian administration under the supervision of Yaʿqūb ibn Killis, an Iraqi merchant who had come to Egypt to serve the Ikshīdid court. Al-Muʿizz appointed Ibn Killis and another official as chief tax-collectors and directors of all financial affairs; they consolidated the collection of taxes in the administrative complex adjacent to the Ibn Ṭūlūn Mosque. This new organization increased tax revenues, especially from the Delta textile towns of Tinnis and Damietta. In addition to centralizing tax collection, Ibn Killis reorganized the administrative *dīwān*s and introduced a system of checks and balances by duplicating administrative functions in more than one *dīwān*. He began to employ north Africans (*maghribī*s) in addition to indigenous Sunnī or Coptic scribes, who were continuously employed by the Fāṭimid state until its demise.

The newly organized *dīwān*s also implemented the Fāṭimids' new monetary policies. Just before the conquest of Egypt, the Ikhshīdid state suffered a monetary crisis and its coinage was seriously debased. Jawhar minted new gold coins, called Muʿizzī *dinars*, of a very high intrinsic value, withdrew the debased coinage from circulation, and demanded that taxes be paid only in the new Muʿizzī *dinars*, a policy that was surely aided by the centralization of the tax collection. The high degree of fineness of their coins was sustained throughout the Fāṭimid period, even during the economic crises of the reign of al-Mustanṣir, and was an important element in maintaining the general economic stability of the state.

The administration of justice was not organized into *dīwān*s, but its functions were divided instead among several offices. As in other states in the medieval Islamic world, a distinction was made between justice based on the religious law (*sharīʿa*), and administrative justice (*maẓālim*), although the two functions were frequently carried out by the chief judge (*qāḍī al-quḍāt*). When the Fāṭimids first came to Egypt, the caliph retained the chief judge already in place. In the reign of al-ʿAzīz, however, the first Ismāʿīlī chief judge was appointed. He was ʿAlī ibn al-Nuʿmān, the son of the great jurist and architect of Ismāʿīlī jurisprudence, al-Qāḍī al-Nuʿmān. From this time on, justice was administered primarily in accordance with Ismāʿīlī law, but Sunnī jurists continued to serve as judges and, in the later Fāṭimid period, on occasion even as chief judge. In the twelfth century, the functions of the chief judge were often assumed by the wazīr, who also held the title *qāḍī al-quḍāt*. At this time, the chief judge was considered to be a deputy of the wazīr.

One of the most frequently used mechanisms for enlisting the assistance of the state and dispensing justice was the petition. Because of the existence in the Cairo Geniza (the treasure trove of documents emanating from the Jewish community of Fusṭāṭ-Cairo in the Fāṭimid and Ayyūbid periods) of a significant number of actual petitions and decrees, we are able to document the composition of petitions and the administrative procedures used in answering them, something which is not possible for most other aspects of Fāṭimid administration, where we must rely almost exclusively on later literary sources. Depending on the structures in place at any given time, petitions were addressed to the caliph, the wazīr, or, sometimes, to judges. Until the introduction of military wazīrs with Badr al-Jamālī, petitions were ordinarily collected outside one of the gates of the palace and then sent to the Chancery, where high officials either made their own decisions or sought the advice of the caliph or wazīr. The petition was then endorsed and the answer was rewritten in a fair copy by an official in the Chancery known as the "secretary of the thick pen" (*ṣāḥib al-qalam al-jalīl*), who inserted all the proper titles and blessings, and it was signed by the caliph. The petition was then either returned with the endorsement to the sender or it was sent to the Chancery where a decree was drawn up. In late Fāṭimid times, the wazīrs held public audiences to receive petitions. The petition was available to both individuals and communities, and almost any dispute or problem might be submitted to the caliph or wazīr. The Geniza documents include, for example, petitions requesting the return of a church to the Christian community and the resolution of a dispute within the Jewish community that led to the closing of a synagogue. But a large number of petitions were submitted by individuals and concern a wide variety of problems. Some of these petitions from individuals requested relief from the actions of the government and its representatives by means of investigation into the impounding of a poor man's property, the granting of various allowances, the release of a man who had been detained, or relief from the poll tax. Some pleaded for justice in the aftermath of criminal activity, as in a petition to the caliph from a father who requested the arrest of the captain and sailors of a Nile boat, who had killed his son and stolen his money and goods. Many petitions asked for the government's intervention in entirely private affairs, such as disputes over the repayment of debts or over property.[6]

The police and market inspectors (*muḥtasib*) of Cairo and Fusṭāṭ were essentially municipal officials, but they were appointed directly by the

[6] On the history of the petition, see Geoffrey Khan, *Arabic Legal and Administrative Documents in the Cambridge Genizah Collections* (Cambridge, 1993), 303ff.; G. Khan, "The historical development of the structure of medieval Arabic petitions," *BSOAS*, 53 (1990), 8–30; S. M. Stern, "Three petitions of the Fāṭimid period," *Oriens*, 15 (1962), 172–209.

central government because they were in the capital. These offices are difficult to characterize: they were held by individuals with a variety of backgrounds, and, although they were not, strictly speaking, religious offices, the functions exercised often converged with religious law and administration. The chief of police, for example, was sometimes a jurist, more often not. Clashes between the chief of police and the chief judge over questions of jurisdiction were not unusual. And some responsibilities, for example, imposing the Qur'anically prescribed punishments (*ḥudūd*) on criminals, were firmly rooted in religious law. The supervision of markets (*ḥisba*) stood at the intersection of religious law, municipal administration, and marketplace ethics. Its authority was expressed in formal religious terms ("to enjoin the good and forbid evil"), though it could scarcely be considered a religious institution; in theory, its jurisdiction ranged from keeping the streets clear, inspecting weights and measures, and controlling quality to ensuring the proper maintenance of mosques and enforcing the requirement that Jews and Christians wear distinctive marks on their clothing; in reality, one of its primary functions was to ensure the availability of grain and bread in the market during times of scarcity and to execute the government's grain policy.[7] More even than policing, the *ḥisba* would have to be characterized as primarily an urban institution, and one of relatively low prestige at that, if we are to judge from the bitter complaint of an official who had just been appointed to the post: "I was a companion of the caliph and the keeper of his purse. Should I now become a *muḥtasib*? I shall not!"[8]

The large and complex Fāṭimid army required substantial economic and administrative resources. As in other parts of the Islamic world from the tenth to the twelfth centuries, a large share of the state's budget and bureaucratic apparatus was dedicated to the military. The Fāṭimid army was administered by the Office of the Army (*dīwān al-jaysh*), which was divided into several sections charged with maintaining complete registers, distributing pay, and administering lands allocated to the army. These different sections display the salient feature of duplication for checks and balances that was typical of Fāṭimid bureaucracies after the tenth century. One section was charged with maintaining complete registers of the soldiers and officers in all regiments, including the district from which the revenues for salaries were drawn, the type of each soldier's equipment, his physical appearance, and his martial skills. These registers were updated through

7 See H. Haji, "Institutions of Justice in Fatimid Egypt," in A. al-Azmeh (ed.), *Islamic Law and Historical Contexts* (London, 1988), 198–214; Lev, *State and Society*, 162–78; Boaz Shoshan, "Fatimid Grain Policy and the Post of Muḥtasib," *International Journal of Middle East Studies*, 13 (1981), 181–89.

8 Al-Musabbiḥī, *Akhbār Miṣr* [Tome Quarantième de la Chronique d'Egypte de Musabbiḥī], ed. Ayman Fu'ād Sayyid and Thierry Bianquis (Cairo, 1978), 14.

periodic military reviews and inspections.[9] Another office registered the names of both civil and military employees who received cash salaries and distributed payments, an arrangement that can perhaps be taken as evidence of the increasing militarization of the state from the middle of the eleventh century onward. At the end of the tenth century, salaries were paid eight times a year, but by the middle of the eleventh century, payment was monthly. In addition to their monthly salaries, soldiers in the capital received special bonuses, and troops generally received a special payment before a campaign or when a new caliph ascended the throne. The *iqṭāʿ* system, which increasingly replaced cash payments to the military, required a very substantial bureaucracy to record and administer the land grants, many of which were in the provinces.

Economic life and economic policy

Egypt was generally prosperous during the Fāṭimid period, and this good fortune was owed largely to geography: the Nile allowed intensive cultivation. When the Nile flooded properly, Egypt produced abundant quantities of wheat and other grains, with surpluses for export. From the early Islamic period on, Egypt had been a significant supplier of wheat to the holy cities of Mecca and Medina, and it was the main food crop. Bread was made primarily from wheat, but a poorer variety was made also from barley, the grain being cultivated mainly to feed beasts of burden.[10] Cotton, which from the nineteenth century has been a staple of Egyptian agriculture, was virtually unknown as a crop, although large quantities of finished cotton goods were imported. The main industrial crop was flax, and twenty-two local varieties of it were cultivated. There is no other cash crop for which we possess such voluminous documentation. The preparation of flax fiber (as opposed to finished linen textiles) was a primary industry, and it was a mainstay of international trade. The quantities were so large that merchants specialized in it, and it was ordinarily traded in bales of 350 to 600 pounds.[11] Linseed oil, commonly used for lighting, was readily available because of the extensive flax cultivation. On the other hand, olive oil, an important ingredient in the daily diet of medieval Egyptians, was almost exclusively an import.

Egypt's flourishing economy in the Fāṭimid period was founded not only upon agriculture but also on international trade. As producer and consumer,

[9] Hamblin, "The Fatimid Army", 106ff.; B. J. Beshir, "Fatimid Military Organization," *Der Islam*, 55 (1978), 37–53; " *ʿarḍ*" *EI2*.

[10] S. D. Goitein, *A Mediterranean Society: The Jewish Communities of the Arab World as Portrayed in the Documents of the Cairo Geniza*, 6 vols. (Berkeley, 1967–1993), I, 116–118.

[11] Goitein, *Mediterranean Society*, I, 104–105, 224.

importer and exporter, Egypt reaped the benefits of sitting at the intersection of two international trade routes and having access to both the Mediterranean Sea and the Indian Ocean. This unique position also helped to protect Fāṭimid trading interests when routes were occasionally shut off. The shift in trade from Ifrīqiya (Tunisia) to Egypt in the tenth century and the migration of traders to Egypt is not unrelated to the Fāṭimid move east. The loss of the Syrian territories to the Crusaders did not deal a death blow to Fāṭimid trade; in fact, the diversion of traffic from the Red Sea to the Nile valley worked in some respects to the advantage of the Fāṭimids. The intensification of Indian Ocean trade in the twelfth century and the Fāṭimids' interest in protecting the Red Sea trade route and trade along the Nile valley should probably be taken as part of the context for the large number of military wazīrs in the twelfth century who came from the Upper Egyptian city of Qūṣ.[12]

But geography alone does not create trade networks. In the Mediterranean of the tenth to the twelfth centuries, men enjoyed an extraordinary degree of freedom of movement. The existence of political boundaries, even hostilities between governments, rarely interfered with the movement of persons or goods around the Mediterranean. Similarly, embargoes on exports or imports were very rare. The governments around the Mediterranean were much more likely to exercise their prerogative by claiming rights as first buyer than by banning merchandise.[13]

In addition to this freedom of movement, the Fāṭimid state produced coins of such fineness and reliability that they were considered to be an international currency (at a time when coins were a commodity as well as a currency). One of the reasons that the Fāṭimids were able to sustain the intrinsic quality of their coins was a plentiful supply of gold. When al-Muʿizz came to Egypt in 361/972, he brought one hundred camels laden with gold bars shaped like millstones. The Fāṭimids also had access to the gold mines of Upper Egypt and Nubia, which they exploited until the costs of production outstripped the yield. Both the mines and the pharaonic tombs, which had been a major source of gold for the Ṭūlūnids, began to run out in the eleventh and twelfth centuries. But until almost the end of the Fāṭimid period, the state maintained the fineness of its coins.[14]

Most international trade was carried out by sea. Overland travel was not a popular mode of transportation for either persons or goods, even for trade

[12] See Jean-Claude Garcin, *Un centre musulman de la Haute-Égypte médiévale: Qūṣ* (Cairo, 1976), 79–118.

[13] Goitein, *Mediterranean Society*, I, 59–70.

[14] J. Devisse, "Trade and trade routes in West Africa," *General History of Africa*, ed. M. El Fasi (London, 1988), III, 367–435; A. S. Ehrenkreutz, "Contributions to the Knowledge of the Fiscal Administration of Egypt in the Middle Ages," *BSOAS*, 16 (1954), 502–14.

between Egypt and Tunisia, where caravan travel would have seemed more likely. While this situation was partly due to exigencies of the times – the Bedouin invasions of the mid-eleventh century increased the danger of piracy – even before these new threats, sea travel had been preferred. The sea posed its own dangers, although merchants made a distinction between the relative calm and safety of the Mediterranean Sea and the greater risks of the Indian Ocean.[15]

International trade posed significant hazards to both men and their merchandise. Merchants in the Fāṭimid period sought to reduce their financial and personal risks by forming partnerships usually limited to a single venture. Partnerships were a substitute for two forms of business association that were viewed with suspicion and only rarely practiced: employment and loans on interest. Free men viewed the dependence inherent in being in the employ of another as a humiliation; borrowing money entailed the same dependency, and, in any case, loans on interest were looked at askance by religious law. Two types of partnership were especially common. The first was *shirka*, in which partners shared profit and loss in direct proportion to their investment. The second was commenda (called *qirāḍ* or *muḍāraba*), in which one or more partners contributed capital or goods, and the other partners did the work; the latter ordinarily took only one-third of the profits, but they assumed no risk for losses. Although such partnerships were common, the most important means of carrying out international commerce was informal business cooperation, or "formal friendship" (*ṣuḥba*). The majority of business transactions were carried out using this elaborate system of exchanging favors, and such relations often lasted throughout the lifetime of the parties involved.[16]

There is little of a general nature that can be said about economic policy in the Fāṭimid period except that it is difficult to generalize about it. Although scholars have generally claimed that the prosperity of the Fāṭimid period was owed largely to a laissez faire policy of the dynasty, it is more accurate to observe that Fāṭimid economic policy fluctuated a great deal, and depended largely on the conditions and demands of any given time and place.[17] Fāṭimid economic policy was a complex phenomenon, the product both of flexibility and responsiveness to change and of a style of interaction between government and merchants, where the lines between commerce and administration, between individuals acting for their own profit and those same men acting on behalf of the government, were often blurred.

The official sources are largely silent when it comes to the business of financial administration, which was carried out by agents and revenue

[15] Goitein, *Mediterranean Society*, I, 43.
[16] Goitein, *Mediterranean Society*, I, 64–179.
[17] Goitein, *Mediterranean Society*, I, 267; Shoshan, "Fatimid Glain Policy," 181.

farmers rather than by employees receiving fixed salaries from the government.[18] These agents and tax-farmers were paid by the job and most of the tax-farmers were attached to a particular locality. Most of them were merchants or industrialists and had intimate knowledge of the industry and its representatives from which they collected revenues. This knowledge was crucial given the relative lack of bureaucratic process in the collection of taxes by the government. That is to say, the government relied on the existing networks and in particular on the knowledge of the agents and tax-farmers who carried out its business. The business of administration was firmly embedded in the day-to-day social and economic life of the country. In general, the financial administration of the Fāṭimid state was carried out less by high-level officials than by merchants and businessmen who acted for, but were not a part of, the government. This system of financial administration was organized to a large extent along the same lines and involved many of the same people as commercial networks. The cooperation between merchants and the government extended beyond the narrow limits of tax collection.

The representative of the merchants (*wakīl al-tujjār*) is perhaps the most striking example of this ambiguity between economic and administrative roles. The *wakīl al-tujjār* was a merchant whose administrative functions derived from his position within the commercial community. He was usually a foreigner, or the son of a foreign merchant, who had settled in a city and had won the respect and trust of his compatriots who were staying there and of the local business community. Initially, he carried out business for merchants from his homeland in their absence, but ultimately he might be entrusted with the business of local merchants as well.[19]

In addition to his commercial activities, the *wakīl al-tujjār* collected taxes, fees, and dues from merchants and conveyed them to the government. But these official functions were not his primary occupation. His ability to act on behalf of the government was not the result of a formal apppointment. Rather, the government was able to exploit the position of the *wakīl al-tujjār* within his community for its own purposes: the collection of taxes.[20] The highly informal nature of the office of representative of the merchants is shown further by the nearly complete silence of Arabic literary, historical, and financial treatises about them. But this office is richly documented in the Cairo Geniza.[21] Although there are references to warehouses (*dār al-wakālas*), there is almost no corresponding information about the men who

[18] Goitein, *Mediterranean Society*, I, 267–72; II, 354.

[19] See Goitein, *Mediterranean Society*, I, 186–92; A. L. Udovitch, "Merchants and Amīrs: Government and Trade in Eleventh-Century Egypt," *Asian and African Studies*, 22 (1988), 53–72.

[20] Udovitch, "Merchants and Amīrs," 65.

[21] See Goitein, *Mediterranean Society*, VI, s.v. "Representative of the merchants."

operated them. The short necrology of a Muslim *wakīl al-tujjār* in the history of the Muslim historian al-Musabbiḥī is an exception. He was one Abū Ismāʿīl Ibrāhīm ibn Tājj, who had "come upon great fortune and turned to acting as a representative of merchants. Commodities and merchandise were brought to him from everywhere. He left an inheritance of great wealth."[22] No other authors make any mention of the *wakīl al-tujjār* in their detailed descriptions of administration in the Fāṭimid and Ayyubid states.

The presence of the government was felt primarily in its role both as producer and as the largest consumer in the country.[23] Agricultural products were bought from or through the government. This was particularly true of flax, the largest export product and the staple of the Egyptian economy in the Fāṭimid period. As a consumer, the government was wealthy enough to buy at prices that were prohibitive for all others. It also had the prerogative of being first buyer of incoming goods, a situation that often resulted in the outright appropriation of goods, even against the will of the merchants, who were forced to sell at artificially low prices and sometimes had difficulty collecting their money. During the reign of al-Mustanṣir, a Commerce Bureau (*matjar*) was established to organize the state's preemptive purchasing rights. In a letter written in the early 1120s, a merchant complains bitterly: "The other item was taken by the governmental wardrobe, may God make permanent his [the ruler's] reign, and, thus far, no payment has been made." The appropriation of the beleaguered merchant's goods was probably not an isolated incident; it occurred at the same time that the government was dramatically increasing its own distributions of ceremonial costumes, which in 516/1122 reached a staggering 14,305 pieces.[24]

Urban life and cultural pluralism

Although Islamic civilization in general and Fāṭimid culture in particular were highly urbanized, the majority of men and women in medieval Egypt lived in the countryside. Egypt's great cities, therefore, while yielding the information that we tend to think of as being characteristic of Fāṭimid culture, were in fact atypical. In the Fāṭimid period, Egypt was, as it continued to be until recent times, primarily agricultural and rural. And though we tend to think of the distinctive categories as urban and rural, there were in fact important differences among Egypt's regions and her major cities. Three urban centers in particular, tied to each other as entrepôts on the vast Mediterranean Sea–Indian Ocean trade continuum, merit

22 See al-Musabbiḥī, *Akhbār Miṣr*, 108.

23 Goitein, *Mediterranean Society*, I, 267.

24 Al-Maqrīzī, *Kitāb al-mawāʿiẓ waʾl-iʿtibār bi-dhikr al-khiṭaṭ waʾl-āthār* (Būlāq, 1853), I, 410; Ibn al-Maʾmūn al-Baṭāiʾḥī, *Nuṣūṣ min akhbār miṣr*, ed. Ayman Fuʾād Sayyid as *Passages de la Chronique d'Egypte d'Ibn al-Maʾmūn* (Cairo 1983), 48–55.

some discussion: Alexandria, Fusṭāṭ-Cairo, and Qūṣ. Each exemplifies a different aspect of urbanism and each had a distinctive character in the Fāṭimid period.

Fusṭāṭ-Cairo was the political and administrative, as well as the financial and commercial, capital of the Fāṭimid state. Although it is appropriate to speak of these twin cities as a single entity with respect to the rest of Egypt and the Fāṭimid empire, Fusṭāṭ and Cairo remained separate and had distinctive characters in relation to one another. As late as the 1240s, when the Maghribī traveler Ibn Saʿīd visited Cairo, the difference was still palpable; he remarked on the graciousness and friendliness of the residents of Fusṭāṭ in contrast to those of Cairo, although the two cities were barely two miles apart.[25]

Early Cairo consisted of two palaces and a congregational mosque, the Azhar, all enclosed by a brick wall. The city had an unmistakably Ismāʿīlī character. By the early eleventh century, Cairo possessed another congregational mosque, the Mosque of al-Ḥākim, which quickly assumed an importance equal to that of the Azhar in ceremonial life. In the late eleventh and early twelfth century, Cairo's walls were extended and rebuilt, and monumental stone gates were added. At this time, Cairo was still essentially a closed city and it had no independent commercial life, but civilians who served the court (like physicians), and even some highly placed Jewish and Christian officials, resided there; the head of the Palestinian academy (*yeshiva*) Maṣlīaḥ Gaon and his entourage of scholars settled in Cairo when he arrived in Egypt in 1127.[26] By the twelfth century, Cairo was beginning to develop its own commercial interests. The Fāṭimid wazīr al-Ma'mūn al-Baṭā'iḥī established a *dār al-wakāla* for Syrian and Iraqi merchants in the 1120s as well as a new mint.

But Cairo could not, and did not, rival its neighboring city Fusṭāṭ as Egypt's economic center, her major emporium, and the site of all important commercial transactions. Customs duties were paid on all imported consignments in Fusṭāṭ; merchants from even the great port cities came to Fusṭāṭ to acquire Mediterranean commodities, including foreign currency; even goods destined for ordinary use (like shoes) were ordered from there.[27] It was, by all accounts, a booming metropolis, an open city where people came and

25 Al-Maqrīzī, *al-Khiṭaṭ*, I, 342, quoting Ibn Saʿīd; cited in Gaston Wiet, *Cairo: City of Art and Commerce*, tr. Seymour Feiler (Oklahoma, 1964), 49; and Goitein, *Mediterranean Society*, IV, 11.

26 Goitein, *Mediterranean Society*, IV, 11. Other heads of the community had houses also in Fusṭāṭ.

27 Goitein, *Mediterranean Society*, I, 4; S. D. Goitein, *Letters of Medieval Jewish Traders* (Princeton, 1973), 24–25; A. L. Udovitch, "A Tale of Two Cities: Commercial Relations between Cairo and Alexandria During the Second Half of the Eleventh Century," in Harry A. Miskimin, David Herlihy, A. L. Udovitch (eds.), *The Medieval City* (New Haven, 1977), 143–62.

went with ease, whose rhythms were determined partly by the ritual calendars of its religious communities and partly by the comings and goings of ships and caravans. Fusṭāṭ maintained the larger and more diverse population, comprised of Sunnī Muslims, Christians, and Jews. Its Mosque of ʿAmr, at the heart of Fusṭāṭ's commercial district, was the Friday mosque for the Muslim population as well as the terminal point for parades on Nawrūz, the Coptic New Year.

Alexandria, like other ports of the Islamic world, was considered to be a frontier fortress (*thaghr*). The ʿAbbāsids built a city wall there in the ninth century which the Fāṭimids, like other dynasties from the tenth to the sixteenth centuries, restored.[28] By the Fāṭimid era, Alexandria had long since ceased to be a capital, having been displaced by Fusṭāṭ at the time of the Arab conquest; but it continued to be sufficiently important for Alexandria along with Fusṭāṭ to be the only cities in Egypt with their own budget and chief judge.

Alexandria possessed two harbors, one for Christian and one for Muslim ships. By the eleventh century, it had both a *dār al-wakāla* (serving as both customs house and warehouse) and a Commerce Bureau (*matjar*), where the government exercised its right of first purchase. The famous Pharos lighthouse, built in the Ptolemaic era, was still standing in 1165, when it was described by the historian al-Balawī. Throughout the twelfth and thirteenth centuries, Alexandria was a center for trading imported spices, slaves, and silk, as well as its own locally produced textiles, for which it was famous. But in spite of its preeminent location on the Mediterranean, and its importance in international trade, Alexandria remained in the Fāṭimid period a "commercial suburb of Fusṭāṭ," and merchants complained continually of the paucity of its markets.[29]

Alexandria was full of foreigners, many of them from around the Mediterranean rim. Unlike Fusṭāṭ, where people tended to settle permanently and marry into local families, Alexandria's foreigners were often temporary residents, and there were many violent clashes between them and the local inhabitants. Indeed, Alexandria was known for its propensity for unruliness and insurrection. In 467/1074, Badr al-Jamālī had to put down the insurrection of a naval regiment in Alexandria. When Badr's son al-Awḥad led a group of soldiers and Bedouins in revolt against his father in

[28] Jamāl al-dīn al-Shayyāl, *Ta'rīkh madīnat al-iskāndariyyah fī al-ʿaṣr al-islāmī* (Cairo, 1967), 41–52; Sayyid ʿAbd al-ʿAzīz Sālim, *Ta'rīkh al-iskāndariyyah wa-ḥaḍāratuhā fī al-ʿaṣr al-islāmī* (Cairo, 1961), 55–66.

[29] See Udovitch, "Tale of Two Cities," esp. 158, and Abraham L. Udovitch, "Medieval Alexandria: Some Evidence from the Cairo Genizah Documents," *Alexandria and Alexandrianism: papers delivered at a symposium organized by the J. Paul Getty Museum and the Getty Center for the History of Art and the Humanties and held at the Museum, April 22–25, 1993* (Malibu, CA, 1996), 273–84.

477/1084, the rebels took refuge in Alexandria. It is not surprising, therefore, that in the aftermath of al-Afḍal's enthronement of al-Mustaʿlī in 487/1094, the displaced Nizār fled to Alexandria, where the local inhabitants took an oath of loyalty to him.

Because of its proximity to north Africa and Spain, Alexandria had a large Maghribī population that increased in the aftermath of the Fāṭimid conquest and the shift of trade to Egypt. Most of its Jewish minority of around 3,000 were Maghribī immigrants. Its Christian community consisted of Copts and Melkites, and it was the seat of the Coptic patriarchate until the early eleventh century. Most probably because of the strong Maghribī presence, it seems to have developed into a center for Sunnī learning, particularly for the Mālikī and Shāfiʿī schools of law. In the late eleventh century, a number of distinguished Mālikīs settled in Alexandria, including the Banū Ḥadīd family of Toledo and the jurist al-Ṭurṭūshī, who wrote a manual of government for the Fāṭimid wazīr al-Maʾmūn al-Baṭāʾiḥī. In the twelfth century, the Fāṭimid wazīrs Riḍwān ibn Walakshī and Ibn al-Sallār established in Alexandria the first of the colleges of law (*madrasas*) that would contribute to the revival of Sunnīsm in Egypt even before the end of the Fāṭimid period.[30]

Qūṣ was a dependency of Aswān in early Fāṭimid times. Aswān was unique among the largely Christian cities of Upper Egypt in having a majority of Muslims among its inhabitants, and it was the site at which commodities brought by caravan from the Red Sea port of ʿAydhāb were transferred to the Nile. Its distance from Cairo and its large Muslim population, however, made it a popular refuge for rebels. In the aftermath of the crises of the eleventh century, Aswān became the haven for the rebellious black troops who had been expelled from the capital. At this troubled moment, Qūṣ was chosen as the new administrative capital of Upper Egypt, probably because its population was largely Christian. In the eleventh and twelfth centuries, the economy of Qūṣ flourished as it displaced Aswān as the Nile terminal for the ʿAydhāb caravan route that was central to the Indian Ocean trade; it became also the favorite stop of Muslim pilgrim caravans which, after the establishment of the Crusader states, no longer had access to the overland routes to the Ḥijāz through Palestine. The city's centrality continued into the Ayyūbid period, when the traveler Ibn Jubayr could say that it "is a city of fine markets and of ample amenities, and it has many beings in it because of the comings and goings of pilgrims and of merchants from India, the Yemen, and Ethiopia. It is a place where all may come upon, a place of alighting for the traveller, a gathering place for companies of wayfarers, and a meeting place for pilgrims from the Maghrib,

30 See Lev, *State and Society*, 139–40 n. 30; Gary Leiser, "The Madrasa and the Islamization of the Middle East. The Case of Egypt," *Journal of the American Research Center in Egypt*, 22 (1985), 29–47.

from Misr, from Alexandria and from adjoining lands. From here they go into the desert of ʿAydhāb, and here they return on their way back from the Hajj [pilgrimage]."[31] In the twelfth century, the town had its own mint (established in 1122) and the power of its governors, who had at their disposal a large military force, rivalled that of the wazīrs. Indeed, a number of the wazīrs of the twelfth century were former governors of Qūṣ. All this benefitted the Christian community there, which was able to build or rebuild during this period dozens of its churches. In the long run, the new administrative and economic importance of Qūṣ would lead to the internal migration of Muslims, the establishment of a judgeship for the northern part of Upper Egypt, and increasing Islamization.[32]

In medieval times, people used the comprehensive term *al-rīf* ("the Province") to refer not only to the rural countryside but also to the many cities, towns, and villages that were to be distinguished from Egypt's great cities of Fusṭāṭ-Cairo and Alexandria. Even large and important cities like Damietta, a major Mediterranean sea port on the eastern arm of the Nile, were part of the Rīf.[33] The Rīf's relative isolation was used to the advantage of defaulting debtors who hoped to elude their creditors, as well as by Christians and Jews who could not afford to pay the poll tax. But the Rīf was not cut off from the major cities. There was continual migration in both directions, and smaller cities and towns were an important part of the large networks of commerce and trade that had as their center the great cities. They were often the terminal point for goods, particularly textiles, peddled by merchants from the large cities; but they were also points for the resale of merchandise to even smaller communities.[34]

Medieval Egyptians shared modern prejudices regarding the sophistication of country people. A man writing to an acquaintance in Cairo complained that he could not find anyone civilized in the small town to which he had been sent. A woman in al-Maḥalla al-Kubrā, a provincial capital and industrial center, complained that she could not bear life in the Rīf and ran away to Cairo. Her husband offered to move to Damietta, which, he said, was the best he could do for her and still make a living; Fusṭāṭ was simply too expensive.[35]

At the beginning of the Fāṭimid period, the majority of Egypt's rural population was still Christian and spoke Coptic. By the end, a large number

[31] Ibn Jubayr, *The Travels of Ibn Jubayr*, trans. R. J. C. Broadhurst (London, 1952), 57–58.

[32] See Garcin, *Un centre musulman*, 120–22.

[33] Goitein, *Mediterranean Society*, IV, 9–10.

[34] Goitein, *Mediterranean Society*, II, 45; IV, 10.

[35] Goitein, *Mediterranean Society*, III, 150, 177; IV, 9–10; Mark Cohen, "Geniza documents concerning a conflict in a provincial Egyptian Jewish Community during the Nagidate of Mevorakh B. Saadya," in S. Morag, I. Ben-Ami, N. A. Stillman (eds.), *Studies in Judaism and Islam* (Jerusalem, 1981), 123–54.

of rural Egyptians were still Christian, but their language was now Arabic. Coptic had disappeared earlier in the cities, and by the ninth and tenth centuries most urban Egyptians knew Arabic.[36] This was especially true of the Christians, who served as financial and administrative officials in the Fāṭimid government, as they had under earlier Islamic regimes. In the tenth century, Sawīrus (Severus) ibn al-Muqaffaʿ, bishop of the Middle Egyptian town of al-Ashmūnayn, complained that nobody now understood Coptic and wrote the first Coptic theological treatise in Arabic. By the eleventh century, the Coptic community was producing large numbers of Arabic texts. Jews, many of whom served the Fāṭimid government, also embraced Arabic, though they ordinarily wrote it in Hebrew characters.[37] By the tenth century, Jews nearly always used Arabic for prose writing, though poetry continued to be written in Hebrew.[38] The first translation of the Hebrew bible into Arabic was completed around 925 by Saadya Gaon (882–942), who originated in the Fayyūm region of Egypt.[39] The Fāṭimid period thus marked the time when the Christian and Jewish communities of Egypt became definitively Arabophone, and when they began to produce significant literary output in Arabic. Arabic was the language of daily life, of the marketplace, and of literary production within communities. It was also the language of debate and polemic between religious communities. The Fāṭimid court itself played a major role in such polemics. There are accounts, for example, of interconfessional debates at the *majlis* (weekly court) of the wazīr Yaʿqūb ibn Killis between a Jew and the Bishop Sawīrus ibn al-Muqaffaʿ, in which the wazīr himself also participated.[40]

The character of Fāṭimid rule

The Fāṭimids ruled a complex state in which much of their energy and attention was necessarily dedicated to balancing factions competing for power. But what characterized the rule of the Fāṭimids, especially given the

[36] Khalif Samir, "Arabic sources for early Egyptian Christianity," in Birger A. Pearson and James E. Goehring (eds.), *The Roots of Egyptian Christianity* (Philadelphia, 1986), 82–97.

[37] See Joshua Blau, The Emergence and Linguistic background of Judaeo-Arabic (Oxford, 1965), esp. 19–50.

[38] This situation should be compared with that of the Jews in Mesopotamia at the same time. In urban areas they spoke Arabic, but in rural areas they continued to speak Aramaic. See Rina Drory, "'Words beautifully put': Hebrew versus Arabic in tenth-century Jewish literature," in Joshua Blau and Stefan Reif (eds.), *Geniza research after ninety years: The case of Judaeo-Arabic* (Cambridge, 1992), 53–66.

[39] This is disputed by Joshua Blau, "On a fragment of the oldest Judaeo-Arabic Bible translation extant," *Geniza research after ninety years*, 31–39, who argues, based on spelling, that Geniza fragment T-S Ar. 53.8 is older.

[40] See Mark Cohen and Sasson Somekh, "In the court of Yaʿqūb ibn Killis: a fragment from the Cairo Genizah," *Jewish Quarterly Review*, 30 (1990), 283–314.

dramatic transition from a civilian to a basically military administration and the rise of military wazīrs whose power by the end of the eleventh century eclipsed that of the caliph? In the face of such changes and such competition, what provided political continuity in the Fāṭimid state?

Patronage was one of the glues that held this political system together, and in employing it the Fāṭimids were like many of their contemporaries who ruled states in the medieval Islamic world.[41] In the early Fāṭimid period, the caliphs commanded sufficient resources, power, and authority to manipulate the elaborate patronage system in their own interests. They did this in several ways: by constructing an elaborate court bureaucracy and central administration staffed with personnel who owed them loyalty, by providing reliably and generously for the Berber tribal armies that had come with them from north Africa, by adding to their army slave troops whose dependence was assumed (often wrongly) to assure their allegiance. For much of the first century of Fāṭimid rule, the resources for pursuing this expensive means of control were considerable, and the Fāṭimid family was able to exploit networks of patronage to keep factions in balance. The administrators who ran the state were also directly dependent upon Fāṭimid royal patronage for their authority. Beginning in the 1020s, administrators under the patronage of different members of the Fāṭimid family and in turn controlling their own patronage networks began to rise to power. This pattern emerged during the reign of al-Ẓāhir, who was a youth when he ascended the throne and was quickly the object of an elaborate struggle for influence between first his aunt Sitt al-Mulk and then his most senior civilian administrators.[42] The patronage system was intensified in the early years of al-Mustanṣir's reign, when al-Sayyida Raṣad, a freed slave and the mother of the caliph, secured an appointment for her former master, Abū Saʿd al-Tustarī, as the head of her *dīwān*; Abū Saʿd then used this position of influence to depose one wazīr and install another, a situation that led to considerable resistance by the army and which led ultimately to Abū Saʿd's murder by the Turkish regiments. Patronage reached its height and became a permanent feature of Fāṭimid political culture in the later years of al-Mustanṣir's reign, when the military wazīrs (beginning with the dynasty of Badr al-Jamālī) of the eleventh and twelfth centuries nurtured their own independent patronage networks that accompanied the increasingly broad military, judicial, and administrative authority that they wielded. They had access to wider networks of patronage to manipulate in their own interests, and these interests often competed with those of the dynasty they served. The second century of Fāṭimid rule, therefore, is characterized not so much by the breakdown of

[41] The most elaborate analysis of this feature of medieval Islamic political culture is in Roy P. Mottahedeh, *Loyalty and Leadership in an Early Islamic Society* (Princeton, 1980).
[42] Lev, *State and Society*, 38–39.

the patronage system, as by the transfer of control of the patronage system from the dynasty to the wazīrs.

Even after their loss of real political and military power, the Fāṭimid caliphs maintained their symbolic position as head of the state and ultimate authority. This fiction of dynastic supremacy was perpetuated largely through ceremonial activity, and with the full complicity of the wazīrs who were denying the caliphs real power. The Fāṭimids participated fully in the general political culture of the Islamic world during the tenth to the twelfth centuries, and they appropriated the highly generalized symbols of authority that most Islamic rulers used to articulate their claims to legitimacy. They wore special costumes (usually white, the dynasty's color) and used the conventional insignia of sovereignty: the specially wound turban called *tāj*, staff, sword, parasol, inkstand, lance, shield, banners, flywhisks, ceremonial arms, drums, and tents. Like other Islamic rulers, they also exercised the prerogatives of pronouncing the caliph's name in the Friday sermon (*khuṭba*) and inscribing his name on coins (*sikka*) and on textiles (*ṭirāz*).[43]

But although the Fāṭimids' court protocol and audiences resembled that of their contemporaries (and most particularly their chief rivals, the ʿAbbāsids), their practices were also distinct in one important way: they made extensive use of urban processions. These processions expressed not only general claims to political and military authority, but also the more specialized claims associated with the Fāṭimids' role as Ismāʿīlī imāms. In fact, the development of the city of Cairo in the Fāṭimid period is partly a function of the role it played in expressing the Fāṭimids' Ismāʿīlism and their evolving relations with the largely Sunnī population that they governed most directly in Cairo and Fusṭāṭ.

In the early years of their rule in Egypt, the Fāṭimids combined architecture, topography, and inscriptions to construct Cairo as an Ismāʿīlī city. The palace stood at the symbolic center of the city, just as the imam stood at the center of Ismāʿīlī belief. The central position of the palace and imāms was expressed in theology and panegyric poetry, as well as in spatial relations. The imam was considered to be an emanation of the divine light, and many epithets described his brilliance and luminosity. As new mosques were constructed in Cairo throughout the Fāṭimid period, they came to be known by names evoking this special quality.

The first mosque to be established by the Fāṭimids, al-Azhar, was not connected to the palace, but stood nearby, to the southeast. The second mosque, begun just outside the original northern brick walls of the city by al-ʿAzīz and finished by al-Ḥākim in 1010, was called both the Mosque of al-Ḥākim and al-Anwar. Its monumental inscribed doorway, the construction of two minarets rather than one, and the monumental inscriptions on

43 See Paula Sanders, *Ritual, Politics, and the City in Fatimid Cairo* (Albany, 1994), ch. 1.

the outside expressed the Fāṭimid ruler's position as the Ismāʿīlī imām.[44] Even in the late eleventh and twelfth centuries, when the Fāṭimids were no longer effectively ruling their state, and when even their armies were mostly Sunnī, they still maintained a firm identity as Ismāʿīlī imams. The Aqmar mosque, built by the wazīr al-Maʾmūn al-Baṭāʾiḥī during the reign of Caliph al-Āmir in 519/1125, had explicitly Ismāʿīlī decorative motifs and inscriptions on its facade.[45] As the mosques were constructed, they were progressively incorporated into the ritual life of the court and were included in the procession routes of the caliphs on special occasions.

Fusṭāṭ, which was not an Ismāʿīlī city, was also incorporated into the ceremonial life of the court. Long after Cairo was established, public life continued to revolve around the two congregational mosques of Fusṭāṭ – the Mosque of ʿAmr and the Mosque of Ibn Ṭūlūn. In the early eleventh century, the Caliph al-Ḥākim began to lead Friday prayer in congregational mosques in both Cairo and Fusṭāṭ. By the twelfth century, Fusṭāṭ's mosques were regularly included in the ritual life of the Fāṭimid court. The caliphs led prayer in its congregational mosques during Ramaḍān and the Festivals, and they went in procession to Fusṭāṭ at the Islamic New Year, on the inundation of the Nile, and during Ramaḍān.

But the Fāṭimids did not present themselves in public solely as Ismāʿīlī imams. In the context of twelfth-century political and social realities – a civilian population and an army that were largely Sunnī – they also began to present themselves in broader terms as Islamic rulers. They reduced their emphasis on the explicitly Ismāʿīlī aspects of their rituals and participated in the public religious culture of the larger population at Fusṭāṭ. From the time of the Jamālī wazīrs, the Festival of Fast-Breaking and the Sacrificial Festival were celebrated with voluminous distributions of food, ceremonial clothing, and money.

In the late Fāṭimid period, the court actively borrowed from the flourishing local religious tradition. In addition to the celebrations of festivals, they patronized the cult surrounding the veneration of the Prophet's family that had been a feature of Egyptian Islamic religious life since early Islamic times. In the twelfth century, their participation in these cultic activities became more systematic, and they built numerous tomb monuments dedicated to various descendants of the family of the Prophet. This presentation of the ruler in ways that could be invested equally with a specifically Ismāʿīlī and a broadly Islamic meaning typified late Fāṭimid court ritual life.[46]

[44] See Irene Bierman, *Writing Signs: The Fāṭimid Public Text*, (Berkeley, 1998).

[45] Bierman, *Writing Signs*; Caroline Williams, "The Cult of ʿAlid Saints in the Fatimid Monuments of Cairo," *Muqarnas*, 1 (1983), 37–52; 3 (1985), 39–60.

[46] See Sanders, *Ritual, politics and the city*, 67–82; Christopher Taylor, "Reevaluating the Shiʿi Role in the Development of Monumental Islamic Funerary Architecture: the Case of Egypt," *Muqarnas*, 9 (1992), 1–10; Williams, "Cult of ʿAlid Saints."

This is not to say that Ismāʿīlism was no longer central to the Fāṭimids' view of themselves or of their state. Indeed, the Fāṭimid caliphs, in the face of two schisms, continued to insist on their special role as Ismāʿīlī imāms until the end of their dynasty. But the regime was characterized also by a certain pragmatism with regard to non-Ismāʿīlī and non-Muslim subjects. As in other Islamic regimes of the same era, Jews and Christians sometimes served in highly visible positions at court, and Sunnīs, especially in the later years of the dynasty, often held high positions in the Fāṭimid administration. After the middle of the eleventh century, even the chief judge of the Fāṭimid state did not have to be an Ismāʿīlī. For a time, these non-Ismāʿīlī judges were constrained to follow Ismāʿīlī law, but by the end of the eleventh century there is evidence to suggest that this was no longer the case. And while the Fāṭimids maintained their large propaganda mission (*daʿwa*) in other parts of the Islamic world, they do not seem to have emphasized their *daʿwa* in Egypt. The reasons for this remain obscure and constitute one of the most difficult and unresolved interpretive issues in Fāṭimid history.

7

The non-Muslim communities: Christian communities[1]

TERRY G. WILFONG

The Christian community in Egypt between 641 and 1517 was an often divided population in a state of constant transition. At the time of the Muslim conquest, the great majority of Egyptians were Christians of some sort, Christianity having been the religion of the Byzantine rulers of Egypt for over 300 years. The gradual transition from majority to minority under Muslim rule was a complex process that had a lasting impact on most aspects of the Christian communities in Egypt. The traditional understanding of Egyptian Christianity after the conquest as being theologically and culturally fixed and moribund is far from the reality of the dynamic religious, social and cultural activities of the Egyptian Christians. Similarly, the traditional notion of the Christian population of Egypt being cut off from the rest of the world is misleading, since there was considerable interaction with the outside world, especially with other Christian populations under Muslim control. Although subject to varying degrees of pressure and persecution from Muslims, the Egyptian Christians suffered equally from internal divisions and sectarian infighting. In spite of their internal

[1] The essential reference for this subject is Aziz S. Atiya, general editor, *The Coptic Encyclopedia*, 8 vols. (New York, 1991); note, though, the review in *JNES*, 52 (1993), 43–47. The major bibliographical reference is the ongoing cumulative bibliography of Tito Orlandi, *Coptic Bibliography* (Rome, 1980–); for earlier works, Winifred Kammerer (ed.), *A Coptic Bibliography*, with the collaboration of Elinor Mullett Husselman and Louise A. Shier, University of Michigan General Library Publications, vol. 7 (Ann Arbor, 1950) is still useful. Most surveys of the Christian communities of Egypt either concentrate on the pre-conquest period or on very recent times; useful overall surveys are Christian Cannuyer, *Les coptes*, Fils d'Abraham (Turnhout, 1990) and Pierre du Bourguet, *Les Coptes*, 2nd edn., Que Sais-Je?, vol. 2398 (Paris, 1989). Aziz S. Atiya, *History of Eastern Christianity* (Notre Dame, IN, 1968), 1–145, is still useful when read with its political biases in mind. Stefan Timm, *Das christlich-koptische Ägypten in arabischer Zeit*, 6 parts, Tübinger Atlas des Vorderen Orients, Reihe B (Geisteswissenschaften), vol. 41/1–6 (Wiesbaden, 1984–92) is an extensive gazetteer of post-conquest Egyptian placenames with Christian associations, and is essential for the study of Christian communities in Egypt.

dissension and dwindling numbers, however, the Egyptian Christians managed to keep a distinctive culture and identity alive and active in the first nine centuries of Muslim rule.

According to later traditions, St. Mark the Apostle brought Christianity to Egypt in the mid-first century. The earliest documentary and archaeological attestations of Christianity in Egypt are considered to be from the second century, but such evidence does not become secure in date or common in occurrence until the third century.[2] The growing Christian population of Egypt in this period was subject to sporadic repression by the Roman authorities; the persecution of Christians under the Roman emperors Decius and Diocletian in the third century was especially severe. Indeed, the impact of the martyrdom of Christians in Egypt under Diocletian was so great that later Christians in Egypt dated events from the accession of Diocletian in 283/4 as being in the "Era of Diocletian" or, more commonly, the "Era of the Martyrs" (usually noted in western scholarly literature as A.M., *Anno martyri*).[3] In spite of these often brutal suppressions, the third century also saw the beginnings of important Christian institutions in Egypt. The early development of Christian monasticism in Egypt in this period had a major impact on the growth of this institution throughout the Mediterranean world and beyond.

By the early fourth century, a significant portion of the population of Egypt had become Christian. The ostensible conversion of Emperor Constantine I to Christianity in 312 and the more gradual institution of Christianity as the official religion of the Eastern Roman (later Byzantine) Empire were signs of the removal of official barriers to conversion. Christianity did not begin to displace the Greco-Roman and indigenous Egyptian religious systems in place in Egypt until the middle to late fourth century, and survivals of the older religions continued well after that period. The traditional assumption that Christianity easily replaced a moribund indigenous religious tradition does not hold up under scrutiny; indeed, the increasing Christian majority in fourth- and fifth-century Egypt persecuted the remaining pagans with the vigor (if not the viciousness) of the earlier persecutors of Christians. Pagan temples were converted into churches and monasteries, or merely destroyed, while the means of writing the indigenous Egyptian language developed from the older script systems (with pagan

[2] For the history of early Christianity in Egypt, C. Wilfred Griggs, *Early Egyptian Christianity: From its Origins to 451 C.E.*, 3rd edn., Coptic Studies, II (Leiden, 1993) is a sometimes useful survey, but is uncritical of sources and should be used with caution. Martiniano Pellegrino Roncaglia, *Histoire de l'Église copte*, 4 vols. (Beirut, Dar al-Kalima, 1966–73) is still useful, although becoming increasingly out of date.

[3] For discussion of the dating systems in use among the Christians, see Walter C. Till, "Die Datierung koptischer Urkunden in der islamischen Zeit," in Adolf Grohmann (ed.), *Arabische Chronologie, Arabische Papyruskunde*, Handbuch der Orientalistik, Erste Abteilung, Ergänzungsband II, Erster Halbband (Leiden, 1966), 39–43.

associations) into an alphabetic system based on Greek letters and Egyptian symbols that came to be known as Coptic. Christian churches and monasteries became important and often wealthy institutions throughout Egypt, while the Church in Alexandria came to exert great political influence. By the time of the Muslim conquest, most of the ancient cults were dead and the majority of the inhabitants of Egypt were Christians (with a significant minority of Jews).

It would not be correct, however, to state that there was a single, unitary "Christianity" in Egypt at this time, or a united Christian community. Although there was a consensus as to the general outlines of the Christian religion in Egypt, there were sharp differences as to the finer points. Egypt was often seen as a hotbed of religious heterodoxy, and relations between Christian groups in Egypt were sometimes extremely fragmented and contentious. In part, these divisions reflected dissident elements within the population of Egypt, but they also reflected the larger divisions within the Byzantine Empire and its official church. The most important division between the Egyptian Christian population and that of the rest of the Byzantine world came about through the Monophysite controversy. Ostensibly a dispute over whether Christ had both a divine and a human nature, or just a single divine nature, the decision of the Council of Chalcedon had set the official policy for Christian doctrine as Christ possessing two natures (the Diophysite, more commonly known later as "Melkite", doctrine). But substantial groups of Christians, including a majority of Egyptians, preferred the Monophysite doctrine of Christ having a single divine nature.[4] This led to a complex situation in which most Egyptians were officially considered "heretics," while the minority who followed official doctrine were often accorded special privileges. It is unlikely, however, that the division in Egypt was as simple as is sometimes suggested: a break between an urban, Hellenized, Greek-speaking Melkite elite and a predominantly rural, Egyptian-speaking Monophysite majority. Relations between these two groups were often bitter and were further complicated by the existence of other Christian minorities in Egypt. The situation became critical in the seventh century, when religious tensions reached breaking point under Heraclius after the Sassanian domination of Egypt. Initially, Heraclius intended to introduce a conciliating doctrine (Monotheletism) as a compromise; this satisfied neither side, however, and the arrival of Heraclius's appointee as governor and Patriarch, Cyrus (known as al-Muqawqas in Arabic sources), in 631 signaled the beginning of fierce official persecution of the Monophysite Christians in Egypt that lasted for ten years.[5]

[4] The theological complexities of this dispute and the resultant religious and political conflicts it engendered are covered in W. H. C. Frend, *The Rise of the Monophysite Movement* (Cambridge, 1972).

[5] The account by Alfred J. Butler, in P. M. Fraser (ed.), *The Arab Conquest of Egypt and*

Thus, at the point of the Muslim conquest of Egypt, the majority of Egyptian Christians belonged to a denomination that had been actively persecuted by the Byzantine rulers of Egypt. So it is not surprising to find no evidence of Monophysite Christians rallying on behalf of these Byzantine rulers or of the minority of Melkite Christians in Egypt. There is indeed little evidence to suggest that the Muslim conquest was seen by the Monophysite Christians of Egypt in a particularly negative light. In contrast to the strong reactions against the Sassanian domination to be found in both documentary and literary sources, and even the literary response to the treatment of Monophysites immediately thereafter, the Muslim conquest has left evidence of relatively little immediate reaction in contemporary Egyptian Christian sources. The actual conquest appears in historical narratives, and it makes its way into biographical and literary narratives by the early eighth century, but does so in a relatively neutral way.[6] No documentary sources are known that directly or indirectly refer to the Muslim conquest; the general impression the evidence conveys is that the Monophysite Christians of Egypt were content or resigned themselves to wait and see what was to happen under the new rulers.

For their part, the new rulers of Egypt were not interested in mass conversion to Islam, large-scale migration of Muslim populations into Egypt or even radical changes in existing administrative structures. The Christians of Egypt, whatever their denomination or doctrinal inclination, were treated as *dhimmī*, falling under the protection extended to the non-Muslim groups that fell under Muslim rule.[7] In theory, distinctions were not made between

the Last Thirty Years of Roman Dominion, Containing Also the Treaty of Miṣr in Ṭabarī (1913) and Babylon in Egypt (1914), With a Critical Bibliography and Additional Documentation, 2nd edn. (Oxford, 1978), 168–93, although in need of minor refinements (note additional bibliography by Fraser on pp. lxiv–lxviii), is still a good narrative account of this period. Note also the references in Mena of Nikiou's life of Isaac of Alexandria (trans. David N. Bell, *Mena of Nikiou: The Life of Isaac of Alexandria and the Martyrdom of Saint Macrobius*, Cistercian Studies, vol. 107 (Kalamazoo, MI, 1988), 10–12, 47–48) and the biography of Samuel of Kalamun (Anthony Alcock, *The Life of Samuel of Kalamun by Isaac the Presbyter* (Warminster, 1983), 6–9, 79–84).

[6] In addition to the lives of Mena of Nikiou and Samuel of Kalamoun cited above, allusions to the Muslim conquest are found in certain Coptic apocalyptic works. See Tito Orlandi, "Un testo copto sulla dominazione araba in Egitto," in Tito Orlandi and Frederik Wisse (eds.), *Acts of the Second International Congress of Coptic Studies Roma 22–26 September 1980* (Rome, 1985), 225–33, and Francisco Javier Martinez, "Eastern Christian Apocalyptic in the Early Muslim Period: Pseudo-Methodius and Pseudo-Athanasius" (Ph.D. dissertation, Catholic University of America, 1985), 261–74.

[7] The standard discussion of Claude Cahen, "D̲himma," *EI2* (Leiden, 1960–65), II, 227–31 has seen some subsequent refinement; see the treatment of the subject in Jørgen Bæk Simonsen, *Studies in the Genesis and Early Development of the Caliphal Taxation System with Special Reference to Circumstances in the Arab Peninsula, Egypt and Palestine* (Copenhagen, 1988), 47–60, and the useful summary in Marlis J. Saleh, "Government Relations with the Coptic Community in Egypt During the Fāṭimid Period

the different denominations, so the Monophysites were no longer at a disadvantage in the way in which they had been under Byzantine rule. However, the conquest did bring new obligations to the Christians of Egypt; as *dhimmī*, they were subject to the payment of a poll tax, in addition to a complex of standard land taxes, fines and work obligations.[8] Thus the large majority of the population of Egypt was subject to special taxes and was a great potential source of revenue; from an economic point of view, it is not surprising that there was no attempt to convert this group of potential taxpayers. The administrative districts and structure of Byzantine Egypt were largely retained, even to the point of keeping Christian scribes and continuing to transact business, at least partially, with Greek documentation up to the beginning of the eighth century.[9] So the Christians of Egypt began life under Muslim rule with at least theoretical doctrinal freedom and many of the familiar forms of life under Byzantine rule.

At this point it becomes necessary to address the issue of terminology for the Christians of Egypt, if only for the purposes of the present chapter. The term most commonly used by Western scholars for Egyptian Christians – Copt(ic) – derives from the Arabic word *qibṭ*, itself derived from either a Greek or Semitic antecedent that ultimately goes back to an ancient Egyptian term for Egyptians.[10] To the Muslims, the term was a designation of specifically Egyptian Christians, but they made no further doctrinal distinctions between the Monophysites, Melkites and any other denomination. The more generic word for Christians – *naṣrānī* – was also used of Egyptian Christians by both Muslim and Christian writers. The modern use of the term "Coptic" has become somewhat more complex; among scholars, it is used to denote the indigenous language of the Egyptian Christians. "Coptic" is also often now used specifically to denote the Monophysite Christians of Egypt, and is also used as a generic term for Egyptian Christians, in addition to having acquired somewhat imprecise usage as chronological, political and cultural designation. The multitude of associations and implications that the term has acquired makes it often difficult to use in an accurate way. In the

(358–567 A.H./969–1171 C.E.)" (Ph.D. dissertation, University of Chicago, 1995), 4–52.

8 Bæk Simonsen, *Studies in the Genesis and Early Development of the Caliphal Taxation System* is the most recent thorough study of this complex subject; see especially pp. 79–112.

9 Evident from the post-conquest Greek papyri, for which see the notes by P. M. Fraser in Butler, *Arab Conquest of Egypt*, 2nd edn., lxxvi–lxxx. The most extensive such evidence is found in the trilingual archive of governor Qurrah ibn Šarrik, for which see (most recently) Adolf Grohmann and Raif Georges Khoury, *Chrestomathie de Papyrologie Arabe: Documents relatifs à la vie privée, sociale et administrative dans les premiers siècles islamiques*, Handbuch der Orientalistik, Erste Abteilung, Ergänzungsband II: Zweiter Halbband (Leiden, 1993), texts 93–94 and notes.

10 See Aziz Suryal Atiya, "Ḳibṭ," *EI2*, V, 90–95 and the more recent discussion in Cannuyer, *Les coptes*, 37–38.

present chapter, use of the term "Coptic" is restricted primarily to the language of the Egyptian Christians or to describe the speakers, readers, or writers of this language. Similarly, the Monophysite Christians of Egypt are often described as "Jacobites," although this term more precisely refers to the Monophysite Christians of Syria after Jacob Baradaeus,[11] and "Monophysites" will be used in the present chapter.

The kinds of evidence available for the Christian communities in Egypt after the Muslim conquest are many and varied; indeed, the very range of the types of sources has contributed to the difficulty of arriving at a satisfactory synthesis of the material. Written histories, chronicles and biographies, mostly in Arabic but in some cases in Coptic, Greek or other languages, are the most significant sources for the political and institutional history of the Egyptian Christians and their churches. There is much important information in the Muslim historians (the *Khiṭaṭ* of al-Maqrīzī being one of the most useful sources), but the most extensive accounts come from the Christians themselves. Of outstanding importance for the history of the Egyptian Christians between the Muslim and Ottoman conquests is the *History of the Patriarchs of Alexandria*, a collection of biographies of the Monophysite patriarchs that provides a detailed history of the Monophysite Church in Egypt from its beginnings, along with much general information about the other Christian denominations in Egypt and the course of interaction between Christians and Muslims throughout the period it covers.[12] Surveys of churches and monasteries in Egypt in Arabic are of great value as well.[13] Other literary sources often provide much incidental detail and help to flesh out the pictures provided by the major histories. Documentary sources in Coptic, Greek and Arabic – papyri, ostraca and to a lesser extent inscriptions – reveal a wealth of information about the society

[11] Frend, *Rise of the Monophysite Movement*, 285–91.

[12] The complex history of this composition is examined in Johannes Den Heijer, *Mawhūb ibn Manṣūr ibn Mufarriǧ et l'historiographie copto-arabe: Étude sur la composition de l'Histoire des Patriarches d'Alexandrie*, Corpus Scriptorum Christianorum Orientalium, Subsidia, vol. 83 (Louvain, 1989). The most accessible publications of text and translation of the Arabic version are: B. Evetts (ed.), *History of the Patriarchs of the Coptic Church of Alexandria I–IV*, Patrologia Orientalis, vol. I, 2, I, 4, V, 1, X, 5 (Paris, 1906–15), Yassā Abd al-Masīḥ, O. H. E. Burmester, Aziz S. Atiya, and Antoine Khater (eds.), *History of the Patriarchs of the Egyptian Church, Known as the History of the Holy Church of Sawīrus ibn al-Mukaffa', Bishop of al-Ašmūnīn, Volumes II–III*, Textes et Documents (Cairo, 1943–1970), and Antoine Khater and O. H. E. KHS-Burmester (eds.), *History of the Patriarchs of the Egyptian Church, Known as the History of the Holy Church According to MS. Arabe 302 Bibliothèque Nationale, Paris, Volume IV, Parts 1–2*, Textes et Documents (Cairo, 1974).

[13] Two of the most important are found in B. T. A. Evetts, and Alfred J. Butler (eds.), *The Churches and Monasteries of Egypt and Some Neighbouring Countries Attributed to Abū Ṣāliḥ, The Armenian* (Oxford, 1895), and Bishop Samuel (ed.), *Abu al Makarem: History of the Churches and Monasteries in Lower Egypt in the 13th Cent* (Cairo, 1992).

and culture of the Christians in Egypt. Such sources provide an important control on the accounts of the historians, and can be especially instructive as to the economic and social lives of the Egyptian Christians. The wealth of written material from the Cairo Geniza provides extensive evidence for the relations between Christians, Jews and Muslims.[14] Finally, archaeological remains often provide important evidence for the material culture of the Egyptian Christians, as well as for their urban and institutional contexts.[15]

From this complex of sources, it is possible to see how the Christian population fared under and reacted to the first centuries of Muslim rule in Egypt. From documentary and archaeological sources, it is evident that life continued to be much as it had been before the conquest. Excepting large administrative centers where Arabic-speaking Muslim administrators settled, most towns and villages remained predominantly Christian, both in the make-up of their population and in the layout and characteristics of the settlement.[16] One of the best-attested Christian towns of the post-conquest period is Jeme in Upper Egypt opposite modern-day Luxor; Jeme was not a large settlement, but its unique combination of documentary and archaeological evidence provides an unparalleled look into a Christian community in this time.[17] The town of Jeme was at the center of a group of villages and monasteries that formed an interacting and interdependent unit. The inhabitants of the region transacted business and continued the agricultural activities that were their main sources of sustenance and income as before the conquest.[18] The major observable changes are in the new taxes and works imposed on the inhabitants of Jeme and environs, and the documentation they generated. In addition to tax receipts themselves, and correspondence relating to taxes, the communal agreements and travel passes issued by local officials show that the Christian population was largely self-regulating. Muslim presence is mostly limited to governors and officials known mostly from legal documents, and a few Arabic names are mentioned in business contexts; direct intervention would occur only when, as a letter

[14] Note especially the discussion in S. D. Goitein, *A Mediterranean Society: The Jewish Communities of the Arab World as Portrayed in the Documents of the Cairo Geniza. Volume II: The Community* (Berkeley, 1971), 273–99.

[15] For an overview, see Alexander Badawy, *Coptic Art and Archaeology: The Art of the Christian Egyptians from the Late Antique to the Middle Ages* (Cambridge, MA, 1978).

[16] See, for example, Qūṣ: Jean-Claude Garcin, *Un centre musulman de la Haute-Égypte médiévale: Qūṣ*, Textes arabes et études islamiques, VI (Cairo, 1976), 48–50.

[17] For discussion of Jeme and survey of available evidence, see Terry G. Wilfong, *The Women of Jēme: Gender and Society in a Coptic Town in Late Antique Egypt*, New Texts from Ancient Cultures, 3 (Ann Arbor, forthcoming), ch. 1.

[18] The extent of the Christian population's involvement in agriculture after the conquest is discussed in Terry G. Wilfong, "Agriculture among the Christian Population of Egypt in the Early Islamic Period: Theory and Practice," in Alan Bowman and Eugene Rogan (eds.), *Land, Settlement and Agriculture in Egypt from Pharaonic to Modern Times*, Proceedings of the British Academy 96 (Oxford, 1998), 217–35.

of the late seventh or early eighth century to a nearby monastic community shows, taxes did not get paid.[19]

This is not to say that Christians did not in general maintain contacts with Muslims in the early years of their rule. In larger urban areas and administrative centers, there was a great variety of interaction, especially on an official level. Both Monophysite and Melkite religious authorities were intent on looking after the interests of their own people, as well as making certain that the other group did not acquire greater status.[20] The pattern of action seen in the *History of the Patriarchs of Alexandria* is set early in the Umayyad period and continues long after, and takes the form of denominational groups and internal dissidents within these groups complaining to the Muslim authorities about their rivals in the hope of penalties or punitive measures. And reprisals were frequently forthcoming based on such complaints, taking the form of the imposition of exile or the imprisonment of individuals, the confiscation of church property, heavy taxation and fines, and in some cases the closure of churches. The important point to note is that such actions toward Christians were not usually part of an official policy of persecution, but were often brought on by rival factions of Christians themselves. This pattern of accusations by Christian groups against each other and subsequent Muslim intervention is especially well-documented for the Fāṭimid period, but is true both before and afterward.[21]

Another recurrent theme in the relations of Muslims and Christians was discontent over taxation. From the Umayyad to the ʿAbbāsid periods, local groups of Christians, especially in the north, staged revolts with considerable regularity, culminating in the Bashmuric revolt of 832, which was dramatically suppressed.[22] Such actions could only create more distrust, both among Christians and between Christians and Muslims. There was considerable interest in keeping the Christians under control, but policies varied on how to do so. It was obvious that the church authorities, especially the respective Monophysite and Melkite patriarchies, exercised considerable power over the Christian populations, and special attention was paid to monitoring and influencing these entities. For example, considerable pressure was applied to the Monophysite patriarch to move the capital to Cairo under the Fāṭimids, making it closer to the center of

[19] H. I. Bell, "Two Official Letters of the Arab Period," *Journal of Egyptian Archaeology*, 11 (1925), 265–81.

[20] C. Detlef G. Müller, "Stellung und Haltung der koptischen Patriarchen des 7. Jahrhunderts gegenüber islamischer Obrigkeit und Islam," in Tito Orlandi and Frederik Wisse (eds.), *Acts of the Second International Congress of Coptic Study Roma 22–26 September 1980* (Rome, 1985), 203–13.

[21] Saleh, "Government Relations with the Coptic Community in Egypt."

[22] See the account in the *History of the Patriarchs*: B. Evetts (ed.), *History of the Patriarchs of the Coptic Church of Alexandria III*, Patrologia Orientalis, V, 1 (Paris, 1910), 600–09.

Fāṭimid rule and easier to watch over.[23] Though the truly severe and contradictory restrictions on Christians imposed by the Fāṭimid Caliph al-Ḥākim were not typical of Muslim attempts to deal with their Christian subjects, such restrictions did often develop from earlier precedents.[24] Beyond such specific interactions of Egyptian Christians with Muslims, it is possible to observe two significant developments in the Christian population of Egypt as a whole: Islamization and Arabicization.

The gradual conversion of portions of the Christian population to Islam was a complex process, often difficult to document. There is no single reason for this process, nor is there any recognizable moment at which Christians become a minority. Initially, it is fairly certain that there was no official attempt to encourage conversion, let alone require it; given the income derived from taxes for which non-Muslims were specifically liable, it seems likely that conversion was at least passively discouraged. The earliest conversions seem to have stemmed directly from the taxation of Christians and also seem to have been tied to issues of land tenure; conversion on this basis occurred as early as the Umayyad period.[25] These earliest conversions, then, were largely economically motivated; so too were conversions for the sake of employment, which seems to have been the other major factor in early conversions to Islam. As the sporadic persecution and regulation of Christians became more frequent through the Umayyad and ʿAbbāsid periods and afterwards, escape from these troubles seems to have become an increasing impetus for Christians to convert to Islam. Rates of conversion during any period, however, are difficult to measure. C. Décobert has rightly pointed out the difficulty in determining whether what is usually taken as evidence of conversion (the use of Arab names, for example) is not, in fact, merely a signal of Arabicization.[26] In any case, most of the evidence that survives is limited primarily to an elite, or at least literate population; the extent and reasons for conversion among non-elite Christians are difficult to track. The violent suppression of the Bashmuric Christian tax revolts in 832 appears to have been an important turning-point for conversions.[27] Subsequent successive periods of Ṭūlūnid, Fāṭimid and Ayyūbid rule were, with

23 Mark R. Cohen, *Jewish Self-Government in Medieval Egypt* (Princeton, 1980), 67–69.

24 Saleh, "Government Relations with the Coptic Community in Egypt," 85–89, for al-Ḥākim's destruction of churches; 98–105 for his dress regulations for Christians and their earlier precedents.

25 Gladys Frantz-Murphy, "Conversion in Early Islamic Egypt: The Economic Factor," in Yusuf Ragib (ed.), *Documents de l'Islam Médiéval: Nouvelle Perspectives de Recherche*, Textes arabes et études islamiques, XXIX (Cairo, 1991), 11–17.

26 Christian Décobert, "Sur l'arabisation et l'islamisation de l'Égypte médiévale," in Christian Décobert (ed.), *Itinéraires d'Égypte: Mélanges offerts au père Maurice Martin S. J.*, Bibliothèque d'Étude, vol. 106 (Cairo, 1992), 273–300.

27 See references in Sam I. Gellens, "Egypt, Islamization of," in Aziz S. Atiya (general ed.), *The Coptic Encyclopedia* (New York, 1991), III, 936–42.

notable exceptions, relatively free of systematic persecution, but still saw enough sporadic action against Christians to account for some conversions.[28] The interest in legendary stories of the conversion of Muslim caliphs to Christianity during this time may be significant in this context.[29] The Mamlūk period saw perhaps the most extensive conversions of Christians; increased tension between Christians and Muslims seems to have been a major factor in the marked increase in conversions during this period.[30] Violence was often directed at Christian officials, thus specifically encouraging conversion among elites, and possibly by example among the rest of the Christian population.[31] Even Christians who converted, though, were often mistrusted and still classed as *qibṭ*.[32]

Perhaps the next most significant change in the Christian communities of Egypt, as depicted in literary evidence, was the decline in the use of the Coptic language and the shift to the use of Arabic by Christians.[33] At the time of the Muslim conquest, Coptic and Greek were the principal languages of Egypt. Greek continued to be used as a literary language in Egypt after the conquest, although much less frequently than before, but Greek as a language of administrative texts had largely disappeared by the early ninth century. Coptic seems to have been the principal language of daily life in Egypt just before the conquest (at least outside the major cities), and certainly became so for the Christians in Egypt afterwards. Similarly, Coptic was the standard literary language for Christians just before and after the conquest; Coptic was never, however, a primary administrative language in

[28] Yaakov Lev, "Persecutions and Conversion to Islam in Eleventh Century Egypt," *Asian and African Studies*, 22 (1988), 73–91.

[29] Johannes den Heijer, "Apologetic Elements in Coptic-Arabic Historiography: The Life of Afrahām ibn Zurʿah, 62nd Patriarch of Alexandria," in Samir Khalil Samir and Jørgen Nielsen (eds.), *Christian Arabic Apologetics during the ʿAbbasid Period (750–1258)*, Studies in the History of Religion, 63 (Leiden, 1994), 192–202.

[30] Donald P. Little, "Coptic Converts to Islam During the Baḥrī Mamlūk Period," in Michael Gervers and Ramzi Jibran Bikhazi (eds.), *Conversion and Continuity: Indigenous Christian Communities in Islamic Lands, Eighth to Eighteenth Centuries*, Papers in Mediaeval Studies, 9 (Toronto, 1990), 263–88.

[31] Linda S. Northrup, "Muslim–Christian Relations During the Reign of the Mamlūk Sultan al-Manṣūr Qalāwūn, AD 1278–1290," in Michael Gervers and Ramzi Jibran Bikhazi (eds.), *Conversion and Continuity: Indigenous Christian Communities in Islamic Lands, Eighth to Eighteenth Centuries*, Papers in Mediaeval Studies, 9 (Toronto, 1990), 253–61.

[32] Carl F. Petry, *The Civilian Elite of Cairo in the later Middle Ages* (Princeton, 1981), 272–74.

[33] For the Coptic language in general, see the articles in the "linguistic appendix" of Aziz S. Atiya (general ed.), *The Coptic Encyclopedia* (New York, 1991), VIII, 13–227. For the shift from Coptic to Arabic, the references in Leslie S. B. MacCoull, "Three Cultures under Arab Rule: The Fate of Coptic," *Bulletin de la Société d'Archéologie Copte*, 27 (1985), 61–70, and Leslie S. B. MacCoull, "The Strange Death of Coptic Culture," *Coptic Church Review*, 10 (1989), 35–45 are of great use, although the accompanying discussion is often highly polemical.

Egypt, and indeed, after the decree of 705 making Arabic the sole official language, it could not legally be used as such. Nevertheless, Coptic continued as an active and developing language for centuries after the conquest. Coptic persisted as a documentary language long after Arabic began to be used for documents; this is illustrated, for example, by an archive of letters and contracts from the town of Teshlot dating to the eleventh century.[34] The presence of Arabic documents is not unusual even for a Christian archive – many bilingual collections are known from earlier periods. However, the Arabic texts in the Teshlot archive are a sign of the shift to Arabic as a documentary language for Christians. Christians had begun to use Arabic for legal purposes by the ninth century, and Arabic contracts became relatively common among Christians by the tenth century.[35] The latest Coptic documentary texts are from the thirteenth century: two marriage contracts.[36] Official church documents in Coptic, such as letters of ordination, are known from the fourteenth century.[37] As a spoken language of daily life, Coptic probably survived somewhat longer, although traditions of spoken Coptic surviving as late as the nineteenth century are probably exaggerated. As a literary language, Coptic survived, developed and even flourished after the conquest, when Bohairic gradually supplanted Sahidic as the standard literary dialect. But the increasing use of Arabic by Egyptian Christians for daily life paved the way for use of Arabic in a literary context as well. Both Arabic translations of Coptic texts and original compositions in Arabic by Christian writers in Egypt are known from the tenth century onwards. The process of transition is apparent in such texts as a tenth-century manuscript of an Arabic version of the *Apophthegmata patrum*, in which the Arabic is phonetically spelled out in Coptic characters.[38] The latest substantial Coptic literary composition is the long poem known as the *Triadon* from the fourteenth century.[39] As with the late documentary texts

[34] Published in Michael Green, "A Private Archive of Coptic Letters and Documents from Teshlot," *Oudhedkundige Mededelingen*, 64 (1983), 61–122; note also the discussion in Leslie S. B. MacCoull, "The Teshlot Papyri and the Survival of Documentary Sahidic in the Eleventh Century," *Orientalia Christiana Periodica*, 55 (1989), 201–06.

[35] Note, for example, the texts published in Nabia Abbott, "Arabic Marriage Contracts among the Copts," *Zeitschrift der Deutschen Morgenländischen Gesellschaft*, 95 (1941), 59–81, one of which is an Arabic contract with a Coptic filing docket.

[36] References in MacCoull, "Strange Death of Coptic Culture," 39–40.

[37] See, for example, the documents published in F. Bilabel and A. Grohmann, *Zwei Urkunden aus dem bischöflichen Archiv von Panopolis in Ägypten*, Quellen und Studien zur Geschichte und Kultur des Altertums und des Mittelalters, Reihe A: Mehrsprachige Texte, I (Heidelberg, 1935).

[38] See O. H. E. KHS-Burmester, "Further Leaves from the Arabic MS. in Coptic Script of the Apophthegmata Patrum," *Bulletin de la Société d'Archéologie Copte*, 18 (1965–66), 51–53 for discussion of this phenomenon, and also its reverse: manuscripts in Coptic transcribed into Arabic.

[39] Most recently translated and discussed in Peter Nagel, *Das Triadon: Ein sahidisches*

mentioned above, the *Triadon* also contains an indication of things to come in a parallel Arabic version of the poem. Indeed, Arabic was in use by some Christians within a century or so of the Muslim conquest and can be seen more as replacing Coptic than filling the gap left by the decline of Coptic. As Coptic went into decline as a literary means of expression, Christian scholars began to compile Arabic-language grammars[40] and word-lists (known to western scholars as *scalae*)[41] to preserve the language.These are the very tools used by the first western scholars to study Coptic. Coptic remained in use as a liturgical language throughout this period and beyond, continuing on to the present; such Coptic was fairly well set and similar to the Latin used in western churches long after the language had ceased to be spoken.

Rates of conversion and language transition seem to have been consistent across denominations for Christians; but common languages and common concerns about the preservation of their religion did not serve to bring the different Christian groups in Egypt together. Rather than serving as a unifying factor, the Muslim conquest of Egypt seems only to have aggravated existing tensions between the Monophysites and the Melkite Christians. In theory, neither group was privileged under Muslim rule, but in practice the situation was quite different. The Monophysites had numerical superiority in their favor; they also lacked the traditional associations with Byzantium of the Melkites and seemed to be the natural favorites of the Muslim administrators of Egypt. And, in fact, this is sometimes how the situation worked out. The Monophysites worked to maintain any advantage they could over the Melkites, and considerable anti-Melkite sentiment appeared in Monophysite histories and polemical writings.[42] The Melkites, however, were traditionally associated with the Byzantine administration in Egypt and, hence, were more likely candidates for such government jobs as were open to Christians. Moreover, the Melkites were quick to turn problems within the Monophysite Church to their advantage. The history of Monophysite–Melkite relations, as far as it can be reconstructed, is one of

Lehrgedicht des 14. Jahrhunderts, Martin-Luther-Universität Halle-Wittenberg Wissenschaftliche Beiträge, 23 (K 7) (Halle [Saale], 1983).

40 Enumerated and discussed in the context of an edition of one of the best-known Arabic grammars of Coptic: Gertrud Bauer, *Athanasius von Qūṣ: Qilādat at-taḥrīr fī ʿilm at-tafsīr: Eine koptische Grammatik in arabischer Sprache aus dem 13./14. Jahrhundert*, Islamkundliche Untersuchungen, 17 (Freiburg im Breisgau, 1972), see especially 7–17.

41 Listed in Adel Sidarus, "Les lexiques onomasiologiques gréco-copto-arabes du Moyen Âge et leurs origines anciennes," in Regine Schulz and Manfred Görg (eds.), *Lingua Restituta Orientalis: Festgabe für Julius Assfalg*, Ägypten und Altes Testament, 20 (Wiesbaden, 1990), 348–59, although the attempt to link the *scalae* with earlier Egyptian onomastic texts is not entirely convincing.

42 See, for example, Gérard Troupeau, "Une réfutation des Melkites par Sévère ibn al-Mouqaffaʿ," in C. Laga, J. A. Munitz, and L. van Rompay (eds.), *After Chalcedon: Studies in Theology and Church History offered to Professor Albert van Roey for his Seventieth Birthday*, Orientalia Lovaniensia Analecta, 18 (Leuven, 1985), 371–80.

frequent conflict and infrequent cooperation. This tension was apparent to the Muslim authorities, who turned it to their advantage when possible. The Melkites maintained their own patriarch at Alexandria and their own religious communities and monasteries. Their history is somewhat less well documented than that of the Monophysites, though, and it is often much more difficult to get an accurate picture of this minority denomination except from the obviously biased Monophysite sources dating from when the two groups came into conflict.[43] It is harder still to enumerate and describe the smaller Christian denominations that coexisted with the Monophysites and Melkites under Muslim rule. Such groups make frequent appearances in the histories, but it is not always possible to know if the groups so described represent distinct denominations or are simply splinter groups of the two main denominations. The pre-conquest tradition of Christian sectarian infighting in Egypt seems only to have intensified with the coming of Islam.

In spite of such dissension, the Christian communities of Egypt shared similar characteristics. In part these communities preserved the society and culture of pre-conquest Egypt, but in a form adapted for life under Muslim rule. Christians tended to live together, in urban settings, in Christian communities or quarters.[44] Trends in rural areas are harder to trace outside Christian monasteries, which were normally in a rural setting. The banding together of Christians in Muslim Egypt resulted in increasing regulation from within, not only in matters of religious doctrine and ritual, but also in terms of an increasing conservatism in social organization and practice. This trend toward more conservative social attitudes can be seen perhaps most clearly in the changing status of women in the Christian population.[45] Although Christian women continued to exercise more autonomy and occupy a more visible position in society than their Muslim contemporaries, the restrictions on their behavior by Christian religious authorities seem to have become more pronounced and more rigidly enforced as more Christians converted to Islam. This change can be viewed both as a concession to the prevailing practices of the Muslims and as an attempt to keep control within the Christian community. In addition to this increasing conservatism in social matters, it is also clear that the declining numbers of Christians in

[43] One of the best sources for the Melkite Church is the history of Eutychios, Michael Breydy, *Das Annalenwerk des Eutychios von Alexandrien*, Corpus Scriptorum Christianorum Orientalium, Scriptores Arabici, 44–45 (Louvain, 1985); what is known of the Melkite Church from the Muslim conquest up to 1095 is synthesized in Stanley H. Skreslet II, "The Greeks in Medieval Islamic Egypt: A Melkite Community under the Patriarch of Alexandria (640–1095)" (Ph.D. dissertation, Yale University, 1988).

[44] Such as the Christian neighborhoods of Fusṭāṭ, for which see Wladyslaw B. Kubiak, *Al-Fusṭāṭ: Its Foundation and Early Urban Development* (Cairo, 1987), 102–08.

[45] See the discussion in Wilfong, *Women at Jēme*, ch. 6.

Egypt resulted in an increasing reliance by those who remained Christian on the central institutions of their religion.

The institutions of post-conquest Christianity in Egypt are known mostly for the Monophysites, although we do have some information about Melkite institutions as well. Central to Christian life in Egypt was the church – both the physical building and the institutional entity it was designed to house.[46] Christian communities in both urban and rural settings tended to cluster physically near the church building, while organizing life around the institution. The church par excellence for Monophysite Christians in Egypt was represented by the church of the patriarch, first at its traditional site of Alexandria, then at Damrū in the early eleventh century and finally at Cairo a few decades later. The activities of the patriarch's church and the other major churches in larger towns, where religious policy was set and official dealings with the Muslim administration were carried out were those which were recorded in historical sources such as the *History of the Patriarchs*. For the individual Christian, the local church was a central institution and individuals organized their lives around its liturgical schedule and activities. The local church served as meeting-place and guide; it was involved in the administration of charity and education, and was essential to Christian life.

The other important Christian religious institution in post-conquest Egypt was the monastery. Monasteries were obviously of great importance to the men or women who lived in them, not only for spiritual reasons, but also as places of employment, learning, refuge and, for some individuals, imprisonment.[47] Monasteries were also of importance to the non-monastic population, serving at times as important factors in the economic life of the Egyptian Christians, especially in the production and circulation of goods, and as owners of land in the countryside. Monasteries were also sometimes centers of theological dispute and even rebellion, making them suspect to local Muslim authorities. Although the local churches and monasteries were the institutions of the most immediate importance to Egyptian Christians, the practice of pilgrimage to monasteries and churches in other parts of Egypt is well-attested and not uncommon in certain periods.[48]

The church and, more especially, the monasteries, also served as foci for the intellectual and cultural life of Christians in post-conquest Egypt. Monasteries were the nexus of literary production and distribution for the

[46] For what follows, in general, see O. H. E. KHS-Burmester, *The Egyptian or Coptic Church: A Detailed Description of her Liturgical Services and the Rites and Ceremonies Observed in the Administration of her Sacraments*, Textes et Documents (Cairo, 1967).

[47] For women in a monastic context, see Iris Habib el-Masih, "A Historical Survey of the Convents for Women in Egypt up to the Present Day," *Bulletin de la Société d'Archéologie Copte*, 14 (1950–57), 63–111, but note also the discussion in Wilfong, *Women of Jēme*, ch. 4.

[48] Survey in Gérard Viaud, *Les pèlerinages coptes en Égypte, d'après les notes de Qommos Jacob Muyser*, Bibliothèque d'Études Coptes, 15 (Cairo, 1979).

Egyptian Christians; they were crucial for the preservation of Christian literature and the continuation and growth of the Christian intellectual tradition within Egypt. Older texts were preserved and recopied in monasteries, while adaptations, translations and new compositions mostly came from a monastic setting.[49] In such a setting, the Coptic language was kept alive probably much later than in the secular world, and when it finally gave way to Arabic for most uses, the preservation of Coptic in grammars, word-lists and the liturgy itself owed much to the activities of monks. Outside a monastic context, the great emphasis on education within the Christian communities of Egypt still attests to the influence of the monasteries, a tradition that persists in the education of Egyptian Christians to this day. None of this is to say that an active intellectual life for an Egyptian Christian was restricted to the monastery; there are many instances of Christian scholars living in a secular urban setting. But the foundation of most Christian intellectual activity in this period lay clearly in the monastic world.

Most of the evidence for the intellectual life of the Egyptian Christians is manifested in the extensive and varied literary production of the period. Much of this activity involved the recopying, adaptation and translation of earlier work, leading some scholars to assume mistakenly that there was little significant original work produced by Christian writers in Egypt after the conquest. This is far from the case; the period saw an extraordinary range and amount of written work in Coptic and later in Arabic.[50] The

[49] The best-documented such activity is from the complex of monasteries at the Wadi Natrun, from which enormous quantities of manuscripts derive; see the specific discussion in Lothar Störk, *Koptische Handschriften: Die Handscriften der Staats- und Universitätsbibliothek Hamburg, Teil 2: Die Handschriften aus Dair Anbā Maqār*, Verzeichnis der orientalischen Handschriften in Deutschland, 22:2 (Stuttgart, 1995), 41–98, and, in general, Hugh G. Evelyn White, *The Monasteries of the Wādi 'n Natrūn, Part I: New Coptic Texts from the Monastery of Saint Macarius, Edited with an Introduction on the Library at the Monastery of Saint Macarius*, Publications of the Metropolitan Museum of Art Egyptian Expedition, II (New York, 1926). Extensive collections of manuscripts attesting to monastic scribal activity are known from other sites, including Sohag and Hamouli; the Sohag manuscripts are scattered across the world, while the Hamouli library is largely preserved in the Pierpont Morgan Library.

[50] For literature in Coptic, see the general discussions in Tito Orlandi, "Literature, Coptic," in Aziz S. Atiya (general ed.) *The Coptic Encyclopedia*, (New York, 1991), V, 1450–60, Tito Orlandi, "Coptic Literature," in Birger A. Pearson and James E. Goehring (eds.), *The Roots of Egyptian Christianity*, Studies in Antiquity and Christianity (Philadelphia, 1986), 51–81, and Martin Krause, "Koptische Literatur," in Wolfgang Helck and Eberhard Otto (eds.) *Lexikon der Ägyptologie, Band III* (Wiesbaden, 1979), 694–728; also still useful Johannes Leipoldt, "Geschichte der koptischen Literatur,' in C. Brockelmann et al., *Geschichte der christlichen Litteraturen des Orients*, 2nd edn., Die Litteraturen des Ostens in Einzeldarstellungen, VII, 2 (Leipzig, 1909), 131–83. For Arabic-language Christian literature, the standard reference is, of course, Georg Graf, *Geschichte der Christlichen Arabischen Literatur*, 5 vols., Studi e Testi, 118, 133, 146, 147, 172 (Città del Vaticano: Biblioteca Apostolica Vaticana, 1944–53), see especially 2:294–475 and 4:114–48. The general discussions

historical works in Coptic and Arabic from this time have already been mentioned above, but the majority of the writing produced was more specifically religious: scriptural commentaries, theological tractates, sermons, the lives of saints, monastic guides and epistles, martyrdoms and liturgical works were composed or adapted during this time. Important writers of the post-conquest period were generally noted clerics if not patriarchs and include Benjamin I, Severus of Ashmunein, Christodulos, Cyril III Ibn Laqlaq, and many others.[51] The transition from Coptic to Arabic in spoken language also led to a very active tradition of translation and elaboration of Coptic texts into Arabic.[52] Whether in Coptic or Arabic, original or translation, the colophons of literary manuscripts often give important information as to the context of the copying of the text, as well as information about the occupation and religious affiliation of the copyist.[53] The eventual replacement of Coptic by Arabic as the main literary language also had the effect of making a much larger body of literature with a much broader range accessible to the Egyptian Christians. Previously, the Coptic (and sometimes Greek) reading population of Christians had access mostly to indigenously written, translated or adapted literature; the coming of Arabic gave potential access to an international body of literature from throughout the Arabic-literate world, and there is considerable indication that this access was not merely theoretical. What might be termed "secular" literature, although ultimately probably also emanating from a monastic context, includes a number of historical "romances" and a variety of poems.[54] The intellectual productions of the Christians in Egypt were not

in Aziz S. Atiya, "Literature, Copto-Arabic," in Aziz S. Atiya (general ed.), *The Coptic Encyclopedia* (New York, 1991), 5:1460–67 and Khalil Samir, "Arabic Sources for Early Egyptian Christianity," in Birger A. Pearson and James E. Goehring (eds.), *The Roots of Egyptian Christianity*, Studies in Antiquity and Christianity (Philadelphia, 1986), 82–97 are useful summaries.

51 An anthology of excepts from relevant major Coptic and Arabic authors is in Cannuyer, *Les coptes*, 107–127.

52 The majority of such translated or adapted works are covered by Graf, *Geschichte der Christlichen Arabischen Literatur*, 1:456–83, 640–52, although not always with reference to or knowledge of the Coptic originals.

53 Colophons of Sahidic manuscripts are collected in Arn van Lantschoot, *Recueil des colophons des manuscrits chrétiens d'Égypte, Tome I: Les colophons coptes des manuscrits sahidiques*, Bibliothèque du Muséon, I (Louvain, 1929); the projected volumes of colophons in other dialects were never published, and, in general, colophons in Greek and Arabic are not collected and are scattered through individual manuscript publications and catalogues. Individual copyists are listed in Atiya, *Coptic Encyclopedia*, under their names, providing a wealth of information not covered in Lantschoot.

54 For the former, see C. D. G. Müller, "Romances," in Aziz S. Atiya (general ed.), *The Coptic Encyclopedia* (New York, 1991), 7:2059–61, and Terry G. Wilfong, "The Coptic Story of Theodosios and Dionysios, CE X-X," in Traianos Gagos et al. (eds.), *P. Michigan Koenen (=P.Mich. XVIII): Michigan Texts Published in Honor of Ludwig Koenen*, Studia Amstelodamensia ad Epigraphicam, Ius Antiquum et Papyrologicam

limited to literary texts; there is a great range of grammatical, scientific, alchemical, medical and magical texts,[55] as well as school texts that show something of the processes of education among the Christian population of Egypt.[56]

In addition to this extensive literary production, Christian culture in Egypt was also visibly manifested in other forms of expression. The visual arts of the Egyptian Christians of this period were distinctive blends of indigenous Egyptian elements with those of Hellenistic, Byzantine and ultimately Islamic artistic traditions.[57] Two-dimensional art of the Egyptian Christians is best typified by painted icons, mural paintings and manuscript illuminations,[58] as well as the ubiquitous "Coptic" textiles.[59] Such produc-

Pertinentia, 36 (Amsterdam, 1996), 351–56; for the latter H. Junker, *Koptische Poesie des 10. Jahrhunderts*, 2 vols. (Berlin, 1908–11).

55 Grammars are discussed above in the context of the shift from Coptic to Arabic. For scientific and alchemical texts, see the references in Leslie S. B. MacCoull, "Coptic Alchemy and Craft Technology in Islamic Egypt: The Papyrological Evidence," in *The Medieval Mediterranean: Cross-cultural Contacts*, Marilyn Chiat and Kathryn Reyerson (eds.), 3 (St. Cloud, MN, 1988), 101–04 (reprinted in Leslie S. B. MacCoull, *Coptic Perspectives on Late Antiquity*, London, 1993, XV); perhaps to be classified with these texts are the "farmers' almanacs" discussed and translated in Wilfong, "Agriculture among the Christian Population." Medical texts are translated in Walter C. Till, *Die Arzneikunde der Kopten* (Berlin, 1951), and see the long papyrus published in Émile Chassinat, *Un papyrus medicale copte*, Mémoires publiés par les membres de l'Institut Français d'Archéologie Orientale, 32 (Cairo, 1921). Coptic-language magical texts are translated and discussed in Marvin Meyer and Richard Smith, *Ancient Christian Magic: Coptic Texts of Ritual Power* (San Francisco, 1994); for a summary discussion of these and Arabic-language Christian magical texts, see Werner Vycichl, "Magic," in Aziz S. Atiya (general ed.), *The Coptic Encyclopedia* (New York, 1991), 5:1499–1509. Note also the text published in Nessim Henry Henein, and Thierry Bianquis, *La magie par les Psaumes: Édition et traduction d'un manuscrit arabe chrétien d'Égypte*, Bibliothèque d'Études Coptes, vol. 12 (Cairo, 1975).

56 Coptic-language school texts collected in Monika R. M. Hasitzka, *Neue Texte und Dokumentation zum Koptisch-Unterricht*, 2 vols., Mitteilungen aus der Papyrussammlung der Österreichischen Nationalbibliothek (Papyrus Erzherzog Rainer), n. s., vol. 18 (Vienna, 1990).

57 See in general Badawy, *Coptic Art and Archaeology*.

58 See Marie-Hélène Rutschowscaya, "La peinture sur bois dans les collections coptes du Musée du Louvre," in Marguerite Rassart-Debergh and Julien Ries (eds.), *Actes du IVe Congrès Copte, Louvain-la-Neuve, 5–10 septembre 1988; I. Art et archéologie* (Louvain-la-Neuve, 1992), 56–62; Jules Leroy, *Les peintures des couvents du désert d'Esna*, published in collaboration with Basile Psiroukis and Bernard Lenthéric, "La peinture murale chez les coptes, 1," Mémoires publiés par les membres de l'Institut Français d'Archéologie Orientale, vol. 94 (Cairo, 1975); and Jules Leroy, *Les manuscrits coptes et coptes-arabes illustrés*, Bibliothèque archéologique et historique, vol. 96 (Paris, 1974).

59 Marie-Hélène Rutschowskaya, *Tissus Coptes* (Paris, 1990) and Annemarie Stauffer, *Spätantike und koptische Wirkereien: Untersuchungen zur ikonographische Tradition im spätantiken und frühmittelalterliche Textilwerkstätten* (Bern, 1992) are useful introductions and guides to the extremely extensive literature on the subject. Karel C. Innemée, *Ecclesiastical Dress in the Medieval Near East*, Studies in Textile and

tions are highly recognizable by their stylized representations and vivid decoration; although they are most often found in a religious context, secular and non-representational motifs are often incorporated as well. Three-dimensional art includes metalwork, stone sculpture and the distinctive traditions of woodwork for which the Egyptian Christians were well known.[60] Architecture became another specialization of Christians in Egypt,[61] and one often put to use by Muslims, as in the case of the Christian architects of Ibn Ṭūlūn and Ṣalāḥ al-Dīn.[62] Music is the best-attested of the performing arts among the Egyptian Christians, specifically religious music.[63] Church services were sung and the music to which these services were set has survived, although often filtered through later traditions. Although often similar to the liturgical music of other eastern Christian groups, Coptic church music retains highly distinctive features of its own; some scholars have seen in this distinction the surviving traces of the music of pharaonic Egypt, but this is largely undocumentable. Secular music of this period has left little trace; lyrics of songs that could be classed as secular are known and these often bear indications of the tune to which they were to be sung, but the music itself was not written down.[64]

The impact of these developments in Egyptian Christian culture after the Muslim conquest was restricted largely to within the borders of Egypt. Egypt's importance to Christianity in general, however, was a matter of considerable interest throughout the Christian and Muslim worlds. Although not as closely associated with the early history of Christianity as the "Holy

Costume History, vol. 1 (Leiden, 1992) is a helpful guide to the uses to which such textiles were put.

60 See Dominique Bénazeth, "Objets de métal de la section copte du Musée du Louvre," in Marguerite Rassart-Debergh and Julien Ries (eds.), *Actes du IVe Congrès Copte, Louvain-la-Neuve, 5–10 septembre 1988; I. Art et archéologie* (Louvain-la-Neuve, 1992), 63–68, John Beckwith, *Coptic Sculpture, 300–1300* (London, 1963) and Marie-Helene Rutschowscaya,*Catalogue des bois de l'Égypte copte au Musée du Louvre* (Paris, 1986).

61 There is no general guide to the architecture of Christians in Egypt, but see Peter Grossmann, *Mittelalterliche Langshauskuppelkirchen und verwandte Typen in Oberägypten*, Abhandlungen des Deutschen Archäologischen Instituts Kairo, Koptische Reihe, 3 (Glückstadt, 1982), Charalambia Coquin, *Les édifices chrétiens du Vieux-Caire, Volume I: Bibliographie et topographie historique*, Bibliothèque d'Études Coptes, 11 (Cairo, 1974) and Hugh G. Evelyn White, *The Monasteries of the Wādi 'n Natrūn, Part III: The Architecture and Archaeology*, ed. Walter Hauser, Publications of the Metropolitan Museum of Art Egyptian Expedition, 8 (New York, 1933). The architecture and decoration specifically of monasteries is surveyed in C. C. Walters, *Monastic Archaeology in Egypt*, Modern Egyptology Series (Warminster, 1974).

62 For Christians as architects for Muslims, see Kubiak, *Al-Fusṭāṭ*, 75.

63 Perhaps the most detailed survey to date is in the complex of articles under "Music, Coptic," in Aziz S. Atiya (general ed.), *The Coptic Encyclopedia* (New York, 1991), 6:1715–47.

64 The "poems" in Junker, *Koptische Poesie*, referred to above, were actually songs, the tune of which was often indicated.

Land" of Syro-Palestine or the sacred sites in Asia Minor or even Rome, Egypt was considered highly important for its contributions to early monasticism. Although pilgrimage by outsiders to holy sites in Egypt was not as common (or indeed as practical) as pilgrimage to these other places, it did still take place, most often by Christians from elsewhere in the Near East. The monasteries of Scetis and Nitria were important pilgrimage sites to devout Christians familiar with the Arabic or Syriac versions of the *Apophthegmata patrum* or the other early monastic histories, and pilgrimage to Upper Egyptian Christian shrines by Syrian monks was not unheard-of. But even more important than visits to these early Egyptian monastic sites was the circulation and use of the monastic literature that they generated. Indeed, the impact of the Egyptian monastic literature was enormous: the Latin translations and versions of the Greek-language stories of the desert fathers and early monastic rules were instrumental in the development of the monastic tradition in western Christianity. Monastic rules were patterned on the Latin versions of Egyptian rules, while the stories and sayings of early Egyptian monks entered into the literature of medieval Europe, recycled into such original works as the plays of the tenth-century nun Hrosiwtha. The writings of Egyptian monasticism in Greek contributed directly to monastic traditions in the Byzantine world. The Arabic, Syriac and Ethiopic versions of such works contributed directly to the development of monastic tradition among Christians throughout the regions in which these languages were used, taking Egyptian traditions of monasticism well beyond Egypt itself.

Contact with other Christian populations was not limited to the occasional pilgrimage or the more passive means of the dissemination of monastic literature. The scholarly tradition that the Muslim conquest effectively cut off Egyptian Christians from direct and sustained contact with other Christian populations is not supported by the evidence: Egyptian Christians interacted on many levels with Christian groups outside Egypt. Not surprisingly, the Christian communities of Egypt had the most direct contact with corresponding communities elsewhere in the Muslim world. In part this was simply a matter of access, but it was also due to doctrinal distribution: Egyptian Christians were mostly Monophysites and the other major Monophysite population was in Syria, so that the interaction between the two groups is not surprising. The *History of the Patriarchs of Alexandria* records very frequent interchange between the Monophysite patriarchs of Alexandria and Antioch, along with considerable indications that such interaction also took place on a more general level as well.[65] This is

[65] See, for example, the events described in the life of Monophysite Patriarch Mennas I, when the patriarch of Antioch is unwittingly involved in a plot against Mennas around 767 (B. Evetts (ed.), *History of the Patriarchs of the Coptic Church of Alexandria III*, Patrologia Orientalis, vol. 5:1 (Paris, 1910), 476–77) or the correspondence between Antiochene patriarch Cyriacus and his Egyptian counterpart about the unity of their

confirmed by the often considerable number of Syrian monks known in Egypt, and best known from the Wādī Naṭrūn monasteries, although individual Syriac-writing monks are known in Upper Egypt relatively early.[66] At Wādī Naṭrūn, the population was considerable enough for one of the monasteries to come to be known as Dayr as-Suriani ("Monastery of the Syrians") and many Syriac manuscripts are known to come from the area.[67] Pilgrimage to holy sites in the Muslim Near East was also an important part of the interaction of Egyptians with other Christian populations. Jerusalem was in particular a pilgrimage site par excellence, a place where Egyptian Christians established a church and monastery; it is in Jerusalem that most of the information on the Egyptian custom of tattooing pilgrims has been preserved.[68]

Egyptian Christians also interacted, mostly on an official level, with nearby Christian populations that were not under Muslim rule. The closest such group was the Christian community in Nubia directly to the south. The relations between the Egyptian and Nubian churches are particularly well-documented, through accounts by contemporary writers and from the extensive documentary and archaeological remains from such Nubian sites as Qasr Ibrim and Faras.[69] The Christian populations of Nubia left behind extensive documentation in Old Nubian, in which both translations of biblical and Patristic texts as well as non-literary documents such as letters and contracts are known.[70] Sources in Coptic, Greek and Arabic are also known from Nubian Christian sites and show how communication was carried out with the Egyptian Christians.[71] Indeed, much of this documenta-

two churches (ibid., 506–08). Much of the interaction described between Egypt and Syria is through the exchange of letters.

66 H. E. Winlock and W. E. Crum, *The Monastery of Epiphanius at Thebes, Part I*, The Archaeological Material by H. E. Winlock, The Literary Material by W. E. Crum, Publications of the Metropolitan Museum of Art Egyptian Expedition, 3 (New York, 1926), 140–42.

67 Hugh G. Evelyn White, *The Monasteries of the Wādi 'n Natrūn, Part II: The History of the Monasteries of Nitria and Scetis*, ed. Walter Hauser, Publications of the Metropolitan Museum of Art Egyptian Expedition, 7 (New York, 1932), 309–21. Also note the translation of Syriac literature into Coptic, whether directly or through Arabic versions; a recently published example with discussion is Paul-Hubert Poirier, "Fragments d'une version copte de la *Caverne des Trésors*," *Orientalia*, 52 (1983), 415–23.

68 See Otto Meinardus, *The Copts in Jerusalem* (Cairo, 1960) and John Carswell, *Coptic Tattoo Designs*, with a foreword by Margaret A. Murray, revised and expanded edn. (Beirut, 1958).

69 See especially Stefan Jakobielski, *A History of the Bishopric of Pachoras on the Basis of Coptic Inscriptions*, Faras, vol. 3 (Warsaw, 1972), which provides a useful summary of the interaction between Egypt and Faras.

70 The Old Nubian texts from Qasr Ibrim provide a good cross-section of the range of documentation in this language; see Gerald M. Browne, *Old Nubian Texts from Qasr Ibrim I-III*, Texts from Excavations, 9–10, 12 (London, 1988–91).

71 See, for example, the bilingual Arabic-Coptic letter of Monophysite patriarch Gabriel

tion shows the dependence of the Nubian Church on the Egyptian for ecclesiastical appointments and guidance. Even farther to the south, the Church in Ethiopia was similarly dependent on the Egyptian Monophysite Church, which chose from its own ranks the successive heads of the Ethiopian church and exerted considerable influence at a distance.[72] Ethiopic translations of Egyptian Christian literature (most often from Arabic versions of Coptic or Greek texts) sometimes remain the only attestations of the now-lost originals, as with the important chronicle of John of Nikiou.[73]

Interaction with Christian populations outside northeastern Africa and the Near East was more problematic for Egyptian Christians, but was still sporadically undertaken. A community of Coptic-literate Egyptians on Cyprus from the twelfth to the sixteenth centuries is perhaps explicable more in terms of Egyptian economic and political interest in Cyprus than formal relations between churches.[74] Relations with the Byzantine Church were not resumed in a significant way after the Muslim conquest, owing no doubt both to the difficulties of communication and to the doctrinal differences that became more acute with the continued lack of contact. Egyptian Christian contacts with the western church based at Rome are much better-known, at least to modern scholars. The crusades, of course, brought about a sort of contact between Egyptian and European Christians, but such interaction could not, on the whole, have been considered positive. Crusader victories in Egypt often resulted in reprisals against the Egyptian Christians, the Muslim rulers of Egypt not distinguishing between the two groups.[75] For their part, western crusaders were not particularly impressed with the state of Christianity in Egypt and considered the Monophysites

IV from 1372 to the Nubian people confirming the appointment of Timotheos as successor to their recently deceased bishop, published J. Martin Plumley, *The Scrolls of Bishop Timotheos: Two Documents from Medieval Nubia*, Texts from Exacavations, 1 (London, 1975).

72 The interrelationship between Egypt and Ethiopia is summarized in Christian Stoffregen-Pedersen, *Les Éthiopiens*, Fils d'Abraham (Turnhout, 1990), 155–56, and Atiya, *History of Eastern Christianity*, 146–57; both of these works are, in addition, useful guides to the history and culture of Christianity in Ethiopia.

73 Robert Henry Charles, *The Chronicle of John (c. 690 AD) Coptic Bishop of Nikiu: Being a History of Egypt Before and During the Arab Conquest Translated from Hermann Zotenberg's Edition of the Ethiopic Version with an Introduction, Critical and Linguistic Notes, and an Index of Names*, Text and Translation Series, 3 (London, 1916).

74 The evidence is discussed in Anne Boud'hors, "Manuscrits coptes 'Chypriotes' à la Bibliothèque Nationale," in *Études coptes: Troisième Journée d'études, Musée du Louvre 23 Mai 1986*, Cahiers de la Bibliothèque copte, 4 (Louvain, 1989), 11–20.

75 Aziz Atiya has written most extensively of Egyptian Christians and the crusades, most recently "Crusades, Copts and the," in Aziz S. Atiya (general ed.), *The Coptic Encyclopedia* (New York, 1991), 3:663–65, but the relevant sections in Norman P. Zacour and H. W. Hazard (eds.), *The Impact of the Crusades on the Near East, A*

there to be schismatics "crippled for a long time by a miserable and lamentable error."[76] Nevertheless, there was some interest in a rapprochement between Egypt and Rome. The presence of European Christian traders and missionaries in Alexandria in the fourteenth and fifteenth centuries doubtless contributed to this renewed interest in contact. There is also evidence of travel by Egyptian Christians into Europe: a phrasebook with the Old French phrases transliterated into Coptic characters was evidently intended for Coptic-literate Christians (most probably monks) traveling in French-speaking Europe.[77] Official interaction between the Egyptian church and Rome seems to have been first initiated in 1237 by Cyril III Ibn Laqlaq, who is thought to have envisioned some sort of union with the Church at Rome.[78] Such a union did not, of course, take place, but the initiative did have the result of setting a precedent for future attempts at reconciliation. The most dramatic attempt occurred as a result of the 1438 Council of Ferrara-Florence, attended by an Egyptian delegate sent by the Monophysite Patriarch Johannes IX at the request of Pope Eugenius IV. This resulted in a papal bull proclaiming the union of the Egyptian Church with that of Rome, but the matter was carried no further.

This attempted alliance with Rome took place during Mamlūk rule of Egypt and it is during this period that the Egyptian Christians were most vulnerable to oppression. During the two and a half centuries of Mamlūk control of Egypt, the status and number of Christians continued to decline. Popular reactions against Christians combined with incidents of official destruction of Christian churches to make the situation difficult for those who did not convert; when groups of Christians did revolt, they were met with quick reprisals. On the face of it, the number of officials identified as "Copts" under the Mamlūks would seem to be a positive indication of the status of Christians. However, it has been shown that most of these "Copts" were in fact Muslim converts identified by their past religion.[79] This identification seems to have been made because of a general distrust of these converts and their loyalty. Such "Copts" occupied only certain kinds of

History of the Crusades, ed. Kenneth M. Setton, 5 (Madison, 1985) present a more balanced account.

[76] As described by Jacques de Vitry; see Christian Cannuyer, "Coptes et 'Jacobites' dans l'*Historia Hierosolimitana* (1220) de Jacques de Vitry, Évêque d'Acre," in Marguerite Rassart-Debergh and Julien Ries (eds.) *Actes du IVe Congrès Copte, Louvain-la-Neuve, 5–10 septembre 1988* (Louvain-la-Neuve, 1992), 198–208.

[77] Gaston Maspero, "Le vocabulaire français d'un copte du XIIIe siècle," *Romania*, 17 (1888), 481–512.

[78] For Egyptian Christian relations with Rome in general, see Petro B. T. Bilaniuk, "Coptic Relations with Rome," in Aziz S. Atiya (general ed.), *The Coptic Encyclopedia* (New York, 1991), 2:609–11 and references therein.

[79] See Carl F. Petry, "Copts in Late Medieval Egypt," in Aziz S. Atiya (general ed.), *The Coptic Encyclopedia* (New York, 1991), 2:618–35 for a detailed listing.

position within the Mamlūk administration, and it is unlikely, given the mistrust with which they were viewed, that they were willing or able to exert much influence in favor of their former co-religionists. Persecution of Christians took place along with heavy taxation, not necessarily as a matter of policy but more often in sporadic bursts. It is against this backdrop of insecurity and declining numbers that the attempts to ally the Egyptian Church with that of Rome took place. Ultimately, the appeal to Rome was to no avail and the Christian communities of Egypt were left on their own.

The situation of the Christian population of Egypt on the eve of the Ottoman conquest was precarious. Decidedly in the minority, their numbers were perhaps the lowest they had ever been, with a large percentage of the remaining Egyptian Christians living in monastic communities. The decline in the population level of Christians in Egypt posed unique challenges to those who still identified with the religion. In particular, the Christian communities of Egypt had to balance the preservation of their cultural and religious traditions with the need to adapt to changing and often adverse political circumstances. Although beyond the chronological scope of this chapter, it is certainly not out of place to conclude by noting that the Christian communities of Egypt did survive and came, in time, to flourish again, retaining their unique cultural identities and religious doctrines while remaining a significant social and economic presence in Egypt through to the present day.

8

The non-Muslim communities: the Jewish community

NORMAN A. STILLMAN

Although by no means the most important Jewish community of the medieval Muslim world either numerically or culturally, Egyptian Jewry is certainly the best-known to modern historical scholarship, or at least the most intimately known with regard to its quotidian life during the Islamic High Middle Ages, owing to the rich documentation that has survived in the Cairo Geniza. The Geniza was a vast repository of discarded written materials – sacred and secular, literary and documentary – that was attached to the Ben Ezra synagogue in Fusṭāṭ (Old Cairo). Emptied of its contents in 1896, the Geniza was found to contain over a quarter of a million manuscripts and fragments dating back as far as the mid-eighth century, although the lion's share of the material dated from the tenth to the thirteenth centuries, that is from the Fāṭimid, Ayyūbid, and early Mamlūk periods.[1]

Egypt had always been the foremost center of Hellenistic Jewry. However, by the time of the Arab conquest, the heyday of the Egyptian Jews had long passed and their numbers were considerably reduced in the suppression of Jewish uprisings during the first two centuries of the Common Era and later, as a result of Byzantine Christian persecution. Still, the number of Jews was large enough to impress the Muslim conquerors from the Arabian desert. According to the early chronicler Ibn ʿAbd al-Ḥakam, there were 40,000 Jews in Alexandria alone when the city fell to the Muslims in 642.[2] Although the actual figure was probably closer to 4,000, it is a good indication of the rude desert Arabs' sense of wonder and amazement at the size and sophistication of the large urban Egyptian Jewish community. In fact the

[1] For a general introduction to the Geniza and a magisterial survey of the social and economic life of medieval Egyptian Jewry based upon its contents, see S. D. Goitein, *A Mediterranean Society: The Jewish Communities of the Arab World as Portrayed in the Documents of the Cairo Geniza*, 6 vols. (Berkeley and Los Angeles, 1967–94).

[2] Ibn ʿAbd al-Ḥakam, *Futūḥ Miṣr* [The History of the Conquest of Egypt, North Africa and Spain], ed. Charles C. Torrey (New Haven, 1922), p. 82.

Jews are listed along with 4,000 gardens, 4,000 bath houses, and 400 royal places of amusement among the marvels of the city.

As tolerated members of a recognized scriptural religion (Arabic, *ahl al-kitāb*), the Jews of Egypt were required to pay tribute, or *jizya*, to the Islamic state for its protection. But the imposition of the *jizya* probably was the cause for no additional hardship since the Egyptian Jews were already paying a poll tax as well as other fiscal impositions to the Byzantine authorities. In fact, the Muslim conquest in all likelihood brought them some relief, since the legal position of the Jews in the Byzantine Empire had been declining for more than a century. The years immediately preceding the Arab takeover had been marked by a policy of outright persecution under the Emperor Heraclius, inflicted because the Jews collaborated with the Persians during the recent round of wars between the two rival empires. These had ended with a Byzantine victory and the expulsion of the Persians from Syria, Palestine and Egypt in 628.

Little is known about Egyptian Jewry until the latter part of the tenth century, which is the time when large numbers of documents begin to be preserved in the Cairo Geniza. The first two centuries of the Islamic era represented a time of far-reaching political, social, and economic change for all of the Middle East and its inhabitants, including the Jews. It is also one of the most obscure periods in Jewish history. But even though the specific course of events in Jewish life during these formative years remains shrouded in darkness, the outcome is eminently clear. During this time, the transformation of the Jews into a primarily urban people, a process which had already begun in late antiquity, was completed. The Babylonian Talmud was disseminated from Iraq throughout the Jewish world to become the constitutional framework of medieval and later Judaism. Jews, along with other peoples in the caliphate, began to take part in the burgeoning commercial revolution that was occurring in the wake of the ʿAbbāsid rise to power. Also during this time Jews began migrating to Egypt from the Islamic east, particularly after the political upheavals of the second half of the ninth century that shook Iraq and Iran. As early as 750, an individual by the name of Abū ʿAlī Ḥasan al-Baghdādī was "Head of the Congregation" (Hebrew *Rosh ha-Qahal*) in Fusṭāṭ.[3]

There was little that distinguished the Jewish community of Egypt during the first three centuries of Islamic rule. The great diocesan centers of Jewish life were in Iraq (called *Bavel*, or Babylonia, in Hebrew) and Palestine, with their great talmudic academies, or yeshivot, headed by officials known as *geʾonim* (sing., *gaʾon*). Because of long-standing historical ties and physical

[3] The Taylor-Schechter Collection, University Library, Cambridge 16.79, l. 3. The document is published with a facsimile, by Israel Abrahams, "An Eighth-Century Genizah Document," *Jewish Quarterly Review*, 17 (1905), 426–30.

propinquity, the Egyptian Jews looked officially to the Palestinian yeshiva for ultimate spiritual and legal authority; the large numbers of Iraqi and Persian Jews and their descendants who followed the Babylonian rite turned to the Babylonian yeshivot of Sura and Pumbeditha for guidance. There were two main congregations in Fusṭāṭ, the capital of Islamic Egypt prior to the building of Cairo, one Palestinian (*kanīsat al-shāmiyyīn*) and one Babylonian (*kanīsat al-ʿirāqiyyīn*). There were two congregations in many other of the larger Egyptian Jewish communities, although not in many of the smaller ones. All in all, more than ninety names of cities, towns, and villages with Jewish populations are mentioned in the Geniza documents.[4]

In addition to the mainstream Palestinians and Babylonians who comprised the so-called Rabbanite Jewish community, there were also the Karaites, who formed a distinct communal group. The Karaite schism was founded in Baghdād during the mid-eighth century by ʿAnan ibn David, but only became a major sect during the ninth century. The Karaites rejected the rabbinic traditions of talmudic Judaism and accepted only the Bible as their sole source of religious law (hence their name in Hebrew, *Qaraʾim*, which means "Scripturalists"). Exactly when the Karaites first became established in Egypt is not known, but they were probably already numerous by the tenth century. Many Karaites at that time belonged to the wealthiest elite of merchants and officials in the government bureaucracy. Despite the significant theological and ritual differences between the Rabbanite and Karaite sects, which were a source of constant friction elsewhere in the Middle East, in Egypt they were able to form more or less a single, larger Jewish community which could act in concert for the purpose of charitable fundraising and in times of emergency. Intermarriage between Rabbanites and Karaites occurred frequently in Egypt at this time, although it was always rare elsewhere and also became less common in Egypt by the end of the Middle Ages.

There was also a Samaritan community in medieval Egypt, which was considered to be part of the Jewish subject population by the Islamic governmental authorities during the later Middle Ages. It had seceded from the main body of Jewry more than a millennium earlier, and Samaritans did not consider themselves, nor were they considered by other Jews to be, part of the greater Jewish community.

Although a spiritual dependency of Palestine and Iraq, Jewish Egypt must have had some educational facilities during this period. The great theologian, exegete, and translator of the Hebrew Bible into Arabic, Saʿadya ben Joseph Gaʿon (882–942), was born in the town of Dilāẓ in the Fayyūm district of Upper Egypt. That he remained in his native land until the age of

[4] See Norman Golb, "The Topography of the Jews of Medieval Egypt," *JNES*, 24 (1965), 251–70, and 33 (1974), 116–49.

twenty-three, before emigrating to Tiberias in Palestine to further his studies, indicates that a person could get at least the foundation of a good rabbinic education in Egypt. That he had already composed his *Sefer ha-Agron*, a Hebrew rhyming dictionary and grammatical treatise, three years before departing for Palestine indicates that the new Hebrew linguistic and philological studies that were inspired by the Arabic language studies (*fiqh al-lugha*) of Muslim scholars were already cultivated among Egyptian Jews at that time. The great Jewish philosopher and physician, Isaac Israeli (ca. 855–955), who spent the second half of his prodigiously long life in Qayrawān and who through the Latin translations of his works came to be known in medieval and Renaissance Europe as *eximius monarcha medicinae*, was also born, brought up, and educated in Egypt. Like his younger contemporary, Saʿadya, he too sought renown outside his homeland in a more flourishing Jewish cultural center.[5]

Only after the Fāṭimid conquest of Egypt and the establishment of the caliphal seat of government in the newly founded city of Cairo in 972 did Egypt become a prominent center of Jewry, even as it became a political, economic, and cultural center of the Islamic world. Many Jews were attracted to the Egyptian capital, as they had been earlier in the century to Qayrawān and al-Mahdiyya in Ifrīqiya, by both the laissez-faire economic policies of the Fāṭimids and the opportunity for service in the Fāṭimid bureaucracy. With the sole exception of the persecutions under the mad Caliph al-Ḥākim between 1007 and 1021, when churches and synagogues were closed or demolished and the sumptuary laws of *ghiyār* (differentiation) were vigorously enforced, the heterodox Ismāʿīlī Fāṭimids showed relatively more tolerance toward their non-Muslim subjects than did most Islamic rulers. They did not normally enforce the requirement for *dhimmīs* to wear distinguishing clothing, nor did they impose the discriminatory tariffs for *dhimmī* merchants prescribed by orthodox Muslim law, and they had even fewer qualms than most other sovereigns over employing nonbelievers in the civil service, even up to the ranks of the *aṣḥāb al-khilʿa*, the royal entourage.[6]

By the turn of the millennium, Egypt had a very sizable Jewish population, and it continued as such until the thirteenth century, when it was decimated by plague and famine. Fusṭāṭ had a Rabbanite community numbering some 3,600 souls. In addition, there were the much smaller Karaite community and a small congregation in nearby Cairo, bringing the total Jewish popula-

[5] For extensive biographies of each of these two figures, see Henry Malter, *Saadia Gaon: His Life and Works* (Philadelphia, 1921), and Alexander Altmann and Samuel M. Stern, *Isaac Israeli: A Neoplatonic Philosopher of the Early Eleventh Century* (London, 1958).

[6] See Norman A. Stillman, *The Jews of Arab Lands: A History and Source Book* (Philadelphia, 1979), 43–44, 52.

tion in the capital to well over 4,000.[7] Alexandria's Jewish community was probably about half as large as the capital's.

There were no Jewish quarters in the major cities and towns of Egypt during this period, except perhaps in al-Maḥalla al-Kubrā, where such a specific quarter (*ḥāra*) is identified in a document from the early thirteenth century.[8] Rather, Jews concentrated in a few neighborhoods. One of these was the Qaṣr al-Shamʿ, the old Byzantine fortified area (also known as Qaṣr al-Rūm) around which the Islamic garrison town evolved. This had been inhabited by Jews and Christians prior to the Muslim conquest and remained heavily *dhimmī* for centuries. Within this section of the city, there was an area known as Suwayqat al-Yahūd (The Little Jewish Market), but this name probably arose from the presence of a Jewish abattoir (*majzarat al-Yahūd*) there, and not because it was a center of Jewish commercial activity.[9] There was also a lane referred to occasionally as Zuqāq al-Yahūd, along which the synagogues of the Palestinians and the Babylonians were both located. Jews lived in other sections of the city as well, including the al-Rāya Quarter, which was named for the troops that had borne the army's standard and was the site of the original area of Muslim settlement near the Mosque of ʿAmr. Nearly half a millennium after the Arab conquest, this was a neighborhood that had become predominantly Christian, but was in the process of being bought up by Jews.[10]

Prior to the Fāṭimid period little is known about either the internal organization of Egyptian Jewry or the mechanism of its administrative relations with the Islamic state. Until the middle of the eleventh century,

[7] This estimate is based on a Goitein's calculations, for which see Goitein, *A Mediterranean Society*, II, 139–140. This figure is considerably higher than Ashtor's estimate of only 1,500, which is probably closer to the mark for the thirteenth century, although Ashtor argues for the validity of his calculations for the earlier period as well – see Eliyahu Ashtor, "Prolegomena to the Medieval History of Oriental Jewry," *Jewish Quarterly Review*, n.s. 50 (1959), 56–57; and Ashtor, "Some Features of the Jewish Communities of Medieval Egypt," *Zion*, 30, 1–2 (1965), 63–64 [Hebrew]. Both Goitein's and Ashtor's estimates are lower than that of the late twelfth-century traveler, Benjamin of Tudela, who reports that 7,000 Jews were living in Fusṭāṭ-Cairo at the time of his visit there. See *The Itinerary of Benjamin of Tudela*, ed. and trans. Marcus Nathan Adler (London, 1907; reprinted, New York, n.d.), 98 (Heb. text), 69–70 (Eng. trans.). However, the numbers in the manuscripts, and indeed the manuscript tradition of Benjamin's travelogue itself, are highly problematic.

[8] Taylor-Schechter 12.166 (dated 1202), Taylor-Schechter Collection, University Library, Cambridge.

[9] See Paul Casanova, "Essai de Reconstitution topographique de la ville d'Al Fousṭāṭ ou Miṣr," *Mémoires de l'Institut Français d'Archéologie Orientale du Caire*, 35 (1913), 18–19; and also E. J. Worman, "Notes on the Jews in Fustāt," *Jewish Quarterly Review*, 18 (1905), 28, 30.

[10] For the Lane of the Jews, see Goitein, *A Mediterranean Society*, II, 291, and the sources cited in ibid., 589, n.7. Concerning al-Rāya, see Norman A. Stillman, "The Jew in the Medieval Islamic City," in Daniel Frank (ed.) *The Jews of Medieval Islam: Community, Society, and Identity*, (Leiden, 1995), 5.

there was no single Egyptian Jewish official recognized by the government as the leader and authoritative representative of the entire Jewish community, including the Karaites and Samaritans. The view long held by many scholars, that the Fāṭimid government set up the office of *Nagid*, or *Ra'īs al-Yahūd* in order to provide an alternative object of Jewish loyalties previously offered to the Exilarch, the Jewish official at the caliphal court in Baghdād, has been shown to be completely erroneous.[11]

In the early years of Fāṭimid rule, the state authorities recognized the *ga'on* of the Palestinian Yeshiva as the supreme communal authority over all of the Jews in the empire. This, however, did not prevent Jews of the Babylonian rite from sending legal queries and donations to their diocesan authorities, the *ge'onim* of the Iraqi academies. The Egyptian capital was in fact the great transfer point for donations and queries sent to both the Palestinian and Babylonian yeshivot by Jews from all over the Islamic Mediterranean and for the return to them of gaonic responsa, religious books and treatises, and other forms of international Jewish communal correspondence. (It is for this reason that the Geniza has proved to be a source of information of tremendous value for the entire Islamic world and not just for Egypt.) During the last decades of the tenth and the first three decades of the eleventh centuries, the official intermediaries in charge of facilitating this flow of letters, documents, and funds were the merchant princes Abū Yūsuf Ya'qūb ibn 'Awkal and his son Abu'l-Faraj Yūsuf.[12]

The highest local Jewish leader in Egypt at this time was the representative of the Palestinian Yeshiva. He was called the *rav rosh*, or chief scholar, and resided in Fusṭāṭ. His primacy was recognized by both the Palestinian and Babylonian congregations. Throughout the first quarter of the eleventh century, the position of *rav rosh* was occupied successively by a father and son, Shemarya ben Elḥanan (died ca. 1012) and Elḥanan ben Shemarya (died ca. 1025). The father established a school of higher Jewish learning in Fusṭāṭ, and his son had access to the caliphal presence and was wont to receive favors from the ruler.[13]

11 Goitein, *A Mediterranean Society*, II, 23–40. Goitein's conclusions have been corroborated and expanded upon by Mark R. Cohen, *Jewish Self-Government in Medieval Egypt: The Origins of the Office of Head of the Jews, ca. 1065–1126* (Princeton, 1980).

12 See Norman A. Stillman, "Quelques renseignements biographiques sur Yōsēf Ibn 'Awkal, médiateur entre les communautés juives du Maghreb et les Académies d'Irak," *Revue des études juives* 132, fasc. 4 (October-December 1973), 529–42; and Stillman, "The Eleventh-Century Merchant House of Ibn 'Awkal (A Geniza Study)," *JESHO*, 16 (1973), 1, 15–88.

13 For biographical data on these two individuals, see Jacob Mann, *The Jews in Egypt and in Palestine under the Fāṭimid Caliphs*, 2 vols. in one, with preface and reader's guide by S. D. Goitein (New York, 1970), passim; Shraga Abramson, *Ba-Merkazim uva-Tefuṣot bitqufat ha-Ge'onim* (Jerusalem, 1965), 105–173; S. D. Goitein, "Shemarya b. Elḥanan: With Two New Autographs," *Tarbiz*, 32 (1963), 3, 266–272 [Hebrew with

After Elḥanan ben Shemarya's death, it would appear that the office of *rav rosh* fell into desuetude and that the chief *dayyanim*, or judges, of the Palestinian Jews acted as communal leaders for all the Rabbanite Jews of Egypt. However, each of the Rabbanite congregations had its own leaders, and each looked toward the Geʾonim in either Jerusalem or Baghdād as its ultimate authorities in Jewish legal, ritual, or exegetical matters. The head of the Palestinian congregation usually bore the title of *ḥaver*, or "member of the academy," and the head of the Babylonians that of *alluf*, or "distinguished member." Despite the not infrequent dissension between Jewish leaders in Fusṭāṭ, the Rabbanite Jews felt a sense of being a single community, and this feeling extended somewhat to the Karaites as well.

Each Egyptian Jewish community had a common chest (called *quppa* in Alexandria, as in much of the Jewish world, *ṣibbur* in the provinical town of Sunbāṭ, and with no specific name in Fusṭāṭ/Cairo) for wide-ranging social services which included philanthropy, the upkeep and maintenance of the houses of worship and communal properties, and the salaries of communal officials. This was in keeping with both the long-standing Jewish tradition of providing for one's own and with the Islamic social system, under which charity and social service were the responsibity of each confessional group and not the state. Thus the Jews had their own pious foundations (*awqāf* or *aḥbās*; in Hebrew, *heqdesh* or *qodesh*), as did the Muslims and Christians. The *aḥbās al-yahūd* were administered by the *dayyanim* of the Jewish court and were legally recognized as *waqf* properties by the state.[14]

Around the year 1065, an office was created for a single supreme Jewish authority over all of Egyptian Jewry that was recognized by the Fāṭimid government. The formal Arabic title of this dignitary was *raʾīs al-yahūd* (head of the Jews). In Hebrew he was referred to as *nagid* (prince), a title which had come into use in the Maghrib and Spain earlier in the century. This new post was created at a time when the Palestinian gaonate was in decline, weakened by internal rivalries. The loss of Palestine to the Seljūk Turks in 1071, together with other factors, caused the Fāṭimids to turn increasingly inward and Egyptocentric. Thus for a Jewish community to be under local leadership was desirable from the point of view of Fāṭimid policy. Furthermore, administrative independence from the Palestinian gaonate probably began to look attractive at this time to the Jews of Egypt themselves, as the Palestinian

English summary]; and Goitein, "Elḥanan b. Shemarya as Communal Leader," in Sidney B. Hoenig and Leon D. Stitskin (eds.) *Joshua Finkel Jubilee Volume* (New York, 1974), 117–37 [Hebrew]. See now also the important doctoral dissertation of Elinoar Bareket, *The Leaders of the Jews in Fusṭāṭ During the First Half of the Eleventh Century*, 2 vols. (Tel Aviv University, 1987) [Hebrew with English abstract].

14 For a detailed picture of the Jewish social services, see Goitein, *A Mediterranean Society*, II, 91–143, 413–510; and Moshe Gil, *Documents of the Jewish Pious Foundations from the Cairo Geniza* (Leiden, 1976). Cf. also Norman A. Stillman, "Charity and Social Service in Medieval Islam," *Societas*, 5, 2 (Spring 1975), 105–15.

yeshiva and its leadership became increasingly tarnished by unseemly and divisive squabbles. The function of the *ra'īs al-yahūd* evolved slowly over the next 200 years under the Fāṭimids and Ayyūbids. By Mamlūk times, the powers and responsibilities of this official were well defined and spelled out in such administrative handbooks as al-ʿUmarī's al-Taʿrīf or al-Qalqashandī's *Ṣubḥ al-Aʿshā*, where it clearly states that:

It is incumbent upon him to unite his community and to gather their various elements in obedience to him. He is to judge them in accordance with the principles of his religion and the customary usages of its religious leaders . . . He must see to it that their persons are protected by their being humble and lowly and by their bowing their heads in submissiveness to the followers of the faith of Islam, by their giving way to Muslims in the streets and when they are intermingled with them in the bath house . . . He is responsible for appointing the various offices of rank among his coreligionists from the rabbis on down according to their degree of merit and in accordance with their agreement. He has the final say in matters pertaining to all of their synagogues.[15]

In other words, the *ra'īs al-yahūd* eventually became the supreme Jewish authority within Egypt with unprecedented powers over every aspect of Jewish communal life, in addition to being the sole representative of his religious community, including the sectarian Karaites. It has been suggested that the office of head of the Jews developed along parallel lines with changes in the Coptic patriarchate at that time, and that the recognition extended to the *ra'īs al-yahūd* by the Fāṭimid government probably came as part of a conscious policy of centralization instituted by the military strongman, Badr al-Jamālī. This hypothesis makes good sense. Unfortunately, the details of the development of the *ra'īs al-yahūd*'s office are still not clear by any means.[16]

Like so many of the senior communal posts in the medieval Islamic world, the position of *ra'īs al-yahūd* in Egypt tended from its very inception to be dominated by a single family. Three of the first four holders of the office were members of a family of physicians who served at the royal court – Judah ben Saʿadya (ca. 1064–78), his brother, Mevorakh (ca. 1078–82 and again in 1094–1114), and the latter's son, Moses (1112–ca. 1126). Their combined rule of more than half a century was interrupted for a little over a decade between 1082 and 1094, when David ibn Daniel, an ambitious member of the Davidic House and a disappointed aspirant to the Palestinian gaonate, was able to usurp the office for himself. From the late twelfth to the early fifteenth century the position was passed on in true dynastic succession from the great Moses Maimonides (died 1207) to his descendants right up to

15 Al-Qalqashandī, *Ṣubḥ al-Aʿshā*, 11 (Cairo, 1913–1919), 390–91, translated in Stillman, *The Jews of Arab Lands*, 269–70.

16 Cohen, *Jewish Self-Government in Medieval Egypt*.

the time of the Ottoman conquest. The office was then given to appointees from Constantinople, but was terminated sometime around 1560 in the wake of local objections to the outsiders.

In addition to the *ra'īs al-yahūd*, many other officials in the Egyptian Jewish community were connected in some way or other with government, and although Muslims always constituted the majority of civil servants, non-Muslims were represented in the bureaucracy out of all proportion to their numbers in the general population. This was partly because of the prevailing tolerance of the Fāṭimid and Ayyūbid regimes, and perhaps also because of the overcompensation for their lesser status often exhibited by members of a minority. However, it may also be attributed to the fact that careers in government were fraught with danger and therefore were not attractive to the majority of people. Furthermore, unlike many pious Muslims, Jews considered government service to be a highly honorable calling.[17] Naturally, the highest offices, such as the vizierate of state, were normally reserved for Muslims. There are two or three notable exceptions of Christians who wielded the power of vizier, sometimes bearing the title and sometimes not. But those individuals of Jewish birth who achieved this exalted office, such as Yaʿqūb ibn Killis (died 991), Ḥasan ibn Ibrāhīm al-Tustarī (died 1064), and Ṣadaqa ibn Yūsuf al-Fallāḥī (died 1048), had all converted to Islam prior to becoming vizier.[18]

The one Jewish courtier who rose to the very pinnacle of power in Fāṭimid Egypt during the third and fourth decades of the eleventh century was Abū Saʿd Ibrāhīm ibn Sahl al-Tustarī, the scion of a wealthy Karaite mercantile and banking house of Persian origin that was established in Egypt during the reign of al-Ḥākim. According to al-Maqrīzī,[19] Abū Saʿd became purveyor of luxury goods to the Caliph al-Ẓāhir, and his star rose still further when a black slave girl he had sold to the royal harem became queen mother and acting regent for her son al-Mustanṣir, who succeeded to the caliphate in 1036 upon the death of his father. The dowager regent relied upon her former master as advisor and confidant. After the death of the Vizier

[17] For a comparison of attitudes toward government in Islam and Judaism, see S. D. Goitein, *Studies in Islamic History and Institutions* (Leiden, 1966), 197–213; and Norman A. Stillman, "Subordinance and Dominance: Non-Muslim Minorities and the Traditional Islamic State as Perceived from Above and Below," in Farhad Kazemi and R. D. McChesney (eds.), *A Way Prepared: Essays on Islamic Culture in Honor of Richard Bayly Winder*, (New York, London, 1988), 132–41.

[18] For the career of Ibn Killis, see Walter J. Fischel, *Jews in the Economic and Political Life of Mediaeval Islam*, rev. edn. (New York, 1969), 45–68; for Ḥasan al-Tustarī, see Ibn Muyassar, *Ta'rīkh Miṣr* [*Annales d'Égypte*], ed. Henri Massé (Cairo, 1919), 32; and also Moshe Gil, *The Tustaris: Family and Sect* (Tel Aviv, 1981), 58; for Ibn al-Fallāḥī, see al-Suyūṭī, *Ḥusn al-Muḥāḍara fī Akhbār Miṣr wa 'l-Qāhira*, II (Cairo, 1968), 201.

[19] al-Maqrīzī, *al-Mawāʿiẓ wa 'l-Iʿtibār bi-Dhikr al-Khiṭaṭ wa'l-Āthār*, I (Bulaq, 1853; reprint, Baghdad, n.d.), 424–25. In addition, see Fischel, *Jews in the Economic and Political Life of Mediaeval Islam*, 68–89 and the sources cited there.

al-Jarjarā'ī in 1044, Abū Sa'd became a veritable power behind the throne with the ability to make or break viziers – something that he actually did. However, he was murdered at the height of his career in a plot involving the Turkish troops and the apostate Jewish vizier Ibn al-Fallāḥī. As was frequently the case when a non-Muslim rose too high and became too conspicuous in the affairs of state in the Islamic world, Abū Sa'd's downfall was preceded by anti-*dhimmī* agitation, and a popular satiric verse by the poet Riḍā ibn Thawb that was circulating prior to his assassination ran:

> The Jews of this time have attained their
> utmost hopes and have come to rule. Honor is
> theirs, wealth is theirs too,
> and from them come the counsellor and ruler.
> People of Egypt, I have good advice for you –
> Turn Jew, for Heaven itself has become Jewish![20]

Abū Sa'd's brother and business partner, Abu Naṣr Hārūn, together with Abū Sa'd's son Abū 'Alī Ḥasan, were both granted protection by the caliph following the assassination. Abū Naṣr himself entered government service shortly thereafter, but his career was short-lived. His property was confiscated, and he died in prison under torture in 1048. Abū Sa'd's son survived, converted to Islam at some point, and became al-Mustanṣir's vizier in 1064.[21]

The fall of the Tustarīs by no means spelled the end of Jews in Fāṭimid government service. A certain Abu'l-Munajjā ibn Sha'yā served under the Vizier al-Afḍal as fiscal inspector of the Province of Damietta (*mushārif al-a'māl al-sharqiyya*) and was responsible for the excavation of a large irrigation canal which was named after him (*khalīj Abī Munajjā*). Another Jewish offical, Ibn Abī Dimm, served as a secretary in the chancery (*dīwān al-inshā'*) under al-'Āmir.[22]

Jews continued to serve in the government bureaucracy under the Ayyūbids, but in lesser numbers and in less conspicuous positions than under the Fāṭimids. The eighty years of Ayyūbid rule marked a period of transition for the Jews of Egypt, as they did for the country as a whole. The Sunnī Ayyūbids began their reign with a wave of orthodox zeal and the anti-*dhimmī* fervor of their counter-Crusade. They moved toward stricter enforcement of the Pact of 'Umar, and by the end of their rule most Jews wore a distinguishing mark (*ruq'a*) on their turbans and cloaks and most

[20] Ibn Muyassar, *Ta'rīkh Miṣr*, 61–62; al-Suyūṭī. *Ḥusn al-Muḥāḍara*, II, 201. Goitein, *A Mediterranean Society*, II, 374, has pointed out that the last verse may contain a punning allusion to Abū Sa'd.

[21] Fischel, *Jews in the Economic and Political Life of Medieval Islam*, 86–87 and the sources cited there.

[22] For Ibn Munajjā, see al-Maqrīzī, Khiṭaṭ, I, 72, 477, 487–88; and for Ibn Abī Dimm, see Ibn Muyassar, *Ta'rīkh Miṣr*, 74.

Christians wore a special outer belt (*zunnār*). For much of the time, however, members of the *dhimmī* upper class were still able to evade fulfilling the requirement, which was considered a mark of humiliation (*dhull*) as well as differentiation (*ghiyār*). Periodic decrees were a means by which the Ayyūbids – like other Muslim rulers in various times and places – reminded the upper-class nonbelievers that they should pay for their exemption, which they readily did.

The Ayyūbid period also witnessed a decline in the Egyptian Jewish population in the wake of the disastrous famine and epidemic of 1201–02 and the lesser epidemics of 1217 and 1235–36. A Geniza letter from 1217 specifically invokes a prayer "May God spare the people of Israel from the plague" that was then ravaging Fusṭāṭ.[23]

The decline in numbers of the Egyptian Jewish community was coupled with its economic decline. The vibrant laissez-faire commercial policies of the Fāṭimids progressively gave way to a Middle Eastern brand of feudalism. High tariffs, debased coinage, the formation of restrictive guilds and the allocation of agriculture lands as fiefs for the military elite – all contributed not only to the declining prosperity, but to the marginalization of the non-Muslims in the economy overall, and this trend was fully realized under the Mamlūks.

Although the Ayyūbid period marks a steady downward spiral in Egyptian Jewish prosperity, it was also the time when the greatest scholar in all of post-Talmudic Jewish history lived in Egypt. Moses Maimonides (1138–1204) came to Egypt from the Islamic west in 1165. There he served as physician to the *qāḍī* al-Fāḍil and later to al-Malik al-Afḍal. He also served as *rāʾis al-yahūd*. It was in Egypt that Maimonides produced an enormous body of responsa and his two greatest works, his great law code, the *Mishneh Torah*, his only work in Hebrew, and his philosophic chef d'oeuvre, *The Guide of the Perplexed* (*Dalālat al-Ḥāʾirīn*). His son, Abraham, who succeeded him as a court physician and as Head of the Jews, founded a pietist circle inspired by Ṣūfī practices, whose members were called *ḥasidim*. He also wrote an important guide to mystical piety, *Kifāyat al-ʿābidīn* (The Complete Guide for Worshippers). Both the senior Maimonides and his son introduced various reforms and tried to shore up the morale of the Egyptian Jewish community which was becoming increasingly desperate during these years, but to no avail.[24]

The general state of Egyptian Jewry deteriorated even more under the

[23] Taylor-Schechter 16.305v, l. 26. See also Michael W. Dols, *The Black Death in the Middle East* (Princeton, 1977), 33–34.

[24] For succint surveys of the lives and oeuvres of the Maimonides father and son, see the articles "Maimonides, Moses," *Encyclopaedia Judaica* 11, cols. 754–81; and "Abraham Ben Moses Ben Maimon," ibid. 2, cols. 150–52. See also now S. D. Goitein's moving protrait of Abraham in *A Mediterranean Society*, V, 474–96.

Mamlūks. The sumptuary laws were enforced with ever-increasing vigor. After all, since the Mamlūks did not allow the native Arabs to dress like Mamlūks or ride horses as they did, they were not going to permit nonbelievers to dress like Muslims. As of 1301, "*dhimmīs* were so-to-speak color coded by their outer garments"; yellow became the identifying color for Jews, blue for Christians, and red for Samaritans.[25] The decree of the Sultan al-Malik al-Ṣāliḥ in 1354 went further in imposing restrictions. Together with Christians, Jews were to now limit the size of their turbans. Non-Muslim men were henceforth to wear a distinctive metal neck ring when visiting the public baths, so that even undressed they could not be mistaken for Believers. Jewish and Christian women were to be barred altogether from bathing with Muslim women.[26]

Sometime during the first century and a half of Mamlūk rule, a humiliating oath for Jews appearing before a Muslim court was reintroduced after a moratorium on such oaths which had lasted more than five hundred years. The tone and intent of this degrading, ludicrously worded adjuration is reminiscent of the notorious oath *More Judaico* in Christian Europe.[27]

One anti-*dhimmī* decree that stood out as truly unusual was made by Sultan Jaqmaq in 1448. This edict banned Jewish and Christian physicians from treating Muslim patients. This was a momentous reversal of the longstanding non-confessional nature of the medical profession in the Islamic world. In the two centuries preceding Jaqmaq's ban, a number of polemical treatises had appeared containing horror stories about the malevolence of *dhimmī* physicians toward their Muslim patients.[28]

European travelers, such as Friar Felix Fabri, who passed through Egypt during the second half of the fifteenth century testify to the serious demographic and social decline of the local Jewry, and European Christian travelers describe a similarly gloomy picture for their Egyptian coreligionists during this period. Obadiah da Bertinoro, who passed through Egypt in 1487 on his way to the Holy Land, mentions Jewish officials selling off ritual ornaments, Torah scrolls, and codices from the synagogues of Cairo and Jerusalem to foreigners, including Gentiles. In one instance related by Obadiah, the beadle of Fusṭāṭ's Ben Ezra Synagogue sold off a Torah scroll and promptly converted to Islam to avoid prosecution. He also notes widespread poverty and an appalling lack of charity toward the Jewish poor (a startling reversal from the highly organized social services of earlier

[25] Yedida K. Stillman, "The Medieval Islamic Vestimentary System: Evolution and Consolidation," in *Kommunikation zwischen Orient und Okzident: Alltag und Sachkultur* (Vienna, 1994), 304.

[26] This decree is translated in Stillman, *The Jews of Arab Lands*, 273–74.

[27] The text of the oath from al-ʿUmarī's *al-Taʿrīf* is translated in Stillman, *The Jews of Arab Lands*, 267–68.

[28] See Stillman, *The Jews of Arab Lands*, 71–72.

periods). His contemporary, Meshullam da Volterra, testifies to the serious decline in population of a number of Jewish communities. He mentions, inter alia, that the Jewish community in Alexandria had dwindled to only sixty families at the time of his visit in 1481.[29]

The Mamlūk period marks the nadir of medieval Egypt Jewry. The community would recover somewhat with the arrival of Iberian exiles at the end of the fifteenth and the beginning of the sixteenth century and with the new prosperity that came in the wake of the Ottoman conquest. However, it would not be until the second half of the nineteenth and the first half of the twentieth century that Egyptian Jewry would enjoy again, albeit for a limited time, the kind of wealth and influence that it had known during the heyday of Fāṭimid rule.

[29] Stillman, *The Jews of Arab Lands*, 74–75.

9

The crusader era and the Ayyūbid dynasty

MICHAEL CHAMBERLAIN

The Ayyūbid period was a turning-point in Egypt's pre-modern history.[1] During it Egypt regained the regional preeminence it had lost under the later Fāṭimids. The period also saw the first appearance of many of the institutions Egypt would maintain until the beginning of the modern era, and in

[1] For general accounts of the Ayyūbid period see C. Cahen, "Ayyūbids," *EI2*; J.-C. Garcin, "Les Zankides et les Ayyubides," in J.-C. Gardin et al. (eds.), *États, sociétés et cultures du monde Musulman médiéval, X^e^–XVe siècle*, I, *L'evolution politique et sociale* (Paris, 1995), 233–55; H. A. R. Gibb, "The Aiyūbids," in *A History of the Crusades*, K. Setton (gen. ed.), II, *The Later Crusades, 1189–1311*, R. L. Wolff and H. W. Hazard (eds.) (Madison, 1969), 693–714. Outdated but not entirely superseded are S. Lane-Poole, *A History of Egypt*, IV: *The Middle Ages* (London, 1901); G. Wiet, *L'Égypte arabe* (Paris, 1937), chs. 10 and 11. Monographs devoted to specific reigns or places include F. J. Dahlmanns, *Al-Malik al-Adil. Ägypten und der Vordere Orient in den Jahren 589/1193 bis 615/1218* (Giessen, 1975), with much attention to social and economic developments in the reign of al-ʿĀdil; H. L. Gottschalk, *Al-Malik al-Kamil von Egypten und seine zeit* (Weisbaden, 1958), which deals with the Ayyūbid who ruled Egypt for nearly half of the period, with an excellent bibliography; R. S. Humphreys, *From Saladin to the Mongols: The Ayyubids of Damascus* (Albany, 1977), the best study of Ayyubid politics, deals with Syria more than Egypt but is indispensable for both; J.-C. Garcin, *Un centre musulman de la haute-Égypte médiévale: Qūṣ* (Cairo, 1976), 125–80, a pioneering study of Upper Egypt; E. E. al-ʿArīnī, *Miṣr fī ʿaṣr al-ayyūbiyīn* (Cairo, 1960); S. D. Goitein, *A Mediterranean Society: The Jewish Communities of the Arab World as Portrayed in the Documents of the Cairo Geniza*, 6 vols. (Berkeley, Los Angeles, 1967–94), the fundamental study of the social and economic history of the period. The major published primary sources include Ibn al-ʿAmīd, *Kitāb al-majmūʿ al-mubārak*, ed. C. Cahen, in "'La Chronique Ayyoubides' d'al-Makīn Ibn al-ʿAmīd," *BEO*, 15 (1955–58), 109–84; also published as *Akhbār al-ayyūbiyīn*, ed. C. Cahen, (Cairo, 1958); Ibn Wāṣil, *Mufarrij al-kurūb fī akhbār banī ayyūb*, ed. G. al-Shayyāl and Ḥ. M. Rabīʿ, 5 vols. (Cairo, 1953–77); Sawīrus ibn al-Muqaffaʾ (continuation of), *Siyar al-bayʿa al-muqaddasa*, published as *History of the Patriarchs of the Egyptian church*, III, 1–3, ed. and trans. Y. ʿAbd al-Masīḥ and O. H. E. KHS-Burmester (Cairo, 1968–70); IV, 1–2, ed. and trans. A. Khater and O. H. E. KHS-Burmester (Cairo, 1974), the English translations are unreliable (references below are to the Arabic text); Abū Shāma, *Tarājim rijāl al-qarnayn al-sādis waʾl-sābiʿ al-maʿrūf biʾl-dhayl ʿalā al-rawḍatayn*, ed. M. al-Kawtharī (Cairo, 1947); Sibṭ Ibn al-Jawzī, *Mirʾāt al-zamān*, facs. edn. by J. R. Jewett (Chicago, 1907);

some cases well into it. Yet Ayyūbid rule lasted only eighty years, under rulers whose interests were often elsewhere. Moreover, in spite of the importance of their institutional models for succeeding periods, the Ayyūbids imposed new institutions haphazardly, and Ayyūbid politics largely escapes study through the examination of its institutional structures. How did such a regime – one that was both shortlived and distant from its subjects – leave so lasting an imprint on an Egypt so rightly known for its continuity?

The Ayyūbids came to power in the long aftermath of the Second Crusade (1147–48). This crusade, having been launched to recover Edessa and fought in central Syria, had little immediate impact on Egypt. Its indirect consequences nonetheless represented a serious threat to Fāṭimid rule. Perhaps the most significant outcome was the centralization of Muslim power in Syria and Mesopotamia. In 549/1154 Nūr al-Dīn Zengī, whose father's conquest of Edessa had set off the crusade, seized Damascus as a result of it. He then organized a state devoted to the prosecution of the

flawed edition based on the Jewett facs. published as VIII, 1, 2 (Hyderabad, 1952); Ibn al-Athīr, *Al-Ta'rīkh al-bāhir fī al-dawla al-atābakiyya*, ed. A. A. Ṭulaymat (Cairo, 1963); Ibn al-Athīr, *Al-Kāmil fī'l-ta'rīkh*, XI, XII, ed. C. J. Thornberg (Leiden, 1867–76; repr. Beirut, 1965); Abū Ṣāliḥ al-Armanī, *The Churches and Monasteries of Egypt and Some Neighboring Countries*, ed. and trans. B. T. A. Evetts (Oxford, 1895). Not to be neglected are later chronicles, biographical dictionaries, and biographies: Ibn ʿAbd al-Ẓāhir, *Al-Rawḍ al-zāhir fī sīra al-malik al-ẓahir*, ed. A. A. al-Khuwayṭir (Riyadh, 1396/1976), especially informative on the reign of al-Ṣāliḥ Ayyūb and his Ṣāliḥī and Baḥrī amīrs; Ibn al-Dawādārī, *Kanz al-durar wa jāmiʿ al-ghurar*, vii: *Al-Durr al-maṭlūb fī akhbār banī ayyūb*, ed. S. A. ʿĀshūr (Cairo, 1972); Yūnīnī, *Dhayl mir'āt al-zamān*, I, II (Hyderabad, 1380/1960); Ibn Taghrībirdī, *Al-Nujūm al-zāhira fī mulūk miṣr wa'l-qāhira*, VI (Cairo, 1355/1936); al-Maqrīzī, *Al-Muwāʿiẓ wa'l-iʿtibār bi-dhikr al-khiṭaṭ wa'l-āthār*, 2 vols. (Cairo, 1270/1853); partial edn., ed. G. Weit, 5 vols. (Cairo, 1911–27); al-Maqrīzī, *Kitāb al-sulūk li-maʿrifat duwal al-mulūk*, ed. M. M. Ziyāda and S. A. ʿĀshūr, 4 vols. (Cairo, 1943–72); Ibn Abī Uṣaybiʿa. *ʿUyūn al-anbā' fī ṭabaqāt al-aṭṭibā'*, 3 vols. in 1, ed. A. Müller (Königsberg, 1884; new edition based on Müller, Beirut, 1965), with numerous biographies of Egyptian physicians and their unique perspectives on sultanal and amiral households; al-Dhahabī, *Ta'rīkh al-Islām wa-wafayāt al-mashāhīr wa'l-aʿlām*, LX–LXIV, ed. B. Maʿrūf et al. (Beirut, 1408/1988); Ibn Khallikān, *Wafayāt al-aʿyān w'anbā abnā' al-zamān*, ed. M. ʿAbd al-Ḥamīd (Cairo, 1948), ed. I. ʿAbbās (Beirut, 1968–72); Ibn Shākir (al-Kutubī), *Fawāt al-wafayāt wa'l-dhayl ʿalayhā*, 2 vols., ed. M. ʿAbd al-Ḥamīd (Cairo, 1951), 4 vols., ed. I. ʿAbbās (Beirut, 1973–74). Travelers' and geographers' accounts include Benjamin of Tudela, *The Travels, 1160–73*, ed. and trans. M. Komroff (London, 1928); Ibn Jubayr, *Tadhkira li-akhbār ʿan ittifāqāt al-asfār (The Travels of Ibn Jubayr)*, ed. W. Wright, Gibb Memorial Series, V (Leiden, 1907, reprint, Beirut, 1964); al-Harawī, *Kitāb al-ishārāt ilā maʿrifat al-ziyārāt*, ed. J. Sourdel-Thomine (Damascus, 1953); al-Ḥamawī, *Muʿjam al-buldān*, iv (Beirut, 1376/1957), esp. 261–66, 301, 413. For documentary evidence see Cahen, "Ayyubids," *EI2*, 804–05. For epigraphic evidence see G. Wiet, *RCEA*, VII–IX; G. Wiet, "Les inscriptions du mausolée al-Shāfiʿī," *BIE*, XV (1933), 167–85; G. Wiet, "Les inscriptions de Saladin," *Syria*, 3 (1922), 307–28; M. Van Berchem, *Corpus inscriptionum arabicarum, Égypte*, I, *MMAF*, 18 (Paris, 1894–1903). For a bibliography and assessment of translations of Arabic sources in European languages see C. Cahen, "Crusades," *EI2*.

war against the Kingdom of Jerusalem.[2] At the same time Baldwin III asserted his power over his nobles, making the kingdom more dangerous to its rivals. With his new freedom of action Baldwin conquered Ascalon in 548/1153, a victory that gave him a short route to the Nile Delta. By the 1160s, in a case of the extension of anchored opposing lines, the two powers found themselves fighting in an Egypt too weak militarily, and too divided by internal rivalries, to do much more than play them off against one another.

In the late 550s/early 1160s, Baldwin's successor Amalric made two raids on Egypt, and between 559/1164 and 564/1168 Nūr al-Dīn dispatched three Syrian expeditions. The first was sent in response to a request by Shāwar, wazīr of the adolescent Fāṭimid Caliph al-ʿĀḍid. After Shāwar was deposed by his rival Ḍirghām in Ramaḍān 558/August 1163 he fled to Damascus, where he promised Nūr al-Dīn a third of Egypt's revenues in return for assistance. In response, Nūr al-Dīn dispatched a small army under the command of his Kurdish amīr Asad al-Dīn Shīrkūh. Shīrkūh, possibly accompanied by his nephew Ṣalāḥ al-Dīn Ibn Ayyūb (known to the west as Saladin), succeeded in killing Ḍirghām and reinstating Shāwar. The Syrians, whatever they hoped to gain from this expedition, now found themselves outmaneuvered by their ally Shāwar. When Shīrkūh appeared reluctant to leave the country, Shāwar invited in Amalric. The ensuing contest between Amalric and Shīrkūh was inconclusive, and after neither side gained an advantage both departed.

Nūr al-Dīn and Amalric were now aware of Fāṭimid weakness and determined to take advantage of it. In 562/1167 Shīrkūh invaded Egypt, this time after more meticulous preparation, and in response Shāwar again invited in Amalric. In the event, the contest between Shīrkūh and the combined Frankish–Egyptian forces was as inconclusive as the first. After several months of maneuvering, expeditions as far south as Qūṣ, and a siege of Alexandria, Amalric and Shīrkūh left the country again. The Syrians were promised a full Frankish withdrawal in return for their own, but the Franks retained control of the gates of Cairo, and received the promise of a large yearly tribute.

This situation, unsatisfactory from the Syrian point of view, might soon have provoked Nūr al-Dīn to react. But in 564/1168, before the Syrians felt compelled to intervene, Amalric broke with Shāwar and marched on Egypt. As a defensive measure Shāwar ordered the burning of Fusṭāṭ, the effects of which have been overestimated – the city regained much of its population and retained its economic importance throughout the Ayyūbid period.

[2] The major study of Nūr al-Dīn, with extensive bibliography, is N. Elisséeff, *Nūr al-Dīn, un grand prince musulman de Syrie au temps des Croisades 511–569 H./1118–1175*, 3 vols. (Damascus, 1967); later additions to the bibliography in N. Elisséeff, "Nūr al-Dīn Maḥmūd b. Zankī," *EI2*.

Alarmed by the Frankish advance, the Fāṭimid Caliph offered Nūr al-Dīn a third of the revenues of Egypt in return for support, and in response Nūr al-Dīn dispatched Shīrkūh at the head of an army much larger than the previous two. The ensuing conflict between Shīrkūh and Amalric was more palpably a contest to gain a permanent position, if not hegemony itself, in the country. Shīrkūh succeeded in forcing Amalric out, and this time he was determined to stay. Shāwar was killed, and the Fāṭimid caliph appointed Shīrkūh as his wazīr.

Fāṭimid caliphs had appointed Sunnī, and indeed Kurdish, wazīrs before, and there is little reason to believe that Shīrkūh's selection was seen as a clean break with the past. Shīrkūh held his title for two months before his death on 22 Jumādā II 564/March 23, 1169. Three days later the Fāṭimid caliph appointed Ṣalāh al-Dīn to the vizierate.[3] Ṣalāḥ al-Dīn, hitherto a fairly minor figure, had recently distinguished himself in the siege of Alexandria. His father Ayyūb, from whom the lineage took its name, was said to be high in Nūr al-Dīn's esteem. But these were not decisive advantages and Ṣalāḥ al-Dīn's position following his appointment was precarious. Although he inherited at least some of his uncle's recruits he had no troops of his own; indeed it may have been the relative fragility of his position that recommended him to al-ʿĀḍid.[4] Moreover, his appointment was resented by a number of Shīrkūh's amīrs, some of whom had hoped for the vizierate themselves. Several of these refused to follow him and returned to Syria; others remained only after an appeal to Kurdish solidarities.[5] In addition, Ṣalaḥ al-Dīn's relations with the palace establishment, and with the Fāṭimid

[3] On the career of Salāḥ al-Dīn the major published sources are the portions of al-Qāḍī al-Fāḍil's *Mutajaddidāt* conveyed in Maqrīzī's *Khiṭaṭ*; Imād al-Dīn al-Iṣfahānī, *Al-Fatḥ al-qussī fi'l-fatḥ al-qudsī*, ed. C. de Landberg (Leiden, 1888), ed. M. M. Ṣubḥ (Cairo, 1951); ʿImād al-Dīn al-Iṣfahānī, *Al-Barq al-shāmī*, surviving fragments published by M. al-Ḥayyārī (Amman, 1987) and F. al-Nabarāwī (Cairo, 1979); an abridged version, al-Bundārī, *Sanā al-barq al-shāmī*, ed. R. Şeşen (Ar.: Shīshīn) (Beirut, 1970), survives intact. Other passages are summarized in Abū Shāma, *Kitāb al-rawḍatayn fī akhbār al-dawlatayn*, ed. H. Aḥmad and M. M. Ziyāda, 2 vols. (Cairo, 1956, 1962), one of the major sources in its own right; an abridgement of debated authorship has recently been published: Abū Shāma, *ʿUyūn al-rawḍatayn fī akhbār al-dawlatayn* (Damascus, 1992); Ibn Shaddād, *Al-Nawādir al-sulṭāniyya wa'l-maḥāsin al-yūsufiyya, sīrat Ṣalāḥ al-Dīn*, ed. J. al-Shayyāl (Cairo, 1962), Ibn Wāṣil, *Mufarrij*, I, II. The definitive modern biography, with full bibliography, is M. C. Lyons and D. E. P. Jackson, *Saladin: The Politics of Holy War* (Cambridge, 1982); still useful are A. S. Ehrenkreutz, *Saladin* (Albany, 1972); H. A. R. Gibb, *The Life of Saladin* (Oxford, 1973); S. Lane-Poole, *Saladin* (London, 1926); other important studies include Ripke, *Saladin und sein Biograph Bahā' al-Dīn Ibn Shaddād* (Bonn, 1988); H. Möring, *Saladin und der dritte Kreuzzug* (Wiesbaden, 1980); V. Minorsky, "The Pre-history of Saladin," in his *Studies in Caucasian history* (London, 1953); D. S. Richards, "The early History of Saladin," *Islamic Quarterly*, 17 (1973), 140–59; D. S. Richards, "Saladin," *EI2*.

[4] Ibn al-Athīr, *Al-Bāhir*, 141–42.

[5] Ibn al-Athīr, *Al-Bāhir*, 142.

armies, were tense throughout this early period: both saw him as a threat to their interests, while he lacked the power to challenge them directly. His status vis-à-vis his masters was equally ambiguous. He was now the wazīr of a Fāṭimid caliph and a lieutenant of Nūr al-Dīn, and a potential rival to both.

A joint expedition by Amalric and Andronicus Contostephanus in Ṣafar 565/October 1169 had the paradoxical effect, seen of later Frankish invasions, of strengthening Ayyūbid power at a difficult moment of transition. The military threat, at least in retrospect, does not appear to have been especially serious. Confronted with superior force, and unable to resolve their own rivalries, the Franks and Byzantines lifted the siege of Damietta and left the country. But the appearance of a threat strengthened Ṣalāh al-Dīn considerably. Fighting it off brought Ṣalāḥ al-Dīn some badly needed prestige, resources in money and men (the caliph sent 10,000,000 dīnārs, a sum that nearly doubled the cost of the campaign; Nūr al-Dīn sent troops), and an excuse to move against internal opposition.

Ṣalāḥ al-Dīn now faced the delicate task of recruiting his own supporters without alarming Nūr al-Dīn. He assigned *iqṭāʿat* to his family and followers and began, for the first time, to purchase his own mamlūks. He also assigned *iqṭāʿat* to Egyptian Bedouin leaders and to amīrs who had opposed him earlier. He came to terms with local powers, as much to forestall opposition as to recruit supporters, and permitted some of them to retain the titles of honor they had held under the Fāṭimids. At the same time Ṣalāḥ al-Dīn began to recruit scholars and secretaries with local knowledge or prestige, and to build charitable foundations to support learned Sunnī shaykhs. A Shāfiʿī jurist was appointed as chief *qāḍī* in Cairo in Jumādā II 566/February 1171, after the dismissal of all Shiʿite judges. The abolition of the Ismāʾīlī religious establishment was accomplished by decree.

A major step in replacing the Fāṭimid ruling elite was the deposition of the Fāṭimid caliph himself. Ṣalāḥ al-Dīn may well have been content with remaining as wazīr. The office gave him useful cover in Egypt and a degree of independence from Nūr al-Dīn. Even so, he could not resist pressure from both Nūr al-Dīn and the ʿAbbāsid Caliph indefinitely; a number of learned shaykhs also agitated for deposition. On 7 Muḥarram 567/September 10, 1171 the *khuṭba* was pronounced at Fusṭāṭ in the name of the ʿAbbāsid caliph. Al-ʿĀḍid died, perhaps of natural causes, three days later, and on the following Friday the ʿAbbāsid *khuṭba* was pronounced in Cairo itself. Ṣalāḥ al-Dīn now moved to dispose of the caliph's family and the palace establishment. In short order the Fāṭimid palace was occupied, its staff dismissed or reemployed, the caliph's family confined, its male and female members segregated, and its property seized.

Ṣalāḥ al-Dīn was less interested in refashioning the institutional structures of the Fāṭimid state than in replacing the Fāṭimid elite with one loyal to him.

Resistance to him, at least in Cairo, came largely from members of the Fāṭimid ruling establishment. Between 565/1169 and 569/1174 there were numerous insurrections raised in the name of the Fāṭimids, some in concert with Franks and Byzantines. Given the state of the evidence it is difficult to assess how much of a threat these movements posed. Ṣalaḥ al-Dīn's may have provoked one or two himself to flush out opposition. Moreover, as Ṣalāḥ al-Dīn seems to have acted forcefully enough to have retained the initiative, he may have been prepared for the timing of these revolts, if not their terrain.

Two revolts were described as especially serious. In 564/1169 the Sudanese foot soldiers and Armenian archers garrisoned in Cairo revolted, only to be defeated by Ṣalāḥ al-Dīn and his brother Tūrānshāh. In 569/1174 Fāṭimid partisans, together with some of Ṣalāḥ al-Dīn's own supporters, plotted to restore the Fāṭimid caliphate. The plan was supposedly coordinated with the Ismāʿīlīs and the kings of Sicily and Jerusalem, and preparations were made for a combined land and sea invasion. In the event the various elements of the attack were poorly synchronized – the fleet did not arrive until after the conspirators in Cairo were arrested – and the revolt failed.

Whether or not these movements constituted a serious threat, Ṣalāḥ al-Dīn appears not to have concerned himself with popular opposition in Cairo. Its largely Sunnī population was indifferent to the fate of Fāṭimid supporters. Resistance in Upper Egypt may have had a wider base, as the implantation of Sunnism was recent and Shiʿism had a communal expression there; the region also sheltered Fāṭimid troops driven from Cairo.[6] In contrast to the Cairo rebellions, however, such local revolts did not threaten Ṣalāḥ al-Dīn's power base directly. Following 569/1174 the Ayyūbids faced insurrections in Cairo, but these appear to have been small messianic movements, and not well-organized attempts to dislodge the ruling dynasty.[7]

As Ṣalāḥ al-Dīn consolidated his power he undertook a building program in Cairo.[8] The citadel was begun in 572/1176–77 on a spur of the Muqaṭṭam hills between Cairo and Fusṭāṭ, and construction of a wall enclosing the two cities commenced. Several explanations have been ad-

[6] Garcin, *Qūṣ*, 130ff.

[7] See for example the movement of 587/1191, raised in the name of the family of ʿAlī, suppressed by a single amīr: Ibn al-Dawādārī, VII: 109–10; for another see Ibn al-Athīr, *Al-Kāmil*, XII: 24.

[8] M. G. Salmon, *Études sur la topographie du Caire*, MIFAO (Cairo, 1902); K. C. Creswell, *The Muslim Architecture of Egypt*, vol. 2, *Ayyubid and Early Bahrite Mamluks AD 1171–1326* (Oxford, 1959); N. O. Rabbat, *The Citadel of Cairo: A New Interpretation of Royal Mamlūk Architecture* (Leiden, 1995), 9–17, 50–84; A. Raymond, *Le Caire* (Paris, 1993), ch. 3. For a list of monuments see N. D. Mackenzie, *Ayyubid Cairo: A Topographical Study* (Cairo, 1992). On Alexandria see M. Müller-Wiener, *Eine Stadtgeschichte Alexandrias von 564/1169 bis in die Mitte des 9./15. Jahrhunderts. Verwaltung und innerstädtische Organisationsformen* (Berlin, 1992).

vanced to explain these new constructions. One obvious reason was to provide protection against the Franks and internal revolt. Another motivation may have been ideological, as Ṣalāḥ al-Dīn seems to have conformed to the pattern set by previous rulers in marking a new dynasty with a major new construction. It also seems logical to look at Ṣalāḥ al-Dīn's background for an explanation. Each large city in Syria had its wall and citadel, and during Ṣalāḥ al-Dīn's residence in Damascus Nūr al-Dīn had made major improvements to its fortifications.

In addition to these large-scale military building programs, the Fāṭimid imperial squares were gradually filled in with smaller buildings. Though this development had its origins in the later Fāṭimid period, and was completed only under the Mamlūks, the Ayyūbids accelerated it; it is from this period that the city acquired the form that was to last for many centuries. As was true of Ayyūbid urbanism in Syria, these were not major imperial constructions, but rather individual buildings that conformed to the existing street plan. This too began (but by no means completed) the assimilation of the topography of Cairo to that of the Syrian cities.

While suppressing internal opposition and holding Amalric and Nūr al-Dīn at bay, Ṣalāḥ al-Dīn inherited Fāṭimid strategic imperatives. The first problem was the resumption of trade, which provided both revenue and war materials. To stabilize relations with European merchants, much disrupted by the recent Latin invasions, he signed treaties with the Italian trading cities and allowed their merchants to settle in Alexandria. After an attempt to oblige Christian and Jewish merchants to pay double tariff, he returned to earlier practice and permitted them to pay the same rate as Muslims. To favor trade in the direction of the Red Sea and the Indian Ocean, Ṣalāḥ al-Dīn and his supporters built facilities for merchants on the major trade routes from the Indian Ocean to the Mediterranean.

Another imperative was to reassert Egyptian power in the region. Ṣalāḥ al-Dīn devoted substantial resources to rebuilding the Egyptian Mediterranean fleet. Perhaps related to this policy was Sharaf al-Dīn Qarāqūsh's expedition to north Africa, which brought much of the coast, with its raw materials and trained seamen, under Ayyūbid control. Ṣalāḥ al-Dīn also asserted Egyptian hegemony over the Red Sea region. Tūrānshāh, after securing Upper Egypt, made use of its revenues to invade the Ḥijāz and the Yemen. The motives for this expedition were mixed. Control over trade routes undoubtedly had some role, though it was not the sole or even the most important factor. Booty was more useful to Ṣalāḥ al-Dīn's immediate political needs, but the amount found in the Yemen was disappointing. Ṣalāḥ al-Dīn also needed a refuge to which he could retire should Nūr al-Dīn decide to attack him. And finally, control over the holy cities of the Ḥijāz was to remain an important basis for Ayyūbid claims to legitimacy. Whatever may have been the immediate motive, the effect, at a point quite early in Ṣalāḥ al-Dīn's reign, was to reestablish Egyptian hegemony in the region.

The year 570/1174 was a turning-point in Ṣalāḥ al-Dīn's career, as it marked his final consolidation of power in Egypt and presented him with an unexpected opportunity in Syria. During the winter of 1173/74 Nūr al-Dīn sent a representative to audit the registers of troops and *iqṭāʿāt*. By the following summer he was mustering troops to put pressure on Ṣalāḥ al-Dīn. Nūr al-Dīn's death on 11 Shawwāl 569/May 15, 1174 not only put an end to these plans, it so weakened the Zangid hold on Syria that Ṣalāḥ al-Dīn was able to take Damascus in Rabīʿ II 570/October 1174. He first posed as a supporter of Nūr al-Dīn's twelve-year-old heir, but soon ruled in his own name. In this year too his father died, leaving Ṣalāḥ al-Dīn with the preeminent position in the house of Ayyūb.

Ṣalāḥ al-Dīn's final good fortune in 1174 was Amalric's death, an event that inaugurated a long period of weakness in the Latin Kingdom. Disputes between regents for the young Baldwin IV and Amalric's adult relatives, followed by Baldwin's leprosy, undermined Latin power just as Ṣalāḥ al-Dīn was consolidating his own. Egypt henceforth was threatened by crusades organized from Europe, but not by the Latin states themselves. For the remainder of the Ayyūbid period the Latin states restricted their military operations to Syria or were junior partners in crusades launched from Europe.

After 570/1174 Ṣalāḥ al-Dīn, now unencumbered by his most serious rivals, was preoccupied with Syria and Mesopotamia. Here, just as he had earlier inherited Fāṭimid strategic imperatives, he now acquired Nūr al-Dīn's. He first tried to continue Nūr al-Dīn's policy of war against the Latin settlements, but realized few tangible gains. As Nūr al-Dīn had recognized, a decisive move against the Latin settlements required the unification of Syria and Mesopotamia. For the next nine years Ṣalāḥ al-Dīn concentrated on gaining ascendancy over his Muslim rivals in these regions. With the seizure of Aleppo in Ṣafar 579/June 1183 he had built a state that included Egypt, Nūr al-Dīn's domains, a portion of Mesopotamia, the Ḥijāz, the Yemen, and the north African coast to the borders of Tunisia. Now, having united the territories of the Fāṭimid and Zangid empires, he could turn to the Latin kingdom. The Battle of Ḥattīn on 24 Rabīʿ II 583/July 4, 1187 won him Jerusalem, Nūr al-Dīn's long-term goal, and most of the coast.

The Third Crusade (1190–92), launched in response to the loss of Jerusalem, had little direct impact on Egypt. Its recovery of the coast, however, discouraged Ṣalāḥ al-Dīn from further attempts to conquer the Latin settlements. The era of aggressive warfare had passed. Henceforth Ayyūbid policies with regard to the Franks were marked by the desire to conclude truces, increase trade, and fight off incursions. Ṣalāḥ al-Dīn's death on 27 Ṣafar 589/March 4, 1193 changed little in the relations between the Latin states and the Ayyūbids.

There is no question that over the long term the Ayyūbid period saw the adaptation, if not the direct adoption, of Syrian political practices to Egypt. In the short term, however, there is little evidence of a concerted attempt to reorder Egyptian state and society through the transplantation of Syrian institutions. Attempts to find an Ayyūbid administrative blueprint obscure the extent to which Ṣalāḥ al-Dīn maneuvered in an ad hoc manner, adapting existing Egyptian revenue sources to the recruitment and support of a new elite.

Ṣalāḥ al-Dīn made an effort to understand the Fāṭimid court and administrative apparatus, had treatises written to explain the Fāṭimid court and revenue system, and employed Fāṭimid secretaries.[9] He also tried to learn about the land revenues upon which his military power depended and had a cadastral survey undertaken. In spite of these measures, Ṣalāḥ al-Dīn ruled less through an institutional apparatus, either imposed or inherited, than by devolving power and revenue sources upon his clients. At local levels there was considerable continuity – and variety – which he, and his successors, did little to change.

Throughout his reign the links between local and central revenue collection, and their connections with revenue consumers, were inefficient. At the level of the sultanate revenue collection was never rationalized. Revenue included booty, duties, tribute, forced loans, one-time exactions, and aid from other rulers or the caliph. To the grief of his secretaries, Ṣalāḥ al-Dīn distributed much of it to his supporters as soon as it arrived. Taxes were a continuing problem. Ṣalāḥ al-Dīn abolished the *mukūs*, taxes which Islamic law deemed illegal. To make up for some of the lost revenue he adopted one interpretation of the *zakāt* to make it an *ad valorem* tax on certain goods. This measure was probably intended to appeal to jurists more than taxpayers, who seem to have resented new taxes no matter how ingeniously their legality was argued.

The succession to Ṣalāḥ al-Dīn proved to be unpredictable, as were most successions in the period. Ṣalāḥ al-Dīn divided his domains among his sons and relatives, designating his eldest son al-Afḍal ʿAlī, ruler of Damascus, as his successor as sultan. There was undoubtedly some notion of loyalty to the Ayyūbid house, if not to single lines of descent within it. But after Ṣalāḥ al-Dīn's death the ties that bound the ruling household together, and those that

[9] These treatises include Ibn al-Ṭuwayr, *Nuzhat al-muqlatayn fī akhbār al-dawlatayn*, ed. A. F. Sayyid (Beirut, Stuttgart, 1412/1992), which discusses bureaucracy and royal ceremonial in the Fāṭimid period; Qāḍī Abū'l-Ḥasan on the land-tax (extracts in Maqrizī's *Khiṭaṭ*); Ibn al-Mammātī, *Qawānīn al-dawāwīn*, ed. A. S. Atiya (Cairo, 1943); al-Makhzūmī, *Kitāb al-minhāj fī ʿilm kharāj Miṣr*, ed. C. Cahen and Y. Ragib, *AI*, 8, supplement (Cairo, 1986); C. Cahen, *Makhzūmiyyāt: Études sur l'histoire économique et financière de l'Égypte médiévale* (Leiden, 1977); C. Cahen, "al-Makhzūmī et Ibn al-Mammātī sur l'agriculture égyptienne médiévale," *AI*, 11 (1972), 141–51; C. Cahen, "Un traité financier inédit d'époque fatimite ayyūbide," *JESHO*, 5 (1962), 139–59.

attached it to its military supporters, unraveled. There soon appeared divisions both within the Ayyūbid house and among the great amīrs, together with conflicts between rulers and the amīrs upon whose military power they depended.

Both al-Afḍal ʿAlī and his brother and rival, al-ʿAzīz ʿUthmān, the ruler of Egypt, faced opposition from powerful amīrs. The most powerful amiral factions were Ṣalāḥ al-Dīn's recruits, the Ṣalāḥiyya, and those of Asad al-Dīn Shīrkūh, the Asadiyya. As the two Ayyūbids fought between themselves and against powerful amīrs, their paternal uncle al-ʿĀdil positioned himself as a mediator. Moving from one hostile camp to another, and for a time not appearing to threaten the interests of any of the senior amīrs, al-ʿĀdil was able to play off the conflicting interests to his benefit. Until late in the day his supporters, and perhaps al-ʿĀdil himself, did not foresee his taking power. The unexpected death of al-ʿAzīz (27 Muḥarram 595/November 29, 1198) gave him an opening in Egypt. The Ṣalāḥiyya amīrs of Egypt, struggling with their Asadiyya rivals, invited al-ʿĀdil to Cairo as regent for al-ʿAzīz's son al-Manṣūr. Al-ʿĀdil entered Cairo and soon thereafter, on 29 Rabīʿ II 596/February 17, 1200, had himself proclaimed sultan.

He now had to face the Ṣalāḥiyya, whose recognition that they were as dangerous to their friends as to their enemies was summed up in the boast: "Every day we make a ruler and every day we dismiss one."[10] It was only in 599/1202 that al-ʿĀdil was able to defeat the Ṣalāḥiyya and assert his authority over the Syrian Ayyūbids, finally putting an end to the succession disputes that had commenced in 589/1193. The dynamic between external threat and internal solidarity was seen here again, as a Latin raid on Egypt in 599–600/1202–03 brought al-ʿĀdil substantial military assistance from al-Ẓāhir, the ruler of Aleppo.[11] In 604/1207 al-ʿĀdil received a patent of investiture from the caliph.

After the long fragmentation of political power following the death of Ṣalāḥ al-Dīn, al-ʿĀdil reconstituted the empire in much the same form in which Ṣalāḥ al-Dīn had left it. He relied, as Ṣalāḥ al-Dīn had done, on his sons to rule the major provinces of the empire (displacing many of Ṣalāḥ al-Dīn's appointees in the process, al-Ẓāhir and the rulers of Ḥimṣ and Ḥamā being the most notable exceptions). He also continued Ayyūbid expansion to the east, taking territories that had not been part of Nūr al-Dīn's original domains. Like Ṣalāḥ al-Dīn after the Third Crusade his attitude toward the Franks was cautious, marked by the signing of treaties, the keeping of truces, and the promotion of trade.[12] He took more particular care with administrative matters than had Ṣalāḥ al-Dīn, though this may reflect changing

10 Ibn Wāṣil, III: 119.
11 Ibn Wāṣil, III: 135.
12 On al-ʿĀdil's reign see Dahlmanns, *Al-Malik al-Adil*; H. A. R. Gibb, "al-ʿĀdil," *EI2*.

circumstances more than a different style of rule. Now that war with the Latin states had ended, and major expansion was out of the question, the finances of Egypt required a sound basis if he were to satisfy his clients.

Although al-ʿĀdil was the sultan in Egypt, and took an active interest in its administration, his son and deputy al-Kāmil was the effective ruler of the country during most of his reign.[13] Al-ʿĀdil and al-Kāmil strengthened their ties with European merchants. They made some reforms to the coinage, though the motives for these reforms are unclear, and their effects uncertain – the sources indicate monetary instability throughout the Ayyūbid period. Al-ʿĀdil and al-Kāmil also reinstituted the non-canonical *mukūs* and applied new taxes called the *ḥuqūq*, which survived well into the Mamlūk period.[14] The relative effectiveness of their rule can be assessed by the recovery of the country following the earthquake of 597/1200 and the low flood of the Nile in 595–98/1199–1202. The drought, described as the second worst since the Fāṭimid conquest, was followed by famine throughout the country and the devastation of rural areas.[15] Al-ʿĀdil and al-Kāmil responded to the depopulation of the countryside by having amīrs, soldiers, and others work the land directly. In contrast to the famines of the mid-eleventh century, which inaugurated a period of political chaos, Egypt maintained its political stability and began an economic recovery.

In comparison with Ṣalāḥ al-Dīn, al-ʿĀdil was unable to wield his military power with confidence. His troops were devoted to the defense of Egypt against Frankish incursions (there were naval raids on Rosetta in 600/1204 and Damietta in 607/1211); they were also of uncertain reliability. The principal instrument of his rule was the distribution of the various provinces to his sons, who then developed, with varying degrees of success, their own cadres of supporters. This policy maintained a relative balance of power

[13] For examples of al-ʿĀdil's direct involvement in administration see Ibn al-ʿAmīd, 6ff.; Sawīrus ibn al-Muqaffāʾ, iv/1: 17–18.

[14] On Ayyūbid coinage and monetary history see P. Balog, *The Coinage of the Ayyubids* (London, 1980); J. L. Bacharach, "Monetary movements in medieval Egypt, 1171–1517," in J. F. Richards (ed.), *Precious Metals in the Later Medieval and Early Modern Worlds* (Durham, 1983); C. Cahen, "La circulation monétaire en Egypte des Fatimides aux Ayyubides," *Revue numismatique*, 6th ser., 26, 208–17; C. Cahen, "Monetary circulation in Egypt at the time of the crusades and the reform of al-Kāmil," in A. L. Udovitch (ed.), *The Islamic Middle East, 700–1900: Studies in Economic and Social History* (Princeton, 1981), 315–33; A. S. Ehrenkreutz, "Contributions to the knowledge of the fiscal administration of Egypt in the middle ages," *BSOAS*, 16 (1954), 502–14; 178–84; A. S. Ehrenkreutz, "The crisis of the *dinar* in the Egypt of Saladin," *JAOS*, 76 (1956), 178–84; S. Goitein, "The exchange rate of gold and silver money in Fatimid and Ayyubid times," *JESHO*, 8 (1965), 1–46.

[15] On the drought and famine see especially the account of the physician al-Baghdādī, *Kitāb al-ifāda waʾl-iʿtibār fiʾl-umūr al-mushāhada waʾl-ḥawādith al-muʿāyana bi-arḍ miṣr*, ed. A. G. Sabānū (Damascus, 1983); also Maqrīzī's later account in A. Allouche, *Mamlūk Economics: A Study and Translation of al-Maqrīzī's Ighāthah* (Utah, 1994), 41–42; Sibṭ Ibn al-Jawzī, VIII, 477ff.; Ibn Wāṣil, III, 127ff.

during his lifetime. However, in the next generation it proved a weak basis for sustaining the unity of the Ayyūbid domains. In al-ʿĀdil's last years no member of the next generation of the house of Ayyūb held decisive power.

The Fifth Crusade, which appeared off Damietta in Rabīʿ I 615/June 1218, preserved Ayyūbid family solidarity at the difficult moment of succession. The crusade was the last to be organized by a medieval pope, and benefited from better planning, and perhaps greater commitment, than any other.[16] Its strategy was sound, at least in contrast to its antecedents: the Latins now realized that the road to Jerusalem ran through Egypt. The ultimate Latin defeat was perhaps due to happenstance more than anything else, as both combatants saw many perilous moments and unexpected reversals. But in retrospect it is possible to discern several Frankish shortcomings that were conducive to, if they did not guarantee, Muslim victory. Among these were failure to exploit initial success, divided command, shifting objectives, ignorance of terrain, and tenuous lines of supply and communication. Perhaps most damaging to the crusader cause was their inability to convert their salt water naval supremacy into brown water superiority. In the enclosed waters of the Nile Delta, which they knew less well than their enemies, their advantages in shipbuilding, seamanship, and numbers counted for less.

The indirect political effects of the crusade were ultimately of greater consequence than the immediate military threat. Al-ʿĀdil opened up a second front in Syria, both to relieve pressure on Egypt and to protect the approaches to Damascus. But the military situation in Egypt deteriorated rapidly. When al-ʿĀdil was informed of the loss of the Chain Tower at Damietta, a stronghold that controlled movement on the river, the shock killed him (7 Jumādā I 615/August 31, 1218).

The succession crisis that was latent in al-ʿĀdil's political arrangements was now joined to an external invasion that somewhat paradoxically ameliorated it. As was typical of Ayyūbid successions – including that following the death of Ṣalāḥ al-Dīn – political power began to fragment following the death of the individual who held the various powers in balance in his lifetime. This dissolution of political power produced what the sources referred to (and condemned) as *fitna*, or atomized conflict. *Fitnas* over the succession usually occurred in two dimensions – horizontally among rulers, and vertically between rulers and the amīrs upon whose military power they depended.[17] In this crisis the vertical split occurred when the preeminent

[16] On the Fifth Crusade, with a recent bibliography of western scholarship, see J. M. Powell, *Anatomy of a Crusade, 1213–1221* (Philadelphia, 1986); from the Ayyūbid perspective, with an extensive bibliography of Muslim sources, see Gottschalk, *Al-Kāmil*, 58–115.

[17] For *fitna* used in this sense see Ibn al-ʿAmīd, 31; Ibn Wāṣil, III: 28, 111, 140, 253; Dhahabī, LXIII: 21, 112; Ibn al-Dawādārī, VII: 142; Sawīrus ibn al-Muqaffāʾ, IV/2: 115;

Kurdish amīr, ʿImād al-Dīn Ibn al-Mashṭūb, tried to replace al-Kāmil with the latter's brother al-Fā'iz.[18] The crusader threat postponed the usual horizontal fracture, however, when al-Kāmil's brothers recognized his sultanate and came to his aid.

Al-Muʿaẓẓam's arrival in Egypt brought Ibn al-Mashṭūb into obedience. But in the confusion the Franks crossed the Nile and laid siege to Damietta. Their seizure of the city the following year so unnerved al-Kāmil that he offered the former territories of the kingdom of Jerusalem in return for a withdrawal and a thirty-year truce. Negotiations broke down over the status of the Transjordan castles of Kerak and Shawbak (Montréal), indispensable to either party because they simultaneously controlled communications between Syria and Egypt and protected the eastern approaches to Palestine. The debates in the crusader camp also suggest that the Italians were more interested in holding on to the port cities of Egypt than in acquiring an economically peripheral Jerusalem. In the event the crusaders were to regret rejecting al-Kāmil's proposal. Instead of marching directly on Cairo they waited for reinforcements, giving al-Kāmil time to fortify and reinforce al-Manṣūra. After a blundering campaign in the direction of Cairo the crusaders opened negotiations, admitted defeat, and permitted Damietta to be reoccupied in Rajab 618/September 1221.

The solidarity of al-ʿĀdil's sons did not survive the passing of the external threat. Throughout his reign al-Kāmil continued to be preoccupied with opposition from his amīrs in Egypt and his rivals in Syria. To offset al-Muʿaẓẓam, whose army was one-quarter the size of his own, but more reliable, and who moreover had the clandestine support of many of his own amīrs, he relied on alliances. One was with al-Ashraf against al-Muʿaẓẓam, which if it did not succeed in deposing the latter at least kept him occupied for a time. Another was his alliance with Frederick II, each of the two parties recognizing, and endeavoring to counter, the other's weakness among his co-religionists.[19] It was only with the death of Muʿaẓẓam in Dhu'l-Qaʿda 624/

Ibn ʿAbd al-Ẓāhir, 50; Ibn Kathīr, *Al-Bidāya wa'l-nihāya fi'l-ta'rīkh* (Beirut, 1982), XIII: 179; Ibn al-Athīr, *Al-Kāmil*, XII: 184; and below, note 18; for approximate synonyms such as ʿaṣabiyya or ikhtilāf see Maqrīzī, *Khiṭaṭ*, I: 94–95; Ibn al-Dawādārī, VII: 142, 317, 330, 343; Ibn Wāṣil, III: 111, 140; Dhahabī, LXIV: 30.

18 For characterizations of this event as *fitna* see Ibn al-ʿAmīd, 11; Dhahabī, lxii: 31; Ibn al-Wardī, *Tatimma al-mukhtaṣar fi akhbār al-bashar*, A. R. Badarāwī ed. (Beirut, 1970), II: 202; for references see Gottschalk, *Al-Kāmil*, 79, to which add Ibn al-Wardī, II: 158, 202; Ibn al-Dawādārī, VII: 198–99; Maqrīzī, *Khiṭaṭ*, II: 375–76; Dhahabī, LXII: 24–25, 397; Ibn Wāṣil, IV: 29–30.

19 On al-Kāmil's relation with Frederick II see T. C. Van Cleve, "The crusade of Frederick II," in K. M. Setton (gen. ed.), *A history of the crusades*, II: *The later crusades, 1189–1311*, R. L. Wolff and H. W. Hazard (eds.) (Madison, 1969), 429–62; the most recent biography of Frederick II, with an account of his relations with al-Kāmil, is D. Abulafia, *Frederick II: A Medieval Emperor* (London, 1988).

November 1227 that al-Kāmil was able to assert his power in Syria, Mesopotamia, and Anatolia directly.

The death of al-Kāmil in Rajab 635/March 1238 left a more complicated political situation than had his father's death, and in this crisis there was no external threat to strengthen family solidarities. Al-Kāmil's successor as sultan was his son al-ʿĀdil Abū Bakr II, who, after receiving the oath of his father's amīrs, eunuchs, and household attendants, quickly lost their loyalties. His fathers' amīrs and eunuchs seized him in Shawwāl 637/May 1240 and invited his brother al-Ṣāliḥ Ayyūb to Cairo, where he was proclaimed sultan.

Al-Ṣāliḥ Ayyūb, much like other Ayyūbids before him, was opposed by established amīrs and members of his family. He was unable to assert his power in Syria after his rival al-Ṣāliḥ Ismāʿil of Damascus made an alliance with Theobald of Champagne and the Templars. Given the narrow base of his military support, amīral rivalries, and the unstable finances of Egypt, it is unlikely that he could have done so even had he wished. Unable to rely on the Egyptian army as he found it, he began to purchase large numbers of mamlūks and to assign them the *iqṭāʿat* of the amīrs of the previous generation. He had a barracks and fortress built for some of these recruits on the island of Rawḍa; henceforth this group – a fraction of the total number of his Ṣāliḥiyya mamlūks – was known as the Baḥrī (bahr: river) mamlūks.[20] To balance al-Ṣāliḥ Ismāʿil's alliance with the Franks, al-Ṣāliḥ Ayyūb made one of his own with the Khwārazmians. With his new troops and allies al-Ṣāliḥ Ayyūb defeated the Franco-Syrian army at al-Ḥarbiyya (La Forbie), near Gaza (Jumādā I 642/October 1244). He was now able to take much of Syria and threaten the rest.

The disorders of the preceding period, and the sack of Jerusalem by the Khwārazmians, played a part in the organization of the Seventh Crusade. This crusade, although well financed and benefiting from the leadership of Louis IX, displayed some of the same defects as earlier invasions. A long wait for reinforcements in Cyprus in 646/1248–49 lost the crusaders the element of surprise; once in Egypt they suffered from the now familiar combination of strategic irresolution and tactical impetuousness. The crusaders took Damietta soon after landing in Ṣafar 647/June 1249. But they failed to follow up on their success and allowed al-Ṣāliḥ Ayyūb to put blocking forces in place at al-Manṣūra.

Once again a Frankish invasion coincided with a succession crisis to shape its outcome. Al-Ṣāliḥ Ayyūb died in Shaʿbān 647/November 1249. The fact of his death was concealed by his slave concubine, Shajar al-Durr, in concert with Fakhr al-Dīn Ibn al-Shaykh, commander of the Baḥriyya, and several of al-Ṣāliḥ Ayyūb's intimates. They took the oath in secret for al-Muʿaẓẓam

[20] D. Ayalon, "Le Régiment Baḥriyya dans l'armée mamlouke," *REI* (1951), 133–41.

Tūrān Shāh, al-Ṣāliḥ Ayyūb's sole surviving son, from some of al-Ṣāliḥ Ayyūb's amīrs, and summoned him from Ḥiṣn Kayfā in Mesopotamia. But there were conflicting interests within both al-Ṣāliḥ Ayyūb's household and the Baḥriyya, conflicts which Tūrānshāh's slow progress from Mesopotamia allowed to come out in the open. Fakhr al-Dīn Ibn al-Shaykh, commander of the Baḥriyya, appears to have acted in a manner similar to that of Ibn al-Mashṭūb in the Fifth Crusade. He seems to have contemplated ruling in the name of a young Ayyūbid until Shajar al-Durr and her Baḥrī supporters had his candidate confined. For a short time he was the effective ruler of the country – it was his orders, which contradicted many of al-Ṣāliḥ Ayyūb's, that made it obvious that the latter had died. But when Fakhr al-Dīn died in a skirmish in the battle of al-Manṣūra, Shajar al-Durr and her Baḥrī supporters were able to control the situation until Tūrānshāh arrived.

Al-Muʿaẓẓam Tūrān Shāh faced the same problems as previous new sultans, and had fewer of his own resources than most. The Baḥriyya were largely responsible for the ultimate defeat of the crusading army, and were in a stronger position than their sultan and his Mesopotamian amīrs. When, in the usual fashion, Tūrān Shāh tried to replace his father's amīrs with his own, the Baḥrīs, in concert with Shajar al-Durr, killed him (27 Muḥarram 648/May 1, 1250). Shajar al-Durr was proclaimed sultana, but in time she too was killed and Ayyūbid rule in Egypt came effectively to an end.[21]

Latin invasion, which brought the Ayyūbids to power and sustained them at difficult moments, thus also contributed to their downfall. This is perhaps less of an irony than it may seem. The Ayyūbid empire was held together by opportunistic alliances among its ruling households. It had few intrusive institutions by which to bridge the gap between the sultan and the lesser rulers, and between rulers and their clients. In the open contests for power that erupted at moments of transition, these rivalries broke out with little to restrain them. Those able to take advantage of invasion therefore had an edge in internal disputes.

The advent of Mamlūk rule was not a decisive break with the past. In the succession crisis both al-Muʿaẓẓam Tūrān Shāh and the Baḥrī amīrs acted much as rulers and amīrs had in *fitnas* before them. The difference was that on this occasion the usual contest between the new sultan and his predecessor's amīrs was resolved in favor of the latter. In a manner recalling other Ayyūbid successions these amīrs first tried to rule in name of a young Ayyūbid. Once they took power in their own name they continued to identify with the house of their master al-Ṣāliḥ Ayyūb, and his name and tomb were revered long thereafter.[22] In any case, the most striking change at

21 G. Schregle, *Die Sultanin von Ägypten. Šağarat al-Durr in der arabischen Geschichtsschreibung und Literatur* (Wiesbaden, 1961).

22 Ibn ʿAbd al-Ẓāhir, 71.

the top was the origin of the new rulers. In this respect the Baḥrī mamlūks resembled previous new rulers of post-Saljūk military-patronage states, including the Ayyūbids and Zengids themselves.

Military organization and recruitment

Ṣalāḥ al-Dīn and his successors built an army on the Syrian pattern, the numbers of cavalrymen fluctuating roughly between 8,500 and 12,000. It was composed largely of free-born Kurds and Turks who were purchased as slaves (*mamlūk*, pl. *mamālīk*); in the early period of Ayyūbid rule there was also a large contingent of Turkoman. Added to these were Arab contingents such as the Kināniyya, largely devoted to the defense of Egypt, Arab auxiliaries, and former Fāṭimid units, especially Nubians. Large numbers of city people volunteered or were drafted to fight in the Fifth and Seventh Crusades. Of the foot soldiers and engineers cited in the sources little is known.

Contemporary sources do not provide enough information to establish the relative proportions of Kurds and Turks, though the balance (if such it was) seems to have shifted from the former to the latter at a fairly early date. Rivalries between the two groups began with the death of Shīrkūh and continued throughout the period, becoming quite bloody at times.[23] However, it is probably an anachronism to characterize these clashes as ethnic conflicts. Kurds and Turks intermarried and seem not to have had ethnic epithets for one another; fighting between them broke out when there was something at stake. Perhaps less important than ethnic identity was factional affiliation, which was determined in part by variations in recruitment paths. Affiliation, therefore, may have had a greater role than ethnicity in the perception of difference. Sultans, in spite of their Kurdish origin, do not seem to have been partial to either group. Al-Ṣāliḥ Ayyūb was an exception to this, but even he continued to have Kurdish amīrs in his service (contrary to a number of statements in later sources), and Kurdish amīrs and contingents are cited well into the early Mamlūk period.

The organization of the army is poorly understood, as it is difficult to ferret out relations between tactical formations (*ṭulb*, pl. *aṭlāb*), soldiers associated for the acquisition of revenue, and those bound together, and known by, their ties to their commanders or their places of origin. This problem may be due to the fact that recruitment and organization were in continuous flux, rather than to any silence in the sources. Perhaps it is fair to say that the Ayyūbids made use of military manpower as they found it or could recruit it, and gave their amīrs considerable freedom of action. Rulers were more interested in winning the loyalties of amīrs than in developing an

[23] See Ibn al-Athīr, *Al-Bāhir*, 142; Ibn al-Dawādārī, VII: 78.

organized and hierarchical army. The army was divided into contingents known by the names of their masters, as Ayyūbid rulers and senior amīrs recruited bodies of troops loyal to them; contingents known by tribe or place or origin, often under their own leadership; and the *ḥalqa* or *ḥalqa sultāniyya*. The *ḥalqa* often occupied the center of the line of battle and was celebrated for its loyalty to the sultan – a characterization confirmed by a number of incidents given in the sources.[24] In contrast to the Mamlūk unit of the same name, the Ayyūbid *ḥalqa* recruited large numbers of Turkish mamlūks.[25]

Naval forces were of lesser importance and less is known of them. Although Ṣalāḥ al-Dīn carried out offensive operations against the Frankish ports, these largely ended as a consequence of the Third Crusade. Throughout the period there were raids on the Egyptian coast against which the Ayyūbids were powerless to defend. There was probably little in any case that Ayyūbid sultans could do to regain Egyptian supremacy in the eastern Mediterranean. Egypt had difficulty keeping up with the pace of innovation in European shipbuilding, and lacked the trained seamen, shipbuilding materials, and eastern Mediterranean ports of the European and Byzantine naval powers. Nonetheless, Ayyūbid naval power did not come to an end with Ṣalāḥ al-Dīn. Al-ʿĀdil is known to have built a small Mediterranean fleet at Alexandria, which seems to have accomplished little before it was wrecked in a storm off Tripoli. When Egyptians were unable to project naval power in the Mediterranean, in the Fifth and Seventh Crusades they deployed warships on the Nile, at least for blocking and cutting-out operations.[26] And finally, the Ayyūbids maintained ships on the Red Sea, many of which were constructed in the Fusṭāṭ shipyards and transported overland.

Land tenure and politics

The Ayyūbids supported their warriors with *iqṭāʿāt*, franchises to collect revenue at source.[27] Ayyūbid *iqṭāʿāt* in Egypt had both Fāṭimid and Zangid

[24] H. A. R. Gibb, "The armies of Saladin," *Cahiers, d'histoire Égyptienne*, 3/4 (1951), 304–20; R. S. Humphreys, "The emergence of the Mamluk army," *SI*, 45 (1977), 67–99, 147–82; D. Ayalon, "From Ayyubids to Mamluks," *REI*, 49 (1981), 43–57; D. Ayalon, "Ḥalḳa," *EI2*.

[25] Sawīrus ibn al-Muqaffā', iv/2: 90–92.

[26] A. S. Ehrenkreutz, "The place of Saladin in the naval history of the Mediterranean sea in the middle ages," *JAOS*, 75 (1955), 100–16. For fleets deployed by al-ʿĀdil, al-Kāmil, and al-Ṣāliḥ Ayyūb see Ibn al-Dawādārī, vii: 159; Sawīrus ibn al-Muqaffā', iv/2: 81; Ibn ʿAbd al-Ẓāhir, 92. For operations on the Nile in the Fifth crusade see especially Ibn Wāṣil, iv: 16, 95.

[27] H. M. Rabie, *The Financial System of Egypt, AH 564–741/AD 1169–1341* (Oxford, 1972); H. M. Rabie, *Al-Nuẓum al-māliyya fī miṣr zaman al-ayyūbiyīn* (Cairo, 1964);

antecedents. The distinction between the two antecedent forms is difficult to discern, in part because Fāṭimid *iqṭāʿ* appears to have been moving in the direction of Syrian practice. One difference from the Fāṭimid use of *iqṭāʿ* is that the Ayyūbids tied it more directly to military service. But the contrast was not absolute. Some clients of Ayyūbid sultans received *iqṭāʿāt* without an obligation to render military service, and *iqṭāʿāt* were also occasionally granted as pensions to defeated rulers and amīrs.[28] Moreover, the military and personal service expected from the *iqṭāʿ* holder was somewhat limited: to take troops on campaign it was necessary to pay them cash. Finally, just as Fāṭimid *iqṭāʿ* had been moving in the direction of Syrian practice, during the Ayyūbid period some *iqṭāʿāt* had distinctively Fāṭimid antecedents, especially the lease of non-surveyed land in return for cash payments to the treasury.

The same caution applies to comparisons between Egyptian and Syrian practice under the Ayyūbids themselves. In Syria, under Nūr al-Dīn and in the early Ayyūbid period, some *iqṭāʿāt* are thought to have been hereditary, while in Egypt, as far as can be determined (which is not very far), they have generally thought not to have been.[29] But here we must be careful not to confuse policy with principle. In both regions *iqṭāʿāt* were assignable at the will of the ruler, and in the case of Syria it is hazardous to derive a hereditary principle from the episodic assignment of *iqṭāʿāt* to the sons of warriors.

Some *iqṭāʿ* holders, or *muqṭaʿ*s, had a role in the organization of agriculture. Many were present in their *iqṭāʿāt* to handle the harvest. Some maintained the smaller dams, distributed seed-stocks, and supervised land reclamation. During the famine of 596–99/1200–03 some *muqṭaʿ*s sent their soldiers to work the land after the peasants fled or died.[30] The sources, however, do not support confident generalizations on this issue. Because *iqṭāʿāt* were often assigned in scattered parcels, and individuals often held more than one, it is clear that agents (*wakīls*) handled at least some management. Moreover, Cairo was the preferred place of residence for the great amīrs, and amīrs who resided there could hold *iqṭāʿāt* as far

H. M. Rabie, "The size and value of the *iqṭāʿ* in Egypt 564–741 AH/1169–1341 AD," in M. A. Cook (ed.), *Studies in the Economic History of the Middle East from the Rise of Islam to the Present Day* (London, 1970), 129–38; I. A. Ṭarkhān, *Al-Nuẓum al-iqṭāʿiyya fī'sharq al-awsaṭ fī'l-ʿuṣūr al-wusṭā* (Cairo, 1968); C. Cahen, "Iḳṭāʿ," *EI2*; C. Cahen, "L'évolution de l'Iqṭāʿ du IXe au XIIe siècle: Contribution à une histoire comparée des sociétés médiévales," *Annales E.S.C.*, 8;1 (1953), 25–52; C. Cahen, "Réflexions sur l'usage du mot 'Féodalité'," *JESHO*, 3 (1960), 7–20; A. N. Poliak, "The Ayyubid feudalism," *JRAS* (1939), 97–109; A. N. Poliak, *Feudalism in Egypt, Syria, Palestine and the Lebanon* (London, 1939); A. K. S. Lambton, "Reflections on the iqṭāʿ," in G. Makdisi ed., *Arabic and Islamic Studies in Honor of Hamilton A. R. Gibb* (Leiden, 1965); Humphreys, *From Saladin to the Mongols*, 42–43, 371–75.

28 See Maqrīzī, *Khiṭaṭ*, ii: 373.

29 In fact in Egypt some sons received their fathers' *iqṭāʿāt*: Ibn al-Dawādārī, vii: 380–81.

30 Baghdādī, *Ifāda*, 252, 254, 262.

away as Syria or Palestine. The same caution applies to generalizations about the relationship of *iqṭāʿ* holders to peasants. In theory *iqṭāʿ* holders held only financial rights. In practice some *muqṭa*ʿs exercised coercion at least some of the time. Some peasants, those known as *al-fallāḥūn al-qarāriyya*, were tied to their villages, and *iqṭāʿ* holders could compel the return of fugitives. Many if not all peasants, moreover, were obliged to perform corvée labor, in the organization of which some *muqṭa*ʿs may have had a role.

In spite of these occasional functions, it remains generally true that the *muqṭaʿ* was "the beneficiary rather than the master of the village."[31] The *iqṭāʿ* was a revenue source before it was anything else. The *muqṭa*ʿs revenue was calculated in a dīnār of account (the *dīnār jayshī*), which included cash and kind. *Muqṭa*ʿs supported their troops from revenue from their personal *iqṭāʿāt* or by assigning them their own smaller *iqṭāʿāt*. In the case of the ordinary *iqṭāʿ* the sultan's agents collected the sultan's share on site. Members of the Ayyūbid house, together with a few great amīrs, had a different form of *iqṭāʿ* called the *iqṭāʿ khāṣṣ*. Recipients of these *iqṭāʿāt* were allowed to keep all revenue, including the shares of the sultan and those of the soldiers. The *iqṭāʿ khāṣṣ* could also include non-agricultural revenue sources. Under al-Kāmil appeared the *iqṭāʿ darbastā*, which allowed the *muqṭaʿ* to collect all taxes and, at least in some cases, to appoint officials and governors.

The variety of forms that the *iqṭāʿ* took, and the various roles that *muqṭa*ʿs exercised, make it difficult to find a pure or final form of Ayyūbid land tenure. To understand the relationship between Ayyūbid politics and land tenure, it is perhaps less productive to search for Zengid or Fāṭimid antecedents, or to attempt to define administrative practices exactly, than to note that *iqṭāʿāt* were assigned and exploited in an ad hoc manner. The Ayyubid *iqṭāʿ* system adapted to local circumstances and fitted into local arrangements. Longstanding relationships, the status of the *iqṭāʿ* holder, and the political circumstances of the time all came into play. The control over land revenue was now more parceled out than it had been before, and more directly tied to the support of a horse-riding military elite, but the forms such parcelization took varied throughout the period. In this respect as in many others, each Ayyūbid ruler supported his clients through a mix of habit and improvisation.

Trade

Rulers regarded trade much as they saw agriculture, as a source of revenue and strategic materials.[32] In both cases they attached more importance to

[31] Goitein, *Mediterranean Society*, I: 117–18.

[32] E. Ashtor, *Levant trade in the Later Middle Ages* (Princeton, 1983); E. Ashtor, "The

extracting revenue from existing arrangements than to managing economic activity directly. The Ayyūbids made money from sultanal monopolies and goods traded on their own account, but they benefited principally from taxes and duties.

The Kārimī merchants, first mentioned in the Fāṭimid period, predominated in the long-distance trade between the Indian Ocean and Egypt. As far as can be determined, the Kārimīs were a loose association based on partnerships, who owned their own ships and enjoyed a poorly understood legal status. The Ayyūbids provided protection and built warehouses and port facilities for them, but otherwise did not interfere in their activities. To handle the Mediterranean end of this trade the Ayyūbids permitted Europeans – mainly Italians, with some French and Catalans – to settle in Alexandria. These seem to have been present in fairly large numbers, if the three thousand European merchants arrested in the Fifth Crusade are any indication. From Africa Egypt imported among other products slaves, ivory, and gold, for which West Africa replaced Nubia as the principal source.

The period also saw an increasing European penetration into local markets. The European presence, though growing, should not be overestimated. The reasons for the growing integration of the Egyptian and European economies are complex in any period of post-Fāṭimid history, and it is difficult to sort out causes from effects or to assess precisely the relative importance of any given factor. That Europeans were beginning to penetrate Egyptian markets is certain; the extent and pace are not.

Nonetheless, it is clear that some European goods began to supplant local production. This is especially true in the case of textiles, which suffered from competition from Flanders and Italy. European raw materials – especially English wool – were cheap and of high quality. Improvements in loom technology and bulk shipping may have given European merchants important, if not decisive, advantages. Europeans also benefited from superior organization and production on a larger scale, especially in comparison with

volume of the medieval spice trade," *Journal of European Economic History*, 9 (1980), 753–63; E. Ashtor, *East-West Trade in the Medieval Mediterranean* (Variorum reprints), ed. B. Kader (London, 1986); C. Cahen, "Doanes et commerce dans les ports méditerranéens de l'Égypte médiévale d'après le Minhādj d'al-Makhzūmī," *JESHO*, 7 (1964), 217–314; S. Goitein, "From the Mediterranean to India," *Speculum*, 24 (1952); S. Goitein, "Letters and documents on the India trade in medieval times," *IC*, 37 (1963), 188–205; S. Goitein, "The beginnings of the Kārim merchants and the character of their organization," in his *Studies in Islamic History and Institutions* (Leiden, 1966), 351–60; S. Labib, "Al-Iskandariyya," *EI2*; S. Labib, "Al-Tujjār al-kārimiyya wa-tijārat miṣr fī'l-'usūr al-wusṭā," *Al-Majalla al-ta'rīkhiyya al-miṣriyya*, 4 (1952), 5–63; S. Labib, *Handelsgeschichte Ägyptens im Spätmittelalter, 1171–1517* (Wiesbaden, 1965), ch. 2; S. Labib, "Kārimī," *EI2*; W. Heyd, *Histoire du commerce du Levant au moyen âge* (Leipzig, 1885–86; reprint, Amsterdam, 1967); M. M. Postan and E. Miller (eds.), *The Cambridge Economic History of Europe*, II: *Trade and industry in the Middle Ages*, 2nd edn. (Cambridge, 1987).

the small and heavily taxed workshops of Egypt. Several of the major centers of Fāṭimid textile production in Egypt closed down by the end of the Ayyūbid period, though the sultanal workshops of Alexandria survived, if they did not thrive, well into the Mamlūk period. In 624/1227, al-Kāmil ordered the destruction of Tinnīs, called "Baghdād the lesser" in the Fāṭimid period for the scale of its textile production. The sources agree that this was a scorched-earth policy in anticipation of a crusader attack, but Tinnīs was not rebuilt; other major textile centers in the period also seem to have declined in importance. One source also refers to the sale of European wheat in bulk (described as superior to the local product), but there is no indication of a massive or sustained presence.[33]

Set against the loss of some local production were new markets gained in Europe for trade goods and raw materials. European economic expansion stimulated an ever rising demand for Indian Ocean products. The Italian textile industry also provided a market for nitre and especially alum, products which also served as ballast in returning vessels. Egypt also benefited – indeed it may have been one of the principal beneficiaries – of the opening up of new silver mines in Tuscany, Germany, and Eastern Europe in the 1160s and 1170s.[34] Finally, continuing European demand for Egyptian cotton and sugar set the stage for later developments.

Urban politics

The Ayyūbids had three principal means of recruiting the learned elites whom they needed to rule their cities and towns. Some shaykhs entered the service of ruling or amiral households and were supported out of household revenues. Others were paid directly out of revenue collected by the *dīwāns*.[35] The third method, which was to have enduring consequences, was the assignment to shaykhs of the revenues of charitable endowments or *waqfs*. Ṣalāh al-Dīn endowed approximately five *madrasas* – *waqfs* that supported learned shaykhs and students – in Cairo and Fusṭāṭ: there were some twenty-five founded throughout the Ayyūbid period, mainly by rulers, amīrs, and secretaries.[36] The Ayyūbids also endowed numerous *khānqāhs* for ṣūfīs.

These foundations have been viewed as the expression in Egypt of a Sunnī

[33] Sawīrus ibn al-Muqaffā', IV/2: 144.

[34] P. Spufford, *Money and its Use in Medieval Europe* (Cambridge, 1988).

[35] See the fragment of al-Qāḍī al-Fāḍil's *Mutajaddidāt* listing *dīwān* revenues in 577: Maqrīzī, *Khiṭaṭ*, I: 86–87.

[36] M. M. Amīn, *Al-Awqāf wa'l-ḥayā al-ijtimā'iyya fī miṣr* (Cairo, 1980); G. Leiser, "The madrasa and the islamization of the Middle East: the case of Egypt," *JARCE* (1985); G. Leiser, "The restoration of sunnism in Egypt: madrasas and mudarrisūn, 495–647/1101–1249," (Ph.D dissertation, University of Pennsylvania, 1976); A. Fikry, *Masājid al-qāhira wa-madārisihā*, 2 vols. (Cairo, 1965–69); on Ayyūbid patronage of the

revival that began in Khurāsān and Iraq in the eleventh century and achieved its final victory in the suppression of Shiʿism in Egypt. The Ayyūbids were undoubtedly attached to Sunnī Islam and exerted themselves to see it flourish. However, the relationship between this general commitment and their patronage of religious institutions is more intricate that the notion of the Sunnī revival can account for. Some evidence indeed hints at an ideological dimension to a few of the early Ayyūbid *madrasas*. An infamous prison was turned into a *madrasa*, and a *madrasa* was built next to the tomb of the great jurist al-Shāfiʿī, evoking, perhaps, both the Fāṭimid shrine and the Syrian *madrasa*-tomb. But insofar as we can discern an ideological objective in Ayyūbid religious policy, it seems to have been directed at Sunnīs as much as Shiʿis. One condition of Ṣalāḥ al-Dīn's *waqf* foundation deeds was that those appointed to *madrasa*s be Ashʿarite in doctrine. Al-ʿAzīz, Ṣalāḥ al-Dīn's son and successor, also seems to have been more concerned with asserting his authority over Sunnīs than with the extirpation of Shiʿism, and tried to have the small Ḥanbalī community of Cairo expelled.[37] There is little evidence that the foundation of *madrasas* was an anti-Fāṭimid policy, or that Sunnism, the religious affiliation of the majority of the Muslim population, required new institutions to flourish on the levels of belief or communal identity. *Madrasas* existed in Egypt well before Ṣalāḥ al-Dīn, some sponsored by Fāṭimid wazīrs.[38]

To understand Ayyūbid patronage of religious institutions, it is perhaps more productive to look at the characteristics it shared with other post-Saljuk military patronage states of the period. The Ayyūbids, together with other such regimes, had relatively few state agencies by which they could penetrate their cities and towns. To link themselves to the learned elite whom they needed to rule, they relied instead on the political use of patronage practices. Through the support by *waqf* of scholars on the eastern pattern, Ṣalāḥ al-Dīn and his successors could simultaneously bring in new men (they came largely from Syria, Iraq, Andalus, North Africa, Mesopotamia, and Iran) and win over established Egyptian learned families. The assignment of *waqf* revenue to the learned thus resembled the assignment of *iqṭāʿāt* to warriors. In both cases it enabled the Ayyūbids to recruit a dependent but not administratively subordinate elite.

The Ayyūbids also supported various religious offices, some of which had clear Zengid antecedents. The clearest example of the transplantation of a Syrian office was the *muḥtasib* or market inspector, which appeared in Egypt for the first time. The *qāḍi*ship of course existed in Fāṭimid Egypt, but the Ayyūbids appointed and made use of *qāḍīs* in the Syrian manner.

ʿulamāʾ see I. Lapidus, "Ayyūbid religious policy and the development of schools of law in Cairo," *Colloque international sur l'histoire du Caire* (Cairo, 1974), 279–86.

37 Ibn Kathīr, *Al-Bidāya*, xiii: 18.

38 Leiser, "Restoration," I: lii–liii, 111–86, 264–67; II: 403, 427–31.

Although *qāḍīs* were supported by salaries out of the *dīwāns*, they also often received *waqf* income as lecturers and administrators of madrasas. *Qāḍīs* also exercized non-judicial functions in a manner reminiscent of some areas of the eastern Islamic world. In the larger towns some *qāḍīs* were superintendents of ports, others collected taxes or served in *dīwāns*, still others were envoys to other rulers or the caliph.[39] In the smaller towns *qāḍīs* were often the most important personages, the office finding the man rather than the other way around.

The duties of these offices are prescribed in the sources, in some cases in great detail. In practice, however, it is difficult to establish the effect that formal jurisdiction or recognized capacity had on behavior. A *qāḍi* could undertake to ensure public order; the *wālī* or governor could intervene in an inheritance case or property dispute. The *muḥtasib* could get involved in questions of law that might fall in the formal jurisdiction of a *qāḍi*, or an issue of public order that might belong to a *wālī* or amīr. Learned shaykhs who were not part of a state apparatus could also involve themselves in social or political issues. And in any case amīrs and secretaries intervened in questions of law, public order, and local administration when they had the power to do so. The formal division of functions was probably of lesser importance than the status and power of particular individuals.

This reliance on dependent but not administratively subordinate religious elites, who were remunerated with franchises to existing revenue sources as much as with stipends or household revenues, also extended to the *dhimmīs*. Christian and Jewish leaders came to have a relationship to the ruling elite much like that of the Muslim *ʿulamāʾ*. Ayyūbid sultans relied on the religious leaders of all three communities for the organization of taxation and occasional corvée labor. Sultans began to make appointments to *dhimmī* religious offices and to intervene in their religious controversies, much as they did among Muslims.[40] A long struggle over the Coptic patriarchate between the bishops and monasteries on the one hand and the patriarch on the other closely resembled Muslim struggles over religious offices. The sultan now laid claims to the authority to make appointments, demanded payoffs for them, and put his power behind the winner.[41] The patriarch began to act in much the same manner as a powerful Muslim shaykh, and to be criticized by his co-religionists much as Muslims criticized shaykhs who associated themselves too closely with rulers.[42] And as Muslims feared open competition as *fitna* now we find Christians doing so as well.[43]

39 Goitein, *Mediterranean Society*, II: 366–71.

40 Goitein, *Mediterranean Society*, II: 405–07; Maqrīzī, *Khiṭaṭ*, I/1: 252; Ibn al-ʿAmīd, 6–7, 20; Sawīrus ibn al-Muqaffāʾ, IV/1: 2–17, 40–41, 64ff.; IV/2: 8, 74ff.

41 Sawīrus ibn al-Muqaffāʾ, IV/2: 73–77.

42 Sawīrus ibn al-Muqaffāʾ, IV/2: 82–83.

43 Sawīrus ibn al-Muqaffāʾ, IV/1: 10, 24; IV/2: 118, 131, 134.

In addition to offices and revenue sources held by the elite, there were a number of smaller functions. The sources cite messengers, spies, guards, police, and agents of various kinds, but are vague with respect to function or importance. It is usually unclear whether these were offices staffed by minor officials (generally the least likely possibility), occasional tasks carried out by retainers, or small services rendered for tips.[44] Each urban area had a *ṣāḥib al-rubʿ*, or head of the quarter, who was more of a watchman than a communal leader or state official: his status was low and he was paid in the form of presents. Others, such as the *ḥāshir* who was used to round up taxpayers, and the *raqqāṣ*, or "runner," must have been very temporary functions. Still other functions, such as the mint, were farmed out, the mint workers being paid by the job instead of receiving a salary.

Assessing the influence of Syrian practice on Ayyūbid Egypt, it appears that the overall pattern of relations between ruling households and the warriors and shaykhs upon whom they depended was more significant than the direct importation of institutions. Great men did not assert power through a structure of differentiated offices; rather, they devolved power and revenue sources on to their clients. These, in turn, did not exercise power as specialists possessed of a defined capacity within an institutional hierarchy. Rather, they asserted themselves as lesser versions of great men themselves.

Dīwāns and the politics of revenue assignment

Keeping track of the politics of revenue assignment were the *dīwa*ns. As in the case of the *iqṭāʿ*, the *dīwāns* drew on both Fāṭimid and Syrian antecedents, adapted to local practice and changing circumstances. The *dīwāns* were relatively small. They do not appear to have been housed in large or permanently designated buildings; indeed the sources rarely mention government buildings.[45] They were also unhierarchical; we read less of promotion than of advancement in the service of an individual or movement to new positions. Occupational terms such as *kātib* or *mushrif* relate loosely to function, and not at all to rank: either can refer to a humble provincial clerk or an intimate of the sultan.[46] Al-Nābulsī's treatise on the Fayyūm suggests that local revenue sources could be recorded down to the last date-

44 S. Goitein, *Mediterranean Society*, II: 368ff.

45 S. Goitein, "Cairo: an Islamic city in the light of the Geniza documents," in I. Lapidus (ed.), *Middle Eastern cities* (Berkeley, 1969), 90–91; Goitein, *Mediterranean Society*, II: 377; al-Kāmil himself interviewed the clerks of the *dīwān al-māl* personally, summoned the *dīwān*s to the palace, and supervised their work in person, additional indications of small numbers: al-Nābulsī, *Kitāb lamʿ al-qawānīn al-muḍiyya*, C. Becker and C. Cahen (eds.), *BEO*, 17 (1958–60), 13; Maqrīzī, *Sulūk*, i/1: 260.

46 Goitein, *Mediterranean Society*, II: 377.

palm.[47] There remained, however, a considerable gap between local revenue collection and the center.

Several treatises on the *dīwāns* have survived.[48] While they do not agree as to either the number or the names of the major *dīwāns* (and this may itself be important), they do give some general indication as to their functions. There were three or four major *dīwāns* at the center. The most important were the chancery (*dīwān al-inshā'*), which handled the ruler's correspondence, petitions, and decrees, and the treasury (*dīwān al-māl*), which funded the sultan's household, recorded revenue sources throughout the country, and estimated expected revenues. The army *dīwān*, (*dīwān al-jaysh* or *dīwān al-juyūsh*) kept rosters of troops (some probably put together by the amīrs) and assigned *iqṭāʿāt* in collaboration with the *dīwān al-māl*. The *dīwān* of the charitable endowments (*dīwān al-aḥbās*), which kept track of *waqf* revenue, was listed by al-Nābulsī as one of the central *dīwāns*. In theory it had the obligation to inspect lecturers, khaṭībs, imāms, ṣūfīs, and Qurʿān readers for their eligibility to receive *waqf* income. Perhaps for this reason the head of the *dīwān* was expected to be a learned and pious man who could meet the chief *qāḍī* on an equal footing. However, the *dīwān al-aḥbās* seems to have had a minor role in the administration of *waqfs* and the assignment of their income, and the chronicles and biographical dictionaries give the office summary treatment.

In addition to the central *dīwāns* there were various lesser ones, each keeping records on a revenue source or, as in the case of the *dīwān* of the armory, storehouses of materials. The great amīrs maintained their own *dīwāns*, staffed by clerks in their service. This made it easier for them to ignore the sultan's *dīwāns* when they had the power to do so: the difference between the staff of the amiral household and the bureaucracy of the sultan was one of size more than kind. The amīrs often emerged as the most important defenders of the *dhimmīs* against the hostility aroused against them by the crusades, a fact attributed to their dependence on *dhimmī* clerks in their service. Finally, the Copts, and perhaps other *dhimmīs* as well, kept records of their own revenue sources, which were open to seizure by agents of the sultan in exceptional circumstances.[49]

The clerks and secretaries who staffed the *dīwāns* were of various origins, and their career paths unstable. There was no bureaucratic path of recruitment or notion of bureaucratic tenure, nor were the secretaries of the *dīwāns* a distinct social type. The heads of the *dīwāns* were generally amīrs or learned shaykhs, and in one case a Coptic monk and ascetic; at lower levels it was not unusual for a lecturer or learned shaykh to serve in a *dīwān* for a

47 al-Nābulsī, *Ta'rīkh al-fayyūm wa-bilādihi*, ed. B. Moritz (Cairo, 1899, reprint, 1974).
48 See above, note 9; H. L. Gottschalk, "*Dīwān*," *EI2*; Nābulsī, *Lam*ʿ; C. Cahen, "Le régime des impôts dans le Fayyūm Ayyubide," *Arabica*, 3/1 (1956), 8–30.
49 See Sawīrus ibn al-Muqaffā', IV/1: 33–34 for an example from the Fifth Crusade.

time.[50] Some *dīwāns* were staffed by members of a particular religious community, the Copts serving in many, and Jews predominating in the *dīwān al-ḥarb*. As a check on the *dīwāns* the sultan sent an amīr or (rarely) a shaykh known as the *shādd* or *mushidd*, whose responsibility was to report to the sultan directly. In practice, however, the power of the sultan to penetrate the *dīwāns* through them was variable. Some mushidds were unable to counter established interests; others, especially in the provinces, were so powerful that they were more a balance than a check. Thus the *dīwāns* provided necessary services in the politics of revenue assignment and the maintenance of powerful households; but sultans could not rule their subjects or coordinate their followers directly through them.

Sovereignty, diplomacy, and the politics of revenue assignment

Ayyūbid rule is often referred to as a family confederation, but this characterization may be more an effect of distance than an accurate reflection of how the Ayyūbids themselves conceived of sovereignty. Recognition of a particular sultan shaped, but usually did not determine, the political behavior of the lesser rulers, except perhaps in the case of fathers and sons. This is not to say that Ayyūbid rulers had nothing in common but descent. Intermarriage, external threat, and the interest of the caliph, amīrs, shaykhs, and lesser Ayyūbids in stability all helped to moderate inter-Ayyūbid conflicts. However, each Ayyūbid ruler generally pursued his own interests, which were advanced on occasion by contracting with outside powers against rivals within the Ayyūbid house. This extended to non-Muslim or heretical powers, as Latins, Khwārazmians, and Mongols were all brought into inter-Ayyūbid conflicts.[51] In addition to such opportunistic alliances several Ayyūbids may have been prepared to recognize the suzerainty of non-Ayyubid rulers. One contemporary source wrote that al-Muʿaẓẓam offered to give the most important signs of sovereignty – having the khuṭba given in his name, and putting his name on the coinage – to Jalāl al-Dīn Khwārazmshāh, while the Ayyūbid sultans of Aleppo seem to have been prepared to recognize Saljūkid suzerainty.[52] These maneuvers were occasionally condemned, especially in the case of Ayyūbids ties to Latin

[50] See Sawīrus ibn al-Muqaffāʾ, IV/1: 65 for a monk summoned to the *dīwān al-naẓr* by al-Kāmil.

[51] Ibn Wāṣil, IV: 204, 209–10; Yūnīnī, *Dhayl*, I: 84–85.

[52] Ibn al-ʿAmīd, 14; but see Humphreys, "Al-Muʿaẓẓam," *EI2*; unfortunately none of al-Muʿaẓẓam's coinage has survived to confirm Ibn al-ʿAmīd's account. On al-Afḍal's and al-Ashraf's relations with the Saljukids see al-Maqrīzī, *Sulūk*, i/1: 254; Dhahabī, LXII: 239; Ibn Wāṣil, III: 263ff.; Ibn al-Athīr, *Al-Kāmil*, XII, 183.

rulers. However, there does not seem to have been much of a notion of treason, as opposed to treachery toward an individual.

Although members of the house were assigned different areas to rule, there was no territorial division of sovereignty in the European sense. The various provinces were regarded less as territorial entities in their own right than as revenue sources, to which Ayyūbid rulers and their clients moved (and were moved) without the issue of sovereignty arising. Moreover, they looked upon external territories in much the same manner as internal ones, as revenue sources that could be integrated into the existing pattern of relations.[53]

The difference between foreign relations and internal politics is thus often difficult to see. To powerful individuals the principal instrument of politics was the assignment of power and revenue sources among allies, lesser rulers, amīrs, and learned shaykhs. Terms such as *ʿiwaḍ* (the substitution of one revenue source for another or for a cash payment), *intizāʿ* (the seizure of a revenue source), *nuzūl* (the bestowal of a revenue source by its holder) and *ʿazl* (dismissal from a revenue source) applied to territorial lordships, governorships, *iqṭāʿāt*, *qāḍī*-ships, lectureships in *madrasas*, and positions in the *dīwāns*. Such revenue sources could be held in shares (*mushāraka*), overseen by a deputy (*nāʾib*), or controlled independently (*istiqlālan*). Their beneficiaries held them by virtue of their competence and power (*istiḥqāq*). An individual had no presumptive right to a revenue source, as weakness (*ʿajz*) – meaning everything from the political weakness of a ruler to the poor preparation of a student – could cause him to lose it.[54] At many levels of politics – wars between rulers, feuds between shaykhs or amīrs, brawls between groups of students, property disputes between religious communities – open competition was represented as *fitna* or *ʿaṣabiyya*. This made for a dynamic tension between the upper and middle levels of politics that is quite different from the European pattern. From above, it may be viewed as a politics of assignment; from below, as one of maneuver. Regarded from either direction, to venture one of the military metaphors of which the sources are so fond, Ayyūbid politics was more a war of movement than one of position.

Political culture and the elite household

The Ayyūbids ruled less through specialized institutions than through practices which today would be considered private, personal, and domestic.

[53] For one striking illustration in the reign of al-Kāmil see Maqrīzī, *Sulūk*, I/1: 248–49; Dhahabī, LXIV: 5–6; Ibn al-ʿAmīd, 19.

[54] Ibn al-Dawādārī, VII: 331; Dhahabī, LXII: 8, 252; LXIV: 15, 20, 21; Maqrīzī, *Khiṭaṭ*, II: 365–66, 387, 377; Ibn Wāṣil, III: 210; iv: 81, 120, 252, 231, 256; Ibn Khallikān, IV: 173, 174, 176; Sibṭ Ibn al-Jawzī, VIII: 771; Ibn ʿAbd al-Ẓāhir, 48–49; Abū Shāma, *ʿUyūn al-rawḍatayn*, i: 265.

Political power was concentrated in, and emanated from, the household (*bayt*). To some extent this was also true of medieval Europe, but the elite household in Ayyūbid Egypt escapes definition in terms of European categories. The *bayt* was not necessarily characterized by consanguinity, as slaves and intimates could acquire great, even supreme, power within it. Nor was co-residence a necessary attribute, as members of households moved from place to place frequently. This mobility was reflected in the physical manifestation of the *bayt*'s unity – the family tomb, rather than the ancestral residence typical of Europe.

The household was held together internally and expanded outwards through acquired ties of intimacy – a term which should be qualified as it implies neither the privacy nor the informality of the modern sense of the word. The sources convey many examples of the experience of political and social bonds as ties of love, friendship, and companionship. Some favored amīrs and shaykhs were integrated directly into the sultan's household, residing in the palace or even in the sultanal bedchamber.[55] Outside the walls of the house, relationships between leaders and followers strongly resembled the other important bonds of the period, including those between husband and wife, master and disciple, teacher and student, and patron and client.

Perhaps the most important of the ties that bound rulers to their supporters were love and service. Love (*ḥubb*, *maḥabba*) referred to the intimate ties of the family and the sentimental attachments of masters and disciples; it also was a means by which the powerful recruited political supporters. There is thus much discussion in the sources of love between rulers, between them and their clients, and between powerful men and their followers in many domains of politics and administration.[56] *Ḥuẓwa* (also *ḥaẓwa*), the state of being in a fortunate or favored relationship, applied as much to leader and follower as to woman and man.[57] *Mayl*, which could mean sentimental love or involuntary attraction, applied equally to relationships between women and men and leaders and followers.[58] Service or *khidma* also united what today would be considered the distinct spheres of the domestic and the political. Within the household it included the service

55 Dhahabī, LXIII: 233; Maqrīzī, *Khiṭaṭ*, III: 337; Maqrīzī, *Sulūk*, I/1: 259.

56 Between secretaries: Sibṭ Ibn al-Jawzī, VIII: 504–05; between rulers; Ibn Wāṣil, III: 121; between al-Kāmil's amīrs and al-Muʿaẓẓam, creating a dangerous situation for al-Kāmil: Ibn Wāṣil: IV: 209, Ibn al-Dawādārī, vii: 287; between rulers and subjects: Dhahabī, lxii: 251; Sibṭ Ibn al-Jawzī, viii: 647, 696, 702.

57 For esteem see Dhahabī, LXII: 252; for a sexual connotation to the word see Ibn al-Dawādārī, VII: 322.

58 For the sense of romantic love of a spouse see Dhahabī, XII: 311; for involuntary attraction see Yūnīnī, ii: 359.

of wives to husbands, the young to the old, and servants to masters; outside it many forms of subordination were represented as *khidma*.[59]

These affectual ties extended to whole households, and the sources convey numerous examples of sons following their fathers in the service of a great *bayt*. A striking example of Ayyūbid dependence on a client lineage was their relationship with the Awlād al-Shaykh, the grandsons of a ṣūfī shaykh who was favored by Nūr al-Dīn in Damascus.[60] The Awlād al-Shaykh, unusually but not uniquely, included both warriors and learned shaykhs. Al-Kāmil was tied to them in various ways. Their mother, a daughter of the famous Damascene *qāḍī* Ibn Abī ʿAṣrūn, suckled al-Kāmil in his infancy, making him their foster brother; in later life one of them became his boon companion. The Awlād al-Shaykh became so important to al-Kāmil and his sons that they constituted a kind of shadow ruling household, making many of the important decisions in successions and forcing solutions to inter-Ayyūbid conflicts. It may be no accident that the end of Ayyūbid rule in Egypt came very soon after the death of the last of this house, who was also the last non-mamlūk commander of the Baḥrī mamlūks, in the crusade of Louis IX.

As power and status were more devolved on clients than channeled through specialized institutions, at each level of politics and social life men and women with any power acted as great men and women themselves. There was thus a premium on extravagant hospitality, lavish gift-giving, and glorified forms of self-presentation.[61] It was difficult to find clients who were not themselves patrons, asserting their power and status through the same practices from which they benefited. The urban poor also derived benefit from gift-giving at feasts and celebrations; if they could not afford a burial shroud, they could be supplied one by the sultan. The periodic waves of gifts, clothing, food, and even medicines emanating from powerful households washed over much of the urban population.

Looking at the household as the center of power can help to explain an apparent paradox – while elite women were closely guarded, some exercised

59 Service of wives to husbands: Ibn al-Athīr, *Al-Bāhir*, 164; Ṣalaḥ al-Dīn's service to his father: Ibn al-ʿAmīd, 13; service of a sultan to an old amīr: Ibn Wāṣil, IV: 255; uses of *khidma* to mean court, personal, or retinue service: Ibn al-Dawādārī, VII: 184–85; Nābulsī, *Lumaʿ*, 13; Dhahabī, LXII: 252, 263, 342; Ibn Wāṣil, III: 44, 92, 95, 234–36; iv: 81, 105, 116, 128, 244, 310, 313–14, 330–31; Ibn Shākir, *Fawāt*, i: 183; service of one Ayyūbid ruler to another: Sibṭ Ibn al-Jawzī, viii: 618, 699; Dhahabī, LXII: 252; shaykhly *khidma*: Dhahabī, LXII: 263; obligations of *khidma*: Dhahabī, LXII: 252; Sibṭ Ibn al-Jawzī, VIII: 689.

60 H. L. Gottschalk, 'Die Aulad Šaiḫ aš šuyuḫ (Banū Ḥamawiya)," *Wiener Zeitschrift für die Kunde des Morgenlandes*, 53 (1956), 57–87, a shorter version in H. L. Gottschalk, "Awlad al-Shaykh," *EI2*.

61 For examples of the exchange of lavish gifts for loyalty or favor see Dhahabī, LXIV: 20; Sibṭ Ibn al-Jawzī, VIII: 721–24; Ibn al-Dawādārī, vii: 312; Ibn Wāṣil, III: 7–8, 184–85; Sawīrus ibn al-Muqaffāʾ, IV/2: 73–74, 79–80.

power assertively, far beyond the walls of the house. Exclusion from what, in other ages and places, would be called the "public" sphere did not mean that elite women were powerless. As power emanated from what we would term the "private" sphere of the household, some women both exercised it independently and had a strong influence on its exercise by others. Given the extent of intermarriage, several Ayyūbid women could draw simultaneously on their roles as wives, mothers, sisters, and daughters of rulers. Mothers of young rulers acted as independent powers, and, in the case of Aleppo, as rulers in their own right. Moreover, as power was asserted through practices that in other periods would be considered private – gift-giving, hospitality, tomb construction, charity and the foundation of charitable institutions – the sources gave some great women as much attention as great men.[62] This accounts for the power even former slave women could wield. Shajar al-Durr was not the only former slave of an Ayyūbid household to exercise power over men. In northern Syria, a manumitted slave whom al-Ẓāhir married off to one of his amīrs seized the citadel which her husband wished to surrender, took oaths from soldiers, handed out robes of honor, and organized resistance to a Saljūkid invasion.[63]

The primacy of the household in politics also helps to explain the power exercized by eunuchs. Within the household eunuchs served as attendants, *ustādārs*, and atabegs. Outside it eunuchs were amīrs, governors, and army commanders. One of Ṣalāḥ al-Dīn's most important supporters was the eunuch Bahā' al-Dīn Qarāqūsh al-Asadī. Bahā' al-Dīn was responsible for the deposition of the Fāṭimid family and the disposition of its property, began construction of the wall around Cairo, and carried out the cadastral survey. After Ṣalāḥḥ al-Dīn's death he continued to be one of the most powerful members of his household, and for a short time following the death of al-ʿAzīz he was regent for al-Manṣūr and the effective ruler of the country. Under Ṣalāḥ al-Dīn's successors eunuchs were commanders and deputy sultans. Shams al-Dīn Ṣawāb, the eunuch commander of al-ʿĀdil and al-Kāmil's armies, was allowed by al-Kāmil to set up his own *dihlīz* (a vestibule to a building or a tent that could serve as a symbol of sovereignty) when he was deputy sultan over Āmid and Diyār Bakr. In 637/1239–40 the commanders of the *ḥalqa* were said to be eunuchs, as was the deputy sultan of Damascus at the end of the Ayyūbid period. Eunuchs could also build up their own households by purchasing their own eunuchs. Shams al-Dīn Ṣawāb was said to have 100 of his own eunuch mamlūks, several of whom went on to become great amīrs, and one a deputy sultan.[64]

[62] For two examples see Ibn al-Dawādārī, VII: 204–05; Dhahabī, LXII: 268.

[63] Ibn al-ʿAmīd, 12.

[64] On eunuchs see Ibn al-ʿAmīd, 20, 25, 26, 30, 33, 34, 36; Sibṭ Ibn al-Jawzī, VIII: 719; Ibn Wāṣil, iii: 238ff.; Dhahabī, lxi: 216; 62: 152ff., 251; lxiv: 86; Sawīrus ibn al-Muqaffā', IV/1: 63, iv/2: 79–80; Ibn Taghrībirdī, VI: 320; Ibn al-Dawādārī, VII: 108,

Conclusion

At the risk of over-generalization, some observations may be hazarded concerning the place of the Ayyūbids in Egypt's medieval history. By the middle of the twelfth century, the Fāṭimid empire – at one time the last Islamic empire to retain numerous late antique imperial features – had lost much of its ideology of universal rule and the bureaucratic organization of its economy and military power. Its internal stability and ability to project power beyond the Nile valley were gone. It was thus at a loss to deal with the two expansionist forms of state organization of the high medieval period, the Franco-Norman states of Europe and the Muslim military patronage states of central and western Asia.

When the attention of the crusaders shifted to Egypt, the country became something of a frontier state. Egypt's politics were now marked by the weak institutions, ever-shifting alliances, and struggles over revenue sources seen in other examples of the penetration of the organizational mode of the frontier into the agrarian regions of the Middle East. Drawn into Egypt by the crusades, their politics shaped by the continuing contest between Muslims and crusaders, the Ayyūbids thus brought the country into what, for lack of a better term, might be termed high medievality. Egypt now shared a number of characteristics with both the post-Saljuk Muslim military patronage states and the Franco-Norman states of Europe. Like these states, its political economy was marked by a relatively weak bureaucracy and ruling establishment, partial control of land revenue by horse warriors and religious leaders, indirect rule through religious and military magnates, and parcelized and derived sovereignties. With its wealth from agriculture and trade now tied to new forms of military power and political organization, Egypt regained its hegemony in the region. But Ayyūbid rule was not imperial, even in the attenuated later Fāṭimid sense, and its political practices were no longer predominantly bureaucratic or institutional.

As we have seen, the combination of affective household ties with the politics of revenue assignment penetrated rulership, military organization, diplomacy, urban administration, education, land tenure, the administration of justice, and bureaucracy. This is why beneath their surface formality and functional differences these domains appear to be so similar. In time – in some cases not until the later Mamlūk period – these domains were to acquire a limited autonomy and predictability. But throughout the period under consideration the politics of Egypt and its provinces remained those of a new frontier region in flux.

184–85, 277, 299–301, 309, 343; Maqrīzī, *Khiṭaṭ*, II: 374; 3: 378; Ibn al-Athīr, *Al-Bāhir*, 156; M. Sobernheim, "Ḳarāḳūsh," *EI2*.

10

The Baḥrī Mamlūk sultanate, 1250–1390

LINDA S. NORTHRUP

When the [ʿAbbāsid] state was drowned in decadence and luxury and donned the garments of calamity and impotence and was overthrown by the heathen Tatars, who abolished the seat of the Caliphate and obliterated the splendor of the lands and made unbelief prevail in place of belief, because the people of the faith, sunk in self-indulgence, preoccupied with pleasure and abandoned to luxury, had become deficient in energy and reluctant to rally in defense, and had stripped off the skin of courage and the emblem of manhood – then, it was God's benevolence that He rescued the faith by reviving its dying breath and restoring the unity of the Muslims in the Egyptian realms, preserving the order and defending the walls of Islam. He did this by sending to the Muslims, from this Turkish nation and from among its great and numerous tribes, rulers to defend them and utterly loyal helpers, who were brought from the House of War to the House of Islam under the rule of slavery, which hides in itself a divine blessing. By means of slavery they learn glory and blessing and are exposed to divine providence; cured by slavery, they enter the Muslim religion with the firm resolve of true believers and yet with nomadic virtues unsullied by debased nature, unadulterated with the filth of pleasure, undefiled by the ways of civilized living, and with their ardor unbroken by the profusion of luxury. The slave merchants bring them to Egypt in batches, like sandgrouse to the watering places, and government buyers have them displayed for inspection and bid for them, raising the price above their value. They do this not in order to subjugate them, but because it intensifies loyalty, increases power, and is conducive to ardent zeal. They choose from each group, according to what they observe of the characteristics of the race and the tribes. Then they place them in a government barracks where they give them good and fair treatment, educate them, have them taught the Qur'ān and kept at their religious studies until they have a firm grasp of this. Then they train them in archery and fencing, in horsemanship, in hippodromes,

> and in thrusting with the lance and striking with the sword until their arms grow strong and their skills become firmly rooted. When the masters know that they have reached the point when they are ready to defend them, even to die for them, they double their pay and increase their grants [*iqṭāʿ*], and impose on them the duty to improve themselves in the use of weapons and in horsemanship, and so also to increase the number of men of their own race in the service for that purpose. Often they use them in the service of the state, appoint them to high state offices, and some of them are chosen to sit on the throne of the Sultans and direct the affairs of the Muslims, in accordance with divine providence and with the mercy of God to His creatures. Thus, one intake comes after another and generation follows generation, and Islam rejoices in the benefit which it gains through them, and the branches of the kingdom flourish with the freshness of youth.
>
> Ibn Khaldūn (d. 1406)[1]

While the strangeness of a slave-king system has a particular fascination in its own right, the Mamlūk sultanate of Egypt and Syria played a more important role in world history than its slave origins or exotic appearance might suggest, as indicated not only by the comments above of the north African historian-philosopher Ibn Khaldūn, a contemporary observer and one of the keenest political analysts of the medieval period, but also by modern historians who have the advantage of hindsight.[2] From the perspective of institutional history, most of what we know about the mamlūk institution itself is based on the relatively well-documented Mamlūk period in which it reached its apogee. In no small measure it was this institution, as embodied in the Mamlūk sultanate of Egypt and Syria, which enabled the Arabic-speaking lands of the Middle East not only to extirpate the crusaders but also to thwart the Mongol advance. The repercussions of these achievements on the surrounding region and on world history in general, were significant. Partly under the pressure of the Mongol invasions, the Baḥrī mamlūks succeeded in bringing about the political and military union of Egypt and Syria which lasted even beyond 1517. The frontier established between Mamlūk and Mongol territory as a result of Mamlūk resistance remains to this day roughly the boundary between the Arabic-speaking and

[1] ʿAbd al-Raḥmān ibn Muḥammad ibn Khaldūn, *Kitāb al-ʿibar wa dīwān al-mubtadā wa'l-khabar* (Bulāq, 1284/1867), V, 371, trans. Bernard Lewis, *Islam from the Prophet Muhammad to the Capture of Constantinople*, I: *Politics and War* (Oxford, 1987), 97–99. Cf. David Ayalon, "Mamlūkiyyāt: (B) Ibn Khaldūn's View of the Mamlūk Phenomenon," in *Jerusalem Studies in Arabic and Islam*, II (Jerusalem, 1980), 340–49, reprinted in*idem*, *Outsiders in the Lands of Islam* (London, 1988), X, 340–49.

[2] For example, David Ayalon, "Aspects of the Mamlūk Phenomenon: a) The Importance of the Mamlūk Institution," *Der Islam*, 53 (1976), 197, reprinted in idem, *The Mamlūk Military Society* (London, 1979), Xa, 197.

the Persian cultural zones. The commercial importance of the Mamlūk period, in which Egypt played a key role in the transit trade in spices and not only harboured its own textile industry, but was the source of many raw materials necessary to that industry and so essential to the development of the west, should not be underestimated. "Much of what we think of as distinctively Islamic was not really the product of some earlier and rather notional 'Golden Age of Islam', under the first four caliphs, or the ʿAbbāsids, or the Fāṭimids. Rather the shape of such things as the layout of Cairo, the structure and content of the Arabian Nights and the development of dervish orders are really products of the Mamlūk age."[3] One might add that some important developments in modern Islam may be traced to the impact of such figures as Ibn Taymiyya who flourished during this period.

Origins of the Mamlūk or military slave institution and the establishment of the Baḥrī Mamlūk sultanate

Among the several words in Arabic for "slave" (such as *ʿabd*, *khādim*, or *ghulām*), the passive participle "*mamlūk*", derived from the verbal root *m-l-k* (to own) and meaning something which is owned, came to denote a slave, and even more particularly a military slave. The Mamlūk sultanate thus refers to the regime which ruled Egypt and Syria from 1250 to 1517 in which mamlūks (military slaves), individuals of servile origin, constituted the ruling élite.

Two conditions favoured the emergence of the Baḥrī Mamlūk sultanate: the evolved state of the mamlūk institution in the thirteenth century,[4] and the nascent political hegemony of Egypt in the region and its vital role in a global trade system. Without several other catalysts of an ad hoc nature, however, the result might have been very different indeed. These catalysts were: al-Ṣāliḥ Najm al-Dīn Ayyūb's responses to the problems of his reign, which altered established patterns of rule; his death in the midst of a military crisis; the subsequent murder of his son and heir to the throne Tūrān-Shāh; and the crusader and Mongol threats.

For a thousand years, from the ninth until the nineteenth century, the mamlūk institution was a prominent feature of nearly all Islamic societies. Young men were recruited from pagan lands to meet the requirements of Muslim rulers for military manpower of a particular kind. With ties to their families and homelands severed not only by distance, but also by the bestowal of new, usually Turkish, names, coupled nearly always with the nondescript Arabic name "ibn ʿAbd Allāh" (son of the slave [or servant] of

[3] Robert Irwin, *The Middle East in the Middle Ages: The Early Mamlūk Sultanate 1250–1382* (Carbondale and Edwardsville, 1986), introduction.

[4] Irwin, *Middle East*, passim.

God), symbolizing the erasure of the past and the humiliating lack of lineage in a lineage-based society, such young recruits were made dependent on, and theoretically fiercely loyal to, their new master, to whom they would henceforth owe whatever fortune they might find in life. In the words of the Seljuk *wazīr* Niẓām al-Mulk (d. 1092) "One obedient slave is better than three hundred sons; for the latter desire their father's death, the former his master's glory."[5] In the best of circumstances these young men were taught the rudiments of Islam, to which they were eventually converted, thus making them "insiders," a factor which distinguishes them from mercenaries who remain "outsiders,"[6] and given military training. During the Mamlūk sultanate, if not before, the training period resulted in conversion and manumission. Yet the bonds between the mamlūk and his master remained strong, and the recruit, now free, retained his mamlūk and, therefore, elite status.

Because of its universality and longevity, some scholars have speculated that the mamlūk system was in some way an outgrowth of Islamic civilization, if not of Islam.[7] A variety of theories for its prominence have been advanced: manpower shortages;[8] technological advances such as the introduction of the stirrup which made cavalry who used this device particularly desirable;[9] Muslim withdrawal from political life because of its failure to approximate an Islamic ideal;[10] a means to preserve nomad vitality;[11] and the evolution of an elite more interested in commercial life than in military affairs.[12] There is no simple answer to the question of why the mamlūk institution gained such importance in Islamic civilization.[13]

The predominance of Turkish mamlūks also seems to result from a combination of factors. The frontier with Turkestan was more permeable to Islamic ideas and population movement than other frontiers established as a

[5] *The Book of Government or Rules for Kings: The Siyar al-Muluk or Siyasat-nama*, trans. Hubert Darke (London, 1960), 117.

[6] Daniel Pipes, *Slave Soldiers and Islam: The Genesis of a Military System* (New Haven, London, 1981), 23.

[7] David Ayalon, "Preliminary Remarks on the *Mamlūk* Military Institution in Islam," in V. J. Parry and M. E. Yapp (eds.), *War, Technology and Society in the Middle East* (Oxford, 1975), 44, reprinted in idem, *Mamlūk Military Society*, IX, 44. See also Pipes, *Slave Soldiers*, 54–102.

[8] Ayalon, "Preliminary Remarks," 44, reprinted in idem, *Mamlūk Military Society*, IX, 44.

[9] Pipes, *Slave Soldiers*, 55–57.

[10] Pipes, *Slave Soldiers*, xviii–xix, 62. See also Patricia Crone, *Slaves on Horses: The Evolution of the Islamic Polity* (Cambridge, 1980), 57, 63.

[11] David Ayalon, "The Muslim City and the Mamlūk Military Aristocracy," *Proceedings of the Israel Academy of Sciences and Humanities*, 14 (1967), 2, 313, reprinted in *idem*, *Studies on the Mamlūks of Egypt (1250–1517)* (London, 1977), VII, 313.

[12] Pipes, *Slave Soldiers*, 71.

[13] Irwin, *Middle East*, 7–10, where these theories are discussed with insight.

consequence of the early Arab conquests.[14] Turkish slaves were used as early as Umayyad times[15] but were not recruited systematically or in large numbers until the ninth century, when Transoxiana was finally subdued and Islamized and the ʿAbbāsid caliph in Baghdād, al-Muʿtaṣim (833–42), carried out military reforms which, among other things, allowed him to replace Arabs with mamlūks, and in particular Turkish mamlūks, whose military qualities and skills – hardiness, horsemanship and archery – were increasingly in demand. The central Asian steppes provided a vast recruiting ground for Turkish (broadly defined) mamlūks who, as pagans, were eligible, according to Muslim law, for enslavement.[16] Although Turkish mamlūks were used in Egypt as early as the Ṭūlūnid period and subsequently by the Ikhshīdids and Fāṭimids, they were not as important an element in the Egyptian armies as in the armies of some other regions of the Islamic world until the Ayyūbid period. Their increased use in Egypt in Ayyūbid times appears to be related to the change which occurred in the structure of Islamic armies during the Seljuk period in Iraq and Persia, when a cavalry-based military organization, which also relied heavily on mamlūks, replaced an infantry-based structure composed of non-mamlūk troops.[17] The cavalry was usually composed of horsemen of Turkish origin, and the Ayyūbids brought their Seljuk heritage, including the cavalry-based army comprised mainly of Turks, with them to Egypt.[18] Thus, from the days of Shirkūh (d. 1169), the Kurdish vassal of the Syrian prince Nūr al-Dīn (hero of the counter-Crusade), and his nephew Ṣalāḥ al-Dīn (d. 1193) on, Turkish mamlūks played an increasingly prominent role in the Ayyūbid army of Egypt.[19]

During the reign of the last Ayyūbid sultan al-Ṣāliḥ Najm al-Dīn Ayyūb (1240–49) the use of Turkish cavalry was further accelerated, to the point that the Turkish predominance countered a previous preference among Muslim rulers for a racially and ethnically diverse army whose various

[14] David Ayalon, "Aspects: a) Importance," 196–204, reprinted in idem, *Mamlūk Military Society*, Xa, 196–204.

[15] Ayalon, "Aspects: a) Importance," 205, reprinted in idem, *Mamlūk Military Society*, Xa, 205. See his "Preliminary Remarks," 46, reprinted in idem, *Mamlūk Military Society*, IX, 46.

[16] Ayalon, "Aspects: a) Importance," 203, reprinted in idem, *Mamlūk Military Society*, Xa, 203. Also David Ayalon, "The European-Asiatic Steppe: A Major Reservoir of Power for the Islamic World," in *Actes du XXVe Congrès International des Orientalistes*, II (Moscow, 1963), 47–52, reprinted in idem, *Mamlūk Military Society*, VIII, 47–52.

[17] David Ayalon, "From Ayyubids to Mamlūks," *REI*, 49 (1981), 43–44, reprinted in idem, *Islam and the Abode of War* (London, 1984), III, 43–44.

[18] Jere L. Barcharach, "African Military Slaves in the Medieval Middle East: The Cases of Iraq (869–955) and Egypt (868–1171)," *IJMES*, 13 (1981), 488–91.

[19] David Ayalon, "Aspects of the Mamlūk Phenomenon: b) Ayyubids, Kurds and Turks," *Der Islam*, 54 (1977), 1–32, reprinted in idem, *Mamlūk Military Society*, Xb, 1–32.

factions might be played off against each other.[20] Al-Ṣāliḥ purchased Turkish mamlūks in larger numbers than any of his predecessors, perhaps out of racial preference, but more likely because horsemanship was now the critical factor in the cavalry-based army, and also because at this moment Turkish slave recruits were in especially abundant supply as a result of the Mongol invasions which were sweeping across the Kipchak steppes of western Asia and southern Russia, creating large pools of captives who found themselves on the slave market. Slaves might, however, also be acquired by other means, such as by purchase from dispossessed peoples who, out of necessity, or hoping to improve their fortune, sold their children into slavery, or as gifts.

Soon after coming to power, al-Ṣāliḥ Ayyūb purchased between 800 and 1,000 mamlūks, primarily of Kipchak Turkish origin, and with them created his elite Baḥrī regiment, so named because it was quartered in the fortress complex built by the sultan on Rawḍa island in the Nile river (Baḥr al-Nīl) near Cairo. They are referred to in the sources both as "al-Baḥriyya" to distinguish them from other of al-Ṣāliḥ's regiments, and as "al-Baḥriyya-al-Ṣāliḥiyya," to indicate their relationship to al-Ṣāliḥ Ayyūb, their master.

In retrospect it is clear that the formation of this regiment, which acted as al-Ṣāliḥ's personal bodyguard, constituted the first step in the ascent of the Baḥriyya mamlūks to the throne. The Baḥrī regiment formed the powerful, élite corps of the emergent Mamlūk army. The Baḥriyya and their descendants (by birth or mamlūk ties) would dominate the ruling structure of Egypt and Syria during the second half of the thirteenth century and all but the last decade of the fourteenth.[21] It is of some interest and importance to note furthermore that at least three members of this regiment, two of whom would attain the sultanate (Baybars and Qalāwūn), hailed from the same Kipchak tribe.

As a consequence of the political and territorial fragmentation of the ʿAbbāsid empire during the ninth and tenth centuries, Egypt gained greater political and economic independence and began to thrive culturally as well. Even prior to the crusades Egypt, because of its location, had begun to play a pivotal role in east–west trade, a role which it continued during the crusades, and which was undoubtedly advanced by them. During the crusading period Egypt also came to be viewed by both sides as the key to their respective political and military goals, which included the domination

20 Amalia Levanoni, "The Mamlūks' Ascent to Power in Egypt," *SI*, 33 (1990), 124–5. On the preference for racially diverse armies see, for example, Clifford Edmund Bosworth, *The Ghaznavids: Their Empire in Afghanistan and Eastern Iran 994/1040* (Edinburgh, 1963), 107.

21 David Ayalon, "Le régiment Bahriya dans l'armée mamelouke," *REI*, 19 (1951), 133–41; R. Stephen Humphreys, "The Emergence of the Mamlūk Army," *Studia Islamica*, 45 (1977), 67–99, and 46 (1977), 147–82.

of Syria.[22] Though the degree of Syro-Egyptian unity achieved by Ṣalāḥ al-Dīn was threatened by his division of the Ayyūbid realm among family members at his death, Egypt emerged ever more strongly during the power struggles which ensued as the dominant power in the region. Under al-Ṣāliḥ Ayyūb power was further centralized in Egypt.[23] Following his death the political status of the mamlūks in Egypt was confirmed by the results of the battle of Kurāʾ in 1251, which brought them victory over the Ayyūbid prince al-Nāṣir Yūsuf of Damascus, and by the treaty subsequently signed in 1253, which gave *de facto* recognition to the ending of Ayyūbid rule and to the Mamlūk claim to Egypt.[24] Syria, however, fell definitively into Egyptian hands only as a result of the Mamlūk victory at ʿAyn Jālūt in 1260. Syria did not accept the situation complacently. Twice, during the reigns of Baybars and Qalāwūn, would-be sultans among their *khushdāshiyya* (comrades in purchase, training and manumission)[25] exploited Syrian regional sentiments to gain support for their bids for the throne by attempting to make Syria independent, or semi-independent, as in Ayyūbid times. Toward the end of his reign al-Nāṣir Muḥammad may have been motivated to cause the demise of his *nāʾib* in Damascus, Tankiz, by the latter's ambitions in Syria, now most probably viewed as a stepping stone to the throne of Egypt.

The crusader presence and Mongol invasions required a military response and the Baḥriyya were positioned to provide it. The regiment first proved its mettle in battle against the crusading forces of the French king Louis IX at Manṣūra on the Egyptian coast in 1249,[26] and even more significantly in their victory over the Mongols at ʿAyn Jālūt in 1260. As a result of these victories the Baḥriyya came to be widely perceived by Muslims as the saviours of Islam. It was al-Ṣāliḥ Ayyūb's death, however, during Louis IX's invasion of Egypt, which propelled the Baḥrī regiment onto the political stage as well. In the political void left by the sultan's death and by that soon thereafter of his general Fakhr al-Dīn ibn Shaykh al-Shuyūkh, and then by

22 David Ayalon, "Egypt as the Dominant Factor in Syria and Palestine during the Islamic Period," in Ammon Cohen and Gabriel Baer (eds.), *Egypt and Palestine – A Millenium of Association (868–1948)* (Jerusalem, 1984), 31–32, reprinted in idem, *Outsiders*, II, 31–32.

23 R. Stephen Humphreys, *Saladin to the Mongols: The Ayyubids of Damascus, 1193–1260* (Albany, 1977), esp. 1–13, and 299–301; Levanoni, "Mamlūks' Ascent," 121, 127–29, 135.

24 On the significance of this battle and treaty see Levanoni, "Consolidation of Aybak's Rule: An Example of Factionalism in the Mamlūk State," *Der Islam*, 71 (1995), 246–47.

25 On *khushdāshiyya*, see David Ayalon, "L'Esclavage du mamelouk," *Oriental Notes and Studies*, 1 (1951), 29–31; reprinted in idem, *Mamlūk Military Society*, I, 29–31. See also Irwin, *Middle East*, 88–90, 154–55.

26 See, for example, David Ayalon, "Studies on the Transfer of the ʿAbbasid Caliphate from Baghdad to Cairo," *Arabica*, 7 (1960), 58, regarding Ibn Wāṣil's assessment of Mamlūk prestige following this battle, and idem, 59, for references to their reputation after ʿAyn Jālūt.

the incompetence of his son and heir Tūrān-Shāh (1249–50), which also led to the latter's murder, the Baḥriyya emerged as a strong factional contender for the throne.[27]

Contemporary sources tend to view Egyptian history as a continuum and the Baḥrī mamlūks as the natural heirs of the Ayyūbids.[28] But how did they see themselves? It has been suggested that the Mamlūks were, in fact, reluctant to admit the end of Ayyūbid rule,[29] while a counter argument runs that the evidence, including the statement found in a contemporary source, that Baybars wished to reestablish the "state" as it had existed during the reign of al-Ṣāliḥ Ayyūb, should not be taken at face value; the Baḥriyya were, in fact, simply exploiting their Ayyubid links to give their claim to rule an air of legitimacy. The decisive event was the murder of Tūrān-Shāh (1250), when the Baḥriyya acted for the first time, but not the last, as a faction. Perhaps initially the Baḥriyya may have sought only to defend their interests (the estates and privileges they had been granted during al-Ṣāliḥ's rule), but with the throne suddenly in view they began quite deliberately to seek the prize.[30] Whatever the case may be, while putting their Ayyūbid heritage to good use, the Baḥrī mamlūks, from at least the reign of Baybars I on, began not only to consolidate their hold on the sultanate, but also to impress it with their own form and style.

The Baḥriyya were not without opposition, however: they would not attain the throne for another decade. First they had to deal with their Ayyūbid opponents as well as with mamlūk rivals. In the meantime, a rather motley assortment of rulers ascended the throne while the factional power struggles, erupting in the wake of the deaths of al-Ṣāliḥ Ayyūb and Tūrān-Shāh, were fought out.[31] With both Tūrān-Shāh and Fakhr al-Dīn ibn Shaykh al-Shuyūkh, commander of al-Ṣāliḥ's armies, dead, Shajarat al-Durr, of Turkish slave origin, a former concubine, then wife, and now widow of al-Ṣāliḥ Ayyūb, assumed control with the appearance of Baḥrī backing. Failing to obtain recognition from al-Nāṣir Yūsuf, the Ayyūbid ruler of Damascus, however, the Baḥriyya in May 1250 appointed a mamlūk amīr, Aybak al-Turkumānī, as *atābak al-ʿasākir* (commander-in-chief of the armies), to rule jointly with Shajarat al-Durr. It now seems clear that Aybak, though a Ṣāliḥī, was not a member of the elite Baḥriyya, and had been chosen by them because he was politically weak and could, they thought, be

27 Levanoni, "Mamlūks' Ascent," 134–44; *idem*, "Consolidation," 243–56.

28 R. S. Humphreys, "Emergence," 67–99 and Ayalon, "Ayyūbids to Mamlūks," 43–57; Levanoni, *Turning Point*, 5–6.

29 Irwin, *Middle East*, 26.

30 Levanoni, "Mamlūks' Ascent," 136–42; *idem*, "Consolidation," 241–54. For other interpretations see Ayalon, "Régiment bahriyya"; Humphreys, "Emergence"; P. M. Holt, "Mamlūks," *EI2*, VI, 321; Crone, *Slaves*, 261, n. 631.

31 Levanoni, "Consolidation," 241–54.

replaced by one of their own as soon as a consensus emerged regarding a candidate. Shajar al-Durr abdicated in July 1250 and Aybak was raised to the sultanate. But only a few days later, perhaps compelled by the Baḥriyya, he stepped down in favour of the even more malleable al-Ashraf Mūsā, a young Ayyūbid prince, who was now nominally recognized as sultan. However, in 1254 Aybak was returned to the sultanate: at some point he had married Shajar al-Durr, thereby strenghthening his grip on power. The marriage, however, was doomed by political jealousy and resulted in their murder in 1257. Aybak's mamlūks, the Muʿiziyya, now led by Quṭuz, installed Aybak's young son by another wife, ʿAlī, as sultan. Using the imminent Mongol invasion as a pretext, however, Quṭuz usurped the sultanate.

In the meantime most of the Baḥriyya had fled Egypt in the wake of the murder in 1254 at Aybak's behest of his rival, the Baḥriyya leader Fāris al-Dīn Aqṭāy al-Jamdār. The Baḥriyya in exile, led by the amīr and future sultan Baybars al-Bunduqdārī, did not forget this treachery. Though these two hostile factions were reconciled in the face of the Mongol invasion of Syria in 1260, the struggle between them was resolved only by the Baḥriyya's murder in 1260 of Quṭuz, who had struck the fatal blow against their former leader Fāris al-Dīn Aqtāy. Though lacking unanimous support even among his *khushdāshiyya*, Baybars, as leader of the Baḥriyya and a participant in the coup, became sultan of Egypt. On the basis of the accomplishments of his relatively long reign (1260–77), Baybars, who took the regnal title "al-Malik al-Ẓāhir," is considered the real founder of the Baḥrī Mamlūk sultanate.

"Baḥrī" is the name commonly assigned to this dynasty by western historians. This name, of course, derives from the Baḥrī regiment whose members dominated the political, economic and military structure of the empire during the last half of the thirteenth century and whose descendants (natural or mamlūk) continued to rule, at least nominally, during most of the fourteenth. On the other hand, as has been recently pointed out, though the beginning of Baḥrī rule is usually dated to 1250, none of the first five sultans were, in fact, members of the Baḥriyya.[32] The Arabic sources for the period refer to the dynasty as the *dawlat al-atrāk*, *dawlat al-turk*, or *al-dawla al-turkiyya* (i.e. dynasty of the Turks), in recognition of the racial or ethnic group which predominated in the mamlūk caste during this period, and to distinguish it from the Burjī sultanate in which mamlūks of Circassian origin were ascendant. Yet, to the extent that two members of the Baḥrī corps, Baybars and Qalāwūn, and their sons and mamlūks dominated the

[32] Irwin, *Middle East*, 26–27. Cf. David Ayalon, "al-Bahriyya," *EI2*, I, 944: P. M. Holt (*The Age of the Crusades: The Near East from the Eleventh Century to 1517* (London and New York, 1986), 84), who identifies Aybak as a Baḥrī.

sultanate for a little over a century, and that the Baḥrī regiment "was the model and inspiration for *al-mamālīk al-sulṭāniyya* (the royal guard) of succeeding generations,"[33] there is perhaps some justification for calling the early period the "Baḥrī Mamlūk sultanate."

Though originally slaves themselves, the Baḥrī sultans and their Circassian successors continued to import slaves, for slavery provided the "framework"[34] for recruitment of young men who could then be molded through military training, religious education and conversion to Islam to the needs of the sultanate. Having been a slave was a condition for eligibility to the highests ranks of military society, for it assured selection of the highest-quality military personnel available. The two basic mamlūk relationships, the *ustādh-mamlūk* and *khushdāshiyya* ties, though they might be modified by other factors such as race, ethnicity, ambition and personal interest, constituted a system of loyalties which shaped the Mamlūk political structure and gave it strength. The military slave institution as embodied in the Mamlūk sultanate represents one of the most highly developed versions of that institution in the Islamic world.

The Baḥrī sultanate may be divided into five periods: 1250–60, the ascent of the Baḥriyya to power; 1260–93, the period of consolidation; 1293–1310, a time of factional struggle and political instability; 1310–41, the third reign of al-Nāṣir Muḥammad ibn Qalāwūn; and 1341–90, a period of increasing socio-economic distress and internal political instability which paved the way for the rise of the Circassian dynasty. The decade which began with al-Ṣāliḥ Ayyūb's death and ended with the murder of Quṭuz gave birth to the Baḥrī sultanate as already described. This period had coincided with the growing Mongol danger and the continued presence of the crusader kingdoms, factors which would continue to dominate events in the region throughout the rest of the century, and which were also, certainly, largely responsible for the character of the regime and its institutions which evolved in response.

Faced by essentially the same problems, the reigns of the sultans al-Ẓāhir Baybars I (1260–77), al-Manṣūr Qalāwūn (1279–90) and al-Ashraf Khalīl (1290–3), which dominate the second period, reflect a certain unity. The crusader presence, the Mongol threat, the incorporation of Syria, the organization of the empire, and the protection of the trade routes to maintain the flow of slaves, war materials and other essential items as well as luxury goods, constituted the major preoccupations of these rulers and to a large extent determined the activities in which these sultans engaged during their reigns. The period as a whole is characterized by incessant warfare against both adversaries and their allies. During their reigns the

[33] Humphreys, "Emergence," 99.
[34] Irwin, *Middle East*, 4.

remnants of the crusader colonies were systematically attacked until Khalīl completed the task with the conquest of Acre in 1291. In the meantime Baybars and Qalāwūn also succeeded in bringing the Mongol advance to a halt while simultaneously hammering away at their allies, including the Armenians and Seljuks of Rūm. Both sultans also sent military expeditions into Upper Egypt and Nubia to secure the trade routes if not to expand the sultanate territorially. At the same time diplomatic relations with friendly and even normally hostile powers were opportunistically cultivated. Under these circumstances the political and institutional structure of Mamlūk rule became increasingly militarized and mamlūkized. Both Baybars and Qalāwūn were members of the original Baḥriyya-Ṣāliḥiyya corps, who had shared common origins and experiences before ascending to the sultanate. Qalāwūn was the last Ṣāliḥī sultan. His son Khalīl, who ascended the throne at his father's death, unable to claim Ṣāliḥī mamlūk ancestry, emphasized instead his Qalāwūnid ties. Before departing to complete the conquest of Acre begun by his father, Khalīl made a state visit to the tomb of his father. Subsequently, Qalāwūn's tomb replaced that of al-Ṣāliḥ Ayyūb as the site of the ceremony in which new mamlūk officers were commissioned. The "cult" of Qalāwūn had been established and outlived Khalīl, who met an untimely end at the hands of some amīrs who felt that they were more entitled to rule.

Khalīl's death inaugurated the third period in which factional quarrels dominated the politics of the realm. Though several of the Baḥriyya-Ṣāliḥiyya survived into the early fourteenth century, the members of this élite corps were now aged, and it is probably partially in light of this fact that younger factions began vying for position. Though Khalīl's eight-year-old brother al-Nāṣir Muḥammad ascended to power in 1293, his position was subsequently usurped twice by mamlūk officers who represented the most powerful factions, now defined it would seem as much by racial and ethnic ties as by mamlūk loyalties. Al-ʿĀdil Kitbughā (1294–96), a Manṣūrī mamlūk and partisan of Khalīl, of Mongol origin, was followed on the throne by the Manṣūrī Ḥusām al-Dīn Lājīn (1296–98) of Prussian or Greek origin[35] and later by the wealthy, cultured and pious al-Muẓaffar Baybars (II) al-Jāshnikīr (1309–10), both of whom are seen as representing Burjī-Circassian interests. Thus this period is notable in the first instance for the light it sheds on ethnic and racial ties as factors which cut across *mamlūk-khushdāshiyya* bonds. Of these three sultans, the sequence of whose reigns was interrupted by the second reign of Qalāwūn's son al-Nāṣir Muḥammad (1299–1309), Lājīn's rule is notable for his attempted *rawk* or redistribution of *iqṭāʿāt*, i.e., the assignment of agricultural revenues, perhaps motivated by his desire to gain the upper hand over rival factions by gaining control over resources.

[35] Irwin, *Middle East*, 70.

The third reign of al-Nāṣir Muḥammad ibn Qalāwūn (1310–41) is often seen as the apogee of the Baḥrī sultanate and Mamlūk rule as a whole. The Mamlūk defeat at the hands of the Īlkhānids in 1299 was not allowed to stand; in subsequent encounters, the last of which occurred in 1313, the Mamlūks were victorious. When the Mamlūk-Mongol conflict finally came to an end, however, with the signing of a peace treaty in 1322, the Baḥrī regime entered a period of relative peace, internal stability and prosperity. Yet it is to this period that the seeds of military decline, and hence the decline of Baḥrī rule, can be traced. Unfortunately, the political, military and economic reforms instituted by al-Nāṣir Muḥammad, although intended to strengthen his political and economic position, led in the long term to the end of Qalāwūnid and Kipchaki-Turkish rule. The Īlkhānid ruler Abū Saʿīd died soon after and with him the Īlkhānid regime faded into oblivion. In its wake several petty kingdoms (Dhu'l-Qadrids, Karamānids, Germiyanids, and Ottomans in Anatolia and Jalāyirids, Muẓaffarids and Sarbadārs in the east) arose on the former Mamlūk–Īlkhānid frontiers, and Mamlūk diplomatic efforts now turned to establishing beneficial relationships with these new entities.

Upon the death of al-Nāṣir Muḥammad the sultanate once again entered a period of political instability in which no fewer than twelve sultans, all descendants of the late monarch, ascended the throne before the dynasty was finally overthrown by the Circassians in 1390. Unlike al-Nāṣir, however, these sultans, with perhaps the exception of al-Nāṣir Ḥasan (1347–51, 1354–61) and al-Ashraf Shaʿbān (1363–77), all ruled in name only, as the mamlūk leaders of the dominant factions wielded the real power in pursuit of their factional interests. Political instability was exacerbated by social and economic difficulties. The bubonic plague arrived in Egypt in 1347–48 and was followed by bouts of the even more pernicious pneumonic plague: the very high mortality rate resulted in significant social and economic changes. Rivalry over trade in the eastern Mediterranean led to Mamlūk attempts to expand into Armenia, which had succeeded Acre as the western commercial bridgehead to the Orient. The Mamlūk effort, however, was disputed by Cyprus. Motivated by commercial, rather than religious, goals, Peter I of Lusignan, ruler of the crusader kingdom of Cyprus and titular ruler of the Latin Kingdom of Jerusalem, attacked Alexandria in 1365. Additional economic difficulties, a shortage of specie and Egypt's deteriorating position in international trade, further undermined the regime and facilitated the circumstances of revolt. Although it took two attempts, Barqūq succeeded in his bid for the throne and encountered little resistance.

Political, military and administrative structure

The Baḥrī Mamlūk political structure is perceived in contemporary sources as having had three main divisions – political-military, financial-administrative and religious-judicial.[36] Military posts were held by "men of the sword" – mamlūks; financial posts by "men of the pen" or scribal class, usually native Arabic-speaking Muslim or Coptic civilians; and religio-judicial posts by "men of the turban," Muslims who normally had some higher training in the religious sciences. In theory, as head of the Muslim community, the caliph stood at the top of the structure. In fact, while the caliph continued to play a symbolic role, it was the sultan in the early Baḥrī period and the leading amīrs in the later Baḥrī period who exercised real power. Recent research on the position of sultan has focused on four main issues: the concept of the sultanate and the role of the sultan, legitimacy, succession, and factionalism.

The concept of the sultanate and the role of the sultan in the Baḥrī period has been studied from at least four perspectives: as seen through events described in the chronicles; as portrayed in royal biographies; as viewed from a legal or juridical point of view through documents such as the *ʿahd* or diploma of investiture; and as reflected in institutional change and court ceremony. The resulting image is one of tension between oligarchy and autocracy. Sultans such as Baybars and Qalāwūn were brought to power by their *khushdāshiyya*. As their peers, *khushdāshiyya* were potential rivals, and sultans brought to power by them ruled only with their consent and were, in fact, restrained by them in their rule.

The early Baḥrī sultans played several roles: they were warriors *par excellence* (demonstrated in their campaigns against crusaders, Mongols, their allies, and others), pseudo-tribal chiefs as leaders of mamlūk *khushdāshiyya* and household groups,[37] and finally, factional leaders.[38] In all roles they were regarded as *primus inter pares*. Qalāwūn's diploma of investiture, however, which contains the caliph's full delegation of executive power to the sultan, projects a more autocratic vision of the sultanate. This diploma may be seen as a forerunner of Badr al-Dīn ibn Jamāʿa's (d. 1333) theoretical legal justification for the absorption of the caliphate by the sultanate.[39] In practice the increasing centralization of power in the sultanate, culminating in the autocracy of the third reign of al-Nāṣir Muḥammad (1310–41), supports such a view. Yet even with a high degree of centralization, the sultan ruled only with the consent of his amīrs. Qalāwūn, for example, was concerned to recognize the status of his Ṣāliḥī *khushdāshiyya* in his diploma,

[36] For an early fourteenth-century statement, see Qirṭāy al-ʿIzzī al-Khazindārī, trans. Linda S. Northrup, in *Slave to Sultan: The Career of al-Manṣūr Qalāwūn and the Consolidation of Mamlūk Rule in Egypt and Syria, 678–689 A.H./1279–1290 A.D.*, Freiburger Islamstudien (Stuttgart, 1998), 198–200.

[37] P. M. Holt, "The Position and Power of the Mamlūk Sultan," *BSOAS*, 28 (1975), 247: idem, "Succession in the Early Mamlūk Sultanate," XXIII, Einar von Schuler (ed.), *Deutscher Orientalistentag, Würzburg, 16–20 September 1985* (Stuttgart, 1989), 145.

[38] Irwin, *Middle East*, 154.

[39] Northrup, *Slave to Sultan*, 170.

and in the diploma of his son al-Ṣāliḥ ʿAlī he counselled seeking their advice.[40] Though autocracy triumphed during al-Nāṣir's reign, it was rejected after his death when factional struggles resulted in rule by mamlūk coalitions and eventually in the "re-mamlūkization" of the sultanate with the ascent of Barqūq to the throne.

Mamlūks, who were of both pagan and slave origin, suffered a double liability with respect to legitimacy in Muslim eyes, a fact which may help to explain the preoccupation with legitimacy shown by the early Baḥrī sultans. Moreover in a society still largely tribal in organization, in which, despite the coming of Islamic egalitarianism, lineage defined a person's status, Mamlūk rulers of, in most cases, unknown ancestry were considered unworthy of their role. Upon the death of al-Ṣāliḥ Ayyūb in 1250 the only possible justification for the mamlūk claim to the throne was the prominent role played by the Baḥriyya in the victory over Louis IX's crusader forces at the Battle of Manṣūra near the Egyptian coast. In fact, those whose rule followed al-Ṣāliḥ groped for ways to establish their title. The Battle of ʿAyn Jālūt served to consolidate their claim arising from military superiority, and it was, indeed, ultimately their exercise of military might in the protection of Islam and the perception that they were the "saviours of Islam" that provided the real moral basis for mamlūk rule and established their right to rulership.

In the meantime, however, it was necessary to provide a veneer of legality for the regime. In addition to their other socio-legal deficiencies Baybars I and Qalāwūn were both usurpers. Both they and their encomiasts used their ties to their *ustādh* al-Ṣāliḥ Ayyūb to bolster their claims. The royal biographies of Baybars, Qalāwūn and Khalīl, modeled on the twelfth-century tradition associated with Ṣalāḥ al-Dīn, portray these sultans as virtuous rulers in the Islamic and Arab tribal tradition, perhaps in an effort to legitimize their status as traditional (and heroic) Islamic rulers.[41] The most flamboyant gesture, however, was Baybars's installation in 1261, following the fall of Baghdad to the Mongols and the caliph's execution, of a refugee ʿAbbāsid as caliph in Cairo with the regnal title al-Mustanṣir (1261), who was succeeded later that year by his kinsman al-Ḥākim I (1261–1302).

The caliph, however, paid a high price for the rescue of his office. In return for this favour, he was obliged to bestow a diploma of investiture on the sultan. While Mamlūk rule gained a semblance of legality, the caliphate existed only by the grace of the sultanate. The caliph was allowed to reign, but not to rule. Although Baybars made a public show of his investiture, it is

[40] Northrup, *Slave to Sultan*, 185, 243.

[41] P. M. Holt, "The Virtuous Ruler in Thirteenth-Century Mamlūk Royal Biographies," *Nottingham Medieval Studies*, 24 (1980), 27–35; idem, "Three Biographies of al-Ẓāhir Baybars," in D. O. Morgan (ed.), *Medieval Historical Writing in the Christian and Islamic Worlds* (London, 1982), 19–29.

less certain that Qalāwūn did so, in spite of the fact that a copy of the latter's diploma has been preserved. Qalāwūn's diploma, with the statement that "everything that God entrusted to our lord, the prince of the believers with respect to sovereignty on earth . . . shall henceforth be delegated to his exalted excellency, the sultan, al-Malik al-Manṣūr . . ."[42] legalizes the sultan's usurpation of caliphal authority. Indeed, during Qalāwūn's reign and much of the rest of the Baḥrī period the caliph lived in a state of honorable house arrest. Al-Nāṣir actually arrested the caliph al-Mustakfī in 1336 and imprisoned him along with his family in a tower at the Citadel before exiling him to Qūṣ.[43] At the accession of al-Nāṣir Aḥmad to the throne in 1342, it was not al-Nāṣir who took the oath of allegiance to the caliph, but the caliph who performed the oath of allegiance (*bayʿa)* to the sultan.[44] By the reign of the last Qalāwūnid sultan Ḥājjī (1389), the caliph was regarded as no more exalted in rank than the chief judges of the four Sunnī *madhhab*s.[45] Though the caliphate apparently remained indispensible as a symbol, the sultanate had gained control over the highest office of the Sunnī religious institution. Legal scholars adjusted the theory of the caliphate accordingly. Badr al-Dīn ibn Jamāʿa (1241–1333) accepted usurpation of caliphal authority, deeming tyranny preferable to disorder.[46] Ibn Taymiyya (d. 1328) ignored the institution altogether; his primary concern was that the "Sharīʿa [be] the supreme authority, the exclusive and complete guide of the ʿummaʾ of Islam . . ." The caliphate was not necessary as long as the ruler, whoever he might be, recognized the authority of the *Sharīʿa*.[47] Ibn Taymiyya perhaps saw the demise of the caliph as an opportunity for the *ʿulamāʾ*: they, rather than the caliph or the sultan, would ultimately determine what the law was.[48]

The mamlūk institution, at least in part originating in the need to preserve nomadic vitality in the interests of military superiority, required that the mamlūk elite continually recreate itself through the importation of fresh recruits. Thus the sultanate was inherently a one-generation military aristocracy. Yet the principle of a non-hereditary nobility can only be inferred, since nothing in the sources indicates the existence of a formal regulation to

42 Aḥmad ibn ʿAbd Allāh al-Qalqashandī, *Ṣubḥ al-aʿshā fī ṣināʿat al-inshāʾ*, 14 vols. (Cairo, 1913–20; reprinted 1963), X, 102: Northrup, *Slave to Sultan*, 167.

43 Hayāt Nāṣir al-Ḥājjī, *The Internal Affairs in Egypt during the Third Reign of al-Sultan al-Nāṣir Muḥammad ibn Qalāwūn, 709–741/1309–1341* (Kuwait, 1978), 27–28.

44 P. M. Holt, "Some Observations on the ʿAbbasid Caliphate of Cairo," *BSOAS*, 47 (1984), 504.

45 P. M. Holt, "The Structure of Government in the Mamlūk Sultanate," in idem (ed.), *The Eastern Mediterranean Lands in the Period of the Crusades* (Warminster, 1977), 45.

46 E. I. J. Rosenthal, *Political Thought in Medieval Islam* (Cambridge, 1962), 44–45.

47 Rosenthal, *Political Thought*, 52.

48 Rosenthal, *Political Thought*, 55–56.

this effect, except perhaps for the statement in the diploma delivered by al-Mustakfī to Baybars I, "that kingship is childless . . ."[49] At the highest political levels, however, the principle was not strictly respected, for it conflicted with the natural desires of mamlūk fathers to bequeath their status and wealth to their non-mamlūk sons *(awlād al-nās)*. Both Baybars and Qalāwūn named their sons as heirs to the throne, though only Qalāwūn was successful in establishing a dynasty. This dynasty eventually included not only his sons and direct descendants but also, in the cases of the sultans Kitbughā, Lājīn and Baybars II al-Jāshnikīr, mamlūks of his household. After the death in 1341 of al-Nāṣir Muḥammad (who is said to have named his son as heir only under duress),[50] Qalāwūn's descendants, excepting perhaps al-Nāṣir Ḥasan (1347–51, 1354–61) and al-Ashraf Shaʿbān (1363–77), ruled in name only; real power was exercised by the leading amīrs of the dominant faction.

The ambiguity inherent in a system in which a nominal sultanate provided a facade for the rule of the amīrs has stimulated discussion over the degree to which succession in the Baḥrī period was hereditary or dynastic as opposed to non-hereditary, elective, and oligarchic.[51] While a written rule regarding the non-hereditary, one-generation elite nature of the sultanate did not exist, and neither did there develop "any explicit theory of hereditary succession, still less of primogeniture,"[52] the theory of the one-generation elite was really put to test, as has been noted, when it came to preventing the elite from passing on economic wealth and influence. Though the Baḥrī sultanate may have tried to institutionalize a non-hereditary system through, for example, centralized control of *iqṭāʿāt* and confiscation, its efforts were not entirely successful, for the mamlūk élite had discovered a loophole provided by the *waqf* (pious endowment) system. Thus the dynastic impulse was stronger than is evident from the point of view of sultani succession alone: "the Baḥrī state, even in its frail last decade . . . had been solidly built on a disproportionate share of the house of Qalāwūn in the wealth of Egypt."[53] Finally, the possibility that Turkish custom regarding regicide played a role in the succession process has been raised. Finding some evidence in this regard for Baybars I's election to the sultanate, Haarmann suggests that the repeated depositions of sultans were, in fact, "regicide" symbolically transformed.[54]

49 Holt, "Some Observations," 505.

50 Amalia Levanoni, "The Mamlūk Conception of the Sultanate," *IJMES*, 26 (1994), 380.

51 The various points of view are well summarized in Levanoni, "Mamlūk Conception," 373–92.

52 Irwin, *Middle East*, 156.

53 Ulrich Haarmann, "The Sons of Mamlūks as Fief-holders in Late Medieval Egypt," in Tarif Khalidi (ed.), *Land Tenure and Social Transformation in the Middle East* (Beirut, 1984), 163.

54 Ulrich Haarmann, "Regicide and the Law of the Turks," in Michel M. Mazzaoui and

Mamlūk politics have frequently been viewed as primarily a function of mamlūk loyalties (i.e. the *khushdāshiyya* and *ustādh-mamlūk* relationships), the glue which bound mamlūk factions. The Baḥriyya, mamlūks of the same master, who were additionally mainly of Kipchak origin and thus also ethnically homogeneous, first acted as a faction when their interests were threatened by Tūrān-Shāh, who too swiftly moved to replace them with his own, junior mamlūks. The generational pattern of the junior amīrs of a new sultan posing a challenge to the political power and economic status of senior mamlūks of the household of a former sultan is seen throughout Mamlūk history. The Baḥriyya, for example, revolted against Tūrān-Shāh because they wanted to preserve their estates.[55] Qalāwūn usurped the sultanate because Baḥrī-Ṣāliḥī interests were again threatened by the ascent of the mamlūks of Baybars's heir al-Malik al-Saʿīd as well as by the Ẓāhiriyya, Baybars's mamlūk corps.[56] Al-Nāṣir Muḥammad hated the Manṣūriyya, his father's mamlūks, and contrived to rid himself of most of them.[57] Usually, though not always (as in the case of Qalāwūn's descendants) raised to the throne by his *khushdāshiyya*, a new sultan's hold on power ultimately depended on his replacing these senior amīrs with mamlūks of his own younger household whose loyalty was, at least in theory, unquestioned. Baybars I, Qalāwūn, and al-Nāṣir Muḥammad (in his third reign) were successful because they had been able to build up large households of mamlūks and knew how to manipulate the factions.

Although mamlūk loyalties were indeed important, they do not explain all factional liaisons. Ethnic ties, for example, often cut across mamlūk factions, as is evident in the alignments which emerged between the death of Khalīl (d. 1293) and the inauguration of al-Nāṣir Muḥammad's third reign in 1310, when Circassian and Mongol mamlūks tended to belong to different coalitions. Qalāwūn, it should be noted, either to counter the Kipchak predominance or possibly to supplement the supply of Kipchaks who were, perhaps, no longer in such abundance, began importing Circassian mamlūks in large numbers. As sultan, he created a new regiment, known as the Burjiyya because it was quartered in the towers (*burj*) of the Cairo citadel, to which he is said to have assigned about 3,700 of his mamlūks of Circassian and Abkhāzī origin. Factions eventually developed within the Manṣūriyya which were supported by other elements in the army and in society at large. Whereas Kitbughā, Qalāwūn's mamlūk of Mongol origin, rose to the sultanate at least in part as a representative of the interests of *wāfidiyya*

Vera B. Moreen (eds.), *Intellectual Studies on Islam: Essays Written in Honor of Martin B. Dickson* (Salt Lake City, 1990), 127–35.

55 Levanoni, "Mamlūks' Ascent," 135, 141.

56 Northrup, *Slave to Sultan*, 73–76, 81.

57 Reuven Amitai-Preiss, "The Remaking of the Military Elite of Mamlūk Egypt by al-Nāṣir Muḥammad ibn Qalāwūn," *Studia Islamica*, 72 (1990), 145–63.

(immigrants or refugees from Mongol territory who had arrived in the Mamlūk realm),[58] disaffected Ẓāhiriyya, Kurdish auxiliaries and *ḥalqa* troops, and non-mamlūk interests, his rival Lājīn gained support from the Manṣūriyya-Burjiyya mamlūk elite.[59] Nevertheless, the two basic mamlūk relationships, the *ustādh-mamlūk* and *khushdāshiyya* ties, though they might be modified by other factors such as race, ethnicity, mamlūk and non-mamlūk affiliations, ambition and interests, constituted a system of loyalties that helped to shape and strengthen the Mamlūk political structure. Still to be determined is whether factions and inter-factional coalitions were simply rooted in ambition and self-interest, as it would now appear, or whether they may ultimately have had some moral or ideological basis.[60]

The basis of sultani power was the army, and the sultan was of course commander-in-chief. The senior amīrs holding the rank of *amīr mi'a muqaddam alf* (amīr of 100 with command on the battlefield of 1,000 ḥalqa troops), ideally twenty-four in number, formed an executive military council. Mamlūks filled all major military posts, positions in the palace administration and senior urban offices. Baybars I, under the threat of Mongol attack, clearly devoted energy to strengthening the Mamlūk army numerically, reorganizing the *barīd* (military post and intelligence system), strengthening fortifications, encouraging military readiness through *furūsiyya* exercises (games and training in horsemanship, archery and other military skills), trying to build a navy, and introducing (unsuccessfully) innovations such as fighting elephants.[61] There is no clear evidence, however, that as sultan either he or his immediate successors undertook a major reorganization of the Mamlūk army, as has sometimes been stated.[62] The early Mamlūk army shows a great deal of continuity with its Ayyūbid predecessor, the mamlūk element, always a minority, constituting in both periods the backbone of the army. The élite ḥalqa corps, composed of such high-ranking free-born troops as *awlād al-nās* and *wāfidiyya*, retained that status in the Mamlūk period until the reign of al-Nāṣir Muḥammad. The

[58] David Ayalon, "The Wafidiyya in the Mamlūk Kingdom," *Islamic Culture*, 25 (1951), 89–104; reprinted in idem, *Studies on the Mamlūks*, VII, 313.

[59] Irwin, *Middle East*, 88–104. For an example of the limits of mamlūk loyalties see Amalia Levanoni, *A Turning Point in Mamlūk History: The Third Reign of al-Nāṣir Muḥammad Ibn Qalāwūn (1310–1341)* (Leiden, 1995), 33.

[60] Irwin, *Middle East*, 152–56; idem, "Factions in Medieval Egypt," *JRAS* (1986), 228–46.

[61] Reuven Amitai-Preiss, *Mongols and Mamlūks: The Mamlūk-Īlkhānid War, 1260–1281* (Cambridge, 1995), 71–75: Peter Thorau, *The Lion of Egypt: Sultan Baybars I and the Near East in the Thirteenth Century*, trans. P. M. Holt (London and New York, 1987), 99: Ayalon, "Ayyubids to Mamlūks," 50; reprinted in idem, *Islam and the Abode of War*, III, 50. On the use of elephants see Bosworth, *Ghaznavids*, 115–19.

[62] Humphreys, "Emergence," *Studia Islamica*, 45 (1977), 67–99 and 46 (1977), 147–8: cf. Ayalon, "Ayyūbids to Mamlūks," 50–55, reprinted in idem, *Islam and the Abode of War*, III, 50–55.

ṭulb remained the basic battle, or parade, formation throughout both periods. The rather loose ranking system characteristic of the Ayyūbid army is also found in the early Mamlūk army. Only gradually did the ranks evolve into the more rigid, three-tiered system of the later period, comprising the highest rank of *amīr mi'a muqaddam alf*, *amīr ṭabalkhāna* (amīr of forty) and *amīr ʿashara* (amīr of ten).[63] Though the mamlūk military chain of command was not as elaborate as that of the Mongol army,[64] the Mamlūk system of loyalties perhaps served the purpose to a degree.

On the other hand, although it is nowhere explicitly stated in the sources, there are indications that Baybars and Qalāwūn systematized the military structure. Whereas the Ayyūbid army had consisted of disparate elements brought together as need arose, Baybars, following ʿAyn Jālūt, created a "discrete framework for a single army which he made subordinate to the central government."[65] Both he and Qalāwūn also introduced changes "which established a clear formal link between a soldier's rank and the size of his *iqṭāʿ*."[66] The early Mamlūk army thus consisted of three main elements: the Royal Mamlūks – the mamlūks belonging to the sultan (*al-mamālīk al-sulṭāniyya*); the mamlūks of the amīrs (*mamālīk al-umarā'* or *al-ajnād*);[67] and the ḥ*alqa* corps.[68] The Royal Mamlūks and *ḥalqa* were made subordinate to the sultan, while the amīr's troops, though under the authority of an amīr, were to be placed at the disposal of the regime whenever necessary.[69] Auxiliary units of free Kurdish, Turkoman and Bedouin Arab troops were also used in battle.[70] Among them the Arabs of northern Syria were most important, as is clear from the fact that they were actually granted an amīrate.[71] The sultan's guard (*khāṣṣakiyya*) was chosen from the Royal Mamlūks.[72] Royal Mamlūks filled most household or palace positions such as those of the *ḥājib* (chamberlain), *ustādār* (major domo), *amīr akhūr* (amīr in charge of the stables), and the *khāzindār* (the official in

[63] Levanoni, *Turning Point*, 10. Cf. David Ayalon, "Studies on the Structure of the Mamlūk Army – II," *BSOAS*, 15 (1954), 467–75, reprinted in idem, *Studies on the Mamlūks*, I, 467–75.

[64] E.g., Amitai-Preiss, *Mongols and Mamlūks*, 214–25.

[65] Levanoni, *Turning Point*, 8–9.

[66] Levanoni, *Turning Point*, 10–11.

[67] Ayalon, "Studies – II," 459–67; reprinted in *idem*, *Studies on the Mamlūks*, I, 459–67.

[68] On the *ḥalqa*, see Ayalon, "Studies – II," 448–59: reprinted in *idem*, *Studies on the Mamlūks*, I, 448–59.

[69] Levanoni, *Turning Point*, 8.

[70] David Ayalon, "The Auxiliary Forces of the Mamlūk Sultanate," *Der Islam*, 45 (1988), 13–37, reprinted in idem, *Mamlūk Military Society*, Xa, 196–225.

[71] M. A. Hiyari, "The Origins and Development of the Amirate of the Arabs during the Seventh/Thirteenth and Eighth/Fourteenth Centuries," *BSOAS*, 38 (1975), 509–24.

[72] David Ayalon, "Studies on the Structure of the Mamlūk Army – I," *BSOAS*, 15 (1953), 213–16, reprinted in idem, *Studies on the Mamlūks*, I, 213–16.

charge of the royal treasure), among others.[73] The superiority of the Royal Mamlūk corps and its elite status were reinforced by the recruitment and selection procedures and the resources available for their training and maintenance, which gave the sultan the advantage over the amīrs who formed their own households, though on a smaller scale. Whether because the supply of Kipchak recruits was drying up or because his aim was to balance Kipchak mamlūks with other ethnic groups, Qalāwūn endeavoured to obtain mamlūks from a variety of sources and is said to have selected them on the basis of merit rather than ethnic origin.[74] Throughout the Baḥrī period the Royal Mamlūks and mamlūk regiments retained their high status, while the *ḥalqa* declined in status and skill during the fourteenth century owing to circumstances discussed below.

The early Baḥrī sultans were concerned to increase the size and strength of the army. This aim is explicitly stated in instructions Qalāwūn left with his son during his absence on campaign.[75] In fact, Qalāwūn advertised for recruits. Baybars, Qalāwūn and al-Nāṣir Muḥammad successively purchased more mamlūks than their predecessors. The army was based on the *iqṭāʿ* system, i.e. the assignment of revenues mainly from agricultural land for the maintenance of a soldier and a certain number of horsemen.[76] The maintenance of such a standing army certainly constituted the major expenditure of the state: the early sultans were thus also concerned to increase revenues.

Two factors led to a weakening of the Mamlūk military structure in the fourteenth century: first, paradoxically, the coming of a period of relative peace and prosperity; and second, the structural changes inadvertently introduced by al-Nāṣir Muḥammad ibn Qalāwūn as he sought to meet the challenges of his reign. The military crises of the thirteenth century had demanded discipline. Galvanized by the Mongol threat and the crusader presence, the new Mamlūk regime had insisted on hard training, slow promotion and gradual pay increases. Discipline had instilled a value system in which individual merit and achievement were eventually well rewarded and which made the early mamlūk army the strongest in the region at that time. But with the elimination of the crusader principalities, the signing of the Mamlūk–Mongol peace treaty in 1322 and the disintegration of the Īlkhānid state soon after, the Baḥrī regime entered a period of peace,

[73] Irwin, *Middle East*, 39. Also, Jonathan Riley-Smith (ed.), *The Atlas of the Crusades* (London, 1991), 110–11.

[74] Northrup, *Slave to Sultan*, 188.

[75] On Baybars; Amitai-Preiss, *Mongols and Mamlūks*, 71–3: Thorau, *Lion of Egypt*, 99; on Qalāwūn; Northrup, *Slave to Sultan*, 188: Levanoni (*Turning Point*, 32), however, claims that al-Nāṣir Muḥammad purchased less than his predecessors.

[76] See Cl. Cahen, "Iḳṭāʿ," *EI2*, III, 1088–91: Robert Irwin, "'Iqṭāʾ and the End of the Crusader States," in P. M. Holt (ed.), *The Eastern Mediterranean Lands in the Period of the Crusades* (Warminster, 1977), 62–77; Hassanein Rabie, *The Financial System of Egypt*, AH 564–741/AD 1169–1341 (London, 1972), 26–72.

prosperity and internal stability. The military ethic that had served so well during a time of crisis began to deteriorate. It was further eroded by the ways in which al-Nāṣir Muḥammad (not himself a mamlūk) tried to gain mastery over the mamlūk elite and greater access to and control over economic resources. Al-Nāṣir's ultimately ill-considered efforts to buy loyalty through more liberal pay, rapid promotions and marriage alliances with mamlūks of his own household rather than high-ranking outsiders such as the *Wāfidiyya* and others encouraged a lapse in discipline.[77] Like his predecessors, he moved as quickly as possible to remove the amīrs of former sultans, and in particular the Manṣūriyya of his father, ruthlessly eliminated potential rivals, and promoted "amirs on whom he could depend, mainly – but not exclusively – his own mamlūks."[78] Al-Nāṣir began promoting non-mamlūks to senior military posts. Not only were civilians appointed to posts formerly held by the military, but a roster of al-Nāṣir's senior amīrs includes several of non-mamlūk origin.[79] This trend toward de-mamlūkization, which became increasingly apparent from al-Nāṣir Muḥammad's reign on, was reinforced by the dislike of al-Nāṣir Ḥasan (1347–51, 1354–61) of the mamlūk institution and his extreme preference for the *awlād al-nās* and other non-mamlūk groups.[80] It was furthered by the arrival of bubonic plague in Egypt in 1347, and subsequently by recurrent epidemics of pneumonic plague that decimated not only the civilian population but the mamlūk ranks of the army.

A second factor that had a negative effect on Mamlūk military organization was the attempt by several sultans to redistribute land and agricultural resources to the benefit of the mamlūk army and to meet the needs of the sultanate. Despite the efforts of Qalāwūn and al-Nāṣir Muḥammad and perhaps others to reclaim unproductive lands, the possibility of agricultural development remained quite limited; the agricultural resources of Egypt were finite. The strain on agricultural resources imposed by a standing army of mamlūk recruits was perhaps felt as early as the end of Qalāwūn's reign, when this sultan launched a program of confiscations so broad in scope that it affected not only the military elite but civilians as well.[81] Qalāwūn's son, Khalīl, at the time of his death seems to have been considering a *rawk* or cadastral survey as a basis for a redistribution,[82] and Lājīn was on the point of implementing such a program when he was assassinated, partly because of it. Al-Nāṣir finally succeeded in implementing a series of *rawk*s in both

[77] Levanoni, *Turning Point*, 28–80.
[78] Amitai-Preiss, "Remaking," 145–63.
[79] Amitai-Preiss, "Remaking," 160.
[80] Levanoni, *Turning Point*, 49, 86; Haarmann, "Sons of Mamlūks," 162.
[81] Northrup, *Slave to Sultan*, 134–39; Jacqueline Sublet, "La folie de la princesse Bint al-Ašraf," *BEO*, 27 (1974), 45–50.
[82] Irwin, *Middle East*, 81–82.

Syria (1313) and Egypt (1315). Rather than strengthening the army, however, al-Nāṣir's *rawk* had the opposite effect. Though it worked to the advantage of the sultan and the Mamlūk elite by giving them a greater share of the revenues, it undermined the military strength and status of the *ḥalqa* corps, which subsequently attracted only riff-raff.[83] Finding his situation desperate as a consequence of the redistribution, the *ḥalqa* soldier now might lease his *iqṭāʿ* and do his best to avoid military service. From al-Nāṣir's reign on military training was no longer a prerequisite for membership in the *ḥalqa*. Its ranks now counted elderly and disabled persons, and, after the plague of 1347, even children.[84]

It has been said that the army of the sultanate was the state. But the core of the army was mamlūk. Therefore, the state was both militarized and mamlūkized. The political structure *was* the mamlūk military structure. Major posts in the administration were filled by mamlūks or by civilians supervised by mamlūks. The Baḥrī sultanate inherited the administrative divisions of the Ayyūbid realm but was much more successful in forging the political and administrative unity of Egypt and Syria by superimposing the more highly centralized Mamlūk military system on the confederational Ayyūbid structure. The mamlūk system with its inherent loyalties and ranks helped to weld these two geographically and historically disparate regions together in what proved to be an extremely durable political union. The nature of rule, previously personal and ephemeral, became institutionalized in the Mamlūk system itself. Mamlūk sultans, unlike Ayyūbid rulers, did not appoint their sons to governorships or to any other administrative positon; ideally they appointed at the beginning of their reigns senior mamlūk officers from among their *khushdāshiyya* to these posts, who were then replaced as opportunities arose by the more loyal mamlūks of their own personal households. Nor did they divide their realm among their sons at death. Cairo was the seat of the sultanate and the only major governmental centre in Egypt. Damascus ranked second in importance to Cairo, and its governor (*nāʾib*), usually either the sultan's *khushdāsh* or a mamlūk of his household, was directly responsible to the sultan as were the governors of all smaller administrative centres and garrisons. The sultan also exercised control by means of his prerogative to appoint and dismiss and the fragmentation of responsibilities. Governors of major fortresses, for example, were appointed by, and were directly responsible to, the sultan rather than by the governor of the province.

The civil administration comprised three branches: finance, chancery and religio-judicial affairs. The *nāʾib al-salṭana* (viceroy) of Egypt was after the

83 Haarmann, "Sons of Mamlūks," 142; idem, "Ḥalḳa," *EI2*, 99; Levanoni, *Turning Point*, 8, esp. n.14, 106–09, 142–43; Ayalon, "Studies – II," 448–59, reprinted in idem, *Studies on the Mamlūks*, I, 448–59.

84 Levanoni, *Turning Point*, 106–07, 128–31.

sultan the second most powerful government official. He was charged with the overall administration of governmental affairs, including some aspects of finance. In the sultan's absence he was often appointed acting sultan. The *wazīr* was responsible for the financial administration which included such important offices as the bureau of sultani properties (*naẓar al-khāṣṣ*) and the army bureau (*dīwān al-jaysh*) which was responsible for the distribution of *iqṭā*ʿs as well as for the offices in charge of tax collection. Previously held by a civilian, the wazīrate was militarized during Qalāwūn's reign with the appointment to the post of his mamlūk ʿAlam al-Dīn Sanjar al-Shujāʿī. Qalāwūn probably sought to increase his control over revenues in this way; indeed, the *wazīr* proved extremely capable, enriching both himself and the sultan in the process. Eventually, however, al-Shujāʿī's efficiency in filling the coffers undermined goodwill toward this sultan. Al-Nāṣir, also searching for ways to increase his personal control over financial resoures, eventually abolished the office altogether. Henceforth, the financial functions of the wazīrate and *niyābat al-salṭana*, which he also abolished, were concentrated in the office of *nāẓir al-khāṣṣ*, thus centralizing control over financial resources in one individual. That individual was usually someone chosen because of his vulnerability, a Copt or Christian convert, whose obedience was assured. Karīm al-Dīn al-Kabīr, a former Copt appointed in 1310, and al-Nashw, also a Coptic convert, appointed in 1333, are prominent examples.[85]

Chancery posts were filled by "men of the pen," who though they had most probably received a religious education, had also frequently served an apprenticeship as a government scribe. Virtual dynasties of professional scribes, such as the ʿAbd al-Ẓāhir and Faḍl Allāh families, served in these posts during the early Mamlūk period. Baybars I, it seems, had relied on a mamlūk officer, the *dawādār* (master of the inkwell) to serve as chief secretary during his reign, but for security reasons eventually appointed a civilian veteran of the chancery to that post. Although the sources are not entirely clear, they tend to indicate that Qalāwūn created the office of *kātib al-sirr* (secretary of the secret) or private secretary to the sultan, also called *ṣāḥib dīwān al-inshā*ʾ (head of the chancery), perhaps as a means to maintain his domination over the mamlūk elite, for this official was not only in charge of state correspondance, but also of the royal post (*barīd*) and, thus, intelligence.

Theoretically, the sultan had no authority over the religious establishment, including the judiciary. In fact, however, not only the sultan but also the amīrs wielded a great deal of control over religious affairs through appointments to the judiciary and the foundation of *madrasa*s (educational institutions which provided higher-level instruction in the Islamic religious

[85] Irwin, *Middle East*, 112–14.

sciences (jurisprudence, *ḥadīth*) and sometimes in other subjects as well (such as rhetoric, literature, poetry, and medicine)), *khanqāh*s (institutions which provided facilities for moderate Ṣūfīs), and other religious establishments which they funded through the *waqf* system. One source claims that Qalāwūn had actually appointed one of his *khushdāshiyya* over the men of religion, but this report has not been substantiated elsewhere.[86] Further aspects of the religio-judicial administration will be considered in the following section. Alongside the religio-judicial administration, however, the existence of a system of secular, administrative justice (the *maẓālim* court), originating in the ʿAbbāsid period or earlier, which functioned parallel to the Sharīʿa courts, should be noted. Held in a Shāfiʿī *madrasa* in Cairo, the *maẓālim* sessions were moved by Baybars I, imitating Nūr al-Dīn's practice, to the *dār al-ʿadl* (palace of justice) just below the citadel, and during Qalāwūn's reign to the ceremonial hall within the Citadel walls (*īwān kabīr*). Originally a means by which injustices or requests might be brought directly to the attention of the ruler, the *maẓālim* functions had by early Mamlūk times become highly bureaucratized and were, in the process, absorbed as one of the ceremonial formalities surrounding the sultan's audiences (*khidma*). Among the wide range of matters dealt with in *maẓālim* sessions were petitions "for offices or *iqṭā*ʿs, the suppression of particular *ʿulamā*ʾ and their teachings, and the implementation of law and order, as well as appeals for justice and the application of *ḳāḍī*s" decisions."[87] Though *qāḍī*s were normally present at these sessions, and indeed, might even be consulted, *maẓālim* cases were nevertheless dealt with by mamlūk officials.

Religious currents

Early Mamlūk Egypt harboured a wide spectrum of Islamic religious expression, a range which included the remnants of Ismāʿīlī Shiʾism, but now increasingly Sunnism and Ṣūfism in all their variety. Less than a century preceding the Mamlūk ascent to power, Egypt under the aegis of the Fāṭimid caliphate had been, if perhaps only nominally, an Ismāʿīlī Shiʾi state. While it may be that the Ismāʿīlism of the Fāṭimids had never put down deep roots among the Egyptian populace as a whole, pockets of Shiʾism remained, especially, perhaps, in areas of Upper Egypt, at least until the early fourteenth century. That Abuʾl-Ḥasan al-Bakrī's fantastical biography of the Prophet, dating to a much earlier period, continued to find an audience in Mamlūk Cairo may be further evidence for the persistence of Shīʿī belief

[86] Northrup, *Slave to Sultan*, 199.

[87] J. S. Nielsen, "Maẓālim," in *EI2*, VI, 932–35; and idem, *Secular Justice in an Islamic State: Maẓālim under the Baḥrī Mamlūks* (Istanbul, 1985), 935.

even in the north, for it incorporated ideas which appealed mainly to Shīʿīs.[88] Social unrest, expressed in religious terms, sometimes with Shīʿī colouring, was also not unknown. Rioters in Cairo protested in the name of ʿAlī in 1260; and in 1297 a revolt was raised against the Mamlūk regime by a Fāṭimid pretender in Upper Egypt.[89] Force was occasionally used to eliminate Shīʿī strongholds: the Ismāʿīlī Assassins, still ensconced in their fortresses in northern Syria, were finally extirpated in 1271, and early in the fourteenth century al-Nāṣir Muḥammad sent an expedition against Shīʿī heretics in Mount Lebanon.[90] Also, Christians still constituted an important minority of the Egyptian population, a minority which had gained renewed strength and vigour as a result of the mostly benign attitude of the Fāṭimid regime. Perhaps as much to counter the revivification of Christianity and the prominence of Christians in Egypt as to erase the traces of Fāṭimid Ismaʿilism, Ṣalāḥ al-Dīn, upon abolishing the Fāṭimid caliphate, embarked upon a religious policy aimed at strengthening Sunnī Islam against these competitors.[91] The religious policies of the Ayyūbids, pursued even more energetically by the Baḥrī mamlūks, would result in a "consciousness-raising," which ultimately created in the Baḥrī period an even more intensely Islamic and Sunnī religious environment.

Sunnī Islam itself included a wide spectrum of religious belief and practice including Ṣūfism, which in its more moderate form had been incorporated within the Sunnī sphere. The relatively well-documented lives and careers of two individuals, the Shādhilī Ṣūfī shaykh Tāj al-Dīn ibn ʿAṭāʾ Allāh (d. 1309) and the Ḥanbalī jurisprudent and scholar Taqī al-Dīn ibn Taymiyya (d. 1328), give some idea of the range of Sunnī religious expression in Egypt at the time. By the thirteenth century Ṣūfism had become widespread among the Egyptian population. The Shādhiliyya, a Ṣūfī order (*ṭarīqa*), or perhaps more precisely, "school," which had coalesced around the teachings of Abuʾl-Ḥasan al-Shādhilī (d. 1258), quickly found wide appeal in Morocco, where al-Shādhilī had originated, in north Africa, and in Egypt, where he finally settled, and even further afield. Although it was not the only Ṣūfī

88 Boaz Shoshan, *Popular Culture in Medieval Cairo* (Cambridge, 1993), 23–39, esp. 38–39.

89 Jean-Claude Garçin, *Un centre musulman de la Haute Egypte médiévale: Qūṣ* (Cairo, 1976), 309, 311. Baybars suppressed a revolt of black slaves in Cairo led by a Shīʿī ascetic and for all practical purposes brought about the downfall of the Syrian Ismāʿīlīs during his reign (Garçin, *Qūṣ*, 101); al-Nāṣir sent an expedition against the Druze and their Shīʿī and Maronite allies in the Lebanese mountains (Holt, "Some Observations," 504).

90 Enumerated by U. Haarmann, "Miṣr, 5. The Mamlūk Period 1250–1517," *EI2*, VII, 169.

91 Gary Leiser, "The Madrasa and the Islamization of the Middle East: The Case of Egypt," *JARCE*, 22 (1985), 29–47: see also Leonor Fernandes, "Mamlūk Politics and Education: The Evidence of Two Fourteenth Century Waqfiyya," *Annales Islamologiques*, 23 (1987), 87–88.

order in early Mamlūk Egypt (the Rifāʿiyya, Badawiyya and others also found adherents), the popularity of the Shādhiliyya is probably to be attributed to its flexibility and lack of real institutional structure, a characteristic which allowed it to adapt to changing conditions and embrace a variety of more local popular practices and beliefs. Combining aspects of Sunnī piety, based on the Qur'an and *ḥadīth*, and Ṣūfī mysticism, al-Shādhilī's teachings provided a middle way.

Representative of Shādhilī Ṣūfism in Egypt in the early Mamlūk period is Ibn ʿAṭāʾ Allāh (d. 1309). Mālikī by birth, Shāfiʿī by later affiliation, and an opponent of Ṣūfism in his early years, Ibn ʿAṭāʾ Allāh was, nevertheless, destined to become the third great shaykh or "master" of the Shādhiliyya. Though more extreme forms of Ṣūfism existed, Ibn ʿAṭāʾ Allāh's career and preaching exemplify the moderate Ṣūfism of the time which melded Sunnī orthodoxy with Ṣūfī spirituality, for Ibn ʿAṭāʾ Allāh was both orthodox scholar and Ṣūfī shaykh. His sermons, addressed to ordinary people, while propagating rather conventional Sunnī themes, also introduced listeners to Ṣūfī ideas which now incorporated elements of popular religion such as saints, miracles, the invocation of God (*dhikr*), and visits (*ziyāra*) to the tombs of saints and the pious.[92]

It was exactly these sorts of ideas and practices that the Ḥanbalī scholar Taqī al-Dīn ibn Taymiyya found most abhorrent. Born in Ḥarrān and raised in Damascus, Ibn Taymiyya, although perhaps not the most typical representative of Sunnī orthodoxy, is without doubt the most prominent religious scholar of the period. His thought illustrates an important strand of Sunnism at the time, still influential today, while his career helps to delineate aspects of the religious outlook of the Mamlūk regime. An adherent of the Ḥanbalī legal rite, yet versed in the doctrines of the other *madhhab*s (schools of legal thought and practice), as well as in heresiographical literature, philosophy, and Ṣūfism, Ibn Taymiyya's irascible personality, his insistence on an extreme, morally rigorist Sunnism based on a literal interpretation of the Qurʾān and Sunna, and his hostility to popular religion brought him into frequent conflict with the regime and with individuals who, for religious or political reasons, did not support his views.[93] In fact, he was imprisoned no fewer than six times, on five occasions with regard to his religious beliefs, which were considered by the regime to pose a threat.[94] Though not opposed to Ṣūfism per se, he denounced all Ṣūfī innovations.

So vehement was Ibn Taymiyya in his attacks on the Shādhiliyya that a clash was inevitable. In 1307 or 1308 Ibn ʿAṭāʾ Allāh joined the shaykh of the Saʿīd al-Suʿadāʾ *khānqāh* and more than 500 commoners in a march to

92 Shoshan, *Popular Culture*, 14–16, and works cited therein.
93 Shoshan, *Popular Culture*, 67.
94 Donald P. Little, "The Historical and Historiographical Significance of the Detention of Ibn Taymiyya," *IJMES*, 4 (1973), 311–13.

the Cairo citadel to protest against Ibn Taymiyya's polemics against *ittiḥādiyya* Ṣūfīs – those who believed in some form of mystical union with God, among whom may be counted Islam's greatest mystic Muḥyī al-Dīn Ibn (al-) ʿArabī (d. 1240) and its greatest Arab mystical poet Ibn al-Fāriḍ (d. 1235), who by the end of the thirteenth century had been accorded sainthood.[95] As Shoshan notes, the incident reveals the widespread influence of Ibn ʿAṭāʾ Allāh's ideas.[96] Ibn al-Fāriḍ's rapid elevation to sainthood likewise indicates the strength of aspects of popular religion such as the cult of saints which, incidentally, found adherents not just among the poor and illiterate, but among all segments of the population.[97] In any case Ibn Taymiyya, taking his Sunnism to an extreme, incurred the wrath of several of his more moderate colleagues and the suspicion of the intrepid traveller and observer, Ibn Baṭṭūṭa, that he was "unbalanced" (*illā anna fī ʿaqlihi shayʾan*).[98]

The Baḥrī Mamlūks embraced Sunnism and Ṣūfism in all its variety out of both personal piety and political expediency. Although Baybars I endowed several Sunnī instititutions, his attachment to the dervish shaykh Khāḍir is well known.[99] Qalāwūn, for whom there is, incidentally, evidence of lingering shamanistic belief, endowed a *madrasa* in his hospital complex; yet it was from Ṣūfīs that he sought comfort at the time of his son's fatal illness. Lājīn and Kitbughā were both pious and the latter was affiliated with at least two Ṣūfī orders.[100] Baybars al-Jāshnikīr sought the counsel of a Ṣūfī shaykh and during his short reign endowed several Ṣūfī institutions. Al-Naṣir Muḥammad likewise sponsored a *madrasa*, but it is perhaps his *khānqāh* at Siryāqūs in which he was personally more interested and which attracted most public attention. Al-Nāṣir Ḥasan (1347–51) not only favoured religious scholars at court but built just below the citadel perhaps the most renowned *madrasa* of the Baḥrī period.

Ascending the throne the Baḥrī mamlūks, continuing Ayyūbid precedents, professed loyalty to the ʿAbbāsid caliph, continued to favour the Shāfiʿī legal school over the other three *madhhab*s (the Mālikī, Ḥanafī and Ḥanbalī legal rites), and founded Sunnī and Ṣūfī religious institutions. However, the course they followed was dictated not just by precedent but also by new

95 T. Emil Homerin, "ʿUmar ibn al-Fāriḍ, a Saint of Mamlūk and Ottoman Egypt," in Grace Martin Smith (ed.), and Carl W. Ernst (assoc. ed.), *Manifestations of Sainthood in Islam* (Istanbul, 1993), 86.

96 Shoshan, *Popular Culture*, 16.

97 Homerin, "ʿUmar ibn al-Fāriḍ," 88–89.

98 Ibn Baṭṭūta, *Riḥla*, as cited by Donald P. Little, "Did Ibn Taymiyya Have a Screw Loose?" *Studia Islamica*, 41 (1975), 95, with discussion of the phrase and its translation.

99 P. M. Holt, "An Early Source on Shaykh Khaḍir al-Mihrānī," *BSOAS*, 46 (1983), 33–39.

100 Irwin, *Middle East*, 95.

circumstances: the strength of the religious currents they found on taking power, the impact of the crusades and the Mongol invasions and of the fall of the caliphate, and their slave origin and consequent need for legitimacy and supremacy. First, the crusades and Mongol invasions had left Egypt as the final redoubt of Islam. To counter the enemy the Baḥrī Mamlūks were compelled to build on the foundations of moral unity which had been laid at least since the days of Nūr al-Dīn, hero of the "counter crusade" (d. 1174). Unity was an essential basis for the enterprise, and so the Baḥrī sultans were compelled to uphold majority views in order to elicit cooperation from the civilian elite and to avoid the disaffection of the masses whose labor ultimately paid for Mamlūk military ventures.

Second, having been introduced to Islamic society under the tutelage of the Ayyūbids, it was only natural that the early Mamlūk sultans should follow the only model they knew, the Sunnism traditionally favoured by the Turks and also by their master al-Ṣāliḥ Ayyūb as well as heroes of the recent past such as Ṣalāḥ al-Dīn. Although personal piety should not be discounted as a factor in Mamlūk support for Sunnī Islam, the "deficient" status of mamlūks in Islamic society[101] as individuals of pagan birth and slave origin, who craved acceptance at the political, and probably at the personal, level must certainly have been a consideration, for faith was an integrating and unifying factor; it was the one thing the Mamlūk elite shared with their subjects. Legitimation, even if only symbolic, was thus a priority. This was sought among other means, as we have seen, through the transfer of the ʿAbbāsid caliphate to Cairo and caliphal recognition. As seat of both the sultanate and the caliphate, Cairo succeeded Baghdad as the religio-political centre of Sunnī Islam.[102]

The Mamlūks also came to wield considerable influence among the scholars and judiciary. From the reign of Ṣalāḥ al-Dīn the Shāfiʿī *madhhab* had enjoyed pre-eminence, symbolized by the selection of the *qāḍī al-quḍāt* (chief judge) from its ranks. Baybars began appointing a chief *qāḍī* for each of the four rites. While the Shāfiʾīs still retained certain privileges, each school now gained increased stature. Baybars's motives can only be surmised. He thought perhaps to meet the needs of an increasingly diverse population who came from regions where other schools were preeminent, or it may be that he wished to promote the more liberal Ḥanafī *madhhab* favored by the Mamlūks. In any case the appointment of an individual from each school to a prestigious judicial post allowed the sultan to exercise patronage in each group and thus more influence over all four legal rites.

Either to demonstrate personal piety, or to gain legitimacy or influence

101 Haarmann, "Miṣr," 165.

102 Shaun Marmon, *Eunuchs and Sacred Boundaries in Islamic Society* (New York, Oxford, 1995), 50–51, for associated titulary and a particularly interesting interpretation of this process viewed through the eunuch institution.

among the scholarly class, the Mamlūks surpassed their predecessors in the number of both Sunnī and Ṣūfī religious institutions they established during their rule. Pious civilians also endowed such institutions, but because of the far greater resources at their disposal, those established by the mamlūk élite dominated in terms of both number and prestige. This activity reached a peak during the fourteenth century, transforming the physical environment of the major urban centers and consequently the religious climate of the entire region as well. The widespread establishment of *madrasa*s assured the creation of an educated Sunnī religious élite with shared values, one which could articulate a response to any challenge to official religion and which also, incidentally, tended to cooperate with the regime. It was also from among the *madrasa* graduates that appointments to the judiciary, to secretarial posts, and to the religious establishment were usually made. But the Mamlūk elite, both through piety and the need to win the support and cooperation of the masses among whom Ṣūfīsm was gaining increasing strength, also endowed Ṣūfī institutions. The *khānqāh*, as opposed to the *ribāṭ* or *zāwiya*, was the institution chosen to promote moderate Ṣūfīsm, i.e. Ṣūfīsm which conformed to the Sharīʿa.[103] Through the pious endowments which funded these institutions and the patronage of the religious scholars appointed to them, the Mamlūk elite exercised enormous influence on religious life. Although the properties donated as endowments (*awqāf*: sing., *waqf*) to fund these institutions were theoretically alienated from private ownership, the donor frequently reserved the right to supervise the foundation during his lifetime. He was thus able to control appointments to educational, legal and spiritual posts and in this way to influence the religious environment of the realm.

Although the Mamlūks appear on the surface to have fostered variety within Sunnism, the parameters of what was acceptable within each particular mode of expression became increasingly circumscribed as the period progressed, at least in part as a result of Mamlūk involvement with the religious institution. This trend, which had begun even prior to the rise of the Mamlūks, was accelerated in the early Mamlūk period when new circumstances, and, perhaps, the increasingly diverse and multi-ethnic population, compelled the Baḥrī regime to seek unity. The more conservative environment, one most receptive to orthodox Islam in its several forms, furthered the process of re-Sunnification, even Islamization in Egypt. Partly through the regime's utilization of these various currents and partly as a result of natural inclinations, it would seem, a certain cross-fertilization or homogenization of Sunnism and Ṣūfīsm occurred in early Mamlūk Egypt

[103] Leonor Fernandes, *The Evolution of a Sufi Institution in Mamlūk Egypt: The Khanqah* (Berlin, 1988), 2.

and Syria. Orthodox scholars were appointed to Ṣūfī institutions[104] and by the end of the fourteenth century the teaching of Ṣūfīsm in *madrasas* had become acceptable.[105] The Shādhilī shaykh Ibn ʿAṭāʾ Allāh, for example, ended his life as a professor in the Manṣūriyya *madrasa*.

At the same time extremism was less tolerated. Ibn Taymiyya's trial and detentions are one indication of the more restrictive environment, as is the fact that in 1306 the dervish shaykh Barāq received at best "a mixed reception" in Damascus and Cairo,[106] whereas, despite some raised eyebrows, al-Ẓāhir Baybars had early in his reign indulged the unsavory dervish shaykh Khāḍir with his patronage and confidence.[107] This growing religious intolerance, characterized by one scholar as an "inquisition," eventually also came to affect the non-Muslim minorities of the Baḥrī sultanate.

Communal interaction

Although by the eleventh century the *dhimmī* population in Egypt had been reduced to a minority, albeit still a significant one, it was probably not until the fourteenth century that this minority was definitively weakened through more massive conversions, forced or otherwise. Only then did Coptic cease to be spoken, relegated to liturgical use. To explain this trend, scholars have adduced several theories: the impact of the crusades and the Mongol invasions on Muslim perceptions of these religious minorities; the employment of Christians in administrative-financial positions which gave them power over the Muslims in contravention of Muslim legal and popular opinion; the social stress created by "an unsympathetic, largely alien, government," which was expressed in protests against Christians;[108] and the flowering of the Sunnī revival in Egypt and Syria since Ayyubid times which had led to a more intensely religious atmosphere. More recently there has been some thought that growing rivalry over trade in the eastern Mediterranean may also have contributed to the hardening of attitudes toward Christians, particularly in Egypt in the Baḥrī period.[109]

During the second half of the thirteenth century, at the peak of the campaigns to oust the crusaders from the Syrian littoral and of the struggle against the Mongols and their Christian allies, the Baḥrī sultans, Baybars, Qalāwūn and Khalīl, displayed a certain ambivalence toward their indi-

104 Shoshan, *Popular Culture*, 14: Fernandes, "Evolution," 101.
105 Garçin, *Qūṣ*, 314: Fernandes, *Evolution*, 2. Also Donald P. Little, "Religion under the Mamlūks," *The Muslim World*, 73 (1983), 177: Shoshan, *Popular Culture*, 11.
106 Little, "Religion," 175–77.
107 Holt, "An Early Source on Shaykh Khaḍir," 33–39.
108 Donald Richards, "The Coptic Bureaucracy under the Mamlūks," in *Colloque international sur l'histoire du Caire, 27 mars–5 avril 1969* (Cairo, n.d.), 377–78.
109 Irwin, *Middle East*, 118.

genous Christian and Jewish (but especially Christian) subjects. Though they continued to depend on Christian bureaucrats, especially in the financial bureaus, they also sometimes bowed to Muslim pressure to impose traditional restrictions on their employment as well as other symbols of subservience. The target of these actions was not the indigenous Christian minority as a whole, but usually the employees of the financial and army bureaus.[110] Paradoxically, in the fourteenth century, long after the fall of Acre and the Mongol invasions had subsided, the attitude of the regime toward the indigenous Christian community hardened. To this period belong, for example, Ghāzī ibn al-Wāsiṭī's, al-Asnāwī's and Ibn Taymiyya's tracts against their employment.[111] A Shāfiʿī jurisprudent "publicly accused the Sultan al-Nāṣir Muḥammad . . . of favoring Copts to the detriment of Muslims: 'You have appointed Copts and Coptic Muslims to office and have given them authority in your *dīwān* and over the money of the Muslims!' "[112] The boiling point seems to have been reached in 1321, when anti-Christian riots broke out. The situation for minorities became so difficult that previously steadfast Christians began converting to Islam in larger numbers. The events of 1321 have been interpreted in various ways. The outbreak of violence has been ascribed to Muslim resentment against Christian employment in the financial and army bureaus, and indeed there is evidence to suggest that much of the anti-Christian sentiment was directed at this specific group.[113] On the other hand it is also suggested that the sultan himself stirred up trouble to divert the anger of those who had suffered from his efforts to redistribute *iqṭāʿ* assignments.[114] But also worth mentioning is that several Coptic converts were involved in administering the *rawk*, giving rise to resentment among those who had suffered.[115] In 1354 yet another wave of rioting swept the country, possibly provoked by the exposure of Ibn Zunbur, a Christian convert to Islam. In his capacity as wazīr, *nāẓir al-khāṣṣ* and *nāẓir al-jaysh* (head of financial administration, supervisor of the privy purse, supervisor of the army bureau) to the sultan al-Ṣāliḥ Ṣāliḥ, Ibn Zunbur concentrated unprecedented fiscal and administrative powers in his

[110] Richard Gottheil, "A Fetwa on the Appointment of Dhimmis to Office," *Zeitschrift für Assyriologie* (1912), 203–14; Donald P. Little, "Coptic Converts to Islam," in Michael Gervers and Ramzi Jibran Bikhazi (eds.), *Conversion and Continuity: Indigenous Christian Communities in Islamic Lands Eighth to Eighteenth Centuries* (Toronto, 1990), 263–88; Linda S. Northrup, "Muslim-Christian Relations during the Reign of the Mamlūk Sultan al-Manṣūr Qalāwūn, AD 1278–1290," in *Conversion and Continuity*, 253–61; Richards, "Coptic Bureaucracy," 373–81.

[111] Richard Gottheil, "An Answer to the Dhimmis," *JAOS*, 41 (1921), 393–457; Moshe Perlmann, "Asnawi's Tract against Christian Officials," in Samuel Lowinger (ed.), *Ignace Goldziher Memorial Volume* (Jerusalem, 1958), II, 172–208.

[112] Little, "Coptic Converts," 265.

[113] Little, "Coptic Converts," 266: also Irwin, *Middle East*, 12–14.

[114] Haarmann, "Miṣr," 170.

[115] Irwin, *Middle East*, 110–12.

hands.[116] Not only Copts, but Christian converts to Islam were dismissed and sumptuary laws were reimposed. The crusade of the Cypriot ruler Peter I of Lusignan, which attacked Alexandria in 1365, causing damage from which that city never really recovered, could not have led to an improvement in intercommunal relations.

Diplomatic and commercial relations

During the reigns of sultans Baybars (1260–77) and Qalāwūn (1279–90), Egypt became the dominant power in the Middle East, but Egypt's hegemony did not go unchallenged. While the Baḥriyya were emerging as a political and military factor in Egyptian politics during the crisis of 1249 in Egypt, the Mongols were already hovering on the horizon. Transoxiana and eastern Iran, including the territory of the Khwarazm-Shah, east of the Caspian Sea, southern Russia including the Kipchak steppes (the recruiting ground for al-Ṣāliḥ Ayyūb's mamlūks), Georgia, Seljuk Rūm (Anatolia), as well as Cilician (Lesser) Armenia with its capital at Sīs, and its ally the crusader principality of Antioch, had all fallen under the Mongol yoke.[117] The Mongols were poised to advance into Iraq, Syria and even Egypt itself. Though the Mamlūks would recover Syria and save Egypt from Mongol overlordship, the Mongol menace would continue to dominate most aspects of Mamlūk foreign and commercial policy into the early years of the fourteenth century.

No sooner had the Mamlūks seized power than Hülegü, grandson of Chingiz Khān, began his advance into Iran. Baghdād was taken in 1258 and the ʿAbbāsid caliph was executed. Mongol forces crossed the Euphrates in 1259. Syria was next. Hülegü, whose armies now also included Georgians, Armenians, and Rūm Seljuks, took Aleppo in January 1260. Ḥamāh and Ḥomṣ offered submission, leaving the way to Damascus open. At this point Hülegü himself withdrew, but left his general Kitbughā with a small army in Syria. Despite his earlier indications of submission to the khān, the Ayyūbid prince of Damascus, al-Nāṣir Yūsuf, now had second thoughts. Caught between the Mongols and his enemy the sultan Quṭuz in Cairo, al-Nāṣir fled into the desert north of Karak, where he was captured by Mongols and later probably executed. Damascus was occupied in February 1260 and Mongol forces raided as far as Gaza and Hebron. Cairo now seemed within Mongol reach. Baybars, leader of the exiled Baḥriyya, and his rival Quṭuz, sultan of Egypt, though bitter adversaries, found this prospect sufficiently frightening that they effected a reconciliation in order to present a united front to the enemy. Baybars at the head of the vanguard led the Mamlūk forces up the

116 Little, "Coptic Converts," 269; Irwin, *Middle East*, 41.
117 Amitai-Preiss, *Mongols and Mamlūks*, 17–25.

Syrian littoral, their passage facilitated by the authorities of the Latin Kingdom of Jerusalem. The victory of the combined Mamlūk forces over the Mongol armies at ʿAyn Jālūt in September 1260 had a tremendous psychological impact; it demonstrated that the Mongols were not invincible. It was also, as we have seen, a rather convincing reason to recognize the legitimacy of Mamlūk rule. One immediate consequence of the Mamlūk victory was that Syria, in the absence of any political authority, was absorbed by the Baḥrī sultanate of Egypt. As a buffer zone and granary and also as a region with some commercial significance, Syria was an important acquisition. Yet its situation was precarious. Bohemond VI of Antioch-Tripoli, allied through marriage with the Armenian ruling family, had cast his lot with the Mongols. Al-Nāṣir Yūsuf in Damascus vacillated. Al-Mughīth ʿUmar at Karak was later accused by Baybars of also treating with the Mongols.

The early Baḥrī sultans Quṭuz, Baybars and Qalāwūn, on the other hand, all successively assumed a defiantly anti-Mongol stance. To do so was their very raison d'être and won them the grudging acceptance, and sometimes even gratitude, of their subjects. Despite continual skirmishing, the Mongols would fail to launch a serious attack on Mamlūk territory during the remainder of Baybars's reign (1260–77). Since Baybars could not have known this he began efforts to strengthen his army, consolidate his rule, and secure the frontiers in Syria. Lulls in the border war with the Mongols were used to gain a firm grip over internal affairs in Syria: rivals – mamlūk or Ayyūbid – were eliminated. The revolt of Baybars's *khushdāsh* Sanjar al-Ḥalabī in Damascus was quashed; the renegade mamlūk al-Barlī's hold on the strategic fortress of al-Bīra on the Euphrates was broken; the Ismāʿīlī fortresses in the north were taken. The Ayyūbid prince al-Mughīth ʿUmar, Baybars's former "employer," and still the lord of the strategically located fortress of Karak at the southern end of the Dead Sea, was treacherously murdered. Relations with the Bedouin Arab tribes of the region were also cultivated.

Like Baybars, Qalāwūn also had to surmount internal challenges to his authority in order to gain a free hand against the Mongols. Initially appointing members of his *khushdāshiyya*, who had helped bring him to power, to important posts in that province, he replaced them as soon as possible with his own, theoretically more loyal, mamlūks. The danger of appointing one's *khushdāshiyya*, among whom one was only first among equals, to posts such as the governorship of Damascus, for example, had been amply demonstrated during Baybars's reign by the revolt of Sanjar al-Ḥalabī. Now, shortly after Qalāwūn had usurped the sultanate, his viceroy in Damascus, his *khushdāsh* Sunqur al-Ashqar, also declared his independence. Taking advantage of the discord between Qalāwūn and Sunqur al-Ashqar, and probably at the latter's urging, the Mongol armies, led by Möngke Temür and assisted as before by Armenians, Georgians and

Rūm, sacked Aleppo. Sunqur al-Ashqar, however, was persuaded by the sultan's allies to stand with the Mamlūks rather than take his chances with the Mongols. Thus, the further progress of the Mongol armies was definitively arrested at the Battle of Ḥomṣ in 1281, when the Mamlūks and their auxilliaries, united under Qalāwūn's personal leadership, were victorious over the invaders. Following the victory, however, Sunqur al-Ashqar was allowed to re-ensconce himself in the fortress of Ṣahyūn (Saone) which dominated strategic routes from the coast to the interior and which Qalāwūn had given to him as an *iqṭāʿ* after putting down his revolt. Thus Sunqur al-Ashqar remained a weak link in the Syrian defenses. Simultaneously, Baybars's sons, exiled to the fortress of Karak in the south, instigated unrest in that region and maintained contact with Sunqur al-Ashqar in the north, further undermining Qalāwūn's hold. It was only during the second half of his reign that both these rebels were subdued. Karak and Ṣahyūn were taken in 1286 and 1287 respectively.

In addition to the internal enemies of the sultan Syria also harbored external foes: Frankish crusader and other western European interests with a presence in the Syrian coastal lands including the military orders (Templars, Hospitallers and Teutonic Knights, the strongest force in rural areas) and the Italian commercial cities, especially Genoa and Venice, whose strength lay in urban centers. Fortunately for the Mamlūks the crusader kingdoms had been weakened by the discord among these various factions which the Mamlūks, of course, sought to exploit. These parties were also at a disadvantage in that they lacked a ready and available supply of manpower. Though in comparison to the Mongols, the crusaders thus presented a minor threat in the short term, their occupation of Syrian soil could not be tolerated for strategic reasons in the long run, for not only might their ports and fortresses serve as bases for future crusading ventures, but experience had confirmed that they should be regarded as potential allies both of internal rivals and of the Mongols themselves. The thirteenth century had been punctuated by numerous efforts on the part of both the western powers and the Īlkhānids to coordinate their military campaigns against the Mamlūks and even to effect an alliance.

Nevertheless, both Baybars and Qalāwūn sought to secure their positions by signing accords with the crusader states. Providing no guarantee of security, the truces did help to buy time and a freer hand and were used to exploit Frankish factionalism. The Frankish parties, in any case, were in the weaker position, so that these agreements, skillfully used in concert with military action, eventually led to the demise of the crusader and Frankish presence in the Syrian littoral. Renewing an existing agreement, Baybars concluded a truce with the Hospitallers of Ḥiṣn al-Akrād (Crac des Chevaliers) in 1267 which was renewed by him in 1271 and by Qalāwūn in 1281. Negotiations which had begun as early as 1261 with Beirut eventually resulted in a truce concluded in 1269 which was renewed by Qalāwūn in 1285, by which Beirut became, in effect, a vassalage of the sultanate. In 1271, the same year that Baybars deprived Bohemond VI of Antioch and was preparing for the conquest of Tripoli itself, the sultan signed a truce with him regarding Tripoli, perhaps because news had reached the sultan of the arrival of King Edward I of England at the head of a crusading army and of the king's rumored collaboration with the Īlkhānids.[118] Qalāwūn renewed the agreement concluded by Baybars with Bohemond VII in 1281. In 1282 Qalāwūn also signed an accord with the Templars and in the following year came to an agreement with the authorities of Acre (now capital of the Latin Kingdom), Sidon and ʿAthlīth (Chateau Pélerin). While imposing bans on the construction of new fortifications and requiring notice of any impending Crusades, these agreements created a semblance of normal relations between the two parties with regard to frontier regions, fugitives, and commerce, and even, surprisingly, the joint administration of some areas where revenues and some responsibilities were shared. Despite the underlying hostilities, it was convenient and eventually advantageous to the sultanate to permit these condominia (*munāṣafāt*), for it allowed the Mamlūks to "whittle away Frankish authority in the border districts."[119]

Mamlūk diplomatic efforts were, however, only a temporary solution. Baybars, Qalāwūn and al-Ashraf Khalīl pursued their objectives militarily as well. Thus soon after his victory at ʿAyn Jālūt, Baybars launched a systematic series of campaigns aimed at reducing crusader strongholds along the Syrian littoral. By the end of his reign Baybars counted among his most important conquests the coastal towns of Caesarea, Haifa and Arsūf (1265), the strategically positioned, interior fortress of Safad (1266), and the Latin Kingdom possessions of Jaffa and Shaqīf Arnūn (Beaufort) (1268), all of which were crowned by the reconquest of Antioch, wrested from Bohemond VI in 1271. Bohemond was left only with Tripoli, whose vicinity Baybars also raided in the last years of his reign.

Obliged to devote the first years of his sultanate to deterring the Mongol threat and eliminating internal opposition, Qalāwūn undertook no major campaigns against the crusader kingdoms. Once he had achieved some stability on these fronts, however, he embarked on a much more aggressive policy toward the Frankish enclaves and nearly completed the task begun by Baybars. The Hospitaller fortress of Marqab (Margat) was recovered in 1285 and thereafter replaced Ḥiṣn al-Akrād as the Mamlūk base for further campaigns in the north, including Tripoli, which fell in 1289. By 1290, however, he felt strong enough to attack the final crusader enclave, Acre, capital of the Latin Kingdom. While encamped outside Cairo in preparation

118 Holt, *Age of the Crusades*, 96.
119 Holt, *Age of the Crusades*, 156–57.

for departure, however, Qalāwūn died. His son Khalīl inherited the task of reducing this last Frankish outpost on Syrian territory. Acre fell in 1291, ending, for all practical purposes, the crusader presence in Syria. Thus by 1291 not only had the Mamlūks stopped the Mongol advance, but they had also rid the region, with the exception of Cyprus, of the two-century-long Frankish presence.

Though the Battle of Ḥomṣ in 1281 would be the last major Mongol-Mamlūk encounter until the end of the century, Qalāwūn, like Baybars, remained on his guard throughout the rest of his reign, never certain that the enemy would not return. In the meantime the sultan received two embassies in Cairo from the Īlkhān, now Tegüder (1282–4), who having converted to Islam had taken the name Aḥmad. In the course of the first a letter was delivered to the sultan which, "far from being a call for friendship or alliance . . . [was] rather an ultimatum to Qalāwūn, urging him to show submission and obedience or risk war . . . in other words . . . to become an obedient vassal of the Ilkhans."[120] Now that he had converted to Islam, Tegüder suggested that there was no longer any reason for the sultan not to submit. Qalāwūn's answer was defiant: "You send us word that if strife is not to cease between us, that we had better choose a battlefield, and that God will give victory to whom He will. Here is our answer: Those of your troops who survived their last defeat are not anxious to revisit the former battlefield. They fear to go there again to renew their misfortunes . . . "[121] By the second embassy, Tegüder had dropped his demand. Although it was perhaps not apparent at the time, the Mongol advance had, in fact, come to a halt, for the possibility of world dominion was dwindling as their empire began to dissolve. Nevertheless, raiding activity, usually initiated by the Mongols, continued into the early fourteenth century. Only once were the Mongols victorious, in 1299 at the Battle of Wādī al-Khazindār near Homs, but by 1300 the Mongols had departed. The last Mongol incursion into Mamlūk territory in 1312–13 ended in a rout. Though hostilities were formally ended by a peace agreement, signed in 1322, the situation remained tense until 1328 when the agreement was confirmed. In the meantime the Mamlūks maintained a state of military preparedness.

The Mongols, however, posed far more than a military threat. The Mongol conquests had created a vast new trade zone, making the northerly overland route to the east an attractive alternative to the southerly sea route which linked eastern lands via the Indian Ocean, the Red Sea, and the Nile with the Mediterranean. For the next century the Mamlūks struggled to maintain trade over the southern route from which they stood to reap large benefits. Even more critical, however, was the threat posed to the slave

[120] Adel Allouche, "Teguder's Ultimatum to Qalāwūn," *IJMES*, 22 (1990), 438.
[121] Allouche, "Teguder's Ultimatum," 442.

trade, vital to the existence of the Mamlūk regime, which was conducted along routes passing through Mongol territory. Increasingly this concern became intertwined with the competition in the region for the east-west trade. Indeed, it is clear that commercial concerns underlay much of Mamlūk diplomatic and even military activity during the Baḥrī period.

Upon seizing power Baybars lost no time in securing access to the recruiting grounds in, and the trade routes which led to, the Kipchak steppes north and east of the Black Sea, now ruled by Berke, Mongol khān of the Golden Horde. Fortunately for the Mamlūks one important circumstance favoured this policy. A power struggle had broken out upon the death of the Great Khan, Möngkē, in 1259. Berke, who had sided with the losing candidate, now sought an alliance with Baybars against their common enemy the Mongol Īlkhānids of Iran. Good relations were also favoured by the fact that Berke had become a Muslim. Embassies were exchanged and favourable relations were established. Though Berke's successor, Möngkē Tëmur, was not a Muslim, mutual interests made it incumbent on him to renew the alliance with the sultanate. Qalāwūn dispatched envoys to Möngkē Tëmur in 1280, who on their return brought news of Möngkë Tëmur's death and the accession of Tödë Möngkē (1280–87), who like Berke converted to Islam, giving the sultan some hope for continued cordial relations.

Two major north-south trade routes linked the Kipchak recruiting grounds under Berke's control with the sultanate: a sea route which passed from the north through Byzantine territory – the Black Sea and the narrow straits to the Mediterranean; and a land route which crossed Anatolia through territory controlled by the Mongol protectorates of the Seljuk sultanate of Rūm and Cilician Armenia. While relations with the Golden Horde remained more or less cordial, relations with Byzantium and the Mongol protectorates of Cilician Armenia and Seljuk Rūm were more complicated. Byzantium, fearing a Mongol advance, was obliged to maintain friendly relations with both the Golden Horde and the Īlkhānids, and because of its shaky position with respect to the Īlkhānids was inclined to seek Mamlūk favour by allowing access to the trade routes. Thus not long after recapturing Constantinople in 1261 from the Latins, Michael VIII Palaeologus (1259–82), emperor of Nicaea, initiated diplomatic contacts with the sultanate. Baybars responded by sending two embassies which returned together in 1262. Incidentally, Baybars's embassy to the Golden Horde, which returned in 1264, had travelled via Constantinople. Because of Michael's need to placate the Īlkhānids, Mamlūk envoys were sometimes detained, especially when Īlkhānid envoys were present or expected in the capital. Qalāwūn, faced with Sunqur al-Ashqar's revolt and Īlkhānid aggression, as well as the growing power of Charles d'Anjou in the eastern Mediterranean early in his reign, was eager to maintain good relations with

Byzantium. Michael, who also viewed Charles d'Anjou as an enemy, saw Qalāwūn as a potential ally. Thus, the result of Qalāwūn's embassy to Michael of 1280 was an agreement reached in 1281, which in addition to clauses of political import contained others intended to secure the slave trade. According to the emperor's text, Michael would abstain from hostilities and guarantee the security of merchants and the free passage of the sultan's ambassadors as well as that of newly recruited mamlūks and slave girls. For his part Qalāwūn also agreed to abstain from hostilities, but did not accede to the emperor's condition that Christian slaves be excluded from the trade.[122]

Relations with Cilician Armenia and Seljuk Rūm, which straddled the overland route linking Mamlūk lands to the Golden Horde-controlled Kipchak steppes, necessitated both diplomatic activity and military action. Armenia had been the most faithful of allies to the Īlkhānids in their campaigns against the Mamlūks. Weakened by the Mamlūk victories at ʿAyn Jālūt and Homs, Cilician Armenia, occupying the southeastern corner of Anatolia, the site of several strategic frontier fortresses, was vulnerable. Seljuk Rūm to the north was also at risk, because of its internal disunity. Having previously led several expeditions against northern Syria, the Armenian King Heth'um sought to conclude a truce with Baybars following the Mamlūk conquest of Ṣafad in 1266. As part of the agreement, however, Baybars sought the surrender of several frontier fortresses, a demand with which the king could not comply out of fear of Mongol reprisal. Baybars was anxious to control these strongholds to secure the frontier and to control the route to central Anatolia.[123] Al-Manṣūr of Ḥamāh, Baybars's Ayyūbid vassal in Syria, led an expedition against Cilician Armenia in 1266 which left its capital Sīs in ruins and the king's son, the future Leo III, temporarily a prisoner. Just two years later Armenia's ally, Antioch, under Bohemond, succumbed to a Mamlūk siege. Subsequently, Mamlūk expeditions against Armenia became increasingly frequent, perhaps because the latter had been harassing Muslim caravans and travellers. Sīs was again punished in 1275. A joint Mamlūk–Turkoman expedition, not reported in the Mamlūk sources, attacked from the northeast in 1276.[124] In 1279 Baybars's son and heir sent an expedition to Armenia under the command of Baysarī and the future sultan Qalāwūn. As sultan, Qalāwūn during the first years of his reign put increasing pressure on the kingdom, partly in retribution for its assistance to the Īlkhānids, but also in an effort to secure the trade routes. He took possession of a number of fortresses and received the tribute formerly paid by the Ismāʿīlīs to the Armenians. Armenian

122 Holt, *Age of the Crusades*, 162.

123 Marius Canard, "Le Royaume d'Arménie-Cilicie et les mamelouks jusqu'au traité de 1285," *Revue des Etudes Arméniennes*, 4 (1967), 242–43.

124 Canard, "Royaume d'Arménie-Cilicie," 241–42.

possessions were attacked in 1283 and 1284, and by 1285 the Armenians were also in a much weaker position externally; their ally Antioch had been taken and Tripoli was under pressure. The Īlkhān Abagha's death in 1282 precluded any help from that quarter. Nor could Armenia expect help from the pope. Perhaps realizing that the Armenians no longer posed a significant military threat, Qalāwūn concluded an agreement with them which achieved many of the objectives of the previous expeditions – not only to punish the Armenians for their Mongol alliance, but also to secure the trade routes. At this moment Qalāwūn also began to pursue a more aggressive policy toward the Frankish strongholds so that the agreement was also perhaps convenient in this respect. The respite for the Armenians was brief, however, for Qalāwūn's son al-Ashraf Khalīl, with the crusades behind him, would make Armenia his next objective. In a letter to the Armenian ruler announcing the conquest of Acre, al-Ashraf Khalīl ominously intimated his intentions and in 1292 Qalʿat al-Rūm, the see of the Armenian patriarch, was besieged and taken. Only al-Ashraf Khalīl's assassination in 1293 saved Armenia from further devastation. Cilician Armenia would, nevertheless, eventually suffer the same fate as the crusader states; in 1375 it became a vassalage of the sultanate.

Baybars, exploiting factional feuding in Seljuk Rūm, was from at least 1272 in diplomatic contact with the *pervāne*, the real power in that state. Nevertheless, Baybars attacked Seljuk Rūm in 1277. Following his victory over a Mongol army at Elbistan, Baybars was actually installed as sultan, but withdrew, fearing Īlkhānid military intervention. Though the Īlkhānids subsequently established their control in the peninsula more firmly, it was temporary. By Qalāwūn's day Rūm seems to have posed a lesser threat.

Complicating this nexus of relations was the expansion of Genoese power in the Black Sea and the eastern Mediterranean during the last half of the thirteenth century, an expansion which was related to the growing competition in the eastern Mediterranean over east-west trade. Not long after the fall of Baghdād to the Mongols, the Genoese had, through an agreement with Michael VIII Palaeologus, established a colony in Kaffa on the Black Sea. As a result the Genoese gained commercial dominance over one of the most important long-distance routes in the eastern Mediterranean, the north–south route, at the expense of the Venetians (1204–61), who were ousted along with their Latin allies. This route connected Kaffa with the Armenian ports, especially Ayās (where notarial records indicate Genoese involvement in the slave trade),[125] with Cyprus and with the ports of the Syrian littoral, especially Acre (also involved in the slave trade), and ultimately with Egypt, where the Genoese were represented as well. Genoese attempts to extend their control to the southern portion of this route were

[125] Amitai-Preiss, *Mongols and Mamlūks*, 210.

bitterly contested by other Italian cities, notably Venice, and eventually also by Qalāwūn, who did his best to exploit Genoese-Venetian rivalry.[126] When, following the death of Bohemond VII in 1287, Tripoli was taken over by the Genoese Embriaco clan (to whom the sultan had previously given assistance) and then nearly incorporated into the Genoese republic, Venice, reacting to this major assertion of strength in the region, may have encouraged the sultan to intervene. No doubt he would have done so anyway. In any case, having concluded a truce with Venice in 1288 which granted Venetian merchants commercial privileges in Syria, Qalāwūn besieged Tripoli, which fell in 1289. Perhaps in retaliation, Benedetto Zaccaria, the Genoese diplomat and admiral, turned corsair and attacked a Muslim ship out of Alexandria. Disclaiming any responsibility for the act, the Genoese authorities sought to reestablish cordial relations with the sultanate. Qalāwūn, dependent on Genoa for the slave trade, had no choice and signed an accord in 1290.

The accession of Arghun (1284–91) to the Īlkhānid throne intensified concern for the trades routes. The thirteenth century had been punctuated by numerous attempts, on the part of both western Christian powers and the Īlkhānids, to coordinate their military campaigns against the Mamlūks if not to form an actual political and military alliance, none of which were realized. Arghun too sent embassies to the pope in 1284, 1287 and in 1289. Significantly, perhaps, the third of these embassies was headed by a Genoese merchant, Buscarello di Ghisolifi, who was also a member of Arghun's guard.[127] In fact, Arghun may have already come to the conclusion that what the Īlkhānids had not been able to accomplish on the battleground might be achieved on the economic field. He would simply undermine the Mamlūk regime through trade. As early as the 1270s Genoese merchants could be found in the Īlkhānid capital, Tabriz. But by the year 1290 the Genoese, with at least the tacit cooperation of the Īlkhānids, were preparing to extend their reach to the Indian Ocean with the aim of ending the Muslim monopoly over trade with the East. In 1290, 700 western Christians spent the winter in Baghdad building the ships that would be launched in Baṣra.[128] The Genoese-Īlkhānid alliance was acquiring a stranglehold over the Mamlūk trade lifelines, with the potential not only to cut the route to the north but also to harrass merchants in the eastern oceans from which western merchants had previously been excluded. In fact, by the late thirteenth and early fourteenth centuries several proposals for imposing a trade embargo against the Mamlūks and thereby cutting their lifeline had been put forward. Among the most detailed were those outlined by the

126 Jonathan Riley-Smith, *The Crusades: A Short History* (New Haven, London, 1987), 201–03.

127 P. Jackson, "Argūn," *Encyclopaedia Iranica*, II (1987), 403.

128 Eliyahu Ashtor, *The Levant Trade in the Later Middle Ages* (Princeton, 1983), 12.

Venetian Marino Sanudo in his *Secreta Fidelium Crucis*,[129] and by the Dominican friar Guillaume Adam in his *De modo Sarracenos extirpandi*.[130] These plans, probably unrealizable in any case, came to nothing when the Īlkhānid ruler Abū Saʿīd signed a peace treaty with the sultan al-Nāṣir Muḥammad in 1322.

As a consequence of the fall of Baghdād to the Mongols in 1258 and the transfer of the caliphate to Cairo, the sultan in Cairo had inherited Baghdād's political and religious role in the region as protector of the two holy cities in Arabia – Mecca and Medina, on the eastern shore of the Red Sea – a responsibility which every sultan took seriously since it served to bolster claims to legitimacy. Thus the sultan sought to demonstrate his interest in the holy cities symbolically through titulary, by sending each year with much pomp and ceremony the *kiswa*, or covering for the Kaʿba, by the construction and repair of monuments, and by making the pilgrimage when possible. The routes also carried pilgrim traffic to the holy sites. Though obliged to secure the safe passage of pilgrims, the sultan also benefited from the important revenues collected from them. The protection of these interests thus involved not only diplomacy but occasionally merited limited military intervention in quarrels between the rulers of the Ḥijāz.

No less important an aspect of the sultanate's interest in the region, however, was Egypt's location at the crossroads of the trade and communications routes with the east, which, extending from China and southeast Asia, hugged the coast of India, branched south along the Arabian coast, turned north through the Red Sea, connecting, via the ports of Aden in southern Arabia, then Dahlak and Suakin on the Nubian shore and Aydhāb in Upper Egypt, with the overland caravan route to Qūṣ on the Nile from where goods were transported by the river to Cairo and beyond. The enormous revenues that accrued to the sultanate from the lucrative trade, especially in spices, ensured that the Red Sea basin and eastern oceans would be a vital sphere of interest to the sultanate. Although it may not have been immediately apparent, this route would suffer from the competing and more attractive northern route now in the hands of the Genoese-Īlkhānid alliance for a century following the Mongol conquest. But there was an additional concern. Not only were the Īlkhānids allowing the Genoese access to the eastern oceans, but they themselves were also involved in the area. Historically Persia had had interests in the Gulf region and along the eastern coast of Arabia. During this period, however, in 1315–16, if not earlier, the Īlkhānids became involved in local rivalries in Mecca and sought to use them, just as the Mamlūks did, to exert influence. Though an effort to conquer the Ḥījāz by the sharīf of Mecca with a force furnished by the

[129] Riley-Smith, *Atlas*, 122–23, for a discussion and map of Sanudo's proposed plan.
[130] David Morgan, *The Mongols* (Oxford, 1986), 186–87.

Īlkhān Khudābanda (Öljeitü) failed, the sharīf did capture Mecca with Mongol assistance two years later, whereupon the name of the Īlkhān Abū Saʿīd (1316–35) was mentioned in the *khuṭba*.[131] Underlying religious and political interests in the region, therefore, was the imperative to protect the sultanate's commercial interests in the lands of the Red Sea basin (Arabia, the Yemen, Upper Egypt and Nubia, Ethiopia) and the Indian Ocean (e.g., Ceylon, Sind, Hind, China). Mamlūk diplomatic and military activities in these lands must be viewed, therefore, at least partially in the light of these concerns.

Upper Egypt and Nubia were on a route which linked Egypt to sources of gold and slaves. Qūṣ was both a military garrison and as a port an important link in the eastern trade. Disturbances which threatened the trade routes were firmly dealt with. Baybars and Qalāwūn were occasionally forced to send embassies or even military forces to end tribal harassment of merchants in the eastern deserts of Egypt and in the region of the major ports of Nubia.[132] These sultans also took advantage of invitations of pretenders to the throne of the Christian Nubian kingdom of al-Maqurra to intervene on their behalf in the frequent disputes over succession, thereby to extend their influence in the region. Diplomacy was often backed up with military force, which, perhaps, rather than territorial acquisition, aimed at ensuring the payment of the *baqt*, the tribute of slaves and gold imposed since early Islamic times,[133] at securing the southern frontier region, and at ensuring the safe passage of merchants and pilgrims. Al-Nāṣir Muḥammad succeeded in 1311–12 in having a Muslim candidate installed on the Nubian throne who actually established Islam as the state religion, but his reign was brief. Mamlūk efforts to assert control, if not sovereignty, in the region, which continued at least until the reign of al-Ashraf Shaʿbān (1363–77), resulted in no permanent control, and by the end of the period the Nubian kingdom had crumbled.

Diplomatic relations with Ethiopia during the reigns of Baybars and Qalāwūn ostensibly concerned the appointment of new bishops to the Ethiopian Church, which was affiliated with the Patriarchate of Alexandria. But these relations were not devoid of commercial importance. Worthy of note is, first, that diplomatic contacts with Ethiopia were carried on not by an overland route through Nubia but through ports on the Red Sea coast,[134] and second, that there was a resident population of Muslim merchants in Ethiopia. The fact that westerners such as Marino Sanudo knew about

[131] Donald P. Little, "The History of Arabia during the Baḥrī Mamlūk Period According to Three Mamlūk Historians," in *Studies in the History of Arabia*. I. *Sources for the History of Arabia*, Part 2 (Riyadh, 1979), 20–21.

[132] Garcin, *Qūṣ*, 211–18; Northrup, *Slave to Sultan*, 141–45.

[133] Holt, *Age of the Crusades* , 131.

[134] Garcin, *Qūṣ*, 220.

Ethiopia and its role in the spice trade with India also indicates the commercial importance of Ethiopia.[135] Both Baybars and Qalāwūn were approached by the negus of Abyssinia to approve the nomination and dispatch of a patriarch. Though we do not know the results of the requests, the two parties had a mutual interest in cooperation, for the safety of the resident merchants might be assured in exchange for compliance with the Ethiopian requests.

While there is no explicit statement in the sources linking increased activity in the Red Sea region and the east during the last decades of the thirteenth century with the appearance of Genoese-Īlkhānid cooperation, it seems quite likely that their grip on the north-south route, coupled with the Genoese push eastward, affected Mamlūk diplomatic and commercial policy in the region in two ways, with regard to the recruitment of mamlūks and to the increasing commercial competition between east and west. While Qalāwūn's deliberate efforts to recruit mamlūks from diverse, non-Kipchak, sources have been attributed to his desire to balance the power of his mainly Kipchak mamlūk forces with other ethnic groups, it also seems probable that the possiblity of a Genoese-Īlkhān'id blockade on trade with the Golden Horde was a second powerful incentive. Thus, Qalāwūn not only recruited mamlūks of Circassian origin from whom he created the Burjī regiment, but he actually advertised for mamlūks and slave girls (*jawārī*) in his famous epistle (*mithāl*) of 1288 addressed to the rulers of Sind, Hind, China and the Yemen, offering trade incentives and proclaiming the virtues of Egypt to merchants who responded.[136]

The foreign and commercial affairs of the Baḥrī sultanate during the fourteenth century, even during the latter half of it, contrast sharply with those in the second half of the thirteenth. During the third reign of al-Nāṣir Muḥammad Egypt attained its greatest stability and prosperity. The conclusion of peace with the Īlkhānids, and their demise upon the death of the khān Abū Saʿīd in 1335, left Egypt the unchallenged power in the region. No military threat of the magnitude of the Mongols or even the crusaders presented itself. Egypt had also survived the economic effects of the Mongol conquests elsewhere and successfully managed its commercial relations. In this regard it is of interest to note that al-Nāṣir Muḥammad took as a bride the daughter of the khān of the Golden Horde. The only clouds on the horizon were the continuing trade war between east and west and the disturbances along the frontier and in Syria caused by the rise of a number of Turkoman principalities in Anatolia.

It is of some interest that peace between the Mongols and the Mamlūks

[135] Taddesse Tamrat, *Church and State in Ethiopia, 1250–1527* (Oxford, 1972), 43–44, 76–85; Garcin, *Qūṣ*, 222–25.
[136] Northrup, *Slave to Sultan*, 147.

was negotiated with the help of one of the sultan's slave merchants, Majd al-Dīn al-Sallāmī. The treaty concluded in 1322 ended the military and commercial threat posed by the Īlkhānids. The potential for an Īlkhānid military and political alliance with the west had never been realized. None of the proposals to cut Mamlūk trade had ever been implemented. During the fourteenth century economics, rather than religion or politics, dictated that trade continue despite papal restrictions and, indeed, despite the prohibitions placed on trade with the Mamlūks by the commercial republics themselves. The struggle for commercial advantage, however, went on even without Īlkhānid assistance to the Genoese. Lacking a navy or merchant marine of its own, the Mamlūk sultanate was dependent on the Kārimī merchants who monopolized the commerce of the sultanate, especially the spice trade, in the Red Sea and the eastern oceans. In the Mediterranean, however, western commercial powers, among which Genoa, Venice and Aragon still figured most prominently, were supreme. The brawl which broke out in Alexandria in 1327 between Muslims and foreign (Christian) merchants may have been fueled by foreign Christian–Muslim (Kārimī) rivalry over trade as much as by religious sentiments. In this case it seems that the Mamlūk regime punished the Kārimīs, perhaps in an effort to diminish their monopoly, and favored the Europeans, from whom it obtained commodities of military importance such as timber and iron.[137] The competition may have been sharpened by the fact that Egypt from about the mid-fourteenth century seems to have regained the Red Sea spice trade carried on as a result of the disruption to the northern routes engendered by Īlkhānid territorial dismemberment.

During the second half of the fourteenth century the struggle continued in the eastern Mediterranean as Egypt fought with Cyprus over Cilician Armenia. Since the fall of Acre in 1291 Armenian ports, in particular Ayās, had become the main outlet in the Mediterranean for trade between the Christian west and the east, and to a certain extent it must have been in competition with Alexandria. The Armenian ports were closely linked with Cyprus. In 1322 the Mamlūks attacked Ayās and received tribute from it. The temporary occupation of the Armenian capital Sīs in 1337 was followed in 1355 by that of the ports of Ṭarsūs, Adhāna, and Maṣṣīṣa on the southern coast of Anatolia. Through these ports flowed commodities of military importance such as wood, iron and of course slaves, but also luxury items such as silk and spices.[138] Mamlūk attempts to extend control over south-eastern Anatolia, coupled with Venetian efforts to establish direct trading relations with the Mamlūk regime in Egypt and along the Syrian coast, left Cyprus, with which the Venetians had previously dealt, at a commercial

[137] Ashtor, *Levant Trade*, 52–54.
[138] Irwin, *Middle East*, 145.

disadvantage. Thus it seems clear that the Cypriot attack led by King Peter I of Lusignan, which rocked Alexandria in 1365, though styled a crusade, was, in fact, fueled by commercial rather than religious interests.[139] Though the Cypriot "Crusade" would have a long-term economic and psychological impact on Egypt, it could not compare with the challenges of the previous century. The Mamlūks, in any case, prevailed; Sīs was conquered during the reign of al-Ashraf Shaʿbān (1363–77), followed by Cyprus during the reign of the Circassian sultan Barsbāy in the early fifteenth century.

Mamlūk efforts to assert control over Anatolia, which were without doubt commercially motivated, led to increasing involvement with various Turkoman groups in the region who now emerged in the wake of Īlkhānid decline. Al-Nāṣir Muḥammad acted decisively against his viceroy in Syria, Tankiz al-Ḥusāmi, when he suspected him of plotting an alliance with the Dhu'l-Qadrids, a Turkoman regime which had risen in the 1330s with Tankiz's help, an alliance which, if allowed to flourish, would have posed a potential danger to the sultanate. The attractiveness of such an alliance to mamlūk would-be rulers was demonstrated once again when in 1352 the renegade governor of Aleppo joined forces with the Dhu'l-Qadrid chief to march on Damascus. The rebels were eventually captured and executed in 1354 with the help of Maḥmūd ibn Eretna, whose father, another Anatolian adventurer, had carved out a principality for himself which included several centers on the slave trade route to the north.[140] The Turkoman principalities of Anatolia continued to cause disturbances along the frontier until the end of Baḥrī rule and beyond. Nevertheless, this period might be considered the calm before the storm, for neither Timūr-Lenk (Tamerlane) nor the Ottomans had yet cast their shadow over the sultanate.

The ascent of the Circassian dynasty

The formative period of Baḥrī rule had coincided with a time of crisis in Egypt and in the region. The institutions and patterns of rule which evolved then were characterized by moral rigor and military discipline. In contrast, the fourteenth century, as a consequence of the Mamlūk-Mongol peace treaty of 1322 and the dissolution of the Īlkhānid regime soon after, brought relative peace and prosperity to the land. Mamlūk resources could now be directed to other than military ends. Paradoxically, although the idea of a Qalāwūnid succession was now accepted, perhaps even, desired by the populace, al-Nāṣir Muḥammad, not himself of slave origin, seems to have been plagued by insecurity with respect to the mamlūk elite. Simultaneously, another aspect of sultani authority, the role of warrior, had evaporated as

139 Irwin, *Middle East*, 145. Cf. Holt, *Age of the Crusades*, 125.
140 Irwin, *Middle East*, 140.

the more peaceful conditions of the century made themselves apparent. These seem to be among the factors which prompted al-Nāṣir to assert autocratic control over the mamlūk elite. In addition to emphasizing his Kipchak ties and purchasing more mamlūks than any of his predecessors, he also sought to buy the support of his own young mamlūks and others with gifts, rapid promotion and marriage alliances, even with his own mamlūks, in contrast to earlier, more spartan, policies. Al-Nāṣir's successful effort to redistribute economic resources to his own advantage and that of the mamlūk elite by the *rawk* of 1315–16 seriously damaged the military caliber of the *ḥalqa* corps which had hitherto constituted an important element of the Mamlūk army, and which, it might be added, had provided a means for the regime to gain the support of important non-Mamlūk groups such as the *awlād al-nās* and *wāfidiyya* for its aims by incorporating them within the mamlūk military structure. These reforms, however, brought about a revolution in mamlūk "ethics" which ultimately resulted in a partial demamlūkization and demilitarization of the mamlūk structure, undermined the bases of Baḥrī rule and made the rise of Barqūq possible.

The negative impact of these reforms, however, was exacerbated by several other factors, namely, factional politics and its interplay with the succession in the post-Nāṣirid period, the arrival of the bubonic plague in Egypt in 1347–48 and subsequent occurrences of pneumonic plague thereafter, the attack on Alexandria in 1365 by the Cypriot crusader forces of Peter I of Lusignan, titular ruler of the Latin Kingdom of Jerusalem, and the worsening economic situation, a consequence in particular of a trade imbalance which Egypt was suffering during the latter half of the century. Following al-Nāṣir's death in 1341 he was succeeded in rapid succession by no fewers than eight sons, two grandsons and two great-grandsons, most of whom, as minors, ruled nominally. Effective power was in the hands of the amīrs of the dominant factions, although the Qalāwūnid sultans still controlled a large share of the wealth of Egypt in allodial lands and *iqṭā*ʿs. The factional feuding of this period no doubt created instability, although one may find a certain logic in these struggles, imbedded as they were in factional interests. Of the post Nāṣirid sultans only al-Nāṣir Ḥasan (1347–51) had a significant impact on events. Although non-Mamlūk elements had, at least since al-Nāṣir's reign, penetrated the mamlūk elite structure, al-Nāṣir Ḥasan actively encouraged this trend, raising *awlād al-nās*, eunuchs and even women to high status, thus further undermining the basis of Baḥrī rule. Perhaps he prepared the way for a mamlūk backlash, which eventually came in the form of Barqūq.

Even more serious was the arrival of the bubonic plague in 1347 at a time when the country was also experiencing famine. Egypt never recovered, for subsequently the country suffered an estimated fifty-five outbreaks of infectious pneumonic plague with even higher mortality levels than those experienced in 1347–8. The civilian population was affected more seriously than the mamlūk elite by the bubonic plague, but the pneumonic plague spared no one. The mamlūk military structure was thus further weakened by the decimation of the mamlūk ranks, and in addition, by the effect of the plague also on agricultural productivity, the main source of revenues for the regime and for the organization of the army. Those most affected were, as Udovitch notes, the mamlūk class and the beneficiaries of rural *waqf*s. Consequently, the Mamlūk regime was forced to make up for losses in agricultural revenues by preying on the profits of the urban market place, which prospered in these conditions. Simultaneously, however, the chronic shortage of specie, which by 1359 had become "fairly acute," compounded by a lack of exports and a consequent imbalance in trade, contributed to a worsening economic situation.[141] Thus despite the relative tranquility of the fourteenth century and the illusion of prosperity, not all was well.

It is against this background that the rise of Barqūq and the Circassian dynasty must be seen. Nevertheless, it was the reforms of al-Nāṣir Muḥammad, which had led to demamlūkization and the possibility of the rapid ascent of junior mamlūks to the highest ranks, which ultimately made the rise of Barqūq possible. Yalbughā al-ʿUmarī, a mamlūk of the sultan al-Nāṣir Ḥasan, having become leader of a faction which resented the favour shown by his master to non-mamlūk groups, killed al-Nāṣir Ḥasan in 1361. As regent for the young sultan Ḥājji (1381–82, 1389–90), whom he deposed, and then of the ten-year-old al-Ashraf Shaʿbān, Yalbughā undertook the remamlūkization of the Mamlūk state and military. In 1366 al-Ashraf Shaʿban threw his support behind a rival mamlūk faction, but Yalbughā was killed in the fighting which ensued. Al-Ashraf Shaʿban ruled in his own right until 1377 when, as he travelled to Mecca to make the pilgrimage, he was captured and later killed by a group of rebellious mamlūks.

Barqūq was not a royal mamlūk as Kitbughā, Lājīn and Baybars al-Jāshnikīr had been. Rather he was the mamlūk of the amīr Yalbughā. Of Circassian origin, Barqūq had been recruited in about 1363–64 and had participated in the overthrow of al-Ashraf Shaʿbān. Thereafter, his rise to power was meteoric. By 1378 he had attained the post of *atābak al-ʿasākir*, which now, in contrast to the earlier period, meant simply "senior amīr." Initially he exercised power with a colleague, but by 1380 had ousted him. Then with the support of Yalbughā's *khushdāshiyya*, Barqūq seized power in 1382. The *cursus honorum* of the thirteenth century was extinct. Barqūq had reached the pinnacle of power in just a little less than twenty years.

141 In Robert Lopez, Harry Miskimin, and Abraham Udovitch, "England to Egypt, 1350–1500: Long-term Trends and Long-distance Trade," in M. A. Cook (ed.), *Studies in the Economic History of the Middle East from the Rise of Islam to the Present Day* (London, 1970), 123–24.

Immediately, he was faced with rebellions in Syria reminiscent of those faced by Baybars I and Qalāwūn. But rather than staying the course as had his predecessors, Barqūq was forced to flee for the time being. Ḥājjī, now with the regnal title al-Muẓaffar, was restored to the throne. In the meantime, however, Barqūq, in exile at Karak, gathered support and seized power once again in 1390, thus establishing the Burjī or Circassian regime.

11

The regime of the Circassian Mamlūks

JEAN-CLAUDE GARCIN

The regime of the Circassian Mamlūks, or the "state of the Circassians" as contemporaries called it to distinguish it from the state of the Turks, formed a bridge between Egypt's most brilliant medieval period and the beginning of the sixteenth century which we, in Europe, see as the beginning of modern times. The use of the ethnic criterion to designate this period shows that the change in the origin of the dominant class had been felt to be a major factor that had to be taken into account in explaining the political evolution. It might also be thought that this change did not explain every aspect of an ongoing process, some results of which were maintained under the Ottoman administration.

The general development

First we shall consider the major phases of this lengthy period (1382–1517), summarizing only briefly the military confrontations and international relations which, while not the subject of this chapter, cannot be overlooked when interpreting internal political changes. Four major phases of varying length are apparent.

This first period saw the restoration of the Mamlūk state under the amīr al-Malik al-Ẓāhir Barqūq (1382–1389). Barqūq, who contrived to impose his exclusive authority from 1378, under the sultanate of the two sons of al-Malik al-Ashraf Shaʿbān (al-Malik al-Manṣūr ʿAlī and then al-Malik al-Ṣāliḥ Ḥajjī, whose *atābak* he was and whose mother he had married) acceded to the sultanate as Qalāwūn had done in former times. Save for a break when he would have to accept the return to the throne of his ousted ward (in 1389–90), he would wield power until his death in 1399. The tradition of the classic Mamlūk regime was restored. The institutions had not changed. The sole innovation possibly attributable to Barqūq, while he was still only *atābak*, was the division of Egypt into three *niyābat al-salṭanat* as in Syria, the better to control the countryside where order was still being threatened by the growing strength of the Bedouin;[1] Berbers from the Delta, the Hawwāra, were moved into Upper Egypt to keep the Arabs in check, and the sultan's authority was reaffirmed.

Barqūq was Circassian and he had promptly purchased mamlūks of that race. From 1383, non-Circassian elements (Kurds and Turks) had been attempting unsuccessfully to overthrow him, with the support of Caliph al-Mutawakkil, who was quickly arrested and replaced in the caliphate. The opposition resumed shortly afterwards, led by Yalbughā al-Nāṣirī, a former mamlūk of al-Malik al-Nāṣir Ḥasan; like Barqūq, he had become a mamlūk of Yalbughā al-ʿUmarī. Senior to Barqūq, and as such feared and clumsily ousted, he was joined by Minṭāsh, a former mamlūk of al-Malik al-Ashraf Shaʿbān, governor of Syria, very hostile to the Circassians. Barqūq was besieged in the Citadel and had to abdicate and serve a term in prison in Syria before returning to eliminate his two rivals. After this episode, which amazed his contemporaries, the sultan's power was not threatened again. His financial resources had increased since the special office (*dīwān al-mufrad*), set up to manage the *iqṭāʿāt* of his son, Muḥammad, had transformed its function, after the prince's death, to enhance the revenues of the private office (*dīwān al-Khāṣṣ*). The sultanate was increasingly well financed.

Externally, the position of the Mamlūk state was beginning to be challenged. In Anatolia in 1387, a Mamlūk army had obliged Sīwās to recognize Egyptian suzerainty. The attitude of the newcomers to the region, the Ak Qoyunlū and Kara Qoyunlū, was closely watched, especially at the approach of Timūr-Lenk; in 1394, Barqūq had confronted him on the Euphrates but Timūr-Lenk had withdrawn. More ominous was the advance of the Ottomans; the Karamānids had been absorbed, an Ottoman protégé had been placed at the head of the Dhu'l-Qadirids and immediately following the sultan's death in 1399, Ottoman troops had penetrated Mamlūk territory in the southeast. The solidity of Mamlūk power was to be put to the test.

In this critical situation, the establishment on the throne of al-Malik al-Nāṣir Faraj, Barqūq's eleven-year-old son, should have led very quickly to his eviction in favour of one of his father's mamlūks. But it was not until 1412 that, from their base in Syria, the rebel amīrs, Tanam, Jakam and then Nawrūz and Shaykh, managed to defeat the young sultan who had defended his power with all the ardour (he led no fewer than seven expeditions against the Syrian amīrs) but also the cruelty, that a struggle of this nature gave rise to. Even then, in order to overthrow him, the amīrs had to acclaim Caliph al-Mustaʿīn as sultan; his indisputable legitimacy cost the sultan, then in

[1] Al-Maqrizi, *Kitāb al-sulūk li-maʿrifat duwal al-mulūk*, ed. Muḥammad Muṣṭafā Saʿīd ʿAbd al-Fattāḥ ʿĀshūr, 4 vols. (Cairo, 1956–72), III, 340, 394.

Damascus, the backing of non-Circassian elements and of the population of the town who supported him. The prolonged nature of this crisis may be explained initially by the dramatic circumstances then affecting the Mamlūk state.

In 1399 Timūr-Lenk had resumed his march westward and taken Aleppo, allowing it to be pillaged. The sultan's entourage, intent on assuring their political fortunes, chose to take the prince back to Cairo, abandoning Damascus to the ravages of Timūr-Lenk. In 1402 the Mongol then withdrew to Ankara so as to break the power of the Ottomans, who posed a strategic threat to him. So, paradoxically, it was the Ottomans who saved Egypt from invasion. But in 1403, a low Nile flood caused famine in the country, followed by plague in 1405. The epidemic, which was more lastingly damaging to Egypt than the outbreak of 1347–8, exacerbated the problem of the amīrs' feuding. The Bedouin, profiting from the fact that the army was entirely taken up with internal conflicts and paralyzed by the external threat, rose in revolt. It seems that from 1401 to 1413 the Mamlūk provincial authorities had been swept right out of Upper Egypt; we know the name of no governor in this period and the taxes that should have supplied the revenues of sultans and amīrs could not be collected.[2] Barqūq's domestic achievements were thus reduced to nothing. On the frontiers, the Ak Qoyunlū who had supported Timūr-Lenk were installed at Diyār Bakr; the Kara Qoyunlū had formed a Mesopotamian domain perilously close by; the only positive point was in Anatolia where there was a long-term reduction in the Ottomans' power, but the Mamlūks had no part in that. Throughout their domains their prestige was tarnished. The only gold coinage still in circulation was that of Venice. The capital, Cairo, was in grievous straits.

It was in the aftermath of this crisis that the main features characteristic of the Circassian state gradually manifested themselves. The situation had first to be restored. After ten years, the regime had regained stability and credibility, and the Mamlūk sultanate had once more become a great and respected power. By common consent, it reached its apogee in the sultanate of Qāytbāy during the first part of his regime, before the hardships of the new conflict with the Ottomans once again compromised the stability of the sultanate. So several stages must be identified in the history of this second Mamlūk age.

The sultanate of Caliph al-Mustaʿīn lasted only six months, time enough for one of the amīrs, Shaykh, to establish himself in power in Cairo before finishing off his former ally, Nawrūz, who had thought to remain master of the situation by taking over the government of the Syrian provinces. One of the tasks of the new sovereign, al-Malik al-Mu'ayyad Shaykh, was to restore

[2] J.-C. Garcin, *Un centre musulman de la Haute Égypte médiévale: Qūṣ* (Cairo, 1976), 465–68.

the authority of the sultanate in a country where the structures for the maintenance of order had disappeared in some regions and where plague again struck in 1415–17 and 1420. It is not clear when a regional financial administration was restored throughout the realm. In order to replenish the royal Treasury, the *ustādār* in charge of the private office (*dīwān al-mufrad*) was made responsible for sweeping fiscal expeditions into the provinces, where taxes were collected by force, a process that resembled outright plunder, under the guise of recouping unpaid taxes.

On the Anatolian border, a reorganized Mamlūk force again intervened from 1417; the sultan led another and the Mamlūk state regained its former role; the temporary removal of the Ottomans had made the task easy for the Mamlūks. It was a sign of renewed Mamlūk authority but there was little indication of new tactics. Shaykh appeared rather a restorer of the old order, even endeavouring to balance the influence of the Circassians in the army by starting to recruit Turks again. Before he died, it was to a Turkish *atābak* that he entrusted the guardianship of his infant son Aḥmad, who was proclaimed sultan despite being aged only twenty months.

Barqūq's Circassian mamlūks did not appreciate this loss of influence. A Circassian amīr, Ṭaṭar, then an officer of the audience (*amīr majlis*), removed the *atābak* and after first affirming the real position of that office by marrying the widow of the late sovereign, was proclaimed sultan. But when he died three months later, it was another of Barqūq's former Circassian mamlūks, the dawādār Barsbāy, who took over the guardianship of Ṭaṭar's young son and subsequently the sultanate (1422–38). So appeared one of the striking features of the new system: it was mamlūks of the most senior age groups who acceded to the sultanate. After Barsbāy, the sultans Jaqmaq (1438–53) and Aynāl (1453–61) had been Barqūq's mamlūks. It was only subsequently that one of Shaykh's mamlūks, Khushqadam, came to power (1461–67), and then one of Jaqmaq's mamlūks, Timurbughā (1467–68). Belonging to senior age groups, they came to power later and later in life: if Ṭaṭar was probably no more than fifty at the start of his sultanate, and Barsbāy no more than forty-five, both Jaqmaq and Aynāl were over seventy at their accession. The sultanate was acquiring the appearance of a military magistrature, no longer threatened by the ambition of the amīrs.

Credit for consolidating the new system falls to Barsbāy. Contemporaries reproached him for his "greed" and some modern historians have adopted this view.[3] It seems, however, that his policies showed a great coherence which cannot be reduced to a single trait of character. Because of the epidemics that returned lethally every six to eight years, there was a drop in

3 A. Darrag, *L'Égypte sous le règne de Barsbay, 825–841/1422–1438* (Damascus, 1961), 436–39.

the total resources that realistically could be expected from the agrarian lands of Egypt. On the other hand, Timūr-Lenk's wars and those of the Turcomans in Mesopotamia and Iraq had made the Red Sea the safest route for the shipment of spices. Barsbāy had the idea of ensuring the exclusive rights of this transit route to Egypt, and to the sultanate the exclusive rights of trade with the Europeans. These, it seems, were the considerations dictating the policy followed in the years 1425–27. To make sure that it would not be the princes of the Yemen who reaped the benefits of this situation, merchants were encouraged to discharge their merchandise at Jedda (where a major customs was set up) rather than at Aden. In Egypt itself, the sultanate's monopoly over the sale of spices was established, a decision that had manifold consequences. It obviously struck a blow at Muslim free trade, in particular that of the spice merchants (*Kārimīs*), and Barsbāy was accused of having played into the hands of the European traders. The caravan trails of the Ḥijāz had to be more assiduously protected against the activities of Bedouin brigands. In the Mediterranean it was necessary to take stronger measures against Catalan and Genoese pirates who descended on the Egyptian coast, and the two campaigns against Cyprus (in 1425 and 1426, in which the king was taken prisoner), on the grounds that it assisted the pirates, must, it seems, be seen in the context of this policy of the sultan. Jaqmaq attempted to pursue the same policy, with less success, against Rhodes between 1440 and 1444. The ransom paid by the Cypriot king had allowed Barsbāy to strike a new gold coinage, whereas from the beginning of the century the ducat had been supplanting the *dīnār* even in Egypt. So the sultan possessed all the resources necessary for consolidating his authority.

Internally, inspectors (*kāshif*, *kushshāf*) were set up over the local governors in order to control the Bedouin more effectively.[4] However, the advantages won by the tribes had to be acknowledged; thus in Upper Egypt it had to be accepted that the Hawwāra amīrs, established by Barqūq, had become a local power, rich from their lands and their trade with central Africa and, in the eyes of some people, good, respectable and educated Muslims. Along the borders, affirmation of Mamlūk greatness had to continue. Even though Ottoman power, restored after 1413, was applied more prudently than in the past, the principalities of Anatolia had to be made to accept that acknowledgment of Mamlūk hegemony constituted a balancing factor. In Iraq, the Ak Qoyunlū, locked in conflict with their rivals, showed little respect for Mamlūk territory. In 1429, the Mamlūk troops sacked Edessa in response to one of their raids; the atrocities committed by the army against civilian Muslim populations scandalized their contemporaries and were of little value as an example. An expedition

[4] Garcin, *Un centre musulman*, 477 et seq.

in 1433, led by Barsbāy in person, against the capital of the Ak Qoyunlū, Amid, failed to take it but ended well with formal recognition of Mamlūk hegemony, though it left the impression that the army had not regained its former efficiency. On the other hand, and this too is one of the features of this period, recruits presented successive sultans, Barsbāy from 1428, Jaqmaq from 1442, Aynāl from 1454 and Khushqadam from 1463, with serious problems of indiscipline in the capital itself. The recurrence of these disturbances, of a kind previously unknown and affecting a fundamental element of the regime, amounted to an indication of fragility that could not be ignored.

The long sultanate of Qāytbāy (1468–1496) is traditionally held to mark the happy culmination of the Circassian regime. On the death of Khushqadam in 1467, two *atābaks*, Yalbāy and Timurbughā, were successively proclaimed sultan; they failed in the difficult task of controlling the pressure groups in the army and it was Qāytbāy, Barsbāy's former mamlūk and now an *atābak* himself, who was raised to the sultanate after the enforced, but agreed and understandable withdrawal of his predecessor. Thanks to his political astuteness, he managed to get control of the situation, keeping a balance between the groups and their representatives, the amīr Azbak on the one hand, who was the new *atābak* and another former mamlūk of Barsbāy's and on the other, the dawādār Yashbak min Maḥdī, a relative of the sultan and former mamlūk of Jaqmaq. Generally a first period of this reign is identified, lasting till 1481. The sultan appeared to have complete confidence in the stability of his position; he would leave the capital for long tours of inspection in Alexandria, the Fayyūm or Syria (four months in 1478). The Bedouin tribes seemed under firmer control. In Upper Egypt, as from 1466, general tribal unrest had seemed to be on the point of disrupting the country; the amīr Yashbak was given a mission of inspection (*kashf*) over the whole of the south and the authority of the sultan was reestablished, at times with great brutality. In 1477 even the Hawwāra amirate was virtually suppressed; this amounted to imposing the law of the Mamlūk state without seeking the support of one tribal group against another. Not since the beginning of the century had a sultan achieved such results. Egypt seemed prosperous once more. In the capital, the sultan invested in buildings, an example followed by Yashbak and Azbak. Cairo had become a beautiful city again.

Yet the problem of the recruits' turbulence had still not been solved, though it did not resurface until 1473. At that date the sultan had already been faced with a resumption of Ottoman pressure. The Karamānid principality, traditionally a vassal of the sultan, was occupied, and a hostile Dhu'l-Qadirid prince, Shāh Sūwār, encouraged by the Ottomans, had been defeated only after several military setbacks to the north of Aleppo in 1468 and 1469. The Mamlūk state had been momentarily relieved of the Ottoman danger by the intervention of the Ak Qoyunlū chieftain Uzun Ḥasan, but support for him was ruled out because of his alliance with the Europeans, and when he was conquered by the Ottomans in 1473 and his empire broke up, the annexation of the Karamānids by the Ottomans became irreversible and a new pro-Ottoman Dhu'l-Qadirid prince was installed in 1479. Conflict with the Ottomans appeared unavoidable. It was probably hastened by a blunder by Qāytbāy; he had thought he could welcome and temporarily shelter in Cairo an Ottoman crown prince removed from power after the death of Mehmet II in 1481. The Ottomans had at first merely stepped up support for their Dhu'l-Qadirid protégé but then joined in the fight themselves from 1483. To face up to what had become a direct confrontation, successive armies had to be equipped and sent to the front in 1484, 1485–86, 1488, 1489 and 1490. The Mamlūks had the last word; they were able to penetrate as far as Kayseri and the peace was signed in 1491, helped by a change of heart on the part of the Dhu'l-Qadirid, now aware that he was in danger of being the next prey to Ottoman ambition. Up to a point, then, the result was positive. The Ottomans, heavily committed elsewhere in the Mediterranean or the Balkans, had resigned themselves to ending their aggressive attitude. But the internal balance of the Mamlūk state had been compromised.

The destabilization had been becoming apparent from the 1480s in several ways. With the army on the borders, the maintenance of order in the provinces was less secure; once again the Bedouin were a power to be reckoned with, and had become virtually uncontrollable from 1485–86 on. In Upper Egypt, the Hawwāra amīrs had reasserted their authority: they were now the natural masters of the country and would remain so. In the capital the sultan had quickly to recruit ever more troops on a continuing basis; they could not immediately be assimilated and pressure from them again became a major problem. From 1481, the dawādār Yashbak, who had incurred their hostility, chose to leave Cairo and Egypt to go and try his luck (it proved fatal) in the Ak Qoyunlū domains, then in complete turmoil. One of his relatives, the amīr Qānṣūh Khamsmiyya, had then been promoted grand amīr akhūr (in charge of the sultan's stables), while the post of dawādār devolved on the amīr Aqbirdi, a relative of the sultan. The insubordination of the recruits intensified from 1486 in the context of price rises that devalued their pay; it reached such a pitch that in 1489 the sultan made a show of abdicating. From 1491, hostility had broken out between Qānṣūh Khamsmiyya and Aqbirdī and the recruits took sides with one or other amīr, thinking that one of them would replace the aging sultan. Qāytbāy was less and less able to dominate the situation. In 1495, the old *atābak* Azbak allowed himself to be drawn into Qānṣūh Khamsmiyya's faction but the coup d'état failed and Azbak was forced into exile in the Ḥījāz. However, even before the old sultan's death, the Qānṣūh Khamsmiyya faction had imposed Qāytbāy's son Muḥammad, with Qānṣūh

Khamsmiyya as *atābak*. The long sultanate ended in political unrest, the price of a conservatism that had been unable to see and overcome its problems.[5]

The end of the state of the Circassians was in fact marked by two crises. There was first a long political crisis (1496–1501), which resulted in the situation left by Qāytbāy and made contemporaries believe that Mamlūk power would not recover. Subsequently, under the sultanate of Qānṣūh al-Ghawrī (1501–16), who had managed to restore the political situation, there was a more damaging crisis, caused by European pressure in the Indian Ocean and the Mediterranean, which, directly and indirectly, sapped the resources of the sultanate. The confrontation with the Ottomans, in which the regime was to disappear, occurred only belatedly and rather unexpectedly, but the weaknesses of the Mamlūk state were decisive by then.

As in the case of Barqūq, Qāytbāy's disappearance was not followed in short order by the swift deposition of his son al-Malik al-Nāṣir Muḥammad in favour of the *atābak* Qānṣūh Khamsmiyya. This claimant came up against the unforeseen opposition of the sultan's immediate entourage, led by the amīr Qānṣūh Qānṣūh (later al-Ẓāhir), a simple palace official but the brother of the concubine who was the sultan's mother; he resisted even though the amīrs had already agreed to the deposition. After some violent fighting in Cairo, Qānṣūh Khamsmiyya was obliged to flee and was killed. Aqbirdī, for his part, had to retire to Syria where he eventually died. Qāytbāy's recruits, gathered round the fifteen-year-old sultan who was said to be unbalanced, remained in control, and demanded that resources be found for the maintenance of the army. The amīrs of Qānṣūh Khamsmiyya's clan finally rallied to the sultan's uncle and, in an attempt to get things under control at the instigation of one of Qāytbāy's mamlūks, the second *dawādar* Tūmānbāy, they had the prince assassinated in 1498 and acclaimed Qānṣūh Qānṣūh as sultan. The new ruler could see no other solution than to tax the elites in order to meet the needs of the recruits, so the amīrs abandoned him and Ṭūmānbāy then pressed the sultanate on the *atābak* Jānbalā, a former mamlūk of Yashbak (1500–01), so as to be in a position to seize power himself in 1501. Since it soon became apparent that Ṭūmānbāy's policies differed little from those of his predecessors, the amīrs then put the *dawādār* Qānṣūh al-Ghawrī on the throne. He alone proved capable of exacting obedience from the recruits and payment of taxes from the notables, a price that had to be paid for a return to tranquility. These five years, marked in addition in the provinces by the rebellion of other amīrs, insecurity, and Bedouin turbulence, as well as a return of plague, formed a tragic epilogue to the sultanate of Qāytbāy.

[5] Carl Petry, *Twilight of Majesty: The Reigns of the Mamlūk Sultans al-Ashraf Qāytbāy and Qānṣūh al-Ghawrī in Egypt* (Seattle, 1993), 234.

The atypical character of the last great Mamlūk sultan, Qānṣūh al-Ghawrī (1501–1516), has been well portrayed.[6] After his accession to power, a few revolts by recruits in 1508 and 1510 must still be recorded; these were the result of deficiencies in the services charged with maintaining the mamlūks, but the sultan was able to stand firm. His chief concern was to keep his treasury well filled, often by highly disreputable means. But the stability of the regime was abruptly compromised in a different way. The threat came, not from the Ottomans who had made no attempt to take advantage of the five years of crisis, but from the Europeans. In 1498, Vasco da Gama had appeared in the Indian Ocean and in 1501 Muslim ships had been sunk off Calicut in Kerala; in 1503 a Portuguese squadron was cruising at the entrance to the Red Sea. The sultan found himself faced simultaneously with an advance that endangered the holy paces, of which he was protector, and a decline in royal revenues. The provinces were again subject almost every year to the same expeditions to collect taxes by force, amounting almost to pillage, as under Shaykh's rule; they were now led by the *dawādār*. From 1505 an armed force had to be dispatched to the Red Sea and the Indian Ocean, and in 1508 trials to create an artillery unit began. The European threat demanded a new type of riposte which appeared unseemly to contemporaries accustomed to the classic Mamlūk army.

The threat was felt too on the Mediterranean shore which Qāytbāy had already started to fortify. Ships began to be built on both seas. The alliance with the Ottomans was strengthened; since 1502, they were themselves confronted by the Ṣafavid movement, also linked with Europe. Egypt was thus able to obtain timber and iron. After the defeat of the Egyptian fleet off Diu in 1500, it was the Red Sea that had to be defended. From 1511, Ottoman consignments of guns and powder reached Alexandria, accompanied by shipwrights and sailors. In the same year, al-Ghawrī created a corps of fusiliers, known as the "Fifth Corps," or corps of the "Fifth Instalment" (of pay), recruited from outside the mamlūk traditions. But had the sultan the means for this policy? The army was now enlarged, and henceforth any way of finding the resources for it was good enough. From 1511, too, delays in paying the troops (distributions of meat, barley, uniforms) reappeared and the recruits were grumbling again. In 1514 came renewed riots. The sultan was accused of having emptied the Treasury for the benefit of a military contingent alien to the mamlūk tradition and so compromising the existence of the army; the mamlūk veterans joined with the recruits and, although afraid of them, stirred them up surreptitiously against the sultan, whom the recruits normally supported.

[6] Petry, *Twilight of Majesty*, 167–73.

It was under these circumstances that the situation changed one last time. In 1512, in order to organize resistance to the Ṣafavids, Salim seized power in Constantinople; in 1514 he led his army into Anatolia where a confrontation took place in August at Chaldiran. But neither al-Ghawrī, despite being aided by the Ottomans in the Red Sea, nor the Dhu'l-Qadirids could bring themselves to rally to his side; they were frightened at the sight of an Ottoman army so close to their domains. Once victory had been won, Salim came back to wreak vengeance, first on the Dhu'l-Qadirids and then he set about the Mamlūk empire which was totally unable to fight against the enemies of Islam. The engagement took place at Marj Dābiq, to the north of Aleppo, on August 24, 1516, where al-Ghawrī lost his life. The mamlūk veterans had borne the brunt, but they felt they were being sacrificed to the recruits who showed little fight and fell back; the Ottoman fusiliers did the rest, since the Mamlūk fusiliers were stationed on the Red Sea. In this engagement the problem of how the army was constituted had come up again and had proved decisive. Syria was easily invaded. The amīr Ṭūmānbāy, a nephew of al-Ghawrī and serving *dawādār*, was proclaimed sultan. He attempted to resist by hastily assembling an artillery field and a fusilier corps, but Cairo's defences were easily outflanked. In April 1517 the last Mamlūk sultan was hanged under Bāb Zuwayla. Khayrbak, governor of Aleppo and long-time supporter of the Ottomans, was put in charge of Cairo, the Delta and Middle Egypt; in Upper Egypt, the Hawwāra amīrs, who had rallied to the Ottoman cause, were acknowledged as masters of the country.

The characteristics of the new Mamlūk system

In the course of the general developments we have described, the Mamlūk system experienced appreciable modifications compared with what it had been in the thirteenth and fourteenth centuries. They are characteristic of the Circassian state.

The political changes in the Mamlūk system seem to be linked to two basic causes: the ethnic solidarity of the Circassians and the steady relative growth, for successive and differing reasons, of the financial means available to the sultans, compared with the revenues of the amīrs as a whole.

When Barqūq came to power after the death of al-Malik al-Ashraf Shaʿbān in 1377, the mamlūk system had not significantly changed. Barqūq probably had some of his former comrades against him but he clashed mainly with the mamlūks of his predecessor Shaʿbān, led by Minṭāsh, who, moreover, was hostile to the Circassians, as we have seen. His political skill enabled him to return to the sultanate. Having learnt from the experience, he bought a great many mamlūks (5,000, it is said) from among the

Circassians (or the Greeks); these were the Ẓāhiris.[7] Their maintenance was soon the chief duty of the *dīwān al-mufrad*, created in 1383.[8] If there had already been a considerable proportional increase in the financial resources of the sultans since the time of al-Nāṣir Muḥammad, the creation of the *dīwān al-mufrad* accentuated this phenomenon. The resources available now allowed any sultan to recruit mamlūks swiftly. This probably partially explains Faraj's long resistance to his father's amīrs; in the classic system, they would have got rid of him quickly and replaced him with one of their own.

Once in power, Shaykh too was able more easily to buy mamlūks: the Mu'ayyadīs. He did so by attempting to return (although not exclusively) to Turkish mamlūks[9] and that was enough to ensure subsequently that the Mu'ayyadīs were the object of lasting mistrust when the Circassians managed to seize power again. This they did in 1421, with the accession of Ṭaṭar.[10] Contemporaries were amazed that within three months the sultan had succeeded in forming an infrastructure of mamlūks:[11] he had the financial means to do so. Barsbāy consolidated his achievement. By keeping the Mu'ayyadīs out of power, the ethnic cohesion of the Circassians created (no doubt unintentionally) the conditions for the formation of an aristocracy consisting of the former Circassian elite, in which those of longest standing were considered the most noble.

Barsbāy's sultanate marks a new stage. Thanks to the sultanate's monopolies, instituted in 1425–27, the sultan's resources grew again (proportionately) through the inflow of revenues not accessible to the amīrs. The sultan took advantage of it to establish his power even more firmly and buy mamlūks (the Ashrafīs). From then on, the training time for mamlūks seems to have been reduced to twelve or eighteen months. From 1428, too, the problem first appeared of recruits who were unruly, not because they were not Circassians (they were, largely), nor because they would not have had a political future in the framework of their integration into the system, but because that integration could not happen fast enough. Faced with the recruits, the amīrs, now with fewer mamlūks, found themselves at a loss. The rift between the old troops and newcomers brought about a corresponding strengthening of the move to form the older ones into an aristocracy. On Barsbāy's death in 1438, the recruits attempted to unite

[7] Abu'l-Maḥāsin ibn Taghrī Birdī, *Al-Nujūm al-zāhira fī mulūk miṣr wa'l-qāhira*, partial edn. W. Popper, University of California Publications in Semitic Philology (Berkeley, 1909–36), V, 597.

[8] B. Martel-Thoumian, *Les civils et l'administration dans l'état mamlūk (IXe–XVe siècle)* (Damascus, 1991), 53.

[9] Ibn Taghrī Birdī, *Nujūm*, VI, 430.

[10] Ibn Taghrī Birdī, *Nujūm*, VI, 503–05.

[11] Ibn Taghrī Birdī, *Nujūm*, VI, 519.

around his young son, Al Malik al-ʿAzīz Yūsuf, who was thirteen. This was a complete reversal of the attitude adopted formerly, when the father's mamlūks had to be wary of the late ruler's son; in 1438 the young prince was obviously just a rallying point, but the situation would recur as would the outcome.

The recruits were more numerous, but, having been recently brought in, they were still only novice soldiers and had little understanding of Mamlūk politics. So they were easily defeated and set aside by Barqūq's mamlūks and it was another of Barqūq's mamlūks, Jaqmaq, who seized power in that same year of 1438. The troubles connected with the rapid recruitment of new mamlūks clearly recurred under Jaqmaq, as did the regrouping of the recruits around his son after Jaqmaq's death in 1453. It was yet another of Barqūq's mamlūks, Aynāl, who took it upon himself to remove them from power, this time by relying, at least temporarily, on Barsbāy's former recruits who had been finally integrated into the system, were no longer the untried mass they had been originally and, after the death of their patron, had become a mamlūk group like any other. So recruits did finally become integrated, but more slowly, when no doubt they were older, and at the cost of serious political disturbances.

The phenomenon recurred, then, with Aynāl's recruits; they had to be forcibly removed in 1461 when they attempted to regroup around his son – an episode that marks the complete integration of the mamlūks of the previous sultan, Jaqmaq. At that date, the group of the feared Mu'ayyadīs no longer constituted a serious force; they had joined the aristocracy, so it was possible to call on two of Shaykh's former mamlūks, Khushqadam and Yalbāy, to assume the sultanate. Through weakness and lack of political astuteness, Yalbāy had been unable to remove his predecessor's recruits so he was replaced by Timurbughā, one of Jaqmaq's mamlūks, who, having proved equally incapable of resisting Kushqadam's recruits, had to cede power in 1468 to Qāytbāy, a former mamlūk of Barsbāy. So a new political mechanism had gradually been imposed: any amīr who rose to be sultan had first to remove his predecessor's recruits, relying on the previous age group that had been kept in the wings until that point, which marked their genuine entry into the political arena. The initial rhythm of Mamlūk political life was thus much slowed down.

If, under Qāytbāy, the usual disturbances caused by the recruits did not recur until 1473, that was probably because the hostilities along the Anatolian border had been responsible for a swifter integration of some and the physical elimination of others. The plague of 1477 had helped, too. There followed a few years of calm. After the departure of the amīr Yashbak, their aggression came into the spotlight again in 1482. The reason was probably that Qāytbāy was engaged in skirmishes with the Ottomans which he thought would become open war, so he began to recruit very large numbers of troops at a pace which precluded their being integrated. Although these troops fought well, an indication that the Mamlūk "matrix" was still training good soldiers, from 1486 the recruits started wanting to cash in on their participation in the fighting. They were the more violent because, though there were not enough resources to pay them regularly and to offset price rises, the Mamlūk aristocracy, now conscious of its status, flaunted excessive luxury. In the face of this aristocracy, the recruits had become mercenaries. However, the sultan continued to recruit, finding the resources in an exceptional system of taxation, justified by the war; he went so far as to levy *iqṭaʿ* revenues (1488) and even *awqāf* (1491), so building up important financial reserves which he tapped only under the threat of riots. Thus the war against the Ottomans marked one more stage in the (relative) growth of royal resources, some of which were saved and some spent recruiting yet more men.

We have seen that the consequences were dramatic. The Mamlūk aristocracy was now dividing into clans (for example the faction of Aqbirdī against that of Qānṣūh Khamsmiyya), foreshadowing the clanṣ of the Ottoman period (their creators might vanish but the groups remained), and the recruits split up between the clans; this was the protracted crisis from 1496 to 1501 that almost brought about the collapse of the sultanate.

Only al-Ghawrī had the ability to bring the "iniquitous effect" of too high a level of recruitment (and inadequate integration) under control. This was made possible by the resources first amassed under a system of "taxation for war." When al-Ghawrī succeeded in restoring order, we are told that there had never been such large numbers of troops (at least, under the Circassians).[12] Bearing in mind the real decline in wealth (plague struck again several times between 1492 and 1514) and the uselessness of the royal spice monopoly, which brought the sultan nothing at all after 1500, this exceptional taxation system was maintained, using the worst of methods: confiscation and extortion of funds under torture in the towns, tax-gathering expeditions in the countryside. This, with a restriction on traditional royal largesse in the form of pensions granted to "the people" (*al-nās*) vouchsafed ten years of internal calm. But when the European presence in the Indian Ocean required additional expenditure, the demands of the recruits were renewed. In the final engagement with the Ottomans, the division of the military class into recruits, more senior mamlūks and military aristocracy, even more than the absence of the mamlūk fusiliers, was the cause of the defeat.

The development we have described explains in broad outline the characteristic features of the Mamlūk system under the Circassians.

[12] Ibn Iyās, *Badāʾiʿ al-Zuhūr fī Waqāʾiʿ al-Duhūr*, ed. Muḥammad Muṣṭafā, (Cairo, 1960–61), IV, 14.

Like the first Mamlūk state, the state of the Circassians was legitimized by the sanction of an ʿAbbāsid caliph. Since the middle of the fourteenth century, the material situation of the ʿAbbāsid caliphs had improved. They were in charge of the sanctuary of Sayyida al-Nafīsa and that associated them with big demonstrations of piety in Cairo life.[13] They had become prominent religious figures. They had even managed to appear to be guarantors of the first Mamlūk tradition against the Circassian seizure of power: al-Mutawakkil, caliph since 1361, had thus been forced by Barqūq to step down in 1382 for having supported anti-Circassian intrigues. In order to replace him, the sultan had recourse to another branch of the ʿAbbāsid family as al-Malik al-Nāṣir Muḥammad had done in the fourteenth century. But the ploy failed; when his power was threatened, Barqūq attempted to rally public opinion by restoring al-Mutawakkil in 1390. The caliph had known better than to get too involved with the rebellious amīrs, and the prestige of the caliphate emerged from the test enhanced when Barqūq returned to power. Al-Mustaʿīn succeeded his father, al-Mutawakkil, in 1405 and we have seen how the amīrs contrived to use the prestige of the caliphate to defeat Faraj in 1412. The sultan-caliph took his role seriously (a decree of al-Mustaʿīn, carved in stone, is preserved at Ghazza)[14] but for the amīrs it was nothing more than a political stratagem which came to an end after six months, when he was deposed simultaneously from the sultanate and the caliphate and exiled to Alexandria. After two other sons of al-Mutawakkil, men of religion who led exemplary lives, al-Qāʾim was invested with the caliphate in 1451 and he too intervened in the political arena by supporting Aynāl in 1453 in his struggle against Jaqmaq's recruits: Aynāl's triumph reflected glory on the caliph who once more enjoyed great prestige. But he allowed himself to get involved in an attempted coup d'état against Aynāl the following year. Al-Qāʾim too was exiled to Alexandria. After that, the caliphs never again stepped out of their role as symbols of Islamic legality, residing now in the Citadel, now in the caliph's palace in the Kabsh district. The sultans made a conventional show of deference to them. The last of them, al-Mutawakkil III, was at al-Ghawrī's side at Marj Dābiq; he was briefly held in great respect by the victor, then deported with other Cairo notables to Constantinople. The caliphate ended with him.[15]

The legal sanction of the caliphate was felt to be less and less necessary since the legitimacy of the sultanate was not established. The Mamlūk sultan even took the title of "sultan of Islam and the Muslims" under Jaqmaq.[16] The quasi-symbolic *modus operandi* of the sultanate was maintained: a

13 Ibn Taghrī Birdī, *Nujūm*, V, 383.
14 M. M. Sadek, *Mamlūkische Architektur der Stadt Gaza* (Berlin, 1991), 98–9.
15 J.-C. Garcin, "Histoire, opposition politique et piétisme traditionaliste dans le Husn al-Muḥāḍarat de Suyūṭī," *AI*, 7 (1967), 56–65.
16 Khalil Al-Zāhirī, *Kitāb zubda kashf al-mamālik*, ed. P. Ravaisse (Paris, 1894), 67.

"royal service" (*khidma*) was held in the morning shortly after sunrise in the presence of the confidential secretary (*kātib al-sirr*) and the amīrs, when decisions were taken concerning the military class, followed by the ceremonial meal with the chief amīrs.[17] Sultans in the second half of the fifteenth century were at pains to give maximum publicity to sessions of the *maẓālim* (royal dispensation of justice and decisions of a juridical nature concerning the administration of the state, taken in conjunction with the *qāḍīs*). The sultan always entered Cairo (and Damascus and Aleppo) in solemn procession, preceded by cantors and the yellow standard of the sultanate.[18] He was sheltered under a parasol which, from 1514, was no longer surmounted by a bird but by a crescent.[19] There were no solemn entries into other towns, where the sultan was officially received on a platform outside the town.[20] The official game of polo continued to offer the populace a rite, which had become a spectacle of mounted amīrs.

However, the locations for displays of power had changed. Within the Citadel the fourteenth century *Qaṣr* was abandoned in favour of the Courtyard (*Ḥawsh*), the great square (*maydān*) at the foot of the Citadel, laid out as a garden by al-Ghawrī, or the mausoleum of Yashbak at al-Maṭariyya where open spaces prevailed.[21] At the foot of the Citadel, the royal stables frequently provided a setting for the *maẓālim* appellate court: the exercise of authority was to be more visible. More and more frequently the sultans would set out without pomp to cross Cairo and visit this grand amīr or that civil administrator, and some showed a flair for contact with the crowd.[22] From 1422, Barsbāy abolished the practice of prostration before the sultan, replacing it with a bow.[23] The sultan's family became more prominent: first the eldest son, who alone with the *atābak* was authorized (in Egypt only) to brandish the royal parasol,[24] but also the sultanas, some of whom were deemed too influential; from Qāytbāy's time, the royal parasol was borne over their heads as well, but only within the Citadel.[25] The residences in the Citadel also accommodated descendants of Qalāwūn and princess consorts, concubines, mothers, sisters, and daughters of former sultans; and if deposed Circassian sultans and their male children were generally relegated to Alexandria, there were occasions when certain of them, even at times former sultans, returned to the Citadel for family visits.

[17] for i., Ibn Taghrī Birdī, *Nujūm*, VI, 540; Khalīl al-Zāhirī, *Zubda*, 86–87.
[18] Ibn Taghrī Birdī, *Nujūm*, VI, 693–94.
[19] Ibn Iyas, *Badā'i'*, IV, 412.
[20] for i., Ibn Taghrī Birdī, *Nujūm*, VI, 376.
[21] J.-C. Garcin, B. Maury, J. Revault and M. Zakaryn, *Palais et maisons du Caire du XIVe au XVIIIe siècle*, I (Paris, 1982), 191, 193–7.
[22] Ibn Taghrī Birdī, *Nujūm*, VI, 627.
[23] Al-Maqrizi, *Sulūk*, VI, 608; Ibn Taghrī Birdī, *Nujūm*, VI, 559.
[24] Ibn Taghrī Birdī, *Nujūm*, VI, 694.
[25] Ibn Iyas, *Badā'i'*, III, 106.

Assassinations of sultans occurred only at times of great political crisis (Faraj at the beginning of the century, al-Nāṣir Muḥamad or Jānbalāṭ at the end). The sultanate had profoundly changed.

We have seen how a Circassian aristocracy began to emerge as a reaction to the resumption of diversified recruitment during Shaykh's reign. The primacy bestowed on Barqūq's former mamlūks, and subsequently on those enfranchized by them, constituted a kind of nobility based on seniority, ever more closely linked to the Mamlūk traditions as the difficulty of integrating recruits from Barsbāy's time seemed to threaten them. This tendency was accentuated under Qāytbāy for the same reasons. It is difficult to assess the overall numbers of mamlūks; wars and plague came along to counteract the effect of purchases. We have seen that Barqūq bought 5,000 royal mamlūks; they numbered more than 3,000 on the eve of the advent of Barsbāy;[26] Barsbāy himself is thought to have bought more than 2,000[27] and Qāytbāy 8,000 mamlūks.[28] The number of royal mamlūks would have been 7,000 just before Marj Dābiq (whereas only about a thousand mamlūks of the amīrs went to fight).[29]

What do these figures imply about the aristocracy of the amīrs? The number of important amīrs seems to have declined appreciably after Barqūq. In 1486, only 15 amīrs of a hundred, 10 amīrs of forty, 60 amīrs of ten and 40 *khaṣṣakīs* remained.[30] It is not until 1502 that we find the traditional count of 24 amīrs of a hundred again, with 75 amīrs of forty, 180 amīrs of ten and 800 *khaṣṣakīs*, soon to be increased to 1,200;[31] and at the end of Ghawrī's reign there were 27 amīrs of a hundred, with 300 amīrs of forty and of ten.[32] Around the sultan, the hierarchy of the amīrs was fixed as follows, in descending order of rank: the *atābak*, the *amīr silāḥ*, the *amīr majlis*, the *amīr akhūr*, the dawādār, the *ra's nawbat al-nuwāb*, the *ḥājib al-ḥujjāb*.[33] In official ceremonies, in particular the royal services, the place of each one in relation to the sultan was strictly laid down: on the right (where the highest rank was occupied by the *atābak*) or on the left (where the sultan's son occupied the highest rank),[34] but it was always meticulously calculated according to the merits of those present and was the subject of subtle contrivances so as to respect the rights of each one; this aristocracy clung passionately to its rights.

Promotions of the grand amīrs generally followed ascending order of rank

26 Ibn Taghrī Birdī, *Nujūm*, VI, 534.
27 Ibn Taghrī Birdī, *Nujūm*, VI, 773.
28 Ibn Iyas, *Badā'i'*, III, 325.
29 Ibn Iyas, *Badā'i'*, V, 44–45.
30 Ibn Iyas, *Badā'i'*, III, 222–23.
31 Ibn Iyas, *Badā'i'*, IV, 30–34.
32 Ibn Iyas, *Badā'i'*, V, 3–4.
33 for i., Ibn Taghrī Birdī, *Nujūm*, VII, 37.
34 for i., Ibn Taghrī Birdī, *Nujūm*, VI, 364.

and one may wonder to what extent in the fifteenth century, as in the European courts of the period, even the most characteristic ones still corresponded to precise functions. It is clear that under Qāytbāy the dawādār Yashbak had frequently led his troops into battle, whereas the *atābak* Azbak was engaged in the maintenance of internal order.[35] Moreover, the dawādārs at the end of the Circassian regime exercised a power that cannot be explained by the hierarchy of rank, but more probably by their role regarding the state finances at that period. Finally there no longer seems to have been any connection between the rank and the political role of a particular amīr who became spokesman for an age group.

Women seem to have played a large part in establishing links between families, whose assets they often managed.[36] Beyond the political confrontations, matrimonial alliances ensured the cohesion of this elite, in which the descendants of the fourteenth-century Turkish mamlūks, no longer seen as a threat, were respected for the antiquity of their origins; there is even mention of a descendant of Baybars in the highest society at the end of the fifteenth century.[37] Under Qāytbāy, the richest families readily provided the spectacle of the sumptuous festivals (weddings, circumcisions), still further provoking the anger, even physical aggression, of the recruits. Wealth was necessary: since the days of Barqūq, nomination to the higher ranks involved payments to the sultan; the revenues that accompanied those ranks would soon allow the new holder to restore his finances.

Below the grand families, all gradations were possible within that mass of descendants of mamlūks who called themselves "the people" (*al-nās*). They always counted to some extent on receiving some sort of pension and royal bounty in order to live when they had no handy family relationship to enable them to obtain positions that only true mamlūks were supposed to occupy.

The Mamlūk state was always run by civilian administrators who made up the various *dīwāns* in the capital.[38] To the traditional *dīwāns* (*dīwān al-wizāra*, *dīwān al-inshā'*, *dīwān al-jaysh*, *dīwān al-khāṣṣ*), a very important new one was added as we have seen, the *dīwān al-mufrad*, entrusted to a civilian who nevertheless bore the military title of *ustādār*. It can be estimated that, at the end of the fourteenth century, the staff of these *dīwāns* numbered around a thousand individuals in the capital.[39] It is clear that the

[35] Ibn Iyas, *Badā'i'*, III, 92.

[36] Carl Petry, "Class Solidarity vs. Gender Gain: Women as Custodians of Property in Later Medieval Egypt," in Nikki Keddie and Beth Baron (eds.), *Women in Middle Eastern History: Shifting Boundaries in Sex and Gender* (New Haven, 1991), 122–41.

[37] Ibn Iyas, *Badā'i'*, III, 257.

[38] C. Petry, *The Civilian Elite of Cairo in the Later Middle Ages* (Princeton, 1981), 202–20; Martel-Thoumian, *Les civils et l'administration*, 35–38.

[39] We can deduce this from Ibn Taghrī Birdī, *Nujūm*, V, 490.

attention paid to the management of resources occupies a growing place in the historical sources and this must correspond to its growing importance. In its early days, the importance of the *dīwān al-mufrad*, where the sultan could find new resources, explains the political role that unscrupulous individuals like Saʿd al-Dīn ibn Ghurāb (d. 1406) or Jamāl al-Dīn Yūsuf al-Bīrī, known as Jamāl al-Dīn al-Ustādār (d. 1409) were able to play in the reign of Faraj.[40] With the stabilization of the political situation, we see great families of varying origins, whose history has been studied, regularly occupying the top posts in the different *dīwāns*: the Banū al-Haysam (converted Copts from Cairo), the Banū Naṣr Allah (Muslims from Lower Egypt), the Banuʾl-Kuwayz (converted Melkite Christians from Jordan), the Banuʾl-Bārizī (Muslims from Ḥamā), the Banū Muẓhir (Muslims from Damascus), the Banū Kātib Jakam (converted Copts from Cairo) and lastly the Banuʾl-Jīʿān (converted Copts from Damietta).[41]

Often allied with the sultans while they were still only amīrs, some of them subsequently acquired real political influence; men such as the confidential secretary (*kātib al-sirr*) from 1413 to 1420, Nāṣir al-Dīn Muḥammad al-Barizī; the supervisor of the army bureau (*nāẓir al-Jaysh*) from 1421 to 1439, Zayn al-Dīn ʿAbd al-Bāsit; the supervisor of the privy fund (*nāẓir al-khāṣṣ*) from 1437 to 1458, Jamāl al-Dīn Yūsuf ibn Kātib Jakam; and the confidential secretary from 1438 to 1452, Kamāl al-Dīn Muḥammad ibn al-Bārizī. As their importance increased, the Christian origin of some of them aroused reactions of which the sultans were aware but which never had lasting consequences. The sultans became accustomed to finding the administrators necessary for the smooth functioning of the system in this milieu that was generally cultivated, wealthy and pious. Sometimes they were allied by marriage to the top ranks of the Circassian aristocracy, even to the families of the sultans. The costume of the civilian official no longer indicated a lower rank and was sometimes preferred to the uniform of the amīr.[42]

From Qāytbāy's reign, however, we note yet another new development. The determination to find the necessary resources by whatever means then led the sultans to turn to men from civilian society and trade (money-changers, retailers, purveyors of meat, furriers) whose know-how and lack of scruples were doubtless appreciated. The traditional sources obviously saw only the dishonesty, low origins and insolence of these uncultured men, who now donned the respectable garb of secretaries of the *dīwāns* and were in their eyes the sultans' condemned souls. They occupied various posts in the royal offices and the market inspectorate (*ḥisba*), like the notorious Zayn

[40] Martel-Thoumian, *Les civils et l'administration*, 99–105.
[41] Martel-Thoumian, *Les civils et l'administration*, 181–325.
[42] Ibn Taghrī Birdī, *Nujūm*, VI, 727.

al-Dīn Bakarāt ibn Mūsā, whose career would continue under the Ottomans.[43]

It may be thought that this civilian elite, even in its last representatives (still an elite?), did not emerge from the social fabric autonomously but that it too was a creation of the mamlūk system. The sultans tolerated the fact that these families grew rich, though their resources could quite clearly not be derived from the tasks entrusted solely to them. It was thus the rule to buy office, just as for the amīrs. When their services were deemed unsatisfactory or when too much money had been accumulated, the sultans had no hesitation in resorting to the most brutal treatment, which they applied to all who served them (prison, beatings). They confiscated property and exacted (often under torture) huge sums which one may suspect were being deducted from moneys already levied in the name of the sultan.

The Circassian Mamlūks and Egypt

The political development of the mamlūk system that we have described was important in a society where the army, as the holder of both political and economic power, could be a driving force or a brake on society as a whole. It is this aspect that is often the most visible in the chronicles. It is still the case that this development has its place in a more general context which transcended it and, in a sense, induced it, a context dominated by the great events that affected Egypt. And first of all the succession of epidemics: those under the Circassians in 1388–89, 1397–98, 1403–07, 1410–11, 1415–19, 1429–30, 1438–39, 1444–49, 1455, 1459–60, 1468–69, 1476–77, 1492, 1498, 1504–05 and 1513–14.[44] These resulted in a decline in wealth production, and an imbalance between the Bedouin, who were less affected, and the settled population. These phenomena also affected other countries to the south of the Mediterranean (in particular the Maghrib) and were not peculiar to Egypt or to the Mamlūk regime. Nor should we overlook the monetary phenomena linked with the production and circulation of certain metals (gold, silver, copper), which concern a zone that is much bigger still. But because our sources of information in Egypt emanate from urban milieus, themselves closely linked to the military society that dominated them and kept them alive, we can only perceive these phenomena through the contacts maintained by the Mamlūk regime with the civilian population.

The concentration of the majority of the amīrs, the holders of power and

[43] Petry, *Twilight of Majesty*, 55, 105, 145, 148–52; C. Petry, *Protectors or Praetorians? The Last Mamlūk Sultans and Egypt's Waning as a Great Power* (Albany, 1994), 131–89.

[44] B. Shoshan, "Notes sur les épidémies de peste en Égypte," *Annales de démographie historique* (1981), 395–403.

wealth, in the capital, and the large size of the population living there (at least 270,000 inhabitants, a considerable figure for the period),[45] as well as the presence there of a significant proportion of the civilian elites, lend political significance to the relations of the Mamlūk state with the people of Cairo. Moreover, this population was in constant touch with the nearby province, whence rural dwellers arrived quite regularly, fleeing insecurity and despotism. The voids created by the epidemics were easily filled in a capital which by that very fact was being ruralized in some aspects at that period, hence the creation of those great courtyard tenements, the *ḥawsh*, where the poor families were herded together.[46]

The political vicissitudes were dangerous for the urban population in that the challenge to a sultan by a party of amīrs left the civilians defenseless, and the triumph of one or other party meant searches in the district where the defeated party's tenants lived and the plundering of residences and possibly neighbouring dwellings. When armed confrontations were limited to the area round the Citadel, it often happened that the town centre was not affected and indeed everyday activities went on as though nothing was happening. But at times of major crisis, Cairo could become a battlefield, as in 1497 when the battle line stretched from Fusṭāṭ in the south to Maṭariyya in the north.[47] The conflicting parties did not hesitate to swell their ranks by offering to pay anyone who wanted to fight. But it might also be that members of the populace would take part in the fighting without payment, perhaps hoping for plunder but giving vent as well to sympathies that had revealed themselves in less dramatic circumstances. Sultans such as Barqūq,[48] Jaqmaq,[49] al-Ẓāhir Qānṣūh,[50] Al-ʿĀdil Ṭūmānbāy,[51] even al-Ghawrī[52] had had their moments of popularity which they tried to exploit in their outings into the town, but these might also earn them unpleasant comments at times of price rises, monetary fluctuations or the imposition of a new market tax. Whether or not this popular opinion was well founded or reliable, the sultans seem to have been concerned about it. The declining numbers and power of the amīrs left them more exposed to the populace.

One element, however, came between the populace and the sultan: the

45 J.-C. Garcin, "The Mamlūk Military System and the Blocking of Medieval Muslim Society," in J. Baechler et al. (eds.), *Europe and the Rise of Capitalism* (Oxford, 1998), 119–23/"Le système militaire mamlūk et le blocage de la société musulmane médiévale," *AI*, 25 (1988), 93–110.
46 Garcin et al., *Palais et maisons*, 202–03.
47 Ibn Iyas, *Badāʾiʿ*, III, 366–67.
48 Ibn Taghrī Birdī, *Nujūm*, V, 544–45.
49 Ibn Taghrī Birdī, *Nujūm*, VII, 116.
50 Ibn Iyas, *Badāʾiʿ*, III, 405.
51 Ibn Iyas, *Badāʾiʿ*, III, 451.
52 Ibn Iyas, *Badāʾiʿ*, IV, 94, 327.

recruits. Living in barracks in the Citadel, they were feared by the people of Cairo. When their pay was delayed, they attacked places where the civilian and military authorities lived, even the sultan's grain stores or the districts (Būlāq, for example) where the amīr aristocracy had invested their fortune in residences, apartments to rent (*rabʿ*) or commercial buildings. But they also took advantage of festivals, when the populace came out in droves, to carry out raids on civilians. Speaking hardly any Arabic, they knew they were despised and they complained to the sultan about the slights isolated individuals received. In 1450 they demanded that their privileges as mamlūks be respected, in particular that of being the only ones allowed to use horses.[53] When the wars with the Ottomans took the army away, the population felt relieved. The sultans were increasingly judged on their ability to keep the recruits in order.

When the recruits finally became an integral part of the mamlūk body as a whole, they were housed in the town in luxurious or modest apartments, according to rank, mostly rented;[54] the main thing was that there should be a stable. The rents often served to sustain the private trusts (*awqāf*) of the ancient families of civilian or military notables. Amīrs, too, could settle in rented accommodation. The greatest among them followed one another in vast newly built residences, for example that of amīr Māmāy, a close friend of Qāytbāy, in the middle of the old town, or of the *atābak* Azbak in the district he had founded which bore his name, Azbakiyya. Or they occupied refurbishments of amīral residences of the thirteenth and fourteenth centuries, like the former palace (*dār*) of Qūṣūn at the foot of the Citadel, updated in the taste of the day by amīr Yashbak, where after him the *dawādār* traditionally resided, just as the *atābaks* lived in Azbakiyya.[55] At times of political disturbance these residences became rallying points for the different parties and consequently might suffer attacks from their opponents. Great civilian state officials also had their residences, like ʿAbd al-Bāsiṭ who had bought back and refurbished the palace of Tankiz, the all-powerful governor of Syria in the fourteenth century.[56] Sultans were not averse to paying them prolonged visits, especially when the residences were close to the Nile and the royal "services" could be held there, while the amīrs took up temporary residence nearby.

These buildings had been enlarged from the fifteenth century on and organized round a large courtyard (as in the Citadel), on to which the loggia known as *maqʿad* opened, prestige areas where senior amīrs received visitors.[57] Around the courtyard lay the large living rooms on the ground

53 Ibn Taghrī Birdī, *Nujūm*, VII, 205.
54 Garcin et al., *Palais et maisons*, 197–201, 203–11.
55 Garcin et al., *Palais et maisons*, 182–85.
56 Martel-Thoumain, *Les civils et l'administration*, 401.
57 Garcin et al., *Palais et maisons*, 211–13.

floor or in upper storeys (*qāʿa*, *riqāq*), mamlūks' apartments, storerooms for precious objects or provisions, even a private prison. Any amīr or civilian notable might find himself given the job of making some other servant of the sultan return ill-gotten goods, often under torture, and the high ranking amīrs had ushers at their door recording requests from possible plaintiffs, whose lawsuits they dealt with more expeditiously than the *qāḍīs*. From these residences the amīrs extended their authority and protection to the neighborhood, to all the inhabitants of the district, who at times were required to give help with building work, to the shopkeepers whose stalls might bear the coat of arms of the amīr protector, to the people of the craft groups (*ḥarāfish*), just coalescing,[58] even to the self-defence groups (*zuʿar*) who came more to the fore as the districts gradually shut themselves in with gates when insecurity increased towards the end of the fifteenth century, due largely to the recruits. The existence of these client links could have led to the setting-up of a feudal system if the rotation of functions had not involved the families occupying the grand residences as well. The common people made use of the protection, marveled at the festivals and felt the vagaries of political life in terms of the generosity or harshness of the protector of the moment.

The religious foundations (mosques, *madrasas*), often close to the residence, also provided all who had been trained in the *madrasas* with paid work of all grades and acceptable odd jobs. The Mamlūk aristocracy did not lack ties (by marriage) to the great families of the *qāḍīs*. Though sources of friction remained, such as the run-of-the-mill justice handed down by the amīrs (the sultan occasionally banned it in time of plague because he knew it was against religious law and gave rise to abuse), or the favor increasingly granted to the Ḥanafī rite, considered to be that of the Turko-Circassian power,[59] yet their interests could often converge, for example when, under Qāytbāy, the royal tax system turned its attention to the income of the *awqāf*, often greater than the needs of the institutions they supported,[60] the surplus going to the families of the founders and administrators. The royal monopolies, the monetary fluctuations, the market taxes were vigorously condemned by the *ʿulamāʾ*. It was to win over this social group, or else to reduce it to silence, that the sultans made play of their concern for justice. But if royal policies or the conduct of a particular amīr were judged

[58] W. M. Brinner, "The Significance of the Harāfīsh and their 'sultan'," *JESHO*, 6 (1963), 190–215.

[59] L. Fernandes, "Mamlūk Politics and Education: The Evidence from two Fourteenth-Century Waqfiyyas," *AI*, 23 (1987), 87–98.

[60] Petry, *Protectors or Praetorians?*, 196–219; J.-C. Garcin and M. Taher. "Enquête sur le financement d'un *waqf* égyptien du XVe siècle: les comptes de Jawhār al-Lālā," *JESHO*, 38 (1995), 262–304.

appropriately,[61] the sultanate itself was not challenged nor was the organization of society. The teaching in the *madrasas* allowed some social mobility in the town, even the integration into urban society of men originating in the country.[62] This can be seen in the rapid expansion of Al-Azhar towards the end of the fifteenth century when the formerly great *madrasas* were affected by the crisis. Amongst those who trained there were many who were foreign to the Mamlūk world, coming from the Maghrib or Anatolia.[63] Mamlūk power had nothing to fear from the *madrasa* environment.

In addition to the client links, piety formed a very strong bond between members of the military class and the civilian population. The pious foundations of the sultans and amīrs ensured public recitations of the Qur'ān and regular mystic exercises (*dhikr*). Alongside the official celebration of Islam, the quest for the intercession of the saints was widespread. In those times of terrifying epidemics which struck military circles even harder then the civilian populations, recourse to the saints was as common among the mamlūks as in the common people. The blessing of the saints (*baraka*) was sought in all circles. It is very significant that Qāytbāy should have been duped by a false saint when his courage failed in the face of the Ottomans in 1488.[64] A man of the people was very sensitive to material difficulties, iniquitous taxes, oppression by the powerful (*ẓālim*) whose generosity was not even legally acceptable. The *zāwiyyas* of the spiritual masters had often been outside the town (the search for the Way was traditionally linked with travel), but the country folk had brought them into urban territory.[65] Each spiritual master was a member of the invisible society of the saints, itself forming a strict hierarchy under the direction of the "Pole" of the time, who in fact mysteriously directed the world. Common acknowledgment of this society of the Invisible minimized tribulations and the ups and downs of politics and made any idea of rebellion pointless. It was in the *zāwiyya* of one saint, Abu'l-Suʿūd al-Jārihī, that the dawādār Ṭūmānbāy accepted the sultanate in 1516 on the eve of the Ottoman invasion, after renouncing unjust taxes, which won him popular support.[66]

It was more usual to solicit the political assent of the civilian population

[61] B. Shoshan, "Grain Riots and the 'Moral Economy': Cairo, 1350–1517," *Journal of Interdisciplinary History*, 10, 3 (1979–80), 459–78.

[62] J.-C. Garcin, "L'insertion sociale de Shaʿrānī dans le milieu cairote," *Colloque international sur l'histoire du Caire* (Cairo, 1969), 159–68.

[63] Petry, *The Civilian Elite*; idem., "Travel Patterns of Medieval Notables in the Near East," *SI*, 62 (1985), 53–88.

[64] J.-C. Garcin, "Deux saints populaires du Caire au debut du XVIe siècle," *BEO*, 29 (1977), 140.

[65] J.-C. Garcin, "Assises matérielles et rôle économique des ordres soufis dans l'histoire des peuples musulmans," in A. Popovic and G. Veinstein (eds.), *Les voies d'Allah* (Paris, 1995), 223.

[66] Garcin, "Deux saints populaires," 135.

in the great official ceremonies using the urban setting, chiefly along the main thoroughfare or *Qaṣabah* lined with the most beautiful monuments from the Bāb al-Naṣr to the Citadel, where the districts were decorated by order. Royal entry processions and the return of victorious armies were the occasions for the finest ceremonies inspiring genuine or feigned enthusiasm, depending on the economic context. These festivals did much to establish the legitimacy of the sultans. The return of the troops after the occupation of Cyprus in 1426 (when many civilian volunteers had accompanied the mamlūks) occasioned one of the greatest demonstrations of the unity of the Muslim population of Cairo, in which delegations from the towns and from the Bedouin of the Delta took part.[67]

Each year, the procession of the symbolic palanquin (*maḥmal*) marking the preeminence of the Mamlūk sultan at the ceremonies of the pilgrimage,[68] the presentation of the covering of the Kaʿba (*kiswa*), woven in Egypt (another Egyptian privilege), which was transformed towards the end of the Circassian period into the presentation of seven hangings to cover the tombs of the prophets in Mamlūk territory (especially the tomb of Abraham in Hebron) marked the sultanate's prominent position in the Muslim world.[69] From Barsbāy's time, the ceremonies of the birth of the prophet or *mawlid al-nabī* (the reading of the Traditions of Bukhārī in the *Ḥawsh* at the Citadel) provided further confirmation of the Muslim character of the sultanate. Barqūq's visits to the tombs of al-Shāfiʿī or al-Sayyida Nafīsa,[70] Qāytbāy's to the sanctuaries of Aḥmad al-Badawī or Ibrahīm al-Dassūqi[71] proclaimed yet again the Egyptian piety of the sultans. If the sultans were well able to make these Islamic celebrations serve their legitimization, they were also adept at exploiting the Nile festivals, involving the entire population at the breaking of the dike, over which the sultan presided. The building by al-Ghawrī alongside the Nilometer (*Miqyās*) of a royal palace where a veil fluttering at a widow announced that the flood had reached its maximum was more than a mere extravagant fantasy on the part of the sultan.[72] Conversely, poor floods brought together all the religious communities in the desert around the plainly dressed sultan to implore God's clemency. In 1419, a ceremony of that nature, followed by al-Muʾayyad Shaykh, who was not in the best of health, swimming across the Nile, resulted in the Nile starting to rise again, after previously ceasing to do so.[73]

67 Ibn Taghrī Birdī, *Nujūm*, VI, 612–13.
68 J. Jomier, *Le Mahmal et la caravane égyptienne des pélerins de La Mecque* (Cairo, 1953).
69 Ibn Iyas, *Badāʾiʿ*, IV, 337.
70 Ibn Taghrī Birdī, *Nujūm*, V, 560–61.
71 Ibn Iyas, *Badāʾiʿ*, III, 156–199.
72 Ibn Iyas, *Badāʾiʿ*, IV, 389.
73 Ibn Taghrī Birdī, *Nujūm*, VI, 414.

If we can accept that, in spite of the epidemics, the figure for the population of the capital remained relatively stable over a long period, it is likely, on the other hand, that the population of some 2,500 localities in Egypt decreased considerably. The yield of agrarian land, and so of the *iqṭāʿs*, had fallen, which explains the growing imbalance between the sultan's resources and those of the amīrs. In Barsbāy's time, large stretches seem still to have been abandoned after the plague of the start of the century and those that followed. The structures for maintaining order had been weakened; it was to escape Bedouin disturbances that the country people flocked into the towns.

The Mamlūk state imposed its authority outside Cairo through boards of amīrs, nominated in the provinces, the eight provinces of Lower Egypt (excluding Alexandria) and the seven provinces of Upper Egypt.[74] Depending on the size of the provinces, amīrs of forty or of ten were nominated. We have seen that, on the eve of Barqūq's accession to the sultanate, an attempt was made to regroup the Egyptian provinces into three *niyābas* (constituencies under the control of a *nāʾib al-salṭana* or delegate of the sultan), each under an amīr of one hundred as in Syria; they were centered on Alexandria, Damanhūr and Asyūṭ. But already for Lower and Upper Egypt the nomination of two amīrs of inspection (*kāshif*) was announced; this was an old-established, temporary mission whereby amīrs were sent into the province to inspect the state of the dikes and canals and see to it that the crops, always under threat from the Bedouin, were safeguarded. After the crisis at the beginning of the century, it is noteworthy that this reform was abandoned. While Alexandria kept its *nāʾib*, it was three *kushshāf* who were sent into Lower Egypt and three into Upper Egypt, over the governors.[75] The need to control the Bedouin was becoming more pressing.

In Upper Egypt, the legacy of the fourteenth century weighed heavily. Traditionally the Egyptian state relied on the tribes from the South (known as "*Qaysī*" – basically the Banū Hilāl and the Banū Kanz) who were responsible for security on the spice trail towards Aydhāb and had backed the Egyptian thrust into Nubia. In the course of the fourteenth century, the Mamlūk state had been unable to prevent the rising power of the Yemeni tribes of Middle Egypt: the Juhayna, ʿArak and Balī, to whom the opening up of the trails to central Africa (*darb al-arbaʿīn*) had brought wealth and a determination to settle more permanently in the valley. The Mamlūk government had recognized this new situation and this change of alliance

[74] Khalīl al-Ẓahiri, *Zubda*, 32–36; W. Popper, *Egypt and Syria under the Circassian Sultans, 1382–1468 AD: Systematic Notes to Ibn Taghrī Birdī's Chronicles of Egypt*. University of California Publications in Semitic Philology, XV–XVI (Berkeley, 1955, 1957), 13–14.

[75] Khalīl al-Ẓahiri, *Zubda*, 129–130.

had led to the insurrection of the southern tribes. The spice route to Aydhāb had had to be abandoned around 1360. As for the Arab tribes of Middle Egypt, the settling of the Berber Hawwāra at Girga to contain them was a risky gamble. All it achieved was the enhanced power of the family of the Banū ʿUmar ibn ʿAbd al-ʿAzīz at Girga, grown rich from the same sources of wealth, and the fifteenth century sultans ultimately had to accept it, as we have seen. In the south, Aswān, under the control of the Banū Kanz, had left the Mamlūk territory proper. After that, the sultans were seeking above all to prevent too many Bedouin from the Delta moving into Upper Egypt, by exerting firm control in the Fayyūm, through which the tribes passed.[76] From the fifteenth century, Upper Egypt, with the spice trade no longer passing through, was less tightly controlled because it was less important. The pigeon post no longer functioned to the south. Fewer families from the south came to Cairo.[77]

It may be assumed that this gradual settling of the Bedouin in strength in the valley (helped by the epidemics that had hit the villages and towns) reached Lower Egypt in turn in the Circassian period. The Bedouin populations were prepared to be managed by dominant families on whom the Mamlūk government conferred the duties of *mashyakha* of the province and to whom they awarded *iqṭāʿāt*, in recognition of their responsibility for controlling the roads and their duty to provide camels and horses for the army. The Bedouin from the centre of the Delta were no real problem. Their dominant families, the Banū Abī-Shawārib from Qalyūbiyya or the Banū Baghdād from Gharbiyya were noteworthy, often cultivated, occasionally builders of *madrasa* like the Hawwāra of Upper Egypt; one of them is mentioned as having taken his fallāḥīn on the pilgrimage in 1513. It was a different story in Buḥayra, where the *mashyakha* fell to the Banū Saqr (of the Banū Hilāl), living near Taruja, and in Sharqiyya, where the *mashyakha* fell to the Banū Baqar (of the Judhām near al-ʿAbbāsa). The fifteenth century cadastre shows that more than 20 percent of the *iqṭāʿs* cited in Buḥayra and 46 percent of the *iqṭāʿs* in Sharqiyya went to the Bedouin. This does not indicate a corresponding proportion of lands; at this period we have no knowledge of the areas actually being worked, or the yields. But it implies a very substantial presence of Bedouin shaykhs who often levied the total of the contributions required of them on the fallāḥīn and on the revenues of the amīral *iqṭāʿs*. In fact they had become official authorities in the Egyptian countryside after the model of the *kāshif*, formerly charged with controlling them. They had entered the Mamlūk system. But when the ruling power was in difficulties because of the army's departure to the borders, some of them rose up and plundered. They would rally to the Ottomans; when Ṭūmānbāy

[76] J. -C. Garcin, "al-Ṣaʿīd," *EI2*, VIII.
[77] J.-C. Garcin, *Un centre musulman*, 432–45.

was fleeing, he could get no support from the amīr of the Hawwāra and was handed over by the amīr of Tarūja. Already they were often just as much the true masters of the fallāḥīn as the Mamlūks were. But, unlike the Upper Ṣa'īd, the Delta would not slip out of the control of Cairo, which was too close by.[78]

It is not surprising that, despite the epidemics, the towns seem to have maintained their importance, due to the role they were able to play in the struggle against the Bedouin or to the protection they gave; hence Bilbeis and Damanhūr in the Delta beside al-Maḥalla, which was less in danger and remained the major center; Madīnat al-Fayyūm, Minya or Asyūṭ in Upper Egypt. On the other hand, in the south, Qūṣ was in decline and would not recover from the abandonment of the Aydhāb route, and Aswān was in ruins. In the north, Alexandria, much afflicted by plagues and too close to the Buḥayra tribes, was just an empty shell, menaced by European pirates. The Portuguese blockade in the Indian Ocean and fiscal pressure to collect still more resources completed its ruin, to the benefit of Rashīd, with easier access on the Nile.[79] Whereas the Christians would remain the majority in Upper Egypt,[80] where the pace of conversion to Islam was slackening in the part of the south no longer linked to the north by the spice route, by contrast Islam was spreading strongly in the Delta. The style of Muslim religious buildings in the south would long continue to reflect Fāṭimid, Ayyūbid and Turkish Mamlūk models from before the advent of the Circassians, whereas the Delta built its mosques in the taste of fifteenth-century Cairo. The appreciable difference between Upper Egypt and the Delta is one of the legacies of the Circassian era.

Conclusion

The increasing imbalance between the revenues of the amīrs and of the sultan, in the context of the internal struggles for influence typical of a military society, led in the fifteenth century to the dysfunction of the system for integrating the mamlūks and to the defeat at Marj Dābiq. The formation of a military aristocracy, which soon had no thought but the defence of its privileges, was another effect of the dysfunction and grew up to destroy the system. When the Circassian state collapsed in 1517, what disappeared was a political and military structure in crisis and too burdensome for the country's resources. The last sultans had sought to keep it going by means of

[78] J.-C. Garcin, "Note sur les rapports entre bédouins et fellahs à l'époque mamluke," *AI*, 14 (1978), 147–63.

[79] M. Müller-Wiener, *Eine Stadtgeschichte Alexandrias von 564/1169 bis in die Mitte des 9./15. Jahrhunderts* (Berlin, 1992), 71–89, 172–233.

[80] Khalīl al-Ẓahiri, *Zubda*, 33.

brutal fiscal extortion;[81] one of their failures was undoubtedly that they were incapable of innovation in that field or of making use of exceptional tax systems that often allowed wars (as happened in the monarchies of western Europe at that period) in order to ensure that the state functioned more smoothly. But that would have militated against the privileges of the regime's notables. Yet the Ottomans would inherit an experience of administration in which the measures taken were already frequently a matter of accepted secular practice and the liberalities of the first Mamlūk state had gradually been abandoned, despite the criticisms of the "avarice" of the sultans. In their way, and under the pressure of circumstances, the Circassians had favoured the emergence of the more modern state of the Ottomans in Egypt. The Circassian aristocracy would remain in place; it was now firmly entrenched. In the course of becoming settled, the Bedouin had imposed their presence in the countryside and, when they could, the rural inhabitants left for the towns, whose population remained constant. The capital was more huddled together and had taken on the more orderly, more compartmentalized appearance of the traditional towns, around a real urban commercial centre and the al-Azhar mosque. The city had its festivals and firmly fixed devotions, in the course of which the population experienced a sense of unity. This Egypt would last a very long time.

[81] Petry, *Protectors or Praetorians?*, 72–101, 131-89.

12

The monetary history of Egypt, 642–1517

WARREN C. SCHULTZ

"The economic, and perhaps even the political history of a country cannot be successfully investigated without a proper knowledge of the means of payment current in the period studied."[1] When it comes to Islamic Egypt, the sentiment behind these words has not fallen on deaf ears. Drawing upon sources – documentary, literary, and numismatic – that can only be described as rich, especially in comparison with other areas of the medieval Islamic world, much work has been produced about the monetary history of Islamic Egypt for the 875 years covered by this volume. Yet using this material is often fraught with difficulty. The research is scattered across the years and found in many journals – some well-known, some obscure – as well as in numerous monographs, collected-study volumes, encyclopedias and the like. Given the fragmented nature of this specialized scholarship, it is not unusual to find that even though many conclusions regarding various aspects of money in Islamic Egypt have trickled into the wider field of Egyptian history, others have remained in the preserve of numismatists. Furthermore, while limited narratives of Egyptian monetary policy – usually divided by dynastic period or type of coin – have been written, as yet no coherent narrative summary of Egyptian monetary developments from the Muslim conquest to the Ottoman takeover has been attempted.[2] This should not be a surprise, for such an undertaking would be huge indeed. It would also be premature prior to the publication of the Fusṭāṭ-Cairo volume of the

Support for research for this chapter was provided by the College of Liberal Arts and Sciences, DePaul University.

[1] S. D. Goitein, "The Exchange Rate of Gold and Silver in Fāṭimid and Ayyūbid Times," *JESHO*, 8 (1965), 1.

[2] Paul Balog, "History of the Dirham in Egypt from the Fāṭimid Conquest until the Collapse of the Mamlūk Empire," *RN*, 6th ser., 3 (1961); 109–46; Hassanein Rabie, *The Financial System of Egypt, AH 564–741/ AD 1169–1341* (London, 1972), ch. 5; Michael L. Bates, "Coins and Money in the Arabic Papyri," *Documents de L'Islam médiéval. Nouvelles perspectives de recherche* (Cairo, 1991), 43–64.

Sylloge Numorum Arabicorum, Tübingen.[3] What follows is necessarily only an overview of the monetary history of Egypt. It consists of two parts. The first discusses some of the basic terminology and the theoretical issues and controversies affecting the analysis of old money in Islamic Egypt. The second section provides an outline of Egyptian monetary history, broken into three periods: from the Muslim conquest to the Fāṭimids (642–969); the Fāṭimids and the Ayyūbids (969–1250); and finally developments in the Mamlūk period (1250–1517). By necessity, this second section does not give a detailed account of each and every coin type or issue, but is restricted to a discussion of general trends and major developments. Readers interested in pursuing detailed accounts are encouraged to delve into the works cited in the notes.

I

It is best to begin with definitions of the terms "money" and "coin." Specifics may vary, but most modern definitions of money explain it in terms of function: money is what money does. It serves as a store of value, a measure of value, and a means of exchange. In other words, while it is common to think of actual objects such as coins or paper bills as money, money is more than these physical items; it is also a system of valuation. This role is usually described by such terms as "accounting unit of value," or "money of account." It should be emphasized that this "money of account" is not an imaginary money. It may lack the physical form of a coin, but it is nonetheless real.[4] Any discussion of the circulation of pre-modern money must take this aspect of "money of account" into consideration.[5] In the case of Islamic Egypt, the evidence suggests that these monies of account were closely linked to units of weight associated with gold and silver coins.[6]

[3] This publication, based on the collection of Islamic Coins at the Forschungsstelle für islamische Numismatik, Tübingen, produces illustrated mint series of Islamic coins. To date, volumes covering Palestine and Khorasan (Ghazna and Kabul) have been published; the Hamah volume is expected in late 1997.

[4] Peter Spufford, *Money and Its Use in Medieval Europe* (Cambridge, 1988), 411–14. For the unit of account known as the *dīnār jayshī*, used to calculate the value of *iqṭā*ʿs in medieval Muslim Egypt, see Richard Cooper, "A note on the *dīnār jayshī*," *JESHO*, 16 (1973), 317–18.

[5] See Spufford, "Appendix: Coinage and Currency," *Cambridge Economic History of Europe*, vol. 3, (Cambridge, 1963), 593. The similarities between Spufford's analysis and that of Goitein are immediate and obvious (*A Mediterranean Society: The Jewish Communities of the Arab World as Portrayed in the Documents of the Cairo Geniza*, I, *Economic Foundations* (Berkeley, 1967).

[6] For the Umayyad and ʿAbbasid eras, see Bates, "Coins and Money in the Arabic Papyri," 54–60; for the Mamlūk period, see W. Schultz, "Mamlūk Money from Baybars to Barquq: A Study Based on the Literary Sources and the Numismatic Evidence" (Ph.D. dissertation, University of Chicago, 1995), 61–84.

A coin, of course, is a piece of metal used to fulfill the monetary roles of medium of exchange and store of value. Before the widespread acceptance of fiduciary money in the modern era, a coin's value – as measured by the money of account – was determined by three elements. The first was the value of its raw materials (bullion), or what is usually called its intrinsic value. The remaining two elements of value are determined by the actual production of the coins. They are the cost of minting and the profit to the coin maker. Together, the intrinsic value of the bullion plus the cost and profit of minting make up the coin's extrinsic or par value. Few would disagree that for coins struck in the precious metals of gold and silver, their bullion content was the main determinant of par value. The situation is somewhat different for coins made of copper and other base metals, or those with an extremely low silver content. These are often called petty, token, or fiduciary money, with the implication that their par value is based not on the extremely low intrinsic value of their metallic content, but on other factors, such as a government-imposed limit on the number of coins produced. (Thus it is easy to understand why such coins are usually of local currency only.) Whether these coins are of precious or base metal, economists assume that coins would circulate at par value once they left the mint if the issuing authority exercised a tight control over the monetary marketplace.

Invariably, however, a coin would encounter both coins like itself and other types of coins in the marketplace. (This is certainly the case in Egypt throughout the period considered here.) How these many coins circulated against each other is usually said to be governed by the principle commonly known as Gresham's law. Gresham's law states that when a coin of low intrinsic value circulates with a coin of equal extrinsic value but higher intrinsic value, the first coin will drive the second out of circulation. As it is sometimes stated, "bad money" (coins of low intrinsic value) drives out "good money" (coins of higher intrinsic value). In other words, if two gold coins are said to be worth the same amount (have the same extrinsic value) but one has more gold – i.e. it is either heavier or of a greater purity – the holder of the two coins will spend the lighter one and save the heavier.

Gresham's law appeals to common sense. It is important to note, however, that this model rests upon the assumption that the authority which issued the coin can enforce its declared extrinsic value once it is in circulation. A substantial body of literature now exists which argues that it is doubtful that any medieval government had to ability to do so. In the absence of this ability, the official extrinsic value of the coin would become meaningless, as once the coin entered circulation it would find its own value in relation to the other coins already present. This resulting value would be determined by a number of factors, such as bullion content and purity, supply of and demand for bullion, whether a coin was acceptable for payment of taxes and other official dues, consumer preference (which for Muslim users could be influenced in part by the presence of objectionable images or inscriptions), and so on. In such a marketplace, Gresham's law would not apply, as there is no "bad money" or "good money," only many different monies, circulating at varying exchange rates.

This "anti-Gresham's law" interpretation of medieval monetary markets is found primarily in discussions of medieval European monetary developments, although it also exists just beneath the surface of the most important analysis of monetary information found in the Geniza material.[7] Among the important exponents of this interpretation for the medieval Islamic world is Gilles Hennequin.[8] His works have been called an "indispensable starting point" for those interested in pre-modern monetary history.[9] His views have been aptly summarized as follows:

> In particular, Hennequin shows convincingly that all coins before the nineteenth century liberal era must be presumed to have circulated at a premium over their intrinsic bullion value, a premium set first by the cost of minting . . . but thereafter varying in the marketplace according to supply and demand. Not only did gold, silver and copper fluctuate in price in relation to the corresponding raw materials, but also against each other; moreover, even the exchange rate of two different coinages in the same metal would fluctuate around a norm set by their relative precious metal content. Hennequin stresses that in the absence of explicit evidence, we cannot assume that any pre-modern government ever effectively guaranteed the exchange rate of any of its issues against bullion or against other coins, by standing ready both to buy and sell at single fixed rate. *In this context, dīnārs* and dirhams, even when issued by the same mint at the same time, were as much two separate currencies as are pounds and dollars today. The operation of Gresham's law takes on a different character in such a situation, and such

[7] See the works of H. Miskimin, especially his "Money and Money Movements in France and England at the End of the Middle Ages," in D. S. Richards (ed.), *Precious Metals in the Later Medieval and Early Modern Worlds* (Durham, NC, 1983), 79–86; and his *Money and Power in Fifteenth Century France*, (New Haven, 1984), 68–72. For an analysis of money in the Geniza material, see Goitein, *Mediterranean Society*, I, 229–66.

[8] For Hennequin, see "Problèmes théoriques et pratiques de la monnaie antique et mediévale," *Annales Islamologiques*, 10 (1972), 1–57, and his other works listed in the bibliography. Cf. the important works of A. Udovitch, review of *Coinage of the Mamlūk Sultans of Egypt and Syria* by Paul Balog, *Journal of the American Oriental Society*, 90 (1970), 288–90; and his section of the important article co-written with Robert Lopez and Harry Miskimin, "England to Egypt, 1350–1500: Long-term Trends and Long-distance Trade," in M. A. Cook (ed.), *Studies in the Economic History of the Middle East* (Oxford, 1970), 124.

[9] Bates, "Islamic Numismatics (pt. 3)," MESA Bulletin, 13, 1 (1979), 13–14. Hennequin is not without his critics, however. The late Claude Cahen described his work as "too theoretical." Cahen, "Monetary Circulation in Egypt at the Time of the Crusades and the Reform of al-Kamil," in A. L. Udovitch (ed.), *The Islamic Middle East, 700–1900* (Princeton, 1981), 317, n. 1.

terms as "gold standard" or "bimetallism" become virtually meaningless [emphasis added].[10]

Lest one think this is an anachronistic application of modern monetary theory to an earlier time, this interpretation jibes well with the contemporary expression *siʿr allah*, "God's price," so frequently encountered in (at least) the Mamlūk sources. Furthermore, there is nothing to suggest that the existence of many types of coins caused any difficulties in the marketplace. Rather it was a known factor taken into account in business transactions. This is reflected, for example, in the contemporary *fiqh* material governing *muʿāmalāt* (pecuniary transactions). It is known that the *Shāfiʿī* school only allowed partnerships when the intermingling of indistinguishable assets was possible. The jurists were aware of the multiplicity of coins available to merchants, and therefore allowed that only coins of the same type satisfied this qualification.[11]

In such a monetary situation, it is easy to see why an important person in any marketplace was the *ṣayrafī*, the moneychanger, whose duty was not so much to make change but to determine the relative value of a coin.[12] There can also be little doubt that the primary characteristic of the coin used by the *ṣayrafī* to determine its value was bullion content. This too was sanctioned by the jurists, who were clearly aware of the differences between intrinsic and extrinsic value, and who rejected any method other than weighing to determine the true value of coins involved in transactions.[13] It seems clear that "the *fiqh*, established in an age of pluralism and monetary fluctuation, commanded that coins not be taken at face value, but according to weight (allowing for alloyage), in order to insure honesty, as one would deal in any other form of merchandise."[14]

The implications of this interpretation for our understanding of medieval Islamic money are important. In particular, the assertion about the meaninglessness of terms such as "gold standard," "silver standard," and so on, deserves further comment. It is quite common to encounter arguments in the literature that are based upon the assumption that such standards existed, where coins of one metal were said to have been "pegged" in value to those of another, that, for example, the Fāṭimids had a bimetallic standard, the Ayyūbids a gold standard, and the Mamlūks first a gold standard supported by silver, then a silver standard supported by copper, and the like. These

10 Bates, "Islamic Numismatics (pt. 3)," 13–14.

11 Udovitch, *Partnership and Profit in Medieval Islam* (Princeton, 1970), 33. In general, the juridical literature about money deserves closer attention, particularly for later periods such as the Mamlūk era.

12 See Cahen, "Monetary Circulation," 17.

13 Brunschvig, "Conceptions monétaires chez les juristes musulmans (VIIIe-XIIIe siècles)," *Arabica*, 14 (1967), 113–43; Udovitch, *Partnership and Profit*, 60–66.

14 Cahen, "Monetary Circulation," 326, citing Brunschvig.

interpretations need to be revisited and the evidence used in them reexamined. The burden is now on those who hold to the existence of metallic standards to prove that the respective governments had the ability to guarantee exchange rates and thus support such standards. In the absence of such proof, the default assumptions should be those mentioned above.

Finally, it is necessary to examine the contemporary vocabulary of money. In the medieval Islamic world the right to mint coins (*sikkah*) was one of two privileges traditionally reserved for a ruler, the other being the right to have the Friday congregational sermon (*khuṭbah*) delivered in his name. The basic terminology of the money issued was remarkably similar from place to place and time to time. While local usage of names for specific coins – bordering on slang – could vary tremendously, the following essentials remained fairly constant: a gold coin was almost always called a *dīnār* (pl. *danānīr*); a silver coin a *dirham* (pl. *dirāhim*); and a base metal coin was usually referred to as a *fals* (pl. *fulūs*).[15] These terms are best understood as generic labels for coins of specific metals; only in quite specific and limited instances should they be understood as denominational designations. Unfortunately for the modern interpreter of this money, while this basic terminology of Islamic coinage rarely changed, the actual coins referred to by these terms frequently did. The *dīnārs* issued during the reign of the Umayyad Caliph ʿAbd al-Mālik, for example, have little in common with the *dīnārs* of the Mamlūk Sultan Barqūq other than the type of metal used. The failure to address this fact of life has been the source of many modern misinterpretations.[16]

A similar situation is encountered with the terminology of metrology. A detailed discussion of Islamic metrology is beyond the scope of this chapter, but the following comments are in order. In usage dating from the Umayyad period, gold *dīnārs* were minted to the *mithqāl*-weight standard, and silver dirhams to the dirham-weight standard. Initially, these units are said to have been 4.25 and 2.97 grams respectively.[17] These values resulted in the oft-cited 7:10 ratio, where seven *mithqāls* amounted to the same total weight as ten dirhams. However, it is clear that these amounts were not constant over the passage of time or across the increasing geographic expanse of the Islamic world.[18] With regard to Islamic Egypt, the numismatic and coin-

[15] All three words are not of Arabic origin, but are derived ultimately from Greek or Latin. *Dīnār* and *dirham* appear in the Qur'ān, *fals* does not.

[16] See Andrew S. Ehrenkreutz's succinct discussion of this in "Monetary Aspects of Medieval Near Eastern Economic History," in M. A. Cook (ed.) *Studies in the Economic History of the Middle East.* (Oxford, 1970), 40–41.

[17] Eliyahu Ashtor, "Makāyīl and Mawāzīn," *EI2*, VI, 117–22; George C. Miles, "Dīnār," *EI2*, II, 297–99; idem, "Dirham," *EI2*, II, 319–20.

[18] Judith Kolbas, for example, has posited the existence of no less than four *mithqāl* standards in the medieval Islamic world, Kolbas, "Mongol Money: The Role of Tabriz from Chingiz Khan to to Uljaytu. 616 to 709 AH/1220 to 1309 AD" (Ph.D. dissertation, New York University, 1992), 8–9.

weight evidence indicates that both the *mithqāl* and the dirham units differed from those "classical" values, regardless of whether one is dealing with the Umayyad period or the Mamlūk period, and that at all times different localized values existed outside Cairo.[19]

Several additional factors add to the confusion surrounding monetary vocabulary. The first is the fact that these words can have multiple meanings dependent on context. This is especially true for the word dirham, which can mean alternatively a silver coin, a weight standard (with different values according to what was being weighed), or even a unit of account.[20] The vocabulary of money is also not used consistently in the contemporary sources. It is common, for example, to encounter the generic words for gold (*dhahab*) or silver (*fiḍḍah*) – or other synonyms – in contexts where coined money is clearly meant. Furthermore, it is clear that terms occasionally changed in meaning over time. A prime example of this is the word *nuqrah*. In Egypt, the label *nuqrah* was traditionally associated with silver coinage. It was used, however, to describe high-quality silver coins in the Fāṭimid-era Geniza documents,[21] "globular" dirhams of lower silver content during the Ayyūbid period,[22] and dirhams of about two-thirds silver purity in the Mamlūk era.[23] The reader of such passages must always be aware of these possibilities, and make every effort to corroborate the written sources with the surviving numismatic evidence.[24] Last but not least, it is clear that in the period in question there was no Arabic word for the abstract concept of money. This "terminological deficiency" undoubtedly "reflected economic realities. Gold and silver coins were means of payment, but were also traded like goods."[25] This factor also underscores the importance of the above observations regarding bullion content as the primary determinant of a coin's value.

19 See note 5 above; for an example of a local variant, in addition to the sources cited in note 16, see Miles, "The Early Islamic Bronze Coinage of Egypt," in Harald Ingholt (ed.), *The American Numismatic Society Centennial Volume*, (New York, 1958), 500.

20 E. Zambaur, "Kirāt," *EI1*, IV, 1023–24; Goitein, *Mediterranean Society*, I, 360.

21 Goitein, *Mediterranean Society*, I, 360.

22 Balog, "History of the Dirham in Egypt," 123–28.

23 Schultz, "Mamlūk Money from Baybars to Barquq," 141–49. Another example is the adjective *kāmilī*. In Egypt it was first used as a name for the silver dirhams introduced during the reign of the Ayyūbid al-Malik al-Kāmil (615–35/1218–38), reflecting the common practice of "naming" coins after the ruler whose name appears on them. Curiously however, the term *kāmilī dirham* reappears, primarily in the works of al-Maqrizi, to describe some of the silver coins circulating in Mamlūk Egypt at the end of the seventh/fourteenth century. The precise implications of this development are not known.

24 Note that Jere L. Bacharach has illustrated the perils of relying on numismatic evidence alone; see his "The Coinage of Kāfūr: A Cautionary Tale," *Israel Numismatic Journal*, 10 (1988–1989), 71–9.

25 Goitein, *Mediterranean Society*, I, 230.

II

From the Muslim conquest to the Fāṭimids[26]

Lacking a tradition of minting coins, as the early Muslim state expanded beyond the Arabian peninsula it simply adopted the coinage traditions of the lands conquered. In Mesopotamia and Iran this meant the coinage of the Sasanids. In Egypt (along with Syria and north Africa), this meant the coinage of the Byzantine empire. The only coins minted in the latter days of Byzantine Egypt were of copper. These large and thick pieces had imperial portraits, crosses, a mint name of ΑΛΕΞ (ALEX) for Alexandria, and the denomination mark IB for 12, standing for twelve *nummia*. Gold and silver coins no doubt circulated in Egypt in the 640s, but they had been minted elsewhere. Reflecting developments across the rapidly expanding Muslim empire, the new rulers of Egypt at first ordered few or no changes to the existing currency.[27] At an unknown date, and possibly reflecting a move of the mint from Alexandria to Fusṭāṭ, some of these "imitations" were struck with the mint name of MACP (MASR), reflecting a colloquial Arabic pronunciation of *Miṣr*, the classical Arabic name for Egypt.[28] Coins of this style continued to be struck until at least the end of the seventh century.[29]

The next major change in the copper coinage struck in Egypt was undoubtedly spurred by the well-known coinage reforms instituted by the Umayyad Caliph ʿAbd al-Malik. These resulted in the issuance of what have been called the "first purely Islamic coins."[30] Beginning in the year 77/697 for gold, and 79/698 for silver, purely epigraphic-style coins were struck (presumably first in Damascus, although the coin legends lack a mint-name), bearing only inscriptions in kufic script. Other than a mention of date, these inscriptions are of religious nature only.[31] There is no evidence to suggest

26 The best analysis of money in this period is found in Bates, "Coins and Money in the Arabic Papyri," 44–53.

27 The most thorough treatment of this early coinage is in a forthcoming article by Lidía Domaszewicz and Michael L. Bates, "The Copper Coinage of Egypt in the Seventh Century," in which they identify at least ten separate types of these coins.

28 First noted by Bacharach and Henri Amin Awad, "Rare Early Egyptian Islamic Coins and Coin weights: The Awad Collection," *JARCE*, 18 (1981), 51–52. Domaszewicz and Bates argue strongly against the use of the word "imitations" for these coins, "The Copper Coinage," 17.

29 Domaszewicz and Bates argue for a late seventh-century date for the (MASR) coins, "The Copper Coinage," 17.

30 Bates, *Islamic Coins*, American Numismatic Society Handbook 2 (New York, 1982), 14. Prior to this reform, monetary policy, such as it was, was determined at the provincial level, and could vary tremendously. See Bates, "History, Geography and Numismatics in the First Century of Islamic Coinage," *Revue Suisse de Numismatique*, 68 (1968), 236.

31 This post-reform coinage remains very regular in appearance. Silver stayed constant in style until about 145, when regional varieties begin to appear. The first substantial

that gold and silver coins of this style were ever minted in Egypt during the Umayyad period, but "Islamic-style" coppers began to appear in the province in the early 700s. These copper coins with Islamic inscriptions continued to be struck in Egypt until 170/786–87, with sporadic issues encountered up to the Ṭūlūnid period.[32] They frequently bear the names of governors and other officials. Most of these copper issues were minted at Fusṭāṭ, although during the governorship of ʿAbd al-Malik ibn Marwān (131–32/749–50), the last Umayyad governor of Egypt, *fulūs* are known from a number of mints, including Fusṭāṭ, Alexandria, the Fayyūm, and Atrīb in the delta. In general, the design and inscriptions of these *fulūs* change slightly over this span of time, and are similar to contemporary copper issues of Syria, but the fabric tends to be thicker.

This last factor raises an interesting possibility. These early *fulūs* of Islamic Egypt seem to have circulated only within Egypt itself.[33] Copper coins are usually assumed to be fiduciary money. Could the thickness and varying weights that are found in early Islamic Egyptian copper coins indicate that these coins had a par value dependant primarily on their copper content? This possibility was first raised thirty years ago in an analysis of the glass coin weights labeled *fals* which survive from the first two centuries of Islamic rule in Egypt.[34] If this is indeed the case, the differences in value between such small increments of weight have yet to be determined.

After the copper issue of the earlier Ṭūlūnid period alluded to above, there are no known specimens of copper coins minted in Egypt until the reign of the Ayyūbid al-Malik al-Kāmil in 622/1225. The reasons for this apparent hiatus in *fulūs* production are not definitely known. Nor has it been clearly established what fulfilled the need for small change in its absence.

As for precious-metal coins, they were not struck in the new Islamic province of Egypt until the ʿAbbāsid period. The first gold *dīnārs* bearing the mint name of Miṣr are dated 199 H, although it is likely that *dīnārs* were struck in Egypt as early as 170 H. Beginning in that year and continuing until 199, a series of *dīnārs* exists that bear a sequence of names that

design changes in gold do not appear until the reigns of the caliphs al-Ma'mūn and al-Muʿtaṣim. For an overview of the reform coinage, see Stephen Album, *Checklist of Popular Islamic Coins* (Santa Rosa, CA, 1993), 10–12.The dates of appearance for these coins are based on the earliest known specimens to have survived.

32 Miles, "The Early Islamic Bronze Coinage of Egypt," 471–502.

33 Bates, "Coins and Money in the Arabic Papyri," 45.

34 Miles, "On Varieties and Accuracy of Eighth Century Arab Coin Weights," *Eretz Israel*, 7 (1963), 83–87; This possibility was also addressed by Bates, "Coins and Money in the Arabic Papyri," 57. Cf. Bacharach and Awad, "The Early Islamic Bronze Coinage of Egypt: Additions," in Dickran J. Kouymjian (ed.), *Near Eastern Numismatics, Iconography, Epigraphy and History: Studies in Honour of George C. Miles* (Beirut, 1974), 188, 190. The glass *fals* weights have been placed in a chronological order by A. H. Morton, *A Catalogue of the Early Islamic Glass Stamps in the British Museum* (London, 1985).

correspond to the known ʿAbbāsid governors of the province.[35] These *dīnārs* are of typical ʿAbbāsid style, and inaugurate a practically unbroken and abundant series of gold issues minted in the Egyptian capital that lasted up to the Fāṭimid conquest. From 215 onwards these *dīnārs* bear the name of the ʿAbbāsid Caliph. From 266–292, the names of Aḥmad ibn Ṭūlūn and his successors also appear on the *dīnārs*, reflecting the (semi-) autonomous stature of the Egyptian province under the Ṭūlūnids. The situation is repeated again from 332–358 with the *dīnārs* of the Ikhshīdid rulers. In the important area of alloy, one study has shown that the standard of fineness of Egyptian *dīnārs* throughout this period was extremely high, with only a slight debasement seen in the *dīnārs* struck by the successors of Aḥmad ibn Ṭūlūn, and a "temporary serious debasement" observed during the period of ʿAbbāsid restoration in Egypt after the fall of the Ṭūlūnids. "But the usual excellent standard of Egyptian gold coinage was re-established by the Ikhshīdids."[36] The figures of 98 percent purity quoted in this study should be revised slightly downward, however, in light of increased awareness of the limitations of the specific gravity method used for testing gold alloy.[37]

It is probable that the minting of silver dirhams in Egypt also began in 170, but the earliest specimen known thus far has the date 171. Dirhams minted in Egypt from the period up to the Fāṭimid conquest are extremely rare in most modern collections, and this has hampered our knowledge of contemporary developments in this coinage. It is likely, however, that most of the silver circulating in Egypt at this time had been minted elsewhere.[38]

The Fāṭimids and Ayyūbids

The Ṭūlūnid and Ikhshīdid periods have been said to inaugurate the separate history of Egypt vis à vis the rest of the Islamic world. This is clearly not the case in monetary developments, where it is the Fāṭimid conquest in 358/969 that marks the important turning point in the history of Egyptian coinage. This is especially evident with developments in gold. Prior to the arrival of the Fāṭimids, the gold coins of Egypt resembled those minted in the other central provinces of the ʿAbbāsid empire. They featured inscriptions arranged in horizontal lines on the central field of both the obverse and reverse

[35] Bates, "Coins and Money in the Arabic Papyri," 50–52.

[36] Ehrenkreutz, "Studies in the Monetary History of the Near East in the Middle Ages: The Standard of Fineness of some types of Dinars," *JESHO*, 2 (1959), 154. In contemporary sources, the gold coins of Aḥmad ibn Ṭūlūn, known as *aḥmadīyah dīnārs*, are described as prized for their purity.

[37] While made in reference to Ehrenkreutz's measurements of Fāṭimid *dīnārs*, the observations of Oddy are applicable here as well. W. A. Oddy, "The Gold Content of Fāṭimid Coins Reconsidered," *Metallurgy in Numismatics*, I, ed. D. M. Metcalf and W. A Oddy. (London, 1980), 99–100.

[38] Bates, "Coins and Money in the Arabic Papyri," 52, 56.

sides. Under the Fāṭimids, however, the *dīnārs* of Egypt became immediately recognizable from those produced in neighboring regions. These Fāṭimid *dīnārs*, minted in both Cairo and Alexandria, sported a striking new design; the inscribed legends – now featuring appropriately ʿAlid sentiments – were arranged in concentric circles.[39] This concentric circle arrangement was kept until the end of the dynasty, albeit with some stylistic and inscriptional modifications.[40] In both style and content, these coins reflect the "Fāṭimid rejection of the sunnī consensus."[41] The ʿAlid nature of Fāṭimid coin inscriptions has attracted much attention, and while it should not be forgotten that the primary purpose of money is economic in nature, the phrases found on these coins represent a clear example of the use of money for propaganda purposes.[42]

In the analyses of alloy that have been conducted to date, Egyptian Fāṭimid *dīnārs* measure consistently high in purity, almost always above 95 percent pure and usually reaching 97–98 percent.[43] Thus it seems that the Fāṭimids met the promise made by their general Jawhar to the notables of Fusṭāṭ during the negotiations leading up to the Fāṭimid occupation to improve the fineness of circulating *dīnārs* in Egypt.[44] During the reigns of al-Mustaʿlī (487–95/1094–1101) and al-Āmir (495–525/1100–30), the fineness is in the 98–99 percent range. This seems to have been the result of a deliberate effort, since from the reign of al-Mustaʿlī onwards, the phrase

39 This style is subsequently imitated by neighboring states, most notably the crusader principalities. See Ehrenkreutz, "Arabic dīnārs struck by the Crusaders," *JESHO*, 7 (1964), 167–82, and A. A. Gordus and D. M. Metcalf, "Neutron Activation Analysis of the Gold Coinages of the Crusader States," *Metallurgy in Numismatics*, 119–50.

40 The Fāṭimids also minted the first Egyptian coin known that has its inscriptions in the *naskhi* script rather than the hitherto ubiquitous kufic. Balog, "Apparition prematurée de l'écriture nashky sur un *dīnār* de l'Imam fatimite Al Moustaly-Billah." *Bulletin de l'Institut d'Egypte*, 31 (1949), 181–85. *Naskhi* was not used again until the coinage of the Ayyubid al-Kāmil Muḥammad.

41 Bates, Islamic Coins, 30.

42 Andrew S. Ehrenkreutz and G. W. Heck, "Additional Evidence of the Fāṭimid Use of Dinars for Propaganda Purposes," in M. Sharon (ed.), *Studies in Islamic History and Civilization in Honour of Professor David Ayalon* (Jerusalem, 1986), 145–51.

43 Oddy, "The Gold Contents of Fāṭimid Coins Reconsidered," 105–107. Cf. Ehrenkreutz, "Studies in the Monetary History of the Near East in the Middle Ages, II: The standard of fineness of western and eastern *dīnārs* before the crusades," *JESHO*, 6 (1963), 257–60.

44 For the circumstances surrounding this promise, and the contemporary numismatic situation, compare the discussions found in Ehrenkreutz, "Studies in Monetary History," 257–58; Rabie, *The Financial System of Egypt*, 163; and John D. Lowe, "A Medieval Instance of Gresham's Law: The Fāṭimid Monetary System and the Decline of Bimetallism," *Jusūr*, 2 (1968), 5. Given that modern studies of purity have shown that Ikhshīdid *dīnārs* were extremely fine, this apparent contradiction between numismatic and chronicle evidence has usually been explained by referring to the presence in Egypt of debased *dīnārs* from Iraq.

ʿālin ghāyah (extremely high) appears on the center of most Egyptian Fāṭimid *dīnārs*.

As for developments in silver, there are few Fāṭimid dirhams found in the published catalogues of major public collections. This lacuna has been cited in support of the existence of a silver famine across the Islamic world in the eleventh and twelfth centuries. The wider debate about the silver famine lies outside the purview of this chapter, but the following comments are in order. Despite the lack of published specimens, the Fāṭimid-era sources themselves are replete with mentions of silver in the course of everyday economic transactions.[45] This is most easily seen in the abundant exchange-rate information found in the Geniza material.[46] Obviously, this silver had to come from somewhere. Some of it may have been in the form of old coins, and some was certainly of foreign origin, but there were also dirhams of contemporary Egyptian origin. On this the numismatic evidence is clear. This was confirmed by archaeological excavations in Fusṭāṭ, which indicated that silver was minted in Egypt from the end of the eleventh century onwards.[47] However, this Egyptian-produced silver was not of the large round flan type with easy-to-read inscriptions produced in earlier periods. Most of these coins were "black" dirhams, so called in the contemporary sources because their low silver alloy (30 percent or less) resulted in a dark appearance. (Silver coins of high fineness were often called "white.") The vast majority were also small, with the result that legends on any individual coin are always only partial, since the coin die used was always larger than the coin blank struck. Some examples of larger flan but also quite debased dirhams are known from the very end of the Fāṭimid period. Modern-day attribution of the smaller coins has been difficult, since many specimens are usually needed to piece together the coin inscriptions. They are, quite frankly, ugly little coins, and have not registered on the interest scale of collectors and curators.[48] Nevertheless, the existence of such dirhams throughout the remainder of the Fāṭimid era and into the early Ayyūbid period is certain.

The same cannot be said about Fāṭimid copper coins. There is no evidence, numismatic or literary, that indicates that the Fāṭimids minted copper coins. Nor is there anything to suggest that the early Ayyubids

45 As was stressed by Cahen, "Monetary Circulation in Egypt," 320–21.

46 Goitein, "The Exchange Rate of Gold and Silver Money."

47 Balog, first pointed this out in "Études numismatiques de l'Égypte musulmane, III," *BIE* 35 (1952–53), 401–29; on the presence of this silver at Fusṭāṭ, see Bates, "The Function of Fāṭimid and Ayyubid Glass Weights," *JESHO*, 24 (1981), 89.

48 With the obvious exception of Balog (see preceding note). The case of these coins is an example of how scholarship was limited by the acquisition tastes behind most collections, which run toward the rare and the gorgeous and ignore the common and the ugly. Such cases led Cahen to remind us that a gap in "our collections does not give us license to deduce systematic conclusions." "Monetary Circulation in Egypt," 321.

minted *fulūs* prior to 622/1225. In light of this absence of copper coins, a debate has simmered in the literature as to what fulfilled the role of small change in Fāṭimid and early Ayyūbid times. At the center of this debate are small glass and glass-paste disks that survive in large numbers from the period in question. They bear inscriptions, and their weights fall in the range of values associated with the dirham, the *mithqāl*, and multiples and fractions thereof. One view argues that these disks – or "jetons" – were the official fiduciary coinage of the Fāṭimid period, and remained so until the copper issue of 622/1225.[49] The opposing view holds that these glass objects were coin weights; necessary to determine the value of coins used in transactions. The need for small change, it is argued, was adequately fulfilled by the base silver dirhams.[50] Underpinning this second view is the complete lack of mention of the use of glass as money in any contemporary or near contemporary source, a point that has not been adequately rebutted. In the light of what is known about medieval Muslim juridical theories of money, a deliberate attempt by the Fāṭimids to introduce glass money would certainly have attracted attention – and probable condemnation – as an innovation, *bida*ʿ. That said, it is entirely possible that these glass disks did circulate as an unofficial token money among the common people. After all, most anything can be used as means of exchange as long as it is accepted for use; al-Maqrīzī himself wrote that in his youth he saw people in Alexandria using bread as money in small transactions.[51] Nonetheless, it is highly unlikely that these "jetons" were ever an official money, acceptable for the payment of taxes, duties and the like.

Ayyūbid *dīnārs* were minted in both Cairo and Alexandria. The first Ayyūbid gold coins featured the concentric circle design initiated by the Fāṭimids.[52] Changes were immediately made in the inscriptions, however. From the beginning of Ṣalāḥ al-Dīn's reign (564–89/1169–93), all Shiʿite sentiments were removed and the name of the ʿAbbāsid caliph replaced that of the Fāṭimid ruler. (The earliest Egyptian *dīnārs* issued under Ṣalāḥ al-Dīn also bear the name of the Zangid Nūr al-Dīn.) A subsequent design change appeared during the reign of al-ʿĀdil Abū Bakr (596–615/1200–18), when the legends were arranged horizontally on a large central field. From the reign of al-Kāmil Muḥammad (615–35/1218–38), these legends were written in the *naskhi* script, which thenceforth appeared on all Ayyūbid and

49 Balog, "The Ayyubid Glass Jetons and Their Use," *JESHO*, 9 (1966), 242–56; "Fāṭimid Glass Jetons: Token Currency or Coin Weights," *JESHO*, 24 (1981), 93–109.

50 Bates, "The Function of Fāṭimid and Ayyubid Glass Weights," *JESHO*, 24 (1981), 63–92.

51 Al-Maqrīzī, *Ighāthat al-ummah bi-kashf al-ghummah* (Cairo,1940), 69.

52 For crusader imitations of Ayyubid gold, see Bates, "Thirteenth Century Imitation of Ayyubid Silver Coinage: A Preliminary Survey," *Studies in Honor of George C. Miles*, 393–409.

Mamlūk coins. The standard of fineness of most Ayyūbid *dīnārs* was also extremely high, usually above 95 percent according to limited data available.[53] The major exception to this observation is the gold coinage of Ṣalāḥ al-Dīn. Out of a sample of 44 *dīnārs* of his reign that were analyzed, 13 (slightly less than 30 percent) had a fineness of less than 90 percent gold. On the basis of these findings, it has been argued that Ṣalāḥ al-Dīn purposely debased the gold coinage of Egypt to finance his military adventures. While this is possible, the decline in alloy may reflect merely a temporary shortage of bullion, brought on in part, no doubt, by the hoarding of money in light of the political and military uncertainty of the last days of Fāṭimid rule. It is unfortunate that the path-breaking work on this issue has not triggered further study.

A final general trend in the issuing of the Egyptian gold coinage of the Fāṭimid and Ayyūbid periods should be noted here, even though it was not at its most developed until the Mamlūk period. Up to the Fāṭimid conquest, the gold minted in Egypt was struck with incredible care regarding to weight. Most surviving specimens are within 0.10 to 0.20 grams of a median range of 4.10 to 4.20 grams.[54] During the Fāṭimid era, however, the range of weights encountered for gold coins begins to grow larger. At first this is seen in variances of 0.2 to 0.3 grams. This development continues into the Ayyūbid period, where variances of a gram or more are common.[55] The degree of variance grows even wider in the Mamlūk period. Mamlūk *dīnārs*, up to the appearance of the *ashrafī dīnār* during the reign of the Sultan al-Ashraf Barsbay (discussed below), range from 3 to more than 15 grams in weight. This apparent carelessness over weight should not be interpreted as the abandonment of gold as a currency, or as an indicator of scarcity.[56] When combined with the observation that glass coin weights, present since the first years of Islamic Egypt, appear in greater numbers during the Fāṭimid period and continued to be produced in large quantities through Mamlūk times, this metrological development leads to one conclusion: since gold coins would be weighed for all but the smallest transactions, the weight of one *dīnār* out of many was not important. What mattered was the total weight of the sum changing hands. In such a situation, there was no longer a need to produce a tightly regulated (by weight) coinage. Not surprisingly, our best source of information regarding the metrological underpinnings of

[53] Ehrenkreutz, "The Crisis of the Dinar in the Egypt of Ṣalāḥ al-Dīn," *JAOS*, 76 (1956), 178–84.

[54] The observations in this paragraph are based on my examination of the gold coins preserved at the American Numismatic Society in New York. No one has yet undertaken a thorough examination of the gold metrology for the Fāṭimid and Ayyūbid periods.

[55] These developments are illustrated in Table I of Ehrenkreutz, "The Crisis of Dinar," 179.

[56] Balog, *The Coinage of the Ayyubids* (London, 1980), 35.

these *dīnārs* are the glass coin weights and not the *dīnārs* themselves. The interesting question remains, however, as to why it took those in control of the mint such a long time to free the minters from the difficult task of preparing coins of consistent weight.

The problems surrounding our understanding of Ayyūbid silver coinage and how it circulated are complicated, and have not yet been successfully untangled. This particular aspect of Egyptian monetary history awaits a thorough analysis based upon the careful examination of the numismatic, documentary, and literary sources.[57] The earliest Ayyūbid silver was similar to its Fāṭimid predecessors. Black dirhams, also called *wariq* in the sources, were struck in Ayyūbid Egypt up to the reign al-Kāmil Muḥammad. In al-Kāmil Muḥammad's reign, a new type of debased silver coin was minted. These coins are known to be only about one-third silver or less, and have occasionally been called "globular" dirhams in reference to their immediately recognizable appearance.[58] The method of preparation of these coins is described in Ibn Baʿra's mint manual.[59] These coins may be the well-known *kāmilī* dirhams described by al-Maqrīzī, but this conclusion is based upon the assertion that a scribal error exists in that historian's account, since al-Maqrīzī's text as we have it describes the *kāmilī* as two-thirds silver and one-third copper.[60]

The numismatic record indicates that coins of this type continued to be struck until the transitional period between the death of al-Malik al-Ṣāliḥ and the accession of al-Ẓāhir Baybars. Black dirhams of the *wariq* type do not seem to have been minted after the appearance of the "globular" coins, yet they undoubtedly continued to circulate. It is clear, however, that poor-quality silver coins were not the only dirhams in circulation. Large, round-flan dirhams with higher silver content were minted during Ṣalāḥ al-Dīn's reign; they were called *nāsirī* dirhams after his *laqab*, al-Mālik al-Nāsir.[61] These coins were said to be 50 percent silver, 50 percent copper, but since few of these coins are known today, this has not been adequately tested by modern analysis. Examples of this large, round-flan dirham are also known from later reigns, especially that of al-ʿĀdil Abū Bakr. Whether these coins

57 The basic sequence of coin issues is known, thanks to the work of Balog, *The Coinage of the Ayyubids*, along with N. D. Nicol, "Paul Balog's *The Coinage of the Ayyubids*: Additions and Corrections," *Numismatic Chronicle*, 146 (1986), 119–54.

58 Balog, "History of the Dirham in Egypt," 130; idem., *Coinage of the Ayyubids*, 37–38.

59 Ibn Baʿra, *Kasf al-asrār al-ʿilmīyah bi-dār al-darb al-misrīyah*. (Cairo, 1966). The relevant passage is discussed by Ehrenkreutz, "Extracts from the technical Manual on the Ayyubid Mint in Cairo," *Bulletin of the School of Oriental and African Studies*, 15 (1959), 430–32. The Ayyubid period is the only one for which we have detailed information about the operation of the mint.

60 Al-Maqrīzī, in L. A. Mayer (ed.), *Shudhūr alʿUqūd* (Alexandria, 1939), 12; Cahen, "Monetary Circulation in Egypt," 328–30.

61 See the discussion and sources cited in Rabie, *Financial System of Egypt*, 173–76.

represent failed attempts to reform the silver coinage as has been asserted, or merely attempts to introduce higher-value dirhams into circulation remains open to debate. It seems clear from the numismatic record that they did not replace the black dirhams, but that by itself is no reason to assert that they lost currency. It is thus probable that silver coins of widely varying type and value were both minted and circulating at the same time throughout the Ayyūbid period.

It is certain, however, that the minting of copper coins in Egypt resumed during the reign of al-Kāmil Muḥammad, most probably in 622/1225 or shortly thereafter.[62] This is supported by both the numismatic evidence and the accounts preserved in accounts by Mamlūk-era historians. These same accounts state that once issued, these *fulūs* underwent large swings in value, a development also quite common in the Mamlūk era.[63] Copper coins of similar style and fabric to those of al-Kāmil Muḥammad are also known from the reign of al-Malik al-Ṣāliḥ Ayyūb (637–47/1240–49). The account of *fulūs* struck during the reign of al-ʿĀdil II (635–37/1238–40) found in al-Maqrīzī's *Kitāb al-Sulūk* has not yet been corroborated by a surviving coin.[64]

The Mamlūk period

The sources available for the study of Mamlūk money are abundant. The chronicles have been mined for their rich veins of monetary information since the nineteenth century. Much of the numismatic evidence has been accessible to scholars since the publication of a corpus of Mamlūk coinage in 1964.[65] As a result, quantitatively we know more about monetary developments in the Mamlūk sultanate than in any earlier period of Islamic Egypt.[66] Only a bare outline of developments is sketched below, discussing first the precious metal coinages, and concluding with copper.

The Mamlūks, like the Ayyūbids before them, minted coins in both Cairo and Alexandria. The surviving numismatic record indicates that the former mint was in almost constant use, the latter only intermittently.[67] It must be stressed that this same numismatic record proves that the Mamlūks minted

62 Balog, "Ayyubid Divisional Currency Issued in Egypt by al-Kāmil Muḥammad," *Gazette numismatique suisse*, 27 (1977), 62–67.

63 Rabie, *The Financial System of Egypt*, 182–83.

64 Al-Maqrīzī, *Kitāb al-Sulūk*, I, 274.

65 Balog, *The Coinage of the Mamlūk Sultans of Egypt and Syria* (New York, 1964).

66 Yet there is still work to be done. The *waqf* documents, for example, have only just begun to be analyzed for their monetary information. Hennequin, "Waqf et monnaie dans l'Égypte mamlūke," *JESHO*, 38 (1995), 305–12.

67 The Alexandria mint seems to have produced mainly gold coins, although it factored heavily in the apparent explosion of copper coinage at the end of the eighth/fourteenth century. Silver from Alexandria is extremely rare today; only a single specimen is known.

gold and silver coins (at least in Cairo) consistently throughout the 267-year period of their rule. Any suspensions of mint activity in either gold or silver should be understood as temporary or short-term disruptions, brought on by factors such as acute bullion shortage, hoarding, political uncertainty, etc.[68] They do not represent the abandonment of a currency as has sometimes been argued. On this observation there can be no doubt. A survey of the Cairo mint issues reveals that precious-metal coins were minted with almost yearly regularity during the reigns of all but the most ephemeral stake-holding sultans.

Developments in Mamlūk gold and silver coinage fall into two periods. The first lasted from the reign of the Sultan al-Ẓāhir Baybars (658–76/1260–77) up to the end of the eighth/fourteenth century. The second began in the early decades of the ninth/fifteenth century, when a major transformation in Mamlūk money occurred and lasted to the end of the sultanate. The Mamlūk *dīnārs* of the first period are easily described. They were coins of high purity and of widely irregular weights.[69] In design they resembled the later Ayyūbid *dīnārs*, consisting of a large central field featuring several lines of text. These coins were valued according to a money of account based on the *mithqāl*, which in Mamlūk Cairo was around 4.3 grams, slightly higher than the "classical" value of 4.25 grams.[70] One *mithqāl* of gold was usually worth about 20 to 25 dirhams' worth of silver (and vice versa), according to the most commonly encountered exchange rates found in the contemporary sources, although wide fluctuations were also mentioned. An example of the latter was the well-known visit of Mansa Mūsā to Cairo in 1324, when, according to al-Maqrīzī, the Malian ruler spent and gave away so much gold that the *mithqāl* temporarily fell in value by six dirhams.[71]

Mamlūk silver coins for this first period are also very recognizable.[72] New dirhams were struck during the reign of the Sultan al-Zāhir Baybars. These coins featured several lines of inscriptions and an image of a lion or panther. With only minor design or inscriptional changes (the animal no longer appeared after the reigns of Baybars's sons), coins of this type were minted until the last reign of al-Ẓāhir Barqūq (792–801/1390–99). Due to their irregular weight, ranging from less than 1 to more than 5 grams, there can be little doubt that they were weighed in transactions. The survival of

68 The international context of bullion flow and regional bullion scarcity has been explored to productive ends by Shoshan in an important series of articles (listed in the bibliography). The Mamlūk demand for bullion clearly outstripped the supply.

69 Bacharach, "Monetary movements in medieval Egypt, 1171–1517," in J. F. Richards (ed.) *Precious metals in the later Medieval and Early Modern Worlds* (Durham, NC, 1983), 174–76.

70 See Schultz, "Mamlūk Money from Baybars to Barquq," 64–71, 85–103.

71 Al-Maqrīzī, *Sulūk*, II, 255.

72 See Schultz, "Mamlūk Money from Baybars to Barquq," 103–62, for a more detailed discussion of the silver developments in this period.

hundreds of glass coin-weights of either 3 or 6 grams not only supports this assertion, but also provides a value for the dirham weight unit in Mamlūk times. The most important new characteristic of these coins, however, was their purity. Both the contemporary chronicles and modern analysis indicate that these coins were consistently 65–75 percent silver, with the remainder copper. They were thus significantly finer dirhams than those issued under the Ayyūbids.[73] There is evidence to suggest that there was a decline in purity by the end of the century, but the matter needs further research.[74] The silver content of Mamlūk dirhams of this era is also the key to understanding the frequent appearance of Armenian silver coins in Mamlūk-era archaeological sites and coin hoards. These Armenian *trams*, which entered the Mamlūk domains as tribute, had the same level of purity as the Mamlūk dirhams, and thus circulated alongside those coins with little difficulty.[75]

By the end of the eighth/fourteenth century in Egypt, both the numismatic and literary evidence indicates that there were many different types of precious metal coins in circulation in Mamlūk Egypt. There were coins from the reigns of earlier Mamlūk sultans and *dīnārs* and dirhams from the Mamlūk Syrian mints, as well as coins from foreign powers. The chronicles in particular mention the increasing frequency with which the Venetian ducat circulated in Muslim marketplaces.[76] The appearance of these foreign coins has usually been cited as the principal reason behind the reforms in Mamlūk money undertaken at the beginning of the subsequent century. As a result of these reform efforts, the Mamlūk gold and silver coinage of 1430 was far different from that of 1390.

These developments have been well described in numerous studies.[77] Briefly, they resulted in the appearance of new and smaller coins, prepared with such care that the sources indicate they could even pass by tale.[78] The new gold coins were called *ashrafīs*, since they first appeared during the

[73] Bacharach and Gordus, "Studies on the Fineness of Silver Coins," *JESHO*, 11 (1968), 308–10. Significantly, coins of this type were struck in both Egypt and Syria.

[74] The chronicle evidence is especially problematic. Al-Maqrīzī makes several references to the appearance of "*kāmilī*" dirhams at this time, but it is not clear what he means by this term. It is highly unlikely that these were dirhams of the Ayyūbid al-Malik al-Kāmil as has been argued by Shoshan ("Exchange-Rate Policies in Fifteenth-century Egypt," *JESHO*, 29 (1986), 44). It is not supported by hoard evidence.

[75] For the silver content of these *trams*, see Alan Stahl, "Italian Sources for the Coinage of Cilician Armenia," *Armenian Numismatic Journal*," 15 (1989), 59–66; and Bacharach, "Monetary Movement," 178.

[76] Bacharach, "The Ducat in Fourteenth Century Egypt," *Res Orientales*, 6 (1994), 95–101.

[77] The reader is referred to the important studies by Bacharach and Shoshan listed in the bibliography.

[78] See, for example, al-Asadi, *Kitāb al-taysīr*, (Cairo, 1968), 127. How successful these reforms were in achieving this convenience is questionable. There are also references to these same coins being weighed.

reign of al-Ashraf Barsbāy (825–841/1422–1438).[79] Coins of this type were struck during the reigns of all subsequent major (and some minor) Mamlūk sultans. They were of high fineness up until the very end of the sultanate. Most notably, however, they were minted to a new weight standard, one not based on the Muslim *mithqāl*, but apparently derived from (or at least influenced by) the weight of the Venetian ducat.[80]

The new silver coins first appeared in the short reign of the ʿAbbāsid Caliph al-Mustaʿīn (815/1412). These coins and those struck by succeeding sultans are smaller, thinner, lighter, and of finer silver than the dirhams of the preceding period. Their silver content was usually 80–90 percent, although there is indication of a slight debasement by the reign of Qānṣūh al-Ghawrī (906–22/1501–16).[81] Many also bore denominational legends, usually identifying the coin as being a fraction (e.g. $\frac{1}{2}$, $\frac{3}{8}$) of a dirham. These coins may be the most understudied body of numismatic evidence that survives from the Mamlūk period. In particular, they await a detailed study of their metrology. In any case, enough survive to remind us that even though they seem to have been in short supply, silver coins were minted throughout the Circassian period.

The numismatic record is not so forthcoming for the study of Mamlūk copper. There are two long periods for which we have few or no surviving coins. The first is the initial half-century of Mamlūk rule, where, once we move beyond a few *fulūs* of Baybars, there are no surviving copper coins that have been definitely attributed to the Cairo mint. It is not until the early years of the eighth/fourteenth century that copper coins are known in any numbers. The second gap falls in the first half of the ninth/fifteenth century, when from the reign of al-Nāṣir Faraj (801–15/1399–1412, with a brief interregnum) up to that of al-Ashraf Aynāl (857–65/1453–61) only a few *fulūs* of Barsbāy are known. In fact, the only coppers minted during the ninth/fifteenth century for which specimens are known in any quantity are the issues of Sultan al-Ashraf Qāytbāy (872–901/1468–96).[82] Nevertheless, the chronicles are replete with references to copper coins, and, for at least one period, these coins survive in the thousands. The following trends are observable.

The chronicle evidence indicates that for most of the eighth/fourteenth century, Egyptian copper coinage was struck to weight standards. When the

[79] Technically only *dīnārs* produced during this sultan's reign should be called by this term, but the label is frequently applied to all coins of this easily recognizable style.

[80] Bacharach, "The Dinar versus the Ducat," *IJMES*, 4 (1973), 77–96.

[81] Bacharach, "Monetary Movements," 178. The data are inconsistent, however, with some dirhams falling in the 70 percent range, and many more reaching 95 percent.

[82] For an important reassessment of late Mamlūk *fulūs*, see John L. Meloy, "The Copper Coinage of Late Mamlūk Cairo, 1468–1517," an unpublished paper from the 1992 American Numismatic Society summer graduate seminar.

numismatic evidence is surveyed it is clear that this was the case.[83] Up to the year 759/1357–58, the *fulūs* were struck close to a mean weight of 3 grams. From that year up until 794/1391–92 they were minted close to a mean weight of 4.3 grams. The reasons for the minting of fixed weight *fulūs* are not explicit in the sources, although it has been argued that weight standards were fixed for these coins in order to aid in their circulation.[84] Whatever the case, the Mamlūk copper coinage of this century is remarkable for its metrological stability. This changed dramatically in the century's last decade, during the second reign of Barqūq.

Beginning in that decade more and more copper coins entered into circulation, to the extent that al-Maqrīzī mentioned many times that they became the dominant currency in the country.[85] The reasons for this development are not completely understood, but it clearly happened. Extrapolating from the thousands of coins from this era that have survived to our own, it has been estimated that they may have been issued in the hundreds of thousands.[86] When, in 806/1403, it was ordered by the chief qāḍī that prices, contracts, and debts were to be recorded in terms of this copper money, Egypt had clearly entered the "age of copper."[87]

The key to understanding developments in copper coinage for the rest of the ninth/fifteenth century is understanding the term *dirham min al-fulūs*, so ubiquitous in the sources. This phrase refers to a money of account. It does not mean an individual copper coin weighing a dirham, but rather the amount of copper coins necessary to equal the value of one silver dirham.[88] Two further comments are necessary. First, exchange rates using this term

83 These developments are discussed in greater detail in Schultz, "Mahmud ibn ʿAli and the New Fulūs: Fourteenth century Egyptian Copper Coinage Reconsidered," forthcoming.

84 Schultz, "Mamlūk Money from Baybars to Barquq," 169–175. For example, al-Maqrizi wrote that the first copper weight standard was fixed at a dirham in the year 695/1295–96 (*Ighāthat al-Umma*, 70, cf. 37–38). In that same year we read that it took one ratl of *fulūs* to buy two silver dirhams. The ratl unit consisted of 144 dirham-weight units. At such an exchange rate, if the copper coins averaged a dirham in weight, then it would take 72 copper coins to buy a silver coin. In such a situation, a merchant who accepted many copper coins by count in a series of small transactions would not have to worry about loss of value when he used those same coppers in bulk for a larger purchase.

85 Al-Maqrīzī, Sulūk, IV, 165, 205, 280, 306. Shoshan's comments regarding the existence of two distinct sectors of economic activity – where gold served the needs of the government and overseas trade and copper was used for domestic concerns – are particularly apt: Shoshan, "From Silver to Copper," 105.

86 Bacharach, "The Ducat in Fourteenth Century Egypt," 99.

87 See al-Maqrīzī, *Sulūk*, III:1117. There is nothing in the passage in question that implies that copper became the standard currency, only the most common one.

88 The assertion by Shoshan (ultimately relying on Popper) that this phrase once meant a copper coin is not supported by numismatic evidence nor by the usage of the phrase in the chronicles: Shoshan, "Money Supply and Grain Prices in Fifteenth Century Egypt," 52, n. 36.

are commonly cited well into the middle of the century. Thus the chronicles attest to copper coins in circulation well into a period for which no copper coins were known to have been minted. How is this to be explained? The possibility must be acknowledged that *fulūs* were minted, but that we have not found them. However, given the tremendous numbers of copper coins that were struck during the ten years on either side of the turn of the ninth/fifteenth century, it is probable that there were enough of these coins to remain in circulation for decades. There are, after all, no known recalls of this coinage. The second comment concerns the value of these copper coins that made up this money of account. Exchange rates cited in the chronicles reveal that the monetary value of copper coins vis-à-vis silver was plummeting, on occasion reaching the floor set by the intrinsic value of copper. That this was undoubtedly so is supported by the following example. In 1982, Israeli archeologists recovered over 100 kilograms of Mamlūk copper coins dating to no later than 1404 from a shipwreck off the Mediterranean coast.[89] Mingled amongst the coins were various uncoined copper items and utensils. It is hard to argue that those coins had any extrinsic value left. They had clearly sunk to their bullion value.

In conclusion, when Qānṣūh al-Ghawrī hauled the Mamlūk treasury all the way to Marj Dabiq in 1516, there can be little doubt that it included Mamlūk-minted coins of gold and silver. His soldiers and retinue undoubtedly had copper coins in their possession. All this money, of course, ended up in the purse of Salīm. After the Ottoman conquest of 1517, Egypt's status changed from that of center of a regional empire to that of an outlying province. In the first decades of Ottoman control, the most common coinage struck in Cairo consisted of heavy copper coins, a situation remarkably analogous to that found by the Muslim conquerors of Egypt some 875 years earlier.

89 *From the Depths of the Sea*, The Israel Museum, Catalogue no. 263 (Jerusalem, 1995), 17–18.

13

Art and architecture in the medieval period

IRENE A. BIERMAN

Cairo's visual culture so impressed the medieval scholar Ibn Khaldūn that he pronounced the city the *umm al-dunya* ("center [lit. "mother",] of the world"). Cities and their buildings stood at the center of the visual culture of medieval Egypt. Recognized as significant forms in themselves, the cities and their buildings both provided a central focus and constituted an underlying structure to which other elements of the visual world related. Medieval authors saw this structure evolving in the visual world they described.

Ibn Khaldūn was overwhelmed by the richness of Cairo's arts, particularly in its architecture and the related arts of woodworking, gilding and masonry. He noted as well those arts he understood as supporting a luxurious lifestyle such as textiles, fine glass, ceramics, costly papers and books, and the working of precious metals. To Ibn Khaldūn, Cairo was the epitome of "sedentary culture," a term he used to highlight the role of cities as the locus of civilization and as a fundamental art form in themselves. The luxury and diversity he found in early fifteenth-century Cairo was something he believed went hand-in-hand with the strong dynasties which had maintained it as the capital from the tenth century on. He noted also that travelers spread its sedentary culture throughout the Mediterranean by bringing Cairene luxuries back to their home towns.[1]

Indeed, Cairo's visual culture overwhelmed its many visitors and caused its own scholars to laud its greatness, and it also expressed the cultural norms dominant in Egypt. Nevertheless, during the medieval period other cities were also important in the cultural life of Egypt. For example, Qūṣ, the provincial capital and seat of the government of the Ṣaʿīd, was the entrepôt of Red Sea and Nubian trade, as well as a way-station for pilgrims on the *ḥajj*. This role, which it assumed from Aswān in the middle of the eleventh century and maintained until the end of the Mamlūk dynasty in 1517,

[1] Ibn Khaldun, *The Muqaddimah*, trans. by Franz Rosenthal. 3 vols. Bolligen Series XLIII, (New York, 1958), vol. 2, pp.233–305.

assured the building of sectarian structures (such as mosques, *khānqāhs*, tombs and churches), of public, commercial structures (such as *wikālas*), and of family houses of great size, as well as the support of the other related arts. Throughout the entire medieval period, Alexandria, while supporting a full range of notable buildings, also remained an important port city. Its wealthy population wore the most luxurious fabrics, and also amassed noteworthy libraries of fine books. Practices current in the capital were brought to these cities by members of the ruling groups who commissioned the construction of new buildings or renovations at important sites, and who endowed institutions. The practice of everyday life in these cities also fostered the development of a visual culture independent of the capital, one that created other visual links, such as the funerary building practices that linked Qūṣ with Aswān in the tenth and eleventh centuries. The visual cultures of these cities are less well known to us than that of Cairo. They have attracted less attention from medieval and modern scholars and visitors, and in these cities far fewer traces of medieval practices have survived.[2]

Understanding the practices in the visual arts in Egypt from 640 to 1517 requires a critical knowledge of the evidence for those practices. Not only is what remains important, but knowledge of the transformations in form, function and meaning that have taken place over time are essential for understanding the past. Cities, buildings, objects, and books that have remained to the present day do so because in some way their forms or functions have served succeeding generations, with the exception, of course, of those elements accidentally buried or abandoned. Understanding Egypt's visual practices also mandates two different strategies for reconstructing visual culture, namely by noting historical change and dynastic change.

Knowledge of the arts of Egypt, its cities, its buildings – the full range of its visual expressions – comes to us from a number of sources. Buildings and artifacts still extant provide a primary body of evidence. Buildings with foundations dating to the medieval period remain in several cities, and to this day many continue to serve social functions. Archaeological excavations have revealed aspects of domestic and commercial life, and have given us insights into building practices for water supply and sanitation systems.[3]

2 Jean-Claude Garcin, *Un centre musulman de la Haute-Égypte médiévale: Qūṣ* (Cairo,1976); Garcin, "Remarques sur un plan topographique de la grande mosquée de Qūṣ," *AI*, 9 (1970), 97–108; K. A. C. Creswell, *Early Muslim Architecture*, 2 vols., 3 parts (New York, 1979), II. A. Udovitch, "A Tale of Two Cities: Commercial Relations between Cairo and Alexandria," in *The Medieval City* (New Haven, 1977).

3 Irene A. Bierman, "Urban Memory and the Preservation of Monuments," in Jere L. Bacharach (ed.), *The Restoration and Conservation of Islamic Monuments in Egypt* (Cairo, 1995), 1–12; Wladyslaw Kubiak, *Al-Fusṭāṭ: Its Foundation and Early Urban Development* (Cairo, 1982); George Scanlon and W. Kubiak, "Excavations at Fusṭāṭ," *JARCE*, 4–21 (1965–78); Roland P. Gayraud, "Iṣṭabl ʿAntar," *AI*, 25–30 (1991–96); A. R. Guest, "The Foundation of Fusṭāṭ," *JRAS*, January 1907.

Objects from the medieval period, whole and in part, are found both in Egypt and in collections and museums around the world. These range from unglazed ceramics, simple metalware, glass, textiles, papyrus and paper to finely worked objects in a wide range of media, and to exquisitely prepared works on paper with elaborate illuminations and illustrations. Egypt is one of the few places in the world where the soil and climate have preserved textiles in significant amounts. In addition to textiles made in Egypt, those fabricated in the Indian Ocean areas are especially well represented in the archaeological finds. When urban growth in Cairo in the twentieth century necessitated the overbuilding of medieval cemetery areas, even more textiles were revealed, increasing our knowledge of medieval Muslim and Christian burial practices.[4]

Drawings, engravings and photographs of cities, buildings and objects as well as maps – all practices of representation – are sources of information that had a profound effect on the understanding of that world, because they have been used as evidence and as illustrations for a large number of widely disseminated academic and popular studies about Egypt, from the eighteenth century until the present day. Two large-scale projects warrant detailed summary here because they provided the bases of the images of medieval Egypt, especially of medieval Cairo, and one brought about substantial changes to the buildings themselves.

The first project, the encyclopaedic *Description de l'Égypte* compiled and illustrated by the scholars who accompanied Napoleon Bonaparte's expedition to Egypt in 1798–1802, consists of twenty-one large-format volumes.[5] Like Ibn Khaldūn before them, the French scholars were captivated by the art of building found in Egypt's cities, and filled the volumes dedicated to the modern period with favored views: city- and street-scapes, skylines, and architectural studies of individual buildings including measured ground plans (see Plate 1). These are invaluable images of Egypt's buildings and cities from the turn of the nineteenth century and in many instances provide the only record of buildings no longer extant. The depictions of Christian

[4] See especially Esin Atıl, *Renaissance of Islam Art of the Mamluks* (Washington, DC, 1981); A. F. Kendrick, *Catalogue of the Muhammadan Textiles of the Medieval Period* (London, 1924); Kendrick, *Catalogue of Textiles from the Burying-Grounds in Egypt*, 3 vols. (London, 1924). See also E. Kühnel and L. Bellinger, *Catalogue of Dated Tiraz Fabrics: Umayyad, ʿAbbasid, Fatimid* (Washington, DC, 1952); Jochen A. Sokoly, "Between Life and Death: The Funerary Context of Tiraz Textiles," in *Islamische Textilkunst des Mittelalters: Aktuelle Probleme* (Riggisberg, 1997), 71–78; Gayraud, "Iṣṭabl ʿAntar," *AI*, 28 (1994), 1–27.

[5] Nine volumes of text and twelve folio volumes of illustrations, Paris,1803–28. Recent volumes have appeared in which the images (but not the text) from these volumes are republished, making them readily available, albeit in significantly smaller scale. For a selection of images with contemporary commentary, see Robert Anderson and Ibrahim Fawzy (eds.), *Egypt Revealed* (Cairo, 1987). For the complete collection of images, without any original text, see *Description de l'Égypte* (Cologne, 1994).

Plate 1 The mosque of al-Ḥākim.

sectarian structures are limited to the monasteries in the Wādī Naṭrūn and that of St. Catherine on Mount Sinai. Urban churches and synagogues were not included.

Mapping, in the modern cartographic mode, was also used in the *Description* and underpins current knowledge of Egypt's cities. Esnē, Qūṣāyr, Suez, Alexandria, as well as Cairo were surveyed in this manner for the first time, and measured maps were produced which indicated major streets, major mosques, and urban agricultural areas. These have served as the base for subsequent cartographic studies of the cities.[6] Several local maps of Cairo helped the reader locate the streets, buildings, and major recreation areas, *birak* or inundation pools, represented in the drawings.

The second large-scale endeavor, the Comité de conservation des monuments de l'art arabe, was launched by the government in 1882 specifically to direct attention to the Arab arts.[7] Although a direct result of the architectural studies launched by the *Description*, it served as a corrective to the intense interest in the pharaonic period that the *Description* had generated in Europe and in Egypt by drawing attention to the Arab period.[8] Over time the Comité's scope expanded to include monuments of Coptic art, and the area of its authority came to include monuments throughout Egypt, but the main focus of its attention remained the monuments of Cairo.[9] The Comité was responsible for making the inventory of buildings designated as monuments of Arab art, for renovating, restoring and rebuilding them, for creating a museum for Arab art, and for commissioning the first illustrated catalogue of Arab art. In the early twentieth century, the Coptic Museum was founded.

The Comité created a collection of Arab art that was first housed in the mosque of al-Ḥākim and then moved to the newly designed building where it still resides. The collection was composed of structural parts and architectural elements taken from the monuments on which the Comité worked. Columns, woodwork, marble revetments and mosaic works were of special interest to the Comité and these elements remain a significant portion of the collection.[10] Later additions included materials from excavations and

6 The *Description* was not the first text to contain maps of Cairo. Piri Reis, in *Kitāb-i Baḥriye* mapped the whole of the urban area of Cairo including the area of the pyramids. His map dates to 962, 1554 and is most readily consulted in Nasser O. Rabbat, *The Citadel of Cairo* (Leiden, 1995), 213, fig. 29.

7 The Comité continued in existence until the 1950s, although the major portion of its work was completed by 1935.

8 For this phenomonon see Jean-Marcel Humbert, Michael Pantazzi and Christiane Ziegler, *Egyptomania: Egypt in Western Art 1730–1930* (Ottawa, 1994).

9 The deliberations of the Comité were published annually in French (and some years were translated into Arabic) as *Exercise* followed by the year, beginning with 1882.

10 *Exercise 1889*, 6th part, no. 34, March 19, 1889 (Cairo, 1890), 13–31; Hassan Hawary and Hussein Rached. *Catalogue Général du Musée Arabe du Caire: Stèles*

objects from individual donors. In the early twentieth century, when the Coptic collection was established, judgments were made about what objects belonged to each classification – Arab, Coptic and Egyptian – and moved among the museums accordingly.[11] The Comité considered the illustrated catalogue of the Arab art collection as fundamentally a portable museum space which made the objects and their order in the museum known and available to audiences beyond museum visitors.[12]

In addition, the Comité adopted a mutli-faceted strategy in specific sections of Cairo to create a living museum. The targeted areas were primarily the main spine of Cairo in the Fāṭimid period, on the streets of *al-Shāriʿ al-Aʿẓam* (today called *al-Shāriʿa Muʿizz li-Dīn Allāh*) and *al-Darb al-Aḥmar*, especially those portions closer to the Bāb Zūwayla and in the area of the complex of Sultan Ḥasan. On both streets they created a vista lined by facades of major buildings, not unlike the then current European designs for city streets. Small wooden shops which abutted the front of major buildings were demolished by the Comité because they hid the facades of the medieval buildings, although ample evidence indicated that the presence of such stores had been a planned part of the street design. Likewise, striped paintwork on the surfaces of major buildings in these areas, a practice begun in the sixteenth century with the Ottoman period, was removed. However, some minarets retain even now the checkered appearance which resulted from continual renewal of the paintwork, and many local shrines continue annually to have their striped painting renewed.

To accomplish so extensive a program of restoration, the Comité standardized by dynastic period missing architectural elements, a procedure especially apparent on Mamlūk buildings. Such features as overhanging awnings, railings, ceilings, and window treatments were prefabricated by the Comité and used throughout the city on all its restoration and rebuilding projects. Design motifs appropriate for each dynasty were established (Ṭūlūnid, Fāṭimid, Ayyūbid and Mamlūk) based on motifs then visible on extant parts of buildings and applied especially to the exteriors of buildings in these areas. Writing in Arabic on the interior of buildings was placed where evidence suggested that it might have been, and appropriate texts were selected for the many absent sections. Structures which were deemed important historically though they had fallen into disuse or were being used

Funéraires, 2 vols. (Cairo, 1932); Jean-David Weill, *Catalogue Général du Musée Arabe du Caire: Les Bois à l'Épigraphes jusqu'à l'Époque Mamlouke* (Cairo, 1931).

11 How to distribute objects according to the newly perceived classifications was an ongoing discussion in the Comité meetings which began in the first year, 1882: *Exercise*, February 1, 1882, 22, where it is recorded that a resolution was approved that "Arab" objects in the Būlāq (or what is today the Egyptian) museum should be moved to the Museum of Arab Art.

12 *Exercise* 34 (March 19, 1889) (Cairo, 1890, 20), 26–7.

for purposes different from their original ones were rebuilt. For example, the mosque of Aḥmad ibn Ṭūlūn was an occupied ruin, and the mosque of al-Ḥākim had become a brick factory (see Plate 1). The Comité restored both, and only the mosque of Aḥmad ibn Ṭūlūn was maintained as such. Often the rebuilding involved was considerable; for example, the portico facade and interior of the mosque of al-Ṣāliḥ Ṭalā'iʿ was constructed anew. Vistas were created in strategic areas by repositioning buildings. Noteworthy is the *zāwiyā* of Faraj ibn Barqūq (1408), which the Comité moved a considerable distance south to its current position, in order to open up the area around Bāb Zuwayla. This living museum, created by the Comité's extensive endeavors, was composed of its newly conserved and rebuilt monuments prominent to the vision of a pedestrian walking the areas, and to the many travellers who recorded these monuments in drawings and photographs.[13]

In the early decades of the twentieth century, the impact of British scholarship altered the basic assumption about Egyptian cities, especially Cairo. The work of the British architect and engineer K. A. C. Creswell who became a member of the Comité, was especially influential. Scholars associated with the *Description* and members of the Comité in the nineteenth century worked from the basic assumption that the Egyptian urban built environment was modern and Arab. To them modern Arab cities were composed of newly erected structures, existing structures of varying ages which were in social use, and ruins, those structures abandoned or fallen out of social use. In contrast, Creswell's perspective, expressed in his two-volume work, *The Muslim Architecture of Egypt*, and that of the Comité in the first three decades of the twentieth century, was that certain buildings and areas of Egypt's cities were medieval and Islamic.[14]

During the early decades of the twentieth century, scholars sponsored by the Metropolitan Museum of Art in New York produced the fundamental study of medieval Coptic visual culture, an analogue to Creswell's study of Muslim architecture.[15] They studied the monasteries of the Wādī Naṭrūn and published measured plans, elevations, and photographs of the interiors and

13 The minaret of the Aḥmad ibn Ṭūlūn mosque was maintained by the Comité as a vista opportunity, and an additional admission fee was charged to ascend it. Scholarly lectures about the main monuments were advertised in the main tourist hotels and held in the mosque of al-Ḥākim and, later, in the Museum of Arab Art, now called the Museum of Islamic Art. *Exercise*, 1890, 78th rapport, 41–2.

14 *The Muslim Architecture of Egypt* (Oxford, 1952 and 1959; reissued New York, 1978). K. A. C. Creswell, "A Brief Chronology of the Muhammadan Monuments of Egypt to 1517," *BIFAO*, XVI (1919), 39–164.

15 Hugh G. Evelyn White, *The Monasteries of the Wadi'n Natrūn*, part 3: *The Architecture and Archaeology*, ed. Walter Hauser (New York, 1936); see also *Part 1: New Coptic Texts from the Monastery of Saint Macarius* (1926); *Part 2: The History of the Monasteries of Nitria and Scetis* (1932).

exteriors of the Coptic monasteries. Studies of the buildings used by other sectarian groups such as the synagogues in Fusṭāṭ and Armenian practices in Cairo and Alexandria were made in the late twentieth century.[16]

In addition to being expressed in buildings and objects and in the drawings and photographs of them, Egypt's visual culture is revealed to us through written descriptions. From the medieval period, visitors such as Nasir-e Khosrow in the eleventh century and Ibn Khaldūn in the fifteenth have left compelling verbal descriptions of Egypt's cities, especially of Cairo, and of its buildings, textiles and ceramic displays. Many of these accounts of urban culture are comparative, enabling us to assess the cities of Egypt in the Middle Ages in relation to other places. Scholars from the Mamlūk period, notably Ibn Duqmāq and Maqrīzī, wrote detailed descriptive histories of the whole urban area now called Cairo.[17] Maqrīzī's history in particular laid the chronological foundation for subsequent studies, and provided the basic topological framework for studying the city by *khiṭaṭ* (urban quarter), a framework largely followed here.[18] The major nineteenth-century historical study of the urban area of Cairo by ʿAlī Bāshā Mubārak continued Maqrīzī's topographical analysis and brought the study of the city up to the contemporary period.[19]

Medieval sources not consciously written to convey a history or description of the urban areas, or of visual culture in general, nevertheless also contribute substantially to our knowledge. Military manuals, for example, not only describe the introduction of new war machinery such as the counter-weighted turbochet, but in so doing indicate the reason why significant changes in the height and thickness of citadel walls became necessary. In the same vein, the documentary Geniza, that is, "papers thrown away" – letters, bills of sale and contracts – is an exceptionally rich source of information for the visual culture of medieval Egypt.[20] Wide-

16 Phyllis Lambert ed., *Fortifications and the Synagogue: The Fortress of Babylon and the Ben Ezra Synagogue, Cairo* (London, 1994). For Armenian practices, see Nairy Hampikian, *Armenian Presence in Cairo and Alexandria* (forthcoming).

17 Ibn Duqmāq, Ibrāhim ibn Muḥammad, *Kitāb al-intiṣār li-wāsiṭat ʿiqd al-amṣār* (*Description de l'Égypte*), vols. 4,5, ed. Karl Vollers, 1893. Reprint, Beirut, n.d. al-Maqrīzī, Taqi al-Dīn. *Ittiʿāẓ al-ḥunafaʾbi-akhbār al-aʾimma al-fāṭimiyyūn al-khulāfaʾ*, vol. 1, ed. Jamal al-din al-Shayyal (Cairo, 1967), vols. 2,3, ed. M. Hilmi and M. Ahmad (Cairo, 1971–73); Al-Maqrīzī, Taqī al-dīn.*Kitāb al-mawāʿiẓ waʾl-iʿtibār bi-dhikr al-khiṭaṭ waʾl-athār*. 2 vols. (Bulaq, 1853; reprint, Beirut, n.d.); Sylvie Denoix, *Décrire le Caire: Fusṭāṭ-Miṣr d'après Ibn Duqmāq et Maqrīzī*. (Cairo, 1992).

18 For the intellectual heritage of writing about Cairo see Nasser Rabbat, "Writing the history of Islamic Architecture in Cairo," *Design Book Review*, 31(XXX):48–51. For a comparison of Maqrīzī and Ibn Duqmāq's vision of Cairo see Denoix, *Décrire le Caire*.

19 ʿAlī Bāshā Mubārak, *al-khiṭaṭ al-jadīda al-tawfīqiyya li-miṣr waʾl-qāhira*, 20 vols. (Cairo, 1882).

20 S. D. Goitein, *A Mediterranean Society*, 6 vols. (Berkeley, 1967–94). The quotation is from vol. 1, *Economic Foundations*, 7.

ranging information about the material culture of daily life of those members of medieval society able to participate in buying and trading goods comes alive in its fragments and in the many analyses of those fragments. Representing a period from roughly the eleventh to the thirteenth centuries, the documents provide especially abundant evidence of the practices of the Jewish communities.

The visual culture of Egypt from 640 to 1517 is reconstructed here from two different perspectives: historical change and dynastic change. Each identifies different types of evidence. Each also relates to the very different interests that led contemporary inquirers to want to know the visual world of those centuries. Historical change emphasizes the social function of the visual world. Buildings, objects, writing practices, processions – all the visual expressions of a society – are considered in relation to the social, political, economic and religious changes in society. From this perspective, the nine centuries covered here from the coming of the Muslim armies in 640 to the Ottoman conquest in 1517, can be divided roughly in half at the date of 1075.

The second perspective divides the 900 years by periods of dynastic rule, beginning with the Ṭūlūnids in 868 and ending with the close of Mamlūk rule in 1517. This approach emphasizes specific signs, symbols, and materials, what is often called style, as related to political rule. Both the categories, historical and dynastic, are used in contemporary reconstructions of the past and are not directly related to categories people living during those times would have used to frame their understanding of the visual world. Nevertheless, the focus here on cities, buildings and institutions, as a separate category from elements of luxury, relates directly to a division of the visual world found in many medieval texts.

The first historical period, 640–1075

During the first period, from 640, when the Muslim armies conquered Egypt, to 1075, when Badr al-Jamālī was appointed *wazir* to the Fāṭimid caliph, the population of Egypt had become predominantly Muslim, even though significant Christian and Jewish minorities remained.[21] With this political change buildings and spaces for Muslim communal practice came to dominate the central core of cities. The Muslim calendar organized the year, and arts associated with Muslim practices, such as providing the *kiswa* – the covering for the Kaʿba in Mecca – for the annual *ḥajj*, as well as

[21] R. Bulliet, *Conversion to Islam in the Medieval Period, An Essay in Quantative History.* (Cambridge and London, 1979); Michael Morony, "The Age of Conversions: A Reassessment," and G. Anawati, "Arabization and Islamization," in Michael Gervers and Ramzi Jibran Bikhazi (eds.), *Conversion and Continuity, Indigenous Christian Communities in Islamic Lands Eighth to Eighteenth Centuries*. Papers in Medieval Studies 9 (Toronto, 1990); P. du Bourguet, *Les Copts* (Paris, 1988).

preparation for the annual pilgrimage itself, played a role in the public life of the capital as well as many other Egyptian cities.

A language change throughout Egypt is linked to this conversion and to Muslim rule. By the end of this first period Arabic had become the dominant spoken language in Egypt. The acquisition of social status required command of the grammar and vocabulary for reading, writing and speaking proper Arabic. Among the Jewish and Coptic Christian communities, variants of Arabic also came into use, namely Judeo-Arabic, Arabic language written in Hebrew characters, and Copto-Arabic using the Coptic alphabet. While these variants existed only in the practices of these two communities, by the end of the first period Arabic inscriptions in Arabic characters came to be displayed throughout Egypt on buildings, objects, tombstones, textiles, and books of all the communities.[22]

Furthermore, by the end of this early period writing in Arabic came to be used as a public art form. Writing appeared on the outside of mosques, on textiles, and on banners and clothing used in official processions in the public areas. In the early years Arabic, beyond its use in books and official and unofficial written documents, was used only in the interior of Muslim communal spaces, in ways that Coptic, Greek and Hebrew were used in the structures of those communities, namely to mark those spaces and objects in them with the language and alphabet of the community. Change in the traditional practice of using writing mainly on the interior of sectarian communal spaces appeared in the practices of the Ismāʿīlī ruling group, the Fāṭimids. In the late tenth century they placed writing on the minarets and portal of the mosque of al-Ḥākim located outside the Ismāʿīlī royal city of al-Qāhira at its formal entrance portal, the Bāb al-Futūḥ. The writing on the exterior of this mosque displayed a message based predominantly in the Qurʾān and addressed to Muslims. To us today, this use of Arabic appears to have been part of the social and religious dialogue taking place between Muslim groups, namely between the ruling Shīʿī Ismāʿīlī Fāṭimids and the majority of the population who were *Sunnī* Muslims. Such an understanding is supported by the use of writing in Arabic on official clothing, banners, the saddle blankets of mounts used in the official Fāṭimid processions in the late tenth and eleventh centuries which took place on days of importance in the Muslim calendar, especially days important to Ismāʿīlī observance, and on days important in Egypt, such as the opening of the Nile canal.[23]

While in this early period, Arabic inscriptions replaced those in Coptic as one form among many motifs for display on textiles and on pottery, by the late ninth and early tenth centuries writing displaying phrases or parts of

[22] Irene A. Bierman, *Writing Signs: The Fāṭimid Public Text* (Berkeley and Los Angeles, 1998).

[23] Ibid., ch. 3.

phrases from the Qur'ān as well as other words conveying an Islamic sensibility began to appear. On pottery, for example, the words *tawakkul taqwā* (Trust [in God]), *kāmila (*Perfect), *shāmila* (Complete) are designs painted on the surface. Writing in Arabic bearing generalized good wishes, such as *surūr* (joy) and *yumm* (good fortune), also appeared on pottery. Whether the audience for these objects was a general urban audience or whether the specific phrases made them appeal to one group rather than another is not clear.[24]

When the Muslim armies came to Egypt in 641, Egypt's major cities were configured according to their Roman military origin. Alexandria, for example, then the largest city in Egypt, represented a Seleucid variant of the ubiquitous Greco-Roman grid plan, and Babylon and Luxor were sites of Roman fortifications. The new city founded by the commander of the Muslim armies, ʿAmr ibn al-ʿĀṣ, was also built for military purposes, as its name, Fusṭāṭ (the tent), suggests, but its construction brought a new mode of urban organization to Egypt. The urban fabric of the new city was a network of *khiṭaṭ* (sing *khiṭṭa*, delimited areas, or, urban quarters) linked together by streets of varying size. A *khiṭṭa* was allotted to a group of soldiers usually related by tribe. The principal focal buildings of Fusṭāṭ were the *jāmiʿ* or Friday mosque, the *dār al-imāra* (house of the commander, lit. "of the princes") and an open area, *raḥbah* or *maydān*, although each neighborhood also had its own Muslim communal space.[25]

What remained of the Roman fortress of Babylon became a Christian and Jewish enclave within greater Fusṭāṭ. The interior of the northernmost tower became part of the Greek Orthodox church of St. George. The Muʿallaqa (the hanging) church of the Coptic community was suspended over the fortress gate. The Coptic churches of Abū Sargah and St. Barbara and two synagogues, the Palestinian and the Babylonian, were built within the

[24] Helen Philon, *Early Islamic: Ceramics Ninth to Late Twelfth Centuries* (Athens, 1980); Geza Fehervari, *Islamic Pottery* (London, 1973); Arthur Lane, *Early Islamic Pottery* (London, 1947). M. Jenkins, "Muslim: An Early Fāṭimid Ceramist," *Bulletin of the Metropolitan Museum of Art* (May 1968), 359–69; M. Jenkins, "Saʿd: Content and Context," in Priscilla P. Soucek (ed.), *Content and Context of the Visual Arts in the Islamic World* (Philadelphia and London, 1988); 359–69.

[25] K. A. C. Creswell, *Early Muslim Architecture*, 2 vols., 3 parts (Oxford, 1932–40; revised 1969; reprint, New York, 1979), 1, pt.1, 35–40, 149–51; Creswell, *A Short Account of Early Muslim Architecture*, revised and supplemented by James W. Allen (Aldershot, 1989), ch. 14 for the mosque of ʿAmr; Roland-Pierre Gayraud, "Isṭabl ʿAntar (Fostat) 1990. Rapport de fouilles," *Annales Islamologiques*, 27 (1993), 230, figs. 12 and 13 for evidence of the city; André Raymond, *Le Caire* (Paris, 1993); Janet Abu-Lughod, *Cairo* (Princeton, 1971). *Raḥbah* and *maydān* do not appear in the medieval Arabic sources to be exactly interchangeable terms for "open area " or "square," although it is hard to judge the use of these terms over time. In Egypt, at least in the Mamlūk period, *maydān* seems to indicate an open area framed by buildings, and *raḥbah* an open area with less clearly defined boundaries.

fortress. This area changed over time from an enclave of minorities to one which, after 1075, i.e., in the second historical period, supported some eighteen mosques and a substantial integrated Muslim community.[26]

In 758, al-ʿAskar, a new *khiṭṭa*, was established to accommodate the military sent by the ʿAbbāsid caliphs to administer Egypt. Located north of Fusṭāṭ, this new *khiṭṭa* elongated the urban fabric of the capital. Its focal elements were again a newly built Friday mosque, a *dār al-imāra* for the new governor, and a square. Some 100 years later, in 868, the ʿAbbāsid general, Aḥmad ibn Ṭūlūn, built a new *khiṭṭa* further north of Fusṭāṭ and east of al-ʿAskar, on the rising ground toward the Muqaṭṭam hills and just south of the *Birkat* (pool) *al-Fīl*. There was an increase in significant elements in this new center of rule, known as al-Qaṭāʾiʿ, and some changes were made in the way the old types were used.[27]

Aḥmad ibn Ṭūlūn built not only the customary mosque with a *dār al-imāra* (see Plate 2), he also built a palace with a large *maydān* and eight gateways. By these actions he changed the traditional function of the *dār al-imāra* from a palace where the governor lived to a space where governors performed ablutions after coming from the palace residence to the mosque. From the *dār al-imāra* in al-Qaṭāʾiʿ, Aḥmad ibn Ṭūlūn and subsequent governors entered the *maqṣūra* (reserved) section of the mosque at the *miḥrāb* area.[28] This change foreshadowed the elimination of the *dār al-imāra* as a functioning unit in the ruling center which occurred in the next expansion of the city.[29]

The many gated streets leading from the palace into the *maydān*, themselves new additions to urban forms in Fusṭāṭ, were used as processional routes to other locations in the capital. The processions were apparently a new form of ruling display in the capital area. One route, known as The Great Street (*al-Shāriʿa al-Aʿẓam*), led from the palace to the mosque of Aḥmad ibn Ṭūlūn and was decorated with lions made of stucco. The name, The Great Street, as well as its destination, the mosque of Aḥmad ibn Ṭūlūn, continued into the Fāṭimid period (969–1171), when it was used to designate the route from the center of Fāṭimid rule to the mosque.[30] Other new institutions and support systems were built in this area of the capital, such as a hospital for civilians and botanical and zoological gardens, while older systems were expanded, namely the aqueduct system to the new

26 Peter Sheehan, "The Roman Fortifications," in Lambert, *Fortifications and the Synagogue*, 51–59.

27 Zaky Muhammad Hasan, *Les Tulunids: Étude de l'Égypte Musulmane à la fin du IXème siècle 868–905*. (Paris, 1933).

28 Cresswell, *A Short Account*, ch. 20.

29 Jere L. Bacharach, "Administrative Complexes, Palaces, and Citadels: Changes in the Loci of Muslim Rule," in Irene A. Bierman, Rifaʿat A. Abou-El-Haj, and Donald Preziosi (eds.), *The Ottoman City and Its Parts* (New Rochelle, 1991), 111–28.

30 Bierman, *Writing Signs: The Fāṭimid Public Text*, ch., 4, 5.

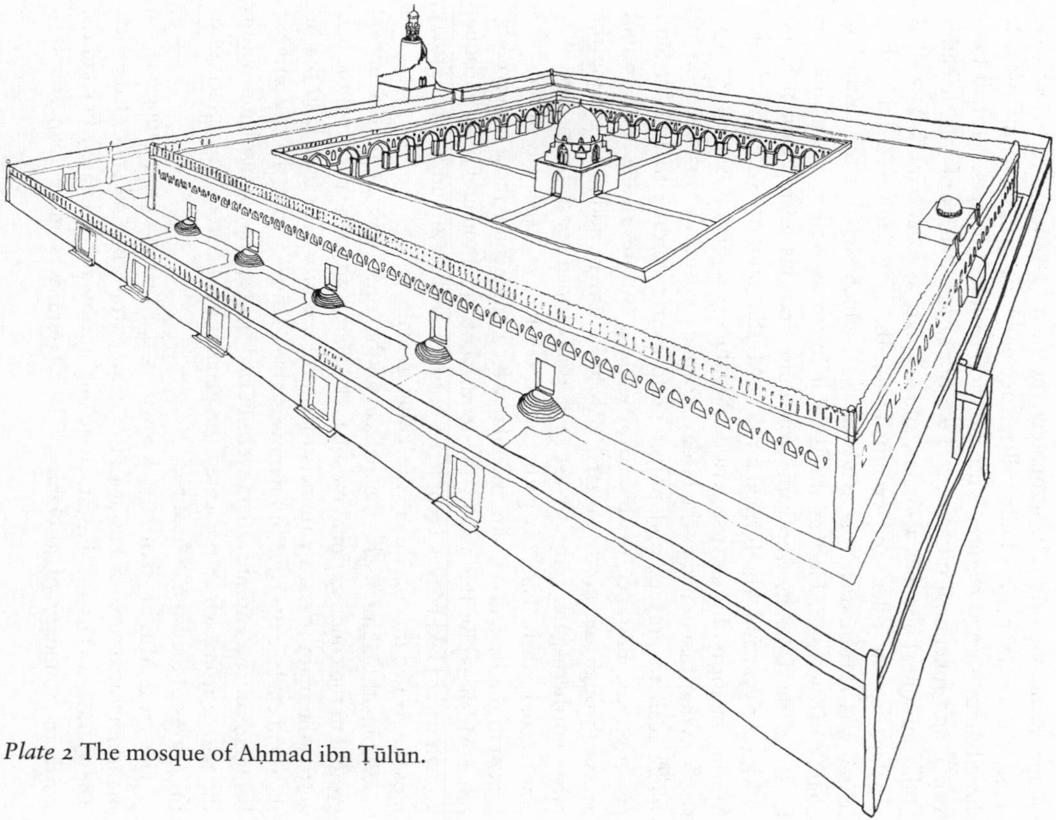

Plate 2 The mosque of Aḥmad ibn Ṭūlūn.

area of building. All that remains of this center of rule is the Friday mosque, for the whole ruling enclave was razed in 905 by the general sent from Baghdād to reclaim Egypt from the far too independent Ṭūlūnids.

The next major addition to the capital city was al-Qāhira, built in 969 by Muslim armies coming to Egypt, this time from the west, from Ifrīqiya. Al-Qāhira ("the Victorious"), ultimately the name given to the whole city, anglicized as Cairo, was built still farther north of the population area. It shared many formal features with the earlier ruling quarters, but had both formal and functional differences. Like the earlier centers of rule, it had a Friday mosque, known as al-Azhar, and a square as focal centers, as well as a palace for the ruler, and eventually for the heir. However, this urban center was surrounded by a symbolic wall which signaled the distinctive quality of the ruler. He was the Ismāʿīlī Imam as well as the caliph, the leader of the Ismāʿīlīs who came with him from his former capital Sabra al-Manṣūriyya, and who formed a ruling Muslim minority within the larger Muslim majority. In this first period, al-Qāhira was a royal Ismāʿīlī enclave, and al-Azhar functioned as the Friday mosque for Ismāʿīlī Muslims, with the *adhān* (call to prayer), and prayer performed according to Ismāʿīlī Shiʿi prescriptions. Entrance to this royal enclave was restricted, with formal access through the northern gate, Bāb al-Futūḥ. In addition, outside the other northern gate, Bāb al-Naṣr, a *muṣalla* (open space for prayer) was constructed where Ismāʿīlīs gathered on feast days, especially those celebrated in the Ismāʿīlī Muslim calendar which augmented those observed by other Muslims. By the end of the tenth century, another Friday mosque, known as al-Ḥākim, was completed outside the Bāb al-Futūḥ. This Friday mosque rivaled that of Aḥmad ibn Ṭūlūn in scale.[31]

Within al-Qāhira itself, the palace of the ruler was connected underground to the congregational mosque, al-Azhar, and to the palace of the heir across the main street, by tunnels that have recently been found, so that in the royal enclave the Ismāʿīlī Imam was able to move within the city without being seen. The Fāṭimid rulers were buried in a special mausoleum within the palace itself, which prevented the general public from having access to the graves of the Ismāʿīlī Imams.

The great Muslim cemetery, known as the Qarāfa, grew alongside the main inhabited area of Fusṭāṭ-Cairo as an extra-urban adjunct of the city. The Qarāfa was east of Fusṭāṭ, stretching northward ultimately beyond the northern boundary of al-Qāhira. The Qarāfa was more than simply a

31 Creswell, *Muslim Architecture of Egypt*, I: 65–106; Jonathan Bloom, "The Mosque of al-Hakim in Cairo," *Muqarnas*, 1 (1983); 15–36. For alternate interpretations see Paula Sanders, *Ritual, Politics and the City in Fāṭimid Cairo* (Albany, 1994) and Bierman, *Writing Signs*, ch. 3. Also, Shlomo D. Goitein, "Cairo: An Islamic City in the Light of the Geniza Documents," in Ira M. Lapidus (ed.), *Middle Eastern Cities* (Berkeley and Los Angles, 1969); 80–96. M. Canard, "Fāṭimids," *EI2*, II, 850–62.

cemetery, it was an inhabited area. Its mosques, large and small, its tomb complexes, public baths and schools served as gathering places for both the residents of the capital and its own residents. This great cemetery complex always functioned for Muslims as an active adjunct to the city proper.[32] Jews and Christians were buried in cemeteries supported by their own communities within the confines of the city.[33] In addition, Coptic Christians supported cultic centers for martyrs in the deserts, such as that of St. Menas at Mareotis in the western desert near Alexandria.

Burial practices of each religious group were varied. Christians were buried in clothing, a practice made known to us through excavations. At least some Jews were buried in new clothing, a practice suggested by the letters of intent recorded in the documentary Geniza. Muslims, on the other hand, were buried in linen shrouds with inscription bands on one end which were wrapped around the head and eyes. The ends of these shrouds, known as *ṭirāz* textiles, are now located in museum collections world-wide. Variations in this practice have been made known to us by excavations early in the twentieth century. Other work indicated that Ismāʿīlī practice required the use of three shrouds rather than one.[34]

During the period in which Cairo was undergoing the changes discussed above, transformations were also under way in Egypt's already existing cities. According to tradition, ʿAmr ibn al-ʿĀṣ sponsored the construction of Friday mosques in the urban cores of Aswān, Qūṣ, Dishna, Bilbeis and Alexandria. In each of these cities, as in Fusṭāṭ, only the site itself remains to indicate the location of the early structures, as over the centuries each mosque has been reconstructed and enlarged many times and houses and palaces have been built over. In Aswān, as in Fusṭāṭ, a Muslim cemetery area existed outside the city. In the cemeteries of both these cities structures with nine domes have been found, suggesting that both citys' cemeteries were used by the Muslim population in similar fashion.

Although mosques, churches and synagogues are mentioned in written sources, few buildings remain from this early period. Those that do have

[32] Christopher Schurman Taylor, "The Cult of the Saints in late Medieval Egypt," (Ph.D. dissertation, Princeton University, 1989); Jonathan Bloom, "The Mosque of the Qarafa in Cairo," *Muqarnas* 4 (1987), 7–20; James Dickie, "Allah and Eternity: Mosques, Madrasas and Tombs," in G. Mitchell (ed.), *Architecture of the Islamic World, Its History and Social Meaning* (London, 1978), 15–47.

[33] Peter Brown, "Christianity and Local Culture in Late Roman Africa," *Journal of Roman Studies*, 58 (1968), 85–95.

[34] Roland-Pierre Gayraud, "Isṭabl ʿAntar 1994," *AI*, 29 (1995), 2–24; Sokoly, "Between Life and Death," 71–78. For Jewish practice in the Geniza material, see the many entries under "deathbed declarations" in S. D. Goitein and Paula Sanders, *A Mediterranean Society: Cumulative Indices* (Berkeley and Los Angeles: University of California Press, 1993). The work of Kendrick in the early twentieth century has been of especial value in understanding Christian practices and variations in Muslim practice.

undergone significant structural changes over the centuries.[35] Yet some general remarks can be made about building practices in this first period. Initially, building materials were mud-brick and plaster with wooden beams (palm or sycamore) laid horizontally in the walls to increase the stability of the building by distributing the weight and enlarging the base of movement. This technique continued into the second period (see Plate 3), and beyond into building practices today. The predominance of such non-durable high-maintenance building materials helps to explain why so little remains from the early centuries of this period. In the tenth century, new materials begin to appear. Stone was used for facing, such as in the mosque of al-Ḥākim, and fired brick with plaster mortar was used for walls. Only the foundations of the Abū Sargah (St. Sergius), St. Barbara and al-Muʿallaqa churches in Fusṭāṭ date from this period and all reveal basilica plans, an adherence to the building practices then current for all rites of Christian churches in Egypt. The foundations of the synagogues date from a later period, although their existence in this period is affirmed by written sources.[36]

At least three different mosque building types existed in this early period, each of which appears to have served a specific function. Friday mosques, whether large like those of Aḥmad ibn Ṭūlūn (Plate 2) or of al-Ḥākim (Plate 1), or small like al-Azhar or the mosque of ʿAmru in Qūṣ, all adhere to a similar spatial arrangement. An outer wall encloses both an open space (*ṣaḥn*) and a roofed area (*ḥaram*, secluded area, or *bayt al-ṣalāt*, house of prayer) on the *qibla* side. Covered porticoes *(riwāq)* usually run along the three other interior sides.[37] The entire building is oriented toward the Kaʿba in Mecca, and the *miḥrāb* (niche) indicating that orientation was in the center of the wall facing the *qibla*. In addition, one other type of prayer space for Muslims, a *musalla*, was delineated and in use in the capital from 969–1171.

The Friday mosque served as the gathering place for Muslims for the Friday mid-day prayer where the *khuṭba* (sermon) was delivered. The *khuṭba* was delivered by the leader of the congregation who sat on the top step of the *minbar* (stepped pulpit) facing the congregation. Each of these mosques had a *minbar* constructed of wood. New *minbar*s were often donated to mosques as pious acts by rulers or members of the ruling family. No *minbar* from this early period in Egypt is extant, but many exist from the second period (see Plate 4). Medieval texts supply what is known about the

[35] For the synagogues see: Charles Le Quesne, "The Synagogue," in Lambert, *Fortifications and the Synagogue*, 79–100.

[36] Abū Ṣāliḥ l'Armenien, *The Churches and Monasteries of Egypt*, ed. and trans. B. T. A. Evetts (London, 1895); De Lacy O'Leary, *The Saints of Egypt* (Amsterdam, 1937).

[37] Dogan Kuban, "The Central Arab Lands," in Martin Frishman and Hassan-Uddin Khan (eds.), *The Mosque* (London, 1994), 77–100.

Plate 3 The *miḥrāb* area in the mausoleum of Sultan al-Ṣāliḥ Najm al-Dīn Ayyūb.

Plate 4 The *minbar* given to the Friday mosque in Qūṣ by the Fāṭimid *wazīr* al-Ṣāliḥ Ṭalāʾiʿ.

formal aspects of the *minbar* in this first period, namely that all of them shared the common feature of five steps leading to the topmost, where the Imām sat facing the congregation. In addition, at least by the ninth century, Friday mosques had one minaret. An exception to this practice was the mosque of al-Ḥākim which had two minarets; communal prayer spaces, since they were not constructed to serve as Friday mosques, had none.

Friday mosques, with one exception, all share one building practice that bears special consideration. The roof of the covered areas and the porticoes of these mosques were supported by columns and capitals gathered as *spolia* from older buildings in the surrounding areas and reused on the interior. The conscious and systematic display of previously used columns and capitals in the Friday mosques was in keeping with the standard building practice in the Friday mosques in all the territories newly acquired by the Muslim armies. In Egypt this practice was continued longer than elsewhere, as the use of Coptic, Hellenistic and pharaonic columns in the Friday mosque of Sultan al-Nāṣir Muḥammad on the citadel (1318) attests. The one notable exception, the use of piers in the mosque of Aḥmad ibn Ṭūlūn, drew considerable negative attention from the Muslim community in its day.

The universal practice of using columns and capitals taken from other sectarian buildings and from ruins to support the roofs of Friday mosques, despite the many resultant structural problems, constitutes evidence for its significance to the Muslim community. The structural problems were obvious. Using columns and capitals gathered from different sites as weight-bearing members inside the Friday mosques forced the architects to devise schemes to compensate for the uneven heights of the columns and capitals and for their varying load bearing capacities. Employing load-bearing units that were uniform, such as piers or columns newly made to standard size and width, is a much more straightforward task.

Understanding the meaning of this practice is a more difficult task because the pattern of use constitutes a major part of the evidence. The practice of reserving the display of reused columns and capitals almost exclusively for the interior of Friday mosques rather than for other constructions suggests a very particular significance to the Muslim community over and above the mere display of spoils of war. It provides a visual emblem of the confirmation of Islam as God's final revelation, and of Muḥammad as the Seal of the Prophets.

The second form used for mosques, that is, what is called *masjid* and refers to communal space for daily prayers, is a walled enclosure totally covered by nine domes. The remains of two such mosques existed into the twentieth century and both appear to have been constructed in the tenth century. The remains of one, known as Ṭabāṭabā, still exist in the Qarāfa, and the other, known as *sabʿa wa-sabʿīn wālī* (seventy-seven governors), located in the cemetery of Aswān, was destroyed in the early twentieth century. Although little is known about the specific function of these mosques at the time of their construction, their location in the cemetery suggests that they were related to funeral rites, and many mausolea were built adjacent to them. No evidence suggests that minarets were attached originally to these mosques.[38]

The mosque of Lu'lu'a is the only example extant of the third type of mosque, also a *masjid* or a space for daily prayer. It is a tower mosque with two small prayer spaces, one above the other (see Plate 5). The Lu'lu'a mosque built in 1015/16 by the Fāṭimid Imam al-Ḥākim is also located in the Qarāfa, which might suggest that it too served a funerary function. However, the spectacular view of the citadel in one direction and of the pyramids in Giza in another offered from its second storey, and especially from its roof, suggests that its form relates to the viewing opportunities of its site, rather than to funeral rituals. In fact, medieval histories report that *manẓara* with prayer spaces, that is, viewing places where prayer space was provided, were built in several locations throughout the greater capital area in the tenth century. Possibly Lu'lu'a is the surviving example of this type of communal prayer space.[39]

The prayer space known as a *muṣalla* is documented in the written record as existing outside the Bāb al-Naṣr of al-Qāhira. It was a space delineated in a fashion not recorded, and was used for major occasions in the Muslim calendar when mosques were not adequate to accommodate the Muslim community from both the city itself and the rural areas. They came together to celebrate occasions in the Muslim calendar such as the Fridays in Ramaḍān or the two major feasts at the end of Ramaḍān or during the month of the *ḥajj*. This space apparently served the Fāṭimid Ismāʿīlī community's expanded observances of Muslim celebrations, such as for the birthdays of the Prophet Muhammad, Ḥusayn and ʿAli, and for the Ismāʿīlī Imams.[40]

Visual culture in the second historical period, 1075–1517

In the second, or late, medieval period the visual arts in cities flourished in an unprecedented manner. This rapid expansion, which made Cairo into the *umm al-dunyā*, was supported by the dramatic changes in the system of supporting Muslim endowments. Revenues from cultivated land were regularly assigned to support pious endowments and the control of the system was centralized. The exact date when these changes were formalized

38 Creswell, *Muslim Architecture of Egypt*, I, 11–18. Ugo Monneret de Villard, *La Necropoli Musulmana di Aswan* (Cairo, 1930).
39 Creswell, *Muslim Architecture of Egypt*, I, 113–15.
40 See Sanders, *Ritual, Politics*, where many references to the role of the *muṣalla* in Fāṭimid practice are discussed.

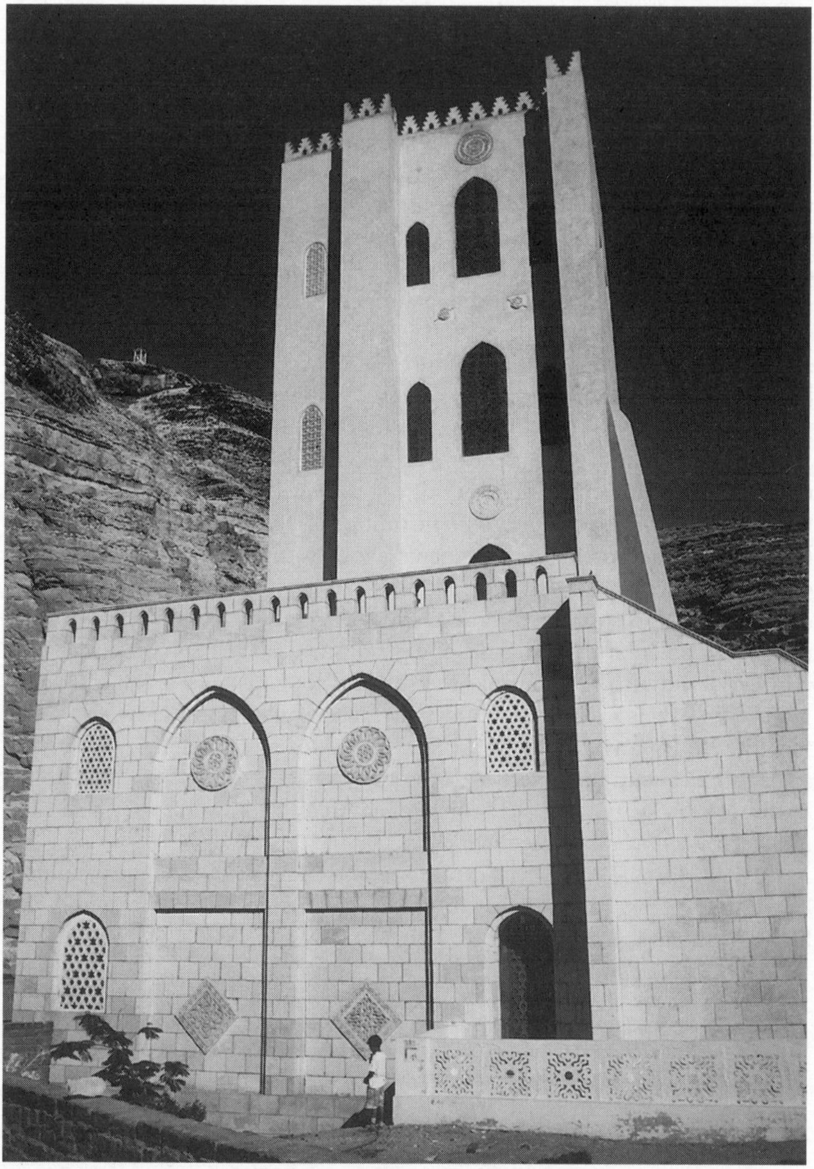

Plate 5 The Lu'lu'a mosque, Qarāfa

is not yet identified clearly, but 1075 was chosen here to mark that date because Badr al-Jamālī became *wazīr* in that year. He and the *wazīr*s who followed him launched extensive building and reconstruction programs, which suggest that the centralized *waqf* system was in the process of being put in place, if it had not actually started. In the first period Muslim, Christian and Jewish communities each had pious foundations that supported charity, helped the poor and funded communal structures. However, the regularization and expansion of the *waqf* endowment system in the hands of the Muslim ruling groups put substantial funds in the service of supporting major Islamic institutional properties throughout Egypt.

This centralization of the *waqf* system and assigning revenues from cultivated land throughout the empire to support urban institutions, particularly those in the capital, made possible a marked expansion in the types, scale and numbers of buildings funded for the general good of the Muslim community. By the fourteenth century Cairo had become the most important university city in the Muslim world, the *umm al-dunyā* described by Ibn Khaldūn. Its streets were lined with institutions large and small, all dedicated to benevolent purposes including many whose usufruct was devoted to all or some of the descendants of the endowers. The extensive revenues for these endowments also supported those processes by which expensive, luxurious materials could be extracted from Egypt, such as quarrying marble and porphyry, and also the control necessary for long-distance trade in luxury materials, such as marble from Italy and lapis lazuli from the east. From the twelfth century onward, as Sunnī law schools came to dominate in Egypt, some families with daughters used the *waqf* system as a means of avoiding seizure of property, and accordingly buildings endowed by foundations founded by women increased markedly.[41]

When Ibn Khaldūn described Cairo as the epitome of sedentary culture, he was responding to the luxury displayed in buildings, in objects and in the lifestyle that he saw around him.[42] Egypt's many cities shared in this culture,

41 For an analysis of the impact of the *waqf* system in Egypt and in particular in Cairo during this second period, Hassanein Rabie, "Some Financial Aspects of the Waqf System in Mamlūk Egypt," in *The Second International Conference on Urbanism in Islam (ICUIT)* (Tokyo, 1990), 1–24, and Carl F. Petry, "Class Solidarity versus Gender Gain: Women as Custodians of Property in Later Medieval Egypt," in Nikki R. Keddie and Beth Baron (eds.), *Women in Middle Eastern History* (New Haven, 1991), 122–42. For descriptions of buildings through endowment records, see Leo A. Mayer, *The Buildings of Qaytbay as Described in His Endowment Deed* (London, 1938); M. M. Amin and Laila A. Ibrahim, *Architectural Terms in Mamluk Documents* (Cairo, 1990).

42 J. A. Williams, "Urbanization and Monument Construction in Mamluk Cairo," *Muqarnas*, 2 (1984), 33–45; K. Stowasser, "Manners and Customs at the Mamluk Court," *Muqarnas*, 2 (1984), 13–20. R. Stephen Humphreys, "The Expressive Intent of Mamluk Architecture in Cairo: A Preliminary Essay," *SI*, 35 (1972), 69–119; Laila ʿAli Ibrahim, "Residential Architecture in Mamluk Cairo," *Muqarnas*, 2 (1984), 47–59; Laila ʿAli Ibrahim and J. M. Rogers, "The Great Hanqah of the Emir Qawsun in

as did Egyptians of all religious groups, according to their ability to support a luxurious lifestyle. The building culture in this second period encompassed more choice in building materials and in materials used for ornamentation, and also in the manner in which these materials were used. Stone became a major construction material. In the late eleventh century, when the area of al-Qāhira was expanded, new defensive gates were constructed of pure stone. Stone was used as two-sided facing for walls, rather than one-sided as in the earlier period. Stone was also used as a rubble fill, and for alternating with courses of brick for the load-bearing walls of buildings. In all these constructions, wooden beams placed horizontally in the coursing of materials continued to assure the stability of buildings, as is shown on the wall of the mausoleum of al-Ṣāliḥ Najm al-Dīn Ayyūb (see Plate 3). Building in stone, or in stone and brick, options available in this second period, enabled architects to construct taller buildings, and to experiment in new ways with vaulting, such as that in the mosque of Sultan Ḥasan.

At the same time it became easier to make more consistent use of decorative surfaces. Luxury materials came to be regularly available, and were thus used consistently in building. In the thirteenth century, beginning with the mausoleum of al-Ṣāliḥ Najm al-Dīn Ayyūb (1250), marble was used for flooring and for lining the *miḥrāb*, a practice continued in ever more elaborate and varied patterns thereafter (see Plate 3).[43] Gold and glass mosaic was used on walls in communal structures and in palaces. Marble and semi-precious stone mosaic was used both in communal structures and palaces both on floors and on walls.

Elaborately carved wood was used as beams in palaces, for screens in churches, *minbar*s in mosques, and on the Holy Ark and pulpits in synagogues. Many of the motifs were shared by all of the communities in Egypt, but their social function varied by community. For example, in the late eleventh and twelfth centuries, images of humans and of animals carved in wood were displayed on screens and on doors in churches where biblical scenes and the lives of saints were appropriate subjects (see Plate 6), and in palaces where courtly and literary scenes were common motifs. Such images were not displayed in mosques or synagogues. In the fourteenth and fifteenth centuries, *minbar*s patterned from carved and assembled expensive woods and ivory were given to many Muslim institutions throughout Egypt.[44]

Cairo," *Mitteilungen des Deutschen Archäologischen Instituts, Abteilung Kairo*, 30,1 (1974), 37–64.

43 Nairy Hampikian, "Restoration of the Mausoleum of al-Ṣāliḥ Najm al-Dīn Ayyūb," in Jere L. Bacharach (ed.), *The Restoration and Conservation of Islamic Monuments in Egypt*, (Cairo, 1995), 46–59. German Institute of Archaeology; *Mausoleum of Sultan a-Saleh Nagm ad-Din Ayyub* (Cairo, 1993).

44 Richard Ettinghausen and Oleg Grabar, *The Art and Architecture of Islam 650–1250* (New York, 1987), 188–208; Gawdat Gabra, *Cairo the Coptic Museum & Old Churches* (Dokki, 1993), esp. 96–101.

Plate 6 A Coptic screen (detail).

Writing in Arabic carved in wood was displayed in mosques, in Hebrew in synagogues and in Coptic in churches of the Coptic community. From the thirteenth century on, a new technique was used on wood to create relief work.[45] A type of gesso was used to cover the surface of the wood, then shaped into letters and floral motifs and painted. This new relief technique almost entirely replaced carving, and is found in many of the Muslim communal structures of the second period. Indeed, wooden boards carved for use in older buildings were often reused by covering the carving with gesso relief work (see Plate 3).

The attention given to surface elaboration in building included details of metalwork devices used in construction. Hinges, braces on the corners of *tābūt*s (wooden cenotaph), metal grillwork, and locks were given elegant form and their surfaces elaborately worked. An outstanding example is the bronze medallion revetment on the doors of the mosque-*madrasa* of Sultan Ḥasan (constructed in 1356–59) (see Plate 7). The basic medallion silhouette was designed to stabilize and hold together the individual planks of wood from which the door was fashioned. However, not only was the silhouette of the medallion elegantly elaborated, its surface was pierced in an exquisite floral pattern that contributed to the aesthetic impact of the buildings.

Beyond the materials for building and elaborating the surfaces of structures, providing for the social use of structures was part of the building culture. In the case of communal structures, whether Muslim, Jewish or Christian, endowing the structure meant providing lamps and candelabras, holy books and book holders, basins, trays for serving residents, wall hangings, mats, and mattresses for sleeping. Thus, along with an expansion in options in construction practices, the arts of paper and book making, enameling glass and metalworking flourished.

The heightened concern for visual presentation was expressed in particular in making copies of the Qur'ān that were given to endowed institutions. Paper produced in Egypt in the fourteenth and fifteenth centuries and destined to be used for making copies of the Qur'ān or *waqfiyya* (pious endowment documents) was of exceptional quality. Likewise, the ways in which the calligraphy was executed on the page were elaborated. Not only black ink, but also gold ink and gold leaf were used for lettering and for illumination. Using gold leaf for writing involved a laborious process whereby glue rather than ink was the medium used for writing, and the gold leaf laid over the writing. Excess gold was then trimmed, leaving the letter

45 For inscriptions: Arabic: Weill, *Les Bois à Épigraphes*. Caroline Williams, "The Qur'anic Inscriptions on the tābūt of al-Ḥusayn in Cairo," *Islamic Art* (1987), 3–26; Hebrew: Menahem Ben-Sasson, "The Medieval Period," in Lambert, *Fortifications and the Synagogue*, 219–23.

Plate 7 A metalwork door revetment from the mosque-*madrasa* of Sultan Ḥasan.

shapes covered with gold leaf which were then outlined in black ink to enhance the visual impact of the writing. Gold, lapis lazuli and carnelian solutions or paints were used in headings and marginalia designs such as medallions and *shamsas* (suns or roundels). The Qur'āns fashioned from precious materials and finely processed and polished paper made for Mamlūk Sultan Shaʿbān (1363–76) and his family are some of the finest illuminated copies ever produced (see Plate 8).[46]

In this second historical period all the cities in Egypt benefited from the expanded ability of pious foundations to fund multi-purpose institutional complexes. Members of the ruling group funded complexes outside the capital and made important gifts both to existing institutions and to newly founded ones. The most elaborate carved wooden minbar of the middle of the twelfth century is found in the Friday mosque of Qūṣ, a gift of the Fāṭimid *wazīr* al-Ṣāliḥ Ṭalā'iʿ.[47] Likewise, the Mamlūk Sultan Qāytbāy sponsored foundations in cities such as Fayyūm which were similar in form to the main building of his complex in the Qarāfa.

Ideas and designs traveled from the capital to other Egyptian cities, and they also traveled from other areas of Egypt to the capital. The mosque of the Fāṭimid *wazīr* al-Ṣāliḥ Ṭalāʿi' built in 1160 outside the Bāb Zuwayla in Cairo with revenue-producing stores built underneath was patterned on a mosque in Upper Egypt.[48] Techniques, as well as structural elements, were brought to the capital from throughout the lands ruled from Cairo. Methods of working in stone were brought to Egypt with Badr al-Jamālī from Egypt's territories in Syria, and the Mamlūk Sultan al-Nāṣr Muḥammad brought the entrance portal used in the construction of his *madrasa*-mausoleum complex from a church in Acre after taking that city from the Latin crusaders.[49]

The shape of the capital city was changed both by the acts of rulers and by nature. Badr al-Jamālī began these changes by opening the royal city of al-Qāhira to residents from throughout the capital area, and by building up the streets linking the various urban areas, and by supporting restoration and rebuilding throughout the greater capital area. Ṣalāḥ al-Dīn, the first Ayyūbid sultan, reinforced these changes by moving the location of the ruling center to the western half of the citadel, that part facing the urban

[46] David James *Qur'ans of the Mamlūks* (London, 1988), see esp. 182–97; David James, "Some Observations on the Calligrapher and Illuminators of the Qur'an of Rukn al-Din Baybars al-Jashangir," *Muqarnas*, 2 (1984), 147–57.

[47] Ed. Pauty, "Le Minbar de Qus," in *Mélanges Maspéro III Orient Islamique* (Cairo, 1940), 41–53.

[48] Creswell, *Muslim Architecture of Egypt*, I, 275–88; Garcin, *Qus*, 88–89, 95.

[49] Creswell, *Muslim Architecture of Egypt*, II, for the details of the building. Lucy-Anne Hunt, "Churches of Old Cairo and Mosques of al-Qahira: A Case of Christian-Muslim Interchange," *Medieval Encounters*, 21(1996), 43–50.

Plate 8 A page of the Qur'ān, from the reign of Sultan Shaʿbān.

population. The Mamlūk rulers continued to build up the area of the citadel.[50]

In addition, the city was shaped by changes in the course of the Nile in the late twelfth century . As a result of these shifts, the area known as Būlāq was permanently above the flood plain, and by the late thirteenth century had become the site of the river port and a bustling population.[51] The Mamlūk sultans encouraged their *amīr*s to build warehouses (*wākālas*) there to support an expanding domestic and international trade. The importance of these two new areas, Bulaq and the Citadel, fostered expansion on the streets linking them with the older urban areas. These changes were particularly noticeable on the *shāriʿa al-darb al-aḥmar* which connected the Bāb Zūwayla area to the Citadel. The former center of rule, the palace area of the Fāṭimid city, became transformed into the site for major residential universities and tombs for the rulers.[52]

In a more programmatic way than in the earlier period, the city of Cairo was transformed on specific occasions by ritual processions which included members of the court, high ranking dignitaries and visitors.[53] Initially, in the eleventh and twelfth centuries, the processions celebrated events in the Muslim calendar as well as events important in the annual cycle of Egypt's economy, such as breaking the dam at the time of the Nile flood. They linked al-Qāhira with the older areas in the city. Not only were members of the processions richly dressed, but the streets along the processional route were elaborately hung with textiles.[54] After a hiatus in the late twelfth and

[50] Bierman, *Writing Signs*, ch. 4 and 5; Paula Sanders, "From Court Ceremony to Urban Language: Ceremonial in Fāṭimid Cairo and Fusṭāṭ," in C. E. Bosworth, Charles Issawi, Roger Savory and A. L. Udovitch (eds.), *The Islamic World from Classical to Modern Times*, (Princeton, 1989), 311–21; Rabbat, *Citadel of Cairo*; Neil D. MacKenzie, *Ayyubid Cairo* (Cairo, 1992); Carl F. Petry, *The Civilian Elite of Cairo in the later Middle Ages.* (Princeton, 1981), esp. the appendices. Nezar Al Sayyad, "Bayn al-Qasrayn: The Street Between the Two Palaces," in Zeynap Celik, Diane Favro and Richard Ingersoll (eds.), *Streets: Critical Perspectives on Public Space*, (Berkeley and Los Angeles, 1994), 71–82; David Ayalon, "The Muslim City and the Mamlūk Military Aristocracy," *Proceedings of the Israel Academy of Sciences and Humanities*, 2 (1968), 311–29.

[51] Nelly Hanna, *An Urban History of Būlāq in the Mamlūk and Ottoman Periods* (Cairo, 1983).

[52] Bierman, "Urban Memory," 2–4; Hampikian, "Restoration of the Mausoleum of al-Salih," 46–59.

[53] Sanders, *Ritual, Politics*. M. Canard, "La procession du nouvel an," *Annales de l'Institut d'Études Orientales, Université d'Alger*, 13 (1955); K. Stowasser, "Manners and Customs at the Mamlūk Court"; Irene A. Bierman and Paula Sanders, *Writing Identity in Medieval Cairo* (Los Angeles, 1995).

[54] Louise W. Mackie, "Toward an Understanding of Mamlūk Silks: National and International Considerations," *Muqarnas*, 2(1984), 127–146; L. A. Mayer, *Mamlūk Costume: A Survey* (Geneva, 1952); D. Behrens-Abouseif, "The Citadel of Cairo," *AI*, 24(1988), 127–146.

thirteenth centuries, processions were revived by the Mamlūk sultans, but with a new route and with some new intentions. The route included the citadel area, the area outside the Bāb al-Naṣr, and the main spine of Cairo. On parade was the military might of the Mamlūk rulers and their amīrs.

Processions much smaller in scale took place regularly as a form of announcement of appointment to high office. Appointees would often proceed from Fusṭāṭ to either al-Qāhira or the Citadel dressed in fine clothing and mounted on richly appointed horses or donkeys, whichever was appropriate to the office.[55] A more local route was followed by the Coptic community in Fusṭāṭ when they made a candle-lit procession to the Nile at Easter. In cities outside the capital, processions were used to celebrate special days commemorating the lives of Muslim as well as Christian holy men and women.[56]

Communal structures

This is the period of expansion not only in number but in type and function of buildings for Muslim communal practice. In addition to the traditional Friday mosque form which continued to be built well into the fourteenth century, beginning in the thirteenth century *madrasa*s (universities), mosques, *khānqāh*s (lodges) and *māristān*s (hospitals) with iwans flanking a courtyard were constructed throughout the capital, in the Qarāfa, and in other Egyptian cities.[57] From the thirteenth century, patrons sponsored the building of complexes which combined areas for several different functions in one large structure with a single main entrance. Most of the larger complexes combined a *madrasa* or a *khānqāh* with the patron's mausoleum. In this manner tombs of Muslim patrons, often the ruler and the ruler's family and members of the government, came to be placed within the city proper, although a significant number of grand complexes were built in the Qarāfa.[58]

The minority communities in Egypt were able to support churches and synagogues and supply them with rich appointments, such as lamps, candelabra, wall hangings, rich fabrics, books and furniture. But by the late fourteenth century the general economy was severely weakened by many factors including the plague, affecting the whole population, and the ability

[55] Irene A. Bierman, "Inscribing the City: Fāṭimid Cairo," in *Islamische Textilkunst des Mittelalters: Aktuelle Probleme* (Riggisberg, 1997): 105–15.

[56] Abū Ṣāliḥ, *Churches and Monasteries.*

[57] Frishman and Khan, *The Mosque*, preface, 11–14.

[58] J. A. Williams, "Urbanization and Monument Construction," and J. A. Williams, " The Khanqah of Siryaqus; A Mamlūk Royal Religious Foundation," in *In Quest of an Islamic Humanism: Studies in Memory of Mohamed al-Nowaihi* (Cairo, 1984).

of the minority communities to afford the use of expensive materials was significantly curtailed.[59]

Visual culture by dynastic period

Understanding visual culture by focusing on ruling groups highlights those visual elements that each ruling group used to distinguish its practices from those of others existing in the cities of Egypt before them. Since artifacts are more ephemeral than major buildings, understanding arts by dynastic period often has meant looking at extant buildings or parts of them. These effects wrought by time on the visual arts appear to support the medieval assumption that cities and their buildings were the most important visual forms in medieval society.

What remains of the architecture of Aḥmad ibn Ṭūlūn's ruling center, al-Qatāʿi', is the Friday mosque (see Plate 2). Several elements of this mosque are unique in Egyptian architecture and relate directly to building practices at Sāmarrā, the capital of the ʿAbbāsid empire from which Aḥmad ibn Ṭūlūn came. These external elements are a *ziyādah*, or an enclosing wall, which surrounded the mosque on all sides except the *qibla* side where the *dār al-imāra* had been built, and a minaret with its staircase partially spiraled on the outside. Internally, designs in the stuccoed walls, especially those carved in a beveled fashion which blurs the contrast between the foreground and background, relate to techniques used in the ornamenting of walls in Sāmarrā. This beveling technique was also used for designing in relief on wood, but it did not remain in use for long after the fall of the Ṭūlūnid rulers.[60]

What remains of the arts of the Ṭūlūnid period are made known to us primarily from excavations at Fusṭāṭ, not from the ruling quarter of al-Qatāʿi'. Those excavations revealed a bath house with depictions of a seated figure and a dancer painted on the stucco-covered *muqarnaṣ*, motifs related to those current at Sāmarrā.[61] The excavations revealed also innumerable fragments of large-scale tapestries designed as hangings. These hangings were variously patterned, some with geometric motifs, some with animals such as lions and water buffalo rendered large in scale, and some with fish. Some also display inscriptions in Arabic. The number of these fragments suggests that a significant portion of the population in Fusṭāṭ was

[59] Donald Little,"Coptic Conversion to Islam under the Baḥrī Mamlūks," *BSOAS*, 39 (1976), 564–70; Le Quesne, "The Synagogue," 84–85. Michael W. Dols, *The Black Death in the Middle East* (Princeton, 1977).

[60] Ettinghausen and Grabar, *Art and Architecture*, 75–124.

[61] Laila ʿAli Ibrahim and ʿAdil Yasin, "A Tulunid Hammam in Old Cairo," *Islamic Archaeological Studies: Museum of Islamic Art, Cairo*, 3 (1988), 35–78.

able to afford these fine furnishings.[62] These tapestries were undoubtedly produced in Egypt during the Ṭūlūnid period, but the excavations also reveal that the residents of Fusṭāṭ enjoyed textiles and weavings fashioned elsewhere. One knotted-pile carpet and fragments of several others have been discovered whose provenence is presumed to be areas further east.[63]

From the Fāṭimid period enough remains of their patronage as Ismāʿīlī Muslim rulers for us to suggest that certain motifs that appear on many of the buildings they sponsored were directly related to their Ismāʿīlī belief. The concentric circle motif appears either on the interior or exterior of most of their extant buildings. This relates directly to their concept of the relationship of Ismāʿīlīsm to the rest of Islam and of man to God and the universe. Often this motif was imbedded in a three-arched format elaborated by bands of writing, such as on the facade of the al-Aqmar mosque (see Plate 9). This format was used on the *qibla* walls of mausolea, on the surface of mosques, and on the *kiswa* (covering for the Kaʿba) the Fāṭimids sent to Mecca for the annual *ḥajj*.[64] In the later Fāṭimid period, monumental inscriptions on the outside of mosques in the city of al-Qāhira displayed the names and titles of the ruling *wazīr* along with that of the Fāṭimid ruler.[65]

Many architectural elements as well as objects and textiles remain from the Fāṭimid period that indicate a significant level of luxury in the arts. Elaborately carved wood was used by all groups of substantial means within Egyptian society (see Plates 4, 6). The wood, usually expensive and imported, was used to fashion doors for mosques, churches and synagogues as well as for palaces and homes of the wealthy. It was also used for furniture within communal structures, such as *minbar*s, portable *miḥrābs*, Holy Arks, pulpits, and altar screens. Wood carving in the range of designs fashionable in the Fāṭimid period has been found in almost all parts of greater Cairo, in the desert monasteries, and in cities such as Qūṣ and Aswān, and even outside Egypt, in Mediterranean cities such as Palermo.[66]

In addition, luster ware ceramics remain in sufficient numbers to attest to the artistry of the Fāṭimid period. The platters, large bowls, plates and jugs

62 I. Bierman, "Medieval Flatweaves in the Urban Middle East," in C. Cootner (ed.), *Flat Weaves, The Arthur D. Jenkins Collection* (Washington, DC, 1981), 161–67.

63 The complete knotted-pile rug is in the collection of the San Francisco Museum, San Francisco, California. Fragments of knotted-pile rugs are in the collection of the Islamic Museum, Cairo. See also A. R. Fahmy, "The Earliest Islamic Rugs in Egypt," *Bulletin of the Faculty of Arts University of Cairo*, 22 (1960), 101–21.

64 See Creswell, *Muslim Architecture of Egypt*, for the numerous mausolea and *mashhads* displaying this motif. See also Bierman, *Writing Signs*, ch. 4.

65 Bierman, *Writing Signs*, chs. 3 and 4; Sanders, *Ritual, Politics*; J. M. Bloom, "The Origins of Fāṭimid Art", *Muqarnas*, 3 (1985), 30–38; Bloom, "The Fāṭimids (909–1171), Their Ideology and Their Art," in *Islamische Textilkunst des Mittelalters:Aktuelle Probleme* (Riggisberg, 1997), 15–26.

66 Gabra, *Cairo the Coptic Museum*; Francesco Gabriele and Umberto Scerrato, *Gli Arabi in Italia* (Milan, 1979), esp. nos. 196–99.

Plate 9 The facade of the mosque of al-Aqmar.

that remain show a refined sense of silhouette and a careful hand in executing the surface designs which included dancers, horsemen, animals and fish, and monks, as well as writing in Arabic. In addition to these luxury ceramic wares, rock crystal was a highly prized medium for small containers such as pitchers and goblets. The rock crystal was carved exquisitely with a range of motifs. Most of the extant examples, now found primarily in church treasuries in Europe, suggest that animals and writing in Arabic with benedictions to the owners who were often named, were favored.[67]

The short reign of the Ayyūbid dynasty left its most traceable marks on the capital city itself. Beginning with the first sultan, Ṣalāḥ al-Dīn, the center of administration was moved to the Citadel, and by the end of the dynasty, the Fāṭimid center of rule on the main spine of al-Qāhira was well on the way to becoming a major university enclave.

The major building complex still extant from this period is the *madrasa* and tomb of Sultan al-Ṣāliḥ Najm al-Dīn Ayyūb (1240–49). Unlike building complexes in the Mamlūk period, this *madrasa* and mausoleum complex were conceived and built at different times by different patrons. Built by the sultan himself, the facade of his *madrasa* provides a sophisticated example of how visual signs important to one dynasty can be altered to signal political change. The general layout of the facade of the *madrasa* relates directly to the facade of the nearby al-Aqmar mosque from the Fāṭimid

[67] Gabrieli, *Gli Arabi*, nos. 521, 538, 540, 587–93.

period. The central hood which divided the facade of the latter was retained on the al-Ṣāliḥiyya *madrasa*, but the concentric circle medallion so important to Ismāʿīlī display was replaced in Ayyūbid practice by a niche filled with writing. The style of the writing, a cursive script, visually signaled the contrast with earlier practice, since the semantic content of the writing, the names and titles of the patron, is equivalent to that on the al-Aqmar mosque.[68] This change of writing style is one of the dominant hallmarks of Ayyūbid visual practices.

The Mamlūk ruling group left a strong and lasting visual mark on Egypt's cities, especially Cairo. All of the buildings sponsored by the ruling group, regardless of differences in construction, composition, and scale, offered a recognizable silhouette to the skyline of the city. They also offered familiar facade elements marking the buildings as belonging to the same dynastic patronage.

Buildings designed for Muslim communal use were constructed so that the domes and the minarets were highly visible to the pedestrian, and on the skyline. In Mamlūk building practice, the dome indicated the mausoleum area of the structure where the patron was buried. Some buildings had two burial areas and therefore two domes. The visual quality of the domes was heightened by elaborate and variously patterned carving on the surfaces. In addition, Mamlūk patrons used minarets in significantly new ways within the capital city. Until the Ayyūbids built the al-Ṣāliḥiyya *madrasa*, minarets had been built primarily on Friday mosques and were used to call the Muslim community to prayer in that mosque. The Mamlūks, in addition to building minarets on Friday mosques, also built minarets on schools and *khānqāh*s where Muslims resided; these were not open to the general Muslim community for Friday prayer. In addition, the Mamlūks used the opportunity provided by the earthquake in 1304 to rebuild fallen minaret tops in their own style. Likewise, in expanding the mosque of al-Azhar by the addition of *madrasa* buildings with attached minarets, the Mamlūks were able to mark that building of the Fāṭimid period with minarets in the style of the Mamlūk dynasty. In those areas of the city where writing on the exterior of buildings had been an important emblem for Fāṭimid and Ayyūbid rule, the new Mamlūk buildings also displayed writing in Arabic. As with earlier practice, a different script style from those previously used was chosen for the presentation of the inscription.

The Mamlūk sultans and their *amīrs* marked their buildings and identified themselves by their emblem (*rank*).[69] On the occasion of major assemblies the emblem of each *amīr* was displayed on the red cloth of the seat back set

[68] Bierman, *Writing Signs*, ch. 5.

[69] Estelle Whelan, "Representations of the Khassakiyah and the origins of Mamlūk Emblems." in Soucek, *Content and Context*, 219–43; Leo Mayer, *Saracenic Heraldry* (Oxford, 1938).

Plate 10 The lion emblem of Sultan al-Ẓāhir Baybars, the Citadel, Cairo.

up for him. The emblems identified the holder of office by the devices, their color, and the type of shield on which they were displayed. About fifty different devices have been identified, from animals (lion, horse and eagle) to signs of office (cup, polo-sticks, sword, bow) and from abstract devices (rosettes, crescents, bars) to written legends. Shields, serving as a background on which these emblems were displayed, occurred in numerous shapes – round, square, multiple-sided, ovoid, and so on – and at different periods were divided into single, double and triple fields. They are the most common single motif in the Mamlūk visual repertoire.

Mamlūk Sultan al-Ẓāhir Baybars (1260–77) used his emblem, a lion walking to the left with a raised forepaw, to mark his coinage and the buildings he sponsored (see Plate 10). He was the sultan who defeated the Mongols in Syria, and his political activities can be measured in part by the places where his emblem appeared. More than eighty lions of al-Ẓāhir Baybars were still in existence in the twentieth century in cities from Turkey to Egypt. His emblem was also used by some of his *amīr*s in combination with their own blazon.

Blazons are found fabricated in all manner of materials: cloth, stone, glass, metalwork and painted wood and stucco. Color played an important role in the presentation of the emblems, enabling those of similar form to be distinguished by placement on a different color field. In the Mamlūk period painted emblems probably displayed the widest range of colors, while those displayed in metalwork were limited by the color range of the materials to silver, gold and reddish copper. Today the greatest color range of emblems is preserved in enameled glass ware and pottery.

The luxury arts of the Mamlūks mentioned by Ibn Khaldūn can be exemplified by textiles and by metalwork. Medieval authors note the extreme care taken by the Mamlūks to wear costumes appropriate to functions and to protocol. The *ʿulamā*ʾ of the different law schools adhered to different codes of dress to signal their roles and different affiliations. Beyond the court costuming, giving textiles and costumes as gifts was a major art form in the Mamlūk period.[70] Elaborate silk brocades and shot-silk fabrics woven in Cairo were an important element of international trade. That trade was especially extensive with Venice, where Mamlūk fabrics and patterns were prized. Individual *wākāla*s (commercial buildings) were dedicated to the storage and sale of expensive textiles. The most significant textile gift was the *kiswa*, the covering for the Kaʿba in Mecca, which was fabricated in Egypt and sent annually at the time of the *ḥajj*. In 1266 Sultan al-Ẓāhir Baybars instituted the *maḥmal* (wooden structure carried on the back of a camel) as the central focus of the Egyptian caravan leaving for Mecca on the *ḥajj*. The *maḥmal*, itself covered with silk embroideries with gold ornament, carried the *kiswa*, and was shown to the people of Cairo in procession before being carried to Mecca.[71]

Metalworking was a major art form in the Mamlūk period. Bronze, brass and copper vessels and door revetments were often inlaid with gold and silver, and gold and silver and gold plated stirrups, pommels and bridles, belt buckles and the like were important part of ceremonial display. Inscriptions in Arabic on the metalwork vessels, using a large-scale *thuluth* script was the means by which these vessels came to be recognized throughout the Mediterranean.[72] Emblems of office present on many of these vessels served to indicate the owner.

This analysis has been organized to facilitate understanding the visual arts of medieval Egypt. Those monuments that remain, and the records of the visual arts that characterized its societies, have been linked here in several different ways to provide a richer understanding of how deeply embedded they were in the culture of medieval Egypt.

70 Mackie, "Mamlūk Silks," 127–46.

71 Jacques Jomier, *Le Mahmal et la caravane égyptienne des pélerins de la mecque XIII-XXe siecles*. (Cairo, 1953).

72 James W. Allan, "Shaʿbān, Barqūq, and the Decline of the Mamlūk Metalworking Industry," *Muqarnas*, 2(1984), 85–94; Mayer, *Saracenic Heraldry*; Atıl, *Renaissance of Islam*.

14

Culture and society during the late Middle Ages

JONATHAN P. BERKEY

As his name indicates, Abū Ḥāmid al-Qudsī, an unprepossessing scholar of the fifteenth century, was a native of Jerusalem. In his youth, however, he moved to Egypt, where he studied with many of the leading traditionists and jurists of his day. Overwhelmed by the splendors of his adopted country, he wrote a treatise extolling its virtues and, in particular, comparing it favorably with his native Syria. Such compositions, celebrating the "wonders" (*faḍā'il*) of a city or region, were of course common in the later medieval Islamic world, and the inhabitants of Damascus or Medina could draw upon comparable works to bolster their civic pride. But Abū Ḥāmid had a strong case when he identified Egypt as the "heartland of Islam," and the last bastion of civilization. He was by no means alone in his admiration: the great historian Ibn Khaldūn, another immigrant to Egypt, had himself been attracted by the reports which reached him in the Islamic west of Egypt's magnificence.[1]

That Egypt should have emerged over the course of the Middle Ages as the fulcrum of the Islamic world is a matter which, despite the antiquity of Egyptian civilization, requires explanation. After all, for much of the first several centuries of Islamic rule, the country was politically and culturally passive, following political developments and decisions taken in the east, the occasional efforts of an Aḥmad Ibn Ṭūlūn or Abu'l-Misk Kāfūr notwithstanding. Moreover, the astounding fertility of the Nile valley cannot obscure the non-agricultural poverty of medieval Egypt. Apart from its vast expanse of unproductive desert land, Egypt consisted of a utilizable land

[1] On Abū Ḥāmid, who was actually born in Ramle, near Jerusalem, see Shams al-Dīn Muḥammad al-Sakhāwī, *al-Ḍaw' al-lāmi' li-ahl al-qarn al-tāsi'*, 12 vols. (Cairo, 1934), 7:234–7, and Ulrich Haarmann, "Rather the Injustice of the Turks than the Righteousness of the Arabs – Changing *'Ulamā'* Attitudes Towards Mamlūk Rule in the Late Fifteenth Century," *Studia Islamica*, 68 (1988), 63–64; on Ibn Khaldūn, see Walter J. Fischel, *Ibn Khaldūn in Egypt: His Public Functions and His Historical Research (1382–1406). A Study in Islamic Historiography* (Berkeley, 1967), 18–19.

area roughly the size of Holland, and was almost completely lacking in those resources which fueled the rapid expansion of late medieval European civilization, such as undeveloped arable, iron and wood, let alone specie.[2] Eventually, the scarcity of natural resources would take its toll.

Under the Fāṭimids, who constructed their capital city of Cairo next to the ancient town of Fusṭāṭ, the political ties binding Egypt to the dominant centers of Islamic culture in the east were broken, at least temporarily, and social and economic patterns began to take forms which would last until the end of the Middle Ages. But it was under their successors, the Ayyūbids, that the groundwork was laid for that cultural order which constituted the greatest glory of medieval Egypt, and which legitimately inspired the admiration of Abū Ḥāmid al-Qudsī and others. Despite economic and demographic crises and profound social tensions, that order found its fullest expression under the Mamlūk regime which ruled Egypt from the middle of the thirteenth century until the beginning of the sixteenth, leading one modern historian to describe Egyptian civilization in this period as "unparalleled since the days of the Ptolemies."[3]

For a variety of reasons, Egyptian society and culture in the later Middle Ages cannot be understood outside a broader international context. With its limited non-agricultural resources, Egypt depended for much of its material wealth on the transit trade of luxury goods which found their way from India and the east, passing through Egypt and Syria en route to European markets. The expansion of the Mongols eventually opened up new trade routes with central Asia to supplement those linking Egypt to the east via the Red Sea; commercial links in the Mediterranean between Egypt and Latin Europe were never completely interrupted, even during the centuries of the crusades. The prosperity generated by that trade supported an urban mercantile class which left a profound mark on social relations, and also financially undergirded the ruling military elite responsible for the religious, academic, and other public monuments which shaped the cultural life of cities such as Cairo. Moreover, after the destruction of Baghdād by the Mongols in 1258, Cairo emerged as the principal center of cultural activity of the Islamic Near East, at least until the Ottomans made Constantinople the seat of their empire in the mid-fifteenth century. Consequently, the Egyptian capital functioned as a cultural magnet, attracting Muslim scholars and others from throughout the Near East, immigrants who lent a profoundly cosmopolitan air to Egyptian society, at least at its higher levels. This international flavor, and Egypt's persistent links to broader patterns of

[2] Jean-Claude Garcin, "The Mamlūk Military System and the Blocking of Medieval Muslim Society," in Jean Baechler, John A. Hall and Michael Mann (eds.), *Europe and the Rise of Capitalism* (Oxford, 1988), 128.

[3] Karl Stowasser, "Manners and Customs at the Mamlūk Court," *Muqarnas*, 2 (1984), 13.

Mediterranean commerce and west Asian politics and culture, must always be borne in mind.

A series of contrasts provides the themes which characterize Egyptian society and culture in this period. The first and most important is that of alterity and inclusion. Most historians have rightly stressed the social segmentation of medieval Islamic societies, and particularly the cities, of the Near East. Muslim writers defined the different layers of Egyptian society in various ways, as we shall see, and the competing demands of religion, wealth, occupation, ethnicity, and educational attainment, let alone gender, resulted in deep social fissures and impeded the emergence of a compelling local identity or political leadership. This social segmentation contributed to, although it was not perhaps the proximate cause of, the dominance of yet another social group, the Kurdish, Turkish, and (later) Circassian military elite which ruled Egypt throughout the period in question. Under the Mamlūks, the social alienation of rulers from the ruled reached its peak, as the legal status of the slave soldiers further distinguished them from the local population. Social identities, therefore, were largely defined in opposition to one another: thus, for example, Muslims were set against non-Muslims, or the Mamlūks against the local population.

Medieval Egyptian society was more, however, than the sum of its parts, and it functioned in such a way as to compensate for, and even to overcome, these various alterities. On the most obvious level, this involved the operation of networks of clientage which bound together various elements of the population, and which gave certain social groups the cohesion and strength necessary to protect themselves and their material and cultural interests.[4] The process went further, however, so that if social identities were characterized by alterity, social experience was characterized more by inclusion. Medieval Egyptian society may have been segmented, but in general it was not fractured: social patterns, cultural activities, even politics, embraced virtually all groups. Much recent research has emphasized the role of less powerful or marginalized sectors of the population, and their ability to assert their interests and make their voices heard, either through direct action or the mediation of more prominent individuals and groups.[5] Such tendencies should not be overstressed, but they did exist, and they contributed to making Egyptian society and culture more inclusive. Above all, we need to understand that widely disparate social groups all contributed to cultural activity at a variety of different levels, and that the interaction of culture, politics, and social relations was correspondingly complex.

[4] A point stressed by Ira M. Lapidus, *Muslim Cities in the Later Middle Ages* (Cambridge, MA, 1967), and Susan Jane Staffa, *Conquest and Fusion: The Social Evolution of Cairo, AD 642–1850* (Leiden, 1977).

[5] See, for example, Boaz Shoshan, "Grain Riots and the 'Moral Economy': Cairo, 1382–1517," *Journal of Interdisciplinary History*, 10 (1979–80), 459–78.

An outstanding example of this complexity can be found in the case of the Ṣūfī Ibn al-Fāriḍ (d. 1235) and the posthumous altercations surrounding his poetry. Already in his own lifetime, Ibn al-Fāriḍ's verse had aroused controversy: many scholars of Islamic law were troubled by what they perceived as the poet's tendency to monism and a belief in divine incarnation (*ḥulūl*). Yet Ibn al-Fāriḍ's popularity grew, both on account of his poetry and a swelling belief in his personal sanctity, as reflected in visits to his tomb by Muslims of all stripes and colors. In the fifteenth century, the doctrinal disputes broke out into open and heated squabbling. Although the controversy involved conflicting and competing forms of Islamic identity – the mystical and the legal, the popular and the academic – the divisions were not drawn clearly along social or professional lines. The opponents of Ibn al-Fāriḍ's poetry included many respectable members of the *ʿulamāʾ*, such as Ibn Ḥajar al-ʿAsqalānī, al-Sirāj al-Bulqīnī, and the historian and jurist Ibn Khaldūn, who wished to see Ibn al-Fāriḍ's books burnt, but also a number of Ṣūfīs, including Ibrāhīm al-Matbūlī, an illiterate chick-pea vendor of enormous popularity, who was himself accused of antinomian ideas and pederasty, among other things. Moreover, Ibn al-Fāriḍ had his supporters among the *ʿulamāʾ*, most notable among them the polymath Jalāl al-Dīn al-Suyūṭī, who wrote a treatise in the poet's defense. Behind the competing social and religious identities one can perceive intense personal quarrels and professional rivalry, but also (and more importantly) a political dimension. The mausoleum erected over Ibn al-Fāriḍ's tomb was endowed and supervised by leading amīrs of the Mamlūk caste, while the controversy engulfed several late Mamlūk sultans, in particular the pious and stern Qāyt Bāy, who found in the dispute an opportunity to reshuffle the higher ranks of the Islamic judiciary.[6]

A second polarity sets various institutional efforts to impose social order and to control religious and cultural expression against the persistent tendency of medieval Egyptian society to function within a structural framework which emphasized personal freedom and choice. As we shall see, Egyptian society, or at least its civilian components, tended to operate in informal ways. Whether in commerce, industry, or scholarship, personal relationships rather than formal institutions set the tone for much social exchange and interaction. This is not to say that institutions did not exist or were unimportant; one of the most important but least understood components of late medieval Egyptian society was the extensive, interlocking

[6] T. Emil Homerin, *From Arab Poet to Muslim Saint: Ibn al-Fāriḍ, His Verse, and His Shrine* (Columbia, SC, 1994), esp. 55–75; Michael Winter, *Society and Religion in Early Ottoman Egypt: Studies in the Writings of ʿAbd al-Wahhāb al-Shaʿrānī* (New Brunswick, NJ, 1982), 160–72; E. M. Sartain, *Jalāl al-Dīn al-Suyūṭī*, vol. 1: *Biography and Background* (Cambridge, 1975), 54–55.

bureaucratic organization through which the government administered the country, and which also served the financial and administrative needs of the ruling elite. On a cultural level, the boom in the construction of *madrasas* during the Middle Ages, most of them at the initiative and expense of the ruling military and political class, represented an effort to give formal structure to and exert control over the social channels by which Islamic religious and legal knowledge was transmitted. But in academic as in other areas, institutional mechanisms of control confronted, and were modified by, the tenacious informality and flexibility of Egyptian social and cultural life.

The final theme concerns the opposition of the public to the private sphere, and the mechanisms by which the "home and the world" dichotomy was bridged. The separation of the public and the private is one of the most familiar motifs of Near Eastern and Islamic history, one fully at work in medieval Egyptian society. Domestic architecture, at least in the towns, reflected the need to protect the private sphere (the *ḥarīm*), whose inviolability was secured through winding, narrow entrances, limited openings to the public street, the use of wooden lattice-work (*mashrabiyya*) to conceal the interior from external viewers, and fully enclosed inner courtyards to provide light, air, and space.[7] But that private space did not define the parameters of social life – even, as we shall see, for those women who were theoretically confined to it. On the contrary, a society as large and complex, and a culture as vibrant as that of medieval Egypt were fundamentally communal affairs – and in almost every case, the impressive historical and literary legacy of the period which allows us to describe that society and culture was a product of open debate, definition, and transmission. The public and the private constantly jostled for position in community life. Higher education, for example, took place both in private teaching circles and in public institutions; those same institutions were founded by a private act. Even the sultans who endowed large religious establishments did so, not as the exercise of public authority, but as an act of private charity.[8]

Population: size and distribution

A study of Egyptian society and culture must identify, first of all, the basic contours of the population: who were the people who lived in the land of Egypt, and where did they live? No scholarly consensus has emerged regarding the size of Egypt's population in the Middle Ages, and it is doubtful that the nature of the sources will ever permit any reasonably

7 Laila ʿAli Ibrahim, "Residential Architecture in Mamlūk Cairo," *Muqarnas*, 2 (1984), 47–50.

8 On the endowments generally, see Muḥammad M. Amīn, *al-Awqāf wa'l-ḥayāh al-ijtimāʿiyya fi miṣr* (Cairo, 1980).

certain estimate.[9] The same is not true for the city of Cairo, for which there is abundant if not unambiguous documentation. Modern estimates tend to cluster around the figure of half a million; one study of the plague and its effects on medieval Egypt, gave a pre-pandemic figure of 451,008. Such estimates may be slightly generous. An extensive analysis based upon the distribution of baths, mosques, and markets, put the population of Cairo at between 150,000 and 200,000 in the early fifteenth century. That figure, of course, reflects the demographic situation *after* the ravages of the plague in the mid-fourteenth century, in which Cairo lost approximately 40 percent of its population, and moreover does not include outlying areas such as Fusṭāṭ (Old Cairo). Even with the slightly lower figures, however, the population of Cairo still eclipsed that of fourteenth-century London or Paris by a factor of three or four.[10] If we assume that the metropolis contained 10 percent of the entire population of Egypt, which was the case in the modern period until the recent explosion in the size of the city, we might suggest a very rough estimate of approximately 3,000,000 for Egypt as a whole.

Whatever the actual figures, there are several important points to be made about the character of Egypt's medieval population. One is that, from a broader perspective, it was probably trapped in a secular decline, one which lasted at least until the end of the Middle Ages. The shrinkage of the population was sharpened by the waves of pestilence which swept over Egypt from the mid-fourteenth century, but it may have been in motion before the first epidemic struck in 1347. Moreover, the population did not recover with the rapidity of that of Europe, in part because the plague recurred at such frequent intervals. A graphic demonstration of the decline in population can be seen in the abandonment of substantial numbers of villages between the Fāṭimid period and the mid-fifteenth century, as attested by a census of 1433–34.[11]

A second point is that groups of immigrants repeatedly left their mark on the people of Egypt and their society, from a cultural if not a demographic perspective. We have already observed how, under the Mamlūks, Cairo emerged as the cultural capital of the Islamic Near East, and attracted to it

[9] Compare David Ayalon, "Regarding Population Estimates in the Countries of Medieval Islam," *Journal of the Economic and Social History of the Orient*, 28 (1985), 1–19, and J. C. Russell, "The Population of Medieval Egypt," *JARCE*, 5 (1966), 69–82.

[10] Michael Dols, *The Black Death in the Middle East* (Princeton, 1977), 197–202; André Raymond, "Cairo's Area and Population in the Early Fifteenth Century," *Muqarnas*, 2 (1984), 21–31.

[11] A. L. Udovitch, Robert Lopez and Harry Miskimin, "England to Egypt, 1350–1500: Long-term Trends and Long-distance Trade," in M. A. Cook (ed.), *Studies in the Economic History of the Middle East* (London, 1970), 93–128, esp. 118–20; David Ayalon, "The Plague and Its Effects upon the Mamlūk Army," *JRAS* (1946), 67–73; Aḥmad Darrağ, *L'Égypte sous le règne de Barsbay, 825–841/1422–1438* (Damascus, 1961), 64.

scholars and others who sought out its intellectual resources and professional opportunities. The phenomenon of immigration, however, was much more widespread. The historian al-Maqrīzī noted that the inhabitants of Egypt were drawn from many races, including Copts (i.e., indigenous Christians and the descendants of those who inhabited the country before the Muslim conquest), Greeks, Arabs, Kurds, Daylamis and Ethiopians.[12] The Mamlūks, of course, primarily Turks and Circassians, represented a constant flow of immigrants; their numbers were supplemented by those known as the *wāfidiyya*, "immigrants," – warriors and tribesmen, many themselves of Tatar origin, who found themselves displaced by the upheavals associated with the Mongol invasions of the thirteenth century and who sought refuge in the Mamlūk empire.[13] The Ayyūbids, finding Sunnī learning in Egypt in a state of decay after 200 years of Ismāʿīlī rule, imported scholars from Syria, Iraq and Iran to staff the educational and religious institutions they established.[14] Under the later Mamlūk sultans, jurists and mystics from Anatolia, the Caucasus and Iran, such as those fleeing the Timurid invasions, occupied a prominent place in Egyptian academic and religious life; at least one *madrasa* was founded specifically to benefit these "foreign Ḥanafī students."[15] Refugees and pilgrims from the Islamic west passed through Egypt en route to the holy cities of the Ḥijāz, and many of them elected to remain; the contingent of Maghribī scholars at the al-Azhar mosque was particularly large and well-defined.[16] As S. D. Goitein's research on the records of the Cairo Geniza has made clear, the tiny Jewish community too knew much immigration, both of merchants from north Africa and Spain who settled in Egypt, and refugees from southern France fleeing persecution in the early thirteenth century.[17] None of this was enough to offset the broader demographic decline, but the immigrants did in many ways enrich Egyptian society and culture.

What of the settled population of the country? Whatever the actual numbers, the vast majority of Egyptians lived in villages in the Nile Delta or in the valley to the south of Cairo, and led an agricultural existence. It is therefore striking that life in the *rīf*, the countryside, represents perhaps the

[12] Taqī ʾl-Dīn Aḥmad al-Maqrīzī, *al-Mawāʿiẓ wa'l-iʿtibār bi-dhikr al-khiṭaṭ wa'l-āthār*, 2 vols. (Būlāq, 1853–4), I, 48.

[13] On the *wāfidiyya*, see David Ayalon, "The Wafidiya in the Mamlūk Kingdom," *Islamic Culture* (1951), 89–104.

[14] Gary L. Leiser, "Notes on the Madrasa in Medieval Islamic Society," *The Muslim World*, 76 (1986), 19; J. Spencer Trimingham, *The Sufi Orders in Islam* (Oxford, 1971), 18.

[15] Jonathan Berkey, *The Transmission of Knowledge in Medieval Cairo: A Social History of Islamic Education* (Princeton, 1992), 91.

[16] Carl F. Petry, *The Civilian Elite of Cairo in the Later Middle Ages* (Princeton, 1981), 161.

[17] S. D. Goitein, *A Mediterranean Society: The Jewish Communities of the Arab World as Portrayed in the Documents of the Cairo Geniza*, 6 vols. (Berkeley, 1967–94), I, 67–68 et passim.

least understood and most under-researched aspect of medieval Egyptian social history. In large part this lacuna reflects the bias of the surviving sources, which were mostly of an urban, even metropolitan provenance. There are important exceptions, of course, such as Kamāl al-Dīn al-Udfuwī's fourteenth-century biographical dictionary of scholars and notables from southern Egypt, from which one of the most comprehensive and insightful modern studies of medieval Egypt has been fashioned.[18] Other sources, such as the endowment deeds (*waqfiyyas*) surviving from the Mamlūk period, contain a wealth of hitherto unexploited information on the *rīf*. But most literary sources, both historical and legal, present the view from the metropolis.

There were, to be sure, close social and economic ties linking the cities to rural life. Townsmen often owned agricultural land, or administered it as tax-farmers. More importantly, aspiring provincials moved from small towns and villages to Cairo in a steady stream, in order to take advantage of its cultural or professional resources, as the *nisbas* (descriptive surnames recording, among other things, place of origin) of the individuals portrayed in the contemporary biographical dictionaries suggest.[19] When an immigrant from the provinces climbed to a high social or political station, he found himself in a position to extend to family, friends and fellow provincials the benefits of his patronage. So, for example, when the famous scholar Ibn Daqīq al-ʿĪd, originally from the town of Qūṣ in the Ṣaʿīd, held the office of Shāfiʿī *qāḍi'l-quḍāṭ* (chief judge) in Cairo at the end of the thirteenth century, numerous other Qūṣīs received appointments in the city as deputy *qāḍīs*, professional witnesses (*shāhids*), and teachers in *madrasas*.[20]

Nonetheless a vast material and mental gulf separated the inhabitants of Cairo from the majority who lived in the rural areas. Popular and sentimental visions of an "eternal Egypt," in which the pace of rural life has changed little over the centuries, should not obscure the enormous vicissitudes and uncertainties to which the peasants, especially, were exposed. The chronicles provide ample evidence of sudden, traumatic climatic and environmental shifts – torrential and unexpected rains that ruined crops, drought, waves of extreme heat or cold, plagues of locusts, and above all variations in the level of the Nile – shifts which had their most immediate, and probably most profound, impact on the peasantry.[21] The rural areas had their small

[18] Kamāl al-Dīn al-Udfuwī, *al-Ṭāliʿ al-saʿīd, jāmiʿ asmāʾ nujabāʾ al-ṣaʿīd*, ed. Saʿd Muḥammad Ḥasan (Cairo, 1966); Jean-Claude Garcin, *Un centre musulman de la Haute-Égypte médiévale: Qūṣ* (Cairo, 1976).

[19] Goitein, *Mediterranean Society*, I, 3; Jean-Claude Garcin, "Le Caire et la province: Constructions au Caire et à Qūs sous les Mamelūks Baḥrides," *AI*, 8 (1969), 47.

[20] Garcin, "Le Caire et la province," 59–60; idem, *Un centre musulman*, 293–96.

[21] William F. Tucker, "Natural Disasters and the Peasantry in Mamlūk Egypt," *JESHO*, 24 (1981), 215–24.

urban centers, towns such as Qūṣ which supported a limited but thriving array of cultural and educational activities, but in general the inhabitants of the agricutural hinterland confronted restricted opportunities. Promising students left the *rīf* for the city, and an outstanding individual such as Ibn Daqīq al-ʿĪd could smooth the way for many an aspiring provincial. Nonetheless, even this outlet may have narrowed over the course of the Middle Ages: a recent study of travel patterns among the Egyptian *ʿulamāʾ* in the fifteenth century indicates that most of those who had interest in and contact with the Delta region and Upper Egypt were low-ranking scholars and religious functionaries, "corroborat[ing] a state of economic and cultural underdevelopment" in the provinces.[22] To the inhabitant of Cairo or Alexandria, the peasant, in particular of Upper Egypt, was a foreigner, an outsider. In part this may have resulted from the suspicions aroused by the Shiʿi sentiments which persisted more resolutely in the Ṣaʿīd than elsewhere in Egypt, or from the lingering concentrations of Coptic Christians in the south. More generally, however, it reflects the urbanite's deep-seated sense of cultural superiority, an attitude which Goitein found rampant in the society that left its mark on the Cairo Geniza. Recalling the demons who had haunted the early church fathers in the Thebaid, Cairenes and foreign visitors alike viewed Upper Egypt as dangerous, a land of mischievous spirits, magicians, and terrifying wonders such as the Nubian with one eye and four fingers protruding from his face whom the chronicler Ibn Iyās records as having been seen in Aswān. That same writer pointedly noted that an individual named Mahdī, executed in Cairo in 1505 for sorcery, atheism, and disregard of the *sharīʿa* (he had performed his ablutions with milk), was "one of the Ṣūfīs of the Ṣaʿīd" (*min fuqarāʾ al-ṣaʿīd*).[23] It is significant that even Ibn Khaldīn, who extolled the contributions of nomadic peoples to human history, could view both the Bedouin and the peasantry as *badw*, "outsiders," i.e., in some respects beyond the pale of (urban) civilization.[24]

The Bedouin represent another under-researched social group in medieval Egypt. Here as elsewhere in the Near East and north Africa, nomadic tribes, Arab and Berber, had constituted a constant and equivocal presence on the edges of settled agricultural regions. Ibn Khaldūn's admiration for the positive force of collective tribal identity (*ʿaṣabiyya*) is well known, although it was not universally shared by those whose livelihood was made precarious by the ever-present threat of Bedouin depredation. In medieval Egypt, as

[22] Carl F. Petry, "Travel Patterns of Medieval Notables in the Near East," *Studia Islamica*, 62 (1985), 61; cf. Garcin, *Un centre musulman*, 433–34.

[23] Muḥammad ibn Aḥmad Ibn Iyās, *Badāʾiʿ al-zuhūr fī waqāʾiʿ al-duhūr*, 5 vols. in 6 parts, ed. Muḥammad Muṣṭafā et al. (Cairo, 1982–84), III, 267 and IV, 87; cf. Garcin, *Un centre musulman*, 432–33.

[24] As noted by Goitein, *Mediterranean Society*, I, 75, citing Ibn Khaldūn, *The Muqaddimah*, trans. Franz Rosenthal, 3 vols. (New York, 1958), I, 249ff.

elsewhere, the Bedouin lived in an ambiguous symbiotic relationship with the cities and the agricultural areas which supported them. On the one hand, they maintained positive and mutually beneficial relations with both the settled population and the state. Arab auxiliaries were employed in military service; some received from the state semi-feudal grants of agricultural income (*iqṭāʿāt*); the Arabs of the eastern desert "protected" the commercial and pilgrimage routes which linked Cairo and the Nile valley to the Red Sea ports of Quṣayr and ʿAydhāb. In certain times and places, as the nomads interacted with and settled among the sedentary population, it could be difficult to distinguish the Bedouin and the peasantry; 20 percent of the individuals named in al-Udfuwī's biographical dictionary possessed *nisbas* indicating a tribal origin. On the other hand, the constant presence of the desert as a refuge, and the existence there of truly nomadic tribes, served as a reminder of a distinct Bedouin identity and as a catalyst to political and cultural tension. If the tribes protected caravans crossing the desert, they could also, in times of mistrust, attack them. One historian noted that many of those Bedouin who settled in agricultural or even urban areas engaged in a process of "opportunistic adaptation," rather than true sedentarization, taking advantage of temporary conditions which drew them from their desert home. And over the course of the Mamlūk period, it seems that the power and identity of the nomadic tribes grew at the expense of the state, with the Bedouin emerging as the effective arbiters of political power in a number of regions in the south.[25]

The Hawwāra, a nomadic tribe of Berber origin, although completely Arabized by this period, provide an instructive example of the role the Bedouin could play. They had migrated to Egypt from further west in the early Middle Ages; some of them had participated in the Fāṭimid conquest of the country. Early in his reign, Sultan Barqūq settled the tribe in Upper Egypt. There they took up agriculture, playing an important role in the cultivation of sugar cane in particular, and their chief was given the *iqṭāʿ* of Girga, a town near Sohag. Increasingly the Hawwāra came to play a political role in the area, maintaining social order; by the early Ottoman period, their chief was recognized as the de facto governing authority for much of Upper Egypt.[26]

Whatever their proportion of the total population, however, it is the cities of medieval Egypt, and Cairo in particular, which loom largest in the view of the social and cultural historian. By far the lion's share of historical studies on medieval Egypt's society and culture focus on the city of Cairo, even those which purport to be studies of Egypt as a whole. In large

[25] A. H. Saleh, "Quelques remarques sur les Bédouins d'Égypte au Moyen Age," *SI*, 48 (1978), 45–70; Garcin, *Un centre musulman*, 360–410, 465–98.

[26] T. Lewicki and P. M. Holt, "Hawwāra," *EI2*; Saleh, "Quelques remarques," 47–8.

measure, this reflects the urban bias of the medieval sources, most of which were produced by scholars, jurists, and functionaries resident in the Egyptian capital, and focus on events and conditions in the metropolis. Even sources which contain extensive data on rural areas often refract that information through the lens of urban institutions or concerns: for example, most of those surviving endowment deeds which record the boundaries, size, and condition of rural properties do so on behalf of religious and academic institutions based in the city. This urban orientation is familiar to students of modern Egypt as well, and in fact reflects older and broader patterns of Mediterranean and Near Eastern social history: it is no fluke that the Cairo Geniza has preserved marriage contracts forbidding the husband to move his family from the city to the *rīf*.[27]

This does not, of course, imply that the city formed a distinctive political or even social unit. The kind of corporate identity which came to characterize the medieval European town had no place in Islamic cities: as Ira Lapidus has demonstrated, it was unnecessary, given the range of political institutions available and the complex social processes at work within Cairo and other urban centers, and inappropriate, given the heterogeneity of the population.[28] Cairo was very much an open city: it was walled, to be sure, but after Ṣalāḥ al-Dīn's ambitious efforts to reconstruct the city's fortifications, which his successors ultimately left unfinished, no further attempt was made to extend the walls to embrace the rapidly growing suburbs.[29] As we have already noted, there was much movement to and especially from the provinces and other regions: whatever social obstacles may have intimidated a young immigrant and blocked his advancement, they did not include a lack of citizenship. The Islamic community, the ʿ*umma*ʾ, granted the city and its inhabitants no exclusive corporate identity.

But Cairo was unique, for its size, the range of its commercial enterprises, and the profusion of its cultural monuments and activities. For the entire period in question, Cairo was the political capital of empires which embraced the whole of Egypt, and usually Syria and the Ḥijāz as well. In contrast to European feudalism, the military institution which ruled Egypt in the late Middle Ages was an essentially urban phenomenon. Even during outbreaks of the plague, when the Mamlūks, an alien (and therefore especially susceptible) elite living close together in their urban households, suffered more grievously than the population as a whole, they did not flee

[27] S. D. Goitein, "Cairo: An Islamic City in the Light of the Geniza Documents," in Ira M. Lapidus (ed.), *Middle Eastern Cities* (Berkeley, 1969), 82–83; idem, *Mediterranean Society*, I, 75.

[28] Lapidus, *Muslim Cities*, passim.

[29] K. A. C. Creswell, *The Muslim Architecture of Egypt*, 2 vols. (Oxford, 1952), II, 41–63, esp. 59.

the confines of the city.[30] Since wealth and political power congregated in the city, so too did culture and learning. It is no surprise, therefore, that we know more about Cairene society than any other in Egypt – arguably, more than any other in the medieval Islamic world.

Social groups and the cultural matrix

Medieval Egyptian society, like most, was deeply hierarchical. Defining the hierarchies into which it was organized, however, is not a clear-cut process. Contemporary Muslim writers (and not only Egyptians) tended to divide the population into four broad categories: the ruling military elite, the civilian notables, the common people and the "lumpenproletariat." The terminology employed, however, was imprecise. Higher social circles might be known as the *khāṣṣa* ("elite"), *aʿyān* ("notables"), and *nās* (literally, "people," but often used in the Mamlūk period to designate the Mamlūk rulers themselves). The standard term for the "common people" was *ʿāmma*, but this vague word really only acquired meaning negatively, in opposition to *khāṣṣa*. At the bottom, the lowest social orders were known by a variety of names (*arādhil*, *awbāsh*, *ghawghāʾ*, *ḥarāfish*), and included those whose activities or occupations put them beyond the reach of polite society: prostitutes, usurers, professional entertainers, tanners, beggars, as well as rambunctious crowds more generally.[31] Taqiʾl-Dīn al-Maqrīzī, a bitter but astute observer of medieval Egyptian society, gave a more comprehensive and nuanced description of the social hierarchy in his treatise on the economy, coinage, and economic decline. At the top, he observed, were those who held the reins of power – in his day, the Mamlūk sultan and amīrs. Below them in the social pecking order came the rich merchants, who lived a life of affluence, followed by retailers, merchants of average means, and small shopkeepers. Interestingly, in the next category he places the peasantry, but the sense is less that they occupied a middle rank in the social order than that al-Maqrīzī did not know quite where to situate them. They were followed by a broad and disparate category, those who receive a stipend – "most of the *fuqarāʾ* and students [of law and theology]," as well as "most of the *ajnād al-ḥalqah* and the like" – thereby lumping together the stipendiaries of schools and Ṣūfī convents with the members of the non-elite military corps which was composed primarily, although not entirely, of the sons of Mamlūks. Below them ranked artisans

[30] David Ayalon, "The Muslim City and the Mamlūk Military Aristocracy," *Proceedings of the Israel Academy of Sciences and Humanities*, 2 (1968), 311–29.

[31] Lapidus, *Muslim Cities*, 79–85. On the *ḥarāfish*, see William M. Brinner, "The Significance of the *Ḥarāfish* and their 'Sultan'," *JESHO*, 6 (1963), 190–215.

and "salaried persons who possess a skill," and at the bottom, paupers and beggars.[32]

Thus the "classes" of medieval Egyptian society are difficult to define, and cannot easily be fit into either feudal or Marxian models. On the one hand, the defining characteristic of the different social gradations was a functional one: one's position in society depended more on what one did than who one was. It is striking that the various categories identified by al-Maqrīzī concern economic function, or (as in the case of the stipendiaries) an individual's dependent relationship to sources of wealth. One of the most important distinguishable social groups, although one which al-Maqrīzī did not identify per se, was the *ʿulamāʾ*, those individuals of varying backgrounds and occupations who had acquired some level of learning in the Islamic religious and legal sciences and who participated in some way in the transmission of knowledge. On the other hand, status as a personal rather than a functional category was at least implicit in the social hierarchy. The Mamlūks were distinguished by their monopoly on military power and most important political offices, but one became a Mamlūk as a result of one's status as a freed slave originally acquired specifically for that purpose. Moreover, behind any functional or economic hierarchy lay the dichotomy of Muslim versus *dhimmī* (a protected non-Muslim, i.e., a Christian or a Jew). Despite the basic egalitarianism of Islamic law, even free Muslim men could be distinguished according to subtle social or even ethnic gradations, as in the law of *kafāʾa* (marital equivalence). And of course if women were restricted to specific social functions, those restrictions resulted fundamentally from their status as women.[33]

The last point should remind us that behind all the social hierarchies discussed or implied by the sources, there lay the institution of the family, which for virtually everyone was the fundamental unit of society. Islamic law of course was deeply concerned with the status and relationship of the different members of the family, and the law-books provide a wealth of detail on the legal institution of marriage, but much of what we know about the actual social condition of the family in medieval Cairo is derived from the Geniza records.[34] This was a society which assumed that its members would be married, that to remain unmarried involved a needless exposure to

[32] Taqī ʾl-Dīn al-Maqrīzī, *Ighāthat al-umma bi-kashf al-ghumma*, ed. Muḥammad Muṣṭafā Ziyāda and Jamāl al-Dīn al-Shayyāl (Cairo, 1957), 72–5; Adel Allouche, *Mamlūk Economics: A Study and Translation of al-Maqrīzī's Ighāthah* (Salt Lake City, 1994), 73.

[33] For cogent remarks on medieval Egyptian social hierarchies, see Goitein, *Mediterranean Society*, I, 75–6. On the Muslim doctrine of *kafāʾa*, see Bernard Lewis, *Race and Slavery in the Middle East* (New York, 1990), 85–88.

[34] Except where noted, the following is drawn from Goitein's *Mediterranean Society*, vol. 3: *The Family* (Berkeley, 1978).

temptation and public disapprobation; it is no slur on the institution of marriage to remark that it formed, in a sense, the primary instrument of social control. In this respect it is important to remember that the "family" or household which underlay social identities was an extended family, generally under the supervision of some patriarch. Individuals married, but match-making was in most cases an impersonal process: marriages were arranged between families, and often involved cousins, both to ensure that wealth remained within the family and to protect the reputation of its women and thus the honor of the family. Reinforcing the element of control was the tendency of related families to live together, either in the same building or in neighboring structures.

It is worth pausing at this point to consider the special position of two groups of people within the structure of the family and its relationship to society at large. The first and most important is that of women. Aside from any restrictions and inequalities to which Muslim women were subject by the law, and with allowance for the enormous variation in individual circumstances which the intimacy and uncertainty of human relations require, it is clear that the position of women within marriage was a precarious one. The circumlocutions by which men referred to their wives, perhaps designed to protect their honor, nonetheless underline their subordinate station: "child" (*ṭifla*), "youth" (*ṣabiyya*), "little one" (*ṣaghīra*). As a general rule, a wife came to live with her husband's family; contact with her own relations might be severely restricted. In that position she was isolated and exposed, since it was to her male relatives – father, uncles, brothers – that a woman looked for protection. The plight of Amina, a central character in Naguib Mahfouz's novel *Bayn al-Qaṣrayn*, is surely one which many medieval Egyptian women faced. This vulnerability could be tempered by, among other things, conditions stipulated in the marriage contract – for example, that the couple live in close proximity to the bride's family; that she be granted easy access to her relatives; that the husband was to take no second wife or concubine without his first wife's approval. But it could never be entirely overcome. Divorce was apparently fairly common (although so, too, was remarriage), and widowhood could be a disaster. The Geniza records indicate that many Jewish widows were thrown back upon the public charity of the Jewish community, and there is no reason to suppose that the situation was any different among other sectors of the population. These records also show that husbands not infrequently deserted their wives and children, because of some marital dispute, or a love affair, or because of debt or business failure – a moral failing to which, presumably, Jewish men were no more predisposed than their Muslim or Christian peers.

Nonetheless, women were able to carve out for themselves spheres of independent action – to achieve freedom in the face of control, to cross the boundary between the private and the public. We will consider below one of the major cultural manifestations of that independence, in the area of the transmission of knowledge; for the moment, it is enough to consider their participation in economic activities. Even within a marriage, most women of necessity played an important economic role, in domestic chores such as spinning or grinding grain. They might also bring income to the family, for example by doing needlework or spinning for other households. Goitein noted that allusions to women working for non-familial clients became much more frequent from the thirteenth century, which may reflect a worsening of the general economic condition.[35] Actual "professions" which were open to women consisted mostly of occupations concerning women's health, such as midwives and wet nurses; services which helped to preserve social boundaries, such as those of match-makers; or occupations which were not socially respectable (even if patronized by men or women of all social levels), such as tattooists, coiffeuses, professional mourners, bath-house attendants and prostitutes.[36] If such activity was more common among the lower classes, wealthier women too played a role in the domestic economy by bringing property to their marriages, and in some cases managing it or administering family endowments.[37]

The extent to which women participated in public economic activity angered many jurists, who were anxious to reinforce those boundaries, such as gender, which in their view undergirded the social order. Ibn al-Ḥājj (d. 1336), for example, who wrote a vitriolic treatise condemning various social and religious practices of which he disapproved, was of the opinion that, following a tradition ascribed to the Prophet's companions, a woman should leave her house on only three occasions: at marriage, to join her husband; for the burial of her parents; and on the occasion of her own death and interment. It is nonetheless clear from his discussion that women led far more extroverted lives than he thought proper, and that in particular they could be found conducting business in the markets – an impression confirmed by numerous tales from the *Thousand and One Nights*, and also by European travelers such as the Venetian Livio Sanuto, who remarked that Egyptian women moved about in the markets and elsewhere with considerable

[35] Goitein, *Mediterranean Society*, III, 132–35.

[36] See, for example, the list of occupations in Aḥmad ʿAbd al-Rāziq, *La femme au temps des Mamlouks en Égypte* (Cairo, 1973), 43–87.

[37] Goitein, *Mediterranean Society*, III, 326–31; Huda Lutfi, "Al-Sakhāwī's *Kitāb al-Nisā*ʾ as a Source for the Social and Economic History of Muslim Women During the Fifteenth Century AD," *The Muslim World*, 71 (1981), 117–19; Carl F. Petry, "A Paradox of Patronage," *The Muslim World*, 73 (1983), 199–201; idem, "Class Solidarity versus Gender Gain: Women as Custodians of Property in Later Medieval Egypt," in Nikki R. Keddie and Beth Baron (eds.), *Women in Middle Eastern History: Shifting Boundaries in Sex and Gender* (New Haven, 1991), 122–42.

freedom.[38] Al-Maqrīzī, like Ibn al-Ḥājj, disdained and feared the free movement of women, and drew upon a deep vein of ethnic prejudice to portray Egyptian women as dominant and their men as weak and emasculated, but such stereotypes should not disguise the wide variation in the restrictions actually faced by women in medieval Egypt.[39] Women of the lower classes necessarily moved about with much greater freedom than did their social betters. Moreover, the chronicles report numerous occasions when the authorities attempted, with varying but never permanent degrees of success, to restrict the public activities of women. In 1438, for example, Sultan Baybars, fearing an outbreak of plague, consulted the *qāḍīs* and leading scholars as to the sins for which God was punishing them. The men of religion identified two – adultery, and that "women adorned themselves and walked through the streets night and day" – and in response, the sultan issued an edict forbidding women to leave their homes.[40]

Another social group best considered under the rubric of the family is that of domestic slaves. In Egypt as in other medieval Islamic societies, slavery was largely an urban phenomenon. As members of the households of the masters who owned them, slaves discharged a variety of functions, ranging from domestic chores to business affairs to (in the case of concubines) satisfying their masters' sexual pleasure and producing offspring. Since Islamic law forbade the enslavement of those born within the Dār al-Islām, most slaves in Egypt were imported from central Asia, Europe, Abyssinia and sub-Saharan Africa. Coming to Egypt as strangers, they were absorbed into their masters' households, in which they were trained, schooled in religion, and acculturated to their new Egyptian homes. Well-known Qur'ānic verses enjoined Muslims to treat their slaves well, influencing the structure of domestic slavery and the strong and personal ties which often bound slaves to their masters. At its best, domestic slavery was thus characterized by a benign paternalism, in which, for example, masters might help to arrange marriages for their slaves. As with the ancient Islamic institution of clientage (*walā'*), close personal ties often survived the emancipation, which was frequently the slave's good fortune; it was not uncommon, for example, for an individual's freed slaves to be beneficiaries of their former master's family *waqf*.[41]

38 Ibn al-Ḥājj, *Madkhal al-shar' al-sharīf*, 4 vols. (Cairo, 1929), I, 244–45; C. Schefer, *Le voyage d'outremer de Jean Thenaud* (Paris, 1884), 33n. See also André Raymond and Gaston Wiet, *Les marchés du Caire: Traduction annotée du texte de Maqrīzī* (Cairo, 1979), 78–80, and Huda Lutfi, "Manners and Customs of Fourteenth-Century Cairene Women: Female Anarchy versus Male Shar'i Order in Muslim Prescriptive Treatises," in Keddie and Baron, *Women in the Middle East*, 99–121.

39 Al-Maqrīzī, *Khiṭaṭ*, I, 49–50.

40 Taqī 'l-Dīn Aḥmad al-Maqrīzī, *al-Sulūk li-ma'rifat duwal al-mulūk*, ed. Muḥammad Muṣṭafā Ziyāda, 4 vols. in 12 parts (Cairo, 1934–73), IV, 1032.

41 Shaun E. Marmon, "Slavery, Islamic World," in Joseph R. Strayer (ed.), *Dictionary of*

The most prominent slaves in medieval Egyptian society were, of course, the Mamlūks, the slave-soldiers who formed an increasingly important military element under the Ayyūbids and who, in the middle of the thirteenth century, came to rule in their own right. Their organization and institution are considered elsewhere in this volume; here we will focus upon their impact on Egyptian society and culture. The attitudes of local Egyptians, and in particular the *'ulamā'*, towards their foreign rulers were decidedly mixed, and reflect the fundamental ambiguity of the Mamlūks' place in Egyptian society. They were distinguished from the local population, first and foremost, by their ethnicities, which were in fact varied, although many local writers thought of them generically as "Turks." As such, they shared in popular conceptions about the characteristics of the Turks, conceptions which in fact have an ancient pedigree in Islamic literary traditions. It was widely held that the Turks were by nature warlike and proficient in arms; some, such as Ibn Khaldūn, credited them with saving Islamic civilization from the twin perils of Frankish crusaders and Mongol heathen. Already in the late twelfth century, before the Mamlūks came to power, the Egyptian-born poet Ibn Sanā' al-Mulk had written a panegyric to Ṣalāḥ al-Dīn, founder of the Ayyūbid dynasty, remarking that "the Arab community has become mighty by the nation of the Turks, and the crusader king has been humbled by Ibn Ayyūb [Ṣalāḥ al-Dīn]. For in the time of Ibn Ayyūb, Aleppo became part of Egypt, and Egypt part of Aleppo" – even though Ṣalāḥ al-Dīn himself was a free-born ethnic Kurd.[42] Others drew less charitable conclusions from the popular stereotypes, seeing in the Turks a boorish, uncultured people; as late as the end of the fifteenth century, the historian and polymath al-Suyūṭī saw the Mamlūks less as the saviors of Islam than as the heirs of the Turkish soldiers who had in the ninth and tenth centuries humiliated and eclipsed the caliphate in Baghdad.[43]

The Mamlūks, whose lingua franca was a Turkish dialect rather than Arabic, deliberately set themselves apart from the native Egyptian population, constructing an ideology of otherness to support their political legitimacy. Their Turkish names distinguished them sharply from their local subjects, a distinction they seem consciously to have maintained: apart from a few Bedouin chiefs, virtually no native Egyptians emulated their masters

the Middle Ages (New York, 1988), XI, 330–3; Goitein, *Mediterranean Society*, I, 130–47; Aḥmad 'Abd al-Rāziq, "Un document concernant le mariage des esclaves au temps des Mamlūks," *JESHO*, 13 (1970), 309–14; Berkey, *Transmission of Knowledge*, 136.

42 Quoted in Homerin, *From Arab Poet to Muslim Saint*, 21.

43 Jean-Claude Garcin, "Histoire, opposition politique et piétisme traditionaliste dans le *Ḥusn al-Muḥādarat* de Suyūṭī," *AI*, 7 (1967), 33–89. On medieval views of the Turks/Mamlūks generally, see Ulrich Haarmann, "Ideology and History, Identity and Alterity: The Arab Image of the Turks from the 'Abbasids to Modern Egypt," *IJMES*, 20 (1988), 175–96, and idem, "Rather the Injustice of the Turks."

by adopting their nomenclature.[44] In dress and comportment, too, the Mamlūks formed a breed apart, enjoying a monopoly on horseback riding, at least within the confines of the city, as well as on sword-bearing. Their clothing instantly marked the Mamlūks as members of the ruling caste; ironically, their taste for fur-trimmed vestments may have contributed to the dissemination of the plague in the mid-fourteenth century, since many of the furs were imported from those central Asian regions from which the plague bacillus spread.[45] Both the sultanic residence in Cairo's Citadel and the smaller amīral households provided forums for a flourishing court culture, one centered around military exercises and activities (*furūsiyya*), from which native Egyptians were excluded, as well as around Turkish literature of both a secular and a religious nature, which most Egyptians could not understand and which many scorned.[46]

It would be seriously misleading, however, to overstress the Mamlūks' alienation from native Egyptian society, or to underestimate the links which bound them to broader, international patterns of Islamic culture. The Mamlūks were, in fact, deeply embedded in the society over which they ruled, and were bound to their subjects by complex ties of patronage, as well as more intimate human relations. In the first place, of course, it was their wealth which provided much of the physical infrastructure for economic and cultural life: the majority of Cairo's mosques and *madrasa*s, for instance, were established and endowed by leading members of the ruling elite.[47] Constructing a mosque or school was not an isolated event: once in operation, a religious or academic institution could support a wide range of urban activities and foundations, from markets to bath-houses. Patterns of growth in the western suburbs of Cairo, such as Būlāq and, later, the quarter known as Azbakiyya, testify to the degree to which even the physical shape of the city depended upon the direction and expenditures of the sultan and leading amīrs.[48] As closely tied as they were to Cairo, the Mamlūks' patronage of cultural monuments was felt throughout the country, and in a provincial town such as Qūṣ, where Mamlūk amīrs were resident, could play

44 Ayalon, "The Muslim City and the Mamlūk Military Aristocracy," 322.

45 Dols, *The Black Death*, 56–57; on their clothing, see L. A. Mayer, *Mamlūk Costume* (Geneva, 1952), esp. 21–35.

46 Doris Behrens-Abouseif, "The Citadel of Cairo: Stage for Mamlūk Ceremonial," *AI*, 24 (1988), 25–79; Karl Stowasser, "Manners and Customs at the Mamlūk Court," *Muqarnas*, 2 (1984), 13–20; A. Bodrogligeti, "Notes on the Turkish Literature at the Mameluke Court," *Acta Orientalia Academiae Scientarum Hungaricae*, 14 (1962), 273–82; Barbara Flemming, "Literary Activities in Mamlūk Halls and Barracks," in Myriam Rosen-Ayalon (ed.), *Studies in Memory of Gaston Wiet* (Jerusalem, 1977), 249–260.

47 Berkey, *Transmission of Knowledge*, 128ff.

48 Nelly Hanna, *An Urban History of Būlāq in the Mamlūk and Ottoman Periods* (Cairo, 1983); Doris Behrens-Abouseif, *Azbakiyya and Its Environs: From Azbak to Ismāʿīl, 1476–1879* (Cairo, 1985).

an important role both in encouraging local cultural life and in linking it to the more cosmopolitan activity of the capital.[49]

The Mamlūks' ties to Egyptian society were by no means limited to recycling the wealth which, as the ruling elite, they extracted from the country. Some Mamlūks married local women, and their children routinely did so. Moreover, their status as rulers, and the political institutions they inherited from earlier regimes, obliged them to take a keen interest in local affairs. Each of the leading amīrs supervised a household which supported a wide variety of retainers, ranging from Mamlūk cadets and domestic slaves to craftsmen and accountants. These households both functioned as semi-contained domestic economies of their own, and also had a profound impact on external economic fortunes. The Mamlūk government itself, it has been suggested, can be seen as simply an enormous extended family or "household economy," distributing food, clothing, and cash to a web of clients "on the basis of political criteria and in accord with state policy rather than economic efficiency."[50] However far we wish to take it, the metaphor suggests a degree of concern and paternalism which should modify the common image of the Mamlūks as a rapacious foreign ruling class.

Perhaps the most surprising and intriguing examples of the ties that bound the Mamlūks to Egyptian society can be found in the intersection of political and religious affairs. Religion was necessarily a matter of great concern to a regime which posed as the defender of Islam against its foreign enemies, and the Mamlūks intervened actively in religious matters. Naturally the Mamlūks left many strictly judicial matters to the Islamic judges (*qāḍīs*) whom they appointed to administer the *sharīʿa*, although it is important to remember that Sultan Baybars profoundly altered the structure of the Islamic judiciary by appointing four chief *qāḍīs*, one for each of the Sunnī schools of law (*madhāhib*), rather than one, as had been the rule in the decades before 1265.[51] Having tied their own interests to those of the society over which they ruled, the Mamlūks found it necessary to intervene directly even in matters which were properly under the purview of the *qāḍīs*, if those matters threatened their control of material resources or the political stability of their state: for example, in questions concerning *awqāf*, or in politically sensitive allegations of unbelief (*kufr*).[52]

It is only natural that much of the Mamlūks' interest in things Islamic grew out of their political concerns. Even the construction of schools,

49 Garcin, *Un centre musulman*, 256–60.

50 Ira M. Lapidus, "The Grain Economy of Mamlūk Egypt," *JESHO*, 12 (1969), 12.

51 Joseph H. Escovitz, "The Establishment of Four Chief Judgeships in the Mamlūk Empire," *JAOS*, 102 (1982), 529–31; Jorgen S. Nielsen, "Sultan al-Ẓāhir Baybars and the Appointment of Four Chief Qāḍīs (663/1265)," *SI*, 60 (1984), 167–76.

52 Jorgen S. Nielsen, *Secular Justice in an Islamic State: Mazālim Under the Baḥrī Mamlūks, 662/1264–789/1387* (Leiden, 1985), esp. 43–45, 99–102.

mosques, and Ṣūfī convents must be viewed in the light of the impact such institutions could have on the course of Mamlūk politics, by conveying status and prestige to the Mamlūk whose name was reflected in that of the building (e.g., the Ẓāhiriyya *madrasa* of Sultan al-Ẓāhir Baybars), and by providing a safe haven, in the institution's endowment, for at least a portion of the founder's wealth.[53] But the Mamlūks were also Muslims; most were unambiguously so, and many were enthusiastic converts to the faith. Religion and learning thereby provided another point of contact with native Egyptian society. Quite a few advanced beyond the basic grounding in Arabic, the Qur'ān, and the religious sciences which formed a part of their initial training, to immerse themselves more deeply in the study of *ḥadīth* or Islamic jurisprudence, and some became noted transmitters of religious knowledge in their own right. Sanjar al-Jāwulī, for example, who established a *madrasa* outside Cairo in 1329, devoted the eight years he spent in prison to copying the Qur'an and other religious volumes, and eventually issued *fatwās* and wrote a commentary on a collection of *ḥadīth* attributed to al-Shāfiʿī. Taghrī Birmish, a fairly typical Mamlūk of the early fifteenth century who died in 1448, was fluent in Arabic and studied with the leading *ḥadīth* transmitters of his day; he was known by contemporaries as *al-Faqīh*, "the Jurist," for the depth and breadth of his religious knowledge.[54] Indeed, virtually all of the important sultans of the last century of Mamlūk rule, including al-Mu'ayyad Shaykh, Jaqmaq, and Qāyt Bāy, were known for their piety and interest in the Islamic sciences – although as a ruler, each one could be as strict and as terrifying as circumstances demanded.

The Mamlūks' interest in things religious provides an important measure of the extent to which they were integrated into local Egyptian cultural patterns. The Mamlūk regime was also, however, tied to an international Sunnī culture which embraced Egypt, Syria, Anatolia and Iran. The dislocations associated with the Timurid invasions provoked a westward migration parallel to that which had occurred a century and a half earlier under the Mongols, and again in the fifteenth century Egypt became a place of refuge for scholars, artists, and craftsmen from places further east. Badr al-Dīn al-ʿAynī, a Turkish-speaking jurist from eastern Anatolia, rose to prominence at the courts of al-Mu'ayyad Shaykh and al-Ashraf Barsbāy, composing a panegyric biography of the former and orally translating his own chronicle into Turkish for the latter; he was not the only scholar to employ his knowledge of the Mamlūk lingua franca to his professional benefit. The

53 Berkey, *The Transmission of Knowledge*, 128–42.

54 Berkey, *The Transmission of Knowledge*, 142–160; idem, "'Silver Threads Among the Coal': A Well-Educated Mamlūk of the Ninth/Fifteenth Century," *SI*, 73 (1991), 109–25; Ulrich Haarmann, "Arabic in Speech, Turkish in Lineage: Mamluks and their Sons in the Intellectual Life of Fourteenth-Century Egypt," *Journal of Semitic Studies*, 33 (1988), 81–114.

secular arts, too, experienced a blossoming in the fifteenth century under the conjunction of Mamlūk patronage and turmoil in the east. Artisans from Tabrīz were, by the second quarter of that century, manufacturing glazed tiles in Fusṭāṭ, while by the end of the century, an Egyptian rug industry had begun with the migration of craftsmen from northwestern Iran. Illustrated Turkish editions of the Alexander romances and the Persian epic, the *Shāhnāmeh*, were among the more popular literary productions of the late Mamlūk court.[55]

For all of their prominence and power, however, the Mamlūks represented only a thin slice of medieval Egyptian society. The civilian population over whom they ruled, and in particular that portion of it concentrated in the major urban centers, was characterized by a fluidity and complexity to which schematic hierarchies such as that of al-Maqrīzī cannot do justice. We can make broad distinctions of socio-economic power (distinguishing, for example, an affluent bourgeoisie from the poorer common people) or identify particular groups by function (such as merchants, bureaucrats and *ʿulamāʾ*). It is important to remember, however, that class lines were not sharply drawn: a merchant might devote much of his time to scholarship, while the population enjoyed, for the medieval world, a surprising degree of social mobility.

Cairo was, above all, a city of commerce. Perhaps al-Maqrīzī exaggerated when he claimed that 12,000 shops were located on the central thoroughfare, Bayn al-Qaṣrayn, but all the sources convey an image of bustling commercial activity. Markets specializing in one product or another were scattered across the city, as were caravanserais (known variously as *funduqs*, *khāns*, *wakālas*, or *qaysāriyyas*) in which both foreign and native businessmen housed their goods and conducted their affairs. Commerce lay at the heart of the city's public life, and its streets were crowded with hawkers, street vendors, and the benches on which merchants sat to make their exchanges. So busy were the thoroughfares that the chroniclers frequently comment on the dangers posed by impassable throngs. Ibn Iyās, for example, reports an incident which occurred in 1508, in which loads of linen on the backs of several camels grazed a merchant's lamp and were accidentally set alight, sending the frightened animals galloping through the crowded streets, crushing numerous passers-by in their flight.[56]

The range of commercial activity, and of the character of those engaged in it, was enormous. At the top, affluent merchants dominated international

[55] Esin Atıl, "Mamluk Painting in the Late Fifteenth Century," *Muqarnas*, 2 (1984), 159–71; Marilyn Jenkins, "Mamluk Underglaze-Painted Pottery: Foundations for Future Study," ibid., 95–114; Ira M. Lapidus, "Mamluk Patronage and the Arts in Egypt: Concluding Remarks," ibid., 173–81.

[56] Raymond and Wiet, *Les marchés du Caire*, passim, esp. 42–48; al-Maqrīzī, *Khiṭaṭ*, I, 374; Ibn Iyās, *Badāʾiʿ al-zuhūr*, IV, 135.

trade. The most prominent of them were the mysterious group known as the Kārimiyya, who conveyed Indian pepper and other spices up the Red Sea to the ports of ʿAydhāb or Quṣayr, and thence overland to Qūṣ and ultimately to Fusṭāṭ and Cairo, until Sultan Baybars in effect eliminated their livelihood by declaring a state monopoly over the lucrative spice trade.[57] But international commerce had an impact on social ranks well below that of the bourgeois elite who controlled it: Jewish brides in Fusṭāṭ in the eleventh and twelfth centuries were loath to be married without at least one Rūmī (European) kerchief in their trousseaux.[58] At the bottom of the commercial ladder, perhaps, were the porters who transported water, on their own backs or on those of camels, from the Nile to the city, a task which grew in importance as the river receded to the west: the traveler Ibn Baṭṭūṭa estimated their number in the early fourteenth century at 12,000.[59] But at all levels, trade and industry were characterized by a high degree of specialization and diversity. The medieval Egyptian economy was capable of supporting workers in such specialized fields as the collection of down for pillows and cushions, or the making of crystal, gold, or silver kohl sticks (an important item in a bride's trousseau); even the production of food was "industrialized," in a sense, as meals were frequently prepared as a commercial activity in the markets for consumption at home. At the same time, the monetization of the economy required a sophisticated system of credit and exchange which produced a wealthy capitalist class and made Cairo a center of international finance for the entire Near East.[60]

The sophistication of the Egyptian economy is important because the commercial class, and the patterns of interaction and exchange characteristic of the commercial enterprise, set the tone for much of the social and cultural order. Goitein described early medieval Egyptian society as fundamentally bourgeois, and although he was correct to note a restriction of opportunity and hardening of class and cultural divisions from the thirteenth century, as a result of economic decline, international conflict, and what he called "intolerance and fanaticism,"[61] nonetheless something of the bourgeois spirit continued to infuse the life of Cairo to the end of the Middle Ages. Oleg Grabar has perceived reflections of this in the monumental architecture of the medieval city, even in those institutions founded and endowed by

[57] On the Kārimiyya, see Walter J. Fischel, "The Spice Trade in Mamlūk Egypt," *JESHO*, 1 (1958), 157–74, and Gaston Wiet, "Les marchands d'épices sous les sultans mamlouks," *Cahiers d'histoire égyptienne*, 7 (1955), 81–147.

[58] Goitein, *Mediterranean Society*, I, 46.

[59] Ibn Baṭṭūṭa, *Travels*, trans. H. A. R. Gibb, 3 vols. (Hakluyt Society, 2nd series, vols. 110, 117, 141) (London, 1958), I, 42; André Raymond, "Les porteurs d'eau," *Bulletin de l'Institut Français d'Archéologie Orientale*, 58 (1958), 183–202; Raymond and Wiet, *Les marchés du Caire*, 62–9.

[60] Goitein, *Mediterranean Society*, I, passim, esp. 75–116 and 229–66.

[61] Goitein, *Mediterranean Society*, I, 29.

Mamlūks, such as the series of *madrasas*, mosques and *khānqāhs* (Ṣūfī convents) which still line the major thoroughfares of the city, and whose facades merge one with the next. With the rare exception of an institution as large and imposing as the *madrasa* of Sultan Ḥasan, Mamlūk-period monuments betray a remarkable similarity and a lack of truly outstanding, individualizing features. They are to be understood, not as expressions of "princely" or imperial grandeur, but as statements of integration into an urban society which valued knowledge and piety, and which relied upon the private exercise of power and wealth to generate its cultural traditions and to protect its social order.[62]

Commercial activity, in fact, blended directly a[6262]nd thoroughly into the broader social and cultural patterns of the city. The mixing of religion and business is of course an ancient motif in Near Eastern cities, as witnessed by Jesus's encounter with the moneychangers at the temple in Jerusalem. In medieval Cairo and other Egyptian towns, too, a religious festival was equally an opportunity for commercial exchange. On a more quotidian level, shops shared virtually every major street with various houses of worship; a *madrasa* such as that founded by Sultan al-Ghawrī was literally built around a warren of commercial stalls which were rented out to provide income for the institution. In one analysis the entire city took the form of a "bazaar," characterized by a "fluid pattern of social interchange and of daily living," in which religious institutions, baths, and commercial establishments were mixed together because the individuals who used them passed easily from prayer and study to work and business, and thence to social interaction and relaxation.[63]

The values and organization of the commercial class impressed themselves upon the civilian population in all its different spheres. Commercial activity, for example, was built around friendship, informal mechanisms of control and contracts freely entered into; at least until the end of the Middle Ages, corporate bodies similar to medieval European guilds were unknown in Cairo and other Islamic cities. It is significant that even the terms used to describe this activity paralleled those in other walks of life, most notably scholarship and the transmission of knowledge. The close personal cooperation which was the mainstay of both international and local trade was known as *ṣuḥba*, "companionship," a word which also described the relationship between a teacher and his closest pupils. The exchange of goods was accomplished in a "sitting" (*majlis*) or a "circle" (*ḥalqa*); the same terms were used to describe the setting of intellectual exchange. The Arabic word *ʿarḍ* represented the offering of goods for sale, and also a student's

62 Oleg Grabar, "Reflections on Mamlūk Art," *Muqarnas*, 2 (1984), 11; cf. R. Stephen Humphreys, "The Expressive Intent of the Mamlūk Architecture of Cairo: A Preliminary Essay," *SI*, 35 (1972), 69–119.

63 Lapidus, *Muslim Cities*, 114.

exposition of a text or problem. Since commercial exchanges were built upon personal relationships, a written contract or deed was, in most instances, unnecessary; books were essential to the academic enterprise, but it was the oral transmission of these texts which was regarded as definitive.[64]

All this reflects a society whose very sophistication was built around a mode of social exchange which emphasized flexibility and personality. This is not to say that there were no mechanisms of institutional control, or, to put it differently, that the public never intruded on the private. Medieval governments frequently tried to impose order on a city which threatened to spiral out of control, for example, by ordering the demolition of recently built structures which had been constructed illegally and which encroached upon the streets and impeded traffic, as Sultan Qāyt Bāy did, with the blessing of a Shāfiʿī *qāḍī*, in 1477.[65] In a densely populated city, fire was an omnipresent threat, one which the government sought to contain by periodically requiring shopkeepers to maintain containers of water to combat any sudden conflagration, although its efforts were largely unavailing. Despite precautions, and despite the organized response of both the Mamlūks and the public, one fire burned out of control in 1321; by the third day, it was "beyond the power of humans" to do anything about it, so that the crowds were convinced that the Day of Resurrection was at hand (although eventually they came to lay the blame on two Coptic monks).[66]

It is important to remember, too, that the Ayyūbid and Mamlūk governments inherited and maintained a sophisticated bureaucratic and financial apparatus, a bureaucracy which produced several compendious manuals outlining administrative forms and procedures, such as that composed by al-Qalqashandī (d. 1418).[67] Both individual amīrs and the state itself required significant numbers of bureaucrats and accountants to administer estates, collect revenues, and supervise the disbursement of funds. These functionaries emerged from a variety of social backgrounds: some were *dhimmīs*, especially Coptic Christians, or recent converts to Islam; many of the high-ranking officials were immigrants from Syria and Palestine; quite a

64 Compare Goitein, *A Mediterranean Society*, I, 164–9 and 192–7, and Berkey, *Transmission of Knowledge*, 21–43.

65 Ibn Iyās, *Badāʾiʿ al-zuhūr*, III, 123–24.

66 Al-Maqrīzī, *al-Sulūk*, II, 220–26, and Abū ʾl-Maḥāsin Yūsuf Ibn Taghrī Birdī, *al-Nujūm al-zāhira fī mulūk miṣr waʾl-qāhira*, 16 vols. (Cairo, 1929–72), IX, 63–72; cf. Raymond and Wiet, *Les marchés du Caire*, 54–57.

67 Aḥmad ibn ʿAlī al-Qalqashandī, *Ṣubḥ al-aʿshā fī ṣināʿat al-inshāʾ*, 14 vols. (Cairo, 1914–28). On the bureaucrats, see Petry, *Civilian Elite*; D. S. Richards, "The Coptic Bureaucracy under the Mamlūks," in André Raymond et al. (eds.), *Colloque international sur l'histoire du Caire* (Cairo, 1969), 373–81; and Bernadette Martel-Thoumian, *Les civils et l'administration dans l'état militaire mamlūk (IXe/XVe siècle)* (Damascus, 1991).

few tied themselves by marriage to amīral families as well as to those of the scholarly and juristic elite, and so occupied a medial position in the diffusion of power, information, and cooperation between the state and the society over which it ruled. Personal relationships and informal contacts often determined the shape of this social group as well – witness the importance of family relationships and ties of clientage to a bureaucratic career – but the bureaucracy provided the institutional mechanism by which the military elite controlled the country and its sources of wealth. Moreover, this administration was centralized in the city of Cairo: all other administrative authorities were firmly subordinated to those at the center.

One of the most important channels of social control, not just in the markets but in society at large, was that of the *muḥtasib*. The title of this official, appointed by the sultan, is often translated as "market inspector," but this rendering fails to convey the full range of his responsibilities or the tensions implicit in his jurisdiction. On the one hand, he was charged with the regulation and supervision of market exchanges, ensuring that they violated neither the law (*sharʿ*) nor accepted custom (*ʿurf*); that money-changers did not short-change their customers, or that butchers did not sell illicit or adulterated meat. But the *ḥisba* (the office of the *muḥtasib*) was also a religious office, one deriving ultimately from the Qurʾanic injunction "to command the lawful and forbid the illicit" (for example, *sūra* 3, verse 104). As such, its holder was responsible for ensuring that Muslims, individually and collectively, properly discharged duties which were spiritual and private in nature: for example, that Muslim parents arranged for the circumcision of their children. More to the point, his mandate extended to investigating actively malfeasances which he himself suspected (as opposed to the *qāḍī* who could act only if some individual brought a formal complaint); his investigations were abetted by the secular authority which he wielded (which one medieval writer described as emanating "from the power of the sultanate," *min salāṭat al-salṭana*).[68] As such, his jurisdiction represents not only a point of contact between secular and spiritual authority, but also one in which the public sphere intruded most aggressively upon the private. It is characteristic of the tensions implicit in the office of the *muḥtasib* in late medieval Egypt that it was held, at different times, by scholars and jurists (such as Taqiʾl-Dīn al-Maqrīzī and his rival Badr al-Dīn al-ʿAynī), and also by Mamlūk amīrs.[69] The *ḥisba* was one of the few offices of which that was true.

68 On the *muḥtasib* and his jurisdiction in medieval Egypt, see Ḍiyāʾ al-Dīn Muḥammad ibn Muḥammad ibn al-Ukhuwwa, *Maʿālim al-qurba fī aḥkām al-ḥisba*, ed. Reuben Levy (Cambridge, 1938) (E. J. W. Gibb Memorial Series, n.s. vol. 12); this final phrase is found on p. 10.

69 Aḥmad ʿAbd al-Rāziq, "La *ḥisba* et le *muḥtasib* en Égypte au temps des Mamlouks," *Annales islamologiques*, 13 (1977), 115–78; idem, "Les *muḥtasibs* de Fosṭāṭ au temps des Mamlūks," *AI*, 14 (1978), 127–46.

This tension in the office of the *muḥtasib* is suggestive of the ambiguities which characterized relations between the *ʿulamāʾ* and the state more generally. Both the social organization of the *ʿulamāʾ* and patterns of cultural transmission were deeply affected by the passing of the Shiʿi Fāṭimid regime at the end of the twelfth century and its replacement by the militantly Sunnī Ayyūbid dynasty and, later, the Mamlūks. While the Fāṭimids apparently never succeeded in converting many Egyptians to their Ismāʿīlī brand of Shiʿism, under their rule Sunnī intellectual life does seem to have stagnated, as an interesting incident from the end of the Fāṭimid period demonstrates. A dispute developed among the Sunnī *ʿulamāʾ* over the old question as to whether human activities were uncreated and pre-existent, and the argument degenerated into violence. To settle the issue, it was agreed to write to the scholars of Baghdād (then the pre-eminent cultural center of the Sunnī world), and ask them to compose *fatwā*s on the matter. Naturally, the Baghdādī scholars issued contradictory opinions, so that the issue was left unresolved; but what is of interest is the intellectual dependence of Egyptian *ʿulamāʾ* at the end of the Fāṭimid period.[70] Ṣalāḥ al-Dīn and his immediate successors recognized their state of under-development, for many of the professors appointed to Ayyūbid *madrasa*s were of foreign origin.[71] Indeed, their policies, and in particular the profusion of new religious institutions which they established and endowed, were designed to strengthen the *ʿulamāʾ* and the channels of Sunnī learning, both to combat a Christian population which had seen a resurgence of status and power under the late Fāṭimids, and, more broadly, to bring to Egypt the renascence of Sunnī identity and culture which had begun in Iraq and Iran and spread eastward into Syria during the eleventh and twelfth centuries.[72]

As a result, a close but always uneasy alliance developed between the *ʿulamāʾ* and the new Sunnī regimes. This relationship was strengthened, of course, by the interest in the religious sciences taken by the military rulers, as described above. From the scholars' perspective, it took the material form of patronage by members of the ruling elite, and also by leading representatives of the bureaucratic class.[73] Much of that patronage centered on the vast network of religious and educational institutions constructed over the course of the Middle Ages. The first Sunnī *madrasa*s in Egypt were established in Alexandria, by the Andalusian Mālikī jurist al-Ṭurṭūshī and later by a Sunnī

70 Gary L. Leiser, "Ḥanbalism in Egypt before the Mamlūks," *Studia Islamica*, 54 (1981), 166.

71 Leiser, "Notes on the Madrasa," 19.

72 Gary L. Leiser, "The *Madrasa* and the Islamization of the Middle East: The Case of Egypt," *JARCE*, 22 (1985), 29–47.

73 On relationships of clientage between bureaucrats and academics, and intercession by the former in favor of the latter, see Martel-Thoumian, *Les civils et l'administration*, 373–82.

vizier, Riḍwān ibn al-Walākhshī, as a result of which that city became a hotbed of rejuvenated Sunnīsm at the end of the Fāṭimid period.[74] Under the Ayyūbids and the Mamlūks, however, it was the sultan and the amīral class who undertook the construction and endowment of many, and virtually all of the most important, of the *madrasas*, Ṣūfī convents, and teaching mosques which provided a new infrastructure for worship and the transmission of religious learning. These were mostly in Cairo, but also in provincial towns such as Alexandria and Qūṣ, the latter functioning as a regional center of education in the Ṣaʿīd. The salaries and stipends (often supplemented by accommodation and meals) which these institutions provided for the teachers and students associated with them became an important source of income for the *ʿulamāʾ*, and the founders often retained for themselves and their descendants some degree of control over appointments to positions in them.[75]

The famous historian and jurist Ibn Khaldūn, an emigré from the Maghrib, provides a noteworthy example of the degree to which a scholar's career might depend upon Mamlūk patronage. His reputation had preceded his arrival in Egypt in 1382, but despite an invitation to lecture at the al-Azhar mosque, he did not receive his first appointment to an official teaching post until 1384, when Sultan Barqūq made him a professor at the Qamḥiyya *madrasa*. His inaugural lecture there is reproduced in his autobiography, and gives a good sense of the ideological support which the Mamlūks' patronage bought them. In it, he lauded the Mamlūks, "this victorious band of Turks," as the protectors of Islam, and praised Barqūq as "the unsheathed sword of God against the infidel enemy."[76] Later, the sultan appointed him to the *madrasa* which he himself had established on Bayn al-Qaṣrayn, although he was soon removed from that post through pressure from rivals within the court. After a reconciliation, however, Barqūq again appointed him professor, this time of *ḥadīth*, at the important *madrasa* established by the amīr Ṣarghitmish in 1356.[77]

The *ʿulamāʾ* found themselves affected by the state in other ways as well. The Ayyūbid sultans consciously fostered the development of the different Sunnī schools of law (*madhāhib*), which had languished under the rule of the Ismāʿīlī Fāṭimids, although they never served in Egypt as a focus for deep and sometimes exclusive social identification as they did further to the east, for example, in Khurāsān.[78] The Ayyūbids promoted in particular the

[74] Leiser, "The *Madrasa* and the Islamization of the Middle East," 37–40.
[75] Berkey, *The Transmission of Knowledge*, 96–107.
[76] ʿAbd al-Raḥmān Ibn Khaldūn, *al-Taʿrīf*, ed. Muḥammad ibn Tāwīt al-Ṭanjī (Cairo, 1951), 279–85.
[77] Fischel, *Ibn Khaldūn in Egypt*, 20–22, 26–27.
[78] Ira M. Lapidus, "Ayyūbid Religious Policy and the Development of the Schools of Law in Cairo," *Colloque international sur l'histoire du Caire* (Cairo, 1969), 279–86.

members of Shāfiʿi school, from among whom they appointed the chief judge. It is significant that Sultan Baybars's appointment in 1265 of four chief *qāḍīs*, one for each of the four Sunnī *madhāhib*, a policy which remained in place to the end of the Mamlūk period, although largely unopposed at the time, was bitterly criticized by the fifteenth-century jurist al-Suyūṭī, who felt that the policy undermined the restorative work of Ṣalāḥ al-Dīn, which had been based upon the primacy of the Shāfiʿī school, and replaced Sunnī unity with division.[79]

The division which these scholars feared was, however, equally a product of competition and rivalry among the *ʿulamāʾ* themselves, a condition which al-Suyūṭī, with his scorn for his colleagues and controversial claim to be the "restorer of the age" (*mujaddid al-ʿaṣr*), did as much as anyone to foster.[80] It is important to remember that the *ʿulamāʾ* were not a homogeneous lot, that there was much diversity and disagreement among them, as exemplified by the persistent controversy over the Ṣūfī poet Ibn al-Fāriḍ, discussed above. Altercations among the scholars were frequent, and generally resulted from a complex mixture of genuine doctrinal or ideological disputes and intense, sometimes vituperative personal or professional animosity. A figure such as the Syrian Ḥanbalī Ibn Taymiyya (d. 1328), who found himself in conflict with his academic colleagues and was hauled before the sultan on more than one occasion, created discord both with his stand on issues such as the literalness of Qur'ānic statements about God sitting on his throne, and also with his undeniably caustic and obstinate personality.[81] The disputes involving Ibn Taymiyya, though perhaps the most famous, were by no means unique for their intensity and color. In the late twelfth century, a Shāfiʿī jurist and poet named Abū ʿAbd Allāh ibn al-Kīzānī, who had a reputation for anthropomorphic beliefs, died and was buried next to the Imām al-Shāfiʿī. Three years after his death, an indignant Ashʿarī theologian named Najm al-Dīn al-Khabūshānī dug up the poet's bones and scattered them about, shouting that "a righteous believer [*ṣiddīq*] and a heretic [*zindīq*] should not be buried in the same place!"[82] Such altercations gave the ruling authorities an opportunity to intervene in matters which otherwise lay beyond their purview, as Sultan al-Nāṣir Muḥammad was forced to do in the matter of Ibn Taymiyya, and Qāytbāy in the controversy surrounding Ibn al-Fāriḍ's poetry.

More generally, the *ʿulamāʾ* as a body represented an enormous range of outlook and accomplishment. Academic enterprise was of course concen-

[79] Garcin, "Histoire, opposition politique et piétisme traditionaliste," 70–71.

[80] On al-Suyūṭī's controversial claims, see Sartain, *Jalāl al-Dīn al-Suyūṭī*, I, 61–71.

[81] Donald P. Little, "Did Ibn Taymiyya Have a Screw Loose?" *SI*, 41 (1975), 93–111; idem, "The Historical and Historiographical Significance of the Detention of Ibn Taymiyya," *IJMES*, 4 (1973), 311–27.

[82] Leiser, "Ḥanbalism in Egypt," 165–66.

trated in Cairo, but minor scholars, preachers and other religious figures could be found in every town, and provided an important channel for the transmission of Islamic learning and ideals to the Muslim Egyptian population beyond the metropolis. At the top of the pyramid were those prominent scholars of Islamic law, *ḥadīth* and the other religious sciences who held professorships at the many academic institutions, and from whose ranks were drawn the judges of the Islamic courts. Such scholars could amass considerable social prestige and power, for example, by acquiring multiple remunerative teaching appointments in which they could install their pupils as substitutes, or which they might transfer to their educated sons.[83] They represented, however, only a fraction of those who could claim to be, in some sense, an *ʿālim* (a learned person, of which the plural is *ʿulamāʾ*). The *ʿulamāʾ* as a group were highly diverse, as a biographical dictionary such as Shams al-Dīn Muḥammad al-Sakhāwī's comprehensive survey of fifteenth-century individuals makes clear.[84] They included a wide variety of minor legal and religious functionaries, such as notaries (*shāhids*), prayer leaders, and professional Qurʾān readers, as well as many bureaucrats and others for whom learning and the transmission of knowledge were more an avocation than a career. The structure of education, in particular the availability of stipends and accommodation for students in *madrasa*s and other institutions, allowed for a fair degree of social mobility, including, as we have seen, the integration of provincial residents into broader patterns of Muslim cultural life. Nonetheless, the diversity of the educated class also mirrors the range of cultural standards: from the cosmopolitanism of the more prominent scholars, whose numbers included many Syrians, Iranians and other foreigners, reflecting the genuinely international Sunnīculture of which Cairo was the center, to low-ranking stipendiaries of mosques, and religious figures of purely local stature whose contact with higher forms of Muslim learning was tangential and superficial.[85]

Part of what made that diversity possible was the flexible character of the transmission of knowledge. Just as the growth in the numbers of religio-academic institutions reflected a "widening of the social base of architectural patronage,"[86] so too did it expand the pool of Muslim Egyptians who had direct contact with, and even professional dependence on, religious and legal education. By the fifteenth century, the number of schools of higher education in Cairo alone numbered well over 100; primary schools must have been even more numerous. Moreover, endowed classes in jurisprudence

83 Berkey, *The Transmission of Knowledge*, 107–27.
84 *Al-Ḍawʾ al-lāmiʿ li-ahl al-qarn al-tāsiʿ*, 12 vols. (Cairo, 1934).
85 On these matters, see especially Petry, *Civilian Elite of Cairo*, passim.
86 Oleg Grabar, "The Architecture of the Middle Eastern City from Past to Present: The Case of the Mosque," in Ira M. Lapidus (ed.), *Middle Eastern Cities* (Berkeley, 1969), 39.

(*fiqh*) and other subjects became standard features, not only of *madrasas*, but of mosques and Ṣūfī convents as well. Nonetheless, the structure of education remained informal and personal, and tied to oral transmission from, and the reputation of, individual teachers. There was no system of institutional degrees; what mattered was the *ijāza*, the attestation by a scholar that a particular student had studied a particular text, or acquired competence in a given field, under his (or her) direction. Since there was no limit to the number of *ijāzas* an individual might acquire, there was a tendency to collect as many as possible; *ijāzas* from older transmitters were especially valued, on the ground that, all things being equal, they would involve fewer links in the "chains of transmission" (*isnāds*) which led back to the original author of a text (or, in the case of *ḥadīth*, to the Prophet himself). The informality and personal nature of the transmission of knowledge, which has direct parallels in the bourgeois culture of commercial exchange, kept the learned class open and flexible, and drew into its ranks people from many different walks of life, including many Mamlūks, who were professional soldiers, not students, but who could nevertheless immerse themselves in the world of learning. Women in particular were able to take advantage of this flexibility to overcome the gender barriers which in theory separated them from most spheres of public life, and quite a number of them became respected transmitters of *ḥadīth*.[87]

There were few issues which so highlighted the diversity of status and opinion among the *ʿulamāʾ*, and few which were so central to the religious culture of the late Middle Ages, as that of Ṣūfīsm. The various forms of Ṣūfī mysticism had engendered much controversy and hostility on the part of many legal scholars, but the later Middle Ages saw its triumph as the dominant form of Sunnī piety and religious experience. In Egypt, a representative figure is Ibn ʿAṭāʾ Allāh, born in Alexandria in the middle of the thirteenth century to a prominent family of jurists. Convinced by a Ṣūfī *shaykh* (master) that mysticism and the law did not exclude each other, he abandoned the hostility to Ṣūfīsm which he had absorbed from his father and grandfather, and taught both *fiqh* and *taṣawwuf* (Ṣūfī mysticism) at al-Azhar mosque in Cairo. He is best remembered as the author of a "breviary" which acquired enormous popularity, in large part because it avoided the extreme incarnationist terminology of controversial Ṣūfīs such as the theosophist Ibn ʿArabī, and spoke of God, and mankind's approach to him, in the direct language of the Qurʾan.[88] To be sure, Ṣūfīsm remained controversial, to the end of the Middle Ages and beyond, as the controversy

[87] On these matters, see Jonathan P. Berkey, "Women and Islamic Education in the Mamlūk Period," in Nikki Keddie and Beth Baron (eds.), *Women in Middle Eastern History: Shifting Boundaries in Sex and Gender* (New Haven, 1991), 143–57.

[88] Paul Nwyia, *Ibn ʿAṭāʾ Allāh (m. 709/1309) et la naissance de la confrérie šādilite* (Beirut, 1972).

surrounding Ibn al-Fāriḍ would indicate, and strict scholars such as Ibn Taymiyya vigorously attacked antinomian excesses in Ṣūfī doctrine and practice. On the other side, a Ṣūfī such as ʿAbd al-Wahhāb al-Shaʿrānī (d. 1565) could scorn the jurists for their obsession with hair-splitting and convoluted argumentation, which ignored the needs of the common people and the spiritual message of Islam (although he, too, was critical of Ṣūfīs who contravened the law).[89] But the rapprochement of Ṣūfism and the juristic culture of the higher *ʿulamāʾ* is one of the defining motifs of late medieval Egyptian society, and one which can be measured in various ways: for example, in the inclusion of a jurisprudence-based curriculum in the program of Ṣūfī convents, and a corresponding introduction of formal Ṣūfī practice into the institutional life of *madrasa*s, and in the fact that Ibn Taymiyya himself turns out to have been a member of a Ṣūfī order.[90]

The Middle Ages saw a boom in the construction and endowment of Ṣūfī *khānqāh*s, along with *madrasa*s and mosques, at the hands of sultans, Mamlūk amīrs, and other leading political and social figures. The most prominent among them were that established by Ṣalāḥ al-Dīn in Cairo (known as Saʿīd al-Suʿadāʾ), and another constructed to the north of the capital at Siryāqūs by Sultan al-Nāṣir Muḥammad in the early fourteenth century, but they were supplemented by dozens of smaller convents providing meals, accommodation, and sometimes stipends to Ṣūfī adepts and masters. Increasingly, these institutions shed the role of providing a forum for spiritual retreat, and turned outward to integrate themselves into broader patterns of social and religious life, and in Cairo, for instance, were located in the central neighborhoods of the city.[91] A concurrent development, although an independent one, was the coalescence of Ṣūfii "orders" (*ṭāʾifas*), which represented paths of spiritual affiliation constructed around hierarchies tracing their authority to some revered eponymous founder, and which provided their members with opportunities for organized meditation and worship (usually built around the practice of *dhikr*, the repetitive oral "remembering" of God's name or other expressive formulae, or *samāʿ*, adoration through music). The leading historian of these *ṭāʾifas* saw their growth as a sign of decline in Ṣūfism, associated with institutionalization and the disappearance of intellectual originality,[92] but they also stand as an important measure of the spread of Ṣūfism among the Muslim population

89 Points emphasized by Winter, *Society and Religion*, esp. 103–05, 230–36.

90 George Makdisi, "Ibn Taimīya: a Ṣūfī of the Qādiriya Order," *American Journal of Arabic Studies*, 1 (1974), 118–29.

91 Doris Behrens-Abouseif, "Change in Function and Form of Mamlūk Religious Institutions," *Annales islamologiques*, 21 (1985), 73–93; on *khānqāhs* generally, see Leonor Fernandes, *The Evolution of a Sufi Institution in Mamlūk Egypt: The Khanqah* (Berlin, 1988).

92 J. Spencer Trimingham, *The Sufi Orders in Islam* (Oxford, 1971), 70, 199–200.

generally. In Egypt, as elsewhere, the orders were polymorphous. Some, such as the Shādhiliyya to which Ibn ʿAṭāʾ Allāh belonged, were moderate and intellectual; they rejected asceticism in favor of an active engagement with society, both through secular occupations and preaching to the masses. Others skirted much more closely the beliefs and practices which the jurists feared and condemned; they included the most popular order in Egypt, the Aḥmadiyya, associated with the famous saint Aḥmad al-Badawī (d. 1276), whose tomb shrine at Ṭanṭa in the Delta is still the object of veneration and pilgrimage. Nor were the orders mutually exclusive: al-Shaʿrānī, for instance, belonged formally to as many as twenty-six orders.[93]

Just as many who were not professional scholars might identify themselves with the transmission of religious knowledge, so too did Ṣūfism reach broadly and deeply into the Muslim Egyptian population. It was popular among the Mamlūks, some of whom may have sensed an affinity between certain aspects of Ṣūfī practice and the shamanism of their central Asian homeland. Sultan al-Ghawrī, for instance, who held a low opinion of many scholars, at one point offering a lieutenant a reward for every drunken jurist he could find, nonetheless had a great respect for Ṣūfī mystics, and when he went to Syria to confront the Ottoman army in 1516, he took with him the head of the Aḥmadī order.[94] Women, too, participated in Ṣūfī rituals, sometimes in leading roles; the chronicles and biographical dictionaries record instances in which women were appointed "*shaykhas*" of hospices reserved for women, as well as several in which a woman succeeded her father or husband as director of a Ṣūfī institution serving, presumably, male adepts.[95]

More broadly, Ṣūfism functioned as a kind of social glue, tying the common people to more elevated forms of religious expression and the inhabitants of rural villages and towns to an urban-dominated cultural order. Mystical practice, at some level, attracted many if not most Muslims, including those who neither lived in a convent nor joined an order nor attached themselves closely to a particular *shaykh*, but who nonetheless found in *dhikr* or *samāʿ* a compelling outlet for their spiritual energies. One historian of late medieval religion has identified the appeal of Ṣūfism as its status as "the sphere of Islam where a ruler, an *ʿālim*, or a commoner could request a personal, or at least a partially creative and active participation in religion."[96] At the lowest social levels, the impact of Ṣūfism is inevitably

93 On the orders generally, see Trimingham, *Sufi Orders in Islam*, passim, and Winter, *Society and Religion*, 88–149.

94 Winter, *Society and Religion*, 19–20, 100.

95 Al-Sakhāwī, *al-Ḍawʾ al-lāmiʿ*, III, 237; Berkey, *Transmission of Knowledge*, 173–75, esp. 175 n. 50; Winter, *Society and Religion*, 130–31; ʿAbd al-Rāziq, *La femme aux temps des mamlouks*, 72–75.

96 Winter, *Society and Religion*, 29; cf. Boaz Shoshan, *Popular Culture in Medieval Cairo* (Cambridge, 1993), 9–22.

more difficult to trace, but organized mysticism may have taken root even among the rabble known as the *ḥarāfīsh*, whose poverty identified with and brought out the asceticism latent in Ṣūfī thought.[97] In rural areas in particular, well-known Ṣūfīs emerged as religious leaders and transmitters of Islam to the peasants and small-townsmen. Links to Cairo and the religious currents there were maintained through education, itinerant mystics, and the *ḥajj*. Abu'l-Ḥasan al-Shādhilī (d. 1258), the eponymous founder of the Shādhilī order, in his repeated performances of the pilgrimage seems to have preferred the more arduous route through Qūṣ and thence to ʿAydhāb, rather than the shorter route to the Red Sea from Cairo, and his disciples, in imitation of the master, often followed suit; the contacts with the Ṣaʿīd which they maintained as a result were of great importance in strengthening the Shādhilī order there.[98] Rural Ṣūfīs who acquired an education and training in Cairo often returned to their home towns and villages, where they supplemented their religious functions such as leading prayer and intercession by filling other compelling social needs: as scribes (copying Qur'āns and other texts for the illiterate villagers), notaries (witnessing wedding contracts), schoolmasters, and occasionally as mediators between the population and the political authorities.[99]

Mediation between native Egyptians and the ruling elite was, in fact, a structural need of the Mamlūk system, one that could be fulfilled by both *ʿulamāʾ* and Ṣūfīs, or by individuals who were both. The *ʿulamāʾ*, including the *qāḍīs* and other leading legal scholars, were especially useful when the issue touched on matters of the *sharīʿa*, as when the sultan attempted to raise cash through extra taxation on merchants or religious endowments.[100] But the *ʿulamāʾ* were also compromised by their own reliance on the Mamlūks, as patrons and as endowers of the institutions from which much of their income and status derived, so that increasingly the role of mediator fell to the Ṣūfīs. This social and political function was linked to the spread, especially in the fifteenth century, of less monumental Ṣūfī institutions, usually known as *zāwiya*s, often little more than neighborhood mosques associated with particular *shaykh*s, and more likely to be independent of patronage by the wealthy and powerful.[101] Revered Ṣūfī *shaykh*s often came

[97] Brinner, "The Significance of the *Ḥarāfīsh*," 204–06, 210–11.

[98] Garcin, *Un centre musulman*, 312–21.

[99] Jean-Claude Garcin, "Histoire et hagiographie de l'Égypte musulmane à la fin de l'époque mamelouke et au début de l'époque ottomane," in *Hommages à la mémoire de Serge Sauneron*, vol. 2: *Égypte post-pharaonique* (Cairo, 1979), 290–300.

[100] See the incidents cited in Carl F. Petry, *Protectors or Praetorians? The Last Mamlūk Sultans and Egypt's Waning as a Great Power* (Albany, 1994), 166–68; on the *ʿulamāʾ* as intermediaries more generally, see Lapidus, *Muslim Cities*, 130–41.

[101] Leonor Fernandes, "The *Zāwiya* in Cairo," *AI*, 18 (1982), 116–21; idem, "Some Aspects of the *Zāwiya* in Egypt at the Eve of the Ottoman Conquest," *AI*, 19 (1983), 9–17.

into conflict with the military elite, as defenders of the local population and their interests, and thereby exercised a certain influence over political processes which were formally the exclusive concern of the ruling authorities.[102] Ṣūfīs may not necessarily have sought such a social and political role: the popular shaykh and powerful intercessor Abu'l-Suʿūd al-Jāriḥī once lamented to al-Shaʿrānī that in his thirty-seven years as a Ṣūfī, no one had come to him asking for guidance on how to reach God, or how to repent of sins; instead they had sought remedy from more worldly complaints: "he who had quit the world saw it flow back towards him."[103] But circumstances cast them in this role, not least the fearful respect in which many Mamlūks held them.

Through Ṣūfīsm we reach the bottom of the social scale. Naturally less is known about the working and poorer classes, let alone rural society, but the sources reveal enough to allow some speculation about their relationship to the broader social and cultural order which we have been tracing. Certainly for many of those in the lower ranks, life was precarious and often miserable. As elsewhere in the Middle Ages, a large portion of a poor family's budget was spent on bread; ʿAbd al-Laṭīf al-Baghdādī (d. 1231–2), an Iraqi physician who settled in Egypt, reports that their diet was supplemented primarily with dates, figs, fish, cheese, and (in the countryside, at least) fieldmice and snakes.[104] Attempts to quantify the misery and misfortune of the poor are difficult, but it is clear that the rampant inflation and periodic shortages of foodstuffs which plagued the Egyptian economy in the later Middle Ages took an especially heavy toll on the more vulnerable members of society. Crisis might be brought on by natural forces, such as a low Nile flood or a wave of pestilence. "This is the Almighty's customary treatment of His creatures," wrote al-Maqrīzī; "whenever they disobey Him and violate His divine law, He calls down a calamity upon them as a punishment for their actions."[105] But al-Maqrīzī had served as *muḥtasib*, and as such had been responsible for overseeing the distribution of grain in Cairo; he accurately perceived that the food shortages which plagued Egypt in the early fifteenth century were more the product of human actions and political decisions, including excessive taxation, failure to maintain the irrigation system, and debasement of the coinage. These calamities brought on the death of most of the peasants, he reported (with some exaggeration);

102 See, for example, Ibn Iyās, *Badāʾiʿ al-zuhūr*, V, 110–13.

103 Jean-Claude Garcin, "Deux saints populaires du Caire au début du XVIe siècle," *BEO*, 29 (1977), 134–36.

104 ʿAbd al-Laṭīf al-Baghdādī, *Kitāb al-ifāda waʾl-iʿtibār fīʾl-umūr al-mushāhada waʾl-ḥawādith al-muʿāyana bi-arḍ miṣr* (Cairo, 1869 [?]), 43, trans. S. de Sacy, *Relation de l'Égypte* (Paris, 1810), 314–15; Eliyahu Ashtor, "The Diet of Salaried Classes in the Medieval Near East," *Journal of Asian History*, 4 (1970), 12, 19.

105 Al-Maqrīzī, *Ighāthat al-umma*, 41; Allouche, *Mamluk Economics*, 50.

more interestingly, he noted that the rise in prices had wiped out the purchasing power of the "stipendiaries," such as the students and minor functionaries at mosques, *madrasa*s and *khānqāh*s, whose stipends were fixed by the deeds of endowment for their institutions, and who therefore were "either dead or wishing death because of the calamity that has befallen them."[106]

Despite their at least potential misery, the common people and the poor were integrated into the social, cultural and even the political order. Artisans and craftsmen, in their relations with each other and with their customers, shared many of the same values and operated in much the same way as bourgeois merchants. As in higher social and economic circles, the hallmarks were flexibility, freedom and personal relationships. With a few exceptions, notably sugar and paper, most industries were organized in small workshops rather than large factories. Partnership was the normal form of industrial cooperation, rather than employment; these partnerships were characterized by a significant degree of freedom of contract, and often produced strong and lasting relationships, stronger in some cases than the ties of family.[107] In general the common people lacked institutional or organizational structures – guilds, for instance – which could effectively represent their interests. As a result, the most common form of expression for their frustrations and grievances was the spontaneous outburst of violence, as in riots. The imprecision of mob violence as a political idiom left the masses open to manipulation by both Mamlūks, in their incessant internecine feuds, and religious leaders. But there was also method in the madness, and urban disruptions could express, however crudely, public feeling on issues ranging from the legitimacy of some particular Mamlūk's claim to the sultanate, to impatience with the government's manipulation of the grain supply and the frequent corruption of those officials (especially the *muḥtasib*) charged with overseeing it.[108]

In the cultural sphere, the common people were not only integrated into the overarching Islamic order, but helped to define it. As we have stressed, the openness and flexibility of the educational system permitted the participation, on some level, of various marginal groups, such as Mamlūks and women; the same was true of the common people, who might also earn *ijāzas* and thereby acquire some stake, however minimal and symbolic, in the transmission of knowledge and the religious order.[109] Cultural transmission was not a one-way street, however, with the ideas and principles of the higher-ranking *ʿulamāʾ* and leading Ṣūfīs trickling down in some attenuated

106 Al-Maqrīzī, *Ighāthat al-umma*, 75; Allouche, *Mamluk Economics*, 75.
107 Goitein, *Mediterranean Society*, I, 80–99.
108 Shoshan, *Popular Culture in Medieval Cairo*, 52–66; see also Lapidus, *Muslim Cities*, 143–84.
109 Berkey, *Transmission of Knowledge*, 201–14.

form to those of lower social rank. Although it is difficult to recover, given the cultural bias of literary sources produced mainly by the academic elite, it is possible to identify a sphere of cultural activity in which the common people – non-scholars – participated as autonomous actors. For instance, despite criticism from the jurists, Muslim Egyptians participated eagerly in the Coptic festival of Nawrūz, a carnivalesque celebration of the new agricultural cycle characterized by excessive eating and drinking, the exchange of gifts, and games and masquerades designed to blur political and gender hierarchies. Although the repeated condemnation of the legal scholars and the obliging edicts of the secular authorities had probably eliminated its public celebration in Cairo by the early fifteenth century, it survived much longer elsewhere in the country, notably in Upper Egypt.[110] On a rather different level, street theater and the popular shadow plays afforded an opportunity for satire and biting social criticism: Ibn al-Ḥājj, for example, described a skit popular with the common people in which the actors lampooned the pretensions of the *qāḍīs* by parading about in oversized turbans and pompous clothing.[111]

The important point, however, is not that the common people had a culture of their own, but that medieval Egyptian culture was a complex tableau consisting of interlocking and overlapping strata, and drawing upon the experiences and insights of Muslims from a variety of different social levels. This becomes apparent from a review of the extensive literature produced in this period which condemned the practice by Muslims of "innovations" (*bidaʿ*), customs and habits which contravened the *sunna* of the Prophet. This polemic was not, of course, peculiar to medieval Egypt, but this society did produce a considerable number of such treatises. Two matters, in particular, concerned the scholars who produced them. One was that certain popular mechanisms for the transmission of religious knowledge, values and culture to the common people, such as unregulated preaching and storytelling, were deceptively similar to "higher" channels, threatening to contaminate the "knowledge" which the masses acquired.[112] But a second was that popular and (in a strict sense) innovative practices were themselves working their way into the fabric of what was accepted, even by many scholars, as "Islam." Perhaps the most prominent example of this tendency was the *ziyārat al-qubūr*, the organized visitation of tombs of

110 Shoshan, *Popular Culture*, 40–51.

111 Ibn al-Ḥājj, *Madkhal al-sharʿ al-sharīf*, I, 146; on the shadow plays, see M. M. Badawi, "Medieval Arabic Drama: Ibn Dāniyāl," *Journal of Arabic Literature*, 13 (1982), 83–107, and Muḥammad Ibn Dāniyāl, *Three Shadow Plays*, ed. Paul Kahle (Cambridge, 1992).

112 See Jonathan P. Berkey, "Tradition, Innovation, and the Social Construction of Knowledge in the Medieval Islamic Near East," *Past & Present*, 146 (1995), 38–65.

pious saints and other venerated folk.[113] The huge cemetery to the south and east of Cairo, known as the Qarāfa, held a vast number of tombs venerated by the Muslim population, and dominated the religious imagination of many Cairenes; but hardly any region of the country was without its own graves of local saints. Indeed, the visitation of tombs is a practice of profound antiquity in Egypt, and jurists such as Ibn al-Ḥājj and Ibn Taymiyya were no doubt correct to question its place in Islam. But what was especially troubling was that the practice seemed to have worked its way into the fabric of Islam in medieval Egypt, in the identification of numerous tombs with various heroes of early Islamic history, thereby claiming a space for the *ziyāra* in the religion's "sacred history," and also in the support it received from prominent religious and legal scholars, such as Taqi'l-Dīn al-Subkī, who wrote a treatise defending the practice.

The cultic visitation of tombs is a fitting place to end this survey, for it brings together the various social strata in a practice which demonstrates the diversity and fluidity of late medieval Egyptian culture. The richness of that culture was a product of many factors, of which the most important were: Egypt's role as a fulcrum of international trade; the presence of an active and engaged ruling elite which, for all its "otherness," effectively identified its own interests with those of the country; and the vigor of the country's network of religious institutions and Cairo's position as the undisputed center of Islamic learning. Those factors did not disappear immediately upon the Ottoman conquest of the country in 1517, but they were seriously, and irretrievably, undermined. From this point on, Egyptian society was tied to imperial Ottoman politics and was increasingly vulnerable to global economic developments, so that its culture grew dependent upon foreign taste.

[113] See Christopher S. Taylor, "The Cult of the Saints in Late Medieval Egypt" (Ph.D. dissertation, Princeton University, 1989), and idem, "Sacred History and the Cult of Muslim Saints in Late Medieval Egypt," *The Muslim World*, 80 (1990), 72–80. See also Muhammad Umar Memon, *Ibn Taimiya's Struggle Against Popular Religion* (The Hague, 1976).

15

Historiography of the Ayyūbid and Mamlūk epochs

DONALD P. LITTLE

As is evident from other chapters of this volume it would be artificial and misleading to try to separate the history of Islamic Egypt from that of its neighbors, especially Syria and Palestine. After all, the geopolitical situation of Egypt throughout the Middle Ages dictated both the necessity to defend its right flank from encroachments by rival powers in Syria and, to a lesser extent, Mesopotamia, and to secure its commercial interests in the Mediterranean through control of the ports of the Levant. These geopolitical factors were not of course peculiar to the Islamic period and are recurring themes of both ancient and modern times. That being the case, it is not surprising that it is also impractical to confine the historiography of the Ayyūbid and Mamlūk periods to writing about Egypt alone or to those composed by Egyptian authors. Although historians resident in Egypt became more and more prominent in the late thirteenth and fourteenth centuries and an Egyptian group of writers flourished in Cairo during the fifteenth century, for the whole of the Ayyūbid period, Syrian and Mesopotamian authors dominated what was recorded about Egypt. Since, moreover, the Egyptian Ayyūbid sultans, including Ṣalāḥ al-Dīn, were involved with building and maintaining an empire with its capital in Cairo but including Syria, Paleṣtine, and other territories, there is no history focusing on Ayyūbid Egypt per se, so that it must be studied as a part of Ayyūbid history in general.

Nevertheless, before examining the historiography of each era separately, it should be useful to ask whether the two periods have any features in common. From the point of view of historiographical genres, the answer is simple: the classical forms of Arabic historical writing were maintained by both Ayyūbid and Mamlūk writers, most notably chronicles and biographies (including biographies of individual personages and biographical dictionaries), but also administrative manuals, though the latter were not used with the same frequency and consistency in both periods. In general, then, the external forms of historiography are marked by conservatism, as is the content, which deals by and large with the activities of the political elites at their courts, in diplomacy, and on battlefields, along with the roles of intellectuals, including religious scholars and mystics, but also the literati, in the life of the times. To a great extent this element of conservatism can be explained by the fact that the historians of both periods had similar backgrounds and were formed by similar influences. Although important exceptions will be noted for the Mamlūk period, basically two types of historians dominated the field for almost 350 years: officials, mainly bureaucrats of both high and low rank, who had access to rulers and/or official documents, and religious scholars, that is *ʿulamāʾ*. The two groups were certainly not mutually exclusive, for most if not all of the former would have had some exposure in the course of their education to the art and science of *ḥadīth* and its transmitters, which continued to influence scholarly historiography from its inception to the time in question. On the other hand many of the *ʿulamāʾ* served in some official capacity or another associated with judicial institutions.

But despite the maintenance of the centuries-old Arabic traditions governing the forms of historical discourse, the historians of our periods have other distinctive characteristics in common. This at least is one thesis, in which it is argued that from the eleventh to the fifteenth centuries a new type of historiography developed and flourished, namely "*siyasa*-oriented historiography,"[1] that is to say historiography without the degree of concern for epistemological and theological implications that had characterized previous works, and with increased emphasis on issues related to the governance of Muslim states. This new orientation, culminating in the Mamlūk "imperial bureaucratic chronicle," resulted in increased reliance on archives and records of various kinds, in an effort not just to lend authenticity to the historical narrative but to expand the subject matter of history to include economic and social processes.[2] Concomitantly, interest in biography became more and more pervasive as historians scrutinized the lives of the governing class and their extended entourages in order to delve more deeply into the day-to-day workings of medieval Muslim principalities. In this respect the *ʿulamāʾ* figure more prominently in the chronicles than had previously been the case, reflecting the fact that the ruling military oligarchies, beginning with the Seljuks but continuing under the Ayyubids and especially the Mamlūks, seeking legitimacy through the support of intellectuals, spent enormous sums on their salaries and patronage, sometimes in return for specific services to the court but often for their function as devotional and educational intermediaries with the public. In addition to the proliferation of biographical works, it has been noted that historians

1 Tarif Khalidi, *Arabic Historical Thought in the Classical Period* (Cambridge, 1994), 184.
2 Ibid., 183.

frequently inserted autobiographical remarks in their narratives, sometimes in the form of moral pronouncements on the conduct of the rulers and their supporters, but more often as casual personal observations. In this respect the emphasis of the bureaucrat historians on *siyāsa* inevitably produced a reaction from historians who deplored the usurpation, both in theory and practice, of the supremacy of the *sharīʿa* in governing and maintaining the state, and advocated a return to it as a remedy for the ills of society.[3]

A final general point needs to be stressed. As is the case with Muslim historiography from the beginning up until the Ottomans in their heyday, virtually no archives have survived. As noted above, historians did occasionally make use of them and sometimes reproduced documents in their texts; it is also true that fragments of chancery and judicial institutions have survived, especially from the Mamlūk period, which historians have recently begun to put to good use.[4] But the fact remains that our knowledge of both Ayyubid and Mamlūk history is based mainly on literary sources. In the following pages only the most important of these will be surveyed.

The historians of Ṣalāḥ al-Dīn and their successors

Given the renown of the founder of the Ayyūbid dynasty in the east and the west, it is not surprising that the sources for his life and career are numerous and that these have been extensively studied by western scholars. As a result of the research of H. A. R. Gibb and others the character of these works and their interrelationship are probably as well known as any for the medieval period of Arabic historiography.[5] Basically there are four major authors, one of whom, Ibn al-Athīr, can be classified as a scholar historian, while the others were bureaucrats.

ʿIzz al-Dīn ʿAlī ibn al-Athīr (555–630/1160–1233), a contemporary of Ṣalāḥ al-Dīn, was born and raised in a small town north of Mosul; in this area he was educated, primarily as a student of *ḥadīth*. Apparently he never held a professional position but remained a private scholar all his life, although he is said to have received the patronage of the atabegs of Mosul and Aleppo. He is also known to have been with Ṣalāḥ al-Dīn's army in an unknown capacity on one or more campaigns against the crusaders in Syria.[6] Although Ibn al-Athīr edited two works related to the science of tradition, his fame rests on his two

[3] *Ibid.*, 200–02.

[4] For references see D. Little, "The Use of Documents for the Study of Mamluk History," *Mamlūk Studies Review*, 1 (1997), 6–12.

[5] See H. A. R. Gibb, "The Arabic sources for the Life of Saladin," *Speculum*, 25 (1950), 58–72, and other works cited below.

[6] D. Richards, "Ibn al-Athīr and the Later Parts of the *Kāmil*: A Study of Aims and Methods," in D. Morgan (ed.), *Medieval Historical Writing in the Christian and Islamic Worlds* (London, 1982), 77.

histories. His voluminous universal history, *al-Kāmil fī al-Ta'rīkh* (*The Perfection of History*), which begins with the Creation and runs to 628/1231, was celebrated by his contemporary Ibn Khallikān "as one of the best productions of its kind."[7] In modern times, Ibn al-Athīr has been acclaimed on the basis of this work as "the only real Arab historian of the period" and "the chief historian of the later crusades."[8] For the events prior to his own lifetime Ibn al-Athīr depended most notably on al-Ṭabarī's *Ta'rīkh al-Rusul wa-al-Mulūk* (*History of the Prophets and Kings*), which he used freely. Besides passages borrowed from works that have not survived in their original form, *al-Kāmil* is interesting primarily for the events of Ibn al-Athīr's own lifetime and the years immediately preceding it, for which he could draw on reports from his father and other eyewitnesses, as well as written sources. These sources are unidentified more often than not. This reluctance to name his sources consistently seems odd for a scholar with training in *ḥadīth* and has been explained as a conscious attempt "to free himself from the Traditionist method followed by his favorite historian, al-Ṭabarī, and by his contemporary Ibn ʿAsākir."[9] Ibn al-Athīr's second history, *al-Bāhir fī Ta'rīkh Atābakāt al-Mawṣil* (*The Dazzling History of the Atabegs of Mosul*), is a local history of the Zengids but includes information on their relations with Egypt. It surveys the years 477–607/1084–1210 and thus covers a century and a quarter recorded also in *al-Kāmil*. Given the fact that the author enjoyed the favor of the Atabegs of Mosul, it is natural that he eulogized them in both of his works and deprecated their enemies, most notably Ṣalāḥ al-Dīn himself. Accordingly in most circles he is regarded as a prejudicial and unreliable source for the career of Ṣalāḥ al-Dīn. More damaging to Ibn al-Athīr's reputation as a historian is Gibb's finding that he relied heavily, even for contemporary events, on the work of his fellow historian ʿImād al-Dīn, rewriting his reports "with an occasional twist or admixture of fiction,"[10] and reminding his readers of God's direction of human affairs.

The main value of Ibn al-Athīr's two histories rests on his account of the period following Ṣalāḥ al-Dīn's death. In fact, for the reign of Ṣalāḥ al-Dīn's nephew, al-Malik al-Kāmil, as sultan of Egypt and Syria (615–35/1218–38), Ibn al-Athīr has been characterized as "the soundest basis of our knowledge."[11] Nevertheless, even for earlier periods he was regarded

[7] *Ibn Khallikān's Biographical Dictionary Translated from the Arabic by Baron MacGuckin de Slane*, 2 (Paris and London, 1843), 289.

[8] F. Gabrieli, *Arab Historians of the Crusades* (Berkeley and Los Angeles, 1969), xxvii, xxviii.

[9] M. Ahmad, "Some Notes on Arabic Historiography during the Zengid and Ayyubid periods (521/1127–648/1250)," in B. Lewis and P. Holt (eds.), *Historians of the Middle East* (London, 1962), 90.

[10] H. A. R. Gibb, "The Achievement of Saladin," in Yusuf Ibish (ed.), *Studies in Islamic History* (Beirut, 1974), 159.

[11] H. Gottschalk, *Al-Malik al-Kāmil von Egypten und seine Zeit* (Wiesbaden, 1948), 6.

as authoritative by the many later historians who borrowed from him, including Abū al-Fidā', Ibn Kathīr, al-Maqrīzī, and Ibn Khaldūn.

Like Ibn al-Athīr, Bahā' al-Dīn ibn Shaddād (539–632/1145–1235) was a native of Mesopotamia and was educated there as a scholar; unlike Ibn al-Athīr, he held various professional appointments as *madrasa* professor, diplomat of the Zangids of Mosul, and judge. Under Ṣalāḥ al-Dīn he held an important position as *Qāḍī al-ʿAskar* (Judge of the Army). After Ṣalāḥ al-Dīn's death Ibn Shaddād served the sultan's surviving sons in Aleppo, one of whom, al-Malik al-Ẓāhir, appointed him Shāfiʿī judge of that city. On the basis of his five-year experience in the company of Ṣalāḥ al-Dīn, Ibn Shaddād composed a biographical study of the sultan, *al-Nawādir al-Sulṭāniyya wa-al-Maḥāsin al-Yūsufiyya* (*Royal Anecdotes and Joseph-like Virtues*). The work is considered to be a sober and authoritative portrait of the sultan despite the author's patent admiration for his subject. In form it is not a conventional biography, being divided into the two parts reflected in the title. The first section is devoted to Ṣalāḥ al-Dīn's virtues, wherein Yūsuf (i.e. Joseph), refers not only to the sultan's given name (Ṣalāḥ al-Dīn Yūsuf) but evokes associations with the biblical Joseph's career in Egypt. In a series of chapters, each beginning with a *ḥadīth* or a verse from the Qur'an in order to link Ṣalāḥ al-Dīn's life with the Prophet Muḥammad's, Ibn Shaddād delineates the sultan's merits, such as justice, generosity, courage, militant zeal, steadfastness, humaneness, and so on. Appropriate anecdotes to illustrate Ṣalāḥ al-Dīn's embodiment of Muslim heroic virtues are narrated in the form of the author's eyewitness accounts. Here Ibn Shaddād's purpose is not just to eulogize the ideal ruler but also to establish Ṣalāḥ al-Dīn as an exemplar worthy of his subjects' emulation. In the second part the author turns to a record of Ṣalāḥ al-Dīn's career from his foray into Egypt in 559/1164 until his death in 589/1193. Although the organization of this section is chronological, it is not annalistic. The most valuable segment is inevitably that covering the years when Ibn Shaddād was in Ṣalāḥ al-Dīn's service. The work is regarded as an authentic record of Ṣalāḥ al-Dīn's deeds during the Third Crusade, thanks largely to Ibn Shaddād's close, but not fawning, relationship with the sultan.[12]

Two other historians enjoyed Ṣalāḥ al-Dīn's confidence as official members of his retinue. The first of these, ʿImād al-Dīn Muḥammad al-Kātib al-Isfāhānī (519–597/1125–1201), is unique as the only non-Arab historian of Ṣalāḥ al-Dīn. Born in Isfahan and reared in Kashan, he received a *madrasa* education in Sāljuk Baghdad and later taught jurisprudence there under the patronage of the Zangid Sultan Nūr al-Dīn. After the death of Nūr al-Dīn, ʿImād al-Dīn fell out of official favor for a short time but regained it in 570/1175 when Ṣalāḥ al-Dīn, campaigning in northern Syria, responded to a

[12] Gabrieli, *Arab Historians*, xxix.

poem written by ʿImād al-Dīn in his honor by appointing him as a deputy scribe (*kātib*) to al-Qāḍī al-Fāḍil, a high official in Ṣalāḥ al-Dīn's service, and, coincidentally, the second "official" historian alluded to above. In this capacity ʿImād al-Dīn drafted much official correspondence on behalf of Ṣalāḥ al-Dīn and gained close and frequent access to the sultan and affairs of state. Both the correspondence and ʿImād al-Dīn's first-hand knowledge figure prominently in his two histories: *al-Fatḥ al-Qussī fī al-Fatḥ al-Qudsī* (*Eloquent Rhetoric on the Conquest of Jerusalem*) and *al-Barq al-Shāmī* (*Syrian Lightning*). Both works are written in a highly ornate (possibly Persianate) style of rhymed prose that embellishes, indeed often obscures, a careful record of Ṣalāḥ al-Dīn's political activities and military campaigns. *Al-Fatḥ* begins with Ṣalāḥ al-Dīn's conquest of Jerusalem in 583/1187, because, the author says, this event opens a new era in Islamic history and thus constitutes a new *hijra* "of more lasting significance than the first."[13] It ends with Saladin's death. Though most of the seven volumes of *al-Barq* are lost, it is a broader work than *al-Fatḥ*, containing a valuable autobiographical record of ʿImād al-Dīn's service under two sultans, Nūrd al-Dīn and Ṣalāḥ al-Dīn, beginning in 562/1166. Besides their stylistic virtuosity, both works are remarkable as melanges of factual narrative, personal observations, and official documents. Both Ibn al-Athīr and the later historian Abū Shāma among others borrowed extensively from ʿImād al-Dīn; Abū Shāma, in fact, abridged *al-Barq* and in the process stripped away its rhetorical excesses.

As already noted, ʿAbd al Raḥmān ibn ʿAlī al-ʿAsqalānī al-Qāḍī al-Fāḍil (529–596/1135–1200) was also a prominent official under Ṣalāḥ al-Dīn, more prominent in fact than the other "official" historian of his reign. Born in Ascalon, he must have had a traditional scholarly education but served an apprenticeship in the Fāṭimid chancery in Cairo and eventually became its director; in this position he caught the attention of Ṣalāḥ al-Dīn when the latter assumed the wazīrate there. Of all this historians of Ṣalāḥ al-Dīn, al-Qāḍī al-Fāḍil was best situated to observe events in Egypt, not least because he acted as Ṣalāḥ al-Dīn's administrative deputy for two years and later returned there after Ṣalāḥ al-Dīn's death to serve under al-Malik al-ʿAzīz. Unfortunately, given al-Qāḍī al-Fāḍil's close association with Ṣalāḥ al-Dīn and his access to official documents, many of which he himself wrote, his work has not survived except in extracts preserved by other historians. This is true of his *Rasāʾil* (*Epistles*) as well as his *Mutajaddidāt* (*Diaries*); nevertheless, these extracts are sufficient in Gibb's opinion to establish al-Qāḍī al-Fāḍil in some respects as "the most valuable of all [the historians of Ṣalāḥ al-Dīn] ..." since his works "... reflect some at least of

[13] Cited by Khalidi, *Historical Thought*, 82; cf. D. Richards, "ʿImād al-Dīn al-Isfahānī: Administrator, Litterateur and Historian," in Maya Shatzmiller (ed.), *Crusaders and Muslims in Twelfth-Century Syria* (Leiden, 1993), 144.

Ṣalāḥ al-Dīn's real purposes and ideals."[14] Be that as it may, it should be noted that as a professional scribe, his works are also marked by rhetorical embellishments, though not to the same extent as ʿImād al-Dīn's.

Three historians might be considered as transitional inasmuch as their works cover both the late Ayyūbid and early Mamlūk periods; for the former, these histories are heavily indebted to the historians of Ṣalāḥ al-Dīn in both form and content. *Mirʾāt al-Zamān fī Taʾrīkh al-Aʿyān* (*Mirror of the Time as Reflected in the History of Notables*) by Sibṭ ibn al-Jawzī (581–654/1185–1256), like Ibn al-Athīr's *al-Kāmil*, is a universal history; it begins with the Creation and ends with the year of the author's death. Trained originally as a Ḥanbalī scholar but converted to Ḥanafism under the influence of his patron, the Sultan al-Malik al-Muʿaẓẓam ʿĪsā of Damascus, Ibn al-Jawzī shows considerably greater interest in the biographies of *ʿulamāʾ* than did his predecessors. But the *Mirʾāt* is regarded mainly as a reworking of the histories of ʿImād al-Dīn, Ibn Shaddāḍ, and others, supplemented by his own first-hand observations. For the years of his own lifetime the work is significant for its focus on the role of Damascus in late Ayyūbid history.[15] ʿAbd al-Raḥmān Abū Shāma (599–665/1203–68), another Damascene scholar, is known primarily for his *al-Rawḍatayn fī Akhbār al-Dawlatayn* (*Two Gardens of Reports on Two Reigns*), a chronicle of the reigns of Nūr al-Dīn and Ṣalāḥ al-Dīn, based on the standard sources. A sequel, *al-Dhayl ʿalā al-Rawḍatayn*, again focuses on events in Damascus as observed by his sources, Ibn al-Jawzī, and eyewitness informants, including himself. Jamāl al-Dīn Muḥammad ibn Wāṣil (604–97/1208–98), though also a scholar trained in Syria, has the distinction of occasional residence in Cairo, where he had access to the courts of both Ayyubid and Mamlūk sultans. In fact, Sultan Baybars sent him as an envoy to King Manfred of Sicily, but Ibn Wāṣil returned to his birthplace in Hama around 663/1264 as a *qāḍī* and remained there until his death.[16] There he wrote his most important historical work, the annalistic *Mufarrij al-Kurūb fī Akhbār Banī Ayyūb* (*The Dissipater of Anxieties about Reports on the Ayyūbids*). One scholar has characterized the work as a reflection of the author's "desire to portray the house of Ayyūb as a kind of ideal Muslim dynasty;"[17] another has deemed it to be "the most important source for the later Ayyūbids."[18] Nevertheless, the *Mufarrij* has been shown to be based

[14] Gibb, "Achievement," 161, 162.

[15] R. Humphreys, *From Saladin to the Mongols: The Ayyubids of Damascus, 1193–1260* (Albany, 1977), 395.

[16] G. Schregle, *Die Sultanin von Ägypten: Šağarat ad-Durr in der arabischen Geschichtsschreibung und Literatur* (Wiesbaden, 1961), 12.

[17] Humphreys, *From Saladin*, 396.

[18] H. Halm, "Quellen und Literatur: IV. Die Ayyubiden," in U. Haarmann (ed.), *Geschichte der arabischen Welt* (Munich, 1987), 639.

largely on Abū Shāma and his sources, including Ibn al-Athīr, until the death of Ṣalāḥ al-Dīn and thereafter, when Ibn Wāṣil's own observations come into play.[19] His experience in Egypt enabled him to write authoritatively about the replacement of the Ayyūbids by the Mamlūks, and his account of the career of Queen Shajar al-Durr was used freely and extensively by later historians.[20]

Besides the chronicles and royal biographies, there were other genres of historiography cultivated under the Ayyūbids which are useful to historians such as biographical dictionaries, the best known being *Wafayāt al-Aʿyān wa-Anbāʾ Abnāʾ al-Zamān* (*Obituaries of Notables and News of the Prominent Men of the Time*) by Aḥmad ibn Muḥammad ibn Khallikān (608–81/1211–82). This is, of course, another transitional work, since Ibn Khallikān flourished during the early Mamlūk period, and served, in fact, as Shāfiʿī *qāḍī* in Cairo and Damascus under various Mamlūk sultans. While the book contains some 3,600 biographies of prominent Muslims who lived from the earliest times, the most valuable ones are those few who were the author's contemporaries, both politicians and intellectuals.

Hardly any documents of Ayyūbid provenance have survived other than a handful of decrees preserved at St. Catherine's monastery in the Sinai.[21] Therefore the chancery and other administrative manuals of the period are of particular value, especially since the authors of the extant works were all Egyptians and served as officials in the Ayyūbid bureaucracy. Most prominent was the Copt al-Asʿad ibn Mammātī (542–606/1147–1209), secretary of government financial bureaus under the first two Ayyūbid sultans of Egypt and author of *Qawānīn al-Dawāwīn* (*Rules for the Bureaux*). This work contains invaluable data on the economic life of Egyptian villages under Sultan ʿAzīz, complete with a cadastral survey. His contemporary, the Shāfiʿī *qāḍī* ʿAlī b. ʿUthmān al-Makhzūmī, was also a bureaucrat in the late Fāṭimid and early Ayyūbid fisc. Drawing on his experience as an expert on taxes, he wrote a manual for the use of other tax officers, entitled *al-Minhāj fī ʿIlm al-Kharāj* (*Methodology of Land Taxation*). Although the book has survived only in fragments, these contain useful information on commerce with the Italian city states and other economic matters.[22] Still another Ayyūbid administrative manual was written by Abū ʿUthmān al-Nābulusī (588–660/1192–1261), who served in administrative capacities under sultans al-Kāmil and al-Ṣāliḥ Ayyūb. To the latter he dedicated his administrative handbook, *Lumaʿ al-Qawānīn al-Muḍīʾa fī Dawāwīn al-Diyār al-*

[19] Ahmad, "Notes," 95.

[20] G. Schregle, *Die Sultanin*, 12.

[21] See A. Atiya, *The Arabic Manuscripts of Mount Sinai* (Baltimore, 1955); cf. S. Stern, "Petitions from the Ayyūbid Period," *BSOAS*, 27 (1964), 1–32.

[22] Conveniently organized by Claude Cahen, *Makhzūmiyyāt: études sur l'histoire économique et financière de l'Égypte médiévale* (Leiden, 1957).

Miṣriyya (*Bright Light on the Rules of the Egyptian Bureaux*). As will be seen below, works designed for chancery clerks became more elaborate and comprehensive during the Mamlūk period.

Mamlūk historiography

With the establishment of the Mamlūk dynasty following the murder of the last Ayyūbid sultan of Egypt in 648/1250 and the short, curious reign of Shajar al-Durr as Queen of the Muslims, the surviving Ayyūbid historians from Syria continued to record political events of the ruling circles in Egypt. Generally, a pro-Ayyūbid attitude is evident in their narratives, since more often than not they had been in the employ of the overthrown rulers. Such a bias can be discerned, for example, when both Ibn Wāṣil and Abū Shāma describe the murder of Turān Shāh and the career of Shajar al-Durr and her consort Aybak with "antipathy toward the Mamlūks who came to power in Egypt."[23] But the Mamlūks soon found their own historians; these, almost without exception during the Baḥrī period (648–784/1250–1382) took a decidedly favorable attitude toward the ruling elite. This is particularly true of the historians who held official positions in the bureaucracy or the army, both in Egypt and in Syria. Here it should be noted that the Mamlūks gave Egypt, Palestine, and Syria a much more pervasive political, economic, and cultural unity than the Ayyūbids had been able to achieve. As a result, even the Syrian historians – scholars for the most part, affiliated with the religious establishment – surpassed their Ayyūbid predecessors in the attention they devoted to affairs in Egypt. In this respect, however, it is curious that Egyptian historians often borrowed heavily from the Syrians, even for reports on events in Egypt.

In addition to the historians of traditional background, be it scholarly or bureaucratic, a new breed flourished under the Mamlūks – historians closely associated with the Mamlūk military institution either as fully-fledged soldiers or as sons of Mamlūks. Although these new historians continued to write in the conventional literary forms – chronicles, biographies, and administrative handbooks – their lack of a rigorous academic training is betrayed by their Arabic prose, which is permeated with colloquialisms. Concomitant with a relaxation of linguistic and literary standards was the use by some historians, including *ʿulamāʾ*, of devices designed to enhance the readability of their works, perhaps in an attempt to entertain or even titillate an expanding, more diversified market for history. Still another trend can be seen in the increased attention given to biography in various forms, to the extent that the space given to obituary notices in chronicles often outweighs the pages devoted to annals. Nevertheless, Mamlūk historiography is so

[23] G. Schregle, *Die Sultanin*, 12–13.

variegated and voluminous that it is difficult to make any generalization about more than just a few works or to find any that would apply to the solitary genius of Ibn Khaldūn. That being the case, the focus will again be on representative historians, chosen primarily on the basis of their originality as primary sources.

Baḥrī historians

Typical of the bureaucrat historians of the Baḥrī period are Muḥyī al-Dīn ibn ʿAbd al-Ẓāhir; his nephew, Shāfiʿ ibn ʿAlī; and ʿIzz al-Dīn Muḥammad ibn al-Shaddād al-Ḥalabī. Of the three, Ibn ʿAbd al-Ẓāhir (620–92/1223–92), a Cairene with a conventional religious education, was undoubtedly the most prominent as confidential secretary (Kātib al-Sirr) and head of chancery (Ṣāḥib Dīwān al-Inshāʾ) under three sultans: Baybars, Qalāwūn, and al-Ashraf Khalīl. During their reigns he wrote numerous royal documents for both domestic and foreign distribution, including letters of appointment, treaties, and diplomatic correspondence. In drafting these he is said to have adopted al-Qāḍī al-Fāḍil as his guide.[24] But his major work, *al-Rawḍ al-Zāhir fī Sīrat al-Malik al-Ẓāhir* (*The Splendid Garden Concerning the Life of al-Malik al-Ẓāhir*), was probably inspired by Bahāʾ al-Dīn ibn Shaddād's biography of Ṣalāḥ al-Dīn, *al-Nawādir*, in that each devoted special sections to a eulogistic enumeration of his subject's merits in an attempt to depict him as an exemplary – and in the case of Baybars, a legitimate – Muslim ruler.[25] But the *Rawḍ* goes a step further in the direction of praise for the sultan: not only was the work known to have been commissioned by Baybars; it was read to him by the author for his approval. In effect it is an official biography with the propagandist aspects which that term implies; indeed, it has been characterized as "almost a ghosted autobiography."[26] Still, thanks to the author's official position and his access to the sultan, the work is an invaluable source and was regarded as such both by Ibn ʿAbd al-Ẓāhir's contemporaries and by later historians. He also wrote biographies in the same vein for his subsequent masters. For Qalāwūn, this was *Tashrīf al-Ayyām wa al-ʿUṣūr fī Sīrat al-Malik al-Manṣūr* (*The Glorious Days and Times of the Life of al-Malik al-Manṣūr*). Although the first part of this work has not survived, the extant portion is again informed by Ibn ʿAbd al-Ẓāhir's first-hand knowledge of events at home and abroad, for he continued to travel as envoy for Qalāwūn, as he had for Baybars. As far as is known from a short extant fragment, the same is true of

[24] *EI2*, III, 679.

[25] P. Holt, "Three Biographies of al-Ẓāhir Baybars," in D. Morgan (ed.), *Medieval Historical Writing in the Christian and Islamic Worlds* (London, 1982), 23.

[26] P. Thorau, *The Lion of Egypt: Sultan Baybars I and the Near East in the Thirteenth Century*, trans. P. Holt (London and New York, 1992), 270.

Ibn ʿAbd al-Ẓāhir's biography of al-Ashraf Khalīl: *al-Alṭāf al-Khafiyya min al-Sīra al-Sharīfa al-Sulṭāniyya al-Malakiyya al-Ashrafiyya* (*Unseen Benevolences in the Noble Life of al-Sultān al-Ashraf*).

Like his uncle, Nāṣir al-Dīn Shāfiʿ ibn ʿAlī al-Miṣrī (649–730/1251–1330) was employed in the Mamlūk chancery in Cairo, but his career was interrupted, though not ended, when he was blinded in battle with the Mongols in Syria in 680/1281. Without attaining Ibn ʿAbd al-Ẓāhir's high rank, he did enjoy access to the sultan, sometimes as assistant to his uncle but also on his own merit. He, too, drafted documents and was privy to the inner political workings of the state. Even as a historian, however, he worked under the shadow of his illustrious relative, and his biography of Baybars, *Ḥusn al-Manāqib al-Sirriyya al-Muntazʿa min al-Sīra al-Ẓāhiriyya* (*The Excellent Secret Virtues Selected from the Life of al-Ẓāhir*), purports to be a condensation of the *Rawḍ*. Nevertheless, perhaps because it was written twenty-five years after Baybars's death, some of the errors and excesses of its model were eliminated by Shāfiʿ ibn ʿAlī, so that the *Ḥusn* often serves a critical corrective.[27] In contrast to the reworking of the Baybars *sīra*, Shāfiʿ ibn ʿAlī's biography of Qalāwūn, *al-Faḍl al-Maʾthūr min Sīrat al-Sulṭān al-Malik al-Manṣūr* (*Virtue Transmitted from the Life of al-Malik al-Manṣūr*), is an original work composed partly during Qalāwūn's lifetime. It, too, however, has the character of an official biography designed to establish the sultan's legitimacy. Be that as it may, it is full of the author's personal observations of the sultan's conduct which lend an air of first-hand authenticity to the work.[28]

The third bureaucrat-biographer of Mamlūk sultans, ʿIzz al-Dīn Muḥammad ibn Shaddād al-Ḥalabī (613–84/1217–85), had served in Ayyūbid chanceries in Syria before he fled from the Mongols to Cairo in 659/1261. Whether he served in any official position in the Mamlūk capital is not known, but he did enjoy the favor of sultans Baybars, Berke, and Qalāwūn.[29] Besides a topographical study of Syria and Mesopotamia, Ibn Shaddād wrote a biography of Baybars – only one volume of two has survived – probably during the reign of Berke, which, curiously, he gave the same title as that by Ibn ʿAbd al-Ẓāhir. He also followed Ibn ʿAbd al-Ẓāhir in devoting a separate section to the sultan's virtues and exploits in an attempt to glorify the Muslim monarch. But even in this section Ibn Shaddād shows his originality by providing anecdotes not to be found in the earlier work, including valuable material on the activities of Mongol and Tur-

27 Holt, "Three Biographies," 26–27.

28 L. Northrup, *From Slave to Sultan: The Career of al-Manṣūr Qalāwūn and the Consolidation of Mamluk Rule in Egypt and Syria (678–689 AH/1279–1290 AD)* (Stuttgart, forthcoming), 36–37.

29 A. Ḥuṭayṭ (ed.), *Die Geschichte des Sultans Baibars von ʿIzz ad-dīn Muḥammad b. ʿAlī b. Ibrāhīm b. Šaddād (st. 684/1285)* (Wiesbaden, 1983), 16.

koman immigrants in the Mamlūk army and state.[30] The annalistic section of the work is distinctive for its inclusion of obituary notices for notables who died in any given year of Baybars's reign.

Higher in rank and status than the bureaucratic historians were two who belonged to the ruling political-military class: one, Abū al-Fidā', was sultan of Ḥamā in his own right; the other, Baybars al-Manṣūrī, was a high-ranking officer in the Mamlūk army. Al-Malik al-Mu'ayyad 'Imād al-Dīn Abū al-Fidā' (672–732/1273–1331) a scion of the Ayyūbid royal family, had an illustrious career as a soldier and prince under the Mamlūks. He is even more famous as a geographer and historian. After military service in such campaigns as the Mamlūk conquest of Acre in 1291, Abū al-Fidā' enjoyed the patronage and company of al-Malik al-Nāṣir Muḥammad, and it was this sultan who, in return for the efforts of Abū al-Fidā' to restore him to the throne in 709/1310, made him governor of Hama and subsequently sultan of that city. Thanks to his high position in Syria, his participation in military and political affairs, and his carefully cultivated friendship with al-Nāṣir Muḥammad, Abū al-Fidā' was in an excellent position to comment on Mamlūk affairs during his lifetime from a Syrian perspective. His history, *al-Mukhtaṣar fī Ta'rīkh al-Bashar* (*Summary of the History of the Mankind*), written, perhaps, under the influence of his teacher, the Syrian historian, Ibn Wāṣil, is a universal chronicle, beginning with Adam and ending in 729/1329; it is supplemented by short obituary notices.

A contemporary of Abū al-Fidā', Rukn al-Dīn Baybars al-Manṣūrī al-Khiṭā'ī (d. 725/1325), served in many military campaigns as a mamlūk before al-Nāṣir Muḥammad assigned him the highest rank in the Mamlūk army – Amīr of a Hundred and Commander of a Thousand. This sultan also rewarded Baybars al-Manṣūrī with several important administrative titles, including chief of chancery and for a short time, viceroy. Given his embroilment in the volatile politics of al-Nāṣir's reign and the sultan's distrust of all his officers, it is not surprising that Baybars al-Manṣūrī fell victim to his master's paranoia and was imprisoned for five years. After his release he devoted himself to study of the Qur'ān and *ḥadīth*, having established a Ḥanafī *madrasa* outside Cairo. He is a rare, but not unique, example of a mamlūk who combined a military career with scholarship and his career shows how effective the Mamlūk educational system must have been for exceptional students. His major historical work, *Zubdat al-Fikra fī Ta'rīkh al-Hijra* (*Choice Thoughts on Hijra History*), is a universal chronicle up to 724/1324 composed in many volumes, apparently with the help of Coptic scribes. While he is generally an authoritative and original source for the reigns of the three sultans under whom he served, beginning with Qalāwūn, recent research has shown that for that sultan and presumably for

[30] Holt, "Three Biographies," 24–25.

earlier sultans, he often relied on Ibn ʿAbd al-Ẓāhir.[31] The annals for al-Nāṣir soon became a favorite source for other historians, both contemporary and later, because, no doubt, of the first-hand experiences the author transcribed. This section cannot be characterized as an encomium of the sultan, but neither is it critical; after all, it was obviously written when al-Nāṣir was in his prime. Later, Baybars al-Manṣūrī epitomized the Mamlūk sections of the *Zubda* in a book entitled *al-Tuḥfa al-Mulūkiyya fī al-Dawla al-Turkiyya* (*The Royal Gem for the Turkish Dynasty*). It ends with the year 711/1312. Although the *Tuḥfa* is a rhymed-prose summary of the earlier material found in the *Zubda*, the author added new data so that the two works should be used in tandem.[32] Curiously, despite the general recognition of Baybars al-Manṣūrī's central importance as a source for early Mamlūk history, only the *Tuḥfa* has so far been published.[33]

One of the most interesting historians of the Baḥrī Mamlūks, Sayf al-Dīn Abū Bakr ibn al-Dawādārī (d. after 736/1335), was a member of the group called *awlād al-nās*, meaning "sons of Mamlūks," who, because they were freeborn Muslims, could not, in theory and normally in practice, become Mamlūks themselves. As a result, some of them turned to belles lettres or to a branch of scholarship as a profession and thus served as a bridge between the native Arabic-speaking *ʿulamāʾ* and the alien, Turkic-speaking Mamlūks. Those who became historians, like Ibn al-Dawādārī, tended to take a more personalized approach to historiography than either the bureaucrats or the scholars, while continuing to write within the traditional genres. Son of a Mamlūk officer of Turkish descent who held several provincial posts in both Egypt and Syria, Ibn al-Dawādārī presents himself as a frequent, if not constant, observer of his father's official activities until the latter's death in 713/1311. Accordingly, Ibn al-Dawādārī constantly cites him as an eye-witness for many of the reports in the two contemporary volumes of his nine-part universal history, *Kanz al-Durar wa-Jāmiʿ al-Ghurar* (*Treasure of Pearls and Trove of the Radiant*), these being the volumes devoted to Baḥrī history until the year 736/1336. Curiously, however, there is ample evidence that Ibn al-Dawādārī deliberately attributed to his father information that he copied from other historians, in an attempt, perhaps, to impart immediacy and interest to his work or maybe to increase its air of authenticity.[34] Or was he simply fond of exaggerating his own and his family's importance

[31] Northrup, *From Sultan*, 36–37.

[32] Little, *An Introduction to Mamlūk Historiography: An Analysis of Arabic Annalistic and Biographical Sources for the Reign of al-Malik an-Naṣir Muḥammad ibn Qalāʾūn* (Wiesbaden and Montreal, 1970), 4–10.

[33] With the exception of excerpts for the years 693–98/1293–98, ed. and trans. in S. Elham, *Kitbuġā und Lāǧīn: Studien zur Mamluken-Geschichte nach Baibars al-Manṣūrī und an-Nuwairī* (Freiburg, 1977), 83–140, Arabic 1–30.

[34] U. Haarmann, *Quellenstudien zur frühen Mamlukenzeit* (Freiburg, 1969), 111.

in the course of events? The possibility that he may have deliberately falsified and enhanced his own genealogy is a case in point.[35] But the distinctiveness of his history lies in what has been persuasively argued to be the efforts of Ibn al-Dawādārī and other toward "literarization" and "dehistorification" of historiography throughout the Mamlūk period.[36] To achieve the popularization of historical writing, in addition to masking the true identity of his sources Ibn al-Dawādārī adopted a number of literary devices, some of which had long been current, since, in fact, the time of the earliest biographies of the Prophet, which were heavily influenced by narrative, anecdotal, and poetic traditions of professional storytellers. Ibn al-Dawādārī, then, was reviving, or, more accurately, making greater quantitative use of anecdotes, folk romance, poetry, and *adab* in general, often couching these elements in a racy colloquial style which also served to bring history closer to the reader than the formal impersonal style adopted by most historians. Thus Ibn al-Dawādārī's chronicles exemplify the attempt to break away from a rigid historiographical framework dominated by *ḥadīth* and *ḥadīth*-trained scholars in favor of annals spiced with anecdotes and mirabilia. In the earlier volumes of the *Kanz* these are often derived from popular legends and myths current among the Turks and Mongols.[37] However, in the two Mamlūk volumes these are not so prominent, as Ibn al-Dawādārī relies more on his father's and his own experiences to enliven the narrative. Nevertheless, emphasis on the stylistic originality of Ibn al-Dawādārī should not be pushed too far, for he did choose the annalistic form as his literary vehicle; equally conventional was his use of lists of rulers and officials to introduce each year and of short obituary notices to end it. Also noteworthy is his liberal borrowing from the work of at least one Syrian-scholar historian, namely al-Jazarī; typically, he does not even mention al-Jazarī, much less acknowledge him as a source. Frequently Ibn al-Dawādārī's written sources can be identified through literary detective work, but there are long passages in the volume devoted to al-Nāṣir Muḥammad concerning events in the kingdom of the Ilkhāns that Ibn al-Dawādārī reports only on the authority of *al-nāqil* (the reporter). These reports, complete with verbatim transcripts of private conversations, are all the more intriguing since they contain information not to be found elsewhere.[38]

[35] Haarmann (ed.), *Die Chronik des Ibn ad-Dawādārī, Achter Teil, Der Bericht über die frühen Mamluken* (Freiburg, 1971), 4.

[36] Haarmann, *Quellenstudien*, 159–81; cf. idem., "Auflösung und Bewahrung der klassichen Formen arabischer Geschichtsschreibung in der Zeit der Mamluken," *Zeitschrift der Deutschen Morgenländischen Gesellschaft*, 121 (1971), 46–60.

[37] See Haarmann, "Turkish Legends in the Popular Historiography of Medieval Egypt," *Proceedings of the VIth Congress of Arabic and Islamic Studies: Visby 13–16 August, Stockholm 17–19 August 1972* (Stockholm and Leiden, 1975), 97–107.

[38] Little, *Introduction*, 118–25.

Mūsā ibn Muḥammad ibn al-Shaykh Yaḥyā al-Yūsufī (676–759/1277–1358) cannot be positively identified either as a mamlūk or as one of the *awlād al-nās*, but he was closely associated with the latter as Muqaddam al-Ḥalqa, *viz.* commander of the non-mamlūk, freeborn corps in which the sons of mamlūks formed a special unit during much of the Baḥrī period. In any event he served in many campaigns waged far away from Egypt, in Syria against the Mongols, for example, and in Yemen, and in Little Armenia. As a result he became acquainted with many prominent Mamlūk officers of high rank and quoted them freely as his sources, both for military engagements and for affairs of state. Al-Yūsufī also had friends in the Mamlūk bureaucracy, including a wazīr, two keepers of the privy purse, and a court physician among many others. These again al-Yūsufī quotes as eyewitnesses of public and private events. In this respect, of course, he had much in common with Ibn al-Dawādārī along with their lack of a traditional scholarly education. In fact, al-Yūsufī occasionally laments his lack of training and proficiency in Arabic grammar and literature, while at the same time acknowledging that his poems were admired and that his prose was adequate for purposes of official correspondence.[39] Be that as it may, his history is written in a highly colloquial style characteristic of Middle Arabic, that is, in classical Arabic influenced by local dialects. His only known work, *Nuzhat al-Nāẓir fī Sīrat al-Malik al-Nāṣir* (*A Spectator's Stroll through the Life of al-Malik al-Nāṣir*), in about a dozen volumes, has survived only in a fragment covering the years 733–38/1332–38, but long passages for other years have been transcribed or recast by contemporary and later historians, most notably al-Shujāʿī and al-ʿAynī.[40] Enough of his original text is retrievable from such sources to establish the *Nuzha* as the fullest, best documented contemporary source for the reign of al-Malik al-Nāṣir Muḥammad. In spite of the title's focus on al-Nāṣir, it is known that the book began with the reign of Qalāwūn and ended with the year 755/1354, thirteen years after the sultan's death. Like Ibn al-Dawādārī's volume on the *sīra* (life, biography) of al-Nāṣir (*al-Durr al-Fākhir fī Sīrat al-Malik al-Nāṣir* (*The Splendid Pearl of the Life of al-Malik al-Nāṣir*), the *Nuzha* is organized as an annalistic chronicle; but there is a major difference between the two works. Whereas Ibn al-Dawādārī pays only perfunctory attention to obituary notices, al-Yūsufī appends to each year detailed, often lengthy, biographies of notables, be they mamlūks, bureaucrats, scholars, or literati. Indeed, al-Yūsufī's keen interest in people is evident on every page as he describes their looks and analyzes their personalities, often from his personal knowledge of them but sometimes from gossip. He does not hesitate to

39 Little, "The Recovery of a Lost Source for Baḥrī Mamlūk History: Al-Yūsufī's *Nuzhat al-Nāẓir fī Sīrat al-Malik al-Nāṣir*," *JAOS*, 94 (1974), 48.

40 Little, "An Analysis of the Relationship between Four Mamlūk Chronicles for 737–45," *Journal of Semitic Studies*, 19 (1974), 252–68.

create private conversations which he could not possibly have heard and to produce melodramatic scenarios marked by an obvious conviction that conspiracy and intrigue lay behind the lives and deaths of al-Nāṣir's retainers and officials. The *Nuzha*, then, is a distinctly personalized version of history; it reads like fiction and is even more "literarized" than Ibn al-Dawādārī's *Kanz al-Durar*. Nevertheless, the *Nuzha* is extremely valuable as the only history of al-Nāṣir Muḥammad's reign that openly criticizes the sultan. Moreover, because it was used so copiously by other historians, it was extremely influential in creating the historical image of al-Nāṣir as an unprincipled megalomaniac that prevails today, despite the encomia of Ibn al-Dawādārī and others.

Among al-Yūsufī's contemporaries, Shams al-Dīn ibn al-Shujāʿī (d. after 756/1355–56) made the fullest use of *Nuzhat al-Nāẓir* in his work *Taʾrīkh al-Malik al-Nāṣir Muḥammad b Qalāwūn al-Ṣāliḥī wa-Awlādihi* (*History of al-Malik al-Nāṣir* [...] *and his Progeny*). Although this work survives only in a fragment for the years 737–745/1337–1345, collation with al-Yūsufī's extant annals for 738 and with passages for later years found in other sources indicate that al-Shujāʿī based his work almost entirely on al-Yūsufī's, without mentioning his name.[41] But the *Taʾrīkh* is extremely important for 741 and following years for preserving data from al-Yūsufī' which is absent from other extant sources.

Another Egyptian historian who lived during the Baḥrī period who should be mentioned is Mufaḍḍal ibn Abī al-Faḍāʾil if only because he was a Copt. Unfortunately, nothing else is known about his life except that he finished his work, *al-Nahj al-Sadīd wa-al-Durr al-Farīd fīmā baʿd Taʾrīkh Ibn al-ʿAmīd* (*The Right Path and Unique Pearl as Sequel to the History of Ibn al-ʿAmīd*) in 759/1358, Contrary to expectations, this work, a history of the Baḥrī dynasty covering the years 658–741/1259–1341, shows little originality beyond a few short references to Coptic patriarchs. Otherwise, it is a typical Mamlūk chronicle and is based almost entirely on Muslim sources, including Baybars al-Manṣūrī, al-Nuwayrī, and al-Yūsufī. Even though at times Mufaḍḍal omitted details from his sources that might have reflected badly on Copts, he occasionally copied Muslim religious formulae into his work![42]

Besides Abu al-Fidāʾ there are several contemporary Syrian historians who, collectively, are of capital importance for Baḥrī Mamlūk historiography. Despite the fact that two of these – Ibn Kathīr (c. 700–774/1300–73) and al-Dhahabī (673–748/1274–1348) – are more famous than their peers, their works, as far as Mamlūk history is concerned, are largely derivative from three of them: al-Birzālī, al-Yūnīnī, and al-Jazarī. All

[41] Ibid. [42] Little, *Introduction*, 37.

five were *hadīth* scholars trained primarily in Syria; most are known to have studied also in Cairo, where they could become acquainted with Egyptian affairs at first hand. Al-Birzālī, al-Yūnīnī, and al-Jazarī were closely associated as teachers, students, and friends. This association was so close and harmonious, in fact, that they lent one another their historical works in draft and felt free to borrow freely from them, sometimes with, sometimes without, acknowledgment. They also served as oral sources to one another, especially al-Birzālī and al-Jazarī. Such close collaboration among scholars has few, if any, parallels in Arabic historiography.

Of the three, the most important in terms of his influence on other historians was Shams al-Dīn Muḥammad al-Jazarī (658–739/1260–1338). His principal work, *Ḥawādith al-Zamān wa-Anbā'uhu wa-Wafāyāt al-Akābir wa-al-Aʿyān min Abnā'ihi* (*Events and News of the Time with Obituaries of Worthies and Notables*), has survived only in fragments, few of which have been published so far. As the title indicates, the work gives equal emphasis to annals and obituaries and is valuable for the attention given to the lives and careers of Syrian scholars. Apparently conceived as a continuation of a twelfth-century Syrian chronicle, the *Ḥawādith* begins with the year 593/1196 and continues until the year of al-Jazarī's death. While the early sections are derived from written sources, most notably al-Yūnīnī's *Dhayl*, beginning with the year 678/1279–80 al-Jazarī writes from his own experience and that of his oral informants, including al-Birzālī, whose written work he probably used also.[43] Thanks to a wide network of informants, al-Jazarī was able to provide reports on events in such remote places as Yemen and the Ilkhānid court in Iran as well as the Mamlūk capital in Cairo. Al-Jazarī's training as a *hadīth* expert may well have induced him to identify these informants, sometimes in the form of a chain of authorities (*isnād*) when he received a report at second- or third-hand. His professional interest is also apparent in the attention given to religious affairs. The space devoted to biographies of religious figures has already been mentioned, and he is one of the main sources for our knowledge of the trials of the celebrated Ḥanbalī jurist, Ibn Taymiyya, conducted in Cairo in 705/1305 by the Mamlūk authorities. Al-Jazarī did not witness the trials himself and had to rely on an Egyptian informant. Oddly enough, this did not prevent Ibn al-Dawādārī and al-Nuwayrī, both of whom were present in Cairo at the time, from dipping into al-Jazarī's second-hand account.[44] But al-Jazarī's interest certainly went beyond religious affairs. By dint of his friendship with mamlūk officers, he was well informed about military campaigns in Syria, Palestine, and Mesopotamia. In addition to reports on political, military and religious affairs, his annals are peppered with digres-

[43] Ibid., 53–57, 60–61. [44] Ibid., 61.

sions and anecdotes about strange and curious events both at home and abroad: for example, a long narration of his visit to the pyramids in Giza. In this respect al-Jazarī serves as Syrian counterpart to Ibn al-Dawādārī for his deliberate introduction of entertaining material expressed, moreover, in a light literary style influenced by Damascus Arabic, all designed to loosen and popularize traditional Arabic historiography while at the same time retaining the traditional chronicle-obituary format.

Like al-Jazarī's, little of the work of ʿAlam al-Dīn al-Qāsim al-Birzālī (665–739/1267–1339) is available. *Al-Muqtafā li-Taʾrīkh al-Shaykh Shihāb al-Dīn Abī Shāma* (*Continuation of the History of* [. . .] *Abū Shāma*) exists only in a manuscript fragment in such poor condition that it can no longer be handled by scholars. As a continuation of *Kitāb al-Rawḍatayn*, it begins with the year of Abū Shāma's death in 665/1267 – also the year of al-Birzālī's birth – and ends with 738/1338. This particular manuscript, located in Istanbul, contains only a rough draft in the form of a diary in which al-Birzālī mixed his notes on daily events with necrologies. In its present state the main value of the *Muqtafā* is the opportunity it affords for comparison with the texts of al-Jazarī and other historians. Collation suggests the interdependence of al-Birzālī and al-Jazarī, but the fragile, fragmentary state of *al-Muqtafā* makes definitive conclusions difficult. Suffice it to say that al-Birzālī's conception and presentation of history had much in common with al-Jazarī's and that both combined a provincial scholarly approach with a lively curiosity in events beyond Damascus.[45]

Quṭb al-Dīn Mūsā al-Yūnīnī (640–726/1242–1326) also wrote a sequel to an Ayyubid work: *Dhayl Mirʾāt al-Zamān* (*Sequel to the Mirror of the Time*), which begins with the year of Sibṭ ibn al-Jawzī's death in 654/1256 and ends with 711/1312. Detailed textual study by several scholars has demonstrated that much, if not most, of the *Dhayl* is a close copy or edition of al-Jazarī's *Ḥawādith*. In fact, the correspondence between the two texts is so close that the most recent scholar to study these authors concludes that a later editor wrongly attributed a section of al-Jazarī's work to al-Yūnīnī![46] Furthermore, he suggests that al-Birzālī, who was a student of al-Yūnīnī's borrowed material from al-Yūnīnī and passed it on to al-Jazarī. Al-Jazarī included it in *Ḥawādith*, and al-Yūnīnī, in turn, used it, twice removed, in his *Dhayl*.[47] Whether or not this particular conclusion can be substantiated is not so important as the incontestable fact that complex mutual borrowing did take place among this small group of Syrian historians. Extensive,

45 Ibid., 56–57.

46 Li Guo, "The Middle Bahrī Mamlūks in Medieval Syrian Historiography: The Years 1297–1302 in the *Dhayl Mirʾāt al-Zamān* Attributed to Quṭb al-Dīn Mūsā al-Yūnīnī: A Critical Edition with Introduction, Annotated Translation, and Source Criticism" (Ph.D. dissertation, Yale University, 1994), I, 105–13.

47 Ibid., 110.

unacknowledged borrowing, as we have seen, is characteristic of Ayyūbid and Mamlūk historiography in general. To label such in practice as plagiarism is sometimes tempting but does not solve the problem faced by modern scholars in trying to trace the original source and to assess its reliability.

Oddly enough, an important chronicle for the Baḥrī period is embedded in an encyclopedia designed for the use of chancery employees: al-Nuwayrī's *Nihāyat al-Arab fī Funūn al-Adab* (*All That Can be Desired in the Scribal Arts*). Shihāb al-Dīn Aḥmad al-Nuwayrī (677–733/1279–1333) was himself a clerk and worked both in Syria and Egypt in the *Dīwān al-Khāṣṣ* (Bureau of the Privy Purse) and, later, the *Dīwān al-Inshā'* (Bureau of Chancery) among other offices. In the former his supervision of some of the royal properties and endowments gave him access to Sultan al-Nāṣir Muḥammad, though he fell for a while into his master's disfavor. His multi-volume encyclopedia is divided into four parts; the first three cover cosmography and natural history, man, and flora and fauna. The last part, comprising two-thirds of the work, is devoted to history, beginning with the Creation and ending in 731/1332. It is arranged chronologically within designated regions and dynasties, including, of course, the Baḥrī Mamlūks of Egypt and Syria. But al-Nuwayrī is noteworthy among his Egyptian contemporaries for his willingness to break the annalistic format whenever he thought an event could not be recounted effectively within a single year: the trials of Ibn Taymiyya, for example.[48] As innocuous as this practice may seem, it is one of the few instances in Baḥrī historiography of innovative experimentation with the rigid annalistic format.[49] Much of the section devoted to the Mamlūks is derivative, of course, from other historians, sometimes identified, sometimes not, but including Ibn ʿAbd al-Ẓāhir, Baybars al-Manṣūrī, and al-Jazarī as well as the standard late Ayyūbid historians. Nevertheless, thanks to the access his position gave him to other administrators and military officers, al-Nuwayrī was able to add material from his own, or his informants' experience, so that his chronicle contains a great deal of original information. Moreover, there is evidence that he did not hesitate to reorganize and reinterpret the material he borrowed when he saw fit.[50] Ibn Faḍl Allāh al-ʿUmarī (700–749/1301–1349), Syrian by birth, was another chancery official in Cairo and Damascus who compiled reference works for scribes that contain material of interest to historians. His *al-Taʿrīf bi-al-Muṣṭalaḥ al-Sharīf* (*Instruction on the Noble Technique*) is a short manual for chancery clerks on drafting decrees and official correspondence. It also contains information on the organization and administration of the Mamlūk state. Though brief, it was a major source for the later encyclopedia

48 Little, *Introduction*, 29. 49 Ibid., 86. 50 Ibid., 32.

compiled by al-Qalqashandī.[51] But al-ʿUmarī's magnum opus was his vast encyclopedia, similar to al-Nuwayrī's *Nihāyat al-Arab* in scope and design, entitled *Masālik al-Abṣār fī Mamālik al-Amṣar* (*Paths of Discernment into the Kingdoms of the Lands*). It, too, contains a historical section of annals, dating from the hijra until 743/1343, but it is disappointing even for the period during which the author lived, being a copy of al-Dhahabī's *Duwal al-Islām* (*Dynasties of Islam*).[52] However, other sections, in particular those devoted to specific regions contiguous to the Mamlūk Empire are of considerable interest, and several of these have been published: for example, those on India, the Mongol empires, Syria, and the Arabian peninsula.

Although Khalīl ibn Aybak al-Ṣafadī (696–764/1297–1363) was not the only author of biographical dictionaries who flourished during the Baḥrī period, he was certainly the most prolific. Like Ibn al-Dawādārī, al-Ṣafadī was the son of a Mamlūk amīr, with an entrée into the elite society of the Mamlūks and its satellites in government, education, and the arts. Al-Ṣafadī's privileged status as a member of *awlād al-nās* was enhanced by his education in Syria, presumably in Safad, where he was born and eventually worked, but also in Damascus, Aleppo, and Cairo, as a student of the Qur'ān, *ḥadīth*, and literature with some of the most prominent scholars of the age, including, apparently, Ibn Taymiyya and al-Dhahabī.[53] As early as 723/1323 he found employment in Safad as a clerk in the chancery. From this post he was promoted to the Damascus chancery, and in this capacity he became a member of the entourage of the famous viceroy Tankiz, whom he frequently accompanied on official visits to Cairo and elsewhere. Inevitably, Tankiz incurred al-Nāṣir Muḥammad's disfavor and was executed; al-Ṣafadī survived and in 745/1345 was appointed to Sultan al-Ṣāliḥ Ismāʿīl's chancery in Cairo. Later he returned to Syria, again as a chancery official, in Aleppo and elsewhere, and died in Damascus. Despite an obviously full professional career and extensive travel, al-Ṣafadī found time to write numerous books on various literary and linguistic subjects as well as a substantial body of poetry. His two massive works, still of major importance as historical sources, are both biographical dictionaries. Ironically, the less original of the two, *al-Wāfī bi-al-Wafāyāt* (*Sufficiency of Obituaries*), has received the major attention of scholars, presumably because of its comprehensiveness as a collection of thousands of biographies (more than 5,500 for the Muḥammads!) of prominent Muslims from the time of the Prophet to the author's contemporaries. Publication of this immense work began in 1931 and

51 R. Veselý, "Zu den Quellen al-Qalqašandī's *Ṣubḥ al-Aʿshā*," *Acta Universitatis Carolinae–Philologica*, 2 (1969), 13–14.
52 Little, *Introduction*, 40.
53 Little, "Al-Ṣafadī as Biographer of His Contemporaries," in D. Little (ed.), *Essays on Islamic Civilization Presented to Niyazi Berkes* (Leiden, 1976), 206–07.

continues today. Al-Ṣafadī's relish for biography was not satisfied by this enormous work, so he devoted a separate dictionary to the lives of his contemporaries, entitled *Aʿyān al-ʿAṣr wa-Aʿwān al-Naṣr* (*Notables of the Age and Supporters of Triumph*), comprising almost 1,900 biographies. some of these were extracted from and embellished with rhymed prose and additional data from *al-Wāfī*, but half or more are completely independent of that work. Notwithstanding its great value as a contemporary source, *Aʿyān* has been published only in facsimile, without critical apparatus. Be that as it may, it is a tour de force almost unparalleled in Arabic historiography for its exploitation of literary sources and the author's vast network of eyewitness informants. Among the former are al-Birzālī's lost dictionary of 3,000 of his teachers, al-Udfuwī's biographical dictionary of notables from Upper Egypt, and a lost history of Egypt by Quṭb al-Dīn ʿAbd al-Karīm.[54] In number and status his oral informants are as impressive as al-Yūsufī's and include colleagues in the bureaucracy (including al-ʿUmarī and Shihāb al-Dīn Abū al-Thanā', who headed the Damascus chancery), the grammarian Abū Ḥayyān, the *ḥadīth* expert Ibn Sayyid al-Nās, and the chief Shāfiʿī qāḍī, Taqī al-Dīn al-Subkī.[55] These are only some of the most eminent of the dozens of informants he cites for first-hand information and anecdotes about his biographees. Unfortunately, only a few women rated his notice, and these are either wives of high-ranking Mamlūks or students of *ḥadīth*. Almost all of the biographies follow a standard, more or less chronological, format and differ from those of *al-Wāfī* only by rhymed-prose introductions in the former, summing up al-Ṣafadī's estimate of the person's character and accomplishments. From a structural point of view the long biography of al-Nāṣir Muḥammad is noteworthy in both dictionaries inasmuch as it is organized as annals, following which al-Ṣafadī appends lists of that sultan's chief officers of state and contemporary rulers.[56] But the influence of chronicles and biographies was clearly reciprocal, for Ibn al-Dawādārī's chronicle-biography of al-Nāṣir Muḥammad's reign has the same format as al-Ṣafadī's shorter version.

Burjī historians

Among many anomalies in the editing, translation, analysis, and publication of Mamlūk histories as conducted by both eastern and western scholars is their uncritical concentration on some historians of the Circassian period at the expense of others, whether Baḥrī or Burjī, irrespective, at times, of the historical value of their works. Thus the chronicles of al-Maqrīzī for the

[54] Ibid., 200–02. [55] Ibid., 202–06. [56] Little, *Introduction*, 100–01.

Baḥrī period were edited and partially translated long before those of his contemporary al-ʿAynī began to be published, despite the fact that the latter are far superior to the former as a source for the period in most respects. Although Ibn Khaldūn's *Muqaddima* (*Prolegomena*) has long been recognized as the acme of Muslim historiography, Ibn Khaldūn's uniqueness as a theorist has served to diminish the attention given to his chronicles. The works of Ibn Taghrī Birdī, like those of al-Maqrīzī, were edited, published, and translated before they were subjected to critical scrutiny. In fact, critical analysis of the originality, sources, and possible interdependence of these and other Burjī historians has not yet approached the level of scholarship on the Baḥrī historians. Many of the observations made here, then, should be regarded as tentative, pending further research and publication.

A case in point is the Egyptian scholar, Nāṣir al-Dīn Muḥammad ibn al-Furāt (735–807/1334–1405), who after being educated in *ḥadīith*, secured positions as a notary. Otherwise, little is known about him, and his universal history, *Ta'rīkh al-Duwal wa-al-Mulūk* (*History of Dynasties and Kings*), has survived only in fragments, a few of which have been published. Of these fragments the Ayyūbid section is described as important because Ibn al-Furāt made extensive use of the lost history by the Aleppan Shīʿī historian, Ibn Abī Ṭayyi' (as did Abū Shāma).[57] The sections on the Baḥrī sultans have been shown to be largely derivative from al-Nuwayrī with additions from al-Jazarī.[58] So far only a single volume has been published for the years of Ibn al-Furāt's own lifetime; arranged as a diary, it covers the period 789–797/1387–1395. Short reports of events are followed by numerous obituary notices. Since Ibn al-Furāt was not in the habit of identifying his sources for this period, it will be impossible to determine his originality for contemporary events until such time as comparison with other sources has been undertaken.

The conventional history of Ibn al-Furāt and other Mamlūk historians does nothing to anticipate the contribution of Ibn Khaldūn. Apparently unappreciated for his genius during his lifetime and for centuries thereafter, he was finally discovered by the Ottoman historian Naʿīma in the eighteenth century and was subsequently recognized and acclaimed in the west as a major figure in the development of the philosophy of history and sociology.

Nor does Ibn Khaldūn's life as set forth in his autobiography account for the originality of his thought. A good case could be made for characterizing him as a careerist because of the multiplicity of his appointments and dismissals at courts stretching from Spain to Cairo; nevertheless, he obviously found time and energy to function as a prolific historian. ʿAbd al-Raḥmān ibn Muḥammad ibn Khaldūn (732–808/1332–1406) was born in

[57] *EI2*, III, 769. [58] Little, *Introduction*, 73–74.

Tunis and studied there with eminent scholars the subjects of the traditional Islamic curriculum; he was deeply influenced by philosophy and theology. When he was seventeen his parents died of plague and he emigrated to Fez. During twenty-three years' residence in the Maghrib he continued his studies and held various positions, including Secretary of the Chancery at the court of the Marinid sultan Abū ʿInān Fāris. He also served time in prison for his alleged involvement in an attempted palace coup. Politics led him to move to Granada in 760/1359, where under the patronage of the famous wazīr and poet Ibn al-Khaṭīb, Ibn Khaldūn was well received at the Nasrid court and served as envoy to the Christians of Seville. After seven years he returned to the Maghrib. There he combined study with political office and intrigue; the latter induced him to return to Spain for a while and back to the Maghrib once more. During a four-year period of seclusion (776–80/1375–79), he worked on the *Muqaddima*. Then he returned to his birthplace as a scholar and teacher. In Tunis he prepared the first edition of his universal history, *Kitāb al-ʿIbar wa-al-Mubtadaʾ wa-al-Khabar* (*Book of Examples and Register of Subjects and Predicates*), a copy of which he presented to the Hafsid sultan. But Ibn Khaldūn apparently enjoyed no peace of mind in Tunis, so in 784/1382 he left, with the sultan's permission, ostensibly to perform the pilgrimage. He landed in Cairo, where he found employment both as a professor of jurisprudence and, in 786/1384, as chief Mālikī *qāḍī* under Sultan Barqūq. From the latter office he was presumably dismissed out of professional envy, later reinstated, again dismissed, until he had served in this capacity six times.[59] But he did manage to retain several important teaching positions and even served as head of a royal Ṣūfī monastery. Perhaps his most illustrious public service under the Mamlūks was as an envoy to Timūr-Lenk, whom he met on several occasions during the siege of Damascus in 1400.

Obviously Ibn Khaldūn's wide experience as a scholar and public servant under many masters should have been beneficial to a history oriented toward *siyāsa* (politics) and the conduct of public affairs, and his cyclical view of the rise and fall of dynasties that originated with nomads imbued with religious fervor, flourished as conquerors, and declined once they had become sedentarized and corrupted by effete urban life, was grounded in Ibn Khaldūn's knowledge of the role of both Arab and Bedouin tribesmen in Maghribi history. Nevertheless, there is little in his biography to explain satisfactorily his unique conceptualization of the nature and function of history within the Islamic arts, sciences, and crafts, though scores of scholars have certainly tried to do so. The relationship of the *Muqaddima* to the *ʿIbar*, or, more precisely, the alleged failure of the latter to meet the standards of the former, is but one of many issues raised by Ibn Khaldūn's

[59] *EI2*, III, 827–28.

work. Since this is a subject of great complexity, it must suffice to point out that two of the most recent students of this question have taken a revisionist stance and argued that the great historian has been misunderstood:

> Because most modern scholarship has taken relatively little interest in the *History*, tending in fact to dismiss it as an incongruous appendage to the *Muqaddima* or as no better or even worse than many typical histories of that age, it serves our interest well here to show ... that Ibn Khaldūn's history was a rigorous and precisely constructed account, arranged by states, of world history as it needs to be understood and rewritten when the principles of the *Muqaddima* are kept in view.[60]

It should also be noted that the *ʿIbar* is recognized as being one of the most important single sources on the history of the Maghrib under Muslim rule. Be that as it may, there are long stretches in the *ʿIbar* derived totally from earlier sources. For the early reign of al-Nāṣir Muḥammad, for example, Ibn Khaldūn was content to summarize al-Nuwayrī and supplement him briefly with material from the standard Syrian sources, al-Jazarī and al-Yūnīnī.[61] Nevertheless, even the standard account of Baḥrī history is dramatically punctuated by Ibn Khaldūn's eloquent passage on the impact of slave soldiers on Islamic history through their defeat of the pagan Mongols.[62] As a historian of his contemporaries, Ibn Khaldūn's history of Sultan Barqūq is particularly valuable from the perspective of an insider under this sultan's patronage. As might be expected, the author is not critical of his patron, and his chronicle of the years of Barqūq's reign (784–801/1382–99) is typical of the court histories of the Mamlūk period.

Ibn Khaldūn's autobiography should also be mentioned as a noteworthy historical source if only because of the rarity of this genre in Muslim literature. *Al-Taʿrīf bi-Ibn Khaldūn wa-Riḥlatuha Gharban was Sharqan* (*Introducing Ibn Khaldūn and His Travel East and West*) was originally intended as an appendix to the *ʿIbar*, but at some point the author decided to publish the work separately as reflections on his life and times until a few months before his death.[63] While the *Taʿrīf* focuses on the major events of Ibn Khaldūn's life, these led him to digressions on the places and people with whom he was involved, often summarizing fuller discussions in the *ʿIbar*. Moreover, the work is enlivened with quotations from poetry and samples of his correspondence composed in rhymed prose. Unfortunately, however,

[60] Tarif Khalidi, *Historical Thought*, 223; cf. Aziz al-Azmeh, *Ibn Khaldūn in Modern Scholarship: A Study in Orientalism* (London, 1981), 201–20.

[61] Little, *Introduction*, 75–76.

[62] D. Ayalon, "Mamlūkiyyāt: (B) Ibn Khaldūn's View of the Mamlūk Phenomenon," *JSAI*, 2 (1980), 340–49.

[63] W. Fischel, *Ibn Khaldūn in Egypt: His Public Functions and His Historical Research* (Berkeley and Los Angeles, 1967), 160–66.

the *Taʿrīf* contains little information about the central issue of the process by which his major work was inspired and composed.

Taqī al-Dīn Aḥmad al-Maqrīzī (766–845/1364–1442) is probably the best-known historian of the Mamlūk period with the obvious exception of Ibn Khaldūn, who may have been one of his 600 teachers. Western scholars have been profuse in their praise of al-Maqrīzī, acclaiming him as "beyond doubt the most eminent of the Mamlūk historians," or judging him to be "the best of the Muslim historians of the fourteenth, fifteenth, and sixteenth centuries," and "the *Sulūk* to be the leading production of the period."[64] It was claimed that this rank could be justified by the fact that "the leading historians of that generation in Egypt were al-Maqrīzī's students," such as Ibn Taghrī Birdī and al-Sakhāwī, and that other contemporaries, such as Ibn Ḥajar al-ʿAsqalānī and al-ʿAynī, "were *ḥadīth* scholars more than historians, since they did not devote their full attention to history as did al-Maqrīzī."[65] Another reason for al-Maqrīzī's fame is undoubtedly the sheer bulk of his historical works; in addition to the several books devoted to the history of Egypt he was author of monographs on such ancillary subjects as famine, tribes, coins, measures, etc. Still another reason for his popularity may well be the accident that his works have been published and widely distributed before those of his unheralded contemporary, al-ʿAynī.

Before he became a professional historian al-Maqrīzī had a varied, if lackluster, career as a teacher and public official. Mainly in Cairo, his birthplace, but also for ten years in Damascus, he served in various capacities such as chancery clerk, judge, prayer leader, *muḥtasib*, financial officer, and professor of *ḥadīth*. Trained in the Islamic curriculum, al-Maqrīzī studied Ḥanafī jurisprudence with his grandfather, but after the latter's death renounced and even attacked it in favor of Shāfiʿism. Around 821/1418, when al-Maqrīzī returned to Cairo from Damascus, he seems to have retired from teaching and public service in order to devote himself to his interest in Egyptian history. Nevertheless, in 833–39/1430–35 he is known to have sojourned in Mecca with his family. There he again taught *ḥadīth* while writing history.[66]

Perhaps, it has been suggested, al-Maqrīzī's several separate historical works should be considered as parts of a comprehensive history of Egypt.[67] The first of these parts, written between 820 and 840/1417 and 1436, is the great *al-Mawāʿiẓ wa-al-Iʿtibār bi-Dhikr al-Khiṭaṭ wa-al-Āthār fī Miṣr wa-al-Qāhira* (*Admonitions and Reflections on the Quarters and Monuments in*

64 Philip Hitti and M. M. Ziyāda are both cited by R. Broadhurst (trans.), *A History of the Ayyubid Sultans of Egypt* (Boston, 1980), xvi–xvii.

65 M. Ziyāda (ed.), *Kitāb al-Sulūk li-Maʿrifa Duwal al-Mulūk* (Cairo, 1934), I, p. *waw*.

66 Ziyāda, *Al-Muʾarrikhūn fī Miṣr fī al-Qarn al-Khāmis ʿAshar al-Mīlādī, al-Qarn al-Tāsiʿ al-Hijrī* (Cairo, 1954), 9.

67 H. A. R. Gibb, *Arabic Literature: An Introduction* (Oxford, 1963), 146.

Fusṭāṭ and Cairo), commonly known as *al-Khiṭaṭ*, a topographical study focusing on Cairo but encompassing Egypt in general. Whether it was plagiarized, as sometimes charged, from an earlier work is not important, since the alleged source is lost and is preserved only in *al-Khiṭaṭ*. It should be noted, moreover, that there were other precedents for Mamlūk topographical history. Ibn ʿAbd al-Ẓāhir, for example, was the author of a lost book on the topography of Cairo, frequently cited by al-Maqrīzī, especially for the Fāṭimid city,[68] and Ibn Faḍl Allāh al-ʿUmarī included many descriptions of monuments in his encyclopedia, *Masālik al-Abṣār*. In any case, the *Khiṭaṭ* has served as a prime source for many aspects of Egyptian history, primarily, it is true, for the architectural history of Islamic edifices but also for the organization and conduct of urban life in Cairo. Building on this core, al-Maqrīzī proceeded to write a series of chronicles and biographies covering the history of Egypt from the Muslim conquest up until his own day. These works include histories of Fusṭāṭ as a province of the caliphate, Cairo under the Fāṭimids, and, finally, Egypt under the Ayyubids and Mamlūks, *al-Sulūk li-Maʿrifat Duwal al-Mulūk* (*The Path to Knowledge of Dynasties and Kings*). Curiously, although parts of this latter book were published and translated at a relatively early date on the strength of scholarly admiration for *al-Khiṭaṭ*, the later, contemporary, sections of *al-Sulūk* were not published until much later. As far as Baḥrī Mamlūk history is concerned, al-Maqrīzī had to rely completely, of course, on earlier sources, and these he adapted freely and sometimes indiscriminately without identifying them. Perhaps the most egregious example of his abuse of sources is found in his distortion of al-ʿUmarī's remarks on the Mongols, whereby al-Maqrīzī inflated and distorted the influence of Mongol law on Mamlūk administrative justice.[69] Unfortunately, until such time as the contemporary annals of *al-Sulūk* have been compared with those of other historians, especially those of al-ʿAynī, al-Maqrīzī's significance as a historian will remain as a compiler and preserver of the work of others.

Badr al-Dīn al-ʿAynī (762–855/1361–1451) also combined a career as public teacher and *fiqh* scholar with a professional interest in history. After a conventional education in Qurʾān, *ḥadīth*, and related disciplines in northern Syria, where he learned Turkish as well as Arabic, al-ʿAynī moved to Cairo in 801/1399. There he was appointed *muḥtasib* to replace al-Maqrīzī. In and out of this office several times he served in other capacities as well, including professor, Supervisor of Pious Endowments, and Chief Ḥanafī Judge.[70] In these high positions al-ʿAynī had access to several sultans and, in fact, composed eulogistic biographies of three of them: al-Muʿayyad Shaykh, al-

[68] *EI2*, III, 679; VI, 194.

[69] Ayalon, "The Great *Yāsa* of Chingiz Khān: A Re-examination. (C-2) Al-Maqrīzī's Passage on the *Yāsa* under the Mamlūks," *Studia Islamica*, 38 (1973), 121–23.

[70] Ziyāda, *Al-Muʾarrikhūn*, 20.

Ẓāhir Ṭaṭar, and al-Ashraf Barsbay.[71] Indeed, al-ʿAyni used to meet regularly with Barsbay to explain to him the intricacies of *fiqh* and to translate his history extemporaneously into Turkish, since Barsbay could not read Arabic. His multi-volume work, *ʿIqd al-Jumān fī Taʾrīkh Ahl al-Zamān* (*A Pearl Necklace of the History of the People of the Time*), is a universal history, beginning with the Creation and proceeding through eight and a half centuries of Muslim dynasties. Inexplicably, the parts concerning the Mamlūks began to be published only in 1987. Inexplicably, because as already stated, *ʿIqd al-Jumān* is superior to al-Maqrīzī's *Sulūk*; this is true in terms both of systematic organization and identification and citation of sources. Moreover, it can be demonstrated in many cases that when al-ʿAynī and al-Maqrīzī used the same source, particularly al-Yūsufī, al-ʿAynī almost invariably gave a fuller, more detailed adaptation of the original than did al-Maqrīzī.[72] In fact, one of the chief merits of *ʿIqd al-Jumān* for the Baḥrī period is his preservation and identification of so much of al-Yūsufī's work. As far as organization and presentation are concerned, al-Maqrīzī follows strict chronological order in his annals, month by month and even day by day when possible. Al-ʿAynī, on the other hand, routinely follows a topical order, starting each annal with a list of rulers and officials, followed by discussion of the most prominent events of the year, and ending with reports of "remaining" events. Both historians append obituary notices to each annal; these are divided roughly into *ʿulamāʾ* and secular personages, with the former normally taking priority unless a ruler such as a sultan happened to die in a given year.

So far only a brief selection of al-ʿAynī's annals for the Burjī period has been published. These cover a period of twenty-six years, 825–50/1421–47, in which the author lived. As preserved, these annals are similar in general to al-Maqrīzī's chronological format, though al-ʿAynī usually prefaces each annal with a lengthy list of rulers and functionaries. Curiously, few topics are developed in the same detail they received in the earlier sections, in which al-ʿAynī had to rely exclusively on written sources; in fact, this contemporary section of the work reads almost like a day book which may have been intended as a first draft of a later work, planned but not completed. Infrequently al-ʿAynī mentions his own observation of events, but for the most part he cites no sources. Again, however, judgment of his significance as a historian, like al-Maqrīzī's, should be suspended until systematic comparison of their works has been undertaken.

Abū al-Maḥāsin Yūsuf ibn Taghrī Birdī (812–74/1409–70) has been praised as a historian for his intimate familiarity "with Mamlūk military society and with the Mamlūk army. His knowledge of these institutions was

[71] ʿA. al-Qarmūṭ (ed.), *ʿIqd al-Juman fī Taʾrīkh Ahl al-Zamān* (Cairo, 1989), 39.
[72] Little, "Analysis," 259–61.

far superior to that of any other Mamlūk historian. But for his writings no detailed and reliable reconstruction of Mamlūk society would be possible".[73]

Son of the highest-ranking Mamlūk officers under sultans Barqūq and Faraj, Ibn Taghrī Birdī was reared after his father died by two of his in-laws, a Ḥanafī judge and a Shāfiʿī judge. They saw to it that Ibn Taghrī Birdī was educated in the Islamic sciences, including the study of history under al-Maqrīzī and al-ʿAynī, before he was taken under the patronage of a group of his father's mamlūks, who apparently undertook to train him in the arts of war.[74] Thus he was one of the privileged few historians whose milieu embraced the military and scholarly worlds. Furthermore, thanks to his status as a member of the elite *awlād al-nās* and his acquaintance with several sultans, including al-Muʾayyad Shaykh, Barsbay, Jaqmaq, and Khushqadam, he naturally had access to the Mamlūk court. But Ibn Taghrī Birdī was a historian by profession, conscious of inheriting al-Maqrīzī's and al-ʿAynī's prestige as premier court historian of his time.[75] He was author of a biographical dictionary (to be discussed later) and two major chronicles. *Al-Nujūm al-Zāhira fī Mulūk Miṣr wa-al-Qāhira* (*Resplendant Stars among the Kings of Miṣr and Cairo*) is a history of Islamic Egypt, beginning with its conquest and ending with 872/1468. It is a work by a courtier for courtiers, or, more specifically, for Sultan Jaqmaq's son, who died before he could succeed his father on the throne. In format the *Nujūm* differs markedly from Ayyūbid and other Mamlūk histories in that it is arranged by reigns of individual rulers rather than strict annalistic chronology. Nevertheless, within each reign chronological order is followed, though there is no formal division of events by years. In keeping with this arrangement, Ibn Taghrī Birdī withheld the obituaries until the end of each sultan's reign, at which point he grouped them by each year. Whatever his purpose may have been, these structural innovations reinforce the biographical emphasis of this work. In contrast, Ibn Taghrī Birdī's second chronicle reverts to the traditional format, perhaps because it was intended as a continuation of al-Maqrīzī's *al-Sulūk*. The title, *Ḥawādith al-Duhūr fī Maḍā al-Ayyām wa-al-Shuhūr* (*Events of the Times within the Passage of Days and Months*), clearly reflects the annalistic structure; the biographies, noticeably longer than those in *al-Sulūk*, are placed conventionally after each annal. This work begins where *al-Sulūk* ends, with 845/1441, and ends with 874/1469, covering the reigns of seven sultans, plus the early years of Qāytbāy. Although there is some overlap between the *Nujūm* and *Ḥawādith*, the former is not as detailed or as comprehensive as the latter. Obviously, given

73 Ayalon, "Notes on the *Furūsiyya* Exercises and Games in the Mamlūk Sultanate," *Scripta Hierosolymitana*, 9 (1961), 32.
74 Ziyāda, *Al-Muʾarrikhūn*, 28.
75 *Ibid.*, 30.

Ibn Taghrī Birdī's access to court circles and his familiarity with the Mamlūk system, the *Ḥawādith* and the contemporary section of the *Nujūm* constitute an invaluable personal commentary on persons, institutions, and events. Just as obviously, Ibn Taghrī Birdī had to rely on earlier written sources for the bulk of *al-Nujūm*, many of which he cited by name. Curiously, al-Maqrīzī is seldom mentioned. But his dependence on earlier sources did not deter Ibn Taghrī Birdī from placing his own interpretations on events, and these are often difficult if not impossible to disentangle from the originals. Despite the fact that even some of his contemporaries, most notably al-Sakhāwī, excoriated him for his failings as a historian and an Arabist, many of his errors have received wide currency until the present day. Recently, however, careful analysis of his texts and collation with other sources have resulted in considerable skepticism toward his version of some events and a recognition of his tendency to idealize the reigns of the Baḥrī sultans, a tendency he shared with al-Maqrīzī.[76] Be that as it may, as a historian of his own generation, specifically of the early reign of Qāytbāy, Ibn Taghrī Birdī's writings have been characterized as expressing "sober judgments of crises and shrewd assessments of character" as well as "musings of a mature thinker whose opinions were tinged with the cynicism of old age."[77]

Although there are several other chroniclers of the Circassian period whose works should not be neglected by present-day students, this survey ends with Muḥammad ibn Aḥmad ibn Iyās al-Ḥanafī (852–930/1448–1524), since both his career and his oeuvre epitomize several salient aspects of Mamlūk historiography. In his life and work Ibn Iyās is reminiscent of Ibn al-Dawādārī and Ibn Taghrī Birdī, in that all three belonged to Mamlūk families and based their histories of contemporaneous events on eyewitness experience – their own and others'. All three, moreover, wrote popularized histories in a conventional format but in a style influenced by the Egyptian vernacular and various literary devices.

Indeed, the *Badā'iʿ az-zuhūr* of Ibn Iyās can be characterized as history in only a very limited way: in its popular thematics and its fabulist embellishments, alien to historical factuality, this last great medieval Arabic chronicle was linked to the historicized folk romance, hence to the light prose that was extremely popular at the time but was not recognized as literature. [This type of prose] had developed as a substratum from the days of earliest Islam until Mamlūk times, next to, or, more accurately, beneath, scholarly historiography, but was now reintegrated with it for the first time since the tenth century.[78]

Whatever Ibn Iyās's shortcomings as a historian may be, his work is of

[76] See Little, *Introduction*, 90–92; Ayalon, "The Circassians in the Mamluk Kingdom," *JAOS*, 69 (1949), 140, 144–45.

[77] C. Petry, *Protectors or Praetorians? The Last Mamlūk Sultans and Egypt's Waning as a Great Power* (Albany, 1994), 5.

[78] Haarmann, "Auflösung," 55.

capital importance for its account of the decline of the Mamlūk state under the sultans Qāytbāy, al-Ghawrī, and Ṭumānbāy, the defeat of the Mamlūks by the Ottomans, and the subsequent occupation of Egypt. Even though Ibn Iyās was a scion of Mamlūks on both sides of his family and held a sizable fief (*iqṭāʿ*), he himself was not prominent enough to be included in any of the biographical notices of the time, perhaps because he held no public office; nor was he, like Ibn Taghrī Birdī and al-ʿAynī, an intimate of sultans. Regarding his education, it is known only that he was a student of the famous scholar al-Suyūṭī and the Ḥanafī jurist ʿAbd al-Bāsiṭ ibn Khalīl.[79] Later, the income derived from his fief enabled him to devote himself at his leisure to his history of Egypt: *Badāʾiʿ al-Zuhūr fī Waqāʾiʿ al-Duhūr* (*Marvellous Blooms among Events of the Times*), which ends with 922/1528. For the period prior to his own lifetime, Ibn Iyās states that he relied on approximately thirty-seven histories.[80] Predictably, the work becomes more detailed for events and biographies of the author's own era, when he divides the annals into monthly records of events interspersed with biographies, almost in the form of a diary. Also remarkable is the frequent citation of verses, sometimes of the historian's own composition. But it is, of course, as an observer and interpreter of the transition from Mamlūk to Ottoman rule that Ibn Iyās gained his status as a worthy successor to the great historians of the Circassian period. With them he shared a propensity to criticize the Circassian sultans in contrast to the Baḥrī Turks, but once the former had been defeated by the Ottomans, "he almost completely forgets all the evils of the *ancien régime*, which he himself had so frequently exposed and castigated, and embarks on an idealization of that regime, turning all his fury against the Ottoman."[81] However, despite Ibn Iyas's shifting subjectivity, his annals of the last years of the Mamlūk sultanate and the inception of Ottoman rule are universally admired by modern historians, who use such language as "a towering figure among chroniclers of the later Middle Ages in Egypt" to characterize Ibn Iyās[82] and "superb chronicle" to judge his work.[83]

The compilation of vast biographical dictionaries continued during the Burjī period. Some of these were highly specialized, focusing, for example, on scholars of a specific legal school, while others, following in the footsteps

79 *EI2*, III, 812.

80 M. Muṣṭafā (ed.), *Unpublished Pages of the Chronicle of Ibn Iyās, AH 857–872/AD 1453–1468*, (Cairo, 1951), 23.

81 Ayalon, "Mamlūk Military Aristocracy during the First Years of the Ottoman Occupation of Egypt," in C. Bosworth (ed.), *The Islamic World, from Classical to Modern Times* (Princeton, 1989), 420.

82 Petry, *Protectors*, 7.

83 Ayalon, "Aristocracy," 413; cf. M. Winter, *Society and Religion in Early Ottoman Egypt: Studies in the Writings of ʿAbd al-Wahhāb al-Shaʿrānī* (New Brunswick and London, 1982), 5.

of al-Ṣafadī, sketched the lives of notable individuals from many spheres of Mamlūk society. Among the latter, the works of Ibn Ḥajar al-ʿAsqalānī, Ibn Taghrī Birdī, and al-Sakhāwī are essential sources for modern historians of the Mamlūks.

Shihāb al-Dīn Aḥmad ibn Ḥajar al-ʿAsqalānī (773–852/1372–1449) was one of the most prominent religious figures in Egypt of his time. An indefatigable scholar of the science of *ḥadīth*, he taught it in numerous Mamlūk educational institutions in Cairo and compiled voluminous works on various aspects of the subject. With his acknowledged expertise on this linchpin of the law, it was inevitable that he should be drafted into the judicial bureaucracy, which, in fact, he headed intermittently as chief Shāfiʿī judge for twenty-one years.[84] Notwithstanding his preoccupation with jurisprudence and the law, Ibn Ḥajar found time to cultivate his interest in history and wrote both a chronicle and a biographical dictionary. *Inbāʾ al-Ghumr fī Abnāʾ al ʿUmr* (*Information for the Uninitiated about the Men of the Time*) comprises an annalistic history of the Mamlūk state during his own lifetime, beginning with the year of his birth to 850/1446, two years before his death. Focus on a limited period is also characteristic of his biographical dictionary entitled *al-Durar al-Kāmina fī Aʿyān al-Miʾa al-Thāmina* (*Hidden Pearls Regarding the Notables of the Eighth Century*). It contains no less than 5,204 biographies of persons from every walk of life, mainly Egyptians and Syrians, who happened to have died between 700 and 799 AH. Given the fact that the author was not born until 773, his data are derived almost exclusively from written sources, most notably al-Ṣafadī. Nevertheless, the accessibility of the work and its integration of a variety of materials make it an indispensable reference for the lives of Baḥrī Mamlūk notables.

Though Ibn Taghrī Birdī is renowned chiefly for his two chronicles, both of which contain obituaries, he was also author of a major biographical dictionary, *al-Manhal al-Ṣāfī wa-al-Mustawfī baʿd al-Wāfī* (*The Pure Pool and Completion of al-Wāfī*). As the title indicates, the work was intended as a companion volume to al-Ṣafadī's *al-Wāfī bi-al-Wafāyāt*, upon which Ibn Taghrī Birdī relied heavily, since *al-Manhal* contains biographies of notables who died during the period 650/1252 to 862/1458. Like al-Ṣafadī, Ibn Taghrī Birdī aimed at comprehensiveness, and the 2,822 biographies cover political and military leaders of the Mamlūk empire and beyond, as well as prominent scholars, writers, scientists, and other celebrities. Obviously *al-Manhal* is valuable primarily for information on the author's contemporaries. Curiously, in the light of his reliance on al-Ṣafadī, Ibn Taghrī Birdī was highly critical of him, berating him as a provincial Syrian litterateur who could not keep track of dates or affairs of state in the capital in Egypt.[85]

[84] Ziyāda, *Al-Muʾarrikhūn*, 19. [85] Little, *Introduction*, 108.

Like Ibn Ḥajar and Ibn Taghrī Birdī, the third main biographer of the period was also an annalist. Abū al-Khayr Muḥammad ibn ʿAbd al-Raḥmān al-Sakhāwī (830–902/1427–97) was the author of continuations of both al-Dhahabī's and al-Maqrīzī's chronicles. The latter, *al-Tibr al-Masbūk fī Dhayl al-Sulūk* (*Refined Gold as Sequel to* [al-Maqrīzī's] *Sulūk*), was commissioned by the amīr Yashbak, a leading officer during the reigns of Khushqadam and Qāytbāy, but his attempts to provide patronage to al-Sakhāwī were not always successful.[86] Al-Sakhāwī's main interest was *ḥadīth*. Like his teacher, Ibn Ḥajar, he wrote numerous books on this subject and taught in various *madrasas* in Cairo. His magnum opus, *al-Ḍawʾ al-Lāmiʿ li-Ahl al-Qarn al-Tāsiʿ* (*Brilliant Light on People of the Ninth Century*), was obviously patterned after Ibn Ḥajar's biographical dictionary of the previous century. Reflecting al-Sakhāwī's professional interest, the majority of his 12,000-plus biographies deal with scholars specialized in some aspect of *ḥadīth*, but again, like Ibn Ḥajar, al-Sakhāwī included notables outside the field of scholarship. In any case, Petry deems the *Ḍawʾ* to be one of the foremost primary sources for research on the *ʿulamāʾ* of the central Islamic lands in pre-modern times.[87] While it is true that the work is written in the Muslim biographical tradition, it is distinctly personal in several respects. First of all, al-Sakhāwī saw fit to include a long and detailed account of his own life. This is highly unusual, though helpful to our understanding of the author. Also unusual are his judgments, often negative and sometimes derisory, of the shortcomings of his biographees, including Ibn Taghrī Birdī and the polymath al-Suyūṭī. Even though the acknowledged purpose of recording biographies was to highlight the positive contribution that a person had made to the Muslim community, al-Sakhāwī did not hesitate to berate those who did not meet his standards of accuracy and reliability in transmitting historical data. Justification for this stance is found in his apologetic essay on historiography as a religious science derived from the science of *ḥadīth*: *al-Iʿlān bi-Taʾbīkh li-Man dhamma Ahl-Taʾrīkh* (*The Open Denunciation of the Adverse Critics of Historians*). Finally, *al-Ḍawʾ* is unique among the biographical dictionaries of the Ayyubid and Mamlūk periods for the attention it gives to women. It is true that both Ibn Ḥajar and Ibn Taghrībirdī wove the lives of a few female scholars and sultans' wives into their alphabetized biographies of men, but al-Sakhāwī devoted a final, separate, volume to eminent women of the ninth century. Admittedly, this volume represents only a twelfth of the total work, but this is substantially more space than that normally assigned to women by medieval Muslim biographers.[88]

86 Ziyāda, *Al-Muʾarrikhūn*, 42–43.
87 *EI*2, VIII, 882.
88 See H. Lutfi, "Al-Sakhāwī's *Kitāb al-Nisāʾ* as a Source for the Social and Economic History of Muslim Women during the Fifteenth Century AD," *The Muslim World*, 71 (1981), 104–24.

A major achievement of medieval Arabic historiography came in the form of *Ṣubḥ al-Aʿshā fī Ṣināʿat al-Inshāʾ* (*Dawn for the Benighted Regarding the Chancery Craft*) by Shihāb al-Dīn Aḥmad al-Qalqashandī (756–821/1355–1418). Despite his education in jurisprudence and his intention of becoming a Shāfiʿī judge, al-Qalqashandī became instead a secretary in the chancery during the reign of the first Burjī sultan, Barqūq.[89] His work in thirteen volumes was designed like those of al-ʿUmarī and al-Nuwayrī of the Baḥrī period as a reference for scribes employed by the chancery and, strictly speaking, was not designed as a historical work at all. Nevertheless, it is invaluable to historians of Fāṭimid, Ayyūbid, and Mamlūk Egypt for the detailed data it contains on the geographical and administrative units of these empires. But the *Ṣubḥ* is indispensable above all for the large number of diplomatic and administrative documents that al-Qalqashandī transcribed and analyzed from the point of view of a chancery official. Since, as noted at the outset, so few documents have survived from medieval archives, these copies are of considerable importance both as substantive sources and as samples for comparison with original Mamlūk documents that have survived in such repositories as Christian monasteries in Jerusalem and the Sinai, the Archives in Cairo, and the Islamic Museum at al-Ḥaram al-Sharīf in Jerusalem.[90]

[89] *EI2*, IV, 509.
[90] See Little, "Documents," 9–12.

16

Egypt in the world system of the later Middle Ages

R. STEPHEN HUMPHREYS

In Islamic times, as in all other phases of its long history, Egypt cannot be comprehended or analyzed in isolation. It was always embedded in a series of larger complexes, whether political, economic, or cultural. Whether it is useful to call the totality of these complexes a "world system" is a question best deferred until a later point in this chapter. Whatever we call them, these complexes were constantly evolving and shifting, as was Egypt's role within them. It is natural but misleading to identify one moment as normative and to judge all other periods against that one. We shall be very badly misled, for example, if we focus on Egypt in the half-century after 1300, when the borders of its empire were secure, its armies were triumphant, its cities were bursting with new construction, it was the linchpin between two flourishing trade zones in the Indian Ocean and the Mediterranean, and its centrality in the intellectual and religious life of the Arabic-speaking Sunnī world was uncontested. There are periods, and they are in fact quite common, when Egypt was but a marginal player, and that within a rather small arena.

An understanding of Egypt's place in its Eurasian and African milieu, then, must begin with some reflections on periodization. The terminal dates for our essay, 641 and 1517, are clear-cut and unambiguous. The first represents the moment at which Egypt was abruptly wrenched out of Constantinople's political, economic, and religious orbit; the second is that moment when it was just as abruptly and unexpectedly dragged back in. Byzantine Egypt and Ottoman Egypt differed from each other in a thousand ways, but there are important structural similarities. Both belonged to empires of remarkably similar shape and size, focused on the intersection of an east–west axis linking Europe and Asia, and a north–south axis connecting the Black Sea and the eastern Mediterranean. Both were politically subordinate and economically tributary to the same imperial capital. Both were influential centers of religious life and thought, but the most powerful and prestigious centers lay elsewhere. Both were vitally important provinces, but provinces nonetheless.

In the 875 years that separated the end of Byzantine domination and the beginning of Ottoman rule and that are conventionally identified as the Middle Ages, however, Egypt was situated within a strikingly different matrix – or rather, a succession of matrices. Sometimes, as in Byzantine and Ottoman times, Egypt was only a subordinate element within a vast empire, but it was an empire of very different shape and character – an immense continental domain stretching across north Africa and southwest Asia, whose political, economic, and cultural focal point was central Iraq. At other times Egypt was part of a much smaller regional complex comprising only Syria-Palestine, the Red Sea littoral, and the eastern Maghrib. Only in the later Middle Ages did Egypt become a major imperial center, with all that implied in the arenas of commerce, religious influence, and cultural expression – and even then it was only one imperial center among many others no less powerful, prestigious, and wealthy.

Egypt's path from conquered province to imperial metropolis was by no means straight and uncomplicated. When Egypt was captured by an Arab Muslim expeditionary force in the 640s, after a remarkably easy campaign, no one could have predicted the size and durability of the new empire ballooning out of Arabia. Indeed, in the late 650s and again in the 680s, that empire seemed on the verge of dissolution. Nor did the Arab Muslim conquerors sink deep roots in Egypt for many decades. The country was garrisoned by a few thousand tribal levies, stationed largely in the military cantonment of Fusṭāṭ at the apex of the Delta. The fiscal administration continued to be carried out in Greek, as it had been for a thousand years. Outside Alexandria (which continued to have many Greek-speakers), the overwhelming majority of the population consisted of native Egyptians, who used Coptic as the language of everyday life and the Church. Apart from the governor's palace and the garrison troops, neither Arabic nor Islam had any significant role in Egyptian life. Moreover, Islam was still a religion in the making; it could hardly compete with the sophisticated theology and liturgical richness of the Coptic or Greek Orthodox Churches.

As the caliphal regime stabilized in the 690s, Egypt found itself embedded within a far larger empire than a century earlier, but its place within that empire was markedly less significant than it had been in Byzantine times. Apart from the garrison troops who helped instigate the revolt against the caliph ʿUthmān in 655–56, Egypt played no real part in the political struggles of the late seventh and eighth centuries. Egypt had ceased to be the granary of Constantinople, and now adopted the more modest role of granary for the holy cities of the Ḥījāz. Egypt was no doubt a vital source of revenue for the Umayyad caliphate in Damascus, but its fiscal importance for the central government was significantly reduced by the transfer of the capital to Baghdad after the ʿAbbāsid seizure of power in 750.

Egypt's role in international commerce likewise shrank markedly in early

Islamic times. The once dynamic Red Sea route to east Africa and India had largely withered away in the course of the sixth century. The Indian Ocean trade was now channeled through the Persian Gulf, and would continue to be so as this commerce burgeoned under ʿAbbāsid and Būyid sponsorship between the eighth and eleventh centuries.[1] In the Mediterranean basin, trade was badly disrupted (though it did not disappear) in the turmoil of the seventh century, no doubt partly because of the naval confrontation between Muslim and Byzantine fleets, but also because of the economic regression of Latin Europe. Such trade as there was between the eastern and western Mediterranean was now channeled through Constantinople rather than Egypt.[2]

Even in the cultural realm Egypt took a step backward. Alexandria had been a major protagonist, often the most important one, in the Trinitarian and Christological debates between the fourth and sixth centuries. That role of course disappeared with the imposition of Arab-Muslim rule, and it was slow to be replaced by any Islamic equivalent. By the early 700s Islam was beginning to articulate its theological doctrines and legal-ethical norms in an increasingly sophisticated fashion, but the key centers of this activity lay in Kūfa and Baṣra, in Damascus and Ḥimṣ, in Mecca and Medina. Until the late eighth century, Egypt was very much a junior partner in this enterprise.

Only in the ninth century did Egypt begin to play a major role in the greater Muslim world. By the end of the eighth century Fusṭāṭ had become a significant center of Islamic learning (though it hardly rivalled Medina or the cities of Iraq), and its position was secured by the fact that Muḥammad ibn Idrīs al-Shāfiʿī (d. 820) spent the later years of his life there. The *madhhab* attached to his name spread and took root in many places throughout the eastern Islamic lands, but Egypt would always remain a key center of Shāfiʿī doctrine.

The growing role of Fusṭāṭ in Islamic thought and practice was certainly connected with demographic and cultural changes within the country as well. By the middle decades of the ninth century, Lower Egypt at least had undergone a considerable process of Arabization and Islamization, owing in part to conversion and acculturation among the native population and in part to large-scale immigration by Arab tribes.[3] Egypt's changing position was also enhanced by the slow consolidation of an Arab Muslim society and culture in north Africa and Spain, for Egypt was the natural conduit for material and intellectual exchange between the eastern and western Islamic

[1] J. I. Miller, *The Spice Trade of the Roman Empire, 29 BC–AD 641* (Oxford, 1969); A. Wink, *Al-Hind. The Making of the Indo-Islamic World* (Leiden, 1990), I, 25–64.

[2] H. Pirenne, *Mohammed and Charlemagne* (New York, 1939), long since superseded but still seminal. A good overview of the debate is given in A. F. Havighurst (ed.), *The Pirenne Thesis: Analysis, Criticism, and Revision*, 3rd edn. (Lexington, MA, 1976).

[3] I. M. Lapidus, "The Conversion of Egypt to Islam," *Israel Oriental Studies*, 2 (1972), 248–62.

lands. (This would be a role of growing importance in the following centuries, culminating perhaps in the thirteenth.) Most of all, Egypt benefited from the weakening of Baghdād's control over the outlying provinces of the ʿAbbāsid empire, and in particular from the catastrophic if temporary collapse of caliphal authority caused by the assassination of al-Mutawakkil in 861. The almost immediate devolution of power into the hands of local governors throughout the empire was replicated in Egypt with the rise of the Ṭūlūnids (reigned 868–905). Although the caliphal government in Baghdād was able to oust the last Ṭūlūnid and reassert direct control over Egypt after 905, it could not maintain its hard-won position for very long, for by the 930s the ʿAbbāsid caliphs had suffered a new and this time irreversible loss of power and prestige. As they became the virtual prisoners of one or another generalissimo in Baghdād, even the caliphate's core provinces became autonomous states under local warlords.

The middle of the tenth century marked a watershed in the history of Islamic Egypt on several levels. In the political arena, the country moved from loose ʿAbbāsid control to autonomy under the Ikhshīdids (935–969), and then to being the central province of a dynamic, expansionist new state, the Fāṭimid caliphate. Had the Fāṭimids succeeded in their program, which was to rule the whole realm of Islam, Egypt might soon have sunk back into its old provincial status. But the new dynasty's failure to advance beyond Damascus ensured that Egypt and its new capital of Cairo would remain the core of the Fāṭimid caliphate until its demise in 1171. The Fāṭimids never ruled a terribly large domain; at its peak between 975 and 1025, their empire reached from Tunisia and Sicily in the west to Ḥimṣ and Tripoli in the east. By the middle of the eleventh century, the Fāṭimids would lose their western possessions, and by the 1070s they were struggling to keep a foothold in Palestine in the face of Turkish incursions. After the coming of the crusaders, of course, they lost even that and retreated within Egypt's traditional frontiers. Even so, the Fāṭimid caliphate was the largest and most durable state to be centered in Egypt since the Ptolemies thirteen centuries earlier. Although the Fāṭimids fell far short of their immense ambitions, they laid both the territorial and institutional foundations for the imperial role that Egypt would assume until the Ottoman conquest.

Fāṭimid propaganda always claimed that the reign of the true Imam would usher in the messianic (or pre-messianic) age of prosperity and security, and for almost a century after the Fāṭimid conquest Egypt seems to have enjoyed that enviable but elusive state of things, though there were obviously ups and downs. A crucial and highly favorable shift in Egypt's position vis-à-vis the international trade routes occurred in the early eleventh century. This shift was perhaps due in part to the conscious policy of the Fāṭimid Imāms and their officials, but its main causes lay beyond the control of any Egyptian government. First of all, there was the slow but unmistakable revival of a market economy in Latin Europe, and this economic revival fed a growth in the seaborne commerce between Italy and the seaports of Egypt. For the first time in many centuries, Egypt began to develop substantial ties not only with the entrepôts of Italy but also (albeit indirectly) with the transalpine lands which these served. These links between Egypt and Latin Europe were reinforced by the continuing trade with the Maghrib, and especially with Tunisia (Ifrīqiya). Via Tunisia, Egypt was connected to Africa, Norman Sicily, and Muslim Andalus.[4] Second, the early eleventh century witnessed a decline, and ultimately a near collapse, in the Persian Gulf route to India and East Africa, probably due in large part to the political turmoil and intensifying economic problems in Iraq and south-western Iran. Under these circumstances, the Indian Ocean trade was rerouted to the Red Sea ports of Egypt.[5] By the middle of the eleventh century, Egypt was the principal hinge between the Indian Ocean and Mediterranean basins, the point at which the complex commercial networks of these two zones were knotted together. Egypt's new (or at least revived) position in the African and Eurasian trade system would endure and grow, and would be a defining element of Egypt's place in the world until the end of Mamlūk times.

The Fāṭimid era also witnessed an ethnic, cultural, and religious transition in Egypt. Essentially, Cairo and the Delta became solidly Arabized and Islamized, though obviously Coptic Christian pockets remained. There was a continuing inflow of nomadic Arab tribes from Arabia (especially the notorious Banū Hilāl and Banū Sulaym), but for the most part we are dealing with conversion to Islam and the adoption of Arabic speech by the indigenous population of the country. The same process was by now well under way in Upper Egypt as far south as Qūṣ, though here Christian communities remained not only prominent but in a majority for many centuries. However, even in Christian areas we see a rapid fading of the Coptic language except as a liturgical language. By the middle of the tenth century, senior churchmen found it necessary to use Arabic for their secular writings. Thus we have the world chronicle composed in the 930s by Eutychius (Saʿīd ibn al-Biṭrīq, 877–940), Melkite Patriarch of Alexandria. In the second half of the century, Severus (Sawīrus ibn al-Muqaffaʿ, d. ca. 980), Coptic bishop of Ashmūnayn, collected and translated Greek and Coptic

[4] S. D. Goitein, "Medieval Tunisia – the Hub of the Mediterranean," in Goitein, *Studies in Islamic History and Institutions* (Leiden, 1966), 308–28; R. S. Lopez, *The Commercial Revolution of the Middle Ages, 950–1350* (Englewood Cliffs, NJ, 1971), 56–84.

[5] A. Wink, *Al-Hind*, I, 56–59; Bernard Lewis, "The Fāṭimids and the route to India," *Revue de la Faculté de Sciences Économiques de l'Université d'Istanbul*, 11e année (Oct. 1949–Jul. 1950); Jean Aubin, "La ruine de Siraf et les routes du Golfe Persique aux XIe et XIIe siècles," *Cahiers de l'Histoire Médiévale*, 10–13 (1959), 187–99.

materials in the monasteries of Egypt for his *History of the Patriarchs of Alexandria*.[6]

Although Fāṭimid religious doctrine seemed deviant (at best) to most Muslims, the Fāṭimid caliphate played a crucial role in Islamic religious thought. Since Ismāʿīlī doctrine in the tenth and eleventh centuries was elaborated under the aegis and sometimes the direct supervision of the Fāṭimid imāms, Egypt came for the first time to have a central place in the definition of Islam, albeit within relatively restricted and highly secretive circles. Fāṭimid Ismāʿīlism was especially influential in Iran, but ultimately it found a home in regions as dispersed as the Yemen and Gujarat.[7] But the Fāṭimid contribution to Islamic thought goes far beyond the development of its own doctrine. The Ismāʿīlī theological challenge demanded and evoked a serious response from leading Imāmi (Twelver) and Sunnī circles, not least Abū Ḥāmid al-Ghazālī (d. 1111). Moreover, the determination of Ṣalāḥ al-Dīn and his Ayyūbid successors not only to root out the Ismāʿīlī infestation in Egypt, but also to make the country a major center of Sunnī learning, is an ironic tribute to the Fāṭimid achievement in this sphere.

At first glance the twelfth century seems an inglorious moment in Egyptian history. The Fāṭimid regime slowly rotted away and lost whatever prestige it had in the Islamic world at large, even among most Ismāʿīlīs. Unable to defend Palestine against the crusaders, the Fāṭimids became progressively unable to defend Egypt itself. The dynasty's demise in 1171 was hardly a shock to any attentive observer. Yet the impression of Egyptian weakness and marginality is very misleading. Egypt continued to be one of the major eastern termini (along with Constantinople and Acre) of the Mediterranean trade, which expanded rapidly throughout the twelfth century. Likewise, the Indian Ocean trade was growing apace, along with European demand for the luxury products of "India." The Fāṭimid fiscal administration was still able to support the costs of a lavish palace establishment and a large if ineffective army. In short, when Ṣalāḥ al-Dīn came to power in 1169 (initially as Fāṭimid wazīr), Egypt could provide him with the financial resources to launch his own ambitious agenda, though perhaps not to complete it.[8]

We need not examine most of Ṣalāḥ al-Dīn's policies in Egypt, since they really affected only the internal affairs of the country. However, some of them had a large and direct impact on Egypt's place in the world outside its

[6] Jean-Claude Garcin, *Un centre musulman de la Haute-Égypte médiévale: Qūṣ* (Cairo, 1976), 71–123; S. Labib, "Ibn al-Muḳaffaʿ"; *EI2*, F. Micheau, "Saʿīd ibn al-Biṭrīḳ," *EI2*.

[7] I. K. Poonawala, *Biobibliography of Ismaʿili Literature* (Malibu, CA, 1977); Nagib Tajdin, *A Bibliography of Ismāʿīlism* (Delmar, NY, 1985).

[8] Claude Cahen, *Makhzūmiyyat* (Leiden, 1977); A. S. Ehrenkreutz, *Saladin* (Albany, NY, 1972), esp. chs. 6, 8, 12.

boundaries. First, he strove to make Egypt a major center of Sunnī religious thought, and in this policy he was energetically followed by the later Ayyūbids. His purpose was in part to root out the vestiges of the Ismāʿīlī heresy, but he was also following the model laid down by Nūr al-Dīn in Syria – namely, demonstrating his profound commitment to the Sunnī cause by surrounding himself with scholars of unimpeachable piety and learning, and by providing generously for the support of these scholars.[9]

In fact Egypt had always remained a predominantly Sunnī country under Fāṭimid rule, and in the twelfth century it produced a fair number of reputable Shāfiʿī and Mālikī scholars. But when Ṣalāḥ al-Dīn seized power, the key centers of Sunnī thought were Damascus, Baghdād, and the cities of Khurāsān. Egypt (or more properly, Cairo) could only move to the forefront as Ṣalāḥ al-Dīn and his successors recruited scholars from Syria, Mesopotamia, Iraq, and Iran and provided them with appropriate livings. By the end of Ayyūbid rule in Egypt (1250), Cairo already rivalled Damascus and probably surpassed Baghdād as the principal center of Sunnī scholarship in the Islamic world. The sacking of Baghdād by the Mongols eight years later served only to confirm Cairo's standing. Although Damascus continued to have scholars of international reputation down through the fourteenth century, it is clear that Cairo had long since become the center of gravity. Under the Ayyūbid aegis, Egypt would quickly produce a strong corps of Sunnī scholars, but now was and would remain a powerful magnet for those from other lands as well. It was thus Ṣalāḥ al-Dīn and his successors who made Cairo an international center of Sunnī thought and education, a role which Cairo would retain down through the Mamlūk period.[10]

Besides being an ardent partisan of Sunnī Islam, Ṣalāḥ al-Dīn was also an empire-builder. Though he never resided in Egypt after 1179, he made it the center of a rapidly expanding empire. At his death, the lands which he ruled either directly or through closely supervised clients comprised not only Egypt and Syria (including most of the territories recently held by the Franks), but Mesopotamia, the Yemen, and Cyrenaica. His forces had penetrated deep into Nubia, though they could not maintain themselves there. Since Ṣalāḥ al-Dīn followed the political custom of his day in distributing these vast territories (the Ayyūbid Cconfederation, to give them a name) to his kinsmen in the form of hereditary and largely autonomous

[9] N. Élisséeff, *Nur al-Din. Un grand prince musulman de Syrie au temps des Croisades*, 3 vols. (Damascus, 1967), III, 750–80.

[10] Damascus has been studied in L. Pouzet, *Damas au VIIe/XIIIe s. Vie et structures religieuses dans une métropole islamique* (Beirut, 1988), and M. Chamberlain, *Knowledge and Social Practice in Medieval Damascus, 1190–1350* (Cambridge, 1994). For the rise of Cairo see J. Berkey, *The Transmission of Knowledge in Medieval Cairo: A Social History of Islamic Education* (Princeton, 1992); on the culmination of the process see Carl Petry, *The Civilian Elite of Cairo in the Later Middle Ages* (Princeton, 1981).

appanages, the whole enterprise carried less weight than one might have surmised. But by any standards Ṣalāḥ al-Dīn's was a large empire, and Egypt was the keystone of the edifice.

In itself, the bloody seizure of power by the Ayyūbid dynasty's mamlūk guards in 1250 changed very little. The new rulers represented a different style of government (rule by military junta rather than by hereditary succession), but there was nothing in their religious or economic policy that deviated from the lines already laid down by the Ayyūbids. This situation was altered by the Mongol invasions, which placed Egypt in a radically new international context. The sack of Baghdād and the destruction of the ʿAbbāsid caliphate in 1258 left Cairo as the only major Muslim metropolis between the Nile and central Asia which was not under Mongol control. When the Mongols swept through Syria almost unopposed in the winter and spring of 1260, Cairo itself seemed on the verge of falling. The Mamlūk victory at ʿAyn Jālūt (September 3, 1260) retrieved the situation for the moment, but it did nothing to end the Mongol threat to Syria and Egypt. For the new and still untried Mamlūk sultans, the crucial military and political challenge for the next half-century would be that of defending their territories against the Mongol armies of Īlkhānid Iran. In facing this challenge, they pursued a policy which on the one hand was cautious and defensive, on the other bold and far-reaching.

Mamlūk foreign policy in the late thirteenth century does much to reveal the complex ties which linked Egypt to the outside world and so requires a fairly close review.[11] This policy rested on three major premises. First, the Mamlūk empire (in contrast to its Ayyūbid predecessor) was a highly centralized state; the empire rested on the fiscal resources of Egypt, and the exploitation of these resources was directed from the Cairo Citadel. In the Mamlūk scheme of things, Syria was regarded chiefly as a strategically vital frontier zone, whose own economic and political interests were of secondary concern. Second, the Mamlūk empire had two enemies, the Mongols of Ilkhānid Iran and the crusaders on the Syro-Palestinian littoral. Assessing the relative danger posed by one or the other was a constant problem. After the humiliating failure of Louis IX's expedition in 1250, the likelihood of new crusades faded markedly, but only a fool would have written off the danger completely. Moreover, there was always the threat of a Frankish–Mongol alliance. Third, the Mamlūks took power at an extremely turbulent moment in the political history of the Mediterranean basin. Two zones were of particular importance. In Italy, the confrontation between the papacy and the Hohenstaufen also involved the ruling house of France, the kingdom of Aragon, the Ḥafṣids of Tūnis, and the Byzantine emperor Michael VIII. In

[11] R. S. Humphreys, "Ayyūbids, Mamlūks, and the Latin East in the Thirteenth Century," *Mamlūk Studies Review*, 2 (1998), 1–17.

the east, the struggles over Constantinople between the Byzantines and their countless enemies were inevitably connected with the bitter rivalries between Genoa, Pisa, and Venice to control the Levant trade.

In the face of all this, the early Mamlūk sultans (specifically Baybars and Qalāwūn) constituted their empire as a fortress. In their judgment, their empire could not hope to pursue an expansionist policy with any prospects of success; indeed, unbridled expansionism would almost surely lead to disaster. What they could do was to secure the borders of Egypt and Syria and convert these lands into a powerful citadel which the enemies of Islam could not penetrate. To the north, the Taurus mountains constituted a deep frontier zone (as they had throughout the interminable wars with Byzantium between the eighth and tenth centuries). To the east, the Euphrates allowed only a few crossing points for the Mongol armies, and these were readily defensible. To the west, the Mediterranean could serve as an effective rampart if the Syro-Palestinian seaports were dismantled. The destruction of these port facilities as they were one by one recaptured from the Franks inevitably crippled the once lucrative seaborne commerce with Syria. From a Mamlūk perspective, however, it made good political as well as military sense to channel the whole Mediterranean trade through Alexandria, since the revenues would go directly to the regime in Cairo, while Syria's provincial governors would be deprived of an independent source of income which they might use for their own purposes.

A fortress which waits passively for the enemy to encamp beneath its gates is ill-defended, and that certainly was not the policy of the early Mamlūk sultans. They pursued an active diplomacy on several fronts, aimed both at frustrating the ambitions of their Frankish and Mongol opponents and at securing the resources that their empire needed for its defense. Thus Baybars's negotiations with the Hohenstaufen and their Angevin successors in Italy and Sicily were meant to check papal efforts to mount a new crusade. His treaties with Byzantium, Genoa, and the Golden Horde secured the vital commerce in Turkish slaves from the north shore of the Black Sea to Egypt. Mamlūk ties with the Golden Horde also helped keep the Īlkhānids preoccupied with their exposed and strategically important Caucasus frontier.

Even this brief review of early Mamlūk diplomacy shows the central place which the early Mamlūk empire (and Egypt in particular) occupied within a vast international arena, and that this place was determined by the intertwined political and economic realities of the period. It is important to stress that these underlying realities lay beyond the control of any Egyptian ruler; the achievement of Baybars and Qalāwūn was to perceive how to bend them to their advantage. Thus, the early Mamlūk empire derived exceptional prestige from the fact that it was the only major Muslim state between the Atlantic Ocean and the Hindu Kush which could hold its own against powerful non-Muslim enemies – the only one which could defend the cause of Islam in a desperate age. The Mongols had overwhelmed every Muslim state in central Asia, Iran, Iraq, and Anatolia. At the other end of the Muslim world, the Almohad Empire had dissolved in the face of the Castilian and Aragonese onslaught. Andalus now lay almost entirely in Christian hands, and although the Marinids in Morocco and the Ḥafṣids in Tūnis gradually shaped viable polities out of the chaos, they were obviously destined to remain minor powers. Only beyond the Hindu Kush and the Indus river was there a Muslim state, that of the Delhi sultans, which in any sense stood at the same level as the Mamlūks of Egypt and Syria. Among his other talents, Baybars was a superb propagandist, and he knew how to exploit the unique position of his empire to the fullest advantage.

The political and military stature of the Mamlūk empire was in the end secured by the wealth at its disposal. To a considerable degree, this was a matter of extracting taxes and dues out of the long-suffering but highly productive Egyptian peasant. The early Mamlūks obviously collected everything they could, but by the standards of their age they were not abusive. Baybars in particular not only insisted on a strict standard of fiscal administration and justice, but made a substantial investment in Egypt's agricultural infrastructure.[12] However, the Mamlūk empire did not have to live off its own resources. Mediterranean commerce grew steadily in volume and institutional sophistication throughout the thirteenth century, and this commerce was more and more closely integrated with the rising manufacturing and commercial economies of the Low Countries and the Baltic. All the evidence we have indicates that the Indian Ocean trade was flourishing in the same way. Egypt was of course the point of intersection between the two trade zones, and the Mamlūk regime (along with many merchants) derived a vast income as a result. But quite apart from the transit trade – essentially a matter of the transshipment of Indian spices and precious woods to Latin Europe – the Mediterranean and Indian Ocean economies were each vital and self-sustaining systems.

We cannot go into any detail on the organization of these commercial systems, but a few comments are necessary.[13] As in centuries past, Egypt continued to supply its own agricultural and manufactured goods (sugar, linen textiles, glass, ceramics, and so on) to European markets. European merchants (largely Italian and Catalan) had manufactured goods of their own to contribute to the exchange, especially fine wools, but their exports fell short of the combined total of Egyptian and Indian imports, and the difference was paid in silver coin. On the other side, Egypt had little to send

[12] P. Thorau, *The Lion of Egypt. Sultan Baybars I and the Near East in the Thirteenth Century*, trans. P. M. Holt (London and New York, 1992), 251–5, gives a balanced assessment.

[13] Wink, *Al-Hind*, II (1996); Lopez, *Commercial Revolution*, chs. 4–6; S. Labib, *Handelsgeschichte Ägyptens im Spätmittelalter, 1171–1517* (Wiesbaden, 1965).

to India except gold; fortunately, Egypt's access to the gold trade of western Africa provided ample quantities of this metal. So long as silver and gold were regarded solely as commodities, and so long as they were adequately available, favorable or unfavorable trade balances posed no significant problems. The system was quite able to sustain itself.

On the other hand, Egypt's merchants no longer traveled on the Mediterranean trade routes, as they had throughout the eleventh and early twelfth centuries. By now, the seaborne legs of this commerce were almost exclusively in the hands of Italian or Catalan merchants, traveling on European ships. For this change, there were several causes. In earlier times, Muslim navies were able to protect Muslim merchant vessels, but by the end of the twelfth century the Italian fleets had obtained a near-monopoly of naval power. In principle, Muslim merchants could have sailed on European ships, and a few did, but in practice that was difficult because the Italian city states did not allow Muslim merchants to reside there. Byzantine Constantinople did permit this, as it had for many centuries, but it no longer lay astride Egypt's principal trade routes (apart from that of the Genoese-dominated Black Sea slave trade). In the Indian Ocean, things were very different; there the western half of that network was largely in the hands of Egyptian and perhaps Yemeni merchants.

From one major commercial network the Mamlūk empire benefited only marginally if at all. In spite of the destruction caused by the Mongol conquests, they did create a kind of *pax mongolica* which revitalized the transcontinental trade routes between China and Anatolia for about a century (ca. 1250–1350).[14] These routes had a great impact in many regions, especially in northern Iran and the lands bordering the Black Sea, but Mamlūk Egypt's main commercial links with Yüan China followed the Indian Ocean sea lanes. The Mamlūk–China trade, though quite extensive, was indirect: Egyptian and Yemeni merchants traveled to the west coast of India, and there their goods were exchanged for Chinese merchandise brought through the South China Sea and the Malacca Straits.

At this point, we need to ask whether early Mamlūk Egypt had become integrated within a "world system."[15] That is a useful concept only if we are content to define a world system in minimal terms, as a set of autonomous but interlocking political and economic zones. Defining these zones can of course be an interesting and frustrating exercise. But in any case, there is no question in this period of any one of these zones being able to impose terms of trade on the others; the concepts of core and periphery, however useful

[14] H. W. Haussig, *Geschichte Zentralasiens und der Seidenstrasse im islamischer Zeit* (Darmstadt, 1988).

[15] Defined originally in I. Wallerstein, *The Modern World System*, I (New York, 1974); re-examined for the later Middle Ages by Janet Abu-Lughod, *Before European Hegemony: The World-System AD 1250–1350* (Oxford, 1989).

for the sixteenth century and later, throw little light on the thirteenth century. In terms of economic production and organization, the most powerful and dynamic zones were surely those in China and India. Both of these were sufficiently vast and complex to be almost self-sufficient, and neither showed any inclination to dominate the political-economic zones lying west of the Indian Ocean. What can be discerned in the late thirteenth century is a far more complex and multilayered set of interactions between the various zones, however defined, than can be found in any earlier period. In fact, the interlocking zones or regions of Eurasia and Africa to be seen in early Mamlūk times are the much same as those we see in the second century, but the intensity and depth of economic, cultural, and religious exchange is far greater.

The dynamic equilibrium of the late thirteenth century could not last, or at least it did not. As we pass into the fourteenth century we begin to confront a far more turbulent and much murkier world. There were vast changes in the demography, economy, and political structures of Eurasia, none of them for the better. Egypt was of course hit as hard by these changes as was any other region. Yet we cannot quite discern just what happened or how changes in one realm of life were related to those in another. Any account of Egypt's role within a "world system" in this period must therefore be provisional and highly conjectural.

We can begin with a group of intriguing parallels in the political life of Eurasia. The death of al-Nāṣir Muḥammad in 1341 opened at least four decades of acute political instability in the Mamlūk empire.[16] The crisis in the Mamlūk regime was mirrored by political breakdown elsewhere, especially in the Mongol successor-states in Iran, central Asia, and China. That is, four of the most powerful empires in Eurasia came unglued almost simultaneously. Each of the Mamlūk, Īlkhānid, Chaghatayid, and Yüan states inevitably had its own dynamic, its own set of political tensions and fault-lines. Even so, it is tempting to ask if there is something more than coincidence in all this. By the last decades of the century, there was some restoration of political order throughout this immense area. The new Ming dynasty in China was by far the most successful in this effort, but the Mamlūk empire experienced a rough and ready consolidation of power under Barqūq (r. 1382–89, 1390–99) and his successors. The "restoration of order" in Iran and central Asia was a far crueler affair, since it was brought about by the bloody empire-building of Timūr-Lenk. Still, by 1400 there was again a relatively stable state system reaching from Egypt to China, and this system would endure more or less intact down to the last decade of the fifteenth century.

[16] Amalia Levanoni, *A Turning Point in Mamlūk History. The Third Reign of al-Nasir Muḥammad Ibn Qalāwūn, 1310–1341* (Leiden, 1995).

Second, in the late 1340s much of Eurasia was ravaged by a pandemic, the so-called Black Death.[17] The plague struck unevenly, but where it took hold the mortality was enormous and sudden – from one-quarter to one-third of the population in many afflicted areas, over a period of only one or two years. After 1350 the great pandemic subsided, but plague remained endemic throughout Europe and the Middle East for some three centuries. Once every ten to twenty years, for example, Cairo and Damascus would be visited by a plague epidemic of several months' duration; though the mortality rate was less severe than in 1347–49, deaths would still number in the many thousands. This pattern of periodic outbreaks was also very common in Europe's larger cities.

It is not difficult to chronicle the appearances of plague, and we can even make a reasonable estimate of the number of deaths caused in any given outbreak. What we cannot yet do in any satisfactory way is to define the impact which these disasters had on the political and economic life of the Mamlūk empire or of Eurasia in general. Historians of western Europe have argued that the drastic fall in population led to a rise in both rural and urban wages (scarce labor commands a higher price) and to a temporary enrichment of many (since existing goods would be distributed among fewer people). On the other hand, it also gave rise to bitter social conflicts as feudal lords struggled desperately to reassert control over a restive peasantry, and masters in the textile trades had to contend with the demands of frustrated and emboldened laborers.

Even if this picture of western Europe is an accurate one (and it is always subject to challenge), it tells us nothing about other plague-stricken regions in Eurasia. In Egypt, the *iqṭāʿ* system and the state fiscal machinery were too powerful to be overturned even by the Black Death, at least in the short term. It is likely that the recurrent plague epidemics had only a limited demographic impact in the countryside. In any case, there is no convincing evidence of any breakdown or transformation of Egypt's rural economy for at least half a century. By the fifteenth century, we do begin to see clear evidence of rural depopulation and village abandonment, but it is by no means certain that these phenomena can be ascribed to the plague.[18]

In Egypt's cities, particularly Cairo, the picture is quite different.[19] There is no doubt whatever that they were severely affected by the Black Death and its aftershocks. Cairo and other urban centers suffered substantial depopulation and urban decay after the middle of the fourteenth century.

17 W. H. McNeill, *Plagues and Peoples* (New York, 1976); Michael Dols, *The Black Death in the Middle East* (Princeton, 1977).

18 H. Halm, *Ägypten nach den mamlūkischen Lehensregistern*, 2 vols. (Wiesbaden 1979–82); R. S. Humphreys, *Islamic History: A Framework for Inquiry* (Princeton, 1991), ch. 7.

19 Dols, *Black Death*, 169–92.

There was also a visible decline in the quantity and quality of Egypt's manufactured goods after this time, and this decline may possibly be linked to plague-induced losses among master craftsmen and their apprentices. The young mamlūk recruits who provided the elite manpower for the Mamlūk armies seem to have been especially susceptible to infection, presumably because they lived in close quarters in their barracks, where the disease could spread rapidly. In any case, mamlūks were extremely expensive to purchase and train, and losses among them must have strained the financial resources of the sultans and senior amīrs. Whether this had some role in causing or aggravating the Mamlūk empire's political crisis between 1341 and 1382 we do not know.

For Egypt, the fifteenth century opened badly – a fitting dénouement to the traumas of the preceding decades. In 1400–01, under the reign of Barqūq's incompetent or unlucky son al-Nāṣir Faraj, Syria was occupied by the armies of Timūr-Lenk. Aleppo and Damascus were sacked, and many of the population (especially skilled craftsmen) were led off into captivity in Samarqand. Egypt was saved only by Timūr-Lenk's withdrawal and then his death in 1405. Almost simultaneously, for reasons which are still being analyzed, Egypt's currency collapsed amidst uncontrolled inflation.[20] Finally, the political order painstakingly restored by Barqūq fell apart under Faraj, who faced constant revolts from his amīrs. It would have seemed simple common sense to predict the imminent demise of the Mamlūk state.

The century's second decade, however, saw a rapid political and financial turnaround under the iron-fisted Sultan al-Mu'ayyad Shaykh (1412–20), and his work was consolidated under al-Ashraf Barsbāy (1422–38).[21] Al-Mu'ayyad in effect rebuilt the Mamlūk army, and Barsbāy used this army to carry out the first important military expedition in over a century, the invasion and subjugation of Cyprus (1426). The military exploits of Barsbāy re-established the Mamlūk empire as the world's preeminent Muslim military power. Perhaps more importantly, Barsbāy was able to establish a reformed gold coinage (the *ashrafī dīnār*), which could compete successfully against such European currencies as the Venetian ducat and which provided a stable foundation for the Mamlūk monetary system down to the Ottoman conquest.[22] By 1438, there was no visible reason to doubt that Egypt and the Mamlūk empire had recovered from the fourteenth-century crisis.

20 J. L. Bacharach, "The Dinar versis the Ducat," *International Journal of Middle East Studies*, 4 (1973), 77–96; idem, "Circassian Monetary Policy: Silver," *Numismatic Chronicle*, 7th ser., 11 (1971), 267–81.

21 Ahmad Darrag, *L'Égypte sous le règne de Barsbāy* (Damascus, 1961); David Ayalon touches on the reforms of al-Mu'ayyad Shaykh in many studies; see "Studies on the Structure of the Mamlūk Army," *Bulletin of the School of Oriental and African Studies*, 15 (1953), 203–38, 448–76; 16 (1954), 57–90.

22 Bacharach, "Dinar versus Ducat."

Nevertheless, the recovery was not as complete and solid as it seemed. Partly this was due to internal factors, such as a population reduced and still periodically ravaged by plague, or the inability of the Mamlūk sultans and their amīrs to maintain a military machine equal in size and quality to that possessed by their thirteenth-century predecessors. There were also policy choices that would prove very damaging in the long run. Barsbāy's expansionist policy was very expensive, and he could not help observing the ample revenues generated by the India trade and by the production and export of sugar. Up till this time, these two sectors of the economy had remained in private hands and had enriched both merchants and the amīrs allied with them. The temptation to subject sugar production and the India trade to royal monopolies was overwhelming, and Barsbāy did not resist it.[23] The precise impact of this monopolization policy is difficult to determine, but it is generally true that monopolies enrich only monopolists and choke off dynamism and growth in the sectors to which they are applied. In any case, it is clear that by the middle of the century the Mamlūk sultans were increasingly hard-pressed to find the revenues they needed to run the army and state administrative machinery in an orderly way. Even a ruler as respected as Qāytbāy (reigned 1468–96) could only keep things together by permitting massive corruption and the looting of the civilian economy through confiscation, protection money, and so on.[24]

In the end, however, the Mamlūk empire's most serious problems lay outside its borders. First of all, by the late fourteenth century international trade was clearly depressed relative to earlier levels, and this would continue until the middle of the fifteenth century. This commercial depression was due to many things. First of all, the breakup of the Mongol empires and the rise of the Ming dynasty in China effectively closed off the overland routes to China and brought to an end the presence of large foreign merchant communities there. A more restricted China trade was henceforth channeled through a few seaports. At the other end of Eurasia, the extraordinary political turmoil in fifteenth-century western Europe – a region which had been an important engine of growth in the twelfth and thirteenth centuries – must have disrupted markets there to some degree. On another level, the depopulation associated with plague simply reduced the overall size of the market throughout Eurasia.

In this altered economic milieu, Egypt found that it could sell fewer and fewer of its own products to western Europe. Europeans were now able to produce better and cheaper versions of most of the things they had once

23 Darrag, *Barsbāy*, chs. 3, 4, 6.

24 Carl Petry, *Protectors or Praetorians? The Last Mamlūk Sultans and Egypt's Waning as a Great Power* (Albany, NY, 1994); D. Ayalon, "Some remarks on the economic decline of the Mamlūk Sultanate," *Jerusalem Studies in Arabic and Islam*, 16 (1993), 108–24.

bought from Egypt; increasingly Egypt was an important trading partner for them only because it was the sole point of access to the "spices of India." This fact made Egypt quite vulnerable to the progress of marine technology in Europe, and particularly in Portugal, whose fifteenth-century monarchs systematically undertook the search for an alternative route to India. And indeed the voyages of Vasco da Gama and his successors at the century's end did provoke a very severe if short-term economic and fiscal crisis in Egypt, and this crisis came at a most inconvenient time. By the time the Indian Ocean trade routes were restructured in the mid-sixteenth century, with Egypt playing a reduced but still very significant role, the country was an Ottoman province.

The Mamlūk empire was also exposed to fundamental political changes in its immediate environment, though the challenge that these posed only became clear in the last decades of the fifteenth century. In the time of Baybars and Qalāwūn, the Mamlūks had had to contend with a powerful and very aggressive Mongol state in Iran and with the threat of a revived crusade. But throughout the fourteenth century, with all its problems, the Mamlūks had been very fortunate in having no foreign enemy who could credibly threaten the regime's existence. The fortress-state erected by Baybars and Qalāwūn proved equal to the task. This happy state of affairs was almost overturned by Tīmūr-Lenk in 1400–1, but he quickly passed from the scene; the old fortress seemed more than adequately repaired by al-Muʾayyad Shaykh and Barsbāy.

But in the second half of the century, the situation changed. The Ottoman Empire had not only arisen from the ashes of Tīmūr-Lenk's invasion in 1402, but had become the paramount power in Anatolia and southeastern Europe.[25] It was the only Muslim state in that era to expand the boundaries of Islam. Moreover, Fatih Muḥammad's brilliant conquest of Constantinople in 1453 only laid the foundations for the real achievement of his thirty-year reign, which was to turn his loose-knit polity into a superbly administered centralized empire. The Ottomans were also building a new-style army which made effective use of gunpowder technology and a well-trained infantry. In view of Ottoman expansion into eastern Anatolia, it was not surprising that the Mamlūks and Ottomans came into conflict along their common frontier in Cilicia and the Taurus mountains. In the inconclusive war fought there in 1485–91, the Mamlūks held their own, but only just. They certainly developed no sense of the possibilities and dangers posed by Ottoman tactics and techniques.[26]

The Mamlūks felt more immediately threatened by the chiliastic Ṣafavid

[25] The consolidation of the Ottoman state is most conveniently presented in Halil Inalcik, *The Ottoman Empire: The Classical Centuries, 1300–1600* (London, 1975).

[26] D. Ayalon, *Gunpowder and Firearms in the Mamlūk Kingdom* (London, 1956).

movement in northwest Iran and eastern Anatolia led by Shah Ismāʿīl in the 1490s and early 1500s.[27] Although this movement had many distinctive elements, it is important to recognize that it was rooted in the political, social, and religious realities of the late fifteenth-century Turco-Iranian world. Among these realities were the great political power wielded by many Ṣūfī leaders, the extraordinary though normally latent military force embodied in the Turkic tribes, and the intense devotion to ʿAlī and his family even among many Sunnīs. In principle, it should not have been surprising (though in practice it always is a surprise) that an intensely charismatic figure like Shah Ismāʿīl should arise and bring all these forces together. The radical theological doctrines espoused by Shah Ismāʿīl, and his uncanny ability to inflame millennarian hopes among the Turkoman tribesmen on the Mamlūk empire's eastern frontier, deeply unsettled the Mamlūk regime. They knew, or thought they knew, how to deal with a rival Sunnī state like the Ottoman empire; they had no idea how to respond to the messianic fervor of the Safavid movement. In the end that problem was solved for them by the Ottoman sultan Yavuz Salīm (r. 1512–20), but the solution quickly turned out to be a problem even more deadly than the one it had replaced.

In 1516 the Mamlūk empire confronted its last and fatal crisis. On one level the crisis was a tragic accident. The Mamlūk regime could not have predicted the Portuguese disruption of the Red Sea route to India, nor was there any reason to suppose that the Ottoman sultan would suddenly turn on them in the midst of the struggle against the Portuguese. But on another level the crisis of 1516 was simply the culmination of world-wide processes that had been going on for more than 150 years. The Mamlūk empire had been constructed in and for the world of the late thirteenth century, and its basic outlook and institutions had changed very little since that time. The army which Qānṣūh al-Ghawrī led to Marj Dābiq in 1516 was not much different in its arms and tactics from the army which Qalāwūn had led to Ḥimṣ in 1281. Likewise, Baybars had based his empire on the fiscal resources provided by Egypt's ancient agrarian economy plus the intersection of the Mediterranean and Indian Ocean trade zones. The last Mamlūk sultans relied on precisely the same foundations. But these foundations were now very weak: Egyptian agriculture was seriously depressed, the Indian Ocean trade routes were in chaos, and Egypt's merchants had few products of their own to contribute to the Mediterranean commerce. In the end, cavalry archers were not quite a match for artillery and muskets, and even had there been the will, there was not the money to build a new army alongside the old.

[27] The stupefyingly complex political and religious affairs of eastern Anatolia and Mesopotamia are carefully analyzed in John E. Woods, *The Aqquyunlu: Clan, Confederation, Empire* (Minneapolis and Chicago, 1976); see esp. chs. 5 and 6.

17

The military institution and innovation in the late Mamlūk period

CARL F. PETRY

Upon the accession of Qānṣūh al-Ghawrī to the Cairo sultanate in 906/1501, the Mamlūk oligarchy over which he presided had ruled Egypt and Syria as a unified imperium for more than 250 years.[1] While no institution of such longevity could remain immune to evolutionary change, the Mamlūk regime was remarkable for its stability in a turbulent international milieu. This stability was sustained in large part because of the Mamlūks' commitment to a static concept of imperialism and their allegiance to conservative values of caste hegemony. To be sure, the Mamlūk oligarchy, during its final decades of sovereignty, exhibited behavioral characteristics that contemporary observers found ominous both for the preservation of the realm's security and ensuring its fiscal solvency. And yet these characteristics were the predictable manifestations of tendencies – positive and negative – in existence since the military elite's inception under the late Ayyūbids.[2]

The last effective Ayyūbid monarch in Cairo, al-Ṣāliḥ Najm al-Dīn, regarded the mamlūk slave-soldiers of his predecessor as a threat, fearing that their loyalty might devolve upon his Syrian rivals. He sought to defend his position by founding a new corps of troops whose officers set up the Mamlūk regime upon his death. They initially regarded their function as custodial, aimed at protecting their own status from Ayyūbid claimants. Rudimentary as their ideas were about statecraft at this early stage, these founders appreciated their vulnerability as usurpers. Installed as bodyguards of a paranoid ruler, they rightly saw their prospects as tenuous if a successor

[1] Hypotheses in this chapter are discussed in the context of fuller documentary evidence in C. Petry, *Protectors or Praetorians? The last Mamlūk Sultans and Egypt's Waning as a Great Power* (Albany, 1994).

[2] On the origins of the Mamlūk institution in Egypt, see D. Ayalon, "Le régiment Bahriya dans l'armée mamelouke," *REI*, 19 (1951), 133–41; "Studies on the Structure of the Mamlūk Army – I, II, III," *BSOAS*, 15 (1953), 203–28, 448–76; 16 (1954), 57–90; "Aspects of the Mamlūk Phenomenon – I & II," *Der Islam*, 53 (1976), 196–225; 54 (1977), 1–32; R. S. Humphreys, "The Emergence of the Mamlūk Army," *SI*, 45 and 46 (1977), 67–99, 147–82.

who resented the privileges their patron had granted them took power. Thus, from the origins of the Mamlūk era, even before its architects had fashioned a distinctive style of governance, these amīrs focused on their self-interest. Over subsequent decades, political adversities and stratagems aimed at surmounting them would vary, but this preoccupation remained constant.

By the end of the seventh/thirteenth century, the band of rebels from the Baḥrī corps had matured into a tradition-bound constabulary regime that regarded its primary duty as guardianship of a fixed territorial appanage confined to the Nile valley, the Syrian littoral, western Arabia (*al-Ḥījāz*), and the marches of southeastern Anatolia. Although suppressing any challenge to its dominance from within this imperial network, the Mamlūk regime eschewed expansion beyond it as a policy fraught with the risks of defeat and the high costs of campaigns. This outlook may seem parochial to contemporary strategists, but it was rooted in practical experience with interstate relations in the central Islamic lands and in the internal idiosyncracies of the Mamlūk institution. The superficial volatility of ties between sovereign polities and their clients did not discredit idealized perspectives they all shared. While competing for suzerainty, regional prominence or dominance of trade routes, few seriously contemplated altering the pattern of interstate politics they had inherited from the High Middle Ages.

In the final decades of the ninth/fifteenth century, concepts of universal empire under the Prophet's caliphal successor, now maintained in Cairo for the sole purpose of legitimating the sultan's office, were manifested in cultural or religious principles mutually respected by most states of the central Muslim world. Previously, local rivalries had not diminished these principles since the temporary ascendance of one regime over its competitors rarely caused profound cultural or religious discontinuity.[3] Indeed, following the invasions from central Asia occurring between 1200 and 1400, resurgent regimes sought to resurrect traditions of cultural unity dating back to the classical era (ca. the seventh to the tenth centuries). Since in the aftermath of this invasion era, change was regarded as more apt to disturb or disorient than to invigorate or renew, most sophisticated governments looked back nostalgically to venerated achievements of a perceived golden age rather than forward toward a future clouded by uncertainties. Maintenance of stasis assured continuity of political systems that promoted the survival of hallowed customs.

Caretaker of the ʿAbbāsid caliph, the Mamlūk sultanate posed as custodian of Sunnism in the tradition of Ṣalāḥ al-Dīn. Although the caliph possessed no tangible authority, his presence sanctified his sovereign's office and enhanced Cairo's claim to primacy of diplomatic protocol over other

[3] See, M. Hodgson, *The Venture of Islam*, II (Chicago, 1974), 329–68, 386–436 for a summation of cultural unity in the central Islamic world during the middle period.

Muslim capitals.[4] Princes or chieftains recently installed by coup often requested formal confirmation of their usurpations from the caliph in Cairo, whose authority to grant such endorsements embellished the sultan's stature as patron-autocrat.[5] During the fourteenth and fifteenth centuries Cairo was acknowledged by Sunnī Muslims as the preeminent seat of legitimate authority, an ironic stature attained by the capital of a regime founded by sedition. Envoys nonetheless ascended to the Citadel to pay their respects and present the sultan with entreaties for support, proposals for regulating trade, requests for safe transit, and pleas for sanctuary from rivals or hostile relatives. When Qānṣūh al-Ghawrī received fourteen emissaries in Rabīʿ II 918/May–June 1512, he no longer ruled a state with unchallenged primacy throughout southwest Asia. Yet so deeply ingrained was Cairo's diplomatic stature that these representatives, ranging from couriers sent by Turkoman aghās concerned over restive neighbors to the French ambassador seeking trade concessions, automatically accorded its ruler the highest rank among Muslim suzerains.[6] Mamlūk sultans, many of whom had seized their thrones by sedition, cherished the prestige they enjoyed in consequence of nurturing the Commander of Believers. His presence in the capital symbolized the esteemed traditions from a past era they sought to emulate.

The military oligarchy ruling Egypt and Syria was composed of slave-soldiers imported from abroad who required years of rigorous training to perform their allotted functions. Due to the expense of their purchase and schooling, the regime guarded its investment by avoiding battlefield losses. The paucity of campaigns abroad by Mamlūk armies after Sultan Qalāwūn's death in 689/1290 underscores the sultanate's reluctance to squander its precious reserve of troops. The Mamlūk regime often brandished its martial readiness in symbolic displays before visiting dignitaries, but exhausted all the diplomatic ploys its chancery could devise in dissuading such dignitaries from pursuing armed conflict. Few doubted the combat effectiveness of the Mamlūk army if the regime were obliged to use it, and theatrically staged shows of strength usually sufficed to dampen a rival's enthusiasm for open confrontation.[7]

[4] P. M. Holt, "Some Observations on the ʿAbbasid Caliphate of Cairo," *BSOAS*, 47 (1984), 501–07; P. Thorau, *Sultan Baibars I. von Ägypten* (Wiesbaden, 1987), 131–42.

[5] Jumādā II 876/November–December 1471: the ambassador from the sultan of Delhi requests a diploma of confirmation from the caliph: al-Ṣayrafī, *Inbāʾ al-Haṣr bi-Abnāʾ al-ʿAṣr* (Cairo, 1970), 362; Ibn Iyās, *Badāʾiʿ al-Zuhūr fī Waqāʾiʿ al-Duhūr*, IV (Cairo, 1963), 65.

[6] *Badāʾiʿ*, IV, 255, 257–58.

[7] Rabīʿ I 873/September–October 1468: Qāytbāy invites emissaries of Uzun Ḥasan, the ruler of the Aqqoyunlū confederacy, the sultan of Ḥind and other foreign princes to attend a troop review; see *Inbāʾ*, 18; D. Ayalon, "Notes on the Furūsiyya Exercises and Games of the Mamlūk Sultanate," *Scripta Hierosolymitana, Studies in Islamic History and Civilization 9 (1961)*, 31–62.

In the light of these motives for caution and restraint, the principles of Mamlūk statecraft acquired their rationale in the circumstances of regional politics prevailing in the sultanate's final decades. These may be summarized as: affirmation of coexistence, negotiation of disputes, acceptance of mutually defined spheres of influence, and acknowledgment of strategic and commercial interests superseding political or doctrinal differences between states. Officials in the Mamlūk chancery observed nuanced distinctions between coexistence and peace. The former implied resignation to the reality of a potential adversary's presence without according it formal recognition. This flexibility of approach enabled the Mamlūk chancery to treat with any state whose objectives coincided with its own, while expending little time soul-searching over that state's ideology or confession. This commitment to coexistence provided the regime with a convenient means of bypassing declaration of jihād, or holy war, against a non-Muslim enemy. As self-proclaimed defenders of orthodoxy, sultans paid lip-service to this venerable principle of communal defense. In practice, they and their aides devised countless means of avoiding it. Implementation of jihād would compromise the regime's imperative of upholding the status quo.

The preceding axioms of statecraft thus aimed at maintaining the balance of power as it had prevailed to the late fifteenth century. Officials of the chancery sought to preserve security by impeding shifts in the established order. The regime wished to sanctify the rank and prerogatives of rulers as they were presently fixed, since the Mamlūk sultan already enjoyed superiority in the hierarchy of regional monarchs and would find his stature diminished in the advent of change. Preservation of equilibrium therefore was cherished as an ideal fundamental to the regime's wellbeing. The sultanate had no taste for deviations from this objective. New ideologies of relations between states, aggressive visions of imperialism, or experiments with untested styles of diplomacy found minimal receptivity. So long as no adversary initiated such experiments, the sultanate managed to maintain a state of equilibrium throughout the central Muslim lands. Yet by the end of the fifteenth century, its competitors were no longer willing to prolong the status quo by playing according to old rules.

Interstate politics during the late sultanate

At the outset of the sixteenth century sweeping changes were transforming the political environment of the eastern Mediterranean and southwest Asia. These changes reflected the ambitions of new actors on the regional stage, energetic polities whose agendas no longer accommodated the Mamlūk sultanate's commitment to stasis. These upstarts in the sultan's view were now converging on Egypt from four fronts: the Ottoman sultanate to the north, restive principalities to the east, and European mariners who asserted themselves in both the Mediterranean and the Red Sea. The Ottomans launched a major campaign against the Mamlūks' vassals in southeastern Anatolia during Sultan Qāytbāy's reign (872–901/1468–96).[8] Although their incursions were repelled, the Sultanate severely strained its already overtaxed resources to equip armies capable of stalling the Ottoman advance. Qāytbāy left his eventual successor al-Ghawrī a bankrupt treasury, the formal resources for which no longer generated revenues sufficient to provide the sums demanded by his troops to maintain security. Few observers in the Citadel expected anything more than a respite from Ottoman expansionism, and when Salīm I succeeded his father Bāyazīd II in 918/1512, he resumed his forebears' pressure against his Muslim neighbors.

Aggression was not monopolized by the Ottomans. Throughout these unsettled decades, ambitious dynasts in Iran sought to alter the political map of southwest Asia. The most prominent of these were Uzun Ḥasan (871–83/1466–78) of the White Sheep (Aqqoyunlū) Principality,[9] and Shāh Ismāʿīl (907–30/1501–24), founder of the Ṣafavid monarchy.[10] While neither posed a challenge comparable to that of the Ottomans, Cairo could not dismiss their hostile stance. Qānṣūh al-Ghawrī resisted his recruits' demands for steep campaign bonuses during much of his reign, but when the Ṣafavids crossed the Euphrates into the northern marches of his realm in Jumādā I 913/September–October 1507, he submitted.[11] The combat readiness of his troops, dependent almost totally on their satisfaction with stipends, could not be jeopardized.

And, finally, the Europeans now posed a menace to Egypt's long-standing monopoly over its lucrative trade in spices and luxury goods imported from South Asia. European pirates had harassed the Levant throughout the ninth/fifteenth century, but when the Portuguese sailed around the African continent to traverse the Indian Ocean and penetrate the Red Sea, the Mamlūk regime saw itself caught in an alien vice. The sultanate devised no

[8] On Ottoman aggression against the Dhu'l-Qādrid principality in southwestern Anatolia see Ibn Taghrī-Birdī, *Ḥawādith al-Duhūr fī Madā al-Ayyām wa'l-Shuhār* 7, part 4 (Berkeley, 1942), 650, 709; *Inbā'*, 69, 162, 199, 214; ʿAbd al-Bāsiṭ al-Malaṭī, *al-Rawḍ al-Bāsim fī Ḥawādith al-ʿUmr wa'l-Tarājim* ms. (Vatican arabo, 729), ff. 221–b, 250–b; S. Har-El, *The Struggle for Domination in the Middle East: the Ottoman-Mamlūk War, 1485–1491* (Leiden, 1995).

[9] J. Woods, *The Aqqoyunlū: Clan, Confederation, Empire* (Chicago, 1976).

[10] H. Rabie, "Political Relations between the Ṣafavids of Persia and the Mamlūks of Egypt and Syria in the early Sixteenth Century," *JARCE*, 15 (1978), 75–81; A. Allouche, *The Origins and Development of the Ottoman-Ṣafavid Conflict* (Berlin, 1983); H. R. Roemer, "The Safavid Period," *CHI*, 6 (New York, 1986), 189–350; W. W. Clifford, "Some Observations on the Course of Mamlūk-Ṣafavī Relations (1502–1516/908–922), *Der Islam*, 70, 2 (1993), 245–65, 266–78; J. Aubin, "La politique orientale de Selim Ier," in Raoul Curiel and Rika Gyselen (eds.), *Res orientales 6: Itinéraires d'orient, hommages à Claude Cahen* (Burres-sur-Yvette, 1994), 203–05.

[11] *Badā'iʿ* IV, 118.

effective strategy for regaining its dominance over the Red Sea.[12] The presence of European ships, which had appeared from regions uncharted by any medieval Islamic state, shook the regime's confidence in its future profits from the commerce that had supplied such copious revenues in the past. Qānṣūh al-Ghawrī was keenly aware of his inability to cope with Portuguese raids against his previously invulnerable southern front.

These forces, converging simultaneously on the Mamlūk sultanate at the close of the fifteenth century, raised challenges the static orientation of Mamlūk foreign policy could not surmount. Despite its long-standing posture as a bulwark of stability in the central Muslim world, the sultanate ultimately succumbed to the Ottoman invaders under the meteoric leadership of Salim I in 922/1516.[13]

Conservatism and adaptation in the military institution

The intensification of foreign threats was not accepted with resignation by the ruling oligarchy in Cairo. Nor did the Mamlūk institution wither away in the aftermath of defeat. Rather, in the face of mounting catastrophe, Qānṣūh al-Ghawrī and his colleagues began experimenting with innovations noteworthy for their short-term ingenuity if not their long-term effectiveness. These experiments demonstrate the capacity of the Mamlūk institution to adapt to trying circumstances. The seeming paradox of creative adaptability by a conservative military caste committed to stasis may, upon examination, shed light on its survival into the future centuries of Ottoman dominion in Egypt.

Why was this paradox of conservatism and adaptability, stasis and innovation, so salient a feature of Mamlūk policy-making? In large measure, it resulted from the military institution's preoccupation with internal factionalism, but in the context of pragmatic self-preferment rather than a rigid commitment to conservatism as an ideology. If judged by its longevity, the Mamlūk sultanate surely ranks among the more successful political experiments in Islamic history. While developing from the ad hoc stratagems of its founders, the military institution did not transcend the personal ties of a barracks culture that delimited its political identity. These ties existed on two levels: between military peers, a relationship of equals, and between military patrons and their civilian clients, a relationship of subordinates. Such bonds proved extremely durable, at once promoting and yet superseding the interfactional rivalries built into the Mamlūk system of power

[12] C. Petry, "Holy War, Unholy Peace? Relations between the Mamlūk Sultanate and European States prior to the Ottoman Conquest," in H. Dajani-Shakeel and R. Messier (eds.), *The Jihad and its Times* (Ann Arbor, 1991), 106–09; J. L. Abu-Lughod, *Before European Hegemony: The World System* AD *1250–1350* (Oxford, 1989).

[13] See Chapter 18.

distribution. Due to its brokerage of power through feuding, the military institution had little incentive to alter its long-standing methods of military training since, first, these had proved effective against foreign enemies and local rebels during the sultanate's ascendant period, and, second, they had augmented the hegemonic status of the ruling caste.[14] For many decades, this political system had sustained the objectives of the ruling elite. Yet by the sultanate's final years, the dilemmas created by Mamlūk conservatism outweighed its benefits, at least from the ruling oligarchy's perspective.

From what conditions did these dilemmas stem? They emerged from the behavior of the sultan's own soldiers, ideally the edifice upon which he relied for the defense of his realm and safety of his person. In fact, by al-Ghawrī's reign, the mamlūk troops had become an interest group whose field reliability was dubious but whose propensity for revolt was endemic. The chronicles compiled from daily accounts of events in Cairo during the sultanate's final decades tell a tale of unremitting pressure on the monarch for payments in return for a modicum of domestic tranquility. Pillaging by his mamlūk recruits (*julbān*) greeted al-Ghawrī on the day of his accession;[15] the trainees burned the palaces of five senior officers, a gesture of their irritation over their perception of low wages they sporadically received, in contrast with the immense fortunes grand amīrs routinely amassed. The recruits' rebellions were invariably linked to calls for stipend increases and bonus payments.

The unrest of these troops in the regime's final decades may bespeak an unresolvable impasse confronting the sultanate. Ever since the time of Ṣalāḥ al-Dīn (564–89/1169–93), Egypt's fisc was organized with funding the army as its first priority. But by the mid-fifteenth century, mamlūk soldiers were progressively less content with the amounts allotted them. Since to them the sultan was no more than a peer, one of their own whom fate and mutual interest had granted ultimate authority, they held him in little regal awe. From their perspective, the sultan served them as a benefactor who assured their monopoly of military force and maintained their expensive stipends as his prime duties. If he failed to fulfill their expectations, the sultan could expect calculated delays to his calls for service, rioting that disrupted commerce, and support for his opponents' plots to supplant him.[16]

Several of the revolts that erupted during al-Ghawrī's reign paralyzed commerce in Cairo and left whole districts in ruins. The message these episodes of sedition conveyed to the autocrat, duty-bound to maintain order

14 D. Ayalon, *Gunpowder and Firearms in the Mamluk Kingdom* (London, 1956), ch. 3; R. Irwin, *The Middle East in the Middle Ages: The Early Mamluk Sultanate, 1250–1382* (London, 1986), 152–59.

15 *Badāʾiʿ*, IV, 5.

16 References to riots, refusals to drill or open revolt occupy roughly a third of Ibn Iyās's annals of al-Ghawrī's reign (*Badāʾiʿ*, IV and V).

for his civilian subjects who bore the regime's costs, was clear. His soldiers now determined the state of domestic peace rather than he. Were their perceptions of underpayment and tarnished prestige to go unredressed, they could make routine administration impossible for the sultan. Regardless of whether the recruits' sense of betrayal was warranted by payments that had fallen precipitously as a consequence of an irreversible decline in the economy, their anger alarmed the autocrat who could no longer garner funds from traditional sources to appease their demands. He therefore had ample reason to fear the restrictions on his own authority imposed by his troopers' hostility and his straitened finances.

The men who presided over the sultanate's final decades were incessantly reminded of their precarious status. In the face of potential sedition from both officers and recruits, they regarded personal survival as their own prime objective. Each sultan of the late Mamlūk period lived with the prospect of deposition, exile and even assassination.[17] Those who eventually consolidated their accessions had themselves plotted to remove opponents who preceded them in ephemeral reigns. Given the ethos of conspiracy permeating the Mamlūk political process, no recently installed autocrat could afford to ignore the likelihood of his own transience. Until the accession of Qānṣūh al-Ghawrī, this paranoia compelled new autocrats to attempt a purge of their predecessors' adjutants and to assemble a host of new retainers recruited from traditional cadres of military personnel. The former had to be disbanded before they could transform their latent antipathy into active revolt, while the latter's cohesion and loyalty had to be coaxed by favoritism lavish enough to dissuade them from heeding the enticements of their patron's competitors.[18]

According to mamlūk caste values, loyalty was conditioned by circumstance rather than rooted in affection. Ever fluctuating according to designs of factions competing for executive supremacy, support by retainers was purchased, just at they themselves had been bought – at high cost. Loyalty carried a price, and the patron who bid the highest readily transcended ties nurtured by years of intimate association between cadets within the barracks.[19] These tensions between ambition and camaraderie had shaped the military elite's concept of power and how it was shared. No autocrat

[17] U. Haarmann, "Miṣr: the Mamlūk Period, 1250–1517," *EI2*, VIII, 174–77; C. Petry, *Protectors*, 88–93.

[18] *Badā'i'* IV, 250 (al-Ghawrī hosts his officers at a lavish reception), 358 (al-Ghawrī rewards his *khaṣṣakī* bodyguards). For background on patron-client relations, see E. Gellner, "Patrons and Clients," in Ernest Gellner and John Waterbury (eds.), *Patrons and Clients in Mediterranean Societies* (London, 1977), 1–6; C. H. Landé, "The Dyadic Basis of Clientism," in Steffen W. Schmidt (ed.), *Friends, Followers and Factions: A Reader in Political Clientism* (Berkeley, 1977), xiii–xxxvii.

[19] See A. Levanoni, *A Turning Point in Mamlūk History: The Third Reign of al-Nāṣir Muḥammad ibn Qalāwūn (1310–1340)* (Leiden, 1995), for an analysis of the

was allowed to rise above the limits placed upon his office by his subordinates. Few before Qānṣūh al-Ghawrī seem to have envisioned the need to do so.

The constraints imposed upon the autocrat's authority in the sultanate's last years were complicated further by subtle changes in his relationship with civilian clients. By the time of al-Ghawrī's enthronement, the autocrat presided over a hierarchy of civil officials whose titles grandiosely proclaimed their formal duties. These overt functions did not embrace the services their patron regarded as essential, however. Bureaucracies of states in the central Muslim regions were composed of malleable coteries of retainers bound to their employers by either camaraderie, if they were military peers, or patronage, if they were learned civilians. Although the relationships underlying such ties did not evolve according to principles of legal interaction as they had developed in medieval Europe, they nonetheless created a finely tuned balance between mutual interest and coercive dependence.

A civilian client was willing to subordinate himself to a military patron because the latter granted him access to influence and wealth otherwise closed to an individual from his social station. A client's usefulness in his patron's service was measured by the information he provided, the social sectors he manipulated or the funds he procured. The extent to which he succeeded at these often clandestine tasks augmented his status in the sultan's bureaucracy. But the higher a client, often of humble origins, rose in royal service the more susceptible he became to his patron's whims. For the power such a client wielded never attained the enforceable authority jealously guarded by the military elite as a prerogative of imperial custodianship over its appanage.

These conditions of service and sponsorship were discernible for centuries before the late Mamlūk period. They were not unique to the imperial bureaucracy based in Cairo. But when Qānṣūh al-Ghawrī consolidated his position after a strenuous probation marked by bitter factional disputes, he regarded his civilian aides in ways that differed from his predecessors' attitudes toward their clients. These contrasts were due to vexing predicaments confronting al-Ghawrī and his senior officers as they attempted to meet the inflating fiscal demands of their soldiers.

Financial dilemmas and the augmentation of clientism

By the late ninth/fifteenth century, the economy of the Mamlūk sultanate delivered lower sums of revenue from its traditional productive sectors than

transformation in recruitment and promotion within the Mamlūk army imposed by this sultan.

in earlier periods. Contemporary chroniclers were aware of this decline, and commented on both processes and perceived causes at length.[20] While the explanations they offered – in particular the deleterious consequences of debased coinage or labor shortages resulting from plague mortality – cannot be discounted, other causes which they glossed over or ignored altogether are detectable upon scrutiny of surviving evidence. By the late fifteenth century, assetholders in the three primary productive sectors of the economy – agriculture, commerce (foreign and domestic) and artisan craftsmanship – had refined their skills at deflecting the regime's demands for revenue and commodities. Their ploys involved procedures of concealment, hoarding and bribery in return for release from taxes. The narrative sources of the late Mamlūk period abound with references to individuals of means summoned before tribunals of inquiry convened by their overlords to investigate disclaimers of secreted wealth.[21] Indeed, the frequency of such protests looms so large in the narrative literature that both contemporary observers and more recent historians have been led to assume a genuine decline in the productivity of the sultanate in the decades preceding the Ottoman conquest.[22]

But in fact, if summations of harvest yields, commercial vitality (before the Portuguese termination of the Mamlūk monopoly over trade from south Asia) or artisan production are considered, the presumption of decline is qualified by an impression of continued wellbeing even in the face of sporadic plague epidemics, Bedouin marauding and foreign encroachment. The narrative sources do indicate a drop in yields from the traditional sources of revenue which were relied on by the sultanate to maintain its military preparedness and sustain its standard of living. Taxes on agrarian districts or urban properties, tolls on caravans arriving at border stations or imposed on ship cargoes in coastal ports were reported as significantly lower than they had been in the sultanate's heyday during the first half of the eighth/fourteenth century.[23]

The ruling oligarchy, which acted as an advisory council of senior officers assembled by the sultan, cannot have been ignorant of either the diminution in formal revenues available to them or the tactics used by assetholders to escape their obligatory payments. It is in this context of the oligarchy's growing consternation over the prospect of monies insufficient to maintain

[20] Petry, *Protectors*, ch. 5; A. Allouche, *Mamlūk Economics, A Study and Translation of al-Maqrīzī's Ighāthah* (Salt Lake City, 1994).

[21] Petry, *Protectors*, 166–73.

[22] E. Ashtor, *A Social and Economic History of the Near East in the Middle Ages* (Berkeley, 1976), 329–31; S. Labib, *Handelsgeschichte Ägyptens im Spätmittelalter (1171–1517)* (Wiesbaden, 1965), chs. 9 and 10.

[23] Ibn Iyās (*Badā'i'*, IV, 423) remarks on the decline of Alexandria in the late Mamlūk period, its condition symptomatic of the regime's diminished revenue base.

the regime that the sultanate's own stratagems for ameliorating its predicament must be examined. The role of the civilian client would be adjusted to meet the altered circumstances of his service. The oligarchy refined a host of clandestine procedures for garnering revenues, in which such clients played a pivotal role. While these measures were not openly discussed in the abstract by contemporary observers, incidents alluding to their practice occurred so frequently that their characteristics may be deduced.[24]

Civilian clients were appointed to high posts in the imperial *dīwān*s because of the lucrative opportunities these offices provided. Illicit gain from a *dīwān* post took many forms. Assetholders might be pressured for kickback payments in return for lowering their tax obligations. Accounts of bureaux dispensing large budgets could be falsified to draw off percentages from their legitimate recipients. Receipts from tariff- or toll-collecting agencies might be reduced, leaving differences to be divided between client and sponsor. Chances for embezzlement, whether minor or substantial, increased if a bureaucrat had mastered the collection techniques of his *dīwān* – and courted the loyalty of his subordinates by sharing his take with them. Whatever his methods, the tactics of such a client deliberately placed by his patron in a *dīwān* to procure funds were enhanced if he controlled several offices at once.

The spread of multiple officeholding during the late Mamlūk period paralleled the heightened importance of covert services *dīwān* staff performed, especially under the conditions of endemic fiscal crisis burdening the sultanate.[25] The same person often administered both the revenue-receiving and dispensing operations of a bureau, laundering accounts with little risk of detection – unless his sponsor were to expose him. Surreptitious hoarding of revenue by *dīwān* staff certainly antedated the late sultanate. Yet the frequency of multiple officeholding reported in the biographical and narrative sources throughout this period implies its integral relationship to the process.

Clients serving as functionaries in the revenue *dīwān*s offered their sponsors large sums on a reliable schedule of delivery. Yet given the prospect of revolts by troops demanding pay increases as an inducement to depart on a campaign, the regime resorted to sweeping confiscations of revenues hoarded by assetholders. The ubiquity of confiscation is a constant in the policies of regimes governing Egypt and Syria throughout the Middle Ages. During the late Mamlūk period, however, the procedures of confiscation were elaborated. Two hypotheses may shed light on this transformation of

24 References to fiscal crisis occupy approximately one-third of total entries in chronicles of the late period.

25 B. Martel-Thoumian, *Les civils et l'administration dans l'état militaire mamlūk (ixe/xve siècle)* (Damascus, 1991), 92–97; C. Petry, *The Civilian Elite of Cairo in the Later Middle Ages* (Princeton, 1981), 201–04.

an ad hoc expedient into a sophisticated policy: that revenue producers had devised an array of tactics to conceal their wealth within a web of institutional shelters, and that the ruling oligarchy was alert to the practice of these ploys.

Historians of Mamlūk society during the later Middle Ages have noted the frequent incidence of practices that sheltered revenue-yielding property from direct taxation by the central government, a phenomenon paralleled by a marked propensity on the part of the ruling elite's own membership to alienate, as personal patrimonies, grants of agrarian land (*iqṭāʿāt*) bestowed temporarily for military service.[26] The former was apparent in the proliferation of endowments (*awqāf*) established ostensibly to support charitable trusts. In the civilian context, the significance of charitable trusts was apparent in the perspective of scholars appointed to the custodianship of the wealthy religio-academic institutions of the capital and elsewhere. During the late Mamlūk period, these scholars (*ʿulamāʾ*) who served as rectors and trust supervisors of the mosques (*jawāmiʿ*), colleges (*madāris*), mystic hospices (*khānaqāh*), hospitals (*bīmāristānāt*), orphanages (*rubuṭ al-aytām*) and retirement hospices (*zawāyā*) of Cairo jealously guarded both the operational autonomy and the fiscal integrity of the institutions entrusted to their stewardship. For its part, the regime increasingly regarded the accumulated endowments of these institutions – most founded by their own membership – as excessively large and thus ripe for mulcting.

From the reign of al-Ashraf Qāytbāy, yields from endowments of religio-academic institutions had been tapped when the sultan could look nowhere else for the means to mitigate his troops' pressure.[27] Al-Ghawrī moved beyond exigency to opportunism as he made mass-scale confiscation a reliable instrument to raise revenue. The system devised by al-Ghawrī's military adjutants involved scrutinizing affluent families who had dexterously hoarded their assets, fining members of Mamlūk lineages previously exempted as untouchable, and extending the reach of extraction to the commons whose seeming poverty had heretofore spared them the government's attention. The first two aspects of this agenda were elaborations of existing tactics. Civilians who profited from their clientship while retaining an aura of respectability had always been subject to extortion in emergencies. But al-Ghawrī placed several eminent families under continual surveillance, extracting their gains without remorse until they were decimated.

Members of the Jīʿān lineage, one of the wealthiest civilian houses in Cairo, were a salient case. For the decade following the arrest of the family's senior member, Ṣalāḥ al-Dīn Yaḥyā, in 908/1502, the sultan fined several

[26] M. Amin, *Al-Awqāf wa'l-Ḥayāt al-Ijtimāʿiyya fī Miṣr* (Cairo, 1980), 338–41; C. Petry, "Fractionalized Estates in a Centralized Regime: The Holdings of al-Ashraf Qāytbāy and Qānṣūh al-Ghawrī," *JESHO*, 39, 4 (1996), 2.

[27] *Ḥawādith*, IV, 633, 635; *Rawḍ*, f. 181–b; *Badāʾiʿ*, III, 13.

Jīʿānīs more than half a million dīnārs without convicting any of them of corruption. Yet al-Ghawrī kept up his intimidation until the family had divulged its assets. The tactic succeeded, since the Jīʿānīs had indeed secreted a vast fortune which they disclosed only under duress. Yet the residual effect of such experiences on the outlook of propertied sectors in Egyptian society long outlasted al-Ghawrī's agenda of confiscation.

Alert to devices for hoarding assets that both producers and collectors were exploiting, al-Ghawrī and his adjutants broadened the range of confiscations, imposed new taxes, and monitored their subordinates more closely. Al-Ghawrī responded to threats of rebellion by his troops at the start of 907/1502 with a confiscation of sweeping scope.[28] The sultan convened his senior officers, each commanding a host of armed retainers, to assign their extorsive duties. The marshal (*atābak*) assumed responsibility for summoning *waqf* supervisors and fief (*iqṭāʿ*) holders. Pensioners, including widows and orphaned daughters, were interrogated by the exchequer (*wakīl bayt al-māl*). Owners of houses, tenements and rented shops were rounded up by the executive adjutant (*dawādār*). Any assetholder who ignored his summons was examined by a tribunal. A group of lesser officers, under the supervision of the aforementioned commanders, proceeded to interrogate wealthy families and canvass Cairo's quarters. Their searches eventually degenerated into a riot of looting by slaves and street gangs following in the extorters' wake. Despite the resultant devastation, these measures produced copious sums.

Al-Ghawrī collected 500,000 dīnārs, a combination of ten months' worth of *waqf* yields turned over by mosques threatened with closure and the pensions of their retirees. His take temporarily covered the troops' stipend demands, and he could complete his consolidation of authority unburdened by further sedition. Disruptions on this scale might depress the economy and traumatize the populace, but the sultan's survival rested on his soldiers' sufferance. Mass confiscations therefore remained a viable option for al-Ghawrī to the end of his reign. Chroniclers of al-Ghawrī's generation and after berated him for oppression of this kind. And yet, objectively considered, his tactics were effective. They generated the revenues necessary to secure his position, and potential clients did not shy away from al-Ghawrī's service, despite the near certainty of their exposure to public censure and draconian punishment. By purging those who succeeded to excess or who failed to share what they had extorted according to their patron's expectations, al-Ghawrī could defuse the ire of his soldiers. So odious were some of his client-agents in their eyes that sham arrests or temporary exiles no longer satisfied the troops' desire for revenge.

By themselves, such tactics could not resolve the broader dilemmas that

[28] *Badāʾiʿ*, IV, 14.

underlay al-Ghawrī's chronic insolvency and consequent insecurity. Assetholders continued to discover new ways of concealing their wealth. To appreciate the complexities of these dilemmas, both the military institution's commitment to beneficence and the innovative policies adopted by al-Ghawrī to turn beneficence to his own profit – and thereby rescue him from reliance on soldiers whom he regarded as a potential nemesis – must be examined.

Beneficence in the late Mamlūk period: public welfare, private insurance

Perhaps even more paradoxical than the simultaneity of intimidation and intimacy in patron-client relations was the concurrence of generosity and extortion by the Mamlūk caste. Often acting as if their realm were a personal fief to be exploited at will, the Mamlūks also sponsored with their plundered assets welfare agencies remarkable for their beneficence in the lean conditions of the late sultanate. As the wealthiest social class, and possessing the largest aggregates of income-yielding property, the military elite functioned as the prime guarantors of charity in medieval Egyptian society. Why were the Mamlūks willing to sustain high levels of patronage in the face of the financial predicaments noted in preceding sections of this chapter? The reasons have to do with the military elite's overt sense of religious obligation, which they took seriously, and their covert fear of destitution through dispossession. Formal custodianship of faith and communal solidarity behind canons of belief endorsed by the *'ulamā'* was, to be sure, a primary duty the Mamlūks assumed from their Ayyūbid predecessors. As self-proclaimed guardians of Sunnī Islam, the Mamlūks regarded themselves as benefactors, a calling enjoined upon them by God. This divine avocation mitigated the origins of their regime in usurpation, and compensated at least in part for the turbulence of their factional rivalries.

The military elite consequently invested in a wide range of charitable foundations, scholastic institutions, houses of worship and welfare services. Scholars have reflected with awe and admiration on the profusion of Sultan Qāytbāy's donations, for example.[29] The legacy of Qāytbāy's charitable endowments confirms the dedication of this pious believer to the idealized responsibilities of his office, a commitment revered in his own time and honored in future centuries.

The beneficent foundations in Cairo established or enhanced by Qāytbāy, al-Ghawrī and their associates continued to engage the most luminous scholars in the central Islamic lands. The satisfaction felt by these men over

[29] Petry, *Protectors*, 158–61; A. W. Newhall, "The Patronage of the Mamluk Sultan Qa'itbay, 872–901/1468–1496" (Ph.D. dissertation, Harvard University, 1987).

their proprietorship of this assemblage of literati cannot be denied. Qāytbāy found his attendance at recitations of canonical Ḥadīth collections during the Prophet's birthday (*ʿĪd al-mawlid*) powerfully inspiring, while al-Ghawrī took pride in hearing the eloquent Friday sermons (*khuṭbas*) preached by respected jurists he invited to grace his mausoleum mosque.[30] Ira Lapidus has noted a diminished capacity of the Mamlūk elite based in the provincial capitals of Damascus or Aleppo to sustain their clerical and scholastic enterprises during the second half of the fifteenth century because of the shrinking assets at their disposal.[31] In Cairo, by contrast, despite the fiscal shortfalls confronting the ruling oligarchy, its sponsorship of religious service and high scholarship did not appreciably decline. The endowment deeds (*ḥujaj al-awqāf*) from this period that were drawn up by senior members of the Mamlūk caste indicate no significant reduction in either posts or stipends aimed at nurturing the *ʿulamāʾ* in Cairo. Even during the sultanate's last decades, so burdened with factional turmoil and sporadic pestilence, the *ʿulamāʾ* sustained their copious output of literary material.

Yet the proliferation of these endowment deeds in the late period, and the increased elaboration of their provisos governing allocation of assets for operational staff and donors' beneficiaries, suggest a heightened concern by the military elite for sheltering their property. This concern, vividly apparent as one reads the carefully scripted stipulations about estate integrity in the *waqf* deeds, underscores the fear of destitution shared by all members of the military institution in the late sultanate. Preserving one's wealth in land or property from the endemic risk of predation by peer rivals became an obsession of the Mamlūk elite. They saw in the charitable trust a measure of insurance that no other legal instrument could offer. The *waqf* endowment therefore had become the military elite's favored repository for assets which they had accumulated by legal purchase or illicit alienation. Sultans Qāytbāy and al-Ghawrī invested massively in such endowments.[32] Formally granted for the welfare of the Muslim community, these documents, under scrutiny, reveal strategies of asset protection their donors did not openly acknowledge. These tactics so closely parallel the fiscal dilemmas confronting both men that their interrelationship cannot be regarded as coincidental.[33] Their implications qualify the charitable purposes for which trusts were set up, as

30 *Badāʾiʿ*, III, 200; IV, 236.

31 I. Lapidus, *Muslim Cities in the Later Middle Ages* (Cambridge, 1967), 34–43, 75–78.

32 M. Amin, *Catalogue des documents d'archives du Caire de 239/853 à 922/1516* (Cairo, 1981): thirty-seven documents for Qāytbāy (twenty-two in support of fourteen foundations), main writ: #475, Wizārat al-Awqāf (WA) 886 *qadīm*; thirty-nine for his spouse Fāṭima al-Khaṣṣbakiyya; 303 for al-Ghawrī, main writ: #652, WA 882 *qadīm*.

33 Amin, *Awqāf*, 320–72 (institutional background); L. Fernandes, "Some Aspects of the Zāwiya in Egypt at the Eve of the Ottoman Conquest," *AI*, 19 (1983), 9–17; *The Evolution of a Sufi Institution in Mamluk Egypt: the Khanqah* (Berlin, 1988).

well as the options for Egypt's creative exploitation of its resources at the end of the Middle Ages.

The clandestine measures for extracting revenues from covert sources discussed previously boded ill for the cohesion of estates. Property holders, civilian or military, were sensitive to such measures since they had applied them themselves. The proliferation of investments in charitable trusts must be interpreted in part as an expression of their alarm. The *waqf* endowment represented the safest haven for fixed assets sanctioned by Islamic law. Once granted to promote the communal welfare, a trust stood above the will of temporal authorities in perpetuity. Ideally, its provisos as set out by its donor could not be obstructed. In practice, Muslim regimes seized the yields from *waqf* properties under circumstances of pressing need such as an impending menace from abroad requiring a costly muster of armed forces. But even in an emergency, a ruler who tampered with *awqāf* invited the condemnation of the religious establishment he was sworn to protect. Moreover, he set a dangerous precedent regarding his own patrimony which he hoped to leave for his descendants. In Mamlūk Egypt, mass *waqf* alienation occurred infrequently until the period under consideration. Until the reign of al-Ghawrī, appropriation of *waqf* deeds occurred intermittently, usually as a response to crisis. Accordingly, in the unsettled financial environment of the late sultanate, locking one's property in a trust with elaborate stipulations governing its supervision by a donor's heirs offered no absolute guarantee of permanence. No formal proviso could preclude interference under some guise by an agent of the regime. But a trust endured as the safest haven available, and the most likely to perpetuate a personal fortune over time.

Given the restriction of an officer's claim to a portion of state domains (*milk* or *dīwān* lands, allotted as *iqṭāʿāt* during the Ayyūbid and Mamlūk periods) to usufruct rather than ownership, the military elite exploited the charitable trust as a convenient means of acquiring title to state properties and thereby providing a legacy for their heirs.[34] That the assets placed under *waqf* were in principle tax-free enhanced their appeal. Yields were spared from or subjected to taxation according to regional policies, but properties stipulated in a deed as the source of such proceeds remained immune to assure the endowment's indefinite productivity.[35] And a charitable trust generated secure income. Only fixed property qualified for investment in a *waqf*, in a fashion assuring a dependable return. The trust was not intended to promote aggressive capital growth, but rather to ensure support of a beneficial service. To individuals, either military patrons or civilian clients, who regarded their wealth as ripe for confiscation by the regime, provision

[34] "Fractionalized Estates," 17–20.
[35] Amin, *Awqāf*, 90–95.

of a dependable legacy for their descendants took precedence over other options for investment that exposed their assets to risk while augmenting their return more aggressively.

This attitude toward the preservation rather than the enlargement of assets thus restricted the options open to the Mamlūk elite and their civilian aides for risk-oriented but high-yielding investments.[36] The exploitation of the charitable trust by all prominent property holders may have contributed to the peculiar course of capital accumulation in the late sultanate. Limited at present to be the object of speculation, this issue merits further investigation as an aspect of Egypt's economic development on the eve of the Ottoman conquest.

The innovations of Qānṣūh al-Ghawrī

When al-Ghawrī was enthroned, his regime could no longer exert its authority according to past procedures. Al-Ghawrī was obliged of necessity to implement tentative, yet daring, innovations in gunpowder weaponry, troop recruitment and revenue enhancement. These experiments had not progressed beyond preliminary phases when al-Ghawrī was forced to place them in abeyance to confront the aggression of Sultan Salīm I (918–26/1512–20). He may not himself have proceeded beyond the inchoate in his own thinking about their applications to issues not directly related to the crises he faced. How alert al-Ghawrī was to their long-range implications for the future development of the military institution in Egypt cannot be determined. The narrative authors, who commented profusely on al-Ghawrī's actions, described no coherent plan when they mentioned his innovations, often as asides to their denunciations of the sultan's oppressive measures.[37] Al-Ghawrī rattled the sensibilities of his contemporaries because he displayed little respect for the privileges that notables, both military and civilian, expected as rights of class. Indeed, one suspects that their ambivalence toward his reign owed more to its disregard for class privilege than to its deviance from established custom.

Qānṣūh al-Ghawrī's career was anomalous. Having attained the sultanate at the age of sixty after years of arduous patrols in Syria and on the Anatolian frontier, he disdained cementing personal ties with colleagues he

[36] See chapter 12; Petry, *Protectors*, 113–17; C. Petry, "Class Solidarity vs. Gender Gain: Women as Custodians of Property in Later Medieval Egypt," in N. R. Keddie and B. Baron (eds.), *Women in Middle Eastern History; Shifting Boundaries in Sex and Gender* (New Haven, 1991), 129–37; J.-C. Garcin and M. A. Taher, "Enquête sur le financement d'un *waqf* égyptien du XVe siècle: les comptes de Jawhar al-Lālā," *JESHO*, 38, 3 (1995), 262–304 for a study of investment strategies employed by the donor of one large *waqf* from the Circasssian period.

[37] al-Ḥalabī, *Kitāb Durr al-Habab fī Ta'rīkh A'yān Ḥalab*, II, pt. 1, 48; *Badā'i'*, IV, 103.

counted as companions as well as advocates. Al-Ghawrī was a solitary, minimally imbued with the values of camaraderie (*khushdāshiyya*) that shaped the outlook of trainees who entered the barracks as adolescents. Yet this man was also a connoisseur of verse who authored respected compositions and invited esteemed poets to recite their work publicly in the Citadel.[38] He understood the symbolic utility of ceremonials and staged them frequently at the court and throughout Cairo. The prolonged adversities al-Ghawrī encountered before he consolidated his position left him a cynical realist, ready to repudiate ties of loyalty or pledges of honor if expedience warranted.[39] But even the sultan's detractors acknowledged his adroit responses to the endemic crises he faced throughout his reign. However draconian al-Ghawrī's methods of pursuing his goals, few disputed their dampening of potential conspiracy. And he was prepared to attempt innovations his predecessors did not contemplate.

Of the three novel policies discernible in al-Ghawrī's actions, his attempts to perfect the use of artillery and muskets (more properly, arquebuses) attracted the most attention from contemporary observers. Trials with artillery predated al-Ghawrī's reign, having been initiated sporadically under Qāytbāy.[40] This tradition-bound sultan marginally appreciated the future advantages of artillery for his own military effectiveness or the potential danger from foreign opponents perfecting its use. Al-Ghawrī, by contrast, was aware of both and allowed neither failure in trials nor derision from his subordinates to deter him. Al-Ghawrī's attempts at achieving a viable artillery unit impressed spectators as absurd, and caused its sponsor vexation. His sustained efforts, however, confirm al-Ghawrī's growing concern over his vulnerability in the context of changes in military technology throughout Europe and in the Ottoman state.[41] Al-Ghawrī persisted with artillery testing despite repeated failures and his adjutants' skepticism. From Rajab 913/November–December 1507 to the last months before he departed for Aleppo in 922/1516 to confront Salīm, al-Ghawrī ordered artillery pieces to be cast at a foundry in Cairo and had them transported to the former sultan al-ʿĀdil Ṭūmānbāy's mausoleum at al-Raydāniyya north of the city where they could be fired. From whom his engineers acquired their models the primary chronicler of al-Ghawrī's reign, Ibn Iyās, did not say. But because of incessant clashes with European mariners whose ships were outfitted with cannons, the sultanate had opportunities to obtain specimens. Although techniques of molding brass or iron pieces capable of withstanding

38 Mehmet Yelsin, "Dīvān-i Qānṣawh al-Ghawrī: A Critical Edition of an Anthology of Turkish Poetry Commissioned by Sultan Qānṣawh al-Ghawrī (1501–1516)" (Ph.D. dissertation, Harvard University, 1993).

39 *Badāʾiʿ*, IV, 19, 23, 67.

40 *Inbāʾ*, 271.

41 Ayalon, *Gunpowder*, 48–52.

discharges without shattering remained elusive, al-Ghawrī did not skimp on materials or personnel. Indeed, the vast size of his early weapons rendered them almost immobile.[42]

Once they arrived at test sites, pieces often failed their trial detonations. When al-Ghawrī invited his entourage to witness a firing two years earlier on 13 Jumādā II 916/September 17, 1510, "not a single unit held up."[43] All fifteen exploded, scattering shrapnel. The debacle so depressed the sultan that he canceled the celebratory banquet he had planned. But tests continued on a regular basis; by mid-917/August 1511 units were withstanding detonations and their accuracy had improved.[44] Al-Ghawrī ordered the casting of large numbers of artillery pieces, and in Muḥarram of 922/February–March 1516 he sent off 200 which had successfully been fired to garrison Alexandria.[45]

Yet given his success at casting cannons, al-Ghawrī equivocated over their purpose. Ready to deploy them in his Suez campaign in concert with the Ottomans against the Portuguese advancing up the Red Sea, he withheld them from his expedition against Salīm in Syria. Since the Ottomans seized the advantage at Marj Dābiq after they fired their artillery and muskets on the Mamlūk cavalry, al-Ghawrī's omission could be interpreted as a strategic error. But so unyielding was opposition to any departure from traditional combat modes within his regular army that the sultan might have feared exacerbating rebellious sentiments already festering if he forced his troops to serve with artillery units. The logistics of hauling such heavy pieces overland may also have caused him to hesitate. Whatever his reasons, al-Ghawrī never tested his elaborate experiment in artillery on the battlefield. But in view of the hostility of his Mamlūk soldiers toward any experiments in new technology, was al-Ghawrī disposed to seek their replacement?

In mid-916/January 1511, Ibn Iyās began mentioning a "Fifth Corps" (*al-ṭabaqa al-khāmisa*) of infantrymen drawn from non-Mamlūk personnel.[46] The narrative sources did not dwell on its presence; Ibn Iyās discussed it primarily in the context of stipend payment, reliance on firearms, venue of service and ambivalence on the part of the sultan's line troops. Although he did not provide an explanation for al-Ghawrī's motives behind its formation, his scattered references are sufficient for conjecture. The corps's title derived from a special fifth pay session following the four days in which

[42] On the hazardous transfer of several pieces weighing more than 100 qinṭārs and measuring several cubits each, see *Badā'i'*, IV, 260; a qinṭār was equivalent to 256.5 kg in Syria; 1 cubit was equivalent to 0.58 meters in Egypt.

[43] *Badā'i'*, IV, 192.

[44] *Badā'i'*, IV, 238.

[45] *Badā'i'*, IV, 14.

[46] *Badā'i'*, IV, 200; Ayalon, *Gunpowder*, 71–83.

regular troops and reservists drew their stipends. Assignment of a day reserved for members of the Fifth Corps emphasized the brigade's status as distinct from that of Mamlūk regulars. Its members were not recruited from traditional divisions of the military, namely the *Sulṭānī* or Royal Mamlūks (including both purchased recruits (*mushtarawāt*) and veterans (*qarāniṣa*) who had seen previous service), the *Sayfiyya* or troopers held by grand amīrs (men of the sword or *sayf*), and reservists (*al-ḥalqa*).[47] Exactly who was impressed into this brigade cannot be specified since the chroniclers often reported derogatory remarks about their quality on the part of regulars who despised them, but provided few details about their origins.[48] Yet behind the vituperation against the recruits one may discern free-born foreigners from Iran or Turkestan, and reservists who had not passed muster on their fitness tests. Al-Ghawrī found their inadequacies in traditional feats of arms no deterrent, since he intended them to practice with arquebuses. While keen eyesight may have mattered in their training, the ability to draw bows or throw lances did not.[49]

The members of the corps, who numbered approximately 300 in their first mobilizations, were not cavalry soldiers and consequently received no *iqṭā*ʿ money. Al-Ghawrī had been reducing his reliance on *iqṭā*ʿ rents to pay troop stipends for some time. In 912/1506, he promoted Arikmās min Ṭarābāy, a former viceroy of Damascus, to the rank of commander (*muqaddam*) and soon bestowed the influential amīrship of council (*imrat al-majlis*) on him.[50] This Arikmās received no fief commensurate to his former rank. Instead, al-Ghawrī paid him a salary of 1,000 dīnārs per month and 1,000 irdabbs of wheat annually from the Dhakhīra reserve bureau.[51]

It is no coincidence that Arikmās was placed in charge of training the Fifth Corps in their new weaponry or maneuvers. Having been separated from the land allotments that, even as usufruct, gave senior officers a sense of autonomy (regarded by the sultan as rivalry), he was al-Ghawrī's natural choice to preside over an experimental unit funded from outside traditional sources. Ibn Iyās noted al-Ghawrī's eroding of *iqṭā*ʿ*āt* parceled out to amīrs in standard service. By Shaʿbān 918/October–November 1512, he was systematically downsizing the grants awarded to even his most senior commanders.[52] Was this money set aside for members of the Fifth Corps?

[47] Ayalon, "Studies – I," 204–05.

[48] 20 Ṣafar 920/April 16, 1514, al-Ghawrī's *khaṣṣakī* bodyguards threatened revolt, accusing their patron of reneging on their stipends to pay his Fifth Corps (*Badāʾi*ʿ IV, 369). Ibn Iyās described them as Turkmān, Persians, reservists and others of low status (*Badāʾi*ʿ, IV, 206).

[49] *Badāʾi*ʿ, IV, 308 (on equipment).

[50] *Badāʾi*ʿ, IV, 100, 308.

[51] An *irdabb* was an Egyptian measure equivalent to 198 liters.

[52] *Badāʾi*ʿ, IV, 283.

Ibn Iyās did not so state, but the possibility exists, since he did remark on the recruits' resentment of Fifth Corps stipends.

In Ṣafar 920/April 1514, the *julbān* positioned themselves outside the courtyard where the corps stood waiting for their payments.[53] As the latter departed, the regulars met them with drawn swords and seized an Ashrafī dīnār from each. "Thus did soldiers of the Fifth Corps suffer severe humiliation that day at the *julbān*'s hands, but the sultan could do nothing to restrain them. Some snatched a corps member's entire stipend, while others took only an Ashrafī and returned the remainder. Those who kept the whole *jamakiyya* fled off with it." The recruits' behavior suggests their anger over being slighted for the benefit of upstarts who might undermine their preferential status if the sultan was unchecked. However valid their alarm, the regulars suspected that al-Ghawrī routinely located funds to pay his new corps, while claiming insolvency in the face of their own bonus requests. Since savings he gained from manipulating *iqṭāʿāt* failed to meet his fiscal needs, the sultan may have raised much of the Fifth Corps's stipend money from expropriated assets, which by this time were substantial.

We therefore can observe a trial military unit funded largely through unofficial channels. This corps received cash only. They could rely on no allotments of property as a means of reducing their dependence on their patron. Having decided that the *iqṭāʿ* system encouraged his regulars' inclinations for conspiracy, al-Ghawrī compensated his new corps with revenues he gleaned from his confiscation network. Members of the Fifth Corps were given reason to believe that their future was directly tied to their benefactor's security. If they wavered, they would fall victim to their enemies.

Al-Ghawrī assigned the Fifth Corps field duties only twice during their brief existence: first as part of the expedition he sent to guard Suez from the Portuguese in mid-919/September–October 1513, and second as a contingent on the naval voyage to India (*al-Hind*) in Jumādā II 921/June–July 1515.[54] The locations of both ventures are significant. Neither involved corps personnel in Cairo, where they might provoke their mamlūk rivals to revolt. Al-Ghawrī may have regarded the Fifth Corps as a more reliable source of personal support, but if so, his deployment of them far from those most likely to dethrone him remains mysterious. Even in these two expeditions, the purpose of the corpsmen's expected service is uncertain. Employment of the sultan's new arquebuses appears to have been their only exclusive duty. Since the Ottoman Janissaries at Suez were outfitted with similar firearms, al-Ghawrī may have hoped to impress upon their admiral, Salmān, that his own soldiers could also field these weapons. But their

[53] *Badāʾiʿ*, IV, 370.
[54] *Badāʾiʿ*, IV, 331, 335, 337, 458–66.

absence from al-Ghawrī's contingents during his march toward Marj Dābiq to confront Salim I discloses a more perplexing mystery.

Ibn Iyās noted several battalions departing Cairo in Rabīʿ II 922/May 1516 for al-Raydāniyya, where they encamped before setting out on the Syrian campaign.[55] The Fifth Corps was not mentioned. The Egyptian force was composed of Sulṭānī recruits or veterans, Sayfiyya troopers and reservists – traditional members of the Mamlūk hierarchy. Why did al-Ghawrī exempt the Fifth Corps from this fateful confrontation? An explanation has been offered that the corps was intended solely for service against Portuguese raiders in the Red Sea.[56] Since their opponents carried firearms, they were of necessity similarly equipped. The Mamlūk regulars on whom al-Ghawrī relied for his campaign against Salīm disdained firearms and tolerated no arquebusiers.

This interpretation may be qualified. If non-Mamlūk arquebusiers ever turned their weapons on their "masters and creators" armed solely with "horses, bows, swords and lances",[57] might the corps's patron not profit from his peers' devastation in a time of crisis? To the end, al-Ghawrī feared deposition by his own soldiers more than any other threat, including that posed by the Ottomans whose victory was not assured. Did he wish to hold back the corps for his own safety at home in the advent of a defeat he might survive, or even of a victory his regular army might exploit to demand a reward beyond his means? The preceding scenarios are possible, and yet each is conjectural. As with al-Ghawrī's other experiments, the sources obscure his real objective in founding the Fifth Corps. Yet their tenuous status is apparent. Beset with dilemmas of bankruptcy, factionalism and menace from abroad, al-Ghawrī could not focus his energies on transforming the Fifth Corps from an ad hoc band of irregulars into a skilled arquebus regiment. To the time of his departure, he may have remained undecided about their use and deployment. The question of whether the ultimate objectives of his covert fiscal experiments were equally vague is also raised.

These experiments can be discerned in al-Ghawrī's investments in *waqf* deeds. His manipulation of them implies his departure from the time-honored means of estate preservation relied upon by his predecessors. The investments reveal al-Ghawrī feeling his way toward construction of a private fisc sheltered by the sanctity of its properties and subject to the sultan's exclusive use. Al-Ghawrī's *waqf* appropriations facilitated two of his overriding goals: securing dependable revenues and attaining the freedom to distribute them as he chose. While examination of the sultan's

55 *Badāʾiʿ*, V, 38–44.
56 Ayalon, *Gunpowder*, 80–82.
57 Ayalon, *Gunpowder*, 82

writs reveals a noticeable intensification of *waqf* appropriation under the guise of licit purchase, al-Ghawrī's experiment seems not to have gone beyond a rudimentary level of execution before it was cut off by his defeat at Marj Dābiq.

Al-Ghawrī's earliest alleged purchases of trust properties date from 907/1501, soon after his accession. From that time until his demise, al-Ghawrī pursued the acquisition of *waqf* properties at a rapid rate. The 300 surviving writs bearing his name as final trustee (*wāqif*) constitute almost a third of archival documents from the independent Mamlūk era. Al-Ghawrī issued only one comprehensive trust deed of his own, however. Despite its vast scope, the writ supports only four charities, with its donations concentrated on the first – the sultan's own mausoleum and mystic hospice (*al-qubba wa'l-khānqāh al-sharīfa*).[58]

From early 907 to the first transaction of his primary *waqf* deed, dated 21 Muḥarram 909/July 16, 1503, al-Ghawrī accumulated a network of properties so extensive that they yielded an estimated annual sum approaching 53,000 Ashrafī dīnārs.[59] By the end of 914/April 1509, he had added holdings whose revenues could exceed 30,000 dīnārs per annum. Thus, by 914, over a period of seven years, this man assembled assets that may have yielded more than 80,000 dīnārs every year – protected in a trust ostensibly dedicated to his mausoleum. Of al-Ghawrī's three other charitable foundations, only the flood gauge, mosque and pavilion of the Nilometer (*Miqyās*) at the southern tip of Rawḍā Island received any significant income (ca. 700 dīnārs annually). The other two were minimal: 12,000 dirhams (ca. 40 dīnārs) paid yearly to the senior eunuch custodian (*shaykh al-khuddām*) of the Holy Sanctuary at Mecca, and some 500 dīnārs every twelve months for

[58] As per note 32: WA 882q, transaction 1, 9–trust (*waqf*) for mausoleum (*qubba*) in Cairo, dated 26 Muḥarram 909/July 21, 1503.

[59] The estimated annual yield was computed from al-Ghawrī's main writ: WA 882q, dated between 26 Muḥarram 909/July 21, 1503 and 18 Rabīʿ II 922/May 20, 1516. In lieu of prices for urban property, which *waqf* writs did not include, item values were estimated at 1,000 dīnārs per unit (averaging three properties each), calculated from prices provided for comparable properties in sale deeds. Annual yield was calculated at 10 percent of this estimated value. Agrarian tracts appearing in WA 882 were located in Heinz Halm, *Lebenregistern*, vols. I and II; annual yields from these were calculated according to shares reported in unit entries from totals in the cadasters of Ibn Duqmāq and Ibn al-Jīʿān (see bibliography), summarized by Halm for each agrarian unit. Trust donors usually purchased shares of a property, a particular tendency with regard to agrarian land. Each village or agrarian district (*nāḥiyya*) placed originally in *iqṭāʿ*, from the Mediterranean to Aswān, was divided as a unit into twenty-four portions according to annual yield computed as "army" (*jayshī*) dīnārs, a currency of account designating rents collected from *iqṭāʿāt* for the Army Bureau and paid out to the amīr assigned the allotment. A *jayshī* dīnār was worth approximately four-fifths of an Ashrafī gold dīnār, the highest value coin of the Circassian period. As these allotments were progressively alienated, the original division of twenty-four was sub-parceled into smaller sections. See Halm, 1, A: Introduction.

the sultan's corpse-washing font below the Citadel. Yet the trove's output greatly exceeded yearly expenditures on al-Ghawrī's mausoleum itself – the principal recipient of his trust. In 914/1509, the most lucrative year of his investment program, slightly less than 6,000 dīnārs covered the annual expenses of al-Ghawrī's tomb-hospice: 7 percent of the total. More than 90 percent seems to have been left unassigned. Al-Ghawrī's primary deed, number 882 in Amīn's notation, does not indicate on what most of its surplus was to be spent. Provisos for the support of al-Ghawrī's wife, son and future descendants allocate modest sums or proportions. Since the deed precisely itemizes its properties and expenditures, oversight may be discounted. This surplus thus presumably passed into the sultan's private domain, without being further accounted for. But by al-Ghawrī's time, narrative and archival sources offer corroborative evidence in support of this possibility.

Al-Ghawrī was compelled to expropriate *waqf* yields to defray his troops' bonus demands soon after his accession. Since Qāytbāy had left him an empty treasury, he had convened his fiscal and legal advisors following the troops' first rebellion in Dhu'l-Ḥijja 906/June–July 1501 to chart a strategy for acquiring the funds.[60] While the four *qāḍī*s initially opposed any tampering with trust monies, the Ḥanafī judge Sarī al-Dīn ibn al-Shiḥna conferred privately with him subsequently to arrange a procedure for taking over *waqf* yields. The sultan's *atābak*, Qāyt al-Rajabī, then took charge of the collection process, assigning to his adjutants quarters throughout Cairo to be mulcted. The chronicler Ibn Iyās described al-Ghawrī's objectives to emphasize his departure from Qāytbāy's policies: "The sultan sought to confiscate *awqāf* of mosques, colleges and other benevolent foundations, leaving them funds sufficient to cover daily operations only. As an incentive to the amīrs responsible for the expropriations, he planned to grant them trust properties in their own names, thereby alienating them permanently."

Despite Ibn Iyās's rancor over this operation, its impact should be considered in light of the disparity between income and expenses noted previously. If the surpluses generated by al-Ghawrī's trust provide a plausible indicator of proportions, his seizure of either a six- or twelve-month cumulative yield from Cairo's *waqf* institutions still left them with most of their assets intact – available for mulcting again when the need arose. The castigation by narrative authors should be tempered by the archival evidence of a large residue surviving allegedly severe extractions. Assaults made upon *waqf* yields of affluent religious institutions during the late sultanate may actually represent a circulation of frozen assets back into the economy. Mamlūk soldiers were big consumers whose purchases kept many crafts in business. But did al-Ghawrī accumulate enough money by means of these

[60] *Badā'i'*, IV, 13–14.

measures to meet his soldiers' demands? Was their appeasement his primary objective? In the course of investigating these queries, the pattern of al-Ghawrī's acquisitions merits examination.

Although al-Ghawrī granted some 300 trust-related documents, only one actually spelled out his charitable donations. The others bearing his name differed in purpose and scope. They certify sale, substitution, transfer and repossession procedures for individual properties. Unlike the primary *waqf*, they indicate the properties' prices – but not in the certificates formalizing al-Ghawrī's acquisition. Many of these documents trace purchase agreements concluded during the preceding century. The certificates associated with al-Ghawrī's assumptions provide dates that are much closer together, suggesting a procedure by which whole series of accumulated writs were transferred to the sultan in a single session. The documents, 262 of which funded the sultan's mausoleum or his other three foundations, listed urban property. The vast rural holdings described in the main deed were absent. Presumably alienated from *iqṭāʿ* allotments, these agrarian properties seem to have been procured in undocumented procedures.[61] Nor can one assume that the dates of al-Ghawrī's acquisition certificates depict every aspect of his expropriation procedure. An indeterminate majority of the documents has been lost, but roughly 60 percent of those that survived resurfaced in the several transactions of Primary Deed 882.[62]

The dates of these purchases by previous buyers extended back more than a century. The first or even second disclosed affluent civilians who were not involved in regime affairs. However, their properties eventually came into the proximity of al-Ghawrī's staff. The key transition phase seems to have occurred when individuals from the bureaucratic and military elites, who themselves speculated in *awqāf*, obtained them. Although 300 deeds were ultimately appropriated by al-Ghawrī's agents, only 115 persons who appeared in the penultimate transaction turned their assets over to him directly. Some 24 percent of them were mentioned in the narrative sources in the context of their confiscation by al-Ghawrī. Former military officers and important bureaucrats figured prominently. Among the most visible was Khayrbak al-Sharīfī, a former confidant and treasurer (*khāzindār*) in al-Ghawrī's service.

Khayrbak immersed himself in ventures implying the privatization of

[61] "Fractionalized Estates," 4–12.

[62] Property items placed in trust yielded rents on a monthly or annual basis. Most common were stalls (*ḥawānīt*) hired by individual shopkeepers. Al-Ghawrī had let more than 1,000 by the end of 914. Other types appearing frequently were markets (*aswāq*), manufacturing halls (*qāʿāt*), caravanserais (*wakālāt*), warehouses (*ḥawāṣil*), dwellings (*ṭibāq*), inns (*khānāt*), magazines (*makhāzin*), merchant emporia (*fanādiq*), sugar kitchens (*maṭābikh*), stables (*iṣṭablāt*), bakeries (*afrān*), baths (*ḥammāmāt*), gardens (*junaynāt*), oil or cane presses (*maʿāṣir*), granaries (*shūnāt*).

waqf properties to his death on 9 Ramaḍān 920/October 28, 1514.[63] Between 20 Muḥarram 910/July 3, 1504 and 6 Rabīʿ I 920/May 1, 1514, the *khāzindār* transferred, via deeds of sale, more than 100 units of property to his sovereign at nominal prices totalling more than 32,000 dīnārs.[64] Many of these were agrarian *iqṭāʿ* tracts he had previously alienated from the army bureau (*dīwān al-jaysh*). Since these legally remained the state's collective property, they could not be publicly auctioned. The cadasters never posted a market price for them, but rather gave their average annual yields. Yet the transfer deeds dated on one day, 27 Shawwāl 914/February 18, 1509 (approximately two-thirds of the total), designated the army bureau chief (*nāẓir al-jaysh*), Muḥyī al-Dīn al-Qaṣrawī, as *wakīl*. It is therefore likely that this individual, whom Khayrbak had recommended for the office, submitted to his pressure and signed over the tracts.

These documents therefore reveal an insight into one aspect of the clandestine process by which the state's properties passed from its jurisdiction into the sultan's personal reserve, sheltered in his trust. While the chroniclers only hinted at this process of alienation, the documents disclosed its occurrence as fully sanctioned by senior legal authorities. Formally, neither Khayrbak nor al-Ghawrī violated any laws as they eroded the realm's store of usufruct properties their competitors coveted for their own power bids.

What do such procedures suggest about al-Ghawrī's development as a creative speculator? Their incidence parallels the councils he convened with his host of client extractors. Although details of their stratagems cannot be recovered, it is clear that al-Ghawrī never lacked astute counselors to assist him in refining his programs or to encourage him once he resolved on a course of action. All of them had risen to the bureaucracy's summit because of their finesse at extortion. Their services, when compared with the pattern of al-Ghawrī's trust acquisitions, would enhance his private reserve in the guise of a huge *waqf* trove of which he was sole sponsor. Since additions to Deed 882 appear as properties hastily grafted on, appended indiscriminately with little attempt at their integration into the expenditure section or at concealment of their insertion, the procedure remained embryonic. Beyond amassment, it does not seem to have progressed to become a more sophisticated means of coordinating acquisitions or augmenting yields. Nonetheless, they yielded a copious income. Al-Ghawrī's *waqf* manipulations thus point to his conception of the charitable trust as a repository available to him alone. No other haven he could devise was less vulnerable to his rivals' conspiracies. And since the discrepancy between yield and outlay was so large, al-Ghawrī's stratagems did not appreciably compromise

[63] *Badāʾiʿ*, IV, 398.
[64] Petry, *Protectors*, ch. 7, n. 46.

his trust's charitable function. Its undesignated income amply served his purpose.

Did al-Ghawrī actually tap this depository to forestall rebellion by his recruits? Despite the correlation between need and appropriation, this question is unanswerable. The narrative sources comment solely on what appear to be his random confiscations to pay bonus demands or expedition costs. Ibn Iyās's only reference to al-Ghawrī's sale of a *waqf* property is noteworthy for the sultan's discomfiture.[65]

> On Sunday the fifth (of Rajab 917/September 2, 1511), the sultan convened only the Julbān recruits in the courtyard. He rebuked them saying: "I shall abdicate the sultanate and you may acclaim whom you will." The stand-off continued into the afternoon until the sultan finally agreed to a bonus for his purchased Mamlūs, but only in the amount of 40 dīnārs each. Several officers remonstrated with the sultan, urging him to avoid worse trouble by raising the bonus to 50. But the sultan responded that he could not now afford that amount. The debate continued until the monarch granted fifty dīnārs per soldier. He was compelled to sell properties and lands he had placed in *waqf* to support his *madrasa*. The sultan had no other choice at this time since the treasuries were empty of funds and he could temporarily find no other means of procuring the money to alleviate the crisis.

Since his survival took precedence over all other priorities, al-Ghawrī took this step, but only with the prospect of deposition. The trauma of this incident may have intensified al-Ghawrī's determination to secure his clandestine fund for more dependent soldiers. One year earlier Ibn Iyās mentioned the Fifth Corps in the context of its stipend payment. The historian referred to revenues he regarded as improperly manipulated: those formerly allotted to Sulṭānī Mamlūks, which the sultan was steadily paring back. He also observed that al-Ghawrī stepped up his reduction of *iqṭāʿāt* at this time. The concurrence of these developments with al-Ghawrī's appropriation of trusts, and his dismay over yielding part of his new reserve to retain his office, lend credibility to his plan for funding from its proceeds units outside the existing military hierarchy.

Can a scheme by which al-Ghawrī intended to dismantle the *iqṭāʿ* system be discerned? Had he accumulated the financial resources to replace its revenues? Was the sultan moving toward neutralization of those within the Mamlūk elite who opposed him most obstinately once he had trained a viable alternative? Did he see an opportunity to surmount the cash shortages that had plagued him from his enthronement with the foundation of a fiscal repository under his exclusive authority? Such possibilities will remain hypothetical unless new sources come to light. They nonetheless offer a rationale for al-Ghawrī's actions that suggests more than the menace his

[65] *Badāʾiʿ*, IV, 241.

contemporaries decried or the capriciousness noted by more recent analysts. For all the condemnation heaped by notables from the literary and military elites on al-Ghawrī's stratagems, in hindsight they warrant respect as innovative means of surmounting crisis.

And beyond dilemmas of the moment, these innovations confirm the tenacity of the Mamlūk oligarchy. Under trying circumstances, the military institution was capable of exploring creative ways of reconstituting its hegemony. The measures discussed in this chapter are indicative of the institution's continued vigor at the end of its independent sovereignty. Rather than resigning itself to an inevitable fate, the Mamlūk oligarchy confronted its final dilemmas with the special combination of pugnacity and élan that had sustained its dominion over Egypt and Syria for so many preceding decades. While surrendering formal authority to the Ottomans after 922/1517, the Mamlūk institution would continue to exhibit the resilience that had overcome the intimidating odds of its last episode of independence. Such resilience would enable the Mamlūk institution to adapt initially to its new condition of subordination, and eventually to assimilate – if not supplant – its conquerors.

18

The Ottoman occupation

MICHAEL WINTER

The sources

The long rivalry between the Mamlūks and the Ottomans that led to war and conquest was a confrontation between two Muslim Sunnī empires, both governed by Turkish-speaking rulers. The predominant language in the central Ottoman provinces was Turkish; the Mamlūk state included Egypt and Syria, with the Ḥijāz – the central Arab lands of the Middle East – within its sphere of influence. In historical perspective, the struggle was over the hegemony of the Sunnī world, which was challenged by the new Shīʿī Ṣafavid state in Iran, and by the Portuguese naval, neo-crusading aggression in the Indian Ocean and the Red Sea. The military power of the Mamlūk state was based on the excellent Mamlūk cavalry and auxiliary forces. Yet it conducted a fundamentally defensive and static strategy; its boundaries were essentially the same as they had been in 1250, when the empire was established. Conversely, the Ottoman empire was an aggressive and dynamic state, which devoted all its energies to conquest and expansion, skillfully integrating all its economic and human resources for further advancement. The outcome of the decisive war, that lasted from August 1516 until January 1517, was the fall of the Mamlūk sultanate.

The conquest of Syria and Egypt by the Ottomans is described in detail by a variety of sources – Arabic, Turkish, European and Hebrew. There are not many instances in which an occupation of one empire by another is recorded so accurately, sometimes day by day, giving a clear picture of confrontations of different traditions, mentalities and attitudes, describing how the Ottoman administration took over after the overthrow of the Mamlūk sultanate.

The best source on the final decades of the Mamlūk sultanate, the Ottoman conquest, and the first six years of Ottoman rule is the excellent chronicle of Muḥammad Ibn Iyās, a native of Cairo and one of the *awlād al-nās* mamlūks' sons. He was familiar with political developments, and deeply identified with the people of Cairo and the fallen regime, without losing his honesty, accuracy and fairness in describing both the Mamlūks and the Ottomans. He was a fine – and the last – representative of the great medieval Egyptian historiographical tradition. As an eyewitness, he is without equal. Ibn Zunbul, another Egyptian, was not a reliable chronicler and his work is a kind of historical romance, yet it is important as a genuine expression of the mamlūks' view of themselves and their ethos. Muḥammad Ibn Ṭūlūn of Damascus was also an eyewitness of the conquest, and his chronicle, as well as his other writings, although inferior to Ibn Iyās's work, complement his account by giving a view from Damascus by a professional *ʿālim*.

There is no Ottoman parallel to the chronicles of Ibn Iyās and Ibn Ṭūlūn. No Ottoman source provides the direct, lively and personal reactions to the great historical events of the late fifteenth and early sixteenth centuries. At that time, the Ottomans did not have the long and glorious historiographical tradition of the Arabs. The Turkish writings that are available are not as detailed, nuanced, and sophisticated as those of the Arab writers. The interesting and well-known chronicle of ʿĀshiqpashazāde that stops in the year 907/1501 covers in detail the Ottoman–Mamlūk rivalry and also attempts to explain its background. Its weakness lies in its naive and anecdotal, sometimes even mythologizing, approach and style. Yet this chronicle presents a clear picture of what can be assumed to be typical Ottoman attitudes. We also have an important Ottoman chronicle which is in fact an official history, although the writer Hoca Saʿdüddīn (d. 1008/1599) was not an official court historian. He wrote on the authority of his father, Ḥāfiẓ Muḥammad, who was one of Sultan Salīm's chamberlains, and who accompanied him on his campaign.

There is a chronicle by a Turkish writer, ʿAbd al-Ṣamad al-Diyārbakrī by name, who came to Egypt with Salīm's army and stayed there to serve as a *qāḍī*. His chronicle is a translation into Turkish of Ibn Iyās's work, with significant changes, and then a detailed continuation for a period of two and a half years. The merit of this work, besides the information it provides, is that it gives an Ottoman point of view of Egyptian affairs seen by a man on the spot. Ferīdūn's *Munsheāt ül-selāṭīn* is a collection of the sultan's correspondence with other monarchs, campaign logbooks, and letters announcing conquests (*fetiḥnāme*). This, of course, is official historiography par excellence (or at least, provides materials for such historiography), and an important source for Ottoman propaganda.

There are even two Hebrew chronicles (Jews were not given to writing history) about early Ottoman Egypt: *Seder Eliyahu Zuta*, written in Crete in 1523, six years after the Ottoman conquest of Egypt, by Rabbi Eliyahu Capsali, describing the conquest of Syria and Egypt, and *Sefer Divrei Yosef* by Yosef ben Yitzhak Sambari, written in Egypt in the second half of the seventeenth century, a work which includes interesting information on the earlier period. We have also contemporary European accounts. By far the most important are the "diaries", *I Diarii* by Marino Sannuto (Venice, 1879–1902 reprinted Bologna, 1969), which is a huge multi-volume collection of reports and letters written by Venetians to their authorities in Venice.

Finally, there are the official documents, which were preserved in the archives. While Ottoman archival materials concerning Egypt become abundant only from about the 1550s, several important documents were preserved in the archives of the Topkapı Palace, mostly concerning relations between the Ottomans and the Mamlūks prior to the conquest. On the Mamlūk side, not many archival documents survived, but there are large collections of *waqf* deeds from the last decades of the Mamlūk regime.[1]

The causes of the conflict and the Ottoman conquest of Syria

The friction between the two empires started during the reign of Muḥammad II, the conqueror of Istanbul (1451–81). Yet it was merely about comparatively minor issues of prestige, as when the Mamlūks zealously guarded their monopoly of the *ḥājj* route and the access to the holy places of Islam against even a symbolic infringement attempted by the Ottomans. Sultan Muḥammad offered to repair at his own expense water wells for the benefit of the pilgrims. His offer was rejected, and his envoys, who were respected *'ulamā'*, were humiliated by the Mamlūk sultan. The conquest of Constantinople (1453) made it clear to everyone that the Ottomans were becoming a great power and a threat to their neighbors. As the Ottomans under Muḥammad and his successor Bayazīd II (1481–1512) consolidated their rule in Anatolia, a fierce struggle for the control of the Turkoman principalities of Qaraman and Dhu'l-Qadr (Elbistan) ensued, since those march zones were considered by Cairo as belonging to its domain.

Qāytbāy, the great Mamlūk sultan (r. 1468–96) fought a long and expensive war between 1468 and 1473 to defend the sultanate's interests against Shāh Suwār, the ruler of Elbistan in eastern Anatolia, an audacious Turkoman chief who challenged Mamlūk suzerainty. Qāytbāy's hard-won victory gave him more than a decade of quiet on his northern border, until he had to confront a mightier enemy, the Ottoman state. The issue of the buffer zones in Anatolia, some of whose chieftains sided with the Ottomans and others, of the same Turkoman families, supported the Mamlūks, caused a series of fierce battles between the two empires (1485–91). Bayazīd was

[1] These have been studied by Carl Petry for an assessment of the last Mamluk sultans' fiscal policies; see Carl F. Petry, *Protectors or Praetorians? The Last Mamlūk Sultans and Egypt's Waning as a Great Power* (Albany, NY, 1994).

deeply preoccupied with the threat of being deposed by Prince Cem, his brother, and did not commit the empire's vast resources to what were for the Ottomans only frontier skirmishes. Thus this long war also ended well for the Mamlūks, but their fears of their stronger neighbor were not allayed.

Bayazīd did not conduct an aggressive policy, however, and the peace between the two empires was maintained through the rest of his reign. Moreover, when the Mamlūk sultan Qānṣūh al-Ghawrī (1501–16) faced the challenge to Muslim trade and security from the Portuguese, Bayezid helped the Mamlūks by sending them war materials to construct ships and even a contingent under an Ottoman captain (1511). The Ottoman sultan refused to accept payment for the materiel he had sent to Egypt. Upon his death, he was eulogized by Ibn Iyās and called "just" (*al-ʿādil*) and "warrior for the faith" (*mujāhid*).[2] Likewise, the Ottomans had a deep respect for Qāytbāy; after the conquest of Egypt, they regarded his administration as ideally suited for Egyptian conditions.

Lesser causes for the Ottoman-Mamlūk conflict can be mentioned. Since the days of Muḥammad II, there had been cases of intentional or unintentional diplomatic insults and breaches of protocol between Cairo and Istanbul.[3] More serious was the affair of the above-mentioned Cem, who after failing in his effort to succeed his father, escaped to Qāytbāy's court in Cairo. The Mamlūk sultan was extremely careful not to provoke Bayazīd's anger, but he was also obliged by the traditions of hospitality in such cases to grant asylum to Cem. The latter attempted again to challenge Bayazīd's rule, but failed. Cem's adventures and death in Europe are well known, but it is important to note here the Ottomans' charge that Qāytbāy tried to "extinguish the Ottoman hearth" by means of Cem, an utterly unfounded accusation against the cautious Qāytbāy. Other Ottoman princes found safe refuge in Cairo against the ruling sultan, notably Qurqud during al-Ghawrī's reign. However, these cases were less serious than that of Cem.

When Sultan Salīm I ascended the Ottoman throne in 1512, he embarked upon a far more warlike and unscrupulous policy than his father. His determination and ferocity won him the appellation "Yavuz" – "the Grim". His name invoked terror. Even the Ottoman sources acknowledge his stern character. Ibn Iyās, who saw Salīm in Cairo after the conquest, describes him as "a clean-shaven, wide-nosed, wide-eyed, short man about forty years old, with a hump on his back. He is agile and tends to turn and glance around when on horseback. He is bad-tempered, irascible and bloodthirsty. He has no royal etiquette (*niẓām*), does not keep his assurances of immunity (*amān*)".[4] Ibn Iyās continues to describe Salīm as a bad Muslim.

2 Muhammad Ibn Iyās, *Badāʾiʿ al-Zuhūr fi waqāʾiʿ al-duhūr*, ed. M Muṣṭafā, (Cairo and Wiesbaden, 1960), IV, 270.

3 See, for example, *ʿĀshiqpashazāde Tāʾrikhi* (Istanbul, 1332/1914), 209–12.

4 Ibn Iyās, V, 150, 152, 207.

It is noteworthy that Ibn Iyās, our principal source for the period, does not mince words in denouncing the character of Qānṣūh al-Ghawrī, his own sultan. Al-Ghawrī, who ruled from 1501 until his death in battle in 1516, was over sixty years of age when he became sultan. He was a strong man and a shrewd ruler. His reign brought relative stability to Mamlūk politics after five tumultuous years and four weak sultans, following the stable period of Qāytbāy. Inevitably, al-Ghawrī was often compared with Qāytbāy and was found wanting. Where Qāytbāy was considered "majestic, serene and dignified, correct in decorum, invariably respected, projecting an aura of majesty," al-Ghawrī is described by Ibn Iyās as an unjust, stingy and greedy despot. He was a *bon vivant*, cultured and talented, but according to Ibn Iyās, who certainly represents the public opinion of Cairo, "each year of his reign weighed down on the people like a thousand years, and his defects outweighed his positive traits."[5] Yet it must be remembered that al-Ghawrī had to face formidable domestic difficulties and foreign threats. He combined caution with originality and imagination and tried to save the empire. He had to deal with the chronic quarrels of the Mamlūk factions and the insubordination of his recruits (*julbān*). The treasury suffered from economic decline brought about by, among other factors, the discovery of the Cape of Good Hope route by the Portuguese (1497), which caused the loss of the Indian transit spice trade through Egypt. Al-Ghawrī had to protect Muslim naval interests in the Indian Ocean against the Portuguese, who also threatened the Red Sea. And, as will be presently shown, he had to maneuver in the face of the fierce Mamlūk-Ṣafavid rivalry. He tried new methods (in contradistinction to Qāytbāy, who did not innovate anything). He realized the importance of artillery, recruited new units from outside the Mamlūk caste and manipulated *waqf* funds to pay them. Even from Ibn Iyās's largely hostile obituary of al-Ghawrī it is obvious that the sultan was a great builder and developer of civil and military projects. He strengthened the fortifications of the sea ports of Alexandria, Rosetta (Rashīd), and Jedda against European and Ottoman enemies, and improved the pilgrims' route to Mecca.

The direct cause of the war between Salīm and al-Ghawrī were the implications of the Ṣafavid threat. Ismāʿīl Shāh, the Ṣafavid ruler, in 1501 united all of Persia and made the Twelver Shīʿa (*Ithnā ʿashariyya*) the state religion. The Ṣafavids posed a danger to the Mamlūks, although in time it was realized that the Ottomans were a much more serious threat. It was reported in Cairo as early as the end of 1501 that Ismāʿīl Shāh had conquered "the lands of Timur Leng" and was invading Mamlūk territories

[5] From Ibn Iyās's obituary of al-Ghawrī, as translated by Carl F. Petry, *Twilight of Majesty: The Reigns of the Mamlūk Sultans al-Ashraf Qāytbāy and Qānṣūh al-Ghawrī in Egypt* (Seattle and London, 1993), 119–22.

in the northeast. The Mamlūks' fears were increased by the association of the Ṣafavids with the redoubtable Timūr-Lenk, who had invaded Syria a century before, inflicting immense destruction. The Mamlūks sent an expeditionary force to Aleppo to observe the Ṣafavids' movements and to defend Syria if necessary. In late summer 1507 the Ṣafavids again invaded Mamlūk territories during their fighting against ʿAlāʾ al-Dawla of Dhuʾl-Qadr. Later Ismāʿīl apologized to the Mamlūks.

The Ṣafavid propaganda won over many Turcomans in Anatolia itself. These (like the adherents in Persia) were known as Qizilbāsh (Red Heads, after their headgear). For the Ottomans, it was no longer merely a matter of a hostile neighbor, but of the control of their own territories in Anatolia. Salīm massacred many Anatolian Qizilbāshs, and then defeated Ismāʿīl's army at Chaldirān in Azerbayjān (August 1514). The Ṣafavids sustained a serious setback, but were not destroyed. They were still regarded as a grave danger both by the Ottomans and the Mamlūks. ʿAlāʾ al-Dawla of Elbistan, the Dhuʾl-Qadrite chieftain, who was Cairo's client, refused to assist the Ottomans as they were crossing his territory during their campaign against Ismāʿīl. Consequently, ʿAlāʾ al-Dawla was killed by Salīm and his region was annexed to the Ottoman empire in 1515, in total disregard of Cairo's rights there. Qānṣūh al-Ghawrī got a taste of Salīm's cruel cynicism when the latter dispatched to him a *fetiḥnāme* (a letter announcing a conquest) along with the severed heads of ʿAlāʾ al-Dawla and several of his sons and his vizier.

The sultan ordered that the heads be given a proper burial. It became obvious that war with Salīm was inevitable. Al-Ghawrī busied himself with military preparations, mustering his troops and instructing the caliph and the four chief *qāḍī*s to get ready for departure to Syria. In order to gain popularity, al-Ghawrī abolished the monthly and weekly taxes he had imposed on grain and other commodities.

The Ottoman historians and propagandists felt obliged to justify the war against a Sunnī Muslim neighbor. Beside recounting many incidents from the distant past of Mamlūk hostility toward the Ottoman state, the Ottoman writers' most serious accusation was the Mamlūks' presumed cooperation with the Ṣafavids and an alleged treaty with them. Saʿdüddīn, the Ottoman chronicler, quotes a verse: "When the Circassian supports the Qizilbāsh, we shall draw our swords also against him."[6]

It is difficult to prove historically the absence of a treaty, but it seems highly improbable that such a treaty ever existed. Sultan al-Ghawrī was very cautious and fully aware of the weakness of his position. His state's economy was in trouble and his army undisciplined and seditious. He was also wary of the Ṣafavids' intentions. It is true that there was an exchange of letters and emissaries between the Mamlūk and the Ṣafavid courts, but there

[6] Muḥammad Saʿdüddīn, *Tāj al-tawārīkh* (Istanbul, AH 1279/80), 328.

is no evidence that al-Ghawrī committed himself to assist Ismāʿīl. After Chaldirān, Ismāʿīl sent letters in a diplomatic offensive to various European and Middle Eastern rulers, attempting to create anti-Ottoman alliances, and one such messenger arrived in Cairo in late 1514.

While Salīm was fortifying strongholds on the passages from Anatolia to Syria, al-Ghawrī was preparing his campaign. Ibn Iyās observes that his army was far smaller and less impressive than that of former Mamlūk sultans who had led their troops northwards in the fifteenth century. There were only 944 royal mamlūks and the whole army numbered approximately 5,000 soldiers, or according to another estimate, some 7,000 men. Numerically, the Ottomans had a huge advantage, in addition to other weaknesses of the Mamlūk side, as will be explained below. The sultan made a special effort to pay his troops, whose salaries had been often in arrears. Even the mamlūks' sons, the *awlād al-nās*, were enlisted, although they were always considered to be inferior fighters, and their pay was much lower than that of the mamlūks. In order to emphasize the religious nature of his regime, the sultan ordered the caliph, the four chief *qāḍī*s, the shaykhs of the most important Ṣūfī orders (*ṭuruq*) and the rectors of Egypt's most revered shrines and sepulchers to join the army on its march. Qāsim ibn Aḥmad ibn Bayazīd, Salīm's young nephew, who had fled to the Mamlūk sultanate to escape death at the hand of Salīm, was also taken along for his symbolic and political value. Many physicians, clerks and artisans were also ordered to go. Al-Ghawrī took with him his huge gold and jewelry treasures; fifty camels were needed to carry all these riches, whose value exceeded more than a million dīnārs. Before he left he appointed Ṭūmānbāy, the *dāwādār*, who was the sultan's nephew, as his deputy during his absence (*nā'ib al-ghayba*).

While al-Ghawrī was still at Raydāniyya, outside Cairo, a courier arrived, carrying a letter from Salīm, which surprisingly offered peace (May 24, 1516). Salīm calls al-Ghawrī "my father", and asks for his forgiveness. He explains that it was ʿAlā' al-Dawla who had instigated the quarrel between his father (Bayazīd) and Sultan Qāytbāy. Salīm promised to return the lands he had seized and also explained that it was not his fault that slavers stopped importing mamlūks to Syria and Egypt, but they were deterred by the debasement of al-Ghawrī's currency. Al-Ghawrī regarded Salīm's missive as a ruse intended to dissuade him from leading his army to Syria, and started his move as planned, leaving Cairo on the next day.

It seems certain that al-Ghawrī's expedition was a defensive move. In addition, he was persuaded to march into northern Syria by false information provided to him by Khāyrbak, the governor of the province of Aleppo, about an incursion of Shāh Ismāʿīl's forces into Mamlūk territories and the occupation of Āmid by them. Khāyrbak had already concluded a secret deal with Salīm to betray his sultan. The warning of the governor of the province of Damascus that no enemy was in sight, and that the economic conditions in Syria would make the presence of a large army difficult, went unheeded. Al-Ghawrī believed that another war between the Ottomans and the Ṣafavids was imminent: he was hoping to stay out of the conflict, but was on his guard.

Al-Ghawrī entered Gaza on June 5, and arrived at Damascus on June 19. On July 11 the sultan entered Aleppo. There he found Rukn al-Dīn, a high-ranking *qāḍī*, and Karaca Aḥmad Pasha, two emissaries sent by Salīm, who was now stationed in Kayseri. Salīm emphasized again his determination to move against the Ṣafavid heretics, and urged al-Ghawrī not to interfere. Indeed, al-Ghawrī sent to Salīm an officer to reassure the Ottomans of his neutrality. When this messenger arrived at Salīm's camp, he was badly mistreated and humiliated, and even threatened with execution, and was then sent back to al-Ghawrī with a message: "Meet me at Marj Dābiq [a place north of Aleppo]!" Al-Ghawrī swore his amīrs to loyalty on the ʿUthmānī Qur'ān and the troops passed under an arch made of two swords, in a Turkish ceremony of pledging allegiance.

One can only speculate about Salīm's real intentions. Were his declared policy of an ideological war against the Ṣafavids at that time and the peace overtures to the Mamlūk sultan only a smokescreen to disguise his plans to destroy the Mamlūks by taking them off-guard? Ibn Iyās believes so. Another version of events, mentioned by al-Ḥalabī, another chronicler, reports that Salīm intercepted a secret message from al-Ghawrī to Ismāʿīl asking for his assistance against the Ottomans. This account, if true, would support the claims of the Ottoman propaganda.

According to an official Ottoman missive, Salīm learned on 4 Rajab/ August 3 that al-Ghawrī had turned to Ismāʿīl for help.[7] On the next day the state council (*dīwān*) was convened and it was decided to attack al-Ghawrī. Even if this version is correct, one should make a distinction between an anti-Ottoman Mamlūk-Ṣafavid alliance (which was not proven) and al--Ghawrī's desperate call for help in the face of an imminent attack by the superior Ottoman forces.

Was Salīm's decision to fight al-Ghawrī, which was made at Elbistan, prompted by his wish to remove a possible threat to his flank before moving against Ismāʿīl? A modern historian argues convincingly that the lesson of the aftermath of the battle of Chaldiran in August 1514, from which Salīm emerged victorious but was forced to retreat due to the severity of the winter in the Iranian plateau and the Shah's scorched earth policy, was not forgotten. When Salīm led his army from Istanbul on June 5, 1516, he was probably thinking of spending the autumn and the winter in a warmer land than Iran.[8]

[7] Ferīdūn, *Munsheāt al-salāṭīn* (Istanbul, AH 1274), 1, 450.

[8] J.-L. Bacqué-Grammont, *Les ottomans, les safavides, et leurs voisins* (Istanbul, 1987),191–94.

There is no doubt that Salīm was fully aware of his decisive military superiority over the Mamlūk sultan. We have clear evidence of his emissary's attending in Cairo the equestrian exercises of the Egyptian army which al-Ghawrī revived and proudly displayed in front of his own subjects and foreign spectators. As one study suggests, one can imagine the kind of report sent by the Ottoman emissary to his sultan about the outdated military ethos of cavalry warfare and the weakness of the Mamlūk army in firearms, the modern weapon already used effectively by the Ottomans.[9] The Mamlūks' numerical weakness in comparison with the Ottomans must also have been known to Salīm. The Ottomans were informed by traitors in the Mamlūk ruling elite; Khāyrbak was only the highest-ranking officer who had secret contracts with the Ottomans; Ibn Iyās mentions other names of important bureaucrats who had betrayed their sultan.

The fate of Syria was decided in a single battle on the plain of Marj Dābiq on Sunday, 25 Rajab 922/August 24, 1516. Al-Ghawrī surrounded himself with forty *ashrāf* bearing copies of the Qur'ān on their heads. The religious dignitaries, *ʿulamā'* and Ṣūfīs and the caliph, stood by the sultan. The sultan's right flank was commanded by Sībāy, the governor of Damascus, and the left flank by Khāyrbak. The commanders of the two main Ottoman flanks were Sinān Pasha, the Grand Vizier, and Yūnus Pasha.

The mamlūks' excellent horsemanship and valor brought them initial success. Yet their cause was doomed from the start. Although exact figures about those periods are rarely known, most sources estimate the size of the Mamlūk army at around 20,000 men, comprising mamlūks, auxiliary forces and many Bedouin Arabs. The Egyptian and Syrian army was probably outnumbered by a ratio of three to one at the very least.[10] The Mamlūk historians were overawed by the size of the huge Ottoman army, the largest that anyone had ever seen.

Al-Ghawrī's force was seriously weakened by treason and disunity. Fulfilling his secret agreement with Salīm, Khāyrbak withdrew with all his troops toward Ḥamā in the heat of the battle. The sultan himself was also to blame for the low morale of his soldiers. During the fighting, he threw into the front lines the veteran mamlūks (*qarāniṣa*), who had been purchased and trained by previous sultans, trying to spare his own mamlūks (*julbān*). As soon as the *qarāniṣa* realized what was happening, they understandably lost their motivation.

9 The classical study of Mamluks and firearms is D. Ayalon's *Gunpowder and Firearms in the Mamlūk Kingdom* (London, 1956).

10 See, for example, Ibn Iyās, V, 123, where more than 60,000 Ottoman troops are mentioned. The figure of 100,000, mentioned by Ibn Ṭūlūn, *Mufākahat al-khullān* (II, p. 30) is certainly an exaggeration. The Ottoman sources (Ferīdūn, p. 479 and Saʿdüddīn, p. 333) estimate the size of the Mamlūk army at the battle of Marj Dābiq at from 20,000 to 30,000 men.

The crucial cause of the Mamlūks' swift defeat, however, was the effective use of firearms – cannon and arquebus – by the Ottomans and the total absence of these modern weapons in the Mamlūk camp. While the Ottomans had already fought efficiently with firearms against the Ṣafavids at Chaldiran, inflicting upon them heavy casualties, the only artillery the Mamlūks had at their disposal were cannons which were used only for defense (at seaports or the Citadel of Cairo), and not on the battlefield. As for handguns (*bunduq raṣāṣ*), the Mamlūks refused to adopt them for psychological and social objections. The ethos of the Mamlūk caste was based on horsemanship (*furūsiyya*). Since the arquebus could not be operated from horseback, its adoption would end a very long and deep-rooted tradition and cause a profound transformation of the structure of the army, and hence of the ruling elite. Ibn Zunbul, the best exponent of that ethos, regarded firearms as un-Islamic and unchivalrous. On the other hand, the Ottoman elite troops (mainly the Janissaries) were infantrymen and had no serious problem getting used to handguns instead of the traditional weapons.

Thus, the battle of Marj Dābiq was over very quickly. The aged sultan fell from the saddle and died, probably of a stroke; his body was never found. The Ottoman soldiers dispersed the mamlūks and killed many of them, including the commander of the army (*atābek*) and the governors of Damascus, Ṭarābulus, Ṣafad and Ḥimṣ. The survivors retreated to Aleppo, but the local inhabitants attacked them and drove them away in revenge for the pillaging and molestation they had suffered from the soldiers during their billeting before the battle. Many soldiers arrived in Damascus disguised as Bedouin and other poor people.

Salīm treated the caliph with respect and promised to return him to Baghdād, the ancestral seat of the ʿAbbāsid caliphate before Sultan Baybars had transferred it to Cairo. Salīm chided the three chief *qāḍīs* of Cairo who had accompanied al-Ghawrī, accusing them of corruption. To demonstrate the completeness of his victory the sultan sent a lame clerk leaning on a cane to take over the forsaken citadel of Aleppo with the huge treasury which al-Ghawrī had deposited there before going to Marj Dābiq. These funds enabled Salīm to cover the costs of his stay in Syria and the campaign to conquer Egypt. Khāyrbak soon reappeared, wearing Ottoman clothes, his beard shaved off after the Ottoman custom.

After appointing an Ottoman pasha as military governor, and a *qāḍī* to administer the province of Aleppo, Salīm resumed his march southwards, and reached the outskirts of Damascus at the end of Shaʿbān/August 23. Twelve days later the sultan entered the city, making efforts to show his respect for local Muslim personages and sites. Later, he built a mosque and a Ṣūfī hospice near the tomb of the famous mystic Muḥyi'l-Dīn Ibn ʿArabī (d. 1240), who is buried in the Ṣāliḥiyya quarter. Inevitably, the descent of such a huge army on Damascus was a traumatic experience for the inhabitants.

Ibn Ṭūlūn, the chronicler, complains of many wrongdoings perpetrated by the soldiery, such as molestation of women, invasion of private houses, and eviction of the owners. Ibn Ṭūlūn himself was forced to leave his home, and his books were thrown out. Many cases of desecration of holy places and brutality toward the inhabitants of the city are reported. Ibn Ṭūlūn, who as a professional *ʿālim* was sensitive to variants in religious practice, notes that the Ottomans had their own customs in performing the religious ordinances, which seemed strange to the local Muslims.

In administrative matters, the Ottomans in Syria followed their usual methods of dealing with newly conquered territories conducting surveys and registration of all sources of revenue for the purpose of taxation, inspecting title deeds of private properties (*amlāk*) and *awqāf*, confiscating those whose holders could not prove their legal claims and reorganizing the judicial system, so that Ottoman, Turkish-speaking *qāḍī*s would be in charge and that litigation and administration would be more centralized and economical to pursue. The local currency was replaced by Ottoman coins, a measure which caused economic suffering; the weights and measures of Istanbul were also enforced. As we shall see, the same methods were later applied in Cairo, and elicited similar negative responses.

Generally speaking, the Ottomans appointed in greater Syria (including Palestine, Lebanon and Transjordan) their own officers as governors in the main cities, but were ready to rely on tribal or local chieftains as their representatives in rural and mountainous areas, as long as they remained loyal or useful. A typical example was Nāṣir al-Dīn ibn Ḥanash, the Bedouin chief of the Biqāʿ.

The only battle in Syria after Marj Dābiq took place in Gaza in Palestine on 27 Dhu'l-Qaʿda, 922/December 22, 1516. Jānbirdī al-Ghazālī, one of the most able and energetic Mamlūk amīrs, and the governor of Ḥamā, had arrived in Cairo as a fugitive following the rout at Marj Dābiq. He was later sent to Gaza in an attempt to create an outpost for an eventual reoccupation of Syria. An Ottoman force headed by Grand Vizier Sinān Pasha easily defeated the Egyptians there; al-Ghazālī succeeded in escaping to Egypt. False rumors about al-Ghazālī's victory prompted inhabitants of Gaza (and according to an Ottoman source, of Ramla as well) to kill Ottoman soldiers and loot their camp. After his victory, Sinān Pasha retaliated by conducting a massacre in the two towns.

The conquest of Egypt

Meanwhile, the Egyptian amīrs elected Ṭūmānbāy to the sultanate. According to Ibn Iyās's account Ṭūmānbāy cuts a truly impressive figure. Already as al-Ghawrī's deputy during the fated Syrian campaign, he showed all the qualities of an ideal ruler. He is described as just, young (he was in his forties), energetic, brave, modest, and pious. As soon as he assumed the responsibility of government he did his utmost to maintain security in the capital and the countryside and to abolish the unjust and oppressive ways by which al-Ghawrī had enriched himself. When it became confirmed that al-Ghawrī had been killed, the grandees compelled the reluctant Ṭūmānbāy to accept the sultanate. He understood the seriousness of the situation: the Ottoman attack was imminent, the treasury was nearly empty, and the amīrs' loyalty was dubious. Ṭūmānbāy made his officers swear allegiance to him, and the ceremony was administered by the Ṣūfī shaykh Abu'l-Suʿūd al-Jāriḥī. The emirs pledged to restore the just regime of Qāytbāy.

Ṭūmānbāy was installed as sultan under the regal name al-Malik al-Ashraf (like al-Ghawrī, but also like Qāytbāy, whose just rule Ṭūmānbāy tried to emulate). The ceremony was modest, since part of the regalia had been lost with Qānṣuh al-Ghawrī. It was Yaʿqūb, Caliph al-Mutawakkil III's father, a former caliph himself, who formally invested Ṭūmānbāy with the office and accepted his vow of allegiance (*bayʿa*), in the name of his son, who was in captivity in Salīm's camp. The people of Cairo accepted their new sultan with jubilation. In a symbolic gesture, Ṭūmānbāy sat to dispense justice on the same couch used by Qāytbāy and not on the *masṭaba* where Qānṣūh al-Ghawrī had sat. The sultan named new chief *qāḍī*s, but unlike former sultans, did not take any money from them for the appointment; instead, he warned them against taking bribes. He ordered the flogging of advisors who suggested imposing unjust taxes on the markets and grain after he had abolished them.

Ṭūmānbāy reviewed his army and made appointments and promotions of officers and bureaucrats. He named al-Ghazālī governor of the province of Damascus. He also reinstated the powerful Arab Bedouin shaykhs of the Banū Baqar clan as governors of the important province of al-Sharqiyya. He was compelled to do so, in spite of the family's notorious turbulence, owing to the region's economic and strategic importance as the gateway to Egypt from the north.

Ṭūmānbāy was desperate for additional manpower for the army, and had to look for it even in questionable places. He called up a great number of Bedouin, traditionally considered unreliable and undisciplined. Young city roughs (*zuʿar*) were encouraged to join, and even criminals in hiding were promised amnesty if they joined the army. Ṭūmānbāy wanted to enlist a thousand men from Cairo's north African (Maghribī) community, but they refused, claiming that they were not accustomed to go with the army, and besides, they were ready to fight Franks, not Muslims.

The Mamlūk high command belatedly realized the importance of fire-arms. In the short time available to him, Ṭūmānbāy focused his energy on providing his army with cannons and handguns. Following the example of Sultan al-Nāṣir Muḥammad ibn Qāytbāy (901–03/1496–98), a frivolous young man who nevertheless did the right thing, Ṭūmānbāy created a unit of black arquebusiers (*ʿabīd nafṭiyya*). Some Maghribīs and Turkomans were also included. As already indicated, it was inconceivable that mamlūks should become infantrymen who carried handguns.

Like the young sultan, Ṭūmānbāy marched through Cairo followed by his new military unit. He also introduced wooden carriages pulled by oxen to carry the soldiers and their handguns, adopting an Ottoman technique observed by Ibn Ṭūlūn in Damascus. Ibn Iyās saw a procession of 100 carriages, each carrying a copper cannon (*mukḥula*) followed by 200 camels laden with gunpowder, lead, iron and other war materials. Ṭūmānbāy prepared for a long siege, and relied on artillery for defense. He ordered a long trench to be dug from Sabīl ʿAllān to al-Jabal al-Aḥmar (the Red Mountain) and the Maṭariyya gardens to protect the heavy guns. He barricaded the positions with a fence; the sultan and his amīrs themselves carried stones to finish it.

Meanwhile, Salīm was pondering his options. Since the possibility of a Mamlūk-Ṣafavid alliance was removed and his hold over Anatolia was firm, he had been in no hurry to carry his campaign into Egypt. Some advisors were apprehensive about the hardships of advancing the army through the Sinai desert with its hostile nomad population. Salīm proposed to Ṭūmānbāy that he govern Egypt as his viceroy. In his letter, which he sent with a small delegation, Salīm emphasized his own royal pedigree as opposed to Ṭūmānbāy's unknown origin, as a former imported slave. The proposal was rejected, and Salīm's emissary was ill-treated (according to Ottoman sources, he was put to death). It was then that the above-mentioned expedition to retake Gaza, which was defeated on December 22, was sent.

Salim therefore decided to proceed with his campaign. The Ottomans realized that Egypt was necessary to control Syria; there is also little doubt that Khāyrbak's advice contributed to Salīm's determination to conquer Egypt. The people of Egypt panicked and many of the inhabitants of Sharqiyya province fled to the capital. In Cairo itself the rich concealed their valuable fabrics and there was also talk of escaping to Upper Egypt. The fallaḥīn refused to pay their taxes before it became clear who would be their ruler, to avoid paying twice.

After visiting the holy places in Jerusalem and Hebron, Salīm led his army through Sinai. A few soldiers were murdered by Bedouin, but the main body of the army arrived without difficulty in Egypt, and on 28 Dhū ʾl-Ḥijja/ January 22 the Ottoman vanguard reached Birkat al-Ḥājj, a few miles north of Cairo. Ṭūmānbāy wished to meet the Ottomans at al-Ṣāliḥiyya, where the desert route entered the confines of the Delta, before they could provision and rest, but his amīrs insisted on making a stand at the fortifications of al-Raydāniyya, immediately outside Cairo.

The battle of Raydāniyya, which sealed the fate of the Mamlūk sultanate, was fought on 29 Dhuʾl-Ḥijja 922/January 23, 1517. The Egyptian army, 20,000-strong by contemporary estimates, was defeated within twenty minutes. The heavy guns, on which Ṭūmānbāy invested so much effort, were utterly useless; an Ottoman force coming from the rear, from the direction of the Red Mountain, attacked his gunners (many of whom were European Christians – Franks – if the Ottoman sources are correct) and seized the cannons, which could not be rotated to fire in the opposite direction. Again, the handguns and light artillery of the Ottomans inflicted heavy casualties in the Egyptians' ranks. The mamlūks fought bravely, and Sinān Pasha himself was killed. Ṭūmānbāy with a handful of his mamlūks and arquebusiers fought for a full eighty minutes until he too had to flee. On the next day, the last of the Muslim year, the *khuṭba* was recited for the Friday prayer in the name of Sultan Salīm. He was called "the Breaker of the Two Armies and the Servitor of the Two Holy Sanctuaries" (*khādim al-ḥaramayn al-sharīfayn*).

The Ottoman soldiers looted homes of amīrs and other wealthy persons, and pillaged the granaries of old Cairo and Būlāq. They also abducted the mamlūks' male servants and black slaves. The looting continued for three days until an official proclamation promised security and peace, and Janissaries were stationed at the gates to enforce it. Yet a systematic manhunt for the Circassians (i.e. mamlūks) started, and those captured were immediately put to death. Many Bedouin and Ḥijāzī Arab residents of Cairo were also executed and their severed heads were suspended from specially erected poles. Anyone of the mamlūks' sons, *awlād al-nās*, wearing the typical Mamlūk headgear, the *takhfīfa* or the red *zamṭ*, was put to death; so that they used the turban (*ʿimāma*) typical of *ʿulamāʾ*.

In the days following the occupation many acts of killing (mainly mamlūks, *zuʿar*, and Bedouins) took place, as well as the pillage and desecration of holy places. Like any other military occupation, the Ottoman conquest of Cairo was traumatic for its inhabitants. Ibn Iyās compares it to the conquest of Egypt by Nebuchadnezzar in antiquity, who supposedly laid waste the whole country, and to the destruction of Baghdād by the Mongols in 1258, which symbolized a disaster of immense magnitude. While such comparisons are gross exaggerations, they reveal the chronicler's attitude toward the Ottomans.

Sultan Salīm preferred to camp at Būlāq on the bank of the river rather than stay in the Citadel. Ṭūmānbāy, who had gathered a force of mamlūks and Bedouin, strengthened by the city toughs, made a sudden night attack (5 Muḥarram/January 28). The bloody streetfighting went on for four days and nights (on Friday, the *khuṭba* was even called in the name of Ṭūmānbāy), until Ṭūmānbāy was forced to flee again. Hundreds of captured mamlūks and Bedouin were beheaded. The executioner, who allegedly was a European Christian or a Jew, separated the heads and threw the bodies into the Nile. In their pursuit of the mamlūks and their allies, the Ottoman soldiers desecrated some of the holiest shrines and mosques of Cairo, such as the mosques of al-Azhar, al-Ḥākim and Ibn Ṭūlūn and the sepulchers of Sayyida Nafīsa, al-Imām al-Shāfiʿī and al-Layth ibn Saʿd. When the fighting was over, it was proclaimed that the mamlūks would be given amnesty if they surrendered; some four hundred did so, and were instantly imprisoned. However, Jānbirdī al-Ghazālī was pardoned, on the assumption that he would henceforth cooperate. The Ottomans also put to death in the Alexandria prison the former sultan al-Ẓāhir Qānṣūh (1498–99) fearing that the Mamlūks might proclaim him their sultan.

Ṭūmānbāy gathered a force of mamlūks and Bedouin at al-Bahnasā in Middle Egypt and sent a message to Salīm offering to act as his deputy in Egypt. Salīm dispatched a delegation consisting of the chief Egyptian *qāḍī*s with a proposal of a treaty. Again, Ṭūmānbāy failed to control some of his hotheaded amīrs, and one of them killed a *qāḍī*, a member of the delegation. Ṭūmānbāy's third battle against the Ottomans took place at a place called Wardān or al-Munāwāt in the Giza desert on 10 Rabīʿ I 923/April 2, 1517. He was again defeated. The Ottomans executed 800 mamlūks who had surrendered after obtaining a promise of quarter. At least 700 mamlūks were chained, brought to Alexandria, and sent to Istanbul. After his defeat, Ṭūmānbāy escaped westward to Buḥayra province, where he took refuge in the house of a Bedouin shaykh who was indebted to him. The Arab swore seven times on the Qurʾān that he would not hand Ṭūmānbāy over to the Ottomans, but immediately broke his oath. The Mamlūk sultan was hanged like a common criminal at Cairo's Zuwayla Gate. The scene of Ṭūmānbāy's execution, during which he proved his courage and piety, is touching. Salīm had achieved his purpose; he scotched the rumors that Ṭūmānbāy was still at large.

Soon afterwards Salīm declared his intention to return to his capital. Meanwhile, he spent his time visiting parts of Cairo and relaxing at the Nilometer (*miqyās*),where he ordered a pavilion erected at the palace that had been built by al-Ghawrī. Later, he left Cairo for fifteen days to visit Alexandria. Before departing, he prayed at al-Azhar and donated presents to mosques and Ṣūfī centers. He also displayed his interest in the *kiswa*, the brocaded carpet covering of the Kaʿba, and the coverings of the Prophet's tomb and Abraham's tomb in Hebron.

Khāyrbak, the first Ottoman governor, and Egyptian views of the occupation

Salīm named Yūnus Pasha as the governor of Egypt, but later changed his mind and appointed Khāyrbak. An Ottoman chronicler writes that Yūnus was guilty of corruption and oppression. Later, on his way northward, Salīm ordered his execution at a place on the Egyptian-Syrian border. The Ottoman sources attribute his fate to an argument he had with the short-tempered sultan. Salīm began his return on 23 Shaʿbān 923/September 10, 1517 stopping to say a prayer at Qāytbāy's tomb. Before he left Cairo, Salīm received the son of Barakāt, the *sharīfi* ruler of Mecca, who demonstrated his submission, since the Ḥijāz fell within Egypt's sphere of influence.

The fifth volume of Ibn Iyās's chronicle, which describes in minute detail the fall of the Mamlūk sultanate and the early years of Ottoman rule, has a winning spontaneity. His description of the suffering of the Egyptian population, that of Cairo in particular, seems credible. Nevertheless, it should be borne in mind that many of the misdeeds perpetrated by unruly soldiers and the oppressive measures against the civilian population did not start with the Ottoman occupation but were common under the Mamlūk sultans, as Ibn Iyās's account of the preceding period makes abundantly clear. However, it is true that the situation worsened after the occupation, since the Ottoman army was much larger than the Mamlūk army. Besides, the Ottoman soldiers were now in a foreign land, far away from their homes and families, and many of them were more culturally and socially alien to the Egyptians than the mamlūks. The latter were also of foreign stock and Turkish-speaking, but the whole of their military and religious education had taken place in Egypt. Many of the Ottoman soldiers were only superficially Islamized, or at least that was the Egyptians' impression of them. Bad Muslims automatically meant bad people, and this stigma was attached to all Ottomans, who were known as *tarākima*, "Turcoman", or *arwām*, "Rumis" (the appellation *atrāk*, "Turks", was reserved for the mamlūks, although most of them were Circassians at the time). According to Ibn Iyās (and other writers, although they were not as vehement), all the Ottomans – Sultan Salīm, his *qāḍīs*, and his soldiers were negligent of the ordinances of Islam. Salīm was described as a drinker and a pederast who did not dispense justice. The Ottoman soldiers generally were depicted as drinkers, hashish addicts, and pederasts; they did not fast during Ramaḍān, and most of them did not pray. They often molested women and boys in the streets.

The Ottoman occupation also altered urban festivities. During Mamlūk times, the people of Cairo had witnessed splendid celebrations and colorful ceremonies at which Mamlūk horsemen displayed their superb skills in war games and parades. Now, the Egyptians were displeased by the apparently egalitarian spirit in the Ottoman army, which "was a rabble, and one could not tell an amīr from an ordinary soldier". It must be mentioned that Ibn Iyās's hatred of the Ottomans carried him too far in his denigration of them. Ibn Ṭūlūn, who went to see the Ottoman camp at Damascus, was favorably impressed by its orderliness; he expressly mentioned the various insignia and rank marks, and he noted that the camp was served by many specialists – physicians, artisans, cooks, and so on.[11] The Mamlūk army may have been more colorful and splendid in appearance than the Ottoman army, but it did not occur to Ibn Iyās that this could be symptomatic of degeneration.

Public religious celebrations were also adversely affected. The first annual celebration of the Prophet's birthday (*mawlid al-nabī*: 11 Rabīʿ al-awwal) passed almost unnoticed. The traditional monthly meeting of the four chief *qāḍī*s and the amīrs in the sultan's court did not take place, and the practice of distributing food to the public was abolished. The Ottomans sold the large tent used in the birthday celebration, which had cost Qāytbāy 30,000 dīnārs, to Maghribī merchants for 400 dīnārs. "The tent," says Ibn Iyās, "was one of the symbols of the kingdom and was sold for the lowest price. The Ottomans did not understand its value . . . It was one of their bad deeds in Egypt."[12]

Ottoman soldiers often stole food from the bazaar and snatched men's headgear in the streets. To protect themselves against the horsemen, people constructed gates across the narrow alleys. Later, Salīm ordered the populace to close all city quarters with gates and to station guards, at the inhabitants' cost. The soldiers took horses and mules from mills and camels from the water carriers, thereby causing shortages of flour and water.

People were forced to pull heavy guns and to load huge stone pillars, which the Ottomans had torn out of some palaces, onto ships bound for Istanbul. Marble was also stripped from buildings and shipped away. Later, in 1522, when the Ottoman navy needed rowers for the galleys headed to conquer the island of Rhodes, people, mostly the city poor and fallāḥīn, were forcibly gathered in from the streets.

The people of Cairo were shocked when they learned of the Ottoman practice of *sürgün*, or deportation, to Istanbul. Groups of notables, artisans needed for construction works in Istanbul, officials, Christians and Jews were deported. The most distinguished exile was the last ʿAbbāsid caliph, al-Mutawakkil ibn al-Mustamsik Yaʿqūb, a respected, though politically powerless figure, who had been captured at Marj Dābiq, and had been brought to Cairo with the Ottomans. Salīm treated him respectfully and gave him a sense of importance and influence that he had hitherto never enjoyed. While everyone was aware that the caliphate was powerless, it still had symbolic importance. The exile of the caliph signaled that Egypt had ceased to be a caliphate, the center of an empire, and had become a province administered from a distant capital.

The *sürgün* caused the exiles and their families, who remained behind, much distress. Some were lost at sea and others were lonely and suffered

[11] Ibn Ṭūlūn, *Mufākahat al-khullān*, II, 30–31.
[12] Ibn Iyās, V, 172.

hardship in Istanbul. A few exiles were allowed to go home for short visits, after the authorities had taken precautions to ensure their return to Istanbul. When Sulaymān became sultan, his benevolence replaced his father's harshness and most of the exiles were permitted to return to Egypt.

From the point of view of Ottoman interests, the choice of Khāyrbak was a success. The appointment of a member of the former ruling elite accorded with the Ottoman principles of administering conquered territories. Khāyrbak resurrected several customs and ceremonies of the Mamlūk sultanate. His official title was *malik al-umarā*ʾ, "the king of amīrs"; he was not a pasha, since he did not come from the Ottoman ruling establishment as did his successors. As already mentioned, he helped to save the mamlūks and employed them in various capacities, primarily in provincial administration, where their familiarity with the irrigation system and with the Bedouin was indispensable. Nevertheless, Khāyrbak remained faithful to his Ottoman masters until his death in October 1522. Fearing that he would not be reappointed at the end of each annual term, he loyally obeyed commands and regulations from Istanbul, where his son was kept as a hostage. He solicited the *ʿulamāʾ* to report favorably to Istanbul about his conduct as governor; he also gave huge gifts of money to Ottoman envoys to strengthen his position.

Khāyrbak was born in Georgia, not in Circassia, like the majority of the mamlūks, and he had never been a slave. Ibn Iyās believed that he hated Circassian mamlūks, but this is not credible, since many mamlūks owed him their lives. He was a shrewd, self-seeking man who was good at assessing situations and adroitly maneuvered to his personal advantage the conflicts among military units in Egypt. Both the mamlūks and the Ottoman soldiers complained that he ill-treated them. He was a notorious miser, and payments due to soldiers and officials were always in arrears, while he continued to enrich himself. Only on his deathbed did he display generosity, donating money to religious institutions. Ibn Iyās characterizes Khāyrbak as bad-tempered, often drunk and cruel. He was capable of sentencing people to death because of a trifle or personal caprice. He once ordered a man to be hanged whose only crime was that he had picked a few cucumbers, *khiyār shanbar*, a crop which was a government monopoly (the vegetable was used as laxative). He also gave the Jewish master of the mint authority over the Muslims' (i.e. public) money, authority which was abused. A Christian official was put in charge of the central government offices. On the other hand, Khāyrbak overthrew the great bureaucratic family of Banū al-Jīʿān, which had been in charge of the fiscal apparatus for over a century.

Khāyrbak demonstrated his prudence when he turned a deaf ear to the governor of Syria, Janbirdī al-Ghazālī, who tried to incite him to fight the Ottomans. Al-Ghazālī was a Mamlūk amīr, who like Khāyrbak had gone over to Salim, but unlike him, cherished his independence; he thought that

Salim's death and the succession of his inexperienced son offered him his opportunity. Khāyrbak sentenced to death Mamlūks who attempted to join the rebels, along with several Cairo commoners who gossiped about the possibility of Khāyrbak's joining the revolt.

It was perhaps characteristic of the transition period that those appointed to high positions were not Mamlūk amīrs, but their progeny (*awlād nās*) and bureaucrats. Such a man was Zayn al-Dīn Barakāt ibn Mūsā, an efficient and ruthless administrator, who had risen under al-Ghawrī from humble origins to become the sultan's most powerful civilian assistant. Under the Ottomans he was given the same power. His proven talent to provide the government with funds which he extorted from the rich, and his popularity with the common people because of his performance as market inspector (*muḥtasib*) made him indispensable. His reappointment to that position under the Ottomans greatly contributed to price stability in the markets. Later, he was charged with the cadastral survey of Upper Egypt, a position that had been assigned under the Mamlūks to *dawādār*s, the most powerful amīrs. He was even appointed commander of the annual pilgrims' caravan to Mecca (*amīr al-ḥājj*), a post held under the Mamlūks by the highest ranking amīrs. This appointment did not denote that the Ottomans had no respect for the pilgrimage, as Ibn Iyās claims, but rather shows Barakāt's power and efficiency. Finally, he was in charge of the state finances, and in addition was given the administration of al-Sharqiyya province as a tax-farm (*iltizām*).

Another man who became prominent during the first years of Ottoman rule was Jānim al-Ḥamzāwī, an amīr of *awlād al-nās* descent. He rendered important services to the Ottomans as a liaison officer with Istanbul and as a successful *amīr al-ḥājj*. He played a role in the capture of Qāsim Bey, the young Ottoman prince, who had fled to Egypt, and after the battle of Marj Dābiq lived as a refugee among the Bedouin. Qāsim was put to death, to Sultan Salīm's relief.

Ibn Iyās repeatedly expressed his resentment at the high-handed bureaucrats (*mubāshirūn)*, who oppressed the people and did not know their place; they married daughters and widows of amīrs, something they would not have dared to do before. Long-established privileges and benefits were abolished. Naturally, the mamlūks' *iqṭāʿāt* were confiscated. Then came the turn of the allotments to the *awlād al-nās*. All title deeds were subject to inspection, and many lost their pensions – first the children and women who had military pensions, then charitable pensions, and, finally, the revenues accruing from villages dedicated to *awqāf* were seized. Later it was decreed that all the *waqf* registers and documents should be deposited in the Citadel rather than be kept with the administrators. A financial official, the *qassām*, "divider," came from Istanbul to impose a tax on bequests. A *defterdār*, chief financial inspector, was sent to the seaports to ensure that the customs duties be transferred directly to Istanbul. All these and similar measures were the beginning of a systematic economic exploitation, in cash and kind, of Egypt, now a province.

The Ottoman monetary innovations caused the population much suffering. Several times the government decreed and proclaimed the abolition of the old (Mamlūk) coinage and the introduction of a new (Ottoman) coinage. The new coins were lighter, and made from inferior metal, and the public, compelled to trade with the new currency, lost as much as a third of the value of their money, and did not trust the debased currency; consequently the fall-off in trade caused the markets to close down. The authorities reacted with threats, and a death sentence was carried out on a Ḥijāzī money-changer who changed coins not according to the official rate. Since these stern measures failed to calm down the markets, the authorities had to resort to moderation and flexibility, several times at the advice of the experienced Barakāt ibn Mūsā. Thus, at one time the value of the gold *ashrafī* dīnār was set at two rates, one for exchange and the other for trade; this brought about the reopening of the markets. In these turbulent times, the mint became an even more sensitive institution than usual. The men who operated it, many of them Jews, were suspected of debasing the coinage. (Again, this kind of accusation had been raised before and would be repeated again.) In August 1521, Khāyrbak appointed an Ottoman *qāḍī* to be in charge of the mint as a supervisor; the master of the mint was a Jew, as before.

As in Damascus, the Ottomans introduced the weights and measures of Istanbul to Cairo by official decree, and the local ones were abolished. Following a custom in Istanbul, the Ottomans ordered that all the dogs in Cairo be killed as a sanitary measure against epidemics. The people regarded the killings as a bad omen and interceded with the governor to stop them.

Yet nothing the Ottomans did provoked as much anger as their legal and juridical innovations, particularly in the sensitive area of personal law. There was much resentment against, though little information about, the non-*sharʿīa* sources of Ottoman administrative law (*qānūn*). The most offensive legal change was the imposition of a tax on marriage contracts called *yasaq*: virgins were required to pay twice as much as women who had been previously married. The Cairene *ʿulamāʾ* denounced the tax as a violation of the Prophet's custom (*sunna*), and for a while the number of marriages decreased. A Maghribī *ʿālim* – the Maghribīs were always the most uncompromising and fearless when religion was at stake – cried into the governor's face: "This is the infidels' law [*yasaq*]!"

In the organization of Egypt's system of justice, the Ottomans adopted an approach of trial and error, but ultimately aimed at Ottomanization and centralization, with the subordination of the local *qāḍī*s to a Turkish-speaking, Istanbul-appointed, chief judge. At first, Salīm reappointed the four senior Egyptian *qāḍī*s, each representing a *madhhab* (legal school). But then a Turkish judge, the *qāḍī al-ʿArab*, namely a *qāḍī* for Arab (Egyptian) affairs, was appointed. He imposed new fees and forbade the Egyptian *qāḍī*s to hear cases or ratify legal transactions at their residences as had been usual. They were warned not to confirm marriage contracts between Ottoman soldiers and women of Mamlūk descent.

The injunction to dismiss or reduce the *qāḍī*s' personnel, such as deputy judges (*nuwwāb*, sing. *nāʾib*), professional witnesses or notaries (*shuhūd*), agents (*wukalāʾ*) and messengers (*rusul*) is reported several times. Then came a reversal order allowing judges to work only in their residences. The Ṣāliḥiyya *madrasa*, which had been "the citadel of the *ʿulamāʾ*", remained deserted. In May 1522, only five years after the conquest, there arrived in Cairo a Turkish chief *qāḍī*, called *qāḍiʾl-ʿaskar* (*kazasker* in Turkish pronunciation, literally "military judge"), putting an end to the tradition, established at the beginning of the Mamlūk period, of four chief *qāḍī*s. This *qāḍī* appointed both Ottoman and Egyptian deputies. Applying Istanbul's standards of morality in Egypt, he forbade women to ride on donkeys. The donkey-drivers sold their animals and bought saddle horses, on which women rode while the drivers held the bridle. The *qāḍiʾl-ʾaskar* also interfered in the stipulations of marriage contracts, again according to the custom of Istanbul, imposing more obligations on women after their wedding. The *qāḍī* supervised all *waqf* deeds, and made the *qassām* ("divider") collect a 20 percent inheritance tax.

All these changes were resented by the people of Cairo, and in particular the *ʿulamāʾ*, whose interests and professional pride were slighted. Ibn Iyās complained again and again that the status of the holy *sharīʿa* law precipitously declined in those days. He called the Ottoman *qāḍī* "more ignorant than an ass, without any knowledge of the Islamic law".

The Mamlūk and Ottoman corps

The most significant changes which took place in Egypt following the Ottoman occupation were related to the military society.[13] Briefly stated, the main developments were the reversal of Salīm's policy of exterminating the mamlūks, and their integration into the Ottoman garrison of Egypt, thereby assuring their survival as a distinct military unit under Ottoman sovereignty (although in time the dividing lines between mamlūks and non-mamlūks were not as clear-cut as under the sultanate). This created unavoidable friction with other, more "organic," Ottoman corps stationed in Egypt. The Mamlūk system of recruitment and training did not end with the overthrow

[13] These changes have been described in detail by D. Ayalon, in "Mamlūk Military Aristocracy During the First Years of the Ottoman Occupation of Egypt," in C. E. Bosworth et al. (eds.), *The Islamic World: From Classical to Modern Times* (Princeton, 1989),413–31.

of the Mamlūk sultanate, and even outlived the system of military slavery in the Ottoman center itself. This, and the emergence of Mamlūk grandees as the virtual rulers of Ottoman Egypt, belongs to a much later period.

The decision to spare the mamlūks, in which Khāyrbak had apparently an important role, was made because the Ottomans realized that it would be a waste to kill those superb warriors (in horsemanship they had no equal even among the Ottomans), who were trained in military slavery like the Ottoman elite troops, and besides were Turkish-speaking and Sunnī Muslims. With the vast increase of the empire's territory and the many challenges it was facing (not least, the Ṣafavid threat), the Ottomans could not afford to forgo this kind of manpower.

The first change in the Ottoman policy toward the mamlūks took place on the eve of Salim's departure from Egypt, when fifty-four Mamlūk amīrs were released from prison. A few days later (September 13, 1517), Khāyrbak declared a general amnesty for the mamlūks, and some 5,000 of them came out from their concealment in a pitiable condition. Two weeks later, they were allowed to ride horses and purchase weapons. Although Khāyrbak was now the governor of Egypt, it is inconceivable that he would have undertaken such a drastic measure against the sultan's wish. Indeed, Salīm himself afterwards sent to Egypt several decrees ordering the payment of salaries as well as the accustomed meat and fodder rations (*laḥm wa-ʿalīq*) to the mamlūks and to *awlād al-nās*. This incurred the envy of the Janissaries, who demanded the same for themselves. The mamlūks' economic conditions, however, were far from enviable: their salaries were always in arrears, sometimes as long as six or seven months, and their meat and fodder rations were canceled. The *iqṭāʿāt* allotted to them were meager – from $\frac{1}{2}$ to $1\frac{1}{2}$ faddān.[14]

A permanent problem facing the authorities was whether and how to demarcate the mamlūks from the Ottoman units (Salīm left in Egypt a garrison of 5,000 horsemen and 500 arquebusiers). In order to discourage any thoughts of mutiny, a policy of Ottomanizing the mamlūks was adopted. They were repeatedly forbidden to wear the customary Mamlūk clothes and headgear, such as *zamṭ* hats and *mallūṭa* coats, and were ordered to wear caftans (*qafṭānāt)* and turbans (*ʿamāʾim*) like the Ottomans. Mamlūks could be distinguished from the Ottomans by their beards, since the Ottoman soldiers were clean-shaven. In an extreme attempt to obliterate the mamlūks' special traits, in December 1521 Khāyrbak dismissed about a thousand mamlūks and *awlād al-nās* from active military service during a parade, and cut off with his own hands half of several mamlūks' beards, handed them over to the mamlūks and said: "Follow the Ottoman rules in cutting your beards, narrowing the sleeves of your dress, and in everything

[14] A feddān was a measure equivalent to about 4,200 sq m.

that the Ottomans do." At about the same time, the Mamlūk amīrs were forbidden to have their servants follow them on a mule when they rode their horses, and were ordered to have them walk in front of them, according to the Ottoman custom.

The dress regulations were also issued to deal with public security in the city. In what seems a lack of consistency on the part of the authorities, the mamlūks were at one time forbidden to dress like Ottomans, the reason being that some mamlūks dressed up like Ottomans to commit acts of robbery against the civilian population. The illegal interference of the soldiers, mamlūks and Ottomans alike, in the lives of the people of Cairo was a chronic problem. Since the occupation, Janissaries sat at the city gates acting as arbiters in private disputes. Orders were issued against these practices, confining the Janissaries to their barracks in the Citadel. Likewise, mamlūks were prohibited from loitering around the *masṭabas* in the city quarters and at the gates of the mosques. Enforcement of these orders proved difficult.

Tensions between the mamlūks and the Ottoman units – and between the different Ottoman units themselves, which were frequent and bloody – were caused to a large degree by the lack of sufficient resources to pay the army. Ibn Iyās mentioned seven military units, whose expenses burdened the treasury: Ottoman emirs, Sipahis (cavalry), Janissaries (infantry), Gönüllū ("volunteer" cavalry), Mamlūk (Circassian) amīrs, Circassian mamlūks, and Khāyrbak's own mamlūks. The governor also gave generous gifts to the sultan's envoys (Istanbul explicitly ordered that practice to be stopped), and cultivated his own mamlūks, whom he quartered in the Citadel in order to strengthen his position. (After his death, they were quickly evicted.) Khāyrbak was extremely stingy and grasping; when his property was evaluated after his death, it was found that he had accumulated the huge sum of 600,000 dīnārs.

So the army was constantly clamoring for pay, threatening and pressing the governor and his officials. The cavalrymen – Sipahis and Gönülluyün – were the most turbulent. They rioted to urge the governor either to pay them properly or to let them return home to their families. It is interesting to notice that the Janissaries, who were better disciplined, did not come up with similar demands, although they too were capable of causing trouble.

On the other hand, Ottoman soldiers found out in the second year after the conquest that service in Egypt meant a relatively quiet and prosperous life (some were already married to Egyptian women). They disobeyed the sultan's orders to prepare for departure, when they would be replaced by fresh troops from the heartland of the empire. Hundreds of soldiers escaped to the countryside or took boats up the Nile to avoid the order. A force, which already included mamlūks, crushed their mutiny, and many Ottoman soldiers were killed. Ibn Iyās observed: "The Circassians and the Turkomans reversed roles; the pursuers have become pursued."

Thus the position of the mamlūks gradually improved. This can be seen from the way in which the official in charge of their salaries addressed them. At first he called them "dogs and *zarābīl* [inferior types of shoes]" and later "masters [*aghāwāt*]." When the news of Sultan Salīm's death arrived in Egypt in June 1520, the mamlūks' morale rose immensely, although, as we have seen, the reversal of the initial attitude toward them was decided by him. Full recognition of their merits as soldiers came in 1522, during the Ottoman siege of Rhodes, when Sultan Sulaymān the Magnificent (Qānūnī) observed them there. (They were a part – some 500 or 800 – of the Egyptian contingent, which numbered 1,500 men.) The sultan was much impressed by them and expressed his amazement at his father's bad judgment in killing such magnificent mamlūks.

Conflicts between Ottoman soldiers and mamlūks were caused also by differences in education and religious attitudes. The contrast between the irreligious Ottoman Turks and the more devout mamlūks is a constant theme in the annals of Ottoman Egypt. Several episodes during the period under study seem to support this view. One example is the opposing attitudes of the two groups at the sight of a Christian who was condemned to death and declared a last-minute conversion to Islam; unlike the mamlūks, the Ottomans were unmoved. Conversely, Ottoman soldiers tried to prevent the execution of a seller of wine and drugs; some were his clients.

Thus, the Ottomans and the mamlūks served in the same army, but it was a very tense coexistence. As they were ordered to take part in the same operations, such as quelling marauding Bedouins guarding the *ḥajj* route, or protecting the Red Sea ports against the Portuguese, and most importantly, going to the siege of Rhodes, they were sent at the same time, but each unit operated separately, under its own commander.

Revolts against the Ottomans and the pacification of Egypt

The overwhelming victory of the Ottomans did not put an end to the political ambitions of the Mamlūk elite. There are indications that even after the conquest, the strength of the Ottoman empire was not fully appreciated, and the yearning to reestablish the defunct sultanate was still vivid. It erupted in three mamlūk revolts – one in Syria (al-Ghazālī's rebellion in November 1520–February 1521, following Sultan Salīm's death), and two in Egypt, in 1523 and 1524. Jānbirdī al-Ghazālī made the fatal mistake of underestimating the empire and the young sultan Sulaymān, who succeeded the redoubtable Salīm. Two Mamlūk *kāshif*s (district governors), Jānim al-Sayfī and Īnāl, made the same error. As we have seen, Khāyrbak was a strong ruler who succeeded in accommodating to some extent Mamlūk traditions and interests to Istanbul's demands. After his death on 5 October 1522, the new governor was Muṣṭafā Pasha, Sultan Sulaymān's brother-in-law. Under him, there was a deliberate policy of the further Ottomanization of Cairo's administration.

Jānim and Īnāl saw their opportunity in the sultan's youth and the governor's weakness. Their revolt, in May–June 1523 was supported by numerous mamlūks and Bedouin Arabs. In an attempt to strengthen the government, Barakāt ibn Mūsā was given the military rank of amīr, but he failed to raise a Bedouin army. According to Diyārbakrī, a contemporary Turkish chronicler, the people of Cairo were amazed at the sight of a Bedouin army, since the Bedouins were believed to fight well only for their subsistence and the honor of their families.

The rebellion was put down easily, with cannons playing an important role in the battle. Jānim was killed and Īnāl disappeared, but Barakāt ibn Mūsā lost his life trying to negotiate with the rebels on behalf of Muṣṭafā Pasha. Many mamlūks joined the rebels and were killed; Diyārbakrī writes that the number of those who fell in battle or were executed afterwards reached 500. Those mamlūks who remained on the government's side infuriated the Ottoman soldiers by their obvious lack of enthusiasm to fight the rebels. It is worth noting that Ottoman policy even during this revolt and afterwards was to appease the mamlūks; an imperial decree ordered that their salaries be paid without delay. It was natural, however, that the pasha would be suspicious of them. He scattered them in the provinces, and allowed only a handful of the mamlūks to stay in Cairo.

The revolt instigated by Aḥmad Pasha, later known as *al-khāʾin*, "the Traitor," was a more serious challenge to Ottoman rule. He was installed as governor of Egypt in August 1523, and soon began preparing his revolt. He confiscated the arquebuses of the Janissaries, because he rightly concluded that they would be the most loyal soldiers to the sultan. Aḥmad urged the "Slaves of the Porte" (Qapi Qulları), namely the Ottoman soldiers, to return to Istanbul. He wooed the mamlūks and pardoned those who were imprisoned for participating in the previous revolt. He dismissed Ottoman officers and appointed his own men in their place. He extorted funds from the rich and demanded an exorbitant sum from the Jewish community, making threats of severe punishment if they failed to raise the money. The pasha ordered ʿAlī ibn ʿUmar, the Arab governor of Upper Egypt, who had been raiding the Nubian territories, to supply him with a thousand black slaves; he intended to train them in the use of firearms to replace the Janissaries. Black slaves were also taken from Cairo households and put into the army. Bedouin Arab shaykhs were pressured to join his revolt.

Aḥmad Pasha restored some of the Mamlūk ceremonies, notably that the senior *qāḍī*s and the caliph should come to the Citadel to greet the ruler at the beginning of each month.[15] Aḥmad identified himself as a Circassian. He

[15] The ʿAbbāsid caliphate passed away with the overthrow of the Mamlūk sultanate. It is

proclaimed himself a sultan, minting his name on the coins. Abraham Castro, the Jewish master of the mint, fled to Istanbul, where he reported Aḥmad's treason.

Aḥmad Pasha is described in contemporary sources as a secret convert to Shīʿism under the influence of Shaykh Qāḍīzāde Ẓahīr al-Dīn al-Ardabīlī. The Ottomans may have feared a Ṣafavid connection. In February the rebels occupied the Citadel, which the Janissaries were holding. Using a secret tunnel, Aḥmad's forces surprised the Janissaries and massacred them. The city mob looted valuables, which had been deposited in the Citadel.

Aḥmad's rule lasted only a few months. Jānim al-Ḥamzāwī and a group of amīrs surprised him in his bathhouse, but the pasha escaped to Sharqiyya province. There he took refuge with Aḥmad ibn Baqar, a Bedouin shaykh, but he was captured and beheaded on March 6, 1524, bringing to an end the last serious effort to separate Egypt from the Ottoman empire until the rebellion of ʿAlī Bey al-Kabīr in 1760. Although the rebellion of Aḥmad Pasha "the traitor" had failed, Egypt remained unsettled because the revolt had stirred up the Arabs throughout the country. The Bedouin Arabs were under the illusion that the Ottomans in Egypt were exhausted and could be defeated easily. The Arabs, however, lacked unity, and their arms and discipline were inferior; fresh reinforcements arrived in Egypt, and Sharqiyya province was finally subdued. On April 2, 1525, Sulaymān's Grand Vizier, Ibrāhīm Pasha, came to Egypt and restored Ottoman authority. He expressed his dissatisfaction with the frequent quarrels between the Ottoman units and the mamlūks, and addressed them saying: "Let us not call one another 'Turcoman' or 'Circassian'. We are all the sultan's servants and brothers in Islam."[16] Arab shaykhs came to the Citadel to pay homage to him, but Ibrāhīm Pasha had them arrested. Those implicated in Aḥmad Pasha's rebellion were hanged, others were set free and reappointed in their provinces.

During Ibrahim's few weeks in Egypt, he promulgated the edict codifying the administrative practice of the province, the *Qānūn-nāme-i Mısır*. The document, whose text has come down to us in full,[17] is of the utmost importance, since it reflects conditions in Egypt shortly after the reconquest, and the principles of Ottoman administration. In the first place, the *Qānūn-nāme* laid the foundations of the military and civil administration, which remained in force, at least in theory, for a long time.

The document casts light on the administration of the sub-provinces by

not clear who this "caliph" was, or whether this piece of information has any basis in reality.

16 Al-Diyārbakrī, *Tarjamat al-nuzha al-saniyya fī dhikr al-khulafāʾ waʾl mulūk al-Miṣriyya* (Ms. Add. 7846, the British Library), fos. 341a, 344b.

17 The text was published by Ö. L. Barkan, *XV ve XVI ncı asırlarda Osmanli Imparatorluğunda zira'î, ekonominin hukukî ve malî esasları* (Istanbul, 1943), I, 355–87.

the *kāshifs*, who were responsible, as formerly, for keeping the irrigation system in working order, maintaining security (protecting villagers against marauding Bedouin), and supervising tax collection. In some provinces, these responsibilities were assigned to Arab shaykhs. Long passages are devoted to the way in which the peasantry were to be treated and their taxes collected. Cadastral surveys, fallow land, land not reached by the Nile floods, *waqf* foundations, granaries, seaports and the mint were also mentioned in the code. The governing pasha, referred to as *malik al-umarāʾ*, should hold regular meetings of the council of state (*dīwān)* four times a week, like the imperial *Dīwān* in Istanbul.

One of the code's outstanding features is the principle of continuity from Mamlūk times, even though the Ottomans had to suppress two serious Mamlūk rebellions and put down Bedouin disturbances. The *Qānūn-nāme* expressly states that laws dealing with taxes, customs duties, and other fiscal and administrative matters promulgated by Sultan Qāytbāy were to remain in force. Measures were taken to ensure that Ottoman supremacy would not be threatened again. Although the document granted the Mamlūks official recognition as one of the cavalry regiments, under the title "the Circassian corps" (*Cherākise Ocağı)*, the government was clearly wary of them. The fifth paragraph of the *Qānūn-nāme* stipulates that their commanding officer and the regimental clerk must be *Rūmlu* – Turks from the Turkish-speaking provinces of the empire (and not Circassians or Arabs). The phrasing of the disciplinary measures to be taken in case of any wrongdoing is particularly severe compared with passages discussing other units in Egypt. No allowance is made for the recruitment of new mamlūks; it is ordered that any vacancy that occurs in the Circassian corps must not be filled, but should revert to the Treasury. It is also forbidden to give certain positions of high command to Circassians, native Egyptians (*fallāḥīn*) or Bedouin (*Aʿrāb*). The policy was clearly to appoint only *Rūmlu*, Turks. As we know, contrary to what was envisaged by the promulgators of the code, the importation of mamlūks continued until the end of Ottoman rule in Egypt three centuries later.

Finally, the *Qānūn-nāme* provided clear evidence of the Ottomans' intention to enhance the status of Islam in Egypt. This is noteworthy, considering Ibn Iyās's view of the Ottomans as bad Muslims. The code orders an ending of religious deviation and moral vices such as drinking and prostitution. The document emphasized the role of the *qāḍī*. It forbade the custom of the common people of Cairo to resort to the *wālī* (the chief of police) for arbitration in their disputes; henceforth all litigation must be brought before the *qāḍī*. The custom that the personnel of the *sharīʿa* courts, namely the deputies and bailiffs, handed out sentences and penalties had to stop; only the *qāḍī* was authorized to pass sentences. There is no doubt that these regulations also reflected Istanbul's determination to centralize and control the judicial and administrative system more firmly than before.

THE RULERS OF EGYPT, 254–922/868–1517

Ṭūlūnids, 254–292/868–905

1	254/868	Aḥmad ibn Ṭūlūn
2	270/884	Khumārawayh, Abū al-Jaysh (son of 1)
3	282/896	Jaysh, Abū al-ʿAsākir (son of 2)
4	283/896	Hārūn, Abū Mūsā (son of 2)
5	292/904	Shaybān, Abū al-Manāqib (son of 1)

292/905 Reconquest by the ʿAbbāsid general Muḥammad ibn Sulaymān

Ikhshīdids, 323–358/935–969

1	323/935	Muḥammad ibn Ṭughj, Abū Bakr al-Ikhshīd
2	334/946	Ūnūjūr, Abū al-Qāsim (son of 1)
3	349/961	ʿAlī, Abū al-Ḥasan (son of 1)
4	355/966	Kāfūr al-Lābī, Abū al-Misk
5	357/968	Aḥmad, Abū al-Fawāris, d. 371/981 (son of 3)

358/969 Conquest of Egypt by Fāṭimids

Fāṭimids, 297–567/909–1171

1	297/909	ʿAbd-Allāh (ʿUbayd-Allāh) ibn Ḥusayn, Abū Muḥammad al-Mahdī
2	322/934	Muḥammad, Abū al-Qāsim al-Qā'im (son of 1?)
3	334/946	Ismāʿīl, Abū Ṭāhir al-Manṣūr (son of 2)
4	341/953	Maʿadd, Abū Tamīm al-Muʿizz (son of 3)
		358/969 Caliph in Egypt
5	365/975	Nizār, Abū Manṣūr al-ʿAzīz (son of 4)
6	386/996	al-Manṣūr, Abū ʿAlī al-Ḥākim (son of 5)
7	411/1021	ʿAlī, Abū al-Ḥasan al-Ẓāhir (son of 6)
8	427/1036	Maʿadd, Abū Tamīm al-Mustanṣir (son of 7)

9	487/1094	Aḥmad, Abū al-Qāsim al-Mustaʿlī (son of 8)
10	495/1101	al-Manṣūr, Abū ʿAlī al-Āmir (son of 9)

524/1130 Interregnum; rule by al-Ḥāfiẓ as regent but not yet as caliph; coins were issued in the name of al-Muntaẓar (the Expected One)

11	525/1131	ʿAbd al-Majīd ibn Muḥammad, Abū al-Maymūn al-Ḥāfiẓ
12	544/1149	Ismāʿīl, Abū al-Manṣūr al-Ẓāfir (son of 11)
13	549/1154	ʿĪsā, Abū al-Qāsim al-Fā'iz (son of 12)
14	555–567/1160–1171	ʿAbd-Allah ibn Yūsuf, Abū Muḥammad al-ʿĀḍid

Ayyūbid Conquest

Ayyūbids, 564–650/1169–1252

1	564/1169	Yūsuf ibn Ayyūb, al-Nāṣir Abū al-Muẓaffar Ṣalāḥ al-Dīn (Saladin)
2	589/1193	ʿUthmān, al-ʿAzīz Abū al-Fatḥ ʿImād al-Dīn (son of 1)
3	595/1198	Muḥammad, al-Manṣūr Nāṣir al-Dīn (son of 2)
4	596/1200	Muḥammad/Aḥmad ibn Ayyūb, al-ʿĀdil Abū Bakr Sayf al-Dīn (brother of 1)
5	615/1218	Muḥammad, al-Kāmil Abū al-Maʿālī Nāṣir al-Dīn (son of 4)
6	635/1238	Abū Bakr, al-ʿĀdil Sayf al-Dīn (son of 5)
7	637/1240	Ayyūb, al-Ṣāliḥ Najm al-Dīn (son of 5)
8	647/1249	Tūrān Shāh, al-Muʿaẓẓam Ghiyāth al-Dīn (son of 7)
9	648–650/	Mūsā ibn Yūsuf, al-Ashraf Muẓaffar al-Dīn

Mamlūk usurpation, al-Ashraf's name retained in *khuṭba* until 652/1254

Mamlūks, 648–922/1250–1517

Baḥrī line, 648–792/1250–1390

1	648/1250	Shajarat al-Durr, Umm Khalīl, widow of al-Ṣāliḥ Ayyūb
2	648/1250	Aybak al-Turkumānī, al-Muʿizz ʿIzz al-Dīn
3	648/1250	Mūsā ibn Yūsuf, al-Ashraf, nominal Ayyūbid sultan
4	652/1254	Aybak, second reign
5	655/1257	ʿAlī I, al-Manṣūr Nūr al-Dīn (son of 4)
6	657/1259	Quṭuz al-Muʿizzī, al-Muẓaffar Sayf al-Dīn

7	658/1260	Baybars I al-Bunduqdārī, al-Ẓāhir Rukn al-Dīn
8	676/1277	Baraka/Berke Khān, al-Saʿid Nāṣir al-Dīn (son of 7)
9	678/1279	Salāmish/Süleymish, al-ʿĀdil Badr al-Dīn (son of 7)
10	678/1279	Qalāwūn al-Alfī, al-Manṣūr Abū al-Maʿālī Sayf al-Dīn
11	689/1290	Khalīl, al-Ashraf Ṣalāḥ al-Dīn (son of 10)
12	693/1293	Muḥammad I, al-Nāṣir Nāṣir al-Dīn (son of 10) (first reign)
13	694/1294	Kitbughā, al-ʿĀdil Zayn al-Dīn
14	696/1296	Lāchīn/Lājīn al-Ashqar, al-Manṣūr Ḥusām al-Dīn
15	698/1299	Muḥammad I, al-Nāṣir (son of 10) (second reign)
16	708/1309	Baybars II al-Jāshnakīr, al-Muẓaffar Rukn al-Dīn
17	709/1310	Muḥammad I, al-Nāṣir (son of 10) (third reign)
18	741/1341	Abū Bakr, al-Manṣūr Sayf al-Dīn (son of 17)
19	742/1341	Kūjūk/Küchük, al-Ashraf ʿAlāʾ al-Dīn (son of 17)
20	742/1342	Aḥmad I, al-Nāṣir Shihāb al-Dīn (son of 17)
21	743/1342	Ismāʿīl, al-Ṣāliḥ ʿImād al-Dīn (son of 17)
22	746/1345	Shaʿbān I, al-Kāmil Sayf al-Dīn (son of 17)
23	747/1346	Ḥajjī I, al-Muẓaffar Sayf al-Dīn (son of 17)
24	748/1347	Ḥasan, al-Nāṣir Nāṣir al-Dīn (son of 17) (first reign)
25	752/1351	Ṣāliḥ, al-Ṣāliḥ Ṣalāḥ al-Dīn (son of 17)
26	755/1354	Ḥasan, al-Nāṣir (son of 17) (second reign)
27	762/1361	Muḥammad II, al-Manṣūr Ṣalāḥ al-Dīn (son of 23)
28	764/1363	Shaʿbān II ibn Ḥusayn, al-Ashraf Nāṣir al-Dīn
29	778/1377	ʿAlī II, al-Manṣūr ʿAlāʾ al-Dīn (son of 28)
30	783/1381	Ḥajjī II, al-Ṣāliḥ/al-Manṣūr Ṣalāḥ al-Dīn (son of 28) (first reign)
31	784/1382	Barqūq al-Yalbughāwī, al-Ẓāhir Sayf al-Dīn (first reign)
32	791–792/ 1389–1390	Ḥajjī II, al-Muẓaffar Ṣalāḥ al-Dīn (son of 28) (second reign)

Burjī (Circassian) line, 784–922/1382–1517

33	784/1382	Barqūq al-Yalbughāwī, al-Ẓāhir (first reign)
34	791/1389	Ḥajjī II, Ṣalāḥ al-Dīn (son of 28) (second reign)
35	792/1390	Barqūq, al-Ẓāhir (second reign)
36	801/1399	Faraj, al-Nāṣir Nāṣir al-Dīn (son of 35) (first reign)
37	808/1405	ʿAbd al-ʿAzīz, al-Manṣūr ʿIzz al-Dīn (son of 35)
38	808/1405	Faraj, al-Nāṣir (son of 35) (second reign)
39	815/1412	al-ʿAbbās ibn al-Mutawakkil, Abū al-Faḍl al-Mustaʿīn, ʿAbbāsid caliph, proclaimed sultan
40	815/1412	Shaykh al-Maḥmūdī al-Ẓāhirī, al-Muʾayyad Sayf al-Dīn
41	824/1421	Aḥmad II, al-Muẓaffar (son of 40)
42	824/1421	Ṭaṭar, al-Ẓāhir Sayf al-Dīn
43	824/1421	Muḥammad III, al-Ṣāliḥ Nāṣir al-Dīn (son of 42)
44	825/1422	Barsbāy, al-Ashraf Abū al-Naṣr Sayf al-Dīn
45	841/1438	Yūsuf, al-ʿAzīz Jamāl al-Dīn (son of 44)
46	842/1438	Chaqmaq/Jaqmaq, al-Ẓāhir Sayf al-Dīn
47	857/1453	ʿUthmān, al-Manṣūr Fakhr al-Dīn (son of 46)
48	857/1453	Aynāl/Ināl al-ʿAlāʾī al-Ẓāhirī, al-Ashraf Abū al-Naṣr Sayf al-Dīn
49	865/1461	Aḥmad III, al-Muʾayyad Shihāb al-Dīn (son of 48)
50	865/1461	Khushqadam, al-Ẓāhir Sayf al-Dīn
51	872/1467	Yalbāy, al-Ẓāhir Sayf al-Dīn
52	872/1467	Timurbughā, al-Ẓāhir
53	872/1468	Qāyit/Qāytbāy al-Ẓāhirī, al-Ashraf Abū al-Naṣr Sayf al-Dīn
54	901/1496	Muḥammad IV, al-Nāṣir (son of 53)
55	904/1498	Qānṣawh/Qānṣūh I, al-Ẓāhir
56	905/1500	Jānbulāṭ/Jānbalāṭ, al-Ashraf
57	906/1501	Ṭūmānbāy I, al-ʿĀdil Sayf al-Dīn
58	906/1501	Qānṣawh/Qānṣūh II al-Ghawrī, al-Ashraf
59	922–923/ 1516–1517	Ṭūmānbāy II, al-Ashraf

923/1517 Ottoman conquest

GLOSSARY

ʿAbbāsid	Pertaining to the Sunnī dynasty of caliphs which reigned over much of the Islamic world in 750–1258 and was installed in Cairo from 1258 until 1517.
ʿabd/ʿabīd	A chattel male slave; during the Mamlūk period referred to domestic slaves; also used in personal names, e.g. Ibn ʿAbd Allāh (Son of God's Servant).
ʿabd nafṭiyya	A black slave employed as an arquebusier (Ottoman period).
Abkhāzī	Christians or Georgians of the Caucasus region east of the Black Sea.
adab	Literature, belles lettres.
Aga Khān	The title by which modern Nizārī imāms are known.
Aghlabids	(800–900) An autonomous Sunni dynasty in Ifrīqiya (Tunisia), loyal to the ʿAbbāsid caliphate.
ʿahd	An injunction, obligation, or agreement of political enactment; a diploma of investiture.
Ahl al-Bayt	Members of the Prophet Muḥammad's family; according to Shīʿīs they include only his descendants through his daughter Fāṭima and her husband ʿAlī.
Aḥmadiyya	A popular Ṣūfī order in Egypt (especially in rural communities), named after the seventh/thirteenth-century saint Aḥmad al-Badawī.
ajnād al-ḥalqa	Originally, the bodyguard of the Ayyūbid sultan; later, a non-elite military corps composed primarily of descendants of mamlūks.

ʿAlid	A descendant of ʿAlī ibn Abī Ṭālib, both Ḥasanid and Ḥusaynid. *See also sharīf.*
ʿālim/ʿulamāʾ	Arabic, "learned [in religious law]"; scholars trained in disciplines regarded as essential to the preservation of the Muslim commonwealth.
amān	Immunity, safe-conduct.
ʿĀmil	The fiscal intendant, usually civilian, of a province (Ṭūlūnid period).
amīr/umarāʾ	Arabic, "commander"; during Mamlūk regime an officer ranked in several grades of authority and according to the size of his slave-soldier contingent.
amīr akhūr	A fourth-rank officer in the military hierarchy (fifteenth c.), responsible for the sultan's stable.
amīr majlis	A third-rank officer in the military hierarchy (fifteenth c.), responsible for court protocol.
amīr miʾa wa-muqaddam alf	The highest-ranking mamlūk officer, entitled to keep 100 horsemen and to command 1,000 *ḥalqa* troops in battle.
amīr silāḥ	A second-rank officer in the military hierarchy (fifteenth c.), responsible for armaments.
amīr ṭabalkhāna	A mamlūk officer entitled to forty horsemen in his service.
amīr al-umarāʾ	The chief of the army in Baghdād (first half of tenth c.), the most powerful man in the ʿAbbāsid state.
ʿāmma	The common people, in contrast to *khaṣṣa*.
appanage	A section of a kingdom or empire, responsibility for which was delegated by a sovereign to a son or other relative; a practice widespread in ʿAbbāsid Caliphate between 800 and 1000. If an appanage holder lived in the capital, he designated a *wālī*.
Aqqoyunlū	Turkish "White Sheep"; an aggressive principality in central Iran during the fifteenth century which challenged Mamlūk suzerainty in southwest Asia.
Aʿrāb/ʿArab	Bedouin.
ʿarḍ	In commerce, the offering of goods for sale; in scholarship, a student's exposition of a text or problem.

arquebus	The predecessor of the musket, employed by soldiers of al-Ghawrī's Fifth Corps.
ʿaṣabiyya	A collective tribal or family identity, a term used by the eighth/fourteenth-century historian Ibn Khaldūn as a social or political force for unity.
ashrāf	*See sharīf.*
Ashrafī (dīnār)	A small gold coin issued by the Mamlūk sultan al-Ashraf Barsbāy and his successors.
ʿĀshūrāʾ	Mourning ceremonies of the tenth of Muḥarram for the martyrs of Karbalāʾ, al-Ḥusayn, the second son of ʿAlī, and his family.
ʿāṣima/ʿawāṣim	Garrison town(s) in north Syria between the Qinnaṣrīn/Ḥalab *jund* and the Cilician *thughūr*, of which the largest was Anṭākiya.
Assassins	An Ismāʿīlī sect, known also as the Nizāriyya, which originated from the dispute over the succession to the Fāṭimid Caliph al-Mustanṣir.
ʿaṭāʾ	The salary paid to members of a *jund* whose names appear in the *dīwān* (Arab conquest period).
atābak	A marshal, after the sultan the second-ranking military officer of the Mamlūk state.
augustulis	an Augustal prefect, the traditional office of the civilian Roman or Byzantine governor of Egypt; a senior civil administrator, normally resident at Alexandria.
awlād al-nās	The sons of mamlūks, some of whom served in an elite unit of the *ḥalqa*.
aʿyān	The notables of society, in reference to both military and civilian elites.
al-Azhar	A principal Friday mosque in Cairo, constructed by the Fāṭimids in the fourth/tenth century.
bāb al-abwāb	"the supreme gate," head of the Ismāʿīlī *daʿwa*, holding a rank immediately under the imām himself; he was also known as "the chief *dāʿī*" (*dāʿī al-duʿāt*).
Badawiyya	*See* Aḥmadiyya.
badw	Bedouin nomads.
Baḥrī	Refers to an elite mamlūk regiment established by the Ayyūbid sultan al-Ṣāliḥ (d. 1249) in barracks near the Nile, hence *baḥr* or "river."
Banū Baqar	An Arab clan in Lower Egypt.
baqṭ	A treaty with Nubia concluded in 652 CE; in the

	Mamlūk period refers to an annual tribute paid to the sultan.
bayʿa	An oath of allegiance to a caliph or sultan.
bidʿa/bidaʿ	Innovation(s), specifically transgressing the Prophet's *sunna*.
bīmāristān(āt)	Hospital(s).
Blue/Green circus factions	Rival groups of chariot racer fans, with special colors.
Bohras	Indian adherents of the Ṭayyibī Ismāʿīlī line.
bunduq raṣāṣ	A hand gun, or arquebus.
Burjī	Pertaining to the predominantly Circassian tower (*burj*) or Citadel Mamlūk regime established in 1390.
Būyids	Dynasty of Daylamite (Shīʿī) amīrs who controlled Baghdād and other eastern ʿAbbāsid territories from 945 to 1055.
caliph	Arabic, *khalīfa*, "Successor [to the Prophet]"; the office held by the ʿAbbāsid dynasty from 750, relocated to Cairo by the Mamlūk sultan al-Ẓāhir Baybars.
Carmatian	*See* Qarmaṭī.
Chalcedonians	Adherents to Christological doctrine of two natures (human and divine) in the one person of Jesus Christ, promulgated at the Council of Chalcedon in 451; see also Melkites.
Chaldirān	The site of the battle in Azerbayjān where the Ottomans defeated the Ṣafavids in 1514.
Circassian	A Caucasian ethnic group which was prominently represented in the Burjī Mamlūk period.
Copts	Indigenous Monophysite Christians of Egypt, retaining their faith after the Muslim conquest; *see also qibṭ*.
Cordobans	Migrants in 818 to Alexandria after a revolt in the district (*rabad*) of Cordoba in Andalus. They remained in Alexandria to 827 and then transferred to Crete, subsequently to Cilicia and to Mount Hermon near Damascus.
dāʿī	A summoner, an agent of the *daʿwa*, organizer and propagandist.
dāʿī al-duʿāt	The chief *dāʿī*, head of the *daʿwa*; an official rank in the Fāṭimid state, apparently synonymous with *bāb al-abwāb*, "the supreme gate."

ḍamān — A guarantee that the issuer will secure the payment of taxes due to the state (Arab conquest period).

dār — Arabic, "house" (fifteenth c.); the residence of an amīr or civil notable.

Dār al-ʿAdl — "Palace of justice."

dār al-hijra — An abode of emigration/immigration; the center of resistance and residence of the leader of an opposition religious movement.

Dār al-Islām — Territory under Muslim dominion, in contrast with *Dār al-Ḥarb*, where war is legitimate.

daʿwa — An appeal or summons to the true religion, to a special cause, to adherence and loyalty to a specific religious leader or imām.

dawādār — Literally "inkstand bearer," the third-ranking military officer of the Mamlūk state after the sultan and the *atābak*, who is formally responsible for the chancery and the *barīd* or royal post.

Daylamis — Individuals from the region of Daylam in Iran, south of the Caspian Sea.

defterdār — The "Keeper of Registers," the head of the treasury in the Ottoman Empire.

dhakhīra — The sultan's personal fiscal reserve (Mamlūk period).

dhikr — Repetitive oral "remembering" of God's name or other expressive formulae, as in Ṣūfī worship.

dhimmī — A protected non-Muslim monotheist, i.e., a Christian or Jew, who receives a recognized, subordinate status in Muslim society in return for payment of a tax (*see also jizya*).

Dhū al-Qadrids — A Turkoman dynasty in eastern Anatolia (Elbistan) during the fourteenth and fifteenth centuries.

dihlīz — The angled entrance to a building. On campaign or a provincial tour, a pavilion symbolic of sovereignty.

dīnār/danānīr — A generic term for gold coin, varying standards of fineness under different dynasties.

dīnār jayshī — The currency of account used to calculate *iqṭāʿ* yields.

dirham/darāhim	The generic term for silver coin of varying values and standards of fineness under different dynasties.
dirham min al-fulūs	During the Mamlūk period, a unit of account giving the amount of copper coins equivalent in value to one silver coin.
dīwān/dawāwīn	(Turkish: *dīvān*) A bureau, ministry of government or senior officer; drafts and stores decrees, correspondence, registers of revenue sources, materials of strategic value; oversees household income and expenditure; in the Arab conquest period, the list of those entitled to receive *ʿaṭāʾ*.
dīwān al-aḥbās	A bureau maintaining records of charitable endowments (*waqfiyyas*).
dīwān al-aḥrāʾ	A bureau of public granaries (Ṭūlūnid period).
dīwān asfal al-Arḍ	The bureau of the Delta (Ṭūlūnid period).
dīwān al-barīd	The postal service linking the capital and provincial towns or garrisons; also used for spying.
dīwān al-inshāʾ	The chancery; the bureau of state correspondence and diplomacy.
dīwān al-jaysh	An army bureau supervising the distribution of *iqṭāʿ* revenues to officers, and responsible for the registration of troops.
dīwān al-kharāj	The bureau of agrarian land taxes (Ṭūlūnid period).
dīwān al-khāṣṣ	Until the Mamlūk period, private bureau of an amīr's treasury; in the fifteenth century, the sultan's bureau overseeing his personal fund that maintained the court, distributed gifts and purchased arms.
dīwān al-māl	The state treasury, occasionally responsible for estimating projected income.
dīwān al-mufrad	A "special" bureau created in the early fifteenth century for the purchase and maintenance of royal mamlūks.
dīwān al-wizāra	The vizierate bureau that supplied royal mamlūks with food and clothing.
Druze	A religious movement, with its origins in Ismāʿīlīsm, that regards the Fāṭimid caliph al-Ḥākim (996–1021) as a manifestation of God on Earth.

Elbistan	A region in southern Anatolia, on the border between the Mamlūk and Ottoman empires.
fals/fulūs	A generic term for base metal coin, usually of copper.
faqīh/fuqahā'	An authority on Islamic jurisprudence.
faqīr/fuqarā'	Literally, "the poor"; by extension, Ṣūfī mystics.
fatwā/fatāwā	A legal opinion issued by a scholar of Islamic law.
fetiḥnāme	An epistle announcing an Ottoman conquest.
fiqh	The science of Islamic jurisprudence.
fitna	Atomized conflict over doctrine, power, revenue sources or the use or occupation of space.
Franks (*Ifranj*)	A collective term for western Europeans.
furūsiyya	Literally, "horsemanship"; martial exercises and recreational activities of the mamlūk elite.
Ga'on	Hebrew, "pride;" the abbreviated title for the "Head of the Academy of the Pride of Jabob," i.e. heads of Yeshivot in Jerusalem and Iraq (Babylonia).
Geniza	A collection of medieval documents (wills, contracts, correspondence, etc.) produced by members of Cairo's Jewish community and located in Fusṭāṭ.
Germiyanids	An Anatolian Turko-Kurdish dynasty, with its capital at Kutahya which emerged after the decline of the Seljuk sultanate of Rūm.
Ghadīr Khumm	The site where, according to the Shī'a, the Prophet announced the designation of his nephew and son-in-law 'Alī as his successor.
ghulām/ghilmān	Arabic, "youth"; in the ninth to fifteenth centuries used to designate a Turkish military slave (*see also mamlūk*).
Golden Horde	The westernmost Khanate of the Mongol empire, based in the Russian steppes.
gönülü	"Volunteer"; a member of a certain cavalry regiment in Ottoman army.
Ḥabūs	See *waqf*.
ḥadīth	The recorded sayings of, and stories about, the Prophet Muḥammad and his companions, introduced by a chain of authorities (*isnād*).
Ḥāfiẓī	An adherent of the imāms who followed

al-Ḥāfiẓ, the eleventh Fāṭimid caliph, in opposition to both Nizārī and Ṭayyibī lines.

ḥājib al-ḥujjāb — A senior chamberlain; the sixth-ranking officer of the military hierarchy (fifteenth c.), who oversaw the military justice applied to mamlūks.

ḥajj — The pilgrimage to Mecca required of every able-bodied Muslim.

ḥalqa — A circle composed of a teacher and his students, or the entourage of a ruler (*see ajnād al-ḥalqa*).

Ḥanafīs — One of four recognized schools of Sunnī Muslim law, widespread in Iran, Central Asia and among Turkish speakers.

Ḥanbalīs — One of four recognized schools of Sunnī Muslim Law, which advocates the literal interpretation of the Qur'ān and of *ḥadīth*.

harāfish — Commoners or craftspersons.

ḥarīm — The private, often secluded section of the household reserved for female members of a family and their domestic servants.

Ḥasanid — A descendant of the second Shīʿī Imām, Ḥasan, the elder son of ʿAlī and Fāṭima.

ḥawsh/aḥwāsh — "Court"; the central courtyard of the Citadel, the site of the sultan's ceremonials (fifteenth c.); it also refers to open spaces in urban quarters inhabited by the poor.

Hawwāra — A nomadic tribe of Berber origin, settled in Upper Egypt.

ḥisba — The office of market inspector (*muḥtasib*), derived from the Qur'ānic injunction to "order the good and forbid evil."

ḥujja/ḥujaj — A deed or document specifying a charitable endowment (*waqf*).

ḥujra/ḥujar — Barracks.

ḥuqūq — Taxes condemned as without basis in Islamic law.

Ḥusaynid — A descendant of the third Shīʿī Imām, al-Ḥusayn, the second son of ʿAlī and Fāṭima.

ʿĪd al-mawlid — The festival of the Prophet's birthday, 11 Rabīʿ I.

ijāza — Certification by a scholar that a student had studied a text, or acquired competence in a given field, under his direction.

Īlkhān	The ruler of the Mongol khanate of Persia and Iraq.
iltizām	Tax farming (Ottoman period).
imām/a'imma	For Sunnis, a prayer leader; for Shī'īs, the religious and spiritual head of their state, a term used interchangeably with that of caliph.
'imāma	Turban.
iqṭā'/iqṭā'āt	Arabic, "apportionment"; a revocable allotment of revenue yield from a tract of agrarian land to provide an officer with resources to support his troop contingent and personal expenses.
Ismā'īl Ṣafavī	(1501–1524) The founder of the Ṣafavid monarchy.
Ismā'īlī	A follower of the seventh Shī'ī Imām, Ismā'īl, descended from al-Ḥusayn.
Ismā'īliyya	A term commonly used in Islamic heresiographical literature to designate the Ismā'īlīs and their movement.
isnād/asānīd	A chain of authorities validating a saying (*ḥadīth*) from or about the Prophet Muḥammad.
ittiḥādiyya	"Becoming one with"; Muslim mystics who believe in a form of union with God.
Jacobite	A common designation of Monophysite Christians in Egypt, derived from Jacob Baradaeus of Syria.
Jalāyirids	A Mongol dynasty in Azerbayjan, the successor regime to the Īlkhānids in the middle of the fourteenth century.
jamakiyya	The salary of mamlūk trainees and troopers, paid monthly.
jāmi'/jawāmi'	A congregational mosque.
Janissaries	The infantry elite corps of the Ottoman Empire, non-Muslim in origin.
jāriya/jawārī	A female slave.
jihād	A holy war against non-Muslims.
jinn	A supernatural being, disposed to tease mortals.
jizya	A poll tax imposed on *dhimmīs* (Christians and Jews).
julbān	Mamlūk cadets or recruits housed in barracks surrounding the sultan's residence in the Cairo Citadel.

jund/ajnād — An army, especially locally recruited militia of Egypt (Arab conquest period); during the Mamlūk period it referred to mamlūks belonging to an amīr.

kafā'a — The legal doctrine of marital equivalence, which protects the social status of the families of the principals in a marriage contract.

Kārimiyya — A syndicate of merchants involved primarily in the lucrative pepper and spice trade until ninth/fifteenth century.

kāshif/kushshāf — A governor or inspector of a sub-province in Mamlūk and Ottoman Egypt, in charge of public security and the irrigation system.

kātib/kuttāb — A clerk or secretary.

kātib al-sirr — The confidential secretary to the sultan; the civilian director of chancery (*dīwān al-inshā'*).

Kayseri — A large town in central Anatolia.

khādim/khuddām — "Servant"; it refers to eunuchs in service to the Mamlūks.

Khādim al-Ḥaramayn al-Sharīfayn — The Servitor of the Two Noble Sanctuaries (Mecca and Medina); the title given to a ruler in charge of the holy cities.

khān — A Mongol ruler.

khānqāh/khānaqāh — A Ṣūfī mystic lodge, larger than a *zāwiya*.

kharāj — A land tax, in place by the end of the century after the Arab conquest.

Khārijīs — Those who abandoned ʿAlī in the battle of Ṣiffīn, who reject both Shiʿism and Sunnism.

khaṣṣa — The social elite; the term indicates either militarists or civilians, or both, and is in contrast with the *ʿāmma*.

khaṣṣakiyya — The bodyguard or entourage of the Mamlūk sultan, chosen from royal mamlūks.

khāzindār — Treasurer; an office held by a senior mamlūk officer.

khidma — A session of the sultan's council attended by amīrs and the *kātib al-sirr* to deal with matters affecting the military class.

khiṭṭa/khiṭaṭ — "District"; in Fusṭāṭ the name given to Muslim groups for settlement (after the Arab conquest).

khiyār shanbar — A type of cucumber found in Egypt, used as laxative.

khushdāshiyya	Persian, "fellowship"; camaraderie, or group identity inculcated during the training of mamlūk soldiers.
khuṭba/khuṭab	The sermon preached (by the *khaṭīb*) in mosques at Friday noon prayer; the acknowledgment of the caliph or ruler.
Khwārazmians	The remnants of the ruling household or military forces of the Khwārazm-Shāh Seljuk successor-state of Iran and Central Asia (ca. 470/1077–628/1231) who arrived in Anatolia, Mesopotamia and Syria in the 1230s.
Kipchak	Pertaining to a group of Turkish tribes inhabiting the Eurasian steppe; the prime origin of mamlūk recruits during the Baḥrī period.
kiswa	A brocaded covering over the Kaʿba shrine in Mecca, which was sent annually from Cairo with the *ḥajj* caravan.
koubikoularios	The imperial palace chamberlain (Byzantine period).
Kurāʾ	The site of a battle in the eastern Delta in February 1251, when Egyptian forces defeated the army of the Ayyūbid ruler of Damascus, al-Nāṣir Yūsuf.
laḥm wa-ʿalīq	Money paid to mamlūks to obtain meat and fodder for their animals.
madhhab/madhāhib	The generic name for any of the four recognized schools or rites of Sunni Muslim law.
madrasa/madāris	A mosque-college with the primary objective of education in the religious law (*Sharīʿa*) and ancillary disciplines.
Maghrib	Arabic, "west," principally referring to modern Morocco.
maḥmal	A richly decorated camel litter for the transport of the *kiswa* in the *ḥajj* caravan.
majlis/majālis	A "sitting" or council, held by amīrs, teachers and students, or Ṣūfīs and their master.
majlis al-ḥikma/ majlis al-daʿwa	A session of wisdom or session of instruction; weekly meetings of Ismāʿīlīs for instruction from their imāms and leaders.
maks/mukūs	Taxes considered contrary to Islamic Law.
Malik al-umarāʾ	"King of the amīrs"; the title of the

Ottoman governor of Egypt following the occupation.

Mālikīs — One of the four recognized schools of Sunni Muslim law; it rejects rational argumentation but is amenable to *istiṣlāḥ* (consideration of the public interest).

mallūṭa — A typical mamlūk coat.

mamlūk/mamālīk — Arabic, "one owned"; slave-soldiers imported to Egypt, primarily from Turkish central Asia or Circassia, but other regions were also represented; see also *ghulām*.

Manṣūra — The site near the Delta coast of a battle in 1250, between the Ayyūbid army and crusader forces of the French King Louis IX.

maqʿad — The reception hall leading to the inner courtyard of a *dār*.

mashyakha — An honorary title bestowed on tribal chief by the sultan (fifteenth c.).

mawlā/mawālī — A non-Arab convert to Islam (Arab conquest period).

mawlid al-nabī — *See ʿĪd al-mawlid.*

maẓālim — An appellate court, apart from *Sharīʿa* jurisdiction, presided over by the sultan or his representative, adjudicating disputes within the military class or cases unresolved by the four *qāḍīs*.

Melkite — A doctrinal designation for Christians following the decision of the Council of Chalcedon that Jesus Christ had both a divine and human nature; Melkites were a minority among Egyptian Christians.

miḥrāb — The niche in a mosque orienting worshippers toward Mecca.

milk/amlāk — Private property.

minbār — The pulpit in a mosque.

Miqyās — The Nilometer, a scale located at the southern tip of Rawḍā Island to measure the Nile flood.

Miṣr — The Arabic name for Egypt; in medieval times, the town of Fusṭāṭ.

mithāl — A written communication, order, or letter.

mithqāl/mathāqīl — A unit of weight in the vicinity of 4.25 g, traditionally associated with gold coins.

Mongol	Pertaining to the mainly pastoral peoples of Mongolia in eastern Asia.
Monophysites	Opponents of doctrines of Chalcedon, believing in the One nature of Jesus Christ; the Coptic, Gregorian, Jacobite, Ethiopian Churches.
Monotheletism	The doctrine that Jesus Christ had only one will, proclaimed by the Emperor Heraclius and the Constantinopolitan Patriarchs Sergios and Pyrrhos; it was rejected by both Chalcedonians and Monophysites (including Copts).
mubāshir	An agent of the treasury, or tax collector.
muezzin (*muʾadhdhin*)	A prayer caller, or reciter of the *qaṣāʾid* or poems honoring the Prophet.
muḥtasib	An inspector of markets, and enforcer of public morality.
mukḥula	A copper cannon.
munāsafāt	Condominia or frontier districts in which the administration and revenues were shared by the Mamlūks and the crusader principalities.
Münsheāt ül-selāṭīn	A famous collection of Ottoman sultans' correspondence.
muqaddam	Commander, the most senior rank in the mamlūk hierarchy of officers: *muqaddam al-ḥalqa*, the commander of the non-slave unit of the Mamlūk army.
muqṭaʿ	An *iqṭāʿ* holder.
murābiṭa	A garrison established in areas subject to attack by non-Muslims (Arab conquest period).
mushidd	An agent, usually a senior amīr, appointed by the sultan to inspect or check on dīwān officials.
mushtarawāt	Arabic, "purchased"; referring to mamlūks bought by a reigning sultan.
muʿtazilī	A Sunnī theological doctrine based on the Greek rationalist concept of primary cause; it asserts the created nature of the Qurʾān.
Muẓaffarids	The Persian successor-state to the Īlkhānid regime (fourteenth c.); its capital was Shirāz.
nāʾib/nuwwāb	A deputy, frequently as in deputy judge.
nāʾib al-ghayba	The acting sultan, during the sovereign's absence.
nāʾib al-salṭana	A deputy sultan, or viceroy.
nāqil	An anonymous reporter.

nās	The "people," in the Middle Ages referring to mamlūks and their descendants.
naṣrānī	A generic Arabic term for Christians.
Nawrūz	The Coptic new year festival.
nāẓir/nuẓẓār	The supervisor of a charitable trust, government bureau or religious institution.
Negus	The sovereign ruler of Abyssinia (Ethiopia).
nisba	A descriptive surname, indicating place of origin, occupation, sectarian affiliation, etc.
niyābat al-salṭana	The office of viceroy (fifteenth c.).
niẓām	Order, etiquette.
Nizārīs	Those Ismāʿilīs who accept a line of imāms descended from Nizār, the son of al-Mustanṣir, the eighth Fāṭimid caliph, in opposition to the line from another of his sons, al-Mustaʿlī.
Nubia	The region along the Nile in extreme south of Egypt.
Ottoman Sultanate	A Sunni Muslim regime founded as a principality (*beylik*) in northwestern Anatolia in the late thirteenth century, evolving into a great power by the fifteenth century, and the prime rival of the Mamlūk sultanate.
Patriarch of Alexandria	The head of the Egyptian Church, Coptic or Chalcedonian/Melkite; the patriarchate is his administrative structure.
pervāne	The title of the assistant to the Seljuk sultan of Rūm (Anatolia).
Praetorian prefecture	A late Roman bureaucratic structure for collecting and districting land tax revenues; important legal jurisdictions.
qāʿa	An appartment with a central dining chamber; the large reception hall of a *dār*.
qāḍī/quḍāt	A judge of an Islamic court.
qāḍī al-ʿaskar (Turkish, *qazalʿasker*)	A military judge; the chief judge in an Ottoman province.
qāḍī al-quḍāt	A chief judge overseeing cases of judges in a *madhhab*.
qā'id	A general, or commander of the army (ʿAbbāsid period).
Qalʿa	The Citadel of Cairo.
qalam	A pen, or writing instrument; *aṣḥāb al-qalam*, or civil bureaucrats, were superior to *aṣḥāb*

al-sayf (sword), or militarists, until the middle of the third/eighth century.

qānūn — Ottoman administrative law, distinct from the *Sharīʿa*.

Qānūnī — The Law Giver, the honorary title of Sultan Sulayman I.

qānūn-nāme — The collection of Ottoman laws and regulations.

Qapı Qulları — "Slaves of the Gate (Porte)"; the Ottoman sultan's military slaves.

Qarāfa — "City of the Dead," a cemetery lying east and south of Cairo, its districts more or less separated by the Citadel.

Qarmaṭī — A pejorative title given first to followers of Ḥamdān Qarmaṭ in Iraq before 899, and second to later groups of Ismāʿīlīs in the eastern regions who refused to recognize the Fāṭimid caliphs as imāms.

qassām — "Divider"; a clerk in the Ottoman treasury in charge of collecting taxes on bequests.

qibla — The wall of a mosque facing Mecca.

qibṭ — The term for specifically Egyptian Christians, derived from the Greek *Aigyptos* and the ancestor of modern "Copt," "Coptic."

Qizilbash — "Red Heads"; the name for supporters of the Ṣafavid shah, after the color of their headgear.

qurnās/qarānisa — Veteran mamlūks purchased by the predecessors of a reigning sultan.

rabʿ — A group of residential lodgings inhabited by families of moderate means (fifteenth c.).

raʾs nawbat al-nuwāb — The fifth-ranking officer in the military hierarchy (fifteenth c.); the chief of the sultan's guard.

Ramla — A town in central Palestine.

rasūl/rusul — A messenger; a bailiff (Ottoman period).

rawk — A cadastral survey to estimate and redistribute yield from *iqṭāʿat*.

ribāṭ/rubuṭ — A stronghold on the frontier of non-Muslim states housing soldiers dedicated to *jihād* (ʿAbbāsid period). During the Mamlūk period, it was the name for a Ṣūfī hospice, often used in conjunction with *khānqāh*; also a residence for the poor, women, or retired mamlūks.

ribāṭ al-aytām	An orphanage.
rīf	The agrarian countryside.
Rifāʿiyya	A Sufi *ṭarīqa* or order.
riwāq/arwiqa	A large reception hall on the upper floor of a *dār*.
Rūm, Rūmī, Rūmlu, Arwām	Turks or Turkish-speakers from the central provinces of the Ottoman Empire.
Ṣafavid monarchy	Founded at the end of the fifteenth century, it attained control over the entire Iranian region by the early sixteenth century, establishing Twelver Shiʿism as the official interpretation of Islam within its boundaries.
Ṣaffārid	A regime in Sijistān, Iran, founded by Yaʿqūb ibn Layth al-Ṣaffār (a coppersmith), 861–910.
Ṣaʿīd	Upper Egypt, south of Cairo.
ṣāḥib dīwān al-inshāʾ	The head of chancery (see *kātib al-sirr*).
ṣāḥib al-kharāj	The official in charge of tax collection (Arab conquest period).
ṣāḥib al-shurṭa	A chief of police, or leader of a *jund*; effectively second-in-command to a governor (Arab conquest period).
Sakellarios	The treasurer of new central Byzantine treasury, the *sacellum*.
Ṣalāḥ al-Dīn (Saladin)	The founder in 1171 of the Ayyūbid dynasty in Cairo, and the restorer of Sunnism as the official interpretation of Islam in Egypt.
Ṣāliḥī	A mamlūk in the corps of the Ayyūbid sultan al-Ṣāliḥ Najm al-Dīn (d. 1249).
al-Ṣāliḥiyya	i) A suburb of Damascus; ii) a town in northeastern Egypt, where the Sinai desert route enters the confines of the Delta.
samāʿ	The adoration of God through music; a Sufi form of worship.
Ṣamānid	An autonomous Sunni dynasty (892–999) in Transoxiana, with its capital at Bukhāra.
Sarbadārs	The Shīʿī successor regime to the Īlkhānids from 1336 to 1381, ruling from their capital, Sabzawār; they were later Timurid vassals.
sayyid	A tribal leader in early Islamic society.
scalae	A western term for Coptic–Arabic word lists.
Seljuks	A Turkish Sunni dynasty that ruled Iraq and western Iran in 1055–1094, Khurāsān in 1038–1157, and Syria in 1078–1183; there was separate branch in Anatolia (Rūm) in the

	eleventh to thirteenth centuries. The Seljuks were the arch-enemies of the Fāṭimids.
shādd	*See mushidd.*
Shādhiliyya	A popular Ṣūfī order (*ṭarīqa*) in Egypt; among its prominent members was Ibn ʿAṭāʾ Allāh.
Shāfiʿīs	One of the four recognized schools of Sunni Muslim Law; it rejects rationalist arguments but accepts *qiyās* or analogy.
shāhid/shuhūd	A notary or witness in the Islamic legal system.
Sharīʿa	The revealed Law of Islam.
sharīf/shurafāʾ, ashrāf	Literally, "noble;" the descendants of the Prophet Muḥammad, either from ʿAlī and Fāṭima or from ʿAbbās ibn ʿAbd al-Muṭṭṭalib, the Prophet's uncle.
Sharīf of Mecca	The title given to rulers of Mecca during the Mamlūk period, members of the Zaydī Shīʿī Banū Qatāda family descended from ʿAlī ibn Abī Ṭālib via his son, Ḥasan.
shaykh	Arabic, "old person"; by extension a respected senior individual such as a Bedouin chief, or a Ṣūfī master or scholar.
Shīʿa (adj. *Shīʿī*)	Arabic, "faction"; those who acknowledge no caliph after ʿAlī (his faction), and regard him and his descendants as true Imāms.
shurṭa	Police.
Silk Road	The route between east Asia and the Mediterranean.
sipahis	Ottoman cavalrymen.
siyāsa	Politics, governance.
Ṣūfī	A Muslim mystic, literally "wool [*ṣūf*] wearer," usually a member of a brotherhood and follower of a "path" defining forms of Islamic mystical experience.
ṣuḥba	"Companionship," as between a teacher and pupil, or a Sufi *shaykh* and his disciple.
Ṣulayḥids	Ismāʿīlī rulers in the Yemen from 1038 to 1138.
sulṭān	A wielder of authority; a secular ruler, initially subordinate to the caliph.
Sulṭānī	Pertaining to royal mamlūks belonging to a reigning sultan.
Sunna (adj. *Sunnī*)	Normative practice of the Prophet Muḥammad; accepts precedent of first four "rightly guided" (*rashīdūn*) Caliphs.

sürgün	Banishment or deportation as practiced by Ottomans.
takhfīfa/takhāfīf	A light hat, worn by mamlūks.
taqlīd/taqālīd	A diploma of endorsement or investiture granted by the ʿAbbāsid caliph in Cairo (Mamlūk period).
ṭārīqa/ṭuruq	An order of Ṣūfī mystics which follows the doctrines or practices of its founding guide.
taṣawwuf	Ṣūfī mysticism.
Ṭaṭars	Pertaining to persons of Mongol stock.
Ṭayyibīs	Adherents of imāms said to descend from al-Ṭayyib, a son of the tenth Fāṭimid caliph al-Āmir, in opposition to both Nizārīs and Ḥāfiẓīs.
thaghr/thughūr	A frontier stronghold protecting against non-Muslim invaders.
Timurid	Pertaining to Tīmūr-Lenk (Tamurlane), in particular the several dynasties which ruled over parts of central Asia and the Middle East afer his death.
Topkapı Sarayı	The sultan's palace in Istanbul, and the center of Ottoman government.
ṭulb/aṭlāb	A cavalry squadron; a tactical military or parade formation (Mamlūk period).
Turkomans	Turkish-speaking nomadic or semi-nomadic tribes.
Twelvers (*Ithnā ʿasharī*)	Shīʿa who accept a legitimate line of only twelve imāms.
ʿulamāʾ	See *ʿālim*.
Umayyads	An Arab caliphal dynasty based at Damascus, which ruled the Islamic world in 661–750.
umma	*Al-umma al-muḥammadiyya*, the Islamic Community.
ʿurf	Popular custom, common social practice.
ustādār (*ustādh al-dār*)	"Master of the household," or major domo; a mamlūk officer in charge of the sultan's court.
ustādh	A purchaser and trainer of a mamlūk; the head of a mamlūk household.
vizier	See *wazīr*.
wāfidiyya	Warriors or tribesmen, many of Tatar origin, displaced by Mongol invasions, who sought refuge in the Mamlūk empire.
wakīl/wukalāʾ	Agent, supervisor or legal representative.

wakīl bayt al-māl	The Exchequer, or the director of the state treasury.
wālī/wulāh	A military governor of a province; the commander of an urban garrison; a chief of police.
waqf/awqāf	A perpetual trust granted by its donor to support charitable services beneficial to the Muslim community.
waqfiyya	The legal document creating a *waqf*.
wāqif	The donor of charitable trust.
wazīr/wuzarā'	The equivalent of a prime minister, subordinate to the caliph (ʿAbbāsid period).
wujūh	Leading members of Muslim society in early Islamic Egypt.
yasaq	A tax levied according to Ottoman administrative law.
Yavuz	"The Stern" or "the Grim"; an appellation of Ottoman Sultan Salīm I.
Ẓāhiriyya	A mamlūk corps of al-Ẓāhir Baybars or later sultans with the same throne title.
zakāt	The pious duty of charitable giving; in many periods the revenue collected as an alms tax.
zamṭ/zumāṭ	A type of red hat (Ottoman period).
Zangids	The Seljuk successor–state ruling portions of Mesopotamia and Syria, 521/1127–619/1222.
zarābīl	A type of inferior shoes (Ottoman period).
zāwiya/zawāya	Pertaining to a small mosque, a corner or section of a larger mosque, or a hospice for Ṣūfī mystics.
Zīrids	Rulers of north Africa on behalf of the Fāṭimids, later to be independent.
ziyāda	The area around a mosque wall to give increased space for those assisting at Friday prayer.
ziyārat al-qubūr	The ritual visitation of tombs, especially in the Qarāfa.
zuʿar	Armed gangs who "protected" urban quarters.
Zuṭṭ	Peasant buffalo herders of Indian origin, living in the marshes of southern Iraq during the third/ninth century.
Zuwayla Gate (*bāb*)	The gate in the southern wall of Fāṭimid Cairo.

BIBLIOGRAPHY

ABBREVIATIONS

AI	*Annales islamologiques*
BEO	*Bulletin d'études orientales*
BIE	*Bulletin de l'Institut d'Egypte*
BIFAO	*Bulletin de l'Institut Français d'Archéologie Orientale du Caire*
BSOAS	*Bulletin of the School of Oriental and African Studies*
EI2	*Encyclopaedia of Islam*, 2nd edition (Leiden, 1960–).
EIR	*Encyclopaedia Iranica*
EPRO	Études préliminaires aux réligions orientales dans l'Empire romain (Leiden)
IJMES	*International Journal of Middle East Studies*
JAOS	*Journal of the American Oriental Society*
JARCE	*Journal of the American Research Center in Egypt*
JESHO	*Journal of the Economic and Social History of the Orient*
JNES	*Journal of Near Eastern Studies*
JRAS	*Journal of the Royal Asiatic Society*
MESA	Middle East Studies Association of North America (Tucson, AZ)
MIFAO	Mémoires publiés par les membres de l'Institut Français d'Archéologie Orientale du Caire
MW	*The Muslim World*
REI	*Revue des études islamiques*
SI	*Studia Islamica*
WO	*Die Welt des Orients*

1 EGYPT UNDER ROMAN RULE: THE LEGACY OF ANCIENT EGYPT

Abbott, Nabia, *The Monasteries of the Fayyūm*, Studies in Ancient Oriental Civilization, 16 (Chicago, 1937).

Abdel Sayed, Gawdat Gabra, *Untersuchungen zu den Texten über Pesyntheus Bischof von Koptos (569–632)* (Bonn, 1984).

Adams, William Y., *Nubia: Corridor to Africa* (London, 1977).
Allam, Schafik, "Geschwisterehe," in W. Helck and E. Otto (eds.), *Lexikon der Ägyptologie*, (Wiesbaden, 1977), vol. II, cols. 568–69.
Atiya, Aziz S. (ed.), *The Coptic Encyclopedia*, 8 vols. (New York 1991).
Baedeker, Karl, *Baedeker's Egypt 1929* (1929; reprint, London, 1974).
Bagnall, R., *Egypt in Late Antiquity*, (Princeton, 1993).
"Religious conversion and onomastic change in early Byzantine Egypt," *The Bulletin of the American Society of Papyrologists* 19 (1982), 105–23.
Bagnall, Roger and B. W. Frier, *The demography of Roman Egypt* (Cambridge, 1994).
Bagnall, R. and K. Worp, *The Chronological Systems of Byzantine Egypt* (Zutphen, 1978).
Bailey, Donald M., "Classical Architecture in Roman Egypt," in Martin Henig (ed.), *Architecture and Architectural Sculpture in the Roman Empire*, Oxford University Committee for Archaeology 29 (Oxford: 1990), 121–37.
Barzanò, A., "Tiberio Giulio Alessandro, Prefetto d'Egitto (66/70)," in Hildegard Temporini (ed.), *Aufstieg und Niedergang der römischen Welt*, vol. 2, §10.1 (Berlin, 1988), 518–80.
Bastianini, G., "Il prefetto d'Egitto (30 a.C.–297 d.C): Addenda (1973–1985)." in Hildegard Temporini (ed.), *Aufstieg und Niedergang der römischen Welt*, vol. 2, §10.1 (Berlin, 1988), 503–17.
"'Έπαρχος Αἰγύπτου nel formulario dei documenti da Augusto a Diocleziano," in Hildegard Temporini (ed.), *Aufstieg und Niedergang der römischen Welt*, vol. 2, §10.1 (Berlin, 1988), 581–97.
Bell, David N., *The Life of Shenute by Besa* (Kalamazoo, MI, 1983).
Betz, H. D., *The Greek Magical Papyri* (Chicago, 1986).
Boas, George, *The Hieroglyphics of Horapollo* (New York, 1900).
Bowersock, G. W., *Hellenism in Late Antiquity* (Ann Arbor, 1990).
Bowman, Alan, *Egypt after the Pharaohs* (Berkeley, 1986).
Bresciani, E. and S. Pernigotti, *Assuan* (Pisa, 1978).
Budge, E. A. Wallis, *Coptic Apocrypha in the Dialect of Upper Egypt* (London, 1913).
Miscellaneous Coptic Texts in the Dialect of Upper Egypt (London, 1915).
Bureth, P., "Le préfet d'Égypte (30 av. J. C.–297 ap. J. C.): État présent de la documentation en 1973," in Hildegard Temporini (ed.), *Aufstieg und Niedergang der römischen Welt*, vol. II, §10.1 (Berlin, 1988), 472–502.
Burstein, S., "The Hellenistic Fringe: The Case of Meroë," in P. Green (ed.), *Hellenistic History and Culture* (Berkeley, 1993), 38–66.
Butzer, Karl W., *Early Hydraulic Civilization in Egypt* (Chicago, 1976).
Capart, Jean, "L'Énigma de Tahta," *Chronique d'Égypte*, 15, no. 29 (1940), 45–50.
Černý, J., "Consanguineous Marriages in Pharaonic Egypt," *Journal of Egyptian Archaeology*, 40 (1954), 23–29.
Chadwick, Henry, *The Early Church* (London, 1967).
Chuvin, Pierre, *A Chronicle of the Last Pagans* (Cambridge, MA, 1990).
Copenhaver, Brian P., *Hermetica* (Cambridge, 1992).

Corcoran, Lorelei H., "Evidence for the Survival of Pharaonic Religion in Roman Egypt: The Portrait Mummy," in Wolfgang Haase (ed.), *Aufstieg und Niedergang der römischen Welt*, vol. II, §18.5 (Berlin, 1995), 3316–32.

Portrait Mummies from Roman Egypt (I–IV Centuries AD), Studies in Ancient Oriental Civilization 56 (Chicago, 1995).

Daris, S., "Documenti minori dell'esercito romano in Egitto," in Hildegard Temporini (ed.), *Aufstieg und Niedergang der römischen Welt*, vol. II, §10.1 (Berlin, 1988), 724–42.

"Le truppe ausiliarie romane in Egitto," in Hildegard Temporini (ed.), *Aufstieg und Niedergang der römischen Welt*, vol. II, §10.1 (Berlin, 1988), 743–66.

David, M. and B. A. van Groningen, *Papyrological Primer*, 4th edn. (Leiden, 1965).

Derchain, Philippe, "A propos de *Claudien* Eloge de Stilichon, II, 424–436," *Zeitschrift für Ägyptische Sprache und Altertumskunde* 81 (1956), 4–6.

De Salvia, Fulvio, "La figura del mago egizio nella tradizione letteraria greco-romana," in A. Roccati and A. Siliotti (eds.), *La Magia in Egitto*, (Milan, 1987), 343–65.

Desanges, Jehan, "Les raids des Blemmyes sous le règne de Valens, en 373–374," *Meroitic News Letter*, 10 (1972), 32–34.

"Les relations de l'Empire romain avec l'Afrique nilotique et érythréenne, d'Auguste à Probus," in Hildegard Temporini (ed.), *Aufstieg und Niedergang der römischen Welt*, vol. II, §10.1 (Berlin, 1988), 2–43.

Drexhage, H.-J., "Eigentumsdelikte in römischen Ägypten (1.-3. Jh. n. Chr.). Ein Beitrag zur Wirtschaftgeschichte," in Hildegard Temporini (ed.), *Aufstieg und Niedergang der römischen Welt*, vol. II, §10.1 (Berlin, 1988), 952–1004.

Dunand, Françoise, "Pratiques et croyances funéraires en Égypte romaine," in Wolfgang Haase (ed.), *Aufstieg und Niedergang der römischen Welt*, vol. II, §18.5 (Berlin, 1995), 3216–32.

El-Saghir, Mohammed et al., *Le camp romain de Louqsor* (Cairo, 1986).

Foraboschi, D., "Movimenti e tensioni sociali nell'Egitto romano," in Hildegard Temporini (ed.), *Aufstieg und Niedergang der römischen Welt*, vol. II, §10.1 (Berlin, 1988), 807–40.

Fowden, Garth, *The Egyptian Hermes* (Cambridge, 1986).

Fraser, P. M., *Ptolemaic Alexandria*, 3 vols. (Oxford, 1972).

Gallo, Paolo, "The Wandering Personnel of the Temple of Narmuthis in the Faiyum and Some Toponyms of the Meris of Polemon," in Janet H. Johnson (ed.), *Life in a Multi-Cultural Society. Egypt from Cambyses to Constantine and Beyond*, Studies in Ancient Oriental Civilization 51 (Chicago, 1992), 119–31.

Gara, A., "Aspetti di economia monetaria dell'Egitto romano," in Hildegard Temporini (ed.), *Aufstieg und Niedergang der römischen Welt*, vol. II, §10.1 (Berlin, 1988), 912–51.

Gardiner, Alan, *Chester Beatty Gift*, 2 vols., Hieratic Papyri in the British Museum 3 (London, 1945).

Garzya, Antonio, "Pancrates," in *Atti del XVII Congresso Internazionale di Papyrologia*, vol. II (Naples, 1984), 319–25.
Gauthier, Henri, *Le Livre des Rois d'Égypte*, vol. 5 "Les Empereurs Romains," MIFAO 21 (Cairo, 1917).
Geraci, G., "'Επαρξία δὲ νῦν ἐστι. La concezione augustea del governo d'Egitto," in Hildegard Temporini (ed.), *Aufstieg und Niedergang der römischen Welt*, vol. II, §10.1 (Berlin, 1988), 383–411.
Gordon, Richard, "Religion in the Roman Empire: the civic compromise and its limits," in Mary Beard and John North (eds.), *Pagan Priests* (Ithaca, 1990), 235–55.
Grégoire, Henri, "L'Énigma de Tahta," *Chronique d'Égypte*, 15, no. 29 (1940), 119–23.
Grenier, Jean-Claude, "L'Empereur et le Pharaon," in Wolfgang Haase (ed.), *Aufstieg und Niedergang der römischen Welt*,vol. II, §18.5 (Berlin, 1995), 3181–94.
"La stèle funéraire du dernier taureau Bouchis (Caire JE 31901 = Stèle *Bucheum* 20)," *BIFAO*, 83 (1983), 197–208.
Griffith, F. Ll., *Catalogue of the Demotic Graffiti of the Dodecaschoenus* (Oxford, 1937).
Stories of the High Priests of Memphis (Oxford, 1900).
Guey, J., "Encore la 'pluie miraculeuse', Mage et Dieu," *Revue de philologie, de littérature et d'histoire anciennes*, 3me sér., vol. XXII (Paris, 1948), 16–62.
Heinen, Heinz, "Vorstufen und Anfänge des Herrscherkultes im römischen Ägypten," in Wolfgang Haase (ed.), *Aufstieg und Niedergang der römischen Welt*,vol. II, §18.5 (Berlin, 1995), 3144–80.
Helck, Wolfgang and Eberhard Otto, *Lexikon der Ägyptologie*, 7 vols. (Wiesbaden, 1975–89).
Hintze, F., "Meroitic Chronology: Problems and Prospects," *Meroitica*, 1 (1973), 127–44.
Hofmann, Inge, "Die meroitische Religion. Staatskult und Volksfrömmigkeit," in Wolfgang Haase (ed.), *Aufstieg und Niedergang der römischen Welt*,vol. II, §18.5 (Berlin, 1995), 2801–68.
Hopkins, K., "Brother–Sister Marriage in Roman Egypt," *Comparative Studies in Society and History*, 22 (1980), 303–54.
van der Horst, P. W., *Chaeremon*. Études préliminaires aux religions orientales dans l'Empire romain 101 (Leiden, 1984).
Hunt, A. S. and C. C. Edgar, *Select Papyri II* (Cambridge, MA, 1934).
Huzar, Elanor G., "Alexandria ad Aegyptum in the Julio-Claudian Age," in Hildegard Temporini (ed.), *Aufstieg und Niedergang der römischen Welt*, vol. II, §10.1 (Berlin, 1988), 619–68.
"Augustus, Heir of the Ptolemies," in Hildegard Temporini (ed.), *Aufstieg und Niedergang der römischen Welt*, vol. II, §10.1 (Berlin, 1988), 343–82.
"Emperor Worship in Julio-Claudian Egypt." in Wolfgang Haase (ed.), *Aufstieg und Niedergang der römischen Welt*,vol. II, §18.5 (Berlin, 1995), 3092–143.

Jackson, Howard M., *Zosimos of Panopolis on the Letter Omega* (Missoula, MT, 1978).
Johnson, Janet H., "Ptolemaic Bureaucracy from an Egyptian Point of View," in M. Gibson and R. D. Biggs (eds.), *The Organization of Power. Aspects of Bureaucracy in the Ancient Near East*, Studies in Ancient Oriental Civilization 46 (2nd edn.) (Chicago, 1991), 123–31.
"The Role of the Egyptian Priesthood in Ptolemaic Egypt," in L. H. Lesko (ed.), *Egyptological Studies in Honor of Richard A. Parker* (Hanover, NH, 1986), 70–84.
Jones, A. H. M., *A History of Rome through the Fifth Century* (London, 1970).
Kákosy, László, "A Christian Interpretation of the Sun-disk," in M. Heerma Van Voss et al. (eds.), *Studies in Egyptian Religion Dedicated to Professor Jan Zandee* (Leiden, 1982), 70–75.
"Probleme der Religion im römerzeitlichen Ägypten," in Wolfgang Haase (ed.), *Aufstieg und Niedergang der römischen Welt*,vol. II, §18.5 (Berlin, 1995), 2894–3049.
Köberlein, E., *Caligula und die ägyptischen Kulte* (Meisenham am Glan, 1962).
Koenen, Ludwig, "Die Prophezeiungen des 'Töpfers'," *Zeitschrift für Papyrologie und Epigraphik*, 2 (1968), 178–209.
"The Prophecies of a Potter: A Prophecy of World Renewal Becomes an Apocalypse," in Deborah H. Samuel (ed.), *Proceedings of the Twelfth International Congress of Papyrology*, American Studies in Papyrology, 7 (Toronto, 1970), 249–54.
"A Supplementary Note on the Date of the Oracle of the Potter," *Zeitschrift für Papyrologie und Epigraphik*, 54 (1984), 9–13.
Krause, Martin, "Blemmyer," in W. Helck and E. Otto (eds.), *Lexikon der Ägyptologie*, II (Wiesbaden, 1975), cols. 827–28.
Lane, Edward W., *An Account of the Manners and Customs of the Modern Egyptians* (New York, 1973; reprint of London: John Murray, 1860).
Law, R. C. C., "Egypt and Cyrenaica under Roman Rule," in J. D. Page (ed.), *The Cambridge History of Africa*, vol. II (Cambridge, 1978), 193–98.
Lepsius, Richard, "Der letzte Kaiser in der hieroglyphischen Inschriften," *Zeitschrift für Ägyptische Sprache und Altertumskunde* 8 (1870), 25–30.
Lewis, Bernard, "The Contribution to Islam," in J. R. Harris (ed.), *The Legacy of Egypt*, 2nd edn. (Oxford, 1971), 456–77.
Lewis, Naphtali, "The demise of the Demotic document: when and why," *Journal of Egyptian Archaeology*, 79 (1993), 276–81.
Greeks in Ptolemaic Egypt (Oxford, 1986).
Life in Egypt under Roman Rule (Oxford, 1983).
"Μερισμὸς ἀνακεχωρηκότων: an aspect of the Roman oppression in Egypt," *Journal of Egyptian Archaeology*, 23 (1937), 63–75.
"A reversal of a tax policy in Roman Egypt," *Greek, Roman, and Byzantine Studies*, 34 (1993), 101–18.
"The Romanity of Roman Egypt: A Growing Consensus," in *On Government and Law in Roman Egypt, Collected Papers of Naphtali Lewis*, American Studies in Papyrology 33 (1984; reprint, Atlanta, 1995), 298–305.

Lexa, François, *La Magie dans l'Égypte Antique*, 2 vols. (Paris, 1925).
Lobel, E. and C. H. Roberts, *The Oxyrhynchus Papyri, Part XXII*. Graeco-Roman Memoirs 31 (London, 1954).
Lyons, H. G. and L. Borchardt, "Eine trilingue Inschrift von Philae," *Sitzungsberichte. Königlich Preussische Akademie der Wissenschaften*, vol. I (Berlin, 1896), 469–82.
Macke, André and Christiane Macke-Ribet, "Paléopathologie osseuse de la population égyptienne d'époque romaine provenant de la Vallée des Reines," in S. Curto et al. (eds.), *Sesto Congresso Internazionale di Egittologia: Atti*, vol. 2 (Turin, 1993), 299–306.
MacMullen, Ramsay, *Christianizing the Roman Empire (AD 100–400)* (New Haven, 1984).
Mahé, Jean-Pierre, *Hermès en haute-Égypte*, 2 vols. (Quebec, 1978–82).
Malaise, Michel, *Les conditions de pénétration et de diffusion des cultes égyptiens en Italie*. EPRO 22 (Leiden, 1972).
Maspero, Jean, "Horapollon et la fin du paganism égyptien," *BIFAO*, 11 (1914), 163–95.
Meyer, Marvin and Richard Smith, *Ancient Christian Magic: Coptic Texts of Ritual Power* (New York, 1994).
Milne, J. G., *A History of Egypt under Roman Rule* (London, 1898).
A History of Egypt under Roman Rule, 2nd revised edn. (London, 1924).
"The Ruin of Egypt by Roman Mismanagement," *Journal of Roman Studies*, 17 (1927), 1–13.
Montevecchi, O., "L'amministrazione dell'Egitto sotto i Guilio-Claudi." in Hildegard Temporini (ed.), *Aufstieg und Niedergang der römischen Welt*, vol. II, §10.1 (Berlin, 1988), 412–71.
"*Graphai hieron*," *Aegyptus*, 12 (1932), 317–28.
Montserrat, Dominic, *Sex and Society in Graeco-Roman Egypt* (London, 1996).
Musurillo, Herbert A., *The Acts of the Pagan Martyrs. Acta Alexandrinorum* (Oxford, 1954).
Oates, J. F., "The Quality of Life in Roman Egypt," in Hildegard Temporini (ed.), *Aufstieg und Niedergang der römischen Welt*, vol. II, §10.1 (Berlin, 1988), 799–806.
Osing, Jürgen, "Horapollo," inW. Helck and E. Otto (eds.), *Lexikon der Ägyptologie*, vol. 2 (Wiesbaden, 1977), col. 1275.
Parker, Richard A., "The Calendars and Chronology," in J. R. Harris (ed.), *The Legacy of Egypt*, 2nd edn. (Oxford, 1971), 13–26.
Pestman, P. W., *Chronologie égyptienne d'après les textes démotiques (322 av. J.-C.–453 ap. J.-C.)*, Papyrologica Lugduno-Batava 15 (Leiden, 1967).
The New Papyrological Primer, Being the Fifth Edition of David and van Groningen's Papyrological Primer (Leiden, 1990).
Piankoff, Alexandre, "The Osireion of Seti I at Abydos during the Greco-Roman Period and the Christian Occupation," *Bulletin de la Société d'Archéologie Copte*, 15 (1958–60), 125–49.
Pomeroy, S. B., "Women in Roman Egypt. A Preliminary Study based on

Papyri," in Hildegard Temporini (ed.), *Aufstieg und Niedergang der römischen Welt*, vol. II, §10.1 (Berlin, 1988), 708–23.

Préaux, Claire, "Greco-Roman Egypt," in J. R. Harris (ed.), *The Legacy of Egypt*, 2nd edn. (Oxford, 1971), 323–54.

Priese, Karl-Heinz, "Zur Ortsliste der römischen Meroe-Expedition unter Nero," *Meroitica*, 1 (1973), 123–26.

Quaegebeur, Jan, "The Genealogy of the Memphite High Priest Family in the Hellenistic Period," in Dorothy J. Crawford, Jan Quaegebeur and Willy Clarysse (eds.), *Studies on Ptolemaic Memphis*, Studia Hellenistica 24 (Leuven, 1980), 43–81.

Rathbone, Dominic, *Economic Rationalism and Rural Society in Third-Century AD Egypt* (Cambridge, 1991).

Rémondon, Roger, "L'Égypte et la suprème résistance au Christianisme (Ve–VIIe siècles)," *BIFAO*, 51 (1952), 63–78.

Reymond, E. A. E., *From the Records of a Priestly Family from Memphis* (Wiesbaden, 1981).

Reymond, E. A. E. and J. W. B. Barns, *Four Martyrdoms from the Pierpont Morgan Coptic Codices* (London, 1973).

Rickman, Geoffrey, *The Corn Supply of Ancient Rome* (Oxford, 1980).

Ritner, Robert K., "Coptic," in Peter T. Daniels and William Bright (eds.), *The World's Writing Systems* (Oxford, 1996), 287–90.

"Egyptians in Ireland: A Question of Coptic Peregrinations," *Rice University Studies*, 62 (1976), 65–87.

"Egyptian Magical Practice under the Roman Empire," in Wolfgang Haase (ed.), *Aufstieg und Niedergang der römischen Welt*, vol. II, §18.5 (Berlin, 1995), 3333–79.

"Horus on the Crocodiles: A Juncture of Religion and Magic in Late Dynastic Egypt," in W. K. Simpson (ed.), *Religion and Philosophy in Ancient Egypt* (New Haven, 1989), 103–16.

"Implicit Modes of Cross-Cultural Interaction: A Question of Noses, Soap, and Prejudice," in J. H. Johnson (ed.), *Life in a Multi-Cultural Society*, Studies in Ancient Oriental Civilization 51 (Chicago, 1992), 283–90.

The Mechanics of Ancient Egyptian Magical Practice, Studies in Ancient Oriental Civilization 54 (Chicago, 1993).

"Poll Tax on the Dead," *Enchoria*, 15 (1988), 205–07.

"A Uterine Amulet in the Oriental Institute Collection," *JNES*, 43 (1984), 209–21.

Roberts, Colin H., *Manuscript, Society and Belief in Early Christian Egypt* (London, 1979).

Sadr, Karim, *The Development of Nomadism in Ancient Northeast Africa* (Philadelphia, 1991).

Sauneron, Serge, "Les querelles impériales vues à travers les scènes du temple d'Ésné," *BIFAO*, 51 (1952), 111–21.

Schäfer, Heinrich, "Zur Inschrift des C. Cornelius Gallus," *Zeitschrift für Ägyptische Sprache und Altertumskunde*, 34 (1896), 91.

Shinnie, P. L., *Meroe: A Civilization of the Sudan* (London, 1967).
Sidebotham, S. E., "Preliminary report on the 1990–1991 seasons of fieldwork at 'Abu Sha'ar (Red Sea coast)," *JARCE*, 31 (1994), 133–58.
Skeat, T. C., "A Letter from the King of the Blemmyes to the King of the Noubades," *Journal of Egyptian Archaeology*, 63 (1977), 159–70.
Smith, John Holland, *The Death of Classical Paganism* (New York, 1976).
Smith, Mark, *The Mortuary Texts of Papyrus BM 10507*, Catalogue of Demotic Papyri in the British Museum III (London, 1987).
Speidel, Michael P., "Augustus' Deployment of the Legions in Egypt," *Chronique d'Égypte*, 57, no. 113 (1987), 120–24.
"Nubia's Roman Garrison," in Hildegard Temporini (ed.), *Aufstieg und Niedergang der römischen Welt*, vol. II, §10.1 (Berlin, 1988), 767–98.
Stead, M., "The high priest of Alexandria and all Egypt," in R. S. Bagnall et al. (eds.), *Proceedings of the XVIth International Congress of Papyrology 1980* (Ann Arbor, MI, 1981), 411–18.
Stern, Ludwig, "Fragmente eines griechisch-ägyptischen Epos," *Zeitschrift für Ägyptische Sprache und Altertumskunde*, 19 (1881), 70–75.
Straus, J. A., "L'esclavage dans l'Égypte romaine," in Hildegard Temporini (ed.), *Aufstieg und Niedergang der römischen Welt*, vol. II, §10.1 (Berlin, 1988), 841–911.
Tait, J. Grafton, "Aemilianus the 'Tyrant'," *Journal of Egyptian Archaeology*, 10 (1924), 80–82.
Tait, W. John, "Demotic Literature and Egyptian Society," in Janet H. Johnson (ed.), *Life in a Multi-Cultural Society. Egypt from Cambyses to Constantine and Beyond*, Studies in Ancient Oriental Civilization 51 (Chicago, 1992), 303–10.
"Theban Magic," in S. P. Vleeming (ed.), *Hundred-Gated Thebes* (Leiden, 1995), 169–82.
Taubenschlag, Raphael, *The Law of Greco-Roman Egypt in the Light of the Papyri 332 BC–640 AD* (New York, 1944).
Till, Walter C., *Koptische Grammatik* (Leipzig, 1955).
Török, L., "Geschichte Meroes. Ein Beitrag über die Quellenlage und den Forschungsstand," in Hildegard Temporini (ed.), *Aufstieg und Niedergang der römischen Welt*, vol. II, §10.1 (Berlin, 1988), 107–341.
Updegraff, R. T., "The Blemmyes I: The Rise of the Blemmyes and the Roman Withdrawal from Nubia under Diocletian," in Hildegard Temporini (ed.), *Aufstieg und Niedergang der römischen Welt*, vol. II, §10.1 (Berlin, 1988), 44–106.
Wallace, Sherman L., *Taxation in Egypt from Augustus to Diocletian* (New York, 1938).
Welsby, Derek A., *The Kingdom of Kush* (London, 1996).
Whitcomb, Donald, "Quseir al-Qadim and the Location of Myos Hormos," *Topoi*, 6 (1996), 747–72.
Whitcomb, Donald and Janet Johnson, *Quseir al-Qadim 1979, Preliminary Report* (Cairo, 1979).
Quseir al-Qadim 1980, Preliminary Report (Malibu, 1980).

Whitehorne, John E. G., "The Pagan Cults of Roman Oxyrhynchus," in Wolfgang Haase (ed.), *Aufstieg und Niedergang der römischen Welt*, vol. II, §18.5 (Berlin, 1995), 3050–91.
"P. Lond. II, 359 and Tuscus' list of temple perquisites," *Chronique d'Égypte*, 53, no. 106 (1978), 321–28.
"Recent Research on the *strategi* of Roman Egypt (to 985)," in Hildegard Temporini (ed.), *Aufstieg und Niedergang der römischen Welt*, vol. II, §10.1 (Berlin, 1988), 598–617.
Wilcken, Ulrich, "Papyrus-Urkunden,"*Archiv für Papyrusforschung*, 5 (1913), 443–44.
Witt, R. E., *Isis in the Graeco-Roman World* (Ithaca, NY, 1971).
Yellin, Janice, "Meroitic Funerary Religion," in Wolfgang Haase (ed.), *Aufstieg und Niedergang der römischen Welt*, vol. II, §18.5 (Berlin, 1995), 2869–92.
Young, Dwight W., "A Monastic Invective Against Egyptian Hieroglyphs," in Dwight W. Young (ed.), *Studies Presented to Hans Jakob Polotsky* (East Gloucester, MA, 1981), 348–60.
Zahrnt, M., "Antinoopolis in Ägypten: Die hadrianische Gründung und ihre Privilegien in der neueren Forschung," in Hildegard Temporini (ed.), *Aufstieg und Niedergang der römischen Welt*, vol. II, §10.1 (Berlin, 1988), 669–706.
Zauzich, K.-Th., "Spätdemotische Papyrusurkunden III," *Enchoria*, 4 (1974), 71–82.
"Spätdemotische Papyrusurkunden IV," *Enchoria*, 7 (1977), 151–80.
Zoega, Georgio, *Catalogus Codicum Copticorum Manuscriptorum*, 2nd edn. (Leipzig, 1903).

2 EGYPT ON THE EVE OF THE MUSLIM CONQUEST

Papyri

BGU = *Ägyptische Urkunden aus den Königlichen Museen zu Berlin, Griechische Urkunden* (Berlin, 1895–98).
CPRF = J. Karabacek, *Corpus Papyrorum Raineri: Führer durch die Ausstellung* (Vienna 1894).
The Oxyrhynchus Papyri. 1898–
SB = F. Preisigke, et al. *Sammelbuch griechischer Urkunden aus Aegypten*. 1915–

It is inappropriate here to survey papyri in detail, but among the important ones of relevance are:

P. Oxy. LVIII 3959, in J. R. Rea (ed.) *The Oxyrhynchus Papyri*, Egypt Exploration Society, Graeco-Roman Memoirs, No. 78 (London, 1991), 48: 116–188, dated to 620. See also note 21.
Crum, W. E., and H. E. Winlock, *The Monastery of Epiphanius* (New York, 1926), I–II.
BGU 314 [Herakleopolis]; 370 [Arsinoe] = *Ägyptische Urkunden aus den*

Königlichen Museen zu Berlin, Griechische Urkunden (Berlin, 1895–1898),vols. 1, 2; *P. Ross.* iii, 51; *SB* 4662, 9461.

P. Lond. i, 113, 6 (b), in F. G. Kenyon (ed.), *Greek Papyri in the British Museum* (London, 1893), 1: 214–15.

P. Flor. 306, in Girolamo Vitelli (ed.), *Papiri Greci Egizii*, 3: *Papiri Fiorentini* (Milan, 1915), No. 306, p. 40 [Oct/Nov 635].

SB 4488; *P. Lond.* 1012, in F. G. Kenyon, H. I. Bell (eds.), *Greek Papyri in the British Museum* (London, 1893), 3: 265–67.

P. Lond. 113, 10, in Kenyon, *Greek Papyri*, 1: 222–24.

SB 6271 = Friedrich Preisigke, Fr. Bilabel, *Sammelbuch griechischer Urkunden aus Ägypten* (Berlin: De Gruyter, 1926): 44–45, which is dated 640/641, from Apollonos Magna [Idfu, in the Thebaid]; esp. *P. Lond.* 113, 10.

CPRF 556; *SB* 9748 = *CPRF* 552; *SB* 9749 = *CPRF* 553; *SB* 9755 = *CPRF* 554; *SB* 9751 = *CPRF* 559; *SB* 9752 = *CPRF* 560; *SB* 9753 = *CPRF* 561, from Friedrich Preisigke, Fr. Bilabel, contd. by Emil Kiessling, *Sammelbuch griechischer Urkunden aus Ägypten* (Wiesbaden: Harrasowitz, 1965), 8: 86–89, 89–90; all of these last are from Herakleopolis Magna, or modern Ihnāsīyat al-madīna, in the Fayyūm area.

Papyri russischer und georgischer Sammlungen. III: *Spätrömische und byzantinische Texte*. Ed. G. Zereteli, P. Jernstedt. 1930.

Other works

Agapius of Membij, *Histoire. Patrologia Orientalis* 8.

Albert, Micheline, R. Beylot, et al., *Christianismes orientaux. Introduction à l'étude des langues et des littératures* (Paris, 1993).

Anastasii Sinaitae Opera. Sermones duo in constitutionem hominis secundem imaginem Dei necnon Opuscula adversus Monotheletas, ed. Karl-Heinz Uthemann, Corpus Christianorum, Series Graeca, 12 (Brepols-Turnhout, 1985).

Borkowski, Z. *Alexandrie II: Inscriptions des factions* (Warsaw, 1981).

Butler, A. J., *The Arab Conquest of Egypt and the Last Thirty Years of Roman Dominion, Containing also the Treaty of Miṣr in Ṭabarī* (1913); *Babylon in Egypt, with a Critical Bibliography and Additional Documentation* (1914; revised edition by P. M. Fraser, Oxford, 1978).

Caetani, L., *Annali dell'Islam*, 10 vols. in 12 (Milan, 1905–26; reprinted Hildesheim, 1972).

Cameron, Av. (ed.), *States, Resources, Armies*, esp. J.-M. Carrié, "L'État à la recherche de nouveaux modes de financement des armées (Rome et Byzance, IVe–VIIIe siècles," 27–60, The Byzantine and Early Islamic Near East, vol. 3 (Princeton, 1996).

Cameron, Av. and L. I. Conrad (eds.), *Problems in the Literary Source Material*, The Byzantine and Early Islamic Near East, 1 (Princeton, 1992).

Conrad, L. I. "Theophanes and the Arabic Historical Transmission: Some Indications of Intercultural Transmission," *Byzantinische Forschungen*, 15 (1990), 1–45.

Dawes, E. and N. H. Baynes, *Three Byzantine Saints* (Oxford, 1948).
Delehaye, H. "Passio sanctorum sexaginta martyrum," *Analecta Bollandiana*, 23 (1904), 289–307.
"Une vie inédite de Saint Jean l'Aumônier," *Analecta Bollandiana*, 45 (1927), 5–74.
Dennis, G. T., ed. trans., *Strategikon* (Philadelphia, 1984).
ed., *Das Strategikon des Maurikios*, trans. E. Gamillscheg (Vienna, 1981).
ed. trans. *Three Byzantine Military Treatises* (Washington, 1985).
Déroche, Vincent, *Études sur Léontios de Néapolis*, Studia Byzantina Upsaliensia, 3 (Uppsala, 1995).
Donner, F. M., *The Early Islamic Conquests* (Princeton, 1981).
Efthymiadis, Stephanos, "Living in a City and Living in a Scetis: The Dream of Eustathios the Banker," *Byzantinische Forschungen*, 21 (1995), 11–29.
Fikhman, I. F. "De nouveau sur la colonat du Bas-Empire," *Miscellanea papyrologica in occasione del bicentenario dell'edizione della Charta Borgiana*, Papyrologica Florentina, 19 (Florence, 1990), 159–179.
Flusin, Bernard, ed. trans., *Saint Anastase le Perse et l'histoire de la Palestine au début du VIII siècle* (Paris, 1992).
Gascou, Jean. "De Byzance à l'Islam," *JESHO*, 26 (1983), 97–109.
Un codex fiscal Hermopolite (P. Sorb. II 69). American Studies in Papyrology, 32 (Atlanta, 1994).
"Les grands domaines, la cité et l'état en Égypte byzantine," *Travaux et Mémoires*, 9 (1985), 1–90.
"L'Institution des bucellaires," *Bulletin de l'Institut français d'archéologie orientale au Caire*, 76 (1976), 143–56.
"Les institutions de l'hippodrome en Égypte byzantine," *BIFAO*, 76 (1976), 185–212.
Gascou, Jean, and Leslie MacCoull, "Le cadastre d'Aphroditô," *Travaux et Mémoires*, 10 (1987), 102–58.
Haas, C. *Alexandria in Late Antiquity. Topography and Social Conflict* (Baltimore, 1997).
Haldon, John, *Byzantium in the Seventh Century*, 2nd edn. (Cambridge, 1997).
"Military Service, Military Lands and the Status of Soldiers," *Dumbarton Oaks Papers* 45 (1993), 1–67.
Hendy, Michael, *Studies in the Byzantine Monetary Economy* (Cambridge, 1985).
Ibn ʿAbd al-Ḥakam, *Kitāb Futūḥ Miṣr wa-Akhbāruhā* (The History of the Conquest of Egypt, North Africa and Spain), ed. C. C. Torrey (New Haven, 1922).
Isaac the Presbyter, *The Life of Samuel of Kalamun by Isaac the Presbyter*, ed. trans. Anthony Alcock (Warminster, 1983).
Jarry, Jean. "L'Égypte et l'invasion musulmane," *AI*, 6 (1966), 1–29.
John of Nikiu, *The Chronicle of John (c. 690 AD) Coptic Bishop of Nikiu: Being a History of Egypt before and during the Arab Conquest, Translated from*

Hermann Zotenberg's Edition of the Ethiopic Version with an Introduction, Critical and Linguistic Notes, and an Index of Names, trans. R. H. Charles (London, 1916).
Jördens, Andrea, *P. Heidelberg* V, in *Vertragliche Regelungen von Arbeiten im späten griechsprachigen Ägypten* (Heidelberg, 1990), 43–48.
Kaegi, W. E. "Byzantine Logistics: Problems and Perspectives," in J. Lynn (ed.), *Feeding Mars* (Boulder, 1993), 39–55.
Byzantine Military Unrest, 471–843: An Interpretation (Amsterdam, Las Palmas, 1981).
Byzantium and the Early Islamic Conquests (Cambridge, 1995).
Keenan, J. G. "A Constantinople Loan, AD 541," *Bulletin of the American Society of Papyrologists*, 29 (1992), 175–82.
"Papyrology and Byzantine Histoirography," *Bulletin of the American Society of Papyrologists*, 30 (1993), 137–144.
"Pastoralism in Roman Egypt," *Bulletin of the American Society of Papyrologists*, 26 (1989), 175–198.
Khoury, R. G., *'Abd Allāh Ibn Lahī'a (97–174/715–790). Juge et grand maître de l'école égyptienne* (Wiesbaden, 1986).
Krüger, Julian, *Oxyrhynchos in der Kaiserzeit: Studien zur Topographie und Literaturrezeption* (Frankfurt, Bern, New York, 1990).
Lapidge, Michael (ed.), *Biblical Commentaries from the Canterbury School of Theodore and Hadrian* (Cambridge, 1994).
Lappa-Zizicas, E., "Un épitomé inédit de la Vie de S. Jean l'Aumônier," *Analecta Bollandiana*, 88 (1970), 265–278.
Leontios of Neapolis, *Vie de Syméon le Fou et Vie de Jean de Chypre*, ed. trans. A. J. Festugière (Paris, 1974).
MacCoull, L. S., *Coptic Perspectives on Late Antiquity* (Aldershot, 1993).
Dioscorus of Aphrodito: His Work and His World (Berkeley, 1988).
Mango, C. "A. Byzantine Hagiographer at Work: Leontios of Neapolis," *Sitzungsberichte, Österreichische Akad. d. Wiss., philosoph.-Hist. Kl.*, 432 (1984), 25–41.
Martindale, F. R., *Prosopography of the Later Roman Empire* III (Cambridge, 1992).
Maspero, Jean, *Organisation militaire de l'Égypte byzantine* (Paris, 1912).
Meyer, Carol, "A Byzantine Gold-Mining Town in the Eastern Desert of Egypt: Bir Umm Fawakhir, 1992–1993," *Journal of Roman Archaeology*, 8 (1995), 192–224.
Meyers, E. M. (ed.), *Oxford Encyclopedia of Archaeology of the Near East*, 5 vols. (Oxford, New York, 1997).
Michael the Syrian, *Chronique*, ed. trans. J.-B. Chabot, 4 vols. (Paris, 1899–1910).
Miracles of St. Artemios, ed. trans. V. S. Crisafulli and John Nesbitt (Leiden, 1997).
Misiu, D. *He diatheke tou Herakleiou* (Thessaloniki, 1985).
Nikephoros, *Short History*, ed. trans. C. Mango (Washington, 1990).

Noth, A., with L. I. Conrad, *The Early Arabic Historical Tradition: A Source-Critical Study*, M. Bonner trans. (Princeton, 1994), 183–184.
Olster, D. M., *The Politics of Usurpation in the Seventh Century* (Amsterdam, Las Palmas, 1993).
Roman Defeat, Christian Response, and the Literary Constuction of the Jew (Philadelphia, 1994).
Pargoire, J., "Les LX soldats martyrs de Gaza," *Échos d'Orient*, 8 (1905), 40–43.
Rémondon, Roger, "P. Hamb. 56 et P. Lond. 1419 (notes sur les finances d'Aphrodito du VIe siècle au VIIIe siècle," *Chronique d'Égypte*, 40 (1965), 401–430).
Relatio motionis factae inter domnum abbatem Maximum et socium ejus atque principes in secretario, ed. J. P. Migne, *Patrologia Graeca*, XC, 109–130.
Rodziewicz, M., *Alexandrie II: La céramique romaine tardive d'Alexandrie* (Warsaw, 1976).
Schiller, A. A., "The Budge Coptic Papyrus of Columbia University and Related Greek Papyri of the British Museum," *Actes du Xe Congrès International des Papyrologues* (Warsaw, 1961), 193–200.
Schmitt, O., "Die *Bucellarii*. Eine Studie zum militärischen Gefolgschaftswesen in der Spätantike," *Tyche*, 9 (1994), 147–174.
Shahid, I. *Byzantium and the Arabs in the Sixth Century*, 2 vols. (Washington, 1995).
Stratos, A., *Vyzantion ston z' aiona*. 6 vols. Athens: Estia, 1965–1978.
Synopsis Chronike, ed. C. Sathas, in his *Mesaionike Bibliotheke*, VII (Paris, 1984; reprint, Athens, 1972), 1–556.
Theophanes, *Chronographia*, ed. C. de Boor, 2 vols. (Leipzig, 1883); *The Chronicle of Theophanes the Confessor*, trans. Cyril Mango and Roger Scott (Oxford, 1997).
Van Dieten, J. L., *Geschichte der Patriarchen von Sergios I. bis Johannes VI.* (Amsterdam, 1972).
Winkelmann, F., "Ägypten und Byzanz vor der arabischen Eroberung," *Byzantinoslavica*, 40 (1979), 161–82, reprinted in Winkelmann, *Studen zu Konstantin den Grossen und zur byzantinischen Kirchengeschichte*, ed. W. Brandes and J. Haldon (Birmingham, 1993).
Wipszycka, E., *Études sur le christianisme dans l'Egypte de l'antiquité tardive*, Studia Ephemeridis Augustinianum, 52 (Rome, 1996).
Zanetti, Ugo, "La vie de Saint Jean Higoumène de Scété au VIIe siècle," *Analecta Bollandiana*, 114 (1996), 273–405.

3 EGYPT AS A PROVINCE IN THE ISLAMIC CALIPHATE, 641–868

Abbot, N., *The Kurrah Papyri from Aphrodito in the Oriental Institute* Studies in Ancient Oriental Civilisation 15 (Chicago, 1938).
"A new papyrus and a review of the administration of ʿUbaid Allāh ibn al-Ḥabḥab," in G. Makdisi (ed.), *Arabic and Islamic Studies in honor of Hamilton A. R. Gibb* (Leiden, 1965), 21–35.

Athamina, K., "Some Administrative, Military and Socio-Political Aspects of Early Muslim Egypt," in Y. Lev (ed.), *War and Society in the Eastern Mediterranean, 7th–15th centuries* (Leiden, 1997), 101–13.

al-Balādhurī, Aḥmad ibn Yaḥyā, *Futūḥ al-Buldān*, ed. M. J. de Goeje (Leiden, 1866).

Bell, H. I., "Organisation of Egypt under the Ummayad Khalifs," *Byzantinische Zeitschrift*, 28 (1929), 278–86.

Butler, A. J., *The Arab Conquest of Egypt and the Last Thirty Years of Roman Dominion, Containing also the Treaty of Miṣr in Tabarī* (1913); *Babylon in Egypt, with a Critical Bibliography and Additional Documentation* (1914; revised edition by P. M. Fraser, Oxford, 1978).

Fahmy, A. M., *Muslim Sea Power in the Eastern Mediterranean from the Seventh to the Tenth Century* (London, 1950).

Forand, P., "Early Muslim Relations with Nubia," *Der Islam*, 48 (1972), 111–21.

Frantz-Murphy, G., "Land tenure and social transformation in early Islamic Egypt," in T. Khalidi (ed.), *Land Tenure and Social Transformation in the Middle East* (Beirut, 1984) 131–39.

Gibb, H. A. R., "The Fiscal Rescript of Omar II," *Arabica*, 2 (1955), 1–16.

Grohmann, A., *From the World of Arabic Papyri* (Cairo, 1952).

Guest, A. R., "The Foundation of Fustat and the Khittahs of that town," *JRAS*, (1907), 49–83.

Hill, D. R., *The Termination of Hostilities in the Early Arab Conquests* (London, 1971).

Hinds, G. M., "The Murder of the Caliph ʿUthmān," *International Journal of Middle East Studues*, 3 (1972), 450–69.

Ibn ʿAbd al-Ḥakam, *Kitāb Futūḥ Miṣr wa-Akhbārihā* (The History of the Conquest of Egypt, North Africa and Spain), ed. C. C. Torrey (New Haven, 1922).

John of Nikiu, *The Chronicle of John (c. 690 AD) Coptic Bishop of Nikiu: Being a History of Egypt before and during the Arab Conquest, Translated from Hermann Zotenberg's Edition of the Ethiopic Version with an Introduction, Critical and Linguistic Notes, and an Index of Names*, trans. R. H. Charles (London, 1916).

Kennedy, H., "Central Government and Provincial Elites in the early ʿAbbasid caliphate," *BSOAS*, 44 (1981), 26–38.

Kennedy, H., *The Prophet and the Age of Caliphates: The Islamic Middle East from the Sixth to the Eleventh Century* (London, 1986).

Al-Kindī, Muḥammad ibn Yūsuf, *The Governors and Judges of Egypt*, ed. R. Guest, Gibb Memorial Series (London, 1912).

Khoury, R. G., "Al-Layth ibn Saʿd (94/713–175/791), grand maître et mecène de l'Egypte," *JNES*, 40 (1981), 189–202.

Kubiak, W., *Al-Fusṭāṭ: Its Foundation and Early Urban Development* (Warsaw, 1982; Cairo, 1987).

Morimoto, K., *The Fiscal Administration of Egypt in the Early Islamic Period*, (Tokyo, 1981).

Noth, A., *The Early Arabic Historic Tradition*, ed. L. I. Conrad (Princeton, 1994).
Rağib, Y. "Lettres nouvelles de Qurra ibn Šarik", *JNES* 40 (1981), 173–88.
Sawīrus ibn al-Muqaffaʿ, *History of the Patriarchs of the Coptic Church of Alexandria*, ed. with English trans. by B. Evetts, *Patrologia Orientalis* I, 99–215; V, 1–216; X, 357–553, text also numbered continuously 1–665; Refs. in notes use this pagination; ed. C. F. Seybold, *CSCO Scriptores Arabici* (Leiden, 1962), vols. 8–9.
Simonsen, J. B., *Studies in the Genesis and Early development of the Caliphal Taxation System with Special Reference to Circumstances in the Arab Peninsula, Egypt and Palestine* (Copenhagen, 1988).
al-Tabarī, Muḥammad ibn Jarīr, *Ta'rīkh al-Rusul wa'l-Mulūk*, ed. M. J. de Goeje *et al.* (Leiden, 1879–1901).

4 AUTONOMOUS EGYPT FROM IBN ṬŪLŪN TO KĀFŪR, 868–969

Gil, Moshe, *A History of Palestine, 634–1099* (Cambridge, 1992), contains an exhaustive bibliography and a useful chronology for Ṭūlūnids and Ikhshīdids.

Abū Ṣāliḥ al-Armanī, *The Churches and Monasteries of Egypt and Some Neighboring Countries attributed to Abū Ṣāliḥ, The Armenian* ed. and trans. B. T. A. Evetts and A. J. Butler (Oxford, 1895).
Ahrweiler, H., *Byzance, les pays et les territoires* (London, 1976).
Études sur les structures administratives et sociales de Byzance (London, 1971).
Bacharach, J. "African Military Slaves in the Medieval Middle East: The Cases of Iraq (869–955) and Egypt (868–1171)," *IJMES* 13 (1981), 471–95.
"The Career of Muḥammad ibn Ṭughj al-Ikhshīd," *Speculum*, 50 (1975), 586–612.
Bahgat, A. and A. Gabriel, *Fouilles d'al-Fusṭāṭ* (Paris, 1921).
al-Balawī, *Sīrat Ibn Ṭūlūn*, ed. M. Kurd ʿAlī (Damascus, 1358 AH).
Becker, C. H., *Beiträge zur Geschichte Ägyptens unter dem Islam* (Strasbourg, 1902).
Bianquis, Th., "L'Acte de succession de Kāfūr d'après Maqrīzī," *AI*, 12 (1974), 263–69.
Damas et la Syrie sous la domination fatimide (359–468/969–1076), 2 vols. (Damascus, 1986, 1989).
"Les derniers gouverneurs ikhchīdides à Damas," *BEO*, 23 (1970), 167–96.
"Ibn al-Nābulusī, un martyr sunnite au IVe siècle de l'Hégire," *AI* 12 (1974), 44–66.
"La prise du pouvoir en Égypte par les Fāṭimides," *AI*, 11 (1972), 50–108.
Bilād al-Shām during the ʿAbbāsid Period, Amman conference 1992, Arabic section edited by M. A. al-Bakhit and M. Y. Abbadi, English and French section edited by M. A. al-Bakhit and R. Schick (Amman, 1992).

Bosworth, C. E., "Abū ʿAmr ʿUthmān al-Ṭarsūsī's *Siyār al-Thughūr* and the last years of Arab rule in Tarsus (fourth/tenth century)," *Graeco-Arabica*, 5 (new edn. Athens, 1993).

"Byzantium and the Arabs; War and Peace between Two World Civilizations," *Journal of Oriental and African Studies* 3, 4 (1991–92), 1–23.

The Islamic Dynasties. 1st edn. (Edinburgh, 1967); 2nd edn. *The New Islamic Dynasties: A Chronological and Genealogical Manual* (New York, 1996).

Busse, H., *Chalif und Grosskönig; Die Buyiden im Iraq* (Beirut, 1969).

Cahen, C. *Les peuples musulmans dans l'histoire médiévale* (Damascus, 1977).

Canard, M., *Byzance et les musulmans du Proche Orient* (London, 1973).

L'Expansion arabo-islamique et ses répercussions (London, 1974).

Histoire de la dynastie des H'āmdanides de Jazīra et de Syrie, vol. 1 (Algiers, 1951).

Casanova, P., *Essai de reconstitution topographique de la ville d'al-Fousṭāṭ ou Miṣr*, MIFAO, 35 (1913).

Chabbi, J. "Ribāṭ," *EI2*.

Chiauzi,G., F. Gabrielli and P.Guichard, *Maghreb médiéval* (Aix-en-Provence, 1991).

Creswell, A. C. *The Muslim Architecture of Egypt* I, (Cairo, 1952).

Dachraoui, F., *Le califat fatimide au Maghreb, 296–362/909–973: histoire, politique et institutions* (Tunis, 1981).

Daftary, F., *The Ismāʿīlīs; Their History and Doctrines* (Cambridge, 1990).

DeGoeje, M. J., *Mémoires d'histoire et de géographie orientales* (Leiden, 1886; reissued as photocopy, Osnabrück, 1977).

Denoix, S., *Décrire le Caire: Fusṭāt-Miṣr d'après Ibn Duqmāq et Maqrīzī: l'histoire d'une partie de la ville du Caire d'après deux historiens égyptiens des XIVe–XVe siècles* (Cairo, 1992).

Ehrenkreutz, A. S. "Kāfūr," *EI2*.

"Numismatico-Statistical Reflections on the Annual Gold Coinage Production of the Ṭūlūnid Mint in Egypt," *JESHO*, 20, 3 (1977), 267–81.

Elisséeff, N., *L'Orient musulman au Moyen Age* (Paris, 1977).

Fu'ad Sayyid, A., *Al-Dawla al-Fāṭimiyya, tafsīr jadīd* (Cairo, 1992).

"Lumières nouvelles sur quelques sources de l'histoire fāṭimide en Égypte," *AI*, 13 (1977), 1–41.

"Nuṣūṣ ḍā'iʿa min Akhbār Miṣr li'l-Musabbiḥī," *AI*, 17 (1981), 1–54, Arabic section.

Garcin, J.-C. *Un centre musulman de la Haute-Égypte médiévale: Qūṣ* (Cairo, 1976).

Espaces, pouvoirs et idéologies de l'Égypte médiévale (London, Variorum Reprints, 1987).

Gayraud, R. P., "Iṣṭabl ʿAntar (Fostat), rapport de fouilles, 1987, 1989, 1990, 1992," *AI*, 25 (1991), 57–88, 88–102; 27 (1993), 225–32; 28 (1994), 1–27.

Goitein, S. D., *A Mediterranean Society: The Jewish Communities of the Arab World as portrayed in the Documents of the Cairo Geniza*, 6 vols. (Berkeley, 1967–94) (bibliography and indices in vol. 6).

Grabar, O. *The Coinage of the Ṭūlūnids* (New York, 1957).
Halm, H., "Nachrichten zu Bautes der Aghlabiden und Fāṭimiden in Libyen und Tunisien," *WO*, 23 (1992), 129–58.
Hassan, Z. M., *Les Tulunides: Études de l'Égypte musulmane à la fin du IXe siècle: 868–905* (Paris, 1933).
Humphreys, R. S., *Islamic History: A Framework for Inquiry* (Princeton, 1992).
Ibn Abī-Uṣaybiʿa, A., *ʿUyūn al-Anbāʾ fī ṭabaqāt al-Aṭibbāʿ*, ed. A. Muller/Umru al-Qays ibn al-Ṭaḥḥān (Cairo, 1882).
Ibn al-ʿAdīm, *Bughyat al-ṭalab fī ta'rīkh Ḥalab*, vols. 1, 2, index, ed. Suhayl Zakkār (Damascus, 1408/1988).
Zubdat al-ḥalab min ta'rīkh Ḥalab, ed. Samī Dahhān (Damascus, 1951).
Ibn al-Athīr, *Al-Kāmil fī al-Ta'rīkh*, VIII: 295–369 H, XI, XII, ed. C. J. Thornberg (Leiden, 1867–76; reprinted Beirut, 1965–67).
Ibn Duqmāq, *Kitāb al-Intiṣār li-Wāsiṭat ʿIqd al-Amṣār*, IV, V, ed. K. Vollers (Cairo, 1893, reprinted Beirut, n.d.).
Ibn Khallikān, *Wafayāt al-aʿyān wa anbāʾ al-zamān*, ed. Iḥsān ʿAbbās (Beirut, 1968).
Ibn Saʿīd al-Andalusī, *Al-mughrib fī ḥūlā al-maghrib; al-jawz al-awal min al-qism al-khāṣṣ bi-Miṣr*, ed. Zakī Muḥammad Ḥasan (Cairo, 1953).
Ibn Taghrī-Birdī, Abū al-Maḥāsin, *Al-Nujūm al-Zāhira fī Mulūk Miṣr wa al-Qāhira*, partial edn. ed. W. Popper, University of California Publications in Semitic Philology, II–III, V–VII (Berkeley, 1909–60); English trans. W. Popper, *History of Egypt, 1382–1469*, same series, XIII–XIV, XVII, XIX, XX–XXIV (Berkeley, 1954–1963); complete edn. 16 vols. (Cairo, 1929–72).
Ibn Zulāq, *Kitāb akhbār Sībawayh al-Miṣrī*, ed. Sa'd, al-Dīb (Cairo, 1933).
Kennedy, Hugh, *The Prophet and the Age of Caliphates; The Islamic Near East from the Sixth to the Eleventh Century* (London, 1986).
Al-Kindī, Muḥammad ibn Y., *Kitāb al-wulāt wa kitāb al-quḍāt*, ed. R. Guest (Beirut, 1908).
Kubiak, W., *Al-Fusṭāṭ: Its Foundation and Early Urban Development* (Warsaw, 1982; Cairo, 1987).
Lane-Poole, S., *A History of Egypt 4: The Middle Ages* (London, 1901).
Lev. Y., *State and Society in Fāṭimid Egypt* (Leiden, 1991).
Lewis, A., *Naval Power and Trade in the Mediterranean,* AD *500–1100* (Princeton, 1951).
Lopez, R. S., *Byzantium and the World Around It: Economic and Institutional Relations* (London, 1978).
al-Maqrīzī, *Kitāb al-Muqaffā al-Kabīr*, ed. Muḥammed Yaʿlāwī, 8 vols. (Beirut, 1991).
al-Mawāʿiẓ wa al-Iʿtibār bi-Dhikr al-Khiṭaṭ wa al-Āthār, 2 vols. (Cairo, 1853–54); partial edn. ed. G. Wiet, 5 vols. (Cairo, 1911–27).
Maspero, J. and Wiet, G., *Matériaux pour servir à la géographie de l'Égypte* (Cairo, 1919).
Rāghib, Y. *Marchands d'étoffe du Fayyoum, 4 vols. (Cairo, 1982, 1985, 1992, 1996).*
Raymond, A., *Le Caire* (Paris, 1993).

Répertoire chronologique d'inscriptions arabes, vols. 3, 4, 5, eds. E. Combe, J. Sauvaget, G. Wiet (Cairo, 1932–35).
Saʿīd ibn Biṭrīq, *Ta'rīkh*, vols. 6, 7, ed. L. Cheikho (second series, Leipzig, 1906, 1909).
Sauneron, S. *Villes et légendes d'Égypte* (Cairo, 1974).
Sawīrus ibn al-Muqaffaʿ, *History of the Patriarchs of the Coptic Church of Alexandria*, ed. with English trans. B. Evetts, *Patrologia Orientalis* I, 99–215; V, 1–216; X, 357–553; Cairo edn. Société d'Archéologie Copte, *History of the Patriarchs of the Egyptian Church, Known as the History of the Holy Church of Sawīrus ibn al-Muḳaffaʿ, Bishop of Ashmūnīn*, II, pt. 1 (AD 849–880, pt. 2 (AD 880–1066); II, pts. 2–3 (textes et documents) ed. and trans. A. Atiya, Y. ʿAbd al-Masīḥ, O. H. E. KHS-Burmester (1943, 1948–1959); III, pts. 1–3; IV, pts. 1–2, A. Khater (1968–70, 1974).
Scanlon, G., "Fusṭāṭ Expedition Preliminary Reports," *JARCE* 5 (1966–).
"Leadership in the Qarmaṭian Sect: Numismatic Evidence," *BIFAO*, 49 (1960), 29–48.
Shaban, A. M., *Islamic History; A New Interpretation*, 2 vols. (Cambridge, 1990).
Sibṭ Ibn al-Jawzī, *Mir'at al-Zamān fi Ta'rīkh al-Aʿyān*, facsimile ed. J. R. Jewett (Chicago, 1907); 2nd edn. based on the above, published as 8/1 and 2 (Hyderabad, 1951–1952); 3rd edn ed. J. Jalīl and M. al-Hamūndī (Baghdad, 1990); partial French trans. "Extraits du Mirāt ez-Zemān," A.-C. Barbier de Meynard, *Historiens orientaux*, III, 517–570.
Sourdel, D., *Le vizirat abbasside de 749 à 936*, 2 vols. (Damascus, 1959, 1960).
Studi orientalistici in onore de Giorgio Levi della Vida. 2 vols. (Rome, 1959). Important articles are by M. Canard ("Quelques 'à côté' de l'histoire des relations entre Byzance et les Arabes"), Cl. Cahen ("Une correspondance būyide inédite") and E. Lévy-Procençal ("Une description arabe inédite de la Crète").
Talbi, M., *L'émirat aghlabide, 184–296h/800–909* (Paris, 1966).
Von Sievers, P., "Military, Merchants and Nomads: The Social Evolution of the Syrian Cities and Countryside during the Classical Period, 780–969/164–358," *Der Islam* 56 (1979), 212–44.
"Taxes and Trade in the ʿAbbāsid Thughūr, 750–962/133–351," *JESHO*, 25,1 (1982), 71–99.
Wiet, G., *L'Égypte arabe*, vol. IV in Gabriel Hanotaux, *Histoire de la nation égyptienne* (Paris, 1937).
Yaḥyā ibn Saʿīd al-Antakī, *Ta'rīkh*, ed. L. Cheikho, vol. 8 (third series, Paris, 1909).

5 THE ISMĀʿĪLĪ DAʿWA AND THE FĀṬIMID CALIPHATE

Bianquis, Thierry, *Damas et la Syrie sous la domination fatimide (359–468/969–1087)*, 2 vols. (Damascus, 1986, 1989).

"La Prise du pouvoir par les Fatimides en Égypte (357–363/968–974)," *AI*, 11 (1972): 48–108.
Bryer, D., "The Origins of the Druze Religion," *Der Islam*, 52 (1975), 47–83, 239–62, 53 (1976), 5–27.
Canard, Marius, "al-Basāsīrī" *EI2*.
"Djawdhar," *EI2*.
"L'impérialisme des Fatimides et leur propagande," *Annales de l'Institut d'Etudes Orientales de la Faculté des Lettres d'Alger*, 6 (1942–47), 156–193 (reprinted, *Miscellanea Orientalia* (London, 1973)).
Dachraoui, Farhat, *Le Califat fatimide au Maghreb, 296–363/909–973: histoire, politique et institutions* (Tunis, 1981).
"Ibn Hāni' al-Andalusī," *EI2*.
Daftary, Farhad, "Carmatians," *EIR*.
"Ḥasan-i Ṣabbāḥ and the Origins of the Nizārī Isma'ili Movement," in Daftary (ed.), *Medieval Isma'ili History & Thought* (Cambridge, 1996), 181–204.
The Ismā'īlīs: Their history and doctrines (Cambridge, 1990).
De Smet, Daniel, *La Quiétude de l'Intellect: Néoplatonisme et gnose ismaélienne dans l'oeuvre de Ḥamīd ad-Dīn al-Kirmānī (Xe/XIe s.)* (Leuven, 1995).
Halm, Heinz, *Das Reich das Mahdi: Der Aufstieg der Fatimiden (875–973)* (Munich, 1991); Eng. trans. M. Bonner as *The Empire of the Mahdi: The Rise of the Fatimids*, (Leiden, 1996).
Hamdani, Abbas, "The Dā'ī Ḥātim Ibn Ibrāhīm al-Ḥāmidī (d. 596 H./1199 AD) and his Book *Tuḥfat al-Qulūb*," *Oriens*, 23–24 (1970–1971), 258–300.
Hamdani, Abbas and F. de Blois, "A Re-examination of Al-Mahdī's Letter to the Yemenites on the Genealogy of the Fatimid Caliphs," *JRAS* (1983), 173–207.
Hamdani, Husayn F., *On the Geneology of the Fatimid Caliphs* (Cairo, 1958).
Hodgson, M. G. S., *The Order of Assassins* (The Hague, 1955).
Ibn al-Athīr, *Al-Kāmil fī al-Ta'rīkh*, ed. C. J. Thornberg (Leiden, 1867–76; reprinted Beirut, 1965–1967).
Ibn Ḥawqal, Abu'l-Qāsim b. 'Alī, *Ṣūrat al-arḍ*, ed. J. H. Kramers (Leiden, 1938); French trans. G. Wiet, as *Configuration de la terre*, 2 vols. (Beirut, Paris, 1964).
Ibn Muyassar, *Akhbār Misr*, ed. A. F. Sayyid (Cairo, 1981).
Idris, H. R., "Buluggīn," *EI2*.
Idris 'Imād al-Dīn, *'Uyūn al-akhbār*, ed. M. al-Ya'lāwī as *Ta'rīkh al-khulafā' al-fātimiyyīn bi'l-maghrib: al-qism al-khāṣṣ min kitāb 'uyūn al-akhbār* (Beirut, 1985).
Ivanow, W., *Ismaili Tradition Concerning the Rise of the Fatimids* (London, Calcutta, Bombay, 1942).
Lewis, Bernard, *The Assasins: A Radical Sect in Islam* (New York, 1968).
Madelung, Wilferd, "Das Imamat in der frühen ismailitischen Lehre," *Der Islam*, 37 (1961), 43–135.
"Fatimiden und Bahrainqarmaten," *Der Islam* 34 (1959); 34–88; slightly revised trans., "The Fatimids and the Qarmaṭīs of Baḥrayn," in

F. Daftary (ed.), *Mediaeval Isma'ili History & Thought* (Cambridge, 1996), 21–73.
"Ḥamdān Ḳarmaṭ," *EI2*.
"Ḳarmatī," *EI21*.
"The Sources of Isma'ili Law," *JNES* 35 (1976), 29–40.
al-Maqrīzī, Taqi'l-Dīn Aḥmad b. 'Alī *Itti'āẓ al-ḥunafā' bi-akhbār al-a 'imma al-fāṭimiyyīn al-khulafā'*, I, ed. Jamāl al-Dīn al-Shayyāl (Cairo, 1967); II and III, ed. Muḥammad Ḥilmī Muḥammad Aḥmad, (Cairo, 1971, 1973).
Kitāb al-muqaffā al-kabīr, ed. Muhammed al-Ya'lāwī, 8 vols. (Beirut, 1991).
Monés, H., "Djawhar al-Ṣiḳillī," *E12*.
Mu'ayyad fi'l-Dīn al-Shīrāzī, *Sīrat al-Mu'ayyad fi'l-Dīn dā'ī al-du'āt*, ed. Muḥammad Kāmil Ḥusayn (Cairo, 1949).
Nāṣir b. Khusraw. *Safarnāma*, ed. with French trans., Charles Schefer, *Sefer nameh: relation du voyage de Nassiri Khosrau* (Paris, 1881); Eng. trans., W. M. Thackston Jr., *Nāṣer-e Khosraw's Book of Travels* (Bibliotheca Persica, 1986).
al-Nawbakhtī, al-Ḥasan b. Mūsā, *Firaq al-Shī'a*, ed. H. Ritter (Istanbul, 1931).
Poonawala, Ismail, *Biobibliography of Ismā'īlī Literature* (Malibu, 1977).
al-Nu'mān b. Muḥammad (al-Qāḍī al-Nu'mān), *Da'ā'im al-Islām*, ed. A. A. A. Fyzee, 2 vols. (Cairo, 1951–60), 1963, 1967).
Iftitāḥ al-da'wa wa ibtidā' al-dawla, ed. Wadad Kadi (Beirut, 1970), Farhat Dachraoui (Tunis, 1975).
al-Qummī, Sa'd b. 'Abdallāh, *al-Maqālāt wa'l-firaq*, ed. M. J. Mashkūr (Tehran, 1963).
Sanders, Paula, "Claiming the Past: Ghadîr Khumm and the Rise of Hâfiẓî Historiography in Late Fâṭimid Egypt," *SI* fasc. 75 (1992), 82–104.
al-Sijillāt al-Mustanṣiriyya, ed. 'A. Mājid (Cairo, 1954).
Sīrat Ja'far al-Ḥājib, Arabic text ed. by W. Ivanow, *Bulletin of the Faculty of Arts*, University of Egypt (Cairo, 1936), 107–33; Eng. trans. Ivanow, in *Ismaili Tradition Concerning the Rise of the Fatimids* (London, Calcutta, Bombay, 1942), 184–223; French trans. M. Canard, "L'autobiographie d'un chambellan du Mahdî 'Obeidallâh le Faṭṭimid," in *Hespéris*, 39 (1952), 279–330 (reprinted in *Miscellanea Orientalia* (London, 1973), no. V.
Sīrat Ustādh Jawdhar, Arabic text ed. M. K. Husayn and M. 'Abd al-Hādī, Sha'īra (Cairo, 1954); French trans. M. Canard, *Vie de l'ustadh Jaudhar*, (Algiers, 1958).
Stern, Samuel M., "Al Mahdī's Reign According to the *'Uyūn al-Akhbār*," in *Studies in Early Ismā'īlism* (Jerusalem, 1983), 96–145.
"The Succession to the Fatimid Imam al-Amir, the Claims of the later Fatimids to the Imamate, and the Rise of Tayyibi Ismailism," *Oriens*, 4 (1951), 193–255.
Talbi, Mohamed, *L'Émirat Aghlabide (184–296/800–909)* (Paris, 1966).

Van Ess, Josef, "Biobibliographische Notizen zur islamischen Theologie," *WO*, 9 (1977/78), 255–61.
Chiliastische Erwartungen und die Versuchung der Göttlichkeit. Der Khalif al-Ḥākim (386–411), Abh. der Heidelberg Akad. der Wiss., Phil. Hist. Kl., 1977. 2 Abhandlung.
Walker, Paul E., *Abū Yaʿqūb al-Sijistānī: Intellectual Misionary* (London, 1996).
"A Byzantine Victory over the Fatimids at Alexandreta (971)," *Byzantion* 42 (1972), 431–40.
Early Philosophical Shiism: the Ismaili Neoplatonism of Abū Yaʿqūb al-Sijistānī (Cambridge, 1993).
"The Ismaili Daʿwa in the Reign of the Fatimid Caliph al-Ḥākim," *JARCE*, 30 (1993), 160–182.
"The Resolution of the Shīʿah," in Clarke (ed.) *The Party of ʿAlī* (forthcoming)
"Succession to Rule in the Shiite Caliphate," *JARCE*, 32 (1995), 239–264.
The Wellsprings of Wisdom (Salt Lake City, 1994).
al-Yaʿlāwī, Muhammad (Mohammed Yalaoui), *Ibn Hāniʾ al-Maghribī al-Andalusī* (Beirut, 1985).
"Ibn Hâniʾ, poète Shîʾîte et chantre des Fâṭʾimides au Maghreb," *Les Africains*, VI (Paris, 1977), 99–125.

6 THE FĀṬIMID STATE, 969–1171

Bierman, Irene, *Writing Signs: The Fāṭimid Public Text* (Berkeley, 1998).
Cahen, Claude, *Makhzūmiyyāt: Études sur l'histoire économique et financière de l'Égypte médiévale* (Leiden, 1977).
Daftary, Farhad, *The Ismāʿīlīs: Their History and Doctrines* (Cambridge, 1990).
Denoix, S., *Décrire le Caire: Fusṭāṭ-Miṣr d'après Ibn Duqmāq et Maqrīzī: l'histoire d'une partie de la ville du Caire d'après deux historiens égyptiens des XIVe–XVe siècles* (Cairo, 1992).
Garcin, Jean-Claude, *Un centre musulman de la Haute-Égypte médiévale: Qūṣ* (Cairo, 1976).
Goitein, S. D., *Letters of Medieval Jewish Traders* (Princeton, 1973).
A Mediterranean Society: The Jewish Communities of the Arab World as portrayed in the Documents of the Cairo Geniza, 6 vols. (Berkeley, 1967–93) (indices in vol. 6).
Halm, Heinz, "Der Treuhänder Gottes, Die Edikte des alifen al-Ḥākim," *Der Islam*, 63 (1986), 11–72.
Hamblin, William, J., "The Fāṭimid Army during the Early Crusades" (Ph.D. dissertation, University of Michigan, 1984).
Ibn Duqmāq, *Kitāb al-intiṣār li-wāsiṭat ʿiqd al-amṣār*, IV, V, ed. K. Vollers (Cairo, 1893; reprinted Beirut, n.d.).
Ibn al-Maʾmūn al-Baṭāʾiḥī, *Nuṣūṣ min akhbār miṣr*, ed. Ayman Fuʾād Sayyid as *Passages de la Chronique d'Egypte d'Ibn al-Maʾmūn* (Cairo, 1983).
Ibn Muyassar, *Akhbār Miṣr* (*Annales d'Égypte*), ed. H. Massé (Cairo, 1919); 2nd edn., *Akhbār Miṣr*, ed. A. F. Sayyid (Cairo, 1981).

Ibn al-Ṣayrafī, Abu'l-Qāsim ʿAlī, *Al-Ishāra ilā man nāla al-wizāra*, ed. ʿAbd Allāh Mukhliṣ (Cairo, 1924–25).
Qānūn dīwān al-rasā'il, ed. ʿAlī Bahjat (Cairo, 1905).
Ibn Taghrī-Birdī, Abū al-Maḥāsin, *Al-Nujūm al-zāhira fī mulūk miṣr wa al-qāhira*, partial edn. ed. W. Popper, University of California Publications in Semitic Philology, II–III, V–VII (Berkeley, 1909–1960); English trans. W. Popper, *History of Egypt, 1382–1469*, same series, XIII–XIV, XVII–XIX, XXII–XXIV (Berkeley, 1954–1963); complete edn., 16 vols. (Cairo, 1929–72).
Ibn al-Ṭuwayr, *Nuzhat al-muqlatayn fī akhbār al-dawlatayn*, ed. A. F. Sayyid (Beirut, 1992).
Ibn Ẓāfir al-Azdī, Abu'l-Ḥasan, *Akhbār al-duwal al-munqaṭiʿa: La section consacrée aux Fatimides*, ed. A. Ferré (Cairo, 1972).
Khan, Geoffrey, *Arabic Legal and Administrative Documents in the Cambridge Genizah Collections* (Cambridge, 1993).
Lev, Yaacov, *State and Society in Fatimid Egypt* (Leiden, 1991).
al-Maqrīzī, *Ittiʿāẓ al-ḥunafā' bi-akhbār al-a'imma al-Fāṭimiyyīn al-khulafā'*, I, ed. J. al-Shayyāl (Cairo, 1967); II–III, ed. M. Ḥilmī M. Aḥmad (Cairo, 1971, 1973).
Kitāb al-muqaffā al-kabīr, ed. Muḥammad Yaʿlāwī, 8 vols. (Beirut, 1991).
al-Mawāʿiẓ wa al-iʿtibār bi-dhikr al-khiṭaṭ wa al-Āthār, 2 vols. (Cairo, 1853–1854); partial edn. ed. G. Wiet, 5 vols. (Cairo, 1911–1927).
al-Musabbiḥī, *Akhbār miṣr* (Tome Quarantième de la Chronique d'Egypte de Musabbiḥī), ed. Ayman Fu'ād Sayyid and Thierry Bianquis (Cairo, 1978).
Nāṣir b. Khusraw, *Safarnāma*, ed. with French trans. Charles Schefer, *Sefer nameh: relation du voyage de Nassiri Khosrau* (Paris, 1881); English trans. W. M. Thackston Jr., *Naser-e Khosraw's Book of Travels* (Albany, 1986).
al-Nuʿmān b. Muḥammad (al-Qāḍī al-Nuʿmān), *Daʿā'im al-islām wa-dhikr al-ḥalāl wa al-ḥarām wa al-qaḍāya wa al-aḥkām*, ed. A. A. A. Fyzee, 2 vols. (Cairo, 1951–60; 2nd edn., 1963, 1967).
al-Qalqashandī, Aḥmad b. ʿAlī, *Ṣubḥ al-aʿshā fī ṣināʿat al-inshā*, 14 vols. (Cairo, 1913–19); indices by M. Qindīl al-Baqlī (Cairo, 1963).
Rabie, Hassanein, *The Financial System of Egypt* AH *564–741* AD *1169–1341* (London, 1972).
Sanders, Paula, *Ritual, Politics, and the City in Fatimid Cairo* (Albany, 1994).
Sayyid, Ayman Fu'ād, *Al-dawlah al-fāṭimiyya fī miṣr: tafsīr jadīd* (Cairo, 1992).
Stern, S. M., *Fāṭimid Decrees: Original Documents from the Fāṭimid Chancery* (London, 1964).
Studies in Early Ismāʿīlism (Jerusalem, Leiden, 1983).
"The Succession to the Fatimid Imam al-Amir, The Claims of the Later Fatimids to the Inamate, and the Rise of Ṭayyibī Ismailism," *Oriens*, 4 (1951), 193–255; reprinted in S. M. Stern, *History and Culture in the Medieval Muslim World* (London, 1984).
Udovitch, A. L. *Partnership and Profit in Medieval Islam* (Princeton, 1970).

7 THE NON-MUSLIM COMMUNITIES: CHRISTIAN COMMUNITIES

Abbott, Nabia, "Arabic Marriage Contracts among the Copts," *Zeitschrift der Deutschen Morgenländischen Gesellschaft*, 95 (1941), 59–81.

The Monasteries of the Fayyūm, Studies in Ancient Oriental Civilization, vol. XVI (Chicago, 1937).

Abd al-Masīḥ, Yassā and O. H. E. KHS-Burmester, *History of the Patriarchs of the Egyptian Church, Known as the History of the Holy Church of Sawīrus ibn al-Muḳaffaʿ, Bishop of al-Ašmūnīn*, Volume II, Pt. 1, Textes et Documents (Cairo, 1943).

Abū Ṣāliḥ al-Armanī, *The Churches and Monasteries of Egypt and Some Neighboring Countries attributed to Abū Ṣāliḥ, The Armenian* ed. and trans. B. T. A. Evetts and A. J. Butler (Oxford, 1895).

Akermann, Philippe, *Le décor sculpté du Couvent Blanc: Niches et Frises*, Bibliothèque d'Études Coptes, 14 (Cairo, 1976).

Alcock, Anthony, *The Life of Samuel of Kalamun by Isaac the Presbyter* (Warminster, 1983).

Anawati, Georges C., "The Christian Communities in Egypt in the Middle Ages," in Michael Gervers and Ramzi Jibran Bikhazi (eds.), *Conversion and Continuity: Indigenous Christian Communities in Islamic Lands, Eighth to Eighteenth Centuries*, Papers in Mediaeval Studies, 9 (Toronto, 1990), 237–51.

Atiya, Aziz S., gen. ed., *The Coptic Encyclopedia*, 8 vols. (New York, 1991).

History of Eastern Christianity (Notre Dame, IN, 1968).

"Ḳibṭ," *EI2*, V, 90–95.

"Literature, Copto-Arabic," in Aziz S. Atiya (general ed.), *The Coptic Encyclopedia* (New York, 1991), 5, 1460–67.

Aziz Suryal Atiya, Yassā Abd al-Masīḥ, and O. H. E. KHS-Burmester, *History of the Patriarchs of the Egyptian Church, Known as the History of the Holy Church of Sawīrus ibn al-Muḳaffaʿ, Bishop of al-Ašmūnīn, Volume II, Parts* 2–3, Textes et Documents (Cairo, 1948–59).

Badawy, Alexander, *Coptic Art and Archaeology: The Art of the Christian Egyptians from the Late Antique to the Middle Ages* (Cambridge, MA, 1978).

Bæk Simonsen, Jørgen, *Studies in the Genesis and Early Development of the Caliphal Taxation System with Special Reference to Circumstances in the Arab Peninsula, Egypt and Palestine* (Copenhagen, 1988).

Bauer, Gertrud, *Athanasius von Qūṣ: Qilādat at-taḥrīr fī ʿilm at-tafsīr: Eine koptische Grammatik in arabischer Sprache aus dem 13./14. Jahrhundert*, Islamkundliche Untersuchungen, 17 (Freiburg im Breisgau, 1972).

Beckwith, John, *Coptic Sculpture, 300–1300* (London, 1963).

Bell, David N. (trans.), *Mena of Nikiou: The Life of Isaac of Alexandria and the Martyrdom of Saint Macrobius*, Cistercian Studies, 107 (Kalamazoo, MI, 1988).

Bell, H. I., "Two Official Letters of the Arab Period," *Journal of Egyptian Archaeology*, 11 (1925), 265–81.

Bell, H. I. and W. E. Crum, *Greek Papyri in the British Museum: Catalogue, with Texts. Vol. IV: The Aphrodito Papyri* (London, 1910).

Bilabel, F. and A. Grohmann, *Zwei Urkunden aus dem bischöflichen Archiv von Panopolis in Ägypten*, Quellen und Studien zur Geschichte und Kultur des Altertums und des Mittelalters, Reihe A: Mehrsprachige Texte, 1 (Heidelberg, 1935).

Bilaniuk, Petro B. T., "Coptic Relations with Rome," in Aziz S. Atiya (general ed.), *The Coptic Encyclopedia* (New York, 1991), II, 609–11.

Boud'hors, Anne, "Manuscrits coptes 'Chypriotes' à la Bibliothèque Nationale," in *Études coptes: Troisième Journée d'études, Musée du Louvre 23 Mai 1986*, Cahiers de la Bibliothèque copte, 4 (Louvain, 1989), 11–20.

Breydy, Michael, *Das Annalenwerk des Eutychios von Alexandrien*, Corpus Scriptorum Christianorum Orientalium, Scriptores Arabici, 44–45 (Louvain, 1985).

Butler, A. J., *The Arab Conquest of Egypt and the Last Thirty Years of Roman Dominion, Containing Also the Treaty of Miṣr in Tabarī* (1913); *Babylon in Egypt with a Critical Bibliography and Additional Documentation* (1914; revised edition by P. M. Fraser, Oxford, 1978).

Cahen, Claude, "Dhimma," *EI2*, II, 227–31.

Cannuyer, Christian, "Coptes et 'Jacobites' dans l'*Historia Hierosolimitana* (1220) de Jacques de Vitry, Évêque d'Acre," in Marguerite Rassart-Debergh and Julien Ries (eds.), *Actes du IVe Congrès Copte, Louvain-la-Neuve, 5–10 septembre 1988* (Louvain-la-Neuve, 1992), 198–208.

Les coptes, Fils d'Abraham (Turnhout, 1990).

Chassinat, Émile, *Un papyrus medicale copte*, Mémoires publiés par les membres de l'Institut Français d'Archéologie Orientale, 32 (Cairo, 1921).

Coquin, Charalambia, *Les édifaces chrétien du Vieux-Caire, Volume I: Bibliographie et topographie historique*, Bibliothèque d'Études Coptes, 11 (Cairo, 1974).

Décobert, Christian, "Sur l'arabisation et l'islamisation de l'Égypte médiévale," in Christian Décobert (ed.), *Itinéraires d'Égypte: Mélanges offerts au père Maurice Martin S. J.*, Bibliothèque d'Étude, 106 (Cairo, 1992), 273–300.

Den Heijer, Johannes, "Apologetic Elements in Coptic-Arabic Historiography: The Life of Afrahām ibn Zur'ah, 62nd Patriarch of Alexandria,' in Samir Khalil Samir and Jørgen Nielsen (eds.), *Christian Arabic Apologetics during the 'Abbasid Period (750–1258)*, Studies in the History of Religion 63 (Leiden, 1994), 192–202.

Mawhūb ibn Manṣūr ibn Mufarriğ et l'historiographie copto-arabe: Étude sur la composition de l'Histoire des Patriarches d'Alexandrie, Corpus Scriptorum Christianorum Orientalium, Subsidia, 83 (Louvain, 1989).

"Une liste d'évêques coptes de l'année 1086," in Christian Décobert (ed.), *Itinéraires d'Égypte: Mélanges offerts au père Maurice Martin S. J.*, Bibliothèque d'Étude, 106 (Cairo, 1992), 147–65.

Diem, Werner, *Arabische Briefe aus dem 7.–10. Jahrhundert*, Corpus Papyrorum Raineri, 16 (Vienna, 1993).

Du Bourguet, Pierre, *Les Coptes*, 2nd edn., Que Sais-Je?, no. 2398 (Paris, 1989).

Habib el-Masih, Iris, "A Historical Survey of the Convents for Women in Egypt up to the Present Day," *Bulletin de la Société d'Archéologie Copte*, 14 (1950–1957), 63–111.

Evelyn White, Hugh G., *The Monasteries of the Wādi 'n Natrūn, Part I: New Coptic Texts from the Monastery of Saint Macarius, Edited with an Introduction on the Library at the Monastery of Saint Macarius*, Publications of the Metropolitan Museum of Art Egyptian Expedition, 2 (New York, 1926).

The Monasteries of the Wādi 'n Natrūn, Part II: The History of the Monasteries of Nitria and Scetis, ed. Walter Hauser, Publications of the Metropolitan Museum of Art Egyptian Expedition, 7 (New York, 1932).

The Monasteries of the Wādi 'n Natrūn, Part III: The Architecture and Archaeology, ed. Walter Hauser, Publications of the Metropolitan Museum of Art Egyptian Expedition, 8 (New York, 1933).

Evetts, B. (ed.), *History of the Patriarchs of the Coptic Church of Alexandria*, Patrologia Orientalis, 1:2 (Paris, 1906).

History of the Patriarchs of the Coptic Church of Alexandria II, Patrologia Orientalis, 1:2 (Paris, 1906).

History of the Patriarchs of the Coptic Church of Alexandria III, Patrologia Orientalis, 5:1 (Paris, 1910).

History of the Patriarchs of the Coptic Church of Alexandria IV, Patrologia Orientalis, 10:5 (Paris, 1915).

Frantz-Murphy, Gladys, "Conversion in Early Islamic Egypt: The Economic Factor," inYusuf Ragib (ed.), *Documents de l'Islam Médiéval: Nouvelle Perspectives de Recherche*, Textes arabes et études islamiques, 29 (Cairo, 1991), 11–17.

Garcin, J.-C., *Un centre musulman de la Haute-Égypte médiévale: Qūṣ* (Cairo, 1976).

Goitein, S. D., *A Mediterranean Society: The Jewish Communities of the Arab World as Portrayed in the Documents of the Cairo Geniza*, 6 vols. (Berkeley, 1967–94) (bibliography and indices in vol. 6).

Graf, Georg, *Geschichte der Christlichen Arabischen Literatur*, 5 vols., Studi e Testi, 118, 133, 146, 147, 172 (Vatican City, 1944–53).

Green, Michael, "A Private Archive of Coptic Letters and Documents from Teshlot," *Oudhedkundige Mededelingen*, 64 (1983), 61–122.

Griggs, C. Wilfred, *Early Egyptian Christianity: From its Origins to 451 C.E.*, 3rd edn., Coptic Studies, 2 (Leiden, 1993).

Grohman, Adolf, "Greek Papyri of the Early Islamic Period in the Collection of Archduke Rainer," *Études de Papyrologie*, 8 (1957).

Grohmann, Adolf and Raif Georges Khoury, *Chrestomathie de Papyrologie Arabe: Documents relatifs à la vie privée, sociale et administrative dans les premiers siècles islamiques*, Handbuch der Orientalistik, Erste Abteilung, Ergänzungsband II: Zweiter Halbband (Leiden, 1993).

Grossmann, Peter, *Mittelalterliche Langshauskuppelkirchen und verwandte Typen in Oberägypten*, Abhandlungen des Deutschen Archäologischen Instituts Kairo, Koptische Reihe, 3 (Glückstadt, 1982).

Hasitzka, Monika R. M., *Neue Texte und Dokumentation zum Koptisch-Unterricht*, 2 vols., Mitteilungen aus der Papyrussammlung der Österreichischen Nationalbibliothek (Papyrus Erzherzog Rainer), n. s., 18 (Vienna, 1990).

Henein, Nessim Henry and Thierry Bianquis, *La magie par les Psaumes: Édition et traduction d'un manuscrit arabe chrétien d'Égypte*, Bibliothèque d'Études Coptes, 12 (Cairo, 1975).

Hölscher, Uvo, *The Excavation of Medinet Habu – Volume V: Post-Ramessid Remains*, ed. and trans. Elizabeth Hauser, Oriental Institute Publications, 66 (Chicago, 1954).

Innemée, Karel C., *Ecclesiastical Dress in the Medieval Near East*, Studies in Textile and Costume History, 1 (Leiden, 1992).

Jakobielski, Stefan, *A History of the Bishopric of Pachoras on the Basis of Coptic Inscriptions*, Faras, 3 (Warsaw, 1972).

John of Nikiu, *The Chronicle of John (c. 690 AD) Coptic Bishop of Nikiu: Being a History of Egypt before and during the Arab Conquest, Translated from Hermann Zotenberg's Edition of the Ethiopic Version with an Introduction, Critical and Linguistic Notes, and an Index of Names*, trans. R. H. Charles (London, 1916).

Kammerer, Winifred, (comp.), *A Coptic Bibliography*, with the collaboration of Elinor Mullett Husselman and Louise A. Shier, University of Michigan General Library Publications, 7 (Ann Arbor, 1950).

Khater, Antoine and O. H. E. KHS-Burmester (eds.), *History of the Patriarchs of the Egyptian Church, Known as the History of the Holy Church of Sawīrus ibn al-Muḳaffaʿ, Bishop of al-Ašmūnīn, Volume III, Parts 1–3*, Textes et Documents (Cairo, 1968–70).

History of the Patriarchs of the Egyptian Church, Known as the History of the Holy Church According to MS. Arabe 302 Bibliothèque Nationale, Paris, Volume IV, Parts 1–2, Textes et Documents (Cairo, 1974).

KHS-Burmester, O. H. E., *The Egyptian or Coptic Church: A Detailed Description of her Liturgical Services and the Rites and Ceremonies Observed in the Administration of her Sacraments*, Textes et Documents (Cairo, 1967).

"Further Leaves from the Arabic MS. in Coptic Script of the Apophthegmata Patrum," *Bulletin de la Société d'Archéologie Copte*, 18 (1965–1966), 51–64.

Krause, Martin, "Koptische Literatur," in Wolfgang Helck and Eberhard Otto (eds.), *Lexikon der Ägyptologie, Band III* (Wiesbaden:, 1979), 694–728.

Kubiak, W. *Al-Fusṭāṭ: Its Foundation and Early Urban Development* (Warsaw, 1982; Cairo, 1987).

Van Lantschoot, Arn, *Recueil des colophons des manuscrits chrétiens d'Égypte, Tome I: Les colophons coptes des manuscrits sahidiques*, Bibliothèque du *Muséon*, 1 (Louvain, 1929).

Leipoldt, Johannes, "Geschichte der koptischen Literatur," in C. Brockelmann, et al. (eds.), *Geschichte der christlichen Litteraturen des Orients*, 2nd edn., Die Litteraturen des Ostens in Einzeldarstellungen, 7:2 (Leipzig, 1909), 131–83.

Leroy, Jules, *Les manuscrits coptes et coptes-arabes illustrés*, Bibliothèque archéologique et historique, 96 (Paris, 1974).

Les peintures des couvents du désert d'Esna, published with the collaboration of Basile Psiroukis and Bernard Lenthéric, La peinture murale chez les coptes, 1; Mémoires publiés par les membres de l'Institut Français d'Archéologie Orientale, 94 (Cairo, 1975).

Lev, Yaakov, "Persecutions and Conversion to Islam in Eleventh Century Egypt," *Asian and African Studies*, 22 (1988) 73–91.

Little, Donald P., "Coptic Converts to Islam During the Baḥrī Mamlūk Period," in Michael Gervers and Ramzi Jibran Bikhazi (eds.), *Conversion and Continuity: Indigenous Christian Communities in Islamic Lands, Eighth to Eighteenth Centuries*, Papers in Mediaeval Studies, 9 (Toronto, 1990), 263–88.

MacCoull, Leslie S. B., "Coptic Alchemy and Craft Technology in Islamic Egypt: The Papyrological Evidence," in Marilyn Chiat and Kathryn Reyerson (eds.), *The Medieval Mediterranean: Cross-cultural Contacts*, 3 (St. Cloud, MN, 1988), 101–104. [Reprinted in Leslie S. B. MacCoull, *Coptic Perspectives on Late Antiquity* (London, 1993) XV.]

"The Strange Death of Coptic Culture," *Coptic Church Review*, 10 (1989), 35–45.

"The Teshlot Papyri and the Survival of Documentary Sahidic in the Eleventh Century," *Orientalia Christiana Periodica*, 55 (1989), 201–06.

"Three Cultures under Arab Rule: The Fate of Coptic," *Bulletin de la Société d'Archéologie Copte*, 27 (1985), 61–70.

Martinez, Francisco Javier, "Eastern Christian Apocalyptic in the Early Muslim Period: Pseudo-Methodius and Pseudo-Athanasius" (Ph.D. dissertation, Catholic University of America, 1985).

Maspero, Gaston, "Le vocabulaire français d'un copte du XIIIe siècle," *Romania*, 17 (1888), 481–512.

Maspero, Jean, "Un diplôme arabe-chrétien du XIIIe siècle," *Annales du Service des Antiquités de l'Égypte*, 11 (1911), 177–85.

Meyer, Marvin and Richard Smith, *Ancient Christian Magic: Coptic Texts of Ritual Power* (San Francisco, 1994).

Müller, C. Detlef G., "Stellung und Haltung der koptischen Patriarchen des 7. Jahrhunderts gegenüber islamischer Obrigkeit und Islam," in Tito Orlandi and Frederik Wisse (eds.), *Acts of the Second International Congress of Coptic Study Roma 22–26 September 1980* (Rome, 1985), 203–13.

Nagel, Peter, *Das Triadon: Ein sahidisches Lehrgedicht des 14. Jahrhunderts*, Martin-Luther-Universität Halle-Wittenberg Wissenschaftliche Beiträge, 23 (K 7) (Halle (Saale), 1983).

Northrup, Linda S., "Muslim–Christian Relations During the Reign of the Mamlūk Sultan al-Manṣūr Qalāwūn, AD 1278–1290," in Michael Gervers and Ramzi Jibran Bikhazi (eds.), *Conversion and Continuity: Indigenous Christian Communities in Islamic Lands, Eighth to Eighteenth Centuries*, Papers in Mediaeval Studies, 9 (Toronto, 1990), 253–61.

Orlandi, Tito, *Coptic Bibliography* (Rome, 1980–).

"Coptic Literature," in Birger A. Pearson and James E. Goehring (eds.), *The Roots of Egyptian Christianity*, Studies in Antiquity and Christianity (Philadelphia, 1986), 51–81.

"Literature, Coptic," in Aziz S. Atiya (general ed.), *The Coptic Encyclopedia* (New York, 1991), 5, 1450–60.

"Un testo copto sulla dominazione araba in Egitto," in Tito Orlandi and Frederik Wisse (eds.), *Acts of the Second International Congress of Coptic Studies Roma 22–26 September 1980* (Rome, 1985), 225–33.

Petry, C. F., *The Civilian Elite of Cairo in the later Middle Ages* (Princeton, 1981).

"Copts in Late Medieval Egypt," in Aziz S. Atiya (gen. ed.), *The Coptic Encyclopedia* (New York, 1991), 2, 618–35.

Plumley, J. Martin, *The Scrolls of Bishop Timotheos: Two Documents from Medieval Nubia*, Texts from Exacavations, 1 (London, 1975).

Poirier, Paul-Hubert, "Fragments d'une version copte de la *Caverne des Trésors*," *Orientalia*, 52 (1983), 415–23.

Richards, D. S., "The Coptic Bureaucracy under the Mamlūks," in *Colloque International sur l'Histoire du Caire* (Cairo, 1969), 373–81.

Roncaglia, Martiniano Pellegrino, *Histoire de l'Église copte*, 4 vols. (Beirut, 1966–73).

Rutschowscaya, Marie-Helene, *Catalogue des bois de l'Égypte copte au Musée du Louvre* (Paris, 1986).

Tissus Coptes (Paris, 1990).

Saleh, Marlis J., "Government Relations with the Coptic Community in Egypt During the Fāṭimid Period (358–567 AH/969–1171 CE)" (Ph.D. dissertation, University of Chicago, 1995).

Samir, Khalil, "Arabic Sources for Early Egyptian Christianity," in Birger A. Pearson and James E. Goehring (eds.), *The Roots of Egyptian Christianity*, Studies in Antiquity and Christianity (Philadelphia, 1986), 82–97.

"Bibliographie copte à l'époque médiévale (1982–1988)," in Marguerite Rassart-Debergh and Julien Ries (eds.), *Actes du IVe Congrès Copte, Louvain-la-Neuve, 5–10 septembre 1988* (Louvain-la-Neuve: Institut Orientaliste, 1992), 82–85.

Samuel, Bishop (ed.), *Abu al Makarem: History of the Churches and Monasteries in Lower Egypt in the 13th Cent.* (Cairo, 1992).

Sawīrus ibn al-Muqaffaʿ, *History of the Patriarchs of the Coptic Church of Alexandria*, ed. with English trans. B. Evetts, *Patrologia Orientalis* I, 99–215; V, 1–216; X, 357–553; Cairo edn., Société d'Archéologie Copte, *History of the Patriarchs of the Egyptian Church, Known as the History of the Holy Church of Sawīrus ibn al-Muḳaffaʿ, Bishop of Ashmūnīn*, II, pt. 1 (AD 849–880), pt. 2 (AD 880–1066); II, pts. 2–3, ed. and trans. A. Atiya, Y. ʿAbd al-Masīḥ, O. H. E. KHS-Burmester (1943, 1948–1959); III, pts. 1–3; IV, pts. 1–2, A. Khater (1968–70, 1974).

Sidarus, Adel, "Les lexiques onomasiologiques gréco-copto-arabes du Moyen Âge et leurs origines anciennes," in Regine Schulz and Manfred Görg (eds.), *Lingua Restituta Orientalis: Festgabe für Julius Assfalg*, Ägypten und Altes Testament, 20 (Wiesbaden, 1990), 348–59.

Skreslet, Stanley H., II, "The Greeks in Medieval Islamic Egypt: A Melkite Community under the Patriarch of Alexandria (640–1095)" (Ph.D. dissertation, Yale University, 1988).

Stauffer, Annemarie, *Spätantike und koptische Wirkereien: Untersuchungen zur ikonographische Tradition im spätantiken und frühmittelalterliche Textilwerkstätten* (Bern, 1992).

Stoffregen-Pedersen, Christian, *Les Éthiopiens*, Fils d'Abraham (Turnhout, 1990).

Störk, Lothar, *Koptische Handschriften: Die Handscriften der Staats- und Universitätsbibliothek Hamburg, Teil 2: Die Handschriften aus Dair Anbā Maqār*, Verzeichnis der orientalischen Handschriften in Deutschland, 22:2 (Stuttgart, 1995).

Till, Walter C., *Die Arzneikunde der Kopten* (Berlin, 1951).

"Die Datierung koptischer Urkunden in der islamischen Zeit," in *I. Arabische Chronologie, II. Arabische Papyruskunde*, Adolf Grohmann, Handbuch der Orientalistik, Erste Abteilung, Ergänzungsband II, Erster Halbband (Leiden, 1966), 39–43.

Timm, Stefan, *Das christlich-koptische Ägypten in arabischer Zeit*, 6 parts, Tübinger Atlas des Vorderen Orients, Reihe B (Geisteswissenschaften), 41/1–6 (Wiesbaden, 1984–92).

Troupeau, Gérard, "Une réfutation des Melkites par Sévère ibn al-Mouqaffa'," in C. Laga, J. A. Munitz and L. van Rompay (eds.), *After Chalcedon: Studies in Theology and Church History offered to Professor Albert van Roey for his Seventieth Birthday*, Orientalia Lovaniensia Analecta, 18 (Leuven, 1985), 371–80.

Viaud, Gérard, *Les pèlerinages coptes en Égypte, d'après les notes de Qommos Jacob Muyser*, Bibliothèque d'Études Coptes, 15 (Cairo, 1979).

Vycichl, Werner, "Magic," in Aziz S. Atiya (general ed.), *The Coptic Encyclopedia* (New York, 1991), 5, 1499–1509.

Walters, C. C., *Monastic Archaeology in Egypt*, Modern Egyptology Series (Warminster, 1974).

Wilfong, Terry G., Review of *The Coptic Encyclopedia*, Aziz S. Atiya (general ed.), *Journal of Near Eastern Studies*, 52 (January 1993), 43–47.

"Agriculture among the Christian Population of Egypt in the Early Islamic Period: Theory and Practice," in Alan Bowman and Eugene Rogan (eds.), *Land, Settlement and Agriculture in Egypt from Pharaonic to Modern Times*, Proceedings of the British Academy, 96 (Oxford, 1998), 217–35.

"The Coptic Story of Theodosios and Dionysios, CE X-X," in Traianos Gagos et al. (eds.), *P. Michigan Koenen (=P.Mich. XVIII): Michigan Texts Published in Honor of Ludwig Koenen*, Studia Amstelodamensia ad Epigraphicam, Ius Antiquum et Papyrologicam Pertinentia, 36 (Amsterdam, 1996), 351–56.

The Women of Jēme: Gender and Society in a Coptic Town in Late Antique Egypt, New Texts from Ancient Cultures, 3 (Ann Arbor, forthcoming).

Winlock, H. E. and W. E. Crum, *The Monastery of Epiphanius at Thebes, Part I*, The archaeological material by H. E. Winlock, the literary material by W. E. Crum, Publications of the Metropolitan Museum of Art Egyptian Expedition, 3 (New York, 1926).

Wüstenfeld, F., *Macrizi's Geschichte der Copten: Aus der Handschriften zu Gotha und Wien mit Übersetzung und Anmerkungen*, Abhandlungen der Königlichen Gesellschaft der Wissenschaften zu Göttingen, 3 (Göttingen, 1845).

8 THE NON-MUSLIM COMMUNITIES: THE JEWISH COMMUNITY

Abrahams, Israel, "An Eighth-Century Genizah Document," *Jewish Quarterly Review*, 17 (1905).

Abramson, Shraga, *Ba-Merkazim uva-Tefuṣot bitqufat ha-Ge'onim* (Jerusalem, 1965).

Altmann, Alexander and Samuel M. Stern, *Isaaac Israeli: A Neoplatonic Philosopher of the Early Eleventh Century* (London, 1958).

Ashtor, Eliyahu, "Prolegomena to the Medieval History of Oriental Jewry," *Jewish Quarterly Review*, n.s. 50 (1959).

"Some Features of the Jewish Communities of Medieval Egypt," *Zion*, 30 (1965), 1–2 [Hebrew].

Bareket, Elinoar, *The Leaders of the Jews in Fusṭāṭ During the First Half of the Eleventh Century*, 2 vols. (doctoral dissertation, Tel Aviv University, 1987). [Hebrew with English abstract].

Benjamin of Tudela, *The Itinerary of Benjamin of Tudela*, ed. and trans. M. N. Adler (New York, n.d.; reprint of 1st London ed., 2nd London edn., *The Travels* 1160–73, ed. and trans. M. Komroff (1928).

Casanova, Paul, "Essai de Reconstitution topographique de la ville d'Al Fousṭāṭ ou Miṣr," in *Mémoires de l'Institut Français d'Archéologie Orientale du Caire*, 35 (1913).

Cohen, Mark R., *Jewish Self-Government in Medieval Egypt: The Origins of the Office of Head of the Jews, ca. 1065–1126*, (Princeton, 1980).

Dols, Michael W., *The Black Death in the Middle East.* (Princeton, 1977).

Encyclopaedia Judaica, 16 vols. (Jerusalem, 1972).

Fischel Walter J., *Jews in the Economic and Political Life of Mediaeval Islam*, revised edn. (New York, 1969).

Gil, Moshe, *Documents of the Jewish Pious Foundations from the Cairo Geniza* (Leiden, 1976).

The Tustaris: Family and Sect (Tel Aviv, 1981) [Hebrew].

Goitein, S. D., "Elḥanan b. Shemarya as Communal Leader," in Sidney B. Hoenig and Leon D. Stitskin (eds.), *Joshua Finkel Jubilee Volume.* (New York, 1974). [Hebrew].

A Mediterranean Society: The Jewish Communities of the Arab World as Portrayed in the Documents of the Cairo Geniza, 6 vols. (Berkeley and Los Angele, 1967–1994).

"Shemarya b. Elḥanan: With Two New Autographs," *Tarbiz*, 32 (1963), 3 [Hebrew].

Studies in Islamic History and Institutions (Leiden, 1966).

Golb, Norman, "The Topography of the Jews of Medieval Egypt," *JNES*, 24 (1965), 33 (1974).

Ibn ʿAbd al-Ḥakam, *Kitāb Futūḥ Miṣr wa-Akhbāruhā* [The History of the Conquest of Egypt, North Africa and Spain], ed. C. C. Torrey. (New Haven, 1922).

Ibn Muyassar, *Ta'rīkh Miṣr* (*Annales d'Égypte*). ed. H. Massé (Cairo, 1919); 2nd edn., *Akhbār Miṣr*, ed. A. F. Sayyid (Cairo, 1981).

Malter, Henry, *Saadia Gaon: His Life and Works* (Philadelphia, 1921).

Mann, Jacob, *The Jews in Egypt and in Palestine under the Fātimid Caliphs*, 2 vols. in 1, with a preface and reader's guide by S. D. Goitein (New York, 1970).

al-Maqrīzī, *al-Mawāʿiẓ wa'l-Iʿtibār di-Dhikr al-Khiṭaṭ wa'l-Āthār*, I (Baghdad, n.d.; reprint of Būlāq edn. 1853).

al-Qalqashandī, Aḥmad ibn ʿAlī, *Ṣubḥ al-Aʿsha fī Ṣināʿat al-Inshā*, 14 vols. (Cairo, 1913–19); indices by M. Qindīl al-Baqlī (Cairo, 1963).

Shaked, Shaul, *A Tentative Bibliography of Geniza Documents*, prepared under the direction of D. H. Baneth and S. D. Goitein, (Paris and The Hague, 1964).

Stillman, Norman A., "Charity and Social Service in Medieval Islam," *Societas* 5 (1975), 2.

"The Eleventh-Century Merchant House of Ibn ʿAwkal (A Geniza Study)," *JESHO*, 16 (1973), 1.

"The Jew in the Medieval Islamic City," in Daniel Frank (ed.), *The Jews of Medieval Islam: Community, Society, and Identity*. (Leiden, 1995).

The Jews of Arab Lands: A History and Source Book (Philadelphia, 1979).

"Quelques renseignements biographiques sur Yōsēf Ibn ʿAwkal, médiateur entre les communautés juives du Maghreb et les Académies d'Irak," *Revue des études juives*, 132 (1973), fasc. 4.

"Subordinance and Dominance: Non-Muslim Minorities and the Traditional Islamic State as Perceived from Above and Below," in Farhad Kazemi and R. D. McChesney (eds.), *A Way Prepared: Essays on Islamic Culture in Honor of Richard Bayly Winder*. (New York, London, 1988).

Stillman, Yedida K., "The Medieval Islamic Vestimentary System: Evolution and Consolidation," in *Kommunikation zwischen Orient und Okzident: Alltag und Sachkultur* (Vienna, 1994).

Strauss [-Ashtor], Eliyahu, *A History of the Jews in Egypt and Syria under the Rule of the Mamlūks*, 3 vols. (Jerusalem, 1944–70) [Hebrew].

al-Suyūṭī, *Ḥusn al-Muḥāḍara fī Akhbār Miṣr wa'l-Qāhira*, II (Cairo, 1968).

Worman, E. J., "Notes on the Jews in Fustāt," *Jewish Quarterly Review*, 18 (1905).

9 THE CRUSADER ERA AND THE AYYŪBID DYNASTY

Abū Ṣāliḥ al-Armanī, *The Churches and Monasteries of Egypt and Some Neighboring Countries attributed to Abū Ṣāliḥ, The Armenian*, ed. and trans. B. T. A. Evetts and A. J. Butler (Oxford, 1895).
Abū Shāma, *Kitāb al-rawḍatayn fī akhbār al-dawlatayn*, 1st edn. 2 vols. (Cairo, 1871–75); 2nd edn. H. Aḥmad and M. M. Ziyāda, 2 vols. (Cairo, 1956, 1962); French trans. A.-C. Barbier de Meynard, "Abou Chamah, Le livre des deux jardins, Histoire de deux règnes. Celui de Nour ed-Dīn et celui de Salah ed-Dīn," *Historiens orientaux*, IV–V (Paris, 1898, 1906), 3–210.
Tarājim rijāl al-qarnayn al-sādis wa'l-sābiʿ al-maʿrūf bi'l-dhayl ʿalā al-rawḍatayn, ed. M. al-Kawtharī (Cairo, 1947).
ʿUyūn al-rawḍatayn fī akhbār al-dawlatayn (Damascus, 1992).
Abulafia, D., *Frederick II: A Medieval Emperor* (London, 1988).
Allouche, A., *Mamlūk economics: A Study and Translation of al-Maqrīzī's Ighāthah* (Salt Lake City, 1994).
Amīn, M. M., *Al-awqāf wa'l-ḥayā al-ijtimāʿiyya fī miṣr* (Cairo, 1980).
ʿArīnī (al-), E. E., *Miṣr fī ʿaṣr al-ayyūbiyīn* (Cairo, 1960).
Ashtor, E., "The volume of the medieval spice trade," *Journal of European Economic History*, 9 (1980), 753–63.
East–West Trade in the Medieval Mediterranean (London, 1986).
Levant Trade in the Later Middle Ages (Princeton, 1983).
Ayalon, D., "From Ayyubids to Mamluks," *REI*, 49 (1981), 43–57.
"Halḳa," *EI2*.
"Le Régiment Baḥriyya dans l'armée mamlouke," *REI* (1951), 133–41.
Bacharach, J. L., "Monetary movements in medieval Egypt, 1171–1517," in J. F. Richards (ed.), *Precious Metals in the Later Medieval and Early Modern Worlds* (Durham, 1983).
Baghdādī (al-), *Kitāb al-ifāda wa'l-iʿtibār fi'l-umūr al-mushāhada wa'l-ḥawādith al-muʿāyana bi-arḍ miṣr*, ed. A. G. Sabānū (Damascus, 1983).
Balog, P., *The coinage of the Ayyubids* (London, 1980).
Benjamin of Tudela, *The Itinerary of Benjamin of Tudela*, ed. and trans. M. N. Adler (New York, n.d., reprint of 1st London edn., 1907); 2nd London edn., *The Travels, 1160–73*, ed. and trans. M. Komroff (1928).
Bundārī (al-), *Ikhtiṣār al-fatḥ Ibn ʿAlī al-Bundārī min kitāb al-barq al-shāmī l'il-ʿImād al-Kātib al-Iṣfahānī*, ed. F. al-Nabarāwī (Cairo, 1979).
Sanā al-barq al-shāmī, ed. R. Şeşen (Ar.: Shīshīn) (Beirut, 1970).
Cahen, C., "Al-Makhzūmī et Ibn al-Mammātī sur l'agriculture égyptienne médiévale," *AI*, 11 (1972).
"Ayyūbids," *EI2*.
"La circulation monétaire en Egypte des Fatimides aux Ayyubides," *Revue numismatique*, 6th series, 26, 208–17.

"Douanes et commerce dans les ports méditerranéens de l'Egypte médiévale d'après le Minhādj d'al-Makhzūmī," *JESHO*, 7 (1964), 217–314.
"L'évolution de l'Iqṭāʿ du IXe au XIIIe siècle: Contribution à une histoire comparée des sociétés médiévales," *Annales E.S.C.*, 8/1 (1953), 25–52.
"Iḳṭāʿ," *EI2*.
Makhzūmiyyāt: Études sur l'histoire économique et financière de l'Égypte médiévale (Leiden, 1977).
"Monetary circulation in Egypt at the time of the crusades and the reform of al-Kāmil," in A. L. Udovitch (ed.), *The Islamic Middle East, 700–1900: Studies in Economic and Social History* (Princeton, 1981), 315–33.
"Réflexions sur l'usage du mot 'Féodalité'," *JESHO*, 3 (1960), 7–20.
"Le régime des impôts dans le Fayyūm Ayyubide," *Arabica* 3/1 (1956), 8–30.
"Un traité financier inédit d'époque fatimite ayyūbide," *JESHO*, 5 (1962), 139–59.
Creswell, A. C., *The Muslim Architecture of Egypt*, 2 vols. (Cairo, 1952).
Dahlmanns, F. J., *Al-Malik al-Adil. Ägypten und der Vordere Orient in den Jahren 589/1193 bis 615/1218* (Giessen, 1975).
Dhahabī (al-), *Ta'rīkh al-Islām wa-wafayāt al-mashāhīr wa'l-aʿlām*, lx–lxiv, ed. B. Maʿrūf et al. (Beirut, 1408/1988).
Ehrenkreutz, A. S., "Contributions to the knowledge of the fiscal administration of Egypt in the middle ages," *BSOAS*, 16 (1954), 502–14; 178–84.
"The crisis of the dinar in the Egypt of Saladin," *JAOS*, 76 (1956), 178–84.
"The place of Saladin in the naval history of the Mediterranean sea in the middle ages," *JAOS*, 75 (1955), 100–16.
Saladin (Albany, 1972).
Elisséeff, N., "Nūr al-Dīn Maḥmūd b. Zankī," *EI2*.
Nūr al-Dīn, un grand prince musulman de Syrie au temps des Croisades 511–569 H./1118–1175, 3 vols. (Damascus, 1967).
Fikry, A., *Masājid al-qāhira wa-madārisuhā*, 2 vols. (Cairo, 1965–69).
Garcin, J.-C., "Les Zankides et les Ayyubides," in Garcin, J.-C. et al. (eds.), *États, sociétés et cultures du monde Musulman médiéval, X^e–XVe siècle*, i: *L'évolution politique et sociale* (Paris, 1995), 233–55.
Un centre musulman de la haute Égypte médiévale: Qūṣ (Cairo, 1976).
Gibb, H. A. R., "The Aiyūbids," in *A History of the Crusades*, K. Setton (gen. ed.), ii: *The Later Crusades, 1189–1311*, R. L. Wolff and H. W. Hazard (eds.) (Madison, 1969), 693–714.
"The armies of Saladin," *Cahiers d'histoire Égyptienne*, 3/4 (1951), 304–20.
The Life of Saladin from the Works of ʿImād al-Dīn (Oxford, 1973).
Goitein, S., "The beginnings of the Kārim merchants and the character of their organization," in his *Studies in Islamic History and Institutions* (Leiden, 1966), 351–60.
"Cairo: an Islamic city in the light of the Geniza documents," in I. Lapidus (ed.), *Middle Eastern Cities* (Berkeley, 1969), 90–91.
"The exchange rate of gold and silver money in Fatimid and Ayyubid times," *JESHO*, 8 (1965), 1–46.

"From the Mediterranean to India," *Speculum*, 24 (1952).

"Letters and documents on the India trade in medieval times," *IC*, 36 (1963), 188–205.

A Mediterranean Society: The Jewish Communities of the Arab World as portrayed in the Documents of the Cairo Geniza, 6 vols. (Berkeley, 1967–94) (bibliography and indices in vol. 6).

Gottschalk, H. L., "Die Aulad Šaiḫ aš šuyuḫ (Banû Ḥamawiya)," *WZKM*, 53 (1956), 57–87.

"Awlad al-Shaykh," *EI*2.

"Dīwān," *EI*2.

Al-Malik al-Kāmil von Egypten und seine zeit (Wiesbaden, 1958).

Ḥamawī (al-), *Muʿjam al-buldān*, iv (Beirut, 1376/1957).

Harawī (al-), *Kitāb al-ishārāt ilā maʿrifat al-ziyārāt*, ed. J. Sourdel-Thomine (Damascus, 1953).

Heyd, W., *Histoire du commerce du Levant au moyen âge*, 2 vols., trans. F. Raynaud (Leipzig, 1885–86; reprinted, Amsterdam, 1967).

Humphreys, R. S., "Al-Muʿaẓẓam," *EI*2.

"The emergence of the Mamlūk army," *SI*, 45 (1977), 67–99, 147–82.

From Saladin to the Mongols: the Ayyubids of Damascus (Albany, 1977).

Ibn Abī Uṣaybiʿa. *ʿUyūn al-anbāʾ fī ṭabaqāt al-aṭibbāʾ*, 3 vols. in 1, ed. A. Müller (Königsberg, 1884; new edition based on Müller, Beirut, 1965).

Ibn al-ʿAmīd, *Kitāb al-majmūʿ al-mubārak*, ed. C. Cahen, in "'La Chronique Ayyoubides' d'al-Makīn Ibn al-ʿAmīd," *BEO*, 15 (1955–58), 109–84; also published as C. Cahen (ed.), *Akhbār al-ayyūbiyīn* (Cairo, 1958).

Ibn al-Athīr, *Al-Kāmil fīʾl-taʾrīkh*, XI, XII, ed. C. J. Thornberg (Leiden, 1867–76; repr. Beirut, 1965).

Al-Taʾrīkh al-bāhir fīʾl-dawla al-atābakiyya, ed. A. A. Ṭulaymat (Cairo, 1963).

Ibn al-Dawādārī, *Kanz al-durar wa jāmiʿ al-ghurar*, vii: *Al-durr al-maṭlūb fī akhbār banī ayyūb*, ed. S. A. ʿĀshūr (Cairo, 1972).

Ibn Jubayr, *Tadhkira li-akhbār ʿan ittifāqāt al-asfār (The travels of Ibn Jubayr)*, ed. W. Wright, Gibb Memorial Series, V (Leiden, 1907, reprint, Beirut, 1964).

Ibn Khallikān, *Wafayāt al-aʿyān wa-anbāʾ abnāʾ al-zamān*, ed. M. ʿAbd al-Ḥamīd (Cairo, 1948), ed. I. ʿAbbās (Beirut, 1968–72).

Ibn al-Mammātī, *Qawānīn al-dawāwīn*, ed. A. S. Atiya (Cairo, 1943).

Ibn Shaddād, *Al-nawādir al-sulṭāniyya waʾl-maḥāsin al-yūsufiyya, sīrat Ṣalāḥ al-Dīn*, ed. J. al-Shayyāl (Cairo, 1962).

Ibn Shākir (al-Kutubī), *Fawāt al-wafayāt waʾl-dhayl ʿalayhā*, 2 vols., ed. M. ʿAbd al-Ḥamīd (Cairo, 1951), 4 vols., ed. I. ʿAbbās (Beirut, 1973–74).

Ibn Taghrī-Birdī, Abū al-Maḥāsin, *Al-Nujūm al-zāhira fī mulūk miṣr waʾl-qāhira*, partial edn. ed. W. Popper, University of California Publications in Semitic Philology, II–III, V–VII (Berkeley, 1909–60); English trans., W. Popper, *History of Egypt, 1382–1469*, same series, XIII–XIV, XVII, XIX, XX–XXIV (Berkeley, 1954–63); complete, edn., 16 vols. (Cairo, 1929–72).

Ibn al-Ṭuwayr, *Nuzhat al-muqlatayn fī akhbār al-dawlatayn*, ed. A. F. Sayyid (Beirut, Stuttgart, 1412/1992).

Ibn al-Wardī, *Tatimma al-mukhtaṣar fī akhbār al-bashar*, ed. A. R. Badarāwī (Beirut, 1970).
Ibn Wāṣil, *Mufarrij al-kurūb fī akhbār banī ayyūb*, ed. G. al-Shayyāl and Ḥ. M. Rabīʿ, 5 vols. (Cairo, 1953–77).
Ibn ʿAbd al-Ẓāhir, *Al-Rawḍ al-zāhir fī sīra al-malik al-ẓahir*, ed. A. A. al-Khuwayṭir (Riyadh, 1396/1976).
Imād al-Dīn al-Iṣfahānī, *Al-Fatḥ al-qussī fī'l-fatḥ al-qudsī*, ed. C. de Landberg (Leiden, 1888), ed. M. M. Ṣubḥ (Cairo, 1370/1951).
ʿImād al-Dīn al-Iṣfahānī, *Sanā al-barq al-shāmī*, surviving fragments published by M. al-Ḥayyārī (Amman, 1987), and F. al-Nabarāwī (Cairo, 1979).
Labib, S., *Handelsgeschichte Ägyptens im Spätmittelalter, 1171–1417* (Wiesbaden, 1965), ch. 2.
"Al-Iskandariyya," *EI2*.
"Kārimī," *EI2*.
"Al-Tujjār al-kārimiyya wa-tijārat miṣr fī'l-ʿuṣūr al-wusṭā," *Al-majalla al-ta'rīkhiyya al-miṣriyya*, 4 (1952), 5–63.
Lambton, A. K. S., "Reflections on the iqṭaʿ," in G. Makdisi (ed.), *Arabic and Islamic studies in honor of Hamilton A. R. Gibb* (Leiden, 1965).
Lane Poole, S., *A history of Egypt*, IV, *The Middle Ages* (London, 1901).
Saladin (London, 1926).
Lapidus, I., "Ayyubid religious policy and the development of schools of law in Cairo," *Colloque international sur l'histoire du Caire* (Cairo, 1974), 279–86.
Leiser, G., "The madrasa and the islamization of the Middle East: the case of Egypt," *JARCE* (1985).
"The restoration of sunnism in Egypt: madrasas and mudarrisūn, 495–647/1101–1249," (Ph.D. dissertation, University of Pennsylvania, 1976).
Lyons, M. C. and D. E. P. Jackson, *Saladin: The Politics of Holy War* (Cambridge, 1982).
MacKenzie, N. D., *Ayyubid Cairo; A Topographical Study* (Cairo, 1992).
Makhzūmī (al-), *Kitāb al-minhāj fī ʿilm kharāj Miṣr*, ed. C. Cahen, and Y. Ragib, in *AI*, 8, supplement (Cairo, 1986).
Maqrīzī (al-), *Al-Mawāʿiẓ wa'l-iʿtibār bi-dhikr al-khiṭaṭ waʾl-āthār*, 2 vols. (Cairo, 1270/1853); partial edn., ed. G. Weit, 5 vols. (Cairo, 1911–27).
Kitāb al-sulūk li-maʿrifat duwal al-mulūk, ed. M. M. Ziyāda and S. A. ʿĀshūr, 4 vols. (Cairo, 1943–72).
Minorsky, V., "The pre-history of Saladin," in his *Studies in Caucasian history* (London, 1953).
Müller-Wiener, M., *Eine Stadtgeschichte Alexandrias von 564/1169 bis in die Mitte des 9./15. Jahrhunderts. Verwaltung und innerstädtische Organisationsformen* (Berlin, 1992).
Nābulsī (al-), *Kitāb lamʿ al-qawānīn al-muḍiyya*, ed. C. Becker and C. Cahen, *BEO*, 17 (1958–60).
Ta'rīkh al-fayyūm wa-bilādihi, ed. B. Moritz (Cairo, 1899, reprint, 1974).
Poliak, A. N., "The Ayyubid feudalism," *JRAS* (1939), 97–109.
Feudalism in Egypt, Syria, Palestine and the Lebanon (London, 1939).

Powell, J. M., *Anatomy of a crusade, 1213–1221* (Philadelphia, 1986).
Rabbat, N. O., *The Citadel of Cairo: A New Interpretation of Royal Mamluk Architecture* (Leiden, 1995), 9–17, 50–84.
Rabie, H. M., *The Financial system of Egypt, AH 564–741/AD 1169–1341* (Oxford, 1972).
Al-Nuẓum al-māliyya fī miṣr zaman al-ayyūbiyīn (Cairo, 1964).
"The size and value of the iqṭās in Egypt 564–741 A.H./1169–1341 A.D.," in M. A. Cook (ed.), *Studies in the Economic History of the Middle East from the Rise of Islam to the Present Day* (London, 1970), 129–38.
Raymond, A., *Le Caire* (Paris, 1993).
Richards, D. S., "The early history of Saladin," *IQ*, 17 (1973), 140–59.
"Saladin," *EI2*.
Ripke, M., *Saladin und sein Biograph Bahā' al-Dīn Ibn Shaddād* (Bonn, 1988).
Salmon, M. G., *Études sur la topographie du Caire, MIFAO* (Cairo, 1902).
Sawīrus b. al-Muqaffaʿ, *History of the Patriarchs of the Coptic Church of Alexandria*, ed. with English trans. B. Evetts, *Patrologie Orientalis* I, 99–215; V, 1–216; X, 357–553; Cairo edn., Société d'Archéologie Copte, *History of the Patriarchs of the Egyptian Church, Known as the History of the Holy Church of Sawīrus ibn al-Muḳaffaʿ, Bishop of Ashmūnīn*, II, pt. 1 (AD 849–80), pt. 2 (A.D. 880–1066); II, pts. 2–3 (textes et documents), ed. and trans. A. Atiya, Y. ʿAbd al-Masīḥ, P. H. E. KHS-Burmester (1943, 1948–59); III, parts. 1–3; IV, pts. 1–2, A. Khater (1968–70, 1974).
Schregle, G., *Die Sultanin von Ägypten. Šağarat al-Durr in der arabischen Geschichtsschreibung und Literatur* (Wiesbaden, 1961).
Sibṭ Ibn al-Jawzī, *Mir'āt al-zamān fī ta'rīkh al-aʿyān*, facsimile ed. J. R. Jewett (Chicago, 1907); 2nd edn. based on the above, published as 8/1 and 2 (Hyderabad, 1951–52); 3rd edn ed. J. Jalīl and M. al-Hamūndī (Baghdad, 1990); partial French trans. "Extraits du Mirāt ez-Zemān," A.-C. Barbier de Meynard, *Historiens orientaux*, III, 517–70.
Ṭarkhān, I. A., *Al-Nuẓum al-iqṭaʿiyya fī'l-sharq al-awsaṭ fī'l-ʿuṣūr al-wusṭā* (Cairo, 1968).
Van Berchem, M., *Corpus Inscriptionum Arabicarum, Égypte*, i, *MMAF*, 18 (Paris, 1894–1903).
Van Cleve, T. C., "The crusade of Frederick II," in K. M. Setton (gen. ed.), *A history of the crusades*, ii: *The later crusades, 1189–1311*, R. L. Wolff and H. W. Hazard (eds.) (Madison, 1969).
Wiet, G., *L'Égypte arabe*, vol. IV in Gabriel Hanotaux, *Histoire de la nation égyptienne* (Paris, 1937).
"Les inscriptions du mausolée al-Shāfiʿī," *BIE*, XV (1933), 167–85.
"Les inscriptions de Saladin," *Syria*, 3 (1922), 307–28.
Yūnīnī (al-), *Dhayl mir' āt al-zamān*, I, II (Hyderabad, 1380/1960).

10 THE BAḤRĪ MAMLŪK SULTANATE, 1250–1390

Abu-Lughod, Janet, *Before European Hegemony: The World System AD 1250–1350* (New York, 1989).

"The World System in the Thirteenth Century: Dead-End or Precursor?" in Michael Adas (ed.), *Islamic and European Expansion: The Forging of a Global Order* (Philadelphia, 1993), 75–102.

Allouche, Adel, "Tegüder's Ultimatum to Qalawun," *IJMES*, 22 (1990), 437–46.

Amīn, Muḥammad Muḥammad, *Al-awqāf wa'l-ḥayāt al-ijtimāʿiyya fī Miṣr, 648–923 AH – 1250–1517 AD* (Cairo, 1980).

Fihrist wathāʾiq al-Qāhira ḥattā nihāyat ʿaṣr salāṭīn al-mamālīk (239–922 AH/853–1516 AD) (Cairo, 1981).

Amitai-Preiss, Reuven, *Mongols and Mamlūks: The Mamlūk-Īlkhānid war, 1260–1281* (Cambridge, 1995).

"The Remaking of the Military Elite of Mamlūk Egypt by al-Nāṣir Muḥammad ibn Qalāwūn," *SI*, 72 (1990), 145–63.

Ashtor, E., *Levant Trade in the Later Middle Ages* (Princeton, 1983).

Studies on the Levantine Trade in the Later Middle Ages (London, 1978).

Atiya, Aziz S., *The Crusade in the Later Middle Ages* (London, 1938).

"Egypt and Aragon: Embassies and Diplomatic Correspondence between 1300 and 1330 AD," *Abhandlungen für Kunde des Morgenlandes*, XXIII, 7 (Leipzig, 1938).

Ayalon, David, "Ḥalḳa," *EI2*, III, 99.

Islam and the Abode of War: Military Slaves and Islamic Adversaries (collected articles) (London, 1994).

"Mamlūk," *EI2*, VI, 314–21.

The Mamlūk Military Society: Collected Studies (London, 1979).

Outsiders in the Lands of Islam: Mamlūks, Mongols and Eunuchs (London, 1988).

Bacharach, Jere L., "African Military Slaves in the Medieval Middle East: The Cases of Iraq (869–995) and Egypt (868–1171)," *IJMES*, 13 (1981), 471–95.

Bosworth, C. E., "Recruitment, Muster, and Review in Medieval Islamic Armies," in V. J. Parry and M. E. Yapp (eds.), *War, Technology and Society in the Middle East* (London, 1975), 59–77.

Brett, Michael, "The Way of the Peasant," *BSOAS*, 47 (1984), 44–56.

Cahen, Claude, "Iḳṭāʿ," *EI2*, III, 1088–91.

Canard, Marius, "Le Royaume d'Arménie-Cilicie et les mamelouks jusqu'au traité de 1285," *Revue des Etudes Arméniennes*, 4 (1967), 217–59.

"Un traité entre Byzance et l'Egypte au XIIIe siècle et les relations diplomatiques de Michel VIII Paléologue avec les sultans mamlūks Baibars et Qalāʾūn," in *Mélanges Gaudefroy-Demombynes* (Cairo, 1934–45), 197–224: reprinted in *idem*, *Byzance et les musulmans du Proche Orient* (London, 1973).

Cooper, R. S., "The Assessment and Collection of Kharaj Tax in Medieval Egypt," *JAOS*, 96 (1976), 365–82.

"Land Classification Terminology and the Assessment of the *Kharaj* Tax in Medieval Egypt," *JESHO*, 17 (1974), 91–102.

Crone, Patricia, *Slaves on Horses: The Evolution of the Islamic Polity* (Cambridge, 1980).
Dols, Michael W., *The Black Death in the Middle East* (Princeton, 1977).
Ehrenkreutz, Andrew S., "Strategic Implications of the Slave Trade between Genoa and Mamlūk Egypt in the Second Half of the Thirteenth Century," in A. L. Udovitch, ed. *The Islamic Middle East, 700–1900*. Princeton: Darwin, 1981, 335–45.
Elham, Shah Morad, *Kitbugā und Lāǧīn: Studien zur Mamlūken-Geschichte nach Baibars al-Manṣūrī und Nuwairī*, "Islamkundliche Untersuchungen," Band 46 (Freiburg, 1977).
Escovitz, J. H., "The Establishment of the Four Chief Judgeships in the Mamlūk Empire," *JAOS*, 102 (1982), 529–531.
The Office of Qāḍī al-Quḍāt in Cairo under the Baḥrī Mamlūks (Berlin, 1984).
Fernandez, Leonor, *The Evolution of the Sufi Institution in Mamlūk Egypt: The Khanqah* (Berlin, 1988).
Garçin, J.-C., *Un centre musulman de la Haute-Egypte médiévale: Qūṣ*, Textes Arabes-Etudes Islamique, VI (Cairo, 1976).
"Ghulām," *EI2*, II, 1079–91.
Gottheil, R. J. H., "An Answer to the Dhimmis," *JAOS*, 41 (1921), 383–457.
"Dhimmis and Muslims in Egypt," in R. F. Harper, et al. (eds.), *Old Testament and Semitic Studies in Memory of W. R. Harper*, 2 vols. (Chicago, 1908), II, 353–414.
"A Fetwa on the Appointment of Dhimmis to Office," *Zeitschrift für Assyriologie*, 26 (1912), 203–14.
Haarmann, Ulrich, "Khalīl, al-Malik al-A*sh*raf Ṣalāḥ al-Dīn" *EI2*, IV, 964–5.
"Miṣr, 5. The Mamlūk Period 1250–1517," *EI2*, VII, 165–172.
"Regicide and the Law of the Turks," in Michel M. Mazzaoui and Vera B. Moreen (eds.), *Intellectual Studies on Islam: Essays Written in Honor of Martin B. Dickson* (Salt Lake City, 1990), 127–35.
"The Sons of Mamlūks as Fief-holders in Late Medieval Egypt," in Tarif Khalidi (ed.), *Land Tenure and Social Transformation in the Middle East* (Beirut, 1984).
al-Hājjī, H. N., *The Internal Affairs in Egypt during the Third Reign of Sultan al-Nāṣir Muḥammad ibn Qalāwūn, 709–741/1309–1341* (Kuwait, 1978).
Halm, Heinz, *Ägypten nach den mamlūkischen Lehenregistern*, 2 vols, Beihefte zum Tübinger Atlas des Vorderen Orients Reihe B, 38 (Wiesbaden, 1979; 1982).
Hanna, N., *An Urban History of Bulāq in the Mamlūk and Ottoman Periods* (Cairo, 1983).
Hiyari, M. A., "The Origins and Development of the Amirate of the Arabs during the Seventh/Thirteenth and Eighth/Fourteenth Centuries," *BSOAS*, 38 (1975), 509–24.
Holt, P. M., *The Age of the Crusades: The Near East from the Eleventh Century to 1517* (London and New York, 1986).

Early Mamlūk Diplomacy (1260–1290): Treaties of Baybars and Qalawun with Christian Rulers (Leiden, 1995).
"An Early Source on Shaykh Khaḍir al-Mihrānī," *BSOAS*, 46 (1983), 33–39.
"The Īlkhān Aḥmad's Embassies to Qalāwūn: Two Contemporary Accounts," *BSOAS*, 49 (1986), 128–32.
"Mamlūks," *EI2*, VI, 321–31.
"The Position and Power of the Mamlūk Sultan," *BSOAS*, 28 (1975), 237–49.
"Some Observations on the ʿAbbāsid Caliphate of Cairo," *BSOAS*, 47 (1984), 501–7.
"The Structure of Government in the Mamlūk Sultanate," in idem (ed.), *The Eastern Mediterranean Lands in the Period of the Crusades* (Warminster, 1977), 44–61.
"Succession in the Early Mamlūk Sultanate," in Deutscher Orientalistentag, XXIII, in Würzburg, September 6–20, 1985; selected papers, ed. Einar von Schuler (Stuttgart, 1989), (*Zeitschrift der Deutschen Morgenländischen Gesellschaft:* Supplement VII), 144–48.
"The Sultanate of Manṣūr Lachīn (696–8/1296–9)," *BSOAS*, 36 (1973), 521–32.
"Three Biographies of al-Ẓāhir Baybars," in D. O. Morgan (ed.), *Medieval Historical Writing in the Christian and Islamic Worlds* (London, 1982), 19–29.
"The Virtuous Ruler in Thirteenth-Century Mamlūk Royal Biographies," *Nottingham Medieval Studies*, 24 (1980), 27–35.
Homerin, T. Emil, "Umar ibn al-Fāriḍ, A Saint of Mamlūk and Ottoman Egypt," in Grace Martin Smith (ed.) and Carl W. Ernst (assoc. ed.), *Manifestations of Sainthood in Islam* (Istanbul, 1993), 85–94.
Humphreys, R. Stephen, "The Emergence of the Mamlūk Army," *SI*, 45 (1977), 67–99; 46 (1977), 69–119.
"The Fiscal Administration of the Mamlūk Empire," in idem, *Islamic History: A Framework for Inquiry*, rev. edn. (Princeton, 1991).
From Saladin to the Mongols: The Ayyubids of Damascus, 1193–1260 (Albany, 1977).
Irwin, Robert. "Factions in Medieval Egypt", *JRAS* (1986), 228–46.
"Iqṭāʿ and the End of the Crusader States," in P. M. Holt (ed.), *The Eastern Mediterranean Lands in the Period of the Crusades* (Warminster, 1977), 62–77.
"The Mamlūk Conquest of the County of Tripoli," in P. W. Edbury (ed.), *Crusade and Settlement* (Cardiff, 1985).
The Middle East in the Middle Ages: The Early Mamlūk Sultanate 1250–1382 (London, 1986).
"The Supply of Money and the Direction of Trade in Thirteenth-Century Syria," in P. W. Edbury and D. M. Metcalf (eds.), *Coinage in the Latin East: The Fourth Oxford Symposium on Coinage and Monetary History*, British Archeological Reports, International Series 77 (Oxford, 1980), 73–104.

Jackson, Peter, "Argūn," in Ehsan Yarshater (ed.), *EIR* (London, New York, II, 1987), 402–04.
"The Dissolution of the Mongol Empire," *Central Asiatic Journal*, 32 (1978), 186–244.
Labib, Subhi, "Egyptian Commercial Policy in the Middle Ages," in M. A. Cook (ed.), *Studies in the Economic History of the Middle East* (London, 1970), 63–77.
Handelsgeschichte Ägyptens in Spätmittelater (1171–1517) (Wiesbaden, 1965).
Lapidus, Ira M., "The Grain Economy of Mamlūk Egypt," *JESHO*, 12 (1969), 1–15.
Muslim Cities in the Later Middle Ages (Cambridge, MA, 1967; new edn., 1984).
Leiser, Gary, "The Madrasa and the Islamization of the Middle East: The Case of Egypt," *JARCE*, 22 (1985), 29–47.
Levanoni, Amalia, "The Consolidation of Aybak's Rule: An Example of Factionalism in the Mamlūk State," *Der Islam*, 71 (1995), 243–56.
"The Mamlūk Conception of the Sultanate," *IJMES*, 26 (1994), 373–92.
"The Mamlūks' Ascent to Power in Egypt," *SI*, 72 (1990), 121–44.
A Turning Point in Mamlūk History: The Third Reign of al-Nāṣir Muḥammad Ibn Qalāwūn, 1310–1341 (Leiden, New York, Cologne, 1995).
Little, D. P., "Coptic Conversion to Islam Under the Bahri Mamlūks, 692–755/1293–1354," *BSOAS*, 39 (1976), 552–69.
"Coptic Converts to Islam during the Bahri Mamlūk Period," in Michael Gervers and Ramzi Jibran Bikhazi (eds.), *Conversion and Continuty: Indigenous Christian Communities in Islamic Lands, Eighth to Eighteenth Centuries* (Toronto, 1990), 263–88.
"Did Ibn Taymiyya Have a Screw Loose?" *SI*, 41 (1975), 95–111.
"The Historical and Historiographical Significance of the Detention of Ibn Taymiyya," *IJMES*, 4 (1973), 311–13.
"Religion under the Mamlūks," *MW*, 73 (1983), 165–81.
Lombard, Maurice, *The Golden Age of Islam*, trans. Joan Spencer (Amsterdam, New York, 1975).
Lopez, Robert, Harry Miskimin and Abraham Udovitch, "England to Egypt, 1350–1500: Long-term Trends and Long-distance Trade," in M. A. Cook (ed.), *Studies in the Economic History of the Middle East from the Rise of Islam to the Present Day* (London, 1970), 93–128.
Mamlūk Studies: A Bibliography. Access through WWW, home page for Middle East Department, Regenstein Library, University of Chicago.
Marmon, Shaun, *Eunuchs and Sacred Boundaries in Islamic Society* (New York, Oxford, 1995).
Memon, M. U., *Ibn Taymiya's Struggle against Popular Religion* (The Hague, 1976).
Montavez, Pedro Martinez, "Relaciones de Alfonso X de Castilla con el Sultan mameluco Baybars y sus Sucesores," *Al-Andalus*, 27 (1962), 343–76.

Nielsen, Jørgen S., *Secular Justice in an Islamic State: Maẓālim under the Baḥrī Mamlūks, 662/1264–789/1387* (Istanbul, 1985).

Northrup, Linda S., "Muslim-Christian Relations during the Reign of the Mamlūk Sultan al-Mansur Qalawun, AD 1278–90," in Michael Gervers and Ramzi Jibran Bikhazi (eds.), *Conversion and Continuity: Indigenous Christian Communities in Islamic Lands, Eighth to Eighteenth Centuries* (Toronto, 1990), 253–61.

From Slave To Sultan: The Career of al-Manṣūr Qalāwūn and the Consolidation of Mamlūk Rule in Egypt and Syria (678–689 AH/ 1279–1290 AD). Freiburger Islamstudien, vol. 18 (Stuttgart, 1998).

Perlman, M., "Asnawi's Tract against Christian Officials," in Samuel Lowinger (ed.), *Ignace Goldziher Memorial Volume* (Jerusalem, 1958), II, 172–208.

"Notes on Anti-Christian Propaganda in the Mamlūk Empire," *BSOAS*, 9 (1940–42), 843–61.

Pipes, D., *Slave Soldiers and Islam: The Genesis of a Military System* (New Haven, London, 1981).

Rabbat, Nasser O., *The Citadel of Cairo: A New Interpretation of Royal Mamlūk Architecture* (Leiden, New York, Cologne, 1995).

Rabie, Hassanein, *The Financial System of Egypt, AH 564–741/AD 1169–1341* (London, 1972).

Richards, D. S., "The Coptic Bureaucracy under the Mamlūks," in *Colloque international sur l'histoire du Caire, 27 mars–5 avril 1969* (Cairo, 1969), 377–81.

Riley-Smith, Jonathan (ed.), *The Atlas of the Crusades* (London, 1991).

Shoshan, Boaz, *Popular Culture in Medieval Cairo* (Cambridge, 1993).

Sublet, Jacqueline, "La folie de la princesse Bint al-Ašraf," *BEO*, 27 (1974), 45–50.

Taylor, Christopher, "The Cult of Saints in Late Medieval Egypt," *Newsletter of the American Research Center in Egypt*, 139 (1987), 13–16.

Thorau, P., *Sultan Baibas I. von Ägypten: Ein Beitrag zur Geschichte des Vorderen Orients im 13. Jahrhundert*, Beihefte zum Tübinger Atlas des Vorderen Orients, Reihe B, no. 63 (Wiesbaden, 1987); English trans. P. M. Holt, *The Lion of Egypt: Sultan Baybars I and the Near East in the Thirteenth Century* (London and New York, 1987).

Udovitch, A. L., "England to Egypt, 1300–1500: Long-term Trends and Long-distance Trade," in M. A. Cook (ed.), *Studies in the Economic History of the Middle East* (London, 1970), 115–28.

11 THE REGIME OF THE CIRCASSIAN MAMLŪKS

Abd ar-Rāziq, A. *La femme au temps des Mamlouks en Égypte* (Cairo, 1973).

"Les gouverneurs d'Alexandrie au temps des Mamlūks," *AI*, 18 (1982), pp. 123–69.

"La ḥisba et le muḥtasib en Égypte au temps des Mamlūks," *AI*, 13 (1977), 115–78.

"Les muḥtasibs de Fosṭaṭ au temps des Mamlūks," *AI*, 17 (1978), 127–46.
"Le vizirat et les vizirs d'Égypte au temps des Mamlūks," *AI*, 16 (1980), 183–239.
Amīn, M. M., *Al-Awqāf wa'l-Ḥayat al-Ijtimā'iyya fī Miṣr* (Cairo, 1980).
Ankawi, A., "The Pilgrimage to Mecca in Mamlūk Times," *Arabian Studies*, 1 (1974), 146–70.
Ashtor, E., "L'évolution des prix dans le Proche-Orient à la basse époque," *JESHO*, 4 (1961), 15–46.
Histoire des prix et des salaires dans l'Orient médiéval (Paris, 1969).
Levant Trade in the Later Middle Ages (Princeton, 1983).
The Medieval Near East: Social and Economic History (London, 1978).
Les métaux précieux et la balance des payements du Proche-Orient à la basse époque (Paris, 1971).
Atıl, E., *Renaissance of Islam: Art of the Mamlūks* (Washington, 1981).
Aubin, J., "La crise égyptienne de 1510–12: Venise, Louis XII et le Sultan," *Moyen Orient et Océan Indien*, 6 (1989), 123–50.
Ayalon, D., "The End of the Mamlūk Sultanate (Why did the Ottomans Spare the Mamlūks of Egypt . . .)," *SI*, 65 (1987), 55–76.
Gunpowder and Firearms in the Mamlūk Kingdom (London, 1956).
"The Plague and its Effects upon the Mamlūk Army," *JRAS* (1946), 67–73.
al-'Aynī, *'Iqd al-Jumān fī Ta'rīkh Ahl al-Zamān*. ed. Muḥammad M. Amīn (Cairo, 1987–).
Bacharach, J., "Circassian Monetary Policy: Copper," *JESHO*, 19 (1976), 32–47.
"Circassian Monetary Policy: Silver," *Numismatic Chronicle*, 11 (1971), 267–81.
"The Dinar versus the Ducat," *IJMES*, 4 (1973), 77–96.
"Monetary Investments in Medieval Egypt, 1171–1517," in *Precious Metals in the Later Medieval and Early Modern Worlds*, ed. J. Richards. Durham, North Carolina, 1983, pp. 159–82.
Bacqué-Grammont, J.-L. and A. Kroell, *Mamlouks, Ottomans et Portugais en Mer Rouge: L'affaire de Djedda en 1517* (Cairo, 1988).
Balog, P., *The Coinage of the Mamlūk Sultans of Egypt and Syria* (New York, 1964).
Behrens-Abouseif, D., *Azbakiyya and its Environs from Azbak to Isma'il, 1476–1879* (Cairo, 1985).
"Change, Function and Form of Mamlūk Religious Institutions," *AI*, 21 (1985), 73–93.
"A Circassian Mamlūk Suburb north of Cairo," *Art and Archaeology Research Papers*, 14 (1978), 17–23.
"The Citadel of Cairo: Stage for Mamlūk Ceremonial," *AI*, 24 (1988), 25–79.
"Locations of Non-Muslim Quarters in Medieval Cairo," *AI*, 22 (1986), 117–32.
"The North-eastern Extension of Cairo under the Mamlūks," *AI*, 17 (1981), 157–89.
"The Qubba, an Aristocratic Type of Zāwiya," *AI*, 19 (1983), 1–7.

"Sufi Architecture in Early Ottoman Cairo," *AI*, 20 (1984), 103–14.
Behrens-Abouseif, D. and L. Fernandes, "An Unlisted Monument of the Fifteenth Century: The Dome of Zāwiyat al-Damirdāsh," *AI*, 18 (1982), 105–22.
Berkey, J., *The Transmission of Knowledge in Medieval Cairo* (Princeton, 1992).
Blanc, B., S. Denoix, J.-C. Garcin, R. Gordiani. "A Propos de la carte du Caire de Matheo Pagano," *AI*, 17 (1981), 203–85.
Bosworth, C. E., "Christian and Jewish Religious Dignitaries in Mamlūk Egypt and Syria," *IJMES*, 3 (1972), 59–74.
"The Protected Peoples (Christians and Jews) in Medieval Egypt and Syria," *Bulletin of the John Rylands Library*, 62 (1979), 11–36.
Brinner, W. M., "The Significance of the Harafish and their 'sultan'," *JESHO*, 6 (1963), 190–215.
Chapoutot-Remadi, M., "L'agriculture dans l'empire mamlūk au Moyen Âge d'après al-Nuwayrī," *Cahiers de Tunisie*, 22 (1974), 23–45.
Cohen, M., "Jews in the Mamlūk Environment: The Crisis of 1441," *BSOAS*, 47 (1984), 44–56.
Cooper, R. S. "Agriculture in Egypt, 640–1800," in B. Spuler (ed.), *Wirtschaftsgeschichte des Vorderen Orients in islamischer Zeit* (*Handbuch der Orientalistik*, Abteilung 1) (Leiden, 1977), 188–204.
Darrag, A., *L'Égypte sous le règne de Barsbay, 825–841/1422–1438* (Damascus, 1961).
Denoix, S. *Décrire le Caire: Fusṭāṭ-Miṣr d'après Ibn Duqmāq et Maqrīzī: l'histoire d'une partie de la ville du Caire d'après deux historiens égyptiens des XIVe–XVe* siècles (Cairo, 1992).
Dols, M., "The Second Plague Pandemic and its Recurrences in the Middle East: 1347–1894," *JESHO*, 22 (1979), 162–89.
Fernandes, L., *The Evolution of a Sufi Institution in Mamluk Egypt: the Khanqah* (Berlin, 1988).
"Mamlūk Politics and Education: The Evidence from two Fourteenth-Century Waqfiyyas," *AI*, 23 (1987), 87–98.
"Some Aspects of the Zāwiya in Egypt at the Eve of the Ottoman Conquest," *AI*, 19 (1983), 9–17.
"Three Sufi Foundations in a 15th-Century Waqfiyya," *AI*, 17 (1981), 141–56.
Frantz-Murphy, G., *The Agrarian Administration of Egypt from the Arabs to the Ottomans* (Cairo, 1986).
Garcin, J.-C., "al-Ṣaʿīd," *EI2*, VIII.
"Assises materielles et rôle économique des ordres soufis dans l'histoire des peuples musulmans," in A. Popovic and G. Veinstein (eds.), *Les voies d'Allah* (Paris, 1995), 213–23, 654–56.
"Le Caire et l'évolution urbaine des pays musulmans à l'époque médiévale," *AI*, 25 (1991), 289–304.
"Deux saints populaires du Caire au début du XIVe siècle," *BEO*, 29 (1977), 133–43.
Espaces, pouvoirs et idéologies de l'Égypte médiévale (London, 1987).

"Histoire, opposition politique et piétisme traditionaliste dans le Ḥusn al-Muḥāḍarat de Suyūṭī," *AI*, 7 (1967), 33–89.

"L'insertion sociale de Sha'rānī dans le milieu cairote," *Colloque international sur l'histoire du Caire* (Cairo, 1969), 159–68.

"The Mamlūk Military System and the Blocking of Medieval Muslim Society," in J. Baechler et al. (eds.), *Europe and the Rise of Capitalism* (Oxford, 1988), 119–23/"Le système militaire mamlūk et le blocage de la société musulmane médiévale," *AI*, 25 (1988), 93–110.

"Note sur la population du Caire en 1517," in *Grandes villes du monde musulman médiéval* (Rome, 1997).

"Note sur les rapports entre bédouins et fellahs à l'époque mamluke," *AI*, 14 (1978), 147–63.

Un centre musulman de la Haute-Égypte médiévale: Qūṣ (Cairo, 1976).

"Une carte du Caire vers le fin du sultanat de Qāytbāy," *AI*, 17 (1982), 272–85.

Garcin, J.-C., M. Balivet, T. Bianquis, H. Bresc, J. Calmard, M. Gaborieau, P. Guichard, J. L. Triaud, *États, sociétés et cultures du monde musulman médiéval, Xe–XVe siècle* (Paris, 1995).

Garcin, J.-C., B. Maury, J. Revault, M. Zakarya. *Palais et maisons du Caire du XIVe au XVIIIe siècle*, I (Cairo, 1982).

Garcin, J.-C., and M. Taher. "Enquête sur le financement d'un *waqf* égyptien du XVe siècle: les comptes de Jawhār al-Lālā," *JESHO*, 38 (1995), 262–304.

Geoffroy, E. *Le soufisme en Égypte et en Syrie sous les derniers mamelouks et les premiers Ottomans* (Damascus, 1995).

Halm, H., *Ägypten nach den Mamlūkischen Lehenregistern: I: Oberägypten und das Fayyūm; II: Das Delta.* Beihefte zum Tübinger Atlas des Vorderen Orients, Reihe B. no. 38 (Wiesbaden, 1979, 1982).

Hanna, N., *An Urban History of Būlāq in the Mamlūk and Ottoman Periods* (Cairo, 1983).

Hess, A. C., "The Ottoman Conquest of Egypt (1517) and the Beginning of the Sixteenth-Century World War," *IJMES*, 4 (1973), 55–76.

Heyd, W., *Histoire du commerce du Levant au Moyen Âge*. 2 vols. trans. Furcy Raynaud (Leipzig, 1885–86); reprinted Amsterdam, 1967).

Holt, P. M., *The Age of the Crusades: The Near East from the Eleventh Century to 1517* (London and New York, 1986).

"Mamlūks," *EI2*, VI.

Ibn Iyās, *Badā'i' al-Zuhūr fī Waqā'i' al-Duhūr*, 5 vols., ed. M. Muṣṭafā (Cairo, 1960–75); French trans. vols. III–V G. Wiet, *Histoire des mamelouks circassiens* (Cairo, 1945); *Journal d'un bourgeois du Caire*, 2 vols. (Paris, 1955, 1960).

Ibn Taghrī-Birdī, Abū al-Maḥāsin, *Al-Nujūm al-Zāhira fī Mulūk Miṣr wa al-Qāhira*, partial edn. ed. W. Popper, University of California Publications in Semitic Philology, II–III, V–VII (Berkeley, 1909–60); English trans. W Popper, *History of Egypt, 1382–1469*, same series, XIII–XIV, XVII, XIX, XX–XXIV (Berkeley, 1954–1963); complete edn., 16 vols. (Cairo, 1929–72).

Ibrahim, L. A., *Mamlūk Monuments of Cairo* (Cairo, 1976).
"Residential Architecture in Mamlūk Cairo," *Muqarnas*, 2 (1984), 49–57.
Jomier, J., *Le Mahmal et la caravane égyptienne des pélerins de La Mecque* (Cairo, 1953).
Labib, S., "Egyptian Commercial Policy in the Middle Ages," in M. Cook (ed.), *Studies in the Economic History of the Middle East* (London, 1970), 63–77.
Handelsgeschichte Ägyptens im Spätmittelalter, 1171–1517 (Wiesbaden, 1965).
Lapidus, I. M., "The Grain Economy of Mamlūk Egypt," *JESHO*, 12 (1969), 1–15.
Muslim Cities in the Later Middle Ages (Cambridge, MA, 1967).
Lopez, R., H. Miskimin, A. Udovitch, "England to Egypt, 1350–1500: Long-Term Trends and Long-Distance Trade," in M. Cook (ed.), *Studies in the Economic History of the Middle East* (London, 1970).
Lutfi, H., "Al-Sakhāwī's *Kitāb al-Nisā'* as a Source for the Social and Economic History of Muslim Women during the Fifteenth Century AD," *The Muslim World*, 71 (1981), 104–24.
al-Maqrīzī, *Kitāb al-Sulūk li-Ma'rifa Duwal al-Mulūk*, ed. M. M. Ziyāda and S. A. 'Āshūr, 4 vols. (Cairo, 1943–72).
Martel-Thoumian, B., *Les civils et l'administration dans l'état militaire mamlūk (IXe/XVe siècle)* (Damascus, 1991).
Meinecke, M., *Die Mamlūkische Architektur in Ägypten und Syrien*, 2 vols. (Glückstadt, 1992).
Meinecke-Berg, V., "Eine Stadtansicht des mamlūkischen Kairo aus dem 16. Jahrhundert," *Mitteilungen des Deutschen Archäologischen Instituts, Abteilung Kairo*, 32 (1976), 113–32.
Michel, N., "Les rizaq iḥbāsiyya, terres agricoles en main morte dans l'Égypte mamlouke et ottomane," *AI*, 30 (1996), 105–98.
Müller-Wiener, M., *Eine Stadtgeschichte Alexandrias von 564/1169 bis in die Mitte des 9./15. Jahrhunderts* (Berlin, 1992).
Petry, C., *The Civilian Elite of Cairo in the Later Middle Ages* (Princeton, 1981).
"Class Solidarity vs. Gender Gain: Women as Custodians of Property in Later Medieval Egypt," in Nikki Keddie and Beth Baron (eds.), *Women in Middle Eastern History: Shifting Boundaries in Sex and Gender* (New Haven, 1991), 122–41.
"A Paradox of Patronage during the Later Mamlūk Period," *The Muslim World*, 73 (1983), 182–207.
Protectors or Praetorians? The Last Mamlūk Sultans and Egypt's Waning as a Great Power (Albany, 1994).
"Travel Patterns of Medieval Notables in the Near East," *SI*, 62 (1985), 53–88.
Twilight of Majesty: The Reigns of the Mamlūk Sultans al-Ashraf Qāytbāy and Qānṣūh al-Ghawrī in Egypt (Seattle, 1993).
Popper, W., *Egypt and Syria under the Circassian Sultans, 1382–1468 AD: Systematic Notes to Ibn Taghrī Birdī's Chronicles of Egypt*. University of

California Publications in Semitic Philology, 15–16, 24 (Berkeley, 1955, 1957, 1963).
Raymond, A., *Le Caire* (Paris, 1993).
"Cairo's Area and Population in the Early Fifteenth Century," *Muqarnas*, 2 (1984), 21–31.
"La population du Caire de Maqrīzī à la *Description de l'Égypte*," *BEO*, 28 (1977), 201–15.
Raymond, A. and G. Wiet, *Les marchés du Caire: Traduction annotée du texte de Maqrīzī* (Cairo, 1979).
Richards, D. S., "The Coptic Bureaucracy under the Mamlūks," in *Colloque international sur l'histoire du Caire, 27 mars–5 avril 1969* (Cairo, 1969), 373–81.
Sadek, M. M., *Die Mamlūkische Architektur der Stadt Gaza* (Berlin, 1991).
Sartain, E., *Jalāl al-Dīn al-Suyūṭī, I: Biography and Background* (Cambridge, 1975).
Saleh, A. "Les relations entre les Mamlūks et les bédouins d'Égypte," *Annali*, Istituto di Napoli (n.s. 30), 40, 3 (1980), 365–93.
Shoshan, B., "From Silver to Copper: Monetary Changes in Fifteenth-Century Egypt," *SI*, 56 (1982), 97–116.
"Grain Riots and the 'Moral Economy': Cairo, 1350–1517," *Journal of Interdisciplinary History*, 10, 3 (1979–80), 459–78.
"Money Supply and Grain Prices in Fifteenth-Century Egypt," *The Economic History Review*, 36 (1983), 47–67.
"Notes sur les épidémies de peste en Égypte," *Annales de démographie historique*, (1981), 387–404.
Sublet, J. "La peste prise aux rêts de la jurisprudence," *SI*, 33 (1971), 141–49.
Wiet, G., *L'Égypte arabe*, vol. 4 in Gabriel Hanotaux, *Histoire de la nation égyptienne* (Paris, 1937).
Winter, M., *Society and Religion in Early Ottoman Egypt: Studies in the Writings of ʿAbd al-Wahhāb al-Shaʿrānī* (New Brunswick, NJ, 1982).
Al-Zāhirī, Khalil, *Kitāb Zubda Kashf al-Mamālik*, ed. P. Ravaisse (Paris, 1894).
Zakarya, M., *Deux palais du Caire médiéval:* waqfs *et architecture* (Paris, 1983).

12 THE MONETARY HISTORY OF EGYPT, 642–1517

General works

Album, Stephen, *A Checklist of Popular Islamic Coins* (Santa Rosa, CA, 1993).
Ashtor, Eliyahu, *East-West Trade in the Medieval Mediterranean* (London, 1986).
Histoire des prix et des salaires dans l'orient médiéval (Paris, 1969).
Levant Trade in the Later Middle Ages (Princeton, 1983).
The Medieval Near East: Social and Economic History (London, 1978).

Les Métaux precieux et la balance des payements du Proche-Orient à la basse époque (Paris, 1971).

A Social and Economic History of the Near East in the Middle Ages (Berkeley, 1976).

Studies on the Levantine Trade in the Middle Ages (London, 1978).

Bacharach, Jere L., "Monetary Movements in Medieval Egypt, 1171–1517," in J. F. Richards (ed.) *Precious Metals in the Later Medieval and Early Modern Worlds* (Durham, NC, 1983), 159–81.

Balog, Paul, *The Coinage of the Ayyubids* (London, 1980).

The Coinage of the Mamluk Sultans of Egypt and Syria (New York, 1964).

"History of the Dirham in Egypt from the Fāṭimid Conquest until the collapse of the Mamlūk Empire, 358 – 922 H/968–1517 AD," *Revue Numismatique*, 6th ser., 3 (1961), 109–46.

"Islamic Bronze Weights from Egypt." *JESHO*, 13 (1970), 233–56.

Bates, Michael L., *Islamic Coins*, American Numismatic Society Handbook no. 2 (New York, 1982).

"Islamic Numismatics." *MESA Bulletin*, 12 2, 3 (1978), 1–16, 2–18; 13, 1, 2 (1979), 3–21, 1–9.

de Bouard, Michel, "Sur l'évolution monétaire de l'Égypte médiévale." *L'Égypte contemporaine*, 30 (1939), 427–59.

Broom, Michael R., *A Handbook of Islamic Coins* (London, 1985).

Brown, Helen W., "The Medieval Mint of Cairo: Some Aspects of Mint Organization and Administration," in N. J. Dayhew and Peter Spufford (eds.), *Later Medieval Mints: Organization, Administration, and Technique* B.A.R International Series no. 389 (1988), 30–39.

Brunschvig, Robert, "Conceptions monétaires chez les juristes musulmans (VIIIe-XIIIe siècles)," *Arabica*, 14 (1967), 113–43.

Dunlap, D. M., "Sources of Gold and Silver in Islam according to al-Hamdani," *Studia Islamica*, 8 (1952), 29–49.

Ehrenkreutz, Andrew S., "Contributions to the Knowledge of the Fiscal Administration of Egypt in the Middle Ages," *Bulletin of the School of Oriental and African Studies*, 16 (1954), 502–514.

"Monetary Aspects of Medieval Near Eastern Economic History," in M. A. Cook (ed.), *Studies in the Economic History of the Middle East* (Oxford, 1970), 37–50.

Monetary Change and Economic History in the Medieval Muslim World, (London, 1992).

"Numismatics Re-Monetized," in L. L. Orlin (ed.), *Michigan Oriental Studies in Honor of George C. Cameron* (Ann Arbor, 1976), 207–218.

Fahmī, ʿAbd al-Raḥmān, *Fajr al-sikkah al-ʿarabīyah* (Cairo, 1965).

Goitein, S. D., *A Mediterranean Society: The Jewish Communities of the Arab World as Portrayed in the Documents of the Cairo Geniza*, 6 vols. (Berkeley, 1967–94) (bibliography and indices in vol. 6).

Grohmann, Adolf, *Einführung und Chrestomathie sur Arabischen Papyruskunde*, part 1, *Einführung* (Prague, 1954).

Hennequin, Gilles P. " 'Bonne' ou 'mauvaise' monnaie? Mutations monétaires et

loi de Gresham avant l'époque moderne," *L'Information historique*, 39 (1977), 203–12.
"De la monnaie antique à la monnaie musulmane." *Annales: Economies, Sociétés, Civilisations* 4 (1975), 890–899.
"An outline of monetary theory with special respect to Medieval Islam (as requested by Michael L. Bates, Curator of Islamic Coins at the ANS)," (unpublished essay, American Numismatic Society, 1975).
"Points de vue sur l'histoire monétaire de l'Égypte musulmane au moyen-āge," *AI*, 12 (1974), 1–36.
"Problems théoriques et pratiques de la monnaie antique et médiévale," *AI*, 10 (1972), 1–57.
Hinz, Walter, *Islamische Masse und Gewichte* (Leiden, 1955).
Labib, Subhi, "Geld und Kredit," *JESHO*, 2 (1959), 225–46.
Miles, George C., "Dīnār," *EI2* II, 297–99.
"Dirham," *EI2* II, 319–20.
Rare Islamic Coins, Numismatic Notes and Monographs no. 118 (American Numismatic Society, 1950).
Nicol, N. D., Raʿfat al-Nabarawi, and Jere L. Bacharach, *Catalogue of the Islamic Coins, Glass Weights, Dies and Medals in the Egyptian National Library*, American Research Center in Egypt Catalogues (Malibu, CA, 1982).
Rabie, H., *The Financial System of Egypt AH 564–741/AD 1169–1341* (London, 1972).
Sauvaire, H., "Matériaux pour servir à l'histoire de la numismatique et de la métrologie musulmanes," *Journal Asiatique* (7th ser.) 14 (1879), 455–533, 15 (1880), 228–77, 421–78, 18 (1881), 499–516, 19 (1882), 23–77, 281–327; (8th ser.) 3 (1884), 368–445, 7 (1886), 124–77, 394–468, 8 (1886), 113–65, 272–97, 479–536.
Sperber, Daniel, "Islamic Metrology from Jewish Sources," *Numismatic Chronicle*, 7th ser., 5 (1965), 231–37.
"Islamic Metrology from Jewish Sources II," in *Numismatic Chronicle*, 7th ser., 12 (1975), 275–82.
Toll, Christopher, "Minting Techniques According to Arabic Literary Sources," *Oriental Suecana*, 19–20 (1970–1971), 125–39.
Udovitch, Abraham L., "Bankers without Banks: Commerce, Banking and Society in the Islamic World of the Middle Ages," *The Dawn of Modern Banking* (New Haven, 1979), 255–73.
Partnership and Profit in Medieval Islam (Princeton, 1970).

From the Muslim conquest to the Fāṭimids

Awad, Henri Amin, "Seventh Century Arab Imitations of Alexandrian Dodecanummia," *American Numismatic Society Museum Notes*, 18 (1972), 113–17.
Bacharach, Jere L., "The Coinage of Kāfūr: A Cautionary Tale," *Israel Numismatic Journal*, 10 (1988–89), 71–79.

"Al-Ikhshīd, the Ḥamdānids, and the Caliphate: The Numismatic Evidence," *Journal of the American Oriental Society*, 94 (1974), 360–70.

Bacharach, Jere L., and Henri Amin Awad, "The Early Bronze Coinage of Egypt: Additions," in Dickran K. Kouymjian (ed.), *Near Eastern Numismatics, Iconography, Epigraphy, and History: Studies in Honor of George C. Miles* (Beirut, 1974), 185–92.

"Rare Early Egyptian Islamic Coins and Coin Weights: The Awad Collection," *JARCE*, 18 (1981), 51–56.

Balog, Paul, "Reference Guide to Arabic Metrology: Umayyad, ʿAbbasid and Tulunid Officials Named on Glass Coin Weights, Weights and Measure Stamps" *Jahrbuch für Numismatik und Geldgeschichte*, 30 (1980), 55–96.

"Table de références des monnaies ikhchidites," *Revue belge de Numismatique*, 103 (1957), 107–34.

Umayyad, ʿAbbasid and Tulunid Glass Weights and Vessel Stamps (New York, 1976).

Bates, Michael L., "Coins and Money in the Arabic Papyri," *Documents de L'Islam médiéval. Nouvelles perspectives de recherche* (Cairo, 1991), 43–64.

"History, Geography and Numismatics in the First Century of Islamic Coinage," *Revue Suisse de Numismatique*, 65 (1986), 231–61.

Berman, Ariel, "Additional Information on the Coinage of Egypt During the Governorship of Muḥammad Ibn Tughj al-Ikhshīd," *Israel Numismatic Journal*, 5 (1981), 69–72.

Domaszewicz, Lidia and Michael L. Bates, "The Copper Coinage of Egypt in the Seventh Century," forthcoming.

Ehrenkreutz, Andrew S., "Numismato-Statistical Reflections on the Annual Gold Coinage Production of the Tulunid Mint in Egypt," *JESHO*, 20 (1977), 267–81.

"Studies in the Monetary History of the Near East in the Middle Ages: (I) The Standard of Fineness of Some Types of Dinars," *JESHO*, 2 (1959), 128–61.

Grabar, Oleg, *The Coinage of the Tulunids*, Numismatic Notes and Monographs no. 139 (New York, 1957).

Miles, George C., "Byzantine Miliaresion and Arab Dirham: Some Notes on Their Relationship," *American Numismatic Society Museum Notes*, 9 (1960), 189–218.

"The Early Islamic Bronze Coinage of Egypt," in Harald Ingholt (ed.), *Centennial Publication of the American Numismatic Society* (New York, 1958), 471–502.

"On the Varieties and Accuracy of Eighth Century Arab Coin Weights." *Eretz Israel*, 7 (1963), 79–87.

"Some Rare and Unpublished ʿAbbasid Coins of the Mint of Misr," (unpublished paper, preserved in the American Numismatic Society Library, New York).

Phillips, J. R., "The Byzantine Bronze Coins of Alexandria in the Seventh Century," *Numismatic Chronicle*, 7th ser., 2 (1962), 225–41.

Walker, John, *Catalogue of the Muḥammadan Coins in the British Museum*, II, *Arab-Byzantine and Post-Reform Umaiyad Coins*, (London, 1956).

The Fāṭimids and Ayyūbids

Balog, Paul, "Ayyubid Divisional Currency Issued in Egypt by al-Kāmil Muḥammad I," *Gazette numismatique suisse*, 27 (1977), 62–67.
"The Ayyubid Glass Jetons and Their Use," *JESHO*, 9 (1966), 242–56.
"The Fāṭimid Glass Jetons: Token Currency or Coin Weights," *JESHO*, 24 (1981), 93–109.
Bates, Michael L., "The Function of Fāṭimid and Ayyūbid Glass Weights," *JESHO*, 24 (1981), 63–92.
"Thirteenth Century Crusader Imitations of Ayyūbid Silver Coinage: a Preliminary Survey," in Dickran K. Kouymjian (ed.), *Studies in Honour of George C. Cameron* (Beirut, 1974), 393–409.
Cahen, Claude, "Circulation monétaire in Égypt des fatimides aux ayyubides," *Revue Numismatique*, 26 (1984), 208–17.
"La Frappe des monnaies en Égypte au VIe/XIIIe siècle d'après le *Minhāj* d'al-Makhzūmī," in L. L. Orlin (ed.), *Michigan Oriental Studies in Honor of George C. Miles* (Ann Arbor, 1976), 335–38.
"Monetary Circulation in Egypt at the Time of the Crusades and the Reform of al-Kāmil," in A. L. Udovitch (ed.), *The Islamic Middle East, 700–1900*, (Princeton, 1981), 315–33.
Cooper, Richard. C., "A Note on the Dīnār Jayshī," *JESHO*, 16 (1973), 317–18.
Ehrenkreutz, Andrew S., "Arabic Dinars Struck by the Crusaders – A case of ignorance or of economic subversion," *JESHO*, 7 (1964), 167–82.
"Byzantine Tertartera and Islamic Dinars," *JESHO*, 7 (1964), 183–90.
"The Crisis of the Dinar in the Egypt of Saladin." *JAOS*, 76 (1956), 178–84.
"The Standard of Fineness of Gold Coins Circulating in Egypt at the Time of the Crusades," *JAOS*, 74 (1954), 162–66.
"Studies in the Monetary History of the Near East in the Middle Ages: II, The Standard of Fineness of Western and Eastern Dinars," *JESHO*, 6 (1963), 243–77.
Ehrenkreutz, Andrew S. and G.W. Heck. "Additional Evidence of the Fāṭimid Use of Dīnārs for Propaganda Purposes," in M. Sharon (ed.), *Studies in Islamic History and Civilisation in Honour of Professor David Ayalon* (Jerusalem, 1986), 145–51.
Goitein, S. D., "The Exchange Rate of Gold and Silver Money in Fāṭimid and Ayyūbid Times. A Preliminary Study of the Relevant Geniza Material," *JESHO*, 8 (1965), 1–46.
Lowe, John D., "A Medieval Instance of Gresham's Law: The Fāṭimid Monetary System," *Jusūr*, 2 (1986), 1–24.
Miles, George C., *Fāṭimid Coins in the Collections of the University Museum*,

Philadelphia, and the American Numismatic Society, Numismatic Notes and Monographs no. 121 (New York, 1951).

Nicol, N. D., "Paul Balog's *The Coinage of the Ayyubids*: additions and corrections," *Numismatic Chronicle*, 146 (1986), 119–54.

Oddy, W. A., "The Gold Content of Fāṭimid Coins Reconsidered," *Metallurgy in Numismatics*, 1. Edited by W. M. Metcalf and W. A. Oddy. (London, 1980), 99–118.

The Mamlūk period

The literature on Mamlūk monetary history is extensive. Only a selection is included here. For a more complete bibliographic listing, the reader is referred to the Numismatic and Economic sections of the Mamlūk Bibliography Project, found on the World Wide Web at the following URL: http://www.lib.uchicago.edu/LibInfo/SourcesBySubject/MiddleEast/MamBib.html.

Ashtor, Eliyahu, "Études sur le système monétaire des mamlouks circassiens," *Israel Oriental Studies*, 6 (1976), 264–87.

Ayalon, David, "The System of Payment in Mamlūk Military Society," *JESHO*, 1 (1958), 37–65, 257–96.

Bacharach, Jere L., "Circassian Mamlūk Historians and Their Economic Data," *JARCE*, 12 (1975), 75–87.

"Circassian Monetary Policy: Copper," *JESHO*, 19 (1976), 32–47.

"Circassian Monetary Policy: Silver," *Numismatic Chronicle*, 7th ser., 11 (1971), 267–81.

"The Dinar versus the Ducat," *IJMES*, 4 (1973), 77–96.

"The Ducat in Fourteenth Century Egypt," *Res Orientales*, 6 (1994), 95–101.

"Foreign Coins, Forgers, and Forgeries in Fifteenth Century Egypt," in Herbert A. Cahn and Georges Le Rider (eds.), *Actes du VIII. Congrès international de numismatique* (Paris, 1976), 501–11.

"A Study of the Correlation Between Textual Sources and Numismatic Evidence for Mamlūk Egypt and Syria, AH 784–872/AD 1382–1468" (Ph.D. dissertation, University of Michigan, 1967).

Bacharach, Jere L., and Adon A. Gordus. "Studies on the Fineness of Silver Coins," *JESHO*, 11 (1968), 298–317.

Balog, Paul, "The Coinage of the Mamlūk Sultans: Additions and Corrections," *American Numismatic Society Museum Notes*, 16 (1970), 113–71.

"I. A Hoard of Late Mamlūk Copper Coins, and II. Observations on the Metrology of the Mamlūk Fals," *Numismatic Chronicle*, 7th ser., 2 (1962), 243–73.

Bedoukian, Paul Z., *Coinage of Cilician Armenia*, Numismatic Notes and Monographs, no. 147 (New York, 1962).

"Some Armenian Coins Overstruck in Arabic," *Armeniaca: mélanges d'études arméniennes* (Venice, 1969), 138–47.

Fahmī, Sāmih ʿAbd al-Raḥmān, *Al-Wihdat al-naqdīyah al-mamlūkīyah* (Jeddah, 1983).

Hennequin, Gilles, "Mamlouks et métaux precieux: à propos de la balance des paiements de l'état syro-egyptien à la fin du moyen-āge. Questions de méthode," *AI*, 12 (1974), 37–44.

"Nouveaux aperçus sur l'histoire monétaire de l'Égypte à la fin du moyan-āge," *AI*, 13 (1977), 179–215.

"*Waqf* et monnaie dans l'Égypte mamlūke," *JESHO*, 38 (1995), 305–12.

Lopez, Robert, Harry Miskimin and Abraham Udovitch, "England to Egypt, 1350–1500: Long-term Trends and Long-distance Trade," in M. A. Cook (ed.), *Studies in the Economic History of the Middle East* (Oxford, 1970), 91–128.

Mayer, L. A., "Lead Coins of Barquq," *Quarterly of the Department of Antiquities in Palestine*, 3 (1934), 20–23.

al-Nabarāwī, Raʿfat, *Al-Sikkah al-islamīyah fi miṣr: ʿaṣr dawlat al-mamālīk al-jirākisah* (Cairo, 1993).

al-Najīdī, Ḥamūd, *al-Nizām al-naqdī al-mamlūkī* (Alexandria, 1993).

Nicol, N. D. and Raʿfat al-Nabarawi, "A Hoard of Mamlūk Copper Coins, c. 770 H (1369 AD) in the Collection of Egyptian National Library," *JARCE*, 21 (1984), 104–18.

Popper, William, *Egypt and Syria Under the Circassian Sultans 1382–1468 AD: Systematic Notes to Ibn Taghri Birdi's Chronicles of Egypt*, University of California Publications in Semitic Philology, XV–XVI. (Berkeley, 1955–57).

Sari, Saleh Khaled, "A Critical Analysis of a Mamlūk Hoard from Karak," (Ph.D. dissertation, University of Michigan, 1986).

Schultz, Warren C., "Mamlūk Money from Baybars to Barquq: A Study Based on the Literary Sources and the Numismatic Evidence" (Ph.D. dissertation, University of Chicago, 1995).

Shoshan, Boaz, "Exchange-Rate Policies in Fifteenth Century Egypt," *JESHO*, 29 (1986), 28–51).

"From Silver to Copper: Monetary Change in Fifteenth Century Egypt," *SI*, 56 (1982), 97–116.

"Money, Prices and Population in Mamlūk Egypt, 1382–1517" (Ph.D. dissertation, Princeton University, 1978).

"Money Supply and Grain Prices in Fifteenth Century Egypt," *Economic History Review*, 36 (1983), 47–67.

13 ART AND ARCHITECTURE IN THE MEDIEVAL PERIOD

Abu-Lughod, J. L., *Cairo: 1001 Years of the City Victorious* (Princeton, 1971).

Abū Ṣāliḥ al-Armanī, *The Churches and Monasteries of Egypt and Some Neighboring Countries attributed to Abū Ṣāliḥ, The Armenian* ed. and trans. B. T. A. Evetts and A. J. Butler (Oxford, 1895).

Allan, James W., "Sha'bān, Barqūq, and the Decline of the Mamlūk Metalworking Industry," *Muqarnas*, 2 (1984), 85–94.

Al Sayyad, Nezar, "Bayn al-Qasrayn: The Street Between the Two Palaces," in Zeynap Çelik, Diane Favro, and Richard Ingersoll (eds.), *Streets: Critical Perspectives on Public Space*, (Berkeley and Los Angeles, 1994).

Amin, M. M. and Laila ʿAli Ibrahim, *Architectural Terms in Mamlūk Documents* (Cairo, 1990).

Anawati, G., "Arabization and Islamization," in Michael Gervers and Ramzi Jibran Bikhazi (eds.), *Conversion and Continuity, Indigenous Christian Communities in Islamic Lands: Eighth to Eighteenth Centuries* (Toronto, 1990).

Anderson, Robert and Ibrahim Fawzy (eds.), *Egypt Revealed* (Cairo, 1987).

Atıl, E., *Renaissance of Islam: Art of the Mamlūks* (Washington, DC, 1981).

Ayalon, David "The Muslim City and the Mamlūk Military Aristocracy," *Proceedings of the Israel Academy of Sciences and Humanities*, 2 (1968), 311–29.

Bacharach, Jere L., "Administrative Complexes, Palaces, and Citadels: Changes in the Loci of Muslim Rule," in Irene A. Bierman, Rifa'at A. Abou-El-Haj, and Donald Preziosi (eds.), *The Ottoman City and Its Parts* (New Rochelle, 1991).

Behrens-Abouseif, D., "The Citadel of Cairo," *Annales Islamologiques*, 24 (1988), 127–46.

Ben-Sasson, Menahem, "The Medieval Period," in Phyllis Lambert (ed.), *Fortifications and the Synagogue: The Fortress of Babylon and the Ben Ezra Synagogue, Cairo* (London, 1994).

Bierman, Irene A., "Inscribing the City: Fāṭimid Cairo," in *Islamische Textilkunst des Mittelalters: Aktuelle Probleme* (Riggisberg, 1997).

"Medieval Flatweaves in the Urban Middle East," in C. Cootner (ed.), *Flat Weaves, The Arthur D. Jenkins Collection* (Washington, DC, 1981), 161–67.

"Urban Memory and the Preservation of Monuments," in Jere L. Bacharach (ed.), *The Restoration and Conservation of Islamic Monuments in Egypt* (Cairo, 1995), 1–12.

Writing Signs: The Fāṭimid Public Text (Berkeley and Los Angeles, 1998).

Bierman, Irene A. and Paula Sanders, *Writing Identity in Medieval Cairo* (Los Angeles, 1995).

Bloom, Jonathan M. "The Fāṭimids (909–1171), Their Ideology and Their Art," in *Islamische Textilkunst des Mittelalters: Aktuelle Probleme* (Riggisberg, 1997), 15–26.

"The Mosque of al-Ḥākim in Cairo," *Muqarnas*, 1 (1983), 15–36.

"The Mosque of the Qarāfa in Cairo," *Muqarnas*, 4 (1987), 7–20.

"The Origins of Fāṭimid Art," *Muqarnas*, 3 (1985), 30–38.

Du Bourguet, P., *Les Coptes* (Paris, 1988).

Brown, Peter, "Christianity and Local Culture in Late Roman Africa," *Journal of Roman Studies*, 58 (1968), 85–95.

Bulliet, R., *Conversion to Islam in the Medieval Period, An Essay in Quantitative History* (Cambridge, MA, and London, 1979).

Canard, M., "Fāṭimids," *EI2*, II.

"La procession du nouvel an," *Annales de l'Institut d'Études Orientales, Université d'Alger*, 13 (1955).
Comité de conservation des monuments de l'art arabe:
Exercise (Cairo), 1 February 1882, 22.
Exercise (Cairo), no. 34 (19 March 1889), 20–7.
Exercise (Cairo), 78th rapport, 1890, 41–2.
Creswell, K. A. C. "A Brief Chronology of the Muhammadan Monuments of Egypt to 1517," *BIFAO*, 16 (1919), 39–164.
Early Muslim Architecture, 2 vols, 3 pts. Oxford, 1932–40; New York: Hacker Art Books, 1979.
The Muslim Architecture of Egypt, 2 vols. (Oxford, 1952 and 1959; New York, 1978).
A Short Account of Early Muslim Architecture. Revised and supplemented by James W. Allen (Aldershot, 1989).
Denoix, Sylvie. *Décrire Le Caire: Fusṭāṭ-Miṣr d'après Ibn Duqmāq et Maqrīzī: l'histoire d'une partie de la ville du Caire d'après deux historiens égyptiens des XIVe–XVe siècles* (Cairo, 1992).
Déscription de l'Égypte. Köln: Benedikt Tashen, 1994.
Dickie, James, "Allah and Eternity: Mosques, Madrasas and Tombs," in G. Mitchell (ed.), *Architecture of the Islamic World, Its History and Social Meaning* (London, 1978), 15–47.
Dols, Michael W. *The Black Death in the Middle East* (Princeton, 1977).
Ettinghuasen, Richard, and Oleg Grabar, *The Art and Architecture of Islam, 650–1250*. New York, 1987).
Fahmy, A. R. "The Earliest Islamic Rugs in Egypt," *Bulletin of the Faculty of Arts, University of Cairo*, 22 (1960), 101–21.
Fehervari, Geza, *Islamic Pottery* (London, 1973).
Frishman, Martin and Hassan-Uddin Khan (eds.) *The Mosque* (London, 1994).
Gabra, Gawdat, *Cairo the Coptic Museum & Old Churches* (Dokki, 1993).
Gabriele, Francesco and Umberto Scerrato, *Gli Arabi in Italia*, (Milan, 1979).
Garcin, J.-C. (ed.), *États, sociétés et cultures du monde musulman médiéval, X^e^–XVe siècles* (Paris, 1992).
"Remarques sur un plan topographique de la grande mosquée de Qūṣ," *Annales Islamologiques*, 9 (1970), 97–108.
Un Centre Musulman de la Haute-Égypte Médiévale: Qūṣ (Cairo, 1976).
Gayraud, Roland-Pierre, "Iṣṭabl ʿAntar," *Annales Islamologiques*, 25–30, 1991–96.
German Institute of Archaeology, *Mausoleum of Sultan as-Saleh Nagm ad-Din Ayyub* (Cairo, 1993).
Goitein, S. D., "Cairo: An Islamic City in the Light of the Geniza Documents," in Ira M. Lapidus (ed.), *Middle Eastern Cities* (Berkeley and Los Angeles, 1969), 80–96.
A Mediterranean Society: The Jewish Communities of the Arab World as Portrayed in the Documents of the Cairo Geniza, 6 vols. (Berkeley, 1967–94) (bibliography and indices in vol. 6).

Guest, A. R., "The Foundation of Fusṭāṭ," *JRAS*, January 1907.

Hampikian, Nairy, *Armenian Presence in Cairo and Alexandria* (forthcoming).

"Restoration of the Mausoleum of al-Salih Najm al-Din Ayyub," in Jere L. Bacharach (ed.), *The Restoration and Conservation of Islamic Monuments in Egypt* (Cairo, 1995), 46–59.

Hanna, Nelly, *An Urban History of Būlāq in the Mamlūk and Ottoman Periods* (Cairo, 1983).

Hasan, Zaky Muhammad, *Les Tulunids: Étude de l'Égypte Musulmane à la fin du IXème siècle 868–905* (Paris, 1933).

Hawary, Hassan and Hussein Rached, *Catalogue Général du Musée Arabe du Caire: Stèles Funéraires*, 2 vols. (Cairo, 1932).

Humbert, Jean-Marcel, Michael Pantazzi and Christiane Ziegler, *Egyptomania: Egypt in Western Art, 1730–1930* (Ottawa, 1994).

Humphreys, R. Stephen, "The Expressive Intent of Mamlūk Architecture in Cairo: A Preliminary Essay," *SI*, 35 (1972), 69–119.

Hunt, Lucy-Anne, "Churches of Old Cairo and Mosques of al-Qahira: A Case of Christian-Muslim Interchange," *Medieval Encounters*, 21 (1996), 43–50.

Ibn Duqmāq, *Kitāb al-Intiṣār li-Wāsiṭat ʿIqd al-Amṣār*, IV, V, ed. K. Vollers (Cairo, 1893; reprinted Beirut, n.d.).

Ibn Khaldūn, *The Muqaddimah*, trans. Franz Rosenthal, 3 vols., Bolligen Series XLIII (New York, 1958).

Ibrahim, Laila ʿAli, "Residential Architecture in Mamlūk Cairo," *Muqarnas*, 2 (1984), 47–59.

Ibrahim, Laila ʿAli and ʿAdil Yasin, "A Tulunid Hammam in Old Cairo," *Islamic Archaeological Studies: Museum of Islamic Art, Cairo*, 3 (1988), 35–78.

Ibrahim, Laila ʿAli and J. M. Rogers, "The Great Hanqah of the Emir Qawsun in Cairo," *Mitteilungen des Deutschen Archäologischen Instituts, Abteilung Kairo*, 30, 1 (1974), 37–64.

James, David, *Qur'āns of the Mamlūks* (London, 1988).

"Some Observations on the Calligrapher and Illuminators of the Qur'an of Rukn al-Din Baybars al-Jashangir," *Muqarnas*, 2 (1984), 147–57.

Jenkins, M, "Muslim: An Early Fāṭimid Ceramist," *Bulletin of the Metropolitan Museum of Art* (May 1968), 359–69.

"Saʿd: Content and Context," in Priscilla P. Soucek (ed.), *Content and Context of the Visual Arts in the Islamic World* (Philadelphia and London, 1988), 359–369.

Jomier, J., *Le mahmal et la caravane égyptienne des pèlerins de La Mecque* (Cairo, 1953).

Kendrick, A. F. *Catalogue of the Muhammadan Textiles of the Medieval Period* (London, 1924).

Catalogue of Textiles from the Burying-Grounds in Egypt, 3 vols. (London, 1924).

Kuban, Dogan, "The Central Arab Lands," in Martin Frishman and Hassan-Uddin Khan (eds.), *The Mosque* (London, 1994), 77–100.

Kubiak, Wladyslaw, *Al-Fusṭāṭ: Its Foundation and Early Urban Development* (Cairo, 1982).

Kühnel, E. and L. Bellinger, *Catalogue of Dated Tiraz Fabrics: Umayyad, ʿAbbasid, Fatimid* (Washington, DC, 1952).

Lambert, Phyllis (ed.), *Fortifications and the Synagogue: The Fortress of Babylon and the Ben Ezra Synagogue, Cairo* (London, 1994).

Lane, Arthur *Early Islamic Pottery* (London, 1947).

Le Quesne, Charles, "The Synagogue," in Phyllis Lambert (ed.), *Fortifications and the Synagogue: The Fortress of Babylon and the Ben Ezra Synagogue, Cairo* (London, 1994), 79–100.

Little, Donald, "Coptic Conversion to Islam under the Baḥrī Mamlūks," *BSOAS*, 39 (1976), 564–70.

MacKenzie, N. D., *Ayyubid Cairo; A Topographical Study* (Cairo, 1992).

Mackie, Louise W., "Toward an Understanding of Mamlūk Silks: National and International Considerations," *Muqarnas*, 2 (1984), 127–46.

al-Maqrīzī, *Ittiʿāẓ al-Ḥunafāʾ bi-Akhbār al-Aʿimma al-Fāṭimiyyīn al-Khulafāʾ*, I, ed. J. al-Shayyāl (Cairo, 1967); II–III, ed. M. Hilmī M. Aḥmad (Cairo, 1971–73).

Kitāb al-mawāʿiẓ wa'l-i-ʾtibar bi-dhikr al-khiṭaṭ wa'l-athār, 2 vols. (Būlāq, 1853; reprinted, Beirut, n.d.).

Mayer, Leo A., *The Buildings of Qaytbay as Described in His Endowment Deed* (London, 1938).

Mamlūk Costume: A Survey (Geneva, 1952).

Saracenic Heraldry (Oxford, 1938).

Morony, Michael, "The Age of Conversions: A Reassessment," in Michael Gervers and Ramzi Jibran Bikhazi (eds.), *Conversion and Continuity, Indigenous Christian Communities in Islamic Lands: Eighth to Eighteenth Centuries* (Toronto, 1990).

Mubarak, Ali Basha, *al-khiṭaṭ al-jadīda al-tawfiqiyya li-miṣr wa'l-qāhira*, 20 vols. (Cairo, 1882).

O'Leary, De Lacy, *The Saints of Egypt* (Amsterdam, 1937).

Pauty, Ed. "Le Minbar de Qūṣ." in *Mélanges Maspero III Orient Islamique*, 41–53 (Cairo, 1940).

Petry, Carl F., *The Civilian Elite of Cairo in the later Middle Ages* (Princeton, 1981).

"Class Solidarity versus Gender Gain: Women as Custodians of Property in Later Medieval Egypt," in Nikki R. Keddie and Beth Baron (eds.), *Women in Middle Eastern History* (Yale, 1991), 122–142.

Philon, Helen, *Early Islamic Ceramics: Ninth to Late Twelfth Centuries* (Athens, 1980).

Rabbat, N. O. *The Citadel of Cairo: A New Interpretation of Royal Mamluk Architecture* (Leiden, 1995).

"Writing the History of Islamic Architecture in Cairo," *Design Book Review*, 31 (XXX), 48–51.

Rabie, Hassanein, "Some Financial Aspects of the Waqf System in Mamlūk

Egypt," in *The Second International Conference on Urbanism in Islam* (Tokyo, 1990), 1–24.
Raymond, André, *Le Caire* (Paris, 1993).
Reis, Piri, *Kitab-i Bahriye*, (n.p., 1554).
Sanders, Paula, "From Court Ceremony to Urban Language: Ceremonial in Fāṭimid Cairo and Fusṭāṭ," in C. E. Bosworth, Charles Issawi, Roger Savoy, and A. L. Udovitch (eds.), *The Islamic World from Classical to Modern Times* (Princeton, 1989), 311–321.
Ritual, Politics and the City in Fāṭimid Cairo (Albany, 1994).
Scanlon, George and W. Kubiak, "Excavations at Fusṭāṭ," *JARCE*, 4–21, 1965–78.
Sheehan, Peter, "The Roman Fortifications," in Phyllis Lambert (ed.), *Fortifications and the Synagogue: The Fortress of Babylon and the Ben Ezra Synagogue, Cairo* (London, 1994), 51–59.
Sokoly, Jochen A, "Between Life and Death: The Funerary Context of Tiraz Textiles," in *Islamische Textilkunst des Mittelalters: Aktuelle Probleme* (Riggisberg, 1997), 71–78.
Stowasser, K, "Manners and Customs at the Mamlūk Court," *Muqarnas*, 2 (1984), 13–20.
Taylor, Christopher Schurman, "The Cult of the Saints in Late Medieval Egypt," (Ph.D. dissertation, Princeton University, 1989).
Udovitch, A. L., "A Tale of Two Cities: Commercial Relations between Cairo and Alexandria," in *The Medieval City* (New Haven, 1977).
De Villard, Ugo Monneret, *La Necropoli Musulmana de Aswān* (Cairo, 1930).
Weill, Jean-David. *Catalogue Général du Musée Arabe du Caire: Les Bois à l'Épigraphes jusqu'à l'Époque Mamlouke* (Cairo, 1931).
Whelan, Estelle, "Representations of the Khassakiyah and the origins of Mamlūk Emblems," in Priscilla P. Soucek (ed.), *Content and Context of the Visual Arts in the Islamic World* (University Park and London, 1988), 219–43.
White, Hugh G. Evelyn, *The Monasteries of the Wadi'n Natrun*, ed. Walter Hauser, 3 parts (New York, 1926–36).
Williams, Caroline, "The Qur'anic Inscriptions on the tabut of al-Husayn in Cairo," *Islamic Art* (1987), 3–26.
Williams, J. A., "The Khanqah of Siryaqus: A Mamlūk Royal Religious Foundation," in *In Quest of an Islamic Humanism: Studies in Memory of Mohamed al-Nowaihi* (Cairo, 1984).
"Urbanization and Monuments Construction in Mamlūk Cairo," *Muqarnas*, 2 (1984), 33–45.

14 CULTURE AND SOCIETY DURING THE LATE MIDDLE AGES

ʿAbd ar-Rāziq, Aḥmad, "Un document concernant le mariage des esclaves au temps des Mamlūks," *Journal of the Economic and Social History of the Orient*, 13 (1970), 309–14.

La femme au temps des mamlouks en Égypte (Cairo, 1973).

"La *ḥisba* et le *muḥtasib* en Égypte au temps des Mamlouks," *AI*, 13 (1977), 115–78.

"Les *muḥtasibs* de Fosṭāṭ au temps des Mamlūks," *AI*, 14 (1978), 127–46.

Allouche, Adel, *Mamlūk Economics: A Study and Translation of al-Maqrīzī's Ighāthat* (Salt Lake City, 1994).

Amīn, Muḥammad M., *al-Awqāf wa'l-ḥayāt al-ijtimā'iyya fī miṣr* (Cairo, 1980).

Ashtor, Eliyahu, "The Kārimī Merchants," *JRAS* (1956), 45–56.

The Medieval Near East: Social and Economic History (London, 1978).

A Social and Economic History of the Near East in the Middle Ages (Berkeley, 1976).

Ayalon, David, *Islam and the Abode of War* (London, 1994).

The Mamlūk Military Society (London, 1979).

Outsiders in the Lands of Islam: Mamlūks, Mongols and Eunuchs (London, 1988).

Badawi, M. M. "Medieval Arabic Drama: Ibn Dāniyāl," *Journal of Arabic Literature*, 13 (1982), 83–107.

Behrens-Abouseif, Doris, *Azbakiyya and Its Environs: From Azbak to Ismā'īl, 1476–1879* (Cairo, 1985).

"Change in Form and Function of Mamlūk Religious Architecture," *AI*, 21 (1985), 73–93.

"The Citadel of Cairo: Stage for Mamlūk Ceremonial," *AI*, 24 (1988), 25–79.

"The North-Eastern Extension of Cairo under the Mamlūks," *AI*, 17 (1981), 157–89.

Berkey, Jonathan, P., "'Silver Threads Among the Coal': A Well-Educated Mamlūk of the Ninth/Fifteenth Century," *SI*, 73 (1991), 109–25.

"Tradition, Innovation, and the Social Construction of Knowledge in the Medieval Islamic Near East," *Past & Present*, 146 (1995), 38–65.

The Transmission of Knowledge in Medieval Cairo: A Social History of Islamic Education (Princeton, 1992).

"Women and Education in the Mamlūk Period," in Nikki R. Keddie and Beth Baron (eds.), *Women in Middle Eastern History: Shifting Boundaries in Sex and Gender* (New Haven, 1991), 143–57.

Bodrogligeti, A., "Notes on the Turkish Literature at the Mameluke Court," *Acta Orientalia Academiae Scientarum Hungaricae* (Budapest), 14 (1962), 273–82.

Brinner, William, "The Significance of the Ḥarāfīsh and their 'Sultan'," *JESHO*, 6 (1963), 190–215.

Cook, Michael A., "Pharaonic History in Medieval Egypt," *SI*, 57 (1983), 67–103.

Creswell, K. A. C., *The Muslim Architecture of Egypt*, 2 vols. (Cairo, 1952).

Darrağ, Ahmad, *L'Égypte sous le règne de Barsbay, 825–841/1422–1438* (Damascus, 1961).

Dols, Michael, *The Black Death in the Middle East* (Princeton, 1977).

Escovitz, Joseph, "The Establishment of Four Chief Judgeships in the Mamlūk Empire," *JAOS*, 102 (1982), 529–31.

The Office of Qāḍī al-Quḍāt in Cairo under the Baḥrī Mamlūks (Berlin, 1984).
Fernandes, Leonor, *The Evolution of a Sufi Institution in Mamlūk Egypt: The Khanqah* (Berlin, 1988).
"The Foundation of Baybars al-Jashnakir: Its Waqf, History, and Architecture," *Muqarnas*, 4 (1987), 21–42.
"Mamlūk Politics and Education: The Evidence from Two Fourteenth Century Waqifiyyas," *AI*, 23 (1987), 87–98.
"Some Aspects of the *Zāwiya* in Egypt at the Eve of the Ottoman Conquest," *AI*, 19 (1983), 9–17.
"Three Ṣufī Foundations in a 15th Century *Waqfiyya*," *AI*, 17 (1981), 141–56.
"The *Zāwiya* in Cairo," *AI*, 18 (1982), 116–21.
Fischel, Walter J., *Ibn Khaldūn in Egypt: His Public Functions and His Historical Research (1382–1406): A Study in Islamic Historiography* (Berkeley, 1967).
"The Spice Trade in Mamlūk Egypt: A Contribution to the Economic History of Medieval Islam," *JESHO*, 1 (1958), 157–74.
Flemming, Barbara, "Literary Activities in Mamlūk Halls and Barracks," in Myriam Rosen-Ayalon (ed.), *Studies in Memory of Gaston Wiet* (Jerusalem, 1977), 249–60.
Garcin, Jean-Claude, "Le Caire et la province: Constructions au Caire et a Qūṣ sous les Mameluks Baḥrides," *AI*, 8 (1969), 47–62.
Un centre musulman de la Haute-Égypte médiévale: Qūṣ (Cairo, 1976).
"Deux saints populaires du Caire au début du XVIe siècle," *BEO* 29 (1977), 131–43.
"Histoire et hagiographie de l'Égypte musulmane à la fin de l'époque mamelouke et au début de l'époque ottomane," in *Hommages à la mémoire de Serge Sauneron*, vol. 2: *Égypte post-pharaonique* (Cairo: 1979), 287–316.
"Histoire, opposition politique et piétisme traditionaliste dans le *Ḥusn al-Muḥāḍarat* de Suyūṭī," *AI* 7 (1967), 33–89.
"The Mamlūk Military System and the Blocking of Medieval Moslem Society," in Jean Baechler, John A. Hall and Michael Mann (eds.), *Europe and the Rise of Capitalism* (Oxford, 1988), 113–30.
"Le Sultan et pharaon (le politique et le religieux dans l'Égypte mamluke)," *Hommages à François Daumas* (Montpellier, 1986), I, 261–72.
Garcin, Jean-Claude et al., *Palais et maisons du Caire, I: Époque mamelouke (XIIIe–XVIe siècles)* (Paris, 1982).
Goitein, S. D., "Cairo: An Islamic City in the Light of the Geniza Documents," in Ira M. Lapidus (ed.), *Middle Eastern Cities* (Berkeley, 1969), 80–95.
A Mediterranean Society: The Jewish Communities of the Arab World As Portrayed in the Documents of the Cairo Geniza, 6 vols. (Berkeley, 1967–93).
"New Light on the Beginnings of the Kārimī Merchants," *JESHO*, 1 (1958), 175–84.

Grabar, Oleg, "Reflections on Mamlūk Art," *Muqarnas*, 2 (1984), 1–12.
Haarmann, Ulrich, "Arabic in Speech, Turkish in Lineage: Mamlūks and their Sons in the Intellectual Life of Fourteenth-Century Egypt," *Journal of Semitic Studies*, 33 (1988), 81–114.
"Ideology and History, Identity and Alterity: The Arab Image of the Turks from the ʿAbbasids to Modern Egypt," *IJMES*, 20 (1988), 175–96.
"Rather the Injustice of the Turks than the Righteousness of the Arabs – Changing ʿUlamāʾ Attitudes towards Mamlūk Rule in the Late Fifteenth Century," *SI*, 68 (1988), 61–77.
Hanna, Nelly, *An Urban History of Būlāq in the Mamlūk and Ottoman Periods* (Supplement aux *Annales islamologiques* no. 3) (Cairo, 1983).
Harīdī, A. A., *Index des Khitat* (Cairo, 1983: I: proper names; II: varied indices; 1984: III: place names).
Homerin, T. Emil, *From Arab Poet to Muslim Saint: Ibn al-Fāriḍ, His Verse, and His Shrine* (Columbia, SC, 1994).
Humphreys, R. Stephen, "The Expressive Intent of the Mamlūk Architecture of Cairo: A Preliminary Essay," *SI*, 35 (1972), 69–119.
Ibrahim, Laila A., "Middle-Class Living Units in Mamlūk Cairo: Architecture and Terminology," *Art and Archeology Research Papers*, 14 (1978), 24–30.
"Residential Architecture in Mamlūk Cairo," *Muqarnas*, 2 (1984), 47–59.
Al-Jammāl, Aḥmad Ṣādiq, *al-Adab al-ʿāmmī fī miṣr fiʾl-aṣr al-mamlūkī* (Cairo, 1966).
Kahle, Paul, "The Arabic Shadow Play in Egypt," *JRAS* (1940), 21–34.
(ed.), *Three Shadow Plays by Muḥammad Ibn Dāniyāl*, prepared for publication by Derek Hopwood and Mustafa Badawi (E. J. W. Gibb Memorial, new series no. 32) (Cambridge, 1992).
King, David A., "The Astronomy of the Mamlūks," *Isis*, 74 (1983), 531–55.
"The Astronomy of the Mamlūks: A Brief Overview," *Muqarnas: An Annual on Islamic Art and Architecture*, 2 (1984), 73–84.
Laoust, Henri, *Essai sur les doctrines sociales et politiques de Taḳī-d-Dīn Aḥmad ibn Taimīya* (Cairo, 1939).
"Le hanbalisme sous les Mamlouks bahrides (658–784/1260–1382)," *REI*, 28 (1960), 1–71.
Lapidus, Ira, "Ayyubid Religious Policy and the Development of Schools of Law in Cairo," in André Raymond et al. (eds.), *Colloque international sur l'histoire du Caire* (Cairo, 1969), 279–86.
"The Grain Economy of Mamlūk Egypt," *JESHO*, 12 (1969), 1–15.
"Mamlūk Patronage and the Arts in Egypt: Concluding Remarks," *Muqarnas: An Annual on Islamic Art and Architecture*, 2 (1984), 173–81.
Muslim Cities in the Later Middle Ages (Cambridge, MA, 1967).
Leiser, Gary, L., "Ḥanbalism in Egypt before the Mamlūks," *SI*, 54 (1981), 155–81.
"The Madrasa and the Islamization of the Middle East: The Case of Egypt," *JARCE*, 22 (1985), 29–47.
"Notes on the Madrasa in Medieval Islamic Society," *The Muslim World*, 76 (1986), 16–23.

Little, Donald P., "Coptic Conversion to Islam under the Baḥrī Mamlūks, 692–755/1293–1354," *BSOAS*, 39 (1976), 552–69.

"Coptic Converts to Islam During the Baḥrī Mamlūk Period," in Michael Gervers and Ramzi Jibran Bikhazi (eds.), *Conversion and Continuity: Indigenous Christian Communities in Islamic Lands, Eighth to Eighteenth Centuries* (Toronto, 1990), 263–88.

"Did Ibn Taymiyya Have a Screw Loose?" *SI*, 41 (1975), 93–111.

"The Historical and Historiographical Significance of the Detention of Ibn Taymiyya," *IJMES*, 4 (1973), 311–27.

"Notes on Aitamiš, a Mongol Mamlūk," in Ulrich Haarmann and Peter Bachmann (ed.), *Die islamische Welt zwischen Mittelalter und Neuzeit. Festschift für Hans Robert Roemer zum 65. Geburtstag* (Beiruter Texte und Studien, 22) (Wiesbaden, 1979), 387–401.

"Religion under the Mamlūks," *MW*, 73 (1983), 165–81.

Lutfi, Huda, "Manners and Customs of Fourteenth-Century Cairene Women: Female Anarchy versus Male Sharʿi Order in Muslim Prescriptive Treatises," in Nikki R. Keddie and Beth Baron (eds.), *Women in Middle Eastern History: Shifting Boundaries in Sex and Gender* (New Haven, 1991), 99–121.

"Al-Sakhāwī's *Kitāb al-Nisā*ʾ as a Source for the Social and Economic History of Muslim Women during the Fifteenth Century AD," *MW*, 71 (1981), 104–24.

Makdisi, George, "Ibn Taymīya: A Ṣūfī of the Qādiriyya Order," *American Journal of Arabic Studies*, 1 (1973), 118–29.

Malti-Douglas, Fedwa, "*Mentalités* and Marginality: Blindness and Mamlūk Civilization," in C. E. Bosworth et al. (eds.), *The Islamic World from Classical to Modern Times: Essays in Honor of Bernard Lewis* (Princeton, 1989), 211–38.

Martel-Thoumian, Bernadette, *Les civils et l'administration dans l'état militaire mamlūk (IXe/XVe siècle)* (Damascus, 1991).

Mayer, L. A., *Mamlūk Costume* (Geneva, 1952).

Memon, Muhammad Umar, *Ibn Taimīya's Struggle against Popular Religion; with an Annotated Translation of his 'Kitāb Iqtiḍāʾ aṣ-Ṣirāt al-Mustaqīm Mukhālafat Aṣḥāb al-Jahīm'* (The Hague, 1976).

Nielsen, Jorgen S., *Secular Justice in an Islamic State: Maẓālim under the Baḥrī Mamlūks 662/1264–789/1387* (Leiden, 1987).

"Sultan al-Ẓāhir Baybars and the Appointment of Four Chief Qāḍīs (663/1265)," *SI*, 60 (1984), 167–76.

Nwiya, Paul, *Ibn ʿAṭāʾ Allāh (m. 709/1309) et la naissance de la confrérie šadilite* (Beirut, 1972).

Petry, Carl, *The Civilian Elite of Cairo in the Later Middle Ages* (Princeton, 1981).

"Class Solidarity versus Gender Gain: Women as Custodians of Property in Later Medieval Egypt," in Nikki R. Keddie and Beth Baron (eds.), *Women in Middle Eastern History: Shifting Boundaries in Sex and Gender* (New Haven, 1991), 122–42.

"A Paradox of Patronage," *MW*, 73 (1983), 182–207.

Protectors or Praetorians? The Last Mamlūk Sultans and Egypt's Waning as a Great Power (Albany, 1994).
"Scholastic Stasis in Medieval Islam Reconsidered: Mamlūk Patronage in Cairo," *Poetics Today*, 14 (1993), 323–48.
"Travel Patterns of Medieval Notables in the Near East," *SI*, 62 (1985), 53–87.
Poliak, A. N., "Les revoltes populaires en Égypte à l'époque des Mamelouks et leur causes économiques," *REI*, 8 (1934), 251–73.
Raymond, André, "Cairo's Area and Population in the Early Fifteenth Century," *Muqarnas: An Annual on Islamic Art and Architecture*, 2 (1984), 21–31.
"Les porteurs d'eau," *BIFAO*, (1958), 183–202.
Raymond, André and Gaston Wiet, *Les marchés du Caire: Traduction annotée du texte de Maqrīzī* (Cairo, 1979).
Richards, D. S., "The Coptic Bureaucracy under the Mamlūks," *Colloque international sur l'histoire du Caire, 27 mars–5 avril 1969* (Cairo, 1969), 373–81.
Russell, J. C., "The Population of Medieval Egypt," *JARCE*, 5 (1966), 69–82.
Saleh, Abdel Hamid, "Quelques remarques sur les Bédouins d'Égypte au Moyen Age," *SI*, 48 (1978), 45–70.
"Les relations entre les Mamlūks et les Bédouins d'Égypte," *Annali: Istituto Orientale di Napoli*, 40 (1980), 365–93.
Sartain, Elizabeth M., *Jalāl al-Dīn al-Suyūṭī*, 2 vols. (Cambridge, 1975).
Shoshan, Boaz, "Grain Riots and the 'Moral Economy': Cairo, 1350–1517," *Journal of Interdisciplinary History* 10 (1979–80), 459–78.
Popular Culture in Medieval Cairo (Cambridge, 1993).
Staffa, Susan Jane, *Conquest and Fusion: The Social Evolution of Cairo,* AD *642–1850* (Leiden, 1977).
Stowasser, Karl, "Manners and Customs at the Mamlūk Court," *Muqarnas*, 2 (1984), 13–20.
Sublet, Jacqueline, "'Abd al-Laṭīf al-Takrītī et la famille des Banū Kuwayk, marchands Kārimī," *Arabica*, 9 (1962), 193–96.
Taylor, Christopher S., "The Cult of the Saints in Late Medieval Egypt," (Ph.D. dissertation, Princeton University, 1989).
"Sacred History and the Cult of the Muslim Saints in Late Medieval Egypt," *MW*, 80 (1990), 72–80.
Trimingham, J. Spencer, *The Sufi Orders in Islam* (Oxford, 1971).
Tucker, William F., "Natural Disasters and the Peasantry in Mamlūk Egypt," *JESHO*, 24 (1981), 215–24.
Udovitch, A. L., Robert Lopez and Harry Miskimin, "England to Egypt, 1350–1500: Long-term Trends and Long-distance Trade," in M. A. Cook (ed.), *Studies in the Economic History of the Middle East* (London, 1970), 93–128.
Wiet, Gaston, "Les marchands d'épices sous les sultans mamlouks," *Cahiers d'histoire égyptienne*, 7 (1955), 81–147.
Williams, John A., "Urbanization and Monument Construction in Mamlūk Cairo," *Muqarnas*, 2 (1984), 33–45.

Winter, Michael, *Society and Religion in Early Ottoman Egypt: Studies in the Writings of ʿAbd al-Wahhāb al-Shaʿrānī* (New Brunswick, NJ, 1982).

15 HISTORIOGRAPHY OF THE AYYŪBID AND MAMLŪK EPOCHS

Primary sources

Abū al-Fidāʾ, "Autobiographie d'Abou ʿl-Fedâ extraite de sa chronique," trans. W. MacGuckin de Slane, *Recueil des historiens des croisades: Historiens orientaux*, I (Paris, 1872), 166–86.

The Memoirs of a Syrian Prince, Abu'l Fidāʾ, Sultan of Ḥamāh (672–732/1273–1331), Translated with an Introduction by P. M. Holt, Freiburger Islamstudien, Band IX, 1983.

Al-Mukhtaṣar fī Taʾrīkh al-Bashar (Cairo, 1907–08).

"Résumé de l'histoire des croisades tiré des annales d'Abou ʿl-Fedâ," ed. and trans. W. MacGuckin de Slane, *Historiens orientaux*, I (Paris, 1872), 2–165.

Abū Shāma, *Kitāb al-Rawḍatayn fī Akhbār al-Dawlatayn*, 1st edn., 2 vols. (Cairo, 1871–75); 2nd edn. H. Aḥmad and M. M. Ziyāda, 2 vols. (Cairo, 1956, 1962); French trans. A.-C. Barbier de Meynard, "Abou Chamah, Le livre des deux jardins, Histoire de deux règnes. Celui de Nour ed-Dīn et celui de Salah ed-Dīn," *Historiens orientaux*, IV–V (Paris, 1898, 1906), 3–210.

Al-ʿAynī, *ʿIqd al-Juman fī Taʾrīkh Ahl al-Zamān*, ed. ʿAbd al-Rāziq al-Ṭanṭāwī al-Qarmūṭ (Cairo, 1989).

ʿIqd al-Jumān fī Taʾrīkh Ahl al-Zamān, ed. Muḥammad Muḥammad Amīn, 4 vols. to date (Cairo, 1987–92).

Baybars al-Manṣūrī, *Kitāb al-Tuḥfa al-Mulūkiyya fī al-Dawla al-Turkiyya*, ed. ʿAbd al-Ḥamīd Ṣāliḥ Ḥamdān (Cairo, 1987).

Zubdat al-Fikra fī Taʾrīkh al-Hijra, MS British Museum, Ar. 1233. Cf. Elham, *Kitbughā*, under "Secondary sources," below.

Al-Birzālī, *al-Muqtafā li-Taʾrīkh al-Shaykh Shihāb al-Dīn Abī Shāma*, MS Topkapi Ahmet III 2591.

Al-Dhahabī, *Kitāb Duwal al-Islām fī al-Taʾrīkh*, 2 vols (Hyderabad, 1944–45).

Ibn ʿAbd al-Ẓāhir, *Baybars I of Egypt*, ed. and trans. Fatima Sadeque (Dacca, 1956).

Al-Rawḍ al-Zāhir fī Sīrat al-Malik al-Ẓāhir, ed. ʿAbd al-ʿAzīz al-Khuwayṭir (Riyadh, 1976).

Tashrīf al-Ayyām wa-al-ʿUṣūr fī Sīrat al-Malik al-Manṣūr (al-Manṣūr Qalāwūn, 678–689 AH), ed. Murād Kāmil (Cairo, 1961).

Ur ʿAbd Allāh b. ʿAbd eẓ-Ẓāhir's biografi över Sultanen el-Melik el-Ašraf Ḫalīl. Arabisk täxt med översättning, inledning ock anmärkningar utjiven, ed. and trans. Axel Moberg (Lund, 1902).

Ibn al-Athīr, *Al-Bāhir fī Taʾrīkh Atābakāt al-Mawṣil*, ed. A. A. Tulaymāt (Cairo, 1963).

Extrait de la chronique intitulée Kamel-Altevarykh par Ibn-Alatyr, ed. and trans. J. T. Renaud and C. F. Defrémy, *Historiens orientaux*, I (Paris, 1872), 189–744, II (Paris, 1876), 3–180.

Histoire des Atabecs de Mosul par Ibn el-Athīr, ed. and trans. W. MacGuckin de Slane, *Historiens orientaux*, II deuxième partie (Paris, 1876), 5–375.

Al-Kāmil fī al-Ta'rīkh, VIII: 295–369 H, XI, XII, ed. C. J. Tornberg (Leiden, 1867–76; reprinted Beirut, 1965–67).

Ibn al-Dawādārī, *Die Chronik des Ibn ad-Dawādārī, Achter Teil, Der Bericht über die frühen Mamluken*, ed. Ulrich Haarmann, Deutsches Archäologisches Institut Kairo Quellen zur Geschichte des islamischen Ägyptens 1h (Freiburg, 1971).

Die Chronik des Ibn ad-Dawādārī, Neunter Teil, Der Bericht über den Sultan al-Malik an-Nāṣir Muḥammad Ibn Qala'un, ed. Hans Robert Roemer, Deutsches Archäologisches Institut Kairo Quellen zur Geschichte des islamischen Ägyptens 1i (Cairo, 1960).

Ibn al-Furāt, *Ayyubids, Mamlukes and Crusaders: Selections from the Tarikh al-Duwal wa'l-Muluk of Ibn al-Furat*, ed. and trans. U. and M. C. Lyons and J. Riley-Smith, 2 vols. (Cambridge, 1971).

Ta'rīkh Ibn al-Furāt, ed. Costi K. Zurayk and Nejla Izzedin, 4 vols. (4, 7, 8, 9) (Beirut, 1936–42).

Ibn Ḥajar al-ʿAsqalānī, *al-Durar al-Kāmina fī Aʿyān al-Mi'a al-Thāmina*, ed. Muḥammad Jādd al-Ḥaqq, 5 vols. (Cairo, 1966).

Inbā' al-Ghumr bi-Abnā' al-ʿUmr fī al-Ta'rīkh, 7 vols. (Hyderabad, 1976).

Ibn Iyās, *An Account of the Ottoman Conquest of Egypt in the Year* AH 922 (AD *1516)*, trans. W. H. Salmon (London, 1921).

Badā'iʿ al-Zuhūr fī Waqā'iʿ al-Duhūr, 5 vols., ed. M. Muṣṭafā (Cairo, 1960–75); French trans. vols. III–V, G. Wiet *Histoire des mamelouks circassiens* (Cairo, 1945); *Journal d'un bourgeois du Caire*, 2 vols. (Paris, 1955, 1960).

Unpublished Pages of the Chronicle of Ibn Iyās, AH 857–872/AD 1453–1468, ed. M. Muṣṭafā, Royal Society of Historial Studies (Cairo, 1951).

Ibn Kathīr, *al-Bidāya wa-al-Nihāya fī al-Ta'rīkh*, 14 vols. (Cairo, 1932–39).

Ibn Khaldūn, *Kitāb al-ʿIbar wa-Dīwān al-Mubtada' wa-al-Khabar fī Ayyām al-ʿArab wa-al-Barbar*, ed. Shaykh Naṣr al-Hārūnī, 7 vols. (Cairo, 1867–68).

The Muqaddimah: An Introduction to History, trans. Franz Rosenthal, Bollingen Series 43 (New York, 1958).

Al-Taʿrīf bi-Ibn Khaldūn wa-Riḥlatuhu Gharban wa-Sharqan, ed. Muḥammad al-Ṭanjī (Cairo, 1951).

Ibn Khallikān, *Ibn Khallikān's Biographical Dictionary Translated from the Arabic by Baron MacGuckin de Slane*, 4 vols. (Paris and London, 1843–71).

Wafāyāt al-Aʿyān fī Anbā' al-Zamān, ed. Ihsan Abbas, 8 vols. (Beirut, 1972).

Ibn Mammātī, *Qawānīn al-Dawāwīn*, ed. A. S. Atiya (Cairo, 1943).

Ibn Shaddād, Bahā' al-Dīn, "Anecdotes et beaux traits de la vie du Sultan Youssof (Salâh ed-Dîn)," ed. and trans. W. MacGuckin de Slane, *Historiens orientaux*, III (Paris, 1884), 3–374.

al-Nawādir al-Sulṭāniyya: Sīrat Ṣīlāḥ al-Dīn, ed. Jamāl al-Dīn al-Shayyāl (Cairo, 1964).

Ibn Shaddād al-Ḥalabī, *Die Geschichte des Sultans Baibars von 'Izz ad-dīn Muḥammad b. 'Alī b. Ibrāhīm b. Šaddād (st. 684/1285)*, ed. Aḥmad Ḥuṭayṭ, Bibliotheca Islamica 31 (Wiesbaden, 1983).

Ibn Taghrī Birdī, Abū al-Maḥāsin, *Al-Nujūm al-Zāhira fī Mulūk Miṣr wa-al-Qāhira*, partial edn. ed. W. Popper, University of California Publications in Semitic Philology, II–III, V–VII (Berkeley, 1909–60); English trans. W. Popper, *History of Egypt, 1382–1469*, same series, XIII–XIV, XVII, XIX, XX–XXIV (Berkeley, 1954–63); complete edn., 16 vols. (Cairo, 1929–72).

Les biographies du Manhal Ṣāfī, French summary by Gaston Wiet, Mémoires présentés à l'Institut d'Égypte 19 (Cairo, 1932).

Extracts from Abu'l Maḥāsin ibn Taghrī Birdī's Ḥawādith al-Duhūr, ed. W. Popper, University of California Publications in Semitic Philology, 8 (Berkeley, 1930–42).

Al-Manhal al-Ṣāfī wa-al-Mustawfī ba'd al-Wāfī, 1 vol. (Cairo, 1956).

Al-Manhal al-Ṣāfī wa-al-Mustawfī ba'd al-Wāfī, ed. Muḥammad Muḥammad Amīn et al., 4 vols. to date (Cairo, 1984–86).

Ibn Wāṣil, *Mufarrij al-Kurūb fī Akhbār Banī Ayyūb*, ed. J. al-Shayyāl, S. A. 'Āshūr, and H. M. Rabī', 5 vols. to date (Cairo, 1953–77).

'Imād al-Dīn al-Kātib al-Isfahānī, *Conquête de la Syrie et de la Palestine par Saladin*, trans. Henri Massé (Paris, 1972).

Al-Fatḥ al-Qussī fī al-Fatḥ al-Qudsī, ed. Carlo de Landberg (Leiden, 1888).

Al-Juz' al-Khāmis min Kitāb al-Barq al-Shāmī: Sīrat al-Sulṭān Ṣalāḥ al-Dīn Yūsuf ibn Ayyūb, ed. Ramazan Sesen (Istanbul, 1979).

Al-Jazarī, *La Chronique de Damas d'al-Jazarī (Années 689–698 H)*, summary trans. Jean Sauvaget, Bibliothèque de l'École des Hautes Études, Sciences historiques et philologiques 394 (Paris, 1949).

Ḥawādith al-Fatra bayn sanatay 682, 687 Hijriyya kamā Dawwanahā Shams al-Dīn Muḥammad b. Ibrāhīm al-Jazarī ... (in Haarmann's Quellenstudien, below, in "Secondary sources").

Ta'rīkh al-Jazarī, Istanbul Köprülü MS 1037.

Al-Makhzūmi, *al-Minḥāj fī 'Ilm Kharāj Miṣr*, MS British Museum Add. 23, 483.

Al-Maqrīzī, *Histoire des sultans mamlouks de l'Égypte écrite en arabe par Taki-eddin-Ahmed-Makrizi*, trans. Etienne Quatremère, 2 vols. (Paris, 1837–45).

A History of the Ayyubid Sultans of Egypt, trans. R. J. C. Broadhurst (Boston, 1980).

Kitāb al-Sulūk li-Ma'rifa Duwal al-Mulūk, ed. M. M. Ziyāda and S. A. 'Āshūr, 4 vols. (Cairo, 1943–72).

al-Mawā'iẓ wa al-I'tibār bi-Dhikr al-Khiṭaṭ wa al-Āthār, 2 vols. (Cairo, 1853–54); partial edn. ed. G. Wiet, 5 vols. (Cairo, 1911–27).

Al-Mufaḍḍal ibn Abī al-Faḍā'il, *Ägypten und Syrien zwischen 1317 und 1341 in der Chronik des Mufaḍḍal ibn Abī'l-Faḍā'il*, ed. and trans. Samira Kortantamer, Islamkundliche Untersuchungen 23 (Freiburg, 1973).

Histoire des sultans mamlouks: Texte arabe publié et traduit en français, Edgar Blochet, Patrologia Orientalis XII, XIV, XX (Paris, 1919–28).

Al-Nābulusī, *Kitāb Luma' al-Qawānīn al-Muḍī'a fī Dawāwīn al-Diyār al-Miṣriyya*, ed. Carl H. Becker and Claude Cahen, *Bulletin d'Études Orientales*, 16 (1958–60), 119–34, 3–78 (Arabic).

Al-Nuwayrī, *Nihāyat al-Arab fī Funūn al-Adab*, ed. Sa'īd 'Āshūr, Fu'ād al-Sayyad et al., 33 vols. to date (Cairo, 1923–98).

Al-Qāḍī al-Fāḍil, *Beiträge zur Ayyubischen Diplomatik* (contains 38 samples of al-Qāḍī al-Fāḍil's writings), ed. and trans. Horst-Adolf Hein (Freiburg, 1968).

Al-Qalqashandī, *Beiträge zur Geschichte der Staatskanzlei im islamischen Ägypten* (summary trans. of *Ṣubḥ*), Walter Björkman (Hamburg, 1928).

Ṣubḥ al-A'shā fī Ṣinā'at al-Inshā, 14 vols. (Cairo, 1913–19); indices by M. Qindīl al-Baqlī (Cairo, 1963).

Al-Ṣafadī, *A'yān al-'Aṣr wa-A'wān al-Naṣr*, facsimile edn., 3 vols. (Frankfurt, 1990).

Das biographische Lexicon des Ṣalāḥaddīn Ḫalīl ibn Aibak aṣ-Ṣafadī, Bibliotheca Islamica, 2nd edn., ed. Hellmut Ritter et al., 22 vols. to date (Wiesbaden, 1963–93).

Al-Sakhāwī, *al-I'lān bi-Tawbīkh li-Man Dhamma Ahl al-Ta'rīkh* (Beirut, 1979).

"Al-Saḫåwî's *I'lān*," trans. Franz Rosenthal, *A History of Muslim Historiography*, 2nd edn. (Leiden, 1968), 263–529.

Shāfi' ibn 'Alī, *al-Faḍl al-Ma'thūr min Sīrat al-Malik al-Manṣūr*, MS Oxford Bodl. Marsh 424.

Kitāb Ḥusn al-Manāqib al-Sirriyya al-Muntaza'a min al-Sīra al-Ẓāhiriyya, ed. 'Abd al-'Azīz al-Khuwayṭir (Riyadh, 1976).

Al-Shujā'ī, *Die Chronik aš-Suğā'īs*, ed. and trans. Barbara Schäfer, 2 vols., Deutsches Archäologisches Institut Kairo Quellen zur Geschichte des islamischen Ägypten 2a–b (Wiesbaden, 1977–85).

Sibṭ Ibn al-Jawzī, *Mir'āt al-Zamān fī Ta'rīkh al-A'yān*, facsimile ed. J. R. Jewett (Chicago, 1907); 2nd edn. based on the above, published as 8/1 and 2 (Hyderabad, 1951–52); 3rd edn ed. J. Jalīl and M. al-Hamūndī (Baghdad, 1990); partial French trans. "Extraits du Mirāt ez-Zemān," A.-C. Barbier de Meynard, *Historiens orientaux*, III, 517–50.

Al-'Umarī, *Masālik al-Abṣār fī Mamālik al-Amṣār*, facs. edn., 27 vols. (Frankfurt, 1988–89).

Masālik al-Abṣār fī Mamālik al-Amṣār d'Ibn Faḍl Allāh al-'Umarī ...: L'Égypte, la Syrie, le-Ḥiğāz et le Yémen, ed. Ayman Fu'ād Sayyid, Textes arabes et études islamiques 23 (Cairo, 1985).

Das mongolische Weltreich: al-'Umarīs Darstellungen des mongolischen Reiches in seinen Werk Masālik al-abṣār fī mamālik al-amṣār. Mit Paraphrase und Kommentar, ed. Klaus Lech, Asiatische Forschungen 22 (Wiesbaden, 1968).

Al-Ta'rīf bi-al-Muṣṭalaḥ al-Sharīf (Cairo, 1895).

Al-'Umarī's Bericht über Anatolien aus dem Masālik al-abṣār, ed. F. Taeschner, Bd. I, Text (Leipzig, 1929).

Al-Yūnīnī, *Dhayl Mir'āt al-Zamān fī Taʿrīkh al-Aʿyān*, 4 vols. (Hyderabad, 1954–61).
Die Jahre 1287–1291 in der Chronik al-Yūnīnīs, ed. and trans. Antranig Melkonian (Freiburg, 1975).
"The Middle Bahrī Mamlūks in Medieval Syrian Historiography: The Years 1297–1302 in the *Dhayl Mir'āt al-Zamān* Attributed to Quṭb al-Dīn Mūsā al-Yūnīnī: A Critical Edition with Introduction, Annotated Translation, and Source Criticism," by Li Guo (Ph.D. dissertation, Yale University, 1994).
Al-Yūsūfī, *Nuzhat al-Nāẓir fī Sīrat al-Malik al-Naṣir*, ed. Aḥmad Ḥuṭayṭ (Beirut, 1986).

Secondary sources

Ahmad, M. Hilmy M., "Some Notes on Arabic Historiography during the Zengid and Ayyubid Periods (521/1127–648/1250)," in Bernard Lewis and P. M. Holt (eds.), *Historians of the Middle East*, Historical Writing on the Peoples of Asia (London, 1962), 79–97.
Ashtor, E., *Levant Trade in the Later Middle Ages* (Princeton, 1983).
"Some Unpublished Sources for the Baḥrī Period," *Scripta Hierosolymitana*, 9 (1961), 11–30.
Atiya, Aziz S., *The Arabic Manuscripts of Mount Sinai* (Baltimore, 1955).
Ayalon, David, "The Circassians in the Mamluk Kingdom," *JAOS*, 59 (1949), 135–47; reprinted in Ayalon, *Studies on the Mamlūks of Egypt (1250–1517)*, no. IV, London, 1977.
"The Great *Yāsa* of Chingiz Khān: A Re-examination. (C2) Al-Maqrīzī's Passage on the *Yāsa* under the Mamlūks," *Studia Islamica*, 38 (1973), 107–56; reprinted in David Ayalon, *Outsiders in the Land of Islam: Mamlūks, Mongols, and Eunuchs* (London, 1988), no. IVd.
"Mamlūk Military Aristocracy during the First Years of the Ottoman Occupation of Egypt," in C. E. Bosworth, C. Issawi, R. Savory, and A. L. Udovitch (eds.), *The Islamic World: From Classical to Modern Times* (Princeton, 1989), 413–31; reprinted in David Ayalon, *Islam and the Abode of War: Military Slaves and Islamic Adversaries* (London, 1994), no. X.
"Mamlūkiyyāt: (B) Ibn Khaldūn's View of the Mamlūk Phenomenon," *Jerusalem Studies in Arabic and Islam*, 2 (1980), 340–49; reprinted in David Ayalon, *Outsiders in the Land of Islam: Mamlūks, Mongols, and Eunuchs* (London, 1988), no. I.
"Notes on the *Furūsiyya* Exercises and Games in the Mamlūk Sultanate," *Scripta Hierosolymitana, Studies in Islamic History and Civilization*, 9 (1961), 31–62; reprinted in David Ayalon, *The Mamlūk Military Society: Collected Studies* (London, 1979), no. II.
Al-Azmeh, Aziz, *Ibn Khaldūn in Modern Scholarship: A Study in Orientalism* (London, 1981).
Berkey, Jonathan, *The Transmission of Knowledge in Medieval Cairo: A Social History of Islamic Education*, Princeton Studies on the Near East (Princeton, 1992).

Cahen, Claude, *Makhzūmiyyāt: Études sur l'histoire économique et financière de l'Égypte médiévale* (Leiden, 1977).
Elham, Shah Morad, *Kitbuġā und Lāǧīn: Studien zur Mamluken-Geschichte nach Baibars al-Manṣūrī und an-Nuwairī* (Freiburg, 1977).
Fischel, Walter J., *Ibn Khaldūn in Egypt: His Public Functions and his Historical Research: A Study in Islamic Historiography* (Berkeley and Los Angeles, 1967).
Gabrieli, Francesco (trans.), *Arab Historians of the Crusades*, The Islamic World Series (Berkeley and Los Angeles, 1969).
"The Arabic Historiography of the Crusades," in Bernard Lewis and P. M. Holt (eds.), *Historians of the Middle East* (London, 1962), 98–107.
Gibb, H. A. R., "The Achievement of Saladin," *Bulletin of the John Rylands Library*, 30 (1952), 44–60; reprinted in Gibb, *Saladin: Studies in Islamic History*, ed. Yusuf Ibish (Beirut, 1974,) 158–76.
Arabic Literature: An Introduction, 2nd (revised) edn. (Oxford, 1963).
"The Arabic Sources for the Life of Saladin," *Speculum*, 25 (1950), 58–72; reprinted in Gibb, *Saladin: Studies in Islamic History*, ed. Yusuf Ibish (Beirut, 1974), 52–75.
"Al-Barq al-Shāmī: The History of Ṣalāḥ al-Dīn by the Kātib 'Imād ad-Dīn al-Isfahānī," *Wiener Zeitschrift für die Kunde des Morgenlandes*, 52 (1953–55), 93–115; reprinted in Gibb, *Saladin: Studies in Islamic History*, ed. Yusuf Ibish (Beirut, 1974), 76–103.
The Life of Ṣalāḥ al-Dīn from the Works of 'Imād ad-Dīn and Bahā' ad-Dīn (Oxford, 1973).
Gottschalk, H. L., *Al-Malik al-Kāmil von Egypten und seine Zeit* (Wiesbaden, 1958).
Graf, Gunhild, *Die Epitome der Universalchronik Ibn ad-Dawādārīs im Verhältnis zur Langfassung: Eine quellenkritische Studie zur Geschichte der ägyptischen Mamluken*, Islamkundliche Untersuchungen 129 (Berlin, 1990).
Haarmann, Ulrich, "Alṭun Ḫān und Čingiz Ḫān bei den ägyptischen Mamluken," *Der Islam*, 51 (1974), 1–36.
"Auflösung und Bewahrung der klassichen Formen arabischer Geschichtsschreibung in der Zeit der Mamluken," *Zeitschrift der Deutschen Morgenländischen Gesellschaft*, 121 (1971), 46–60.
"L'édition de la chronique mamelouke syrienne de Shams ad-Dīn Muḥammad al-Jazarī," *Bulletin d'Études Orientales*, 27 (1974), 195–203.
Quellenstudien zur frühen Mamlukenzeit (Freiburg, 1969).
"Turkish Legends in the Popular Historiography of Medieval Egypt," *Proceedings of the VIth Congress of Arabic and Islamic Studies: Visby 13–16 August, Stockholm 17–19 August 1972* (Stockholm and Leiden, 1975), 97–107.
Halm, Heinz, "Quellen und Literatur: IV. Die Ayyubiden," in Ulrich Haarmann (ed.), *Geschichte der arabischen Welt* (Munich, 1987), 638–40.
Holt, P. M., *The Age of the Crusades: The Near East from the Eleventh Century to 1517* (London and New York, 1986).

"The Presentation of Qalāwūn by Shāfiʿ ibn ʿAlī," in C. E. Bosworth, C. Issawi, R. Savory, and A. L. Udovitch (eds.), *The Islamic World, from Classical to Modern Times* (Princeton, 1989), 141–50.

"Shams al-Shujāʿī: A Chronicler Identified?" *BSOAS*, 58 (1995), 532–34.

"Some Observations on Shāfiʿ ibn ʿAlī's Biography of Baybars," *Journal of Semitic Studies*, 29 (1984), 123–30.

"Three Biographies of al-Ẓāhir Baybars," in David O. Morgan (ed.), *Medieval Historical Writing in the Christian and Islamic Worlds* (London, 1982), 19–29.

"The Virtuous Ruler in Thirteenth-Century Mamluk Royal Biographies," *Nottingham Medieval Studies*, 24 (1980), 27–35.

Humphreys, R. Stephen, *From Ṣalāḥ al-Dīn to the Mongols: The Ayyubids of Damascus, 1193–1260* (Albany, 1977).

Khalidi, Tarif, *Arabic Historical Thought in the Classical Period* (Cambridge, 1994).

Little, Donald P., "An Analysis of the Relationship between Four Mamlūk Chronicles for 734–45," *Journal of Semitic Studies*, 19 (1974), 252–68; reprinted in Little, *History and Historiography of the Mamlūks*, (London, 1986), no. III.

A Catalogue of the Islamic Documents from al-Ḥaram aš-Šarīf in Jerusalem, Beiruter Texte und Studien 29 (Beirut, 1984).

An Introduction to Mamlūk Historiography: An Analysis of Arabic Annalistic and Biographical Sources for the Reign of al-Malik an-Nāṣir Muḥammad ibn Qalā'ūn, Freiburger Islamstudien, 2 (Wiesbaden and Montreal, 1970).

"The Recovery of a Lost Source for Baḥrī Mamlūk History: Al-Yūsufī's *Nuzhat al-Nāẓir fī Sīrat al-Malik al-Nāṣir*," *JAOS*, 94 (1974), 42–54; reprinted in Little, *History*, No. II.

"Al-Ṣafadī as Biographer of His Contemporaries," in Little (ed.), *Essays on Islamic Civilization Presented to Niyazi Berkes* (Leiden, 1976), 190–210; reprinted in Little, *History*, no. I.

"The Significance of the Ḥaram Documents for the Study of Medieval Islamic History," *Der Islam*, 57 (1980), 189–212; reprinted in Little, *History*, no. XI.

"The Use of Documents for the Study of Mamluk History," *Mamluk Studies Review*, 1 (1996), 1–13.

Lutfi, Huda, "Al-Sakhāwī's *Kitāb al-Nisā'* as a Source for the Social and Economic History of Muslim Women during the Fifteenth Century AD," *MW*, 71 (1981), 104–24.

Northrup, Linda S., *From Slave to Sultan: The Career of al-Manṣūr Qalāwūn and the Consolidation of Mamluk Rule in Egypt and Syria (678–689 AH/1279–1290 AD)*, Freiburger Islamstudien, 18 (Stuttgart, 1998).

Petry, Carl F., *The Civilian Elite of Cairo in the Later Middle Ages* (Princeton, 1981).

Protectors or Praetorians? The Last Mamlūk Sultans and Egypt's Waning as a Great Power (Albany, 1994).

Richards, D. S., "Ibn al-Athīr and the Later Parts of the *Kāmil*: A Study of Aims and Methods," in D. O. Morgan (ed.), *Medieval Historical Writing in the Christian and Islamic Worlds* (London, 1982), 76–108.
"ʿImād al-Dīn al-Isfahānī: Administrator, Litterateur and Historian," in Maya Shatzmiller (ed.), *Crusaders and Muslims in Twelfth-Century Syria* (Leiden, 1993), 133–46.
Schäfer, Barbara, *Beiträge zur mamlukischen Historiographie nach dem Tode al-Malik an-Nāṣirs. Mit einer Teiledition der Chronik Šams ad-Dīn aš-Šuǧāʿīs*, Islamkundliche Untersuchungen 15 (Freiburg, 1971).
Schregle, Götz, *Die Sultanin von Ägypten: Šaǧarat ad-Durr in der arabischen Geschichtsschreibung und Literatur* (Wiesbaden, 1961).
Stern, Samuel, "Petitions from the Ayyūbid Period," *BSOAS*, 27 (1964), 1–32; reprinted in Stern, *Coins and Documents from the Medieval Middle East* (London, 1986), no. VIII.
Thorau, P., *Sultan Baibars I. von Ägypten: Ein Beitrag zur Geschichte des Vorderen Orients im 13. Jahrhundert*, Beihefte zum Tübinger Atlas des Vorderen Orients, Reihe B. no. 63 (Wiesbaden, 1987); English trans. P. M. Holt, *The Lion of Egypt: Sultan Baybars I and the Near East in the Thirteenth Century* (London and New York, 1992).
"Zur Geschichte der Mamluken und ihrer Erforschung: Peter Malcolm Holt zum 70. Geburtstag," *WO*, 20/21 (1989/90), 227–39.
Van Ess, Josef, "Ṣafadī-Splitter," *Der Islam*, 53 (1976), 242–66, and 54 (1977), 77–108.
Veselý, Rudolf, "Zu den Quellen al-Qalqašandī's *Ṣubḥ al-Aʿshā*," *Acta Universitatis Carolinae–Philologica* 2 (1969), 13–24.
Winter, Michael, *Society and Religion in Early Ottoman Egypt: Studies in the Writings of ʿAbd al-Wahhāb al-Shaʿrānī* (New Brunswick and London, 1982).
Ziyāda, M. M., *Al-Muʾarrikhūn fī Miṣr fī al-Qarn al-Khāmis ʿAshar al-Mīlādī, al-Qarn al-Tāsiʿ al-Hijrī* (Cairo, 1954).

16 EGYPT IN THE WORLD SYSTEM OF THE LATER MIDDLE AGES

Abu-Lughod, J. L., *Before European Hegemony. The World System AD 1250–1350* (Oxford, 1989).
Cairo: 1001 Years of the City Victorious (Princeton, 1971).
Ashtor, E., *Histoire des prix et des salaires dans l'orient médiéval* (Paris, 1969).
The Levant Trade in the Later Middle Ages (Princeton, 1983).
A Social and Economic History of the Near East in the Middle Ages (Berkeley and Los Angeles, 1976).
Braudel, Fernand, *La Méditerranée et le monde méditerranéen à l'époque de Philippe II*, 2nd rev. edn. 2 vols. (Paris, 1966), trans. Sian Reynolds, *The Mediterranean and the Mediterranean World in the Age of Philip II*, 2 vols. (New York, 1971).

Cahen, Claude, *Makhzūmiyyāt. Études sur l'histoire économique et financière de l'Égypte médiévale* (Leiden, 1977).

Chaudhuri, K. N., *Trade and Civilisation in the Indian Ocean. An Economic History from the Rise of Islam to 1750.* (Cambridge, 1985).

Cipolla, Carlo M., *Money, Princes, and Civilization in the Mediterranean World, Fifth to Seventeenth Century.* (Princeton, 1956).

Dols, Michael W., *The Black Death in the Middle East* (Princeton, 1977).

Goitein, S. D., *A Mediterranean Society. The Jewish Communities of the Arab World as Portrayed in the Documents of the Cairo Geniza*, 6 vols. (Berkeley and Los Angeles, 1967–94) (bibliography and indices in vol. 6).

Studies in Islamic History and Institutions (Leiden, 1966).

Hall, Kenneth R., *Maritime Trade and State Development in Early Southeast Asia* (Honolulu, 1985).

Haussig, H. W., *Die Geschichte Zentralasiens und der Seidenstrasse im islamischer Zeit* (Darmstadt, 1988).

Heyd, W., *Histoire du commerce du Levant au moyen-âge*, 2 vols., (Leipzig, 1885–86; reprinted, Amsterdam, 1967).

Hodgson, Marshall G. S., *The Venture of Islam. Conscience and History in a World Civilization*, 3 vols., vol. II: *The Expansion of Islam in the Middle Periods* (Chicago, 1974).

Hourani, George F., *Arab Seafaring in the Indian Ocean in Ancient and Early Medieval Times* (Princeton, 1951; revised edn., John Carswell, Princeton, 1995).

Labib, Subhi, *Handelsgeschichte Ägyptens im Spätmittelalter, 1171–1517* (Wiesbaden, 1965).

Lane, Frederic C., *Venice, a Maritime Republic* (Baltimore, 1973).

Lopez, Robert S., *The Commercial Revolution of the Middle Ages, 950–1350* (Englewood Cliffs, NJ, 1971).

McNeill, William H., *Plagues and Peoples* (New York, 1976).

Miller, J. Innes, *The Spice Trade of the Roman Empire, 29 BC–AD 641* (Oxford, 1969).

Miskimin, Harry A., *The Economy of Early Renaissance Europe, 1300–1460* (Englewood Cliffs, NJ, 1969).

Postan, M. M., and E. E. Rich (eds.), *Trade and Industry in the Middle Ages*, vol. 2 of *Cambridge Economic History of Europe* (Cambridge, 1952).

Postan, M. M., E. E. Rich, and Edward Miller (eds.), *Economic Organization and Politics in the Middle Ages*, vol. 3 of *Cambridge Economic History of Europe* (Cambridge, 1971).

Richard, Jean, *Orient et Occident au moyen âge: contacts et relations (XIIIe-XVe siecles)* (London, 1976.

La Papauté et les missions d'Orient au moyen âge (XIIIe-XVe siécles) (Rome, 1977).

Les relations entre l'Orient et l'Occident au moyen âge: études et documents (London, 1977).

Richards, Donald S. (ed.), *Islam and the Trade of Asia. A Colloquium* (Philadelphia, 1970).

Rossabi, Morris (ed.), *China among Equals. The Middle Kingdom and its Neighbors, 10th–14th Centuries* (Berkeley and Los Angeles, 1983).
Tibbetts, G. R., *Arab Navigation in the Indian Ocean before the Coming of the Portuguese* (London, 1981).
Udovitch, Abraham L. (ed.) *The Islamic Middle East, 700–1900. Studies in Economic and Social History* (Princeton, 1981).
Wallerstein, Immanuel, *The Modern World System*, 2 vols. (New York, 1974–79).
Wheatley, Paul, *The Golden Khersonese. Studies in the Historical Geography of the Malay Peninsula before AD 1500* (Kuala Lumpur, 1961).
Wink, André, *Al-Hind. The Making of the Indo-Islamic World*, 2 vols. (Leiden, 1990–96).

17 THE MILITARY INSTITUTION AND INNOVATION IN THE LATE MAMLŪK PERIOD

Primary sources

Ibn Duqmāq, *Kitāb al-Intiṣār li-Wāsiṭat ʿIqd al-Amṣār*, IV, V, ed. K. Vollers (Cairo, 1893; reprinted Beirut, n.d.).
al-Ḥalabī, Muḥammad ibn Ibrāhīm, *Durr al-Ḥabab fī Taʾrīkh Aʿyān Ḥalab*, ed. Maḥmūd al-Fakhūrī and Yaḥyā ʿAbbāra, 2 vols. (Damascus, 1972–74).
Ibn Iyās, *Badāʾiʿ al-Zuhūr fī Waqāʾiʿ al-Duhūr*, 5 vols., ed. M. Muṣṭafā (Cairo, 1960–75); French trans. vols. III–V G. Wiet *Histoire des mamelouks circassiens* (Cairo, 1945); *Journal d'un bourgeois du Caire*, 2 vols. (Paris, 1955, 1960).
Ibn al-Jīʿān, *Al-Tuḥfat al-Saniyya bi-Asmāʾ al-Bilād al-Miṣriyya*, ed. B. Moritz (Cairo: Būlāq, 1316/1898).
ʿAbd al-Bāsiṭ al-Malaṭī, *al-Rawḍ al-Bāsim fī Ḥawādith al-ʿUmr waʾl-Tarājim*, ms. Vatican arabo, 729.
al-Jawharī al-Ṣayrafī, *Inbāʾ al-Haṣr fī Abnāʾ al-ʿAṣr*, ed. Ḥasan Ḥabashī (Cairo, 1970).
Ibn Taghrī-Birdī, *Ḥawādith al-Duhūr fī Madā al-Ayyām waʾl-Shuhūr*, ed. William Popper, VII, University of California Publications in Semitic Philology 1–4 (Berkeley, 1930–42).

Archival sources

Amīn: M. Amīn, *Catalogue des documents d'archives du Caire de 239/853 à 922/1516* (Cairo, 1981).
WA: Wizārat al-Awqāf, Cairo; q: qadīm.
Amīn #475. WA 886q (main *waqf* writ of Qāytbāy).
Amīn #652. WA 882q (main *waqf* writ of al-Ghawrī).

Secondary sources

Abu Lughod, Janet L., *Before European Hegemony; The World System AD 1250–1350* (Oxford, 1989).
Allouche, Adel, *Mamlūk Economics: A Study and Translation of al-Maqrīzī's Ighāthah* (Salt Lake City, 1994).
The Origins and Development of the Ottoman-Ṣafavid Conflict (Berlin, 1983).
Amīn, Muḥammad M., *Al-Awqāf wa'l-Ḥayat al-Ijtimāʿiyya fī Miṣr* (Cairo, 1980).
Catalogue des documents d'archives du Caire de 239/853 à 922/1516 (Cairo, 1981).
Ashtor, Eliyahu, *Histoire des prix et des salaires dans l'orient mediévale* (Paris, 1969).
Levant Trade in the Later Middle Ages (Princeton, 1983).
A Social and Economic History of the Near East in the Middle Ages (Berkeley, 1976).
Technology, Industry and Trade: The Levant vs Europe, 1250–1500, ed. B. Z. Kedar (Brookfield, VT, 1992) (collected articles).
Aubin, Jean, "La politique orientale de Selim Ier," in Raoul Curiel and Rika Gyselen (eds.), *Itinéraires d'orient: hommages à Claude Cahen, Res Orientales* 6 (Bures-sur-Yvette, 1994), 197–216.
Ayalon, David, "Aspects of the Mamlūk Phenomenon: I. The Importance of the Mamlūk Institution; II. Ayyūbids, Kurds and Turks," *Der Islam*, 53 (1976), 196–225; 54 (1977), 1–32.
"The Circassians in the Mamlūk Kingdom," *JAOS*, 69 (1949), 135–47.
"Egypt as a Dominant Factor in Syria and Palestine during the Islamic Period," in Amnon Cohen and Gabriel Baer (eds.), *Egypt and Palestine; A Millennium of Association* (New York, 1984), 17–47.
"L'esclavage du Mamlouk," *Oriental Notes and Studies 1* (Jerusalem, 1951).
Gunpowder and Firearms in the Mamlūk Kingdom (London, 1956).
"The Mamlūks and Naval Power: A Phase of the Struggle between Islam and Christian Europe," *Proceedings of the Israel Academy of Sciences and Humanities*, 1, 8 (1967), 1–12.
"Notes on the Furūsiyya Exercises and Games of the Mamlūk Sultanate," *Scripta Hierosolymitana, Studies in Islamic History and Civilization*, 9 (1961), 31–62.
"Le régiment Bahriya dans l'armée mamelouk," *REI*, 19 (1951), 133–41.
"Some Remarks on the Economic Decline of the Mamlūk Sultanate," *Jerusalem Studies in Arabic and Islam*, 16 (1993), 108–24.
"Studies on the Structure of the Mamlūk Army – I, II, III" *BSOAS*, 15 (1953), 203–28, 448–76; 16 (1954), 57–90.
"The Wafidīya in the Mamlūk Kingdom," *Islamic Culture*, 25 (1951), 89–109.
Bacqué-Grammont, Jean-Louis, *Les Ottomans, les Safavides et leurs voisins.*

Contribution à l'histoire des relations internationales dans l'Orient islamique de 1514 à 1524, Publications de l'Institut Historique et Archéologique Néerlandais de Stamboul 57 (Istanbul, 1987).
Bacqué-Grammont, Jean-Louis and Anne Kroell, *Mamlouks, Ottomans et Portugais en Mer Rouge: l'affaire de Djedda en 1517* (Cairo, 1988).
Cahen, Claude, *Makhzūmiyyāt, études sur l'histoire économique et financiere de l'Égypte mediévale* (Leiden, 1977).
Canard, Marius, "Le traité de 1281 entre Michel Paléologue et le Sultan Qalā'ūn," *Byzantion*, 10 (1935), 669–80.
"Un traité entre Byzance et l'Égypte au xiiie siecle et les relations diplomatiques de Michel viii Paléologue avec les sultans mamlouks Baibars et Qalā'ūn," *Mélanges Gaudefroy-Demombynes* (Cairo, 1934–45), 197–224.
Cattan, Henry, "The Law of Waqf," *Law in the Middle East*, vol. 1, *Origins and Development of Islamic Law*, ed. M. J. Khadduri and H. J. Liebesny (Washington, 1955), ch. 8.
Clifford, Winslow W., "Some Observations on the Course of Mamlūk-Safavi Relations (1502–1516/908–922), I and II," *Der Islam*, 70, 2 (1993), 245–65, 266–78.
Cooper, Richard, "Agriculture in Egypt, 640–1800," *Handbuch der Orientalistik*, Abteilung 1: *Der Nahe und der Mittelere Osten* bd. 6: *Geschichte der Islamischen Länder*, Abschnitt 6: *Wirtschaftsgeschichte des Vorderen Orients in Islamischer Zeit*, part 1, ed. Berthold Spuler (Leiden, 1977), 188–204.
"A Note on the Dīnār Jayshī, *JESHO*, 16 (1973), 317–18.
Darrag, Ahmad, *L'Égypte sous le règne de Barsbay, 825–841/1422–1438* (Damascus, 1961).
"Les relations commerciales entre l'état mamlouk et la France," *Majallat Kulliyyat al-Ādāb, Jāmi'at al-Iskandariyya*, 25, 2 (1963), 1–21.
Dölger, Franz, "Der Vertrag des Sultans Qalā'ūn von Ägypten mit dem Kaiser Michael VIII. Palaiologos," *Serta Monacensia Franz Babinger* (Leiden, 1952), 60–79.
Ehrenkreutz, Andrew S., *Salāh al-Dīn* (Albany, 1972).
Escovitz, Joseph H., *The Office of Qāḍī al-Quḍāt in Cairo under the Baḥrī Mamlūks* (Berlin, 1984).
Fernandes, Leonor, *The Evolution of a Sufi Institution in Mamlūk Egypt: The Khanqah* (Berlin, 1988).
"Some Aspects of the Zāwiya in Egypt at the Eve of the Ottoman Conquest," *AI*, 19 (1983), 9–17.
Garcin, Jean-Claude, "The Mamlūk Military System and the Blocking of Medieval Muslim Society," in J. Baechler et al. (eds.), *Europe and the Rise of Capitalism* (Oxford, 1988), 113–30.
Garcin, Jean-Claude and Mustapha A. Taher, "Enquête sur le financement d'un *waqf* égyptien du XVe siècle: les comptes de Jawhār al-Lālā," *JESHO*, 38, 3 (1995), 262–304.
Gellner, Ernest, "Patrons and Clients," in Ernest Gellner and John Waterbury (eds.), *Patrons and Clients in Mediterranean Societies* (London, 1977), 1–6.

Haarmann, Ulrich, "Miṣr: 5. The Mamlūk Period," *EI2*, VIII, 174–77.

"Mit dem Pfeil, dem Bogen: Fremde und einheimishche Stimmen zur Kriegkunst der Mamluken," *Kommunikation zwischen Orient und Okzident: Alltag und Sachkultur, Internationaler Kongress* (Vienna, 1994), 223–49.

"The Sons of Mamlūks as Fief-holders in Late Medieval Egypt," in Tarif Khalidi (ed.), *Land Tenure and Social Transformation in the Middle East* (Beirut, 1984), 141–68.

Halm, H., *Ägypten nach den Mamlūkischen Lehenregistern: I: Oberägypten und das Fayyūm; II: Das Delta.* Beihefte zum Tübinger Atlas des Vorderen Orients, Reihe B. no. 38 (Wiesbaden, 1979, 1982).

Hanna, Nelly, *An Urban History of Būlāq in the Mamlūk and Ottoman Periods* (Cairo, 1983).

Har-El, Shai, *The Struggle for Domination in the Middle East: The Ottoman-Mamlūk War, 1485–1491* (Leiden, 1995).

Heffening, W., "Waḳf," *EI2*, IV, 1096–1103.

Hennequin, Giles, "Mamlouks et métaux précieux à propos de la balance de paiements de l'état Syro-Égyptienne à la fin du Moyen Âge – question de méthode," *AI*, 12 (1974), 37–44.

Hess, Andrew, "The Ottoman Conquest of Egypt (1517) and the Beginning of the Sixteenth-Century World War," *IJMES*, 4 (1973), 55–76.

Heyd, W., *Histoire du commerce du Levant au moyen âge*, 2 vols., trans. F. Raynaud (Leipzig, 1885–1886; reprinted, Amsterdam, 1967).

Hodgson, Marshall, *The Venture of Islam*, II (Chicago, 1974).

Holt, P. M., *The Age of the Crusades: The Near East from the Eleventh Century to 1517* (London and New York, 1986).

Early Mamlūk Diplomacy, 1260–1290: Treaties of Baybars and Qalawun with Christian Rulers (Leiden, 1995).

"Qalawun's Treaty with Genoa in 1290," *Der Islam*, 57 (1980), 101–08.

"Some Observations on the ʿAbbasid Caliphate of Cairo," *BSOAS*, 47 (1984), 501–07.

"The Treaties of the Early Mamlūk Sultans with the Frankish States," *BSOAS*, 43 (1980), 67–76.

Humphreys, R. Stephen, "The Emergence of the Mamlūk Army," *SI*, 45 (1977), 67–99; 46 (1977), 147–82.

"Mamlūk Dynasty," in Joseph R. Strayer (ed.), *Dictionary of the Middle Ages* (New York, 1987), VIII, 73–74.

Irwin, Robert, "Factions in Medieval Egypt," *JRAS*, 1986 (3rd ser.), 228–46.

The Middle East in the Middle Ages: The Early Mamlūk Sultanate, 1250–1382 (London, 1986).

Johansen, Baber, *The Islamic Law on Land Tax and Rent: The Peasants' Loss of Property Rights as Interpreted in the Hanafite Legal Literature of the Mamlūk and Ottoman Periods* (New York: 1988).

Jomier, Jacques, "Le mahmal du Sultan Qānsūh al-Ghūrī (début xvie siècle)," *AI*, 11 (1972), 183–88.

Kahle, Paul, "Die Katastrophe des Mittelalterlichen Alexandria," *Mélanges Maspero*, III: Orient Islamique (MIFAO 68) (Cairo, 1935–40), 137–54.
Kammerer, A., *La Mer Rouge, l'Abyssinie et l'Arabie depuis l'antiquité* (Cairo, 1935).
Labib, Subhi Y., "Ein Brief des Mamlūken Sultans Qā'itbey an dem Dogen von Venedig aus dem Jahre 1473," *Der Islam*, 32 (1957), 324–29.
Handelsgeschichte Ägyptens im Spätmittelalter (1171–1517) (Wiesbaden, 1965).
"Medieval Islamic Maritime Policy in the Indian Ocean Area," *Recueils de la Société Jean Bodin*, 32 (1974), 225–41.
Landé, Carl H., "The Dyadic Basis of Clientism," in Steffen W. Schmidt (ed.), *Friends, Followers and Factions: A Reader in Political Clientism* (Berkeley, 1977), xiii–xxxvii.
Lapidus, Ira M., *Muslim Cities in the Later Middle Ages* (Cambridge, MA, 1967).
Levanoni, Amalia, *A Turning Point in Mamlūk History: The Third Reign of al-Nāṣir Muḥammad ibn Qalāwūn (1310–1340)* (Leiden, 1995).
Little, Donald P., "Relations between Jerusalem and Egypt during the Mamlūk Period according to Literary and Documentary Sources," in Amnon Cohen and Gabriel Baer (eds.), *Egypt and Palestine; A Millennium of Association* (New York, 1984), 73–93.
Lyons, M. C. and D. E. P. Jackson, *Ṣalāḥ al-Dīn: The Politics of the Holy War* (New York, 1982).
Martel-Thoumian, Bernadette, *Les civils et l'administration dans l'état militaire mamlūk (IXe/XVe siècle)* (Damascus, 1991).
Mayer, L. A., *The Buildings of Qāytbāy as Described in His Endowment Deed*, fasc. I: text and index (London, 1938).
Minorsky, Vladimir, "The Aq-quyunlu and Land Reforms," *BSOAS*, 17 (1955), 449–62.
Mordtmann, J. and L. Menage, "Dhū'l-Ḳadr," *EI2*, II, 239.
Mottahedeh, Roy P., *Loyalty and Leadership in an Early Islamic Society* (Princeton, 1980).
Newhall, Amy Whittier, "The Patronage of the Mamlūk Sultan Qa'it Bay, 872–901/1468–1496" (Ph.D. dissertation, Harvard University, 1987).
Petry, Carl F., *The Civilian Elite of Cairo in the Later Middle Ages* (Princeton, 1981).
"Class Solidarity vs. Gender Gain: Women as Custodians of Property in Later Medieval Egypt," in Nikki Keddie and Beth Baron (eds.), *Women in Middle Eastern History: Shifting Boundaries in Sex and Gender* (New Haven, 1991), 122–42.
"Fractionalized Estates in a Centralized Regime: The Holdings of al-Ashraf Qāytbāy and Qānṣūh al-Ghawrī in Egypt," *JESHO*, 39, 4 (1996), 1–21.
"Holy War, Unholy Peace? Relations between the Mamlūk Sultanate and European States prior to the Ottoman Conquest," in H. Dajani-Shakeel and R. Messier (eds.) *The Jihad and Its Times* (Ann Arbor, 1991), 106–09.

"A Paradox of Patronage during the Later Mamlūk Period," *MW*, 53 (1983), 182–207.

Protectors or Praetorians? The Last Mamlūk Sultans and Egypt's Waning as a Great Power (Albany, 1994).

Popper, William, *Egypt and Syria under the Circassian Sultans*, University of California Publications in Semitic Philology 15 (Berkeley, 1955).

Rabie, Hassanein, *The Financial System of Egypt*, AH *564–741*/AD *1169–1341* (Oxford, 1972).

"Political Relations between the Safavids of Persia and the Mamluks of Egypt and Syria in the Early Sixteenth Century," *JARCE*, 15 (1978), 75–81.

"Some Technical Aspects of Agriculture in Medieval Egypt," in A. L. Udovitch (ed.), *The Islamic Middle East, 700–1900: Studies in Economic and Social History* (Princeton, 1981), 59–90.

Raymond, André, *Artisans et commerçants du Caire au XVIII*[e] *siècle* (Damascus, 1973).

Roemer, H. R., "The Safavid Period," in P. Jackson (ed.), *The Cambridge History of Iran* (New York, 1986), VI, 189–350.

Rogers, J. Michael, "To and Fro: Aspects of Mediterranean Trade and Communication in the Fifteenth and Sixteenth Centuries," *Revue du monde musulman et de la Méditerranée*, 55/56 (1990), 57–74.

Sato, Tsugitaka, "The Evolution of the *Iqṭā*ʿ System under the Mamlūks: An Analysis of *al-Rawk al-Ḥusāmī* and *al-Rawk al-Nāṣirī*," *Memoirs of the Research Department of the Toyo Bunko (The Oriental Library)*, 37 (1979), 99–131.

*State and Rural Society in Medieval Islam; Sultans, Muqṭa*ʿ*s and Fallāḥūn* (Leiden, 1997).

Schimmel, Annemarie, "Kalif und Kadi im Spätmittelalterlichen Ägypten," *Die Welt des Islams*, 24 (1942), 1–128.

Serjeant, R. B., *The Portuguese off the South Arabian Coast* (London, 1963).

Shoshan, Boaz, "On the Relations between Egypt and Palestine, 1382–1517 AD," in Amnon Cohen and Gabriel Baer (eds.), *Egypt and Palestine: A Millennium of Association* (New York, 1984), 94–101.

Thorau, P., *Sultan Baibars I. von Ägypten: Ein Beitrag zur Geschichte des Vorderen Orients im 13. Jahrhundert*, Beihefte zum Tübinger Atlas des Vorderen Orients, Reihe B, no. 63 (Wiesbaden, 1987); English trans. P. M. Holt, *The Lion of Egypt: Sultan Baybars I and the Near East in the Thirteenth Century* (London and New York, 1992).

Wallerstein, Immanuel, *The Modern World System: Capitalist Agriculture and the Origins of the European World-Economy in the Sixteenth Century* (New York, 1976).

Wansbrough, John, "A Mamlūk Commercial Treaty concluded with the Republic of Florence," in Samuel Stern (ed.), *Documents from Islamic Chanceries* (Oxford, 1965), 39–79.

"The Safe-Conduct in Muslim Chancery Practice," *BSOAS*, 34 (1971), 20–35.

"Venice and Florence in the Mamlūk Commercial Privileges," *BSOAS*, 28 (1965), 483–523.

Waterbury, John, "An Attempt to Put Patrons and Clients in their Place," in Ernest Gellner and John Waterbury (eds.), *Patrons and Clients in Mediterranean Societies* (London, 1977), 329–42.
Wiet, Gaston, *L'Égypte arabe*, vol. 4 of Gabriel Hanotaux (ed.), *L'Histoire de la nation égyptienne* (Paris, 1937), 589–636.
Winter, Michael, *Society and Religion in Early Ottoman Egypt: Studies in the Writings of ʿAbd al-Wahhāb al-Shaʿrānī* (New Brunswick, 1982).
Woods, John, *The Aqqoyunlu: Clan, Confederation, Empire* (Chicago, 1976).
Yelsin, Mehmet, "Dīvān-i Qānṣawh al-Ghawrī: A Critical Edition of an Anthology of Turkish Poetry Commissioned by Sultan Qānṣawh al-Ghawrī (1501–1516)" (Ph.D. dissertation, Harvard University, 1993).

18 THE OTTOMAN OCCUPATION

Primary sources

ʿĀshiqpashazade Ta'rikhi (Istanbul 1332/1914).
Capsali, Rabbi Eliyahu, *Seder Eliyahyu Zuta*, ed. A. Shmuelevitz, Sh. Simonson, M. Benayahu, 3 vols. (Jerusalem and Tel Aviv, 1975, 1977, 1983).
al-Diyārbakrī, ʿAbd al-Ṣamad, *Tarjamat al-nuzha al-saniyya fī dhikr al-khulafā' wa'l-mulūk al-Miṣriyya*, Ms. add 7846 (The British Library).
Ferīdūn, *Munsheāt al-salāṭīn* (Istanbul AH 1274).
Ibn Ṭūlūn, Muḥammad Shams al-Dīn. *Mufākahat al-khullān fī ḥawādith al-zamān*, (ed. M. Muṣṭafā, 2 vols. (Cairo 1962–64).
Ibn Zunbul, Aḥmad al-Rammāl, *Ākhirat al-mamālīk* (Cairo 1962).
Saʿdüddīn, Muḥammad, *Tāj al-tawārīkh* (Istanbul AH 1279/80).

Secondary sources

Ayalon, David, "The End of the Mamlūk Sultanate (Why did the Ottomans spare the Mamlūks of Egypt and wipe out the Mamlūks of Syria?)", *SI*, 65 (1987), 125–48.
Gunpowder and Firearms in the Mamluk Kingdom (London, 1956).
"Mamlūk Military Aristocracy During the First Years of the Ottoman Occupation of Egypt," in C. E. Bosworth, C. Issawi, R. Savory, and A. L. Udovitch(eds), *The Islamic World: From Classical to Modern Times; Essays in Honor of Bernard Lewis* (Princeton, 1989), 413–31.
Bacqué-Grammont, Jean-Louis, *Les ottomans, les safavides, et leurs voisins*, Nederlands Historisch-Archaelogisch Instituut (Istanbul 1987).
Fisher, Sydney N., *The Foreign Relations of Turkey, 1481–1512* (Urbana, IL, 1948).
Hess, A. C., "The Ottoman Conquest of Egypt (1517) and the Beginning of the Sixteenth-century World War," *IJMES*, 4, 1 (1973), 55–76.
Holt, P. M., *The Age of the Crusades: The Near East from the Eleventh Century to 1517* (London and New York, 1986).

Egypt and the Fertile Crescent 1516–1922: A Political History (Ithaca and London 1966).
"A Notable in the Age of Transition: Jānim Bey al-Ḥamzāwī (d. 944/1538)," in C. Heywood and C. Imber (eds.), *Studies in Ottoman History in Honour of Professor V. L. Menage* (Istanbul, 107–115).
Petry, Carl F., *Protectors or Praetorians? The Last Mamlūk Sultans and Egypt's Waning as a Great Power* (Albany, 1994).
Twilight of Majesty: The Reigns of the Mamlūk Sultans al-Ashraf Qāytbāy and Qanṣūh al-Ghawrī in Egypt (Seattle and London, 1993).
Schimmel, Annemarie, "Kalif und Kadi in spätmittelalterlichen Ägypten," *Die Welt des Islams*, 24 (1942), 1–128.
Stripling, G. W. F., *The Ottoman Turks and the Arabs, 1511–1574* (Urbana, IL, 1942).
Wiet, G., *L'Égypte arabe*, vol. 4 of Gabriel Hanotaux (ed.), *Histoire de la nation égyptienne* (Paris 1937).
Winter, Michael, *Egyptian Society Under Ottoman Rule, 1517–1798* (London and New York, 1992).
Society and Religion in Early Ottoman Egypt: Studies in the Writings of ʿAbd al-Wahhab al-Shaʿrani (New Brunswick, 1982).

INDEX

Abagha, Ilkhanid, 280
ʿAbbās, uncle of Prophet, 131, 146, 537
al-ʿAbbās, son of Ibn Ṭūlūn, 92, 96–7, 100–1, 104
al-ʿAbbāsa, 315
ʿAbd Allāh ibn ʿAbd al-Malik, 33
ʿAbd Allāh ibn ʿAbd al-Raḥmān ibn Muʿāwiya, 66, 77, 78
ʿAbd Allāh ibn ʿAmr ibn al-ʿĀṣ, 69
ʿAbd Allāh ibn al-Fatḥ, 102
ʿAbd Allāh ibn Ḥulays al-Hilālī, 83
ʿAbd Allāh ibn Jaʿfar, 122
ʿAbd Allāh ibn Marwān, 72, 77
ʿAbd Allāh ibn Saʿd ibn Abī Sarḥ, 67, 68
ʿAbd Allāh ibn Ṭāhir, 66, 80–3, 85
ʿAbd al-ʿAziz ibn Marwān, 65, 70, 71, 72, 73, 76, 77, 78
ʿAbd al-ʿAzīz ibn al-Wazīr al-Jarawī, 80–1
ʿAbd al-Bāsiṭ ibn Khalīl, 310, 441
ʿAbd al-Laṭīf al-Baghdādī, 408
ʿAbd al-Majīd, reigned as al-Ḥāfiẓ, 153–4
ʿAbd al-Malik, Umayyad, 323, 325
ʿAbd al-Malik ibn ʿAṭṭāsh, 145
ʿAbd al-Malik ibn Marwān, 71–2, 77, 326
ʿAbd al-Malik ibn Rifāʿa al-Fahmī, 73–4
ʿAbd al-Raḥmān ibn Muʿāwiya ibn Ḥudayj, 66, 71–2
ʿAbd al-Raḥmān ibn ʿUtba al-Fihrī, 70
ʿAbd al-Salām ibn Abiʾl-Māḍī, 83
ʿAbd al-Ṣamad al-Diyārkbakrī, 491
ʿAbd al-Wāḥid, 66
ʿAbd al-Ẓāhir family, 264
ʿAbdān, 123, 125
ʿAbdallāḥ, 125
Abī-Shawārib tribe, 315
ʿĀbis ibn Saʿīd al-Murādī, 70–1
Abkhāzī mamlūks, 258, 521
Abourni, king of the Noba, 31
Abraham, 313
  tomb of, 504
Abraham, son of Maimonides, 208
Abraham Castro, 515
Abuʾl-ʿAbbās, 124, 127–30
Abū ʿAbdallāh al-Shīʿī, 124–5, 127–30, 132n, 133
Abū ʿAlī, *see* Ḥamdān Qarmaṭ
Abū ʿAlī Ḥasan, 207
Abū ʿAlī Kutayfāt, 154
Abū ʿAwn, 76–7
Abū Bakr, 45, 69
Abuʾl-Faraj Yūsuf, 203
Abū al-Fidāʾ, al-Malik al-Muʾayyad ʿImād al-Dīn, 416, 423, 427
Abū Ḥāmid al-Qudsī, 375–6
Abū Ḥanīfa, 66
Abuʾl-Ḥasan al-Bakrī, 265
Abū Ḥayyān, 432
Abū ʿInān Fāris, 434
Abū Isḥāq, 83
Abū Ismāʿīl Ibrāhīm ibn Tājj, 165
Abū Jaʿfar Aḥmad ibn Naṣr, 137
Abuʾl-Khaṭṭāb ibn Daḥiyya, 108n
Abū Manṣūr Aḥmad ibn ʿAbd Allāh, 98

Abū Muḥammad al-Farghānī ʿAbd Allāh ibn Aḥmad ibn Jaʿfar, 98
Abu'l-Munajjā ibn Shaʿyā, 207
Abū Naṣr Hārūn, 207
Abu'l-Qāsim, *see* al-Qā'im
Abū Rūḥ Sukun, 93
Abū Sargah (St Sergius), 349, 354
Abū Saʿīd, Ilkhan, 253, 282–4
Abū Saʿīd al-Jannābī, 124
Abū Shāma, ʿAbd al-Raḥmān, 417–20, 429, 433
Abu'l-Suʿūd al-Jārihī, 312, 408, 501
Abū Ṭāhir al-Jannābī, 114, 135
Abū ʿUbāda al-Buḥtūrī, 106
Abū ʿUthmān al-Nābulsī, 419
Abū Yazīd Makhlad ibn Kaydād, "al-Dajjāl", 133
Abū Yūsuf Yaʿqūb ibn ʿAwkal, 203
Abū Zākī, 129
Abukir, 131
Abydos, 28
Abyssinia, *see* Ethiopia
Achaemenids, 89
Acre (ʿAkkā), 99, 153, 155, 253, 276, 280, 365, 450
  Mamlūk conquest of, 252, 272, 277, 280, 285, 423
Adam, 123, 423
Adana, 102
Aden, 87, 282, 294
Adhana, 285
al-ʿĀdid, Fāṭimid caliph, 154, 213–15
al-ʿĀdil (sultan), *see* Kitbughā; Tūmānbāy
al-ʿĀdil, Ayyūbid, 211n, 220–3, 227, 240, 332
al-ʿĀdil Abū Bakr II, Ayyūbid, 224, 333
Adriatic Sea, 53, 87
Aegean, 87
Aemilianus, 23
al-Afḍal ʿAlī, Ayyūbid, 208, 219–20, 236n
al-Afḍal ibn Amīr al-Juyūsh, wazīr, 148, 153–4, 156, 168, 207
Africa, central, sub-Saharan, etc., 37, 50, 54, 59, 60, 63, 66, 73, 77, 87, 93, 115, 118, 230, 294, 314, 390, 445, 447, 449, 455–6
  see also Maghrib, Ifrīqiyya, Libya
Africa Proconsularis, 42
al-Afshīn, 83
Aga Khans, 121, 149, 521
Agapius of Membij, 45, 59
al-Aghlab ibn Sālim, 77
Aghlabids, 87, 94, 96, 107, 127–33, 521
Aḥmad, 125
Aḥmad ibn ʿAlī, 117
Aḥmad al-Badawī, 406
  sanctuary of, 313
Aḥmad ibn Baqar, 515
Aḥmad (ibn) Kayghulugh, 110–11
Aḥmad ibn al-Muwaffaq, *see* al-Muʿtaḍid
Aḥmad Pasha al-Khā'in, 514–15
Aḥmad ibn Saʿīd al-Kilābī, Abu'l-ʿAbbās, 113
Aḥmad ibn Shaykh, 293
Aḥmad ibn Ṭūlūn, *see* Ibn Ṭūlūn
Aḥmadī order, 406, 521
al-Aḥsā', 107
al-Akdar ibn Hamām, 70
Akhmīm, 14, 39n, 142
Akhū Muḥsin, 142
ʿAlā al-Dawla, 495–6
Alamanni, 20
Alamut, 147
Aleppo, 89, 95–6, 102–3, 107, 113–15, 218, 220, 236, 240, 273, 275, 286, 292, 295, 299, 391, 304, 414–16, 431, 433, 458, 476, 479, 495–7, 499, 523
Alexander the Great, 13, 395
Alexander, patriarch, 74
Alexandretta, 43, 52
Alexandria, Alexandrians, 2–3, 6–7, 9, 12–14, 16–21, 28–9, 32–3, 35–7, 51–3, 55–6, 59, 62–4, 67–9, 71–2, 76, 80–83, 85, 87–8, 90, 92–3, 96–8, 106, 108, 110–12, 127, 130–2, 141, 166–9, 196, 198, 202, 204, 210, 213, 217, 227, 230–1, 253, 273, 281, 285–7, 295, 298, 303–4, 314, 316, 325–6, 328, 330, 333, 340, 343, 346, 349, 353, 383, 400–1, 404, 446–7, 453, 471n, 480, 494, 504, 524
  patriarchate of, 177, 187–8, 193, 283, 449–50
Algeria, 120, 124, 140n

ʿAlī ibn ʿAbd al-ʿAzīz al-Jarawī, 81, 83
ʿAlī ibn Abī Ṭālib, 68, 69, 89, 107, 112, 120–1, 145, 151, 266, 358, 461, 522, 523
ʿAlids, 77, 84–5, 86, 93, 137, 216n, 328, 522, 527–8, 530, 537
ʿAli ibn Aḥmad ibn Ṭūlūn, 108
ʿAlī ibn Badr, 112
ʿAlī Basha Mubārak, 346
ʿAlī Bey al-Kabīr, 515
ʿAlī ibn al-Faḍl, 123, 127
ʿAlī ibn al-Ikhshīd, 115–17
ʿAlī ibn al-Nuʿmān, 158
ʿAlī, son of Aybak, 250
ʿAlī ibn ʿUmar, 514
ʿAlī ibn ʿUthmān al-Makhzūmī, 419
Almohads, 454
Amājūr, 94–6
Amalric, 213–15, 217–18
Amente, 21
Āmid, 240, 295, 496
al-Amīn, 80
Amir, Buyid, 144
al-Āmir, Fatimid, 149, 153, 156, 173, 207, 328
amīr: ākhūr, 260, 296, 305, 522
a. ʿashara, 260
a. al-ḥājj, 508
a. al-juyūsh, 153, 156
a. mi'a muqaddam alf, 259–60, 423, 522
a. ṭabalkhāna, 260, 522
a. al-ʿumarā', 98
ʿAmīr al-Majnūn, 112
Ammonius, 30
Amon, 13
ʿAmr ibn al-ʿĀṣ, 33, 41, 44–6, 54, 57, 61, 62, 64, 67, 69, 349, 353
mosque of, 64, 69, 99, 109–10, 137, 139, 167, 173, 202
ʿAmr ibn Qaḥzam al-Khawlānī, 66, 68, 70, 76
ʿAmru, mosque (Qūṣ), 354
ʿAnan ibn David, 200
Anatolia, Asia Minor, 25, 42, 49, 52–5, 58, 60, 86, 95, 105, 115, 193, 224, 253, 273, 278–9, 284–6, 291–4, 299, 301, 312, 381, 394, 454–5, 460–1, 463, 466n, 478, 492, 495–6, 502, 525, 527, 530–1, 534, 536
ʿAnbasa ibn Isḥāq al-Dabbī, 84
Andalūs, Andalusians, 80–2, 87–8, 98, 104, 141, 232, 400, 449, 454, 524
see also Spain
Andronicus Contostephanus, 215
Angevins, 453
Ankara, 292
Antinopolis, 6, 15–16
Antinous, 15
Antioch, 20, 51, 74, 96, 138, 193n, 523
crusader principality of, 273–4, 276, 279–80
Antoninus Pius, 16, 18
Anūshtakīn al-Dizbirī, 103
al-Anwār mosque, *see* al-Ḥākim
Apis bull, 14–15
Appianus, 22
Aqaba, 80
Aqbirdī, 296–7, 302
al-Aqmar mosque, 173, 370, 371, 372
Aqqoyunlu, Ak Qoyunlu, 291–2, 294–6, 464n, 466, 522
Arabia, 51, 53, 87–8, 115, 118, 135, 142, 198, 282–3, 325, 431, 446, 449, 463
Arabic language, speech, 4, 33, 56, 88, 144, 148, 170, 181, 183–6, 189–91, 193, 200–1, 204, 243–4, 254, 310, 323n, 324–5, 348, 369, 371–2, 374, 391, 394, 397, 424, 426, 437–8, 440, 445–6, 449, 536
sources and texts, 37, 44n, 45, 59, 62–4, 69, 72, 149, 164, 170, 177, 180, 185, 189–90, 194–5, 212n, 244, 250, 344, 348, 349, 363, 490
Arabissos, 42–3
Arabs, 3, 44n, 50–2, 54, 56, 58, 64, 68, 75, 76, 79, 82–4, 87–9, 91, 93, 98, 106, 117, 128–9, 136, 151, 167, 209, 246, 260, 268, 381, 384, 391, 490, 501, 503, 510, 514–16, 522, 538
Arab tribes, 46, 49, 64, 74, 78, 80, 86, 88, 91, 93, 115–16, 146, 198, 226, 255, 274, 291, 315, 383–4, 434, 447, 449, 498, 514, 524
see also Bedouin
Arab conquest, 33, 49, 51, 54, 57,

Arabs (*cont*)
59, 90, 104, 183, 198–9, 202, 246, 446
Arab historiography, 45, 86, 98, 106, 180, 190, 412–16, 420, 428–9, 432, 440, 444, 491
Aragon, 285, 452, 454
ʿArak tribe, 314
Aramaic language, 170n
Arcadius, 30
Archimedes screw, 3
Arghun, 281
Arianism, 27–9
Arikmās min Ṭarābāy, 481
Arkadios, 55–8
Armant, 12–14, 16, 18, 22, 25, 26
Armenia, Armenians, 40, 42, 46, 48, 55, 82, 94, 153, 155, 216, 252, 253, 273–4, 278–80, 285, 335, 346, 426
ʿArqa, 113
Arsinoe, 18
Arsūf, 276
Artemius, 28
al-Asʿad ibn Mammātī, 419
Asadiyya mamlūks (of Shirkuh), 220
al-Aṣbagh, 71
Ascalon, 213, 417
Ashʿarite doctrine, 232, 402
Ashinās, 82
ʿĀshiqpashazāde, 491
Ashmunayn, 63, 115, 170, 449
ashrāf, *sharīf*s, 101, 107, 137, 139, 142, 498, 537
al-Ashraf (Mamlūk sultan), *see* Khalīl, Qāytbāy, Shaʿban
al-Ashraf, Ayyūbid, 223, 236n
al-Ashraf Mūsā, Ayyūbid, 250
Ashrafī mamlūks, 300
ʿĀshūrāʾ, 139, 523
al-ʿAskar, 350
Asklepiades, 31
al-Asnāwī, 272
Aspagurios, 57–8
ʿAssāma ibn ʿAmr al-Maʿāfirī, 66, 76, 77
Assyria, Assyrians, 1
Aswān, 11, 13, 18, 24, 68, 76, 81, 87, 93, 116, 168, 315–16, 339, 340, 353, 357, 370, 383, 484n
Asyūṭ, 314, 316
ʿaṭāʾ, 65–6, 69, 71, 80, 84, 526
atābak, 240, 290, 293, 295–7, 304–6, 310, 414, 474, 485, 499, 523
al-ʿasākir, 249, 288
Athanasius, 27, 28
Athlīth (Chateau Pélerin), 276
Athribis, 13
Atrīb, 326
Augustus, 2, 5, 7, 10, 12, 15, 20, 22, 24, 26
Aurelius, 17, 19
Aurelius Horion, 27
Auxum, 13n
Avar, 43
Avidius Cassius, 17
al-Awḥad, 167
awlād al-nās, 257, 259, 262, 287, 302, 306, 424, 426, 431, 439, 490, 496, 503, 508, 511, 523
Awlad al-Shaykh, 239
Ayās, 280, 285
Aybak al-Turkumānī, al-Muʿizz Aybak, 249–50, 420
ʿAydhāb, 87, 168–9, 282, 314–16, 384, 396, 407
Ayla, 53, 68, 70, 105
ʿAyn Jālūt, 248, 255, 260, 274, 276, 279, 452
ʿAyn Shams (Heliopolis), 51, 54, 61, 69, 139
Aynāl, 293, 295, 301, 303, 336
al-ʿAynī, Badr al-Dīn, 426, 433, 436–9, 441
Ayyūb, father of Ṣalāḥ al-Dīn, 214
Ayyūb ibn Shurāḥbīl, 73
Azbak, 295–6, 306, 310
Azbakiyya district, 310, 392
Azd tribe, 64
Azerbaijan, 495, 524, 529
al-Azhar, mosque, 139, 166, 172, 312, 317, 352, 354, 373, 381, 401, 404, 504, 523
al-ʿAzīz ʿUthmān, Ayyūbid, 220, 240, 417
al-ʿAzīz billāh, Fāṭimid caliph, 114, 140, 152–5, 158, 172
al-ʿAzīz Yūsuf, Mamlūk, 301, 419

Bāb al-Futūḥ, 139, 348, 352
Bāb al-Naṣr, 313, 352, 358, 368

Bāb Zuwayla, 139, 299, 344, 345, 365, 367. 504, 539
Babylon (Old Cairo), 36n, 50, 54, 55, 59, 61, 62, 64, 349
Babylonian rite, Jewry, 199–200, 203–4
Badawiyya order, 267
Badja of Nubia, 93
Badr al-Dīn al-ʿAynī, 394, 399
Badr al-Jamālī, 148–9, 153, 155–7, 159, 167, 171, 205, 347, 360, 365
Badr al-Muʿtaḍidī, 106
Baghdād, 65, 77–80, 82, 86–9, 94–5, 97, 98, 104, 106–14, 117, 132, 136–8, 141–2, 145–7, 200, 204, 231, 246, 281–2, 352, 391, 400, 416, 446, 448, 451, 499, 522, 524
  fall to the Mongols, 255, 269, 273, 280, 282, 376, 451–2, 503
Baghdād tribe, 315
Bahāʾ al-Dīn Qarāqūsh al-Assadī, 240
al-Bahnasā, 504
Baḥrayn, 86, 107, 124–5, 135
Baḥrī mamlūks, 212n, 224–6, 239, 242–89, 420–1, 424, 426–7, 430–3, 437, 440–2, 444, 463, 523, 531
Bajkam, 112
Bākbāk, 91–2
Bakkār ibn Quṭayba, 101–2, 116
al-Balawī, 167
Baʿlbakk, 107, 114
Balbilla, 15
Balbinus, 21
Baldwin III, 213
Baldwin IV, 218
Balī tribe, 314
Balkans, 38, 60, 296
Baltic, 454
Baqar tribe, 315, 501, 524
Baradān river, 102
Barakāt, Sharīf of Mecca, 505
Barakāt ibn Mūsā, Zayn al-Dīn, 508–9, 514
Barāq, shaykh, 271
barīd, 92, 97, 259, 264, 525
al-Bārizī tribe, 307
Barka, 92–3, 105, 112, 130
Barka (al-Marj), 51
al-Barlī, 274
Barmakids, 79
Barqūq, al-Ẓāhir, 253, 255, 287–9, 290–4, 297, 299, 301, 303, 305–6, 309, 313–14, 323, 334, 337, 384, 401, 434–5, 439, 444, 456, 458
Barsbāy, 286, 293–5, 300–1, 313–14, 331, 336, 363, 394, 438–9, 458–9, 523
al-Basāsīrī, 146–8
Bashmuric revolt, 182–3
Basilicus, 32
Baṣra, 77, 86, 88, 100, 142, 281, 447
Baybars I al-Bunduqdārī, al-Ẓāhir, 247–52, 254–5, 257–61, 264–6, 268–9, 271, 273–80, 283–4, 289, 332, 334, 336, 373, 374, 390, 393–4, 396, 402, 418, 421–3, 453–4, 460–1, 499, 524, 539
Baybars II al-Jāshnikīr, 252, 257, 268, 288
Baybars al-Manṣūri al-Khiṭāʾī, Rukn al-Dīn, 423–4, 427, 430
Bāyezīd II, 466, 492–3, 496
Bayn al-Qaṣrayn, 395, 401
Baysarī, 279
Bedouin, 56, 64, 91, 96, 100, 105, 107, 116, 142, 167, 215, 260, 274, 291–2, 294–7, 304–6, 308, 313–17, 383–4, 391, 434, 471, 498–504, 507–8, 513–16, 522, 523, 537
  see also Arabs
Beirut, 275–6
Benedetto Zaccaria, 281
Ben Ezra synagogue, 198, 209
Benjamin, patriarch, 38, 44, 45, 190
Benjamin of Tudela, 202n
Benvenuto, 14
Berbers, 93, 108–9, 112, 116, 118, 124, 128–30, 133, 136, 138, 152–5, 171, 291, 315, 383–4, 528
Berenike, 15
Berke, 278, 422
Bes, 28
Bilbeis, 54, 316, 353
*bīmāristān*s, hospitals, 100, 268, 368, 473
Biqāʿ valley, 500
Bir Umm Fawakhir, 44
al-Bīra, fortress, 274

Birkat al-Fīl, district, 350
Birkat al-Ḥabash, 111
Birkat al-Ḥājj, 502
Birkat Qārūn, 116
al-Birzālī, ʿAlam al-Dīn al-Qāsim, 427–9, 432
Bishr ibn Ṣafwān al-Kalbī, 73
Black Sea, 53, 278, 280, 445, 453, 455
Blemmyes, 12, 22–4, 26, 29–33
Bohairic dialect, 185
Bohemond VI, 274, 276, 279
Bohemond VII, 276, 281
Bonosus, 42
Bosphorus, 26
Bosra, 108
Buchis, 22, 26, 28
Buḥayra, 315–16, 504
Bukhān, Traditions of, 313
Bukhārā, 91, 536
Būlāq, 301, 344n, 367, 392, 503
Buluggīn, 140
Burjī mamlūks, 250, 252, 258–9, 284, 289, 432–3, 441, 444, 524
  see also Circassians
Buscarello di Ghisolifī, 281
Būsīr, 76
Butler, A. J., 37–8, 57
Buwīṭ, 79
Buyids, 114, 117, 144, 447, 523
Byzantium, Byzantine, 3, 26, 32, 35–8, 40, 41, 43, 45–7, 49–61, 62, 64, 67, 82, 84, 86, 88–9, 91, 95–6, 100–1, 103, 110, 114–16, 118, 132, 136, 138, 152, 175–9, 186, 191, 193, 195, 198–9, 202, 215–16, 227, 278–9, 325, 445–6, 452–3, 455, 523, 531, 536

cadastral surveys, 10, 74, 219, 240, 419, 484n, 487, 508, 516, 535
  see also rawk
Caesarea, 51, 276
Caetani Leone, 38
Calicut, 298
Caligula, 12–13
caliphate, caliphs, 303, 463–4
  ʿAbbāsid, 66, 76–84, 86–91, 94–5, 99, 101–8, 110–14, 117–19, 129, 131, 145, 147, 199, 203, 215, 220, 233, 236, 151, 154, 184, 242, 246, 268, 273, 326n, 327, 330, 336, 350, 391, 448, 452, 463, 499, 515n, 522
  at Cairo, 254–6, 269, 282, 291–2, 464, 495–6, 498–9, 501, 506, 514, 538
  Fāṭimid, 103, 107, 118, 120–1, 125, 129–30, 136, 139–40, 148, 152–60, 171–4, 201, 203, 206–7, 213–15, 265–6, 347, 352, 437, 448, 450, 523, 526, 528, 535, 538
  Rashidūn & Umayyad, 41, 54, 65, 68–78, 93, 244, 323, 325, 446, 537
Canopus, 29
Cape of Good Hope, 494
Capsali, Rabbi Eliyahu, 491
Caracalla, 18–20
Carinus, 23
Carthage, 51
Carus, 23
Caspian Sea, 114, 155, 273, 525
Castile, 454
Catalans, 230, 294, 454–5
Caucasus, 45, 381, 453
Cem, prince, 493
central Asia, 104, 241, 246, 376, 390, 392, 406, 452, 454, 456, 463, 528, 531–2, 538
Ceylon, 86, 283
Chaeremon, 13
Chagatayids, 456
Chain Tower, Damietta, 222
Chalcedon, Council of, 31–2, 177, 524, 532–3
  Chalcedonians, 34, 50, 67, 524, 533–4
Chaldiran, 299, 495–7, 499, 524
Charles d'Anjou, 278–9
China, 282–4, 455–6
Chingiz Khan, 273
Christian sources, 24, 63, 69, 72, 74, 178, 180–1, 185
Christianity, Christians
  Byzantine and Armenian, 138, 155, 279, 532
  of Egypt, 3, 8–9, 12–13, 19, 21, 22, 25–32, 36, 38, 41, 49, 54, 64, 69, 72, 73, 83, 85, 92–3, 99–100, 102–4, 116, 119, 152, 159–60, 166–70, 174, 175–97, 198, 202, 204, 206, 208–9, 217, 233, 264,

266, 271–3, 307, 316, 341, 347–9, 353–4, 360, 363, 368, 381, 383, 387–8, 398, 400, 444, 449, 506–7, 513, 524, 525, 529, 532, 534–5
European, 132, 195–6, 209, 217, 281, 285, 434, 454, 503
of Mesopotamia and Syria, 99, 100
of Nubia, 283
Christodulos, 190
Christology, 57, 447, 524
Cilicia, 91, 95, 103–4, 108, 110, 114, 117, 131, 279, 285, 460, 523, 524
Cilician Gates, 43
Circassian mamlūks, 250–3, 258, 284, 286, 288–9, 336, 377, 381, 432, 440–1, 478n, 484n, 495, 503, 505, 507, 512, 514–16, 524, 532
Circassian units under the Ottomans, 512, 516
circus factions of Constantinople, 49
Citadel of Cairo, 216, 256, 258, 265, 268, 291, 303–4, 309–10, 313, 357, 365, 367–8, 373, 392, 452, 464, 466, 479, 485, 499, 508, 512, 514–15, 524, 528–9, 534–5
Claudian, 30
Claudius Gothicus, 23
Claudius, 12
Cleopatra, 1, 6
Coma (Qiman al-Arus), 22
Commodus, 17–18
Companions of the Prophet, 62, 64, 66, 389, 527
Constans II, emperor, 47, 48, 50, 59, 61
Constantia, 56–8
Constantine I, 25–7, 176
Constantine III, *see* Heraclius Constantine
Constantine, city, 124n
Constantinople, 26–7, 31–2, 36–8, 40–1, 47–50, 52, 54, 58–9, 90, 104, 117, 132, 206, 278, 299, 303, 376, 445–7, 450, 455, 460
Constantius Chlorus, 23
Constantius, 28
conversion to Christianity
by Byzantines, 32, 36, 38, 176
by caliphs, 184
pagans, 32, 36, 38, 176
conversion to Islam
by Christians, 67, 72–3, 104, 178, 183–4, 187, 196, 264, 271–3, 307, 316, 398, 513, 532
by Ilkhans, 277
by Jews, 206–7, 209
by mamlūks, 242, 245, 251
in Nubia, 93
conversion to Shīʿism, 107, 119, 515
Coptic Christianity
Church, 3, 21, 24, 33, 167–8, 170, 205, 233, 410, 446, 533–5
Coptic art, 33, 191–2, 343–5, 349, 357
Coptic language, script, 9, 33, 34, 45, 169–70, 177, 180, 184–6, 189–91n, 195–6, 271, 344, 348, 446, 449, 536
sources, 29, 33, 41, 45, 59, 64, 178n, 180, 185, 189–90, 194, 449–50
Coptos, 13, 15–16, 23–4
Copts, 24, 28, 38, 43, 45, 65, 67, 71n, 72, 74, 83, 85, 100, 117, 158, 168, 179, 196, 235–6, 254, 264, 272–3, 307, 381, 383, 398, 419, 423, 427, 449, 524
Cordobans of Alexandria, 87, 524
Cornelius Gallius, 11
Creswell, K. A. C., 345
Crete, 82, 87, 103, 117, 491, 524
crusades, crusaders, 154, 156, 162, 168, 195, 207, 211, 218, 222–5, 231, 235, 241, 243, 244, 246–8, 251–5, 261, 269, 271, 275–7, 280, 284, 328n, 330n, 391, 414–15, 448, 450, 453, 460
Second, 212
Third, 218, 220, 227, 416
Fifth, 222, 225–7, 230, 235n
Seventh, 224, 226–7, 239
Cypriot, 1365 AD, 273, 286–7
Ctesiphon, 90
Cyprus, 37, 41, 52, 55–8, 103, 117, 195, 224, 253, 273, 277, 280, 285–7, 294, 313, 458
Cyrenaica, Cyrenaican Pentapolis, 51, 59, 130n, 451
Cyrene, 14
Cyriacus, patriarch, 193n

Cyril 'the Great', 30
Cyril III Ibn Laqlaq, 190, 196
Cyrus, *see* Kyros
Cyzicus, 18

daftardār, 508, 525
Dahlak, 282
Dakhleh Oasis, 13–14
Dakka, 12
Damanhūr, 314, 316
Damascus, 65, 71, 92, 94, 100–3, 106–8, 112–14, 116–18, 138, 212–13, 217–19, 221–4, 239–40, 248, 249, 263, 267, 271, 273–4, 286, 292, 304, 307, 325, 375, 418–19, 429, 431–2, 434, 436, 446–8, 451, 457, 476, 481, 491, 496–9, 501–2, 505, 509, 524, 531, 536, 538
Damietta, Dimyaṭ, 84, 88, 107, 158, 169, 207, 215, 306
Damrū, 188
Danube, 17, 21
dār al-ʿadl, 265, 525
dār al-imāra, 69, 100, 349–50, 369, 370
David ibn Daniel, 205
dawādār, 264, 293, 296–9, 305–6, 310, 312, 474, 496, 508, 525
Daylam, Daylamites, 114, 117, 155, 381, 524, 525
Dayr al-Suriani, 194
Dead Sea, 56, 274
Debod, 12–13
Decian, 176
Decrius, Trajanus, 12, 21, 33
Décobert, C., 183
Deir el-Medineh, 12
Delhi sultans, 454
Delta, 50, 53–5, 61, 62, 81, 83, 85, 88, 93, 105, 116, 118, 139, 141–2, 158, 213, 222, 291, 299, 313, 315–16, 326, 381, 383, 406, 446, 449, 526, 531–2, 536
Demotic language, 5, 8–9, 17, 19, 21–2, 28, 31
Dendera, 12–14, 16, 17, 29
Dendur, 12, 15
Derʿa, 108
dervishes, *see* Ṣūfīs
Description de l'Egypte, 341, 343, 345
al-Dhahabī, 427, 431, 443
Dhaka al-A'war, 110
Dhakhīra reserve bureau, 481
dhimmī status, 104, 178–9, 201–2, 207–9, 233, 235, 271, 387, 398, 525, 529
see also Christians, Jews
Dhu'l-Qadrids, 253, 286, 291, 295–6, 299, 466n, 492, 495, 525
Diadumenianus, 20n
Didius Julianus, 18
Diḥyā ibn Muṣʿab, 78–9
Dilāẓ, 200
Diocletian, 2, 11, 22–4, 26, 28, 30–1, 176
Dionysus, 21
Diophysite, 177
Dioscorus I, 30–2
Dioskoros of Aphrodito, 35
Diospolis Parva (Hū), 13
Ḍirghām, 213
Dishna, 353
Diu, battle of, 298
dīwān, 64–5, 72, 75, 78, 109, 155, 157–8, 171, 231, 233–7, 272, 306–7, 472, 477, 497, 516, 523, 526, 533
al-aḥbās, 235
al-ahrā', 97, 526
al-ḥarb, 236
al-inshā', 207, 235, 264, 306, 421, 430, 526, 530
al-jaysh, 92, 160, 235, 264, 306, 487, 526
al-khāṣṣ, 97, 291, 306, 430, 526
al-māl, 109, 234–5, 526
al-mufrad, 291, 293, 300, 306–7, 526
al-wizāra, 306
asfal al-arḍ, 97, 526
Diyār Bakr, 240, 292
Diyār Mudar, 96, 105–6
Diyār Rabīʿa, 105
Diyārbakrī, 514
Dodecaschoenus, 11, 22
Domentianus, 47
Dominicans, 282
Domitian, 14
Druze, 143, 152, 266n, 526

Edessa, 91, 212, 294
Edfu, 13
Edict of Milan, 26
Edward I, 276
El-Gabaal, 20
Elagabalus, 20
Elbistan, 280, 492, 495, 496, 525, 527
Elephantine, 11–12
Elḥanan ben Shemarya, 203–4
Embriaco clan, 281
Emesa, 20
England, 276
Epagathus, 20
eparchos, 1
Ephesus, councils of, 30–1
Epiphanius, monastery of, 39n
Esmet the elder, 31
Esna, Esnē, 13–14, 16–19, 21, 29, 93
Ethiopia, Ethiopians, Ethiopic, Abyssinia, 13n, 40, 62n, 168, 193, 195, 283–4, 381, 390, 533–4
Eugenius IV, pope, 196
eunuchs, 101, 106, 114–15, 117, 224, 240, 269n, 287, 484
Euphrates, 42, 101, 105, 108, 273–4, 291, 453, 466
Europe, Latin, 193, 196, 201, 209, 218, 231, 237–8, 241, 275, 290, 294, 306, 317, 321, 344, 376, 380, 385, 390, 396–7, 445, 449–50, 454, 457, 459–60, 479, 493, 527
European merchants, travelers, 196, 209, 217, 221, 230–1, 294, 389, 454, 465–7, 479
  conflict with, 227, 296–8, 302, 316, 447, 494
  in Mamlūk service, 503
  sources, 490, 492
Eusebius, 19, 24
Eutychios (Saʿīd ibn al-Biṭrīq), 30, 32, 41, 187n, 449

Fabia/Eudocia, 48, 59
al-Fāḍil, *qāḍī*, 208
Faḍl Allāh family, 264
al-Faḍl ibn Mūsā ibn ʿIsā, 80
al-Faḍl ibn Sahl, 81
al-Fā'iz, Ayyūbid, 223
al-Fā'iz, Fāṭimid, 154
Fakhr al-Dīn ibn Shaykh al-Shuyūkh, 224–5, 248–9
Faraj, Mamlūk sultan, 291, 300, 303, 305, 307, 336, 345, 439, 458
Faramā, 81
Faras, in Nubia, 194
Farghana, Farghanians, 98, 112
Fāris al-Dīn Aqṭāy al-Jamdār, 250
Fars, 94, 105
Fāṭima, daughter of Muḥammad, 145, 151, 528, 537
Fāṭima al-Khāṣṣbakiyya, 476n
Fayyūm, 4n, 9, 17–18, 22, 39n, 62n, 111, 131–2, 137, 170, 200, 234, 295, 316, 326, 365
Felix Fabri, 209
Feridūn, 491
Ferrara-Florence, Council of, 196
fetihname, 491, 495, 527
Fez, 128n, 434
Fifth Corps, 298, 480–3, 488, 522
Firmus, 23
Fīrūz, 126–7
Flanders, 230
Flavian dynasty, 13–14
Florian, 23
France, French, 196, 230, 248, 341, 381, 452, 464, 532
Franks, 156, 213–18, 220–1, 223–4, 227, 391, 451–3, 501, 503, 527
  see also crusaders
Frederick II, 223
al-Furāt tribe, 106
furūsiyya, 242–3, 259, 392, 499
Fusṭāṭ, 63, 65–6, 68–72, 75–6, 78–9, 81–2, 84–5, 88, 91–4, 96–100, 102–4, 106, 108–19, 131, 136–9, 151–2, 159, 166–7, 169, 172–3, 187n, 198–204, 208–9, 213, 215–16, 227, 231, 309, 318, 325–6, 328–9, 346, 350, 352–4, 368, 369, 370, 376, 395, 396, 437, 446–7, 527, 530, 532

Gabriel IV, patriarch, 194n
Gaius Turranius, 7
Galba, 13
Galerius, 23–5
Gallienus, 22–3
Gaza, 41, 46, 224, 273, 497, 500, 502

Geniza, 87, 159, 164, 181, 198–200, 203, 208, 321, 324, 329, 346, 353, 381, 383, 385, 387–8, 527
Genoa, Genoese, 275, 280–1, 284–5, 294, 453–5
  alliance with Ilkhanids, 281–2, 284
George, Arian bishop, 28
Georgia, Georgians, 73–4, 507
Germanicus, 12
Germany, Germans, 21–2, 29, 32, 231
Germiyanids, 253, 527
Geta, 18–19
Ghabun, 115
Ghadīr Khumm, festival, 139, 527
Gharbiyya, 315
al-Ghazālī, Abū Ḥāmid, 147, 450
al-Ghazālī, Jānbirdī, 501, 504, 507, 513
Ghāzī ibn al-Wāsiṭī, 272
Ghazna, 319n
Ghazza, 303
Gibb, H. A. R., 414–15, 417
Gil, Moshe, 103
Girga, 315, 384
Giza, 109, 116, 131, 137, 358, 504
Goitein, S. D., 381, 383, 398, 396
Golden Horde, 278–9, 284, 453, 527
Gönüllü, 512, 527
Gordian I, 21
Gordian II, 21
Gordian III, 21
Goths, 21–2
Grabar, Oleg, 396
Granada, 434
Greek, 10, 18, 533
  Greeks of Egypt, 4–6, 9, 10, 12, 14, 25, 34–5, 381
  language, 5, 8, 31, 34, 68, 177, 179–80, 184, 190, 193, 194–5, 323n, 348, 446, 535
  mamlūks, 252, 300
  Orthodox Church, 349, 446
  recruits, 94, 105
  sources, 449–50
Gregoria, 58
Gresham's law, 320–1
Guillaume Adam, 282
Gujarat, 450

Haarmann, Ulrich, 257
al-Ḥabashī, 112
Ḥadīd tribe, 168
al-Ḥadītha, 101
Hadrian, 7, 15–16, 18
al-Ḥāfiẓ, 149, 528
Ḥāfiẓ Muḥammad, 491
Ḥāfiẓī line, Ḥāfiẓī Ismāʿīlīs, 149, 527–8, 538
Ḥāfṣ ibn al-Walīd al-Ḥadramī, 75–6
Ḥāfṣids of Tunis, 434, 452, 454
Ḥāfṣiyya, 75–6
Haifa, 276
ḥājib, *ḥājib al-ḥujjāb*, 260, 305, 528
ḥajj, *see* pilgrimage
Ḥajji I, al-Muẓaffar, 256, 288–9
Ḥajji II, al-Ṣaliḥ, 290
al-Ḥākim I, ʿAbbāsid caliph, 255
al-Ḥākim, Fatimid caliph, 103, 140, 142–3, 152–3, 155, 172–3, 183, 201, 206, 358
  mosque of, 166, 172, 343, 345, 348, 354, 357, 504, 526
al-Ḥalabī, 497
ḥalqa corps, 227, 240, 259–61, 263, 287, 386, 426, 481, 521–2, 523, 528, 533
Ḥamāh, 95, 107, 220, 273, 279, 307, 319n, 418, 423, 498
Ḥamdan Qarmāṭ (Abū ʿAlī), 106, 122–3, 125–7, 132, 535
Ḥamdānids, 113–15, 117–18
Ḥamdūnids, 140
Hamitic language, 93n
Hamouli, 189n
al-Ḥamrāʾ al-Quṣwā quarter, 99
Ḥamza ibn ʿAlī, 143
Ḥanafī rite, Ḥanafīs, 88, 101, 129, 134, 268–9, 311, 381, 418, 423, 436–7, 439, 441, 485, 528
Hanbalī rite, Hanbalīs, 232, 266–8, 402, 418, 428, 528
Ḥanīfa tribe, 121
Ḥanẓala, 73
ḥarāfish, 311, 407, 528
al-Ḥaram al-Sharīf, Jerusalem, 444
al-Ḥarbiyya (La Forbie), 224
Ḥarīth ibn Yazīd al-Hadramī, 45
Harnuphis, 17
Harpocration, 27
Ḥarrān, 96, 267
Hārūn ibn Khumārawayh, Abū Mūsā, 106, 108, 111

Hārūn al-Rashīd, 79, 82
Ḥasan, 129n, 537
Ḥasanids, 94, 137, 139, 522, 528
al-Ḥasan ibn al-Aʿṣam, 114
Ḥasan al-Baghdādī, Abū ʿAlī, 199
Ḥasan ibn Ibrāhīm al-Tustarī, 206
al-Ḥasan al-Kalbī, 140–1
Ḥasan ibn al-Ṣabbaḥ, 145, 147–9
al-Ḥasan ibn al-Takhtākh, 80
al-Ḥasan ibn ʿUbayd Allāh ibn Ṭughj, 118
Hāshim, 66
Ḥassān ibn ʿAṭāhiya, 75
Ḥassān ibn Nuʿmān al-Ghassānī, 71
Hathor, 14
Ḥaṭṭīn, battle, 218
Ḥawf, 74–5, 78–9, 80, 83
Hawthara ibn Suhayl al-Bāhilī, 75–6
Hawwāra tribe, amīrate, 291, 294, 296, 299, 315–16, 384, 528
al-Haysam tribe, 307
Hebrew language, sources, 170, 199–201, 204, 208, 348, 363, 490–1
Hebron, 273, 313, 502, 504
Heliopolis, *see* ʿAyn Shams
Hellenistic Jewry, 198
Hennequin, Gilles, 321
Henoticon, 32
Heraclian dynasty 38–42, 48–49
Heraclius, 33, 36–7, 40, 42–5, 47–8, 51–2, 54–5, 57–61, 177, 199, 533
Heraclius, Exarch of Africa, 37
Heraclius Constantine III, 37, 48, 58
Heraiskos, 31–2
Herakleopolis Magna (Ihnasiyat al-madina), 39
Hermetism, 25
Hermopolite, 10
Heroninos archive, 22
Heth'um, Armenian king, 279
hieroglyphs, 8–9, 32
Hilāl, 110
Hilāl tribe, 314–15, 449
Hind, *see* India
Hindu Kush, 453–4
Hishām, 73–5
Hit, 105
Hohenstaufen, 452–3
holy cities, 88, 217, 282, 298, 381, 446, 484, 503, 530
see also Mecca, Medina
Holy Land, 209
Horapollo: the elder, 31; the younger, 31–2
Hospitallers, 275–6
hospitals, *see bimaristan*
Hrosiwtha, nun, 193
Ḥijāz, 53, 75, 94, 135, 168, 217–18, 282, 294, 296, 381, 385, 446, 463, 490, 503, 505, 509
Ḥimṣ, *see* Ḥomṣ
Ḥimyar, 64
ḥisba, *see muḥtasib*
Ḥiṣn al-Akrād (Crac des Chevaliers), 275–6
Ḥiṣn Kayfā, 225
Ḥomṣ, 95–6, 107, 113–14, 220, 273, 275, 277, 279, 447–8, 461, 499
Hubayra, 66
Ḥudayj tribe, 81
Ḥujariyya regiment, 156
Hülegü, 273
Hulwa, 55
Ḥulwān, 71
Ḥumayd ibn Qaḥṭbā, 77
al-Ḥurr ibn Yūsuf, 74
Ḥusām al-Dīn Lājīn, 252
Ḥusayn ibn ʿAlī, 121, 129n, 358, 523
Ḥusaynids, 107, 137, 139, 142, 522, 528–9
al-Ḥusayn Ṣāhib al-Shāma, 107
al-Ḥusayn ibn Saʿīd al-Ḥamdānī, Abū ʿAbd Allāh, 113
Hypathia, 30

Ibadites, 77, 96
Iberian textiles, 210
Ibn al-ʿAbbās, chief, 96
Ibn ʿAbd al-Ḥakam, 37, 40, 41, 45, 60, 63, 198
Ibn ʿAbd al-Kān, Abū Jaʿfar Muḥammad, 97
Ibn ʿAbd al-Ẓāhir, Muḥyī al-Dīn, 421–2, 424, 430, 437
Ibn Abī ʿAṣrūn, 239
Ibn Abī Dimm, 207
Ibn Abī Ḥudhayfa, 68
Ibn Abi'l-Sāj, Muḥammad, 105
Ibn Abī Ṭayyi, 433

Ibn Amājūr, 95
Ibn ʿAmmār, 155
Ibn al-ʿArabī, Muḥyī al-Dīn, 268, 404, 499
Ibn al-Arqaṭ, 85
Ibn ʿAsākir, 415
Ibn al-Aswad, 122n
Ibn ʿAṭāʾ Allāh, Tāj al-Dīn, 266–8, 271, 404, 406, 537
Ibn al-Athīr, ʿIzz al-Dīn ʿAlī, 93, 96, 109, 414–19
Ibn Baʿra, 332
Ibn Baṭṭūṭa, 268, 396
Ibn Daqīq al-ʿId, 382–3
Ibn al-Dawādārī, Sayf al-Dīn Abū Bakr, 424–9, 431–2, 440
Ibn al-Dāya, Aḥmad, 97–8
Ibn Duqmāq, 346, 484n
Ibn Falāḥ, Jaʿfar, 138
Ibn al-Fallāḥī, Ṣadaqa ibn Yūsuf, 206–7
Ibn al-Fāriḍ, 268, 378, 402, 405
Ibn al-Furāt, Abuʾl-Khaṭṭāb Jaʿfar, wazīr, 98, 112, 117–18, 138, 158
Ibn al-Furāt, Nāṣir al-Dīn Muḥammad, 433
Ibn Ḥajar al-ʿAsqalānī, Shihāb al-Dīn Aḥmad, 378, 436, 442–3
Ibn al-Ḥājj, 389–90, 410–11
Ibn Hanbal, 88
Ibn Hānī, 141
Ibn Ḥawqal, 126, 127n
Ibn Ḥawshab, 123–5, 127, 146
Ibn Ḥinzāba, Abuʾl-Fatḥ al-Faḍl, 98, 112
Ibn Hubayra, 76
Ibn Iyās al-Ḥanafī, Muḥammad ibn Aḥmad, 383, 395, 440–1, 468n, 479–83, 485, 488, 490–1, 493–4, 496–8, 500, 502–3, 505–8, 510, 512, 516
Ibn Jamāʿa, Badr al-Dīn, 254, 256
Ibn al-Jaṣṣāṣ, Abū ʿAbd Allāh al-Jawharī, 106
Ibn al-Jawzī, Sibṭ, 418, 429
Ibn al-Jīʿān, 484n
Ibn Jubayr, 168
Ibn Kathīr, 416, 427
Ibn Kātib al-Farghānī, 100
Ibn Khaldūn, ʿAbd al-Raḥman ibn Muḥammad, 243, 339, 341, 346, 360, 374, 375, 378, 383, 391, 401, 416, 421, 433–6, 523
Ibn Khallikān, Aḥmad ibn Muḥammad, 415, 419
Ibn al-Khaṭīb, 434
Ibn Khurradādhbih, 87
Ibn Killis, Yaʿqūb, 114, 117, 158, 170, 206
Ibn al-Kīzānī, Abū ʿAbd Allāh, 402
Ibn Kundāj, Isḥāq, 101, 105
Ibn Lahīʿa, 40, 45, 63
Ibn al-Mashṭūb, ʿImād al-Dīn, 223, 225
Ibn al-Mudabbir Aḥmad ibn Muḥammad al-Rastisānī, 92, 94–6, 100
Ibn Rāʾiq, Muḥammad, 98, 112–13
Ibn Saʿīd, historian, 98, 113, 166
Ibn al-Sallār, 168
Ibn Sanāʾ al-Mulk, 391
Ibn Sayyid al-Nās, 432
Ibn Shaddād, Bahāʾ al-Dīn, 416, 418, 421
Ibn al-Shaykh, ʿIsā ibn al-Shaykh al-Shaybānī, 94, 105
Ibn al-Ṣūfī, Ibrahim ibn Muḥammad, 93
Ibn al-Ṭabāṭabā, Aḥmad ibn Muḥammad, Bughā al-Aṣghar, 93
Ibn Taghrī Birdī, Abū al-Maḥāsin Yūsuf, 433, 436, 438–43
Ibn Taymiyya, Taqī al-Dīn, 244, 256, 266–8, 271–2, 402, 405, 411, 428, 430–1
Ibn Ṭughj, *see* al-Ikhshīd
Ibn Ṭūlūn, Aḥmad, 85, 89–104, 106, 108, 113–14, 116–18, 192, 350, 369
  mosque of, 108, 137, 139, 158, 173, 327, 345, 350, 351, 352, 354, 357, 375, 504
Ibn Ṭūlūn, Muḥammad, 491, 500, 502, 505
Ibn ʿUbaydūs al-Fihrī, 83
Ibn Wāṣil, Jamāl al-Dīn Muḥammad, 248n, 418–20, 423
Ibn al-Zubayr, 70, 71
Ibn Zunbul, 491, 499
Ibn Zunbur, 272
Ibrāhīm III, 96
Ibrāhīm al-Dassūqī, sanctuary of, 313
Ibrāhīm al-Matbūlī, 378

Ibrāhīm Pasha, 515
Ibrāhīm ibn Sahl al-Tustarī, Abū Saʿd, 171, 206–7
Ibrāhīm ibn Ṣāliḥ, 78
Ifrīqiya (Tunisia), 87, 93–4, 96, 104, 107, 111–12, 117–18, 120, 131, 133, 136, 139, 151, 162–3, 201, 218, 352, 448–9
al-Ikhshīd, 89–90, 97–8, 109–15, 118
Ikhshīdids, 100, 103, 105, 112, 114–19, 132, 137–9, 157–8, 246, 327, 328n, 448
Īkjān, 124
Īlkhānids (*see also* Mongols), 253, 261, 275–86, 425, 428, 452–3, 456, 529, 533, 536
Ilyās ibn Asad ibn Sāmān Khūdā, 82
Ilyās ibn Manṣūr al-Nafūsī, 96
ʿImād al-Dīn Muḥammad al-Kātib al-Iṣfahānī, 415–18
Īnal, 513–14
India, Hind, Indians, 15–16, 86–7, 123, 142, 148–9, 168, 282, 283–4, 396, 431, 447, 449–50, 454–6, 459–61, 464n, 482, 524, 539
Indian Ocean, 86, 118, 162–3, 165, 168, 217, 230–1, 277, 281, 283, 297–8, 392, 316, 341, 445, 447, 449–50, 454–6, 460–1, 466, 490, 494
Indus river, 454
iqṭāʿ, *iqṭāʿāt*, 109, 117, 156, 161, 215, 218, 224, 227–9, 232, 234–5, 237, 243, 252, 257, 260, 261, 264–5, 272, 275, 287, 291, 302, 314–15, 384, 441, 457, 473–4, 477, 481–2, 484n, 486–8, 508, 511, 525–6, 529, 533–4
Iran, Iranians; Persia, Persians, 1–2, 21–2, 33, 35, 37–9, 42–6, 49–51, 55–7, 80, 82, 85–6, 88–9, 98, 104–5, 114, 117, 120, 123–4, 142–5, 147–9, 152, 199–200, 206, 232, 243, 246, 273, 278, 282, 381, 394–5, 400, 403, 428, 449–52, 454–6, 460–1, 481, 494–5, 497, 522, 525, 528–9, 531, 533, 536
Iraq, 39, 64, 66, 77, 79, 80, 82, 85, 86–9, 94–5, 97, 101–2, 104–7, 109–10, 114–15, 117, 120, 123–6, 135, 142–8, 158, 166, 199–200, 203, 232, 246, 273, 294, 328n, 381, 400, 446–7, 449, 451, 454, 527, 529, 535–6, 539
ʿĪsā al-Julūdī, 83
ʿĪsā ibn Luqmān, 78
ʿĪsā ibn Muḥammad (Mūsā) al-Nūsharī, 103, 108–10
ʿĪsā ibn Yazīd al-Julūdī, 82
Isaac of Alexandria, 178n
Isaac Israeli, 201
Isaakios, 55–8
Iṣfahān, 105, 416
Isḥāq ibn Andūna al-Sayyid, 72
Isidorus, 17
Isis, 12, 14, 26, 30–1
Islamic law, *see Sharīʾa*
Ismāʿīl, 7th imam, 107, 121–2, 151, 529
Ismāʿīlīs, 86, 106, 117, 119, 120–30, 132–45, 147–50, 151–2, 158, 166, 172–4, 201, 215–16, 265–6, 274, 279, 348, 352–3, 358, 370, 381, 400–1, 450–1, 523–4, 526, 529, 531, 534–5, 537
Ismāʿīl, Shah, 461, 466, 494–7, 529
Ismāʿīl ibn al-Yasaʿ al-Kindī, 66
Iṣṭabl, 72
Istanbul, 429, 492–3, 497, 500, 504, 506–10, 512–16, 538
see also Constantinople
Ītakh, 82
Italy, Italian cities, Italians (*see also* Genoa, Venice), 14, 25, 59, 132, 217, 223, 230–1, 275, 280, 360, 419, 449, 452–5
ʿIzz al-Dīn Muḥammad ibn al-Shaddād al-Ḥalabī, 421–2

Jabal Nafuīsa, 97
Jabal Yashkur, 99
al-Jabalayn, 14
Jābir ibn al-Walīd, 85
Jacob Baradæus, 180, 529
Jacobites, 117, 180, 529, 533
Jaʿfar, *see also* al-Muwaffad
Jaʿfar, servant of Saʿīd, 126–7
Jaʿfar al-Ṣādiq, 107, 121–3
Jaffa, 276

al-Jahshiyārī, 79
Jakam, rebel amīr, 291
Jalāl al-Dīn Khwārazmshāh, 236
Jalāyirids, 253, 529
Jamāl al-Dīn Yūsuf al-Bīrī, *ustādār*, 307
Jamāl al-Dīn Yūsuf ibn Kātib Jakam, 307
Jamāli wazīrs, 173
jamakiyya, 482, 429
Jānbalāt, 297, 305
Jānbirdī, *see* al-Ghazālī
Jānim al-Ḥamzāwī, 508, 515
Jānim al-Sayfī, 513–14
Janissaries, 482, 499, 503, 511–12, 514–15, 529
Jaqmaq, 209, 293–5, 301, 303, 309, 394, 439
al-Jarjarā'ī, wazīr, 207
al-Jarrāḥ tribe, 106
Jawhar, 92, 118–19, 120, 136–41, 151, 157–8, 328
Jaysh ibn Khumarawayh, 106, 108
al-Jazarī, Shams al-Dīn Muḥammad, 425, 427–30, 433, 435
Jazīra, *see* Mesopotamia
Jedda, 294, 494
Jeme, 181
Jerusalem, 14, 47, 103, 107, 110, 117–18, 154, 204, 218, 222–4, 375, 397, 417, 444, 502, 527
  see also Latin Kingdom
Jesus Christ, 14n, 25, 27, 177, 397, 524, 532–3
Jews, Jewish community, 12–14, 35, 36, 87, 98–9, 102–4, 117, 119, 152, 159–50, 166–70, 174, 177, 181, 198–210, 217, 233, 236, 272, 347–9, 353, 360, 363, 381, 387–8, 396, 491, 503, 506–7, 509, 514–15, 524, 527, 529
Jīʿān lineage, 473–4
al-Jīʿān tribe, 307, 507
Johannes IX, patriarch, 196
John Kateas, 40, 57
John Moschus, 38
John of Barka, Barkaines, 47, 51
John of Nikiou, 39, 40, 46, 62n, 195
John Philoponus, 32
John the Almsgiver, patriarch, 38, 51, 55–9
Jordan, al-Urdunn, Transjordan, 56, 74, 92, 94–5, 105, 114, 223, 307, 500
Joseph (Yūsuf), 416
Jovian, 28
Judah ben Sa'adya, 205
Judean revolt, 13–14
Judeo-Arabic language, 348
Judhām, 80, 84, 315
Juhayna tribe, 314
julbān, 468, 482, 488, 494, 498, 529
Julia Maesa, 18, 20
Julian, 28
Julius Cæsar, 3
Jusiyya, 114
Justin I, 32
Justin II, 33
Justinian, 32, 34, 44
Juyūshiyya troops, of Badr al-Jamālī, 156

Kaʿba, 107, 111, 135, 282, 313, 347, 354, 370, 374, 504, 531
Kabsh district, 303
Kabul, 319n
Kaffa, 280
Kāfūr, Abu'l-Misk, 90, 103, 114–19, 375
Kāfūrids, 103, 117–18, 138
Kalabsha (Talmis), 12, 14, 18, 22, 31
Kalb tribe, 108, 114, 116
Kamāl al-Dīn Muḥammad ibn al-Bārizī, 307
al-Kāmil Muḥammad, Ayyūbid, 221, 223–4, 227n, 229, 231, 234n, 236–40, 324n, 326, 330, 332–3, 335n, 415, 419
Kanz tribe, 314–15
Karīm al-Dīn al-Kabīr, 264
Kara Qoyunlū, 291–2
Karaca Aḥmet Pasha, 497
Karaite Jews, 200–1, 203–6
Karak, 223, 273–5, 289
Karamānids, 253, 291, 295–6
Karanis, 13
Kārimī merchants, 230, 285, 294, 396, 530
  see also spice trade
Karnak, 13
Kashan, 416

kāshif, *kushshāf*, 294, 314–15, 513, 515, 530
Kātib Jakam tribe, 307
kātib al-sirr, 264, 304, 307, 421, 530
Kayserī, 296, 497, 530
Kendrick, 353n
Kerala, 298
al-Khabūshānī, Najm al-Dīn, 402
Khāḍir, shaykh, 268, 271
Khā'il III, patriarch, 100
al-Khalanjī, Ibrāhīm, 110
Khālid ibn Ḥumayd, 40, 47, 60n
Khālid ibn Yazīd ibn Mazyad, 81
khalīj Abī Munajja, 207
Khalīl, al-Ashraf, 251–2, 255, 258, 262, 271, 276–7, 280, 421–2
*khānqāh*s, 231, 265, 267–8, 270, 340, 368, 372, 397, 405, 409, 473, 484, 530, 535
Kharga Oasis, 29
Kharibtā, 69
Khārijites, 70, 79, 94, 129, 133, 530
khāṣṣakī mamlūks, *khāṣṣakiyya*, 260, 305, 469n, 481, 530
Khatkīn al-Ḍayf, 142
Khayrbak al-Sharīfī, 299, 486–7, 496, 498–9, 502, 504, 507–9, 511–13
khāzindār, 260, 486–7, 530
khiṭṭa, *khiṭaṭ*, 64, 99, 346, 349, 350, 530
Khudābanda (Öljeitü), 283
Khumārawayh ibn Aḥmad ibn Ṭūlūn, 90–1, 97, 101, 104–6
Khurasan, Khurasanis, 76, 77, 80, 83, 105, 123, 144, 232, 319n, 401, 451
khushdāshiyya, 248, 250–2, 254, 258–9, 263, 265, 274, 288, 479, 531
Khushqadam, 293, 295, 301, 439, 443
khuṭba, 65, 101, 113, 137–8, 147, 172, 215, 236, 283, 323, 354, 476, 503, 531
Khwārazm-Shah, territory of; Khwārazmians, 224, 236, 273, 531
Kilāb tribe, 96, 113–14
Kināniyya Arabs, 226
Kinda, 64
al-Kindī, 70, 72, 73, 79, 80, 84, 109
Kipchak steppes, 247, 273, 278–9
Kipchak Turks, 247, 253, 258, 261, 284, 287, 531
al-Kirmānī, Ḥāmid al-Dīn, 142–3
kiswa, 282, 313, 347, 370, 374, 504, 531
Kitbughā, Mongol general, 273
Kitbughā, Mamlūk sultan, 252, 257–8, 268, 288
Kom Ombo (Ombos), 13–14, 17–18, 20, 32
Kom Sharik, 55
Kūfa, 66, 86, 106–7, 123–4, 127, 145, 447
Kūm al-Shiqāf (Qom es-Shugafa), 9
Kurā', battle of, 248, 531
Kurds, 117, 213–14, 223, 226, 246, 259, 260, 291, 377, 381, 391, 527
Kutāma Berber tribe, 112, 124, 127–30, 136, 154–5
al-Kuwayz tribe, 307
Kyros (Cyrus, al-Muqawqas), Monothelete Patriarch of Alexandria, 40, 44–6, 48, 54–8, 177

Labda, 96
Lājīn, 257, 259, 262, 268, 288
Lakhm, Lakhmis, 64, 70, 80, 81, 84
Lamak ibn Malik al-Ḥammādī, 145
Lapidus, Ira, 385, 476
Latin Kingdom of Jerusalem, 213, 216, 218, 221, 223, 253, 274, 276, 287
  Latins in Levant, 217–18, 220–2, 225, 236, 278, 365
  see also crusades
Latin language, sources, 8, 40, 193, 201, 323n
al-Layth ibn al-Faḍl, 79, 80
al-Layth ibn Sa'd, 63
  tomb of, 504
Lebanon, Lebanese mountains, 43, 266, 500
Leo I, 32
Leo III, 279
Leontios of Neapolis, 37, 55, 57
Leontopolite, 14
Lesser Kabylia, 124
Libya, Libyans, 1, 15, 51, 93, 104, 118, 120, 130n
Licinius, 25–6

Livio Sanuto, 389
London, 380
Louis IX, 224, 239, 248, 255, 452, 532
Low Countries, 454
Lu'lu', commander, 96, 100, 102, 108
Lu'lu'a, mosque of, 358, 359
Lucius Domitius Domitianus, 24
Luxor, 13, 29, 39n, 181, 349
Lycia, 67

Ma'āfir, 64
Ma'arrat al-Nu'mān, 107
Macarius, 27
Macedonia, Macedonians, 1–3
Macrianus, 22
Macrinus, 20
al-Mādharā'ī family, 105
al-Mādharā'ī, Abū 'Alī Ḥusayn, Abū Zunbur, 111–12
al-Mādharā'ī, Abū Bakr al-Atrash, Aḥmad ibn Ibrāhīm, 97
al-Mādharā'ī, Abū Bakr Muḥammad ibn 'Alī, 109
Madianites, 56
*madrasa*s, 168, 231–3, 237, 264–5, 268, 270–1, 311–12, 315, 363, 365, 368, 371–2, 379, 381–2, 392, 394, 397, 400–1, 403–5, 409, 416, 423, 443, 473, 485, 488, 531
Maghrib, *see* north Africa
al-Maḥalla al-Kubrā, 169, 202, 316
Maharraga (Hiera Sykaminos), 12
Mahdī, sorcerer, 383
al-Mahdī, 66, 77, 78, 111–12, 120–2, 125, 129–30, 132, 135
al-Mahdiyya, 133, 201
Mahfouz, Naguib, 388
Maḥfūẓ ibn Sulaymān, 79
maḥmal, 313, 374, 531
Maḥmūd ibn Eretna, 286
Maimonides, Moses (al-Mu'izz ibn Maymūn), 98, 205, 208
Majd al-Dīn al-Sallāmī, 285
Malacca Straits, 455
Mali, Malians, 334
Mālik al-Ashtar, 68
al-Malik al-Sa'īd, 258
Mālikī rite, Mālikīs, 88, 129, 134, 146, 168, 267–8, 400, 434, 451, 532
Māmāy, 310
al-Ma'mūn, 72, 80–2, 88, 91, 326n
al-Ma'mūn al-Bataihī, 153, 166, 168, 173
Manfred of Sicily, 418
Manichaeism, 24
Mansa Mūsā, 334
al-Manṣūr, *see* Qalāwūn
al-Manṣūr, 'Abbāsid caliph, 77–9
al-Manṣūr, Ayyūbid, son of al-'Azīz, 220, 240
al-Manṣūr, Fatimid, 127n, 133, 136, 139
al-Manṣūr, of Ḥamāh, 279
al-Manṣūr 'Alī, 290
al-Manṣūra, 223–5
  battle of, 248, 255, 532
Manṣūri mamlūks (of Qalāwūn), Manṣūriyya, 252, 258, 262
al-Manṣūriyya, 133n, 139, 141
Manṣūriyya *madrasa*, 271
Manuel the Augustulis, 47, 55, 59, 61
al-Maqrīzī, Taqī al-Dīn, 100, 108, 180, 206, 221n, 324, 330, 332–4, 335n, 337, 346, 381, 386–7, 390, 395, 399, 408, 416, 432–3, 436–40, 443
al-Maqurra, Nubian kingdom, 283
Marcian, 31
Marcus Aurelius, 8, 17, 19
Mareotis, 353
Marianos, 47
Marinids, 434, 454
Marino Sannuto, 282–3, 492
Marj Dābiq, 299, 303, 305, 316, 338, 461, 480, 483–4, 497–9, 500, 506, 508
Marj Rāhiṭ, 75
Maronites, 266n
Marqab (Margat), 276
Martina, 47, 48, 57, 61
Marwān ibn al-Ḥakam, 70, 76, 83
Marwān ibn Muḥammad, 75
Masīla, 140
Maslama ibn Muhkallad al-Anṣārī, 65, 68–70
Maṣlīaḥ Gaon, 166
Maspero, J., 52
Massisa, 102, 285
Maṭariyya, 304, 309, 502
Maurice, emperor, 33, 37

Mauricius *strategikon*, 49
mawlid al-nabī, 313, 476, 506, 528
Mawṣil, *see* Mosul
Maxentius, 25
Maximian, 23, 25
Maximin Daia, 25
Maximinus, 21
Maximus the Confessor, 50, 51, 57, 60
maẓālim court, 158, 265, 304, 532
Mecca, 70–1, 86, 93, 107, 111, 114, 124, 135, 144, 151, 161, 282–3, 288, 347, 354, 370, 374, 436, 447, 484, 494, 505, 508, 528, 530–2, 535, 537
Medamud, 16
Medina, 42, 64, 68, 69, 77, 93, 151, 161, 282, 375, 447, 530
Medinet Habu, 13–14, 16, 29
Mediterranean, 203, 308, 339, 370, 374, 385, 453, 484n
  coasts and ports, 36, 38, 64, 115, 169, 227, 298, 338
  trade and rivalry in, 38, 104, 162–3, 165–7, 217, 227, 230, 253, 271, 278, 280, 285, 294, 296–7, 308, 376–7, 412, 445, 447, 449–50, 452, 454–5, 461, 465–6, 537
Meḥmet II (Muḥammad II, Fātiḥ), 296, 460, 492–3
Meletian schism, 27
Melkite Church, Melkites, 43, 55, 116, 168, 177–9, 182, 186–8, 307, 449, 532, 534
Memnon, 15, 18
Memphis, 7, 14
Mena of Nikiou, 178n
Mennas I, patriarch, 193n
Meroe, Meroitic kingdom, 11–13, 22
Meshullam da Volterra, 210
Mesopotamia, 39, 42–4, 46, 49, 50, 53, 57, 78, 85, 86–7, 94, 100, 103, 104–5, 114–15, 117, 170n, 212, 218, 224–5, 232, 292, 294, 412, 416, 428, 451, 461n, 531, 539
Mevorakh ben Sa'adya, 205
Michael the Syrian, 45
Michael VIII Palælogus, 278–80, 452
miḥna, 84
Milan, edict of, 26
Milne, 6, 21
Milvian Bridge, battle, 25
Min, 27
Ming dynasty, China, 456, 460
Minṭāsh, 291, 299
Minya, 316
miqyās, Nilometer, 313, 484, 504, 532
monasteries, monasticism, monks, 22, 27, 29–30, 32, 35, 39, 50, 56, 73, 92, 100, 176–7, 180–1, 187–90, 192n, 193–4, 197, 233, 235, 345–6, 370, 398, 444
Möngke, 278
Möngke Temür, 274, 278
Mongol mamlūks, 252, 258
Mongols, 236, 376, 391, 394, 425, 431, 437, 456, 459–60, 527, 529, 533, 538
  invasions of, 149, 243, 244, 247, 248, 250–5, 259–61, 269, 271–80, 282–4, 292, 373, 376, 381, 422, 435, 426, 451–5, 503
  peace treaty with, 253, 261, 282, 284–6
  see also Ilkhanids
Monophysism, Monophysites, 30, 32, 34, 49, 59, 67, 177–80, 182, 186–8, 193, 194n, 195–6, 524, 529, 533
Monotheletism, 44, 50, 177, 533
Morocco, 128n, 266, 454, 531
Moses, son of Mevorakh, 205
Mosul (Mawṣil), 87, 94, 101, 105, 113, 145, 414–16
Muʿallaqa church, 349, 354
Muʿāwiya ibn ʿAbd al-Raḥmān ibn Muʿāwiya ibn Ḥudayj, 73
Muʿāwiya ibn Abī Sufyān, 65, 68–9, 102
Muʿāwiya ibn Ḥudayj al-Tujībī, 66, 68–9, 83
al-Mu'ayyad Shaykh, *see* Shaykh
Mu'ayyad fi'l-Dīn, *see* al-Shīrāzī
Mu'ayyadī mamlūks (of Shaykh), 300–1
al-Muʿaẓẓam ʿIsā, Ayyūbid, 223, 236, 418
al-Mubārak ibn ʿAlī al-ʿAbdī, 122
al-Mubarākiyya, 122
Muḍar ibn Aḥmad ibn Ṭūlūn, 106

Mudlij tribe, 85
Mufaḍḍal ibn Abī al-Faḍā'il, 427
al-Mufawwaḍ, Jaʿfar ibn al-Muʿtamid, 94–5, 105
al-Mughīth, ʿUmar, 274
al-Muhājir tribe, 97
Muhallabī, 77
Muḥammad, Prophet, 64, 66, 88, 99, 107, 119, 120–1, 123, 137, 151, 173, 265, 313, 357–8, 389, 404, 410, 416, 431, 463, 476, 504, 506, 509, 524, 527–9, 533, 537–8
Muḥammad ibn Abi'l-Layth al-Khwārazmī, 84
Muḥammad ibn Abī Yaʿqūb, 108n
Muḥammad ibn ʿAlī al-Khalij, 110
Muḥammad ibn Asb āṭ, 81
Muḥammad ibn al-Ashʿath, 77
Muḥammad ibn Barqūq, 291
Muḥammad ibn Bughā, 94
Muḥammad ibn al-Faraj al-Farghānī, 93
Muḥammad ibn Ḥudhayfa, 68
Muḥammad ibn Ismāʿīl, 122–6, 135
Muḥammad ibn Ismāʿīl al-Darazī, 143
Muḥammad the Pure Soul, 77
Muḥammad ibn Qāytbāy, 296
Muḥammad ibn Qurhub, 96
Muḥammad ibn Shādhan al-Jawharī, 102
Muḥammad ibn Sulaymān al-Kātib. 107–8, 110
Muḥammad ibn Takīn, 110–11
Muḥammad ibn Ṭughj, *see* al-Ikhshīd
Muḥammad ibn Yūsuf al-Kindī, 63
al-Muhtadī, caliph, 94
muḥtasib, *ḥisba*, 159–60, 232–3, 307, 399–400, 408–9, 436–7, 508, 528, 533
Muḥyī al-Dīn al-Qaṣrawī, 487
al-Muʿizz ibn Bādīs, 146
al-Muʿizz li-Dīn Allāh, Fatimid, 118, 120, 127n, 133–7, 139–42, 151–2, 158, 162
Muʿizziyya mamlūks, 250
al-Muktafī, 107, 110
al-Munāwāt, 504
Mu'nis, 110–12
al-Muntaṣir, 82, 84
Muqaṭṭam district, 99–100, 103–4, 116, 216, 350
muqarnaṣ, 369, 370
al-Muqaddasī, 99
Muqawqas, *see* Kyros
al-Muqtadir, 110
Mūsā ibn Atāmish, 96
Mūsā ibn Bughā, 94–5
Mūsā ibn Jaʿfar, 122
Mūsā ibn Kaʿb, 77
Mūsā ibn Muṣʿab al-Khathʿamī, 78
Mūsā ibn Nuṣayr, 71
al-Musabbiḥī, 165
muṣallā, 109, 352, 354, 358
Muṣṭafā Pasha, 513–14
al-Mussannāh, 69
al-Mustaʿīn, ʿAbbāsid caliph, 91
al-Mustaʿīn, caliph, Mamlūk sultan, 291–2, 303, 336
al-Mustaʿlī, Fāṭimid, 145, 148–9, 153, 168, 328, 534
Mustaʿlī Ismāʿīlis, 145, 148, 154
al-Mustakfī, caliph, 256–7
al-Mustanṣir, caliph in Cairo, 255
al-Mustanṣir, Fāṭimid, 108, 147–8, 152–3, 155, 158, 165, 171, 206–7, 523, 534
al-Muʿtaḍid billāh, Aḥmad ibn al-Muwaffaq, 105–6
al-Muʿtamid ʿalā Allāh, Abū'l-ʿAbbās Aḥmad ibn al-Mutawakkil, 94–6, 101–2, 105
al-Mutannabī, 115
al-Muʿtaṣim, 82, 83, 84, 246, 326n
al-Mutawakkil III ibn al-Mustamsik Ya'qub, Mamlūk caliph, 303, 501, 506
al-Mutawakkil, Abu'l-Faḍl Ja'far ibn Muḥammad, Abbāsid caliph, 84–5, 88, 92, 106, 448
al-Mutawakkil, Mamlūk caliph, 291, 303
Muʿtazilite, 88, 533
al-Muʿtazz, caliph, 91, 94
al-Muttaqī, caliph, 113–14
al-Muwaffaq, Abū Aḥmad, caliph, 89, 94–6, 101–2, 104–5
al-Muẓaffar, *see* Baybars II al-Jāshnikīr, Ḥajjī
Muẓaffarids, 253, 533
Muzāḥim ibn Khāqān, 85
Muzāḥim ibn Muḥammad ibn Rā'iq, 113

Muzhir tribe, 307
Myos Hormos, 16
mysticism, 5, 381, 413, 529
 see also Sufism

al-Nābulsī, 234–5
nā'ib al-ghayba, 496, 533
nā'ib al-salṭana, 248, 263–4, 290, 305, 314, 533
Naʿīma, 433
Najʿ Ḥammādī, 3
al-Najīramī, 98
Napata, 11
Napoleon Bonaparte, 341
Narmuthis (Medinet Madi), 9
al-Nashw, 264
al-Nāṣir, caliph, 102
al-Nāṣir Aḥmad, 256
Nāṣir al-Dawla, 113
Nāṣir al-Dīn ibn Ḥanash, 500
Nāṣir al-Dīn Muḥammad al-Bārizī, 307
Nāṣir al-Dīn Shafi' ibn ʿAlī al-Miṣrī, 422
al-Nāṣir Faraj, *see* Faraj
al-Nāṣir Ḥasan, 253, 257, 262, 268, 287–8, 291
 madrasa complex of, 344, 361, 364, 397
Nāṣir-i Khusraw, 143–4, 152, 346
al-Nāṣir Muḥammad ibn Qalāwūn, 248, 251–9, 261–4, 266, 268, 272, 282–4, 286–8, 300, 303, 357, 365, 402, 405, 423–7, 430–2, 435, 456, 501
al-Nāṣir Muḥammad ibn Qāytbāy, 297, 305
al-Nāṣir Yūsuf, 248–9, 273–4, 531
Naṣr, Abū Ghānim, 108
al-Naṣr Allāh tribe, 307
Naṣrids, 434
Naucratis, 6
al-Nawbakhtī, 122n
Nawrūz, rebel amīr, 291–2
Nawrūz festival, 167, 410, 534
naẓar al-khāṣṣ, nāẓir al-khāṣṣ, 264, 272, 307, 534
naẓir al-jaysh, 272, 307, 487
Nea Aphrodite, 14
Nebuchadnezzar, 503
Neguev, 46
Nero, 7, 13
Nerva, 14
Nessana, 46
Nestorius, 30
Nicaea, 278
 Council of, 27
Nikephoros, 40, 45, 59
Niketas, 51, 55–6, 58
Nikiu, 55, 61
Nikopolis, 2n
Nile, Nile valley, 2–3, 15, 53, 61, 64, 81, 87–8, 93, 98–9, 101, 109, 111n, 117–18, 131, 133, 137, 139, 152, 159, 161–2, 168–9, 173, 213, 221–3, 227, 241, 247, 277, 282, 292, 310, 313, 315–16, 348, 367, 368, 375, 381–2, 384, 396, 408, 452, 463, 504, 512, 516, 523, 532, 534
 see also Delta
Nitria, monastery, 193
Niẓām al-Mulk, 147, 245
Niẓār, 148–9, 153, 168, 534
Niẓārī Ismāʿīlīs, 145, 148–50, 153–4, 523, 528, 534, 538
Noba, 24, 31, 32
Normans, 241, 449
north Africa, Maghrib, 18, 39, 41, 45, 47, 50, 59, 63, 66, 71, 74, 75, 83, 85, 87, 93, 104, 110, 118, 120, 124–5, 127–8, 131–4, 136, 138, 139n, 140, 141n, 146, 154, 158, 166, 168, 171, 204, 217–18, 232, 308, 312, 325, 381, 383, 401, 434–5, 446–7, 449, 501–2, 506, 509, 539
Nubia, Nubians, 1, 11–12, 22–4, 68, 93, 100, 115–16, 118, 162, 194–5, 226, 230, 252, 282–3, 314, 339, 383, 451, 514, 523, 534
Numayr tribe, 114
Numerian, 23
Numidia, 38, 50–1, 60
Nūr al-Dīn Zengī, 212–15, 217–18, 220, 228, 239, 246, 265, 269, 330, 416–18, 451
al-Nuwayrī, Shihāb al-Dīn Aḥmad, 427–8, 430–1, 433, 435, 444

Obadiah da Bertinoro, 209
Octavian, 1, 5, 7, 11

Odoacer, 32
Olympiodorus of Thebes, 31
Olympius, 29
Onias, 14
Origen, 19
Osiris, 15, 30
Osrhoene, 40, 57
Otho, 13
Ottomans, 180, 197, 253, 286, 290–9, 301–2, 308, 310, 312, 315, 317, 376, 384, 406, 411, 414, 441, 445–6, 460–1, 465–7, 478–80, 482–3, 489, 490–516, 524–5, 527, 529–30, 532–9
  conquest, 206, 210, 318, 338, 347, 411, 441, 448, 458, 467, 471, 527
  historians, sources, 433, 491, 495, 498n, 503, 505
Oxyrhynchus, 9, 15, 27

Pachomius, 26
paganism, 12, 17, 25, 28–32, 36, 176
  and shamanism among Mamlūks, 246, 268–9, 406
  Mongol, 391, 435
Palestine, 36, 38, 42–3, 46–7, 49–50, 52–3, 62, 70, 80, 81, 92, 94–5, 99, 105, 110, 112–14, 116, 118, 138, 156, 168, 199–201, 204, 223, 229, 319n, 349, 398, 412, 420, 428, 448, 450, 452–3, 500, 535
Palestinian yeshiva, 166, 199–200, 203–5
Palmyra, 23, 52
Pancrates, 15
Panopolis, 24, 27
papacy, pope, 7, 30, 32, 196, 222, 280, 285, 452–3
Paris, 380
Parthians, 14
Pelusium (al-Faramā), 36, 54
Persia, Persians, *see* Iran
Persian Gulf, 86–7, 107, 447, 449
Persian languages, writing, epics, 144, 148, 395, 417
Pertinax, 18
Pescennius Niger, 18
Petearbeshinis, 27
Peter I of Lusignan, 253, 273, 286–7
Peter, bishop, 28
Peter, commander, 50
Petinakht junior, 31
Petronius, 11
Petry, Carl, 443
Petublast IV, 7
Pharaoh, 13, 17, 22
Pharos lighthouse, 167
Phasis, 44
Philae, 11–14, 16–18, 24, 28, 30–1, 33
Philagrios, 48–9, 51, 54, 57, 61
Philip the Arab, 21–2
Philo, 13
Philumenos, 27
Phocas, Phokas, 33, 37, 38, 42, 51
Phonen, 31
pigeon post, 315
pilgrimage, pilgrims, 283
  Christian, 188, 193–4
  Muslim (*ḥajj*), 88, 94, 107, 111, 118, 124, 135, 137, 144, 168–9, 282, 313, 315, 339, 347–8, 358, 370, 374, 381, 384, 407, 434, 492, 494, 508, 513, 528, 531
  to sites in Egypt, 36, 142, 406
Pims, 16
Piri Reis, 343n
Pisa, 453
Pisentius of Quft, 31
plague, 17, 34–5, 71, 74, 208, 253, 262–3, 287–8, 292–3, 297–302, 305, 308–9, 311–12, 314–16, 368, 380, 385, 390, 392, 408, 434, 457–9, 471
Pliny the Younger, 6n, 13n
Plotina, 14
Portuguese, 298, 316, 460–1, 466–7, 471, 480, 482–3, 390, 493–4, 513
praefectus, 1, 11, 17–18
Premis (Qasr Ibrāhīm), 11
Probus, 23
Propontis, 18
Proterius, 32
Prussian mamlūks, 252
Psenamoun II, 7
Ptah, 12
Ptolemais, Ptolemies, Ptolemaic, 1–8, 11, 14–15, 23, 40, 89–90, 167, 376, 448
Pumbeditha, 200
Pupienus, 21
Pyrrhos, Patriarch, 48, 61, 533

Q. Aemilius Saturninus, 18
qāḍī, 63, 66, 84, 90, 96, 101–2, 105–6, 116, 137–8, 145, 208, 215, 232–3, 235, 237, 239, 265, 311, 337, 382, 390, 393, 398–9, 402, 407, 410, 418–19, 432, 434, 436–7, 485, 491, 495–7, 499–501, 504–6, 509–10, 514, 516, 532, 534
q. al-ʿArab, 510
q. al-ʿaskar, 416, 510, 534
q. al-quḍāt, 157–8, 269, 382, 534
al-Qāḍī al-Fāḍil, ʿAbd al-Raḥmān ibn ʿAlī al-ʿAsqalānī, 417, 421
al-Qāḍī al-Nuʿmān, 134–5, 144, 158
al-Qādir, Abbāsid caliph, 102
al-Qāhir, Abbāsid caliph, 111
Qāḍīzāde Ẓāhir al-Dīn al-Ardabīlī, 515
al-Qā'im, Abbāsid caliph, 147
al-Qā'im, Mamlūk caliph, 303
al-Qā'im bi-Amr Allāh, Abu'l-Qāsim, Fāṭimid, 111–13, 127n, 130–3
Qalʿat al-Rum, 280
Qalāwūn, 247–8, 250–2, 254, 255–8, 260–2, 264–5, 268, 271, 273–81, 283–4, 289, 290, 304, 421–3, 426, 453, 460–1, 464
Qalāwūnid line, 252–3, 256–7, 286–7
al-Qalqashandī, Shihāb al-Dīn Aḥmad, 205, 398, 431, 444
Qalyūbiyya, 315
Qamḥiyya *madrasa*, 401
Qānṣūh al-Ghawrī, 297–9, 302–5, 309, 313, 336, 338, 397, 406, 441, 461, 462, 464, 466–70, 473–89, 493–4, 495–501, 504, 508, 522
Qānṣūh Khamsmiyya, al-Ẓāhir, 296–7, 302, 309, 504
Qānūn-nāme-i Mıṣır, 515–16, 535
Qarāfa, cemetery, 99, 352, 357–9, 365, 368, 411, 535, 539
Qaramān, 492
Qarāmiṭa, Qarmatians, 86, 106–8, 111, 114, 116, 118, 122–6, 133–40, 142, 535
al-Qarqisiyya, 96
al-Qāsim, wazīr, 106
Qāsim ibn Aḥmet ibn Bāyezīd, 496
Qāsim Bey, 508
Qaṣr Ibrim, Nubia, 31, 194n
Qaṣr al-Shamʿ (Qaṣr al-Rūm), 202
al-Qaṭāʾiʿ, town, 99–101, 108, 350, 369–70
Qaṭr al-Nadā, 106
Qayrawān, 127–9, 132–3, 201
Qays Arabs, 64, 74–6, 78, 83, 314
Qays ibn Saʿd al-Anṣārī, 68
Qaysariyya, 99
Qāyt al-Rajabī, 485
Qātbāy, al-Ashraf, 292, 295–8, 301, 304–7, 310–13, 336, 378, 394, 398, 402, 439–41, 443, 459, 464n, 466, 473, 475–6, 479, 485, 492–4, 496, 501, 505–6, 516
Qinnasrīn, 96, 113, 523
Qirwash ibn al-Muqallad, 145
Qizilbash, 495, 535
Quietus, 23
Quintillus, 23
Quraysh, 64
Qurqud, 493
Qurra ibn Sharīk al-ʿAbsī, 72–3, 179n
Qūṣ, 87, 118, 162, 166, 168–9, 213, 256, 282–3, 316, 339, 340, 353, 354, 356, 370, 382–3, 392, 396, 401, 407, 449
Qūṣayr, 16, 87, 100, 343, 384, 396
Qūṣūn palace, 310
Quṭuz, 250–1, 273–4

Rabbanite Jews, 200–1, 204
Rabīʿa tribe, 93
Rabīʿa ibn Aḥmad ibn Ṭūlūn, 108
al-Rāḍī billāh, Abu'l-ʿAbbās, caliph, 98, 110, 112
Rāfiqa, 106
Ra'īs al-Yahūd (*Nagid*), 203–6, 208
Ramla, 80, 94–5, 112–14, 126, 375n, 500, 535
Raphia, 14–15
Raqqa, 95, 107–8, 113–14
Raqqada, 126n, 128–9, 131, 133, 137
al-Rasad heights, 99
Rawḍa island, 98, 112, 118, 224, 247, 484, 532
Rawḥ ibn Ḥātim, 77
rawk (cadaster), 252, 262–3, 272, 287, 535
al-Rāya quarter, 202
al-Raydāniyya, 479, 483, 496, 502–3

Rayy, 105
Red Mountain, al-Jabal al-Aḥmar, 502–3
Red Sea, 15–16, 53, 87, 115, 118, 162, 168, 217, 227, 277, 282–5, 294, 298–9, 339, 376, 384, 396, 407, 446–7, 449, 461, 466–7, 480, 483, 490, 494, 513
Rhine, 20
Rhinocolura (al-ʿArish), 56
Rhodes, 52, 55, 294, 506, 513
Riḍā ibn Thawb, 207
Riḍwān ibn al-Walakhshī, 168, 401
Rifāʿiyya order, 267, 536
Romanus I, 98
Rome, Romans, Roman Church, 1–2, 6, 10, 13–15, 19, 22–4, 31, 34, 37, 38, 43, 89–90, 176, 193, 195–7, 349, 523, 534
Rosetta (Rashīd), 111, 221, 316, 494
Royal mamlūks, *see* sulṭaniyya
Rukn al-Dīn, *qāḍī*, 497
Rūm, *see* Seljuk Rūm
Russia, 247, 273, 527
Rustamids, 97

Saʿad al-Dīn ibn Ghurāb, 307
Saʿadyā ben Joseph Gaʿon, al-Fayyūmī, 98, 170, 200–1
sab'a wa sab 'in walī, 357
Sabīl ʿAllān, 502
Sabina, empress, 15
Sabra al-Manṣūriyya, 352
Sabta mosque, 93
Saʻd ibn Aysar, 105
Saʿdüddīn, Ottoman chronicler, 491, 495
Ṣafad, 276, 279, 431, 499
al-Ṣafadī, Khalīl Aybak, 431–2, 442
Safavids, 298–9, 460–1, 466, 490, 494–5, 497, 499, 502, 511, 515, 529, 535–6
Ṣaffārids, 86, 94, 105, 536
Saharan Africa, 93, 118
Ṣāḥib al-Nāqa, 107
ṣāḥib al-shurta, 65–6, 69–73, 76–7, 79, 82, 85, 90, 536
Sahidic dialect, 185
Ṣahyūn fortress (Saone), 275
Ṣaʿīd, *see* Upper Egypt
Saʿīd ibn al-Ḥusayn, 125–7
Saʿīd al-Suʿadāʾ *khanqah*, 267, 405
Saʿīd ibn Yazīd al-Fihrī, 70
St Anthony, 22
monastery, 56
St Barbara, 349, 354
St Catherine, 343
monastery, 419
St George, church of, 349
St John the Baptist, church, 29
St Mark the Apostle, 176
St Menas, 353
St Michel, 31
Sakellarios, 48, 536
al-Sakhāwī, Abū al-Khayr Muḥammad ibn ʿAbd al-Raḥmān, 436, 440, 442–3
al-Sakhāwī, Shams al-Dīn Muḥammad, 403
Ṣalāḥ al-Dīn ibn Ayyūb, 96, 140, 154, 156, 192, 213–22, 226–7, 231–2, 239–40, 246, 248, 255, 266, 269, 330–2, 365, 371, 385, 391, 400, 402, 405, 412, 414–19, 421, 450–2, 463, 468, 536
Ṣalāḥ al-Dīn Yaḥyā, 473
Salamiyya, 107, 120, 123–7
al-Ṣāliḥ ʿAlī, 255
Ṣāliḥ ibn ʿAlī, 76
al-Ṣāliḥ Ismāʿīl, Ayyūbid, 224, 431
al-Ṣāliḥ Najm al-Dīn Ayyūb, 212n, 224–7n, 244, 246–52, 255, 269, 273, 332–3, 419, 462, 523, 536
mausoleum of, 355, 361, 371
al-Ṣāliḥ Ṣāliḥ, 272
al-Ṣāliḥ Ṭalāʿiʾ, 365
mosque of, 345, 356, 365
Ṣāliḥi mamlūks, Ṣāliḥiyya (of Ṣālāḥ al-Dīn), 212n, 220, 224, 249, 252, 254, 258, 536
al-Ṣāliḥiyya, Egypt, 502
al-Ṣāliḥiyya, Syria, 372, 499, 536
Ṣāliḥiyya *madrasa*, 510
Salīm I, 299, 338, 461, 466–7, 478, 480, 483, 491, 493–9, 510–11, 513, 539
Salmān, admiral, 482
Ṣamānids, 105, 536
Samaritan Jews, 200, 203
Samaritans, 209
Samarqand, 82, 458

Samarrā, 82, 84, 85, 87, 89, 91–2, 94, 97, 99–101, 104, 369–70
Sambarī, Yosef ben Yitzhak, 491
Samos, 11
Samuel of Kalamoun, 178n
Sanjar al-Ḥalabī, 274
Sanjar al-Jāwulī, 394
saqīa, 2, 3n
Ṣaqr tribe, 315
Saray ibn Sahl, 102
Sarbadārs, 253, 536
Ṣarghitmish, 401
Sarī al-Dīn ibn al-Shiḥna, 485
al-Sarī ibn al-Ḥakam ibn Yūsuf al-Balkhī, 80, 81, 97
Sasanians, 43–4, 86, 104, 177, 325
Satrius Arrianus, 24
Sawīrus, *see* Severus
Sayf al-Dawla, 113–15, 118
Sayyida al-Nafisa sanctuary, 100, 303, 313
al-Sayyida Rasad, 171
Scete, 36
Scetis, monastery, 193
Sebeos, 40
Secreta Fidelium Crucis, 282
Seleucids, 349
Seljuks, 146–8, 204, 226, 232, 241, 245, 246, 413, 416, 536–7, 539
  of Rum, 204, 236, 240, 252, 273, 275, 278–80, 527, 534
Serapeum, 28–30
Serapis, 13–14
Seta I, 32
Setif, 124n, 140n
Severan dynasty, 18–20
Severus (Sawīrus ibn al-Muqaffaʿ), 45, 59, 63, 64, 73, 74, 83, 190, 449
Severus Alexander, 20, 21
Severus II, 25
Severus, Septimus, 17n, 18–19
Seville, 434
Shaʿbān, al-Ashraf, 253, 257, 283, 286, 288, 290–1, 299, 365–6
shādd, mushidd, 236, 537
al-Shādhilī, Abu'l-Ḥasan, 266–7, 407
Shādhili order, Shādhiliyya, 266–7, 271, 406–7, 537
Shāfiʿ ibn ʿAlī, 421–2
al-Shāfiʿī, Muḥammad ibn Idrīs, 394, 402, 447
  tomb of, 232, 313, 504
Shāfiʿī rite, 88, 168, 215, 265, 267–9, 272, 322, 382, 398, 402, 416, 419, 432, 436, 439, 442, 444, 447, 451, 537
Shāh Sūwār, 295, 492
Shāhnāmeh, 395
Shahrbaraz, 42–5, 51
Shajar al-Durr, 224–5, 240, 249–50, 419–20
Shams al-Dīn Ṣawāb, 240
Shanūda I, patriarch, 100
Shapur I, 21–2
Shapur II, 29
Shaqīf Arnūn (Beaufort), 276
Sharaf al-Dīn Qarāqūsh, 217
al-Shaʿrānī, ʿAbd al-Wahhāb, 405–6, 408
al-Shāriʿ al-Aʿẓam, 344, 350
Sharīʿa, 158, 256, 265, 270, 393, 407, 414, 477, 509–10, 516, 531–2, 535, 537
Sharīf of Mecca, 282–3, 505, 537
Sharqiyya province, 315, 501–2, 508, 515
Shāwar, 213–14
Shawbak (Montréal), 223
Shayban ibn Aḥmad ibn Ṭūlūn, 108
Shaykh, al-Mu'ayyad, 291–3, 298, 300–1, 305, 313, 394, 437, 439, 458, 460
Shemarya ben Elḥanan, 203
Shenhūr, 12–13
Shenute of Atripe, 28–30
Shihāb al-Dīn Abū al-Thanā', 432
Shiʿites, 88, 106, 112, 119, 120–2, 129, 131–4, 138–41, 143, 146–7, 151, 215–16, 232, 265–6, 330, 348, 352, 383, 400, 433, 490, 515, 524, 527–30, 536–7
  Twelvers, 114, 119, 122, 134, 145, 154, 450, 494, 536–8
  see also Ismāʿīlīs
al-Shīrāzī, Mu'ayyad fi'l-Dīn, 143–4, 146
Shīrkūh, Asad al-Dīn, 213–14, 220, 226, 246
Shoshan, Boaz, 268
al-Shujāʿī, ʿAlam al-Dīn Sanjar, 264
al-Shujāʿī, Shams al-Dīn (ibn), 426–7
Shukayr, 92

Sībāy, 498
Sicily, 59, 87, 94, 120, 132, 140, 216, 418, 448–9, 453
Sidon, 276
Sijilmasa, 126n, 128–9
al-Sijistānī, Abū Ya'qūb, 135
Silko, 31
Silsileh, 14
Sīmā al-Ṭawīl, 96
Sinai, 52, 56, 343, 419, 444, 502, 536
Sinān Pasha, 498, 500, 503
Sind, 283–4
Sipahis, 512, 537
al-Sirāj al-Bulqīnī, 378
Siryāqūs, 268, 405
Sīs, 273, 279, 285–6
Sitt al-Mulk, 152, 171
Siwa oasis, 14
Sīwās, 291
Sobek, 9
Sohag, 28, 189n, 384
Sophronios, 56
Sosigenes, 3
Sossianus Hierocles, 24
Sothic Cycle, 16
Sousse, 94
South China Sea, 455
Spain, 63, 71, 132, 168, 204, 210, 381, 433–4, 447
see also Andalūs
spice trade, 15, 100, 167, 244, 282, 284–5, 294, 302, 314–16, 396, 454, 460, 466, 494, 530
Stoics, 13
Straetegikon, 49
Suakin, 282
Subaytila, 67
al-Subkī, Taqī al-Dīn, 411, 432
Sudanese, soldiers, 216
Suez, 75, 343, 480, 482
Ṣūfism, Sufis, dervish orders, 208, 231, 235, 239, 244, 265–71, 312, 378, 383, 386, 394, 397, 401–2, 404–9, 434, 461, 496, 498–9, 501, 504, 525, 527, 530–1, 535–9
Sufyānids, 69
al-Ṣulayḥī, 'Alī ibn Muḥammad, 145
Ṣulayḥids, 146, 537
Sulaym tribe, 116, 449
Sülaymān, sultan, 507, 513, 515, 535
Sulaymān, Umayyad caliph, 73
Sultan Ḥasan *madrasa*, 397
see also al-Nāṣir Ḥasan
Sulṭānī mamlūks, royal guard, 251, 260–1, 288, 305, 481, 483, 526, 530, 537
Sultays, 55
Sunbāṭ, 204
Sunnism, Sunnis, 88, 101, 103–4, 106, 114, 117, 119, 129, 131, 134, 139, 142, 146–7, 151–2, 158, 167–8, 172–4, 207, 214–16, 231–2, 256, 265–71, 348, 360, 381, 393–4, 400–4, 445, 450–1, 461, 463–4, 475, 490, 495, 511, 528–34, 536–7
Sunqur al-Ashqar, 274–5, 278
Sura, yeshiva of, 200
sürgün, deportation, 506, 538
Suwayqat al-Yahūd, 202
Suyūṭ, 111
al-Suyūṭī, Jalāl al-Dīn, 378, 391, 402, 441, 443
Syria, Syrians, 17–18, 22, 36, 39, 40, 42–54, 58–60, 62, 64, 68–73, 75, 79, 81, 85, 86–7, 89, 92, 94, 98–101, 103–5, 107, 112–18, 120, 123–6, 136–8, 142, 144–9, 152, 154, 156, 162, 166, 180, 193–4, 199, 211–14, 217–20, 222–4, 226, 228–9, 232, 234, 240, 246, 248, 250–1, 260, 263, 266, 271, 273–7, 279, 280–1, 284–6, 289, 290–2, 295, 297, 299, 310, 314, 325–6, 335, 365, 373, 375–6, 381, 385, 394, 398, 400, 402–3, 406, 412, 414–16, 418, 420, 422–31, 437, 442, 446, 451–4, 458, 463, 478, 480, 483, 490–1, 495–8, 500, 502, 505, 507, 513, 523, 529, 531, 536, 539
Syrian historians, 427, 429, 435
Syriac writings, 193–4

al-Ṭabarī, 41, 63, 79, 98, 415
Ṭabaristān, 94
Tabennesi, 26
Tabrīz, 281, 395
Tacitus, 23
Taghrī Birmish, 394

Tahert, 97
Ṭāhirids, 82
Tahta, 25
Takīn, 103, 110–11
Takrīt, 110
Talmud, Talmudic Judaism, 199–200
Tamerlane, *see* Timūr-Lenk
Tanam, rebel amīr, 291
Tankiz al-Ḥusamī, viceroy of Syria, 248, 286, 431
  palace of, 310
Tannūr Firʿawn, 100
Ṭanṭa, 406
Tarsus, 91, 95–6, 101–2, 105, 114, 285
Taruja, 315–16
Ṭaṭar, al-Ẓahrī, 293, 300, 438
Tatars, 242, 381, 538
Taurus mountains, 55, 453, 460
Taweret (Thoeris), 9
Ṭayy tribe, 116
al-Ṭayyib, 149, 153–4, 538
Ṭayyibī Ismāʿīlīs (Bohras), 149–50, 154, 524, 528, 538
Tegüder (Aḥmad), 277
Tehneh (Akoris), 13
Templars, 224, 275–6
Tendunias, 54
Terenuthis, 55
Teshlot, 185
Tetrarchy, 23, 25–6
Teutonic Knights, 275
thaghr, *thughūr*, 108, 167, 523
Theadelphia, 22
Thebaid, 11, 19, 22, 23, 55, 383
Thebes, 15, 17, 19, 27
Theobald of Champagne, 224
Theodora, 32
Theodore, 72
Theodore, patriarch, 103
Theodorus, commander, 61
Theodosios I, 28–9
Theodosius II, 30
Theophanes (George the Syncellus), 40, 45, 59, 60n
Theophilus of Edessa, 40, 45, 59
Theophilus, patriarch, 29
Teophylact Simocatta, 35, 42
Thessalos, 19
Thrace, 26, 38, 47
Tiber, 16
Tiberiad, Tiberias, 92, 94–5, 108, 114, 201
Tiberius II, 33
Tiberius Julius Alexander, 13
Tiberius, 12–13
Timotheos, bishop, 195n
Timothy "the Cat", 32
Timūr-Lenk (Tamerlane), 86, 291–2, 294, 434, 456, 458, 460, 494–5, 538
Timurbughā, 293, 295, 301
Timurids, 381, 394, 536, 538
Tinnīs, 88, 107, 158, 231
Titus, 14
Tod, 16
Töde Möngke, 278
Toledo, 168
Topkapi Palace, 492, 538
Toth, 30
Trajan, 6n, 9, 14–15
Trajanus Decius, *see* Decius, Trajanus
Transoxiana, 98, 105, 246, 273, 536
Triadon, 185–6
Trinitarian debate 447
Tripoli, Syrian
  crusader principality of, 274, 276, 280–1
  Ṭarābulūs, 114–15, 118, 227, 448, 499
Tripoli, western, 96–7, 115, 127, 129–30
  Tripolitania, 67
Ṭughj ibn Juff, 107–8
Tughril, 146
Tujīb, 64
ṭulb, 226, 260, 538
Ṭūlūnids, 93, 95, 101, 103–10, 112, 162, 183, 246, 326–7, 344, 347, 352, 369, 370, 448, 526
Tūmānbāy, 297, 299, 309, 312, 315–16, 441, 496, 500–4
  mausoleum of, 479
Tunis, 133n, 434, 452, 454
Tunisia, *see* Ifrīqiyya
Tūrānshāh, al-Muʿaẓẓam, 216–17, 224–5, 244, 249, 258, 420
Turcomans, Turkmans, 226, 260, 279, 284, 286, 294, 461, 464, 481n, 492, 495, 502, 505, 512, 515, 525, 538
Turkestan, 245, 481

Turkish language, 244, 391, 394, 424, 437–8, 490–1, 500, 505, 509–11, 516, 528, 536, 538
  sources, literature, 392, 395, 490–1, 514
Turks, 82, 143, 146–7, 257, 269, 290, 291, 293, 300, 306, 311, 316, 391, 425, 448, 461, 497, 505, 510, 516, 527, 531–12, 536
  slaves, mamlūks, 82, 85, 87–9, 91, 94, 98, 100, 103, 105, 110, 152–5, 171, 207, 226–7, 242, 244–7, 249–50, 377, 381, 391, 401, 453, 527
  see also Ottomans
al-Ṭurṭūshī, 168, 400
Tuscany, 231
Tustarī family, 206–7

ʿUbayd Allāh, *see* al-Mahdī
ʿUbayd Allāh ibn al-Ḥabḥāb, 74–5, 78
ʿUbayd Allāh ibn al-Sarī, 81
ʿUbayd Allāh ibn Sulaymān ibn Wahb, 106–7
ʿUbayd Allāh ibn Ṭughj, 114
al-Udfuwī, Kamāl al-Dīn, 382, 384, 432
Udovitch, Abraham, 288
ʿUlayy ibn Ribāḥ al-Lakhmī, 66
ʿUmar ibn ʿAbd al-ʿAzīz tribe, 315
ʿUmar ibn ʿAlī ibn Abī Ṭālib, 93
ʿUmar ibn Mihrān, 79
ʿUmar, caliph, 41, 54, 64, 67, 73, 207
al-ʿUmarī, Abū ʿAbd Allah ibn ʿAbd al-Ḥamīd, 93
al-ʿUmarī, Ibn Faḍl Allāh, 205, 430–2, 437, 444
ʿUmayr ibn al-Walīd, 83
Umayyada, 33, 62, 65, 67, 69–75, 77, 87, 182, 183, 246, 319n, 323–6, 538
  of Spain, 140
  Umayyad mosque, 101
  umm al-dunyā, 339, 360
Unūjār, 112, 114, 116
Upper Egypt, Ṣaʿīd, 11, 23, 32, 39n, 62n, 67, 74, 93, 118, 131, 142, 162, 168–9, 181, 193, 200, 211n, 216–17, 252, 265–6, 282–3, 291–2, 294–6, 299, 314–16, 339, 365, 382–3, 384, 401, 407, 410, 432, 449, 502, 508, 514, 528, 536
ʿUqayl tribe, 114, 116
ʿUqaylids, 145
ʿUqba ibn Nafiʿ, 83
Usāma, governor, 73n
ustādār, 240, 260, 293, 306–7, 538
Ustādh Jawdhar, 141
ʿUtba ibn ʿĀmir, 69
ʿUtba ibn Abī Sufyān, 69
ʿUthmān ibn Saʿīd al-Kilābī, Abu'l-Fatḥ, 113
ʿUthmān, caliph, 89, 66–8, 446
Uzun Ḥasan, 296, 464n, 466

Vaballatus, 23
Valens, 28
Valentinos, general, 47–8, 55
Valerian, 22
Vandals, 60
Vasco de Gama, 298, 460
Venice, Venetians, 275, 280–2, 285, 292, 335–6, 374, 389, 453, 458, 492
Vespasian, 13–14
Vitellius, 13

Wadi Hammamat, 16
Wadī Khāzindār, battle of, 277
Wadī Naṭrūn, 27, 132, 189n, 194, 343, 345
Wadi Tumaylat, 54
wāfidiyya, 258–9, 262, 287, 381, 538
wakīl bayt al-māl, 474, 539
wakīl al-tujjār, 164–5
al-Walīd, 71, 72, 74
waqf, *awqāf*, 99, 102, 109, 111, 204, 231–3, 235, 240, 257, 265, 270, 288, 302, 310–11, 333n, 360, 363, 382, 390, 393, 437, 473–4, 476–8n, 483–8, 492, 494, 500, 508, 510, 516, 526, 528, 539
Wardān, 504
Wāsiṭ, 76, 97
al-Wāsiṭī, Aḥmad ibn Muḥammad, 91, 96, 104
al-Wāthiq, caliph, 84, 92, 95
wazīr, vizierate, 81, 88–9, 96–8, 106, 109, 111, 117, 137–8, 147, 153–4, 156–9, 162, 166, 168–9, 171–3, 206–7, 213–15, 232, 245,

264, 272, 306, 347, 356, 360, 365, 370, 401, 417, 426, 434, 450, 495, 498, 500, 515, 526, 539
women, 102, 187, 188n, 209, 238–40, 287, 306, 379, 387–90, 404, 406, 409, 432, 443, 500, 505, 508, 510, 512, 528–9, 535
wujūh, 64, 66, 69, 70, 77, 79, 80, 81

Yüan China, 455–6
Yaḥyā ibn Ayyūb, 40, 47, 60n
Yaḥyā ibn al-Jarawī, 84
Yalbugha al-Nāṣirī, 291
Yalbughā al-ʿUmarī, 288, 291
Yaʿqūb, caliph, 501
Yaʿqūb ibn Killis, *see* Ibn Killis
al-Yaʿqūbī, 87
Yārjākh (Yārūj), 92, 95
Yarmūk, battle of, 47, 57
Yashbak min Mahdī, 295, 297, 301, 304, 306, 310, 443
Yashmak, 296
Yazīd II, 296
Yazīd ibn ʿAbd Allāh ibn Turkī, 85
Yazīd ibn Ḥātim, 77
Yazīd ibn Muʿāwiya, 69–70
Yazmān, 101–2, 105
Yemen, Yemenis, 64, 75, 78, 80, 81, 85, 87, 99, 111n, 115, 118, 120, 122, 123–5, 127, 135, 142, 145–6, 148–50, 154, 168, 217–18, 283–4, 294, 314, 426, 428, 450–1, 451, 455, 537
Yilbāy, 294, 301
Yumgān, 144
al-Yūnīnī, Quṭb al-Dīn Mūsā, 427–9, 435
Yūnus Pasha, 498, 504
al-Yūsufī, Mūsā ibn Muḥammad ibn al-Shaykh Yaḥyā, 426–7, 432, 438

al-Ẓāfir, Fatimid, 154
al-Ẓāhir (Mamlūk sultan), *see* Baybars I; Qānṣūh Khamsmiyya
al-Ẓāhir, Ayyūbid of Aleppo, 220, 240, 416
al-Ẓāhir, Fāṭimid caliph, 152–3, 171, 206
Ẓāhirī mamlūks (of Baybars), Ẓāhiriyya, 258–9, 300, 539
Ẓāhiriyya *madrasa*, 394
Zanāta berbers, 133, 140
Zanj rebellion, 86, 94–6, 102, 106
Zanzibar, 86
zāwiya, 270, 312, 345, 407, 473, 530, 539
Zaydān, 112
Zaydites, 94, 537
Zayn al-Dīn ʿAbd al-Bāsiṭ, 307
Zayn al-Dīn Barakāt ibn Mūsā, 307–8
Zengids, 218, 226–7, 229, 232, 330, 415–16, 539
Zeno, 3
Zenobia, 23
Zikrawayh, 125–6
Zīrī ibn Manād, 140
Zīrids, 146, 539
Ziyādat Allāh, 110
ziyārah, visitation of tombs, 378, 410
Zosimos, 27
zuʿar, 311, 501, 503, 539
Zubayr ibn al-ʿAwwām, 62
Zuqāq al-Yahūd, 202
Zuṭṭ buffalo breeders, 86, 539